SHOWCASE PRESENTS

DC COMICS PRESENTS

SUPERMAN TEAM-UPS

VOLUME 1

SUPERMAN CREATED BY JERRY SIEGEL AND JOE SHUSTER

Dan DiDio Senior VP-Executive Editor
Julius Schwartz Editor-Original Series
Georg Brewer VP-Design & DC Direct Creative
Bob Harras Group Editor-Collected Editions
Bob Joy Editor
Robbin Brosterman Design Director-Books

DC COMICS
Paul Levitz President & Publisher
Richard Bruning Senior VP-Creative Director
Patrick Caldon Executive VP-Finance & Operations
Amy Genkins Senior VP-Business & Legal Affairs
Jim Lee Editorial Director-WildStorm
Gregory Noveck Senior VP-Creative Affairs
Steve Rotterdam Senior VP-Sales & Marketing
Cheryl Rubin Senior VP-Brand Management

Cover illustration by Jose Luis Garcia-Lopez.
Cover colored by Allen Passalaqua.

SHOWCASE PRESENTS: DC COMICS PRESENTS: THE SUPERMAN TEAM-UPS VOL. ONE
Published by DC Comics. Cover and compilation Copyright © 2009 DC Comics.
All Rights Reserved. Originally published in single magazine form in
DC COMICS PRESENTS 1-26 © 1978, 1979, 1980 DC Comics.
All Rights Reserved. All characters, their distinctive likenesses and
related elements featured in this publication are trademarks of DC Comics.
The stories, characters and incidents featured in this publication are entirely fictional.
DC Comics does not read or accept unsolicited submissions of ideas, stories or artwork.

DC Comics, 1700 Broadway, New York, NY 10019
A Warner Bros. Entertainment Company
First Printing
ISBN: 978-1-4012-2535-3
Printed by Transcontinental Gagne, Louiseville, QC, Canada 9/23/09

TABLE OF CONTENTS

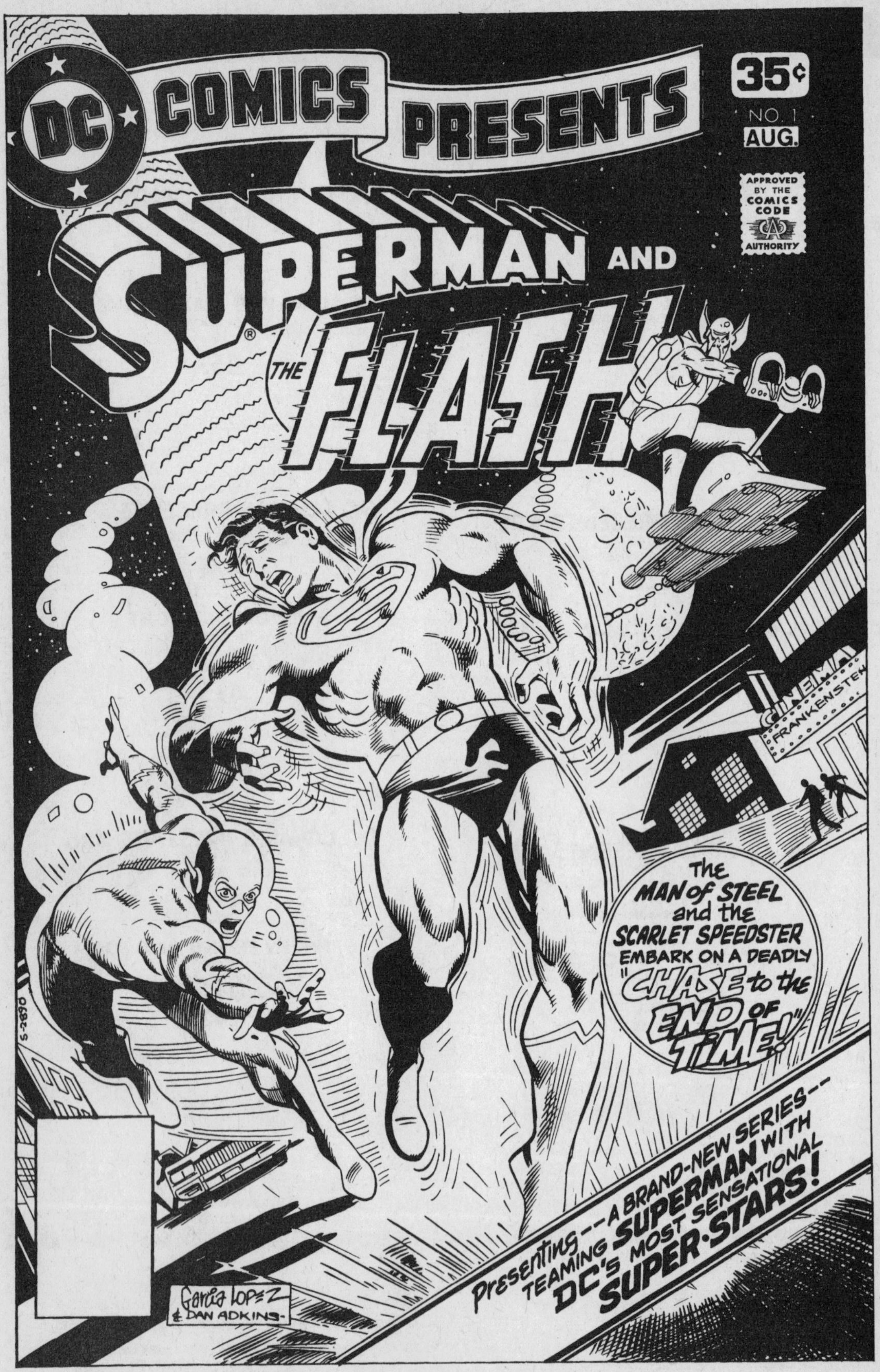
DC COMICS PRESENTS
35¢
NO. 1
AUG.
APPROVED BY THE COMICS CODE AUTHORITY
SUPERMAN AND THE FLASH!
CINEMA
FRANKENSTEIN
The MAN of STEEL and the SCARLET SPEEDSTER EMBARK ON A DEADLY "CHASE to the END OF TIME!"
Presenting---A BRAND-NEW SERIES--- TEAMING SUPERMAN WITH DC's MOST SENSATIONAL SUPER-STARS!
Garcia Lopez & DAN ADKINS

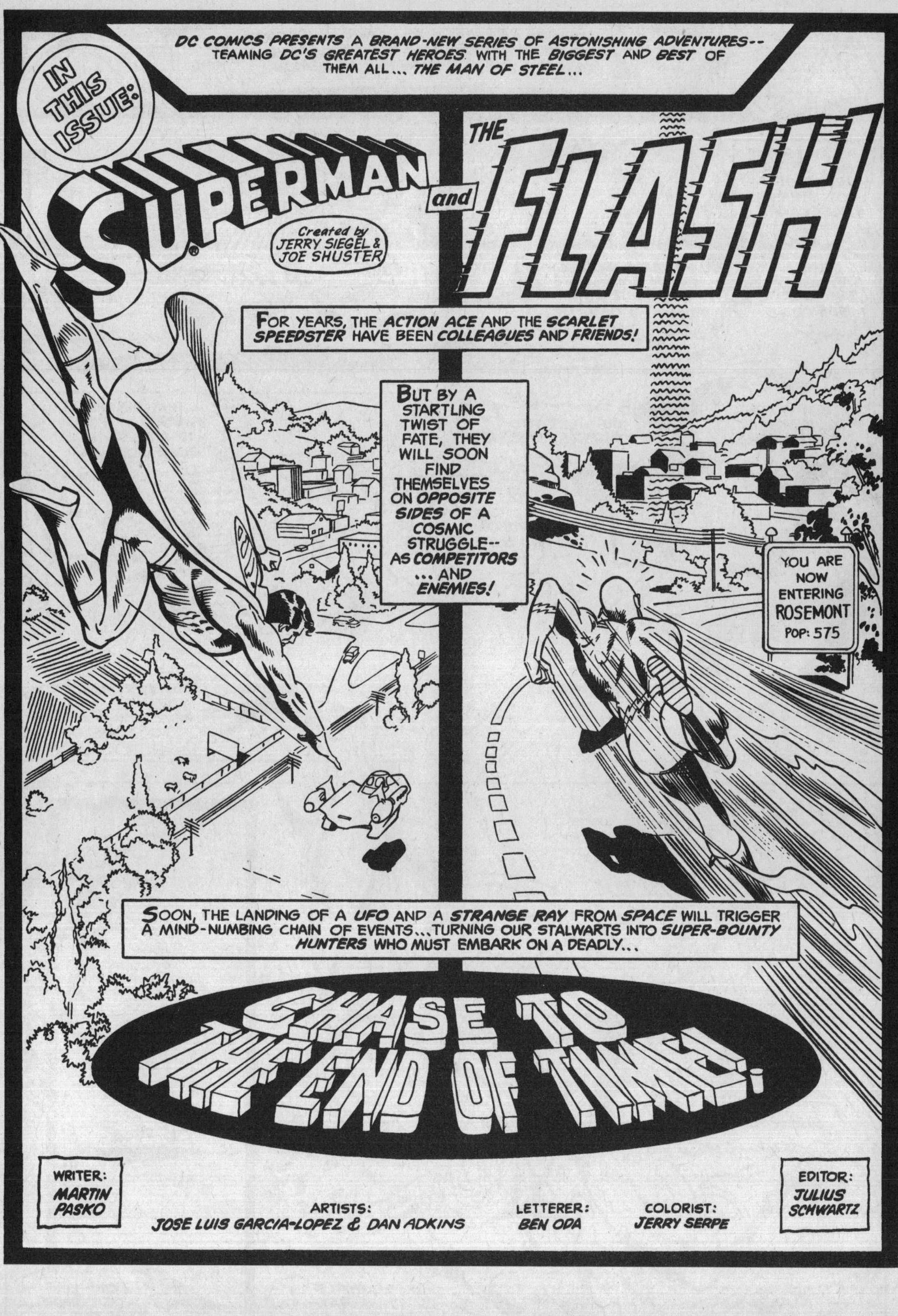
DC COMICS PRESENTS A BRAND-NEW SERIES OF ASTONISHING ADVENTURES-- TEAMING DC'S GREATEST HEROES WITH THE BIGGEST AND BEST OF THEM ALL... THE MAN OF STEEL...
IN THIS ISSUE:
SUPERMAN and THE FLASH
Created by JERRY SIEGEL & JOE SHUSTER
FOR YEARS, THE ACTION ACE AND THE SCARLET SPEEDSTER HAVE BEEN COLLEAGUES AND FRIENDS!
BUT BY A STARTLING TWIST OF FATE, THEY WILL SOON FIND THEMSELVES ON OPPOSITE SIDES OF A COSMIC STRUGGLE-- AS COMPETITORS ...AND ENEMIES!
YOU ARE NOW ENTERING ROSEMONT POP: 575
SOON, THE LANDING OF A UFO AND A STRANGE RAY FROM SPACE WILL TRIGGER A MIND-NUMBING CHAIN OF EVENTS...TURNING OUR STALWARTS INTO SUPER-BOUNTY HUNTERS WHO MUST EMBARK ON A DEADLY...
CHASE TO THE END OF TIME!
WRITER: MARTIN PASKO
ARTISTS: JOSE LUIS GARCIA-LOPEZ & DAN ADKINS
LETTERER: BEN ODA
COLORIST: JERRY SERPE
EDITOR: JULIUS SCHWARTZ

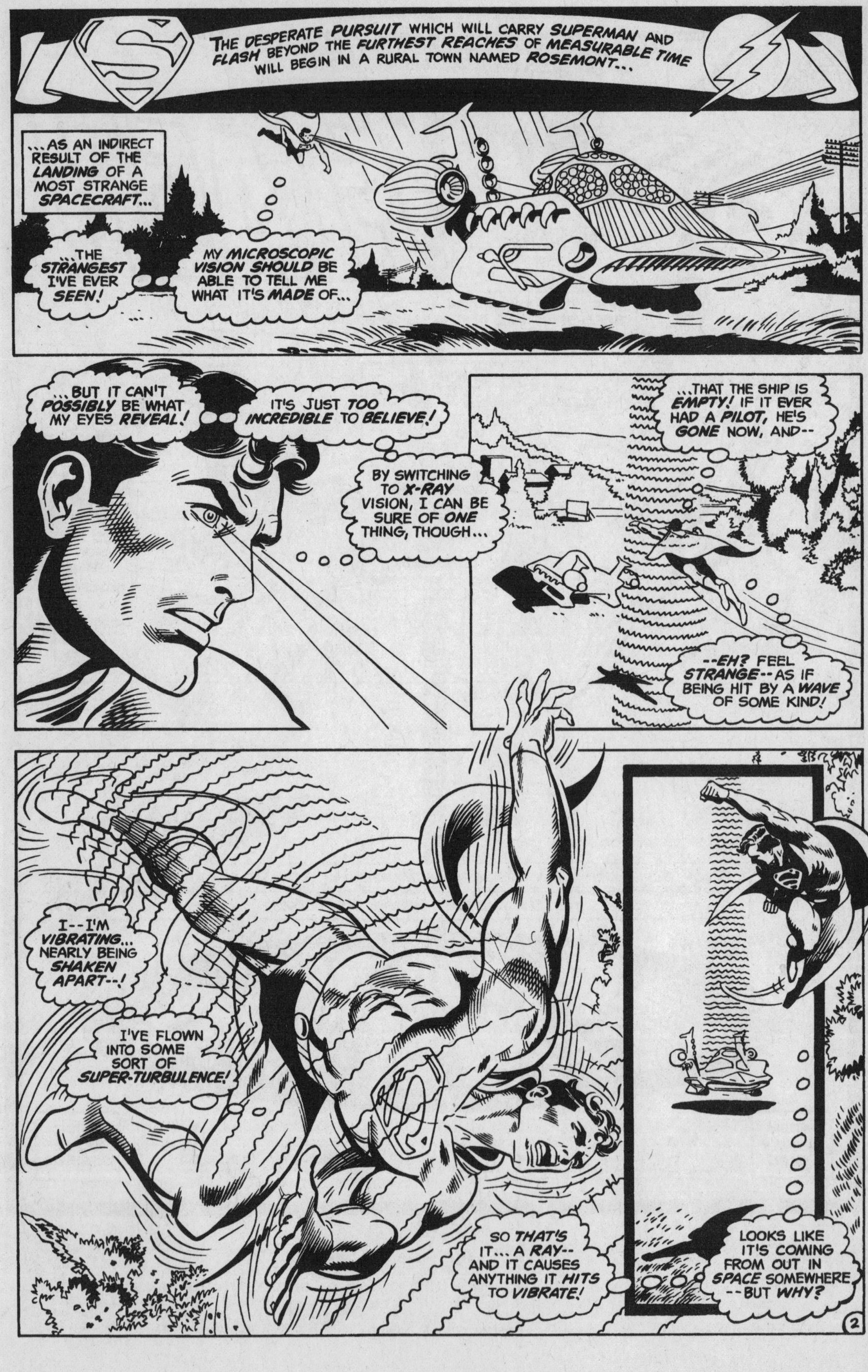
THE DESPERATE PURSUIT WHICH WILL CARRY SUPERMAN AND FLASH BEYOND THE FURTHEST REACHES OF MEASURABLE TIME WILL BEGIN IN A RURAL TOWN NAMED ROSEMONT...
...AS AN INDIRECT RESULT OF THE LANDING OF A MOST STRANGE SPACECRAFT...
...THE STRANGEST I'VE EVER SEEN!
MY MICROSCOPIC VISION SHOULD BE ABLE TO TELL ME WHAT IT'S MADE OF...
...BUT IT CAN'T POSSIBLY BE WHAT MY EYES REVEAL!
IT'S JUST TOO INCREDIBLE TO BELIEVE!
BY SWITCHING TO X-RAY VISION, I CAN BE SURE OF ONE THING, THOUGH...
...THAT THE SHIP IS EMPTY! IF IT EVER HAD A PILOT, HE'S GONE NOW, AND--
--EH? FEEL STRANGE--AS IF BEING HIT BY A WAVE OF SOME KIND!
I--I'M VIBRATING... NEARLY BEING SHAKEN APART--!
I'VE FLOWN INTO SOME SORT OF SUPER-TURBULENCE!
SO THAT'S IT... A RAY-- AND IT CAUSES ANYTHING IT HITS TO VIBRATE!
LOOKS LIKE IT'S COMING FROM OUT IN SPACE SOMEWHERE --BUT WHY?
2

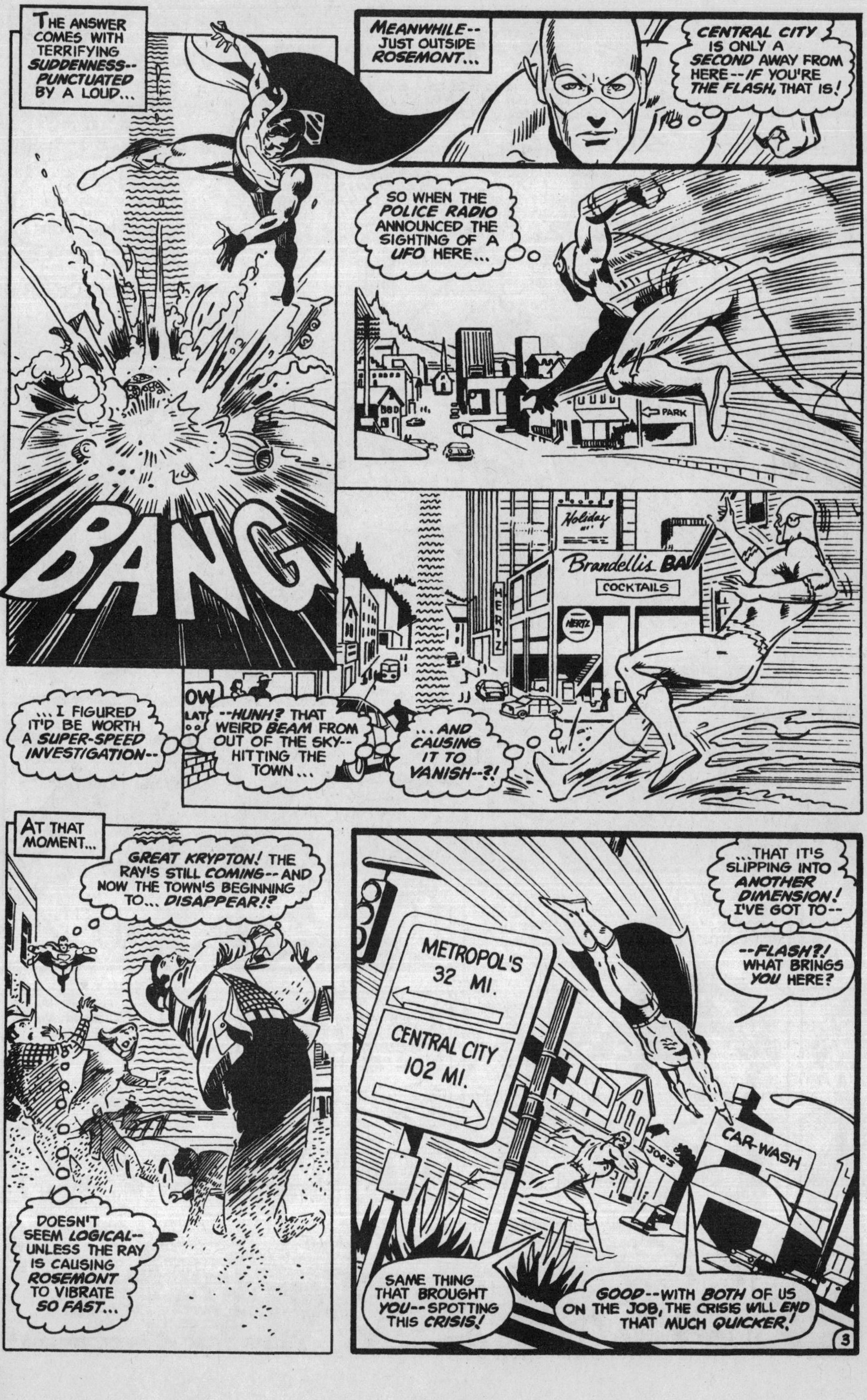

THE ANSWER COMES WITH TERRIFYING SUDDENNESS-- PUNCTUATED BY A LOUD...
BANG
MEANWHILE-- JUST OUTSIDE ROSEMONT...
CENTRAL CITY IS ONLY A SECOND AWAY FROM HERE--IF YOU'RE THE FLASH, THAT IS!
SO WHEN THE POLICE RADIO ANNOUNCED THE SIGHTING OF A UFO HERE...
PARK
Holiday
Brandellis BA
COCKTAILS
HERTZ
...I FIGURED IT'D BE WORTH A SUPER-SPEED INVESTIGATION--
--HUNH? THAT WEIRD BEAM FROM OUT OF THE SKY-- HITTING THE TOWN...
...AND CAUSING IT TO VANISH--?!
AT THAT MOMENT...
GREAT KRYPTON! THE RAY'S STILL COMING--AND NOW THE TOWN'S BEGINNING TO... DISAPPEAR!?
DOESN'T SEEM LOGICAL-- UNLESS THE RAY IS CAUSING ROSEMONT TO VIBRATE SO FAST...
...THAT IT'S SLIPPING INTO ANOTHER DIMENSION! I'VE GOT TO--
METROPOL'S 32 MI.
CENTRAL CITY 102 MI.
--FLASH?! WHAT BRINGS YOU HERE?
JOE'S
CAR-WASH
SAME THING THAT BROUGHT YOU--SPOTTING THIS CRISIS!
GOOD--WITH BOTH OF US ON THE JOB, THE CRISIS WILL END THAT MUCH QUICKER!
3

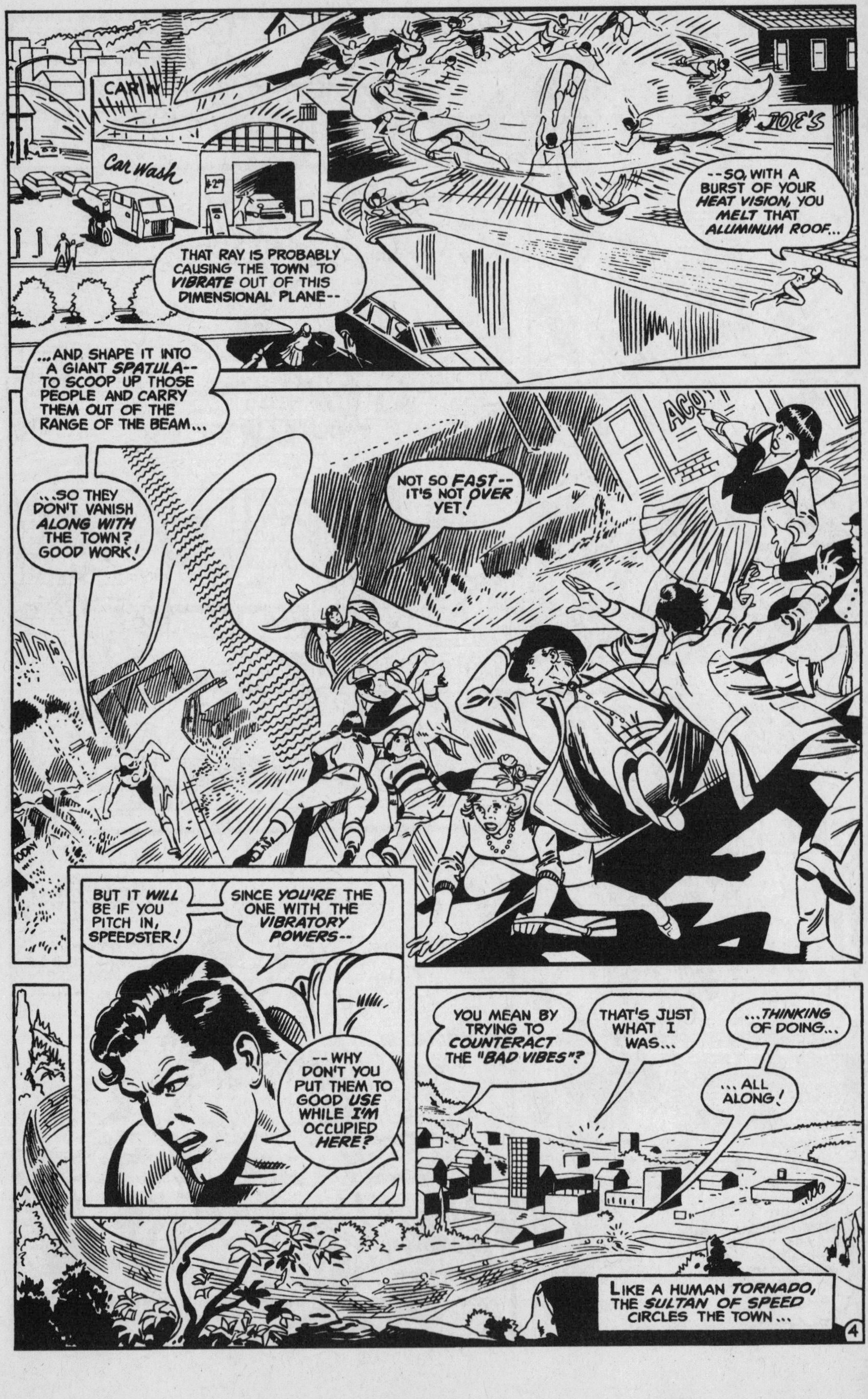
CAR W
Car Wash
JOE'S
--SO, WITH A BURST OF YOUR HEAT VISION, YOU MELT THAT ALUMINUM ROOF...
THAT RAY IS PROBABLY CAUSING THE TOWN TO VIBRATE OUT OF THIS DIMENSIONAL PLANE--
...AND SHAPE IT INTO A GIANT SPATULA--TO SCOOP UP THOSE PEOPLE AND CARRY THEM OUT OF THE RANGE OF THE BEAM...
...SO THEY DON'T VANISH ALONG WITH THE TOWN? GOOD WORK!
NOT SO FAST--IT'S NOT OVER YET!
BUT IT WILL BE IF YOU PITCH IN, SPEEDSTER!
SINCE YOU'RE THE ONE WITH THE VIBRATORY POWERS--
--WHY DON'T YOU PUT THEM TO GOOD USE WHILE I'M OCCUPIED HERE?
YOU MEAN BY TRYING TO COUNTERACT THE "BAD VIBES"?
THAT'S JUST WHAT I WAS...
...THINKING OF DOING...
...ALL ALONG!
LIKE A HUMAN TORNADO, THE SULTAN OF SPEED CIRCLES THE TOWN...
4

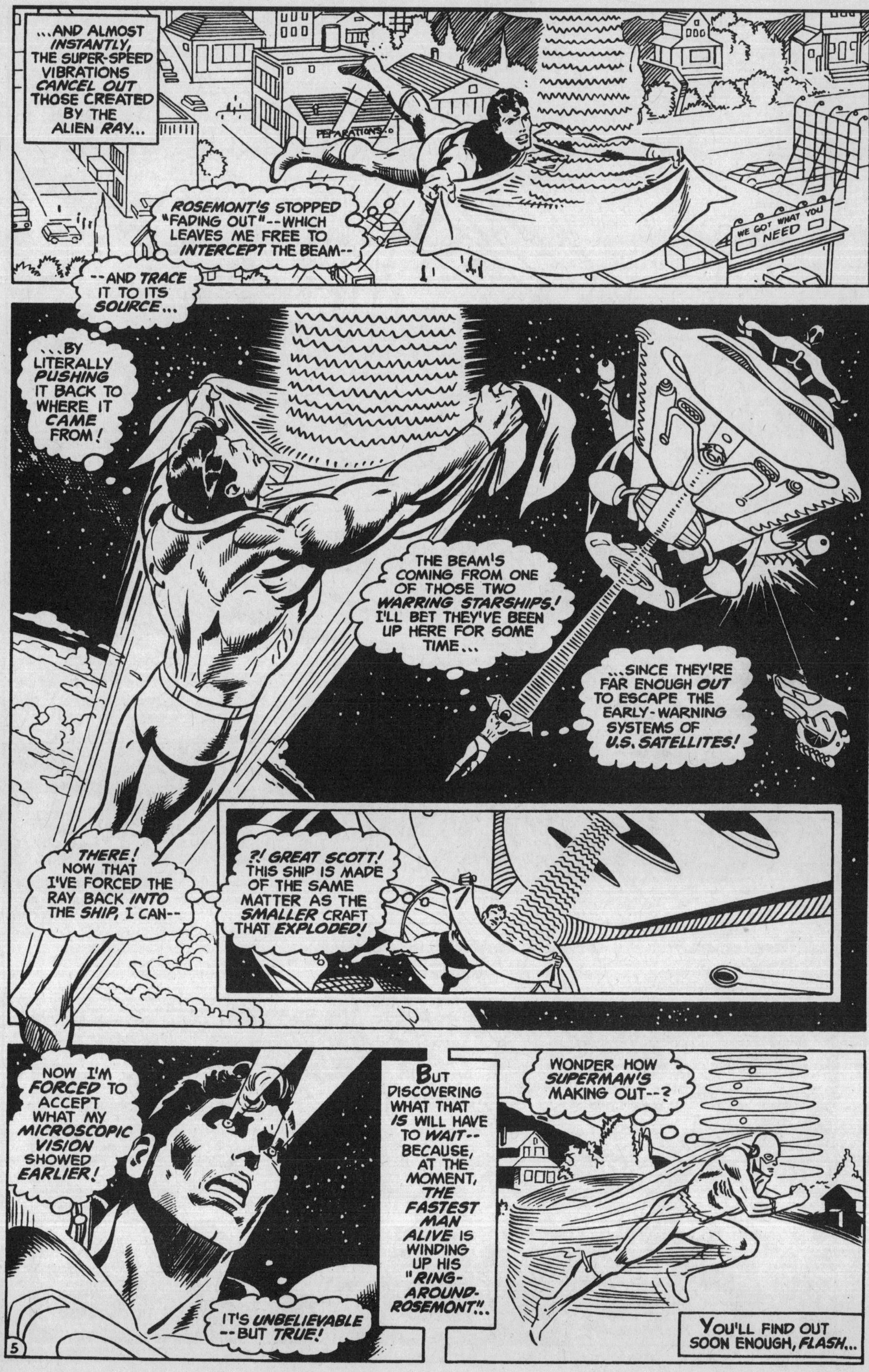
...AND ALMOST INSTANTLY, THE SUPER-SPEED VIBRATIONS CANCEL OUT THOSE CREATED BY THE ALIEN RAY...
REPARATIONS
ROSEMONT'S STOPPED "FADING OUT"--WHICH LEAVES ME FREE TO INTERCEPT THE BEAM--
WE GOT WHAT YOU NEED
--AND TRACE IT TO ITS SOURCE...
...BY LITERALLY PUSHING IT BACK TO WHERE IT CAME FROM!
THE BEAM'S COMING FROM ONE OF THOSE TWO WARRING STARSHIPS! I'LL BET THEY'VE BEEN UP HERE FOR SOME TIME...
...SINCE THEY'RE FAR ENOUGH OUT TO ESCAPE THE EARLY-WARNING SYSTEMS OF U.S. SATELLITES!
THERE! NOW THAT I'VE FORCED THE RAY BACK INTO THE SHIP, I CAN--
?! GREAT SCOTT! THIS SHIP IS MADE OF THE SAME MATTER AS THE SMALLER CRAFT THAT EXPLODED!
NOW I'M FORCED TO ACCEPT WHAT MY MICROSCOPIC VISION SHOWED EARLIER!
IT'S UNBELIEVABLE --BUT TRUE!
5
BUT DISCOVERING WHAT THAT IS WILL HAVE TO WAIT-- BECAUSE, AT THE MOMENT, THE FASTEST MAN ALIVE IS WINDING UP HIS "RING-AROUND-ROSEMONT"!..
WONDER HOW SUPERMAN'S MAKING OUT--?
YOU'LL FIND OUT SOON ENOUGH, FLASH...

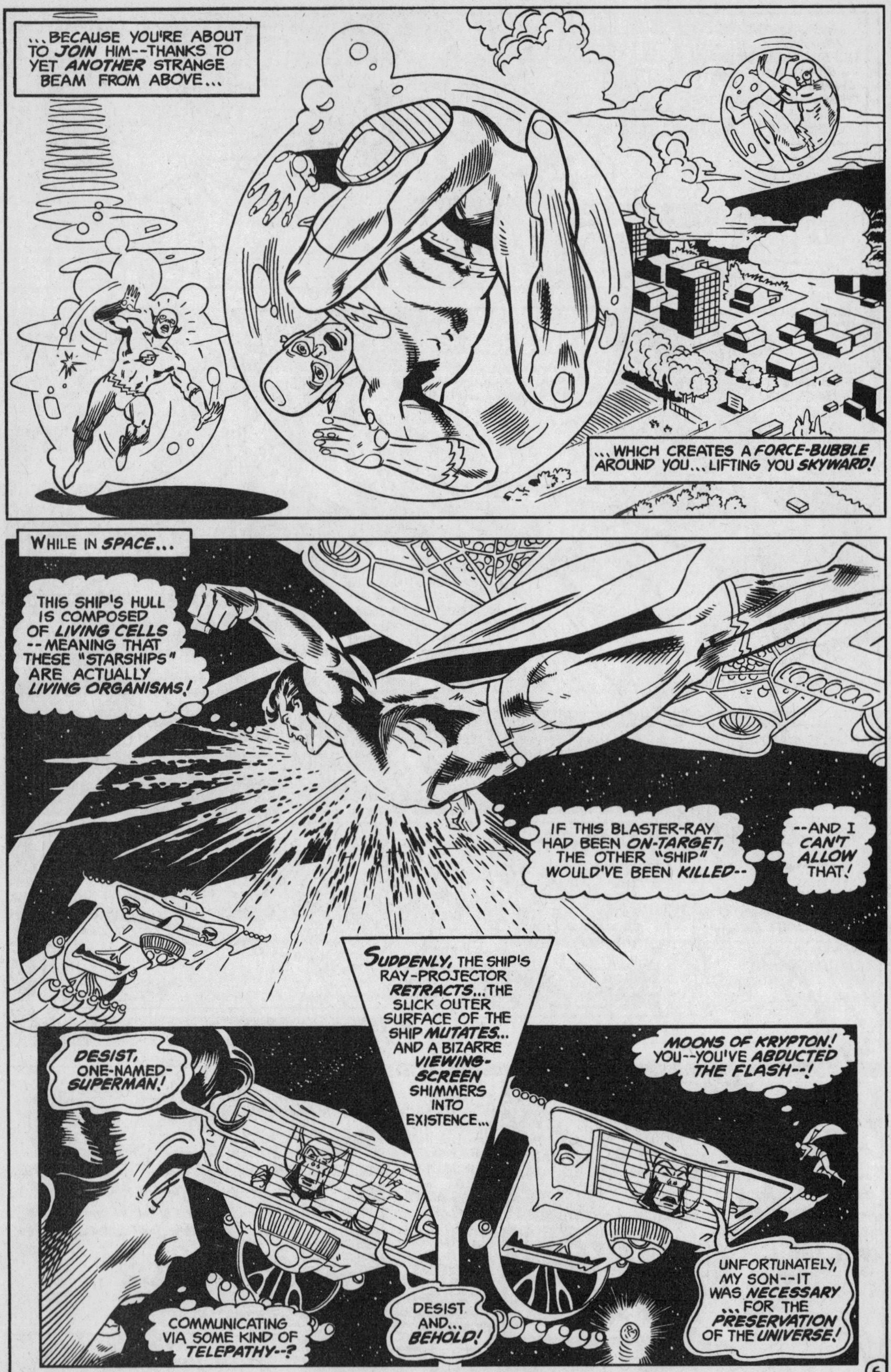
...BECAUSE YOU'RE ABOUT TO JOIN HIM--THANKS TO YET ANOTHER STRANGE BEAM FROM ABOVE...
...WHICH CREATES A FORCE-BUBBLE AROUND YOU... LIFTING YOU SKYWARD!
WHILE IN SPACE...
THIS SHIP'S HULL IS COMPOSED OF LIVING CELLS --MEANING THAT THESE "STARSHIPS" ARE ACTUALLY LIVING ORGANISMS!
IF THIS BLASTER-RAY HAD BEEN ON-TARGET, THE OTHER "SHIP" WOULD'VE BEEN KILLED--
--AND I CAN'T ALLOW THAT!
SUDDENLY, THE SHIP'S RAY-PROJECTOR RETRACTS... THE SLICK OUTER SURFACE OF THE SHIP MUTATES... AND A BIZARRE VIEWING-SCREEN SHIMMERS INTO EXISTENCE...
DESIST, ONE-NAMED-SUPERMAN!
COMMUNICATING VIA SOME KIND OF TELEPATHY--?
DESIST AND... BEHOLD!
MOONS OF KRYPTON! YOU--YOU'VE ABDUCTED THE FLASH--!
UNFORTUNATELY, MY SON--IT WAS NECESSARY ...FOR THE PRESERVATION OF THE UNIVERSE!
6

BUT BEFORE ANOTHER THOUGHT CAN BE TELEPATHICALLY "VOICED"...

WHAT?! YOU TRICKED ME--?!

AGAIN-- YES, IT CANNOT BE HELPED.

I AM SORRY, MY SON.

SUDDENLY, SUPERMAN FINDS HIS STRENGTH GONE--AND HE CAN ONLY WATCH HELPLESSLY AS STRANGE APPENDAGES GROW OUT OF THE BOWS OF THE LIVING SHIPS...

...AND SLOWLY...GRACEFULLY...THEY GLIDE TOWARD ONE ANOTHER...

...AS IF PERFORMING SOME WEIRD CEREMONY ...A KIND OF COSMIC MATING RITUAL BEFORE THEIR CAPTIVE AUDIENCE OF ONE...

BUT THE CAPED KRYPTONIAN CAN SEE THE MANEUVER FOR WHAT IT IS --A DOCKING IN SPACE...

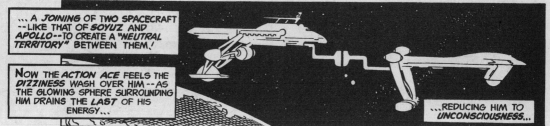

...A JOINING OF TWO SPACECRAFT --LIKE THAT OF SOYUZ AND APOLLO--TO CREATE A "NEUTRAL TERRITORY" BETWEEN THEM!

NOW THE ACTION ACE FEELS THE DIZZINESS WASH OVER HIM -- AS THE GLOWING SPHERE SURROUNDING HIM DRAINS THE LAST OF HIS ENERGY...

...REDUCING HIM TO UNCONSCIOUSNESS...

...FROM WHICH HE IS STIRRED BY THE STRIDENT VOICE OF AN ALIEN MARTINET...

WELCOME ABOARD, ONE-NAMED-SUPERMAN. I AM ISLAYN-- LEADER OF THE VOLKIR AND CAPTAIN OF THE VESSEL WHICH CAPTURED YOU!

WE ARE ALSO RESPONSIBLE FOR THE VIBRATIONAL-BEAM WHICH STRUCK THE PLACE YOU CALL ROSEMONT!

7

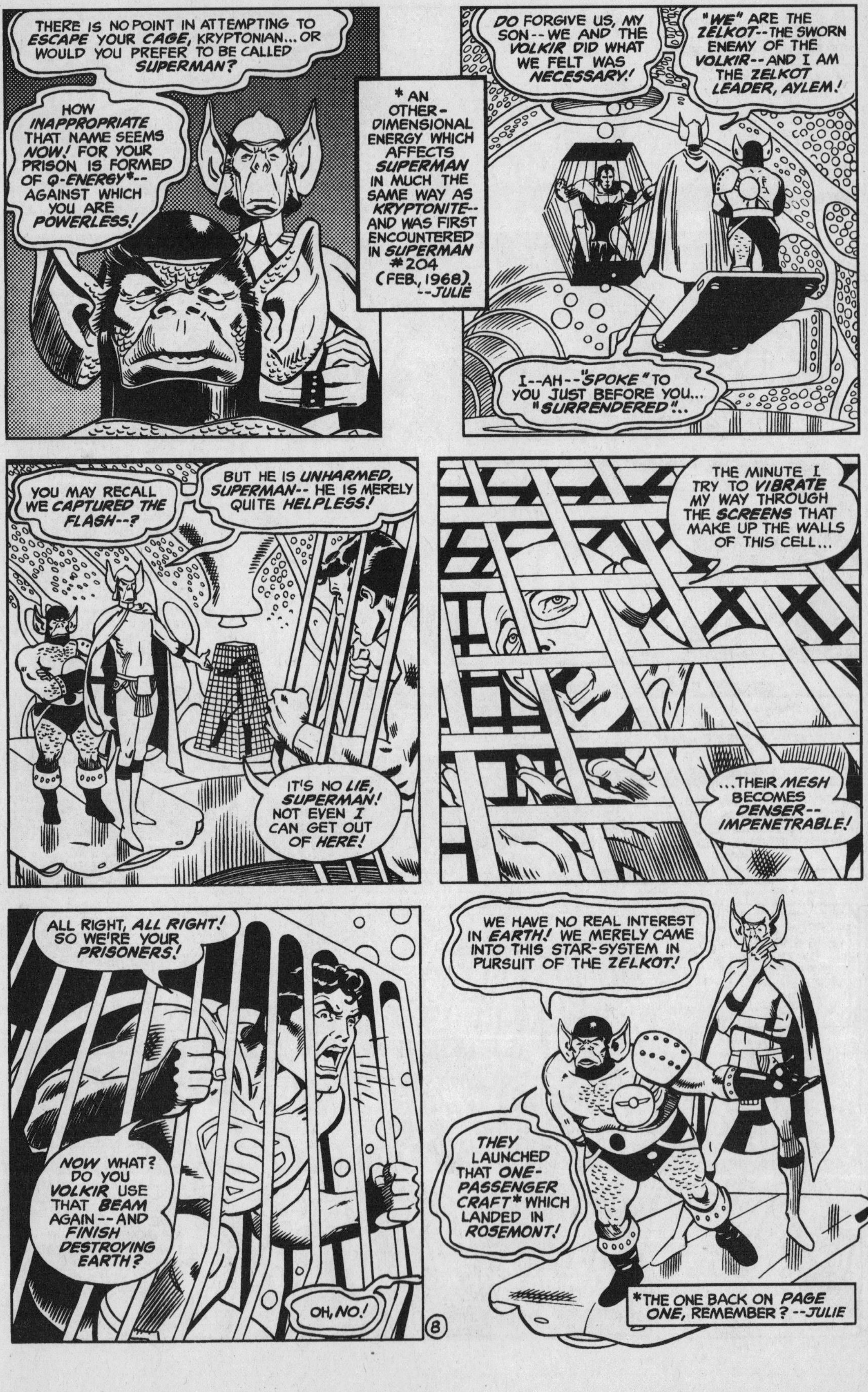
THERE IS NO POINT IN ATTEMPTING TO ESCAPE YOUR CAGE, KRYPTONIAN... OR WOULD YOU PREFER TO BE CALLED SUPERMAN?
HOW INAPPROPRIATE THAT NAME SEEMS NOW! FOR YOUR PRISON IS FORMED OF Q-ENERGY*-- AGAINST WHICH YOU ARE POWERLESS!
* AN OTHER-DIMENSIONAL ENERGY WHICH AFFECTS SUPERMAN IN MUCH THE SAME WAY AS KRYPTONITE-- AND WAS FIRST ENCOUNTERED IN SUPERMAN #204 (FEB., 1968). --JULIE
DO FORGIVE US, MY SON--WE AND THE VOLKIR DID WHAT WE FELT WAS NECESSARY!
"WE" ARE THE ZELKOT--THE SWORN ENEMY OF THE VOLKIR--AND I AM THE ZELKOT LEADER, AYLEM!
I--AH--"SPOKE" TO YOU JUST BEFORE YOU... "SURRENDERED"!..
YOU MAY RECALL WE CAPTURED THE FLASH--?
BUT HE IS UNHARMED, SUPERMAN-- HE IS MERELY QUITE HELPLESS!
IT'S NO LIE, SUPERMAN! NOT EVEN I CAN GET OUT OF HERE!
THE MINUTE I TRY TO VIBRATE MY WAY THROUGH THE SCREENS THAT MAKE UP THE WALLS OF THIS CELL...
...THEIR MESH BECOMES DENSER-- IMPENETRABLE!
ALL RIGHT, ALL RIGHT! SO WE'RE YOUR PRISONERS!
NOW WHAT? DO YOU VOLKIR USE THAT BEAM AGAIN--AND FINISH DESTROYING EARTH?
OH, NO!
8
WE HAVE NO REAL INTEREST IN EARTH! WE MERELY CAME INTO THIS STAR-SYSTEM IN PURSUIT OF THE ZELKOT!
THEY LAUNCHED THAT ONE-PASSENGER CRAFT* WHICH LANDED IN ROSEMONT!
*THE ONE BACK ON PAGE ONE, REMEMBER? --JULIE

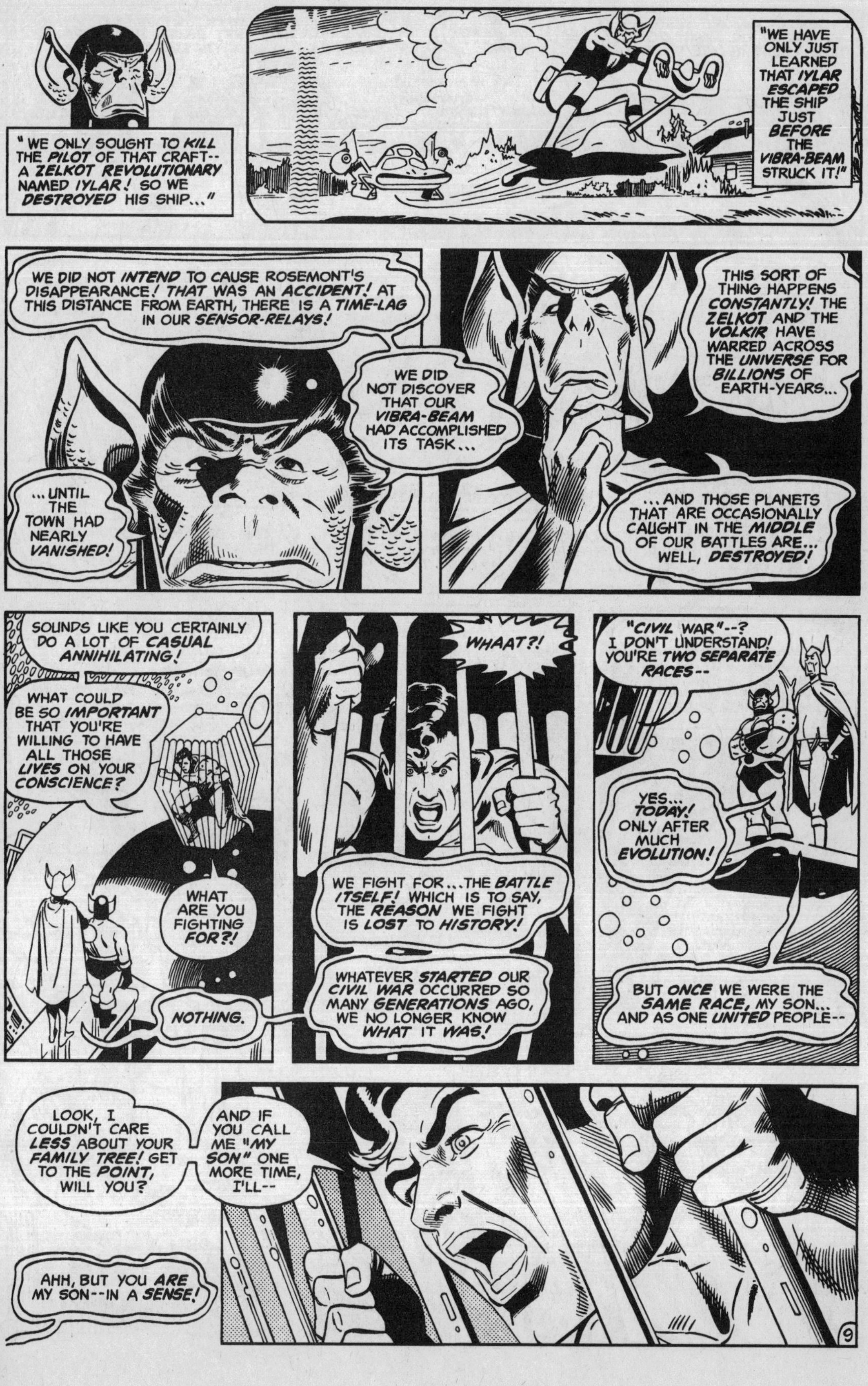
"WE ONLY SOUGHT TO KILL THE PILOT OF THAT CRAFT-- A ZELKOT REVOLUTIONARY NAMED IYLAR! SO WE DESTROYED HIS SHIP..."
"WE HAVE ONLY JUST LEARNED THAT IYLAR ESCAPED THE SHIP JUST BEFORE THE VIBRA-BEAM STRUCK IT!"
WE DID NOT INTEND TO CAUSE ROSEMONT'S DISAPPEARANCE! THAT WAS AN ACCIDENT! AT THIS DISTANCE FROM EARTH, THERE IS A TIME-LAG IN OUR SENSOR-RELAYS!
WE DID NOT DISCOVER THAT OUR VIBRA-BEAM HAD ACCOMPLISHED ITS TASK...
...UNTIL THE TOWN HAD NEARLY VANISHED!
THIS SORT OF THING HAPPENS CONSTANTLY! THE ZELKOT AND THE VOLKIR HAVE WARRED ACROSS THE UNIVERSE FOR BILLIONS OF EARTH-YEARS...
...AND THOSE PLANETS THAT ARE OCCASIONALLY CAUGHT IN THE MIDDLE OF OUR BATTLES ARE... WELL, DESTROYED!
SOUNDS LIKE YOU CERTAINLY DO A LOT OF CASUAL ANNIHILATING!
WHAT COULD BE SO IMPORTANT THAT YOU'RE WILLING TO HAVE ALL THOSE LIVES ON YOUR CONSCIENCE?
WHAT ARE YOU FIGHTING FOR?!
NOTHING.
WHAAT?!
WE FIGHT FOR...THE BATTLE ITSELF! WHICH IS TO SAY, THE REASON WE FIGHT IS LOST TO HISTORY!
WHATEVER STARTED OUR CIVIL WAR OCCURRED SO MANY GENERATIONS AGO, WE NO LONGER KNOW WHAT IT WAS!
"CIVIL WAR"--? I DON'T UNDERSTAND! YOU'RE TWO SEPARATE RACES--
YES... TODAY! ONLY AFTER MUCH EVOLUTION!
BUT ONCE WE WERE THE SAME RACE, MY SON... AND AS ONE UNITED PEOPLE--
LOOK, I COULDN'T CARE LESS ABOUT YOUR FAMILY TREE! GET TO THE POINT, WILL YOU?
AND IF YOU CALL ME "MY SON" ONE MORE TIME, I'LL--
AHH, BUT YOU ARE MY SON--IN A SENSE!
9

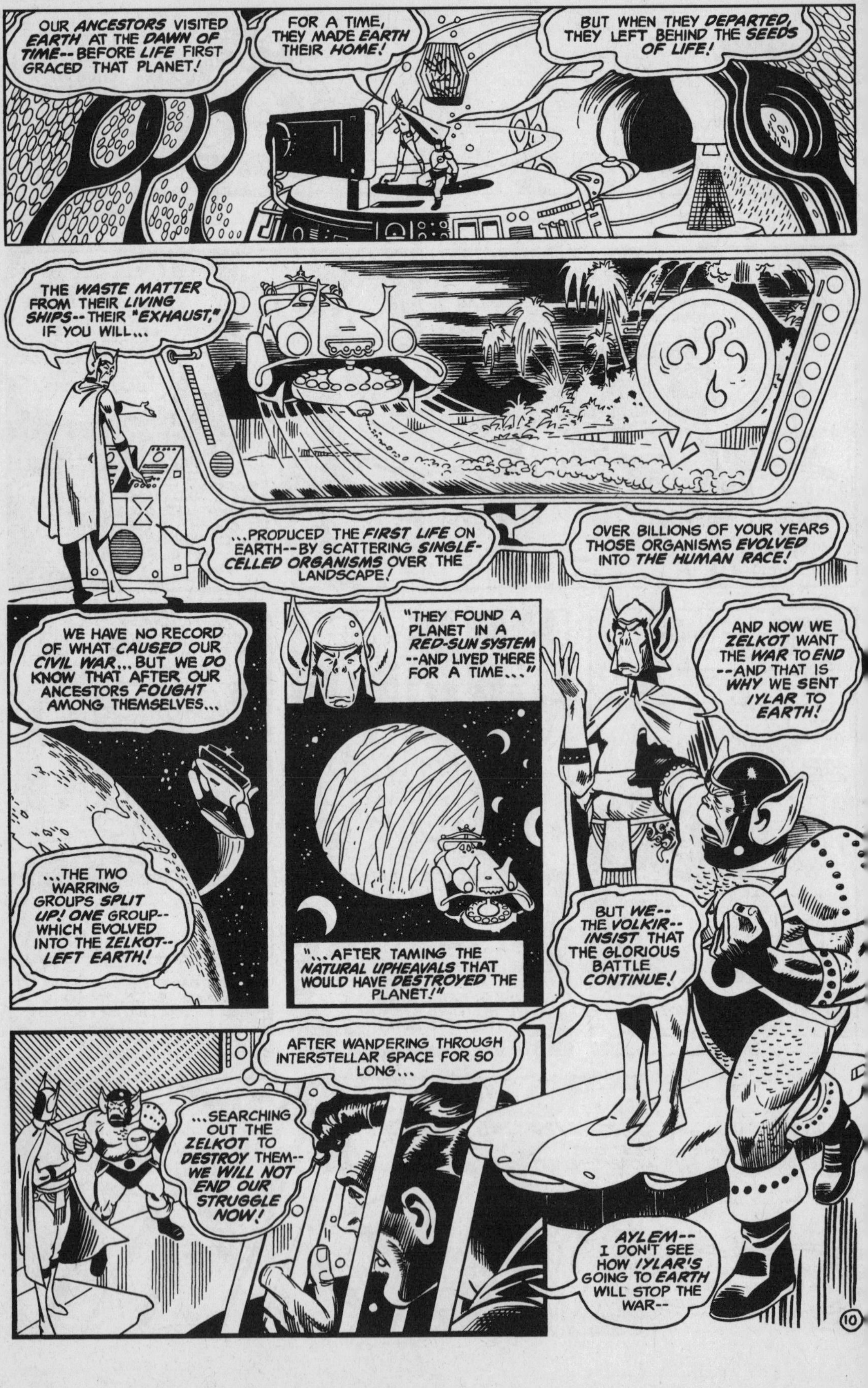
OUR ANCESTORS VISITED EARTH AT THE DAWN OF TIME-- BEFORE LIFE FIRST GRACED THAT PLANET!
FOR A TIME, THEY MADE EARTH THEIR HOME!
BUT WHEN THEY DEPARTED, THEY LEFT BEHIND THE SEEDS OF LIFE!
THE WASTE MATTER FROM THEIR LIVING SHIPS-- THEIR "EXHAUST," IF YOU WILL...
...PRODUCED THE FIRST LIFE ON EARTH--BY SCATTERING SINGLE-CELLED ORGANISMS OVER THE LANDSCAPE!
OVER BILLIONS OF YOUR YEARS THOSE ORGANISMS EVOLVED INTO THE HUMAN RACE!
WE HAVE NO RECORD OF WHAT CAUSED OUR CIVIL WAR... BUT WE DO KNOW THAT AFTER OUR ANCESTORS FOUGHT AMONG THEMSELVES...
...THE TWO WARRING GROUPS SPLIT UP! ONE GROUP-- WHICH EVOLVED INTO THE ZELKOT-- LEFT EARTH!
"THEY FOUND A PLANET IN A RED-SUN SYSTEM --AND LIVED THERE FOR A TIME..."
"...AFTER TAMING THE NATURAL UPHEAVALS THAT WOULD HAVE DESTROYED THE PLANET!"
AND NOW WE ZELKOT WANT THE WAR TO END --AND THAT IS WHY WE SENT IYLAR TO EARTH!
BUT WE-- THE VOLKIR-- INSIST THAT THE GLORIOUS BATTLE CONTINUE!
AFTER WANDERING THROUGH INTERSTELLAR SPACE FOR SO LONG...
...SEARCHING OUT THE ZELKOT TO DESTROY THEM-- WE WILL NOT END OUR STRUGGLE NOW!
AYLEM-- I DON'T SEE HOW IYLAR'S GOING TO EARTH WILL STOP THE WAR--
10

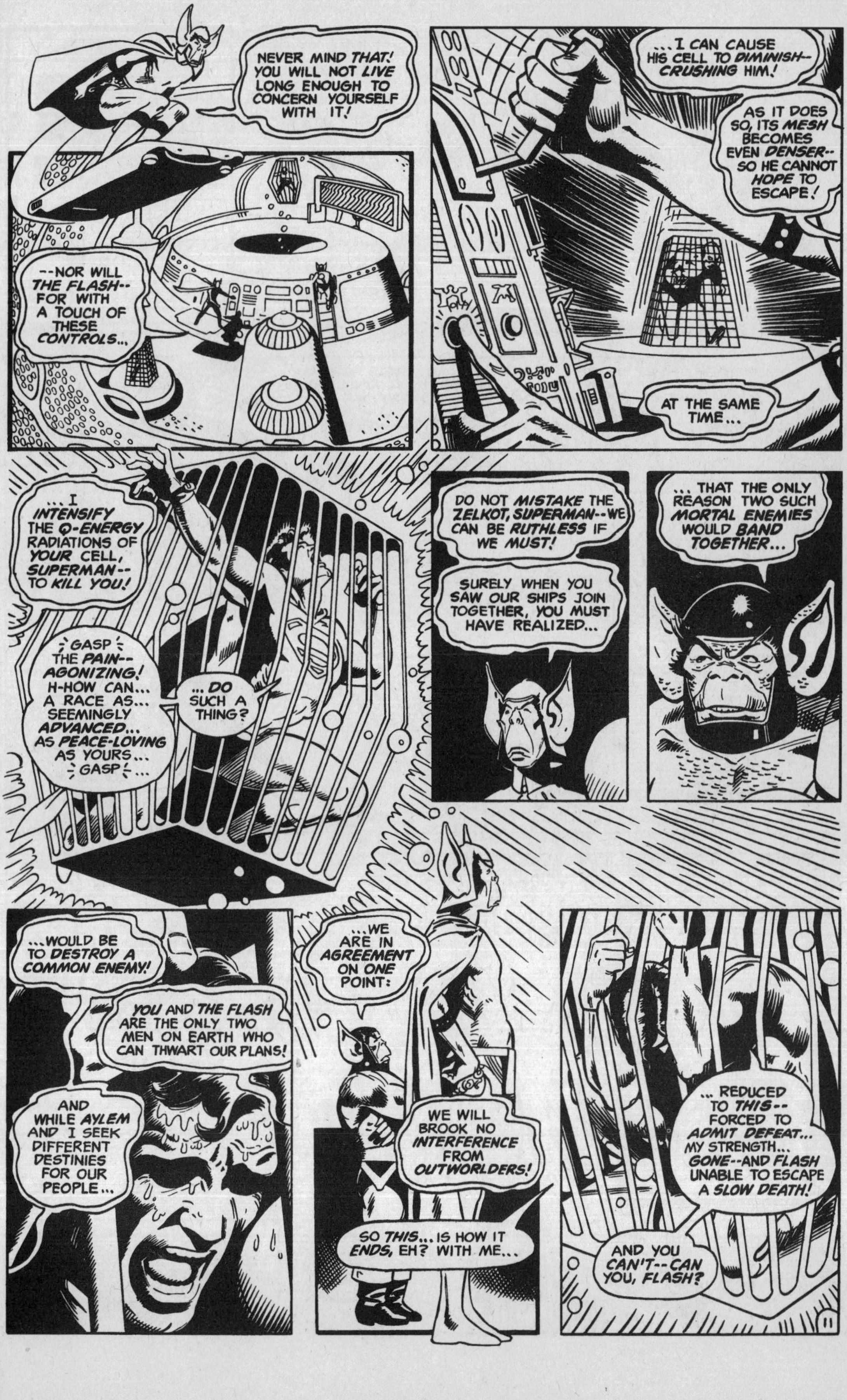
NEVER MIND THAT! YOU WILL NOT LIVE LONG ENOUGH TO CONCERN YOURSELF WITH IT!
--NOR WILL THE FLASH--FOR WITH A TOUCH OF THESE CONTROLS...
...I CAN CAUSE HIS CELL TO DIMINISH--CRUSHING HIM!
AS IT DOES SO, ITS MESH BECOMES EVEN DENSER--SO HE CANNOT HOPE TO ESCAPE!
AT THE SAME TIME...
...I INTENSIFY THE Q-ENERGY RADIATIONS OF YOUR CELL, SUPERMAN--TO KILL YOU!
GASP THE PAIN--AGONIZING! H-HOW CAN... A RACE AS... SEEMINGLY ADVANCED... AS PEACE-LOVING AS YOURS... GASP...
...DO SUCH A THING?
DO NOT MISTAKE THE ZELKOT, SUPERMAN--WE CAN BE RUTHLESS IF WE MUST!
SURELY WHEN YOU SAW OUR SHIPS JOIN TOGETHER, YOU MUST HAVE REALIZED...
...THAT THE ONLY REASON TWO SUCH MORTAL ENEMIES WOULD BAND TOGETHER...
...WOULD BE TO DESTROY A COMMON ENEMY!
YOU AND THE FLASH ARE THE ONLY TWO MEN ON EARTH WHO CAN THWART OUR PLANS!
AND WHILE AYLEM AND I SEEK DIFFERENT DESTINIES FOR OUR PEOPLE...
...WE ARE IN AGREEMENT ON ONE POINT:
WE WILL BROOK NO INTERFERENCE FROM OUTWORLDERS!
SO THIS... IS HOW IT ENDS, EH? WITH ME...
...REDUCED TO THIS--FORCED TO ADMIT DEFEAT... MY STRENGTH... GONE--AND FLASH UNABLE TO ESCAPE A SLOW DEATH!
AND YOU CAN'T--CAN YOU, FLASH?
11

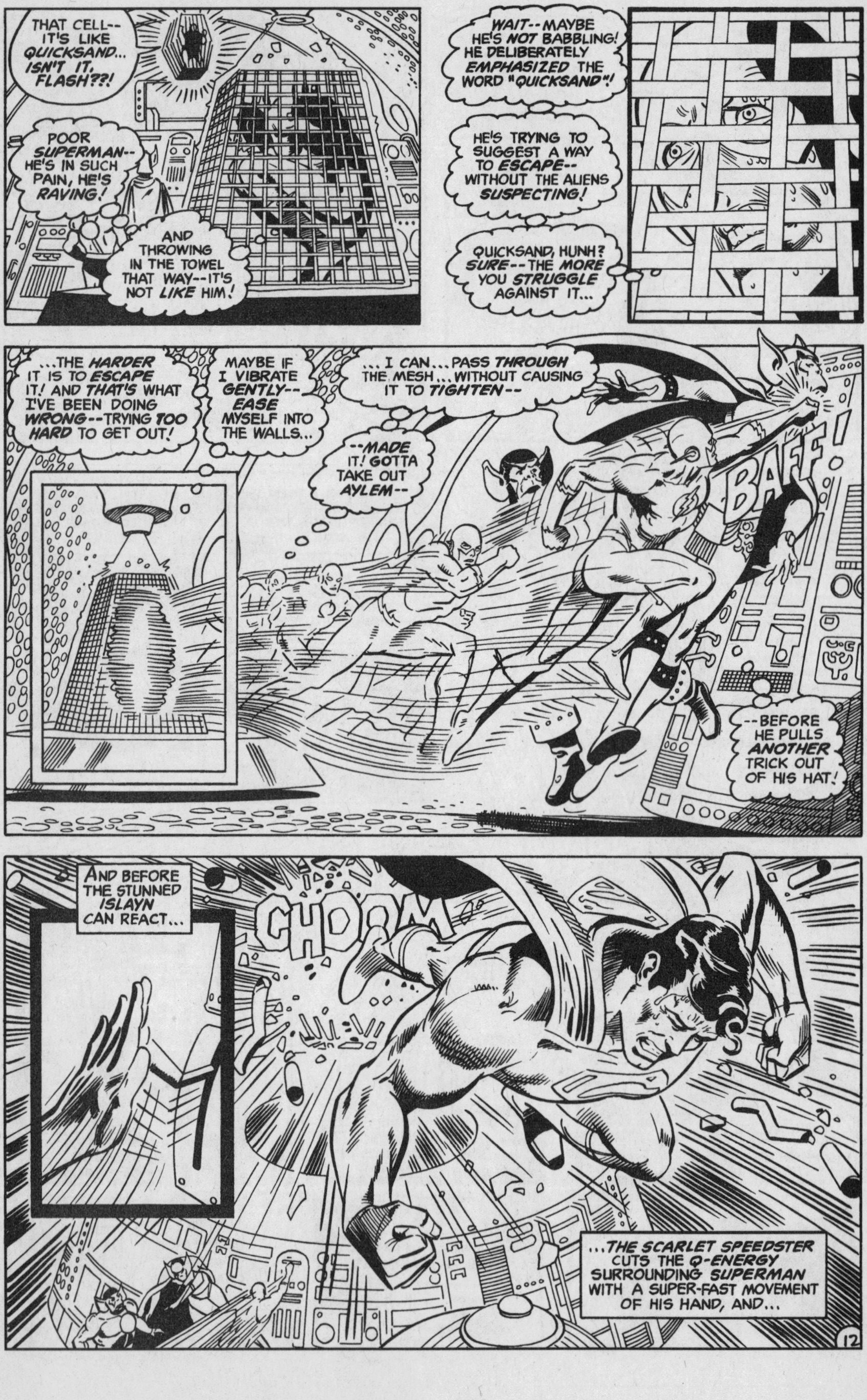
THAT CELL-- IT'S LIKE QUICKSAND... ISN'T IT, FLASH??!
POOR SUPERMAN-- HE'S IN SUCH PAIN, HE'S RAVING!
AND THROWING IN THE TOWEL THAT WAY--IT'S NOT LIKE HIM!
WAIT--MAYBE HE'S NOT BABBLING! HE DELIBERATELY EMPHASIZED THE WORD "QUICKSAND"!
HE'S TRYING TO SUGGEST A WAY TO ESCAPE-- WITHOUT THE ALIENS SUSPECTING!
QUICKSAND, HUNH? SURE--THE MORE YOU STRUGGLE AGAINST IT...
...THE HARDER IT IS TO ESCAPE IT! AND THAT'S WHAT I'VE BEEN DOING WRONG--TRYING TOO HARD TO GET OUT!
MAYBE IF I VIBRATE GENTLY-- EASE MYSELF INTO THE WALLS...
...I CAN...PASS THROUGH THE MESH...WITHOUT CAUSING IT TO TIGHTEN--
--MADE IT! GOTTA TAKE OUT AYLEM--
BAFF!
--BEFORE HE PULLS ANOTHER TRICK OUT OF HIS HAT!
AND BEFORE THE STUNNED ISLAYN CAN REACT...
CHOOM
...THE SCARLET SPEEDSTER CUTS THE Q-ENERGY SURROUNDING SUPERMAN WITH A SUPER-FAST MOVEMENT OF HIS HAND, AND...
12

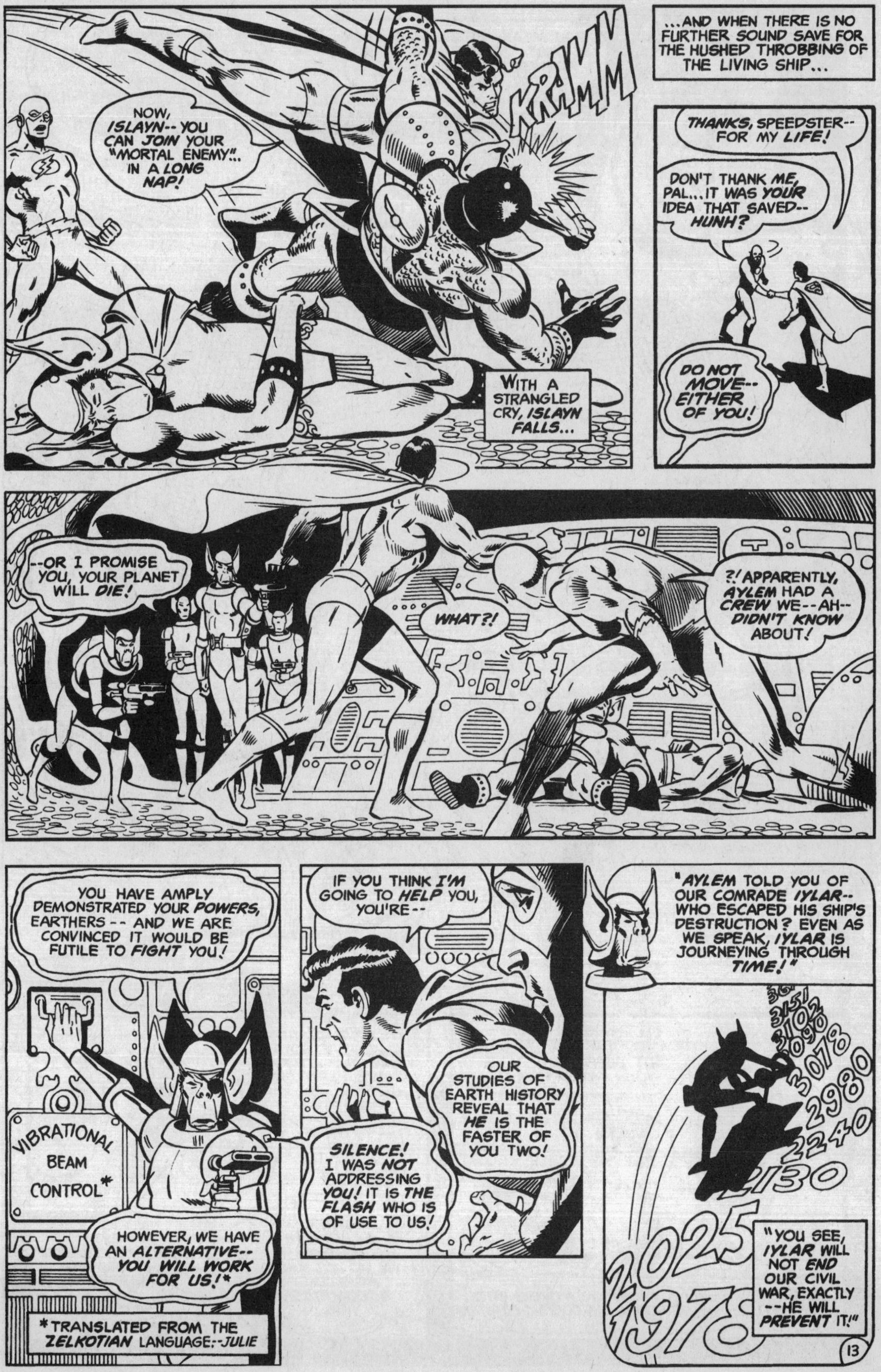
NOW, ISLAYN-- YOU CAN JOIN YOUR "MORTAL ENEMY"... IN A LONG NAP!
KRAMM
WITH A STRANGLED CRY, ISLAYN FALLS...
...AND WHEN THERE IS NO FURTHER SOUND SAVE FOR THE HUSHED THROBBING OF THE LIVING SHIP...
THANKS, SPEEDSTER-- FOR MY LIFE!
DON'T THANK ME, PAL...IT WAS YOUR IDEA THAT SAVED-- HUNH?
DO NOT MOVE-- EITHER OF YOU!
--OR I PROMISE YOU, YOUR PLANET WILL DIE!
WHAT?!
?! APPARENTLY, AYLEM HAD A CREW WE--AH-- DIDN'T KNOW ABOUT!
YOU HAVE AMPLY DEMONSTRATED YOUR POWERS, EARTHERS -- AND WE ARE CONVINCED IT WOULD BE FUTILE TO FIGHT YOU!
VIBRATIONAL BEAM CONTROL*
HOWEVER, WE HAVE AN ALTERNATIVE-- YOU WILL WORK FOR US!*
*TRANSLATED FROM THE ZELKOTIAN LANGUAGE.--JULIE
IF YOU THINK I'M GOING TO HELP YOU, YOU'RE--
OUR STUDIES OF EARTH HISTORY REVEAL THAT HE IS THE FASTER OF YOU TWO!
SILENCE! I WAS NOT ADDRESSING YOU! IT IS THE FLASH WHO IS OF USE TO US!
"AYLEM TOLD YOU OF OUR COMRADE IYLAR-- WHO ESCAPED HIS SHIP'S DESTRUCTION? EVEN AS WE SPEAK, IYLAR IS JOURNEYING THROUGH TIME!"
3151 3102 3090 3078 2980 2240 2130 2025 1978
"YOU SEE, IYLAR WILL NOT END OUR CIVIL WAR, EXACTLY --HE WILL PREVENT IT!"
13

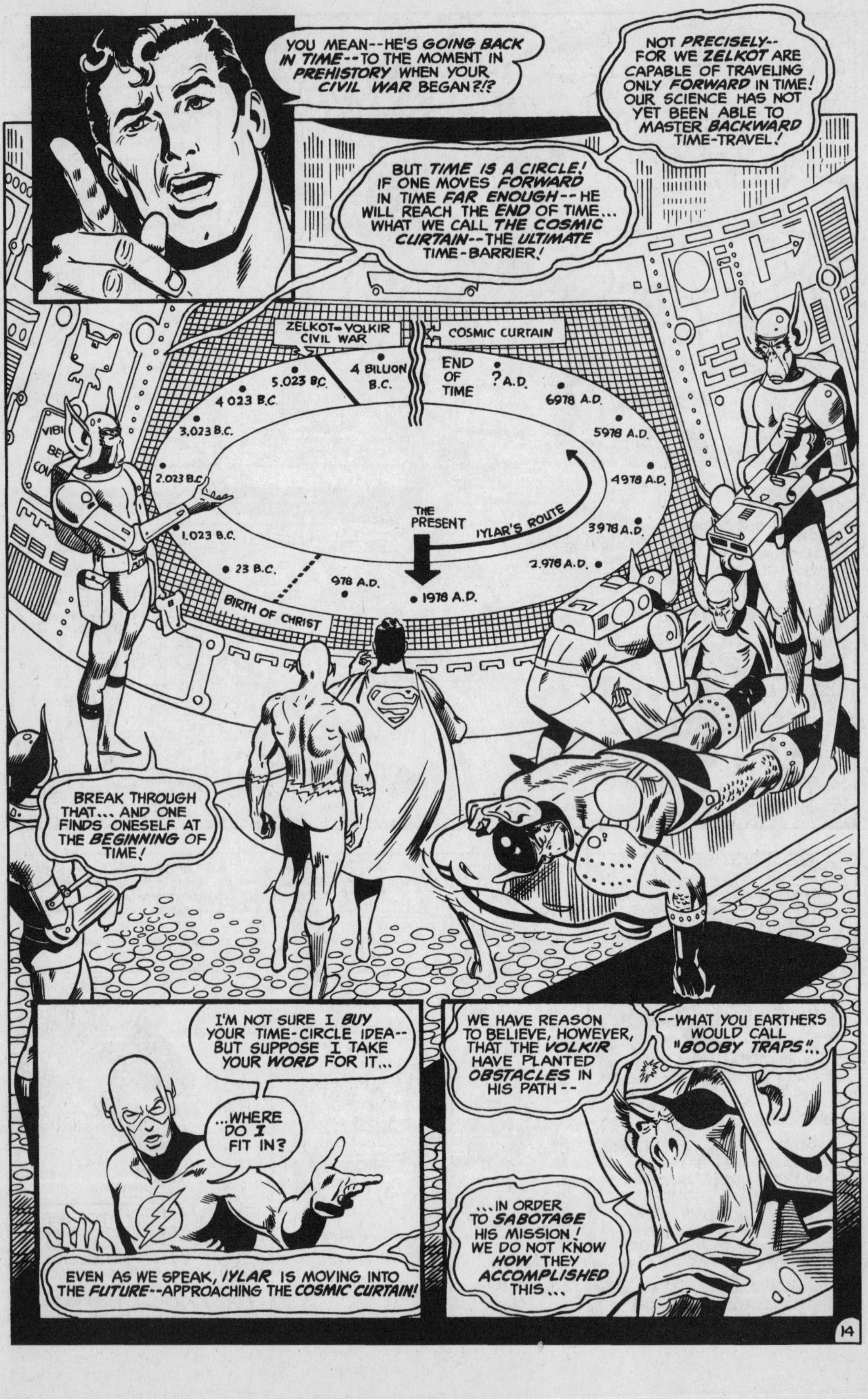
YOU MEAN--HE'S GOING BACK IN TIME--TO THE MOMENT IN PREHISTORY WHEN YOUR CIVIL WAR BEGAN?!?
NOT PRECISELY--FOR WE ZELKOT ARE CAPABLE OF TRAVELING ONLY FORWARD IN TIME! OUR SCIENCE HAS NOT YET BEEN ABLE TO MASTER BACKWARD TIME-TRAVEL!
BUT TIME IS A CIRCLE! IF ONE MOVES FORWARD IN TIME FAR ENOUGH--HE WILL REACH THE END OF TIME... WHAT WE CALL THE COSMIC CURTAIN--THE ULTIMATE TIME-BARRIER!
ZELKOT-VOLKIR CIVIL WAR
COSMIC CURTAIN
4 BILLION B.C.
END OF TIME
? A.D.
5,023 B.C.
4,023 B.C.
3,023 B.C.
2,023 B.C.
1,023 B.C.
23 B.C.
978 A.D.
1978 A.D.
2,978 A.D.
3,978 A.D.
4,978 A.D.
5,978 A.D.
6,978 A.D.
THE PRESENT
IYLAR'S ROUTE
BIRTH OF CHRIST
BREAK THROUGH THAT... AND ONE FINDS ONESELF AT THE BEGINNING OF TIME!
I'M NOT SURE I BUY YOUR TIME-CIRCLE IDEA--BUT SUPPOSE I TAKE YOUR WORD FOR IT...
...WHERE DO I FIT IN?
EVEN AS WE SPEAK, IYLAR IS MOVING INTO THE FUTURE--APPROACHING THE COSMIC CURTAIN!
WE HAVE REASON TO BELIEVE, HOWEVER, THAT THE VOLKIR HAVE PLANTED OBSTACLES IN HIS PATH--
--WHAT YOU EARTHERS WOULD CALL "BOOBY TRAPS"...
...IN ORDER TO SABOTAGE HIS MISSION! WE DO NOT KNOW HOW THEY ACCOMPLISHED THIS...
14

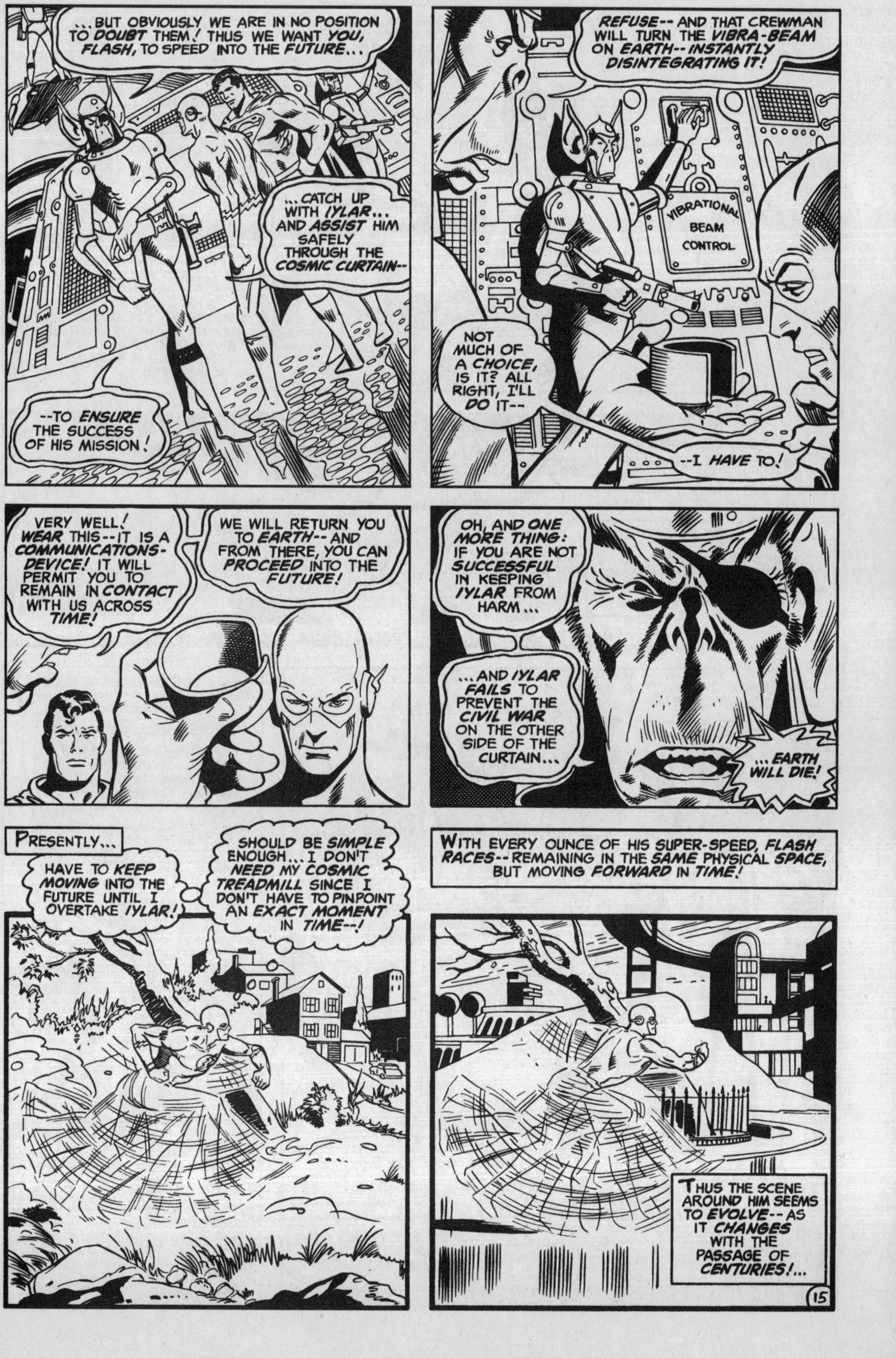
...BUT OBVIOUSLY WE ARE IN NO POSITION TO DOUBT THEM! THUS WE WANT YOU, FLASH, TO SPEED INTO THE FUTURE...
...CATCH UP WITH IYLAR... AND ASSIST HIM SAFELY THROUGH THE COSMIC CURTAIN--
--TO ENSURE THE SUCCESS OF HIS MISSION!
REFUSE-- AND THAT CREWMAN WILL TURN THE VIBRA-BEAM ON EARTH-- INSTANTLY DISINTEGRATING IT!
VIBRATIONAL BEAM CONTROL
NOT MUCH OF A CHOICE, IS IT? ALL RIGHT, I'LL DO IT--
--I HAVE TO!
VERY WELL! WEAR THIS--IT IS A COMMUNICATIONS-DEVICE! IT WILL PERMIT YOU TO REMAIN IN CONTACT WITH US ACROSS TIME!
WE WILL RETURN YOU TO EARTH-- AND FROM THERE, YOU CAN PROCEED INTO THE FUTURE!
OH, AND ONE MORE THING: IF YOU ARE NOT SUCCESSFUL IN KEEPING IYLAR FROM HARM...
...AND IYLAR FAILS TO PREVENT THE CIVIL WAR ON THE OTHER SIDE OF THE CURTAIN...
...EARTH WILL DIE!
PRESENTLY...
HAVE TO KEEP MOVING INTO THE FUTURE UNTIL I OVERTAKE IYLAR!
SHOULD BE SIMPLE ENOUGH... I DON'T NEED MY COSMIC TREADMILL SINCE I DON'T HAVE TO PINPOINT AN EXACT MOMENT IN TIME--!
WITH EVERY OUNCE OF HIS SUPER-SPEED, FLASH RACES-- REMAINING IN THE SAME PHYSICAL SPACE, BUT MOVING FORWARD IN TIME!
THUS THE SCENE AROUND HIM SEEMS TO EVOLVE-- AS IT CHANGES WITH THE PASSAGE OF CENTURIES!...
15

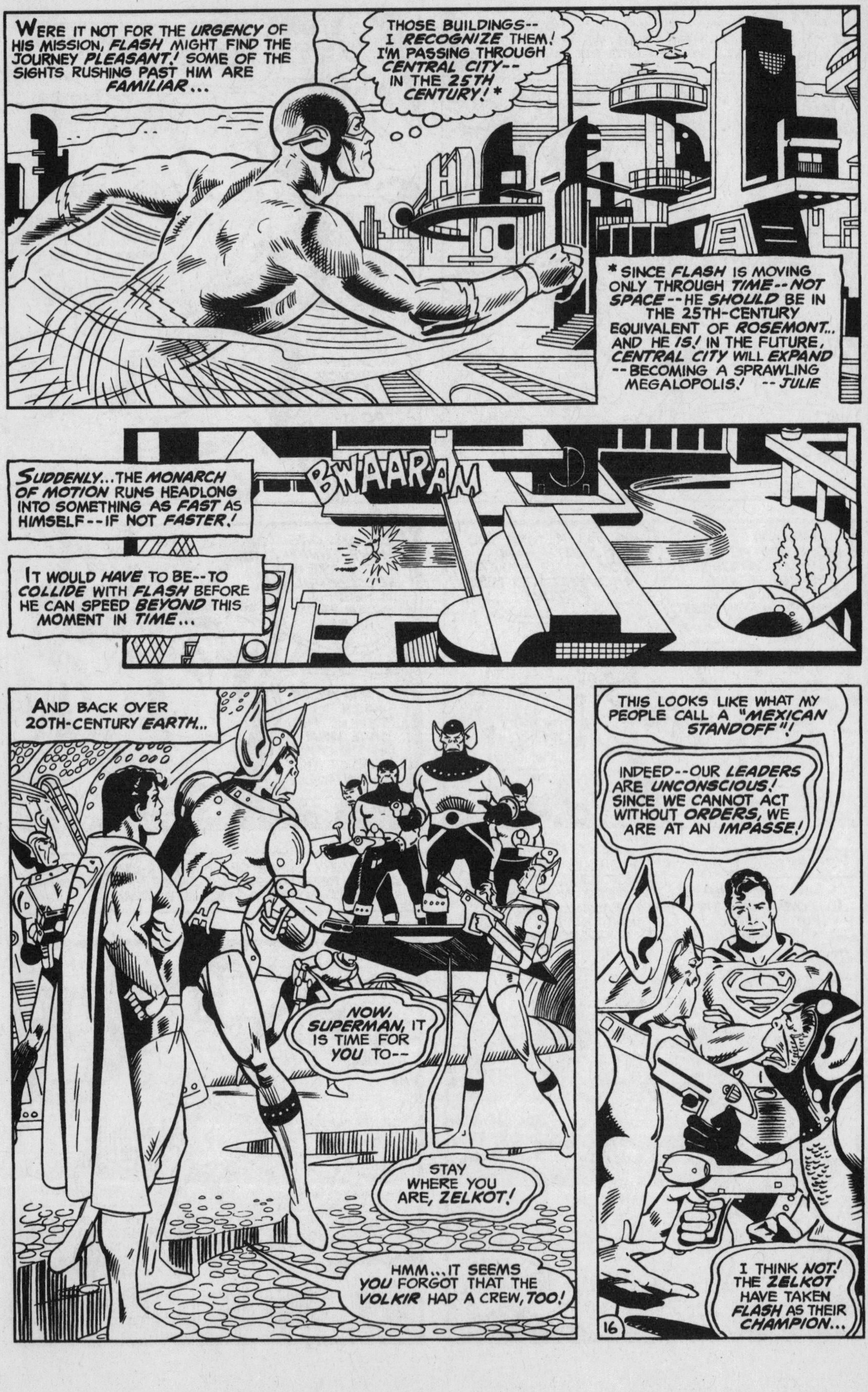
WERE IT NOT FOR THE URGENCY OF HIS MISSION, FLASH MIGHT FIND THE JOURNEY PLEASANT! SOME OF THE SIGHTS RUSHING PAST HIM ARE FAMILIAR...
THOSE BUILDINGS-- I RECOGNIZE THEM! I'M PASSING THROUGH CENTRAL CITY-- IN THE 25TH CENTURY! *
* SINCE FLASH IS MOVING ONLY THROUGH TIME--NOT SPACE--HE SHOULD BE IN THE 25TH-CENTURY EQUIVALENT OF ROSEMONT... AND HE IS! IN THE FUTURE, CENTRAL CITY WILL EXPAND --BECOMING A SPRAWLING MEGALOPOLIS! --JULIE
SUDDENLY...THE MONARCH OF MOTION RUNS HEADLONG INTO SOMETHING AS FAST AS HIMSELF--IF NOT FASTER!
BWAARAM
IT WOULD HAVE TO BE--TO COLLIDE WITH FLASH BEFORE HE CAN SPEED BEYOND THIS MOMENT IN TIME...
AND BACK OVER 20TH-CENTURY EARTH...
NOW, SUPERMAN, IT IS TIME FOR YOU TO--
STAY WHERE YOU ARE, ZELKOT!
HMM...IT SEEMS YOU FORGOT THAT THE VOLKIR HAD A CREW, TOO!
THIS LOOKS LIKE WHAT MY PEOPLE CALL A "MEXICAN STANDOFF"!
INDEED--OUR LEADERS ARE UNCONSCIOUS! SINCE WE CANNOT ACT WITHOUT ORDERS, WE ARE AT AN IMPASSE!
I THINK NOT! THE ZELKOT HAVE TAKEN FLASH AS THEIR CHAMPION...
16

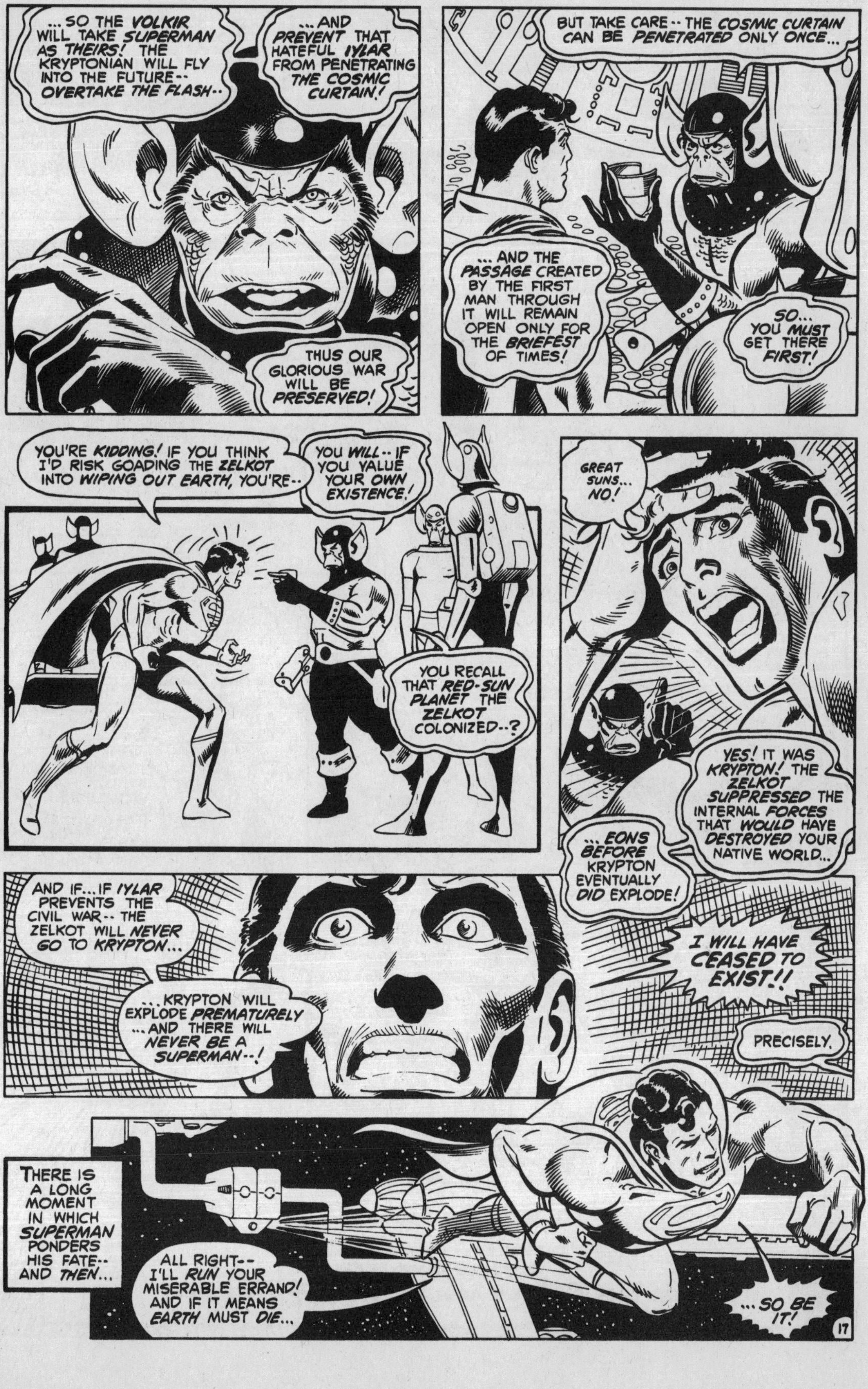
...SO THE VOLKIR WILL TAKE SUPERMAN AS THEIRS! THE KRYPTONIAN WILL FLY INTO THE FUTURE-- OVERTAKE THE FLASH--
...AND PREVENT THAT HATEFUL IYLAR FROM PENETRATING THE COSMIC CURTAIN!
THUS OUR GLORIOUS WAR WILL BE PRESERVED!
BUT TAKE CARE-- THE COSMIC CURTAIN CAN BE PENETRATED ONLY ONCE...
...AND THE PASSAGE CREATED BY THE FIRST MAN THROUGH IT WILL REMAIN OPEN ONLY FOR THE BRIEFEST OF TIMES!
SO... YOU MUST GET THERE FIRST!
YOU'RE KIDDING! IF YOU THINK I'D RISK GOADING THE ZELKOT INTO WIPING OUT EARTH, YOU'RE--
YOU WILL-- IF YOU VALUE YOUR OWN EXISTENCE!
YOU RECALL THAT RED-SUN PLANET THE ZELKOT COLONIZED--?
GREAT SUNS... NO!
YES! IT WAS KRYPTON! THE ZELKOT SUPPRESSED THE INTERNAL FORCES THAT WOULD HAVE DESTROYED YOUR NATIVE WORLD...
...EONS BEFORE KRYPTON EVENTUALLY DID EXPLODE!
AND IF... IF IYLAR PREVENTS THE CIVIL WAR-- THE ZELKOT WILL NEVER GO TO KRYPTON...
...KRYPTON WILL EXPLODE PREMATURELY ...AND THERE WILL NEVER BE A SUPERMAN--!
I WILL HAVE CEASED TO EXIST!!
PRECISELY.
THERE IS A LONG MOMENT IN WHICH SUPERMAN PONDERS HIS FATE-- AND THEN...
ALL RIGHT-- I'LL RUN YOUR MISERABLE ERRAND! AND IF IT MEANS EARTH MUST DIE...
...SO BE IT!
17

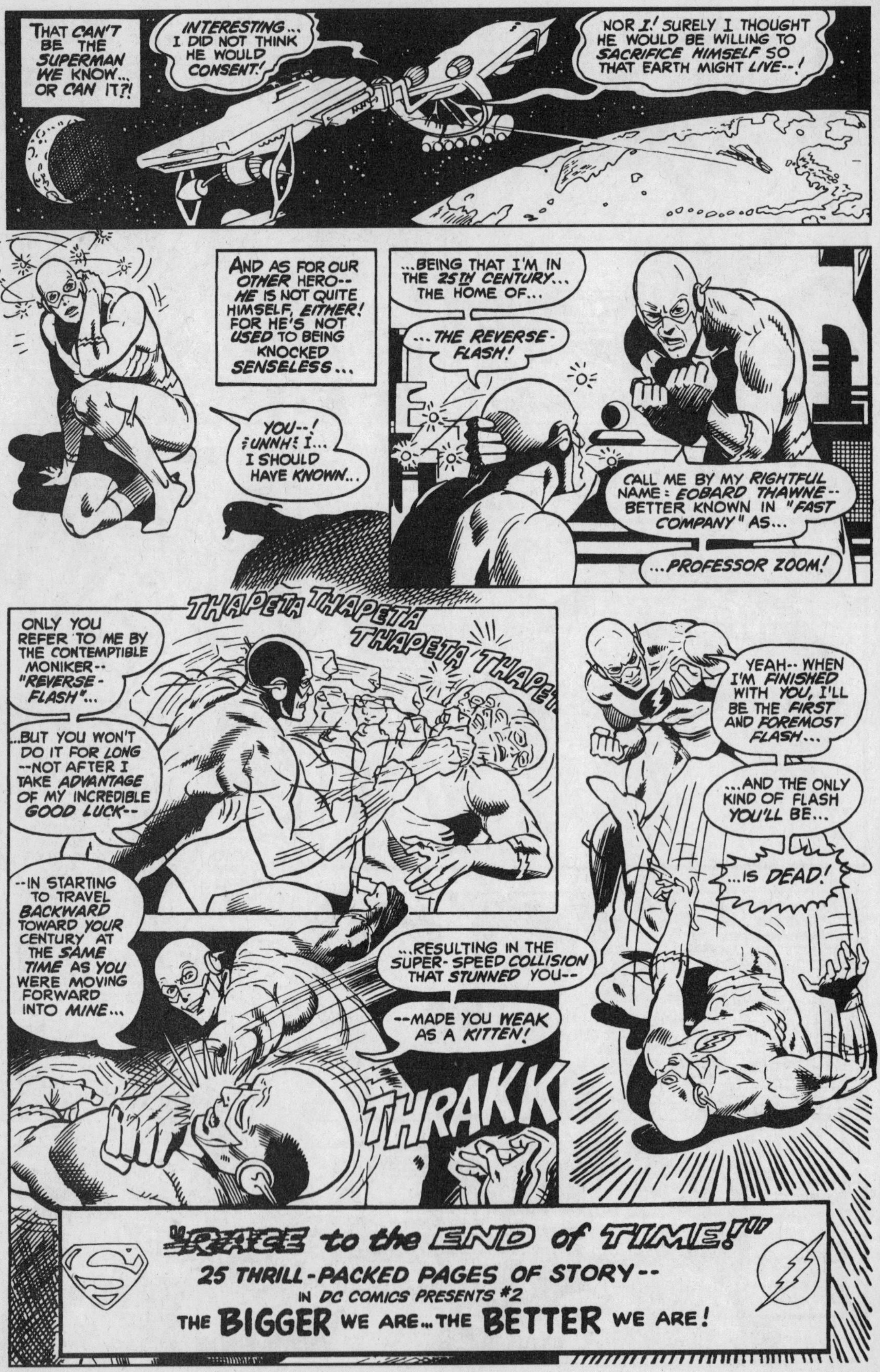
THAT CAN'T BE THE SUPERMAN WE KNOW... OR CAN IT?!
INTERESTING... I DID NOT THINK HE WOULD CONSENT!
NOR I! SURELY I THOUGHT HE WOULD BE WILLING TO SACRIFICE HIMSELF SO THAT EARTH MIGHT LIVE--!
AND AS FOR OUR OTHER HERO-- HE IS NOT QUITE HIMSELF, EITHER! FOR HE'S NOT USED TO BEING KNOCKED SENSELESS...
YOU--! UNNH! I... I SHOULD HAVE KNOWN...
...BEING THAT I'M IN THE 25TH CENTURY... THE HOME OF...
...THE REVERSE-FLASH!
CALL ME BY MY RIGHTFUL NAME: EOBARD THAWNE-- BETTER KNOWN IN "FAST COMPANY" AS...
...PROFESSOR ZOOM!
THAPETA THAPETA THAPETA THAPET
ONLY YOU REFER TO ME BY THE CONTEMPTIBLE MONIKER-- "REVERSE-FLASH"...
...BUT YOU WON'T DO IT FOR LONG --NOT AFTER I TAKE ADVANTAGE OF MY INCREDIBLE GOOD LUCK--
--IN STARTING TO TRAVEL BACKWARD TOWARD YOUR CENTURY AT THE SAME TIME AS YOU WERE MOVING FORWARD INTO MINE...
...RESULTING IN THE SUPER-SPEED COLLISION THAT STUNNED YOU--
--MADE YOU WEAK AS A KITTEN!
THRAKK
YEAH-- WHEN I'M FINISHED WITH YOU, I'LL BE THE FIRST AND FOREMOST FLASH...
...AND THE ONLY KIND OF FLASH YOU'LL BE...
...IS DEAD!
"RACE to the END of TIME!"
25 THRILL-PACKED PAGES OF STORY--
IN DC COMICS PRESENTS #2
THE BIGGER WE ARE... THE BETTER WE ARE!

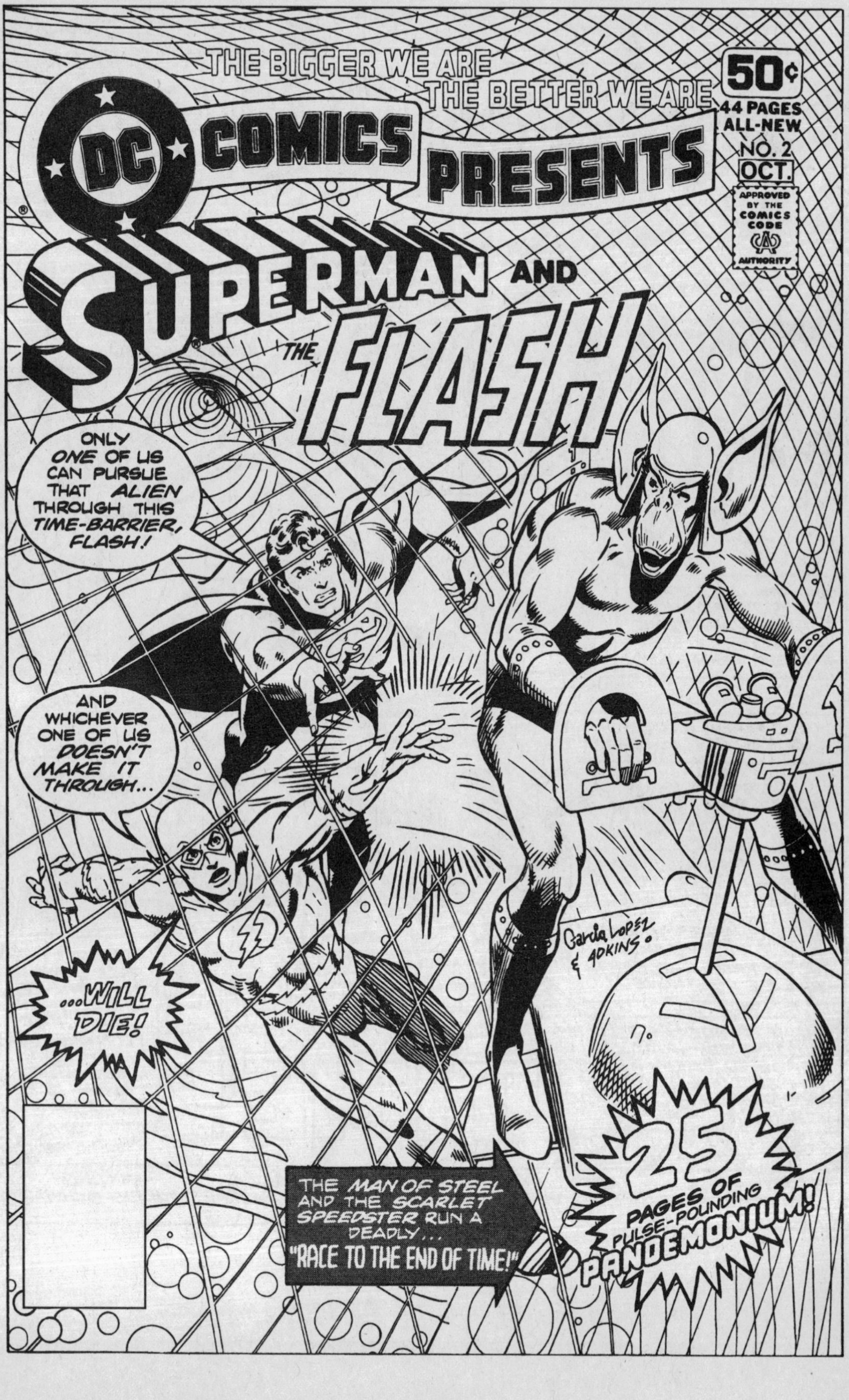
THE BIGGER WE ARE THE BETTER WE ARE
50¢
44 PAGES ALL-NEW
NO. 2
OCT.
APPROVED BY THE COMICS CODE AUTHORITY
DC COMICS PRESENTS
SUPERMAN AND THE FLASH
ONLY ONE OF US CAN PURSUE THAT ALIEN THROUGH THIS TIME-BARRIER, FLASH!
AND WHICHEVER ONE OF US DOESN'T MAKE IT THROUGH...
...WILL DIE!
Garcia Lopez & ADKINS
THE MAN OF STEEL AND THE SCARLET SPEEDSTER RUN A DEADLY... "RACE TO THE END OF TIME!"
25 PAGES OF PULSE-POUNDING PANDEMONIUM!

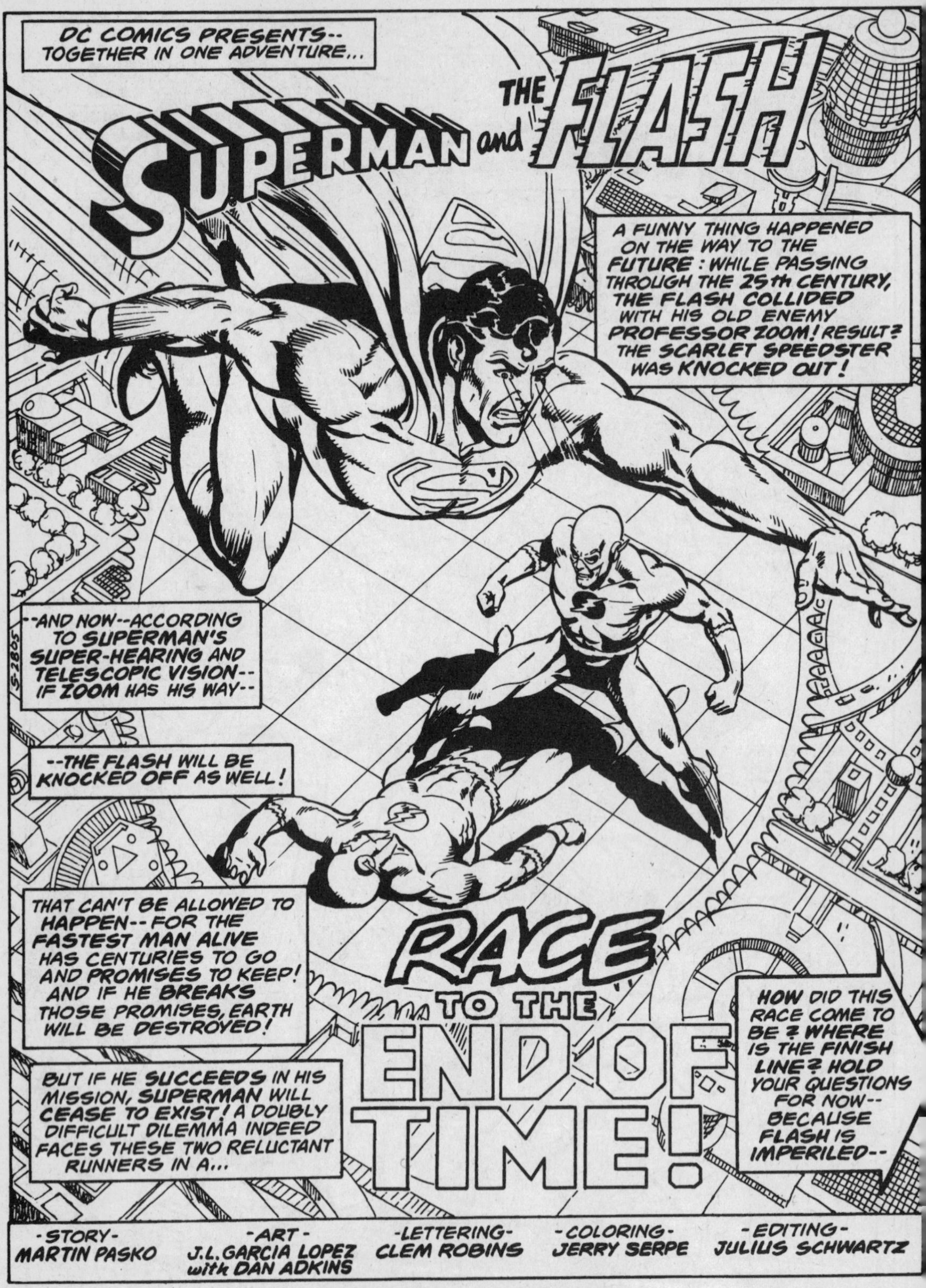
DC COMICS PRESENTS-- TOGETHER IN ONE ADVENTURE...
SUPERMAN and THE FLASH
A FUNNY THING HAPPENED ON THE WAY TO THE FUTURE: WHILE PASSING THROUGH THE 25th CENTURY, THE FLASH COLLIDED WITH HIS OLD ENEMY PROFESSOR ZOOM! RESULT? THE SCARLET SPEEDSTER WAS KNOCKED OUT!
--AND NOW--ACCORDING TO SUPERMAN'S SUPER-HEARING AND TELESCOPIC VISION-- IF ZOOM HAS HIS WAY--
--THE FLASH WILL BE KNOCKED OFF AS WELL!
THAT CAN'T BE ALLOWED TO HAPPEN--FOR THE FASTEST MAN ALIVE HAS CENTURIES TO GO AND PROMISES TO KEEP! AND IF HE BREAKS THOSE PROMISES, EARTH WILL BE DESTROYED!
BUT IF HE SUCCEEDS IN HIS MISSION, SUPERMAN WILL CEASE TO EXIST! A DOUBLY DIFFICULT DILEMMA INDEED FACES THESE TWO RELUCTANT RUNNERS IN A...
RACE TO THE END OF TIME!
HOW DID THIS RACE COME TO BE? WHERE IS THE FINISH LINE? HOLD YOUR QUESTIONS FOR NOW-- BECAUSE FLASH IS IMPERILED--
-STORY- MARTIN PASKO
-ART- J.L. GARCIA LOPEZ with DAN ADKINS
-LETTERING- CLEM ROBINS
-COLORING- JERRY SERPE
-EDITING- JULIUS SCHWARTZ

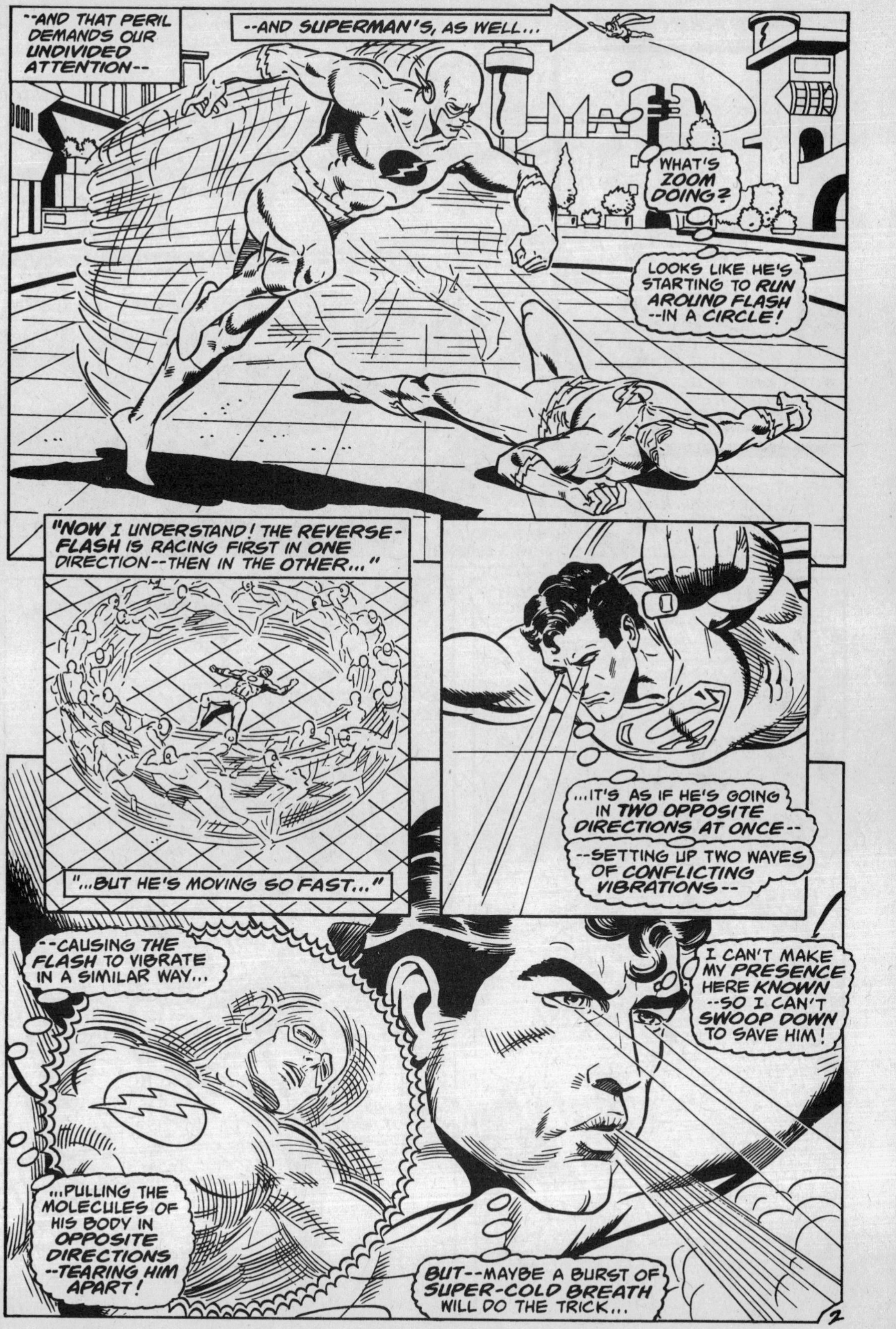
--AND THAT PERIL DEMANDS OUR UNDIVIDED ATTENTION--
--AND SUPERMAN'S, AS WELL...
WHAT'S ZOOM DOING?
LOOKS LIKE HE'S STARTING TO RUN AROUND FLASH --IN A CIRCLE!
"NOW I UNDERSTAND! THE REVERSE-FLASH IS RACING FIRST IN ONE DIRECTION--THEN IN THE OTHER..."
"...BUT HE'S MOVING SO FAST..."
...IT'S AS IF HE'S GOING IN TWO OPPOSITE DIRECTIONS AT ONCE--
--SETTING UP TWO WAVES OF CONFLICTING VIBRATIONS--
--CAUSING THE FLASH TO VIBRATE IN A SIMILAR WAY...
I CAN'T MAKE MY PRESENCE HERE KNOWN --SO I CAN'T SWOOP DOWN TO SAVE HIM!
...PULLING THE MOLECULES OF HIS BODY IN OPPOSITE DIRECTIONS --TEARING HIM APART!
BUT--MAYBE A BURST OF SUPER-COLD BREATH WILL DO THE TRICK...
2

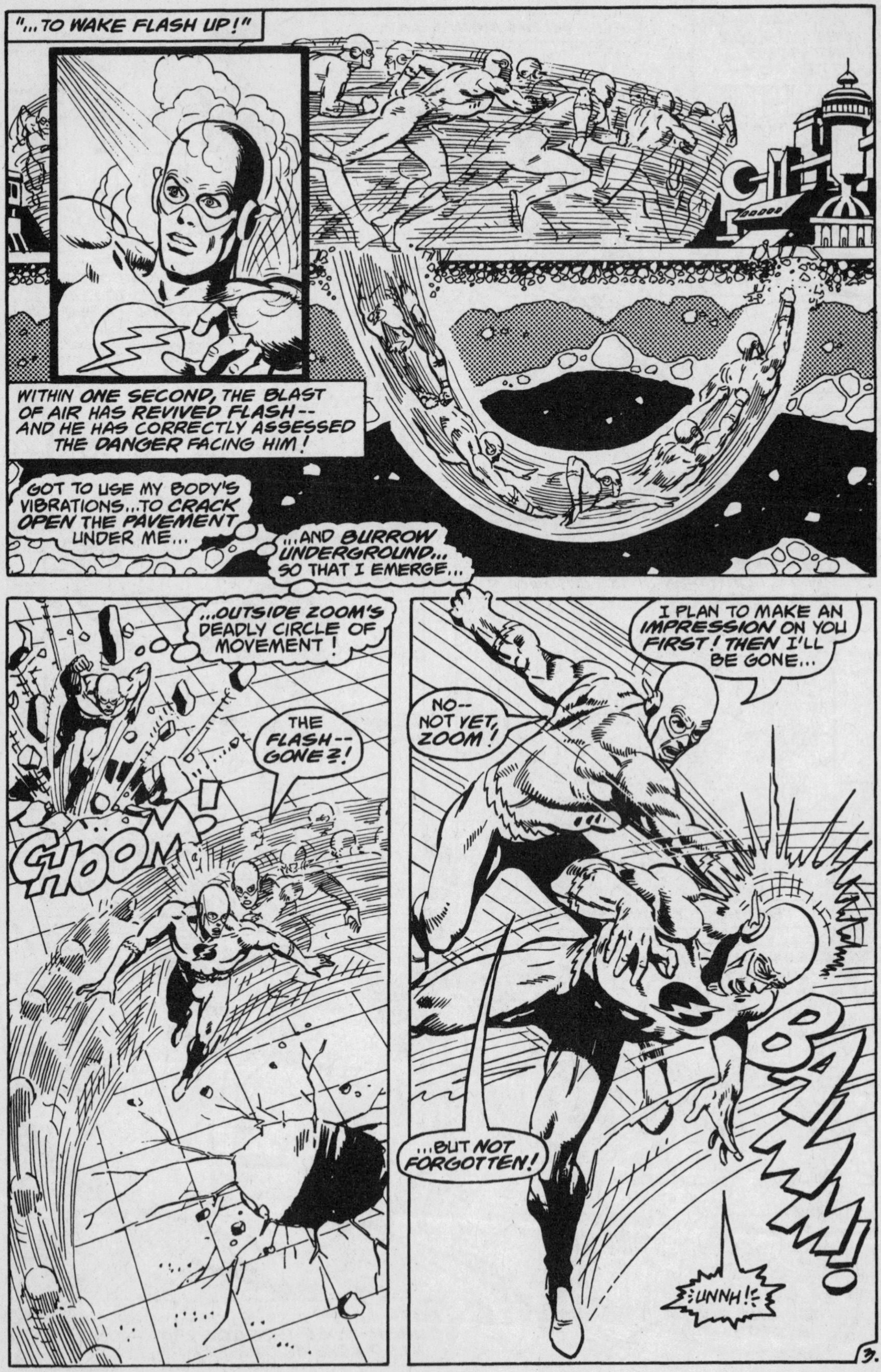
"...TO WAKE FLASH UP!"
WITHIN ONE SECOND, THE BLAST OF AIR HAS REVIVED FLASH-- AND HE HAS CORRECTLY ASSESSED THE DANGER FACING HIM!
GOT TO USE MY BODY'S VIBRATIONS...TO CRACK OPEN THE PAVEMENT UNDER ME...
...AND BURROW UNDERGROUND... SO THAT I EMERGE...
...OUTSIDE ZOOM'S DEADLY CIRCLE OF MOVEMENT!
THE FLASH-- GONE?!
CHOOM!
I PLAN TO MAKE AN IMPRESSION ON YOU FIRST! THEN I'LL BE GONE...
NO-- NOT YET, ZOOM!
...BUT NOT FORGOTTEN!
BAMM!
UNNH!
3.

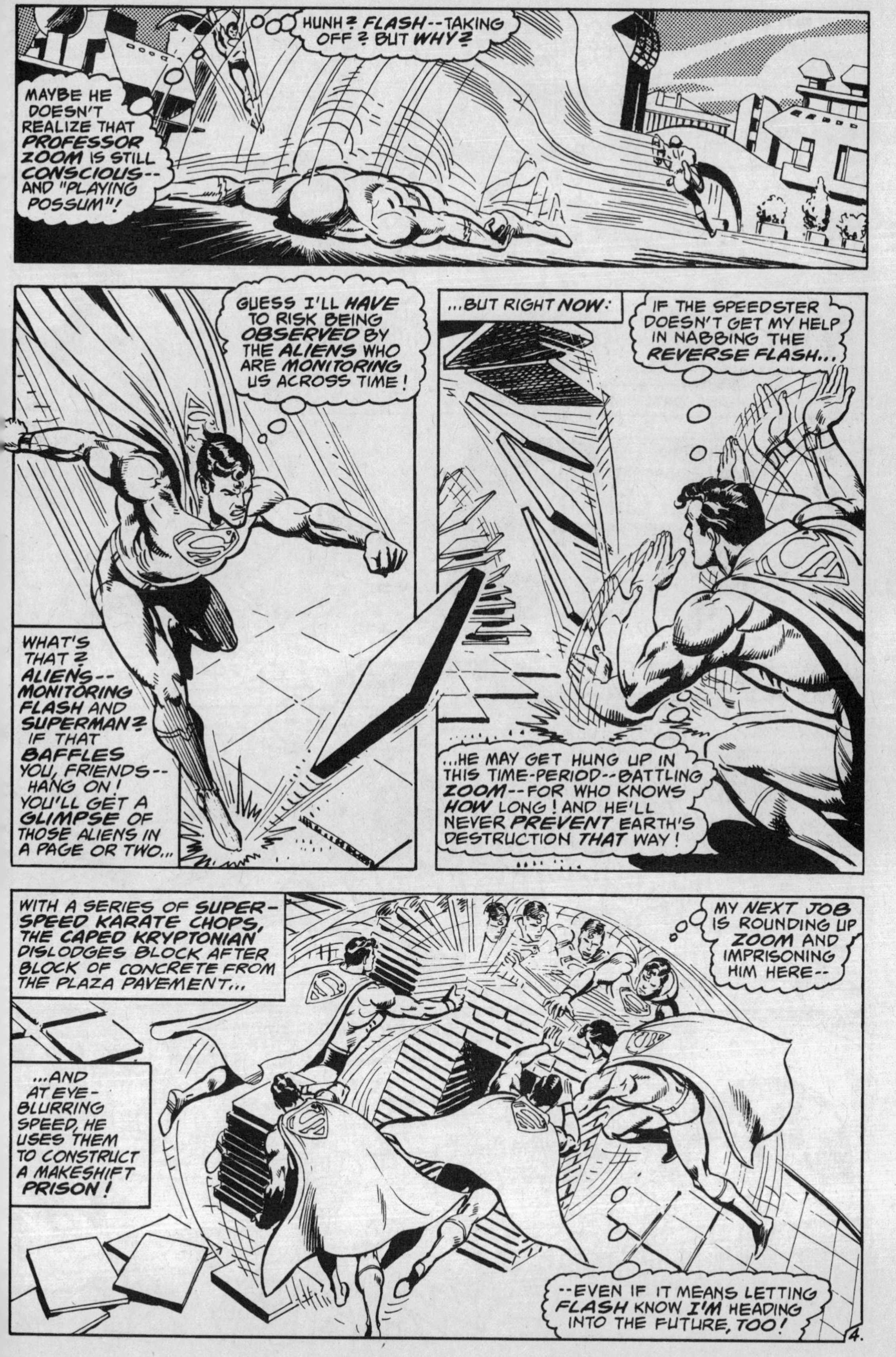
HUNH? FLASH--TAKING OFF? BUT WHY?
MAYBE HE DOESN'T REALIZE THAT PROFESSOR ZOOM IS STILL CONSCIOUS--AND "PLAYING POSSUM"!
GUESS I'LL HAVE TO RISK BEING OBSERVED BY THE ALIENS WHO ARE MONITORING US ACROSS TIME!
WHAT'S THAT? ALIENS--MONITORING FLASH AND SUPERMAN? IF THAT BAFFLES YOU, FRIENDS--HANG ON! YOU'LL GET A GLIMPSE OF THOSE ALIENS IN A PAGE OR TWO...
...BUT RIGHT NOW:
IF THE SPEEDSTER DOESN'T GET MY HELP IN NABBING THE REVERSE FLASH...
...HE MAY GET HUNG UP IN THIS TIME-PERIOD--BATTLING ZOOM--FOR WHO KNOWS HOW LONG! AND HE'LL NEVER PREVENT EARTH'S DESTRUCTION THAT WAY!
WITH A SERIES OF SUPER-SPEED KARATE CHOPS, THE CAPED KRYPTONIAN DISLODGES BLOCK AFTER BLOCK OF CONCRETE FROM THE PLAZA PAVEMENT...
...AND AT EYE-BLURRING SPEED, HE USES THEM TO CONSTRUCT A MAKESHIFT PRISON!
MY NEXT JOB IS ROUNDING UP ZOOM AND IMPRISONING HIM HERE--
--EVEN IF IT MEANS LETTING FLASH KNOW I'M HEADING INTO THE FUTURE, TOO!
4.

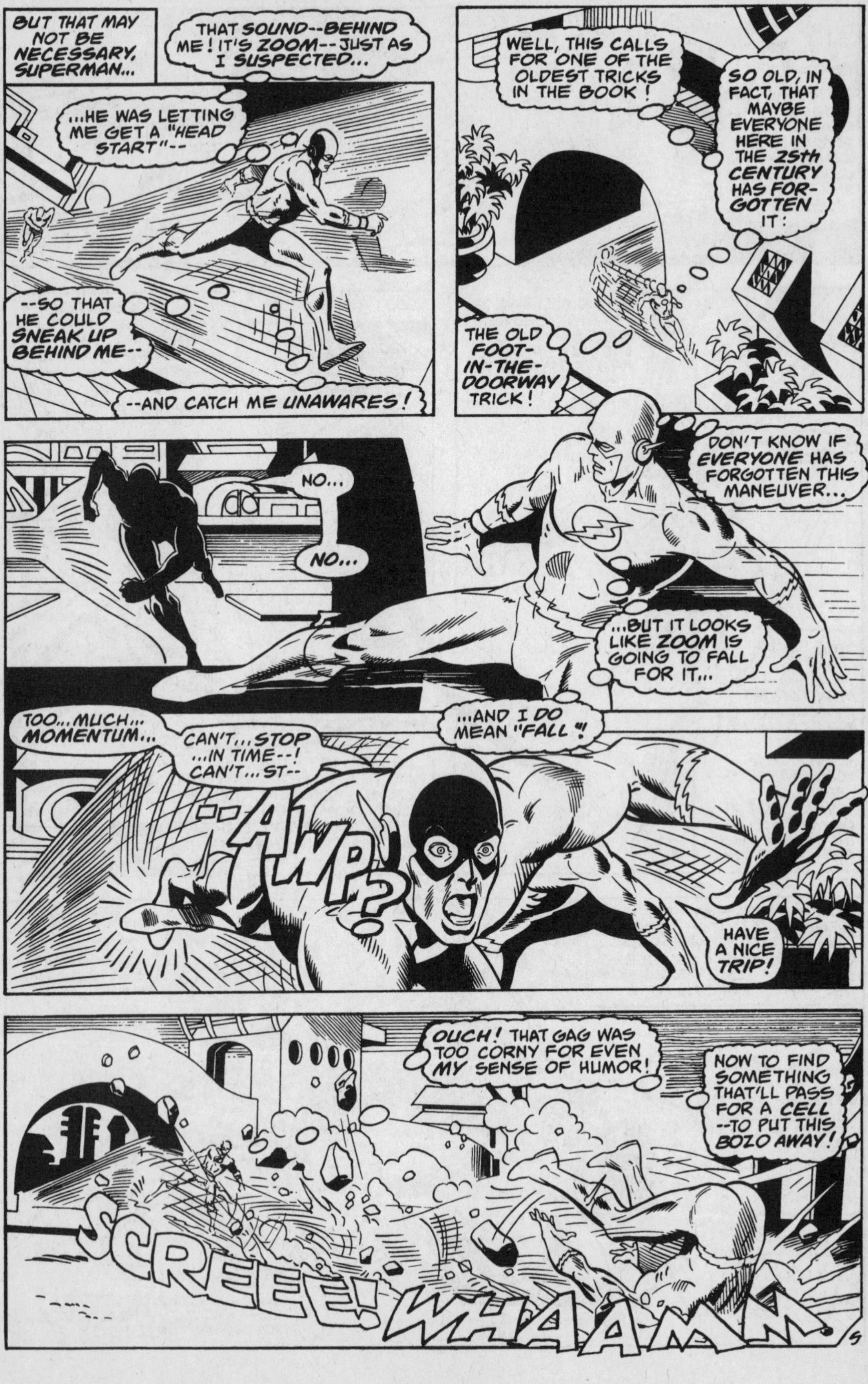
BUT THAT MAY NOT BE NECESSARY, SUPERMAN...
THAT SOUND--BEHIND ME! IT'S ZOOM--JUST AS I SUSPECTED...
...HE WAS LETTING ME GET A "HEAD START"--
--SO THAT HE COULD SNEAK UP BEHIND ME--
--AND CATCH ME UNAWARES!
WELL, THIS CALLS FOR ONE OF THE OLDEST TRICKS IN THE BOOK!
SO OLD, IN FACT, THAT MAYBE EVERYONE HERE IN THE 25th CENTURY HAS FORGOTTEN IT:
THE OLD FOOT-IN-THE-DOORWAY TRICK!
NO...
NO...
DON'T KNOW IF EVERYONE HAS FORGOTTEN THIS MANEUVER...
...BUT IT LOOKS LIKE ZOOM IS GOING TO FALL FOR IT...
TOO...MUCH... MOMENTUM...
CAN'T...STOP ...IN TIME--! CAN'T...ST--
...AND I DO MEAN "FALL"!
--AWP?
HAVE A NICE TRIP!
OUCH! THAT GAG WAS TOO CORNY FOR EVEN MY SENSE OF HUMOR!
NOW TO FIND SOMETHING THAT'LL PASS FOR A CELL --TO PUT THIS BOZO AWAY!
SCREEEE!
WHAAMM
5

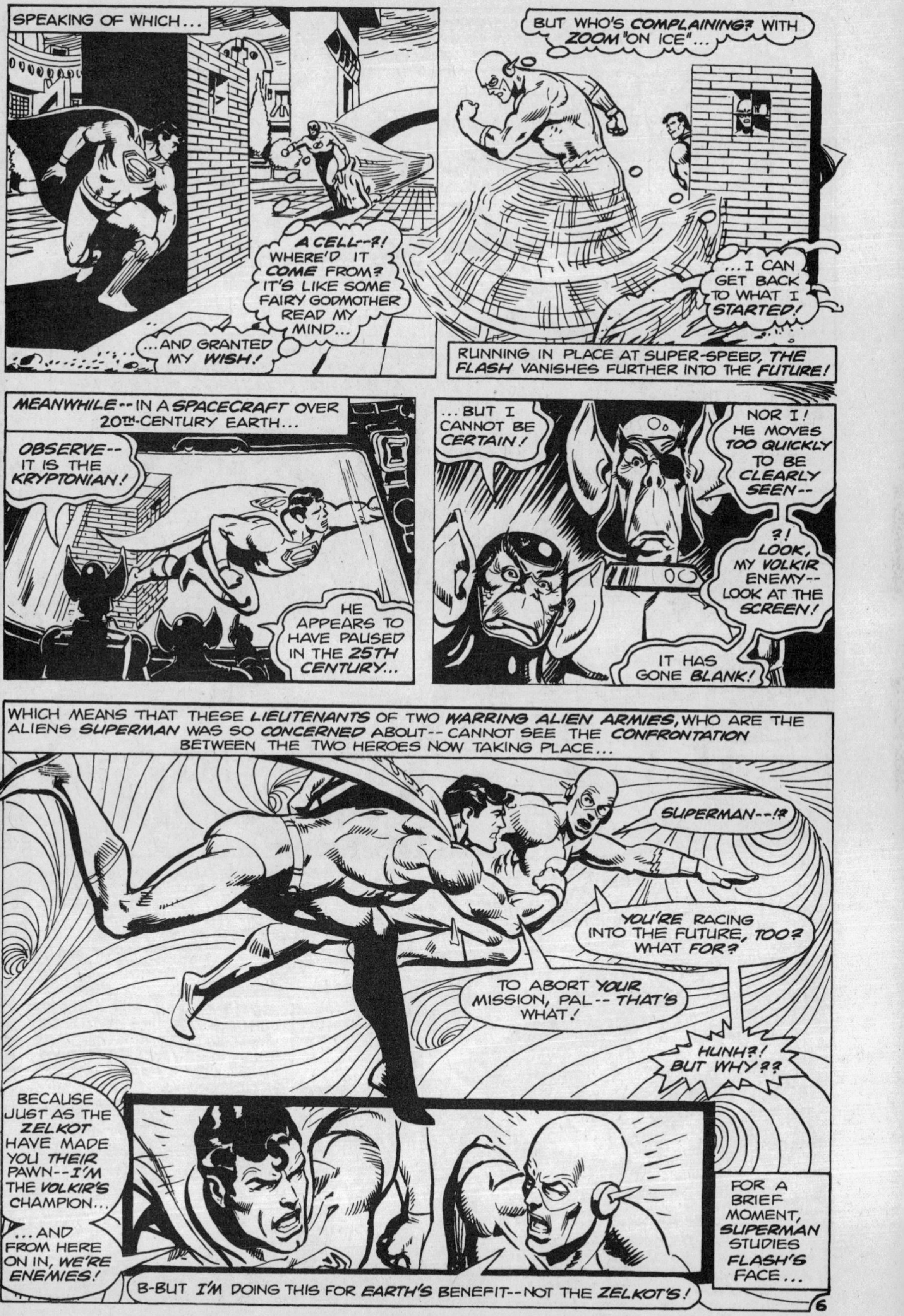
SPEAKING OF WHICH...
A CELL--?! WHERE'D IT COME FROM? IT'S LIKE SOME FAIRY GODMOTHER READ MY MIND...
...AND GRANTED MY WISH!
BUT WHO'S COMPLAINING? WITH ZOOM "ON ICE"...
...I CAN GET BACK TO WHAT I STARTED!
RUNNING IN PLACE AT SUPER-SPEED, THE FLASH VANISHES FURTHER INTO THE FUTURE!
MEANWHILE--IN A SPACECRAFT OVER 20TH-CENTURY EARTH...
OBSERVE-- IT IS THE KRYPTONIAN!
HE APPEARS TO HAVE PAUSED IN THE 25TH CENTURY...
...BUT I CANNOT BE CERTAIN!
NOR I! HE MOVES TOO QUICKLY TO BE CLEARLY SEEN--
?! LOOK, MY VOLKIR ENEMY-- LOOK AT THE SCREEN!
IT HAS GONE BLANK!
WHICH MEANS THAT THESE LIEUTENANTS OF TWO WARRING ALIEN ARMIES, WHO ARE THE ALIENS SUPERMAN WAS SO CONCERNED ABOUT-- CANNOT SEE THE CONFRONTATION BETWEEN THE TWO HEROES NOW TAKING PLACE...
SUPERMAN--!?
YOU'RE RACING INTO THE FUTURE, TOO? WHAT FOR?
TO ABORT YOUR MISSION, PAL-- THAT'S WHAT!
HUNH?! BUT WHY??
BECAUSE JUST AS THE ZELKOT HAVE MADE YOU THEIR PAWN--I'M THE VOLKIR'S CHAMPION...
...AND FROM HERE ON IN, WE'RE ENEMIES!
B-BUT I'M DOING THIS FOR EARTH'S BENEFIT--NOT THE ZELKOT'S!
FOR A BRIEF MOMENT, SUPERMAN STUDIES FLASH'S FACE...
6

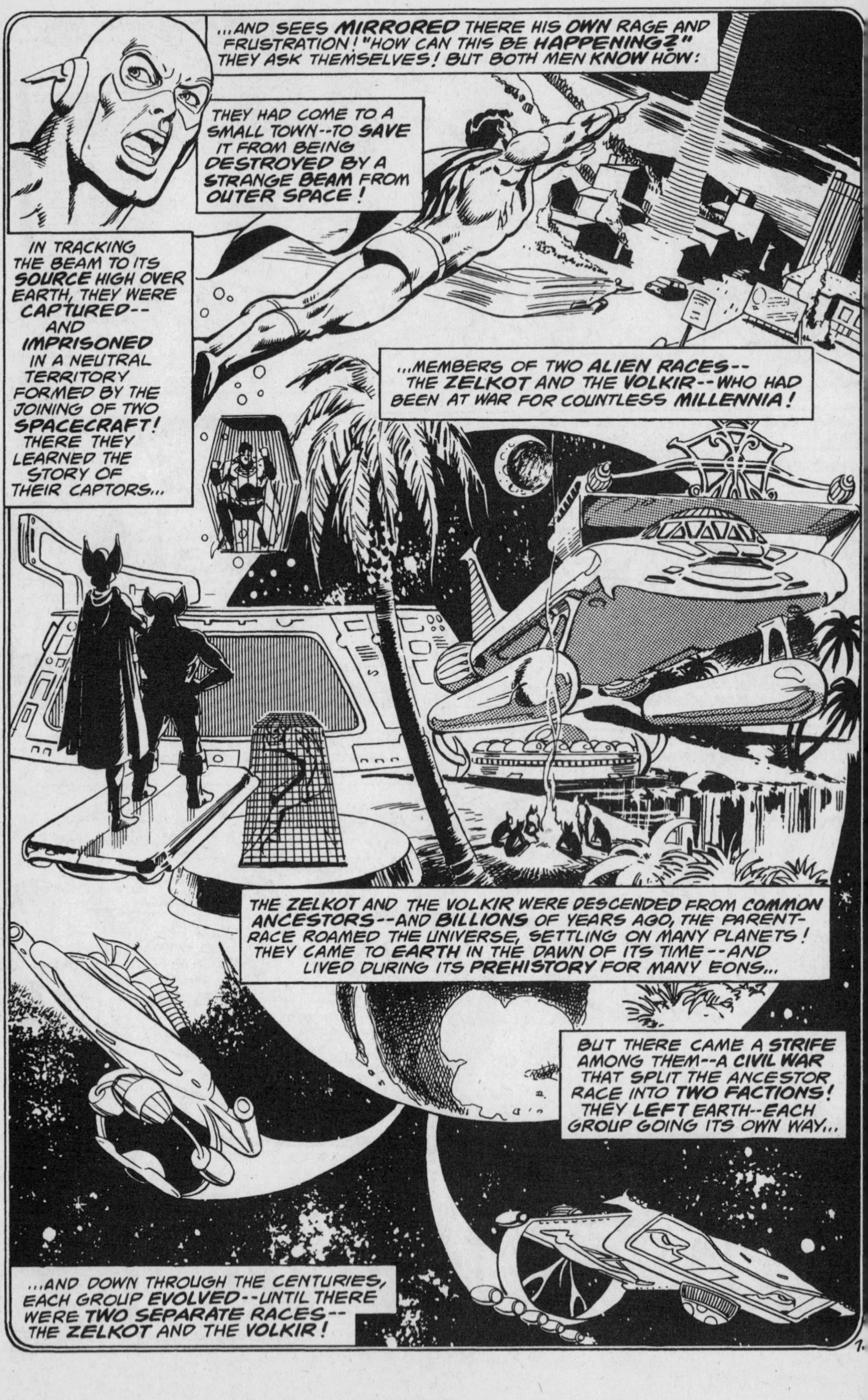
...AND SEES MIRRORED THERE HIS OWN RAGE AND FRUSTRATION! "HOW CAN THIS BE HAPPENING?" THEY ASK THEMSELVES! BUT BOTH MEN KNOW HOW:
THEY HAD COME TO A SMALL TOWN--TO SAVE IT FROM BEING DESTROYED BY A STRANGE BEAM FROM OUTER SPACE!
IN TRACKING THE BEAM TO ITS SOURCE HIGH OVER EARTH, THEY WERE CAPTURED-- AND IMPRISONED IN A NEUTRAL TERRITORY FORMED BY THE JOINING OF TWO SPACECRAFT! THERE THEY LEARNED THE STORY OF THEIR CAPTORS...
...MEMBERS OF TWO ALIEN RACES-- THE ZELKOT AND THE VOLKIR--WHO HAD BEEN AT WAR FOR COUNTLESS MILLENNIA!
THE ZELKOT AND THE VOLKIR WERE DESCENDED FROM COMMON ANCESTORS--AND BILLIONS OF YEARS AGO, THE PARENT-RACE ROAMED THE UNIVERSE, SETTLING ON MANY PLANETS! THEY CAME TO EARTH IN THE DAWN OF ITS TIME--AND LIVED DURING ITS PREHISTORY FOR MANY EONS...
BUT THERE CAME A STRIFE AMONG THEM--A CIVIL WAR THAT SPLIT THE ANCESTOR RACE INTO TWO FACTIONS! THEY LEFT EARTH--EACH GROUP GOING ITS OWN WAY...
...AND DOWN THROUGH THE CENTURIES, EACH GROUP EVOLVED--UNTIL THERE WERE TWO SEPARATE RACES-- THE ZELKOT AND THE VOLKIR!
7.

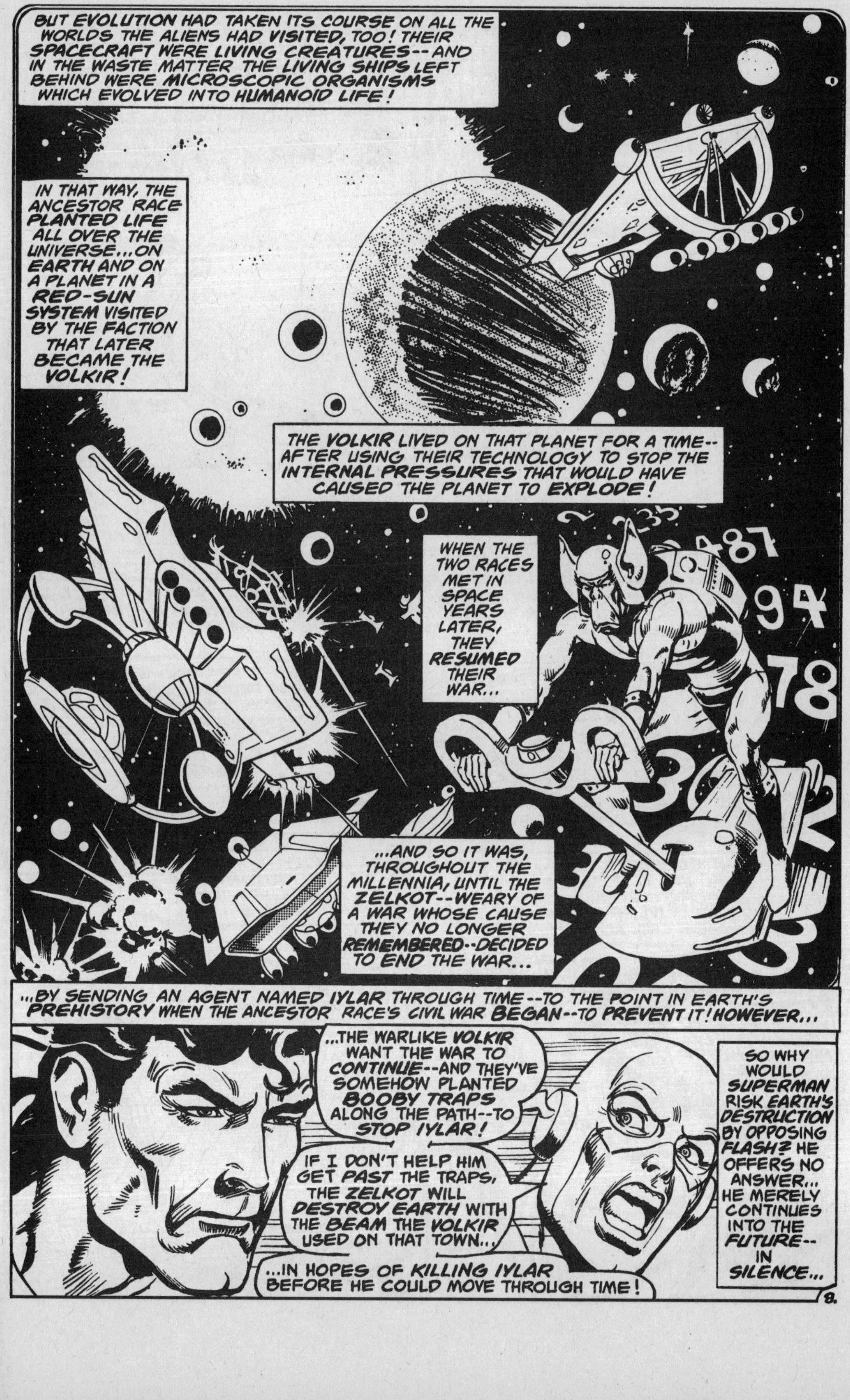
BUT EVOLUTION HAD TAKEN ITS COURSE ON ALL THE WORLDS THE ALIENS HAD VISITED, TOO! THEIR SPACECRAFT WERE LIVING CREATURES-- AND IN THE WASTE MATTER THE LIVING SHIPS LEFT BEHIND WERE MICROSCOPIC ORGANISMS WHICH EVOLVED INTO HUMANOID LIFE!
IN THAT WAY, THE ANCESTOR RACE PLANTED LIFE ALL OVER THE UNIVERSE...ON EARTH AND ON A PLANET IN A RED-SUN SYSTEM VISITED BY THE FACTION THAT LATER BECAME THE VOLKIR!
THE VOLKIR LIVED ON THAT PLANET FOR A TIME-- AFTER USING THEIR TECHNOLOGY TO STOP THE INTERNAL PRESSURES THAT WOULD HAVE CAUSED THE PLANET TO EXPLODE!
WHEN THE TWO RACES MET IN SPACE YEARS LATER, THEY RESUMED THEIR WAR...
...AND SO IT WAS, THROUGHOUT THE MILLENNIA, UNTIL THE ZELKOT--WEARY OF A WAR WHOSE CAUSE THEY NO LONGER REMEMBERED--DECIDED TO END THE WAR...
...BY SENDING AN AGENT NAMED IYLAR THROUGH TIME --TO THE POINT IN EARTH'S PREHISTORY WHEN THE ANCESTOR RACE'S CIVIL WAR BEGAN--TO PREVENT IT! HOWEVER...
...THE WARLIKE VOLKIR WANT THE WAR TO CONTINUE--AND THEY'VE SOMEHOW PLANTED BOOBY TRAPS ALONG THE PATH--TO STOP IYLAR!
IF I DON'T HELP HIM GET PAST THE TRAPS, THE ZELKOT WILL DESTROY EARTH WITH THE BEAM THE VOLKIR USED ON THAT TOWN...
...IN HOPES OF KILLING IYLAR BEFORE HE COULD MOVE THROUGH TIME!
SO WHY WOULD SUPERMAN RISK EARTH'S DESTRUCTION BY OPPOSING FLASH? HE OFFERS NO ANSWER... HE MERELY CONTINUES INTO THE FUTURE-- IN SILENCE...
8.

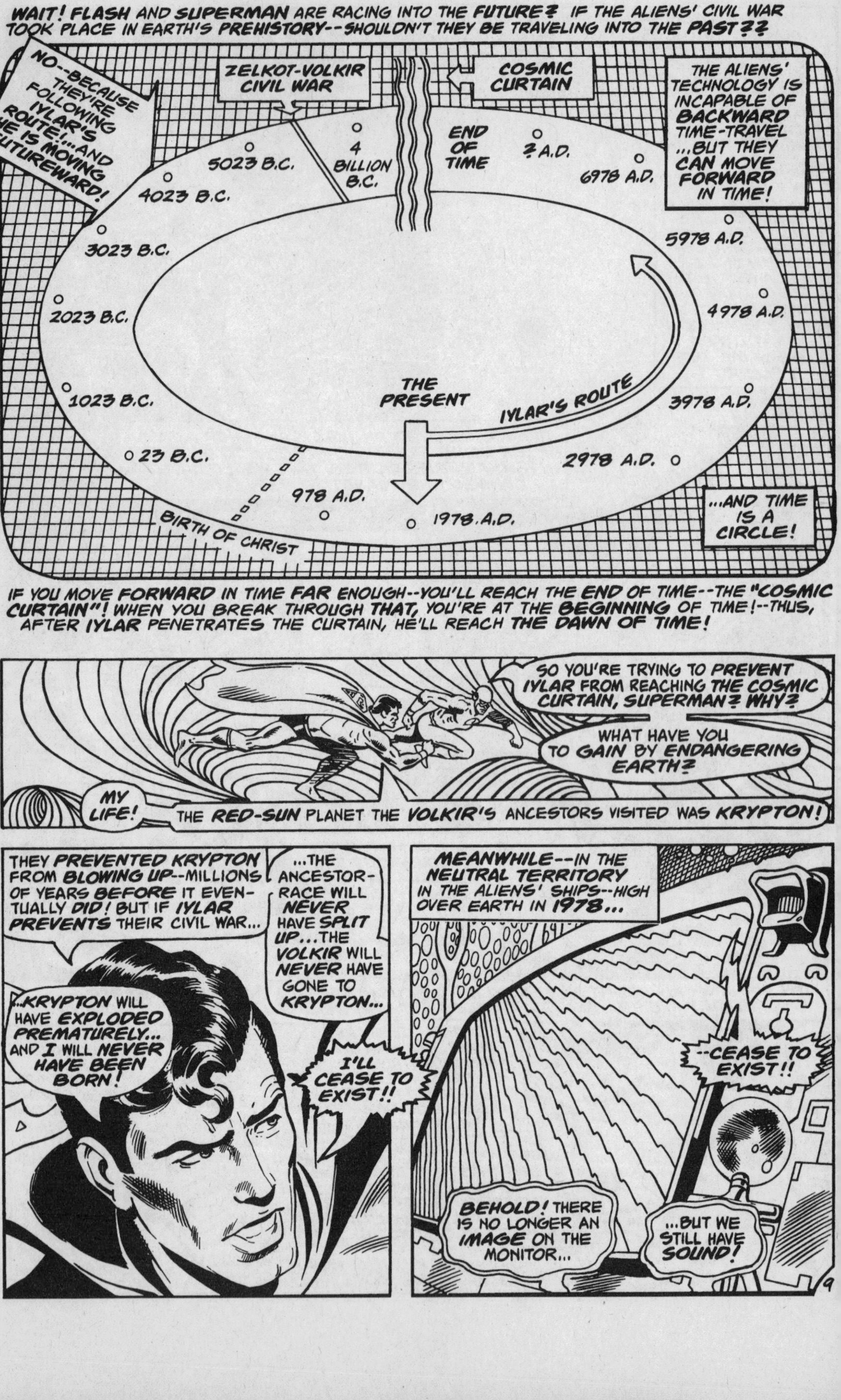
WAIT! FLASH AND SUPERMAN ARE RACING INTO THE FUTURE? IF THE ALIENS' CIVIL WAR TOOK PLACE IN EARTH'S PREHISTORY--SHOULDN'T THEY BE TRAVELING INTO THE PAST??
NO--BECAUSE THEY'RE FOLLOWING IYLAR'S ROUTE!...AND HE IS MOVING FUTUREWARD!
ZELKOT-VOLKIR CIVIL WAR
COSMIC CURTAIN
THE ALIENS' TECHNOLOGY IS INCAPABLE OF BACKWARD TIME-TRAVEL ...BUT THEY CAN MOVE FORWARD IN TIME!
END OF TIME
4 BILLION B.C.
5023 B.C.
4023 B.C.
3023 B.C.
2023 B.C.
1023 B.C.
23 B.C.
BIRTH OF CHRIST
978 A.D.
1978 A.D.
THE PRESENT
IYLAR'S ROUTE
2978 A.D.
3978 A.D.
4978 A.D.
5978 A.D.
6978 A.D.
? A.D.
...AND TIME IS A CIRCLE!
IF YOU MOVE FORWARD IN TIME FAR ENOUGH--YOU'LL REACH THE END OF TIME--THE "COSMIC CURTAIN"! WHEN YOU BREAK THROUGH THAT, YOU'RE AT THE BEGINNING OF TIME!--THUS, AFTER IYLAR PENETRATES THE CURTAIN, HE'LL REACH THE DAWN OF TIME!
SO YOU'RE TRYING TO PREVENT IYLAR FROM REACHING THE COSMIC CURTAIN, SUPERMAN? WHY?
WHAT HAVE YOU TO GAIN BY ENDANGERING EARTH?
MY LIFE!
THE RED-SUN PLANET THE VOLKIR'S ANCESTORS VISITED WAS KRYPTON!
THEY PREVENTED KRYPTON FROM BLOWING UP--MILLIONS OF YEARS BEFORE IT EVENTUALLY DID! BUT IF IYLAR PREVENTS THEIR CIVIL WAR...
...THE ANCESTOR-RACE WILL NEVER HAVE SPLIT UP...THE VOLKIR WILL NEVER HAVE GONE TO KRYPTON...
...KRYPTON WILL HAVE EXPLODED PREMATURELY... AND I WILL NEVER HAVE BEEN BORN!
I'LL CEASE TO EXIST!!
MEANWHILE--IN THE NEUTRAL TERRITORY IN THE ALIENS' SHIPS--HIGH OVER EARTH IN 1978...
--CEASE TO EXIST!!
BEHOLD! THERE IS NO LONGER AN IMAGE ON THE MONITOR...
...BUT WE STILL HAVE SOUND!
9

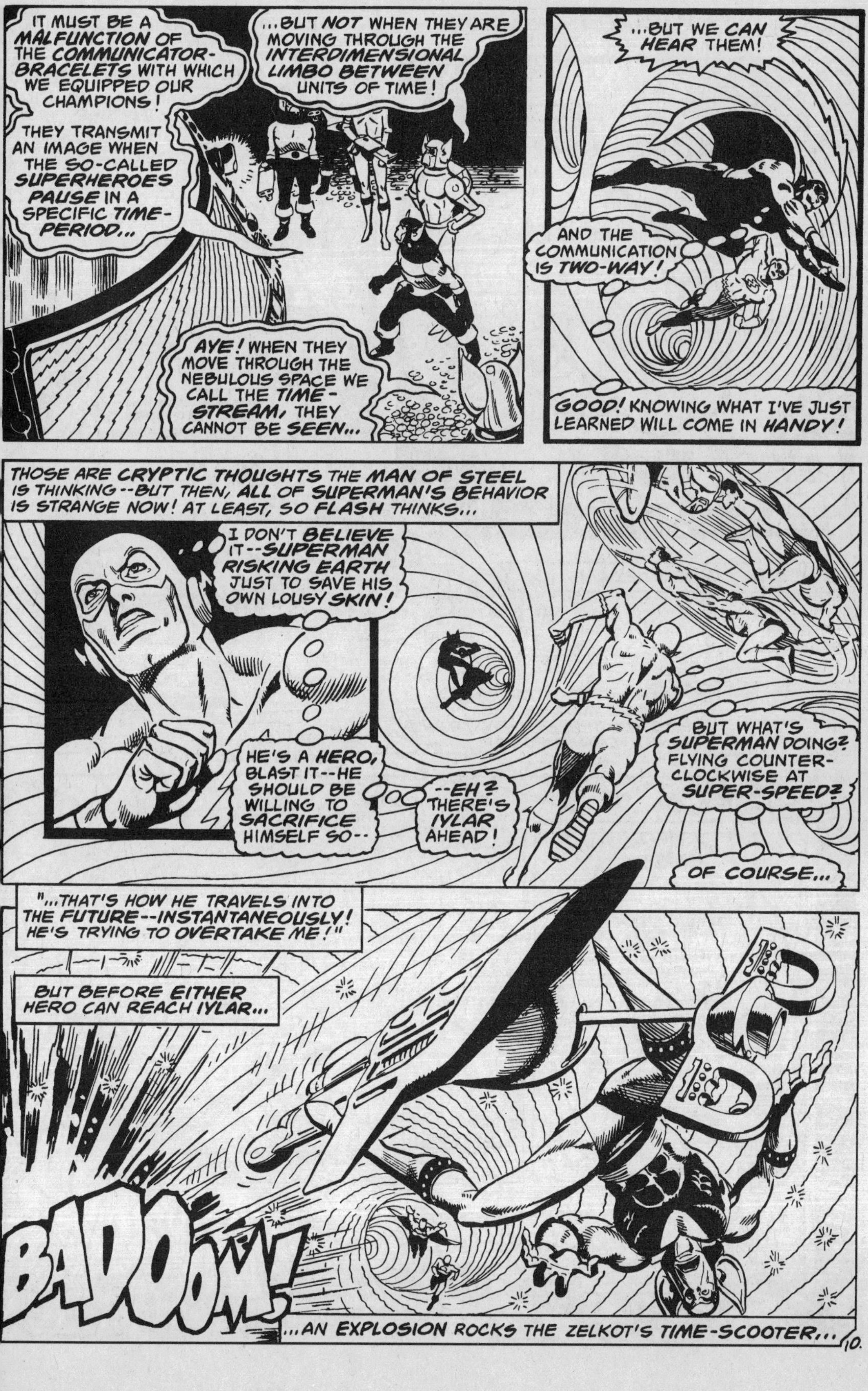
IT MUST BE A MALFUNCTION OF THE COMMUNICATOR-BRACELETS WITH WHICH WE EQUIPPED OUR CHAMPIONS!
THEY TRANSMIT AN IMAGE WHEN THE SO-CALLED SUPERHEROES PAUSE IN A SPECIFIC TIME-PERIOD...
...BUT NOT WHEN THEY ARE MOVING THROUGH THE INTERDIMENSIONAL LIMBO BETWEEN UNITS OF TIME!
AYE! WHEN THEY MOVE THROUGH THE NEBULOUS SPACE WE CALL THE TIME-STREAM, THEY CANNOT BE SEEN...
...BUT WE CAN HEAR THEM!
AND THE COMMUNICATION IS TWO-WAY!
GOOD! KNOWING WHAT I'VE JUST LEARNED WILL COME IN HANDY!
THOSE ARE CRYPTIC THOUGHTS THE MAN OF STEEL IS THINKING--BUT THEN, ALL OF SUPERMAN'S BEHAVIOR IS STRANGE NOW! AT LEAST, SO FLASH THINKS...
I DON'T BELIEVE IT--SUPERMAN RISKING EARTH JUST TO SAVE HIS OWN LOUSY SKIN!
HE'S A HERO, BLAST IT--HE SHOULD BE WILLING TO SACRIFICE HIMSELF SO--
--EH? THERE'S IYLAR AHEAD!
BUT WHAT'S SUPERMAN DOING? FLYING COUNTER-CLOCKWISE AT SUPER-SPEED?
OF COURSE...
"...THAT'S HOW HE TRAVELS INTO THE FUTURE--INSTANTANEOUSLY! HE'S TRYING TO OVERTAKE ME!"
BUT BEFORE EITHER HERO CAN REACH IYLAR...
BADOOM!
...AN EXPLOSION ROCKS THE ZELKOT'S TIME-SCOOTER...
10.

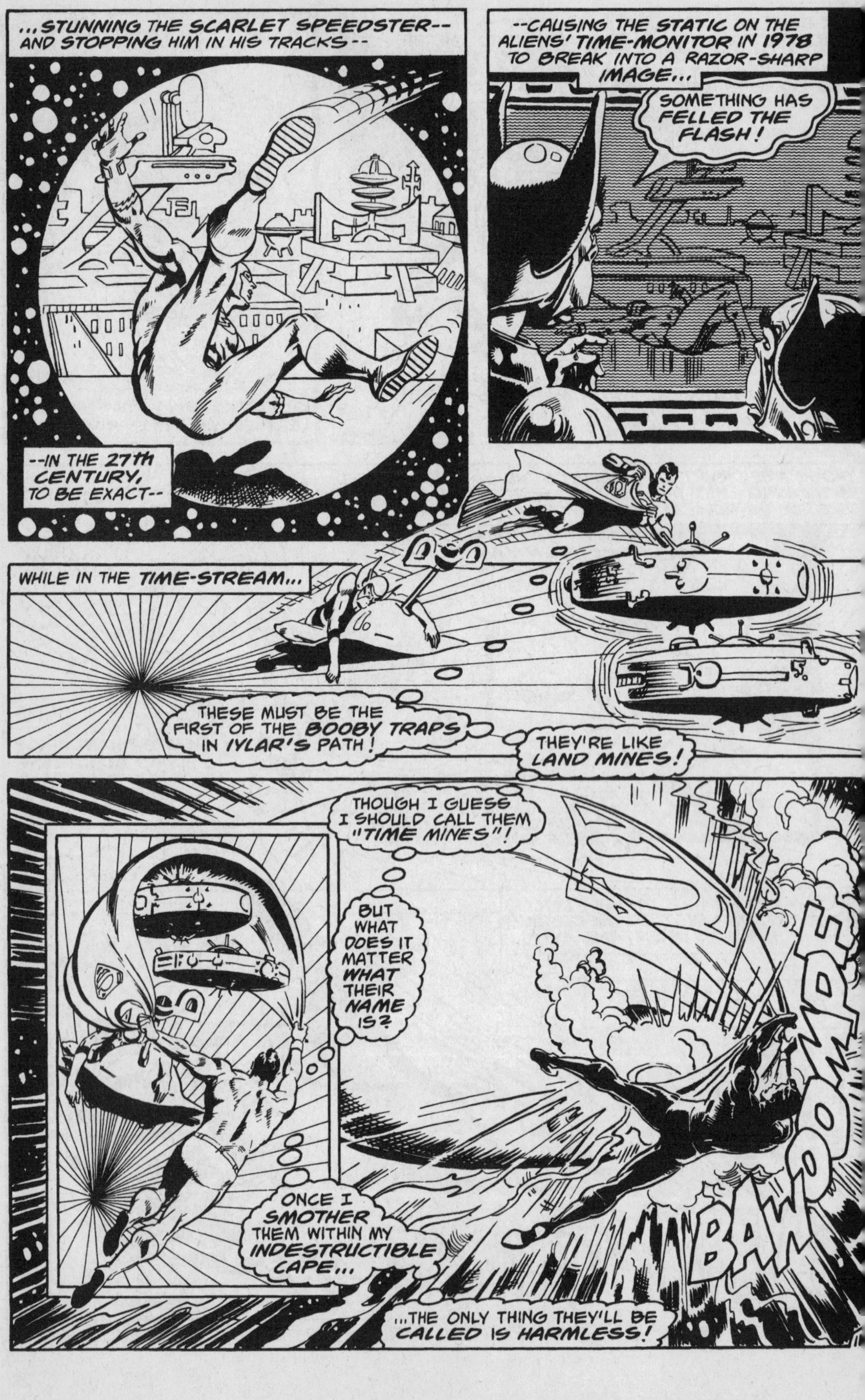
...STUNNING THE SCARLET SPEEDSTER--
AND STOPPING HIM IN HIS TRACKS--
--IN THE 27th CENTURY, TO BE EXACT--
--CAUSING THE STATIC ON THE ALIENS' TIME-MONITOR IN 1978 TO BREAK INTO A RAZOR-SHARP IMAGE...
SOMETHING HAS FELLED THE FLASH!
WHILE IN THE TIME-STREAM...
THESE MUST BE THE FIRST OF THE BOOBY TRAPS IN IYLAR'S PATH!
THEY'RE LIKE LAND MINES!
THOUGH I GUESS I SHOULD CALL THEM "TIME MINES"!
BUT WHAT DOES IT MATTER WHAT THEIR NAME IS?
ONCE I SMOTHER THEM WITHIN MY INDESTRUCTIBLE CAPE...
...THE ONLY THING THEY'LL BE CALLED IS HARMLESS!
BAWOOMPF

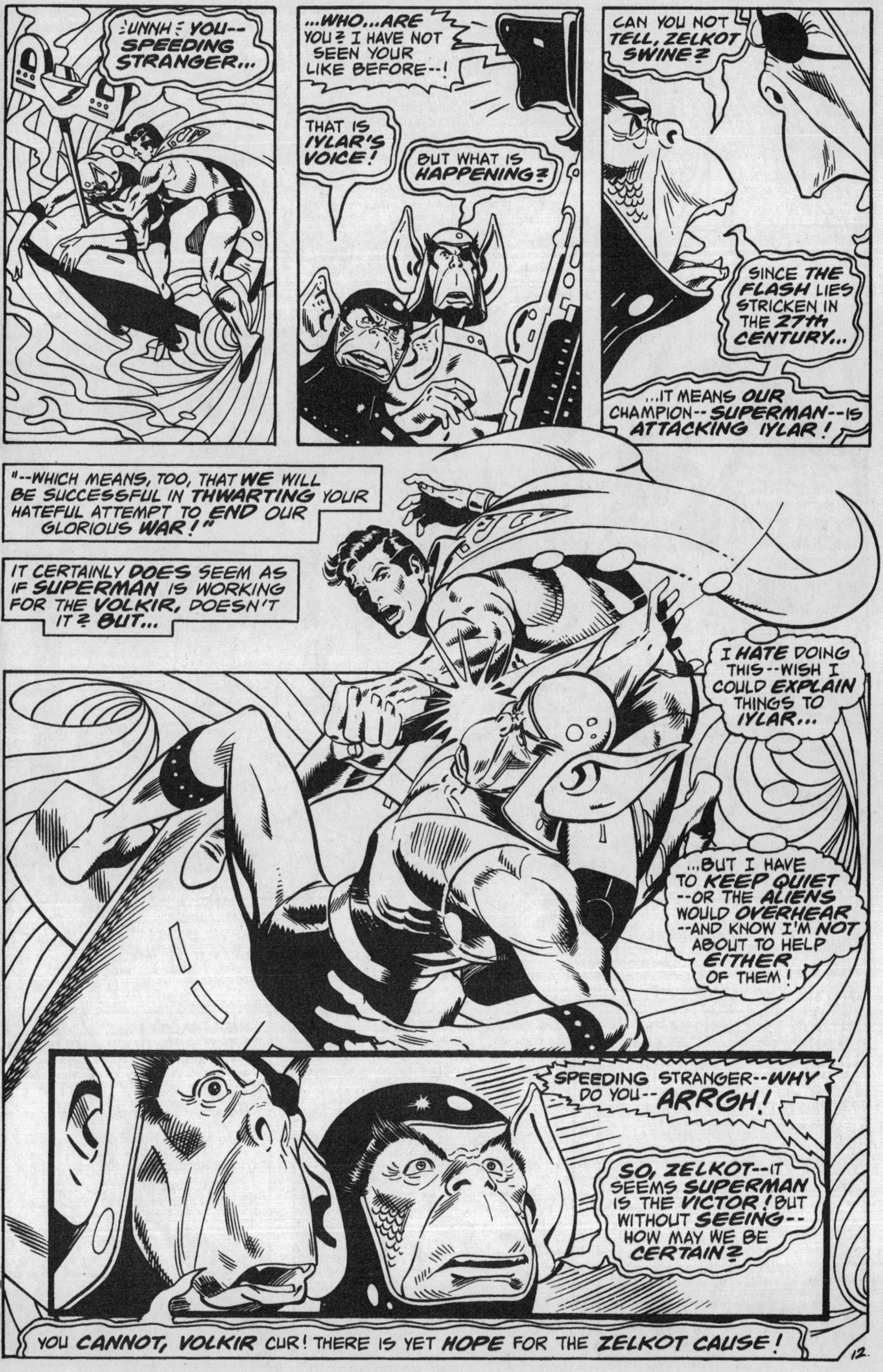
UNNH? YOU--SPEEDING STRANGER...
...WHO...ARE YOU? I HAVE NOT SEEN YOUR LIKE BEFORE--!
THAT IS IYLAR'S VOICE!
BUT WHAT IS HAPPENING?
CAN YOU NOT TELL, ZELKOT SWINE?
SINCE THE FLASH LIES STRICKEN IN THE 27th CENTURY...
...IT MEANS OUR CHAMPION--SUPERMAN--IS ATTACKING IYLAR!
"--WHICH MEANS, TOO, THAT WE WILL BE SUCCESSFUL IN THWARTING YOUR HATEFUL ATTEMPT TO END OUR GLORIOUS WAR!"
IT CERTAINLY DOES SEEM AS IF SUPERMAN IS WORKING FOR THE VOLKIR, DOESN'T IT? BUT...
I HATE DOING THIS--WISH I COULD EXPLAIN THINGS TO IYLAR...
...BUT I HAVE TO KEEP QUIET --OR THE ALIENS WOULD OVERHEAR --AND KNOW I'M NOT ABOUT TO HELP EITHER OF THEM!
SPEEDING STRANGER--WHY DO YOU--ARRGH!
SO, ZELKOT--IT SEEMS SUPERMAN IS THE VICTOR! BUT WITHOUT SEEING--HOW MAY WE BE CERTAIN?
YOU CANNOT, VOLKIR CUR! THERE IS YET HOPE FOR THE ZELKOT CAUSE!
12.

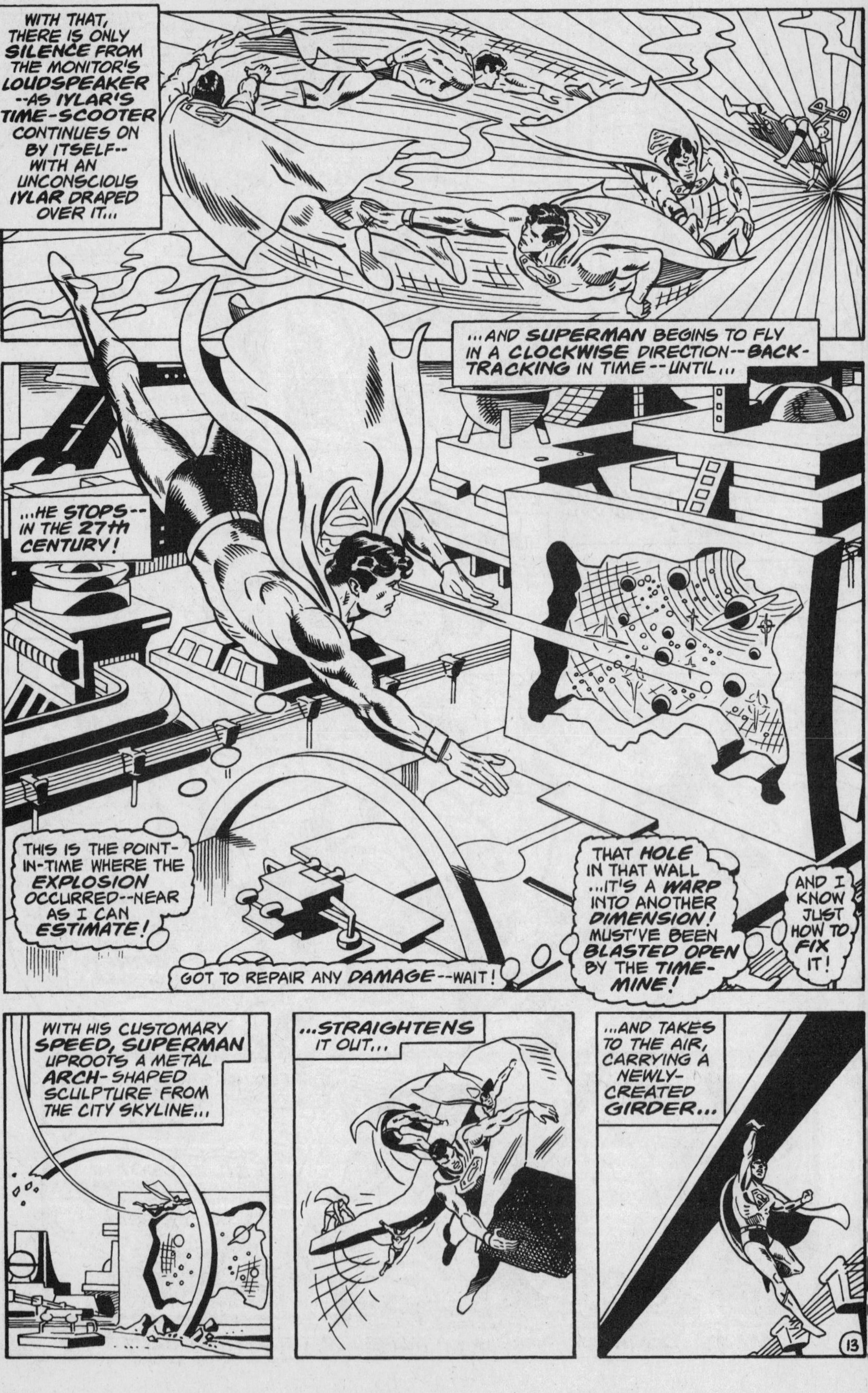
WITH THAT, THERE IS ONLY SILENCE FROM THE MONITOR'S LOUDSPEAKER --AS IYLAR'S TIME-SCOOTER CONTINUES ON BY ITSELF-- WITH AN UNCONSCIOUS IYLAR DRAPED OVER IT...
...AND SUPERMAN BEGINS TO FLY IN A CLOCKWISE DIRECTION--BACK-TRACKING IN TIME--UNTIL...
...HE STOPS-- IN THE 27th CENTURY!
THIS IS THE POINT-IN-TIME WHERE THE EXPLOSION OCCURRED--NEAR AS I CAN ESTIMATE!
GOT TO REPAIR ANY DAMAGE--WAIT!
THAT HOLE IN THAT WALL ...IT'S A WARP INTO ANOTHER DIMENSION! MUST'VE BEEN BLASTED OPEN BY THE TIME-MINE!
AND I KNOW JUST HOW TO FIX IT!
WITH HIS CUSTOMARY SPEED, SUPERMAN UPROOTS A METAL ARCH-SHAPED SCULPTURE FROM THE CITY SKYLINE...
...STRAIGHTENS IT OUT...
...AND TAKES TO THE AIR, CARRYING A NEWLY-CREATED GIRDER...
13

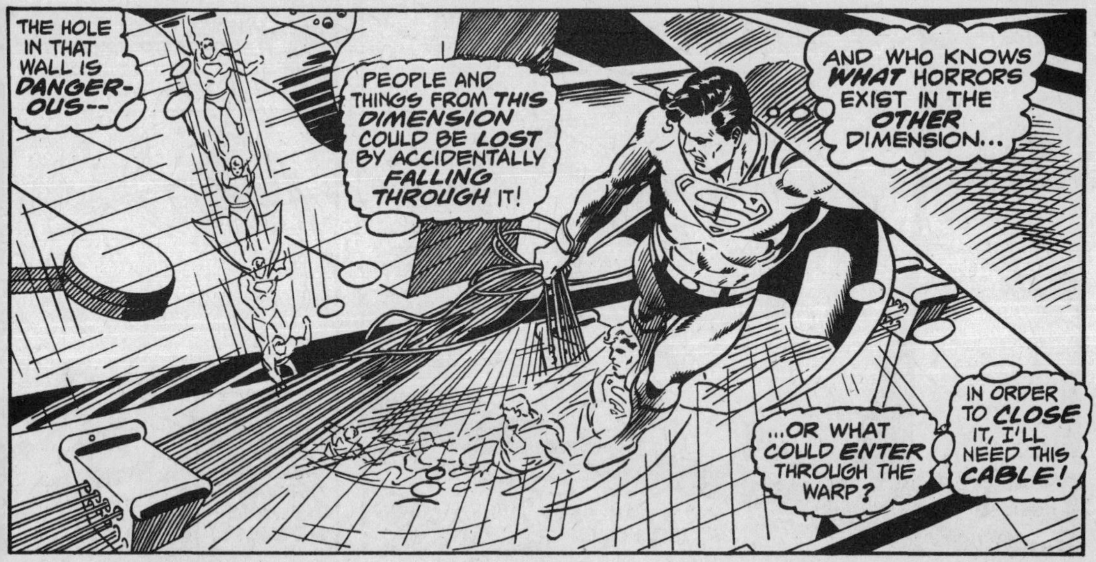
THE HOLE IN THAT WALL IS DANGER-OUS--
PEOPLE AND THINGS FROM THIS DIMENSION COULD BE LOST BY ACCIDENTALLY FALLING THROUGH IT!
AND WHO KNOWS WHAT HORRORS EXIST IN THE OTHER DIMENSION...
...OR WHAT COULD ENTER THROUGH THE WARP?
IN ORDER TO CLOSE IT, I'LL NEED THIS CABLE!

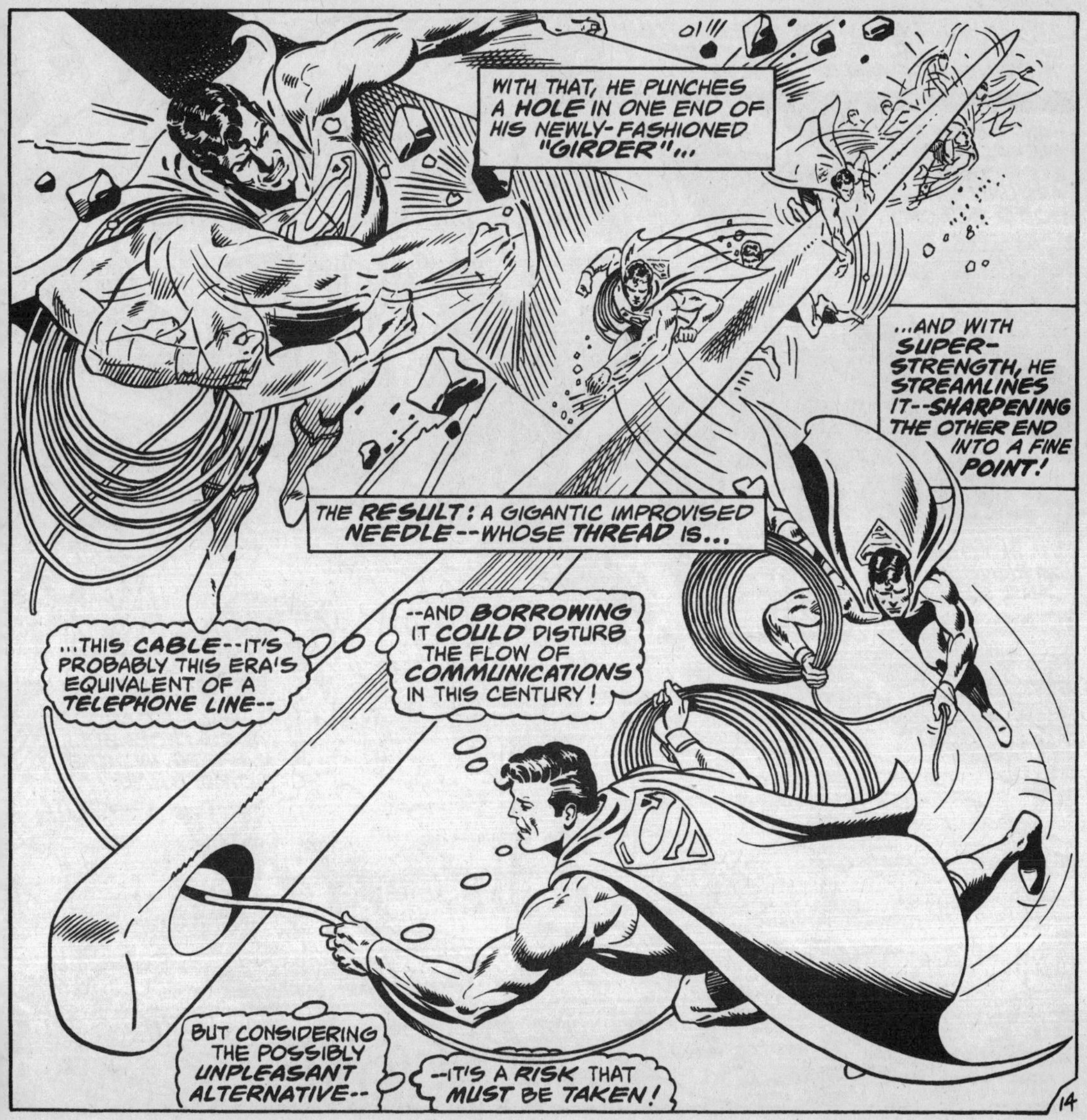
WITH THAT, HE PUNCHES A HOLE IN ONE END OF HIS NEWLY-FASHIONED "GIRDER"...
...AND WITH SUPER-STRENGTH, HE STREAMLINES IT--SHARPENING THE OTHER END INTO A FINE POINT!
THE RESULT: A GIGANTIC IMPROVISED NEEDLE--WHOSE THREAD IS...
...THIS CABLE--IT'S PROBABLY THIS ERA'S EQUIVALENT OF A TELEPHONE LINE--
--AND BORROWING IT COULD DISTURB THE FLOW OF COMMUNICATIONS IN THIS CENTURY!
BUT CONSIDERING THE POSSIBLY UNPLEASANT ALTERNATIVE--
--IT'S A RISK THAT MUST BE TAKEN!
14

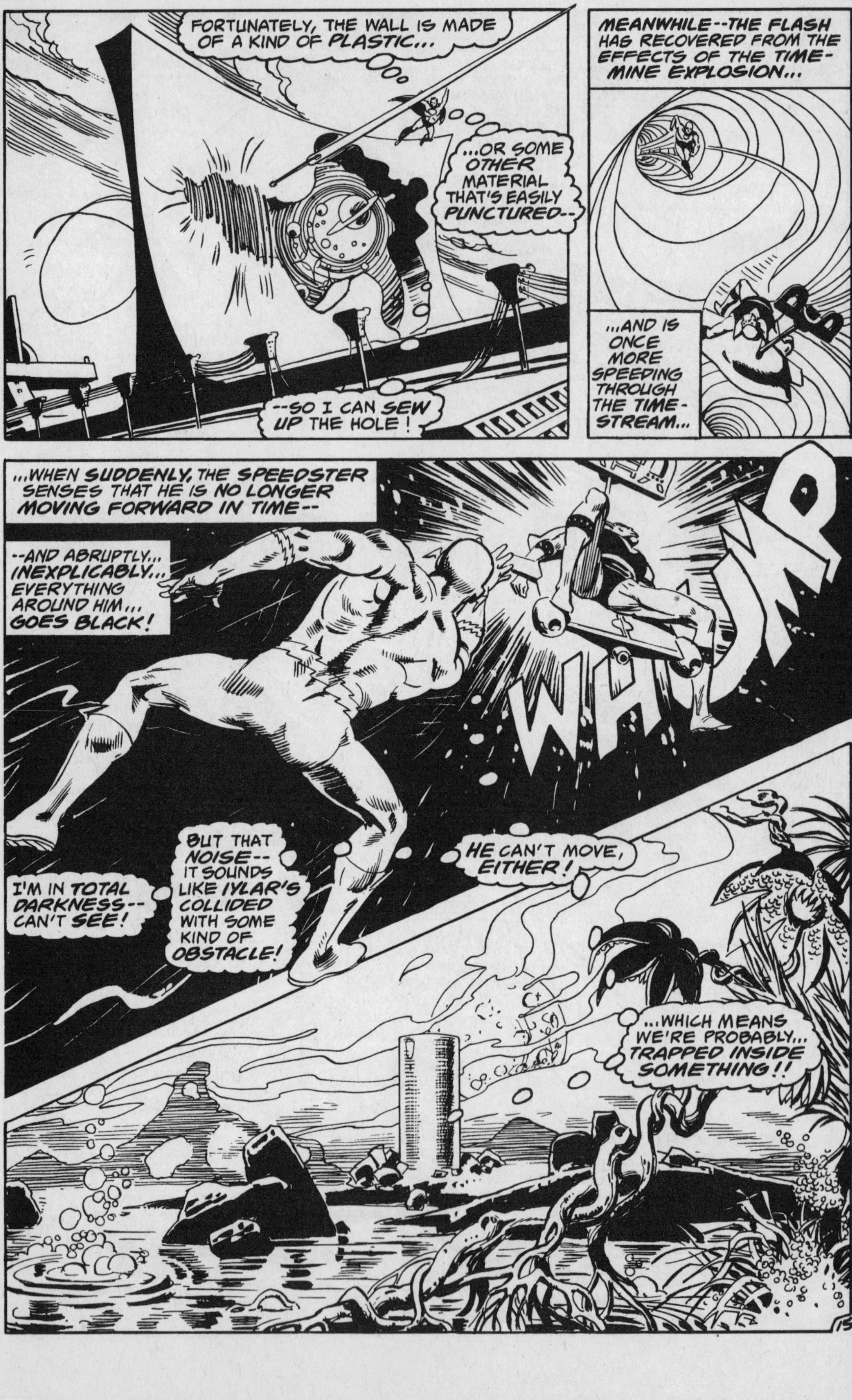
FORTUNATELY, THE WALL IS MADE OF A KIND OF PLASTIC...
...OR SOME OTHER MATERIAL THAT'S EASILY PUNCTURED--
--SO I CAN SEW UP THE HOLE!
MEANWHILE--THE FLASH HAS RECOVERED FROM THE EFFECTS OF THE TIME-MINE EXPLOSION...
...AND IS ONCE MORE SPEEDING THROUGH THE TIME-STREAM...
...WHEN SUDDENLY, THE SPEEDSTER SENSES THAT HE IS NO LONGER MOVING FORWARD IN TIME--
--AND ABRUPTLY... INEXPLICABLY... EVERYTHING AROUND HIM... GOES BLACK!
WHUMP
I'M IN TOTAL DARKNESS-- CAN'T SEE!
BUT THAT NOISE-- IT SOUNDS LIKE IYLAR'S COLLIDED WITH SOME KIND OF OBSTACLE!
HE CAN'T MOVE, EITHER!
...WHICH MEANS WE'RE PROBABLY... TRAPPED INSIDE SOMETHING!!
15.

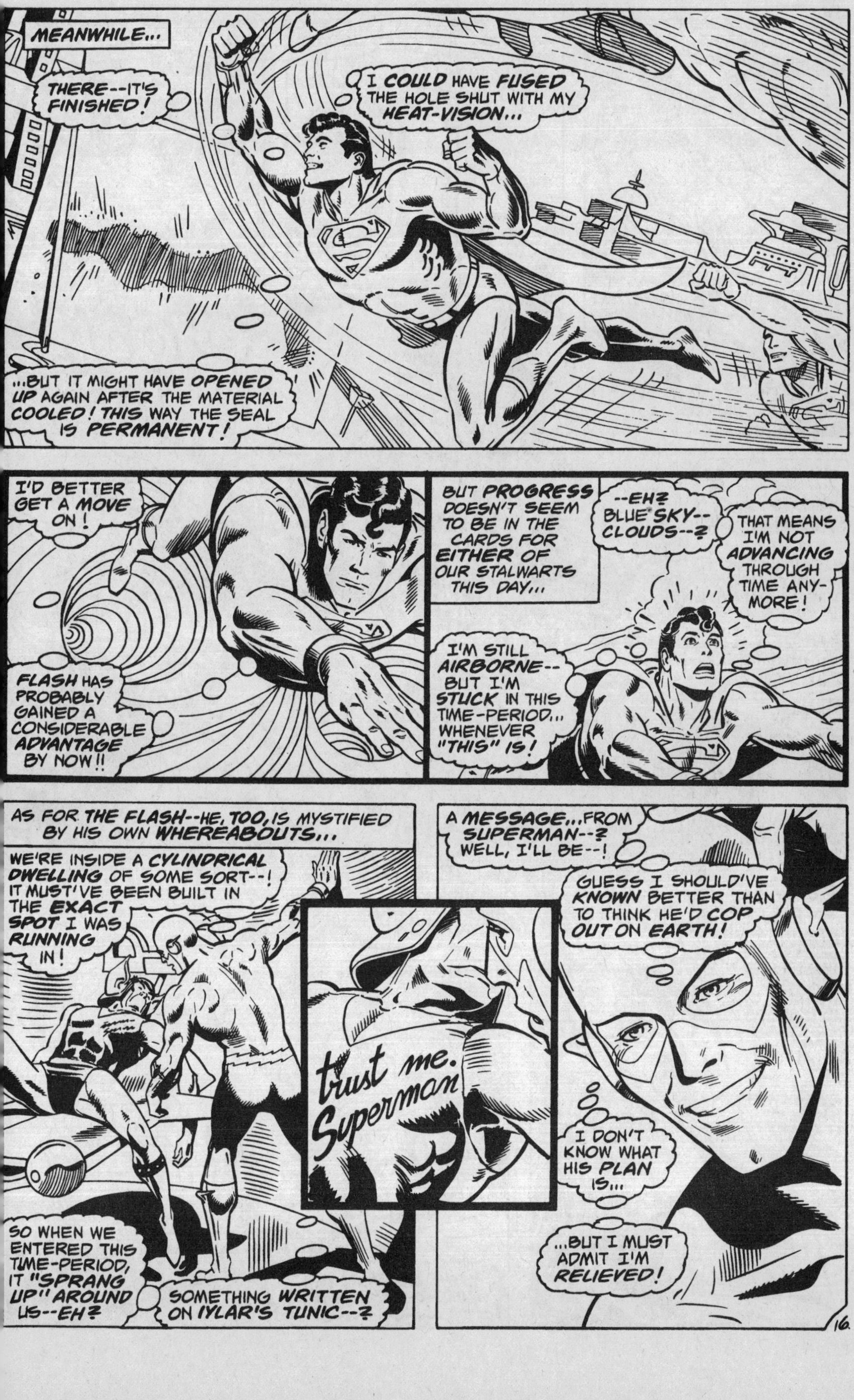
MEANWHILE...
THERE--IT'S FINISHED!
I COULD HAVE FUSED THE HOLE SHUT WITH MY HEAT-VISION...
...BUT IT MIGHT HAVE OPENED UP AGAIN AFTER THE MATERIAL COOLED! THIS WAY THE SEAL IS PERMANENT!
I'D BETTER GET A MOVE ON!
FLASH HAS PROBABLY GAINED A CONSIDERABLE ADVANTAGE BY NOW!!
BUT PROGRESS DOESN'T SEEM TO BE IN THE CARDS FOR EITHER OF OUR STALWARTS THIS DAY...
--EH? BLUE SKY--CLOUDS--?
THAT MEANS I'M NOT ADVANCING THROUGH TIME ANY-MORE!
I'M STILL AIRBORNE--BUT I'M STUCK IN THIS TIME-PERIOD... WHENEVER "THIS" IS!
AS FOR THE FLASH--HE, TOO, IS MYSTIFIED BY HIS OWN WHEREABOUTS...
WE'RE INSIDE A CYLINDRICAL DWELLING OF SOME SORT--! IT MUST'VE BEEN BUILT IN THE EXACT SPOT I WAS RUNNING IN!
SO WHEN WE ENTERED THIS TIME-PERIOD, IT "SPRANG UP" AROUND US--EH?
SOMETHING WRITTEN ON IYLAR'S TUNIC--?
trust me. Superman
A MESSAGE... FROM SUPERMAN--? WELL, I'LL BE--!
GUESS I SHOULD'VE KNOWN BETTER THAN TO THINK HE'D COP OUT ON EARTH!
I DON'T KNOW WHAT HIS PLAN IS...
...BUT I MUST ADMIT I'M RELIEVED!
16

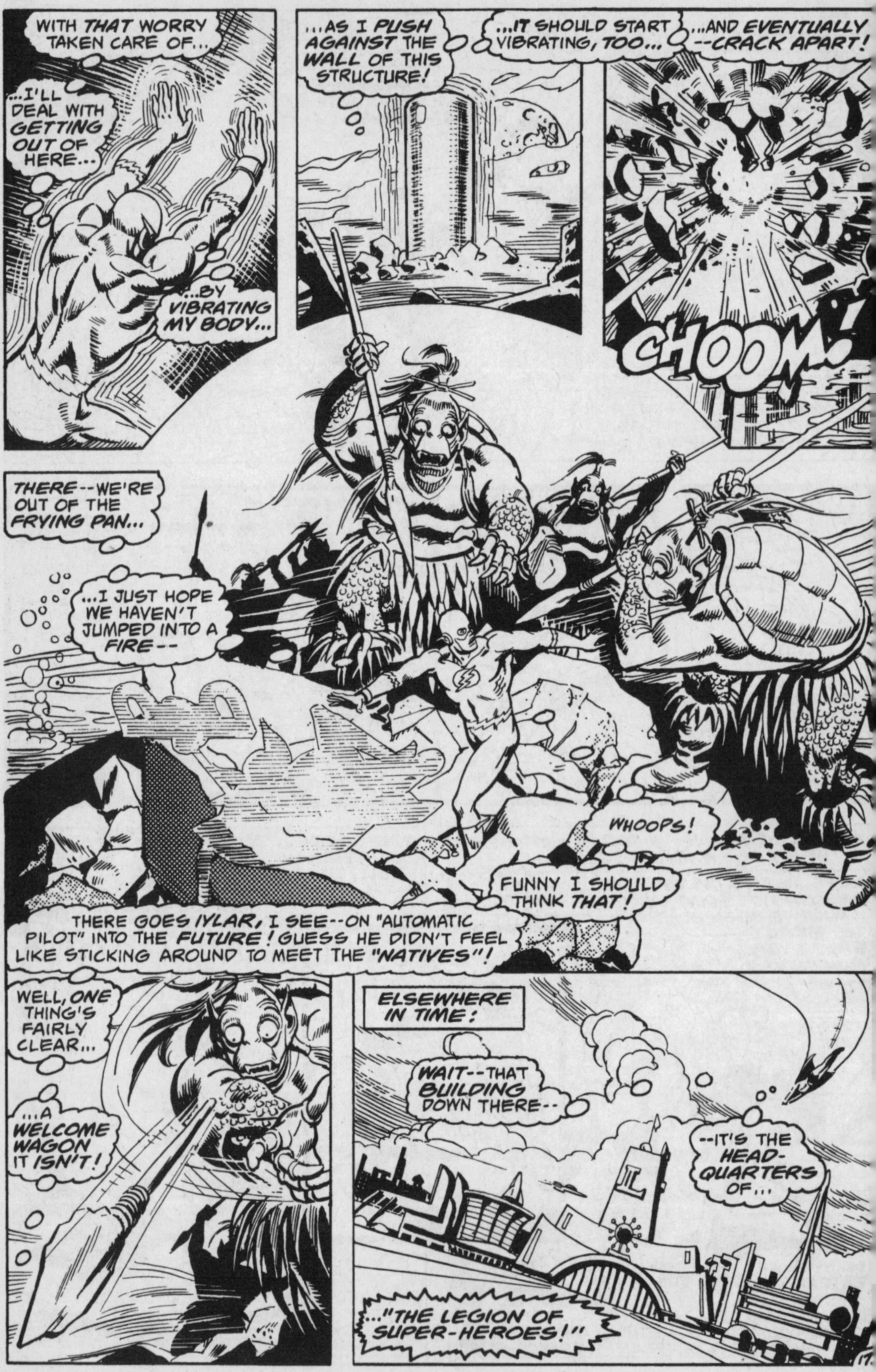
WITH THAT WORRY TAKEN CARE OF...
...I'LL DEAL WITH GETTING OUT OF HERE...
...BY VIBRATING MY BODY...
...AS I PUSH AGAINST THE WALL OF THIS STRUCTURE!
...IT SHOULD START VIBRATING, TOO...
...AND EVENTUALLY --CRACK APART!
CHOOM!
THERE--WE'RE OUT OF THE FRYING PAN...
...I JUST HOPE WE HAVEN'T JUMPED INTO A FIRE--
WHOOPS!
FUNNY I SHOULD THINK THAT!
THERE GOES IYLAR, I SEE--ON "AUTOMATIC PILOT" INTO THE FUTURE! GUESS HE DIDN'T FEEL LIKE STICKING AROUND TO MEET THE "NATIVES"!
WELL, ONE THING'S FAIRLY CLEAR...
...A WELCOME WAGON IT ISN'T!
ELSEWHERE IN TIME:
WAIT--THAT BUILDING DOWN THERE--
--IT'S THE HEAD-QUARTERS OF...
..."THE LEGION OF SUPER-HEROES!"
17

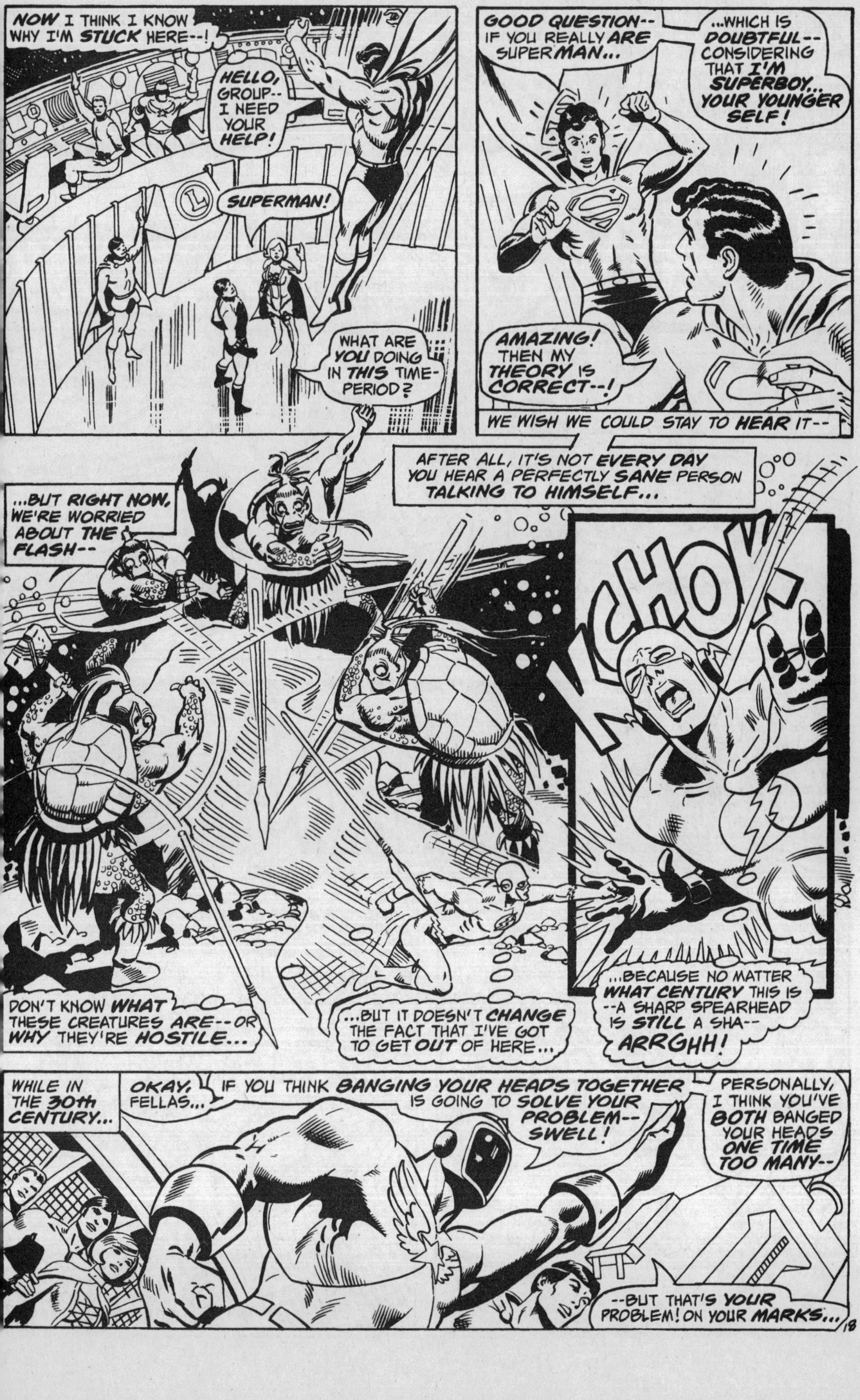
NOW I THINK I KNOW WHY I'M STUCK HERE--!
HELLO, GROUP-- I NEED YOUR HELP!
SUPERMAN!
WHAT ARE YOU DOING IN THIS TIME-PERIOD?
GOOD QUESTION-- IF YOU REALLY ARE SUPERMAN...
...WHICH IS DOUBTFUL-- CONSIDERING THAT I'M SUPERBOY... YOUR YOUNGER SELF!
AMAZING! THEN MY THEORY IS CORRECT--!
WE WISH WE COULD STAY TO HEAR IT--
AFTER ALL, IT'S NOT EVERY DAY YOU HEAR A PERFECTLY SANE PERSON TALKING TO HIMSELF...
...BUT RIGHT NOW, WE'RE WORRIED ABOUT THE FLASH--
KCHOK
DON'T KNOW WHAT THESE CREATURES ARE-- OR WHY THEY'RE HOSTILE...
...BUT IT DOESN'T CHANGE THE FACT THAT I'VE GOT TO GET OUT OF HERE...
...BECAUSE NO MATTER WHAT CENTURY THIS IS --A SHARP SPEARHEAD IS STILL A SHA-- ARRGHH!
WHILE IN THE 30th CENTURY...
OKAY, FELLAS...
IF YOU THINK BANGING YOUR HEADS TOGETHER IS GOING TO SOLVE YOUR PROBLEM-- SWELL!
PERSONALLY, I THINK YOU'VE BOTH BANGED YOUR HEADS ONE TIME TOO MANY--
--BUT THAT'S YOUR PROBLEM! ON YOUR MARKS...
18

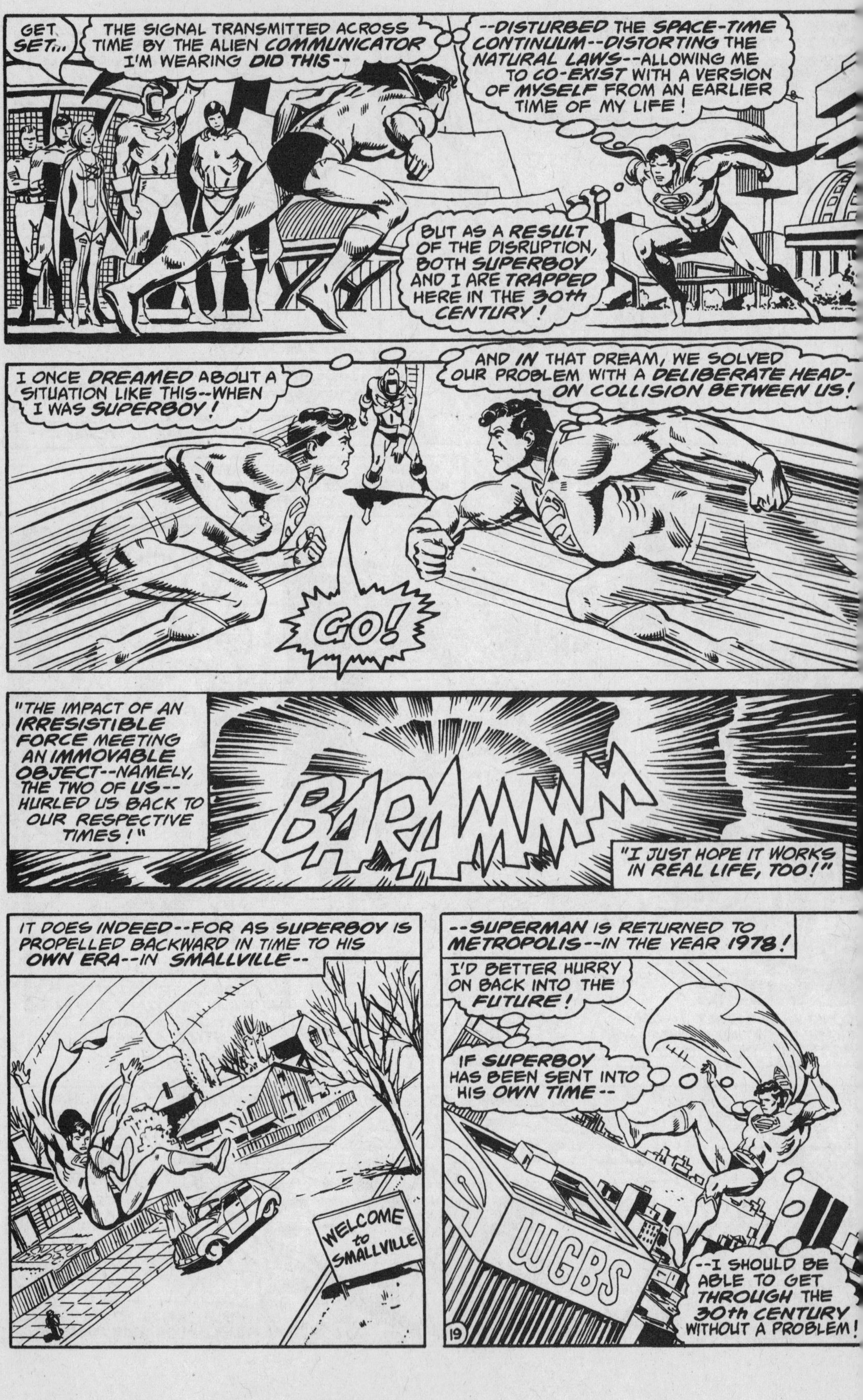
GET SET...
THE SIGNAL TRANSMITTED ACROSS TIME BY THE ALIEN COMMUNICATOR I'M WEARING DID THIS--
--DISTURBED THE SPACE-TIME CONTINUUM--DISTORTING THE NATURAL LAWS--ALLOWING ME TO CO-EXIST WITH A VERSION OF MYSELF FROM AN EARLIER TIME OF MY LIFE!
BUT AS A RESULT OF THE DISRUPTION, BOTH SUPERBOY AND I ARE TRAPPED HERE IN THE 30th CENTURY!
I ONCE DREAMED ABOUT A SITUATION LIKE THIS--WHEN I WAS SUPERBOY!
AND IN THAT DREAM, WE SOLVED OUR PROBLEM WITH A DELIBERATE HEAD-ON COLLISION BETWEEN US!
GO!
"THE IMPACT OF AN IRRESISTIBLE FORCE MEETING AN IMMOVABLE OBJECT--NAMELY, THE TWO OF US--HURLED US BACK TO OUR RESPECTIVE TIMES!"
BARAMMM
"I JUST HOPE IT WORKS IN REAL LIFE, TOO!"
IT DOES INDEED--FOR AS SUPERBOY IS PROPELLED BACKWARD IN TIME TO HIS OWN ERA--IN SMALLVILLE--
WELCOME to SMALLVILLE
--SUPERMAN IS RETURNED TO METROPOLIS--IN THE YEAR 1978!
I'D BETTER HURRY ON BACK INTO THE FUTURE!
IF SUPERBOY HAS BEEN SENT INTO HIS OWN TIME--
WGBS
--I SHOULD BE ABLE TO GET THROUGH THE 30th CENTURY WITHOUT A PROBLEM!
19

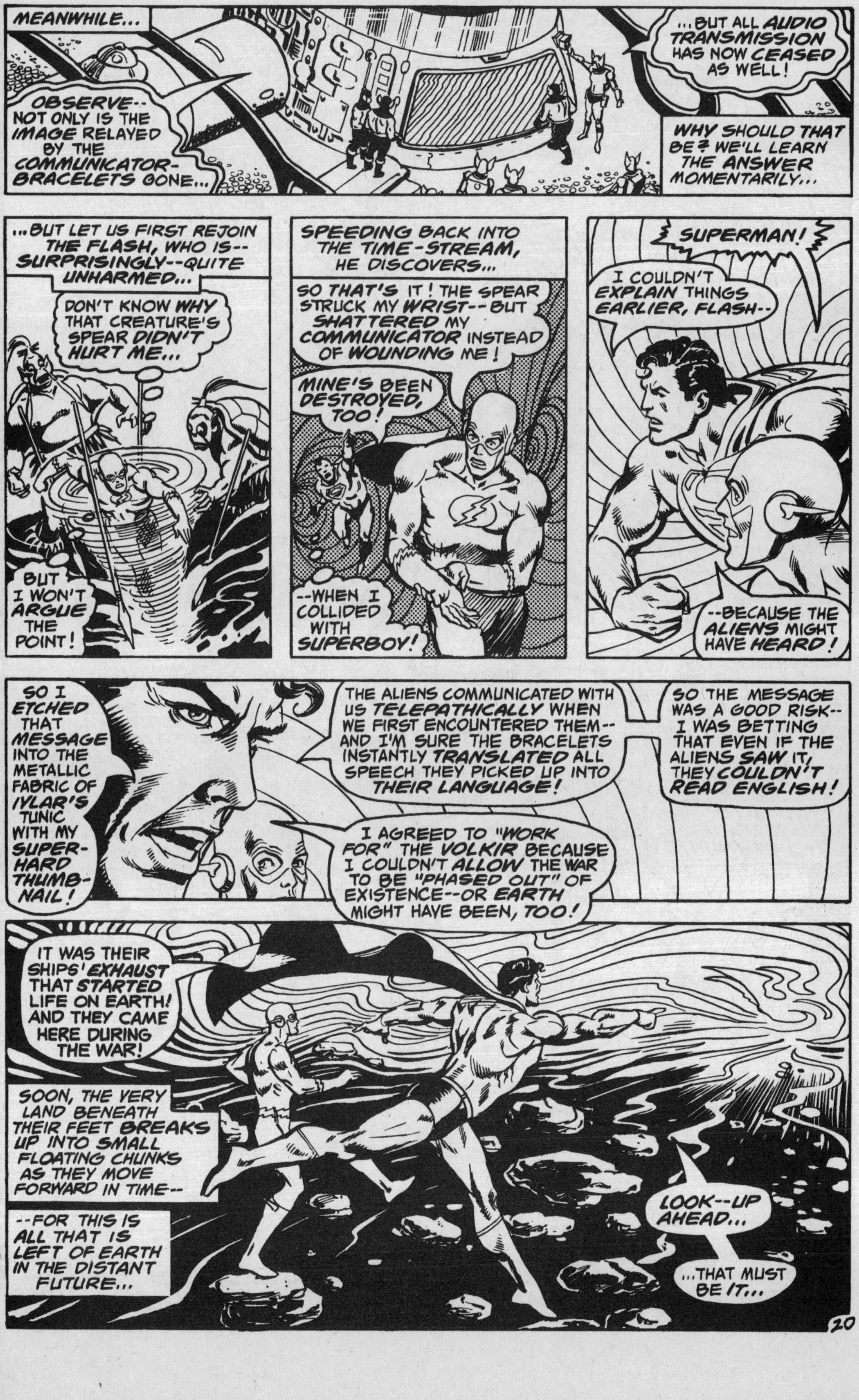
MEANWHILE...
OBSERVE-- NOT ONLY IS THE IMAGE RELAYED BY THE COMMUNICATOR-BRACELETS GONE...
...BUT ALL AUDIO TRANSMISSION HAS NOW CEASED AS WELL!
WHY SHOULD THAT BE? WE'LL LEARN THE ANSWER MOMENTARILY...
...BUT LET US FIRST REJOIN THE FLASH, WHO IS--SURPRISINGLY--QUITE UNHARMED...
DON'T KNOW WHY THAT CREATURE'S SPEAR DIDN'T HURT ME...
BUT I WON'T ARGUE THE POINT!
SPEEDING BACK INTO THE TIME-STREAM, HE DISCOVERS...
SO THAT'S IT! THE SPEAR STRUCK MY WRIST--BUT SHATTERED MY COMMUNICATOR INSTEAD OF WOUNDING ME!
MINE'S BEEN DESTROYED, TOO!
--WHEN I COLLIDED WITH SUPERBOY!
SUPERMAN!
I COULDN'T EXPLAIN THINGS EARLIER, FLASH--
--BECAUSE THE ALIENS MIGHT HAVE HEARD!
SO I ETCHED THAT MESSAGE INTO THE METALLIC FABRIC OF IYLAR'S TUNIC WITH MY SUPER-HARD THUMB-NAIL!
THE ALIENS COMMUNICATED WITH US TELEPATHICALLY WHEN WE FIRST ENCOUNTERED THEM--AND I'M SURE THE BRACELETS INSTANTLY TRANSLATED ALL SPEECH THEY PICKED UP INTO THEIR LANGUAGE!
SO THE MESSAGE WAS A GOOD RISK--I WAS BETTING THAT EVEN IF THE ALIENS SAW IT, THEY COULDN'T READ ENGLISH!
I AGREED TO "WORK FOR" THE VOLKIR BECAUSE I COULDN'T ALLOW THE WAR TO BE "PHASED OUT" OF EXISTENCE--OR EARTH MIGHT HAVE BEEN, TOO!
IT WAS THEIR SHIPS' EXHAUST THAT STARTED LIFE ON EARTH! AND THEY CAME HERE DURING THE WAR!
SOON, THE VERY LAND BENEATH THEIR FEET BREAKS UP INTO SMALL FLOATING CHUNKS AS THEY MOVE FORWARD IN TIME--
--FOR THIS IS ALL THAT IS LEFT OF EARTH IN THE DISTANT FUTURE...
LOOK--UP AHEAD...
...THAT MUST BE IT...
20

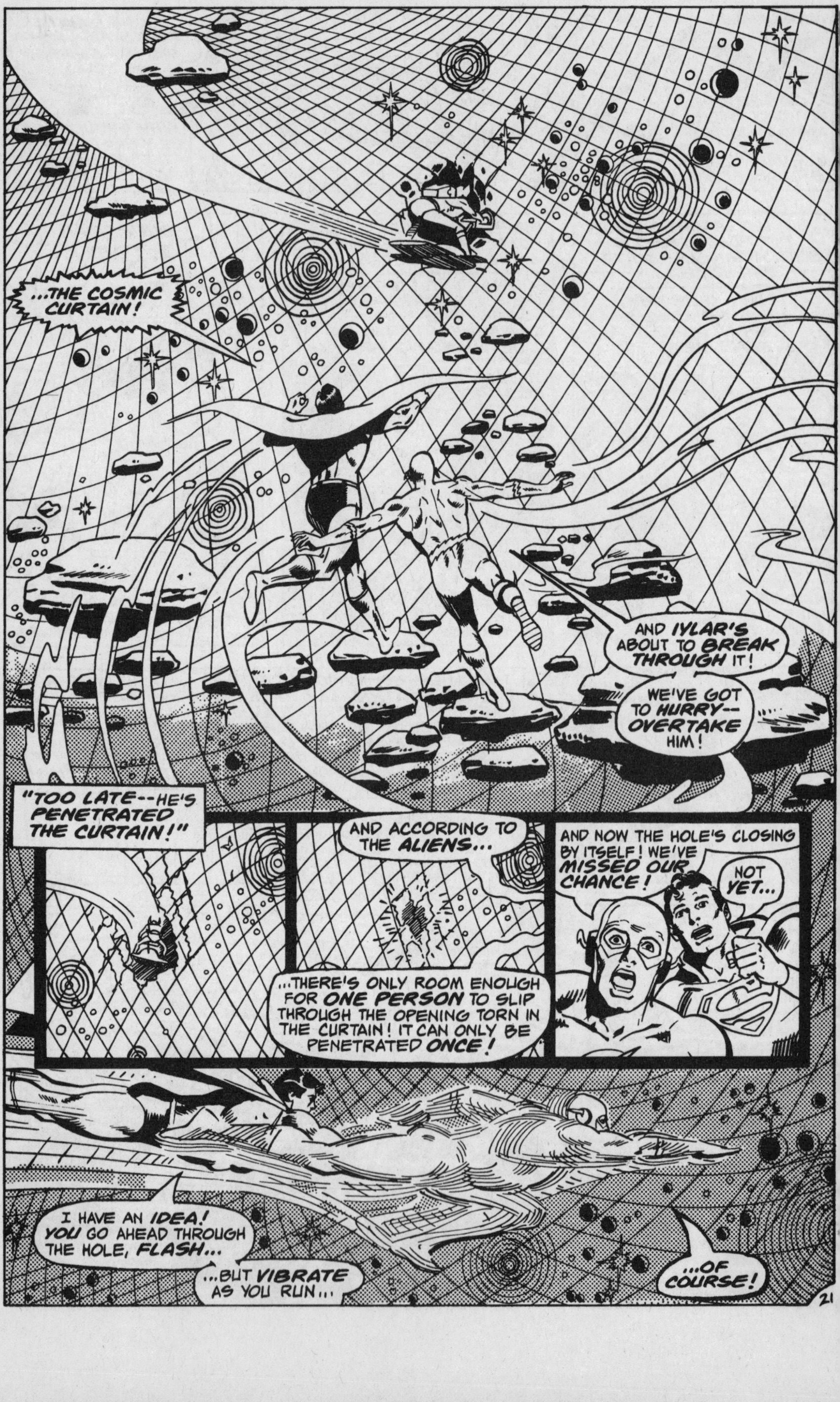
...THE COSMIC CURTAIN!
AND IYLAR'S ABOUT TO BREAK THROUGH IT!
WE'VE GOT TO HURRY-- OVERTAKE HIM!
"TOO LATE--HE'S PENETRATED THE CURTAIN!"
AND ACCORDING TO THE ALIENS...
...THERE'S ONLY ROOM ENOUGH FOR ONE PERSON TO SLIP THROUGH THE OPENING TORN IN THE CURTAIN! IT CAN ONLY BE PENETRATED ONCE!
AND NOW THE HOLE'S CLOSING BY ITSELF! WE'VE MISSED OUR CHANCE!
NOT YET...
I HAVE AN IDEA! YOU GO AHEAD THROUGH THE HOLE, FLASH...
...BUT VIBRATE AS YOU RUN...
...OF COURSE!
21

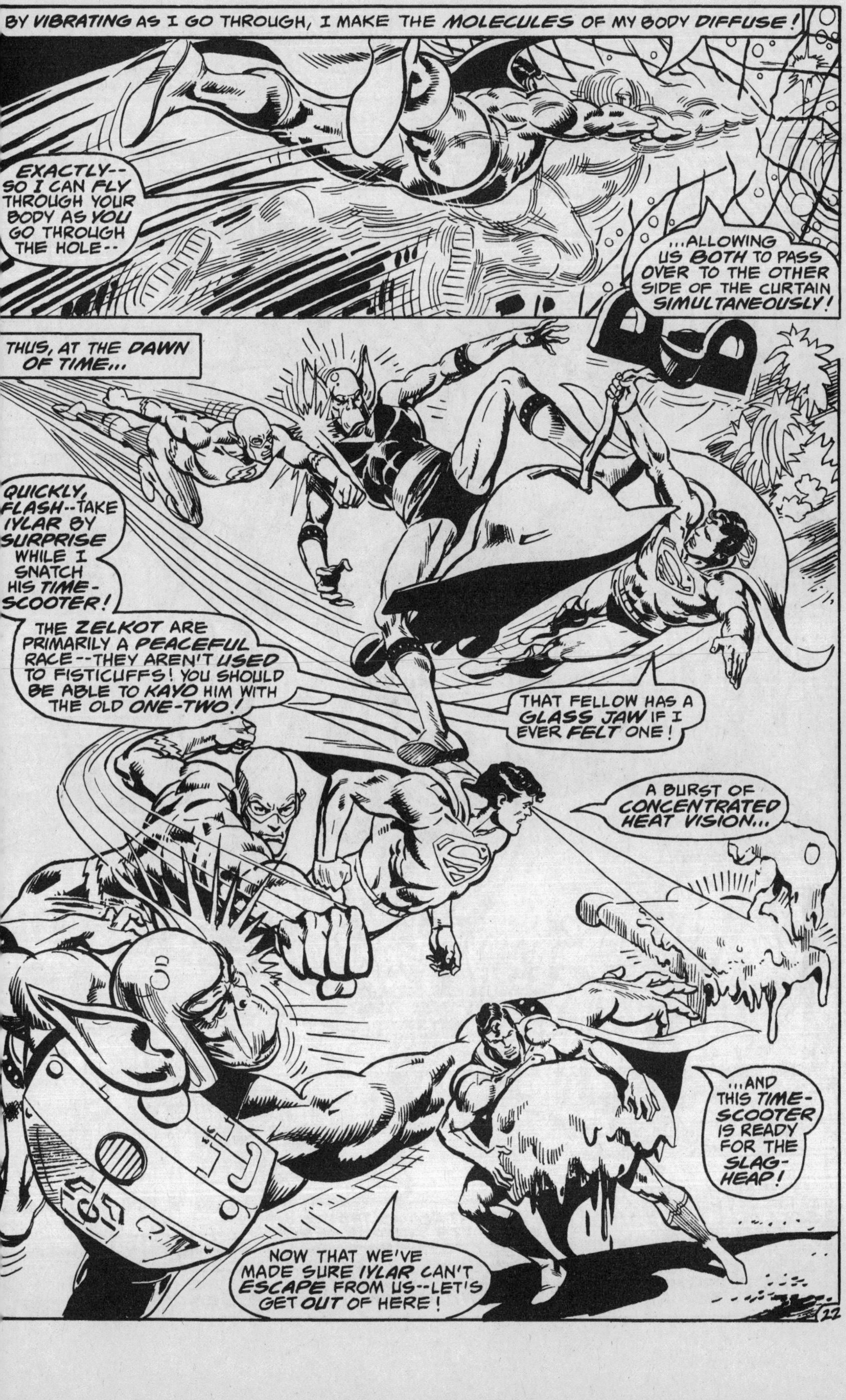
BY VIBRATING AS I GO THROUGH, I MAKE THE MOLECULES OF MY BODY DIFFUSE!
EXACTLY-- SO I CAN FLY THROUGH YOUR BODY AS YOU GO THROUGH THE HOLE--
...ALLOWING US BOTH TO PASS OVER TO THE OTHER SIDE OF THE CURTAIN SIMULTANEOUSLY!
THUS, AT THE DAWN OF TIME...
QUICKLY, FLASH--TAKE IYLAR BY SURPRISE WHILE I SNATCH HIS TIME-SCOOTER!
THE ZELKOT ARE PRIMARILY A PEACEFUL RACE --THEY AREN'T USED TO FISTICUFFS! YOU SHOULD BE ABLE TO KAYO HIM WITH THE OLD ONE-TWO!
THAT FELLOW HAS A GLASS JAW IF I EVER FELT ONE!
A BURST OF CONCENTRATED HEAT VISION...
...AND THIS TIME-SCOOTER IS READY FOR THE SLAG-HEAP!
NOW THAT WE'VE MADE SURE IYLAR CAN'T ESCAPE FROM US--LET'S GET OUT OF HERE!
22

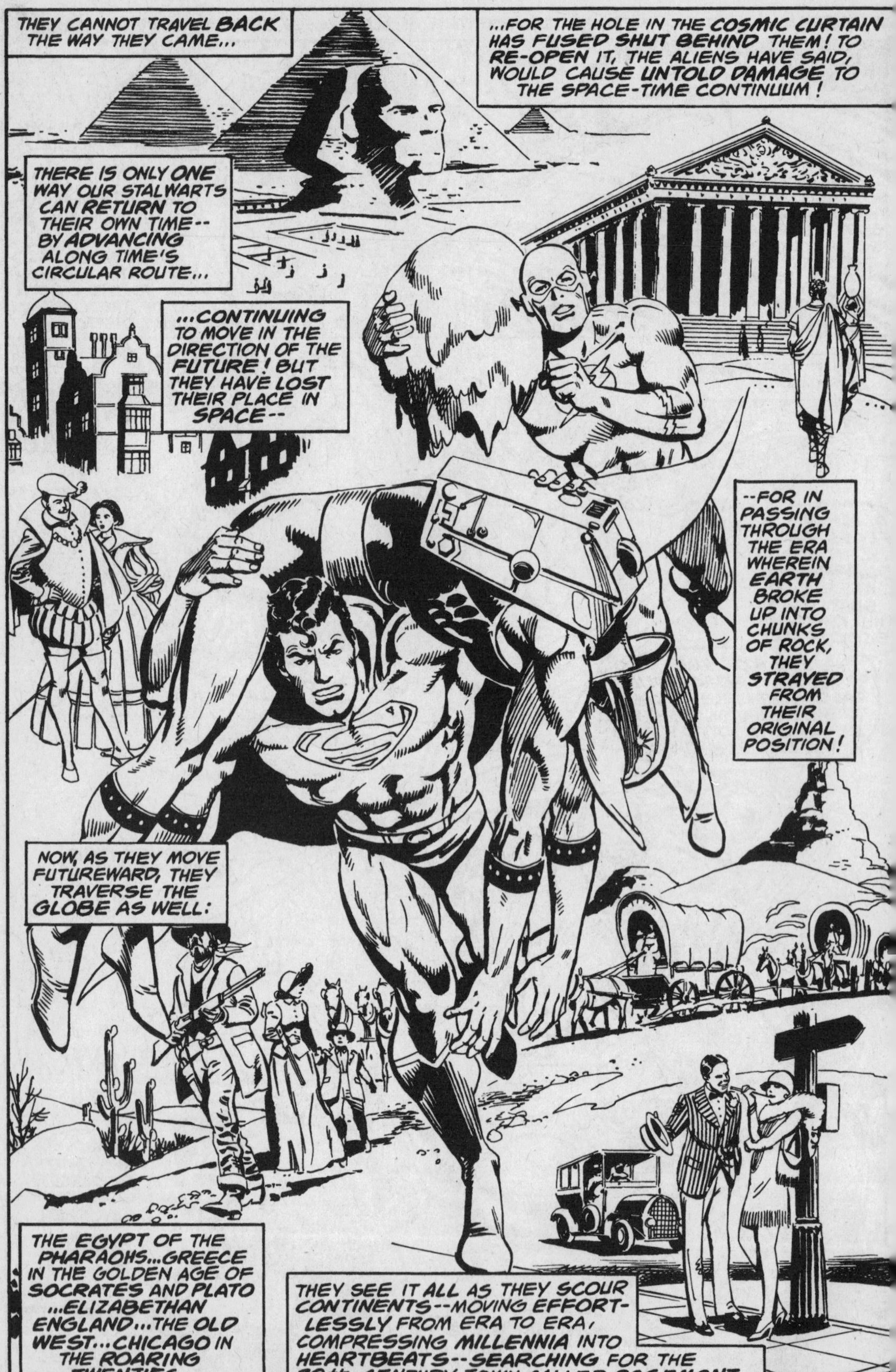
THEY CANNOT TRAVEL BACK THE WAY THEY CAME...
...FOR THE HOLE IN THE COSMIC CURTAIN HAS FUSED SHUT BEHIND THEM! TO RE-OPEN IT, THE ALIENS HAVE SAID, WOULD CAUSE UNTOLD DAMAGE TO THE SPACE-TIME CONTINUUM!
THERE IS ONLY ONE WAY OUR STALWARTS CAN RETURN TO THEIR OWN TIME--BY ADVANCING ALONG TIME'S CIRCULAR ROUTE...
...CONTINUING TO MOVE IN THE DIRECTION OF THE FUTURE! BUT THEY HAVE LOST THEIR PLACE IN SPACE--
--FOR IN PASSING THROUGH THE ERA WHEREIN EARTH BROKE UP INTO CHUNKS OF ROCK, THEY STRAYED FROM THEIR ORIGINAL POSITION!
NOW, AS THEY MOVE FUTUREWARD, THEY TRAVERSE THE GLOBE AS WELL:
THE EGYPT OF THE PHARAOHS...GREECE IN THE GOLDEN AGE OF SOCRATES AND PLATO ...ELIZABETHAN ENGLAND...THE OLD WEST...CHICAGO IN THE ROARING TWENTIES...
THEY SEE IT ALL AS THEY SCOUR CONTINENTS--MOVING EFFORTLESSLY FROM ERA TO ERA, COMPRESSING MILLENNIA INTO HEARTBEATS--SEARCHING FOR THE 20TH-CENTURY TOWN CALLED ROSEMONT...

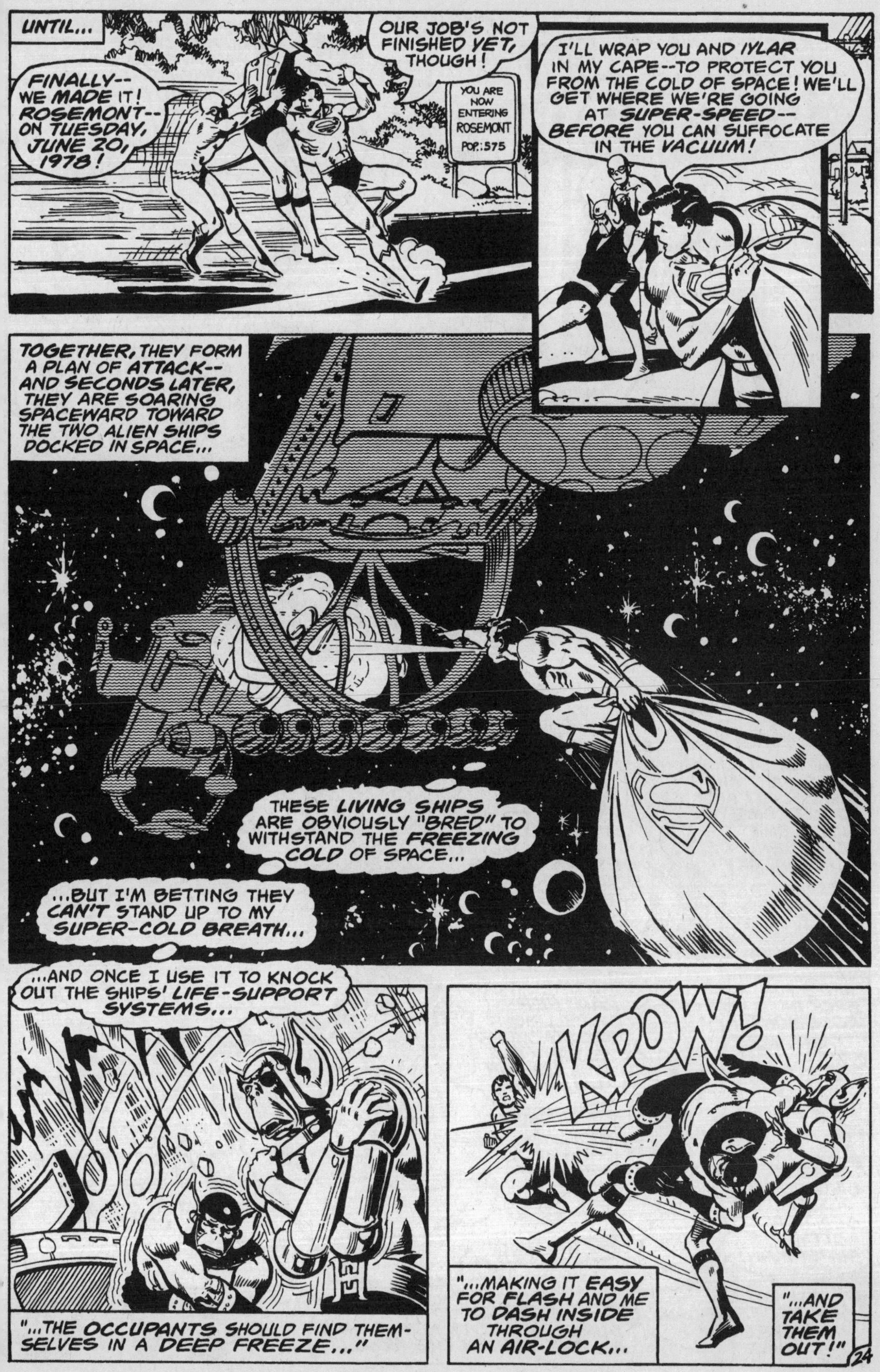
UNTIL...
FINALLY-- WE MADE IT! ROSEMONT-- ON TUESDAY, JUNE 20, 1978!
OUR JOB'S NOT FINISHED YET, THOUGH!
YOU ARE NOW ENTERING ROSEMONT POP.: 575
I'LL WRAP YOU AND IYLAR IN MY CAPE--TO PROTECT YOU FROM THE COLD OF SPACE! WE'LL GET WHERE WE'RE GOING AT SUPER-SPEED-- BEFORE YOU CAN SUFFOCATE IN THE VACUUM!
TOGETHER, THEY FORM A PLAN OF ATTACK-- AND SECONDS LATER, THEY ARE SOARING SPACEWARD TOWARD THE TWO ALIEN SHIPS DOCKED IN SPACE...
THESE LIVING SHIPS ARE OBVIOUSLY "BRED" TO WITHSTAND THE FREEZING COLD OF SPACE...
...BUT I'M BETTING THEY CAN'T STAND UP TO MY SUPER-COLD BREATH...
...AND ONCE I USE IT TO KNOCK OUT THE SHIPS' LIFE-SUPPORT SYSTEMS...
"...THE OCCUPANTS SHOULD FIND THEM-SELVES IN A DEEP FREEZE..."
KPOW!
"...MAKING IT EASY FOR FLASH AND ME TO DASH INSIDE THROUGH AN AIR-LOCK...
"...AND TAKE THEM OUT!"
24

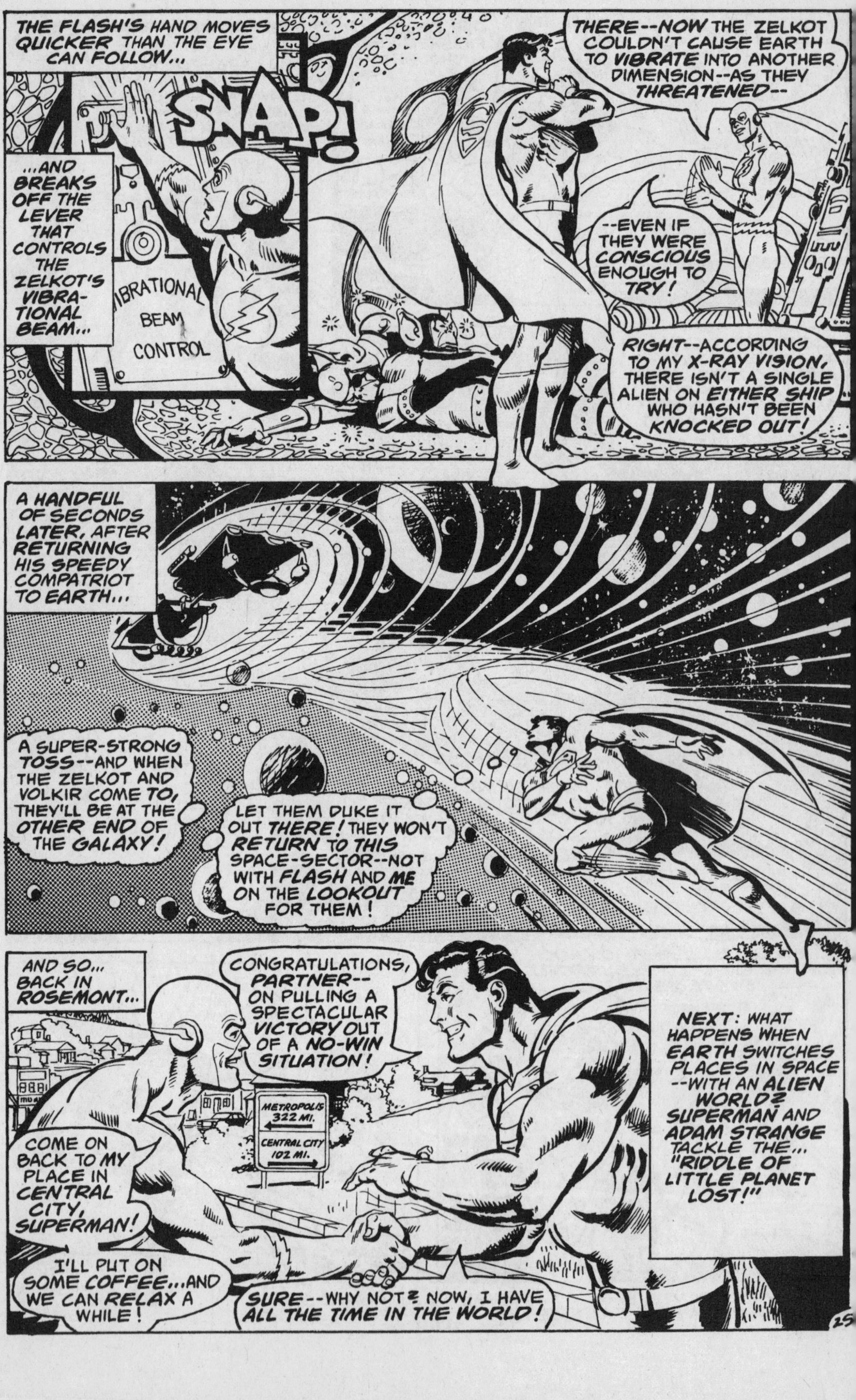
THE FLASH'S HAND MOVES QUICKER THAN THE EYE CAN FOLLOW...
SNAP!
...AND BREAKS OFF THE LEVER THAT CONTROLS THE ZELKOT'S VIBRATIONAL BEAM...
VIBRATIONAL BEAM CONTROL
THERE--NOW THE ZELKOT COULDN'T CAUSE EARTH TO VIBRATE INTO ANOTHER DIMENSION--AS THEY THREATENED--
--EVEN IF THEY WERE CONSCIOUS ENOUGH TO TRY!
RIGHT--ACCORDING TO MY X-RAY VISION, THERE ISN'T A SINGLE ALIEN ON EITHER SHIP WHO HASN'T BEEN KNOCKED OUT!
A HANDFUL OF SECONDS LATER, AFTER RETURNING HIS SPEEDY COMPATRIOT TO EARTH...
A SUPER-STRONG TOSS--AND WHEN THE ZELKOT AND VOLKIR COME TO, THEY'LL BE AT THE OTHER END OF THE GALAXY!
LET THEM DUKE IT OUT THERE! THEY WON'T RETURN TO THIS SPACE-SECTOR--NOT WITH FLASH AND ME ON THE LOOKOUT FOR THEM!
AND SO... BACK IN ROSEMONT...
CONGRATULATIONS, PARTNER-- ON PULLING A SPECTACULAR VICTORY OUT OF A NO-WIN SITUATION!
METROPOLIS 322 MI.
CENTRAL CITY 102 MI.
COME ON BACK TO MY PLACE IN CENTRAL CITY, SUPERMAN!
I'LL PUT ON SOME COFFEE...AND WE CAN RELAX A WHILE!
SURE--WHY NOT? NOW, I HAVE ALL THE TIME IN THE WORLD!
NEXT: WHAT HAPPENS WHEN EARTH SWITCHES PLACES IN SPACE --WITH AN ALIEN WORLD? SUPERMAN AND ADAM STRANGE TACKLE THE... "RIDDLE OF LITTLE PLANET LOST!"
25

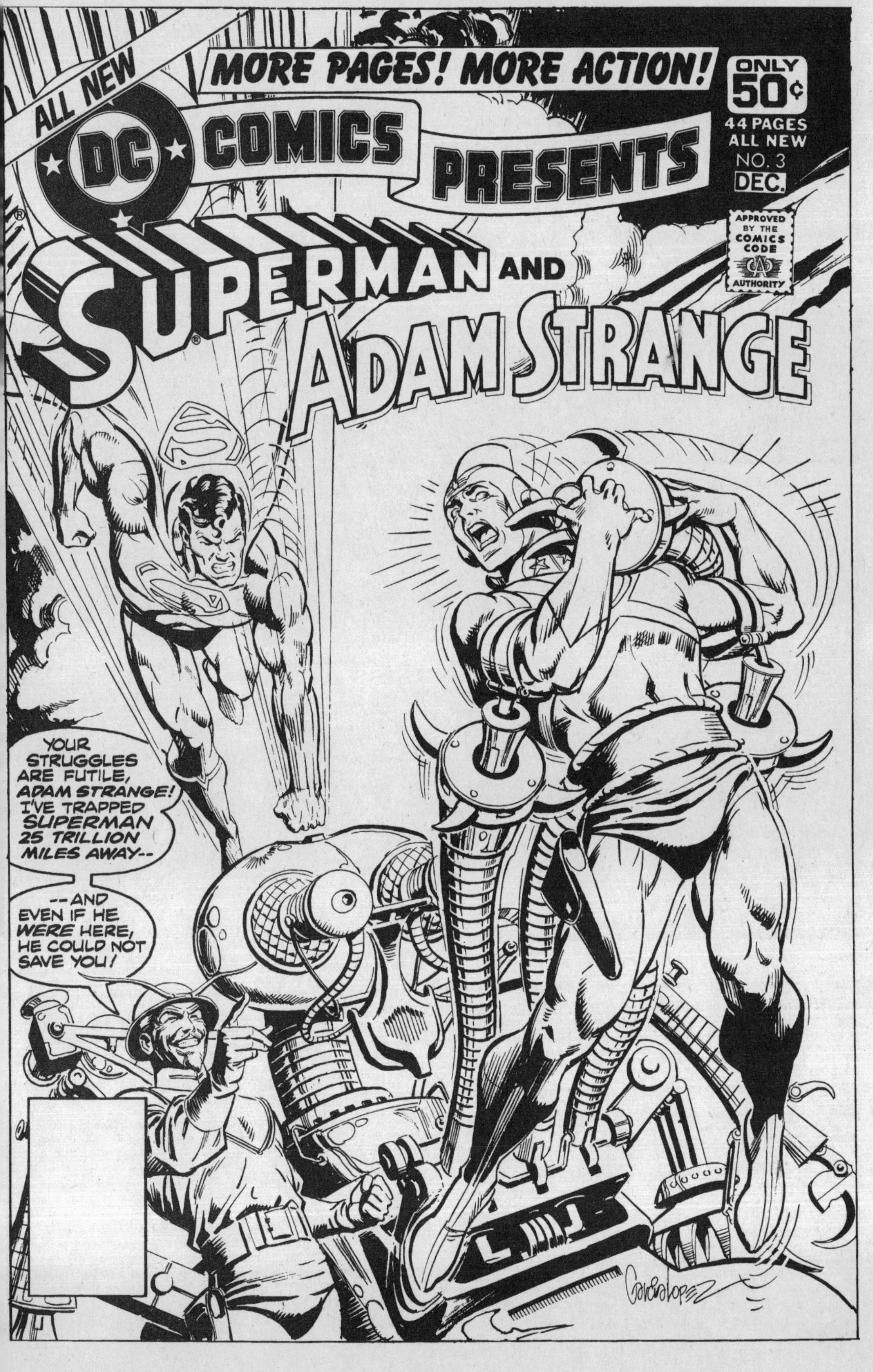
ALL NEW
MORE PAGES! MORE ACTION!
ONLY 50¢
44 PAGES ALL NEW
NO. 3
DEC.
DC COMICS PRESENTS
APPROVED BY THE COMICS CODE AUTHORITY
SUPERMAN AND ADAM STRANGE
YOUR STRUGGLES ARE FUTILE, ADAM STRANGE! I'VE TRAPPED SUPERMAN 25 TRILLION MILES AWAY--
--AND EVEN IF HE WERE HERE, HE COULD NOT SAVE YOU!
GARCIA LOPEZ

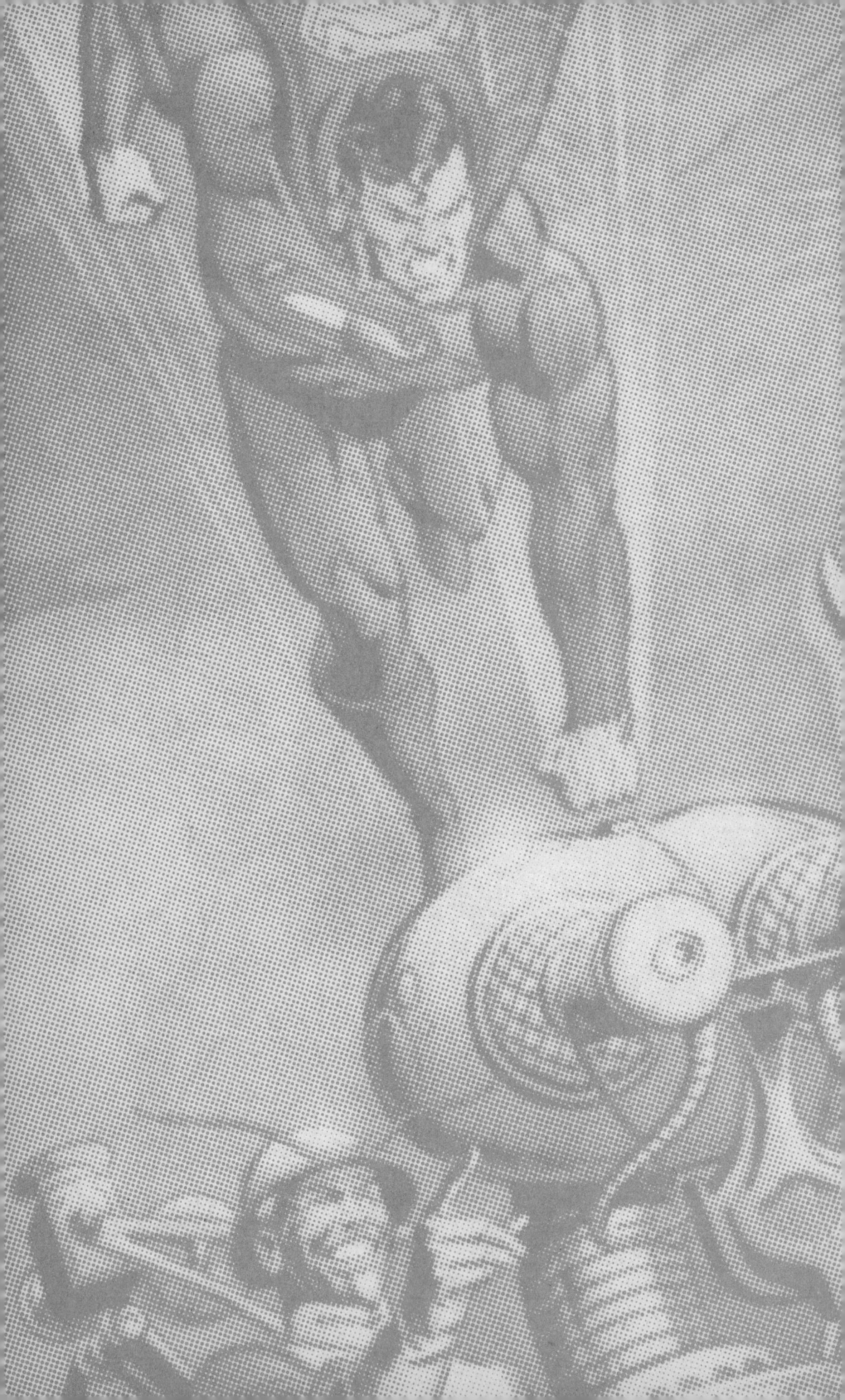

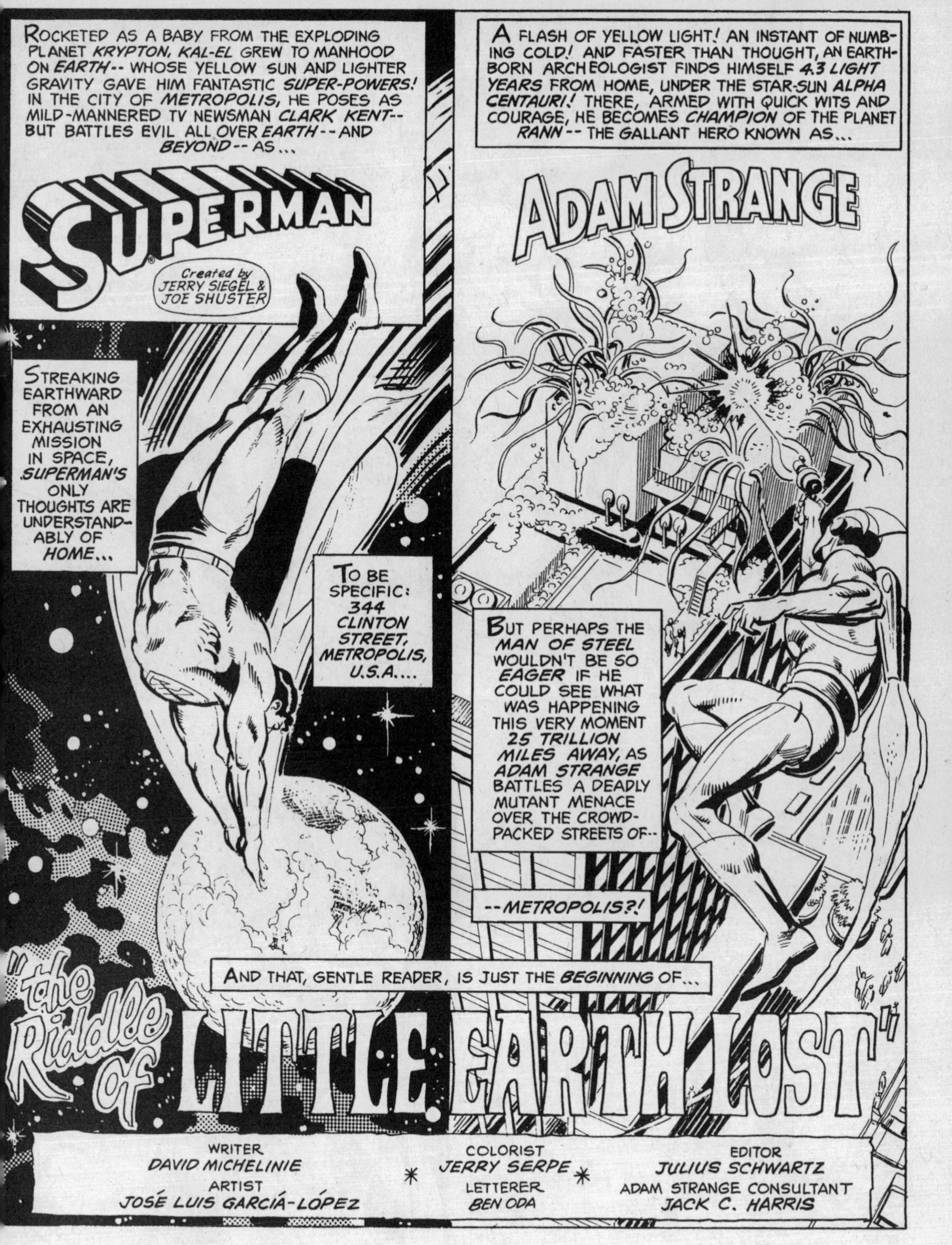
ROCKETED AS A BABY FROM THE EXPLODING PLANET KRYPTON, KAL-EL GREW TO MANHOOD ON EARTH-- WHOSE YELLOW SUN AND LIGHTER GRAVITY GAVE HIM FANTASTIC SUPER-POWERS! IN THE CITY OF METROPOLIS, HE POSES AS MILD-MANNERED TV NEWSMAN CLARK KENT-- BUT BATTLES EVIL ALL OVER EARTH--AND BEYOND--AS...
SUPERMAN
Created by JERRY SIEGEL & JOE SHUSTER
A FLASH OF YELLOW LIGHT! AN INSTANT OF NUMBING COLD! AND FASTER THAN THOUGHT, AN EARTH-BORN ARCHEOLOGIST FINDS HIMSELF 4.3 LIGHT YEARS FROM HOME, UNDER THE STAR-SUN ALPHA CENTAURI! THERE, ARMED WITH QUICK WITS AND COURAGE, HE BECOMES CHAMPION OF THE PLANET RANN-- THE GALLANT HERO KNOWN AS...
ADAM STRANGE
STREAKING EARTHWARD FROM AN EXHAUSTING MISSION IN SPACE, SUPERMAN'S ONLY THOUGHTS ARE UNDERSTANDABLY OF HOME...
TO BE SPECIFIC: 344 CLINTON STREET, METROPOLIS, U.S.A....
BUT PERHAPS THE MAN OF STEEL WOULDN'T BE SO EAGER IF HE COULD SEE WHAT WAS HAPPENING THIS VERY MOMENT 25 TRILLION MILES AWAY, AS ADAM STRANGE BATTLES A DEADLY MUTANT MENACE OVER THE CROWD-PACKED STREETS OF--
--METROPOLIS?!
AND THAT, GENTLE READER, IS JUST THE BEGINNING OF...
"the Riddle of LITTLE EARTH LOST"
WRITER DAVID MICHELINIE
ARTIST JOSÉ LUIS GARCÍA-LÓPEZ
COLORIST JERRY SERPE
LETTERER BEN ODA
EDITOR JULIUS SCHWARTZ
ADAM STRANGE CONSULTANT JACK C. HARRIS

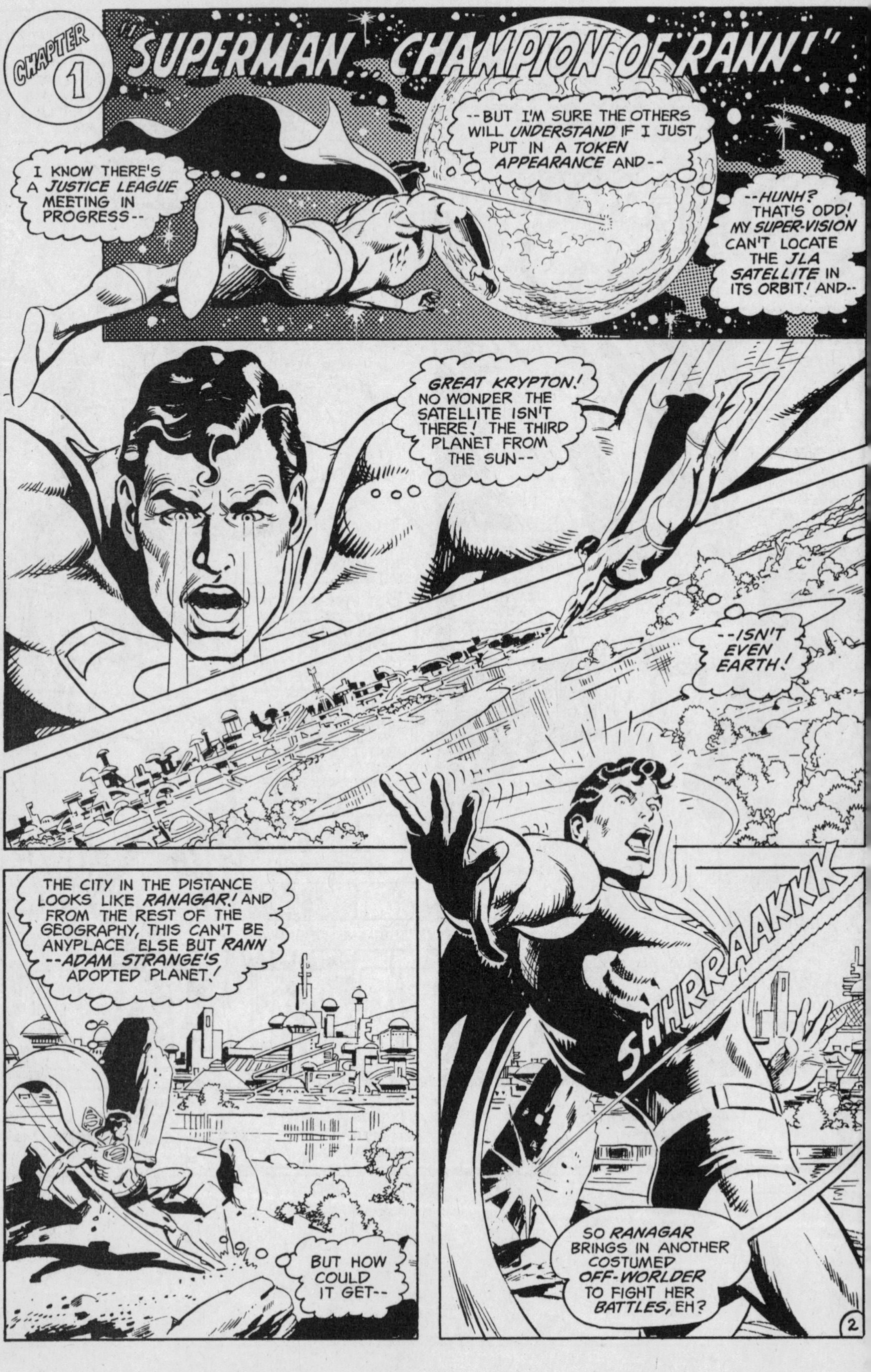
CHAPTER 1
"SUPERMAN... CHAMPION OF RANN!"
I KNOW THERE'S A JUSTICE LEAGUE MEETING IN PROGRESS--
--BUT I'M SURE THE OTHERS WILL UNDERSTAND IF I JUST PUT IN A TOKEN APPEARANCE AND--
--HUNH? THAT'S ODD! MY SUPER-VISION CAN'T LOCATE THE JLA SATELLITE IN ITS ORBIT! AND--
GREAT KRYPTON! NO WONDER THE SATELLITE ISN'T THERE! THE THIRD PLANET FROM THE SUN--
--ISN'T EVEN EARTH!
THE CITY IN THE DISTANCE LOOKS LIKE RANAGAR! AND FROM THE REST OF THE GEOGRAPHY, THIS CAN'T BE ANYPLACE ELSE BUT RANN --ADAM STRANGE'S ADOPTED PLANET!
BUT HOW COULD IT GET--
SHHRRAAKKK
SO RANAGAR BRINGS IN ANOTHER COSTUMED OFF-WORLDER TO FIGHT HER BATTLES, EH?
2

THEN LET'S SHOW THE OUTSIDER THE *PRICE* FOR MEDDLING IN AFFAIRS NOT HIS *OWN!*

VERY WELL, GENTLEMEN, CONSIDER ME *SHOWN!*

ZZZTT BRRAKZ

HNF?!

AND CONSIDER YOUR "PRICE"--

--PAID IN FULL!

SK.D.MASH

KRUK

I'D HEARD THIS PLANET WAS AT *WAR* AGAIN --BUT I NEVER THOUGHT *I'D* BE CAUGHT IN THE *MIDDLE* OF IT!

GOT TO *DISSUADE* THESE OVERZEALOUS WARRIORS WITHOUT *HURTING* THEM--AND A BLAST OF *SUPER-SUCTION* SHOULD DO THE TRICK!

BY SLOWLY CREATING A *VACUUM* BENEATH THOSE ROCKET SLEDS, I CAN "GROUND" THEM WITHOUT SHAKING UP THE *PILOTS* TOO MUCH!

SKKRRRCHH

CRA-KASH

NOW TO *IMMOBILIZE* THEM WITH THE HELP OF THIS NEARBY *LAKE!*

③

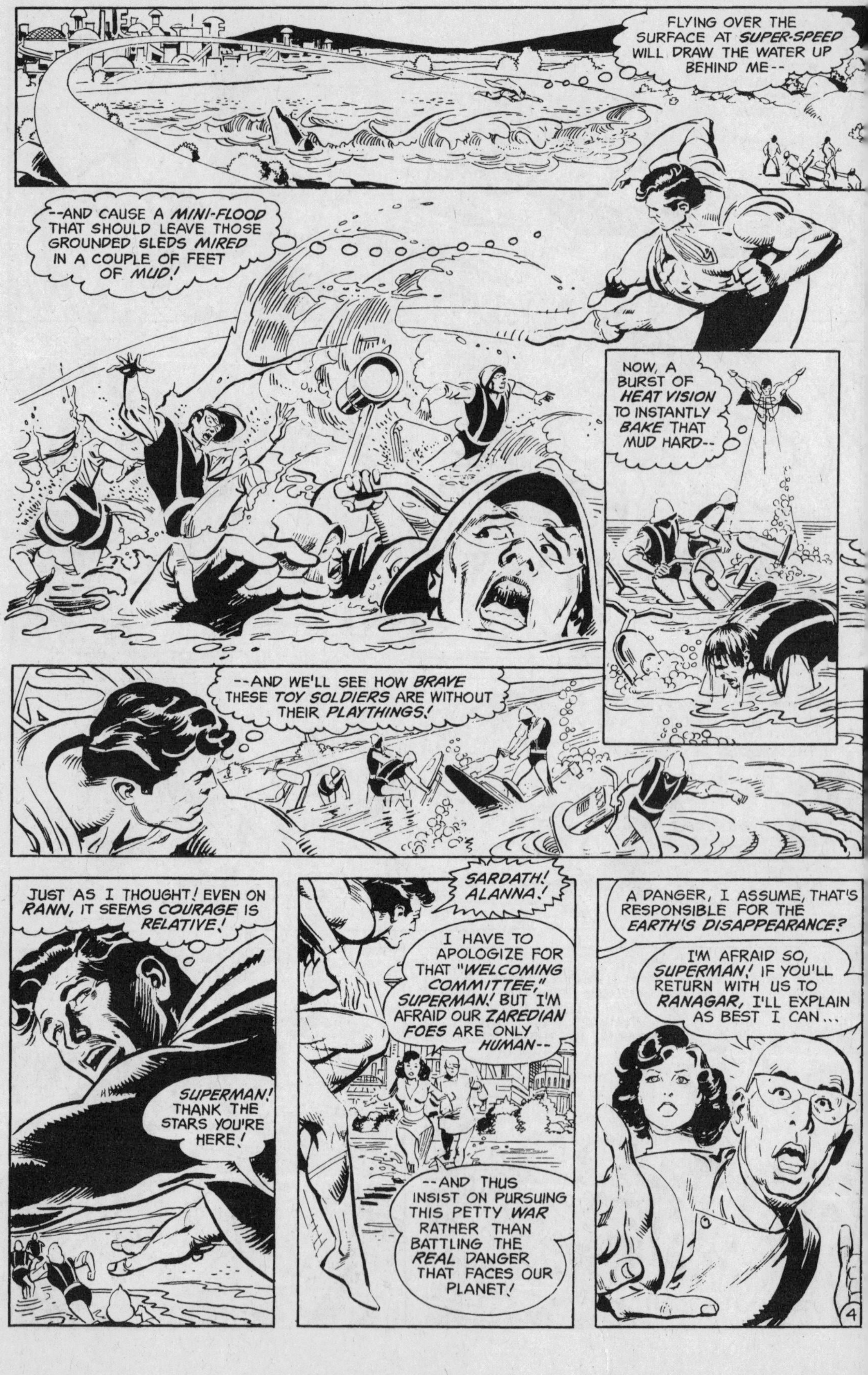
FLYING OVER THE SURFACE AT SUPER-SPEED WILL DRAW THE WATER UP BEHIND ME--
--AND CAUSE A MINI-FLOOD THAT SHOULD LEAVE THOSE GROUNDED SLEDS MIRED IN A COUPLE OF FEET OF MUD!
NOW, A BURST OF HEAT VISION TO INSTANTLY BAKE THAT MUD HARD--
--AND WE'LL SEE HOW BRAVE THESE TOY SOLDIERS ARE WITHOUT THEIR PLAYTHINGS!
JUST AS I THOUGHT! EVEN ON RANN, IT SEEMS COURAGE IS RELATIVE!
SUPERMAN! THANK THE STARS YOU'RE HERE!
SARDATH! ALANNA!
I HAVE TO APOLOGIZE FOR THAT "WELCOMING COMMITTEE," SUPERMAN! BUT I'M AFRAID OUR ZAREDIAN FOES ARE ONLY HUMAN--
--AND THUS INSIST ON PURSUING THIS PETTY WAR RATHER THAN BATTLING THE REAL DANGER THAT FACES OUR PLANET!
A DANGER, I ASSUME, THAT'S RESPONSIBLE FOR THE EARTH'S DISAPPEARANCE?
I'M AFRAID SO, SUPERMAN! IF YOU'LL RETURN WITH US TO RANAGAR, I'LL EXPLAIN AS BEST I CAN...

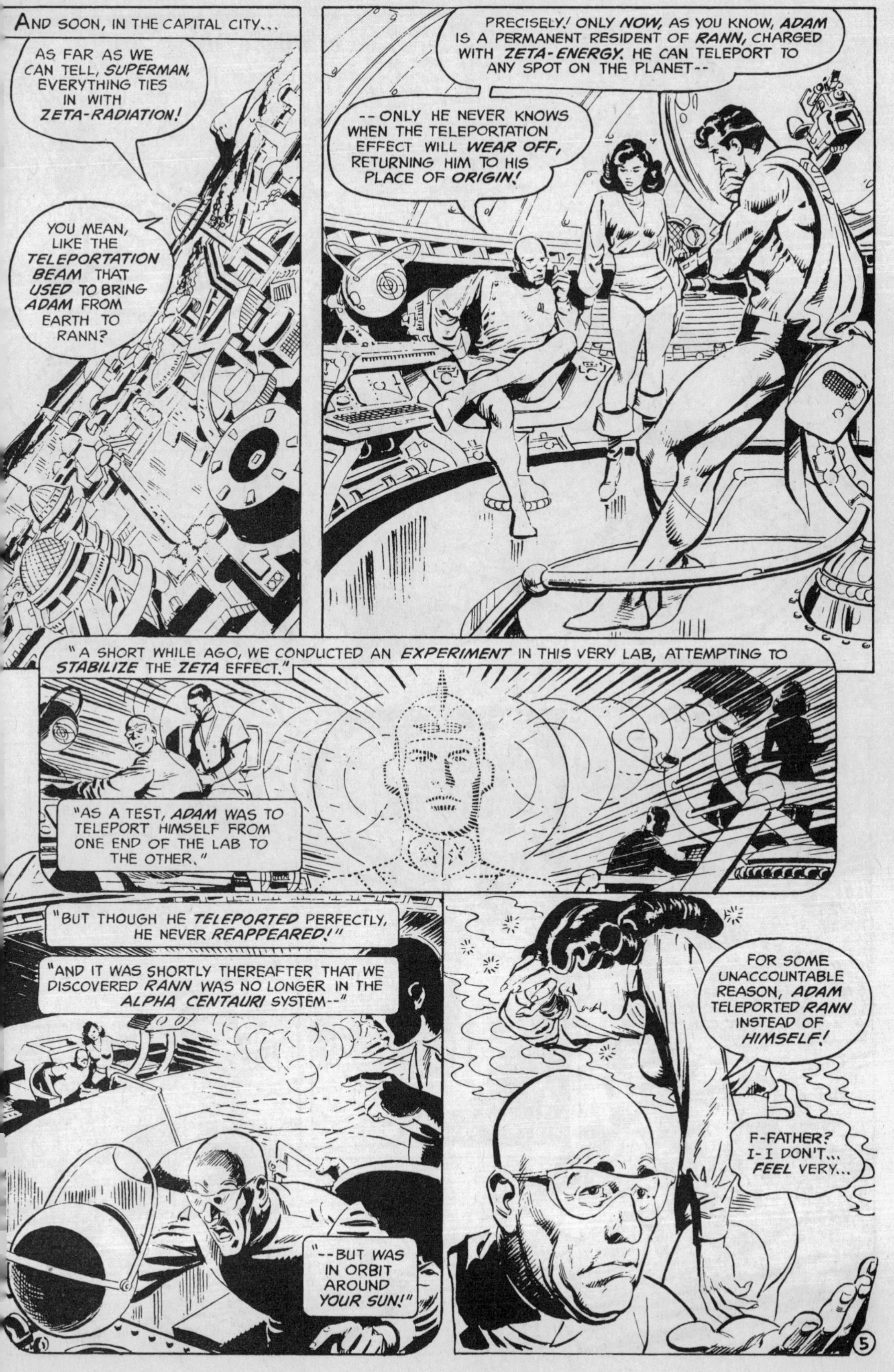
AND SOON, IN THE CAPITAL CITY...
AS FAR AS WE CAN TELL, SUPERMAN, EVERYTHING TIES IN WITH ZETA-RADIATION!
YOU MEAN, LIKE THE TELEPORTATION BEAM THAT USED TO BRING ADAM FROM EARTH TO RANN?
PRECISELY! ONLY NOW, AS YOU KNOW, ADAM IS A PERMANENT RESIDENT OF RANN, CHARGED WITH ZETA-ENERGY. HE CAN TELEPORT TO ANY SPOT ON THE PLANET--
--ONLY HE NEVER KNOWS WHEN THE TELEPORTATION EFFECT WILL WEAR OFF, RETURNING HIM TO HIS PLACE OF ORIGIN!
"A SHORT WHILE AGO, WE CONDUCTED AN EXPERIMENT IN THIS VERY LAB, ATTEMPTING TO STABILIZE THE ZETA EFFECT."
"AS A TEST, ADAM WAS TO TELEPORT HIMSELF FROM ONE END OF THE LAB TO THE OTHER."
"BUT THOUGH HE TELEPORTED PERFECTLY, HE NEVER REAPPEARED!"
"AND IT WAS SHORTLY THEREAFTER THAT WE DISCOVERED RANN WAS NO LONGER IN THE ALPHA CENTAURI SYSTEM--"
"--BUT WAS IN ORBIT AROUND YOUR SUN!"
FOR SOME UNACCOUNTABLE REASON, ADAM TELEPORTED RANN INSTEAD OF HIMSELF!
F-FATHER? I-I DON'T... FEEL VERY...
5

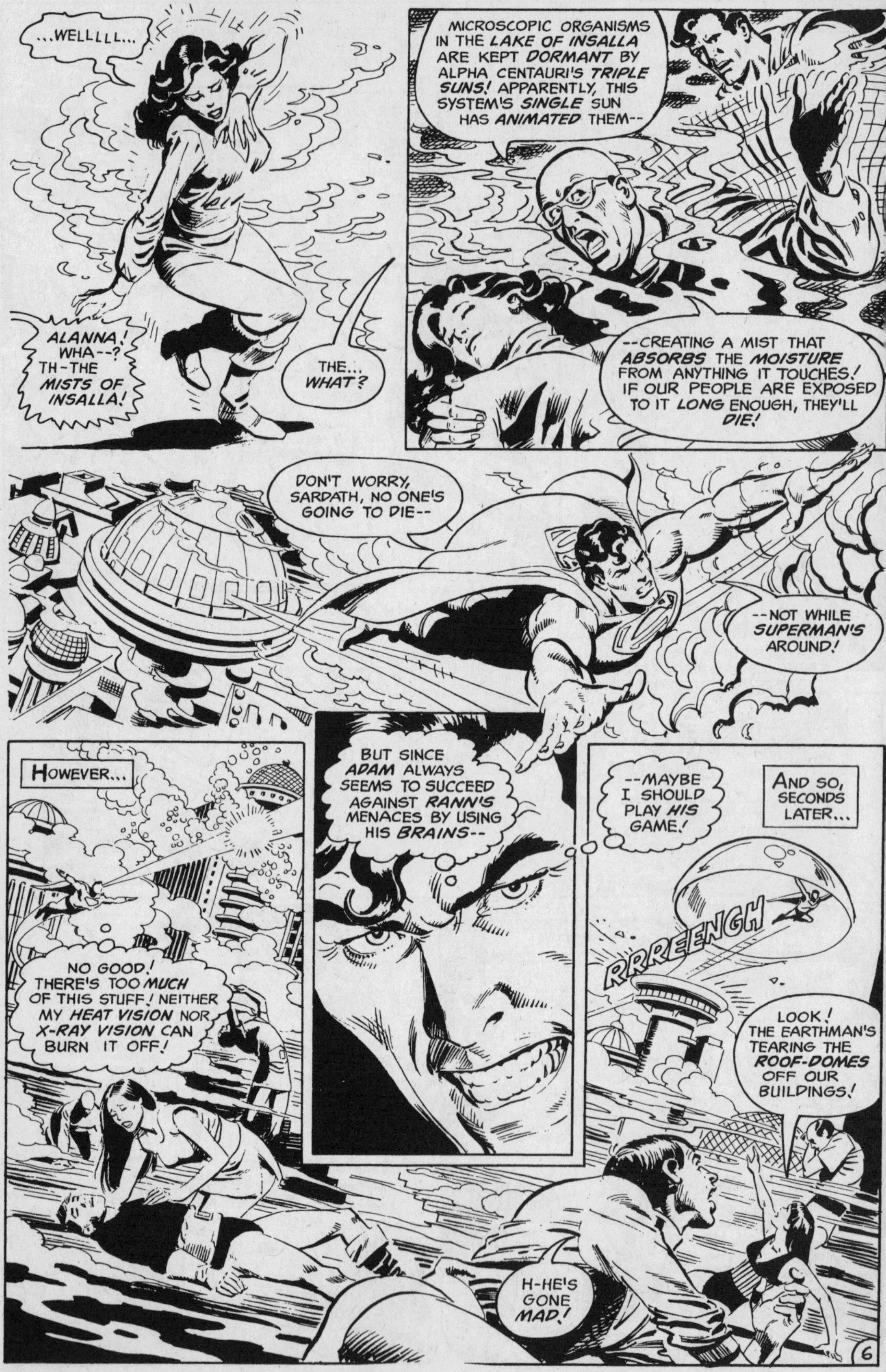
...WELLLLL...
ALANNA! WHA--? TH-THE MISTS OF INSALLA!
THE... WHAT?
MICROSCOPIC ORGANISMS IN THE LAKE OF INSALLA ARE KEPT DORMANT BY ALPHA CENTAURI'S TRIPLE SUNS! APPARENTLY, THIS SYSTEM'S SINGLE SUN HAS ANIMATED THEM--
--CREATING A MIST THAT ABSORBS THE MOISTURE FROM ANYTHING IT TOUCHES! IF OUR PEOPLE ARE EXPOSED TO IT LONG ENOUGH, THEY'LL DIE!
DON'T WORRY, SARDATH, NO ONE'S GOING TO DIE--
--NOT WHILE SUPERMAN'S AROUND!
HOWEVER...
NO GOOD! THERE'S TOO MUCH OF THIS STUFF! NEITHER MY HEAT VISION NOR X-RAY VISION CAN BURN IT OFF!
BUT SINCE ADAM ALWAYS SEEMS TO SUCCEED AGAINST RANN'S MENACES BY USING HIS BRAINS--
--MAYBE I SHOULD PLAY HIS GAME!
AND SO, SECONDS LATER...
RRREENGH
LOOK! THE EARTHMAN'S TEARING THE ROOF-DOMES OFF OUR BUILDINGS!
H-HE'S GONE MAD!
6

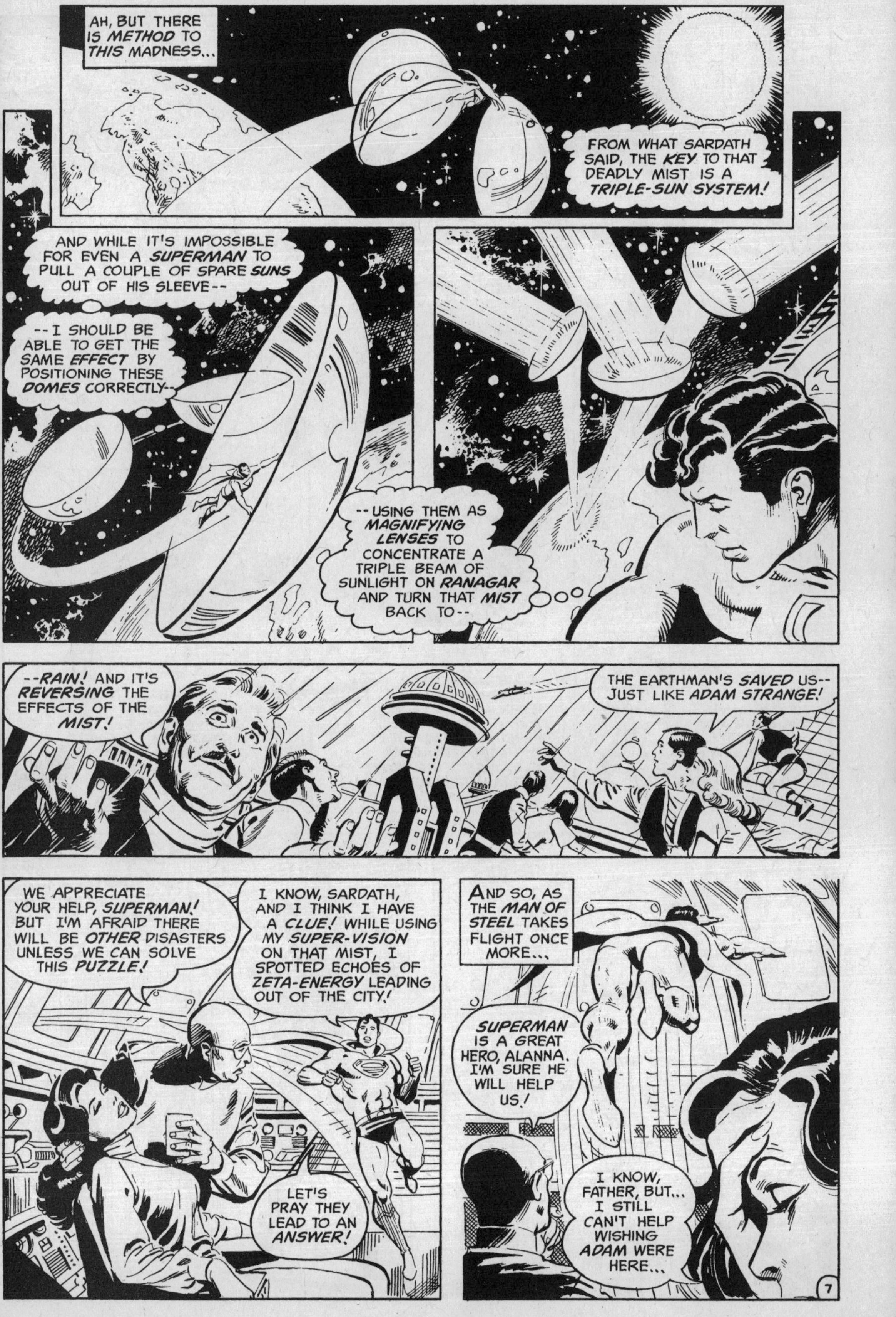
AH, BUT THERE IS METHOD TO THIS MADNESS...
FROM WHAT SARDATH SAID, THE KEY TO THAT DEADLY MIST IS A TRIPLE-SUN SYSTEM!
AND WHILE IT'S IMPOSSIBLE FOR EVEN A SUPERMAN TO PULL A COUPLE OF SPARE SUNS OUT OF HIS SLEEVE--
--I SHOULD BE ABLE TO GET THE SAME EFFECT BY POSITIONING THESE DOMES CORRECTLY--
--USING THEM AS MAGNIFYING LENSES TO CONCENTRATE A TRIPLE BEAM OF SUNLIGHT ON RANAGAR AND TURN THAT MIST BACK TO--
--RAIN! AND IT'S REVERSING THE EFFECTS OF THE MIST!
THE EARTHMAN'S SAVED US-- JUST LIKE ADAM STRANGE!
WE APPRECIATE YOUR HELP, SUPERMAN! BUT I'M AFRAID THERE WILL BE OTHER DISASTERS UNLESS WE CAN SOLVE THIS PUZZLE!
I KNOW, SARDATH, AND I THINK I HAVE A CLUE! WHILE USING MY SUPER-VISION ON THAT MIST, I SPOTTED ECHOES OF ZETA-ENERGY LEADING OUT OF THE CITY!
LET'S PRAY THEY LEAD TO AN ANSWER!
AND SO, AS THE MAN OF STEEL TAKES FLIGHT ONCE MORE...
SUPERMAN IS A GREAT HERO, ALANNA. I'M SURE HE WILL HELP US!
I KNOW, FATHER, BUT... I STILL CAN'T HELP WISHING ADAM WERE HERE...
7

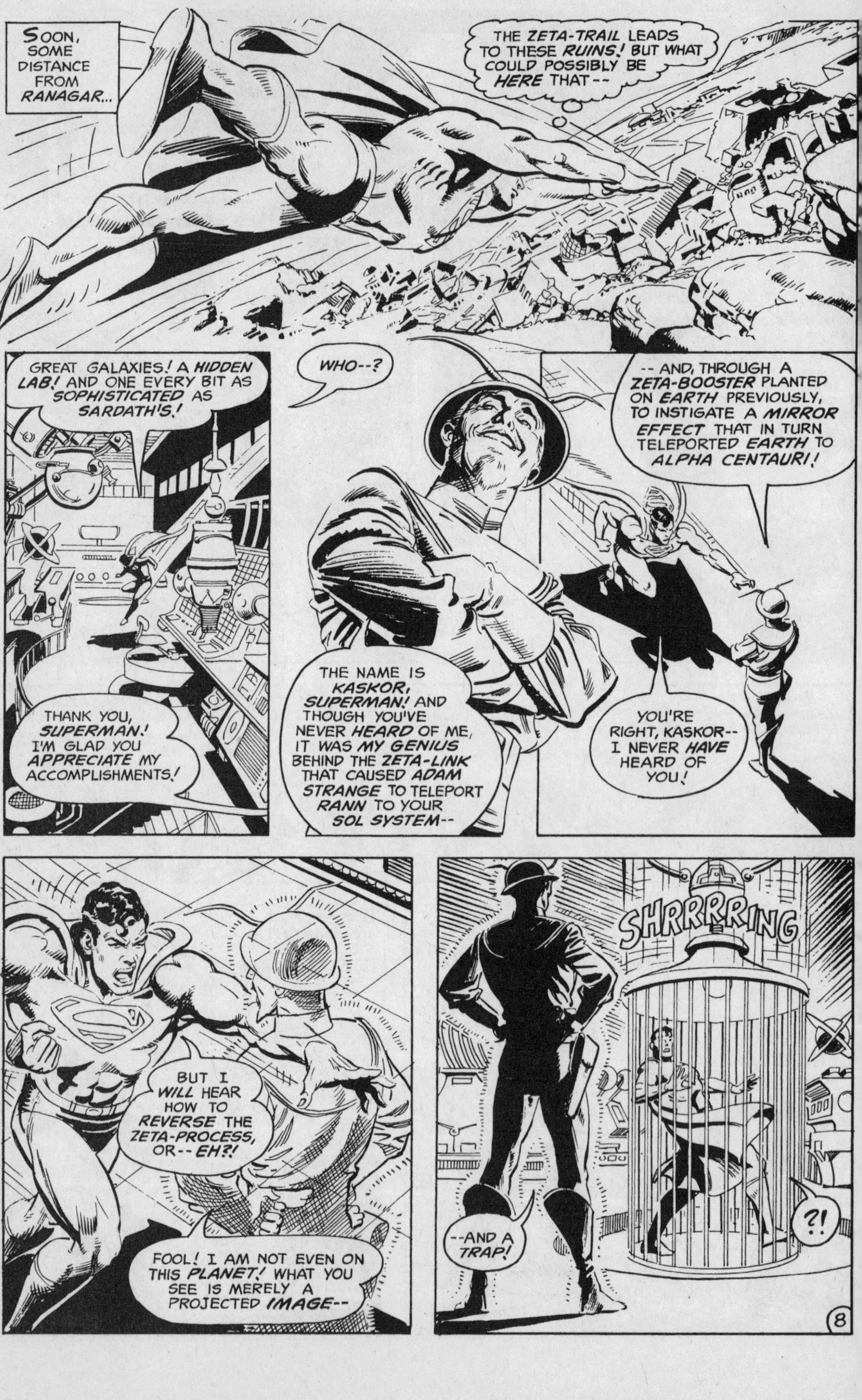
SOON, SOME DISTANCE FROM RANAGAR...
THE ZETA-TRAIL LEADS TO THESE RUINS! BUT WHAT COULD POSSIBLY BE HERE THAT--
GREAT GALAXIES! A HIDDEN LAB! AND ONE EVERY BIT AS SOPHISTICATED AS SARDATH'S!
THANK YOU, SUPERMAN! I'M GLAD YOU APPRECIATE MY ACCOMPLISHMENTS!
WHO--?
THE NAME IS KASKOR, SUPERMAN! AND THOUGH YOU'VE NEVER HEARD OF ME, IT WAS MY GENIUS BEHIND THE ZETA-LINK THAT CAUSED ADAM STRANGE TO TELEPORT RANN TO YOUR SOL SYSTEM--
-- AND, THROUGH A ZETA-BOOSTER PLANTED ON EARTH PREVIOUSLY, TO INSTIGATE A MIRROR EFFECT THAT IN TURN TELEPORTED EARTH TO ALPHA CENTAURI!
YOU'RE RIGHT, KASKOR-- I NEVER HAVE HEARD OF YOU!
BUT I WILL HEAR HOW TO REVERSE THE ZETA-PROCESS, OR-- EH?!
FOOL! I AM NOT EVEN ON THIS PLANET! WHAT YOU SEE IS MERELY A PROJECTED IMAGE--
SHRRRRING
--AND A TRAP!
?!
8

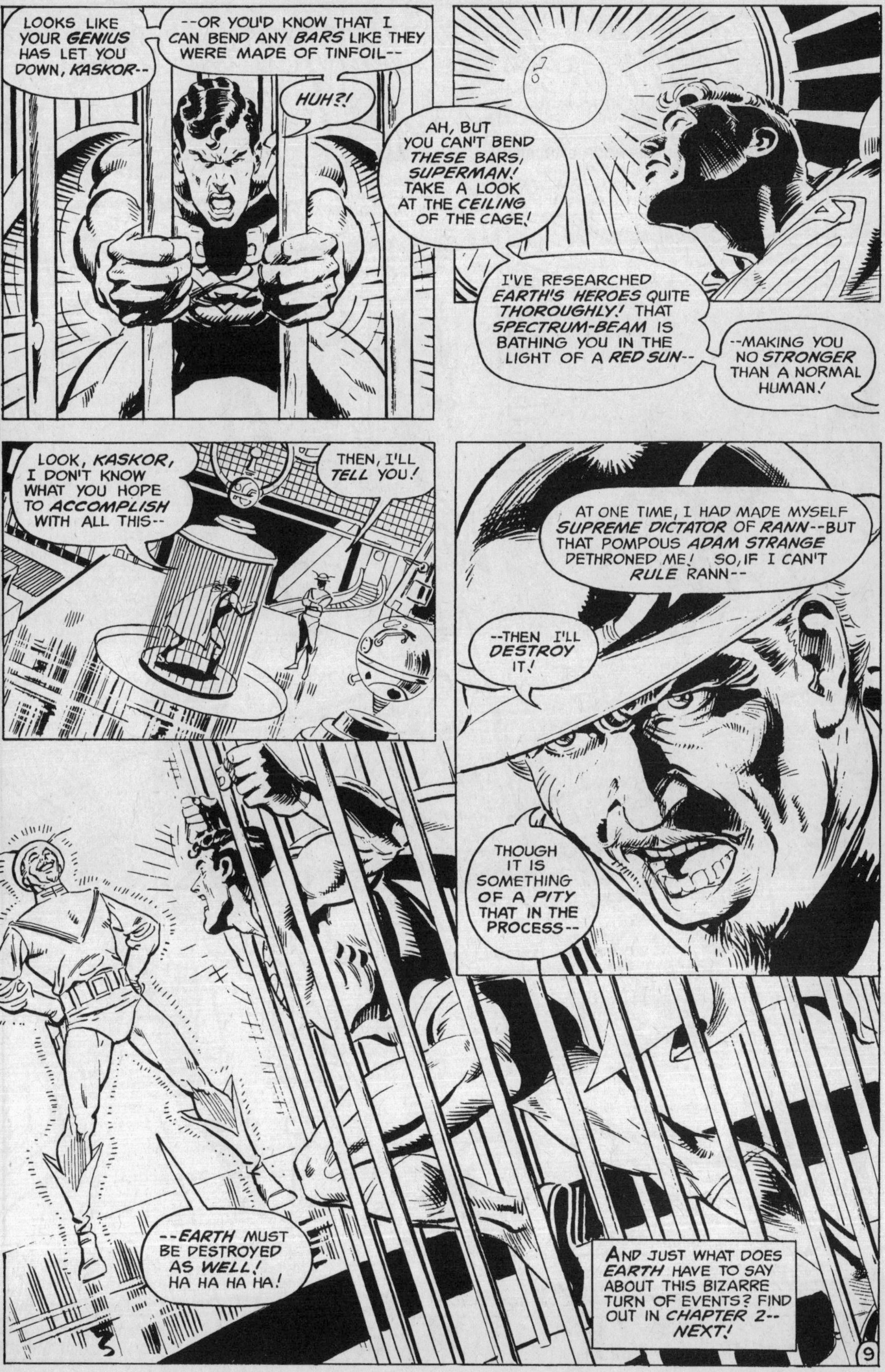
LOOKS LIKE YOUR GENIUS HAS LET YOU DOWN, KASKOR--
--OR YOU'D KNOW THAT I CAN BEND ANY BARS LIKE THEY WERE MADE OF TINFOIL--
HUH?!
AH, BUT YOU CAN'T BEND THESE BARS, SUPERMAN! TAKE A LOOK AT THE CEILING OF THE CAGE!
I'VE RESEARCHED EARTH'S HEROES QUITE THOROUGHLY! THAT SPECTRUM-BEAM IS BATHING YOU IN THE LIGHT OF A RED SUN--
--MAKING YOU NO STRONGER THAN A NORMAL HUMAN!
LOOK, KASKOR, I DON'T KNOW WHAT YOU HOPE TO ACCOMPLISH WITH ALL THIS--
THEN, I'LL TELL YOU!
AT ONE TIME, I HAD MADE MYSELF SUPREME DICTATOR OF RANN--BUT THAT POMPOUS ADAM STRANGE DETHRONED ME! SO, IF I CAN'T RULE RANN--
--THEN I'LL DESTROY IT!
THOUGH IT IS SOMETHING OF A PITY THAT IN THE PROCESS--
--EARTH MUST BE DESTROYED AS WELL! HA HA HA HA!
AND JUST WHAT DOES EARTH HAVE TO SAY ABOUT THIS BIZARRE TURN OF EVENTS? FIND OUT IN CHAPTER 2--NEXT!
9

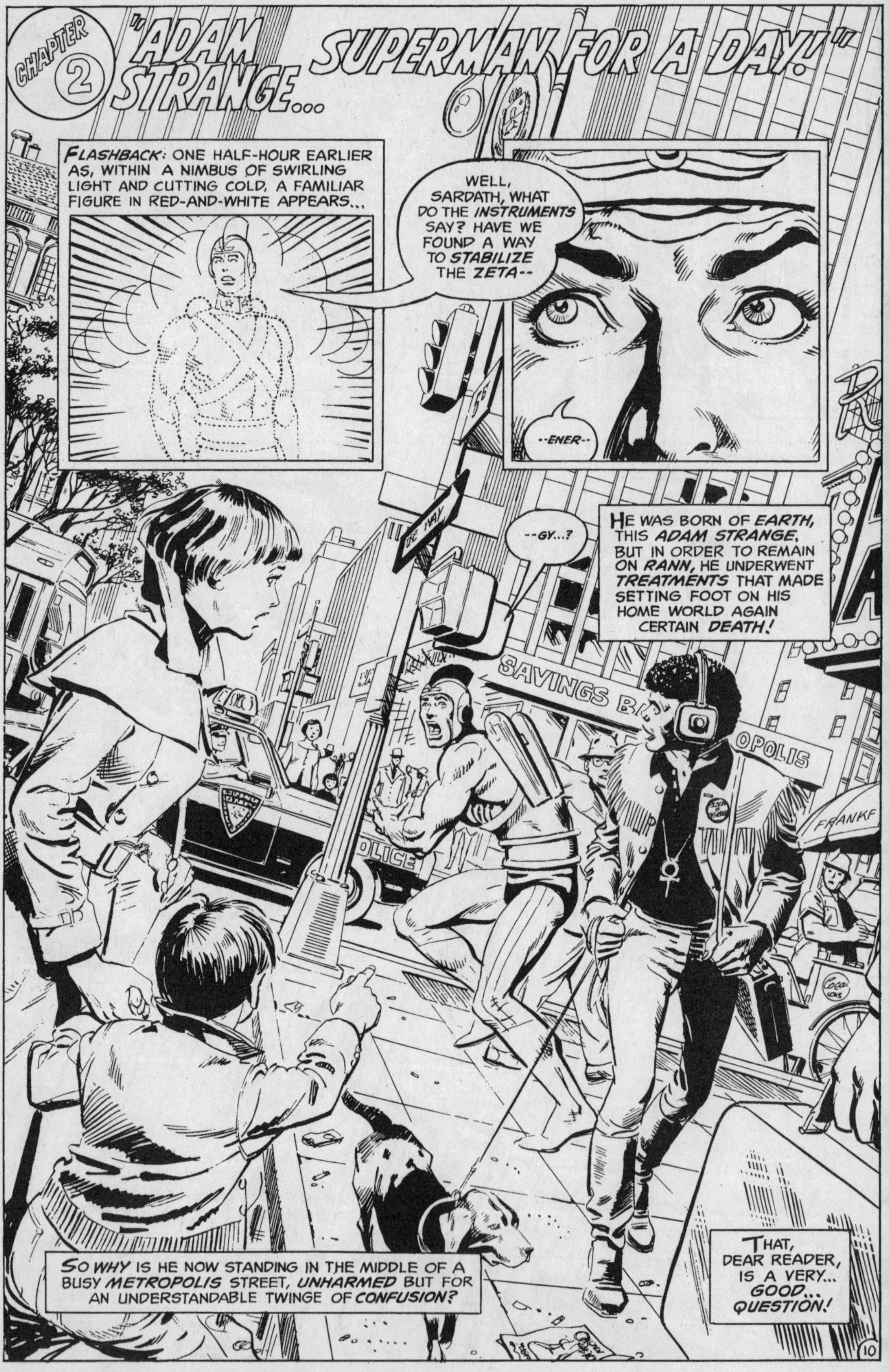
CHAPTER 2
"ADAM STRANGE... SUPERMAN FOR A DAY!"
FLASHBACK: ONE HALF-HOUR EARLIER AS, WITHIN A NIMBUS OF SWIRLING LIGHT AND CUTTING COLD, A FAMILIAR FIGURE IN RED-AND-WHITE APPEARS...
WELL, SARDATH, WHAT DO THE INSTRUMENTS SAY? HAVE WE FOUND A WAY TO STABILIZE THE ZETA--
--ENER--
--GY...?
HE WAS BORN OF EARTH, THIS ADAM STRANGE, BUT IN ORDER TO REMAIN ON RANN, HE UNDERWENT TREATMENTS THAT MADE SETTING FOOT ON HIS HOME WORLD AGAIN CERTAIN DEATH!
SAVINGS B
OPOLIS
POLICE
FRANKF
SO WHY IS HE NOW STANDING IN THE MIDDLE OF A BUSY METROPOLIS STREET, UNHARMED BUT FOR AN UNDERSTANDABLE TWINGE OF CONFUSION?
THAT, DEAR READER, IS A VERY... GOOD... QUESTION!
10

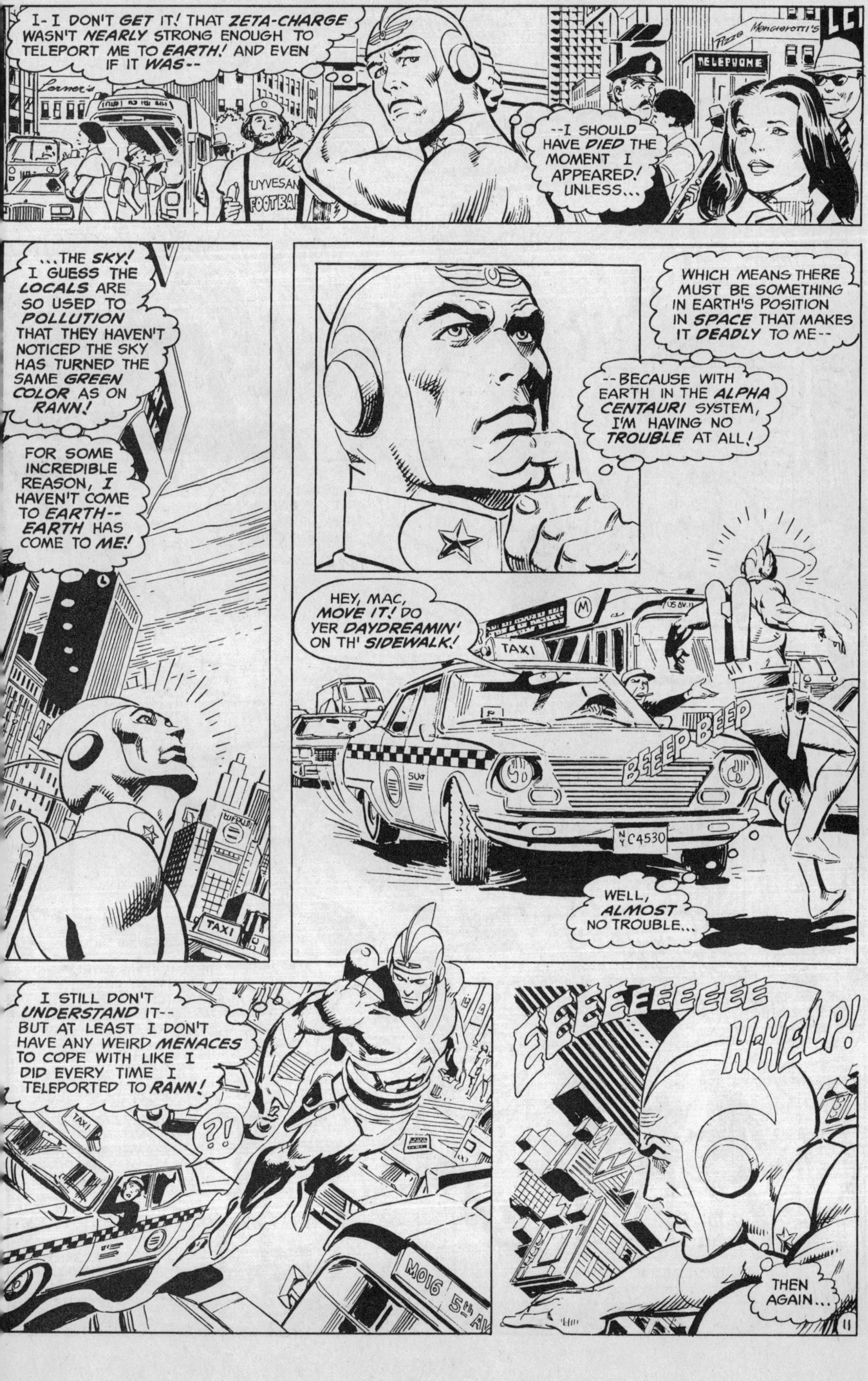
I- I DON'T GET IT! THAT ZETA-CHARGE WASN'T NEARLY STRONG ENOUGH TO TELEPORT ME TO EARTH! AND EVEN IF IT WAS--
--I SHOULD HAVE DIED THE MOMENT I APPEARED! UNLESS...
...THE SKY! I GUESS THE LOCALS ARE SO USED TO POLLUTION THAT THEY HAVEN'T NOTICED THE SKY HAS TURNED THE SAME GREEN COLOR AS ON RANN!
FOR SOME INCREDIBLE REASON, I HAVEN'T COME TO EARTH-- EARTH HAS COME TO ME!
TAXI
WHICH MEANS THERE MUST BE SOMETHING IN EARTH'S POSITION IN SPACE THAT MAKES IT DEADLY TO ME--
--BECAUSE WITH EARTH IN THE ALPHA CENTAURI SYSTEM, I'M HAVING NO TROUBLE AT ALL!
HEY, MAC, MOVE IT! DO YER DAYDREAMIN' ON TH' SIDEWALK!
TAXI
BEEEP BEEP
WELL, ALMOST NO TROUBLE...
I STILL DON'T UNDERSTAND IT-- BUT AT LEAST I DON'T HAVE ANY WEIRD MENACES TO COPE WITH LIKE I DID EVERY TIME I TELEPORTED TO RANN!
?!
EEEEEEEEEE
H-HELP!
THEN AGAIN...
11

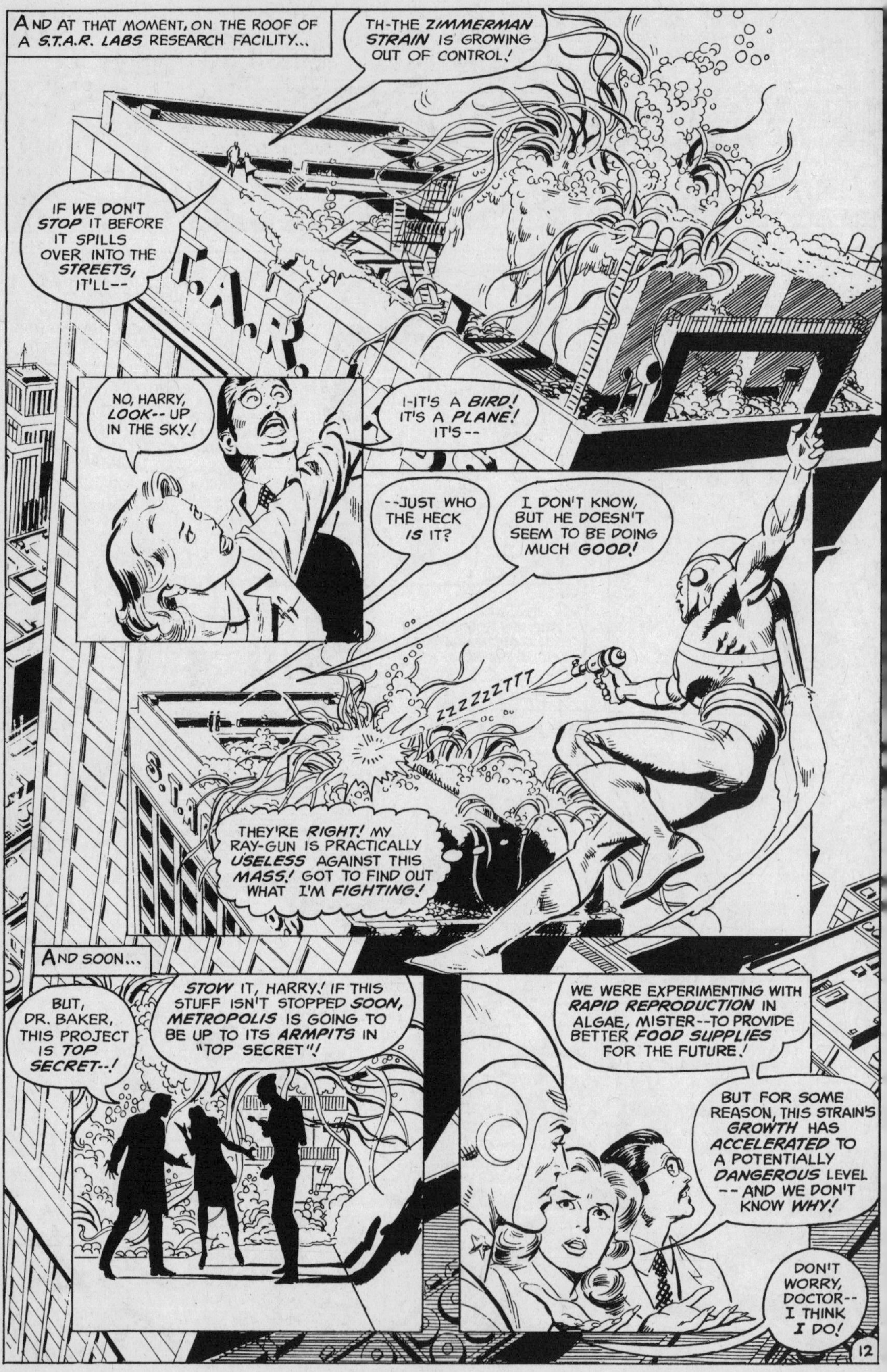
AND AT THAT MOMENT, ON THE ROOF OF A S.T.A.R. LABS RESEARCH FACILITY...
TH-THE ZIMMERMAN STRAIN IS GROWING OUT OF CONTROL!
IF WE DON'T STOP IT BEFORE IT SPILLS OVER INTO THE STREETS, IT'LL--
NO, HARRY, LOOK-- UP IN THE SKY!
I-IT'S A BIRD! IT'S A PLANE! IT'S--
--JUST WHO THE HECK IS IT?
I DON'T KNOW, BUT HE DOESN'T SEEM TO BE DOING MUCH GOOD!
ZZZZZZZTTT
THEY'RE RIGHT! MY RAY-GUN IS PRACTICALLY USELESS AGAINST THIS MASS! GOT TO FIND OUT WHAT I'M FIGHTING!
AND SOON...
BUT, DR. BAKER, THIS PROJECT IS TOP SECRET--!
STOW IT, HARRY! IF THIS STUFF ISN'T STOPPED SOON, METROPOLIS IS GOING TO BE UP TO ITS ARMPITS IN "TOP SECRET"!
WE WERE EXPERIMENTING WITH RAPID REPRODUCTION IN ALGAE, MISTER--TO PROVIDE BETTER FOOD SUPPLIES FOR THE FUTURE!
BUT FOR SOME REASON, THIS STRAIN'S GROWTH HAS ACCELERATED TO A POTENTIALLY DANGEROUS LEVEL -- AND WE DON'T KNOW WHY!
DON'T WORRY, DOCTOR-- I THINK I DO!
12

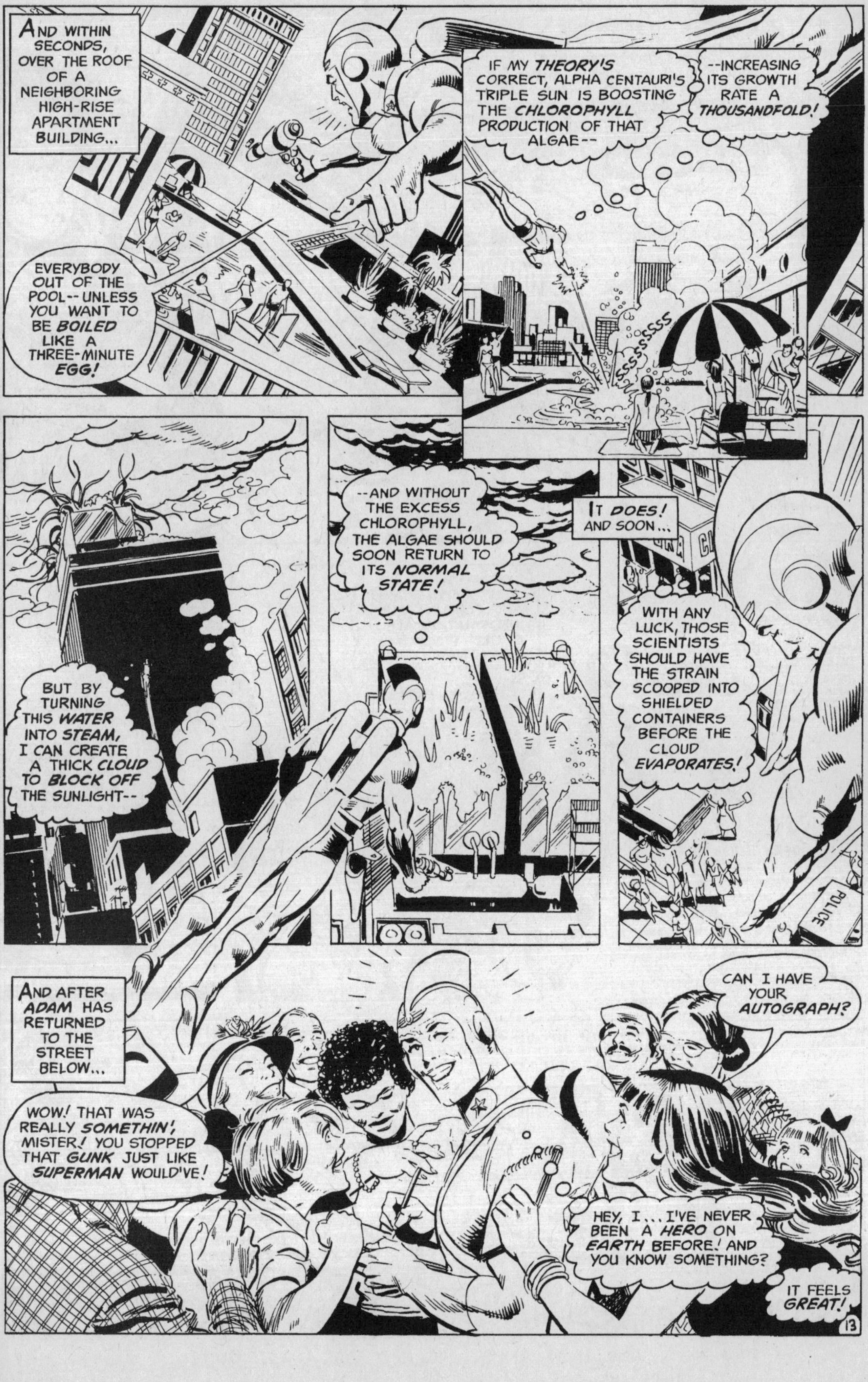
AND WITHIN SECONDS, OVER THE ROOF OF A NEIGHBORING HIGH-RISE APARTMENT BUILDING...
EVERYBODY OUT OF THE POOL-- UNLESS YOU WANT TO BE BOILED LIKE A THREE-MINUTE EGG!
IF MY THEORY'S CORRECT, ALPHA CENTAURI'S TRIPLE SUN IS BOOSTING THE CHLOROPHYLL PRODUCTION OF THAT ALGAE--
--INCREASING ITS GROWTH RATE A THOUSANDFOLD!
SSSSSSSSS
BUT BY TURNING THIS WATER INTO STEAM, I CAN CREATE A THICK CLOUD TO BLOCK OFF THE SUNLIGHT--
--AND WITHOUT THE EXCESS CHLOROPHYLL, THE ALGAE SHOULD SOON RETURN TO ITS NORMAL STATE!
IT DOES! AND SOON...
WITH ANY LUCK, THOSE SCIENTISTS SHOULD HAVE THE STRAIN SCOOPED INTO SHIELDED CONTAINERS BEFORE THE CLOUD EVAPORATES!
POLICE
AND AFTER ADAM HAS RETURNED TO THE STREET BELOW...
CAN I HAVE YOUR AUTOGRAPH?
WOW! THAT WAS REALLY SOMETHIN', MISTER! YOU STOPPED THAT GUNK JUST LIKE SUPERMAN WOULD'VE!
HEY, I... I'VE NEVER BEEN A HERO ON EARTH BEFORE! AND YOU KNOW SOMETHING?
IT FEELS GREAT!
13

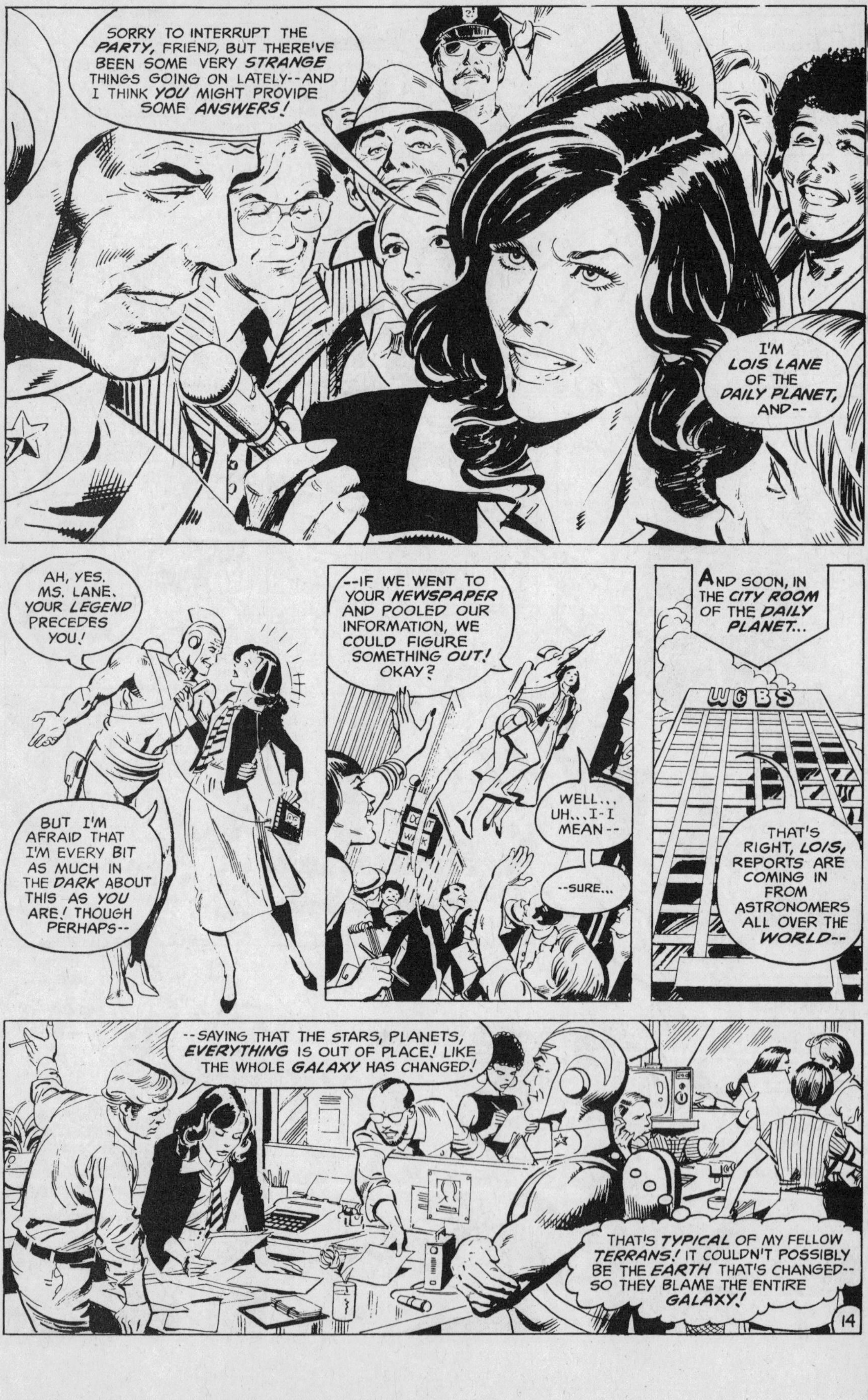
SORRY TO INTERRUPT THE PARTY, FRIEND, BUT THERE'VE BEEN SOME VERY STRANGE THINGS GOING ON LATELY--AND I THINK YOU MIGHT PROVIDE SOME ANSWERS!
I'M LOIS LANE OF THE DAILY PLANET, AND--
AH, YES. MS. LANE. YOUR LEGEND PRECEDES YOU!
BUT I'M AFRAID THAT I'M EVERY BIT AS MUCH IN THE DARK ABOUT THIS AS YOU ARE! THOUGH PERHAPS--
--IF WE WENT TO YOUR NEWSPAPER AND POOLED OUR INFORMATION, WE COULD FIGURE SOMETHING OUT! OKAY?
WELL... UH...I-I MEAN--
--SURE...
AND SOON, IN THE CITY ROOM OF THE DAILY PLANET...
WGBS
THAT'S RIGHT, LOIS, REPORTS ARE COMING IN FROM ASTRONOMERS ALL OVER THE WORLD--
--SAYING THAT THE STARS, PLANETS, EVERYTHING IS OUT OF PLACE! LIKE THE WHOLE GALAXY HAS CHANGED!
THAT'S TYPICAL OF MY FELLOW TERRANS! IT COULDN'T POSSIBLY BE THE EARTH THAT'S CHANGED--SO THEY BLAME THE ENTIRE GALAXY!
14

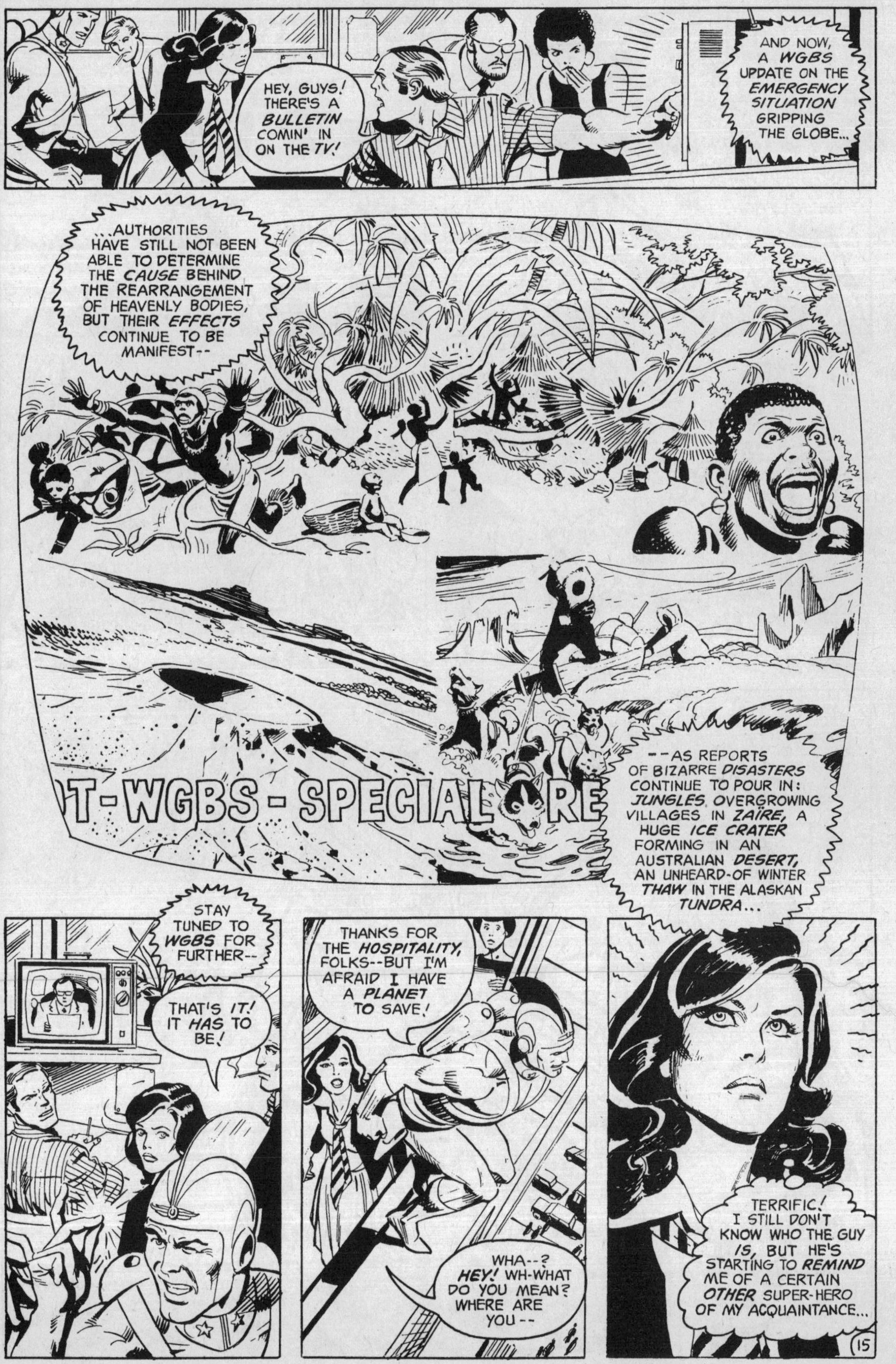
HEY, GUYS! THERE'S A BULLETIN COMIN' IN ON THE TV!
AND NOW, A WGBS UPDATE ON THE EMERGENCY SITUATION GRIPPING THE GLOBE...
...AUTHORITIES HAVE STILL NOT BEEN ABLE TO DETERMINE THE CAUSE BEHIND THE REARRANGEMENT OF HEAVENLY BODIES, BUT THEIR EFFECTS CONTINUE TO BE MANIFEST--
DT-WGBS-SPECIAL RE
--AS REPORTS OF BIZARRE DISASTERS CONTINUE TO POUR IN: JUNGLES OVERGROWING VILLAGES IN ZAÏRE, A HUGE ICE CRATER FORMING IN AN AUSTRALIAN DESERT, AN UNHEARD-OF WINTER THAW IN THE ALASKAN TUNDRA...
STAY TUNED TO WGBS FOR FURTHER--
THAT'S IT! IT HAS TO BE!
THANKS FOR THE HOSPITALITY, FOLKS--BUT I'M AFRAID I HAVE A PLANET TO SAVE!
WHA--? HEY! WH-WHAT DO YOU MEAN? WHERE ARE YOU--
TERRIFIC! I STILL DON'T KNOW WHO THE GUY IS, BUT HE'S STARTING TO REMIND ME OF A CERTAIN OTHER SUPER-HERO OF MY ACQUAINTANCE...
15

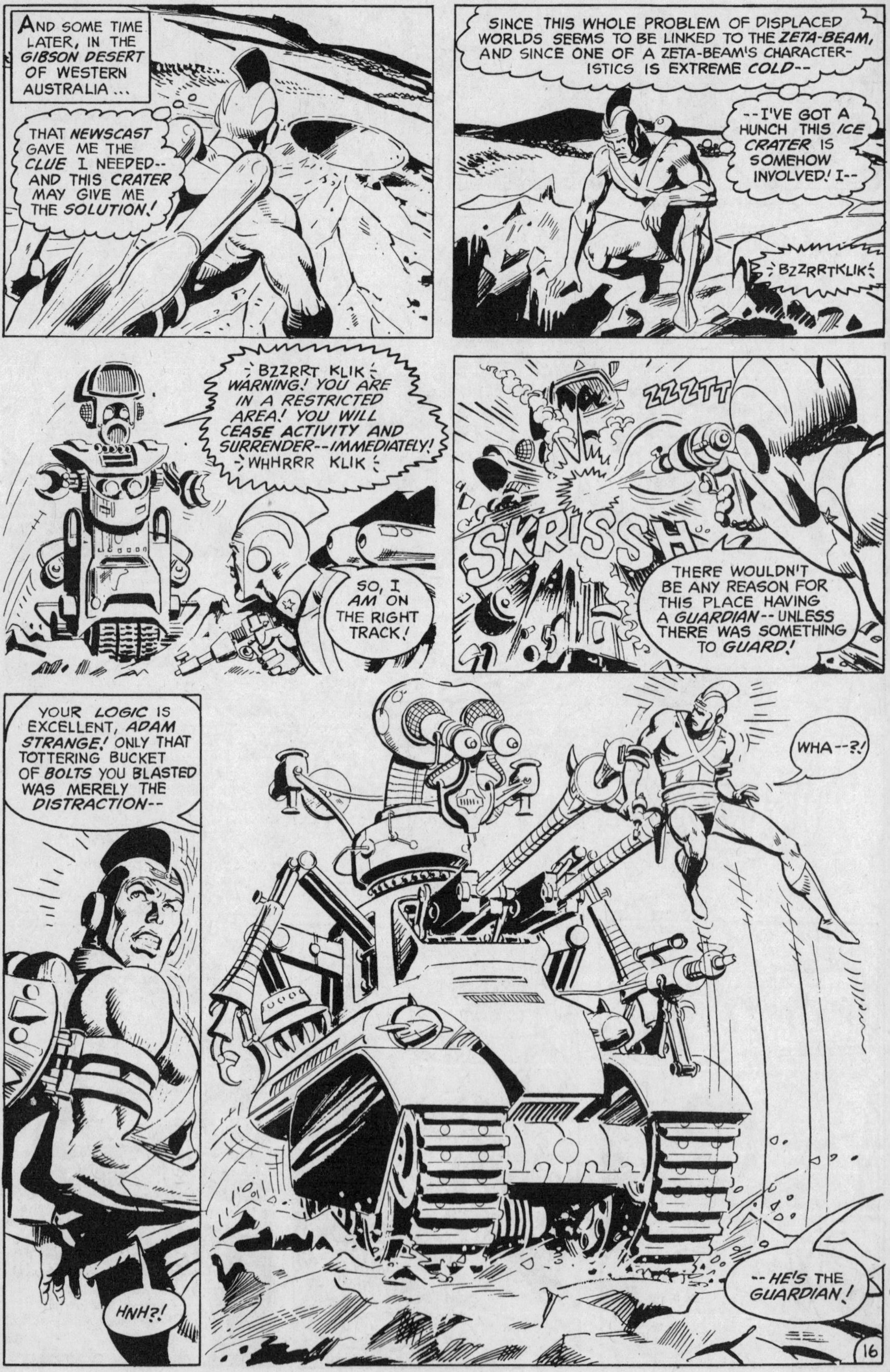
AND SOME TIME LATER, IN THE GIBSON DESERT OF WESTERN AUSTRALIA ...
THAT NEWSCAST GAVE ME THE CLUE I NEEDED-- AND THIS CRATER MAY GIVE ME THE SOLUTION!
SINCE THIS WHOLE PROBLEM OF DISPLACED WORLDS SEEMS TO BE LINKED TO THE ZETA-BEAM, AND SINCE ONE OF A ZETA-BEAM'S CHARACTER-ISTICS IS EXTREME COLD--
--I'VE GOT A HUNCH THIS ICE CRATER IS SOMEHOW INVOLVED! I--
BZZRRTKLIK
BZZRRT KLIK WARNING! YOU ARE IN A RESTRICTED AREA! YOU WILL CEASE ACTIVITY AND SURRENDER--IMMEDIATELY! WHHRRR KLIK
SO, I AM ON THE RIGHT TRACK!
ZZZTT
SKRISSH
THERE WOULDN'T BE ANY REASON FOR THIS PLACE HAVING A GUARDIAN--UNLESS THERE WAS SOMETHING TO GUARD!
YOUR LOGIC IS EXCELLENT, ADAM STRANGE! ONLY THAT TOTTERING BUCKET OF BOLTS YOU BLASTED WAS MERELY THE DISTRACTION--
HNH?!
WHA--?!
--HE'S THE GUARDIAN!
16

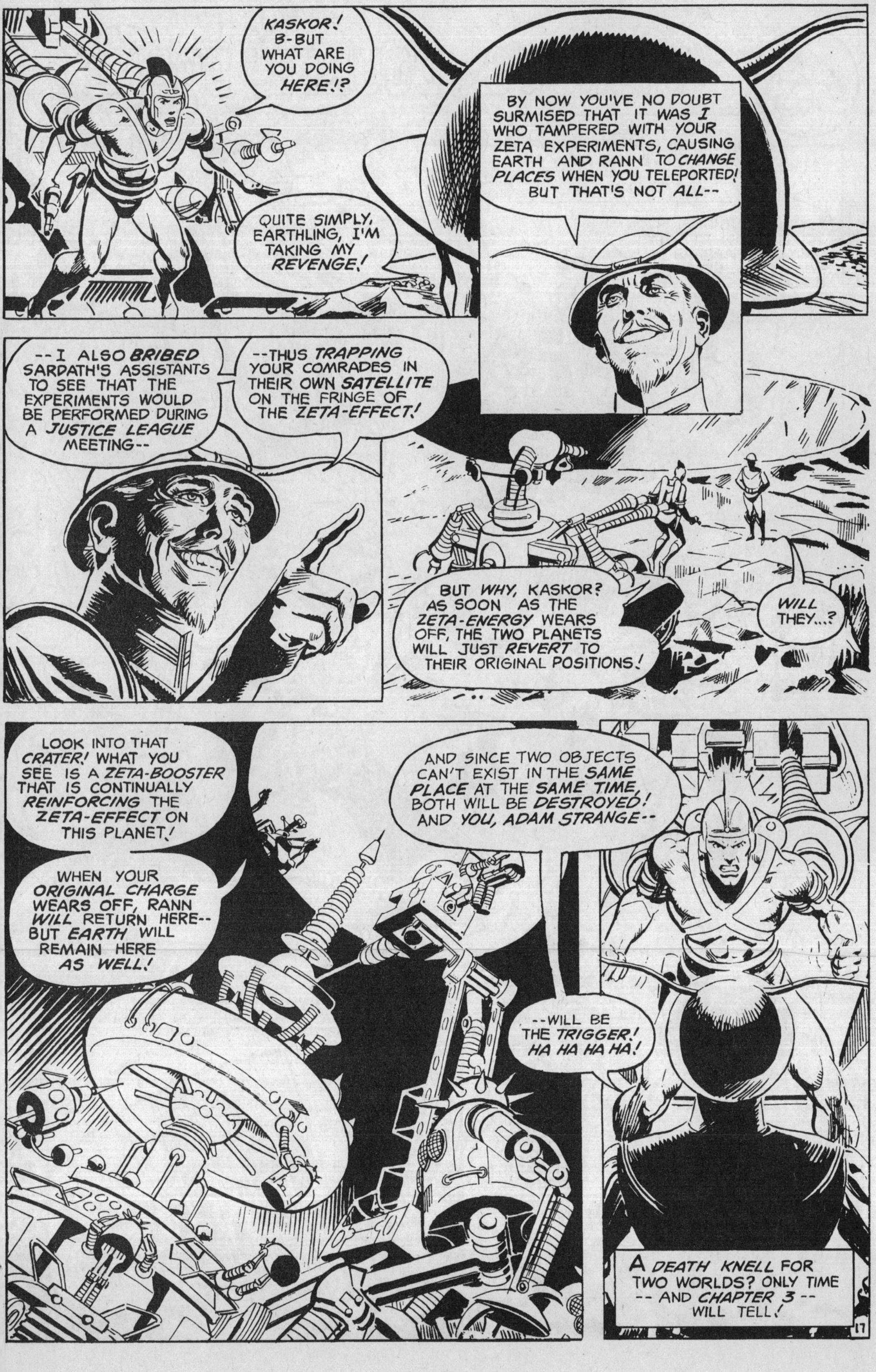
KASKOR! B-BUT WHAT ARE YOU DOING HERE!?
QUITE SIMPLY, EARTHLING, I'M TAKING MY REVENGE!
BY NOW YOU'VE NO DOUBT SURMISED THAT IT WAS I WHO TAMPERED WITH YOUR ZETA EXPERIMENTS, CAUSING EARTH AND RANN TO CHANGE PLACES WHEN YOU TELEPORTED! BUT THAT'S NOT ALL--
--I ALSO BRIBED SARDATH'S ASSISTANTS TO SEE THAT THE EXPERIMENTS WOULD BE PERFORMED DURING A JUSTICE LEAGUE MEETING--
--THUS TRAPPING YOUR COMRADES IN THEIR OWN SATELLITE ON THE FRINGE OF THE ZETA-EFFECT!
BUT WHY, KASKOR? AS SOON AS THE ZETA-ENERGY WEARS OFF, THE TWO PLANETS WILL JUST REVERT TO THEIR ORIGINAL POSITIONS!
WILL THEY...?
LOOK INTO THAT CRATER! WHAT YOU SEE IS A ZETA-BOOSTER THAT IS CONTINUALLY REINFORCING THE ZETA-EFFECT ON THIS PLANET!
WHEN YOUR ORIGINAL CHARGE WEARS OFF, RANN WILL RETURN HERE-- BUT EARTH WILL REMAIN HERE AS WELL!
AND SINCE TWO OBJECTS CAN'T EXIST IN THE SAME PLACE AT THE SAME TIME, BOTH WILL BE DESTROYED! AND YOU, ADAM STRANGE--
--WILL BE THE TRIGGER! HA HA HA HA!
A DEATH KNELL FOR TWO WORLDS? ONLY TIME -- AND CHAPTER 3 -- WILL TELL!
17

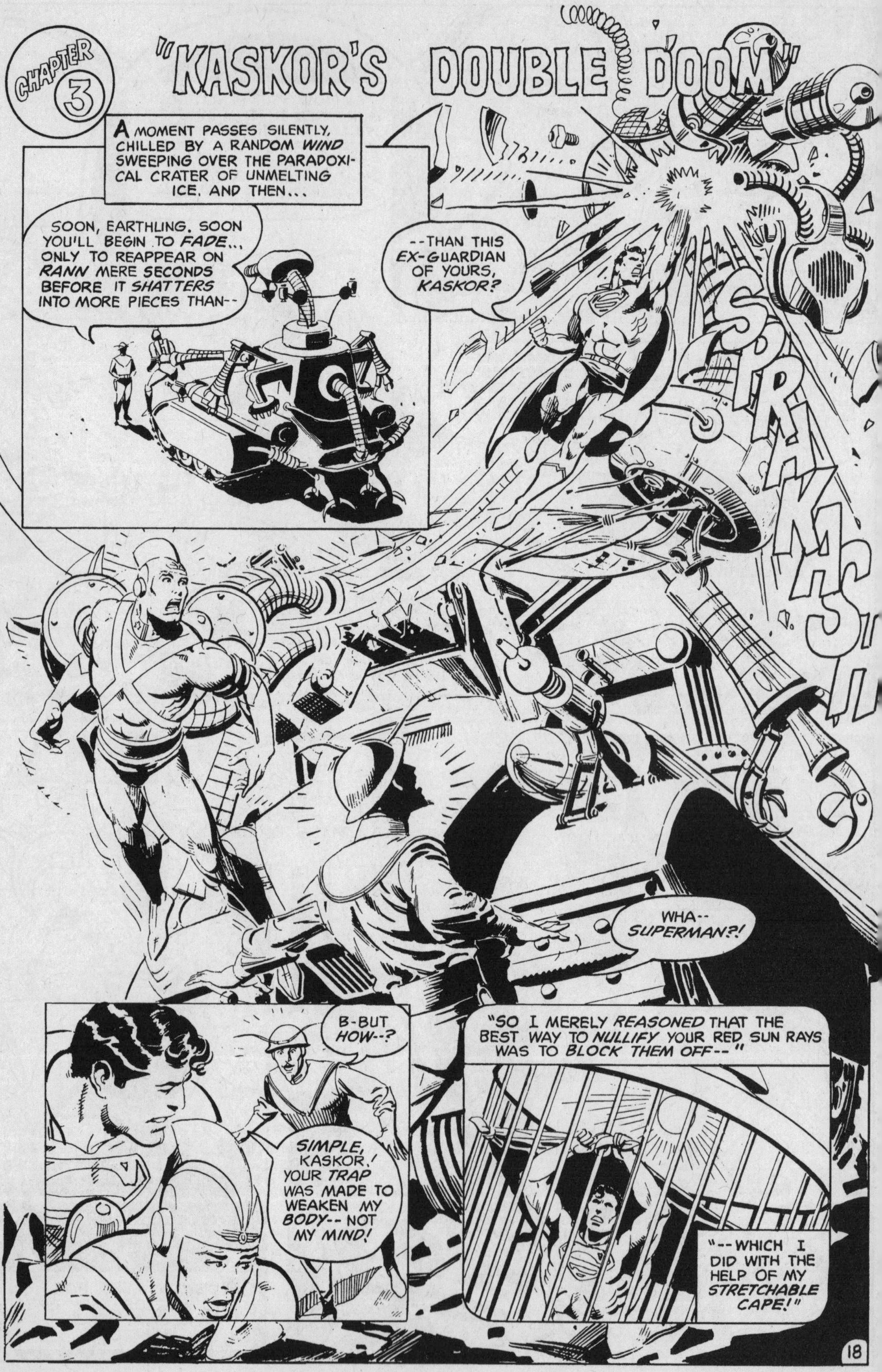
CHAPTER 3
"KASKOR'S DOUBLE DOOM"
A MOMENT PASSES SILENTLY, CHILLED BY A RANDOM WIND SWEEPING OVER THE PARADOXICAL CRATER OF UNMELTING ICE. AND THEN...
SOON, EARTHLING. SOON YOU'LL BEGIN TO FADE... ONLY TO REAPPEAR ON RANN MERE SECONDS BEFORE IT SHATTERS INTO MORE PIECES THAN--
--THAN THIS EX-GUARDIAN OF YOURS, KASKOR?
SPRAKASH!!
WHA-- SUPERMAN?!
B-BUT HOW--?
SIMPLE, KASKOR! YOUR TRAP WAS MADE TO WEAKEN MY BODY-- NOT MY MIND!
"SO I MERELY REASONED THAT THE BEST WAY TO NULLIFY YOUR RED SUN RAYS WAS TO BLOCK THEM OFF--"
"--WHICH I DID WITH THE HELP OF MY STRETCHABLE CAPE!"
18

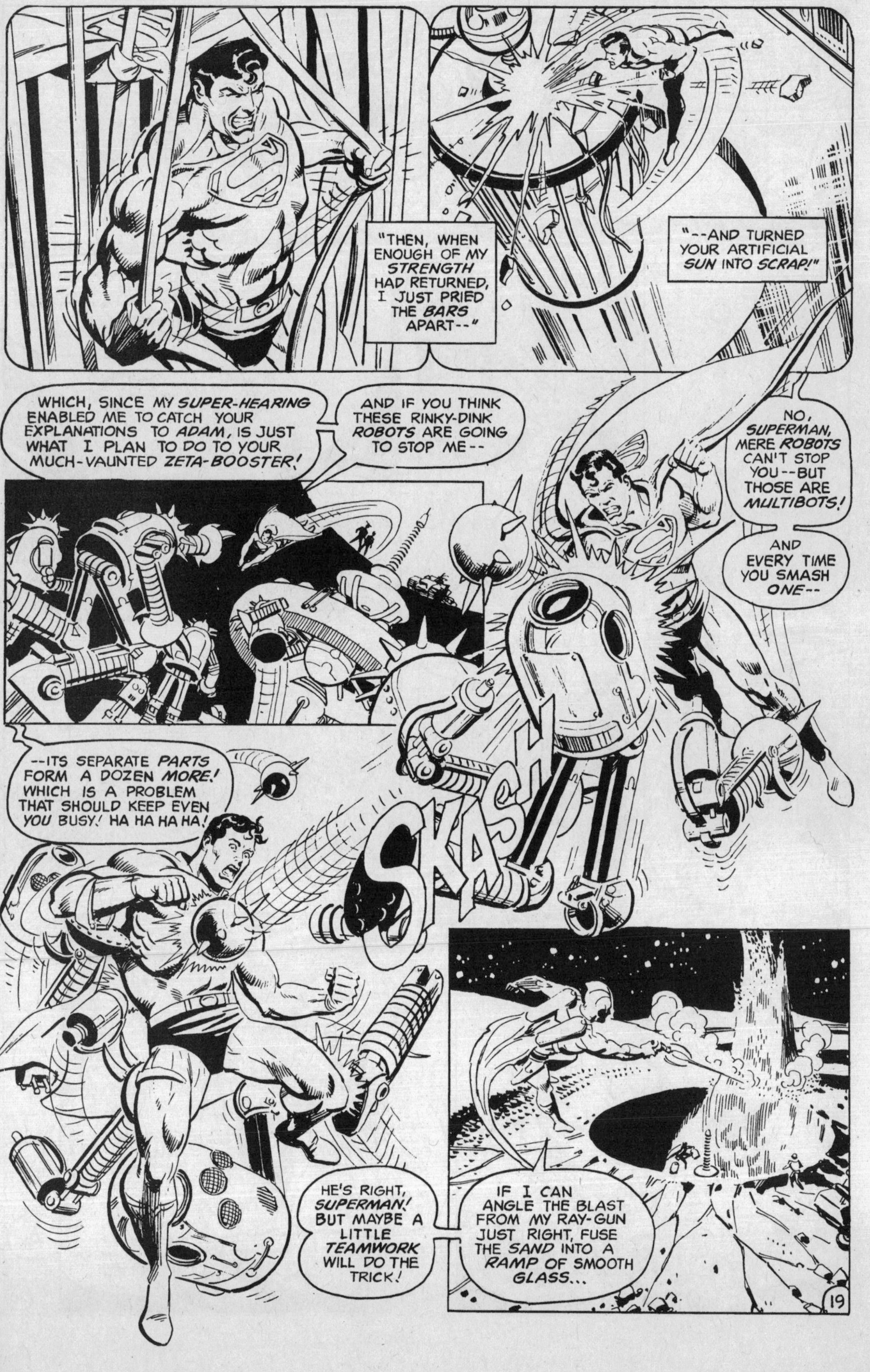
"THEN, WHEN ENOUGH OF MY STRENGTH HAD RETURNED, I JUST PRIED THE BARS APART--"
"--AND TURNED YOUR ARTIFICIAL SUN INTO SCRAP!"
WHICH, SINCE MY SUPER-HEARING ENABLED ME TO CATCH YOUR EXPLANATIONS TO ADAM, IS JUST WHAT I PLAN TO DO TO YOUR MUCH-VAUNTED ZETA-BOOSTER!
AND IF YOU THINK THESE RINKY-DINK ROBOTS ARE GOING TO STOP ME--
NO, SUPERMAN, MERE ROBOTS CAN'T STOP YOU--BUT THOSE ARE MULTIBOTS!
AND EVERY TIME YOU SMASH ONE--
--ITS SEPARATE PARTS FORM A DOZEN MORE! WHICH IS A PROBLEM THAT SHOULD KEEP EVEN YOU BUSY! HA HA HA HA!
SKASH
HE'S RIGHT, SUPERMAN! BUT MAYBE A LITTLE TEAMWORK WILL DO THE TRICK!
IF I CAN ANGLE THE BLAST FROM MY RAY-GUN JUST RIGHT, FUSE THE SAND INTO A RAMP OF SMOOTH GLASS...
19

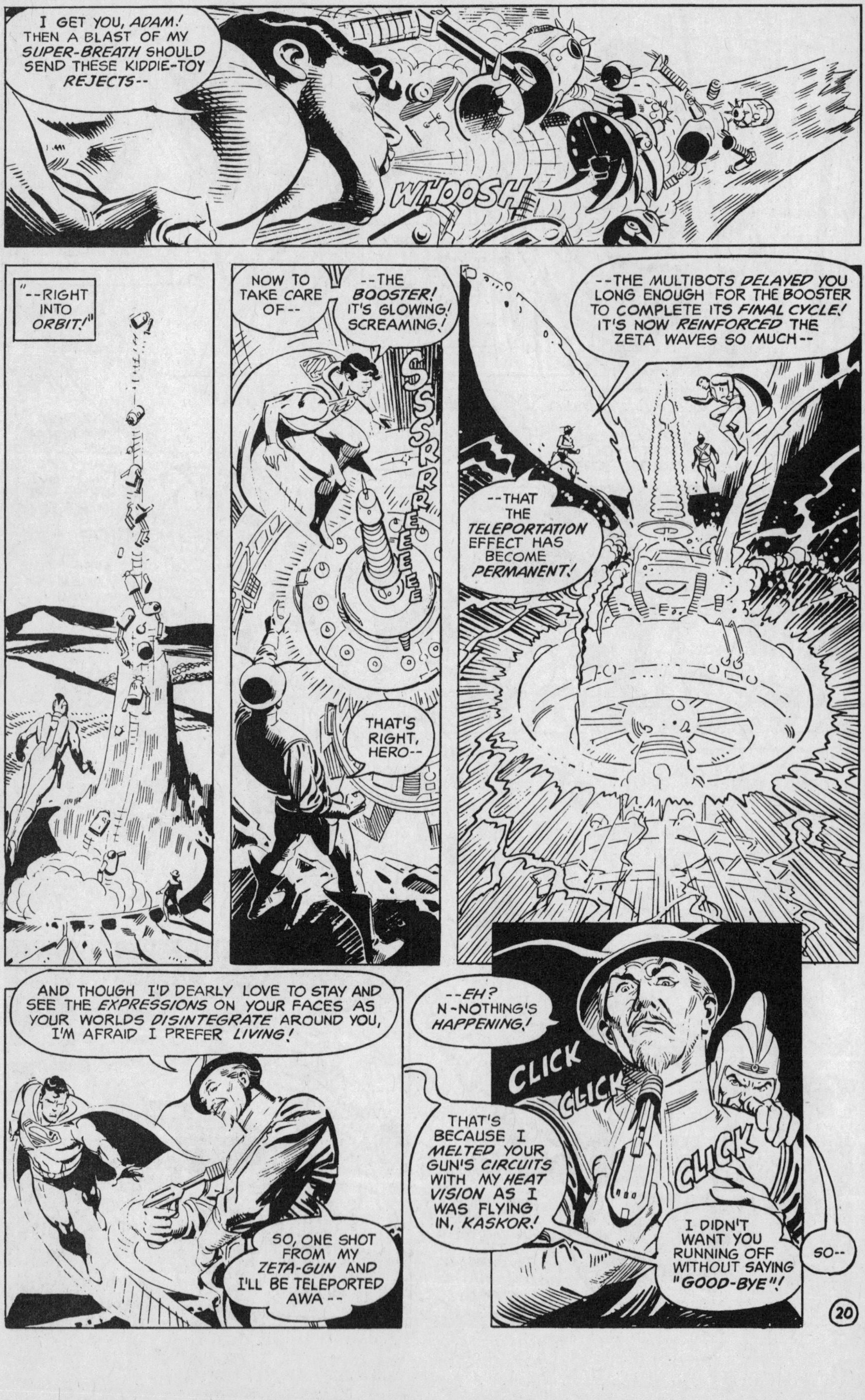
I GET YOU, ADAM! THEN A BLAST OF MY SUPER-BREATH SHOULD SEND THESE KIDDIE-TOY REJECTS--
WHOOSH
"--RIGHT INTO ORBIT!"
NOW TO TAKE CARE OF--
--THE BOOSTER! IT'S GLOWING! SCREAMING!
SSSRRREEEE
THAT'S RIGHT, HERO--
--THE MULTIBOTS DELAYED YOU LONG ENOUGH FOR THE BOOSTER TO COMPLETE ITS FINAL CYCLE! IT'S NOW REINFORCED THE ZETA WAVES SO MUCH--
--THAT THE TELEPORTATION EFFECT HAS BECOME PERMANENT!
AND THOUGH I'D DEARLY LOVE TO STAY AND SEE THE EXPRESSIONS ON YOUR FACES AS YOUR WORLDS DISINTEGRATE AROUND YOU, I'M AFRAID I PREFER LIVING!
SO, ONE SHOT FROM MY ZETA-GUN AND I'LL BE TELEPORTED AWA--
--EH? N-NOTHING'S HAPPENING!
CLICK
CLICK
CLICK
THAT'S BECAUSE I MELTED YOUR GUN'S CIRCUITS WITH MY HEAT VISION AS I WAS FLYING IN, KASKOR!
I DIDN'T WANT YOU RUNNING OFF WITHOUT SAYING "GOOD-BYE"!
SO--
20

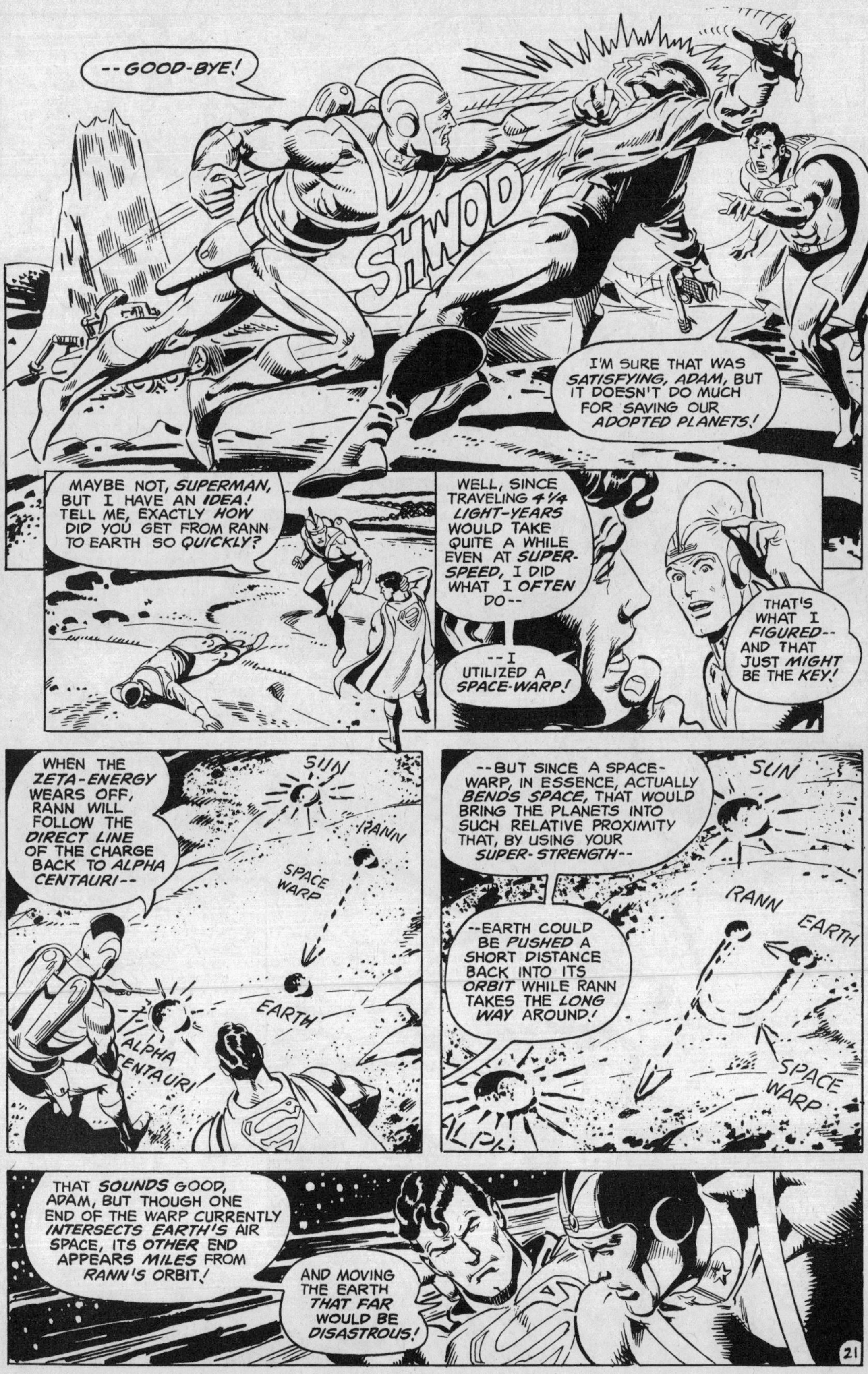
--GOOD-BYE!
SHWOD
I'M SURE THAT WAS SATISFYING, ADAM, BUT IT DOESN'T DO MUCH FOR SAVING OUR ADOPTED PLANETS!
MAYBE NOT, SUPERMAN, BUT I HAVE AN IDEA! TELL ME, EXACTLY HOW DID YOU GET FROM RANN TO EARTH SO QUICKLY?
WELL, SINCE TRAVELING 4 1/4 LIGHT-YEARS WOULD TAKE QUITE A WHILE EVEN AT SUPER-SPEED, I DID WHAT I OFTEN DO--
--I UTILIZED A SPACE-WARP!
THAT'S WHAT I FIGURED--AND THAT JUST MIGHT BE THE KEY!
WHEN THE ZETA-ENERGY WEARS OFF, RANN WILL FOLLOW THE DIRECT LINE OF THE CHARGE BACK TO ALPHA CENTAURI--
SUN
RANN
SPACE WARP
EARTH
ALPHA CENTAURI
--BUT SINCE A SPACE-WARP, IN ESSENCE, ACTUALLY BENDS SPACE, THAT WOULD BRING THE PLANETS INTO SUCH RELATIVE PROXIMITY THAT, BY USING YOUR SUPER-STRENGTH--
SUN
--EARTH COULD BE PUSHED A SHORT DISTANCE BACK INTO ITS ORBIT WHILE RANN TAKES THE LONG WAY AROUND!
RANN
EARTH
SPACE WARP
THAT SOUNDS GOOD, ADAM, BUT THOUGH ONE END OF THE WARP CURRENTLY INTERSECTS EARTH'S AIR SPACE, ITS OTHER END APPEARS MILES FROM RANN'S ORBIT!
AND MOVING THE EARTH THAT FAR WOULD BE DISASTROUS!
21

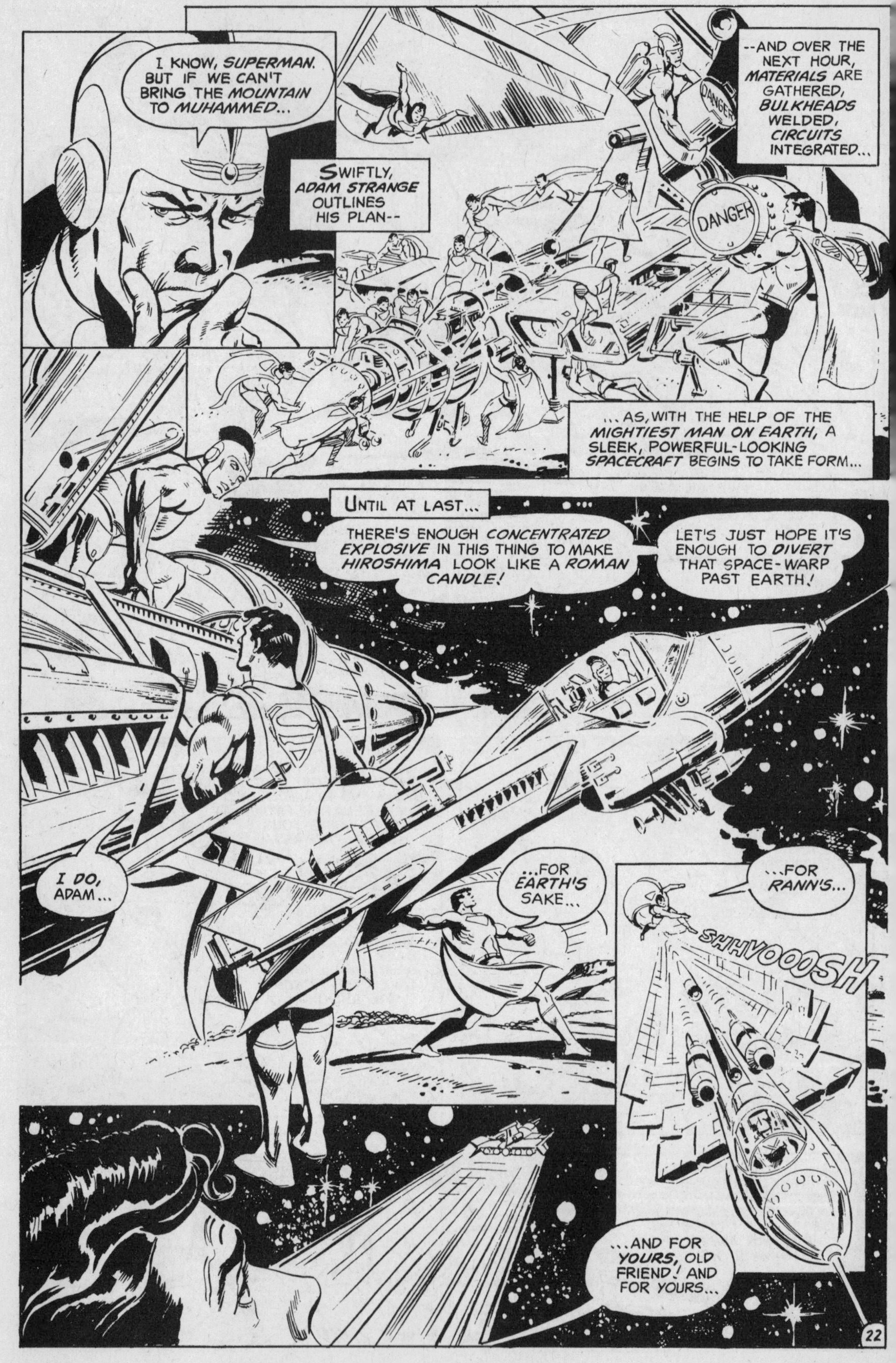
I KNOW, SUPERMAN. BUT IF WE CAN'T BRING THE MOUNTAIN TO MUHAMMED...
SWIFTLY, ADAM STRANGE OUTLINES HIS PLAN--
--AND OVER THE NEXT HOUR, MATERIALS ARE GATHERED, BULKHEADS WELDED, CIRCUITS INTEGRATED...
DANGER
DANGER
...AS, WITH THE HELP OF THE MIGHTIEST MAN ON EARTH, A SLEEK, POWERFUL-LOOKING SPACECRAFT BEGINS TO TAKE FORM...
UNTIL AT LAST...
THERE'S ENOUGH CONCENTRATED EXPLOSIVE IN THIS THING TO MAKE HIROSHIMA LOOK LIKE A ROMAN CANDLE!
LET'S JUST HOPE IT'S ENOUGH TO DIVERT THAT SPACE-WARP PAST EARTH!
I DO, ADAM...
...FOR EARTH'S SAKE...
...FOR RANN'S...
SHHVOOOSH
...AND FOR YOURS, OLD FRIEND! AND FOR YOURS...
22

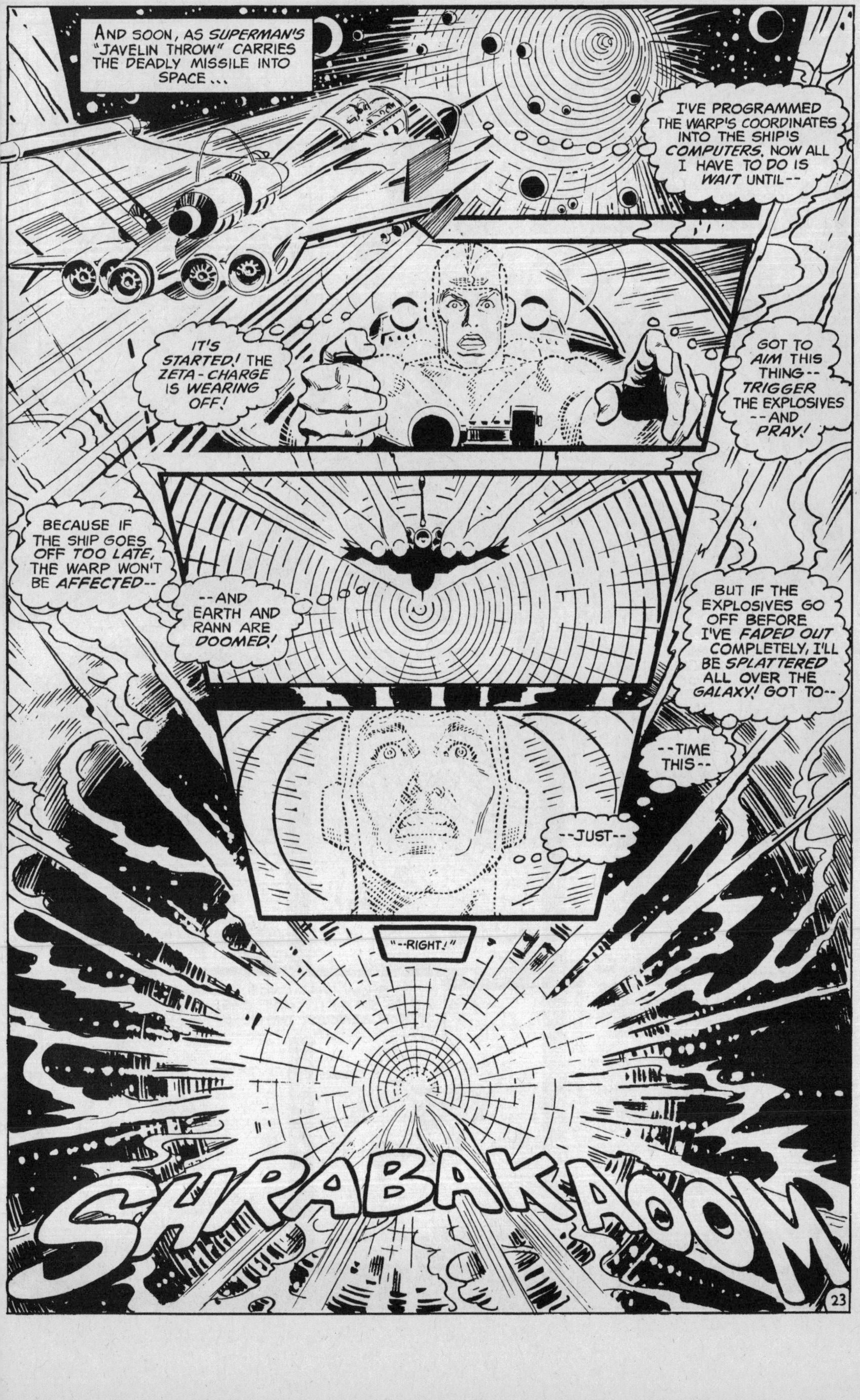
AND SOON, AS SUPERMAN'S "JAVELIN THROW" CARRIES THE DEADLY MISSILE INTO SPACE...
I'VE PROGRAMMED THE WARP'S COORDINATES INTO THE SHIP'S COMPUTERS. NOW ALL I HAVE TO DO IS WAIT UNTIL--
IT'S STARTED! THE ZETA-CHARGE IS WEARING OFF!
GOT TO AIM THIS THING--TRIGGER THE EXPLOSIVES--AND PRAY!
BECAUSE IF THE SHIP GOES OFF TOO LATE, THE WARP WON'T BE AFFECTED--
--AND EARTH AND RANN ARE DOOMED!
BUT IF THE EXPLOSIVES GO OFF BEFORE I'VE FADED OUT COMPLETELY, I'LL BE SPLATTERED ALL OVER THE GALAXY! GOT TO--
--TIME THIS--
--JUST--
"--RIGHT!"
SHRABAKAOOM
23

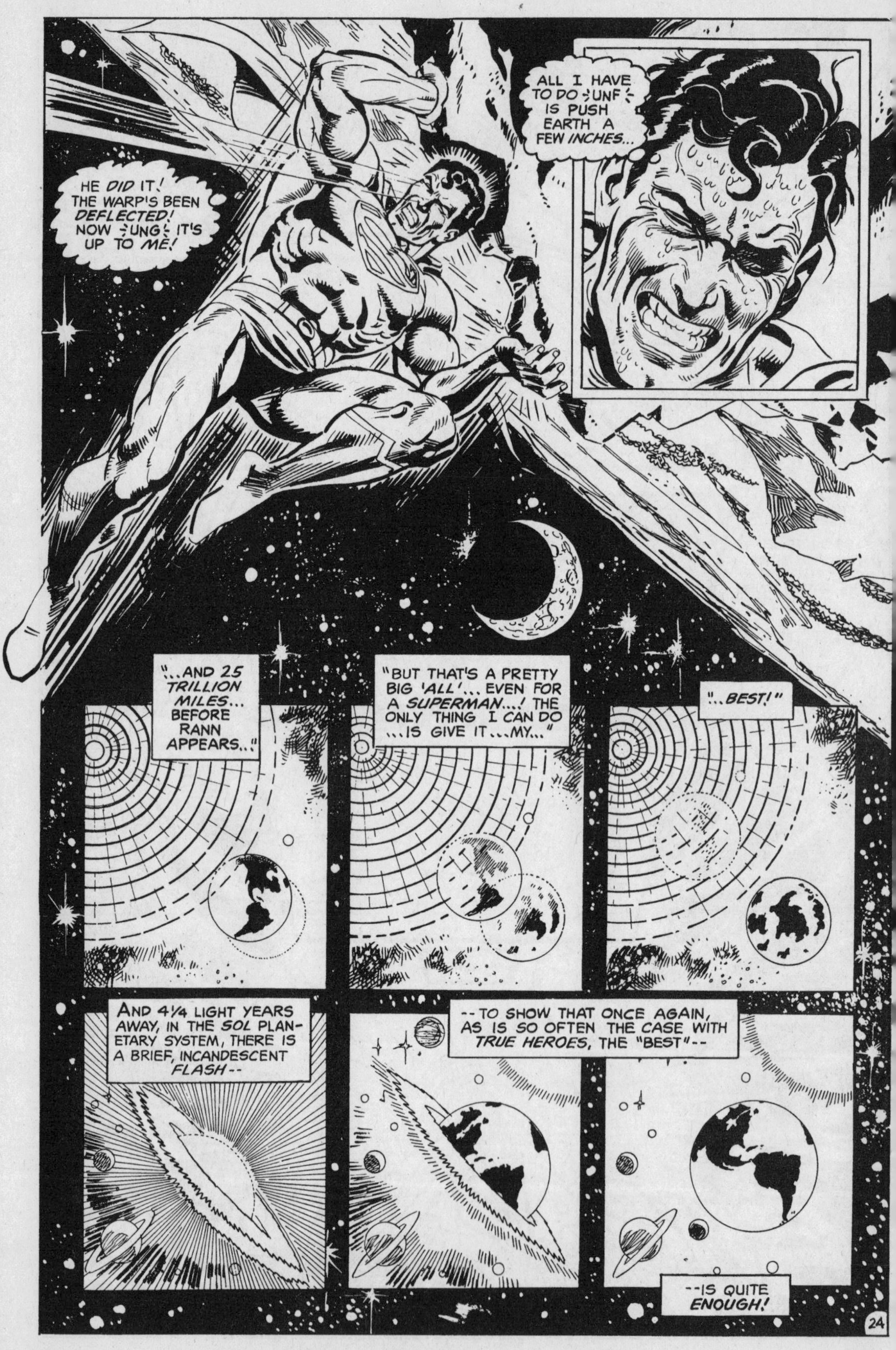
HE DID IT! THE WARP'S BEEN DEFLECTED! NOW -UNG- IT'S UP TO ME!
ALL I HAVE TO DO -UNF- IS PUSH EARTH A FEW INCHES...
"...AND 25 TRILLION MILES... BEFORE RANN APPEARS..."
"BUT THAT'S A PRETTY BIG 'ALL'... EVEN FOR A SUPERMAN...! THE ONLY THING I CAN DO ...IS GIVE IT...MY..."
"...BEST!"
AND 4¼ LIGHT YEARS AWAY, IN THE SOL PLANETARY SYSTEM, THERE IS A BRIEF, INCANDESCENT FLASH--
--TO SHOW THAT ONCE AGAIN, AS IS SO OFTEN THE CASE WITH TRUE HEROES, THE "BEST"--
--IS QUITE ENOUGH!
24

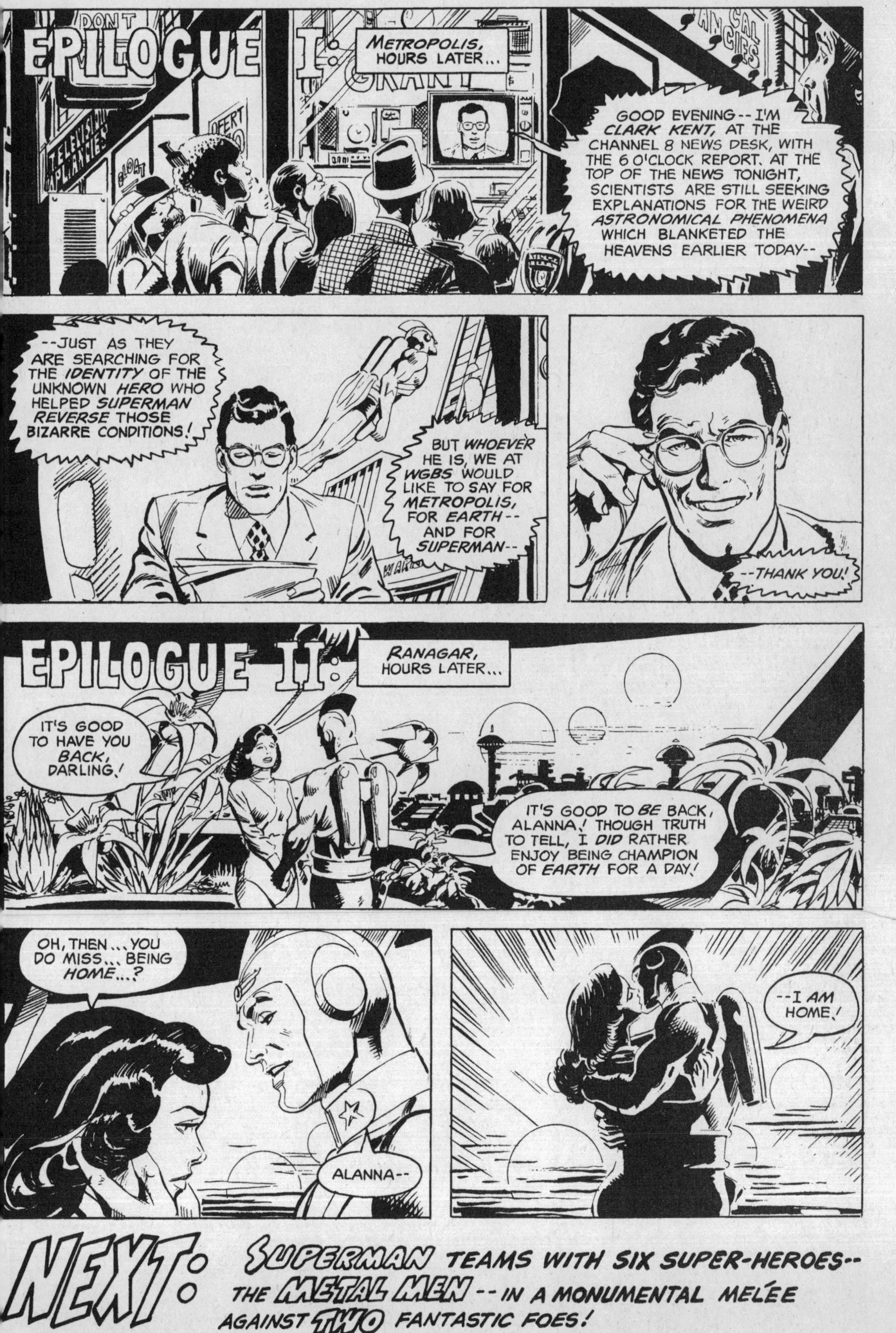
EPILOGUE I:
METROPOLIS, HOURS LATER...
GOOD EVENING--I'M CLARK KENT, AT THE CHANNEL 8 NEWS DESK, WITH THE 6 O'CLOCK REPORT. AT THE TOP OF THE NEWS TONIGHT, SCIENTISTS ARE STILL SEEKING EXPLANATIONS FOR THE WEIRD ASTRONOMICAL PHENOMENA WHICH BLANKETED THE HEAVENS EARLIER TODAY--
--JUST AS THEY ARE SEARCHING FOR THE IDENTITY OF THE UNKNOWN HERO WHO HELPED SUPERMAN REVERSE THOSE BIZARRE CONDITIONS!
BUT WHOEVER HE IS, WE AT WGBS WOULD LIKE TO SAY FOR METROPOLIS, FOR EARTH--AND FOR SUPERMAN--
--THANK YOU!
EPILOGUE II:
RANAGAR, HOURS LATER...
IT'S GOOD TO HAVE YOU BACK, DARLING!
IT'S GOOD TO BE BACK, ALANNA! THOUGH TRUTH TO TELL, I DID RATHER ENJOY BEING CHAMPION OF EARTH FOR A DAY!
OH, THEN... YOU DO MISS... BEING HOME...?
ALANNA--
--I AM HOME!
NEXT:
SUPERMAN TEAMS WITH SIX SUPER-HEROES--THE METAL MEN--IN A MONUMENTAL MELÉE AGAINST TWO FANTASTIC FOES!

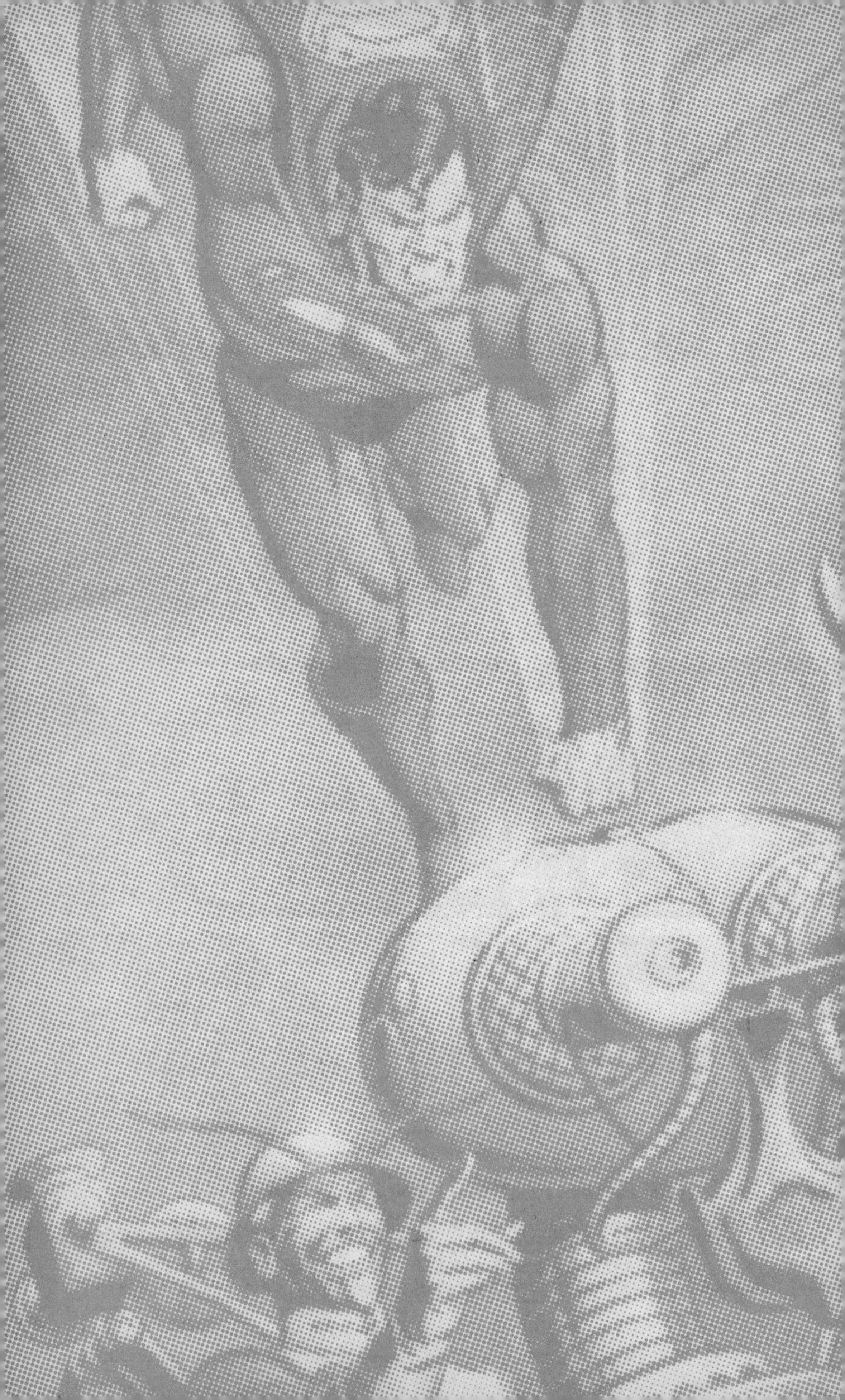

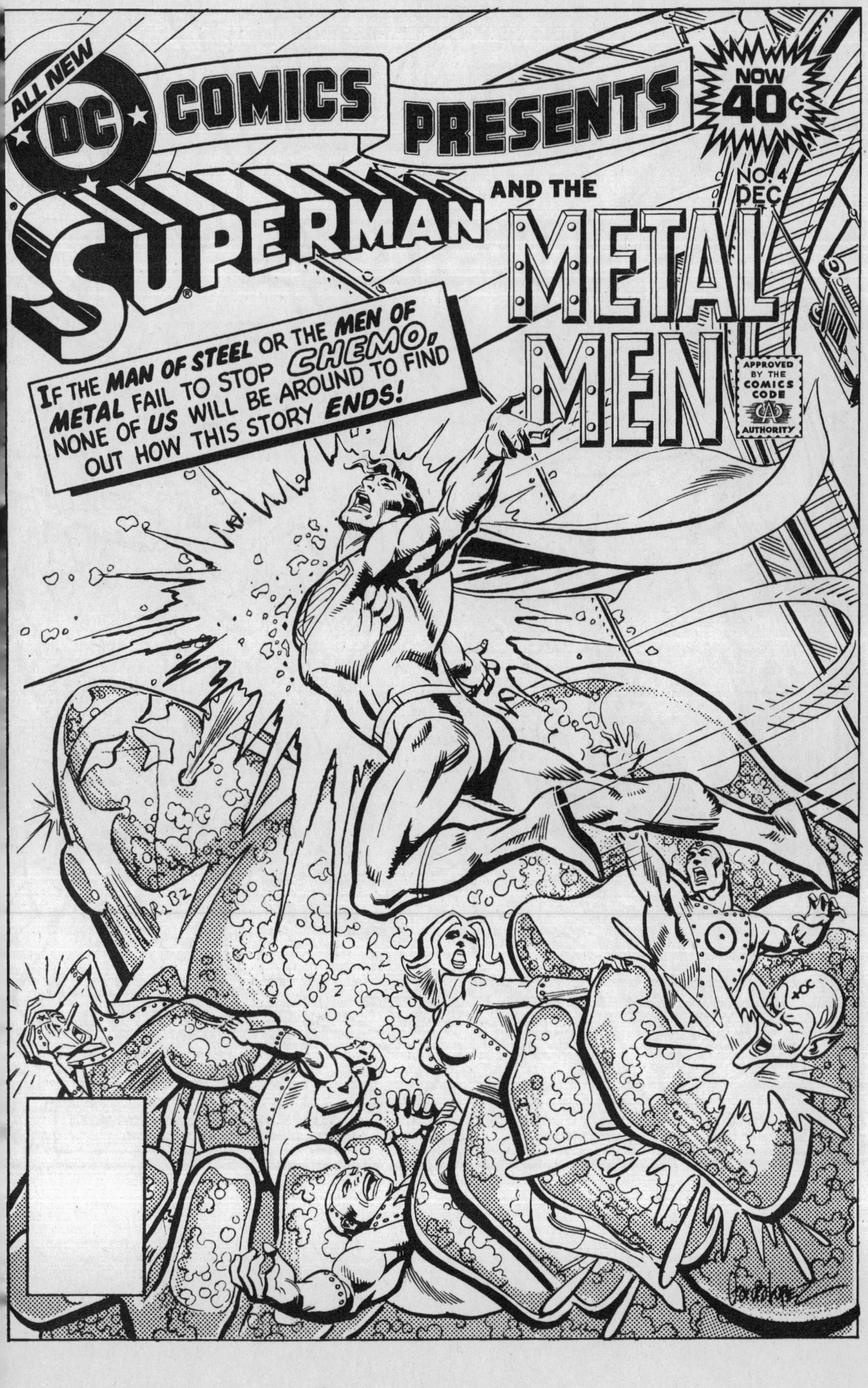
ALL NEW
DC
COMICS PRESENTS
NOW 40¢
NO. 4 DEC
SUPERMAN
AND THE
METAL MEN
IF THE MAN OF STEEL OR THE MEN OF METAL FAIL TO STOP CHEMO, NONE OF US WILL BE AROUND TO FIND OUT HOW THIS STORY ENDS!
APPROVED BY THE COMICS CODE AUTHORITY

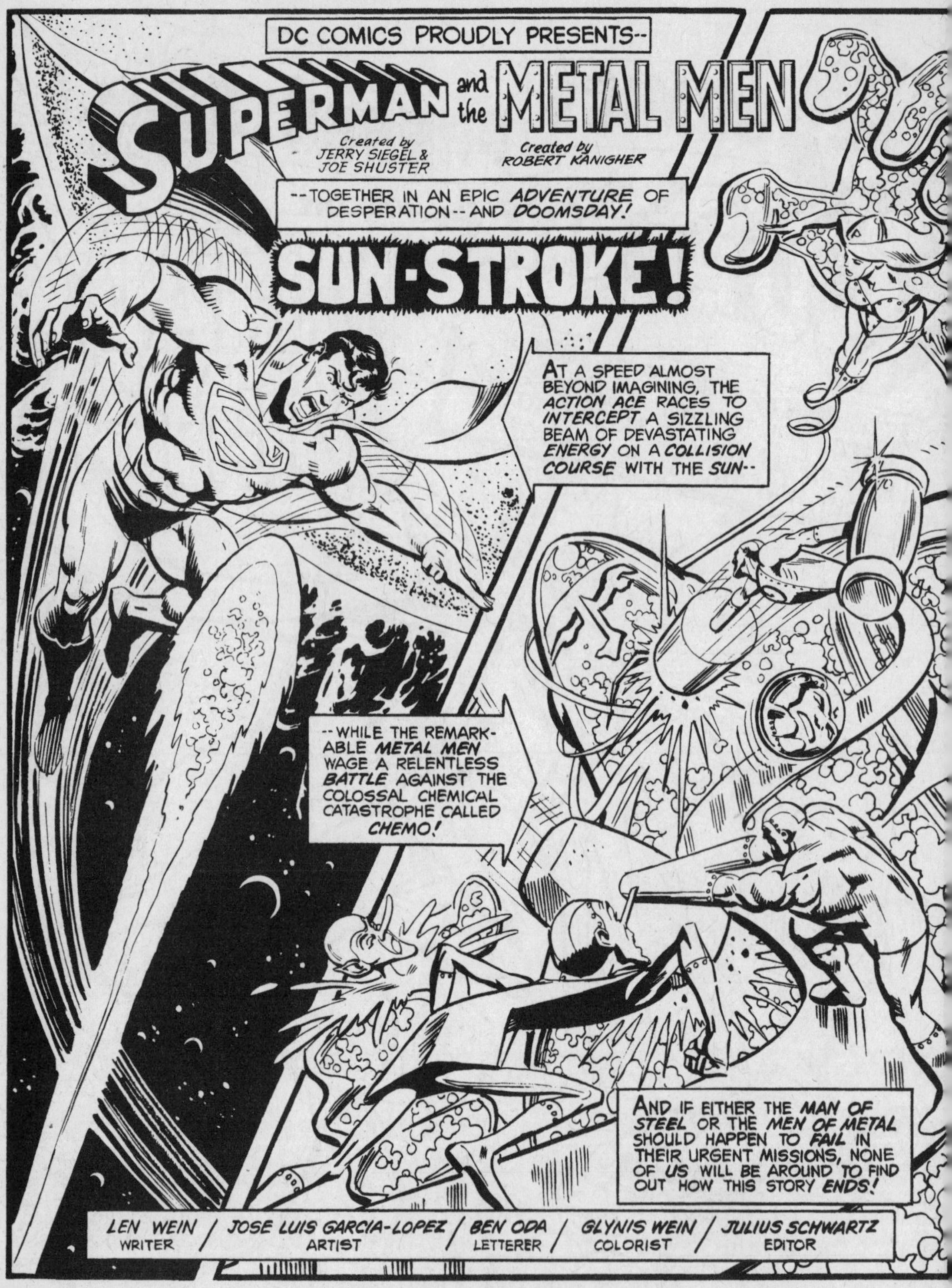
DC COMICS PROUDLY PRESENTS--
SUPERMAN and the METAL MEN
Created by JERRY SIEGEL & JOE SHUSTER
Created by ROBERT KANIGHER
--TOGETHER IN AN EPIC ADVENTURE OF DESPERATION--AND DOOMSDAY!
SUN-STROKE!
AT A SPEED ALMOST BEYOND IMAGINING, THE ACTION ACE RACES TO INTERCEPT A SIZZLING BEAM OF DEVASTATING ENERGY ON A COLLISION COURSE WITH THE SUN--
--WHILE THE REMARKABLE METAL MEN WAGE A RELENTLESS BATTLE AGAINST THE COLOSSAL CHEMICAL CATASTROPHE CALLED CHEMO!
AND IF EITHER THE MAN OF STEEL OR THE MEN OF METAL SHOULD HAPPEN TO FAIL IN THEIR URGENT MISSIONS, NONE OF US WILL BE AROUND TO FIND OUT HOW THIS STORY ENDS!
LEN WEIN WRITER / JOSE LUIS GARCIA-LOPEZ ARTIST / BEN ODA LETTERER / GLYNIS WEIN COLORIST / JULIUS SCHWARTZ EDITOR

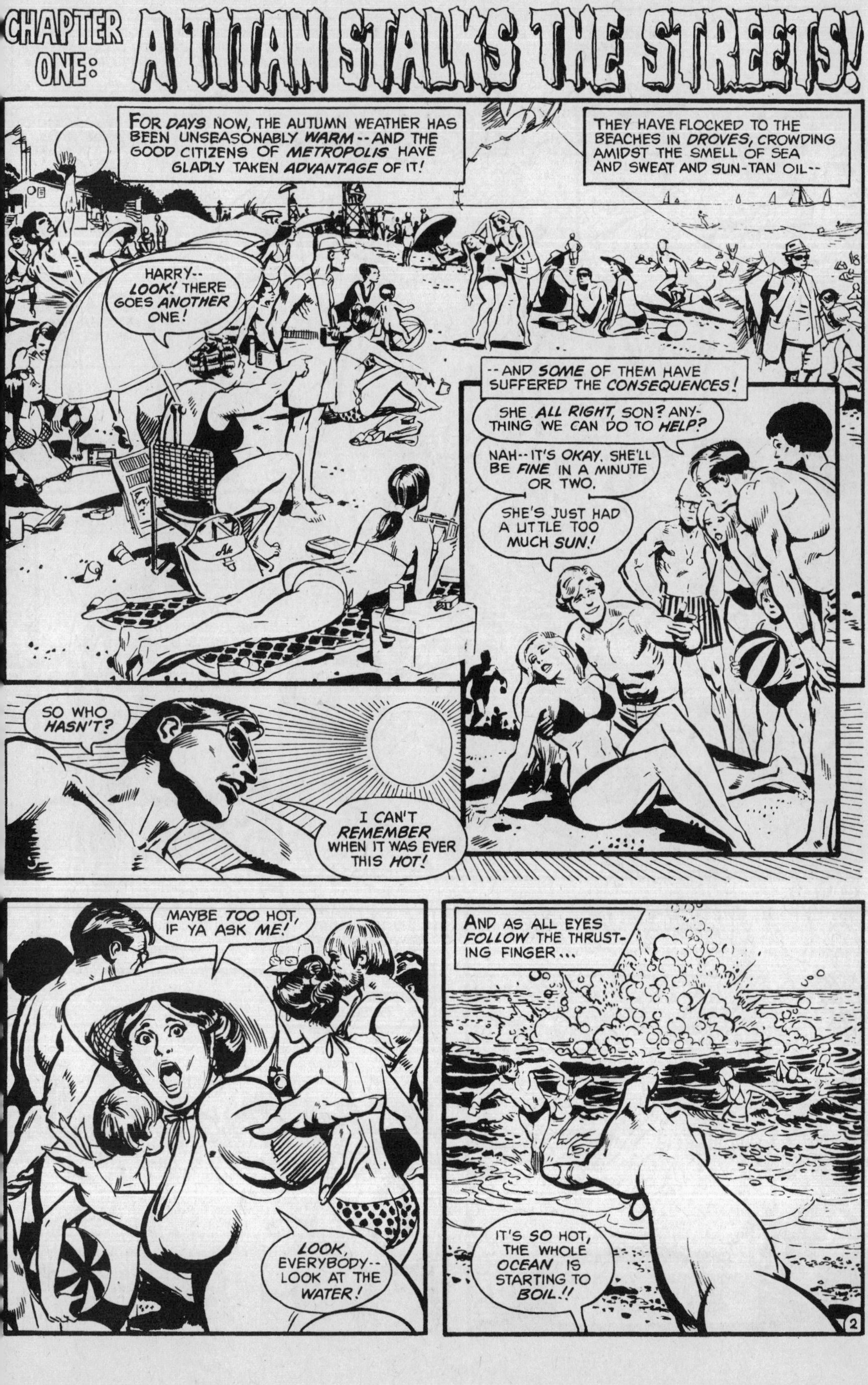
CHAPTER ONE: A TITAN STALKS THE STREETS!
FOR DAYS NOW, THE AUTUMN WEATHER HAS BEEN UNSEASONABLY WARM--AND THE GOOD CITIZENS OF METROPOLIS HAVE GLADLY TAKEN ADVANTAGE OF IT!
THEY HAVE FLOCKED TO THE BEACHES IN DROVES, CROWDING AMIDST THE SMELL OF SEA AND SWEAT AND SUN-TAN OIL--
HARRY--LOOK! THERE GOES ANOTHER ONE!
--AND SOME OF THEM HAVE SUFFERED THE CONSEQUENCES!
SHE ALL RIGHT, SON? ANYTHING WE CAN DO TO HELP?
NAH--IT'S OKAY. SHE'LL BE FINE IN A MINUTE OR TWO.
SHE'S JUST HAD A LITTLE TOO MUCH SUN!
SO WHO HASN'T?
I CAN'T REMEMBER WHEN IT WAS EVER THIS HOT!
MAYBE TOO HOT, IF YA ASK ME!
LOOK, EVERYBODY--LOOK AT THE WATER!
AND AS ALL EYES FOLLOW THE THRUSTING FINGER...
IT'S SO HOT, THE WHOLE OCEAN IS STARTING TO BOIL!!
2

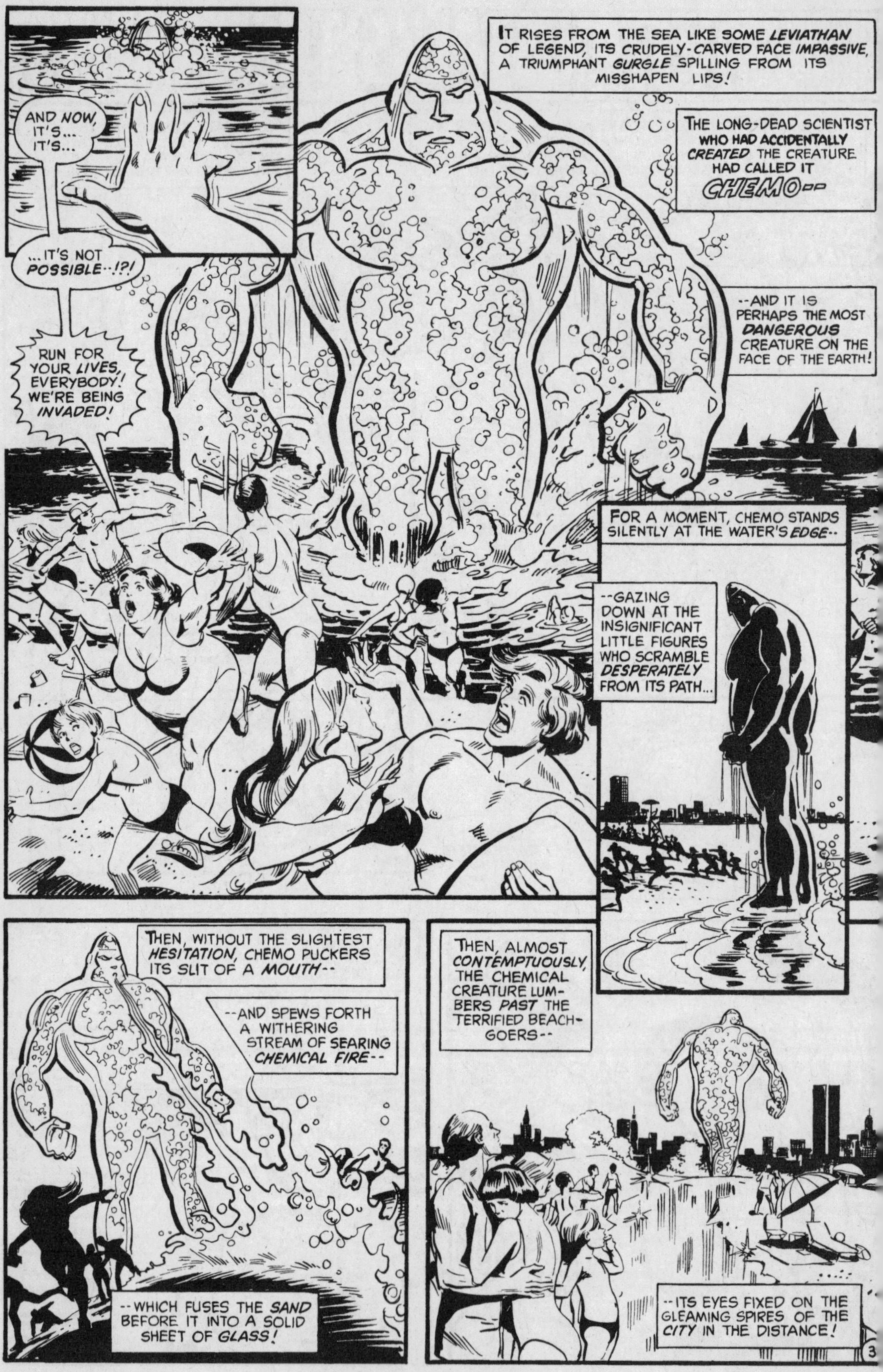
IT RISES FROM THE SEA LIKE SOME LEVIATHAN OF LEGEND, ITS CRUDELY-CARVED FACE IMPASSIVE, A TRIUMPHANT GURGLE SPILLING FROM ITS MISSHAPEN LIPS!
AND NOW, IT'S... IT'S...
THE LONG-DEAD SCIENTIST WHO HAD ACCIDENTALLY CREATED THE CREATURE HAD CALLED IT CHEMO--
...IT'S NOT POSSIBLE--!?!
--AND IT IS PERHAPS THE MOST DANGEROUS CREATURE ON THE FACE OF THE EARTH!
RUN FOR YOUR LIVES, EVERYBODY! WE'RE BEING INVADED!
FOR A MOMENT, CHEMO STANDS SILENTLY AT THE WATER'S EDGE--
--GAZING DOWN AT THE INSIGNIFICANT LITTLE FIGURES WHO SCRAMBLE DESPERATELY FROM ITS PATH...
THEN, WITHOUT THE SLIGHTEST HESITATION, CHEMO PUCKERS ITS SLIT OF A MOUTH--
--AND SPEWS FORTH A WITHERING STREAM OF SEARING CHEMICAL FIRE--
--WHICH FUSES THE SAND BEFORE IT INTO A SOLID SHEET OF GLASS!
THEN, ALMOST CONTEMPTUOUSLY, THE CHEMICAL CREATURE LUMBERS PAST THE TERRIFIED BEACH-GOERS--
--ITS EYES FIXED ON THE GLEAMING SPIRES OF THE CITY IN THE DISTANCE!
3

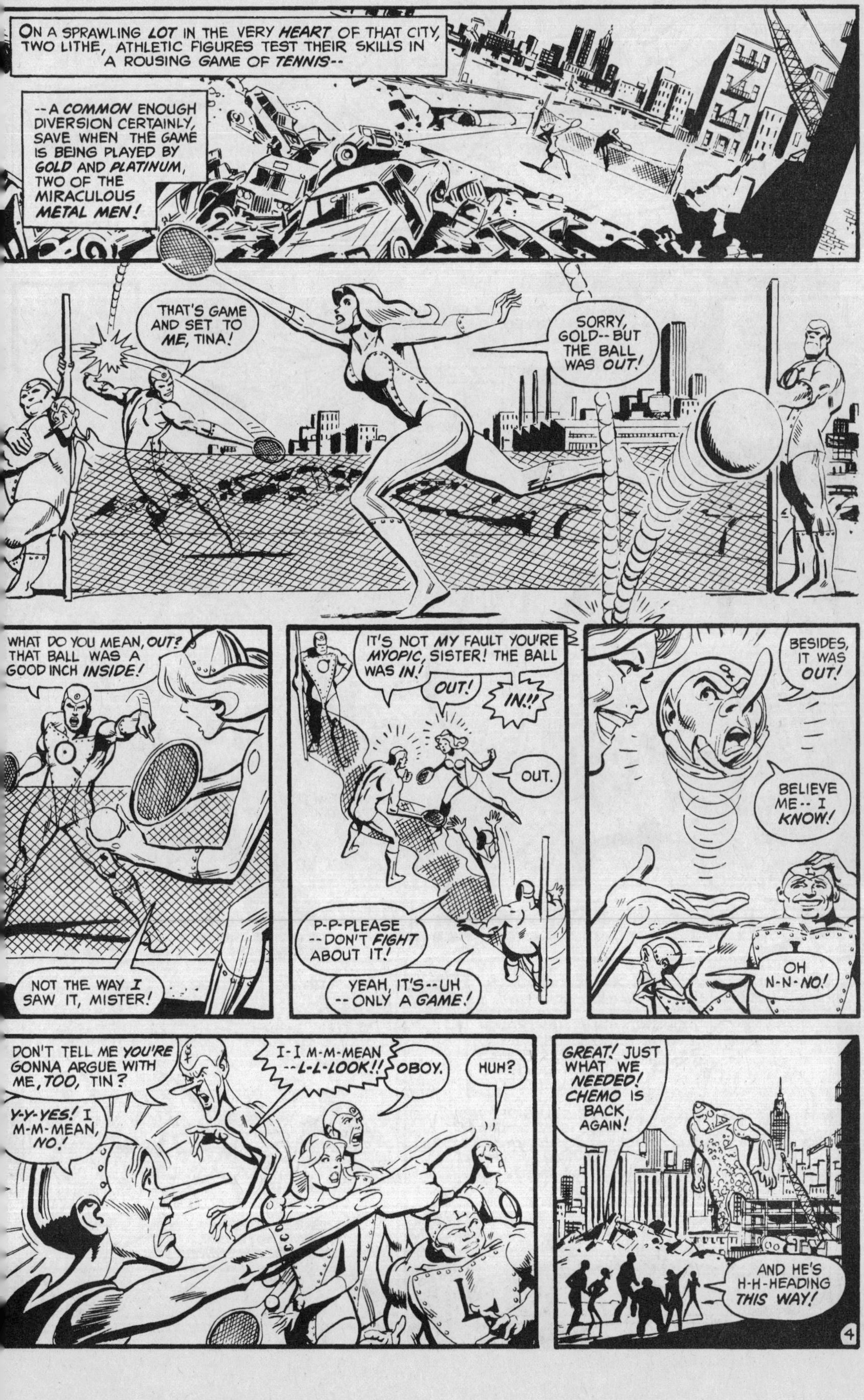
ON A SPRAWLING LOT IN THE VERY HEART OF THAT CITY, TWO LITHE, ATHLETIC FIGURES TEST THEIR SKILLS IN A ROUSING GAME OF TENNIS--
--A COMMON ENOUGH DIVERSION CERTAINLY, SAVE WHEN THE GAME IS BEING PLAYED BY GOLD AND PLATINUM, TWO OF THE MIRACULOUS METAL MEN!
THAT'S GAME AND SET TO ME, TINA!
SORRY, GOLD-- BUT THE BALL WAS OUT!
WHAT DO YOU MEAN, OUT? THAT BALL WAS A GOOD INCH INSIDE!
NOT THE WAY I SAW IT, MISTER!
IT'S NOT MY FAULT YOU'RE MYOPIC, SISTER! THE BALL WAS IN!
OUT!
IN!!
OUT.
P-P-PLEASE --DON'T FIGHT ABOUT IT!
YEAH, IT'S--UH --ONLY A GAME!
BESIDES, IT WAS OUT!
BELIEVE ME-- I KNOW!
OH N-N-NO!
DON'T TELL ME YOU'RE GONNA ARGUE WITH ME, TOO, TIN?
Y-Y-YES! I M-M-MEAN, NO!
I-I M-M-MEAN --L-L-LOOK!!
OBOY.
HUH?
GREAT! JUST WHAT WE NEEDED! CHEMO IS BACK AGAIN!
AND HE'S H-H-HEADING THIS WAY!
4

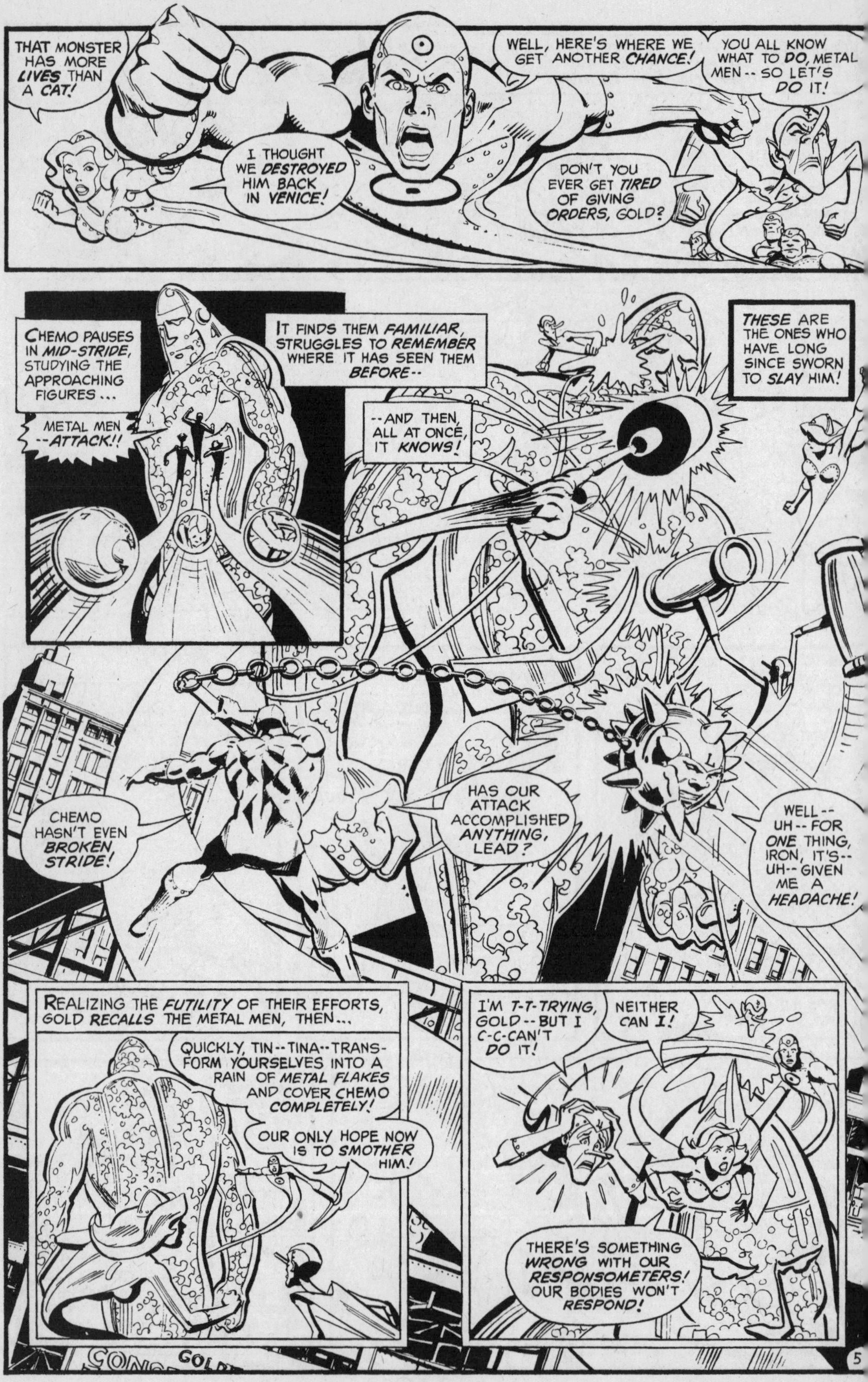
THAT MONSTER HAS MORE LIVES THAN A CAT!
I THOUGHT WE DESTROYED HIM BACK IN VENICE!
WELL, HERE'S WHERE WE GET ANOTHER CHANCE!
YOU ALL KNOW WHAT TO DO, METAL MEN -- SO LET'S DO IT!
DON'T YOU EVER GET TIRED OF GIVING ORDERS, GOLD?
CHEMO PAUSES IN MID-STRIDE, STUDYING THE APPROACHING FIGURES ...
METAL MEN --ATTACK!!
IT FINDS THEM FAMILIAR, STRUGGLES TO REMEMBER WHERE IT HAS SEEN THEM BEFORE--
--AND THEN, ALL AT ONCE, IT KNOWS!
THESE ARE THE ONES WHO HAVE LONG SINCE SWORN TO SLAY HIM!
CHEMO HASN'T EVEN BROKEN STRIDE!
HAS OUR ATTACK ACCOMPLISHED ANYTHING, LEAD?
WELL -- UH -- FOR ONE THING, IRON, IT'S-- UH-- GIVEN ME A HEADACHE!
REALIZING THE FUTILITY OF THEIR EFFORTS, GOLD RECALLS THE METAL MEN, THEN...
QUICKLY, TIN--TINA--TRANSFORM YOURSELVES INTO A RAIN OF METAL FLAKES AND COVER CHEMO COMPLETELY!
OUR ONLY HOPE NOW IS TO SMOTHER HIM!
I'M T-T-TRYING, GOLD -- BUT I C-C-CAN'T DO IT!
NEITHER CAN I!
THERE'S SOMETHING WRONG WITH OUR RESPONSOMETERS! OUR BODIES WON'T RESPOND!
5

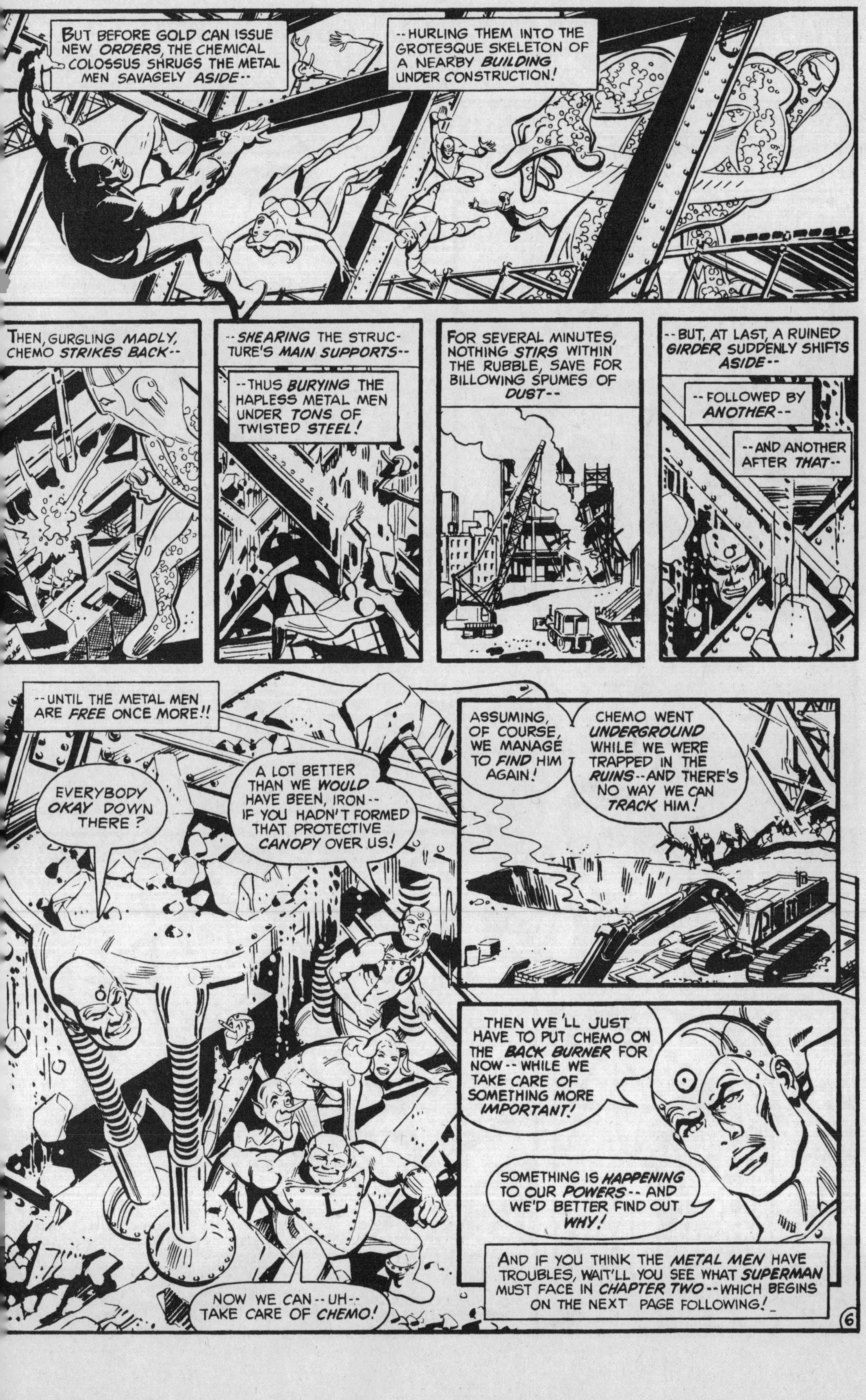
BUT BEFORE GOLD CAN ISSUE NEW ORDERS, THE CHEMICAL COLOSSUS SHRUGS THE METAL MEN SAVAGELY ASIDE--
--HURLING THEM INTO THE GROTESQUE SKELETON OF A NEARBY BUILDING UNDER CONSTRUCTION!
THEN, GURGLING MADLY, CHEMO STRIKES BACK--
--SHEARING THE STRUCTURE'S MAIN SUPPORTS--
--THUS BURYING THE HAPLESS METAL MEN UNDER TONS OF TWISTED STEEL!
FOR SEVERAL MINUTES, NOTHING STIRS WITHIN THE RUBBLE, SAVE FOR BILLOWING SPUMES OF DUST--
--BUT, AT LAST, A RUINED GIRDER SUDDENLY SHIFTS ASIDE--
--FOLLOWED BY ANOTHER--
--AND ANOTHER AFTER THAT--
--UNTIL THE METAL MEN ARE FREE ONCE MORE!!
EVERYBODY OKAY DOWN THERE?
A LOT BETTER THAN WE WOULD HAVE BEEN, IRON-- IF YOU HADN'T FORMED THAT PROTECTIVE CANOPY OVER US!
NOW WE CAN--UH-- TAKE CARE OF CHEMO!
CHEMO WENT UNDERGROUND WHILE WE WERE TRAPPED IN THE RUINS--AND THERE'S NO WAY WE CAN TRACK HIM!
ASSUMING, OF COURSE, WE MANAGE TO FIND HIM AGAIN!
THEN WE'LL JUST HAVE TO PUT CHEMO ON THE BACK BURNER FOR NOW-- WHILE WE TAKE CARE OF SOMETHING MORE IMPORTANT!
SOMETHING IS HAPPENING TO OUR POWERS-- AND WE'D BETTER FIND OUT WHY!
AND IF YOU THINK THE METAL MEN HAVE TROUBLES, WAIT'LL YOU SEE WHAT SUPERMAN MUST FACE IN CHAPTER TWO--WHICH BEGINS ON THE NEXT PAGE FOLLOWING!
6

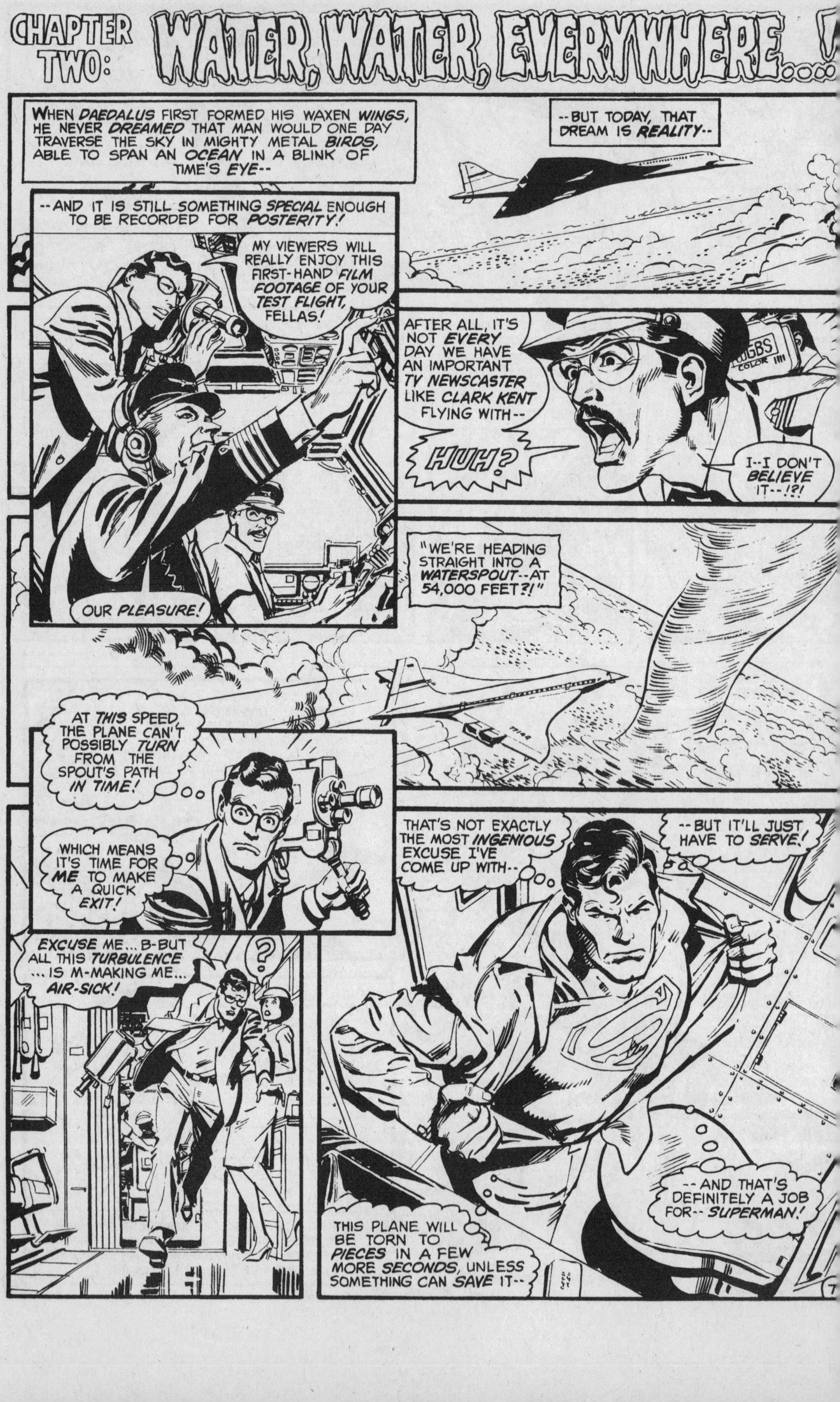
CHAPTER TWO: WATER, WATER, EVERYWHERE...!
WHEN DAEDALUS FIRST FORMED HIS WAXEN WINGS, HE NEVER DREAMED THAT MAN WOULD ONE DAY TRAVERSE THE SKY IN MIGHTY METAL BIRDS, ABLE TO SPAN AN OCEAN IN A BLINK OF TIME'S EYE--
--BUT TODAY, THAT DREAM IS REALITY--
--AND IT IS STILL SOMETHING SPECIAL ENOUGH TO BE RECORDED FOR POSTERITY!
MY VIEWERS WILL REALLY ENJOY THIS FIRST-HAND FILM FOOTAGE OF YOUR TEST FLIGHT, FELLAS!
OUR PLEASURE!
AFTER ALL, IT'S NOT EVERY DAY WE HAVE AN IMPORTANT TV NEWSCASTER LIKE CLARK KENT FLYING WITH--
HUH?
I--I DON'T BELIEVE IT--!?!
"WE'RE HEADING STRAIGHT INTO A WATERSPOUT--AT 54,000 FEET?!"
AT THIS SPEED, THE PLANE CAN'T POSSIBLY TURN FROM THE SPOUT'S PATH IN TIME!
WHICH MEANS IT'S TIME FOR ME TO MAKE A QUICK EXIT!
EXCUSE ME... B-BUT ALL THIS TURBULENCE ...IS M-MAKING ME... AIR-SICK!
?
THAT'S NOT EXACTLY THE MOST INGENIOUS EXCUSE I'VE COME UP WITH--
--BUT IT'LL JUST HAVE TO SERVE!
THIS PLANE WILL BE TORN TO PIECES IN A FEW MORE SECONDS, UNLESS SOMETHING CAN SAVE IT--
--AND THAT'S DEFINITELY A JOB FOR-- SUPERMAN!

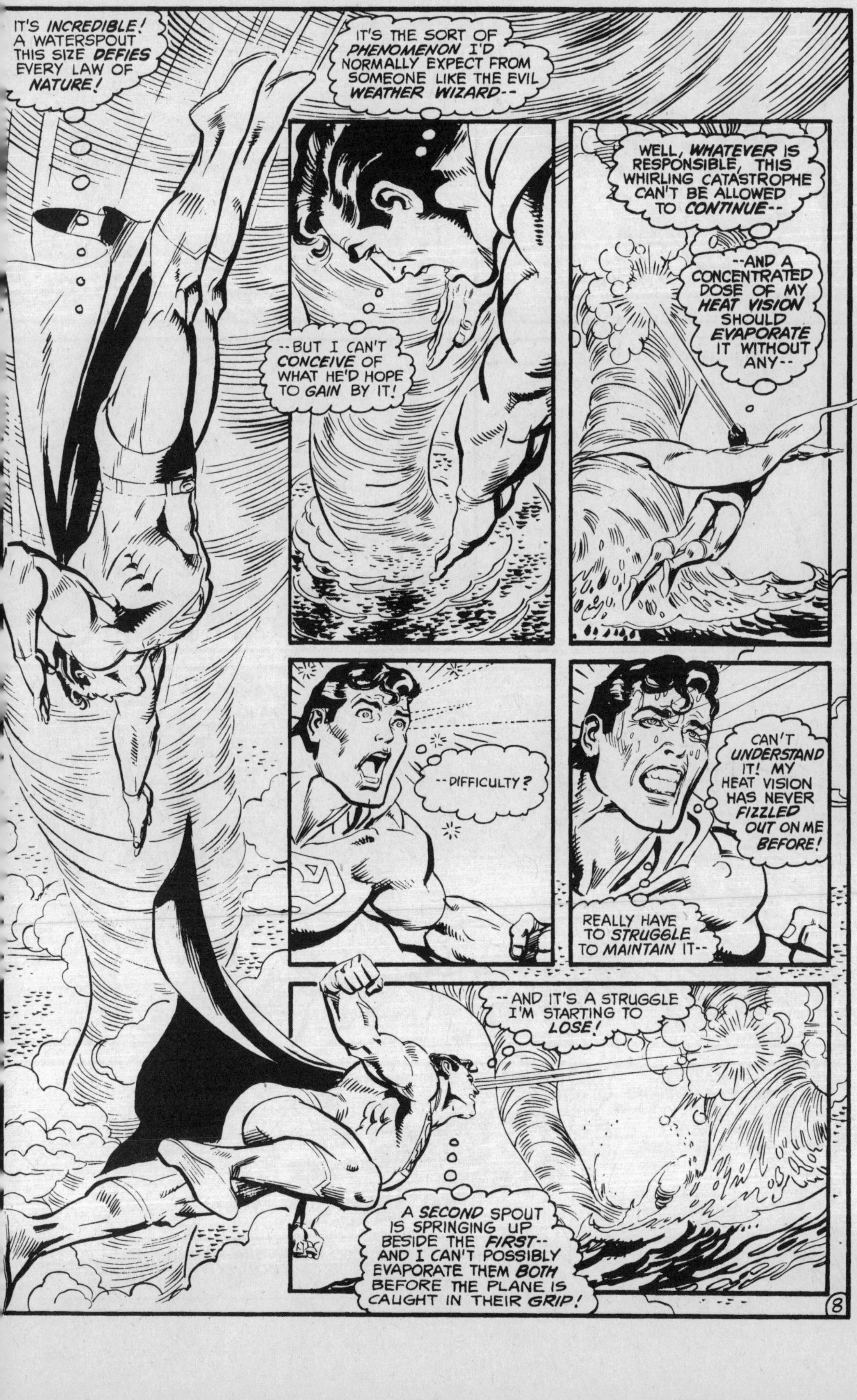
IT'S INCREDIBLE! A WATERSPOUT THIS SIZE DEFIES EVERY LAW OF NATURE!
IT'S THE SORT OF PHENOMENON I'D NORMALLY EXPECT FROM SOMEONE LIKE THE EVIL WEATHER WIZARD--
--BUT I CAN'T CONCEIVE OF WHAT HE'D HOPE TO GAIN BY IT!
WELL, WHATEVER IS RESPONSIBLE, THIS WHIRLING CATASTROPHE CAN'T BE ALLOWED TO CONTINUE--
--AND A CONCENTRATED DOSE OF MY HEAT VISION SHOULD EVAPORATE IT WITHOUT ANY--
--DIFFICULTY?
CAN'T UNDERSTAND IT! MY HEAT VISION HAS NEVER FIZZLED OUT ON ME BEFORE!
REALLY HAVE TO STRUGGLE TO MAINTAIN IT--
--AND IT'S A STRUGGLE I'M STARTING TO LOSE!
A SECOND SPOUT IS SPRINGING UP BESIDE THE FIRST-- AND I CAN'T POSSIBLY EVAPORATE THEM BOTH BEFORE THE PLANE IS CAUGHT IN THEIR GRIP!
8

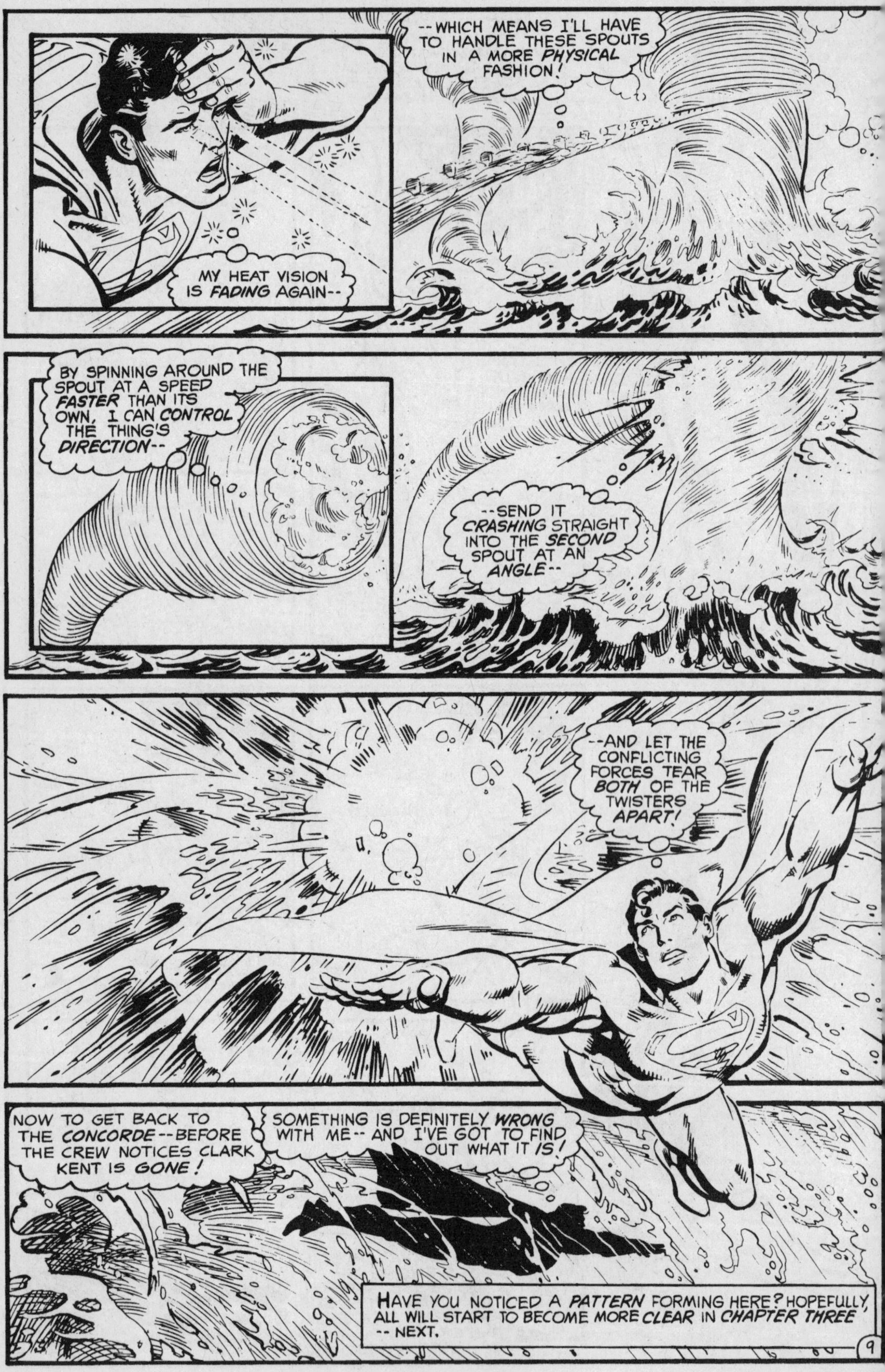
MY HEAT VISION IS FADING AGAIN--
--WHICH MEANS I'LL HAVE TO HANDLE THESE SPOUTS IN A MORE PHYSICAL FASHION!
BY SPINNING AROUND THE SPOUT AT A SPEED FASTER THAN ITS OWN, I CAN CONTROL THE THING'S DIRECTION--
--SEND IT CRASHING STRAIGHT INTO THE SECOND SPOUT AT AN ANGLE--
--AND LET THE CONFLICTING FORCES TEAR BOTH OF THE TWISTERS APART!
NOW TO GET BACK TO THE CONCORDE--BEFORE THE CREW NOTICES CLARK KENT IS GONE!
SOMETHING IS DEFINITELY WRONG WITH ME-- AND I'VE GOT TO FIND OUT WHAT IT IS!
HAVE YOU NOTICED A PATTERN FORMING HERE? HOPEFULLY, ALL WILL START TO BECOME MORE CLEAR IN CHAPTER THREE -- NEXT.
9

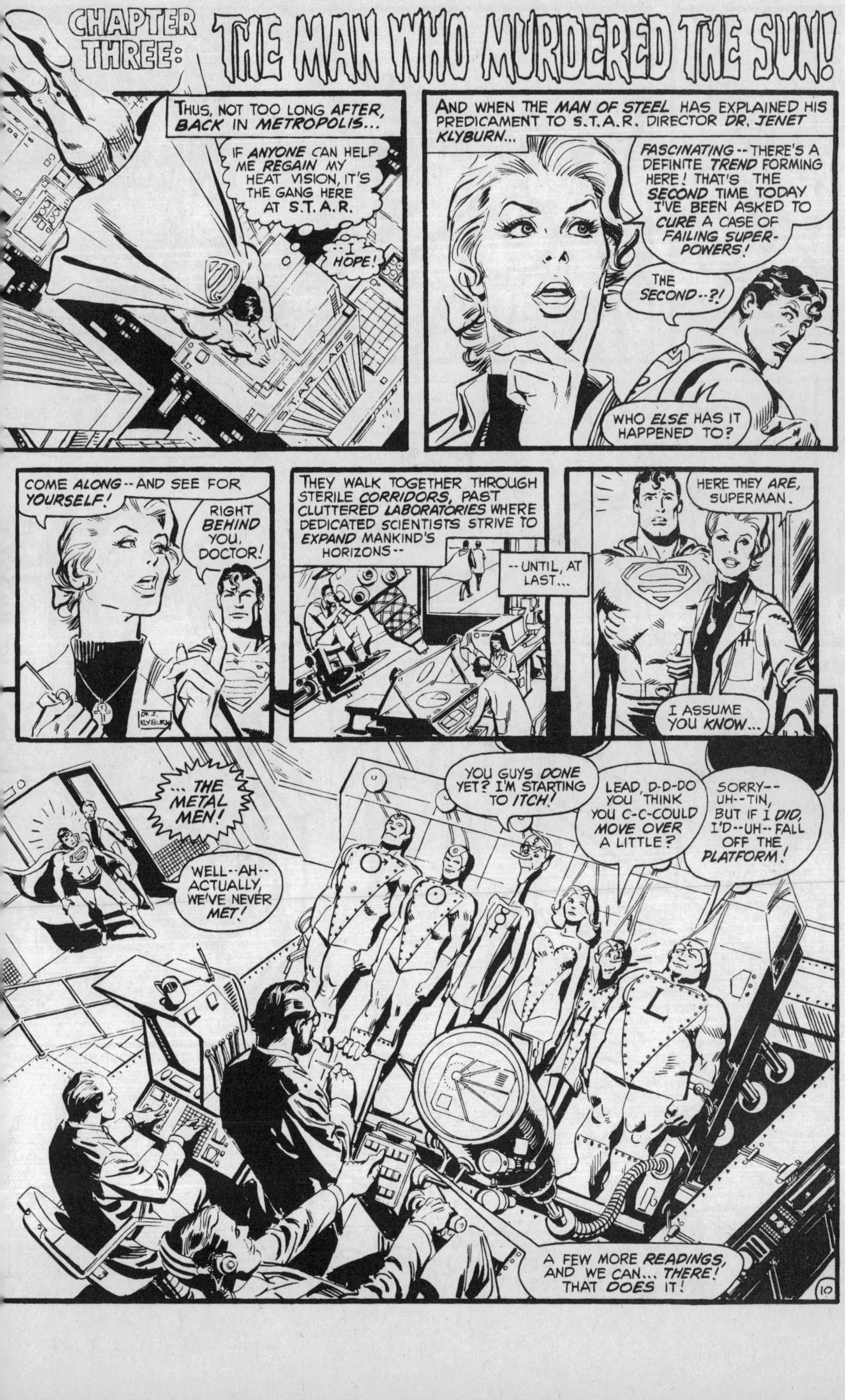
CHAPTER THREE: THE MAN WHO MURDERED THE SUN!
THUS, NOT TOO LONG AFTER, BACK IN METROPOLIS...
IF ANYONE CAN HELP ME REGAIN MY HEAT VISION, IT'S THE GANG HERE AT S.T.A.R.
--I HOPE!
S.T.A.R. LABS
AND WHEN THE MAN OF STEEL HAS EXPLAINED HIS PREDICAMENT TO S.T.A.R. DIRECTOR DR. JENET KLYBURN...
FASCINATING--THERE'S A DEFINITE TREND FORMING HERE! THAT'S THE SECOND TIME TODAY I'VE BEEN ASKED TO CURE A CASE OF FAILING SUPER-POWERS!
THE SECOND--?!
WHO ELSE HAS IT HAPPENED TO?
COME ALONG--AND SEE FOR YOURSELF!
RIGHT BEHIND YOU, DOCTOR!
DR. J. KLYBURN
THEY WALK TOGETHER THROUGH STERILE CORRIDORS, PAST CLUTTERED LABORATORIES WHERE DEDICATED SCIENTISTS STRIVE TO EXPAND MANKIND'S HORIZONS--
--UNTIL, AT LAST...
HERE THEY ARE, SUPERMAN.
I ASSUME YOU KNOW...
...THE METAL MEN!
WELL--AH--ACTUALLY, WE'VE NEVER MET!
YOU GUYS DONE YET? I'M STARTING TO ITCH!
LEAD, D-D-DO YOU THINK YOU C-C-COULD MOVE OVER A LITTLE?
SORRY--UH--TIN, BUT IF I DID, I'D--UH--FALL OFF THE PLATFORM!
A FEW MORE READINGS, AND WE CAN... THERE! THAT DOES IT!
10

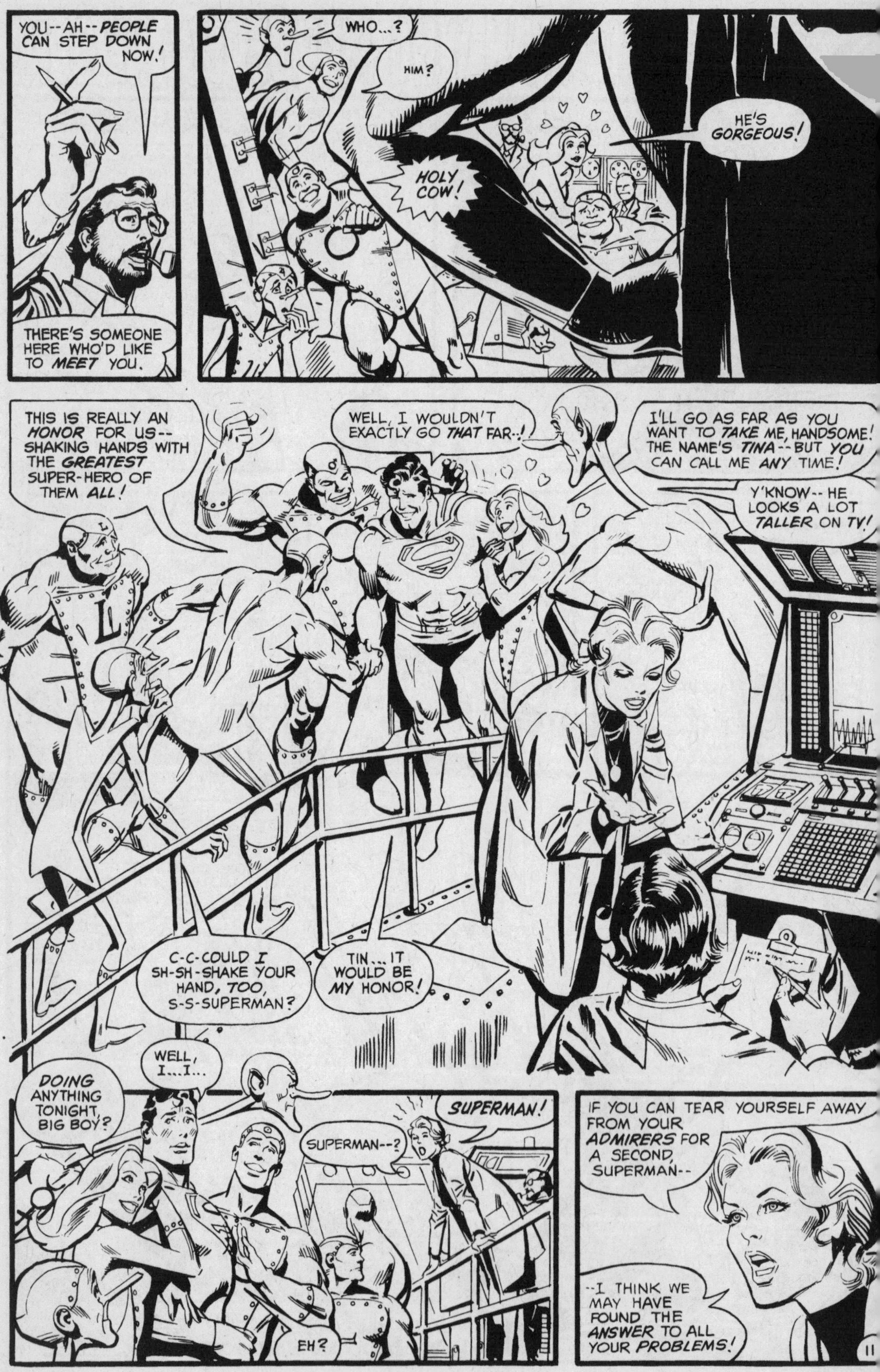
YOU--AH--PEOPLE CAN STEP DOWN NOW!
THERE'S SOMEONE HERE WHO'D LIKE TO MEET YOU.
WHO...?
HIM?
HOLY COW!
HE'S GORGEOUS!
THIS IS REALLY AN HONOR FOR US-- SHAKING HANDS WITH THE GREATEST SUPER-HERO OF THEM ALL!
WELL, I WOULDN'T EXACTLY GO THAT FAR--!
I'LL GO AS FAR AS YOU WANT TO TAKE ME, HANDSOME! THE NAME'S TINA--BUT YOU CAN CALL ME ANY TIME!
Y'KNOW--HE LOOKS A LOT TALLER ON TV!
C-C-COULD I SH-SH-SHAKE YOUR HAND, TOO, S-S-SUPERMAN?
TIN... IT WOULD BE MY HONOR!
DOING ANYTHING TONIGHT, BIG BOY?
WELL, I...I...
SUPERMAN!
SUPERMAN--?
EH?
IF YOU CAN TEAR YOURSELF AWAY FROM YOUR ADMIRERS FOR A SECOND, SUPERMAN--
--I THINK WE MAY HAVE FOUND THE ANSWER TO ALL YOUR PROBLEMS!
11

AND MOMENTS LATER, IN AN ADJOINING *LAB*...

SEVERAL DAYS AGO, OUR *SENSORS* DETECTED AN INCREDIBLY POWERFUL BEAM OF *MAGNETIC ENERGY* BEING BROADCAST FROM SOMEWHERE HERE ON *EARTH*--

--DIRECTLY INTO THE *HEART* OF THE *SUN!*

"THE *RESULT* OF THIS AWESOME MAGNETIC BOMBARDMENT APPEARS TO BE DRASTICALLY-INCREASED *SUNSPOT ACTIVITY*--

"--AND A SERIES OF *SOLAR PROMINENCES* THAT HAVE BLOWN THE *MEASURING NEEDLE CLEAN OFF THE SCALE!*

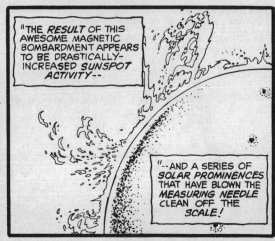

"SINCE YOUR *NON-MUSCULAR POWERS*-- SUCH AS *HEAT VISION*-- ARE A PRODUCT OF THE SUN'S *YELLOW RAYS*, SUPERMAN...

"... AND SINCE THE *RESPONSOMETERS* WHICH CONTROL THE METAL MEN'S *SHAPE-CHANGING ABILITIES* ARE SUSCEPTIBLE TO *MAGNETIC INTERFERENCE*...

"...IT DOESN'T REALLY TAKE A GREAT DEAL OF *EFFORT* TO FIGURE OUT WHAT'S BEEN GOING *WRONG* WITH ALL OF YOU!"

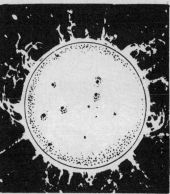

AND *NOW* IT SEEMS THE INCREASED *ULTRA-VIOLET* RADIATION BEING GIVEN OFF BY THE SUN HAS BEGUN TO AFFECT *EVERYONE!*

PEOPLE RUSHING TO THE *BEACHES* DUE TO THE UNSEASONABLY WARM WEATHER ARE TAKING *ILL* AT AN ALARMING *RATE!*

LOGICALLY, THE MOST *DIRECT* METHOD OF *REVERSING* THE SOLAR DISTURBANCES--

--IS TO LOCATE THE *SOURCE* OF THE MAGNETIC RAY THAT *CAUSED* THEM IN THE *FIRST* PLACE!

AND SINCE MOST OF MY *SUPER-SENSES* ARE PRETTY *SUSPECT* AT THE MOMENT, I COULD USE A LITTLE *HELP* IN THAT DEPARTMENT...

...IF YOU *METAL MEN* ARE WILLING TO *PROVIDE* IT!

WE'RE *WITH* YOU, SUPERMAN-- *ALL THE WAY!!*

WHOOPEE!

12

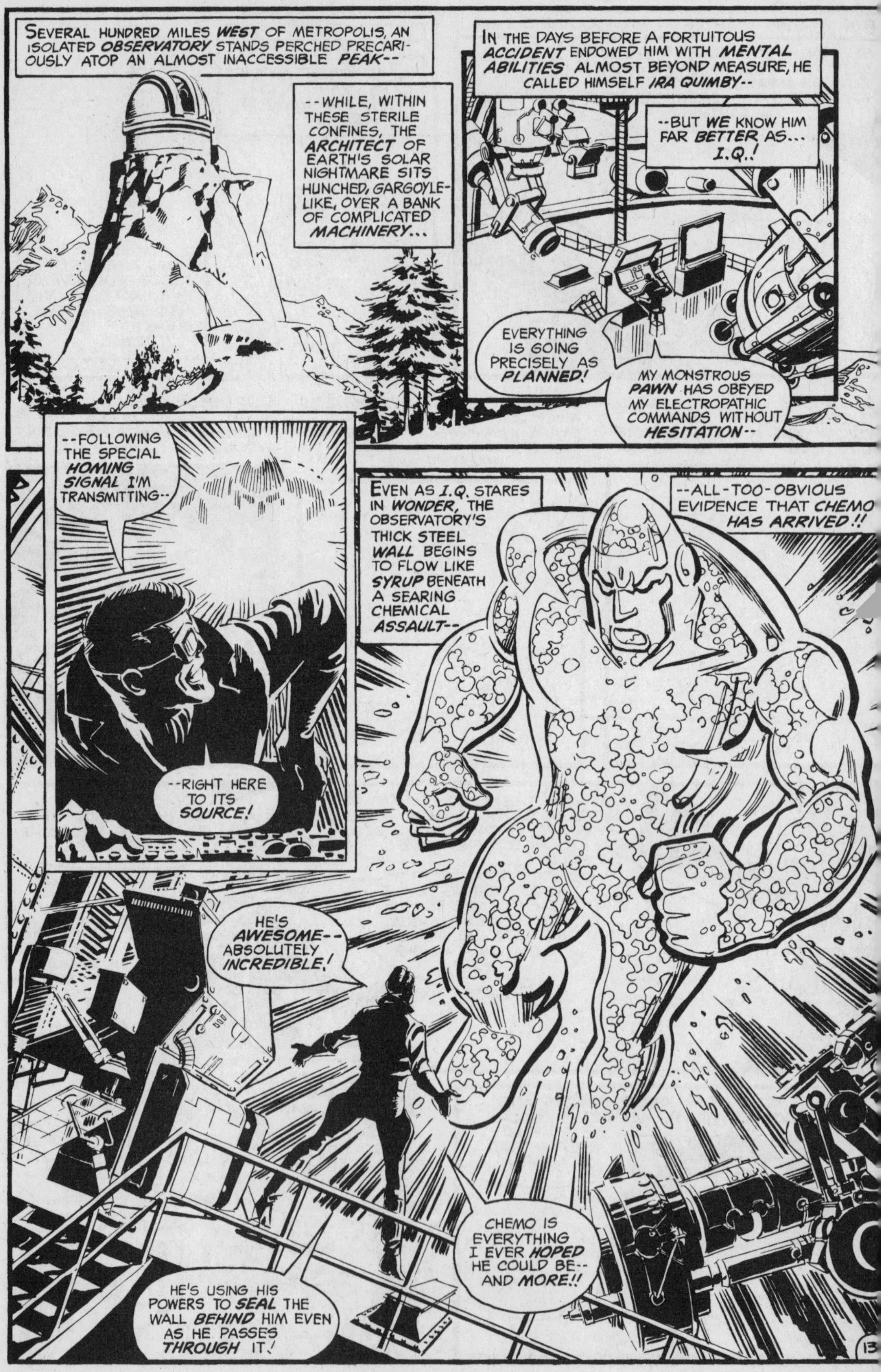

SEVERAL HUNDRED MILES WEST OF METROPOLIS, AN ISOLATED OBSERVATORY STANDS PERCHED PRECARIOUSLY ATOP AN ALMOST INACCESSIBLE PEAK--
--WHILE, WITHIN THESE STERILE CONFINES, THE ARCHITECT OF EARTH'S SOLAR NIGHTMARE SITS HUNCHED, GARGOYLE-LIKE, OVER A BANK OF COMPLICATED MACHINERY...
IN THE DAYS BEFORE A FORTUITOUS ACCIDENT ENDOWED HIM WITH MENTAL ABILITIES ALMOST BEYOND MEASURE, HE CALLED HIMSELF IRA QUIMBY--
--BUT WE KNOW HIM FAR BETTER AS... I.Q.!
EVERYTHING IS GOING PRECISELY AS PLANNED!
MY MONSTROUS PAWN HAS OBEYED MY ELECTROPATHIC COMMANDS WITHOUT HESITATION--
--FOLLOWING THE SPECIAL HOMING SIGNAL I'M TRANSMITTING--
--RIGHT HERE TO ITS SOURCE!
EVEN AS I.Q. STARES IN WONDER, THE OBSERVATORY'S THICK STEEL WALL BEGINS TO FLOW LIKE SYRUP BENEATH A SEARING CHEMICAL ASSAULT--
--ALL-TOO-OBVIOUS EVIDENCE THAT CHEMO HAS ARRIVED!!
HE'S AWESOME-- ABSOLUTELY INCREDIBLE!
CHEMO IS EVERYTHING I EVER HOPED HE COULD BE-- AND MORE!!
HE'S USING HIS POWERS TO SEAL THE WALL BEHIND HIM EVEN AS HE PASSES THROUGH IT!
13

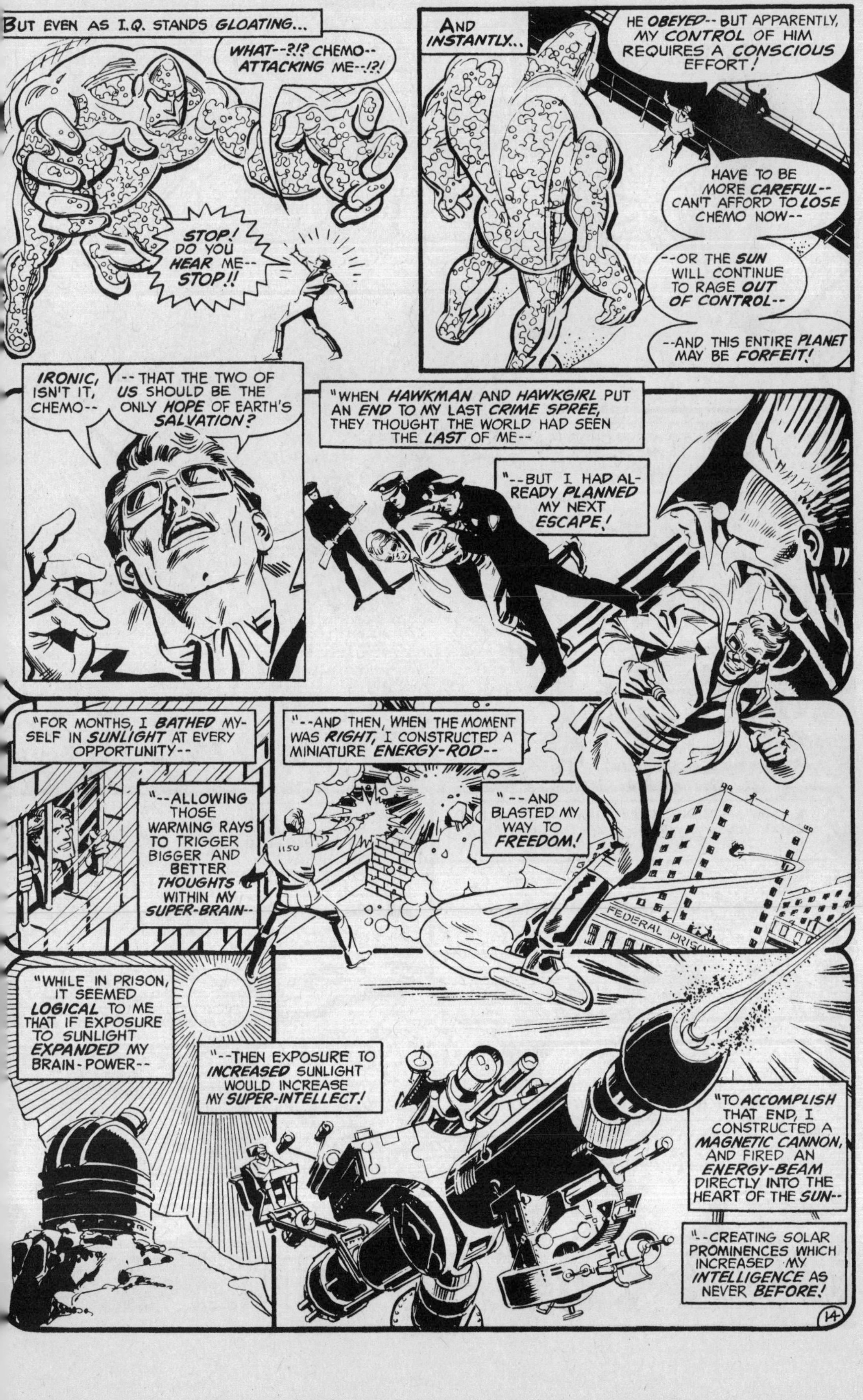
BUT EVEN AS I.Q. STANDS GLOATING...
WHAT--?!? CHEMO-- ATTACKING ME--!?!
STOP! DO YOU HEAR ME-- STOP!!
AND INSTANTLY...
HE OBEYED-- BUT APPARENTLY, MY CONTROL OF HIM REQUIRES A CONSCIOUS EFFORT!
HAVE TO BE MORE CAREFUL-- CAN'T AFFORD TO LOSE CHEMO NOW--
--OR THE SUN WILL CONTINUE TO RAGE OUT OF CONTROL--
--AND THIS ENTIRE PLANET MAY BE FORFEIT!
IRONIC, ISN'T IT, CHEMO--
--THAT THE TWO OF US SHOULD BE THE ONLY HOPE OF EARTH'S SALVATION?
"WHEN HAWKMAN AND HAWKGIRL PUT AN END TO MY LAST CRIME SPREE, THEY THOUGHT THE WORLD HAD SEEN THE LAST OF ME--
"--BUT I HAD AL-READY PLANNED MY NEXT ESCAPE!
"FOR MONTHS, I BATHED MY-SELF IN SUNLIGHT AT EVERY OPPORTUNITY--
"--ALLOWING THOSE WARMING RAYS TO TRIGGER BIGGER AND BETTER THOUGHTS WITHIN MY SUPER-BRAIN--
"--AND THEN, WHEN THE MOMENT WAS RIGHT, I CONSTRUCTED A MINIATURE ENERGY-ROD--
"--AND BLASTED MY WAY TO FREEDOM!
1150
FEDERAL PRISON
"WHILE IN PRISON, IT SEEMED LOGICAL TO ME THAT IF EXPOSURE TO SUNLIGHT EXPANDED MY BRAIN-POWER--
"--THEN EXPOSURE TO INCREASED SUNLIGHT WOULD INCREASE MY SUPER-INTELLECT!
"TO ACCOMPLISH THAT END, I CONSTRUCTED A MAGNETIC CANNON, AND FIRED AN ENERGY-BEAM DIRECTLY INTO THE HEART OF THE SUN--
"--CREATING SOLAR PROMINENCES WHICH INCREASED MY INTELLIGENCE AS NEVER BEFORE!
14

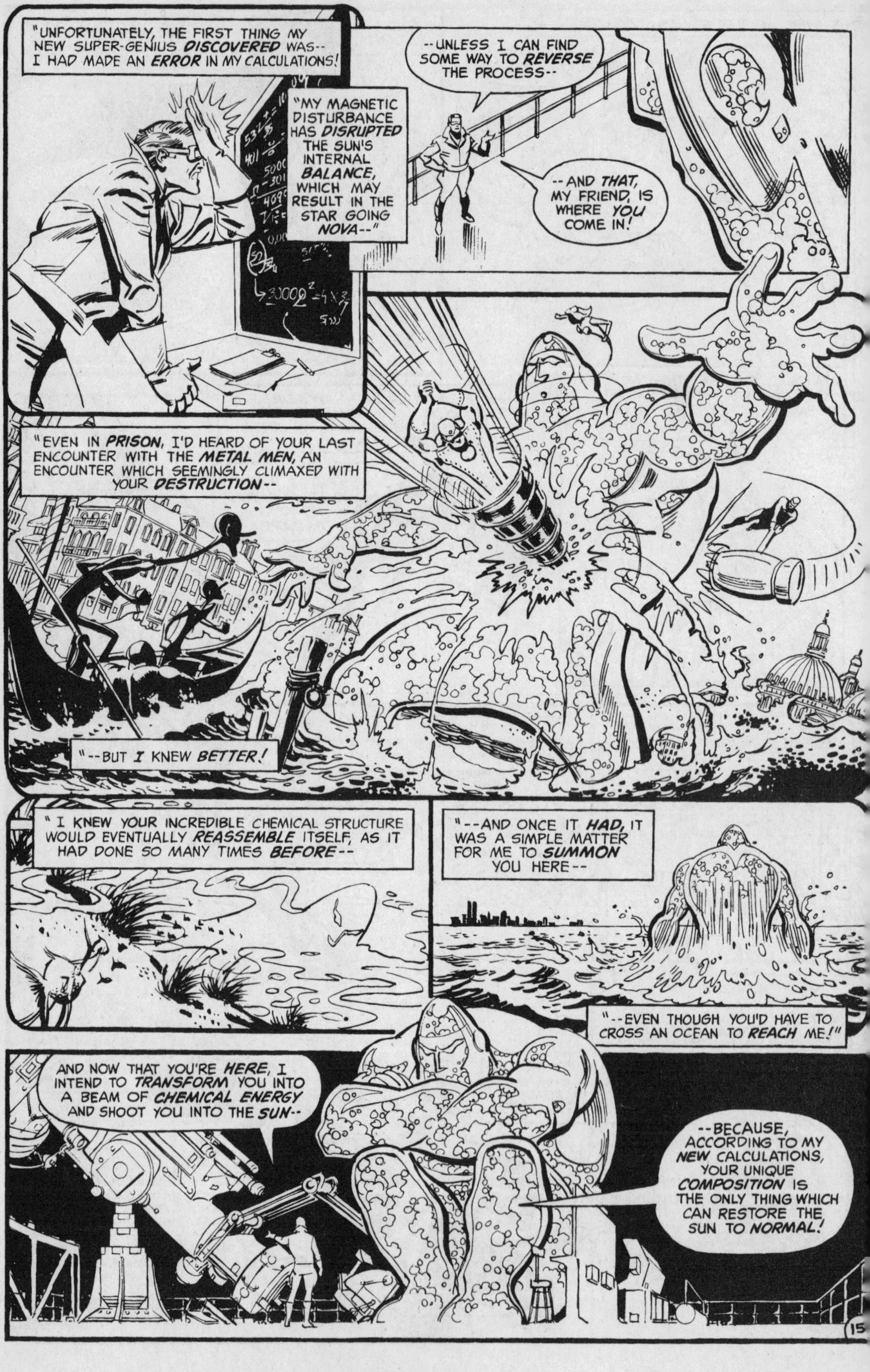
"UNFORTUNATELY, THE FIRST THING MY NEW SUPER-GENIUS DISCOVERED WAS-- I HAD MADE AN ERROR IN MY CALCULATIONS!
"MY MAGNETIC DISTURBANCE HAS DISRUPTED THE SUN'S INTERNAL BALANCE, WHICH MAY RESULT IN THE STAR GOING NOVA--"
--UNLESS I CAN FIND SOME WAY TO REVERSE THE PROCESS--
--AND THAT, MY FRIEND, IS WHERE YOU COME IN!
"EVEN IN PRISON, I'D HEARD OF YOUR LAST ENCOUNTER WITH THE METAL MEN, AN ENCOUNTER WHICH SEEMINGLY CLIMAXED WITH YOUR DESTRUCTION--
"--BUT I KNEW BETTER!
"I KNEW YOUR INCREDIBLE CHEMICAL STRUCTURE WOULD EVENTUALLY REASSEMBLE ITSELF, AS IT HAD DONE SO MANY TIMES BEFORE--
"--AND ONCE IT HAD, IT WAS A SIMPLE MATTER FOR ME TO SUMMON YOU HERE--
"--EVEN THOUGH YOU'D HAVE TO CROSS AN OCEAN TO REACH ME!"
AND NOW THAT YOU'RE HERE, I INTEND TO TRANSFORM YOU INTO A BEAM OF CHEMICAL ENERGY AND SHOOT YOU INTO THE SUN--
--BECAUSE, ACCORDING TO MY NEW CALCULATIONS, YOUR UNIQUE COMPOSITION IS THE ONLY THING WHICH CAN RESTORE THE SUN TO NORMAL!
15

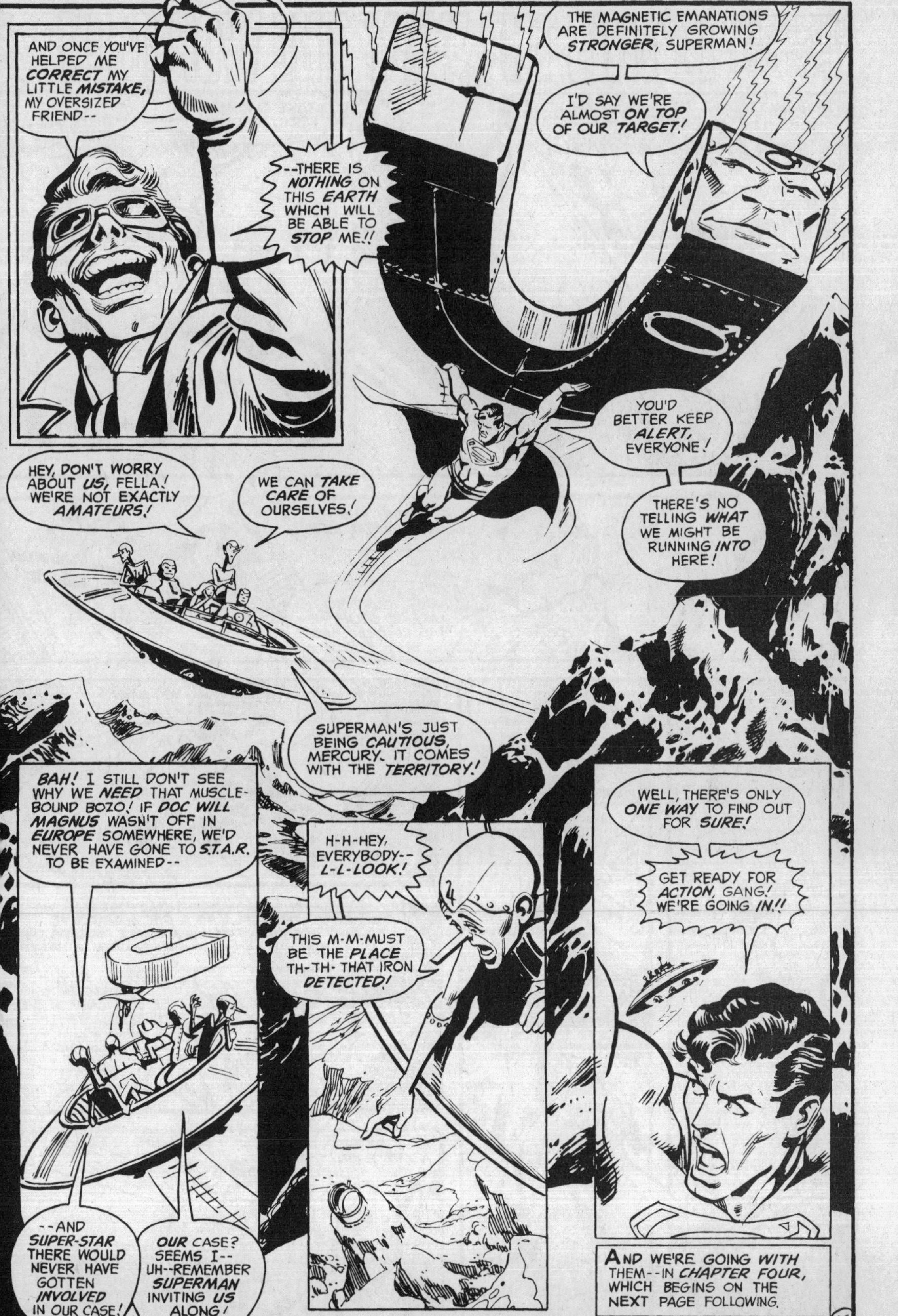
AND ONCE YOU'VE HELPED ME CORRECT MY LITTLE MISTAKE, MY OVERSIZED FRIEND--
--THERE IS NOTHING ON THIS EARTH WHICH WILL BE ABLE TO STOP ME!!
THE MAGNETIC EMANATIONS ARE DEFINITELY GROWING STRONGER, SUPERMAN!
I'D SAY WE'RE ALMOST ON TOP OF OUR TARGET!
HEY, DON'T WORRY ABOUT US, FELLA! WE'RE NOT EXACTLY AMATEURS!
WE CAN TAKE CARE OF OURSELVES!
YOU'D BETTER KEEP ALERT, EVERYONE!
THERE'S NO TELLING WHAT WE MIGHT BE RUNNING INTO HERE!
SUPERMAN'S JUST BEING CAUTIOUS, MERCURY. IT COMES WITH THE TERRITORY!
BAH! I STILL DON'T SEE WHY WE NEED THAT MUSCLE-BOUND BOZO! IF DOC WILL MAGNUS WASN'T OFF IN EUROPE SOMEWHERE, WE'D NEVER HAVE GONE TO S.T.A.R. TO BE EXAMINED--
--AND SUPER-STAR THERE WOULD NEVER HAVE GOTTEN INVOLVED IN OUR CASE!
OUR CASE? SEEMS I--UH--REMEMBER SUPERMAN INVITING US ALONG!
H-H-HEY, EVERYBODY--L-L-LOOK!
THIS M-M-MUST BE THE PLACE TH-TH- THAT IRON DETECTED!
WELL, THERE'S ONLY ONE WAY TO FIND OUT FOR SURE!
GET READY FOR ACTION, GANG! WE'RE GOING IN!!
AND WE'RE GOING WITH THEM--IN CHAPTER FOUR, WHICH BEGINS ON THE NEXT PAGE FOLLOWING.
16

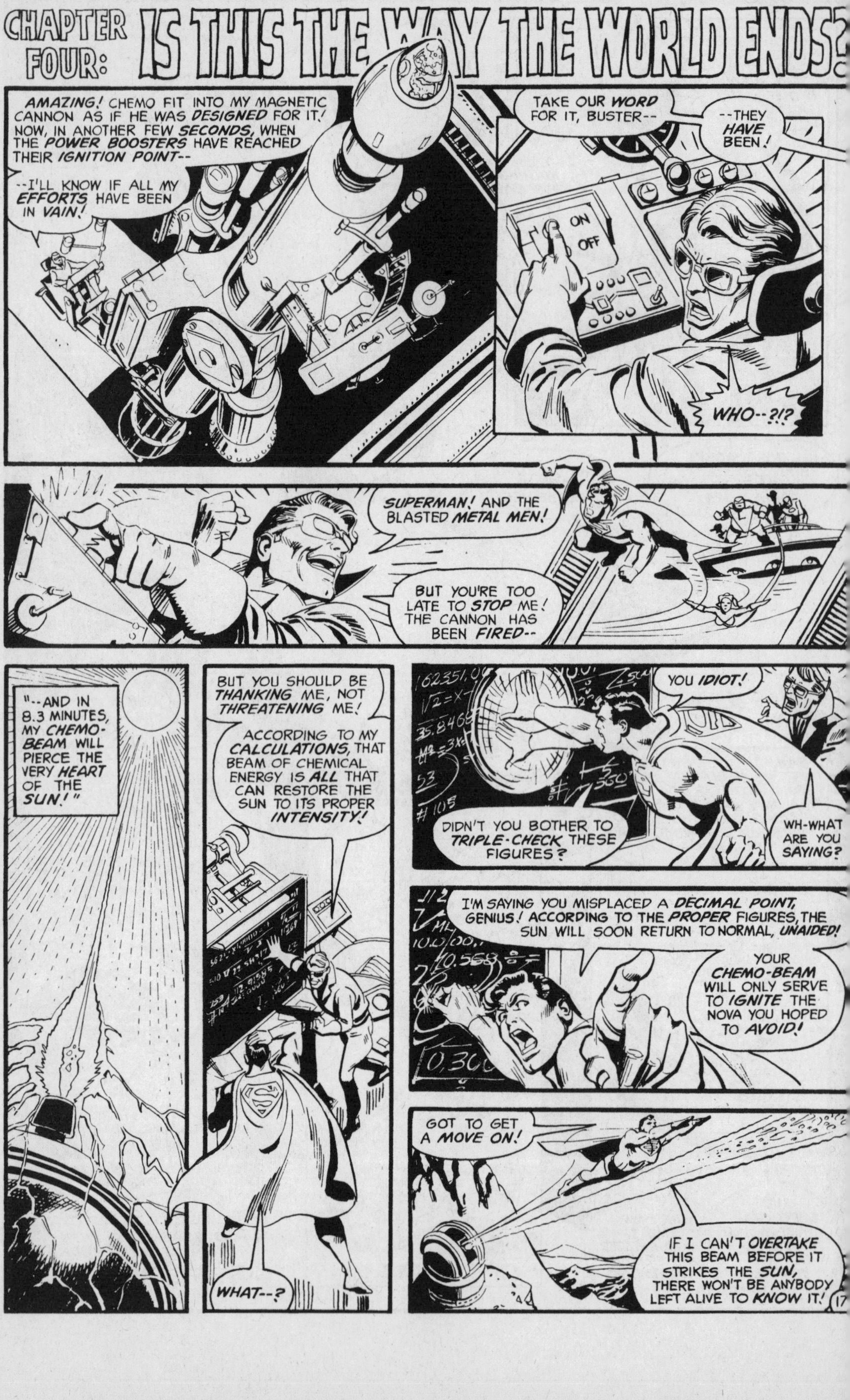
CHAPTER FOUR: IS THIS THE WAY THE WORLD ENDS?
AMAZING! CHEMO FIT INTO MY MAGNETIC CANNON AS IF HE WAS DESIGNED FOR IT! NOW, IN ANOTHER FEW SECONDS, WHEN THE POWER BOOSTERS HAVE REACHED THEIR IGNITION POINT--
--I'LL KNOW IF ALL MY EFFORTS HAVE BEEN IN VAIN!
TAKE OUR WORD FOR IT, BUSTER--
--THEY HAVE BEEN!
ON
OFF
WHO--?!?
SUPERMAN! AND THE BLASTED METAL MEN!
BUT YOU'RE TOO LATE TO STOP ME! THE CANNON HAS BEEN FIRED--
"--AND IN 8.3 MINUTES, MY CHEMO-BEAM WILL PIERCE THE VERY HEART OF THE SUN!"
BUT YOU SHOULD BE THANKING ME, NOT THREATENING ME!
ACCORDING TO MY CALCULATIONS, THAT BEAM OF CHEMICAL ENERGY IS ALL THAT CAN RESTORE THE SUN TO ITS PROPER INTENSITY!
WHAT--?
YOU IDIOT!
DIDN'T YOU BOTHER TO TRIPLE-CHECK THESE FIGURES?
WH-WHAT ARE YOU SAYING?
I'M SAYING YOU MISPLACED A DECIMAL POINT, GENIUS! ACCORDING TO THE PROPER FIGURES, THE SUN WILL SOON RETURN TO NORMAL, UNAIDED!
YOUR CHEMO-BEAM WILL ONLY SERVE TO IGNITE THE NOVA YOU HOPED TO AVOID!
GOT TO GET A MOVE ON!
IF I CAN'T OVERTAKE THIS BEAM BEFORE IT STRIKES THE SUN, THERE WON'T BE ANYBODY LEFT ALIVE TO KNOW IT!
17

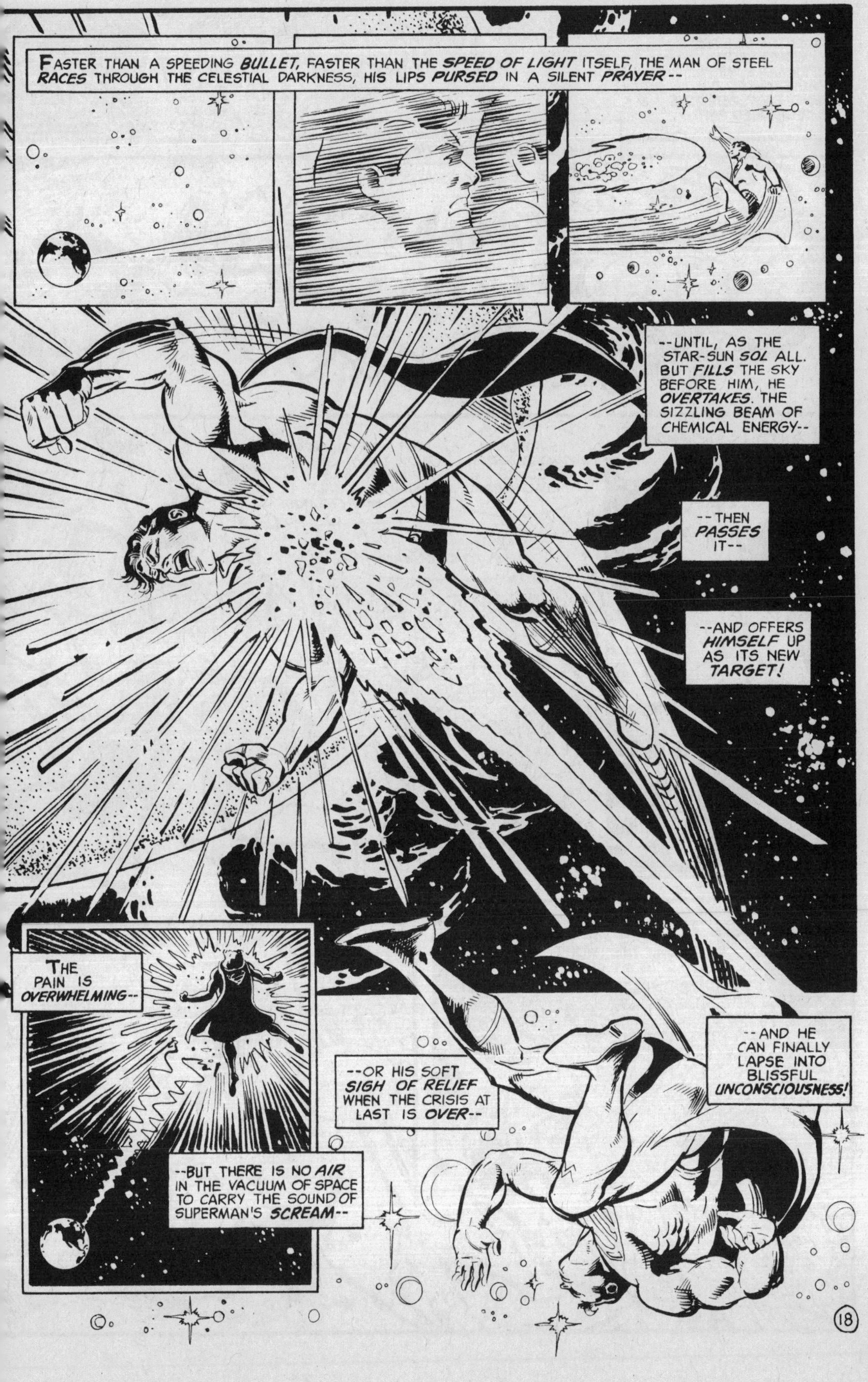
FASTER THAN A SPEEDING BULLET, FASTER THAN THE SPEED OF LIGHT ITSELF, THE MAN OF STEEL RACES THROUGH THE CELESTIAL DARKNESS, HIS LIPS PURSED IN A SILENT PRAYER--
--UNTIL, AS THE STAR-SUN SOL ALL. BUT FILLS THE SKY BEFORE HIM, HE OVERTAKES. THE SIZZLING BEAM OF CHEMICAL ENERGY--
--THEN PASSES IT--
--AND OFFERS HIMSELF UP AS ITS NEW TARGET!
THE PAIN IS OVERWHELMING--
--BUT THERE IS NO AIR IN THE VACUUM OF SPACE TO CARRY THE SOUND OF SUPERMAN'S SCREAM--
--OR HIS SOFT SIGH OF RELIEF WHEN THE CRISIS AT LAST IS OVER--
--AND HE CAN FINALLY LAPSE INTO BLISSFUL UNCONSCIOUSNESS!
18

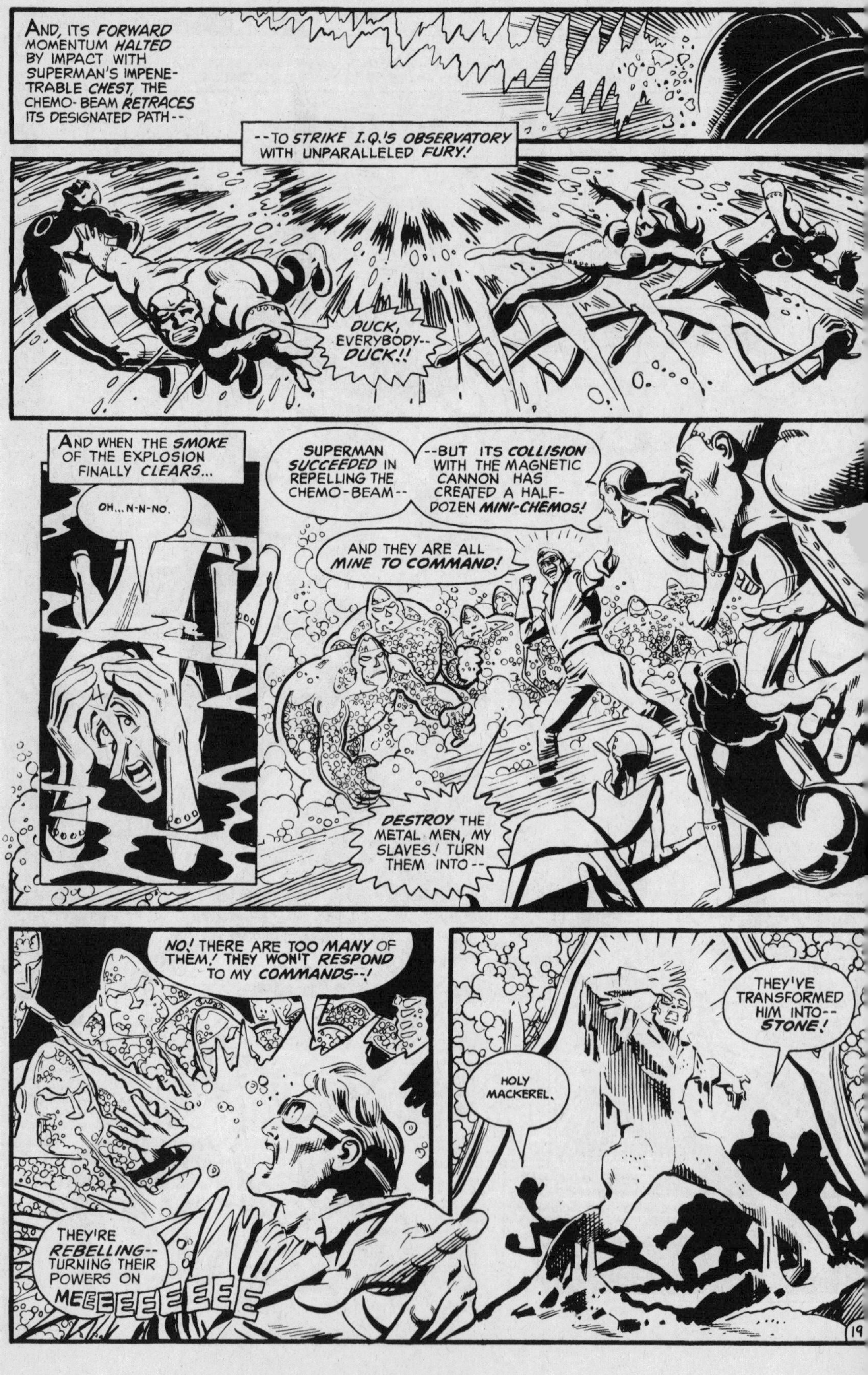
AND, ITS FORWARD MOMENTUM HALTED BY IMPACT WITH SUPERMAN'S IMPENETRABLE CHEST, THE CHEMO-BEAM RETRACES ITS DESIGNATED PATH--
--TO STRIKE I.Q.'S OBSERVATORY WITH UNPARALLELED FURY!
DUCK, EVERYBODY--DUCK!!
AND WHEN THE SMOKE OF THE EXPLOSION FINALLY CLEARS...
OH... N-N-NO.
SUPERMAN SUCCEEDED IN REPELLING THE CHEMO-BEAM--
--BUT ITS COLLISION WITH THE MAGNETIC CANNON HAS CREATED A HALF-DOZEN MINI-CHEMOS!
AND THEY ARE ALL MINE TO COMMAND!
DESTROY THE METAL MEN, MY SLAVES! TURN THEM INTO--
NO! THERE ARE TOO MANY OF THEM! THEY WON'T RESPOND TO MY COMMANDS--!
THEY'RE REBELLING--TURNING THEIR POWERS ON MEEEEEEEEE
HOLY MACKEREL.
THEY'VE TRANSFORMED HIM INTO--STONE!
19

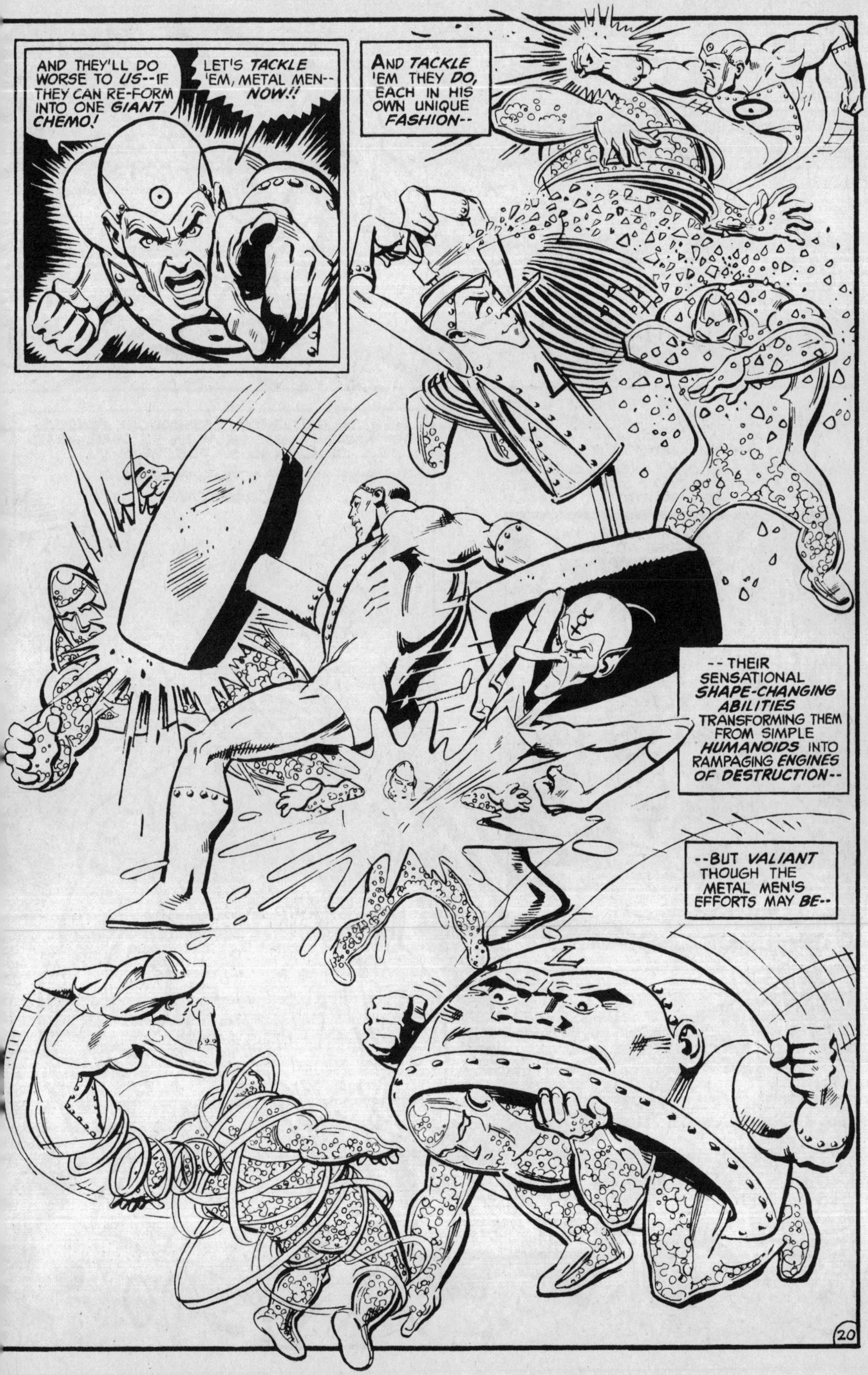
AND THEY'LL DO WORSE TO US--IF THEY CAN RE-FORM INTO ONE GIANT CHEMO!
LET'S TACKLE 'EM, METAL MEN--NOW!!
AND TACKLE 'EM THEY DO, EACH IN HIS OWN UNIQUE FASHION--
--THEIR SENSATIONAL SHAPE-CHANGING ABILITIES TRANSFORMING THEM FROM SIMPLE HUMANOIDS INTO RAMPAGING ENGINES OF DESTRUCTION--
--BUT VALIANT THOUGH THE METAL MEN'S EFFORTS MAY BE--
20

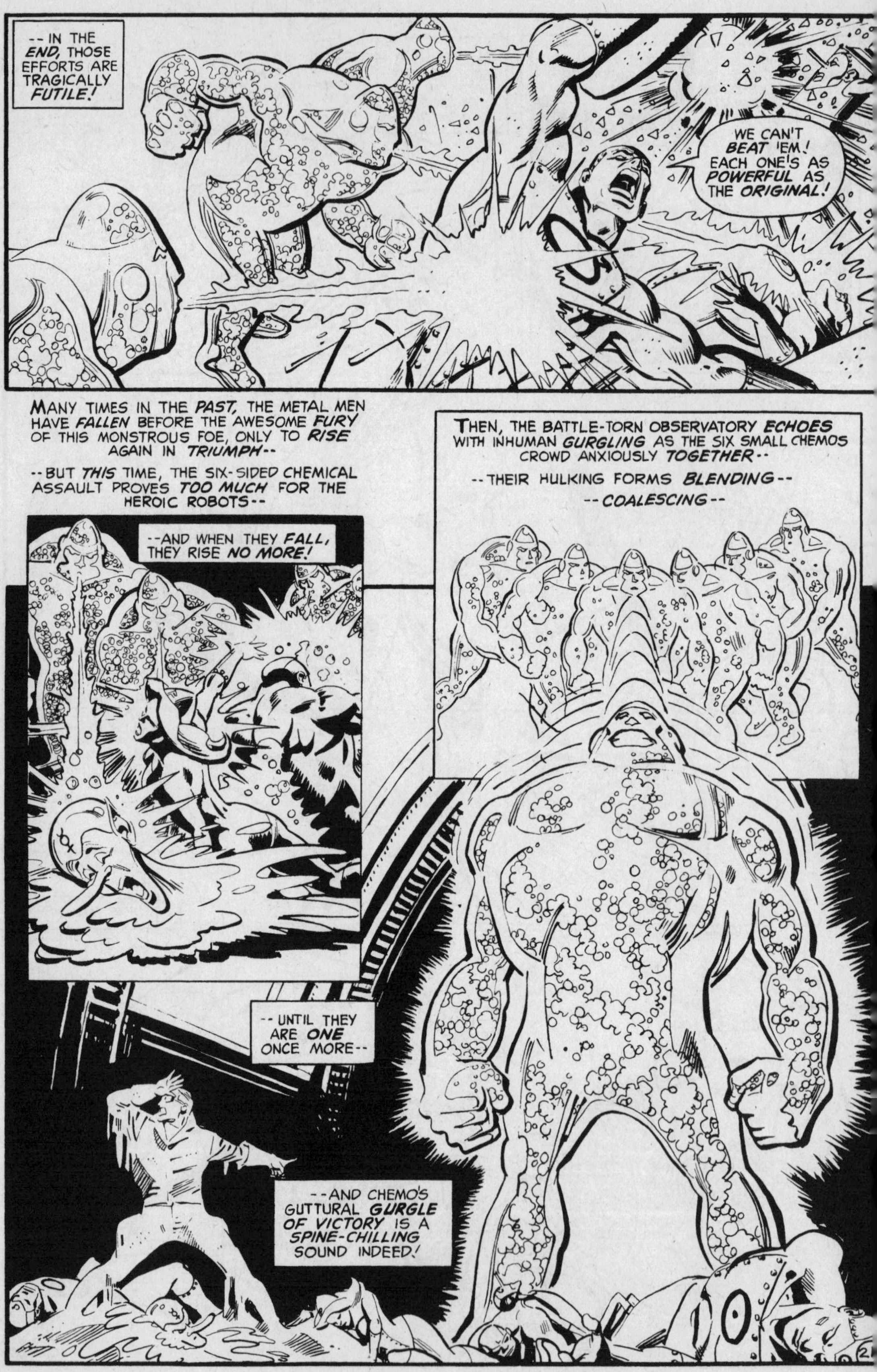
-- IN THE END, THOSE EFFORTS ARE TRAGICALLY FUTILE!
WE CAN'T BEAT 'EM! EACH ONE'S AS POWERFUL AS THE ORIGINAL!
MANY TIMES IN THE PAST, THE METAL MEN HAVE FALLEN BEFORE THE AWESOME FURY OF THIS MONSTROUS FOE, ONLY TO RISE AGAIN IN TRIUMPH--
--BUT THIS TIME, THE SIX-SIDED CHEMICAL ASSAULT PROVES TOO MUCH FOR THE HEROIC ROBOTS--
--AND WHEN THEY FALL, THEY RISE NO MORE!
THEN, THE BATTLE-TORN OBSERVATORY ECHOES WITH INHUMAN GURGLING AS THE SIX SMALL CHEMOS CROWD ANXIOUSLY TOGETHER--
--THEIR HULKING FORMS BLENDING--
--COALESCING--
--UNTIL THEY ARE ONE ONCE MORE--
--AND CHEMO'S GUTTURAL GURGLE OF VICTORY IS A SPINE-CHILLING SOUND INDEED!

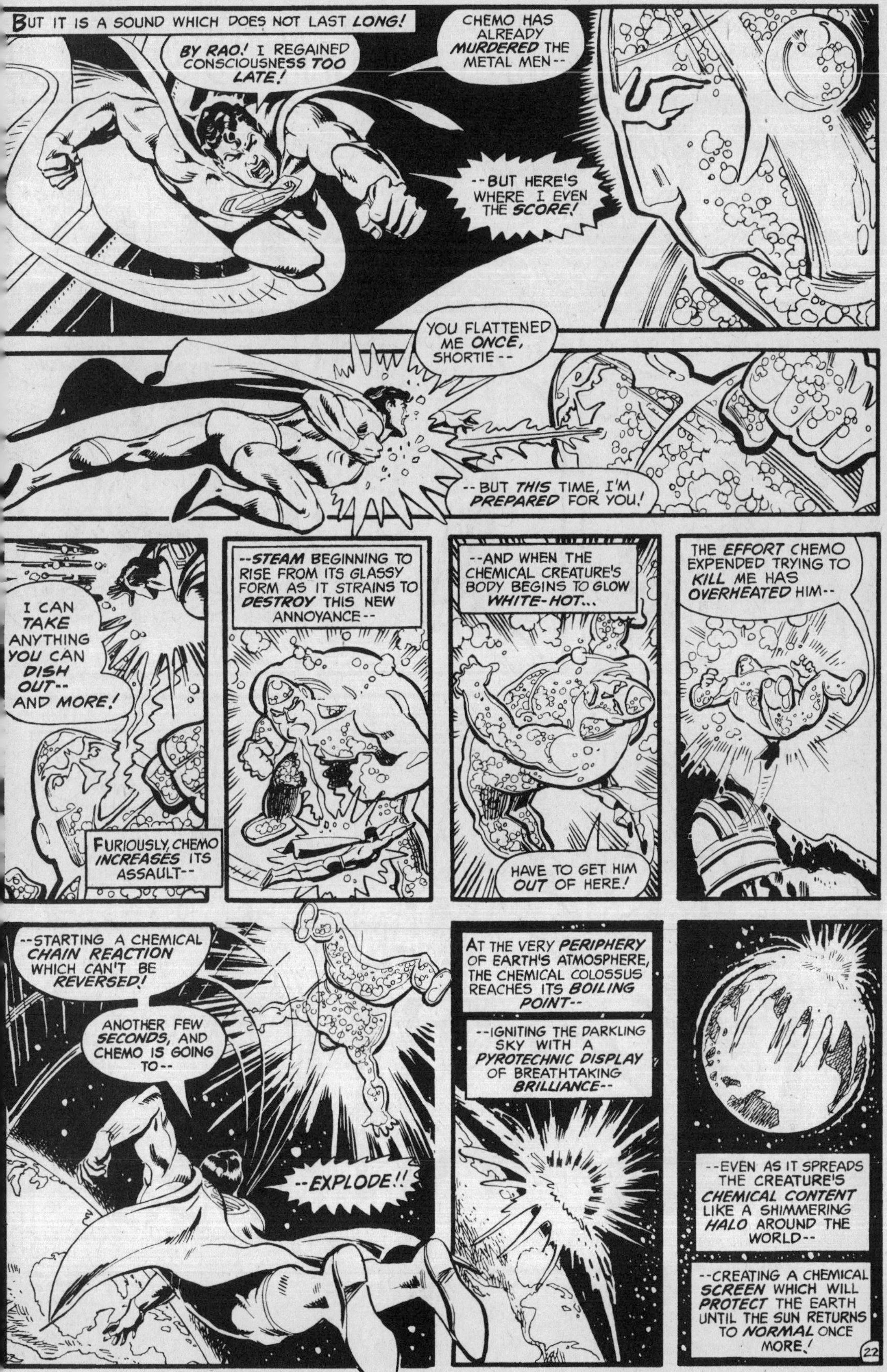
BUT IT IS A SOUND WHICH DOES NOT LAST LONG!
BY RAO! I REGAINED CONSCIOUSNESS TOO LATE!
CHEMO HAS ALREADY MURDERED THE METAL MEN--
--BUT HERE'S WHERE I EVEN THE SCORE!
YOU FLATTENED ME ONCE, SHORTIE--
--BUT THIS TIME, I'M PREPARED FOR YOU!
I CAN TAKE ANYTHING YOU CAN DISH OUT-- AND MORE!
FURIOUSLY, CHEMO INCREASES ITS ASSAULT--
--STEAM BEGINNING TO RISE FROM ITS GLASSY FORM AS IT STRAINS TO DESTROY THIS NEW ANNOYANCE--
--AND WHEN THE CHEMICAL CREATURE'S BODY BEGINS TO GLOW WHITE-HOT...
HAVE TO GET HIM OUT OF HERE!
THE EFFORT CHEMO EXPENDED TRYING TO KILL ME HAS OVERHEATED HIM--
--STARTING A CHEMICAL CHAIN REACTION WHICH CAN'T BE REVERSED!
ANOTHER FEW SECONDS, AND CHEMO IS GOING TO--
--EXPLODE!!
AT THE VERY PERIPHERY OF EARTH'S ATMOSPHERE, THE CHEMICAL COLOSSUS REACHES ITS BOILING POINT--
--IGNITING THE DARKLING SKY WITH A PYROTECHNIC DISPLAY OF BREATHTAKING BRILLIANCE--
--EVEN AS IT SPREADS THE CREATURE'S CHEMICAL CONTENT LIKE A SHIMMERING HALO AROUND THE WORLD--
--CREATING A CHEMICAL SCREEN WHICH WILL PROTECT THE EARTH UNTIL THE SUN RETURNS TO NORMAL ONCE MORE!
22

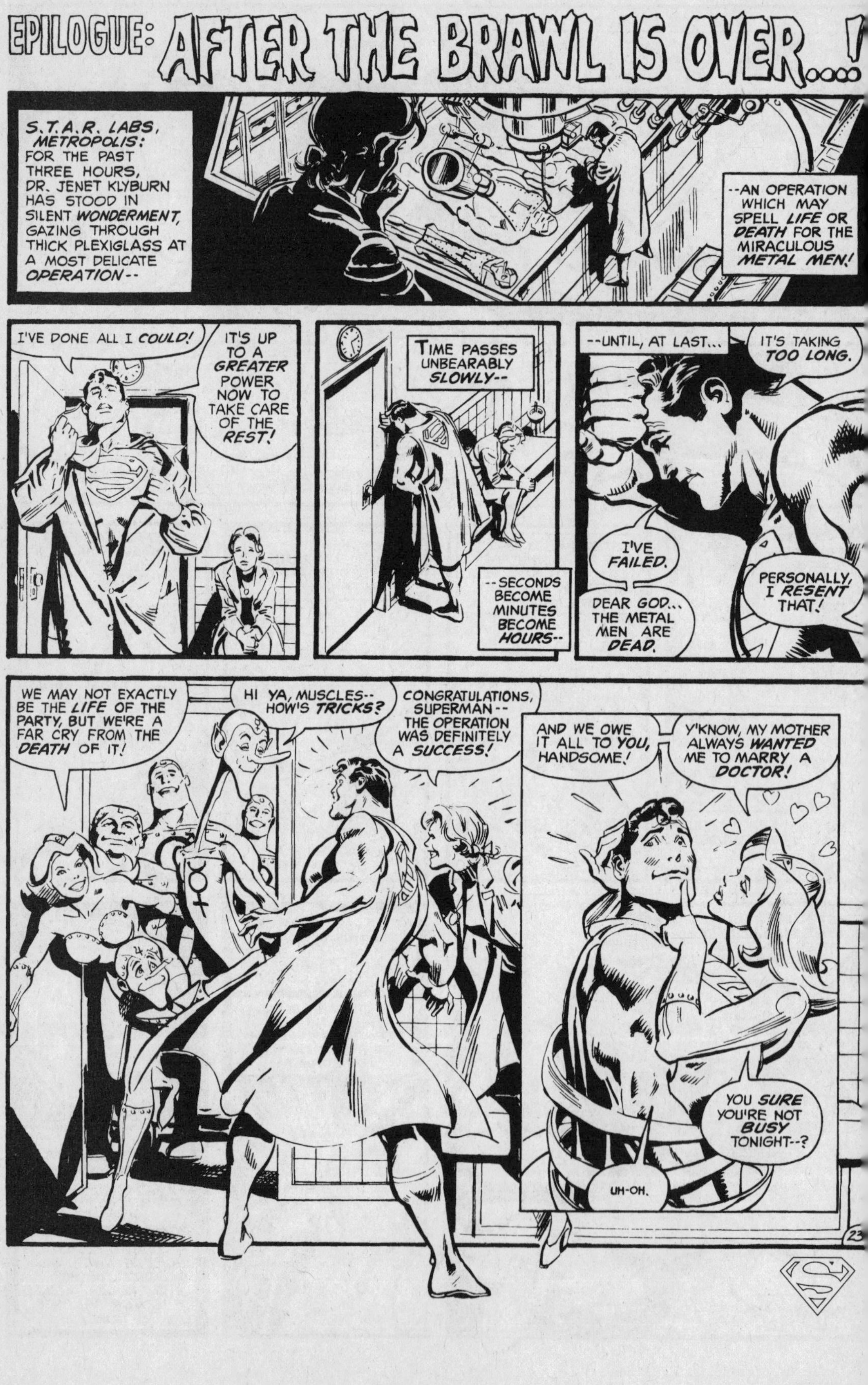
EPILOGUE: AFTER THE BRAWL IS OVER...!
S.T.A.R. LABS, METROPOLIS: FOR THE PAST THREE HOURS, DR. JENET KLYBURN HAS STOOD IN SILENT WONDERMENT, GAZING THROUGH THICK PLEXIGLASS AT A MOST DELICATE OPERATION--
--AN OPERATION WHICH MAY SPELL LIFE OR DEATH FOR THE MIRACULOUS METAL MEN!
I'VE DONE ALL I COULD!
IT'S UP TO A GREATER POWER NOW TO TAKE CARE OF THE REST!
TIME PASSES UNBEARABLY SLOWLY--
--SECONDS BECOME MINUTES BECOME HOURS--
--UNTIL, AT LAST...
IT'S TAKING TOO LONG.
I'VE FAILED.
DEAR GOD... THE METAL MEN ARE DEAD.
PERSONALLY, I RESENT THAT!
WE MAY NOT EXACTLY BE THE LIFE OF THE PARTY, BUT WE'RE A FAR CRY FROM THE DEATH OF IT!
HI YA, MUSCLES-- HOW'S TRICKS?
CONGRATULATIONS, SUPERMAN-- THE OPERATION WAS DEFINITELY A SUCCESS!
AND WE OWE IT ALL TO YOU, HANDSOME!
Y'KNOW, MY MOTHER ALWAYS WANTED ME TO MARRY A DOCTOR!
YOU SURE YOU'RE NOT BUSY TONIGHT--?
UH-OH.
23

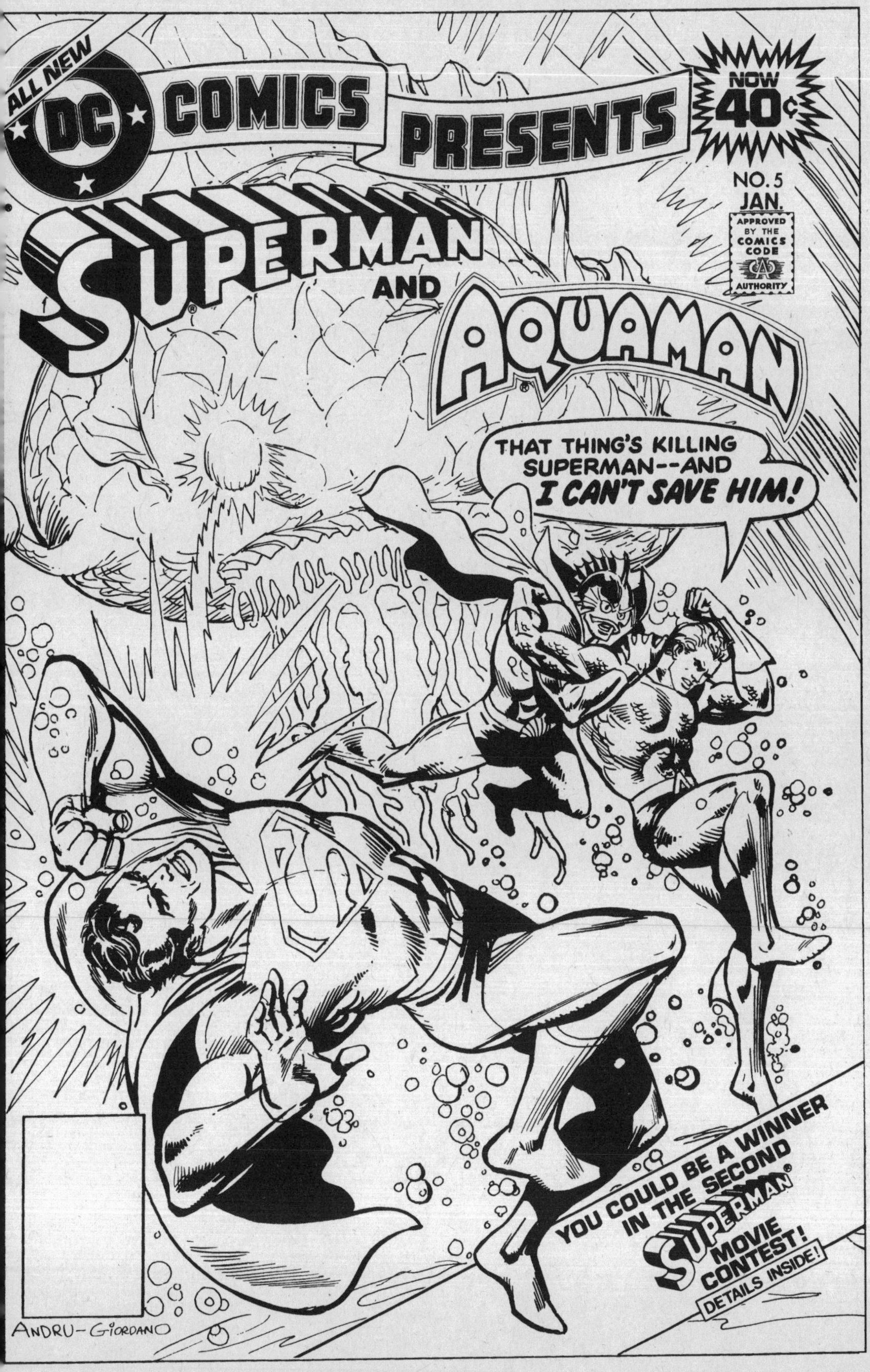
ALL NEW
DC
COMICS PRESENTS
NOW 40¢
NO. 5
JAN.
APPROVED BY THE COMICS CODE AUTHORITY
SUPERMAN AND AQUAMAN
THAT THING'S KILLING SUPERMAN--AND I CAN'T SAVE HIM!
YOU COULD BE A WINNER IN THE SECOND SUPERMAN MOVIE CONTEST!
DETAILS INSIDE!
ANDRU-GIORDANO

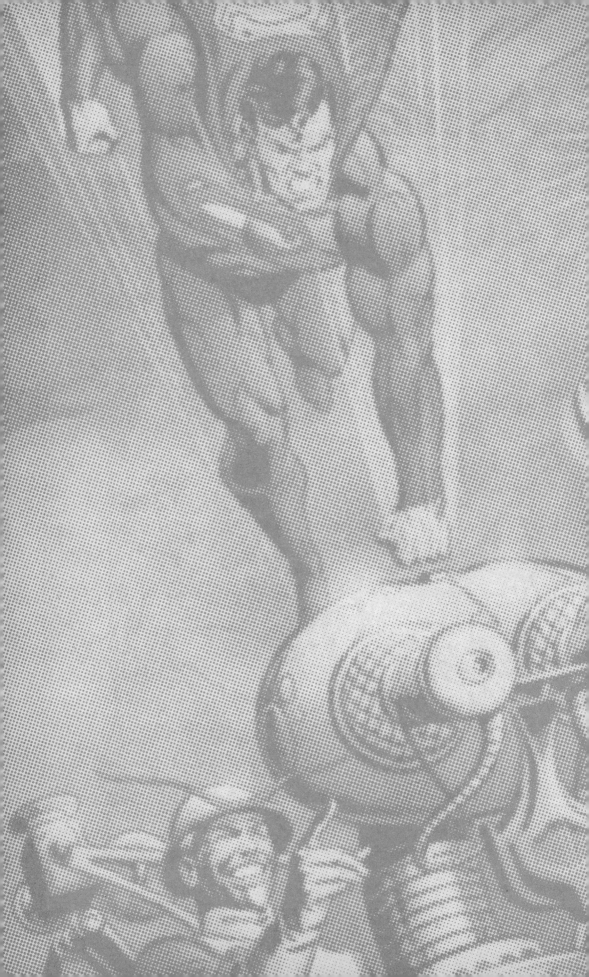

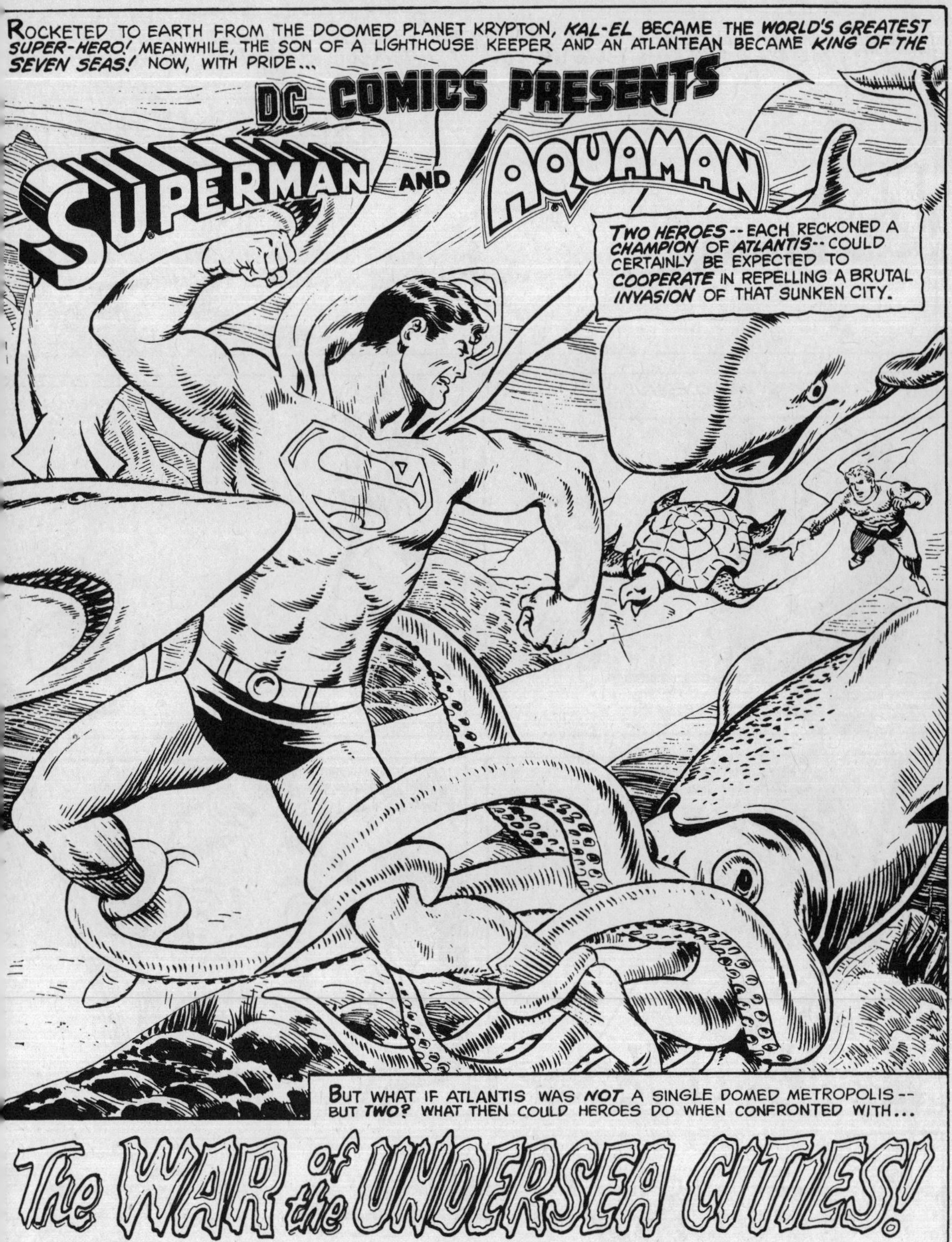
ROCKETED TO EARTH FROM THE DOOMED PLANET KRYPTON, KAL-EL BECAME THE WORLD'S GREATEST SUPER-HERO! MEANWHILE, THE SON OF A LIGHTHOUSE KEEPER AND AN ATLANTEAN BECAME KING OF THE SEVEN SEAS! NOW, WITH PRIDE...
DC COMICS PRESENTS
SUPERMAN AND AQUAMAN
TWO HEROES -- EACH RECKONED A CHAMPION OF ATLANTIS -- COULD CERTAINLY BE EXPECTED TO COOPERATE IN REPELLING A BRUTAL INVASION OF THAT SUNKEN CITY.
BUT WHAT IF ATLANTIS WAS NOT A SINGLE DOMED METROPOLIS -- BUT TWO? WHAT THEN COULD HEROES DO WHEN CONFRONTED WITH...
The WAR of the UNDERSEA CITIES!
LEN WEIN — PLOT
PAUL LEVITZ — DIALOGUE
MURPHY ANDERSON — ARTIST
BEN ODA — LETTERER
JERRY SERPE — COLORIST
ROSS ANDRU — EDITOR

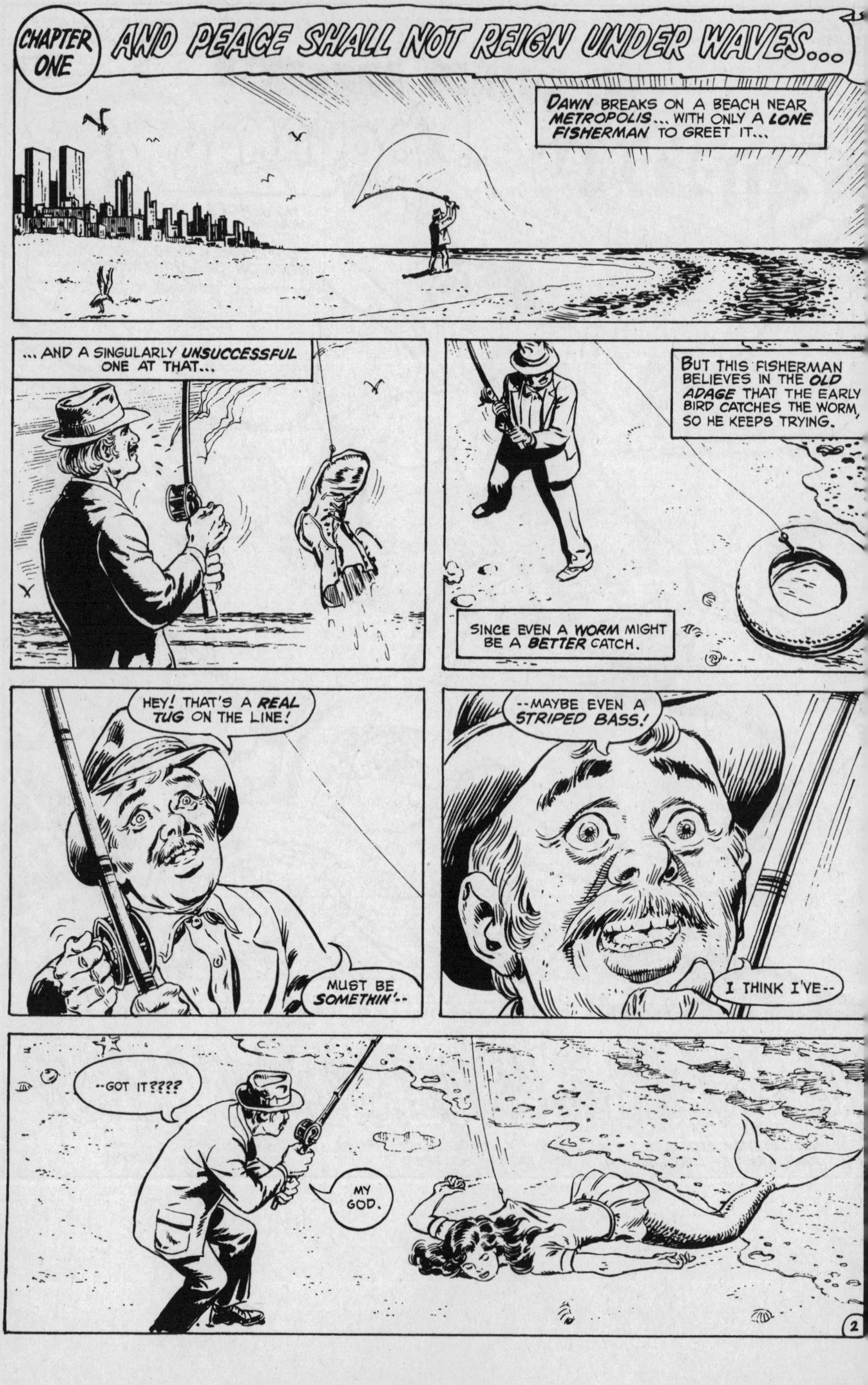
CHAPTER ONE
AND PEACE SHALL NOT REIGN UNDER WAVES...
DAWN BREAKS ON A BEACH NEAR METROPOLIS... WITH ONLY A LONE FISHERMAN TO GREET IT...
... AND A SINGULARLY UNSUCCESSFUL ONE AT THAT...
BUT THIS FISHERMAN BELIEVES IN THE OLD ADAGE THAT THE EARLY BIRD CATCHES THE WORM, SO HE KEEPS TRYING.
SINCE EVEN A WORM MIGHT BE A BETTER CATCH.
HEY! THAT'S A REAL TUG ON THE LINE!
MUST BE SOMETHIN'--
--MAYBE EVEN A STRIPED BASS!
I THINK I'VE--
--GOT IT????
MY GOD.
2

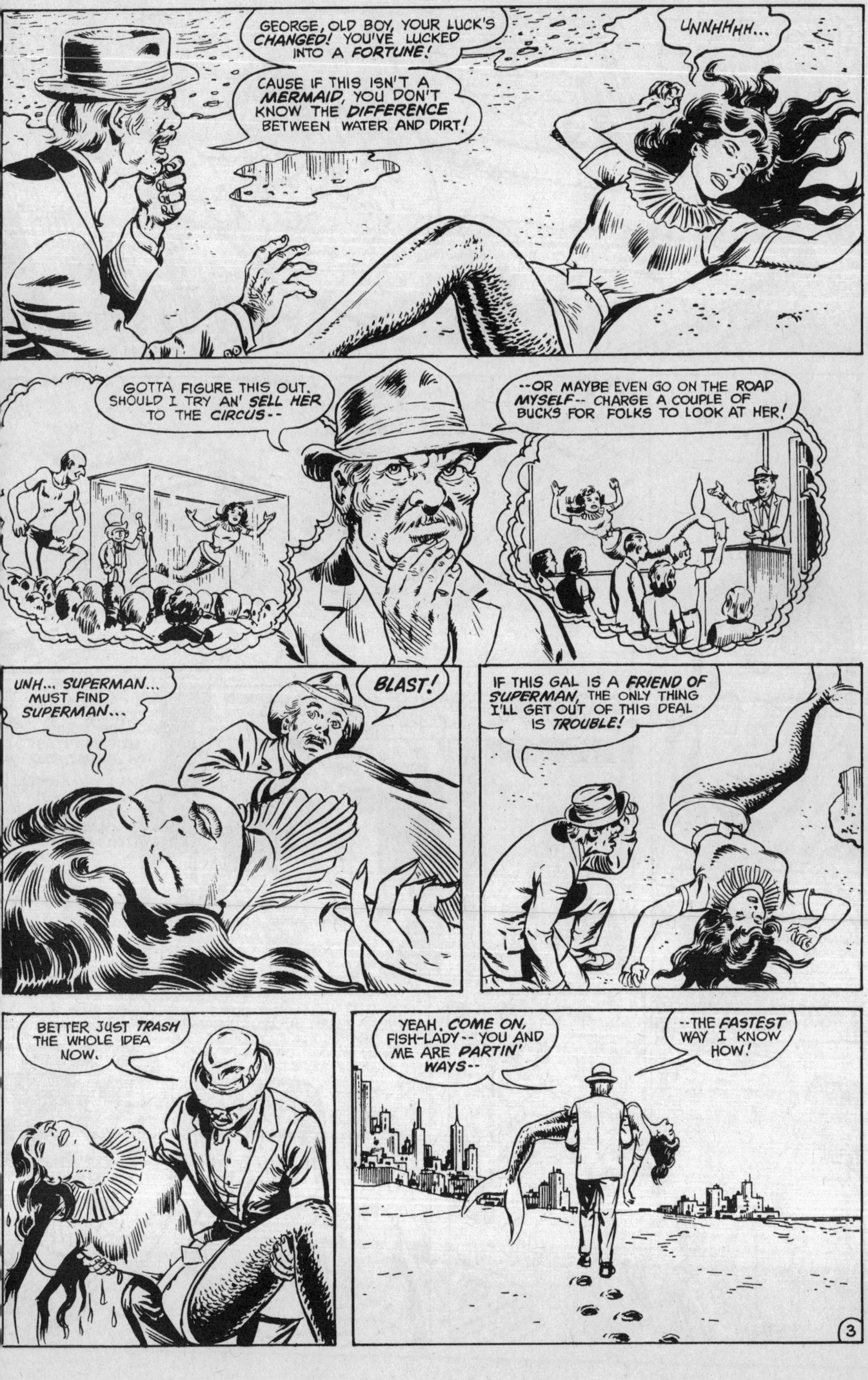
GEORGE, OLD BOY, YOUR LUCK'S CHANGED! YOU'VE LUCKED INTO A FORTUNE!
CAUSE IF THIS ISN'T A MERMAID, YOU DON'T KNOW THE DIFFERENCE BETWEEN WATER AND DIRT!
UNNHHHH...
GOTTA FIGURE THIS OUT. SHOULD I TRY AN' SELL HER TO THE CIRCUS--
--OR MAYBE EVEN GO ON THE ROAD MYSELF-- CHARGE A COUPLE OF BUCKS FOR FOLKS TO LOOK AT HER!
UNH... SUPERMAN... MUST FIND SUPERMAN...
BLAST!
IF THIS GAL IS A FRIEND OF SUPERMAN, THE ONLY THING I'LL GET OUT OF THIS DEAL IS TROUBLE!
BETTER JUST TRASH THE WHOLE IDEA NOW.
YEAH. COME ON, FISH-LADY-- YOU AND ME ARE PARTIN' WAYS--
--THE FASTEST WAY I KNOW HOW!
3

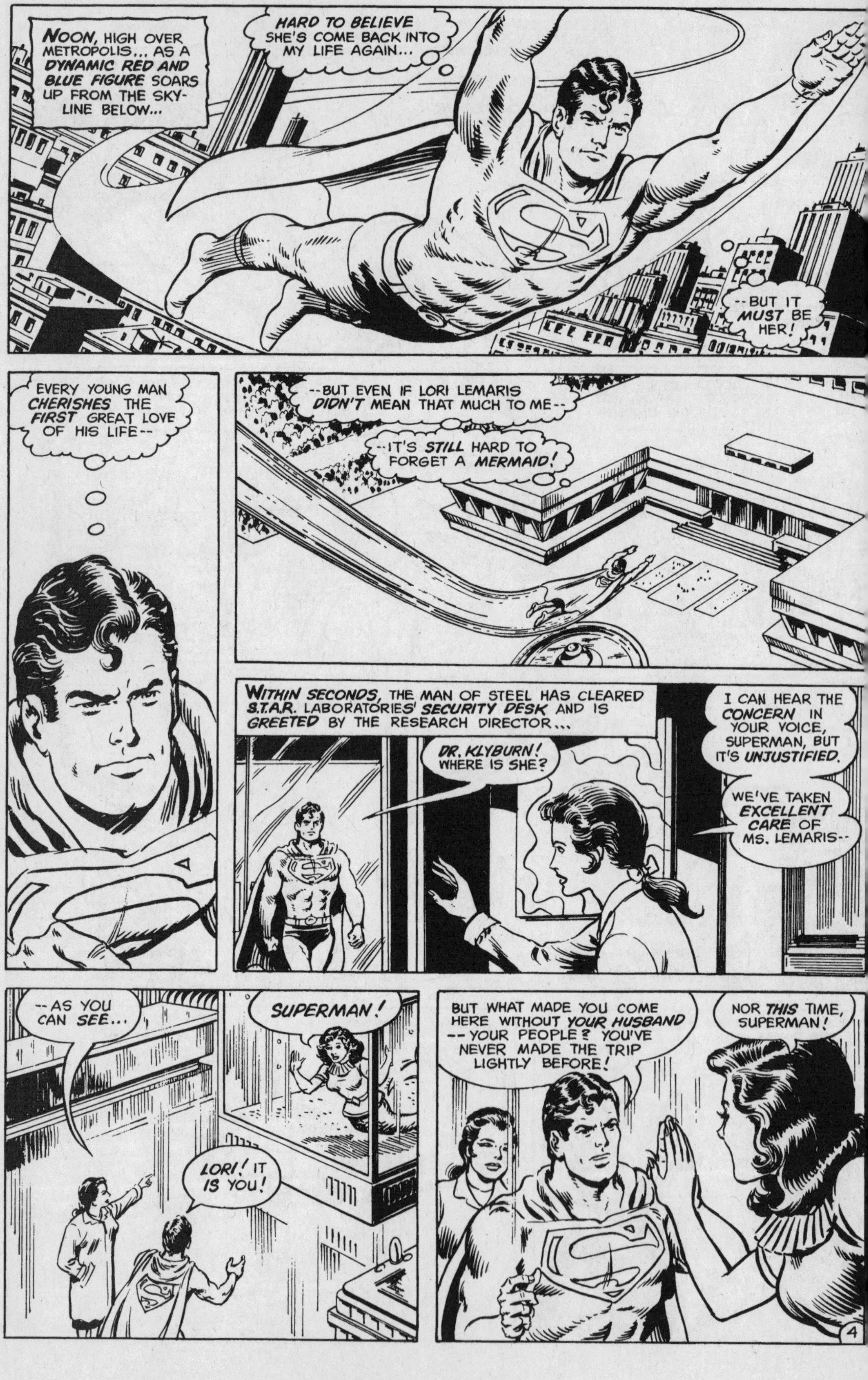
NOON, HIGH OVER METROPOLIS... AS A DYNAMIC RED AND BLUE FIGURE SOARS UP FROM THE SKY-LINE BELOW...
HARD TO BELIEVE SHE'S COME BACK INTO MY LIFE AGAIN...
--BUT IT MUST BE HER!
EVERY YOUNG MAN CHERISHES THE FIRST GREAT LOVE OF HIS LIFE--
--BUT EVEN IF LORI LEMARIS DIDN'T MEAN THAT MUCH TO ME--
--IT'S STILL HARD TO FORGET A MERMAID!
WITHIN SECONDS, THE MAN OF STEEL HAS CLEARED S.T.A.R. LABORATORIES' SECURITY DESK AND IS GREETED BY THE RESEARCH DIRECTOR...
DR. KLYBURN! WHERE IS SHE?
I CAN HEAR THE CONCERN IN YOUR VOICE, SUPERMAN, BUT IT'S UNJUSTIFIED.
WE'VE TAKEN EXCELLENT CARE OF MS. LEMARIS--
--AS YOU CAN SEE...
SUPERMAN!
LORI! IT IS YOU!
BUT WHAT MADE YOU COME HERE WITHOUT YOUR HUSBAND --YOUR PEOPLE? YOU'VE NEVER MADE THE TRIP LIGHTLY BEFORE!
NOR THIS TIME, SUPERMAN!
4

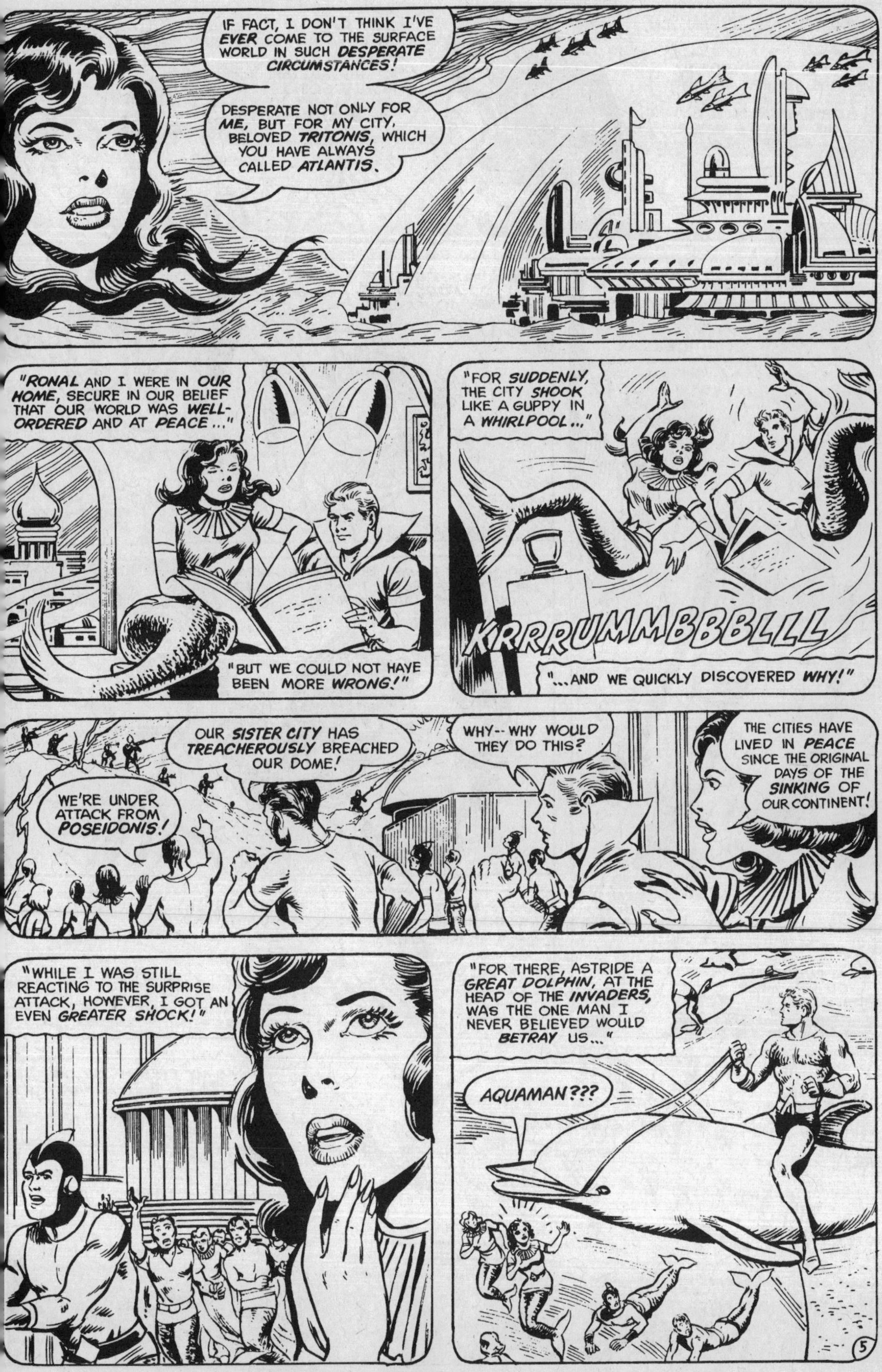
IF FACT, I DON'T THINK I'VE EVER COME TO THE SURFACE WORLD IN SUCH DESPERATE CIRCUMSTANCES!
DESPERATE NOT ONLY FOR ME, BUT FOR MY CITY, BELOVED TRITONIS, WHICH YOU HAVE ALWAYS CALLED ATLANTIS.
"RONAL AND I WERE IN OUR HOME, SECURE IN OUR BELIEF THAT OUR WORLD WAS WELL-ORDERED AND AT PEACE..."
"BUT WE COULD NOT HAVE BEEN MORE WRONG!"
"FOR SUDDENLY, THE CITY SHOOK LIKE A GUPPY IN A WHIRLPOOL..."
KRRRUMMBBBLLL
"...AND WE QUICKLY DISCOVERED WHY!"
WE'RE UNDER ATTACK FROM POSEIDONIS!
OUR SISTER CITY HAS TREACHEROUSLY BREACHED OUR DOME!
WHY-- WHY WOULD THEY DO THIS?
THE CITIES HAVE LIVED IN PEACE SINCE THE ORIGINAL DAYS OF THE SINKING OF OUR CONTINENT!
"WHILE I WAS STILL REACTING TO THE SURPRISE ATTACK, HOWEVER, I GOT AN EVEN GREATER SHOCK!"
"FOR THERE, ASTRIDE A GREAT DOLPHIN, AT THE HEAD OF THE INVADERS, WAS THE ONE MAN I NEVER BELIEVED WOULD BETRAY US..."
AQUAMAN???
5

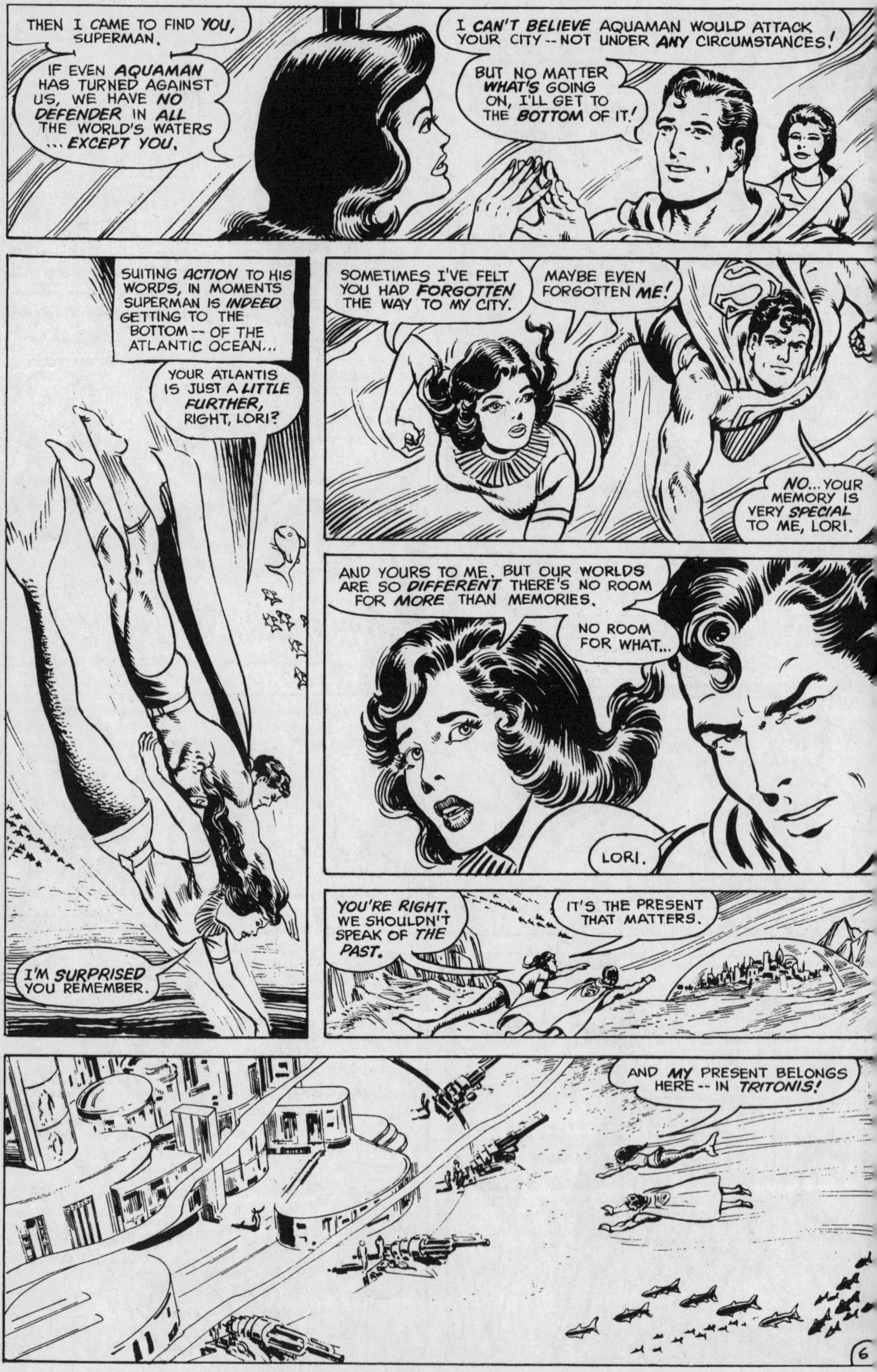
THEN I CAME TO FIND YOU, SUPERMAN.
IF EVEN AQUAMAN HAS TURNED AGAINST US, WE HAVE NO DEFENDER IN ALL THE WORLD'S WATERS ...EXCEPT YOU.
I CAN'T BELIEVE AQUAMAN WOULD ATTACK YOUR CITY -- NOT UNDER ANY CIRCUMSTANCES!
BUT NO MATTER WHAT'S GOING ON, I'LL GET TO THE BOTTOM OF IT!
SUITING ACTION TO HIS WORDS, IN MOMENTS SUPERMAN IS INDEED GETTING TO THE BOTTOM -- OF THE ATLANTIC OCEAN...
YOUR ATLANTIS IS JUST A LITTLE FURTHER, RIGHT, LORI?
I'M SURPRISED YOU REMEMBER.
SOMETIMES I'VE FELT YOU HAD FORGOTTEN THE WAY TO MY CITY.
MAYBE EVEN FORGOTTEN ME!
NO... YOUR MEMORY IS VERY SPECIAL TO ME, LORI.
AND YOURS TO ME. BUT OUR WORLDS ARE SO DIFFERENT THERE'S NO ROOM FOR MORE THAN MEMORIES.
NO ROOM FOR WHAT...
LORI.
YOU'RE RIGHT. WE SHOULDN'T SPEAK OF THE PAST.
IT'S THE PRESENT THAT MATTERS.
AND MY PRESENT BELONGS HERE -- IN TRITONIS!
6

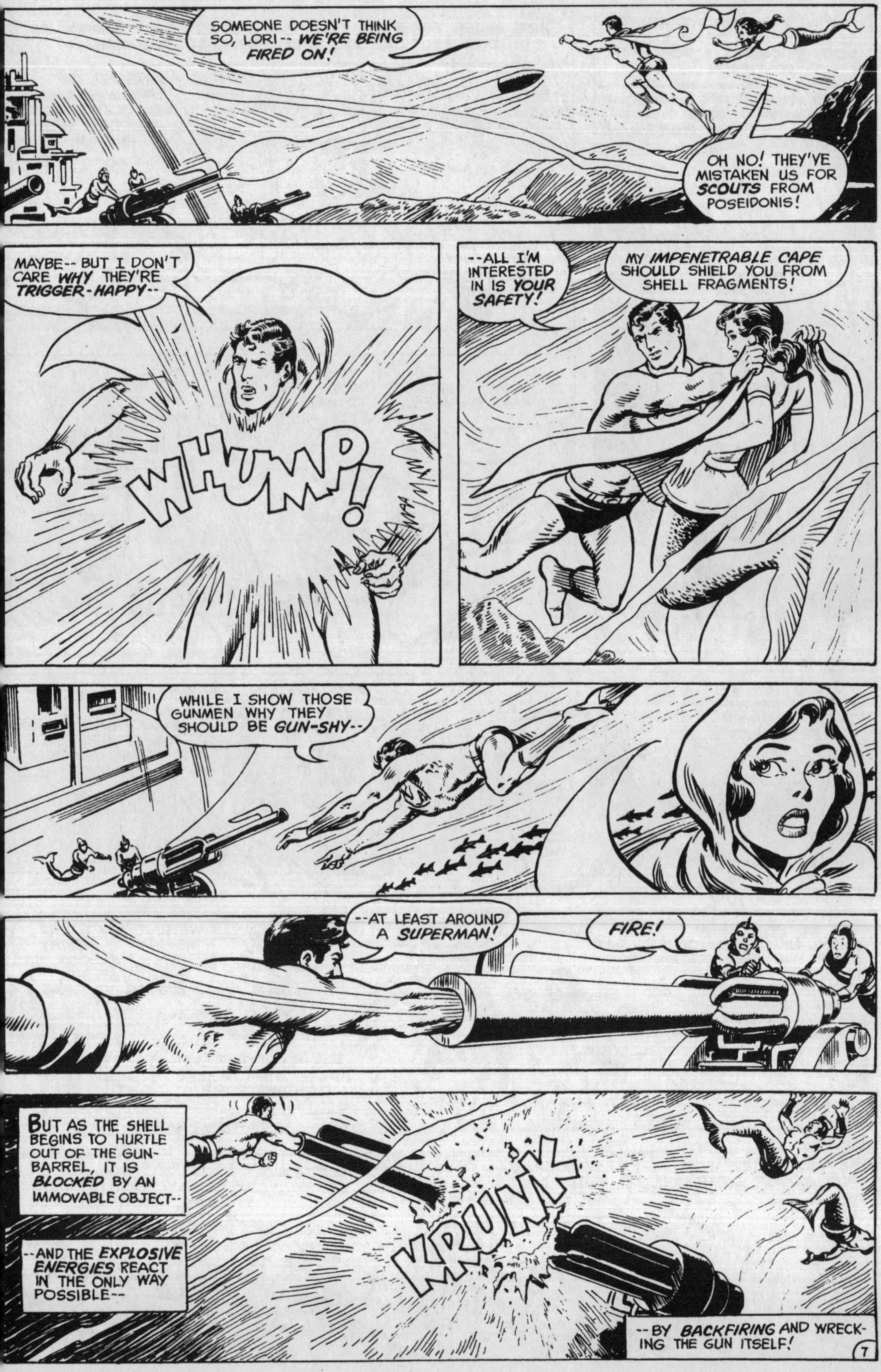
SOMEONE DOESN'T THINK SO, LORI-- WE'RE BEING FIRED ON!
OH NO! THEY'VE MISTAKEN US FOR SCOUTS FROM POSEIDONIS!
MAYBE-- BUT I DON'T CARE WHY THEY'RE TRIGGER-HAPPY--
WHUMP!
--ALL I'M INTERESTED IN IS YOUR SAFETY!
MY IMPENETRABLE CAPE SHOULD SHIELD YOU FROM SHELL FRAGMENTS!
WHILE I SHOW THOSE GUNMEN WHY THEY SHOULD BE GUN-SHY--
--AT LEAST AROUND A SUPERMAN!
FIRE!
BUT AS THE SHELL BEGINS TO HURTLE OUT OF THE GUN-BARREL, IT IS BLOCKED BY AN IMMOVABLE OBJECT--
--AND THE EXPLOSIVE ENERGIES REACT IN THE ONLY WAY POSSIBLE--
KRUNK
--BY BACKFIRING AND WRECKING THE GUN ITSELF!
7

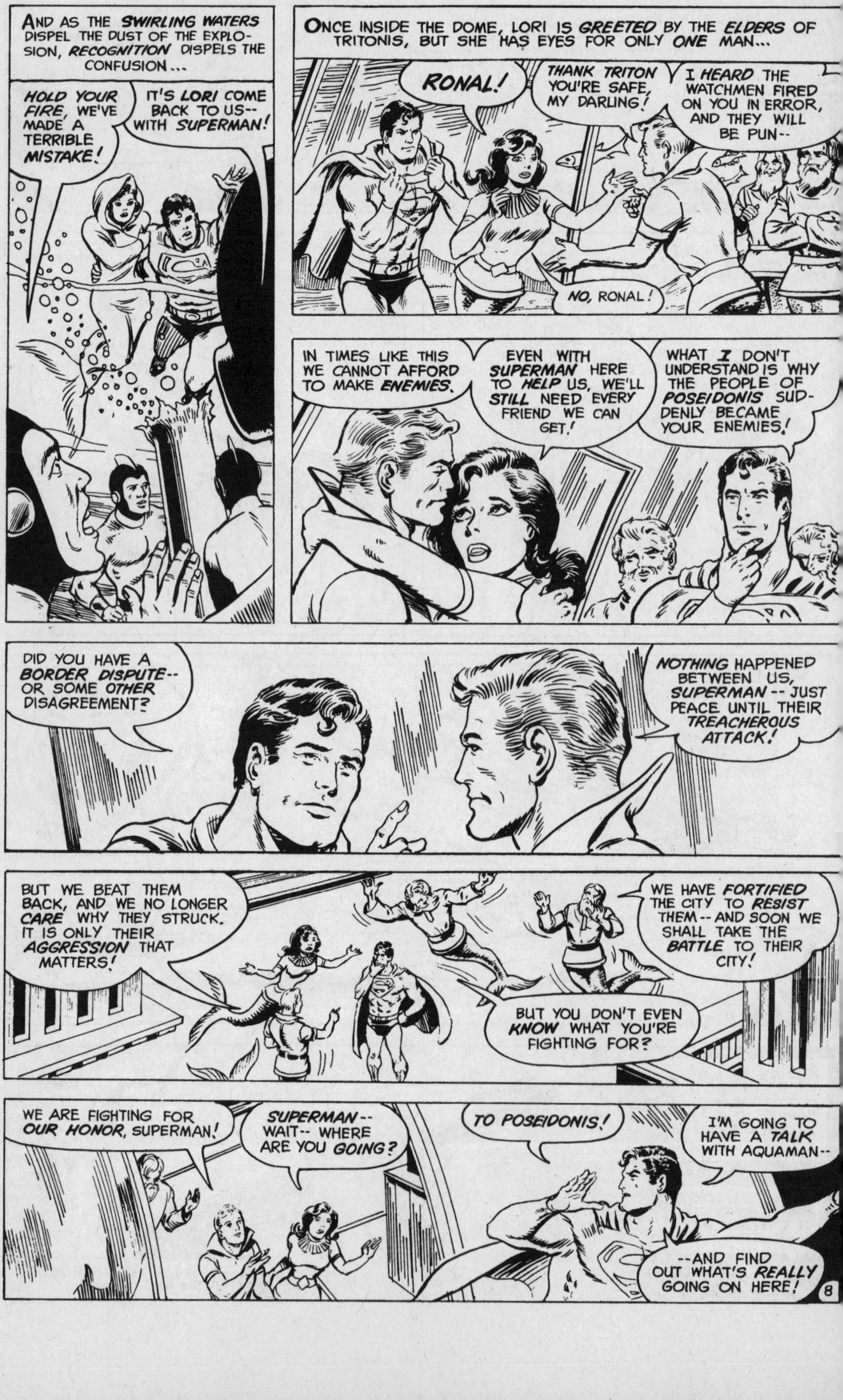
AND AS THE SWIRLING WATERS DISPEL THE DUST OF THE EXPLOSION, RECOGNITION DISPELS THE CONFUSION...
HOLD YOUR FIRE, WE'VE MADE A TERRIBLE MISTAKE!
IT'S LORI COME BACK TO US-- WITH SUPERMAN!
ONCE INSIDE THE DOME, LORI IS GREETED BY THE ELDERS OF TRITONIS, BUT SHE HAS EYES FOR ONLY ONE MAN...
RONAL!
THANK TRITON YOU'RE SAFE, MY DARLING!
I HEARD THE WATCHMEN FIRED ON YOU IN ERROR, AND THEY WILL BE PUN--
NO, RONAL!
IN TIMES LIKE THIS WE CANNOT AFFORD TO MAKE ENEMIES.
EVEN WITH SUPERMAN HERE TO HELP US, WE'LL STILL NEED EVERY FRIEND WE CAN GET!
WHAT I DON'T UNDERSTAND IS WHY THE PEOPLE OF POSEIDONIS SUDDENLY BECAME YOUR ENEMIES!
DID YOU HAVE A BORDER DISPUTE-- OR SOME OTHER DISAGREEMENT?
NOTHING HAPPENED BETWEEN US, SUPERMAN -- JUST PEACE UNTIL THEIR TREACHEROUS ATTACK!
BUT WE BEAT THEM BACK, AND WE NO LONGER CARE WHY THEY STRUCK. IT IS ONLY THEIR AGGRESSION THAT MATTERS!
WE HAVE FORTIFIED THE CITY TO RESIST THEM -- AND SOON WE SHALL TAKE THE BATTLE TO THEIR CITY!
BUT YOU DON'T EVEN KNOW WHAT YOU'RE FIGHTING FOR?
WE ARE FIGHTING FOR OUR HONOR, SUPERMAN!
SUPERMAN-- WAIT-- WHERE ARE YOU GOING?
TO POSEIDONIS!
I'M GOING TO HAVE A TALK WITH AQUAMAN--
--AND FIND OUT WHAT'S REALLY GOING ON HERE!
8

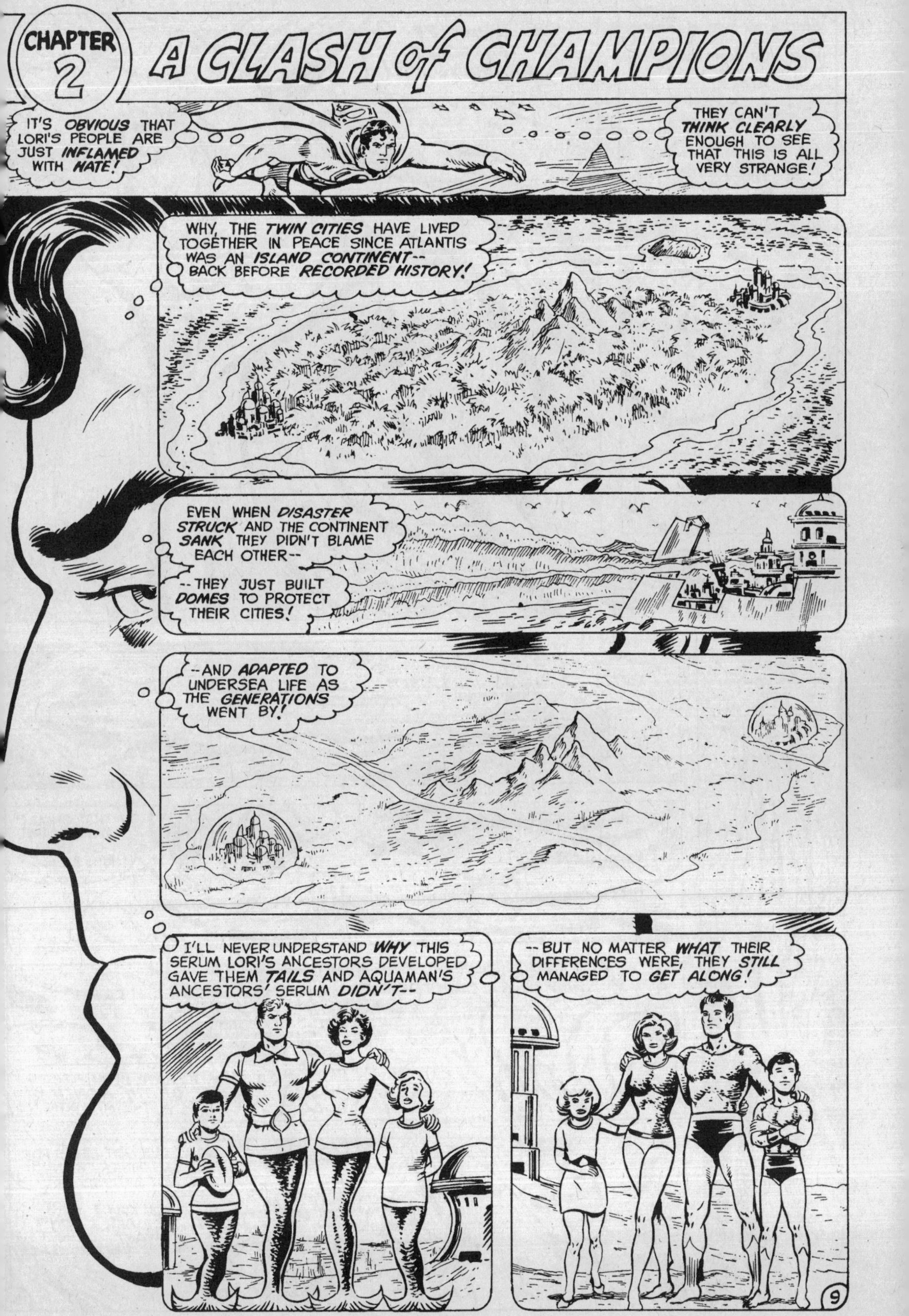
CHAPTER 2
A CLASH of CHAMPIONS
IT'S OBVIOUS THAT LORI'S PEOPLE ARE JUST INFLAMED WITH HATE!
THEY CAN'T THINK CLEARLY ENOUGH TO SEE THAT THIS IS ALL VERY STRANGE!
WHY, THE TWIN CITIES HAVE LIVED TOGETHER IN PEACE SINCE ATLANTIS WAS AN ISLAND CONTINENT-- BACK BEFORE RECORDED HISTORY!
EVEN WHEN DISASTER STRUCK AND THE CONTINENT SANK THEY DIDN'T BLAME EACH OTHER--
--THEY JUST BUILT DOMES TO PROTECT THEIR CITIES!
--AND ADAPTED TO UNDERSEA LIFE AS THE GENERATIONS WENT BY!
I'LL NEVER UNDERSTAND WHY THIS SERUM LORI'S ANCESTORS DEVELOPED GAVE THEM TAILS AND AQUAMAN'S ANCESTORS' SERUM DIDN'T--
--BUT NO MATTER WHAT THEIR DIFFERENCES WERE, THEY STILL MANAGED TO GET ALONG!
9

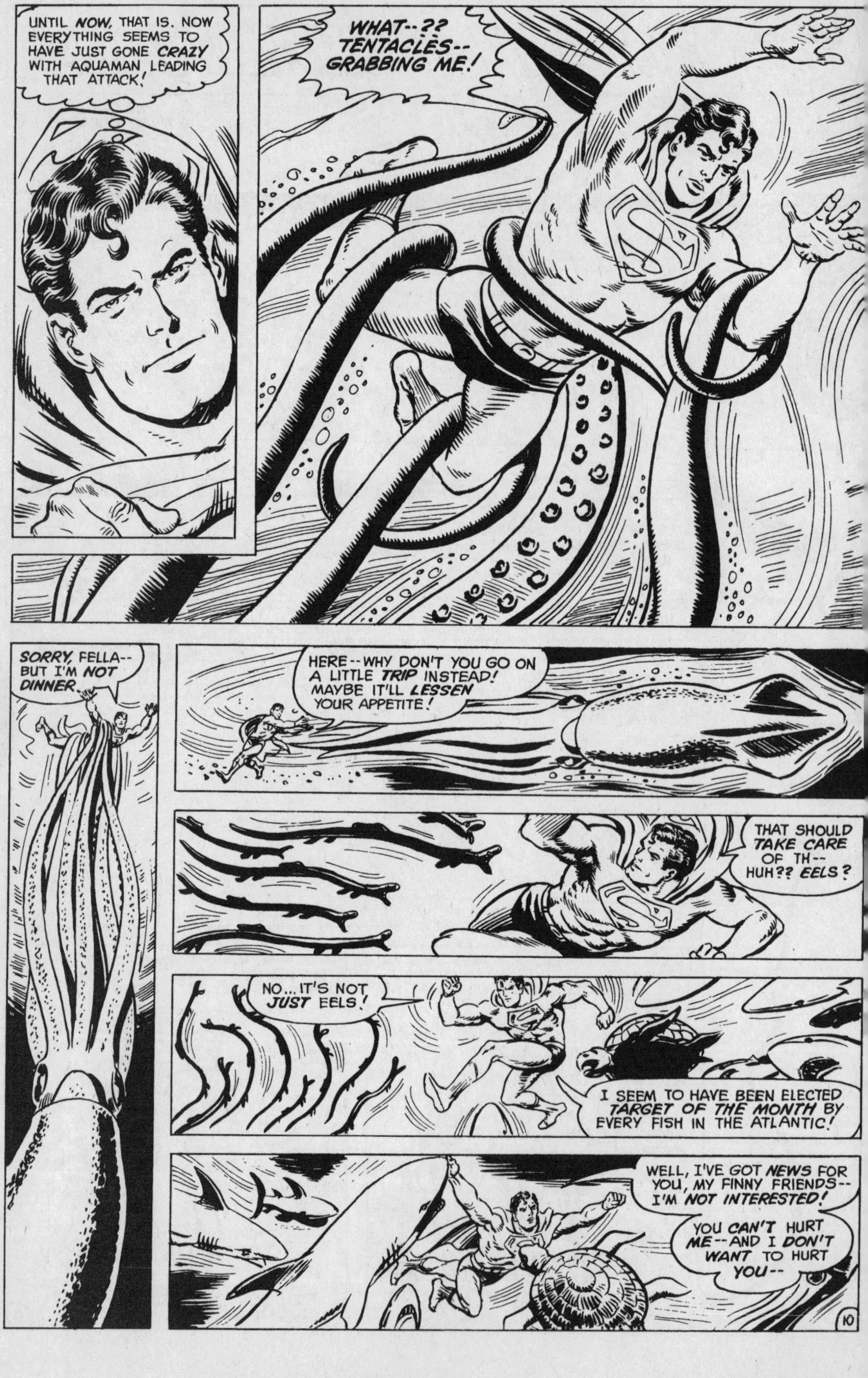
UNTIL NOW, THAT IS. NOW EVERYTHING SEEMS TO HAVE JUST GONE CRAZY WITH AQUAMAN LEADING THAT ATTACK!
WHAT--?? TENTACLES--GRABBING ME!
SORRY, FELLA--BUT I'M NOT DINNER.
HERE--WHY DON'T YOU GO ON A LITTLE TRIP INSTEAD! MAYBE IT'LL LESSEN YOUR APPETITE!
THAT SHOULD TAKE CARE OF TH-- HUH?? EELS?
NO... IT'S NOT JUST EELS!
I SEEM TO HAVE BEEN ELECTED TARGET OF THE MONTH BY EVERY FISH IN THE ATLANTIC!
WELL, I'VE GOT NEWS FOR YOU, MY FINNY FRIENDS-- I'M NOT INTERESTED!
YOU CAN'T HURT ME--AND I DON'T WANT TO HURT YOU--
10

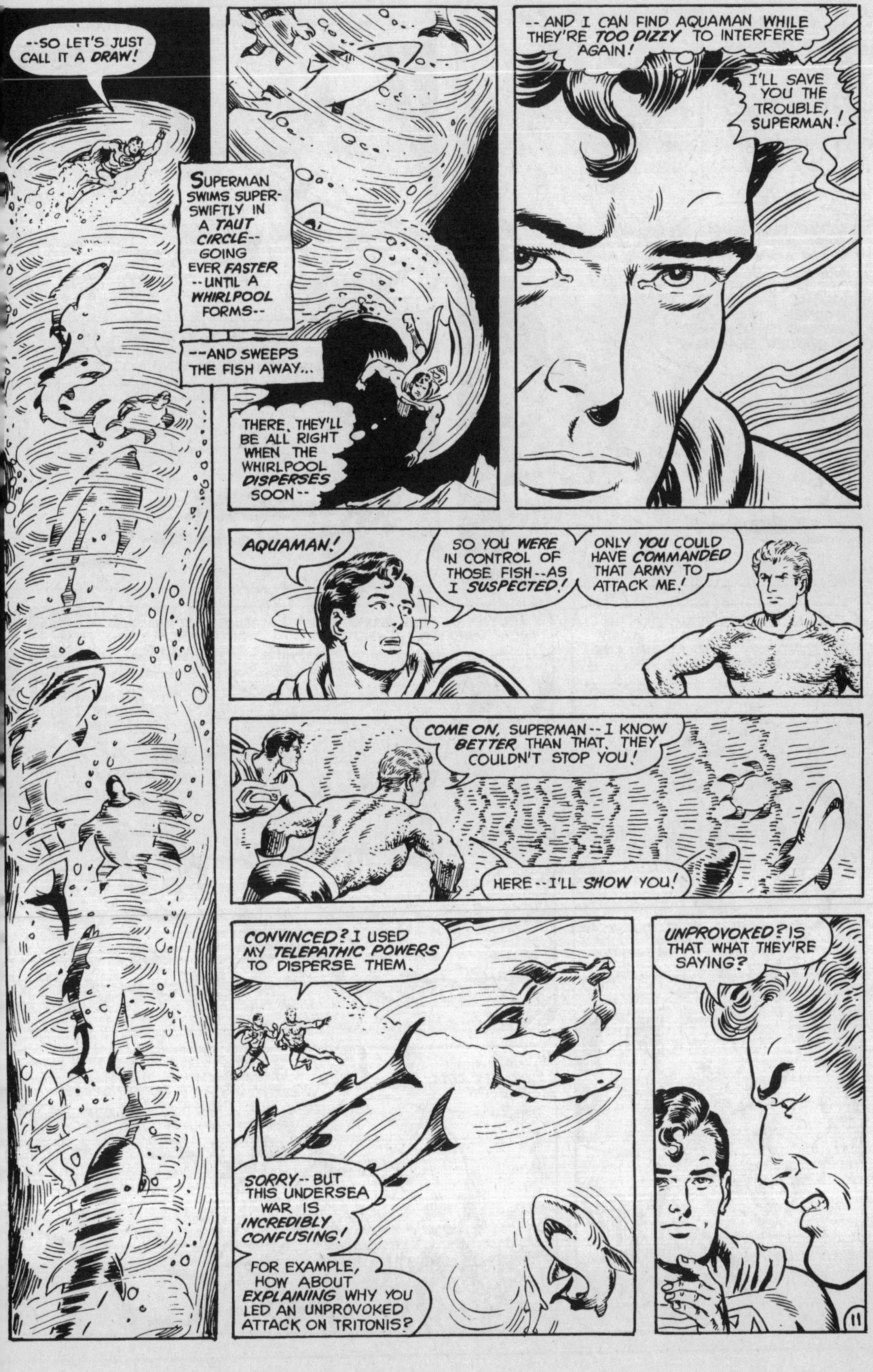
--SO LET'S JUST CALL IT A DRAW!
SUPERMAN SWIMS SUPER-SWIFTLY IN A TAUT CIRCLE--GOING EVER FASTER --UNTIL A WHIRLPOOL FORMS--
--AND SWEEPS THE FISH AWAY...
THERE, THEY'LL BE ALL RIGHT WHEN THE WHIRLPOOL DISPERSES SOON--
--AND I CAN FIND AQUAMAN WHILE THEY'RE TOO DIZZY TO INTERFERE AGAIN!
I'LL SAVE YOU THE TROUBLE, SUPERMAN!
AQUAMAN!
SO YOU WERE IN CONTROL OF THOSE FISH--AS I SUSPECTED!
ONLY YOU COULD HAVE COMMANDED THAT ARMY TO ATTACK ME!
COME ON, SUPERMAN--I KNOW BETTER THAN THAT. THEY COULDN'T STOP YOU!
HERE--I'LL SHOW YOU!
CONVINCED? I USED MY TELEPATHIC POWERS TO DISPERSE THEM.
SORRY--BUT THIS UNDERSEA WAR IS INCREDIBLY CONFUSING!
FOR EXAMPLE, HOW ABOUT EXPLAINING WHY YOU LED AN UNPROVOKED ATTACK ON TRITONIS?
UNPROVOKED? IS THAT WHAT THEY'RE SAYING?
11

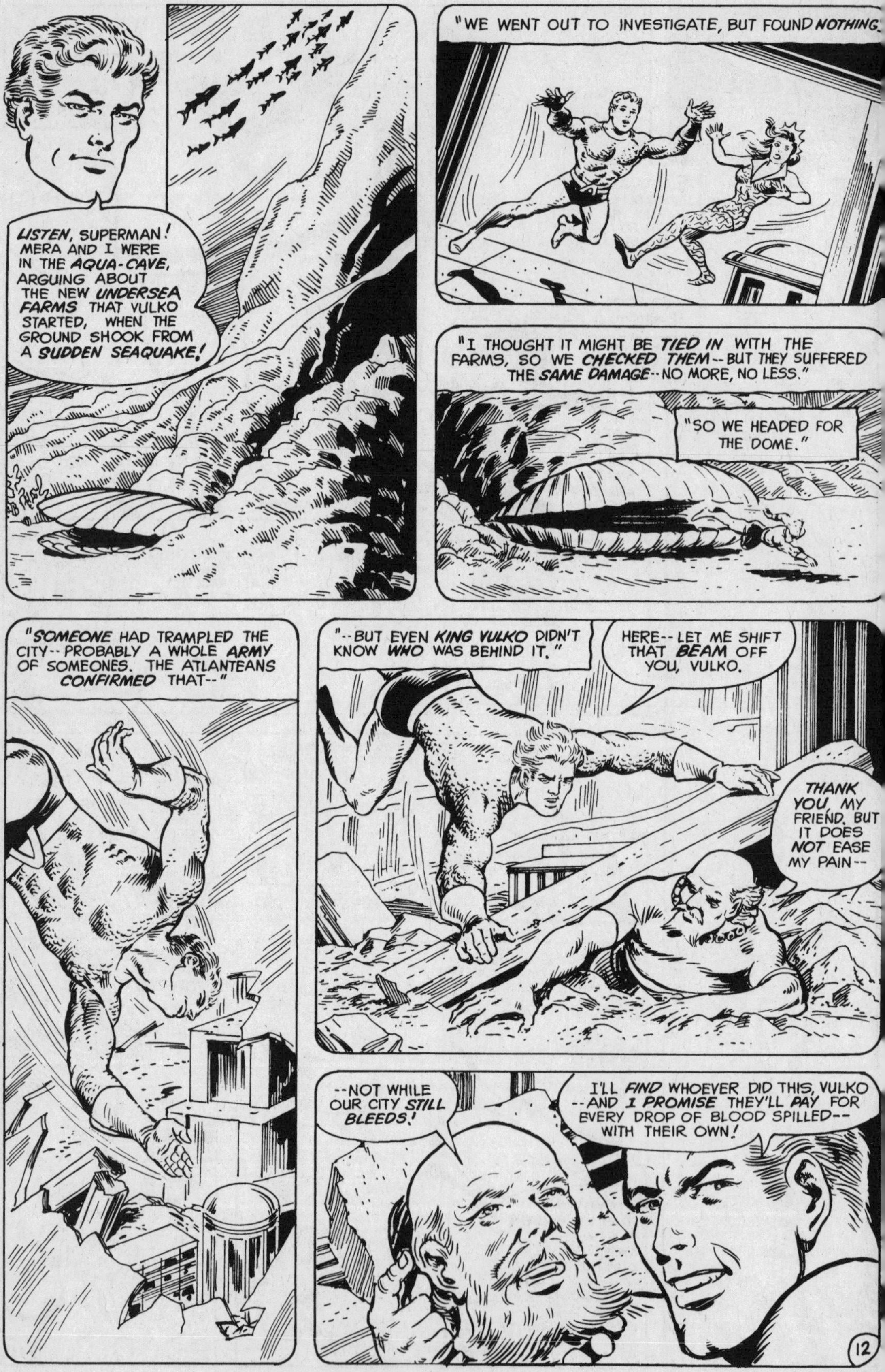
LISTEN, SUPERMAN! MERA AND I WERE IN THE AQUA-CAVE, ARGUING ABOUT THE NEW UNDERSEA FARMS THAT VULKO STARTED, WHEN THE GROUND SHOOK FROM A SUDDEN SEAQUAKE!
"WE WENT OUT TO INVESTIGATE, BUT FOUND NOTHING.
"I THOUGHT IT MIGHT BE TIED IN WITH THE FARMS, SO WE CHECKED THEM--BUT THEY SUFFERED THE SAME DAMAGE--NO MORE, NO LESS."
"SO WE HEADED FOR THE DOME."
"SOMEONE HAD TRAMPLED THE CITY--PROBABLY A WHOLE ARMY OF SOMEONES. THE ATLANTEANS CONFIRMED THAT--"
"--BUT EVEN KING VULKO DIDN'T KNOW WHO WAS BEHIND IT."
HERE--LET ME SHIFT THAT BEAM OFF YOU, VULKO.
THANK YOU, MY FRIEND, BUT IT DOES NOT EASE MY PAIN--
--NOT WHILE OUR CITY STILL BLEEDS!
I'LL FIND WHOEVER DID THIS, VULKO--AND I PROMISE THEY'LL PAY FOR EVERY DROP OF BLOOD SPILLED--WITH THEIR OWN!
12

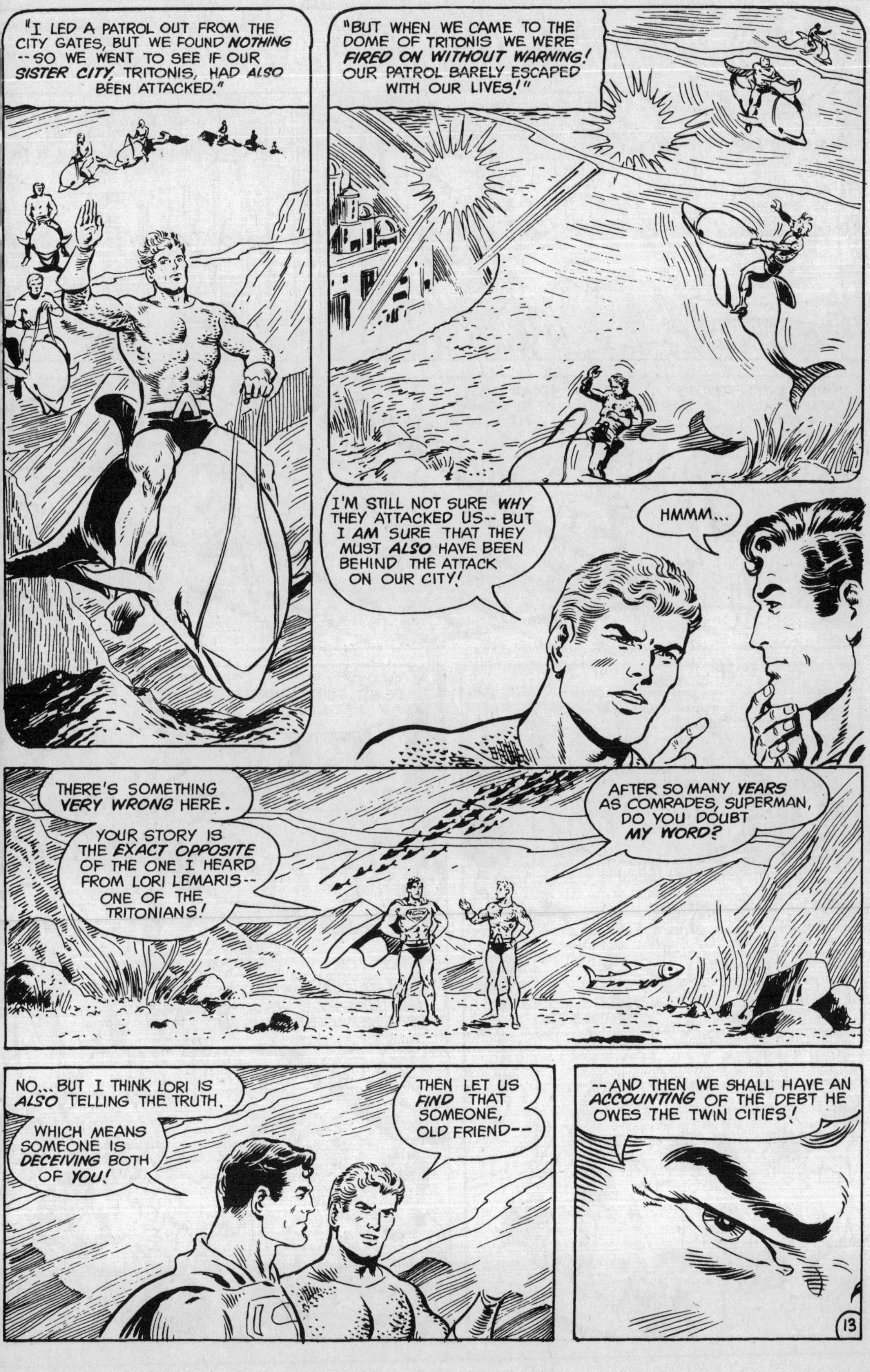
"I LED A PATROL OUT FROM THE CITY GATES, BUT WE FOUND NOTHING --SO WE WENT TO SEE IF OUR SISTER CITY, TRITONIS, HAD ALSO BEEN ATTACKED."
"BUT WHEN WE CAME TO THE DOME OF TRITONIS WE WERE FIRED ON WITHOUT WARNING! OUR PATROL BARELY ESCAPED WITH OUR LIVES!"
I'M STILL NOT SURE WHY THEY ATTACKED US-- BUT I AM SURE THAT THEY MUST ALSO HAVE BEEN BEHIND THE ATTACK ON OUR CITY!
HMMM...
THERE'S SOMETHING VERY WRONG HERE.
YOUR STORY IS THE EXACT OPPOSITE OF THE ONE I HEARD FROM LORI LEMARIS-- ONE OF THE TRITONIANS!
AFTER SO MANY YEARS AS COMRADES, SUPERMAN, DO YOU DOUBT MY WORD?
NO... BUT I THINK LORI IS ALSO TELLING THE TRUTH.
WHICH MEANS SOMEONE IS DECEIVING BOTH OF YOU!
THEN LET US FIND THAT SOMEONE, OLD FRIEND--
--AND THEN WE SHALL HAVE AN ACCOUNTING OF THE DEBT HE OWES THE TWIN CITIES!
13

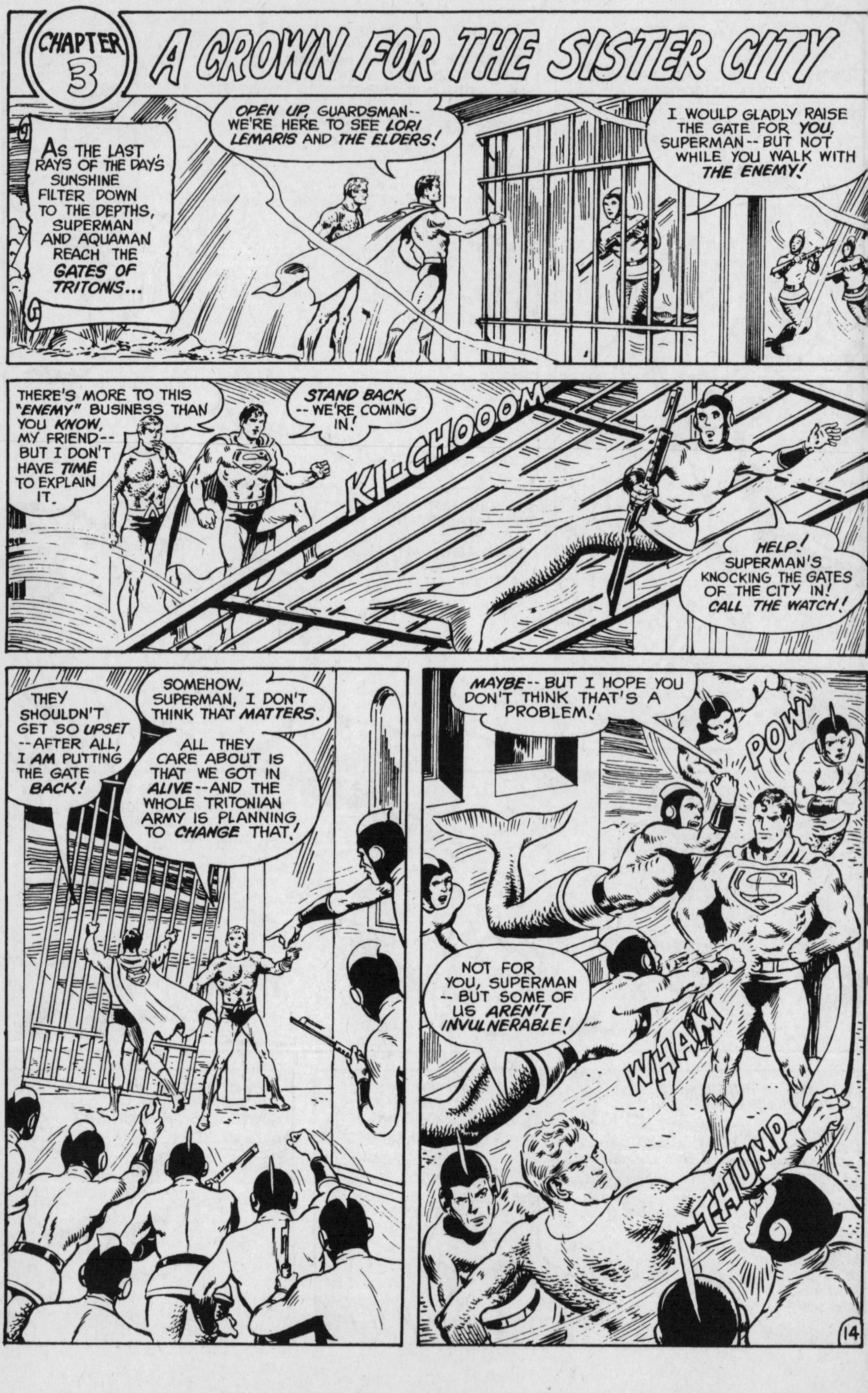
CHAPTER 3
A CROWN FOR THE SISTER CITY
AS THE LAST RAYS OF THE DAY'S SUNSHINE FILTER DOWN TO THE DEPTHS, SUPERMAN AND AQUAMAN REACH THE GATES OF TRITONIS...
OPEN UP, GUARDSMAN-- WE'RE HERE TO SEE LORI LEMARIS AND THE ELDERS!
I WOULD GLADLY RAISE THE GATE FOR YOU, SUPERMAN-- BUT NOT WHILE YOU WALK WITH THE ENEMY!
THERE'S MORE TO THIS "ENEMY" BUSINESS THAN YOU KNOW, MY FRIEND-- BUT I DON'T HAVE TIME TO EXPLAIN IT.
STAND BACK -- WE'RE COMING IN!
KI-CHOOOM
HELP! SUPERMAN'S KNOCKING THE GATES OF THE CITY IN! CALL THE WATCH!
THEY SHOULDN'T GET SO UPSET --AFTER ALL, I AM PUTTING THE GATE BACK!
SOMEHOW, SUPERMAN, I DON'T THINK THAT MATTERS.
ALL THEY CARE ABOUT IS THAT WE GOT IN ALIVE--AND THE WHOLE TRITONIAN ARMY IS PLANNING TO CHANGE THAT!
MAYBE-- BUT I HOPE YOU DON'T THINK THAT'S A PROBLEM!
POW
NOT FOR YOU, SUPERMAN -- BUT SOME OF US AREN'T INVULNERABLE!
WHAM
THUMP
14

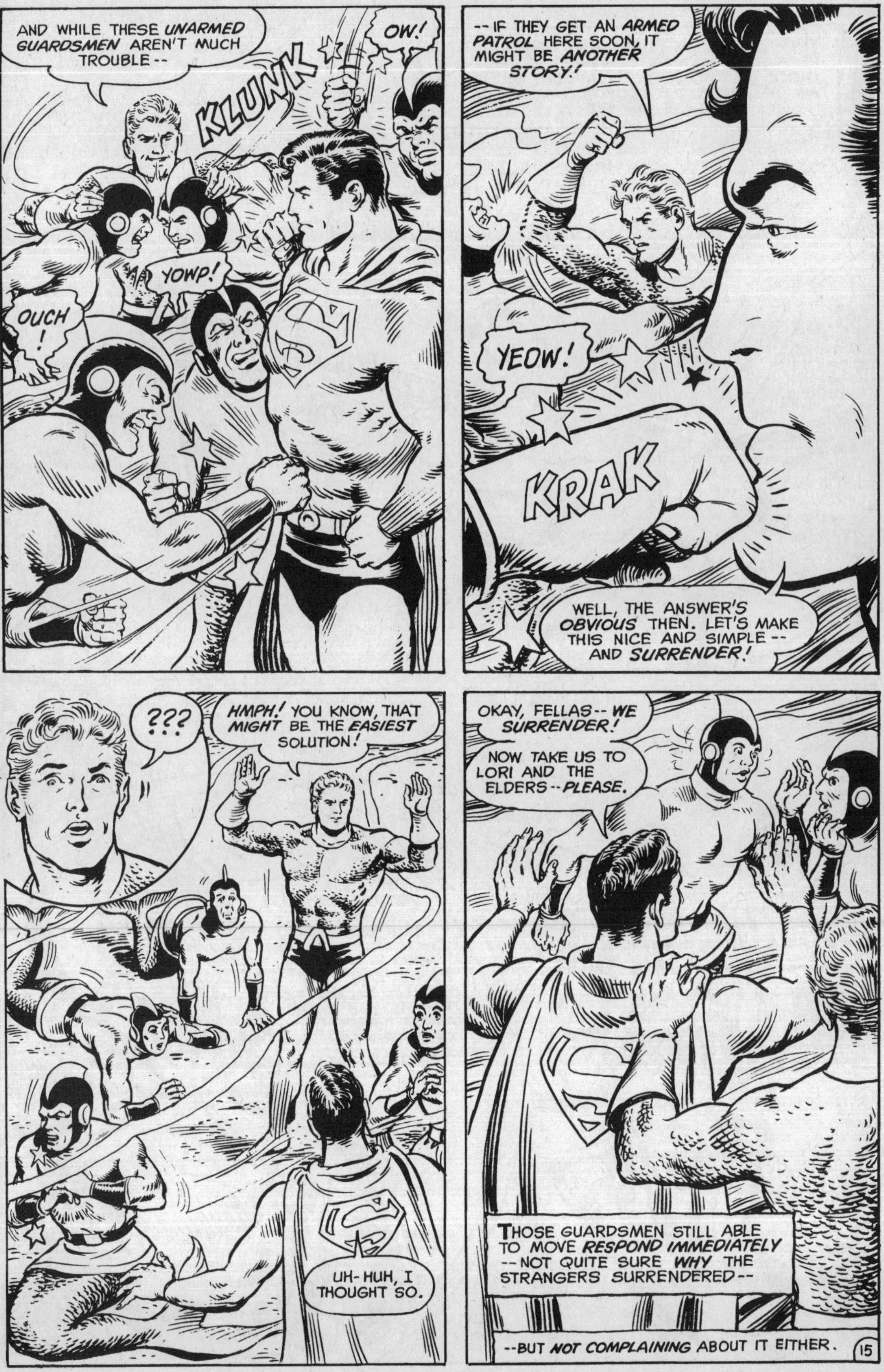
AND WHILE THESE UNARMED GUARDSMEN AREN'T MUCH TROUBLE --
KLUNK
OW!
YOWP!
OUCH!
-- IF THEY GET AN ARMED PATROL HERE SOON, IT MIGHT BE ANOTHER STORY!
YEOW!
KRAK
WELL, THE ANSWER'S OBVIOUS THEN. LET'S MAKE THIS NICE AND SIMPLE -- AND SURRENDER!
???
HMPH! YOU KNOW, THAT MIGHT BE THE EASIEST SOLUTION!
UH-HUH, I THOUGHT SO.
OKAY, FELLAS -- WE SURRENDER!
NOW TAKE US TO LORI AND THE ELDERS -- PLEASE.
THOSE GUARDSMEN STILL ABLE TO MOVE RESPOND IMMEDIATELY -- NOT QUITE SURE WHY THE STRANGERS SURRENDERED --
-- BUT NOT COMPLAINING ABOUT IT EITHER.
15

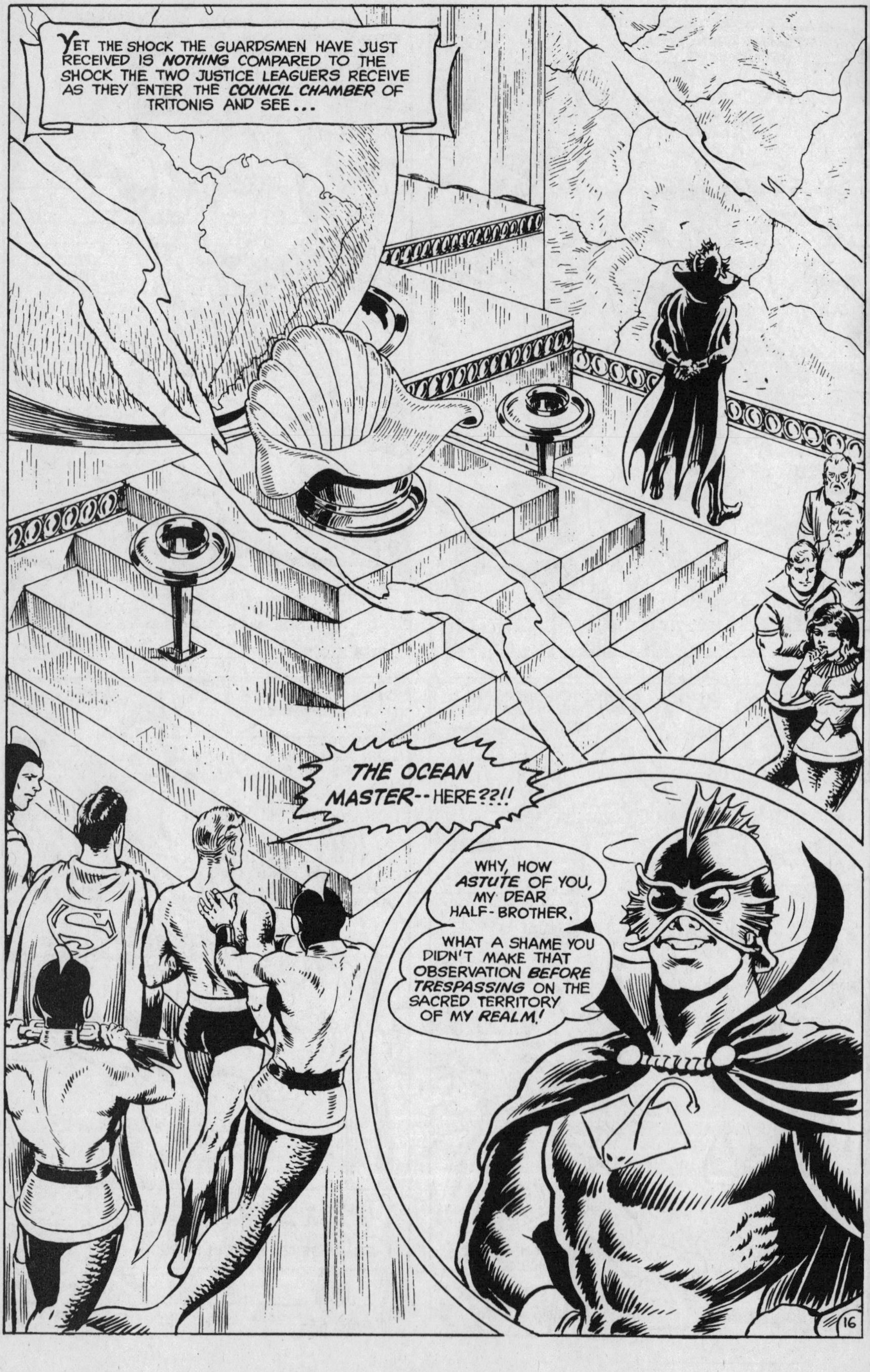
YET THE SHOCK THE GUARDSMEN HAVE JUST RECEIVED IS NOTHING COMPARED TO THE SHOCK THE TWO JUSTICE LEAGUERS RECEIVE AS THEY ENTER THE COUNCIL CHAMBER OF TRITONIS AND SEE...
THE OCEAN MASTER--HERE??!!
WHY, HOW ASTUTE OF YOU, MY DEAR HALF-BROTHER.
WHAT A SHAME YOU DIDN'T MAKE THAT OBSERVATION BEFORE TRESPASSING ON THE SACRED TERRITORY OF MY REALM!
16

WHAT DID YOU--??? YOUR REALM??

IT'S QUITE *SIMPLE,* AQUAMAN.

THE TRITONIANS HAVE MADE ME THEIR *KING* IN EXCHANGE FOR MY *PROTECTION.*

I HAVE SHOWN THEM *CONCLUSIVE PROOF* THAT I AM THEIR *ONLY HOPE* OF DEFENSE --

--AGAINST YOU AND YOUR *MARAUDING ARMY* FROM POSEIDONIS!

YOU'RE *MAD,* ORM, TO THINK YOU CAN *GET AWAY* WITH THIS!

AND *YOU,* LORI-- YOU ACTUALLY *WENT ALONG* WITH THIS?

WE ARE *GENTLE PEOPLE,* SUPERMAN --NOT READY FOR WAR!

WE ARE *GRATEFUL* TO THE OCEAN MASTER FOR AIDING US IN OUR HOUR OF NEED.

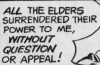

ALL THE ELDERS SURRENDERED THEIR POWER TO ME, *WITHOUT QUESTION* OR APPEAL!

AND AS THE *RIGHTFUL RULER* OF TRITONIS, I SENTENCE YOU TO *DEATH,* AQUAMAN! I CANNOT *ENFORCE* MY DECREE WITH SUPERMAN HERE--

--BUT *BOTH* OF YOU ARE TO LEAVE TRITONIS-- NOW AND *FOREVER.* SHOULD YOU *RETURN,* MY BROTHER, *THEN* YOU SHALL DIE.

FOR A SECOND THE HEROES *PAUSE,* AQUAMAN *TENSING,* PREPARING TO *LEAP* AT HIS HALF-BROTHER'S THROAT.

THEN THE MOMENT *PASSES,* AND REASON RETURNS...

WE *HAVE* TO GO, AQUAMAN --MAD OR NOT, HE *IS* THE LAW HERE.

HMPH.

HA HA·HA HA

17

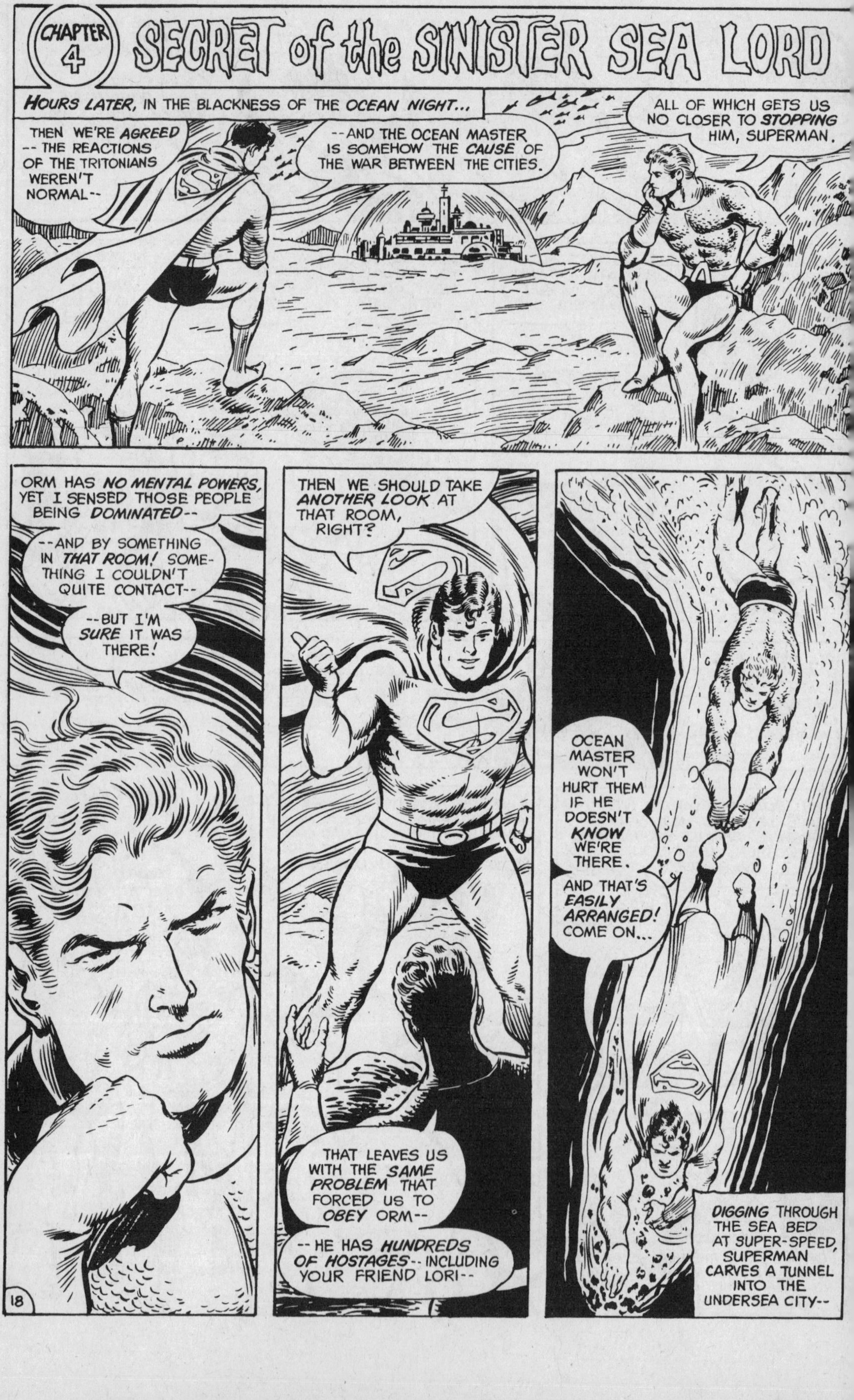
CHAPTER 4
SECRET of the SINISTER SEA LORD
HOURS LATER, IN THE BLACKNESS OF THE OCEAN NIGHT...
THEN WE'RE AGREED -- THE REACTIONS OF THE TRITONIANS WEREN'T NORMAL--
--AND THE OCEAN MASTER IS SOMEHOW THE CAUSE OF THE WAR BETWEEN THE CITIES.
ALL OF WHICH GETS US NO CLOSER TO STOPPING HIM, SUPERMAN.
ORM HAS NO MENTAL POWERS, YET I SENSED THOSE PEOPLE BEING DOMINATED--
--AND BY SOMETHING IN THAT ROOM! SOMETHING I COULDN'T QUITE CONTACT--
--BUT I'M SURE IT WAS THERE!
THEN WE SHOULD TAKE ANOTHER LOOK AT THAT ROOM, RIGHT?
THAT LEAVES US WITH THE SAME PROBLEM THAT FORCED US TO OBEY ORM--
-- HE HAS HUNDREDS OF HOSTAGES-- INCLUDING YOUR FRIEND LORI--
OCEAN MASTER WON'T HURT THEM IF HE DOESN'T KNOW WE'RE THERE.
AND THAT'S EASILY ARRANGED! COME ON...
DIGGING THROUGH THE SEA BED AT SUPER-SPEED, SUPERMAN CARVES A TUNNEL INTO THE UNDERSEA CITY--
18

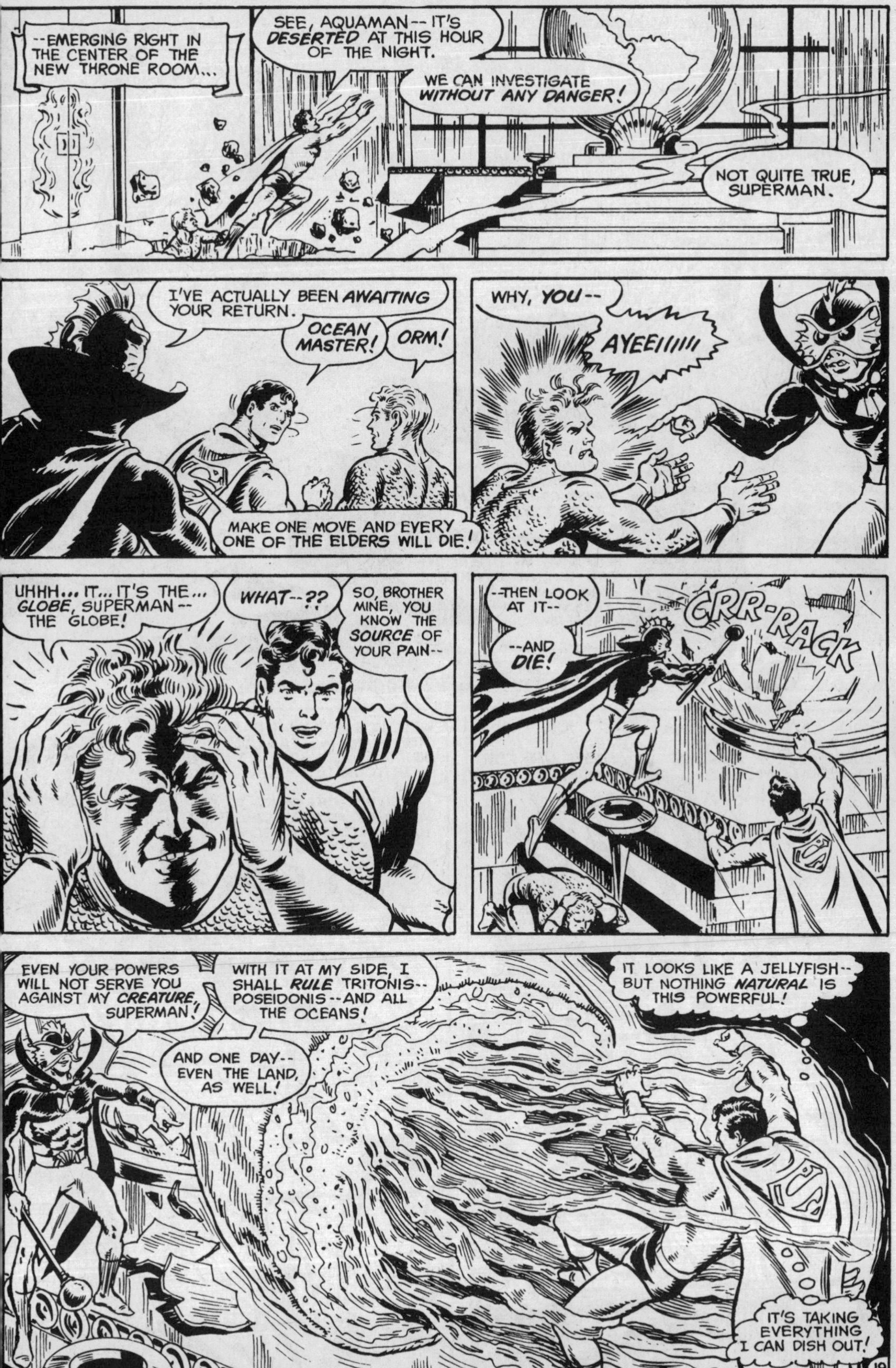
--EMERGING RIGHT IN THE CENTER OF THE NEW THRONE ROOM...
SEE, AQUAMAN--IT'S DESERTED AT THIS HOUR OF THE NIGHT.
WE CAN INVESTIGATE WITHOUT ANY DANGER!
NOT QUITE TRUE, SUPERMAN.
I'VE ACTUALLY BEEN AWAITING YOUR RETURN.
OCEAN MASTER!
ORM!
MAKE ONE MOVE AND EVERY ONE OF THE ELDERS WILL DIE!
WHY, YOU--
AYEE!!!!!!
UHHH... IT... IT'S THE... GLOBE, SUPERMAN-- THE GLOBE!
WHAT--??
SO, BROTHER MINE, YOU KNOW THE SOURCE OF YOUR PAIN--
--THEN LOOK AT IT--
--AND DIE!
CRR-RACK
EVEN YOUR POWERS WILL NOT SERVE YOU AGAINST MY CREATURE, SUPERMAN!
WITH IT AT MY SIDE, I SHALL RULE TRITONIS--POSEIDONIS--AND ALL THE OCEANS!
AND ONE DAY--EVEN THE LAND, AS WELL!
IT LOOKS LIKE A JELLYFISH--BUT NOTHING NATURAL IS THIS POWERFUL!
IT'S TAKING EVERYTHING I CAN DISH OUT!
19

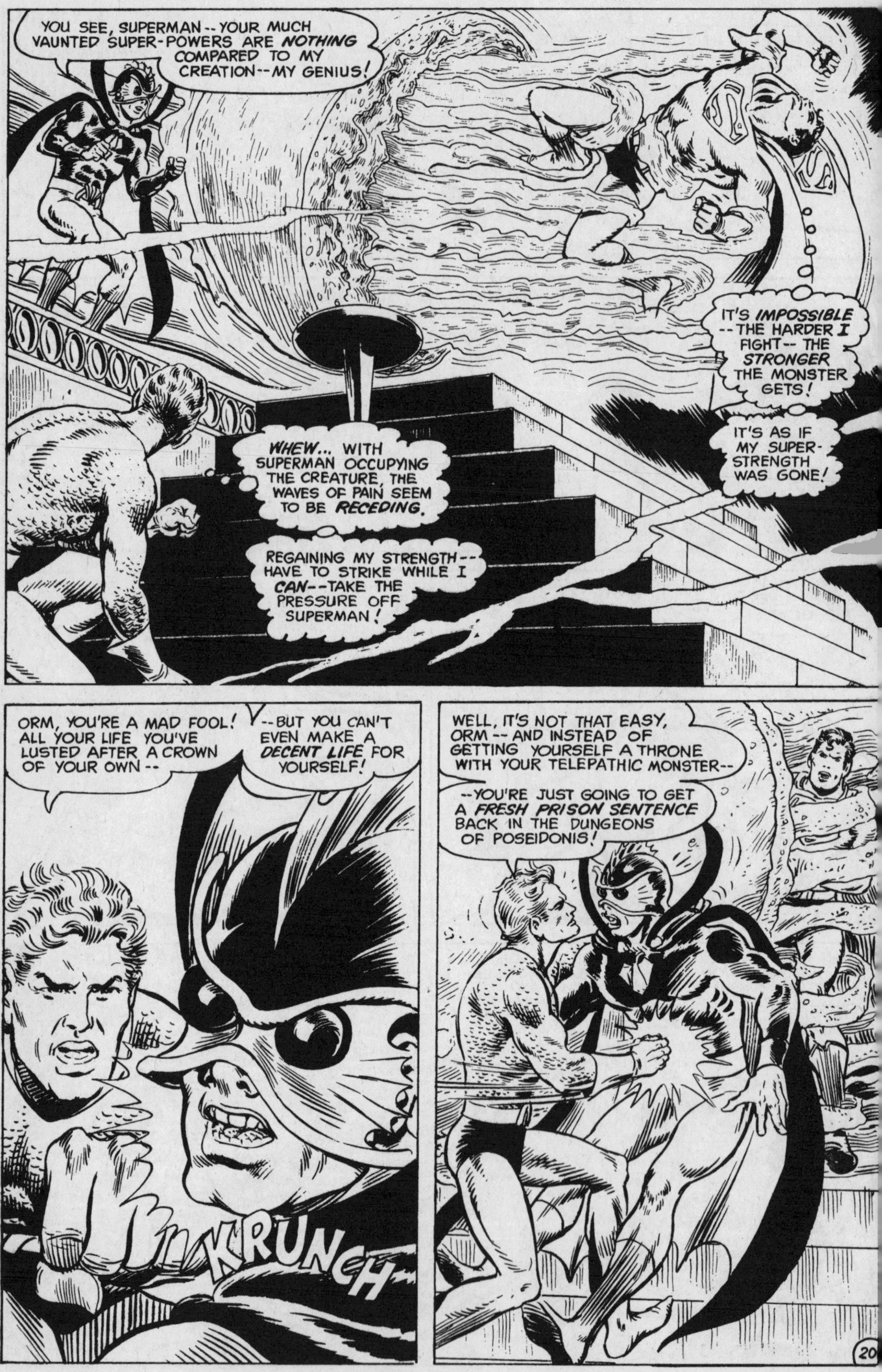
YOU SEE, SUPERMAN -- YOUR MUCH VAUNTED SUPER-POWERS ARE NOTHING COMPARED TO MY CREATION -- MY GENIUS!
IT'S IMPOSSIBLE -- THE HARDER I FIGHT -- THE STRONGER THE MONSTER GETS!
IT'S AS IF MY SUPER-STRENGTH WAS GONE!
WHEW... WITH SUPERMAN OCCUPYING THE CREATURE, THE WAVES OF PAIN SEEM TO BE RECEDING.
REGAINING MY STRENGTH -- HAVE TO STRIKE WHILE I CAN -- TAKE THE PRESSURE OFF SUPERMAN!
ORM, YOU'RE A MAD FOOL! ALL YOUR LIFE YOU'VE LUSTED AFTER A CROWN OF YOUR OWN --
-- BUT YOU CAN'T EVEN MAKE A DECENT LIFE FOR YOURSELF!
KRUNCH
WELL, IT'S NOT THAT EASY, ORM -- AND INSTEAD OF GETTING YOURSELF A THRONE WITH YOUR TELEPATHIC MONSTER--
--YOU'RE JUST GOING TO GET A FRESH PRISON SENTENCE BACK IN THE DUNGEONS OF POSEIDONIS!
20

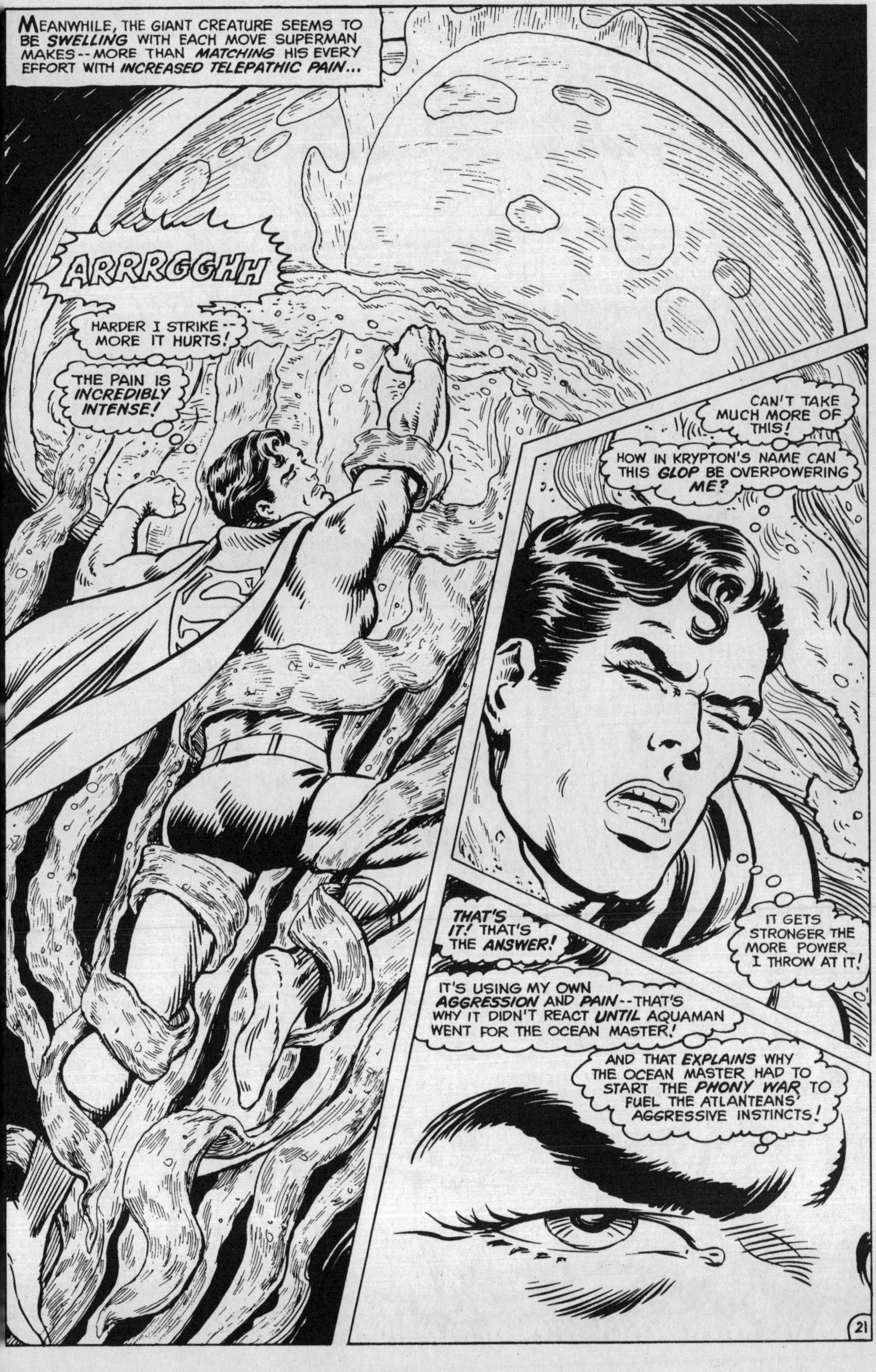
MEANWHILE, THE GIANT CREATURE SEEMS TO BE SWELLING WITH EACH MOVE SUPERMAN MAKES--MORE THAN MATCHING HIS EVERY EFFORT WITH INCREASED TELEPATHIC PAIN...
ARRRGGHH
HARDER I STRIKE--MORE IT HURTS!
THE PAIN IS INCREDIBLY INTENSE!
CAN'T TAKE MUCH MORE OF THIS!
HOW IN KRYPTON'S NAME CAN THIS GLOP BE OVERPOWERING ME?
THAT'S IT! THAT'S THE ANSWER!
IT GETS STRONGER THE MORE POWER I THROW AT IT!
IT'S USING MY OWN AGGRESSION AND PAIN--THAT'S WHY IT DIDN'T REACT UNTIL AQUAMAN WENT FOR THE OCEAN MASTER!
AND THAT EXPLAINS WHY THE OCEAN MASTER HAD TO START THE PHONY WAR TO FUEL THE ATLANTEANS' AGGRESSIVE INSTINCTS!
21

THEN MY *ONLY CHANCE* IS TO *QUIT FEEDING* IT POWER-- *GO LIMP*-- EVEN SUPPRESS MY CONSCIOUSNESS AND EMOTIONS...

FOR A SECOND, THE CREATURE *CONTINUES* ITS PRODIGIOUS ASSAULT *WITHOUT* ANY FRESH SUPPLY OF ENERGY FROM SUPERMAN--

--THEN IT SUDDENLY *COLLAPSES*-- HAVING USED ALL ITS RESERVES IN A SINGLE SECOND, AND UNABLE TO RE-COVER WITH ONLY THE COMPARATIVELY *MEAGER* ENERGIES FROM AQUAMAN AND THE OCEAN MASTER!

IT WORKED!

WH-WHAT'S HAPPENING? MY CREATION-- MY BEAUTY--

IS THAT ALL THAT'S BOTHERING YOU, ORM?

I'VE LOST OUR LINK!

HERE-- I'LL *FIX* THAT!

POW

YOU CAN *JOIN* YOUR LITTLE PET -- IN *UNCONSCIOUSNESS!*

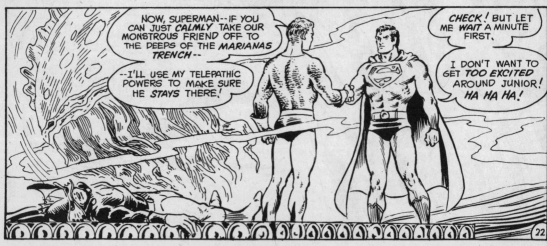

NOW, SUPERMAN--IF YOU CAN JUST *CALMLY* TAKE OUR MONSTROUS FRIEND OFF TO THE *DEEPS* OF THE *MARIANAS TRENCH*--

--I'LL USE MY TELEPATHIC POWERS TO MAKE SURE HE *STAYS* THERE!

CHECK! BUT LET ME *WAIT* A MINUTE FIRST.

I DON'T WANT TO GET *TOO EXCITED* AROUND JUNIOR! HA HA HA!

22

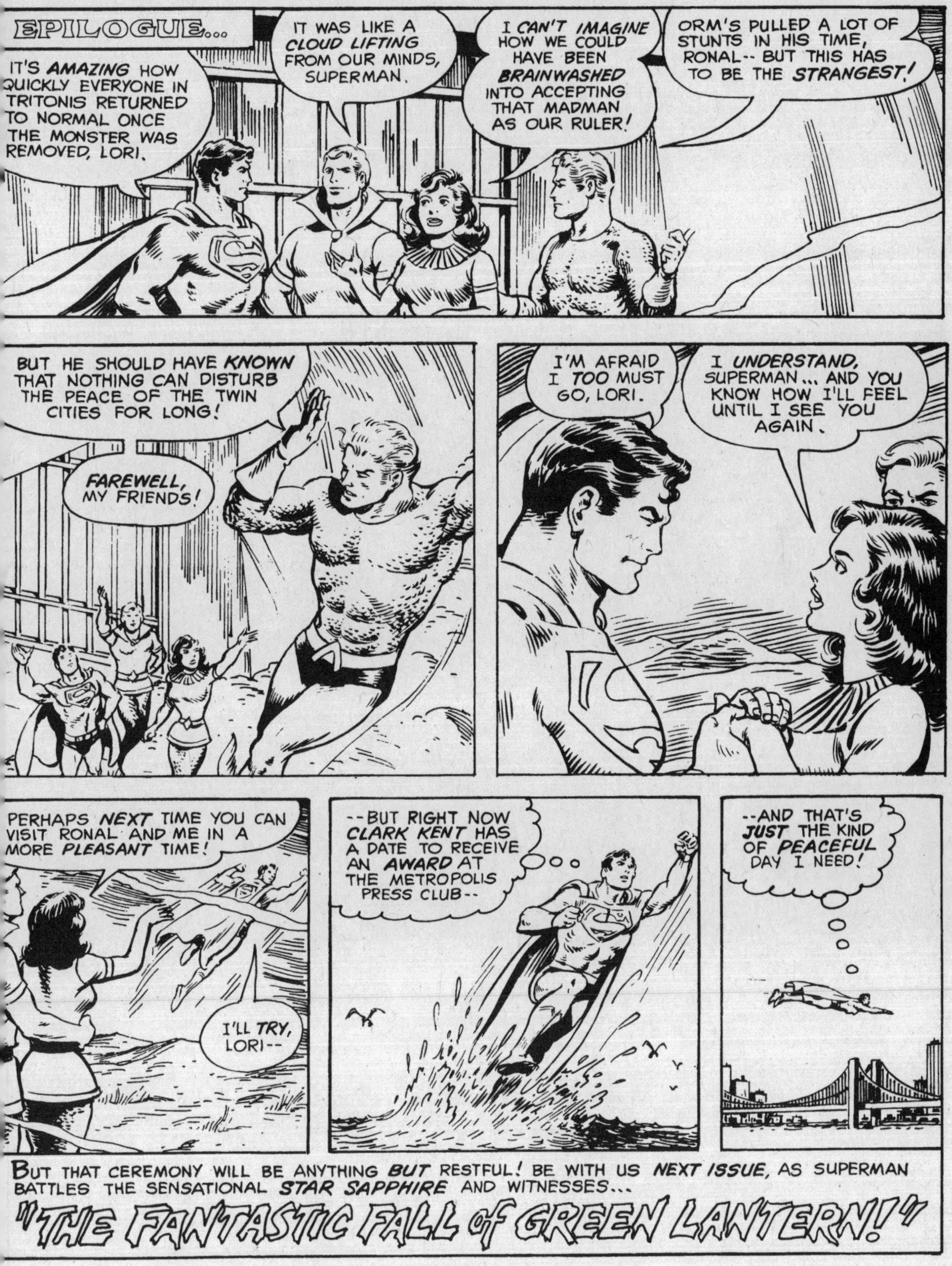
EPILOGUE...
IT'S AMAZING HOW QUICKLY EVERYONE IN TRITONIS RETURNED TO NORMAL ONCE THE MONSTER WAS REMOVED, LORI.
IT WAS LIKE A CLOUD LIFTING FROM OUR MINDS, SUPERMAN.
I CAN'T IMAGINE HOW WE COULD HAVE BEEN BRAINWASHED INTO ACCEPTING THAT MADMAN AS OUR RULER!
ORM'S PULLED A LOT OF STUNTS IN HIS TIME, RONAL-- BUT THIS HAS TO BE THE STRANGEST!
BUT HE SHOULD HAVE KNOWN THAT NOTHING CAN DISTURB THE PEACE OF THE TWIN CITIES FOR LONG!
FAREWELL, MY FRIENDS!
I'M AFRAID I TOO MUST GO, LORI.
I UNDERSTAND, SUPERMAN... AND YOU KNOW HOW I'LL FEEL UNTIL I SEE YOU AGAIN.
PERHAPS NEXT TIME YOU CAN VISIT RONAL AND ME IN A MORE PLEASANT TIME!
I'LL TRY, LORI--
--BUT RIGHT NOW CLARK KENT HAS A DATE TO RECEIVE AN AWARD AT THE METROPOLIS PRESS CLUB--
--AND THAT'S JUST THE KIND OF PEACEFUL DAY I NEED!
BUT THAT CEREMONY WILL BE ANYTHING BUT RESTFUL! BE WITH US NEXT ISSUE, AS SUPERMAN BATTLES THE SENSATIONAL STAR SAPPHIRE AND WITNESSES...
"THE FANTASTIC FALL of GREEN LANTERN!"

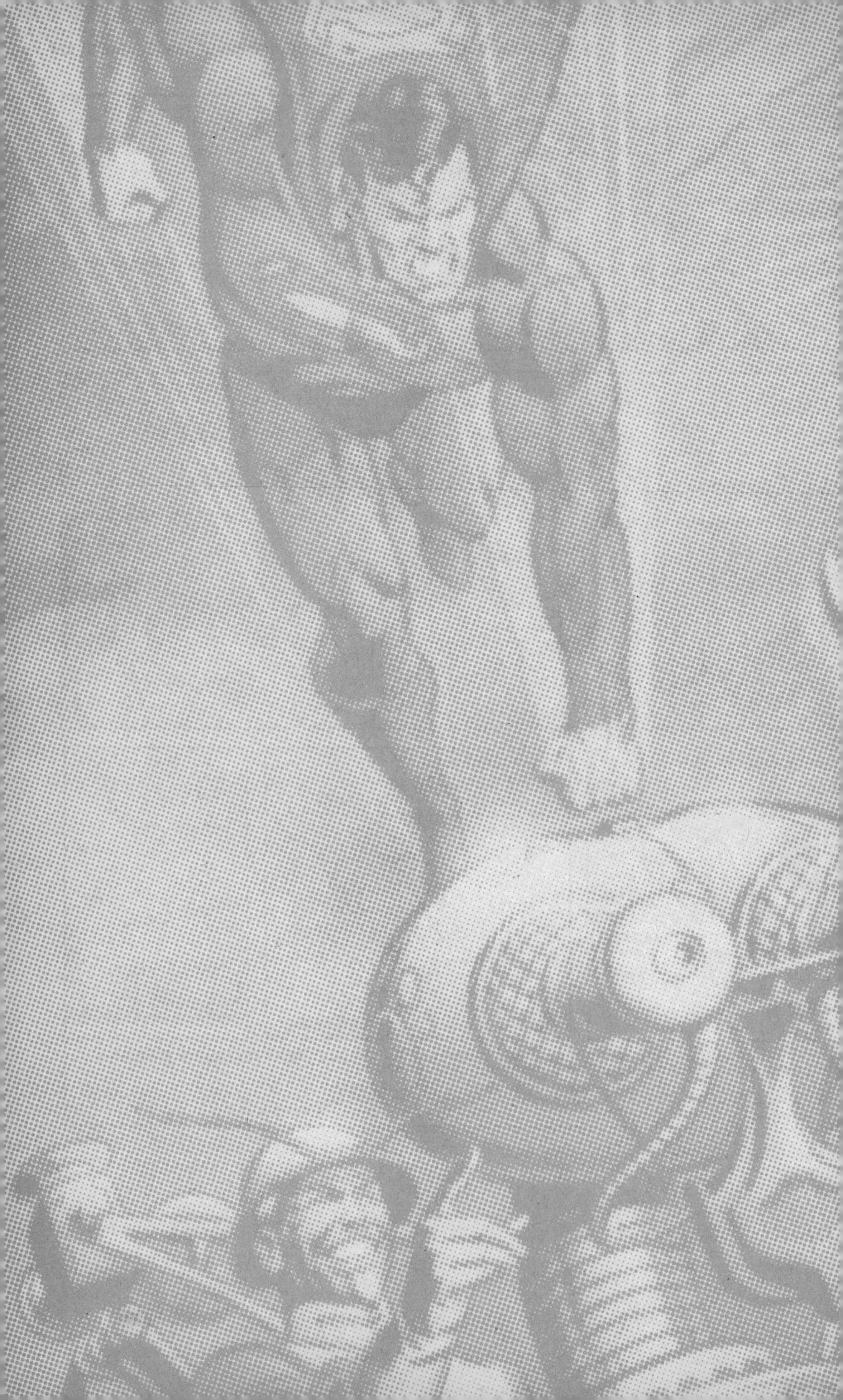

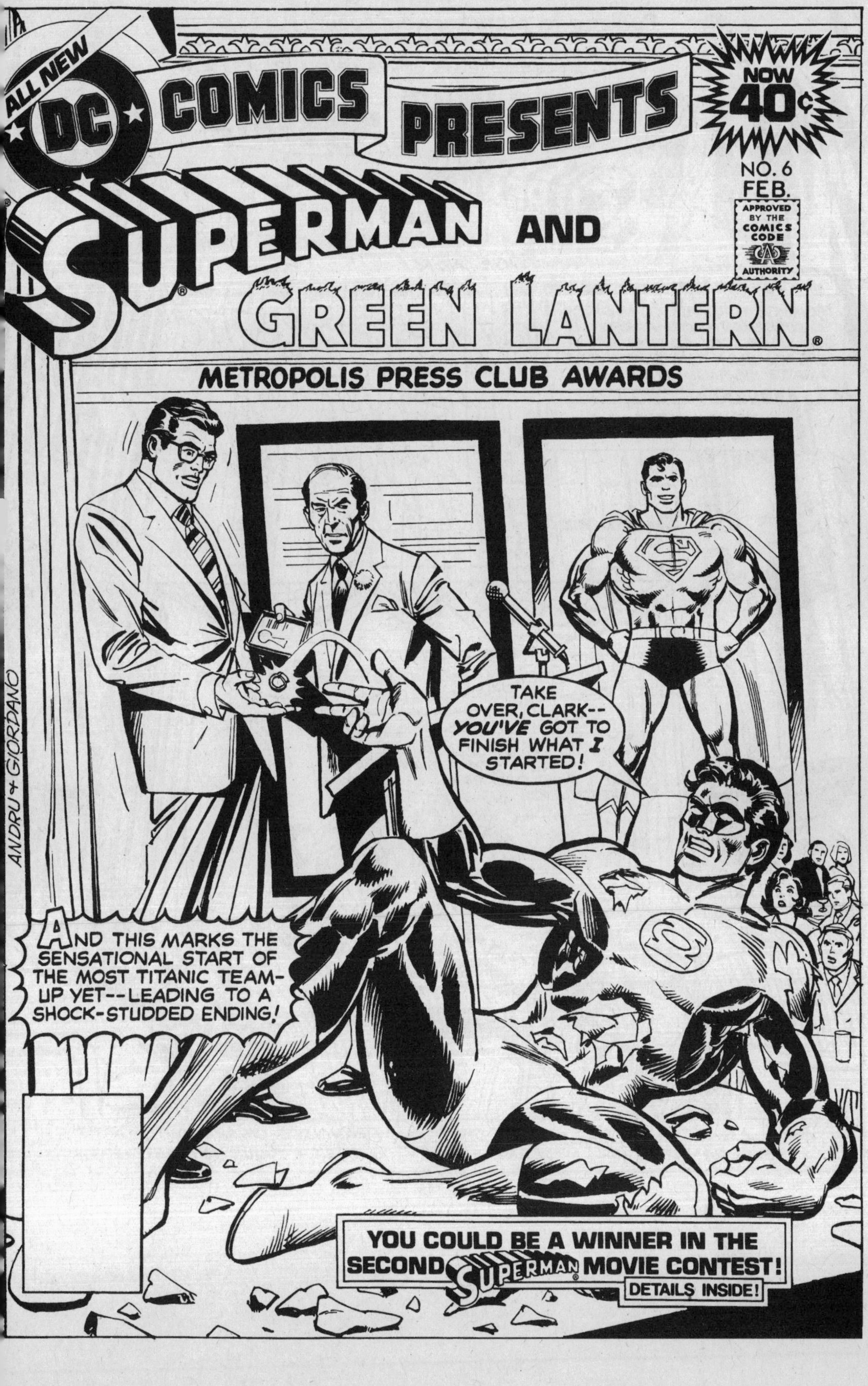
ALL NEW
DC COMICS PRESENTS
NOW 40¢
NO. 6
FEB.
APPROVED BY THE COMICS CODE AUTHORITY
SUPERMAN AND GREEN LANTERN
METROPOLIS PRESS CLUB AWARDS
TAKE OVER, CLARK-- YOU'VE GOT TO FINISH WHAT I STARTED!
AND THIS MARKS THE SENSATIONAL START OF THE MOST TITANIC TEAM-UP YET--LEADING TO A SHOCK-STUDDED ENDING!
ANDRU + GIORDANO
YOU COULD BE A WINNER IN THE SECOND SUPERMAN MOVIE CONTEST!
DETAILS INSIDE!

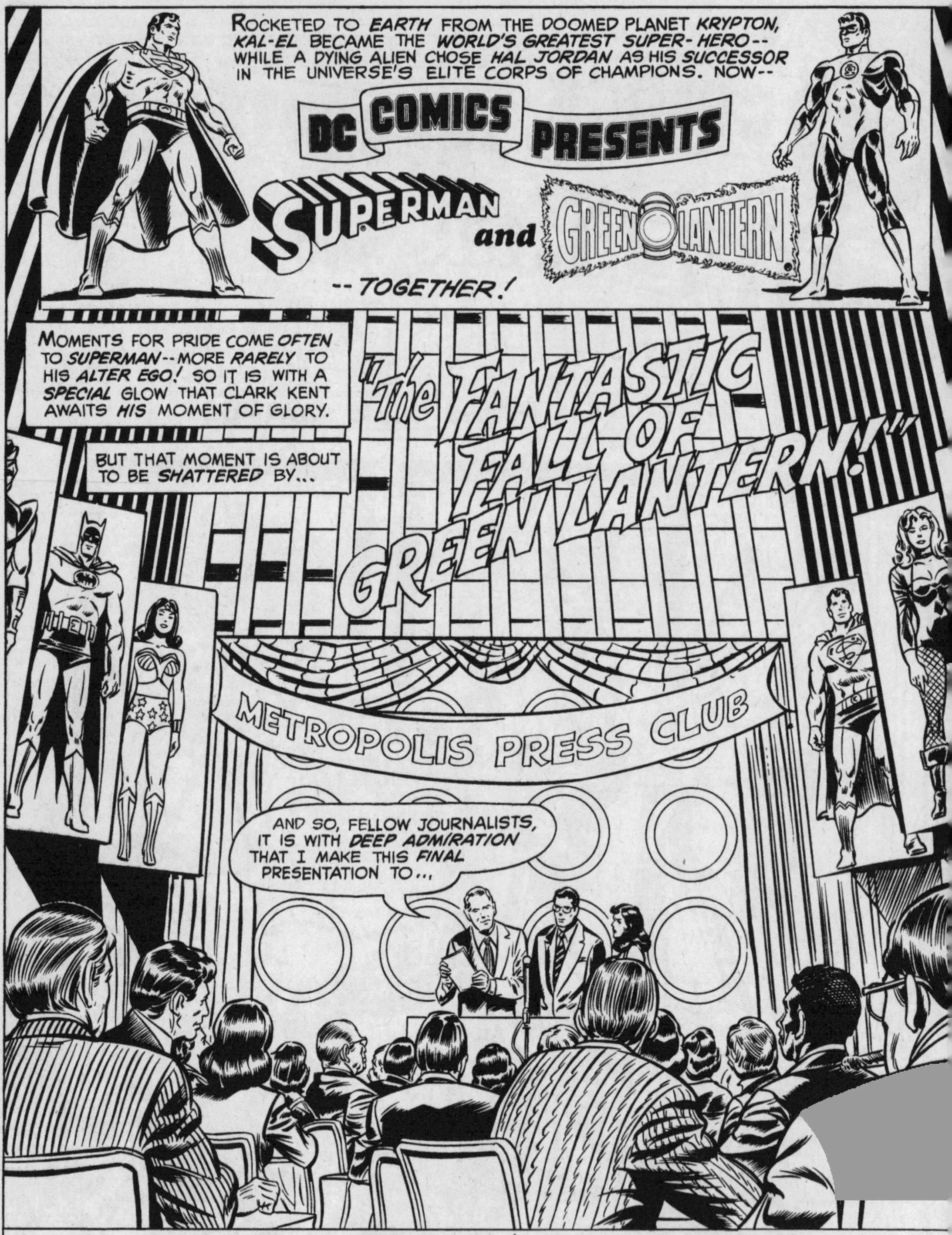
ROCKETED TO EARTH FROM THE DOOMED PLANET KRYPTON, KAL-EL BECAME THE WORLD'S GREATEST SUPER-HERO-- WHILE A DYING ALIEN CHOSE HAL JORDAN AS HIS SUCCESSOR IN THE UNIVERSE'S ELITE CORPS OF CHAMPIONS. NOW--
DC COMICS PRESENTS
SUPERMAN and GREEN LANTERN
--TOGETHER!
MOMENTS FOR PRIDE COME OFTEN TO SUPERMAN--MORE RARELY TO HIS ALTER EGO! SO IT IS WITH A SPECIAL GLOW THAT CLARK KENT AWAITS HIS MOMENT OF GLORY.
BUT THAT MOMENT IS ABOUT TO BE SHATTERED BY...
"The FANTASTIC FALL OF GREEN LANTERN!"
METROPOLIS PRESS CLUB
AND SO, FELLOW JOURNALISTS, IT IS WITH DEEP ADMIRATION THAT I MAKE THIS FINAL PRESENTATION TO...
PAUL LEVITZ – WRITER • CURT SWAN and FRANCISCO CHIARAMONTE – ARTISTS
BEN ODA – LETTERER • JERRY SERPE – COLORIST • JULIUS SCHWARTZ – EDITOR

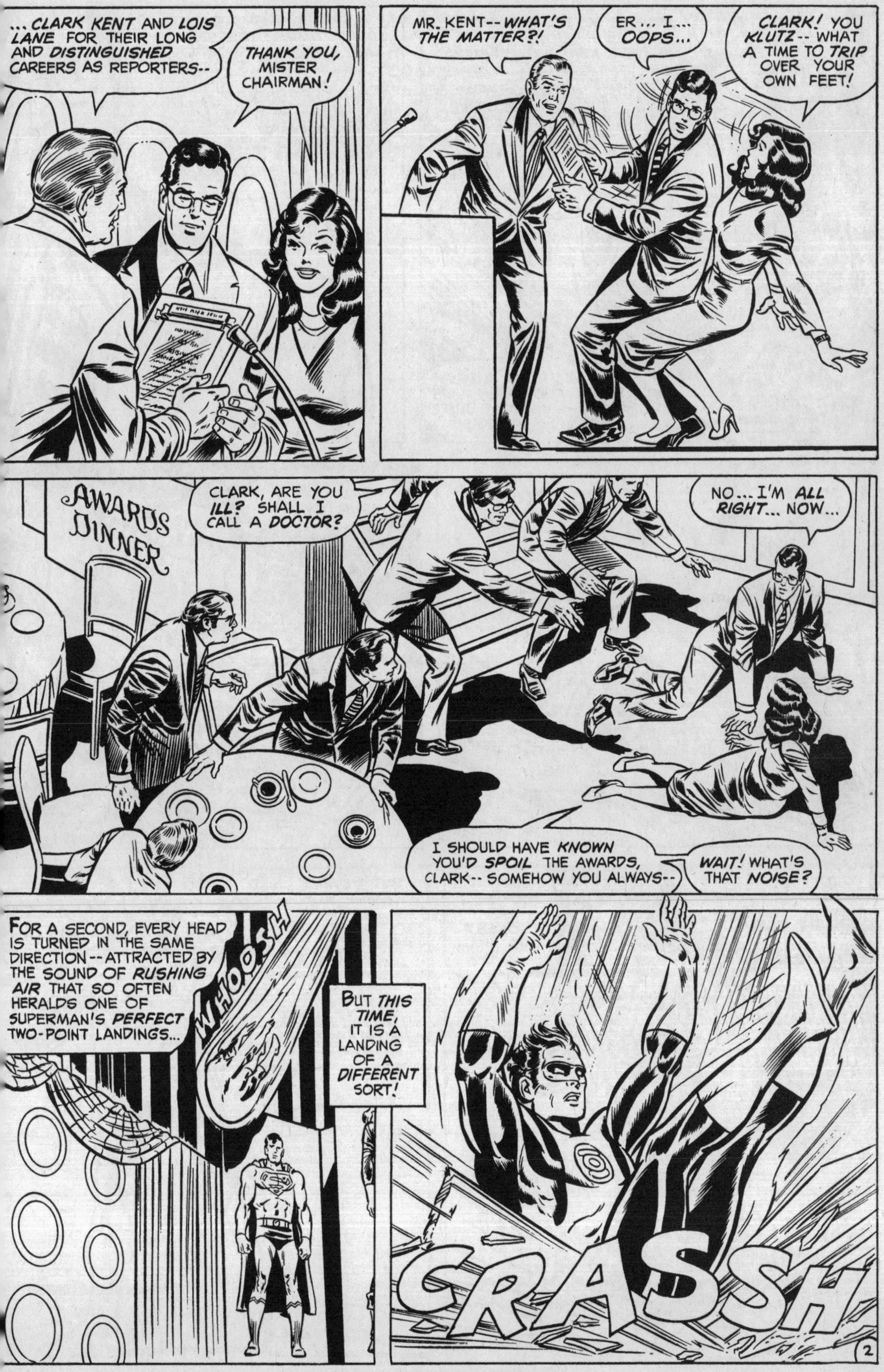
...CLARK KENT AND LOIS LANE FOR THEIR LONG AND DISTINGUISHED CAREERS AS REPORTERS--
THANK YOU, MISTER CHAIRMAN!
MR. KENT--WHAT'S THE MATTER?!
ER... I... OOPS...
CLARK! YOU KLUTZ--WHAT A TIME TO TRIP OVER YOUR OWN FEET!
AWARDS DINNER
CLARK, ARE YOU ILL? SHALL I CALL A DOCTOR?
NO... I'M ALL RIGHT... NOW...
I SHOULD HAVE KNOWN YOU'D SPOIL THE AWARDS, CLARK-- SOMEHOW YOU ALWAYS--
WAIT! WHAT'S THAT NOISE?
FOR A SECOND, EVERY HEAD IS TURNED IN THE SAME DIRECTION--ATTRACTED BY THE SOUND OF RUSHING AIR THAT SO OFTEN HERALDS ONE OF SUPERMAN'S PERFECT TWO-POINT LANDINGS...
WHOOSH
BUT THIS TIME, IT IS A LANDING OF A DIFFERENT SORT!
CRASSH
2

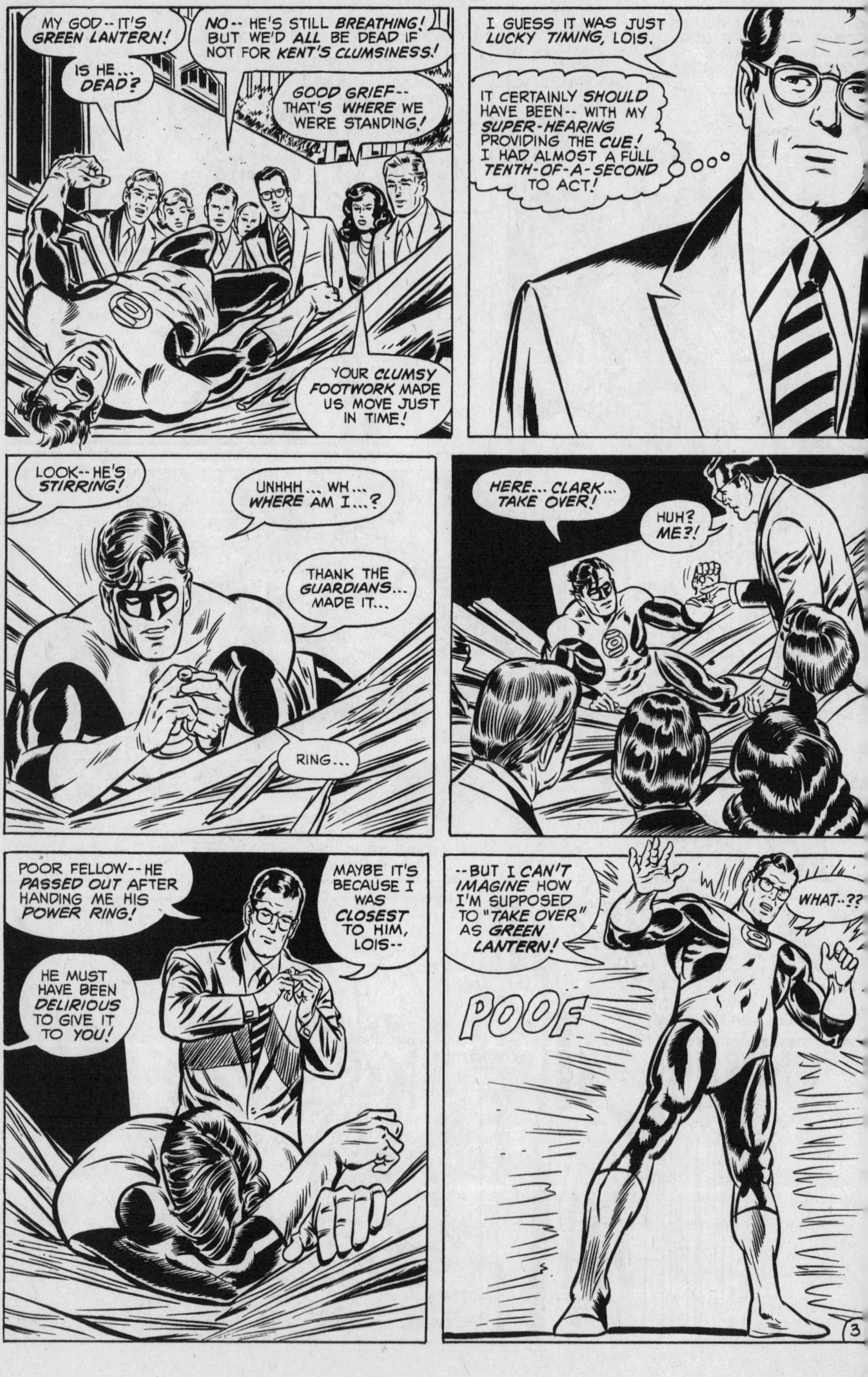
MY GOD -- IT'S GREEN LANTERN!
IS HE... DEAD?
NO -- HE'S STILL BREATHING! BUT WE'D ALL BE DEAD IF NOT FOR KENT'S CLUMSINESS!
GOOD GRIEF -- THAT'S WHERE WE WERE STANDING!
YOUR CLUMSY FOOTWORK MADE US MOVE JUST IN TIME!
I GUESS IT WAS JUST LUCKY TIMING, LOIS.
IT CERTAINLY SHOULD HAVE BEEN -- WITH MY SUPER-HEARING PROVIDING THE CUE! I HAD ALMOST A FULL TENTH-OF-A-SECOND TO ACT!
LOOK -- HE'S STIRRING!
UNHHH... WH... WHERE AM I...?
THANK THE GUARDIANS... MADE IT...
RING...
HERE... CLARK... TAKE OVER!
HUH? ME?!
POOR FELLOW -- HE PASSED OUT AFTER HANDING ME HIS POWER RING!
HE MUST HAVE BEEN DELIRIOUS TO GIVE IT TO YOU!
MAYBE IT'S BECAUSE I WAS CLOSEST TO HIM, LOIS --
-- BUT I CAN'T IMAGINE HOW I'M SUPPOSED TO "TAKE OVER" AS GREEN LANTERN!
POOF
WHAT..??
3

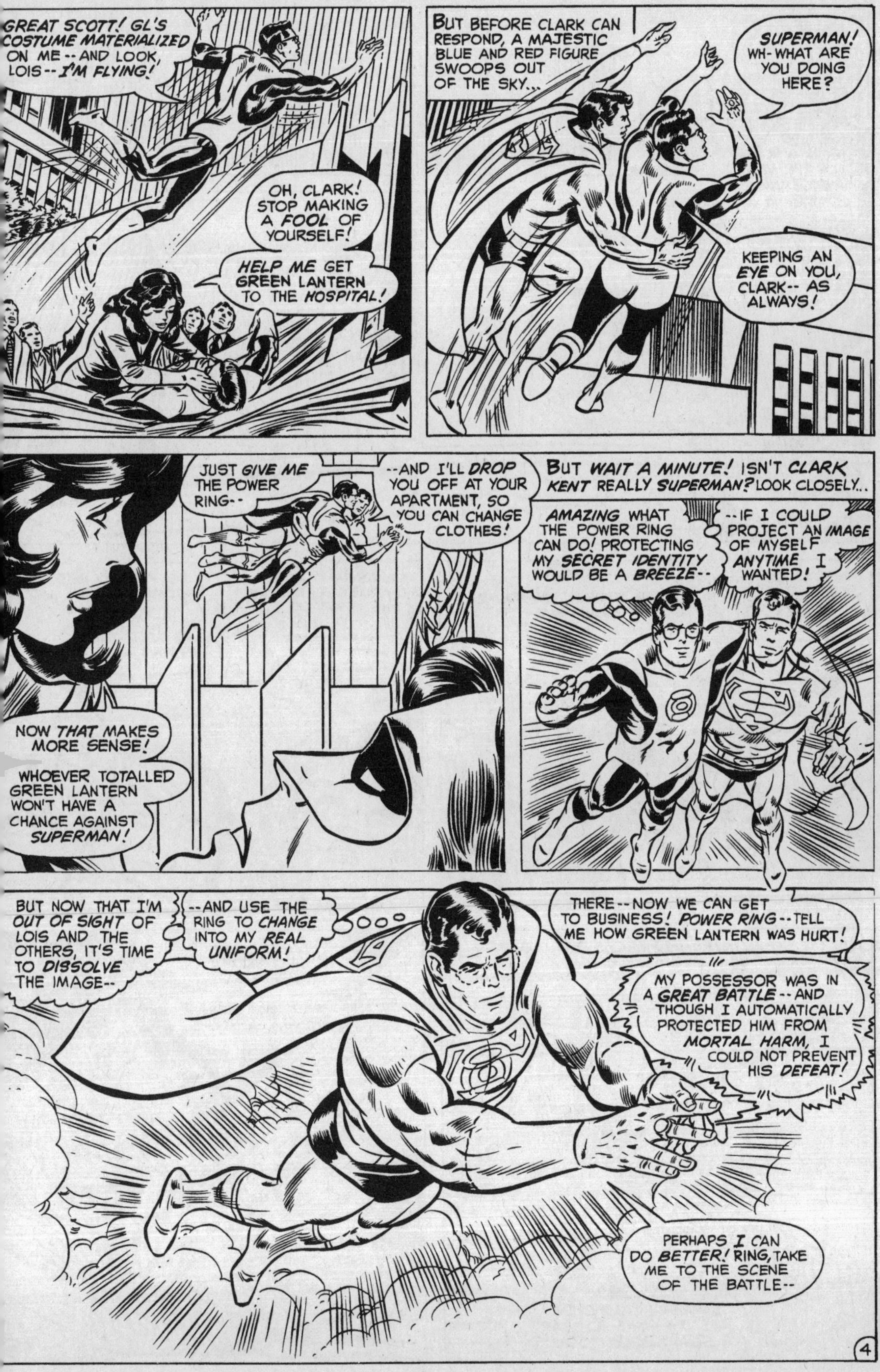
GREAT SCOTT! GL'S COSTUME MATERIALIZED ON ME -- AND LOOK, LOIS -- I'M FLYING!
OH, CLARK! STOP MAKING A FOOL OF YOURSELF!
HELP ME GET GREEN LANTERN TO THE HOSPITAL!
BUT BEFORE CLARK CAN RESPOND, A MAJESTIC BLUE AND RED FIGURE SWOOPS OUT OF THE SKY...
SUPERMAN! WH-WHAT ARE YOU DOING HERE?
KEEPING AN EYE ON YOU, CLARK-- AS ALWAYS!
NOW THAT MAKES MORE SENSE!
WHOEVER TOTALLED GREEN LANTERN WON'T HAVE A CHANCE AGAINST SUPERMAN!
JUST GIVE ME THE POWER RING--
--AND I'LL DROP YOU OFF AT YOUR APARTMENT, SO YOU CAN CHANGE CLOTHES!
BUT WAIT A MINUTE! ISN'T CLARK KENT REALLY SUPERMAN? LOOK CLOSELY...
AMAZING WHAT THE POWER RING CAN DO! PROTECTING MY SECRET IDENTITY WOULD BE A BREEZE--
--IF I COULD PROJECT AN IMAGE OF MYSELF ANYTIME I WANTED!
BUT NOW THAT I'M OUT OF SIGHT OF LOIS AND THE OTHERS, IT'S TIME TO DISSOLVE THE IMAGE--
--AND USE THE RING TO CHANGE INTO MY REAL UNIFORM!
THERE--NOW WE CAN GET TO BUSINESS! POWER RING--TELL ME HOW GREEN LANTERN WAS HURT!
MY POSSESSOR WAS IN A GREAT BATTLE--AND THOUGH I AUTOMATICALLY PROTECTED HIM FROM MORTAL HARM, I COULD NOT PREVENT HIS DEFEAT!
PERHAPS I CAN DO BETTER! RING, TAKE ME TO THE SCENE OF THE BATTLE--
4

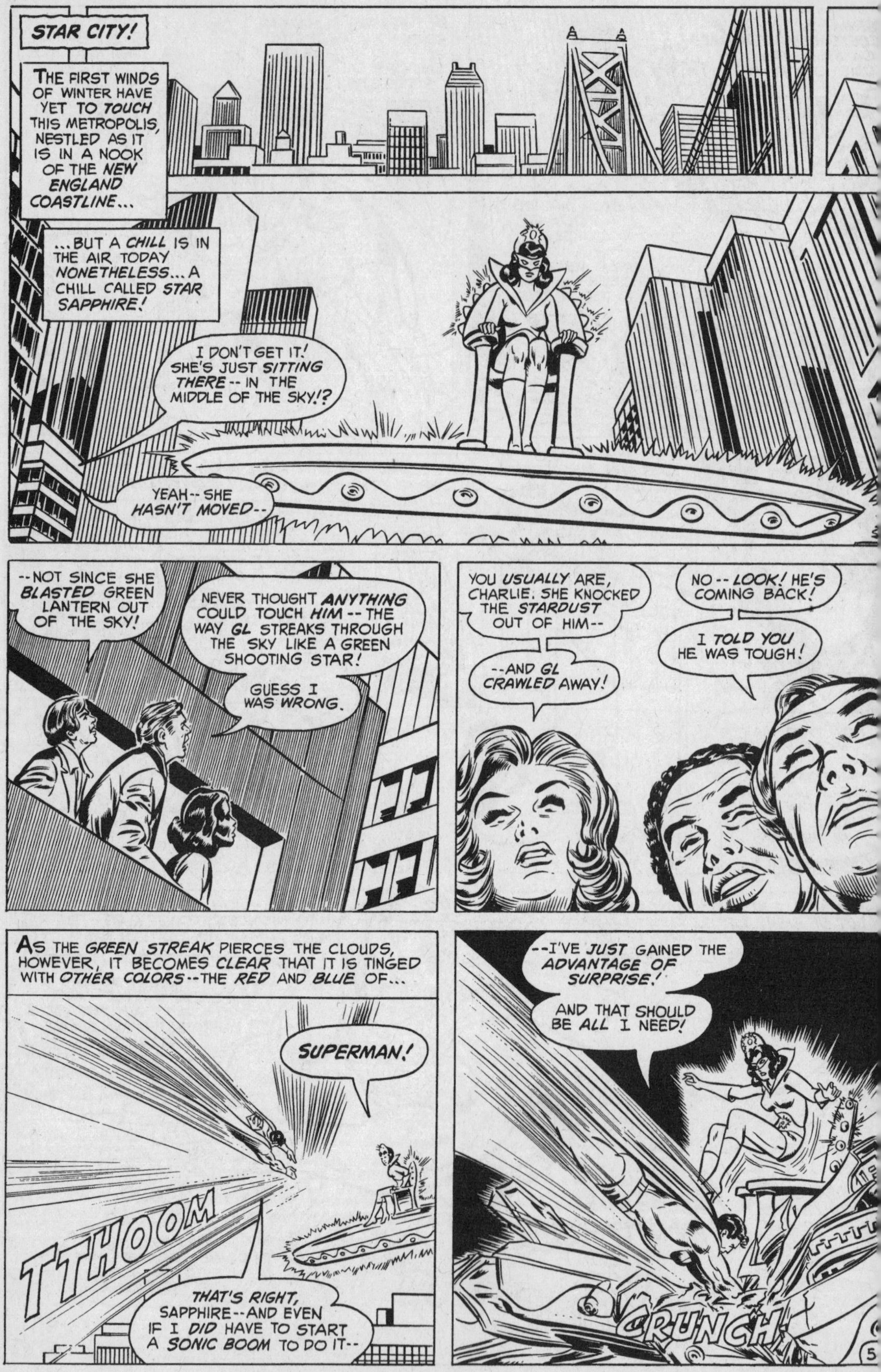
STAR CITY!
THE FIRST WINDS OF WINTER HAVE YET TO TOUCH THIS METROPOLIS, NESTLED AS IT IS IN A NOOK OF THE NEW ENGLAND COASTLINE...
...BUT A CHILL IS IN THE AIR TODAY NONETHELESS... A CHILL CALLED STAR SAPPHIRE!
I DON'T GET IT! SHE'S JUST SITTING THERE -- IN THE MIDDLE OF THE SKY!?
YEAH -- SHE HASN'T MOVED--
--NOT SINCE SHE BLASTED GREEN LANTERN OUT OF THE SKY!
NEVER THOUGHT ANYTHING COULD TOUCH HIM -- THE WAY GL STREAKS THROUGH THE SKY LIKE A GREEN SHOOTING STAR!
GUESS I WAS WRONG.
YOU USUALLY ARE, CHARLIE. SHE KNOCKED THE STARDUST OUT OF HIM--
--AND GL CRAWLED AWAY!
NO -- LOOK! HE'S COMING BACK!
I TOLD YOU HE WAS TOUGH!
AS THE GREEN STREAK PIERCES THE CLOUDS, HOWEVER, IT BECOMES CLEAR THAT IT IS TINGED WITH OTHER COLORS -- THE RED AND BLUE OF...
SUPERMAN!
TTHOOM
THAT'S RIGHT, SAPPHIRE -- AND EVEN IF I DID HAVE TO START A SONIC BOOM TO DO IT--
--I'VE JUST GAINED THE ADVANTAGE OF SURPRISE!
AND THAT SHOULD BE ALL I NEED!
CRUNCH!
5

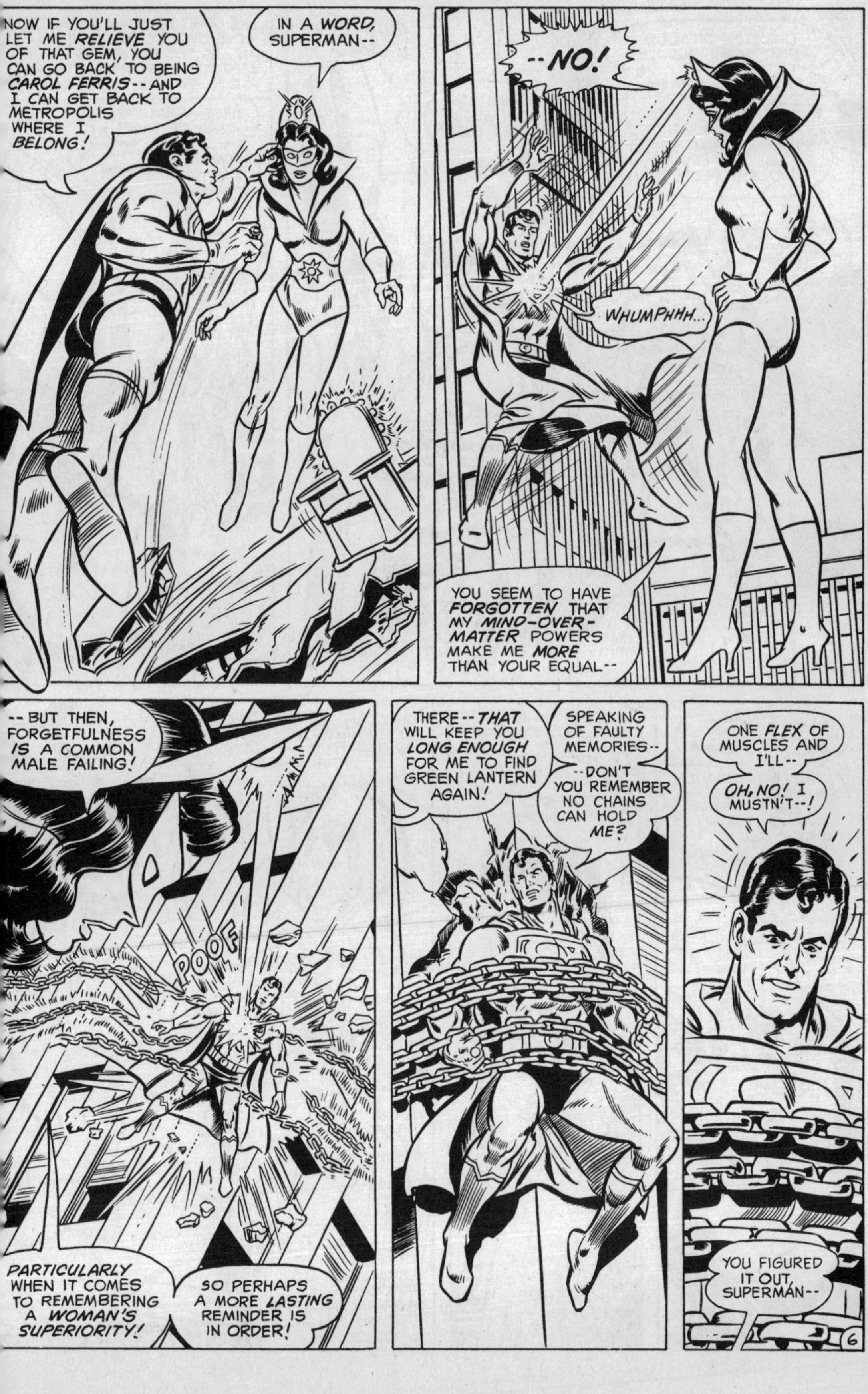
NOW IF YOU'LL JUST LET ME RELIEVE YOU OF THAT GEM, YOU CAN GO BACK TO BEING CAROL FERRIS--AND I CAN GET BACK TO METROPOLIS WHERE I BELONG!
IN A WORD, SUPERMAN--
--NO!
WHUMPHHH...
YOU SEEM TO HAVE FORGOTTEN THAT MY MIND-OVER-MATTER POWERS MAKE ME MORE THAN YOUR EQUAL--
--BUT THEN, FORGETFULNESS IS A COMMON MALE FAILING!
POOF
PARTICULARLY WHEN IT COMES TO REMEMBERING A WOMAN'S SUPERIORITY!
SO PERHAPS A MORE LASTING REMINDER IS IN ORDER!
THERE--THAT WILL KEEP YOU LONG ENOUGH FOR ME TO FIND GREEN LANTERN AGAIN!
SPEAKING OF FAULTY MEMORIES--
--DON'T YOU REMEMBER NO CHAINS CAN HOLD ME?
ONE FLEX OF MUSCLES AND I'LL--
OH, NO! I MUSTN'T--!
YOU FIGURED IT OUT, SUPERMAN--
6

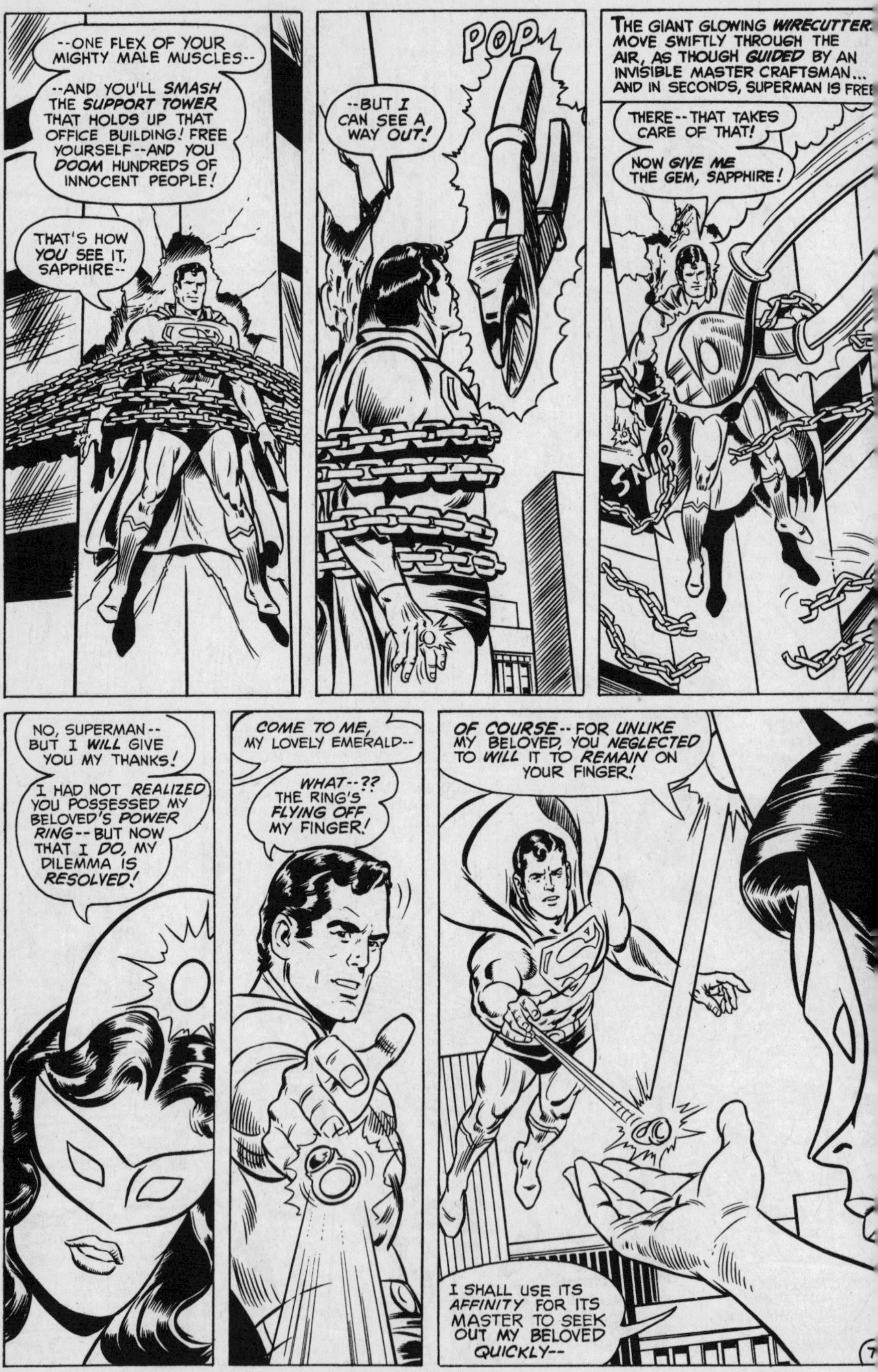
--ONE FLEX OF YOUR MIGHTY MALE MUSCLES--
--AND YOU'LL SMASH THE SUPPORT TOWER THAT HOLDS UP THAT OFFICE BUILDING! FREE YOURSELF--AND YOU DOOM HUNDREDS OF INNOCENT PEOPLE!
THAT'S HOW YOU SEE IT, SAPPHIRE--
POP
--BUT I CAN SEE A WAY OUT!
THE GIANT GLOWING WIRECUTTERS MOVE SWIFTLY THROUGH THE AIR, AS THOUGH GUIDED BY AN INVISIBLE MASTER CRAFTSMAN... AND IN SECONDS, SUPERMAN IS FREE
THERE--THAT TAKES CARE OF THAT!
NOW GIVE ME THE GEM, SAPPHIRE!
SNIP
NO, SUPERMAN-- BUT I WILL GIVE YOU MY THANKS!
I HAD NOT REALIZED YOU POSSESSED MY BELOVED'S POWER RING--BUT NOW THAT I DO, MY DILEMMA IS RESOLVED!
COME TO ME, MY LOVELY EMERALD--
WHAT--?? THE RING'S FLYING OFF MY FINGER!
OF COURSE--FOR UNLIKE MY BELOVED, YOU NEGLECTED TO WILL IT TO REMAIN ON YOUR FINGER!
I SHALL USE ITS AFFINITY FOR ITS MASTER TO SEEK OUT MY BELOVED QUICKLY--

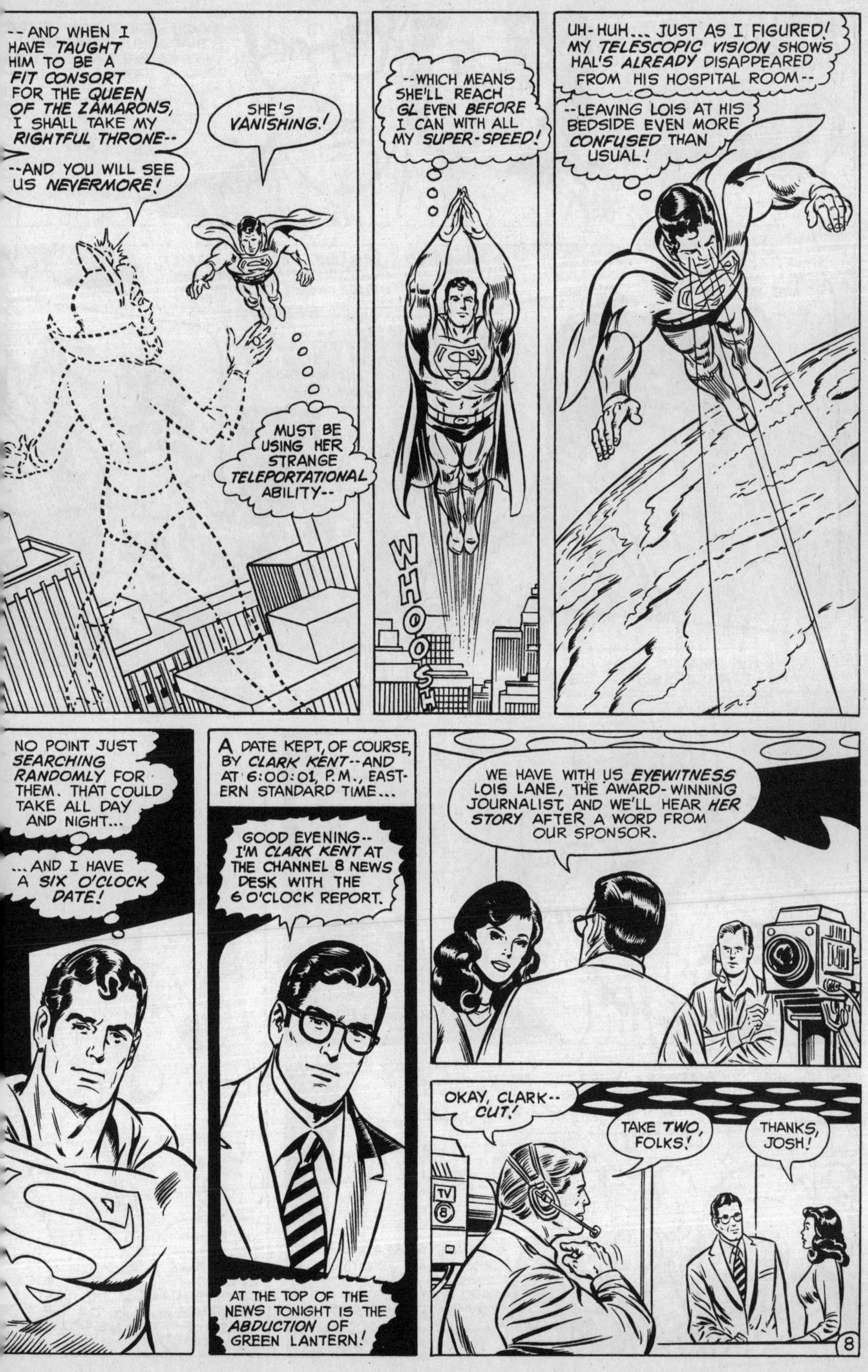
--AND WHEN I HAVE TAUGHT HIM TO BE A FIT CONSORT FOR THE QUEEN OF THE ZAMARONS, I SHALL TAKE MY RIGHTFUL THRONE--
--AND YOU WILL SEE US NEVERMORE!
SHE'S VANISHING!
MUST BE USING HER STRANGE TELEPORTATIONAL ABILITY--
--WHICH MEANS SHE'LL REACH GL EVEN BEFORE I CAN WITH ALL MY SUPER-SPEED!
WHOOSH
UH-HUH... JUST AS I FIGURED! MY TELESCOPIC VISION SHOWS HAL'S ALREADY DISAPPEARED FROM HIS HOSPITAL ROOM--
--LEAVING LOIS AT HIS BEDSIDE EVEN MORE CONFUSED THAN USUAL!
NO POINT JUST SEARCHING RANDOMLY FOR THEM. THAT COULD TAKE ALL DAY AND NIGHT...
...AND I HAVE A SIX O'CLOCK DATE!
A DATE KEPT, OF COURSE, BY CLARK KENT--AND AT 6:00:01, P.M., EASTERN STANDARD TIME...
GOOD EVENING-- I'M CLARK KENT AT THE CHANNEL 8 NEWS DESK WITH THE 6 O'CLOCK REPORT.
AT THE TOP OF THE NEWS TONIGHT IS THE ABDUCTION OF GREEN LANTERN!
WE HAVE WITH US EYEWITNESS LOIS LANE, THE AWARD-WINNING JOURNALIST, AND WE'LL HEAR HER STORY AFTER A WORD FROM OUR SPONSOR.
OKAY, CLARK-- CUT!
TAKE TWO, FOLKS!
THANKS, JOSH!
TV 8
8

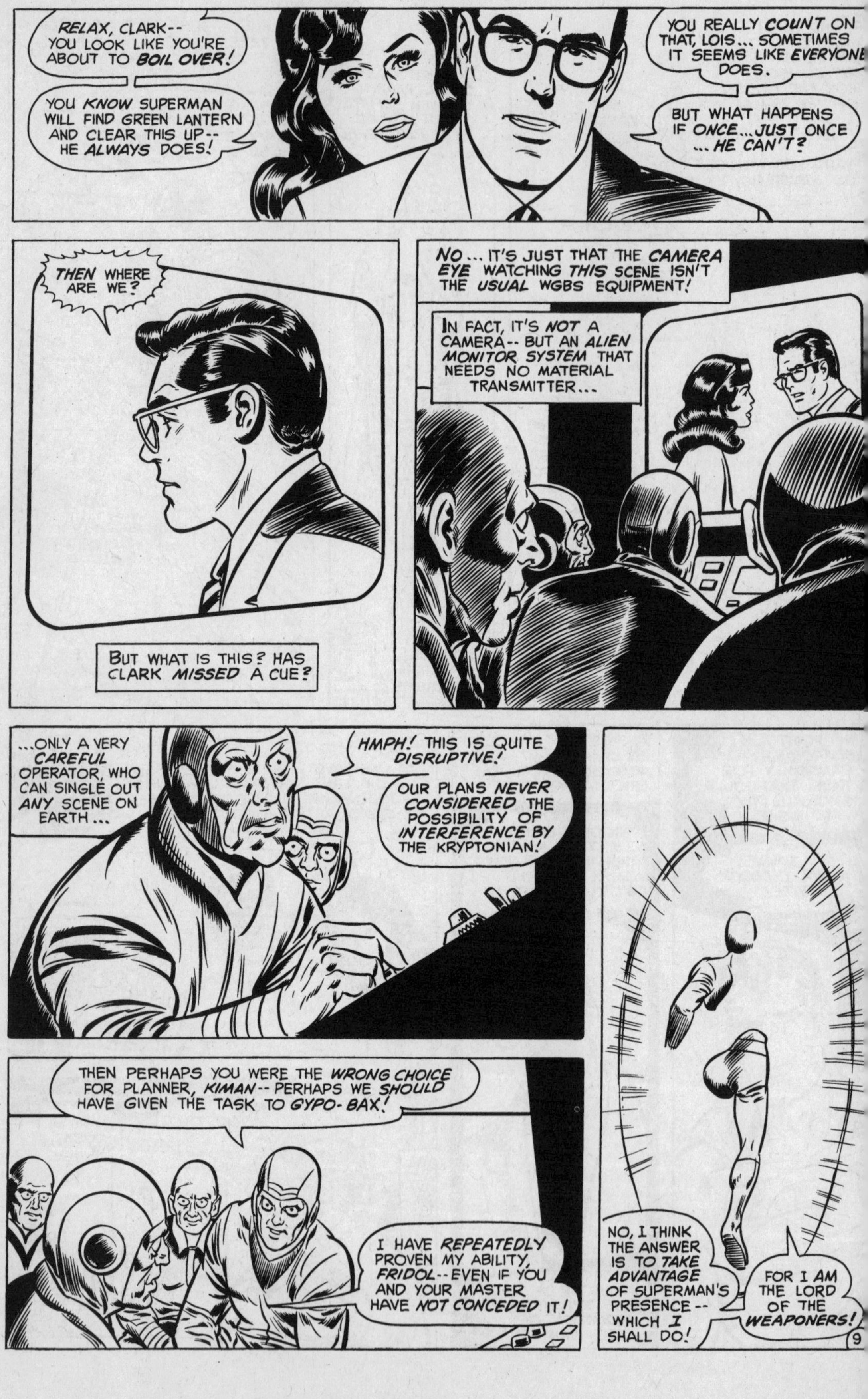
RELAX, CLARK-- YOU LOOK LIKE YOU'RE ABOUT TO BOIL OVER!
YOU KNOW SUPERMAN WILL FIND GREEN LANTERN AND CLEAR THIS UP-- HE ALWAYS DOES!
YOU REALLY COUNT ON THAT, LOIS... SOMETIMES IT SEEMS LIKE EVERYONE DOES.
BUT WHAT HAPPENS IF ONCE... JUST ONCE ... HE CAN'T?
THEN WHERE ARE WE?
BUT WHAT IS THIS? HAS CLARK MISSED A CUE?
NO... IT'S JUST THAT THE CAMERA EYE WATCHING THIS SCENE ISN'T THE USUAL WGBS EQUIPMENT!
IN FACT, IT'S NOT A CAMERA-- BUT AN ALIEN MONITOR SYSTEM THAT NEEDS NO MATERIAL TRANSMITTER...
...ONLY A VERY CAREFUL OPERATOR, WHO CAN SINGLE OUT ANY SCENE ON EARTH...
HMPH! THIS IS QUITE DISRUPTIVE!
OUR PLANS NEVER CONSIDERED THE POSSIBILITY OF INTERFERENCE BY THE KRYPTONIAN!
THEN PERHAPS YOU WERE THE WRONG CHOICE FOR PLANNER, KIMAN-- PERHAPS WE SHOULD HAVE GIVEN THE TASK TO GYPO-BAX!
I HAVE REPEATEDLY PROVEN MY ABILITY, FRIDOL-- EVEN IF YOU AND YOUR MASTER HAVE NOT CONCEDED IT!
NO, I THINK THE ANSWER IS TO TAKE ADVANTAGE OF SUPERMAN'S PRESENCE -- WHICH I SHALL DO!
FOR I AM THE LORD OF THE WEAPONERS!
9

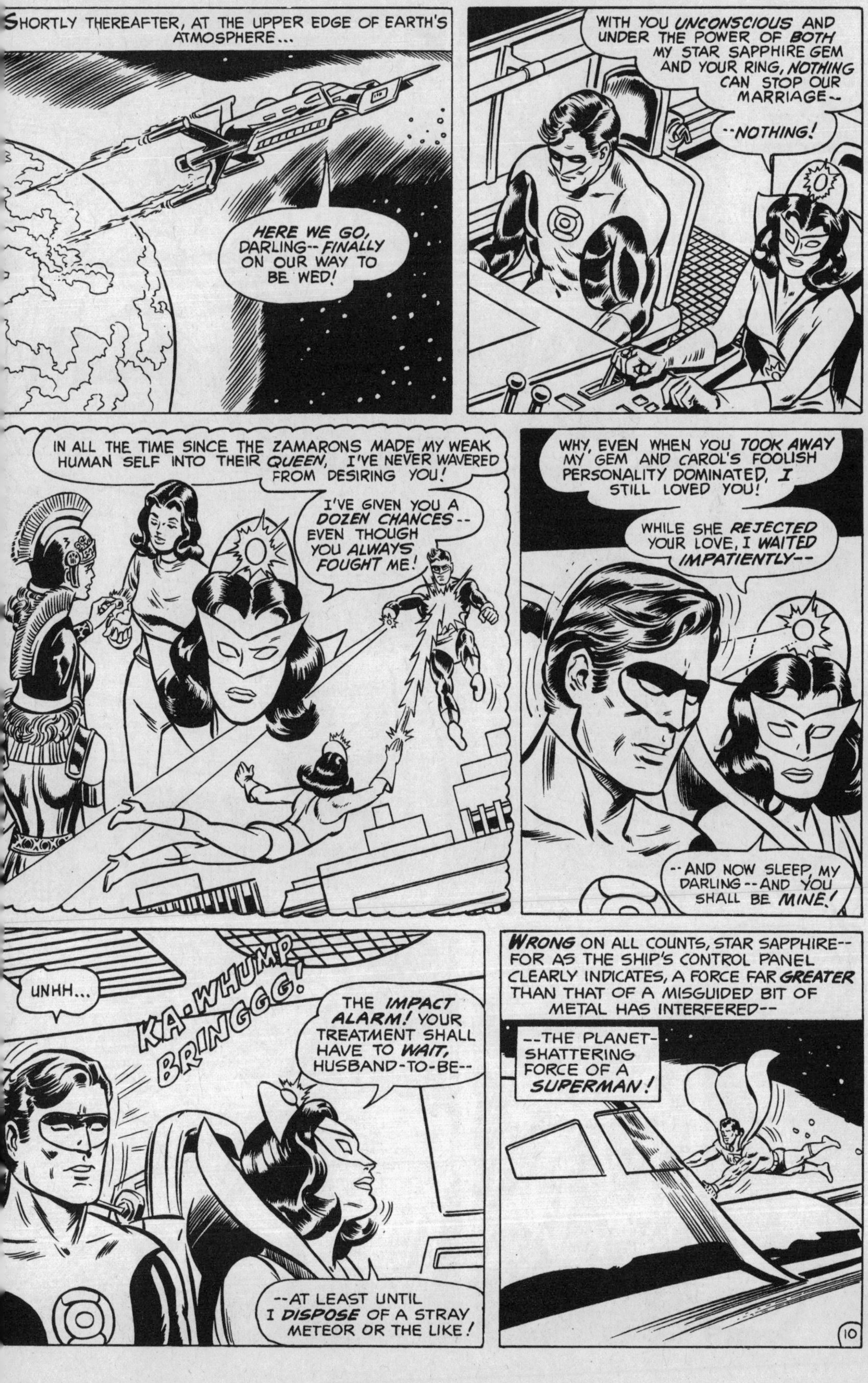
SHORTLY THEREAFTER, AT THE UPPER EDGE OF EARTH'S ATMOSPHERE...
HERE WE GO, DARLING-- FINALLY ON OUR WAY TO BE WED!
WITH YOU UNCONSCIOUS AND UNDER THE POWER OF BOTH MY STAR SAPPHIRE GEM AND YOUR RING, NOTHING CAN STOP OUR MARRIAGE--
--NOTHING!
IN ALL THE TIME SINCE THE ZAMARONS MADE MY WEAK HUMAN SELF INTO THEIR QUEEN, I'VE NEVER WAVERED FROM DESIRING YOU!
I'VE GIVEN YOU A DOZEN CHANCES -- EVEN THOUGH YOU ALWAYS FOUGHT ME!
WHY, EVEN WHEN YOU TOOK AWAY MY GEM AND CAROL'S FOOLISH PERSONALITY DOMINATED, I STILL LOVED YOU!
WHILE SHE REJECTED YOUR LOVE, I WAITED IMPATIENTLY--
--AND NOW SLEEP, MY DARLING --AND YOU SHALL BE MINE!
UNHH...
KA-WHUMP BRINGGG!
THE IMPACT ALARM! YOUR TREATMENT SHALL HAVE TO WAIT, HUSBAND-TO-BE--
--AT LEAST UNTIL I DISPOSE OF A STRAY METEOR OR THE LIKE!
WRONG ON ALL COUNTS, STAR SAPPHIRE-- FOR AS THE SHIP'S CONTROL PANEL CLEARLY INDICATES, A FORCE FAR GREATER THAN THAT OF A MISGUIDED BIT OF METAL HAS INTERFERED--
--THE PLANET-SHATTERING FORCE OF A SUPERMAN!
10

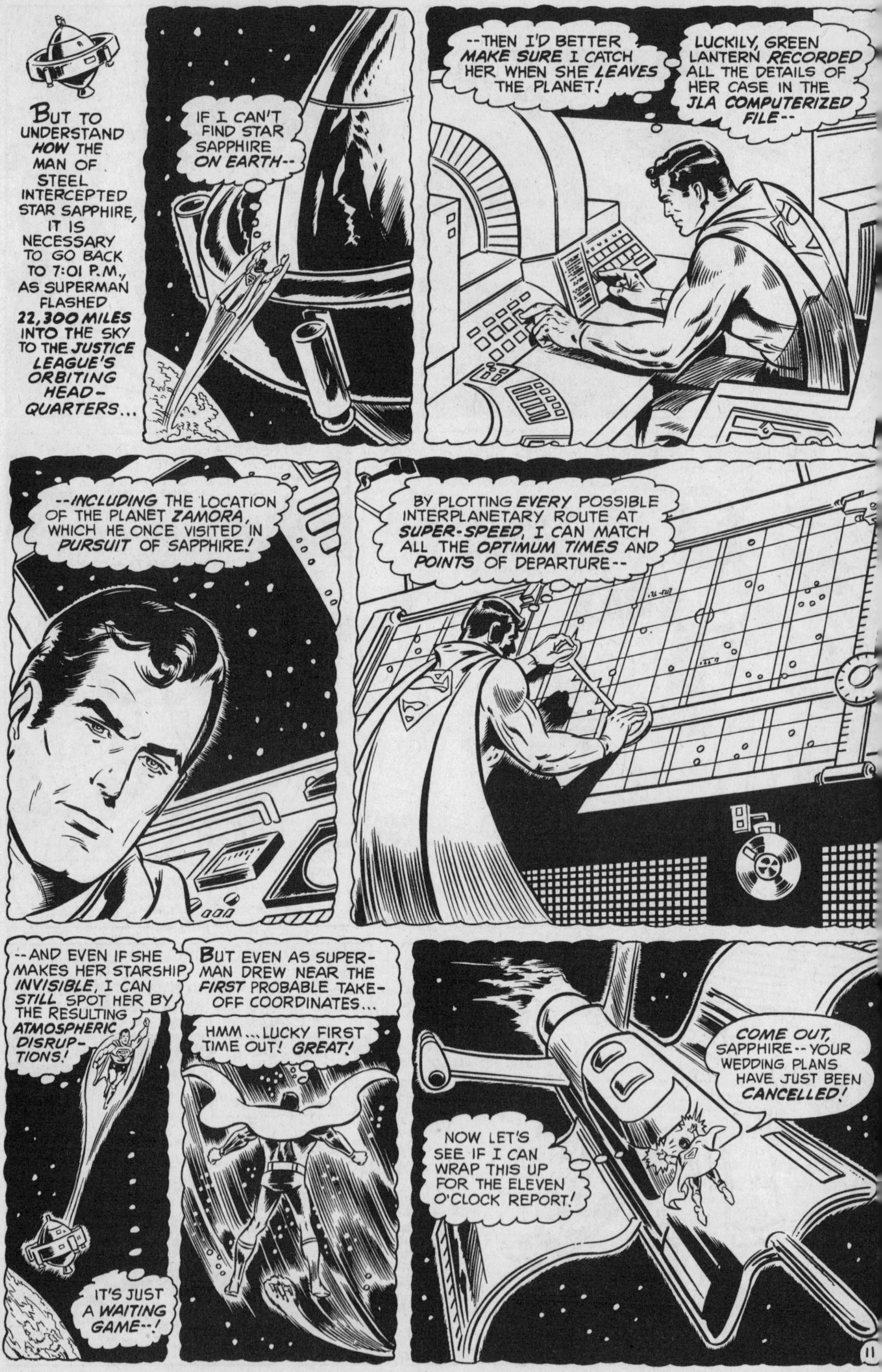
BUT TO UNDERSTAND HOW THE MAN OF STEEL INTERCEPTED STAR SAPPHIRE, IT IS NECESSARY TO GO BACK TO 7:01 P.M., AS SUPERMAN FLASHED 22,300 MILES INTO THE SKY TO THE JUSTICE LEAGUE'S ORBITING HEAD-QUARTERS...
IF I CAN'T FIND STAR SAPPHIRE ON EARTH--
--THEN I'D BETTER MAKE SURE I CATCH HER WHEN SHE LEAVES THE PLANET!
LUCKILY, GREEN LANTERN RECORDED ALL THE DETAILS OF HER CASE IN THE JLA COMPUTERIZED FILE--
--INCLUDING THE LOCATION OF THE PLANET ZAMORA, WHICH HE ONCE VISITED IN PURSUIT OF SAPPHIRE!
BY PLOTTING EVERY POSSIBLE INTERPLANETARY ROUTE AT SUPER-SPEED, I CAN MATCH ALL THE OPTIMUM TIMES AND POINTS OF DEPARTURE--
--AND EVEN IF SHE MAKES HER STARSHIP INVISIBLE, I CAN STILL SPOT HER BY THE RESULTING ATMOSPHERIC DISRUP-TIONS!
IT'S JUST A WAITING GAME--!
BUT EVEN AS SUPER-MAN DREW NEAR THE FIRST PROBABLE TAKE-OFF COORDINATES...
HMM...LUCKY FIRST TIME OUT! GREAT!
COME OUT, SAPPHIRE--YOUR WEDDING PLANS HAVE JUST BEEN CANCELLED!
NOW LET'S SEE IF I CAN WRAP THIS UP FOR THE ELEVEN O'CLOCK REPORT!
11

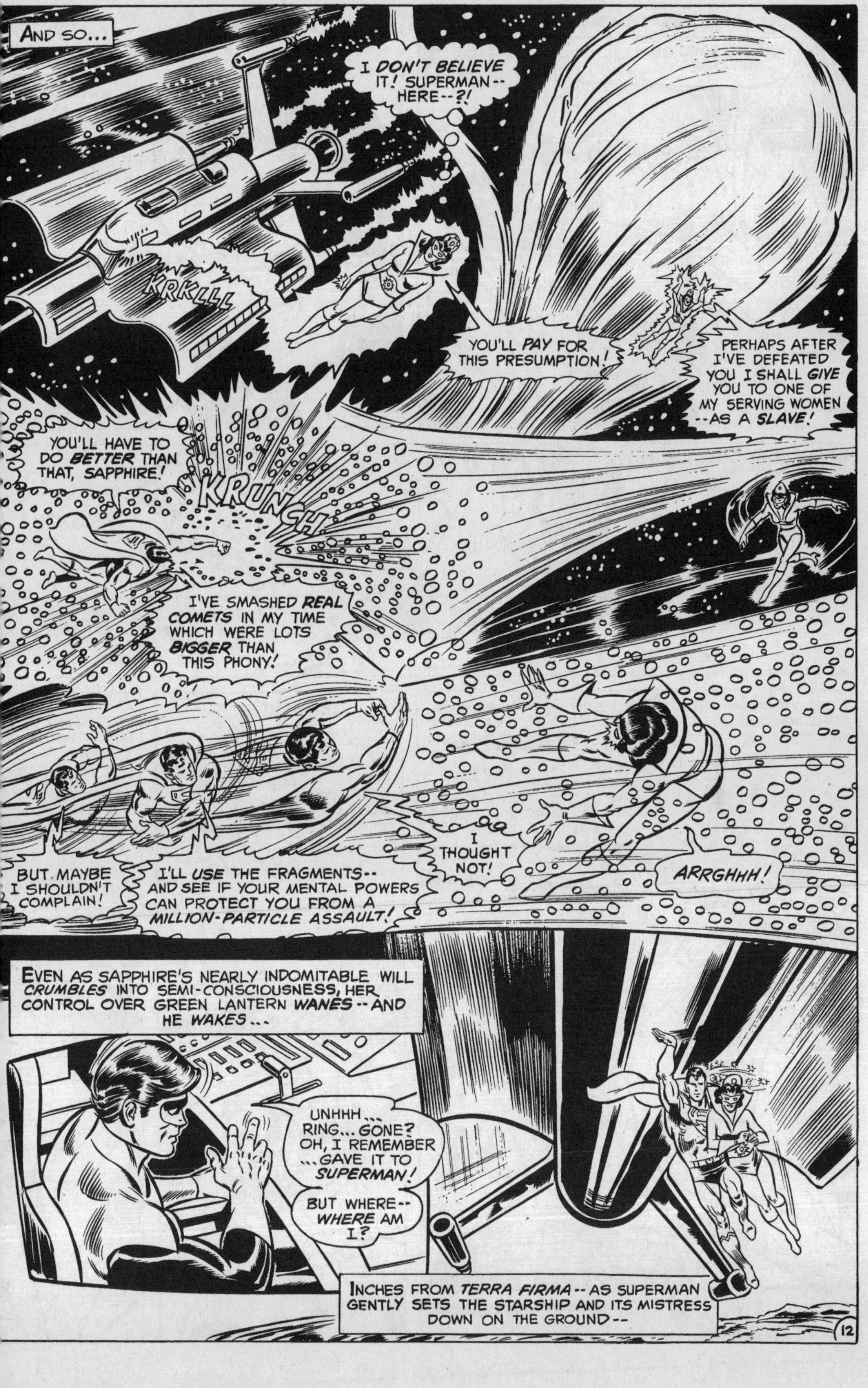
AND SO...
I DON'T BELIEVE IT! SUPERMAN--HERE--?!
KRKLLL
YOU'LL PAY FOR THIS PRESUMPTION!
PERHAPS AFTER I'VE DEFEATED YOU I SHALL GIVE YOU TO ONE OF MY SERVING WOMEN --AS A SLAVE!
YOU'LL HAVE TO DO BETTER THAN THAT, SAPPHIRE!
KRUNCH
I'VE SMASHED REAL COMETS IN MY TIME WHICH WERE LOTS BIGGER THAN THIS PHONY!
BUT MAYBE I SHOULDN'T COMPLAIN!
I'LL USE THE FRAGMENTS--AND SEE IF YOUR MENTAL POWERS CAN PROTECT YOU FROM A MILLION-PARTICLE ASSAULT!
I THOUGHT NOT!
ARRGHHH!
EVEN AS SAPPHIRE'S NEARLY INDOMITABLE WILL CRUMBLES INTO SEMI-CONSCIOUSNESS, HER CONTROL OVER GREEN LANTERN WANES--AND HE WAKES...
UNHHH... RING... GONE? OH, I REMEMBER ...GAVE IT TO SUPERMAN!
BUT WHERE--WHERE AM I?
INCHES FROM TERRA FIRMA--AS SUPERMAN GENTLY SETS THE STARSHIP AND ITS MISTRESS DOWN ON THE GROUND--
12

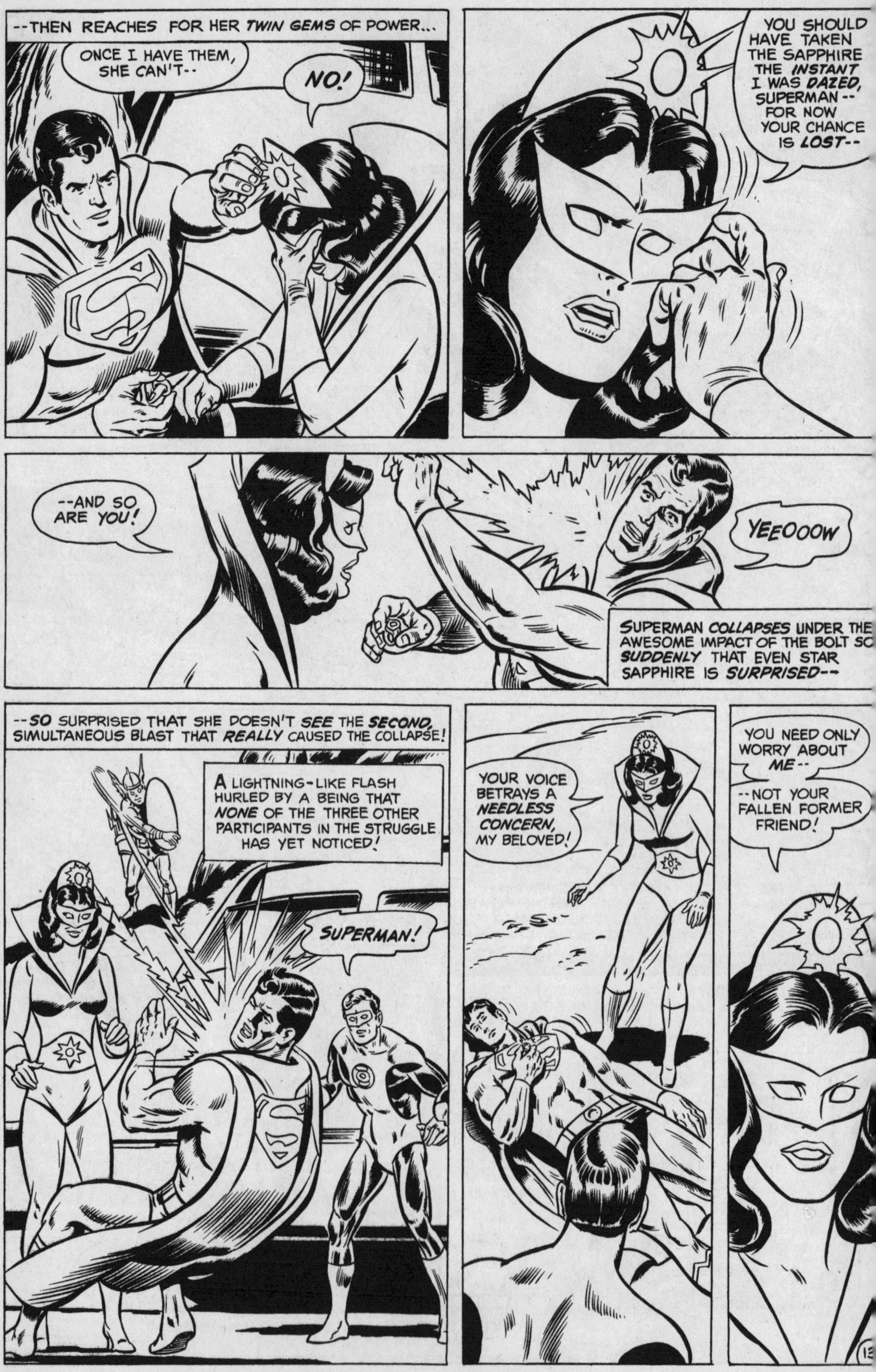
--THEN REACHES FOR HER TWIN GEMS OF POWER...
ONCE I HAVE THEM, SHE CAN'T--
NO!
YOU SHOULD HAVE TAKEN THE SAPPHIRE THE INSTANT I WAS DAZED, SUPERMAN -- FOR NOW YOUR CHANCE IS LOST--
--AND SO ARE YOU!
YEEOOOW
SUPERMAN COLLAPSES UNDER THE AWESOME IMPACT OF THE BOLT SO SUDDENLY THAT EVEN STAR SAPPHIRE IS SURPRISED--
--SO SURPRISED THAT SHE DOESN'T SEE THE SECOND, SIMULTANEOUS BLAST THAT REALLY CAUSED THE COLLAPSE!
A LIGHTNING-LIKE FLASH HURLED BY A BEING THAT NONE OF THE THREE OTHER PARTICIPANTS IN THE STRUGGLE HAS YET NOTICED!
SUPERMAN!
YOUR VOICE BETRAYS A NEEDLESS CONCERN, MY BELOVED!
YOU NEED ONLY WORRY ABOUT ME--
--NOT YOUR FALLEN FORMER FRIEND!

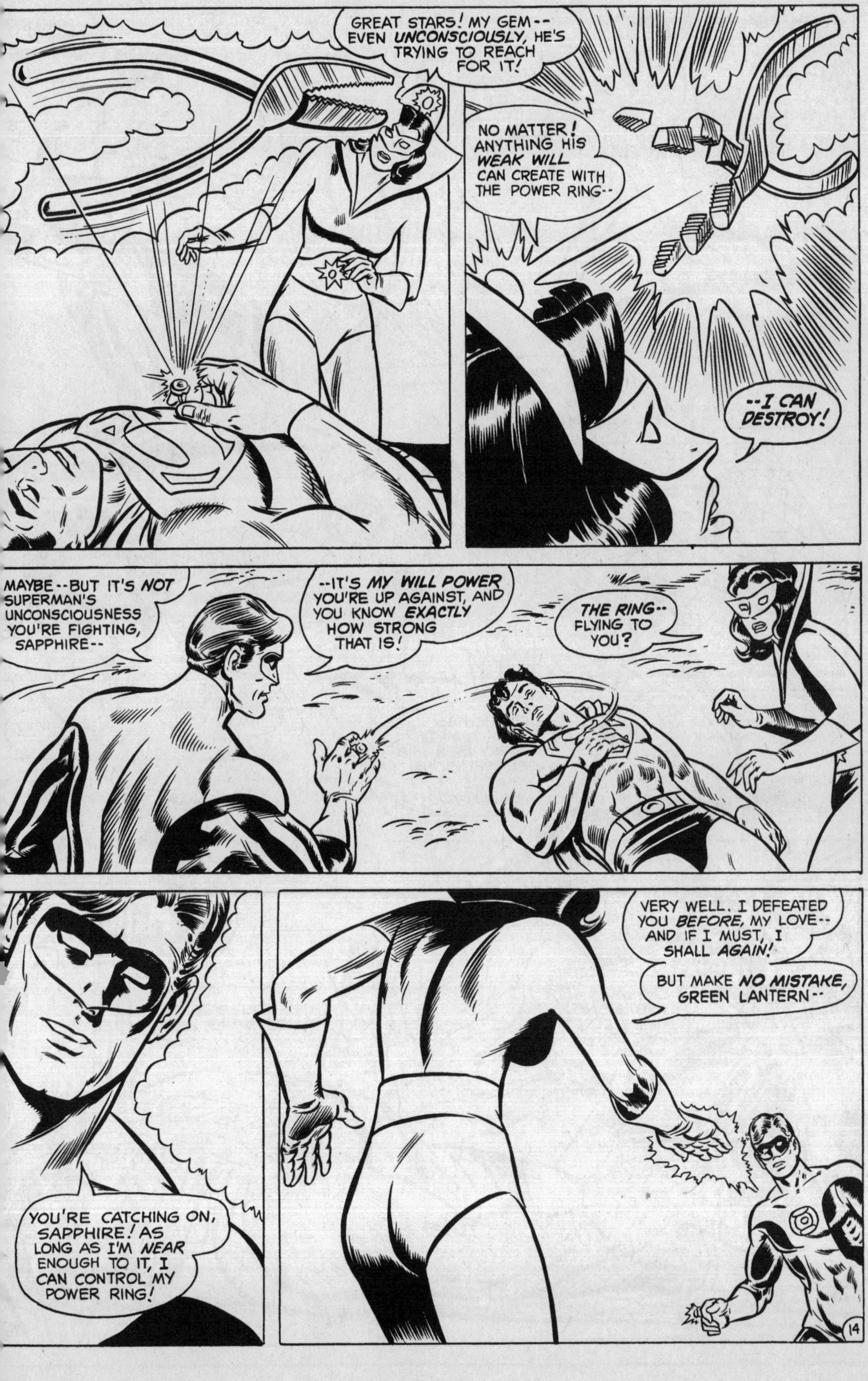
GREAT STARS! MY GEM-- EVEN UNCONSCIOUSLY, HE'S TRYING TO REACH FOR IT!
NO MATTER! ANYTHING HIS WEAK WILL CAN CREATE WITH THE POWER RING--
--I CAN DESTROY!
MAYBE--BUT IT'S NOT SUPERMAN'S UNCONSCIOUSNESS YOU'RE FIGHTING, SAPPHIRE--
--IT'S MY WILL POWER YOU'RE UP AGAINST, AND YOU KNOW EXACTLY HOW STRONG THAT IS!
THE RING-- FLYING TO YOU?
YOU'RE CATCHING ON, SAPPHIRE! AS LONG AS I'M NEAR ENOUGH TO IT, I CAN CONTROL MY POWER RING!
VERY WELL. I DEFEATED YOU BEFORE, MY LOVE-- AND IF I MUST, I SHALL AGAIN!
BUT MAKE NO MISTAKE, GREEN LANTERN--
14

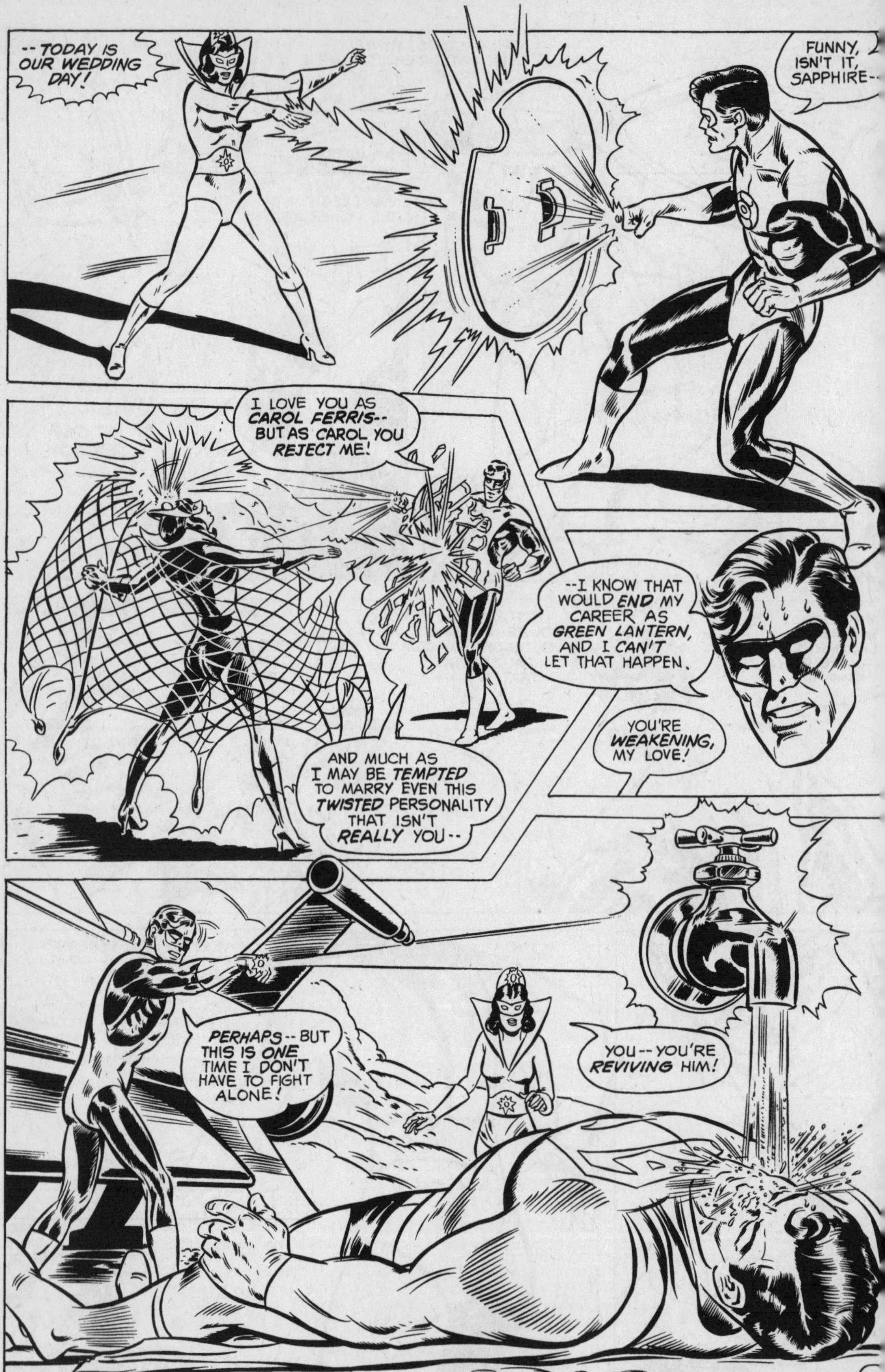
--TODAY IS OUR WEDDING DAY!
FUNNY, ISN'T IT, SAPPHIRE--
I LOVE YOU AS CAROL FERRIS-- BUT AS CAROL YOU REJECT ME!
AND MUCH AS I MAY BE TEMPTED TO MARRY EVEN THIS TWISTED PERSONALITY THAT ISN'T REALLY YOU--
--I KNOW THAT WOULD END MY CAREER AS GREEN LANTERN, AND I CAN'T LET THAT HAPPEN.
YOU'RE WEAKENING, MY LOVE!
PERHAPS--BUT THIS IS ONE TIME I DON'T HAVE TO FIGHT ALONE!
YOU--YOU'RE REVIVING HIM!
15

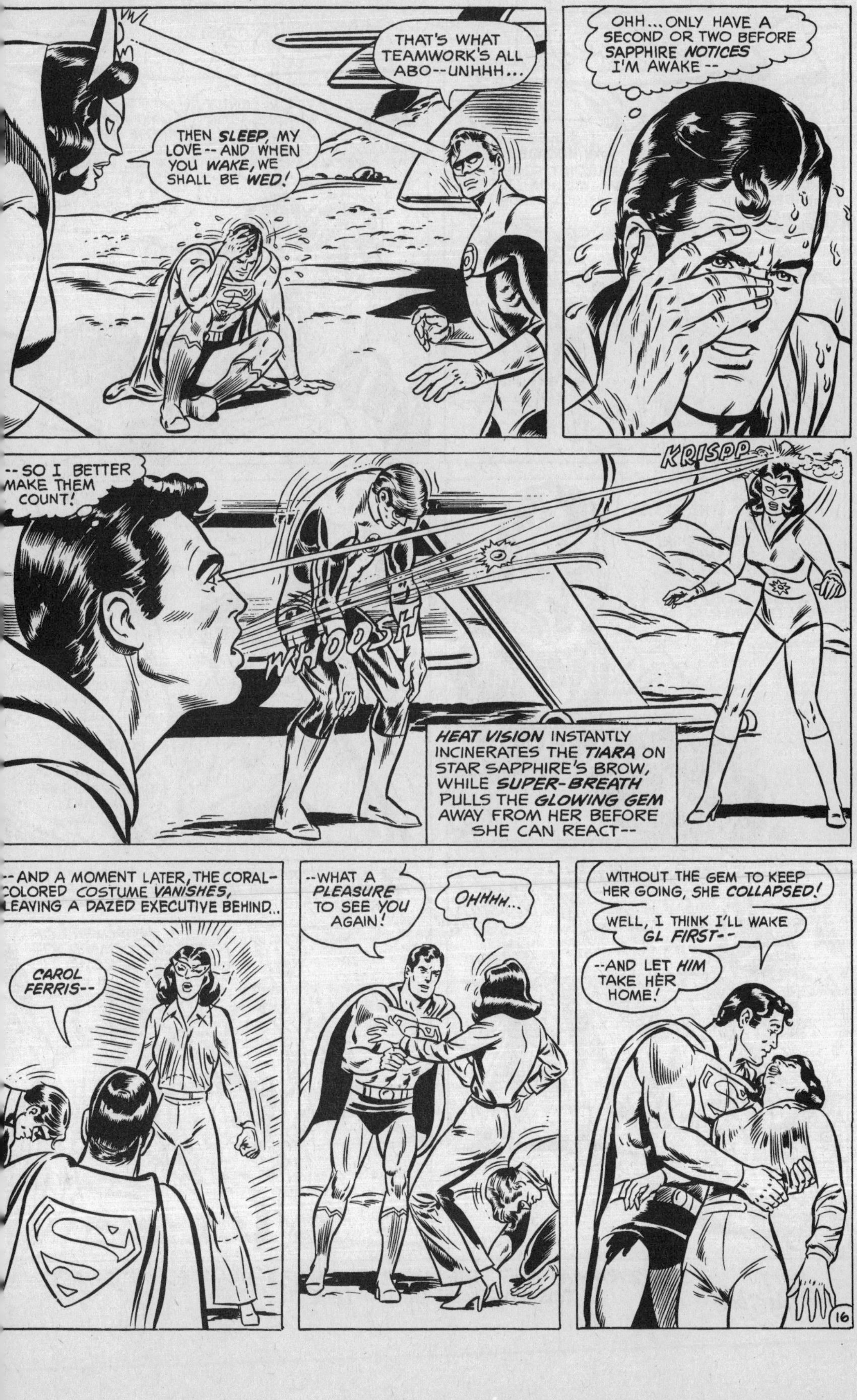
THAT'S WHAT TEAMWORK'S ALL ABO--UNHHH...
THEN SLEEP, MY LOVE--AND WHEN YOU WAKE, WE SHALL BE WED!
OHH...ONLY HAVE A SECOND OR TWO BEFORE SAPPHIRE NOTICES I'M AWAKE --
--SO I BETTER MAKE THEM COUNT!
KRISPP
WHOOOSH
HEAT VISION INSTANTLY INCINERATES THE TIARA ON STAR SAPPHIRE'S BROW, WHILE SUPER-BREATH PULLS THE GLOWING GEM AWAY FROM HER BEFORE SHE CAN REACT--
--AND A MOMENT LATER, THE CORAL-COLORED COSTUME VANISHES, LEAVING A DAZED EXECUTIVE BEHIND...
CAROL FERRIS--
--WHAT A PLEASURE TO SEE YOU AGAIN!
OHHHH...
WITHOUT THE GEM TO KEEP HER GOING, SHE COLLAPSED!
WELL, I THINK I'LL WAKE GL FIRST--
--AND LET HIM TAKE HER HOME!
16

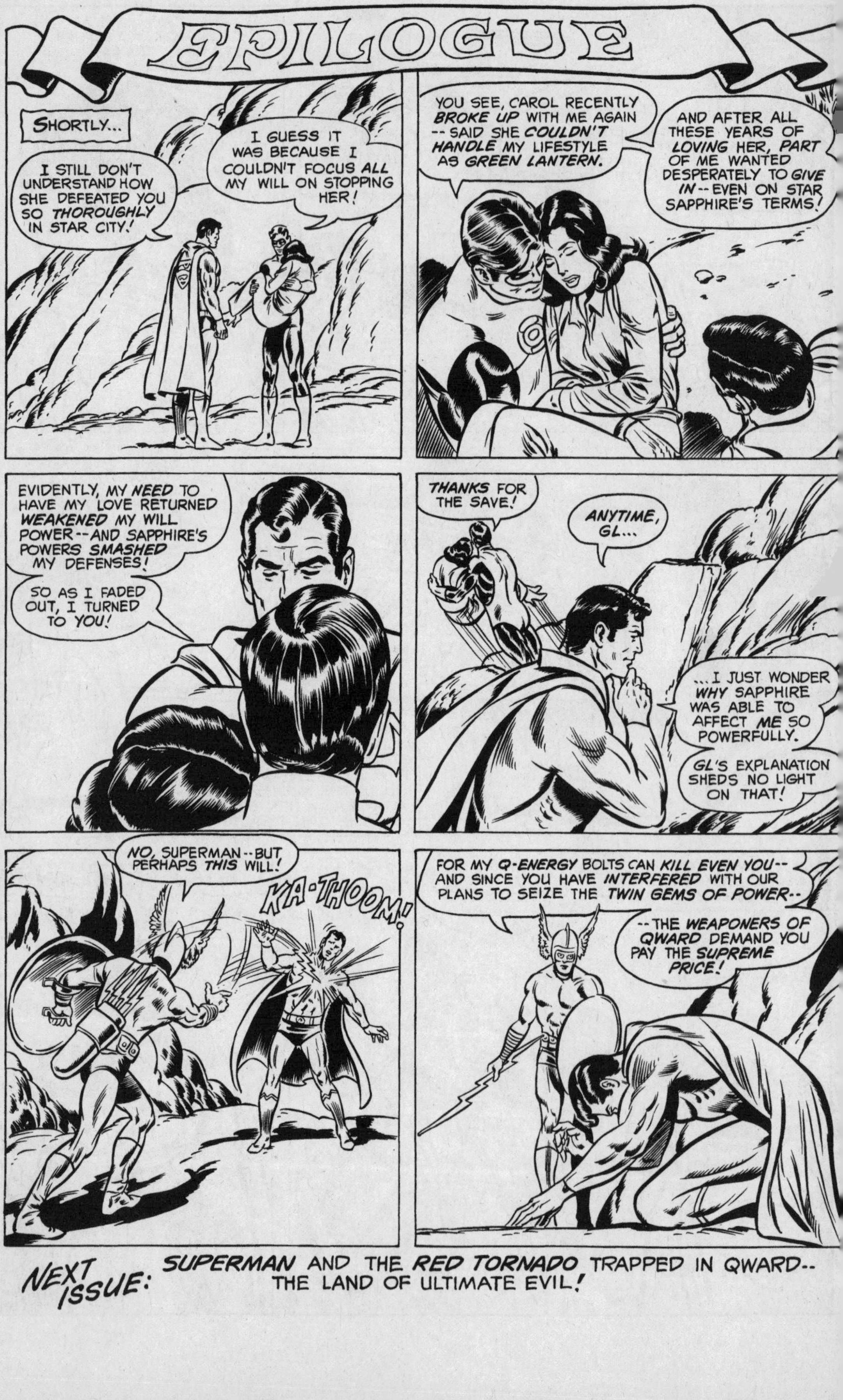
EPILOGUE
SHORTLY...
I STILL DON'T UNDERSTAND HOW SHE DEFEATED YOU SO THOROUGHLY IN STAR CITY!
I GUESS IT WAS BECAUSE I COULDN'T FOCUS ALL MY WILL ON STOPPING HER!
YOU SEE, CAROL RECENTLY BROKE UP WITH ME AGAIN -- SAID SHE COULDN'T HANDLE MY LIFESTYLE AS GREEN LANTERN.
AND AFTER ALL THESE YEARS OF LOVING HER, PART OF ME WANTED DESPERATELY TO GIVE IN -- EVEN ON STAR SAPPHIRE'S TERMS!
EVIDENTLY, MY NEED TO HAVE MY LOVE RETURNED WEAKENED MY WILL POWER -- AND SAPPHIRE'S POWERS SMASHED MY DEFENSES!
SO AS I FADED OUT, I TURNED TO YOU!
THANKS FOR THE SAVE!
ANYTIME, GL...
...I JUST WONDER WHY SAPPHIRE WAS ABLE TO AFFECT ME SO POWERFULLY.
GL'S EXPLANATION SHEDS NO LIGHT ON THAT!
NO, SUPERMAN -- BUT PERHAPS THIS WILL!
KA-THOOM!
FOR MY Q-ENERGY BOLTS CAN KILL EVEN YOU -- AND SINCE YOU HAVE INTERFERED WITH OUR PLANS TO SEIZE THE TWIN GEMS OF POWER --
-- THE WEAPONERS OF QWARD DEMAND YOU PAY THE SUPREME PRICE!
NEXT ISSUE: SUPERMAN AND THE RED TORNADO TRAPPED IN QWARD -- THE LAND OF ULTIMATE EVIL!

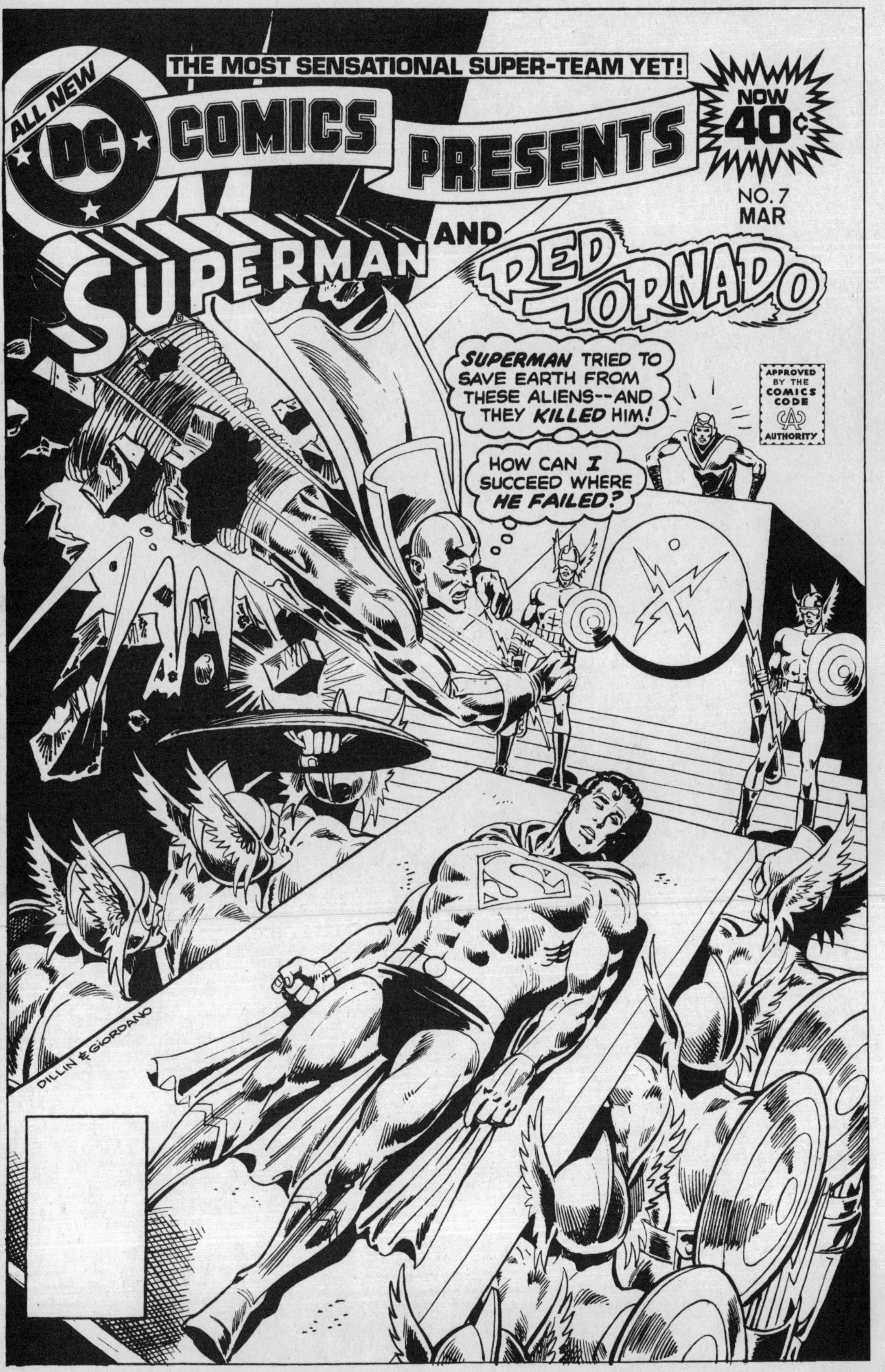
THE MOST SENSATIONAL SUPER-TEAM YET!
ALL NEW
DC
COMICS PRESENTS
NOW 40¢
NO. 7
MAR
SUPERMAN AND RED TORNADO
SUPERMAN TRIED TO SAVE EARTH FROM THESE ALIENS--AND THEY KILLED HIM!
HOW CAN I SUCCEED WHERE HE FAILED?
APPROVED BY THE COMICS CODE AUTHORITY
DILLIN & GIORDANO

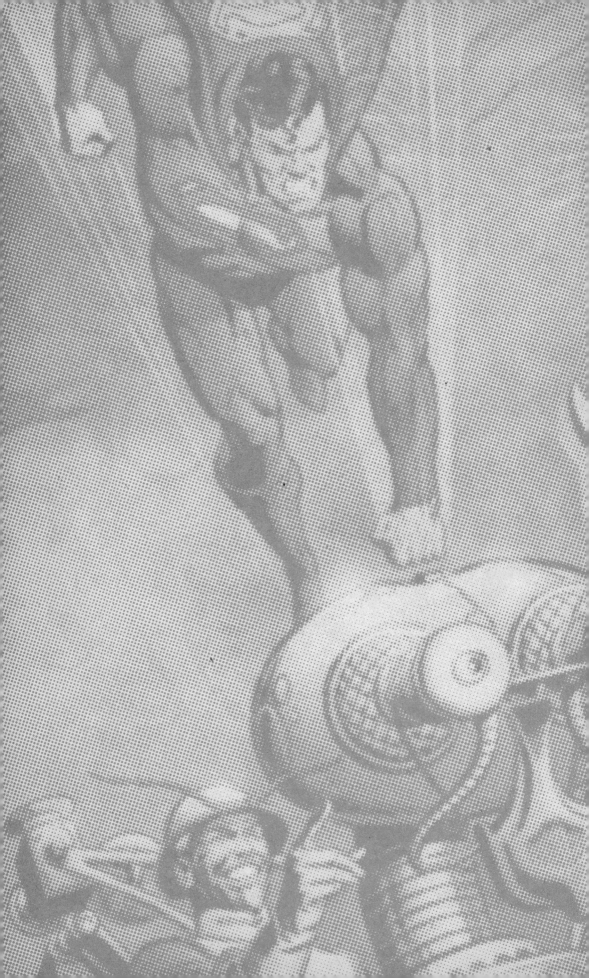

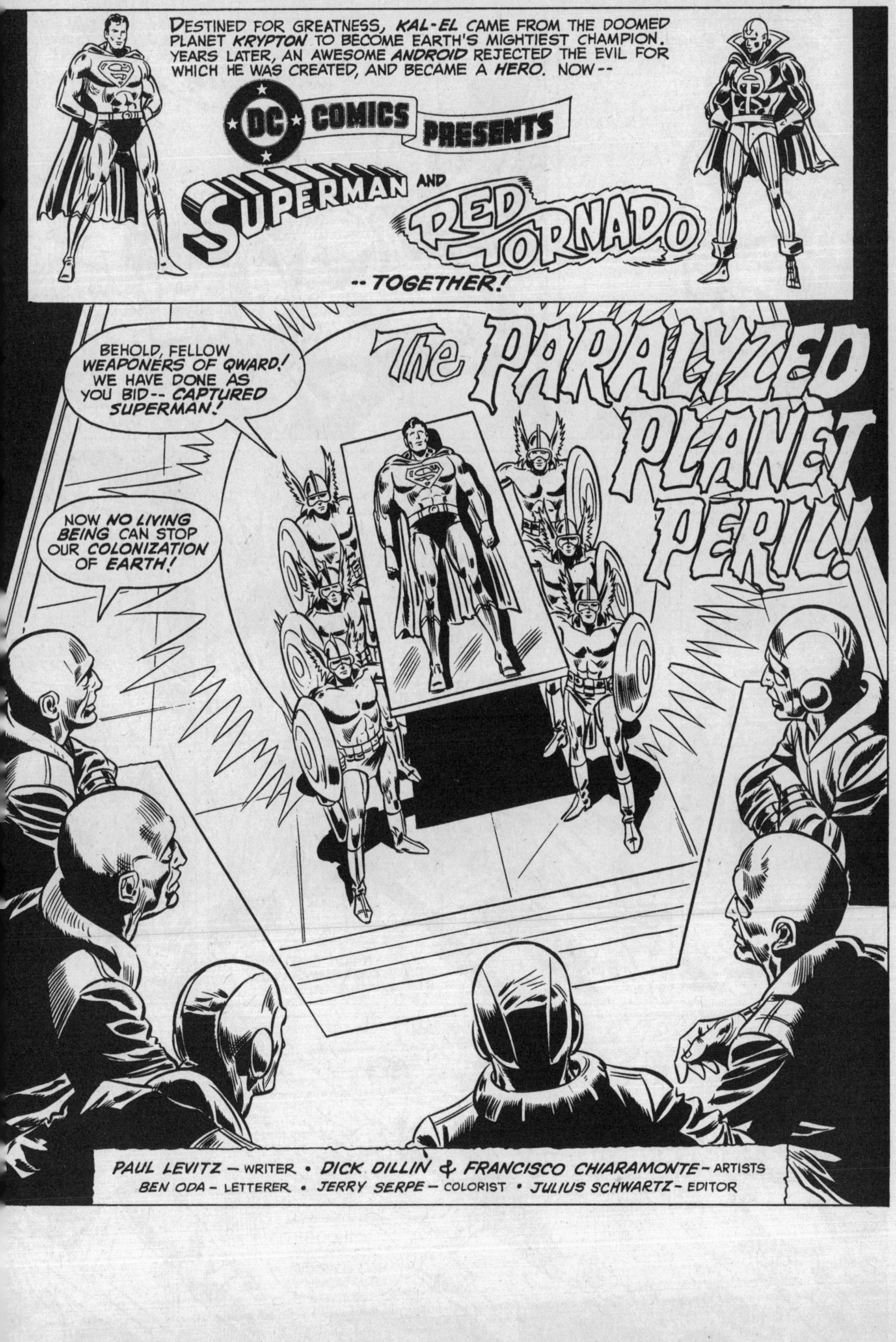
DESTINED FOR GREATNESS, KAL-EL CAME FROM THE DOOMED PLANET KRYPTON TO BECOME EARTH'S MIGHTIEST CHAMPION. YEARS LATER, AN AWESOME ANDROID REJECTED THE EVIL FOR WHICH HE WAS CREATED, AND BECAME A HERO. NOW--
DC COMICS PRESENTS
SUPERMAN AND RED TORNADO
--TOGETHER!
BEHOLD, FELLOW WEAPONERS OF QWARD! WE HAVE DONE AS YOU BID-- CAPTURED SUPERMAN!
NOW NO LIVING BEING CAN STOP OUR COLONIZATION OF EARTH!
The PARALYZED PLANET PERIL!
PAUL LEVITZ — WRITER • DICK DILLIN & FRANCISCO CHIARAMONTE - ARTISTS
BEN ODA - LETTERER • JERRY SERPE — COLORIST • JULIUS SCHWARTZ - EDITOR

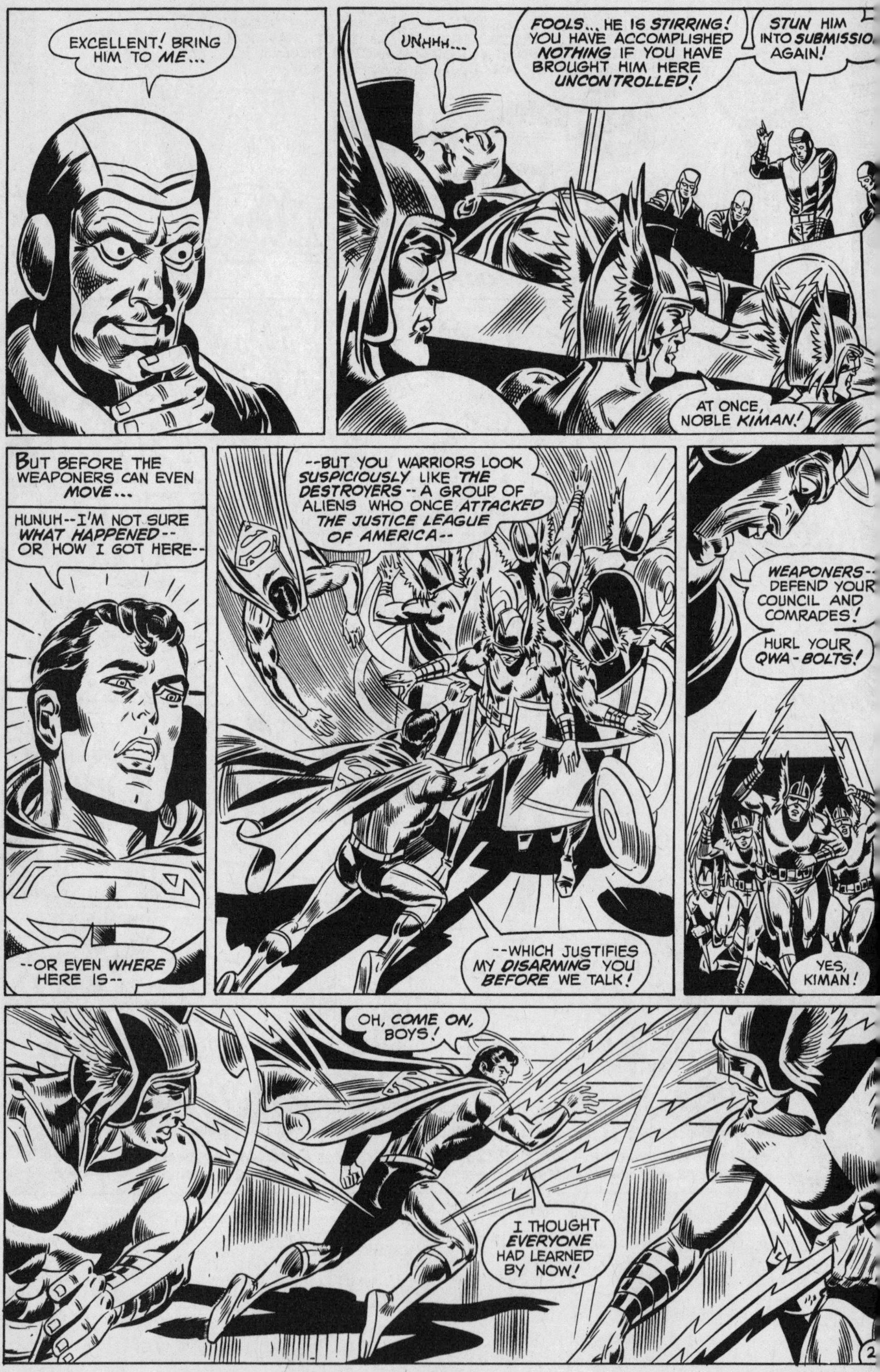
EXCELLENT! BRING HIM TO ME...
UNHHH...
FOOLS... HE IS STIRRING! YOU HAVE ACCOMPLISHED NOTHING IF YOU HAVE BROUGHT HIM HERE UNCONTROLLED!
STUN HIM INTO SUBMISSIO AGAIN!
AT ONCE, NOBLE KIMAN!
BUT BEFORE THE WEAPONERS CAN EVEN MOVE...
HUNUH--I'M NOT SURE WHAT HAPPENED--OR HOW I GOT HERE--
--OR EVEN WHERE HERE IS--
--BUT YOU WARRIORS LOOK SUSPICIOUSLY LIKE THE DESTROYERS--A GROUP OF ALIENS WHO ONCE ATTACKED THE JUSTICE LEAGUE OF AMERICA--
--WHICH JUSTIFIES MY DISARMING YOU BEFORE WE TALK!
WEAPONERS--DEFEND YOUR COUNCIL AND COMRADES!
HURL YOUR QWA-BOLTS!
YES, KIMAN!
OH, COME ON, BOYS!
I THOUGHT EVERYONE HAD LEARNED BY NOW!

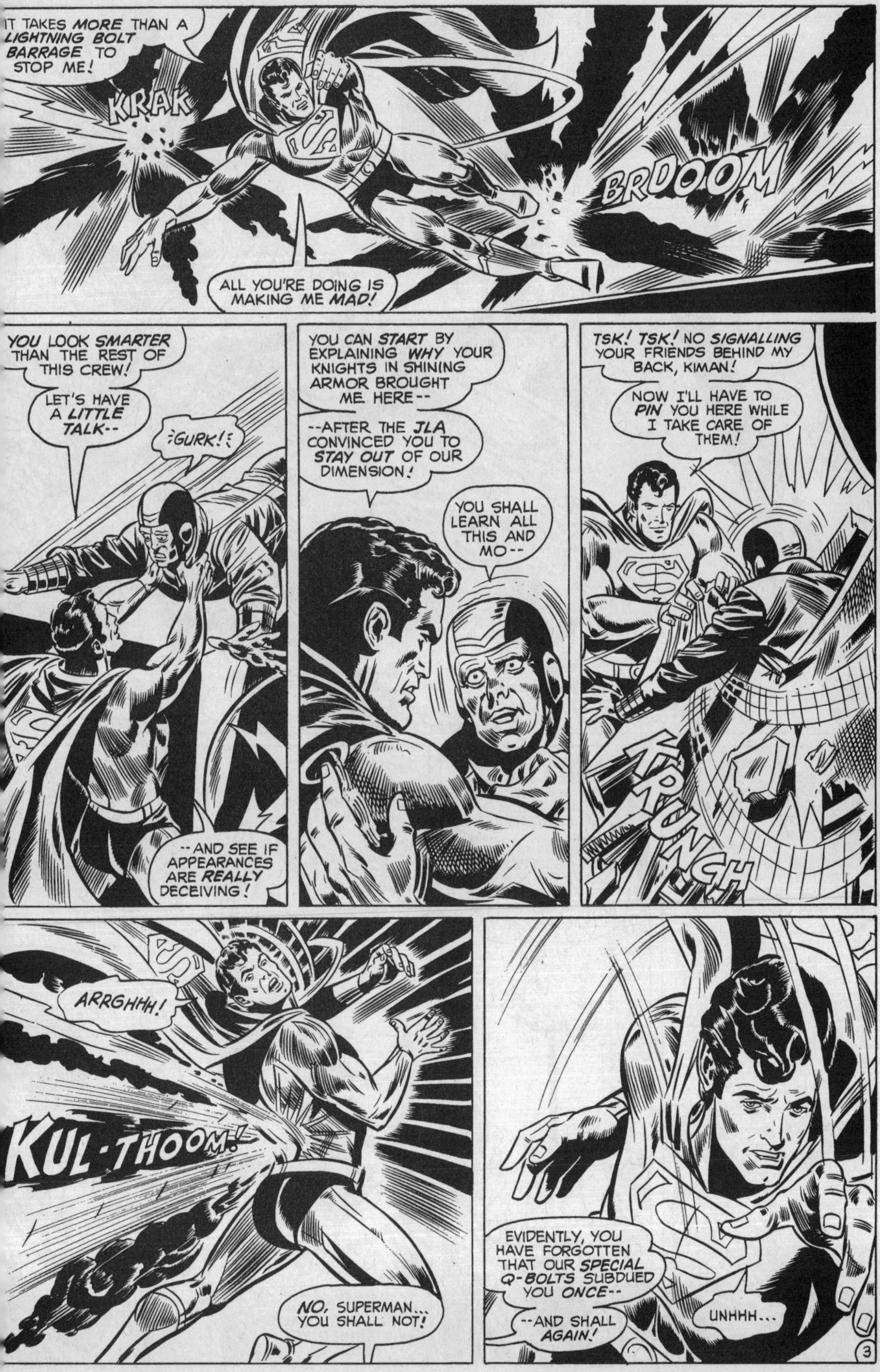
IT TAKES MORE THAN A LIGHTNING BOLT BARRAGE TO STOP ME!
KRAK
BRDOOM
ALL YOU'RE DOING IS MAKING ME MAD!
YOU LOOK SMARTER THAN THE REST OF THIS CREW!
LET'S HAVE A LITTLE TALK--
GURK!
--AND SEE IF APPEARANCES ARE REALLY DECEIVING!
YOU CAN START BY EXPLAINING WHY YOUR KNIGHTS IN SHINING ARMOR BROUGHT ME HERE--
--AFTER THE JLA CONVINCED YOU TO STAY OUT OF OUR DIMENSION!
YOU SHALL LEARN ALL THIS AND MO--
TSK! TSK! NO SIGNALLING YOUR FRIENDS BEHIND MY BACK, KIMAN!
NOW I'LL HAVE TO PIN YOU HERE WHILE I TAKE CARE OF THEM!
KRUNCH
ARRGHHH!
KUL-THOOM!
NO, SUPERMAN... YOU SHALL NOT!
EVIDENTLY, YOU HAVE FORGOTTEN THAT OUR SPECIAL Q-BOLTS SUBDUED YOU ONCE--
--AND SHALL AGAIN!
UNHHH...
3

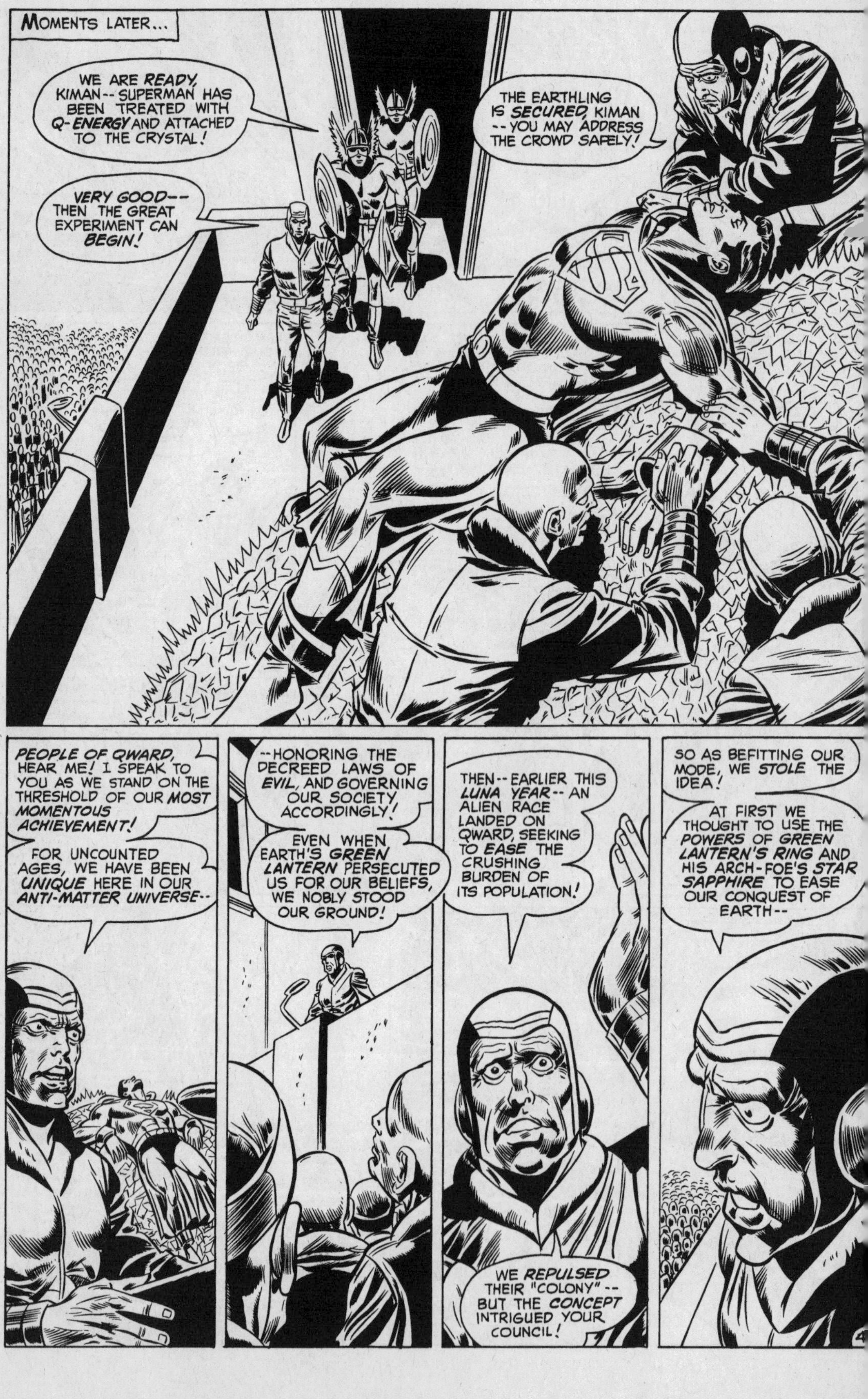
MOMENTS LATER...
WE ARE READY, KIMAN -- SUPERMAN HAS BEEN TREATED WITH Q-ENERGY AND ATTACHED TO THE CRYSTAL!
VERY GOOD-- THEN THE GREAT EXPERIMENT CAN BEGIN!
THE EARTHLING IS SECURED, KIMAN -- YOU MAY ADDRESS THE CROWD SAFELY!
PEOPLE OF QWARD, HEAR ME! I SPEAK TO YOU AS WE STAND ON THE THRESHOLD OF OUR MOST MOMENTOUS ACHIEVEMENT!
FOR UNCOUNTED AGES, WE HAVE BEEN UNIQUE HERE IN OUR ANTI-MATTER UNIVERSE--
--HONORING THE DECREED LAWS OF EVIL, AND GOVERNING OUR SOCIETY ACCORDINGLY!
EVEN WHEN EARTH'S GREEN LANTERN PERSECUTED US FOR OUR BELIEFS, WE NOBLY STOOD OUR GROUND!
THEN--EARLIER THIS LUNA YEAR-- AN ALIEN RACE LANDED ON QWARD, SEEKING TO EASE THE CRUSHING BURDEN OF ITS POPULATION!
WE REPULSED THEIR "COLONY" -- BUT THE CONCEPT INTRIGUED YOUR COUNCIL!
SO AS BEFITTING OUR MODE, WE STOLE THE IDEA!
AT FIRST WE THOUGHT TO USE THE POWERS OF GREEN LANTERN'S RING AND HIS ARCH-FOE'S STAR SAPPHIRE TO EASE OUR CONQUEST OF EARTH--

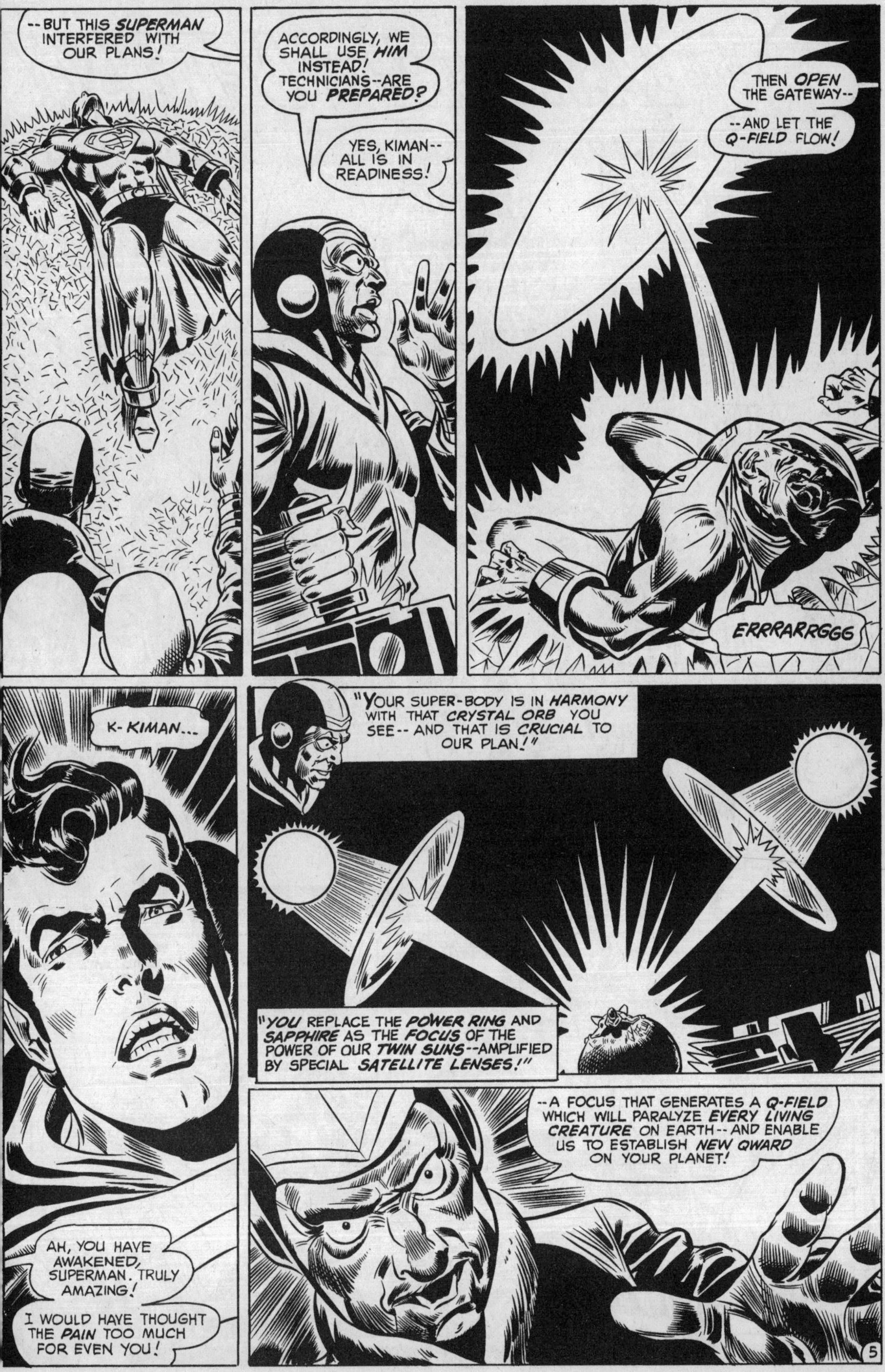
--BUT THIS SUPERMAN INTERFERED WITH OUR PLANS!
ACCORDINGLY, WE SHALL USE HIM INSTEAD! TECHNICIANS--ARE YOU PREPARED?
YES, KIMAN-- ALL IS IN READINESS!
THEN OPEN THE GATEWAY--
--AND LET THE Q-FIELD FLOW!
ERRRARRGGG
K-KIMAN...
"YOUR SUPER-BODY IS IN HARMONY WITH THAT CRYSTAL ORB YOU SEE-- AND THAT IS CRUCIAL TO OUR PLAN!"
"YOU REPLACE THE POWER RING AND SAPPHIRE AS THE FOCUS OF THE POWER OF OUR TWIN SUNS--AMPLIFIED BY SPECIAL SATELLITE LENSES!"
AH, YOU HAVE AWAKENED, SUPERMAN. TRULY AMAZING!
I WOULD HAVE THOUGHT THE PAIN TOO MUCH FOR EVEN YOU!
--A FOCUS THAT GENERATES A Q-FIELD WHICH WILL PARALYZE EVERY LIVING CREATURE ON EARTH--AND ENABLE US TO ESTABLISH NEW QWARD ON YOUR PLANET!
5

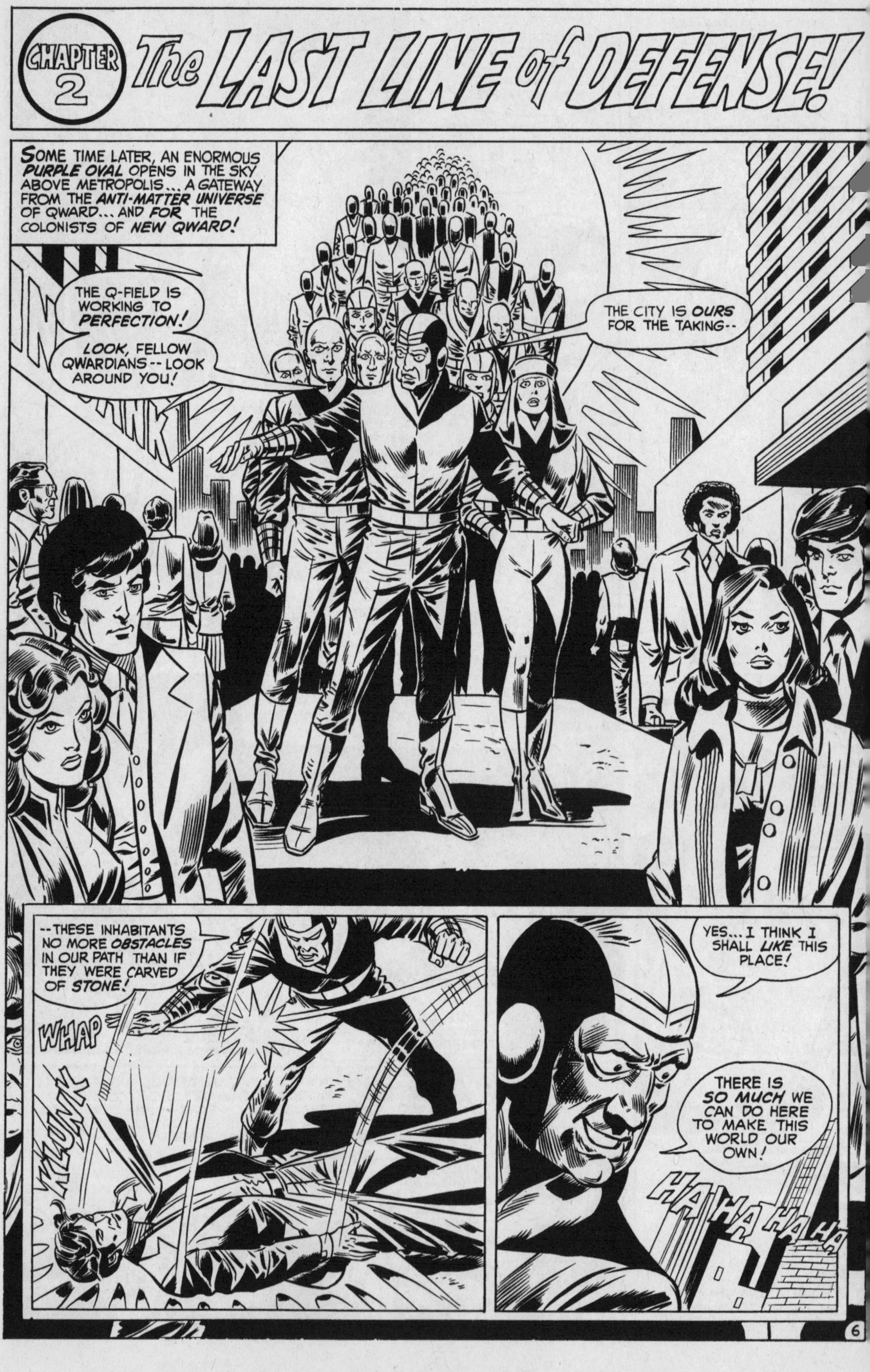
CHAPTER 2
The LAST LINE of DEFENSE!
SOME TIME LATER, AN ENORMOUS PURPLE OVAL OPENS IN THE SKY ABOVE METROPOLIS... A GATEWAY FROM THE ANTI-MATTER UNIVERSE OF QWARD... AND FOR THE COLONISTS OF NEW QWARD!
THE Q-FIELD IS WORKING TO PERFECTION!
LOOK, FELLOW QWARDIANS -- LOOK AROUND YOU!
THE CITY IS OURS FOR THE TAKING--
--THESE INHABITANTS NO MORE OBSTACLES IN OUR PATH THAN IF THEY WERE CARVED OF STONE!
WHAP
KLUNK
YES... I THINK I SHALL LIKE THIS PLACE!
THERE IS SO MUCH WE CAN DO HERE TO MAKE THIS WORLD OUR OWN!
HA HA HA HA HA
6

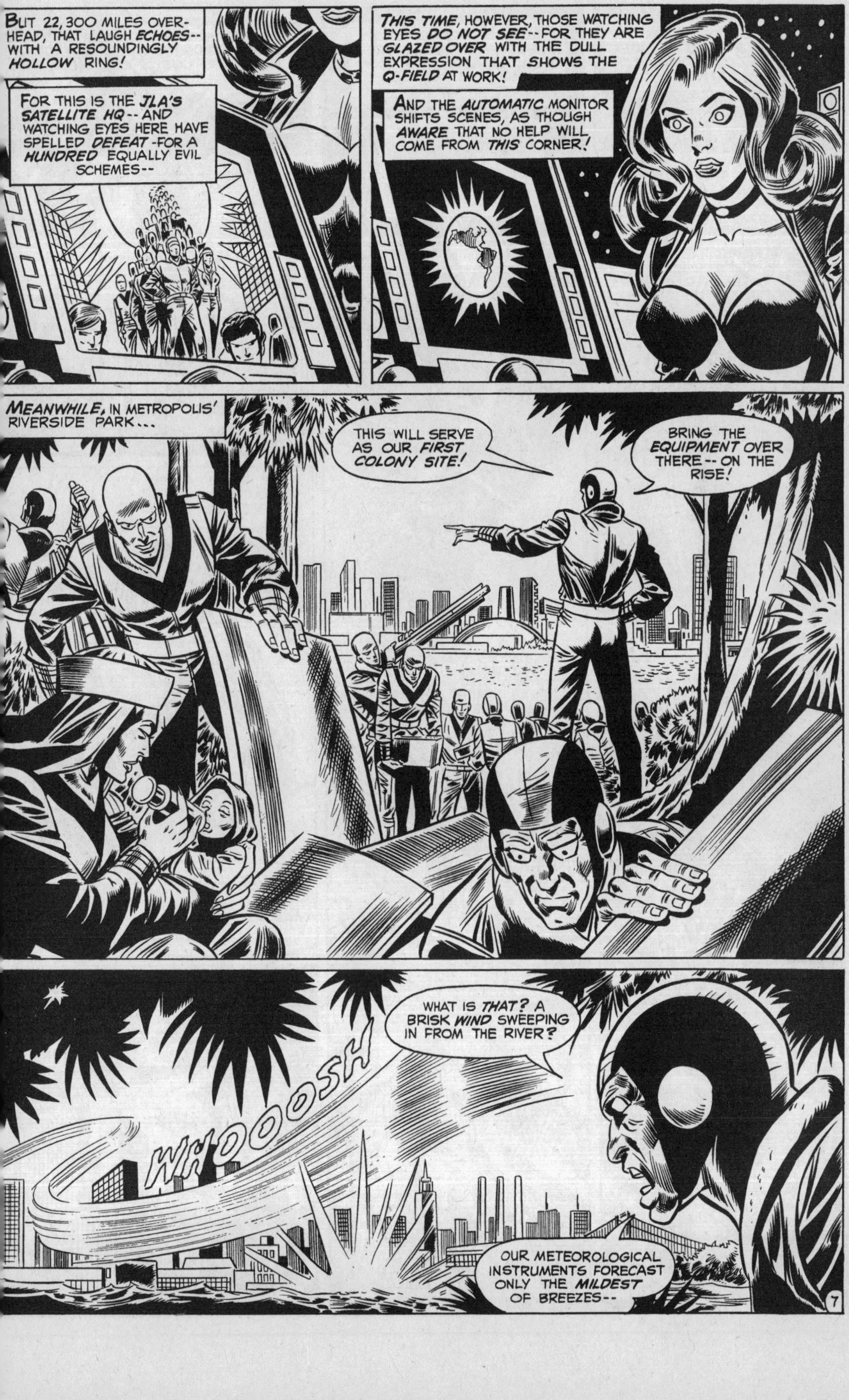
BUT 22,300 MILES OVERHEAD, THAT LAUGH ECHOES-- WITH A RESOUNDINGLY HOLLOW RING!
FOR THIS IS THE JLA'S SATELLITE HQ -- AND WATCHING EYES HERE HAVE SPELLED DEFEAT -FOR A HUNDRED EQUALLY EVIL SCHEMES--
THIS TIME, HOWEVER, THOSE WATCHING EYES DO NOT SEE -- FOR THEY ARE GLAZED OVER WITH THE DULL EXPRESSION THAT SHOWS THE Q-FIELD AT WORK!
AND THE AUTOMATIC MONITOR SHIFTS SCENES, AS THOUGH AWARE THAT NO HELP WILL COME FROM THIS CORNER!
MEANWHILE, IN METROPOLIS' RIVERSIDE PARK...
THIS WILL SERVE AS OUR FIRST COLONY SITE!
BRING THE EQUIPMENT OVER THERE -- ON THE RISE!
WHAT IS THAT? A BRISK WIND SWEEPING IN FROM THE RIVER?
WHOOOOSH
OUR METEOROLOGICAL INSTRUMENTS FORECAST ONLY THE MILDEST OF BREEZES--
7

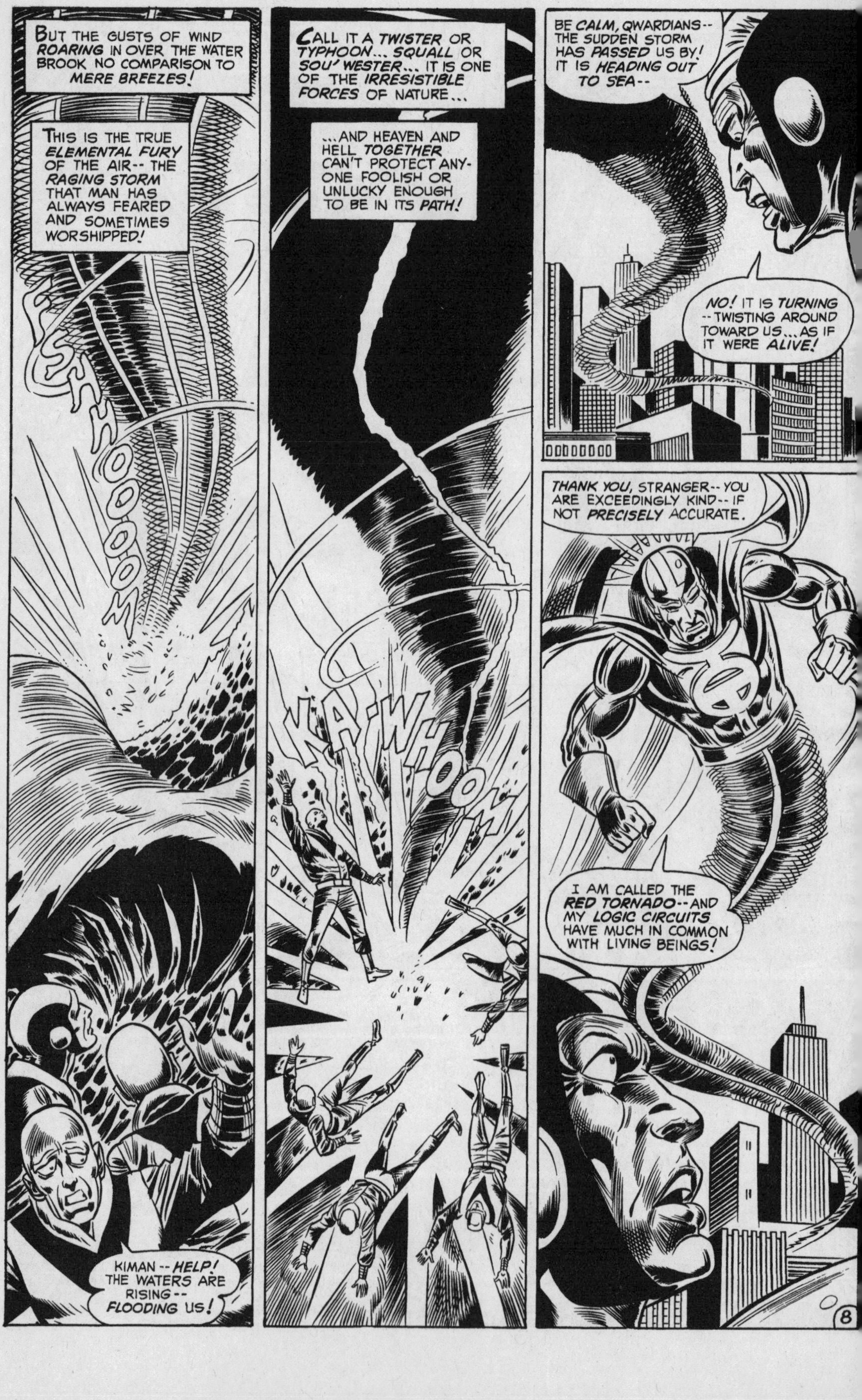
BUT THE GUSTS OF WIND ROARING IN OVER THE WATER BROOK NO COMPARISON TO MERE BREEZES!
THIS IS THE TRUE ELEMENTAL FURY OF THE AIR-- THE RAGING STORM THAT MAN HAS ALWAYS FEARED AND SOMETIMES WORSHIPPED!
SHHOOOOOOM
KIMAN -- HELP! THE WATERS ARE RISING -- FLOODING US!
CALL IT A TWISTER OR TYPHOON... SQUALL OR SOU' WESTER... IT IS ONE OF THE IRRESISTIBLE FORCES OF NATURE...
...AND HEAVEN AND HELL TOGETHER CAN'T PROTECT ANYONE FOOLISH OR UNLUCKY ENOUGH TO BE IN ITS PATH!
KA-WHOOM
BE CALM, QWARDIANS-- THE SUDDEN STORM HAS PASSED US BY! IT IS HEADING OUT TO SEA--
NO! IT IS TURNING -- TWISTING AROUND TOWARD US... AS IF IT WERE ALIVE!
THANK YOU, STRANGER-- YOU ARE EXCEEDINGLY KIND-- IF NOT PRECISELY ACCURATE.
I AM CALLED THE RED TORNADO-- AND MY LOGIC CIRCUITS HAVE MUCH IN COMMON WITH LIVING BEINGS!
8

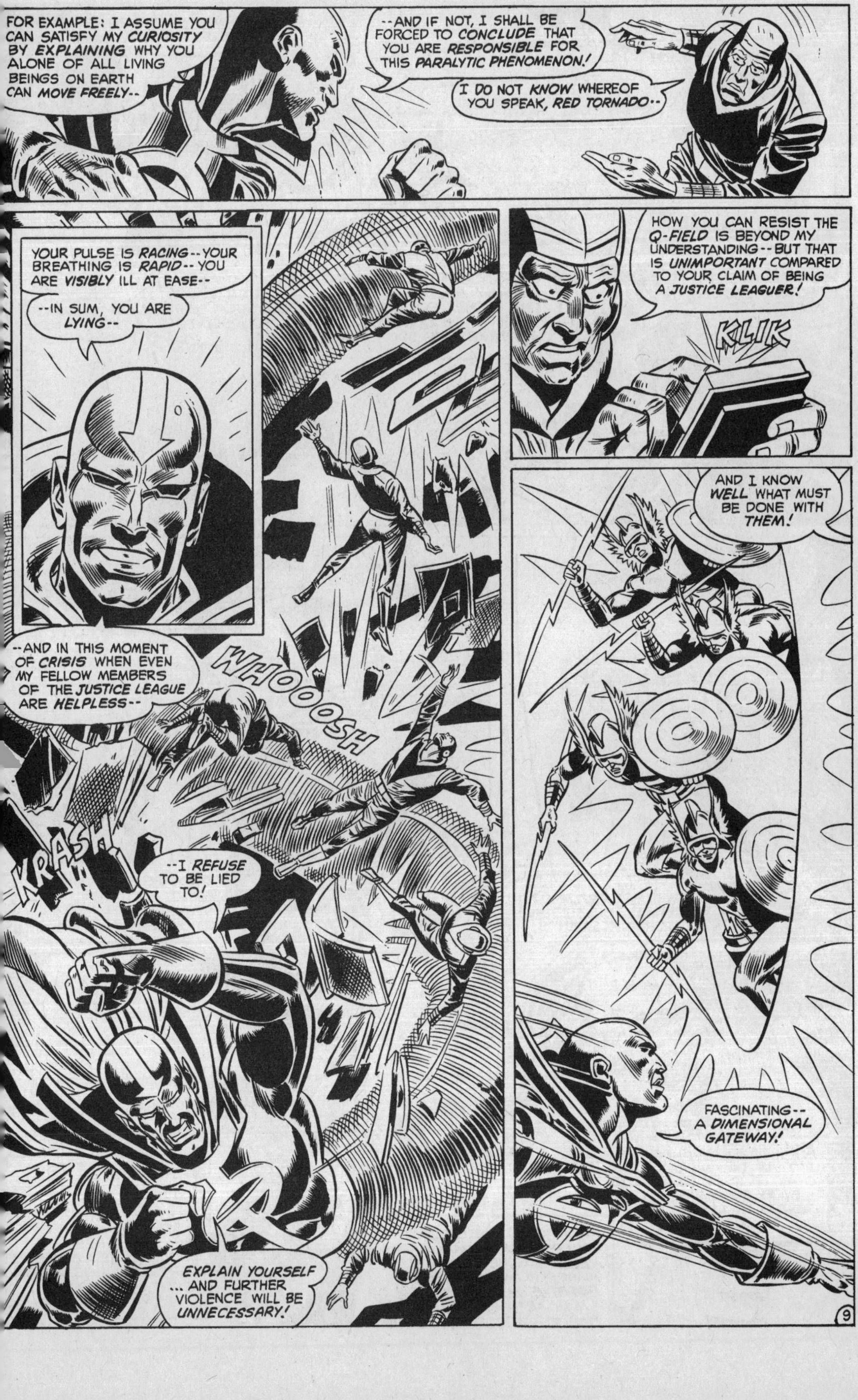
FOR EXAMPLE: I ASSUME YOU CAN SATISFY MY CURIOSITY BY EXPLAINING WHY YOU ALONE OF ALL LIVING BEINGS ON EARTH CAN MOVE FREELY--
--AND IF NOT, I SHALL BE FORCED TO CONCLUDE THAT YOU ARE RESPONSIBLE FOR THIS PARALYTIC PHENOMENON!
I DO NOT KNOW WHEREOF YOU SPEAK, RED TORNADO--
YOUR PULSE IS RACING--YOUR BREATHING IS RAPID--YOU ARE VISIBLY ILL AT EASE--
--IN SUM, YOU ARE LYING--
--AND IN THIS MOMENT OF CRISIS WHEN EVEN MY FELLOW MEMBERS OF THE JUSTICE LEAGUE ARE HELPLESS--
WHOOOSH
KRASH
--I REFUSE TO BE LIED TO!
EXPLAIN YOURSELF ... AND FURTHER VIOLENCE WILL BE UNNECESSARY!
HOW YOU CAN RESIST THE Q-FIELD IS BEYOND MY UNDERSTANDING--BUT THAT IS UNIMPORTANT COMPARED TO YOUR CLAIM OF BEING A JUSTICE LEAGUER!
KLIK
AND I KNOW WELL WHAT MUST BE DONE WITH THEM!
FASCINATING--A DIMENSIONAL GATEWAY!
9

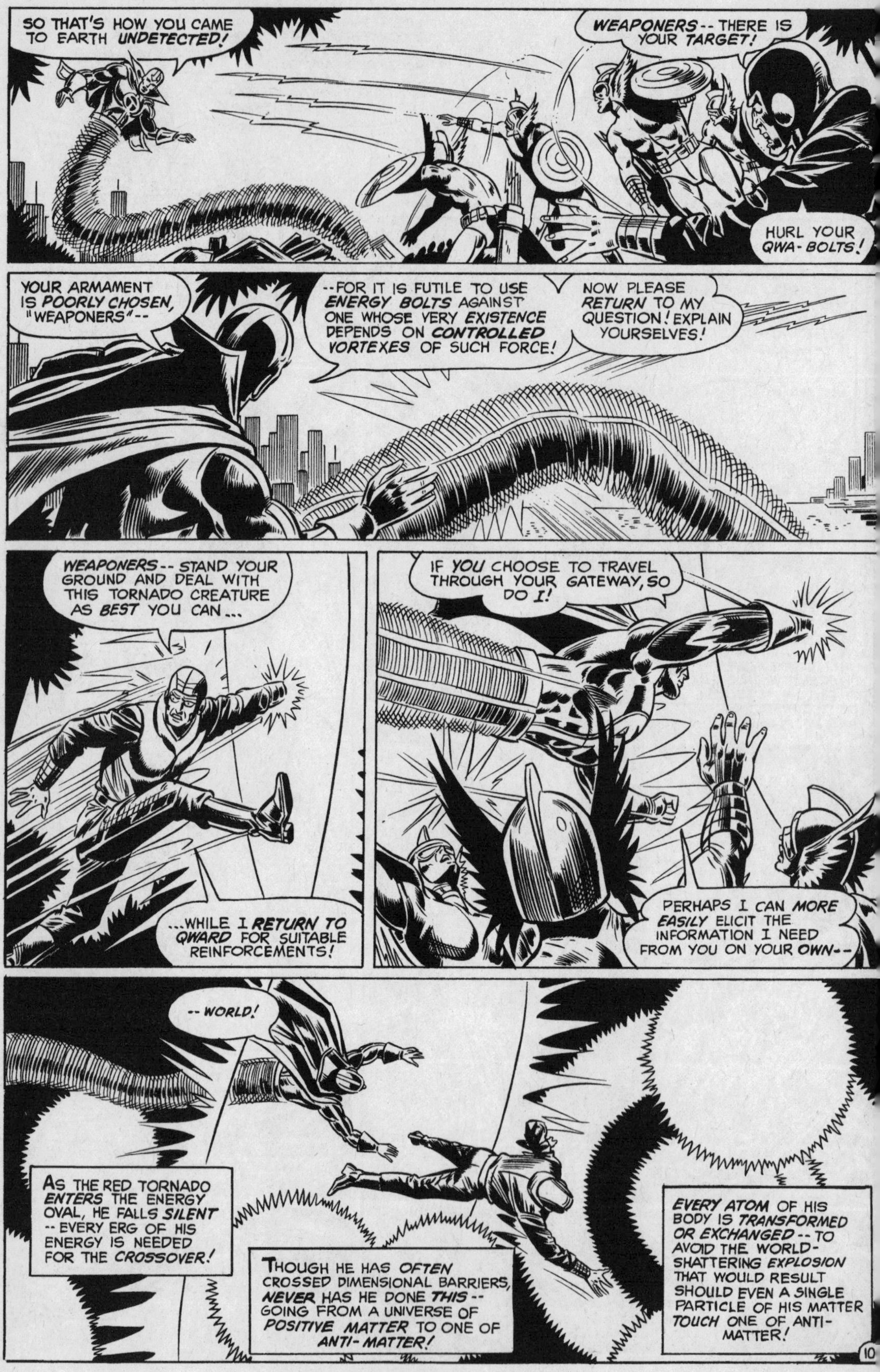
SO THAT'S HOW YOU CAME TO EARTH UNDETECTED!
WEAPONERS -- THERE IS YOUR TARGET!
HURL YOUR QWA-BOLTS!
YOUR ARMAMENT IS POORLY CHOSEN, "WEAPONERS" --
-- FOR IT IS FUTILE TO USE ENERGY BOLTS AGAINST ONE WHOSE VERY EXISTENCE DEPENDS ON CONTROLLED VORTEXES OF SUCH FORCE!
NOW PLEASE RETURN TO MY QUESTION! EXPLAIN YOURSELVES!
WEAPONERS -- STAND YOUR GROUND AND DEAL WITH THIS TORNADO CREATURE AS BEST YOU CAN ...
... WHILE I RETURN TO QWARD FOR SUITABLE REINFORCEMENTS!
IF YOU CHOOSE TO TRAVEL THROUGH YOUR GATEWAY, SO DO I!
PERHAPS I CAN MORE EASILY ELICIT THE INFORMATION I NEED FROM YOU ON YOUR OWN --
-- WORLD!
AS THE RED TORNADO ENTERS THE ENERGY OVAL, HE FALLS SILENT -- EVERY ERG OF HIS ENERGY IS NEEDED FOR THE CROSSOVER!
THOUGH HE HAS OFTEN CROSSED DIMENSIONAL BARRIERS, NEVER HAS HE DONE THIS -- GOING FROM A UNIVERSE OF POSITIVE MATTER TO ONE OF ANTI-MATTER!
EVERY ATOM OF HIS BODY IS TRANSFORMED OR EXCHANGED -- TO AVOID THE WORLD-SHATTERING EXPLOSION THAT WOULD RESULT SHOULD EVEN A SINGLE PARTICLE OF HIS MATTER TOUCH ONE OF ANTI-MATTER!
10

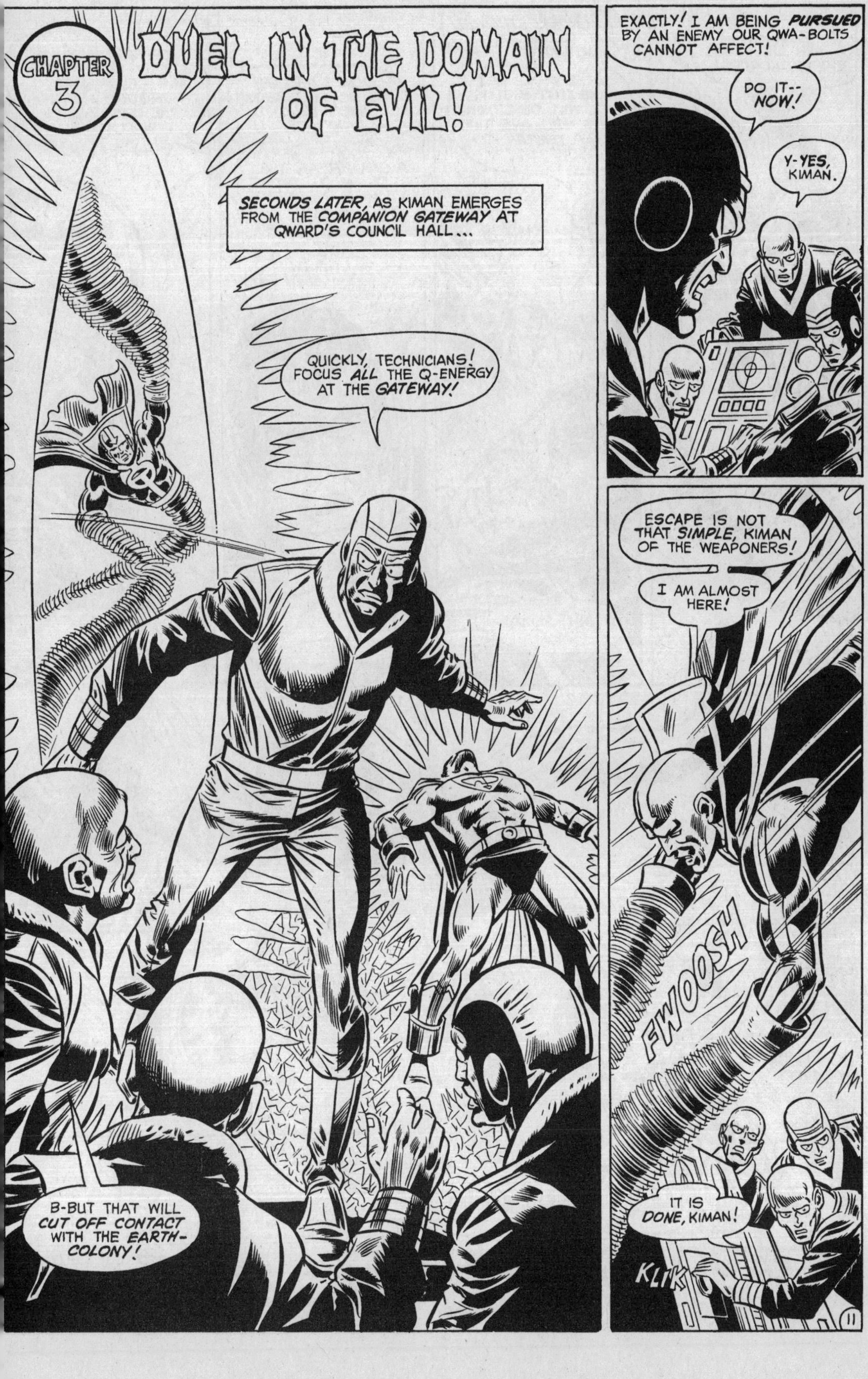
CHAPTER 3
DUEL IN THE DOMAIN OF EVIL!
SECONDS LATER, AS KIMAN EMERGES FROM THE COMPANION GATEWAY AT QWARD'S COUNCIL HALL...
QUICKLY, TECHNICIANS! FOCUS ALL THE Q-ENERGY AT THE GATEWAY!
B-BUT THAT WILL CUT OFF CONTACT WITH THE EARTH-COLONY!
EXACTLY! I AM BEING PURSUED BY AN ENEMY OUR QWA-BOLTS CANNOT AFFECT!
DO IT-- NOW!
Y-YES, KIMAN.
ESCAPE IS NOT THAT SIMPLE, KIMAN OF THE WEAPONERS!
I AM ALMOST HERE!
FWOOSH
IT IS DONE, KIMAN!
KLIK
11

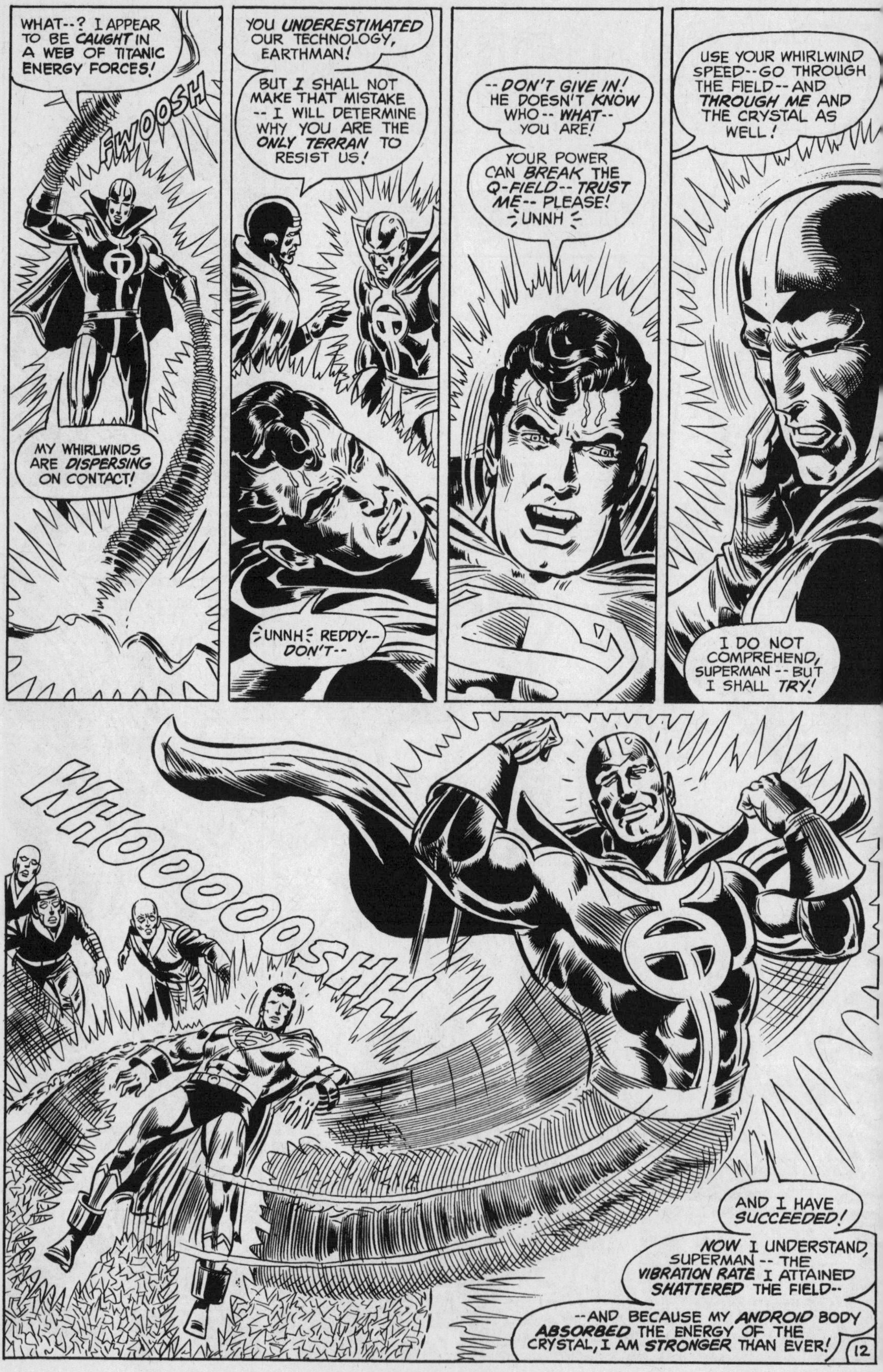
WHAT--? I APPEAR TO BE CAUGHT IN A WEB OF TITANIC ENERGY FORCES!
FWOOSH
MY WHIRLWINDS ARE DISPERSING ON CONTACT!
YOU UNDERESTIMATED OUR TECHNOLOGY, EARTHMAN!
BUT I SHALL NOT MAKE THAT MISTAKE -- I WILL DETERMINE WHY YOU ARE THE ONLY TERRAN TO RESIST US!
UNNH REDDY-- DON'T--
--DON'T GIVE IN! HE DOESN'T KNOW WHO-- WHAT-- YOU ARE!
YOUR POWER CAN BREAK THE Q-FIELD-- TRUST ME-- PLEASE! UNNH
USE YOUR WHIRLWIND SPEED--GO THROUGH THE FIELD--AND THROUGH ME AND THE CRYSTAL AS WELL!
I DO NOT COMPREHEND, SUPERMAN -- BUT I SHALL TRY!
WHOOOOOSHH
AND I HAVE SUCCEEDED!
NOW I UNDERSTAND, SUPERMAN -- THE VIBRATION RATE I ATTAINED SHATTERED THE FIELD--
--AND BECAUSE MY ANDROID BODY ABSORBED THE ENERGY OF THE CRYSTAL, I AM STRONGER THAN EVER!
12

LISTEN TO ME, REDDY... ≈UNNH≈ GO INTO *SPACE*...

...*DESTROY* THEIR *ORBITING LENSES*... BEFORE THEY FIND A WAY TO GRAB YOU... AND HOLD YOU!

THE ENERGY THEY COMMAND... ALMOST UNLIMITED... ≈ARRGH!≈

I'M ON MY WAY, SUPERMAN! YOUR ADVICE WORKED OUT SO WELL, I SHALL FOLLOW IT ONCE AGAIN!

BUT ON MY *RETURN*, I SHALL FOLLOW THE DICTATES OF *MY LOGIC CIRCUITS* -- AND SET YOU *FREE!*

BUT WHEN THE *RED TORNADO* STRIKES THE *SATELLITE* ABOVE QWARD...

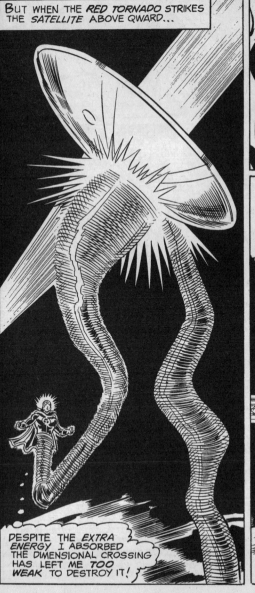

DESPITE THE *EXTRA ENERGY* I ABSORBED THE DIMENSIONAL CROSSING HAS LEFT ME *TOO WEAK* TO DESTROY IT!

REASON DICTATES, THEREFORE, THAT I USE THE *SATELLITE* TO *DESTROY ITSELF*--

--OR IN THIS CASE, ITS *TWIN*--SINCE I OBSERVE *TWO IDENTICAL LENSES!*

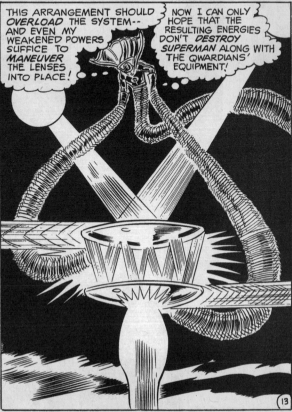

THIS ARRANGEMENT SHOULD *OVERLOAD* THE SYSTEM-- AND EVEN MY *WEAKENED POWERS* SUFFICE TO *MANEUVER* THE LENSES INTO PLACE!

NOW I CAN ONLY HOPE THAT THE RESULTING ENERGIES DON'T *DESTROY SUPERMAN* ALONG WITH THE QWARDIANS' EQUIPMENT!

⑬

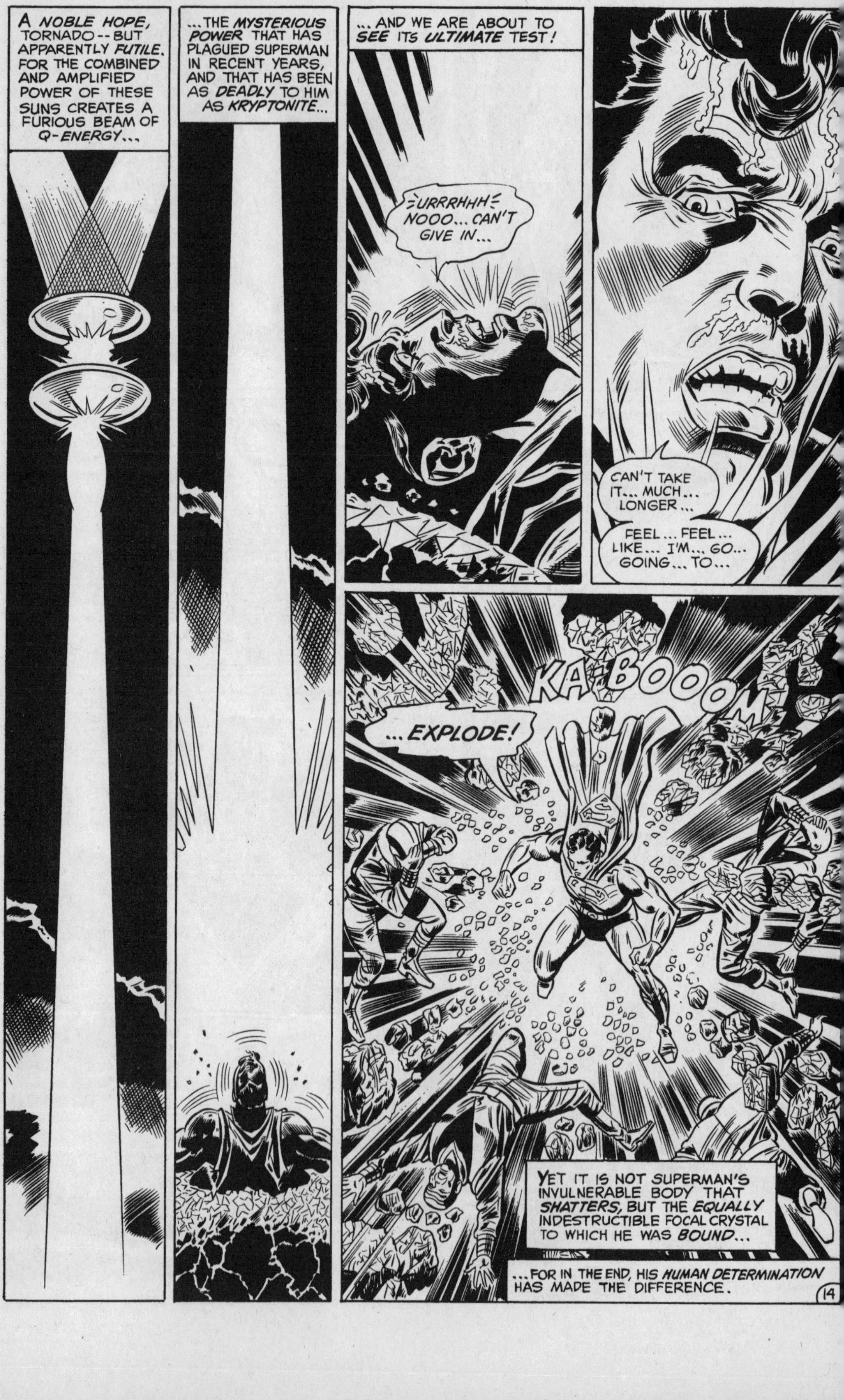
A NOBLE HOPE, TORNADO -- BUT APPARENTLY FUTILE. FOR THE COMBINED AND AMPLIFIED POWER OF THESE SUNS CREATES A FURIOUS BEAM OF Q-ENERGY...
...THE MYSTERIOUS POWER THAT HAS PLAGUED SUPERMAN IN RECENT YEARS, AND THAT HAS BEEN AS DEADLY TO HIM AS KRYPTONITE...
...AND WE ARE ABOUT TO SEE ITS ULTIMATE TEST!
URRRHHH NOOO... CAN'T GIVE IN...
CAN'T TAKE IT... MUCH... LONGER...
FEEL... FEEL... LIKE... I'M... GO... GOING... TO...
KA-BOOOOM
...EXPLODE!
YET IT IS NOT SUPERMAN'S INVULNERABLE BODY THAT SHATTERS, BUT THE EQUALLY INDESTRUCTIBLE FOCAL CRYSTAL TO WHICH HE WAS BOUND...
...FOR IN THE END, HIS HUMAN DETERMINATION HAS MADE THE DIFFERENCE.
14

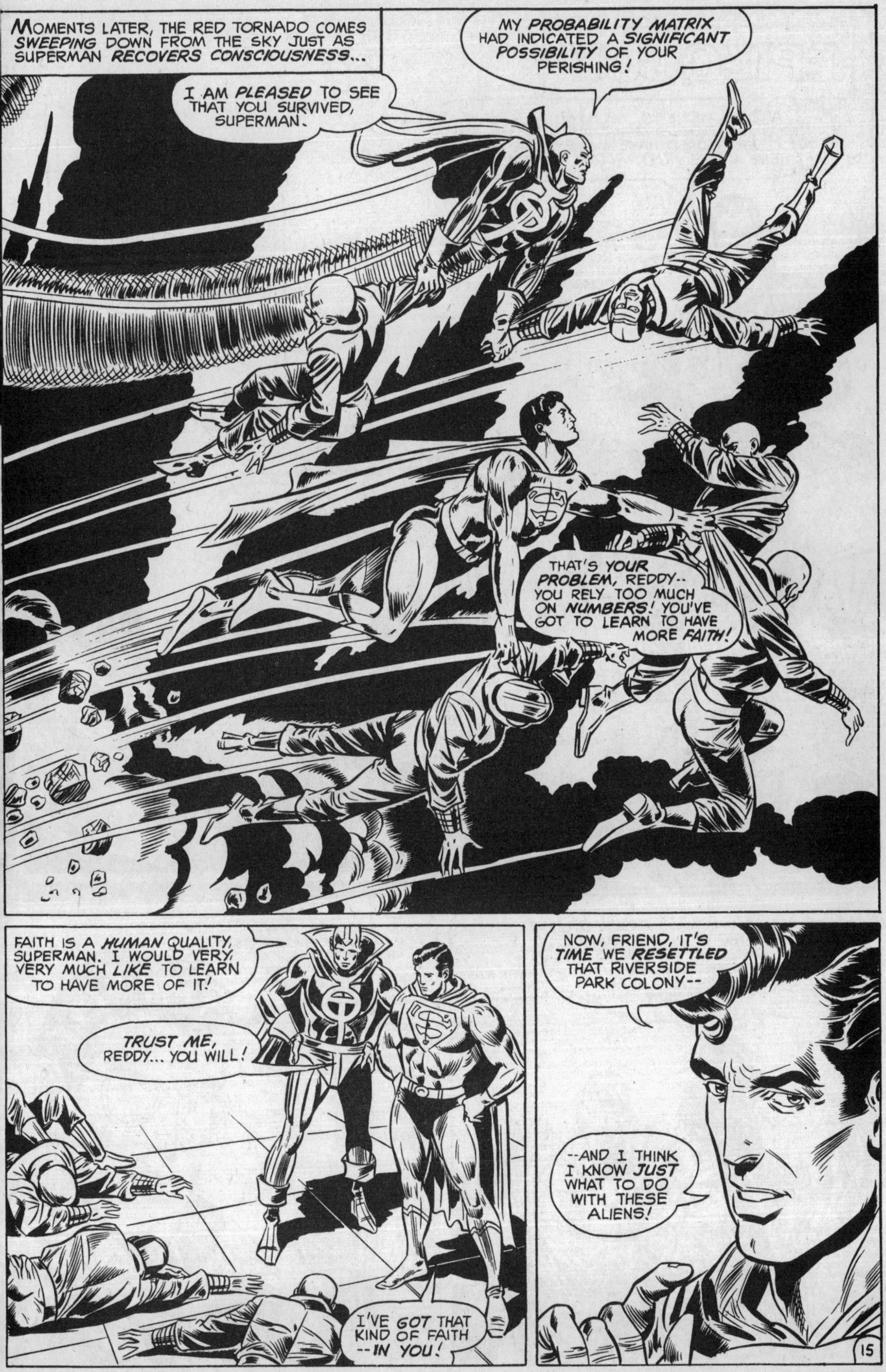
MOMENTS LATER, THE RED TORNADO COMES SWEEPING DOWN FROM THE SKY JUST AS SUPERMAN RECOVERS CONSCIOUSNESS...
I AM PLEASED TO SEE THAT YOU SURVIVED, SUPERMAN.
MY PROBABILITY MATRIX HAD INDICATED A SIGNIFICANT POSSIBILITY OF YOUR PERISHING!
THAT'S YOUR PROBLEM, REDDY-- YOU RELY TOO MUCH ON NUMBERS! YOU'VE GOT TO LEARN TO HAVE MORE FAITH!
FAITH IS A HUMAN QUALITY, SUPERMAN. I WOULD VERY, VERY MUCH LIKE TO LEARN TO HAVE MORE OF IT!
TRUST ME, REDDY... YOU WILL!
I'VE GOT THAT KIND OF FAITH --IN YOU!
NOW, FRIEND, IT'S TIME WE RESETTLED THAT RIVERSIDE PARK COLONY--
--AND I THINK I KNOW JUST WHAT TO DO WITH THESE ALIENS!
15

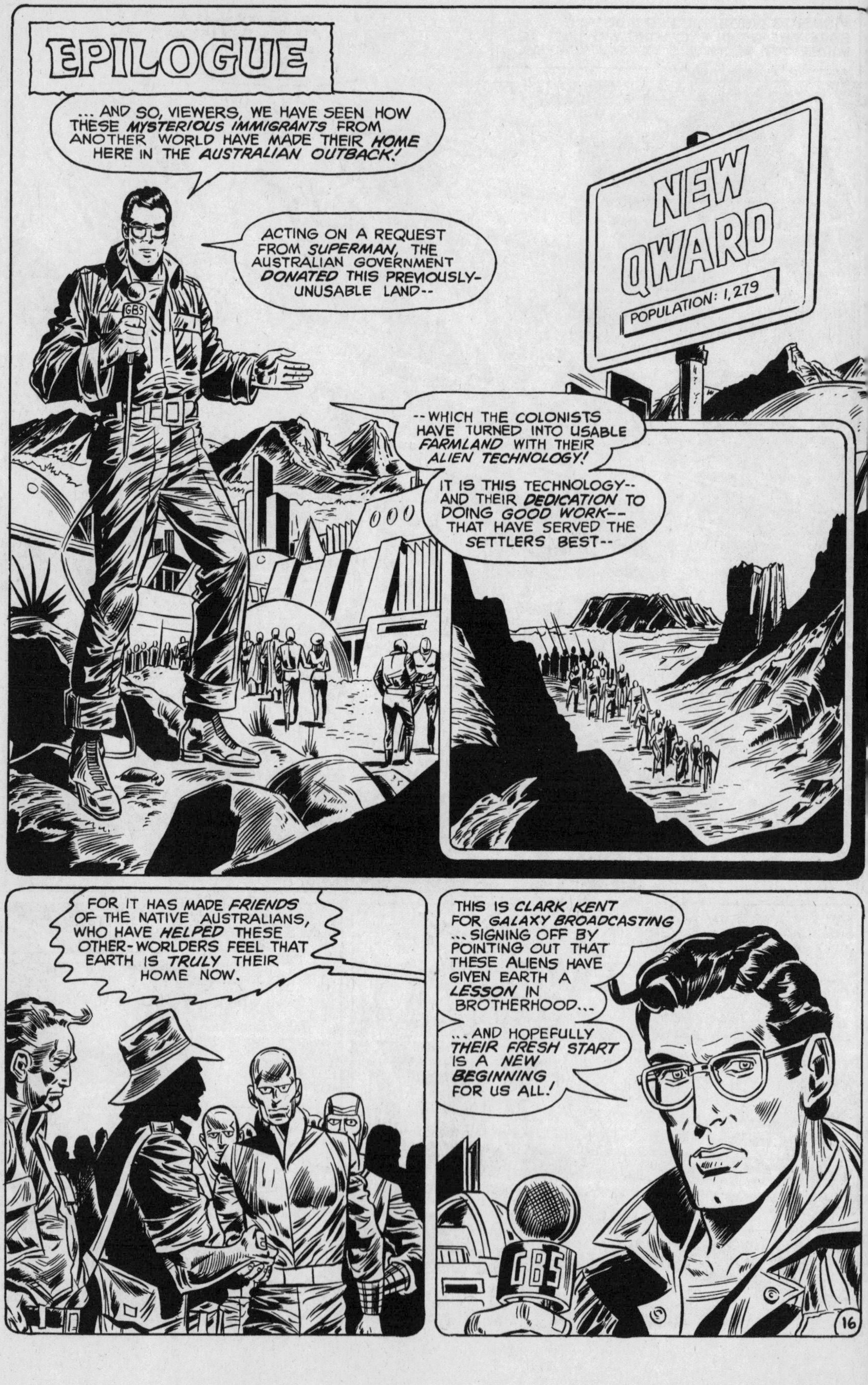
EPILOGUE
... AND SO, VIEWERS, WE HAVE SEEN HOW THESE MYSTERIOUS IMMIGRANTS FROM ANOTHER WORLD HAVE MADE THEIR HOME HERE IN THE AUSTRALIAN OUTBACK!
ACTING ON A REQUEST FROM SUPERMAN, THE AUSTRALIAN GOVERNMENT DONATED THIS PREVIOUSLY-UNUSABLE LAND--
NEW QWARD
POPULATION: 1,279
--WHICH THE COLONISTS HAVE TURNED INTO USABLE FARMLAND WITH THEIR ALIEN TECHNOLOGY!
IT IS THIS TECHNOLOGY-- AND THEIR DEDICATION TO DOING GOOD WORK-- THAT HAVE SERVED THE SETTLERS BEST--
FOR IT HAS MADE FRIENDS OF THE NATIVE AUSTRALIANS, WHO HAVE HELPED THESE OTHER-WORLDERS FEEL THAT EARTH IS TRULY THEIR HOME NOW.
THIS IS CLARK KENT FOR GALAXY BROADCASTING ... SIGNING OFF BY POINTING OUT THAT THESE ALIENS HAVE GIVEN EARTH A LESSON IN BROTHERHOOD...
... AND HOPEFULLY THEIR FRESH START IS A NEW BEGINNING FOR US ALL!
GBS
16

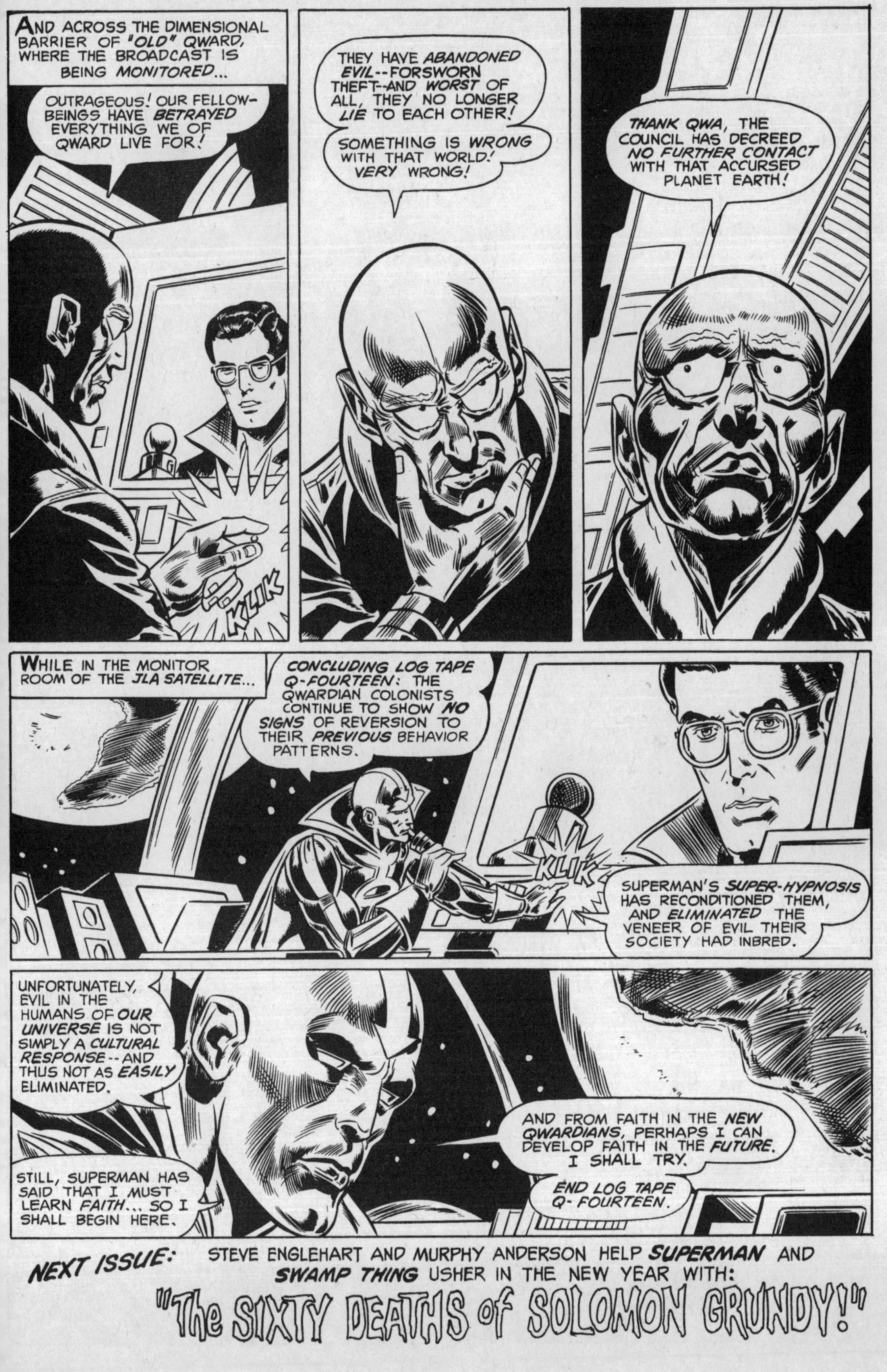
AND ACROSS THE DIMENSIONAL BARRIER OF "OLD" QWARD, WHERE THE BROADCAST IS BEING MONITORED...
OUTRAGEOUS! OUR FELLOW-BEINGS HAVE BETRAYED EVERYTHING WE OF QWARD LIVE FOR!
KLIK
THEY HAVE ABANDONED EVIL--FORSWORN THEFT--AND WORST OF ALL, THEY NO LONGER LIE TO EACH OTHER!
SOMETHING IS WRONG WITH THAT WORLD! VERY WRONG!
THANK QWA, THE COUNCIL HAS DECREED NO FURTHER CONTACT WITH THAT ACCURSED PLANET EARTH!
WHILE IN THE MONITOR ROOM OF THE JLA SATELLITE...
CONCLUDING LOG TAPE Q-FOURTEEN: THE QWARDIAN COLONISTS CONTINUE TO SHOW NO SIGNS OF REVERSION TO THEIR PREVIOUS BEHAVIOR PATTERNS.
KLIK
SUPERMAN'S SUPER-HYPNOSIS HAS RECONDITIONED THEM, AND ELIMINATED THE VENEER OF EVIL THEIR SOCIETY HAD INBRED.
UNFORTUNATELY, EVIL IN THE HUMANS OF OUR UNIVERSE IS NOT SIMPLY A CULTURAL RESPONSE--AND THUS NOT AS EASILY ELIMINATED.
STILL, SUPERMAN HAS SAID THAT I MUST LEARN FAITH... SO I SHALL BEGIN HERE.
AND FROM FAITH IN THE NEW QWARDIANS, PERHAPS I CAN DEVELOP FAITH IN THE FUTURE. I SHALL TRY.
END LOG TAPE Q-FOURTEEN.
NEXT ISSUE: STEVE ENGLEHART AND MURPHY ANDERSON HELP SUPERMAN AND SWAMP THING USHER IN THE NEW YEAR WITH:
"The SIXTY DEATHS of SOLOMON GRUNDY!"

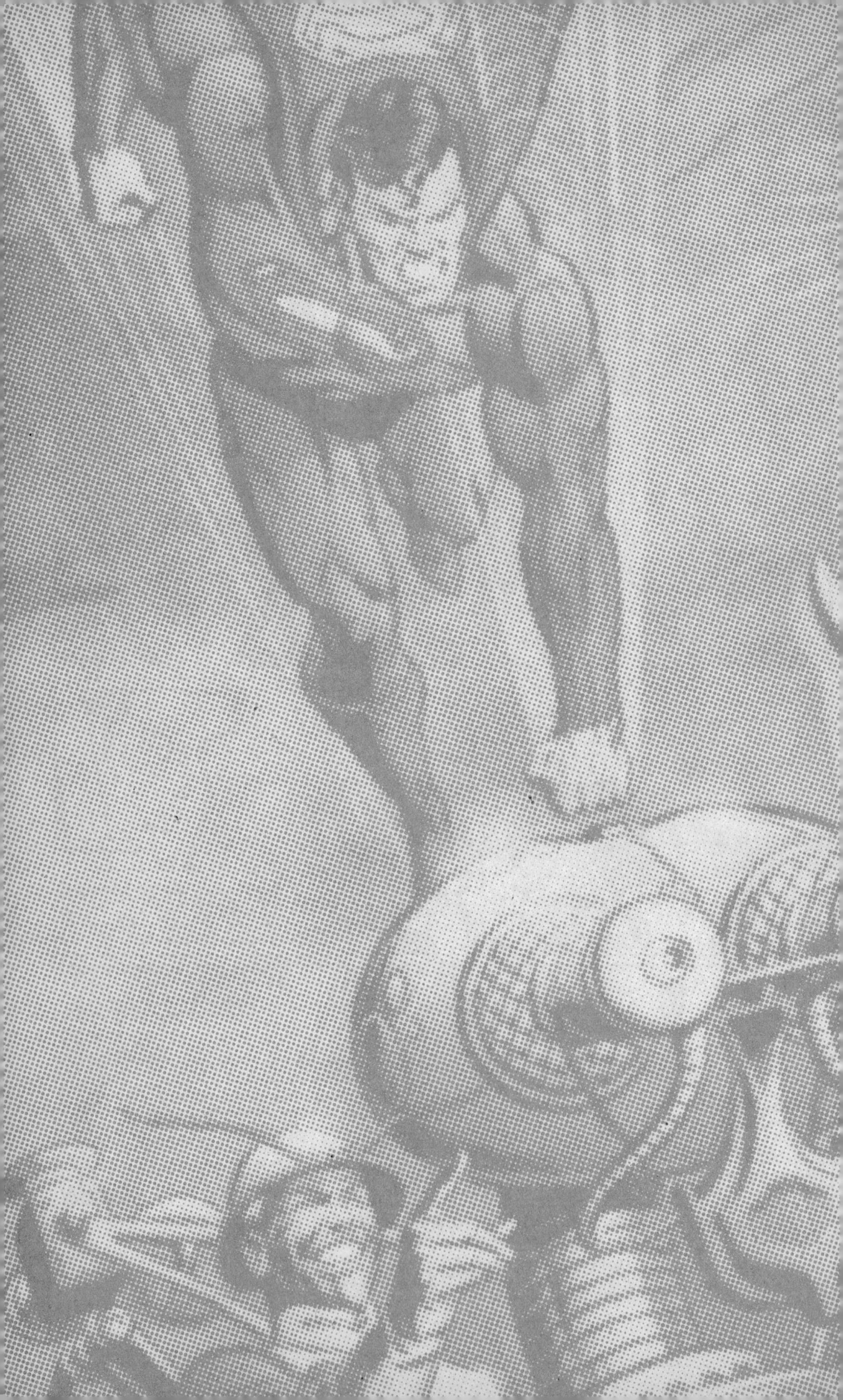

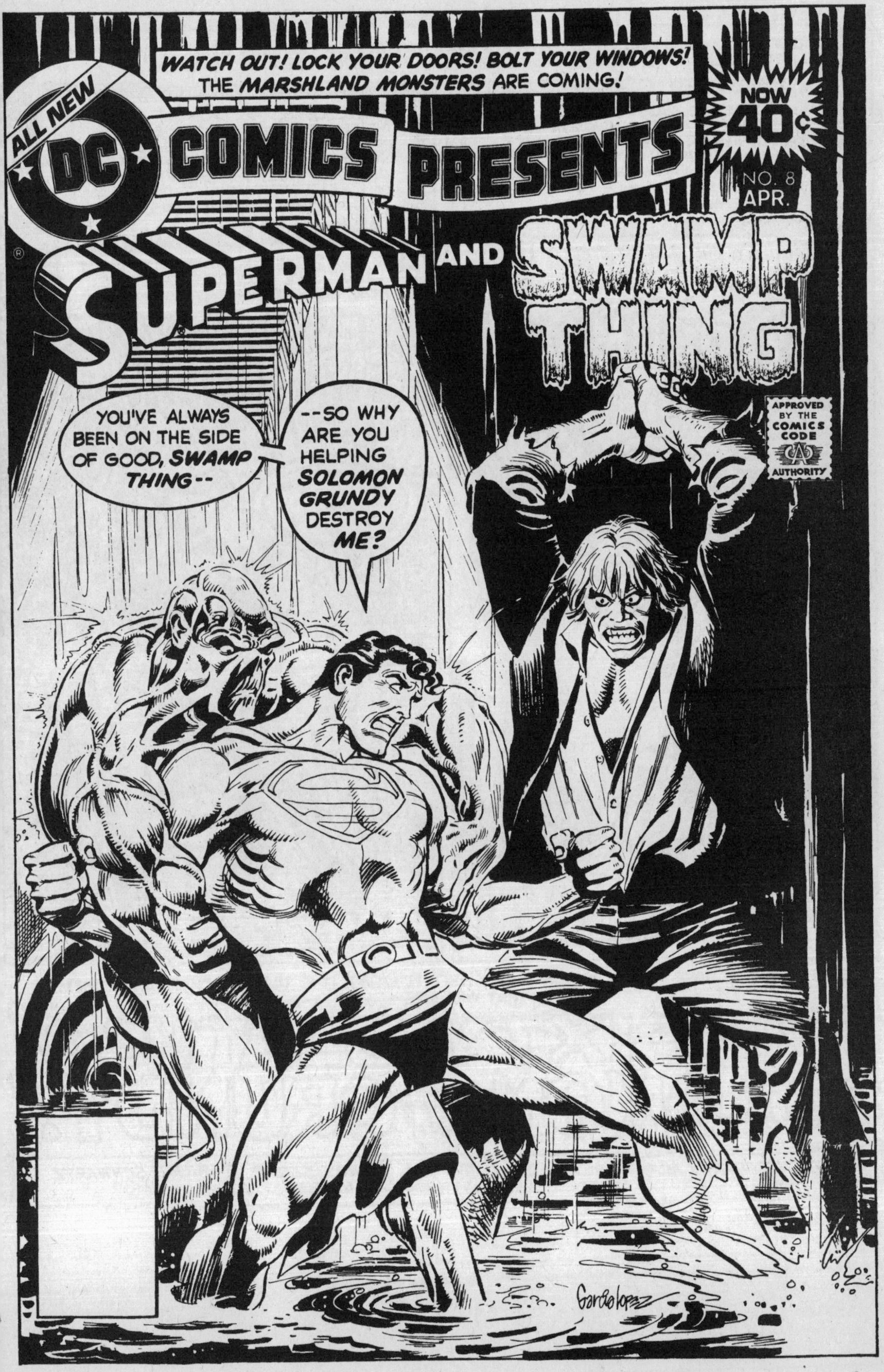
WATCH OUT! LOCK YOUR DOORS! BOLT YOUR WINDOWS! THE MARSHLAND MONSTERS ARE COMING!
ALL NEW
DC COMICS PRESENTS
NOW 40¢
NO. 8 APR.
SUPERMAN AND SWAMP THING
APPROVED BY THE COMICS CODE AUTHORITY
YOU'VE ALWAYS BEEN ON THE SIDE OF GOOD, SWAMP THING--
--SO WHY ARE YOU HELPING SOLOMON GRUNDY DESTROY ME?
Garcia-Lopez

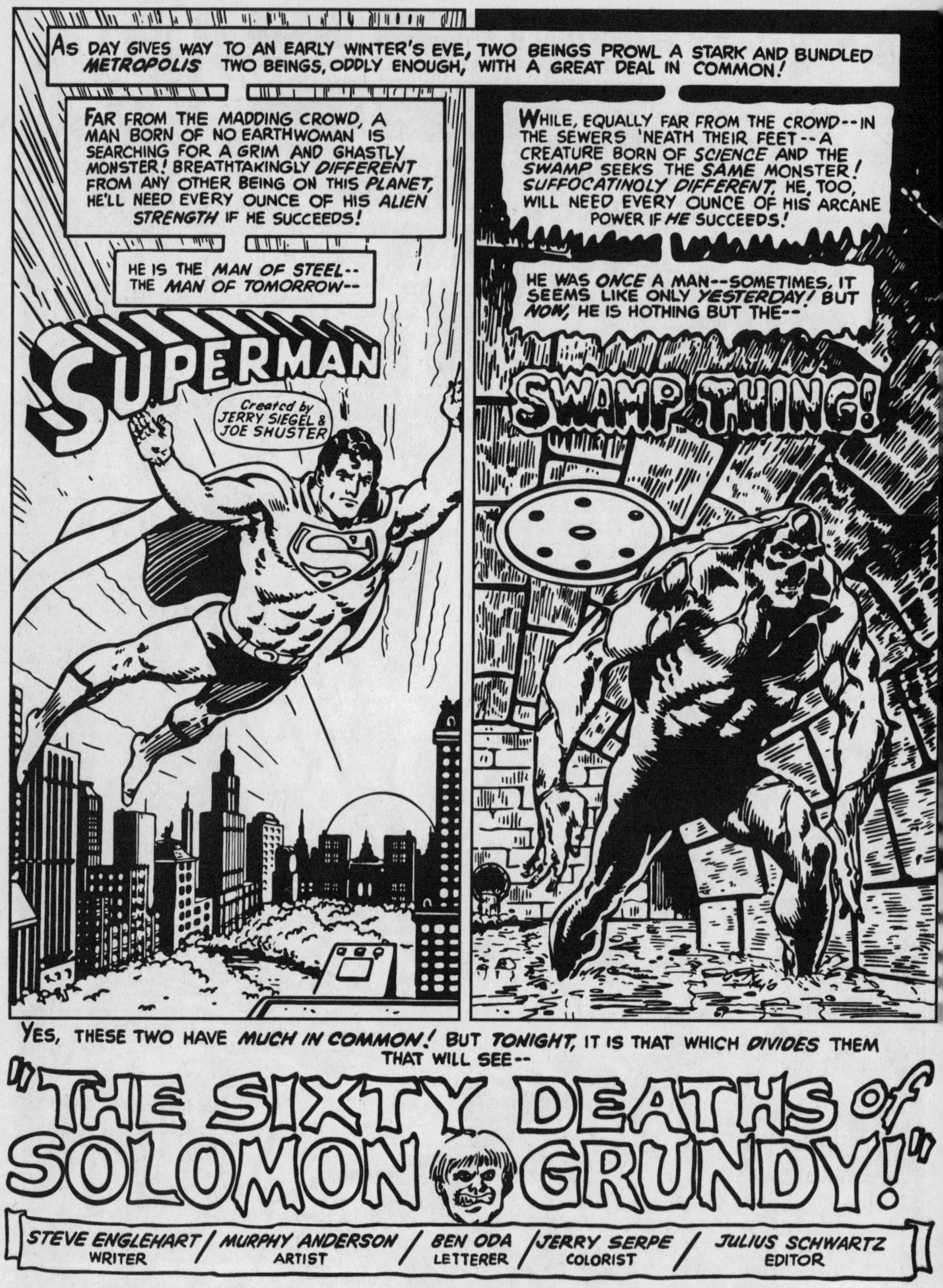
AS DAY GIVES WAY TO AN EARLY WINTER'S EVE, TWO BEINGS PROWL A STARK AND BUNDLED METROPOLIS TWO BEINGS, ODDLY ENOUGH, WITH A GREAT DEAL IN COMMON!
FAR FROM THE MADDING CROWD, A MAN BORN OF NO EARTHWOMAN IS SEARCHING FOR A GRIM AND GHASTLY MONSTER! BREATHTAKINGLY DIFFERENT FROM ANY OTHER BEING ON THIS PLANET, HE'LL NEED EVERY OUNCE OF HIS ALIEN STRENGTH IF HE SUCCEEDS!
HE IS THE MAN OF STEEL-- THE MAN OF TOMORROW--
SUPERMAN
Created by JERRY SIEGEL & JOE SHUSTER
WHILE, EQUALLY FAR FROM THE CROWD--IN THE SEWERS 'NEATH THEIR FEET--A CREATURE BORN OF SCIENCE AND THE SWAMP SEEKS THE SAME MONSTER! SUFFOCATINOLY DIFFERENT, HE, TOO, WILL NEED EVERY OUNCE OF HIS ARCANE POWER IF HE SUCCEEDS!
HE WAS ONCE A MAN--SOMETIMES, IT SEEMS LIKE ONLY YESTERDAY! BUT NOW, HE IS HOTHING BUT THE--
SWAMP THING!
YES, THESE TWO HAVE MUCH IN COMMON! BUT TONIGHT, IT IS THAT WHICH DIVIDES THEM THAT WILL SEE--
"THE SIXTY DEATHS of SOLOMON GRUNDY!"
STEVE ENGLEHART / WRITER
MURPHY ANDERSON / ARTIST
BEN ODA / LETTERER
JERRY SERPE / COLORIST
JULIUS SCHWARTZ / EDITOR

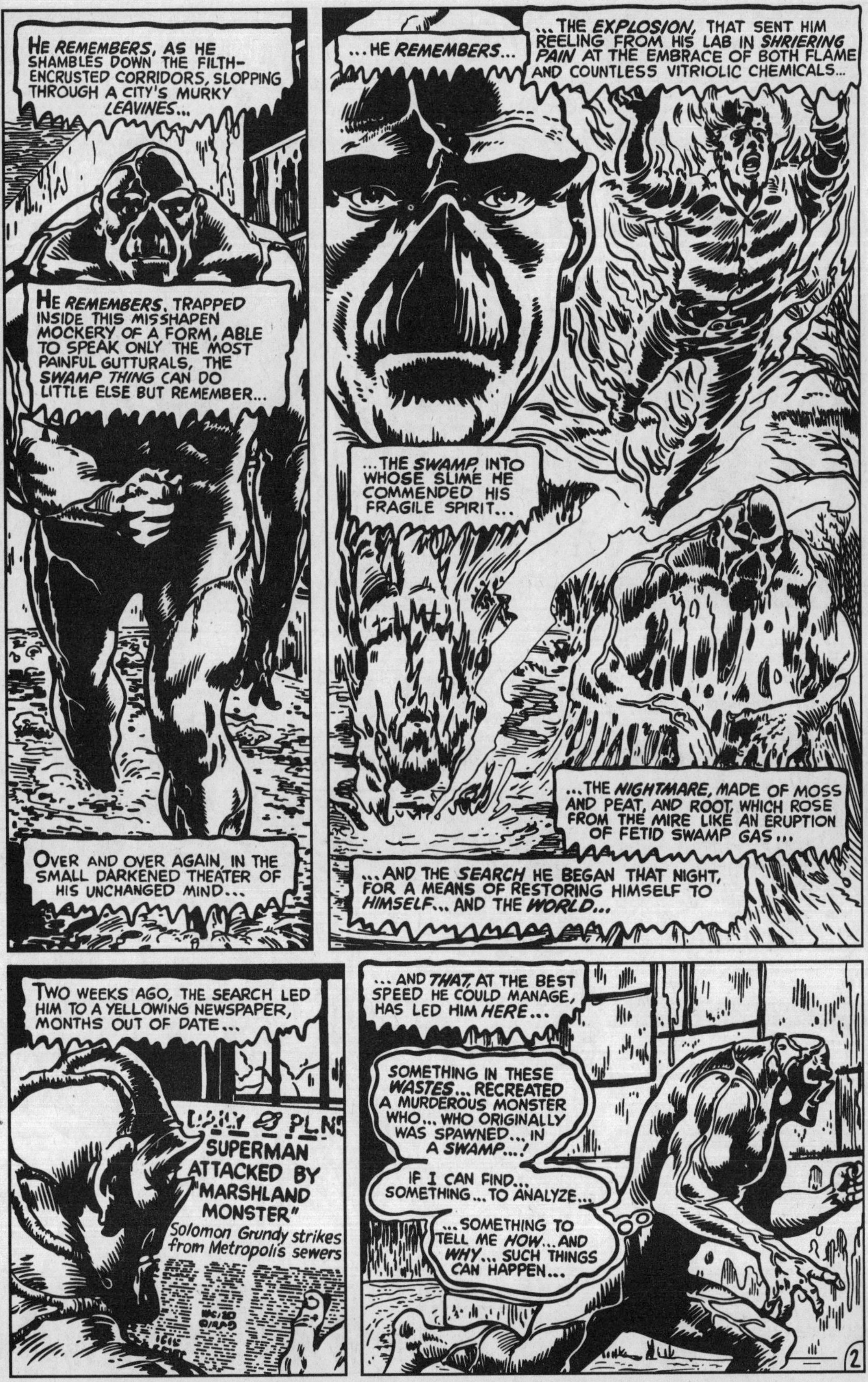
HE REMEMBERS, AS HE SHAMBLES DOWN THE FILTH-ENCRUSTED CORRIDORS, SLOPPING THROUGH A CITY'S MURKY LEAVINES...
HE REMEMBERS, TRAPPED INSIDE THIS MISSHAPEN MOCKERY OF A FORM, ABLE TO SPEAK ONLY THE MOST PAINFUL GUTTURALS, THE SWAMP THING CAN DO LITTLE ELSE BUT REMEMBER...
OVER AND OVER AGAIN, IN THE SMALL DARKENED THEATER OF HIS UNCHANGED MIND...
...HE REMEMBERS...
...THE EXPLOSION, THAT SENT HIM REELING FROM HIS LAB IN SHRIERING PAIN AT THE EMBRACE OF BOTH FLAME AND COUNTLESS VITRIOLIC CHEMICALS...
...THE SWAMP, INTO WHOSE SLIME HE COMMENDED HIS FRAGILE SPIRIT...
...THE NIGHTMARE, MADE OF MOSS AND PEAT, AND ROOT, WHICH ROSE FROM THE MIRE LIKE AN ERUPTION OF FETID SWAMP GAS...
...AND THE SEARCH HE BEGAN THAT NIGHT, FOR A MEANS OF RESTORING HIMSELF TO HIMSELF... AND THE WORLD...
TWO WEEKS AGO, THE SEARCH LED HIM TO A YELLOWING NEWSPAPER, MONTHS OUT OF DATE...
SUPERMAN ATTACKED BY "MARSHLAND MONSTER"
Solomon Grundy strikes from Metropolis sewers
...AND THAT, AT THE BEST SPEED HE COULD MANAGE, HAS LED HIM HERE...
SOMETHING IN THESE WASTES... RECREATED A MURDEROUS MONSTER WHO... WHO ORIGINALLY WAS SPAWNED... IN A SWAMP...!
IF I CAN FIND... SOMETHING... TO ANALYZE...
...SOMETHING TO TELL ME HOW... AND WHY... SUCH THINGS CAN HAPPEN...
2

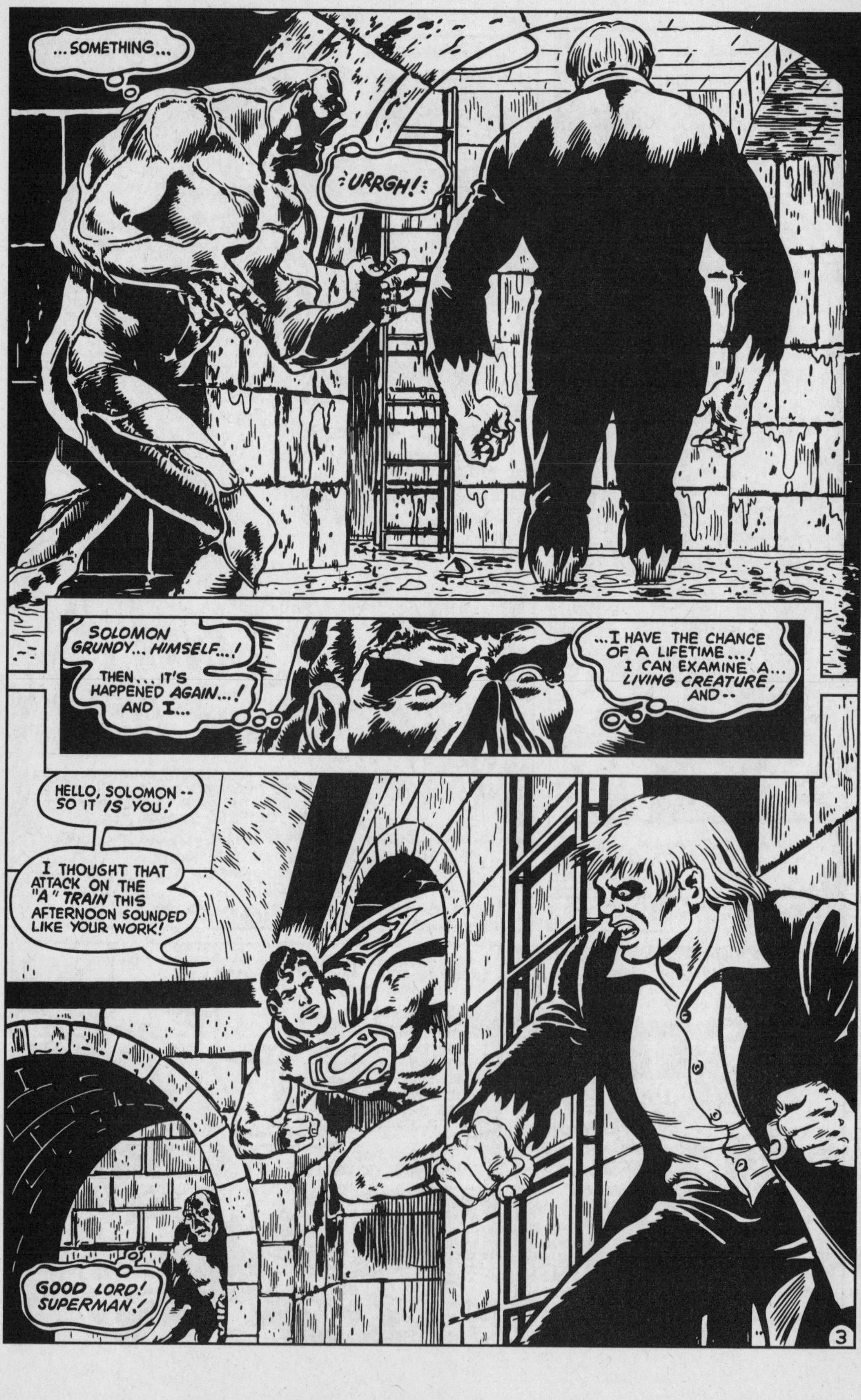
...SOMETHING...
URRGH!
SOLOMON GRUNDY... HIMSELF...!
THEN... IT'S HAPPENED AGAIN...! AND I...
...I HAVE THE CHANCE OF A LIFETIME...! I CAN EXAMINE A... LIVING CREATURE, AND--
HELLO, SOLOMON -- SO IT IS YOU!
I THOUGHT THAT ATTACK ON THE "A" TRAIN THIS AFTERNOON SOUNDED LIKE YOUR WORK!
GOOD LORD! SUPERMAN!
3

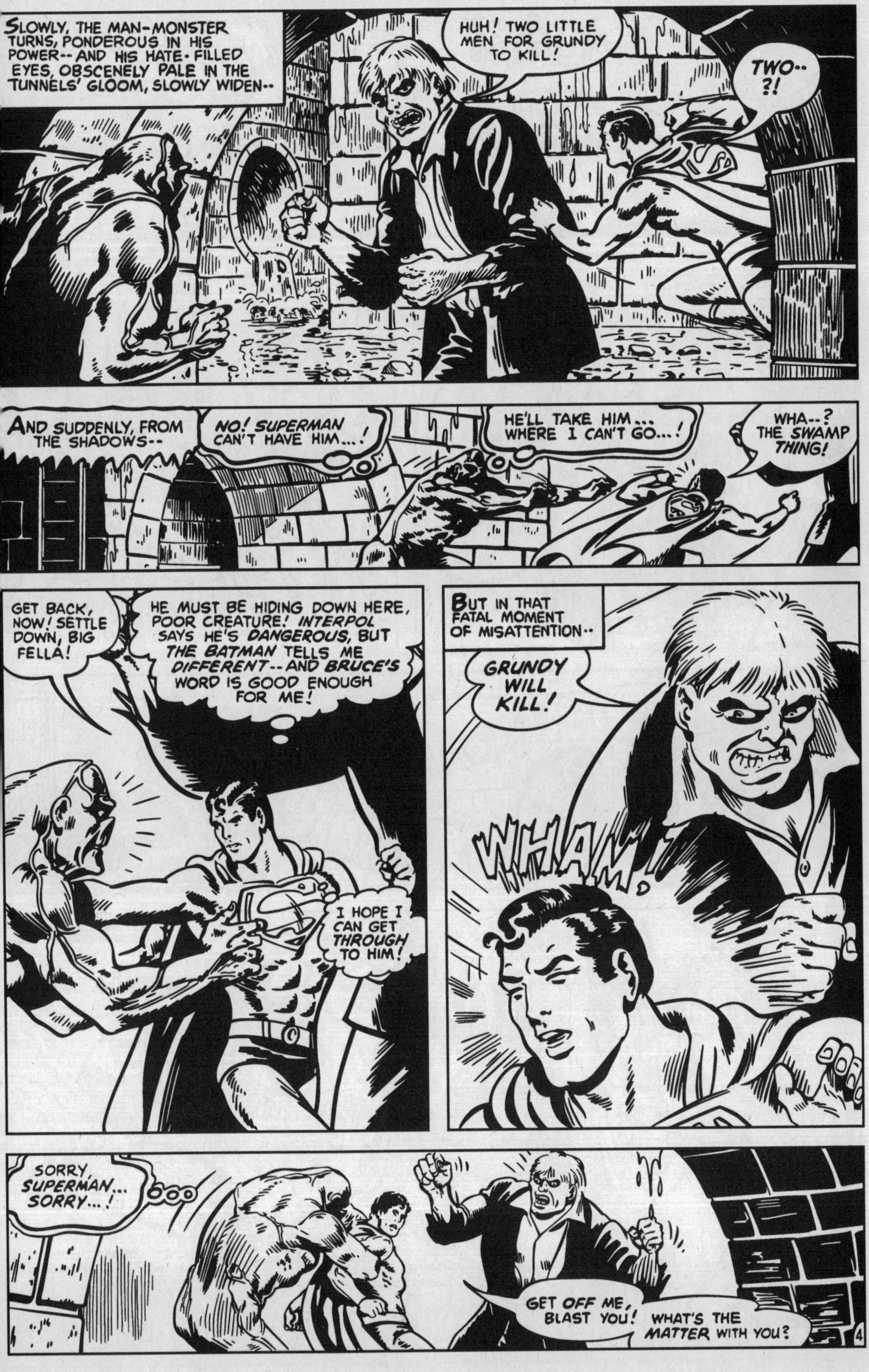
SLOWLY, THE MAN-MONSTER TURNS, PONDEROUS IN HIS POWER-- AND HIS HATE-FILLED EYES, OBSCENELY PALE IN THE TUNNELS' GLOOM, SLOWLY WIDEN--
HUH! TWO LITTLE MEN FOR GRUNDY TO KILL!
TWO-- ?!
AND SUDDENLY, FROM THE SHADOWS--
NO! SUPERMAN CAN'T HAVE HIM...!
HE'LL TAKE HIM... WHERE I CAN'T GO...!
WHA--? THE SWAMP THING!
GET BACK, NOW! SETTLE DOWN, BIG FELLA!
HE MUST BE HIDING DOWN HERE, POOR CREATURE! INTERPOL SAYS HE'S DANGEROUS, BUT THE BATMAN TELLS ME DIFFERENT--AND BRUCE'S WORD IS GOOD ENOUGH FOR ME!
I HOPE I CAN GET THROUGH TO HIM!
BUT IN THAT FATAL MOMENT OF MISATTENTION--
GRUNDY WILL KILL!
WHAM!
SORRY, SUPERMAN... SORRY...!
GET OFF ME, BLAST YOU!
WHAT'S THE MATTER WITH YOU?
4

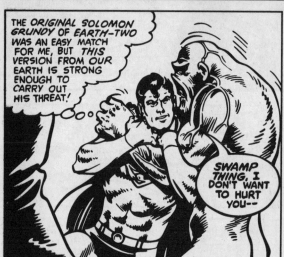

THE *ORIGINAL* SOLOMON *GRUNDY* OF EARTH-TWO WAS AN EASY MATCH FOR ME, BUT *THIS* VERSION FROM OUR EARTH IS STRONG ENOUGH TO CARRY OUT HIS THREAT!

SWAMP THING, I DON'T WANT TO HURT YOU--

--BUT I HAVE TO GET *FREE!*

UUHN! DIDN'T MEAN TO DO *THAT!* BUT IT DOESN'T SEEM TO *HURT* HIM!

NOW, GRUNDY..!

KRAM!

BLUM!

KRAK!

GRUNDY WILL *KILL!*

5

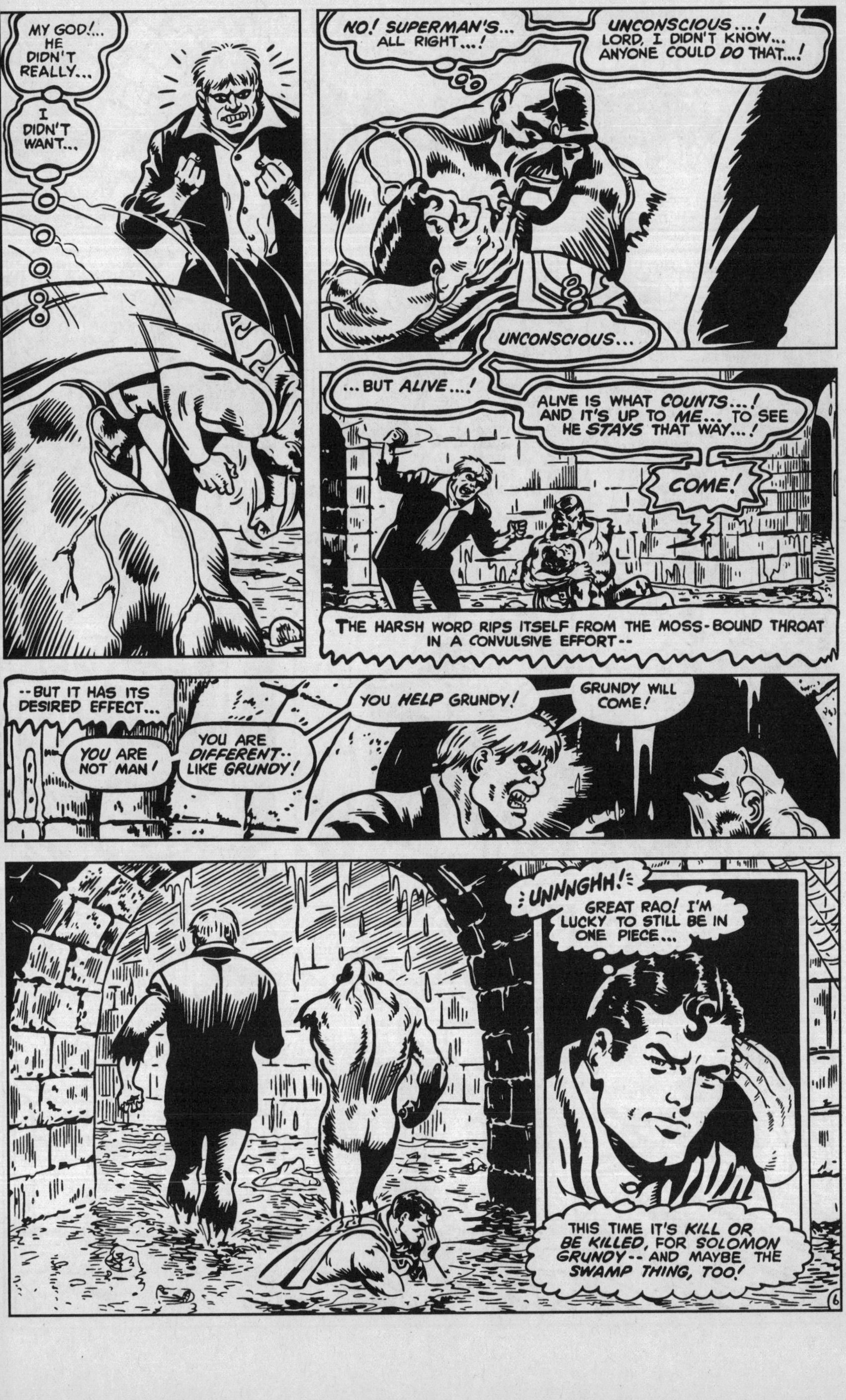
MY GOD!... HE DIDN'T REALLY...
I DIDN'T WANT...
NO! SUPERMAN'S... ALL RIGHT...!
UNCONSCIOUS....! LORD, I DIDN'T KNOW... ANYONE COULD DO THAT...!
UNCONSCIOUS...
...BUT ALIVE...!
ALIVE IS WHAT COUNTS...! AND IT'S UP TO ME... TO SEE HE STAYS THAT WAY...!
COME!
THE HARSH WORD RIPS ITSELF FROM THE MOSS-BOUND THROAT IN A CONVULSIVE EFFORT--
--BUT IT HAS ITS DESIRED EFFECT...
YOU ARE NOT MAN!
YOU ARE DIFFERENT.. LIKE GRUNDY!
YOU HELP GRUNDY!
GRUNDY WILL COME!
UNNNGHH!
GREAT RAO! I'M LUCKY TO STILL BE IN ONE PIECE...
THIS TIME IT'S KILL OR BE KILLED, FOR SOLOMON GRUNDY--AND MAYBE THE SWAMP THING, TOO!
6

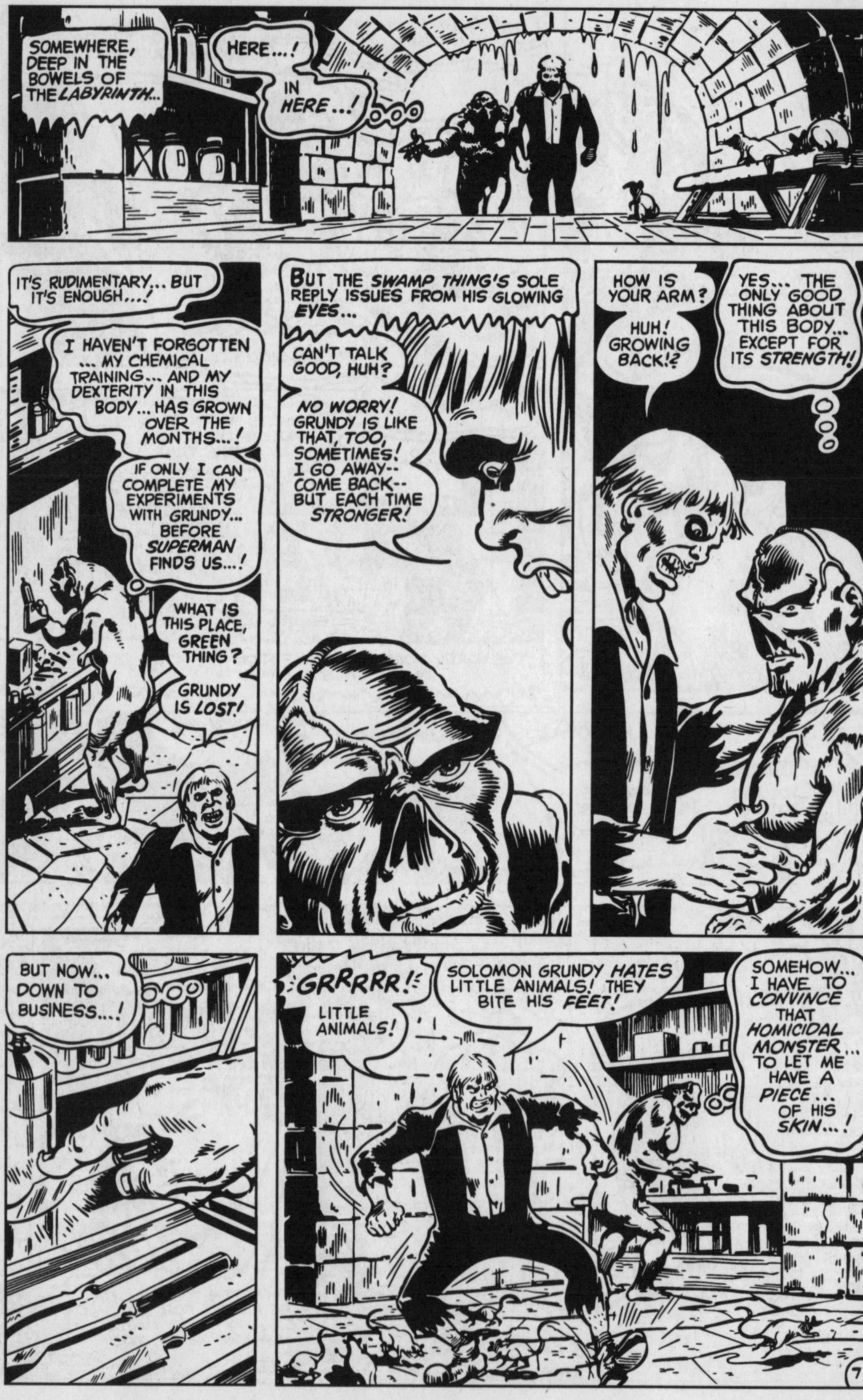
SOMEWHERE, DEEP IN THE BOWELS OF THE LABYRINTH...
HERE...!
IN HERE...!
IT'S RUDIMENTARY... BUT IT'S ENOUGH...!
I HAVEN'T FORGOTTEN ... MY CHEMICAL TRAINING... AND MY DEXTERITY IN THIS BODY... HAS GROWN OVER THE MONTHS...!
IF ONLY I CAN COMPLETE MY EXPERIMENTS WITH GRUNDY... BEFORE SUPERMAN FINDS US...!
WHAT IS THIS PLACE, GREEN THING?
GRUNDY IS LOST!
BUT THE SWAMP THING'S SOLE REPLY ISSUES FROM HIS GLOWING EYES...
CAN'T TALK GOOD, HUH?
NO WORRY! GRUNDY IS LIKE THAT, TOO, SOMETIMES! I GO AWAY-- COME BACK-- BUT EACH TIME STRONGER!
HOW IS YOUR ARM?
HUH! GROWING BACK!?
YES... THE ONLY GOOD THING ABOUT THIS BODY... EXCEPT FOR ITS STRENGTH!
BUT NOW... DOWN TO BUSINESS...!
GRRRRR!
LITTLE ANIMALS!
SOLOMON GRUNDY HATES LITTLE ANIMALS! THEY BITE HIS FEET!
SOMEHOW... I HAVE TO CONVINCE THAT HOMICIDAL MONSTER... TO LET ME HAVE A PIECE... OF HIS SKIN...!
7

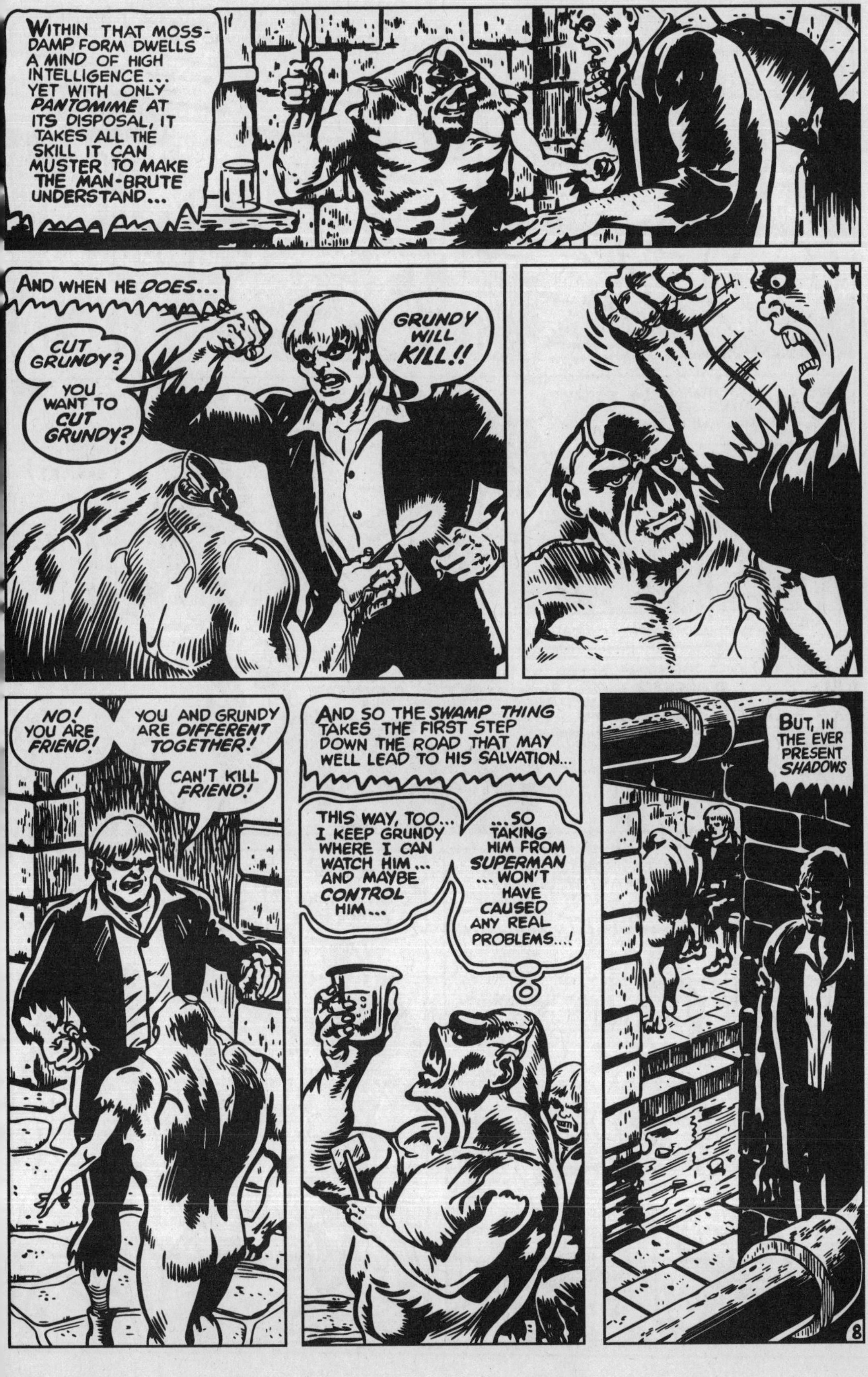
WITHIN THAT MOSS-DAMP FORM DWELLS A MIND OF HIGH INTELLIGENCE... YET WITH ONLY PANTOMIME AT ITS DISPOSAL, IT TAKES ALL THE SKILL IT CAN MUSTER TO MAKE THE MAN-BRUTE UNDERSTAND...
AND WHEN HE DOES...
CUT GRUNDY?
YOU WANT TO CUT GRUNDY?
GRUNDY WILL KILL!!
NO! YOU ARE FRIEND!
YOU AND GRUNDY ARE DIFFERENT TOGETHER!
CAN'T KILL FRIEND!
AND SO THE SWAMP THING TAKES THE FIRST STEP DOWN THE ROAD THAT MAY WELL LEAD TO HIS SALVATION...
THIS WAY, TOO... I KEEP GRUNDY WHERE I CAN WATCH HIM... AND MAYBE CONTROL HIM...
...SO TAKING HIM FROM SUPERMAN ...WON'T HAVE CAUSED ANY REAL PROBLEMS...!
BUT, IN THE EVER PRESENT SHADOWS
8

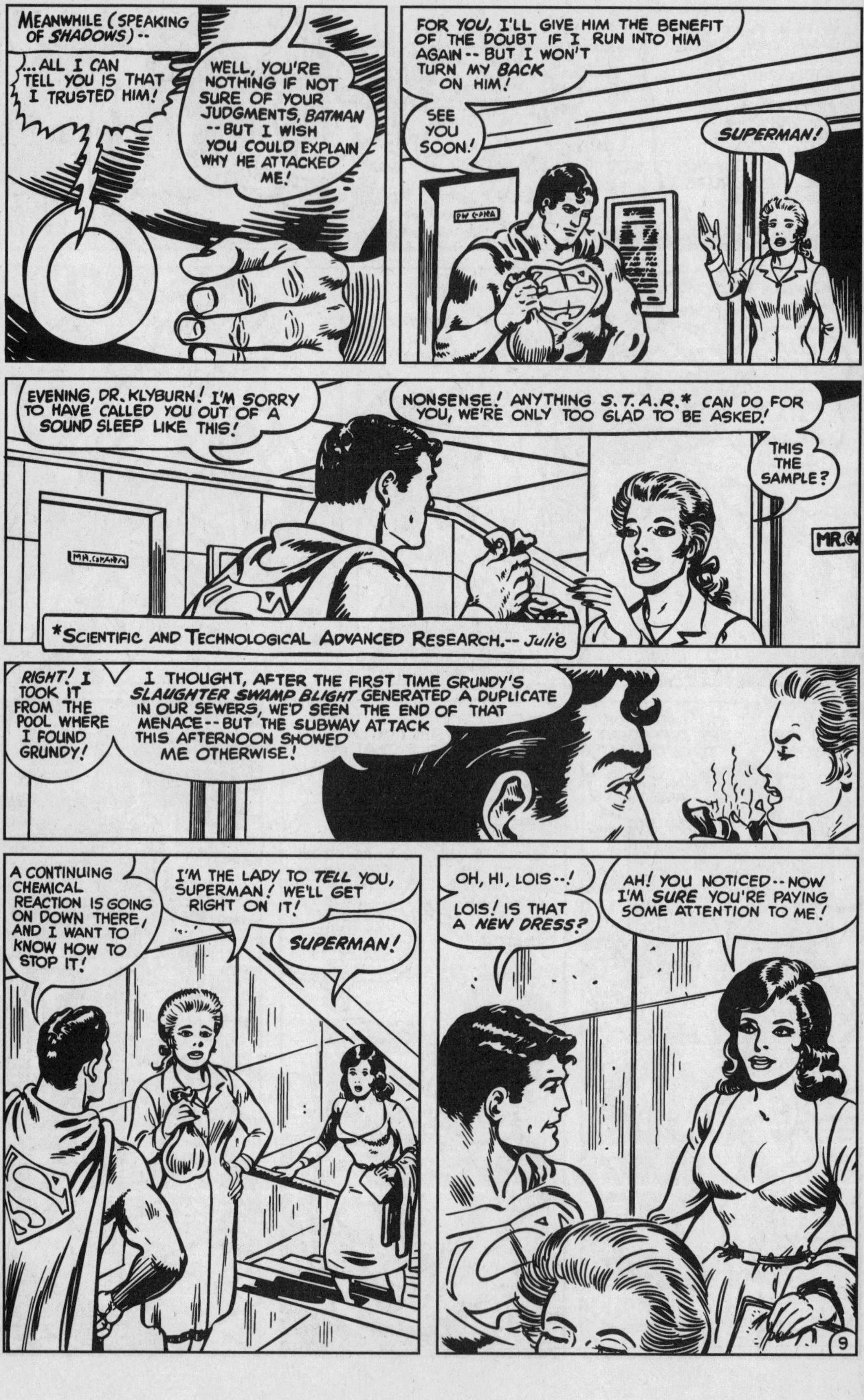
MEANWHILE (SPEAKING OF SHADOWS)--
...ALL I CAN TELL YOU IS THAT I TRUSTED HIM!
WELL, YOU'RE NOTHING IF NOT SURE OF YOUR JUDGMENTS, BATMAN --BUT I WISH YOU COULD EXPLAIN WHY HE ATTACKED ME!
FOR YOU, I'LL GIVE HIM THE BENEFIT OF THE DOUBT IF I RUN INTO HIM AGAIN--BUT I WON'T TURN MY BACK ON HIM!
SEE YOU SOON!
SUPERMAN!
EVENING, DR. KLYBURN! I'M SORRY TO HAVE CALLED YOU OUT OF A SOUND SLEEP LIKE THIS!
NONSENSE! ANYTHING S.T.A.R.* CAN DO FOR YOU, WE'RE ONLY TOO GLAD TO BE ASKED!
THIS THE SAMPLE?
*SCIENTIFIC AND TECHNOLOGICAL ADVANCED RESEARCH.-- Julie
RIGHT! I TOOK IT FROM THE POOL WHERE I FOUND GRUNDY!
I THOUGHT, AFTER THE FIRST TIME GRUNDY'S SLAUGHTER SWAMP BLIGHT GENERATED A DUPLICATE IN OUR SEWERS, WE'D SEEN THE END OF THAT MENACE--BUT THE SUBWAY ATTACK THIS AFTERNOON SHOWED ME OTHERWISE!
A CONTINUING CHEMICAL REACTION IS GOING ON DOWN THERE, AND I WANT TO KNOW HOW TO STOP IT!
I'M THE LADY TO TELL YOU, SUPERMAN! WE'LL GET RIGHT ON IT!
SUPERMAN!
OH, HI, LOIS--!
LOIS! IS THAT A NEW DRESS?
AH! YOU NOTICED--NOW I'M SURE YOU'RE PAYING SOME ATTENTION TO ME!
9

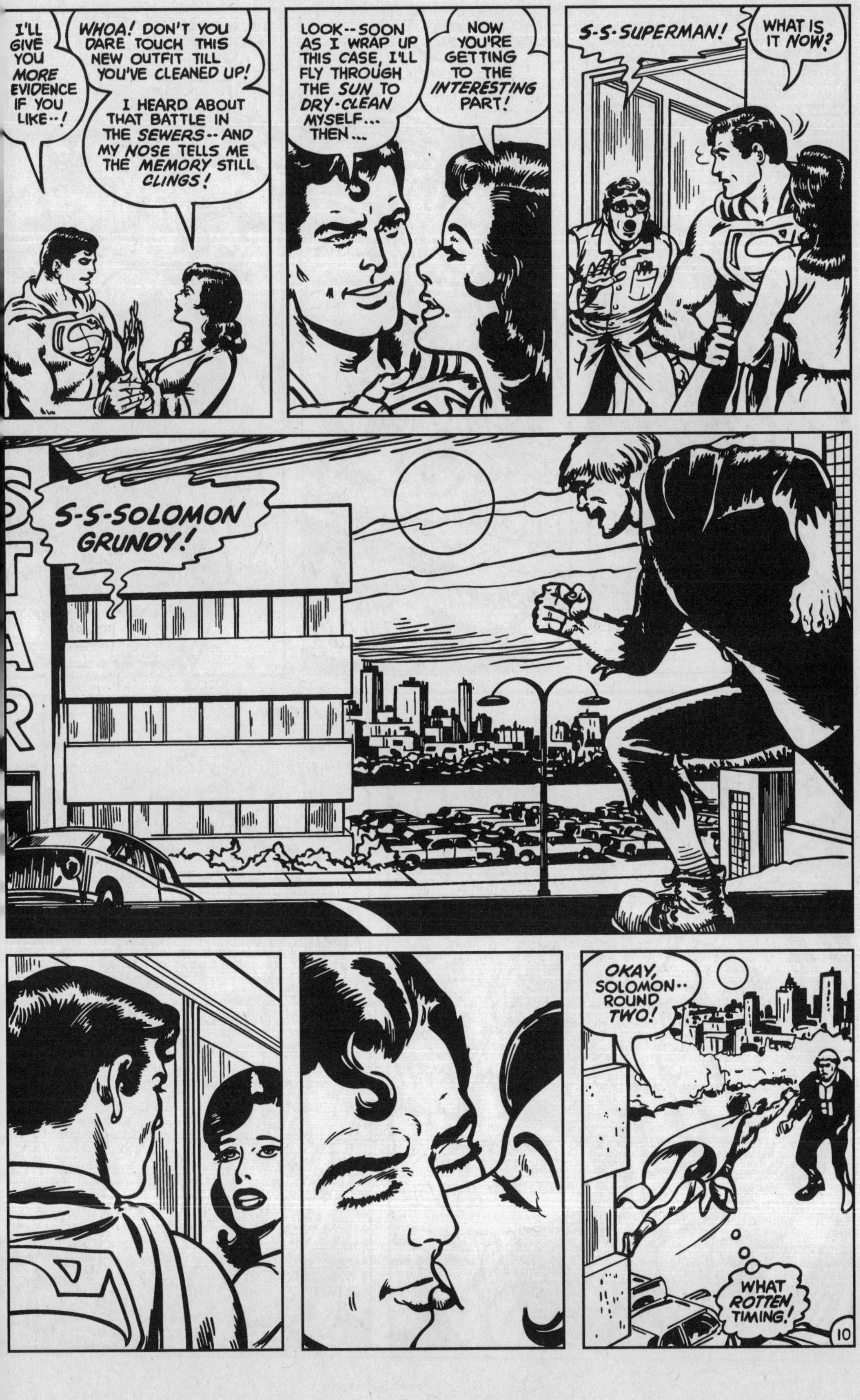
I'LL GIVE YOU MORE EVIDENCE IF YOU LIKE--!
WHOA! DON'T YOU DARE TOUCH THIS NEW OUTFIT TILL YOU'VE CLEANED UP!
I HEARD ABOUT THAT BATTLE IN THE SEWERS--AND MY NOSE TELLS ME THE MEMORY STILL CLINGS!
LOOK--SOON AS I WRAP UP THIS CASE, I'LL FLY THROUGH THE SUN TO DRY-CLEAN MYSELF... THEN...
NOW YOU'RE GETTING TO THE INTERESTING PART!
S-S-SUPERMAN!
WHAT IS IT NOW?
S-S-SOLOMON GRUNDY!
OKAY, SOLOMON-- ROUND TWO!
WHAT ROTTEN TIMING!
10

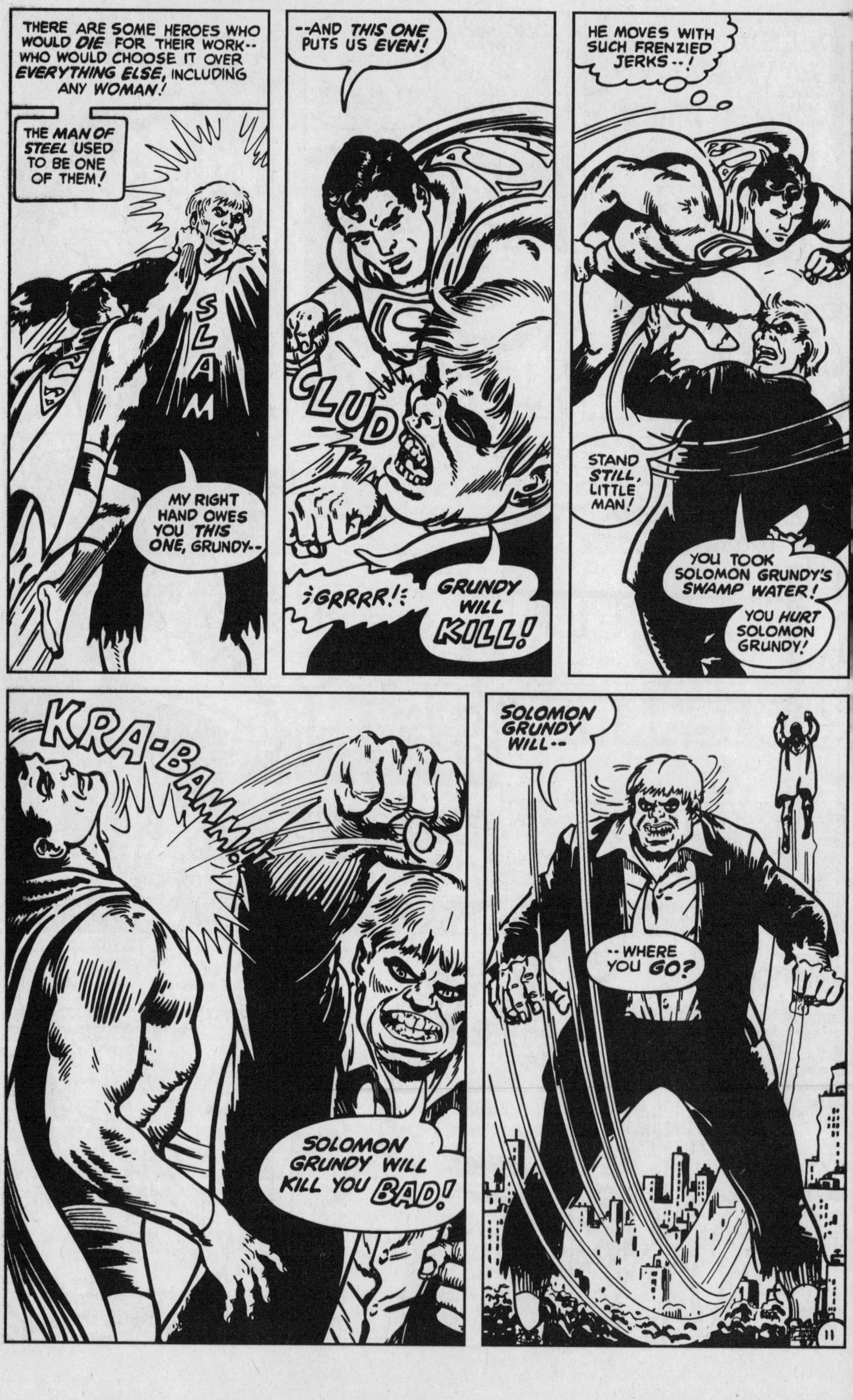
THERE ARE SOME HEROES WHO WOULD DIE FOR THEIR WORK-- WHO WOULD CHOOSE IT OVER EVERYTHING ELSE, INCLUDING ANY WOMAN!
THE MAN OF STEEL USED TO BE ONE OF THEM!
SLAM
MY RIGHT HAND OWES YOU THIS ONE, GRUNDY--
--AND THIS ONE PUTS US EVEN!
CLUD
GRRRR!
GRUNDY WILL KILL!
HE MOVES WITH SUCH FRENZIED JERKS--!
STAND STILL, LITTLE MAN!
YOU TOOK SOLOMON GRUNDY'S SWAMP WATER!
YOU HURT SOLOMON GRUNDY!
KRA-BAM
SOLOMON GRUNDY WILL KILL YOU BAD!
SOLOMON GRUNDY WILL--
--WHERE YOU GO?
11

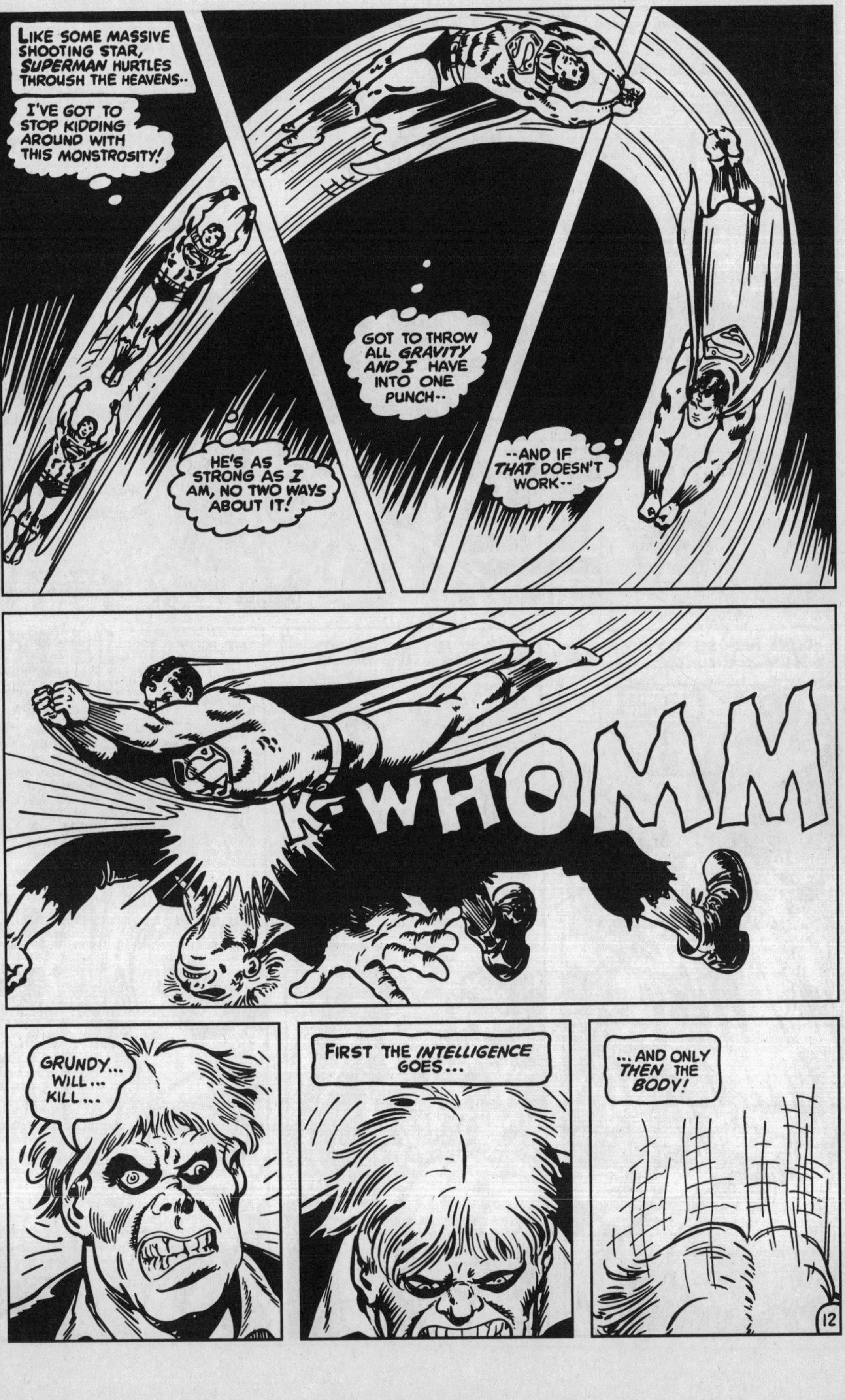
LIKE SOME MASSIVE SHOOTING STAR, SUPERMAN HURTLES THROUSH THE HEAVENS..
I'VE GOT TO STOP KIDDING AROUND WITH THIS MONSTROSITY!
HE'S AS STRONG AS I AM, NO TWO WAYS ABOUT IT!
GOT TO THROW ALL GRAVITY AND I HAVE INTO ONE PUNCH..
--AND IF THAT DOESN'T WORK--
K-WHOMM
GRUNDY... WILL... KILL...
FIRST THE INTELLIGENCE GOES...
... AND ONLY THEN THE BODY!
12

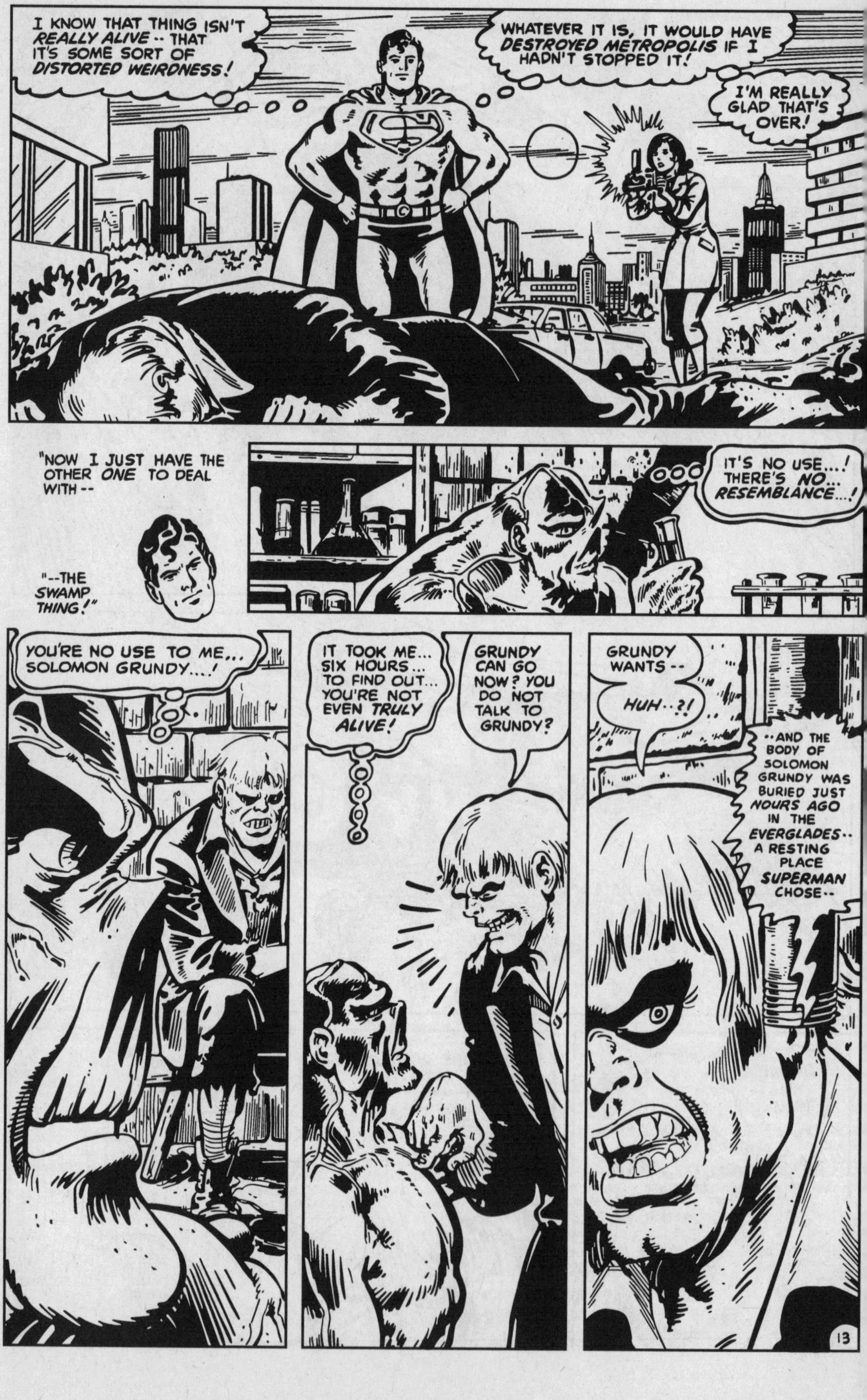
I KNOW THAT THING ISN'T REALLY ALIVE -- THAT IT'S SOME SORT OF DISTORTED WEIRDNESS!
WHATEVER IT IS, IT WOULD HAVE DESTROYED METROPOLIS IF I HADN'T STOPPED IT!
I'M REALLY GLAD THAT'S OVER!
"NOW I JUST HAVE THE OTHER ONE TO DEAL WITH --
"--THE SWAMP THING!"
IT'S NO USE....! THERE'S NO... RESEMBLANCE....!
YOU'RE NO USE TO ME... SOLOMON GRUNDY....!
IT TOOK ME... SIX HOURS... TO FIND OUT... YOU'RE NOT EVEN TRULY ALIVE!
GRUNDY CAN GO NOW? YOU DO NOT TALK TO GRUNDY?
GRUNDY WANTS --
HUH..?!
..AND THE BODY OF SOLOMON GRUNDY WAS BURIED JUST HOURS AGO IN THE EVERGLADES.. A RESTING PLACE SUPERMAN CHOSE..
13

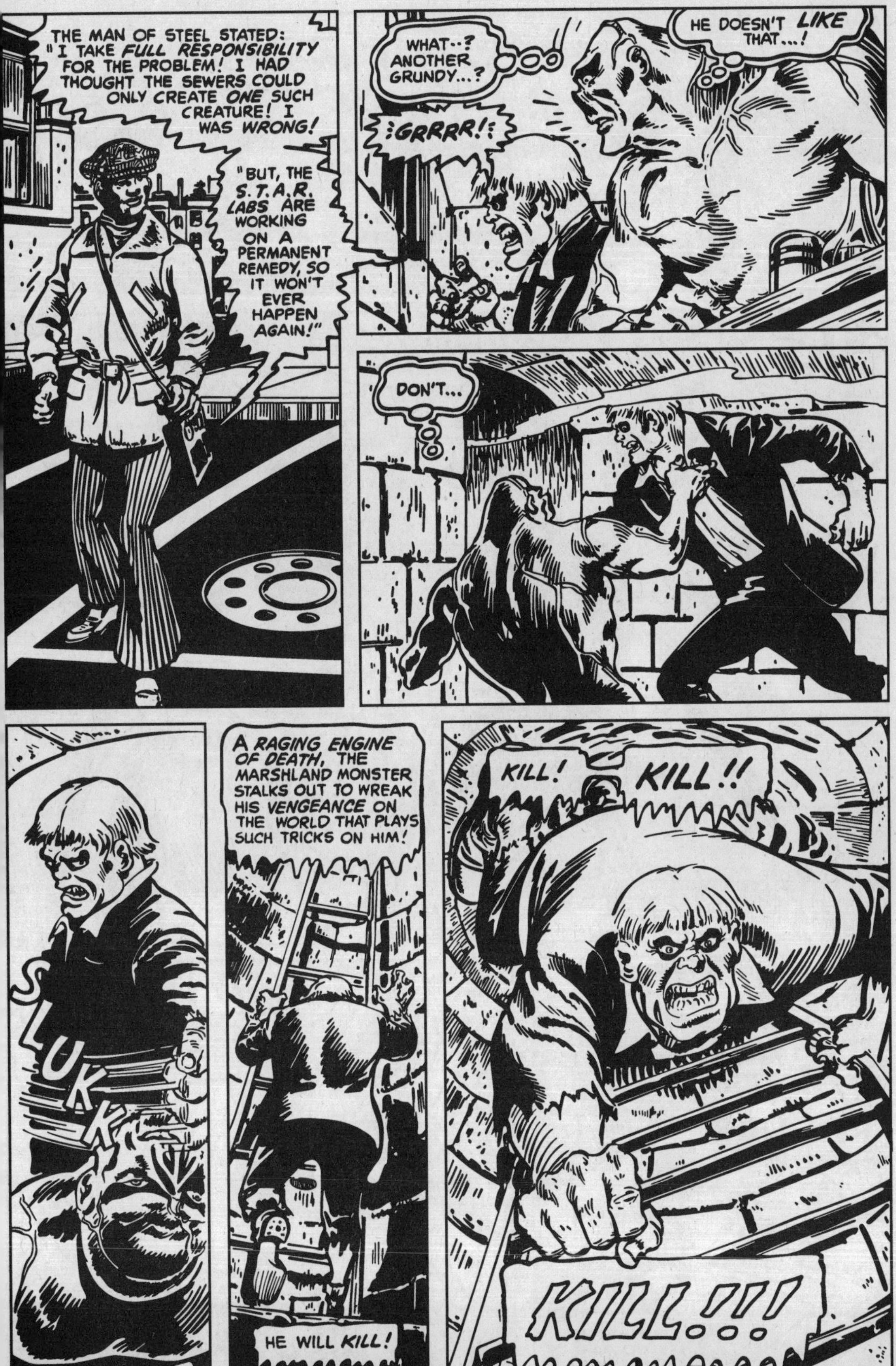
THE MAN OF STEEL STATED: "I TAKE FULL RESPONSIBILITY FOR THE PROBLEM! I HAD THOUGHT THE SEWERS COULD ONLY CREATE ONE SUCH CREATURE! I WAS WRONG!
"BUT, THE S.T.A.R. LABS ARE WORKING ON A PERMANENT REMEDY, SO IT WON'T EVER HAPPEN AGAIN!"
WHAT..? ANOTHER GRUNDY...?
GRRRR!
HE DOESN'T LIKE THAT...!
DON'T...
SLUK
A RAGING ENGINE OF DEATH, THE MARSHLAND MONSTER STALKS OUT TO WREAK HIS VENGEANCE ON THE WORLD THAT PLAYS SUCH TRICKS ON HIM!
HE WILL KILL!
KILL!
KILL!!
KILL...!!!
14

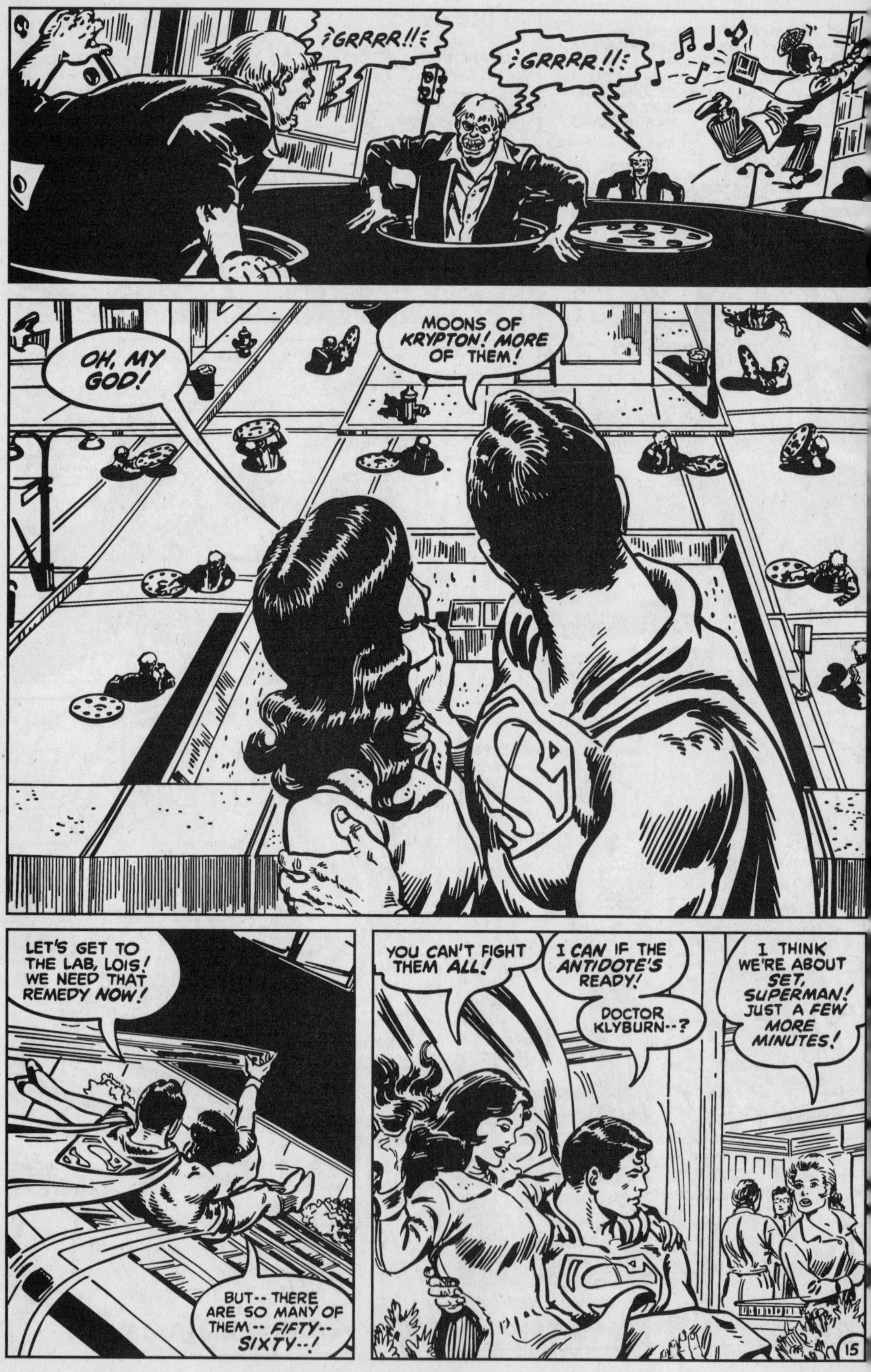
GRRRR!!
GRRRR!!
OH, MY GOD!
MOONS OF KRYPTON! MORE OF THEM!
LET'S GET TO THE LAB, LOIS! WE NEED THAT REMEDY NOW!
BUT-- THERE ARE SO MANY OF THEM -- FIFTY-- SIXTY--!
YOU CAN'T FIGHT THEM ALL!
I CAN IF THE ANTIDOTE'S READY!
DOCTOR KLYBURN--?
I THINK WE'RE ABOUT SET, SUPERMAN! JUST A FEW MORE MINUTES!
15

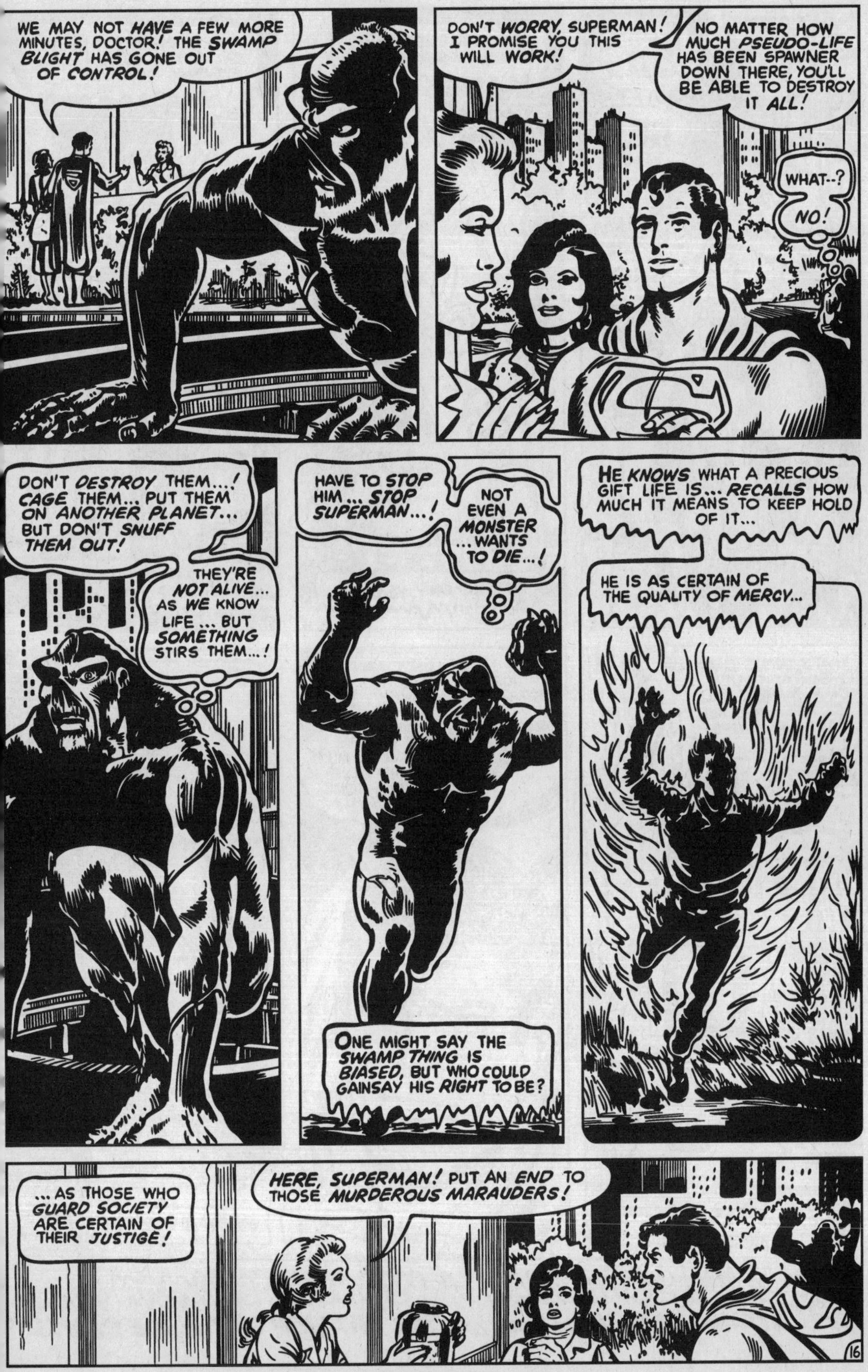
WE MAY NOT HAVE A FEW MORE MINUTES, DOCTOR! THE SWAMP BLIGHT HAS GONE OUT OF CONTROL!
DON'T WORRY, SUPERMAN! I PROMISE YOU THIS WILL WORK!
NO MATTER HOW MUCH PSEUDO-LIFE HAS BEEN SPAWNER DOWN THERE, YOU'LL BE ABLE TO DESTROY IT ALL!
WHAT--?
NO!
DON'T DESTROY THEM....! CAGE THEM... PUT THEM ON ANOTHER PLANET... BUT DON'T SNUFF THEM OUT!
THEY'RE NOT ALIVE... AS WE KNOW LIFE ... BUT SOMETHING STIRS THEM...!
HAVE TO STOP HIM ... STOP SUPERMAN...!
NOT EVEN A MONSTER ...WANTS TO DIE...!
ONE MIGHT SAY THE SWAMP THING IS BIASED, BUT WHO COULD GAINSAY HIS RIGHT TO BE?
HE KNOWS WHAT A PRECIOUS GIFT LIFE IS... RECALLS HOW MUCH IT MEANS TO KEEP HOLD OF IT...
HE IS AS CERTAIN OF THE QUALITY OF MERCY...
...AS THOSE WHO GUARD SOCIETY ARE CERTAIN OF THEIR JUSTICE!
HERE, SUPERMAN! PUT AN END TO THOSE MURDEROUS MARAUDERS!
16

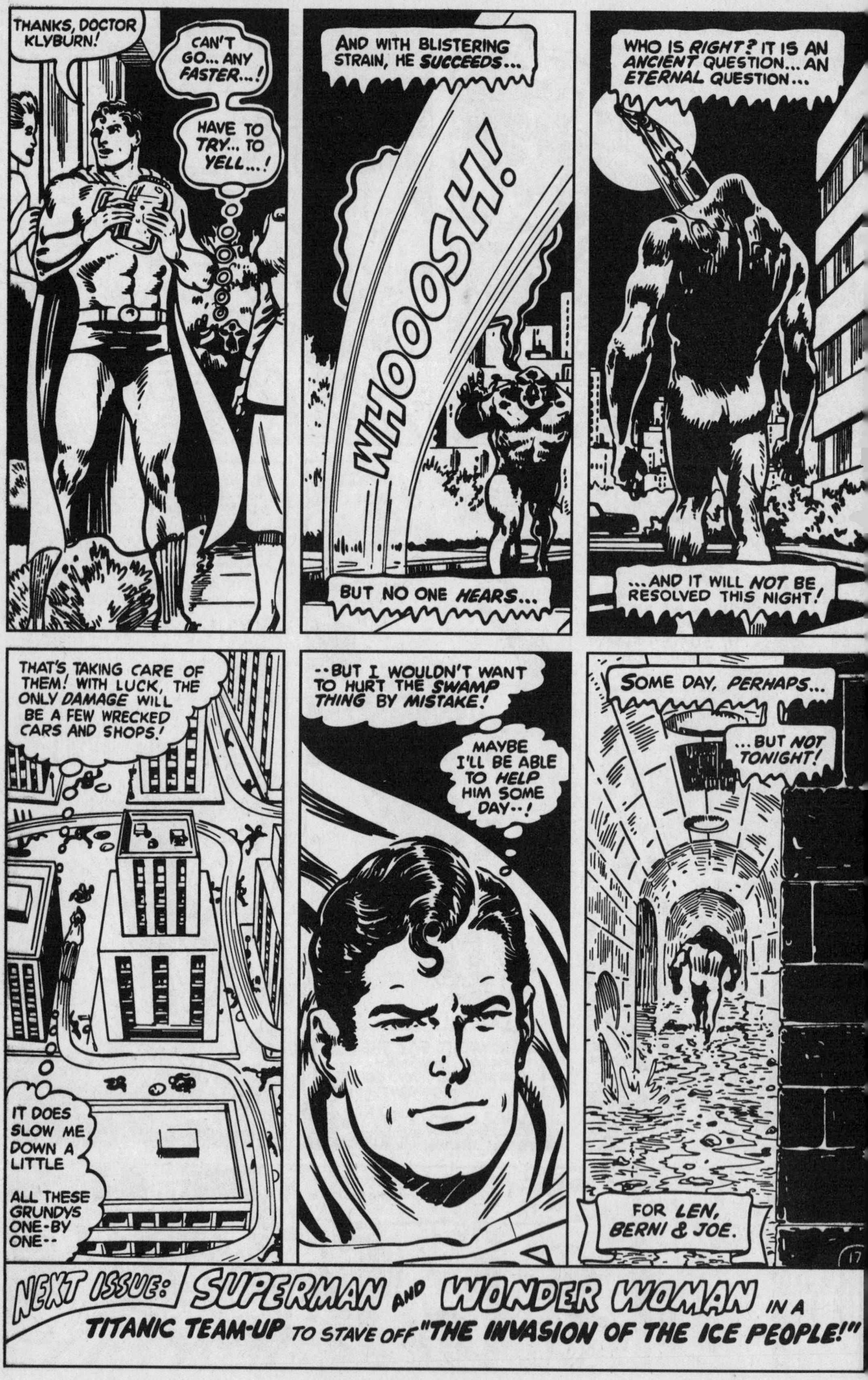
THANKS, DOCTOR KLYBURN!
CAN'T GO... ANY FASTER...!
HAVE TO TRY... TO YELL...!
AND WITH BLISTERING STRAIN, HE SUCCEEDS...
WHOOOSH!
BUT NO ONE HEARS...
WHO IS RIGHT? IT IS AN ANCIENT QUESTION... AN ETERNAL QUESTION...
...AND IT WILL NOT BE RESOLVED THIS NIGHT!
THAT'S TAKING CARE OF THEM! WITH LUCK, THE ONLY DAMAGE WILL BE A FEW WRECKED CARS AND SHOPS!
IT DOES SLOW ME DOWN A LITTLE
ALL THESE GRUNDYS ONE-BY ONE--
--BUT I WOULDN'T WANT TO HURT THE SWAMP THING BY MISTAKE!
MAYBE I'LL BE ABLE TO HELP HIM SOME DAY--!
SOME DAY, PERHAPS...
...BUT NOT TONIGHT!
FOR LEN, BERNI & JOE.
17
NEXT ISSUE: SUPERMAN AND WONDER WOMAN IN A TITANIC TEAM-UP TO STAVE OFF "THE INVASION OF THE ICE PEOPLE!"

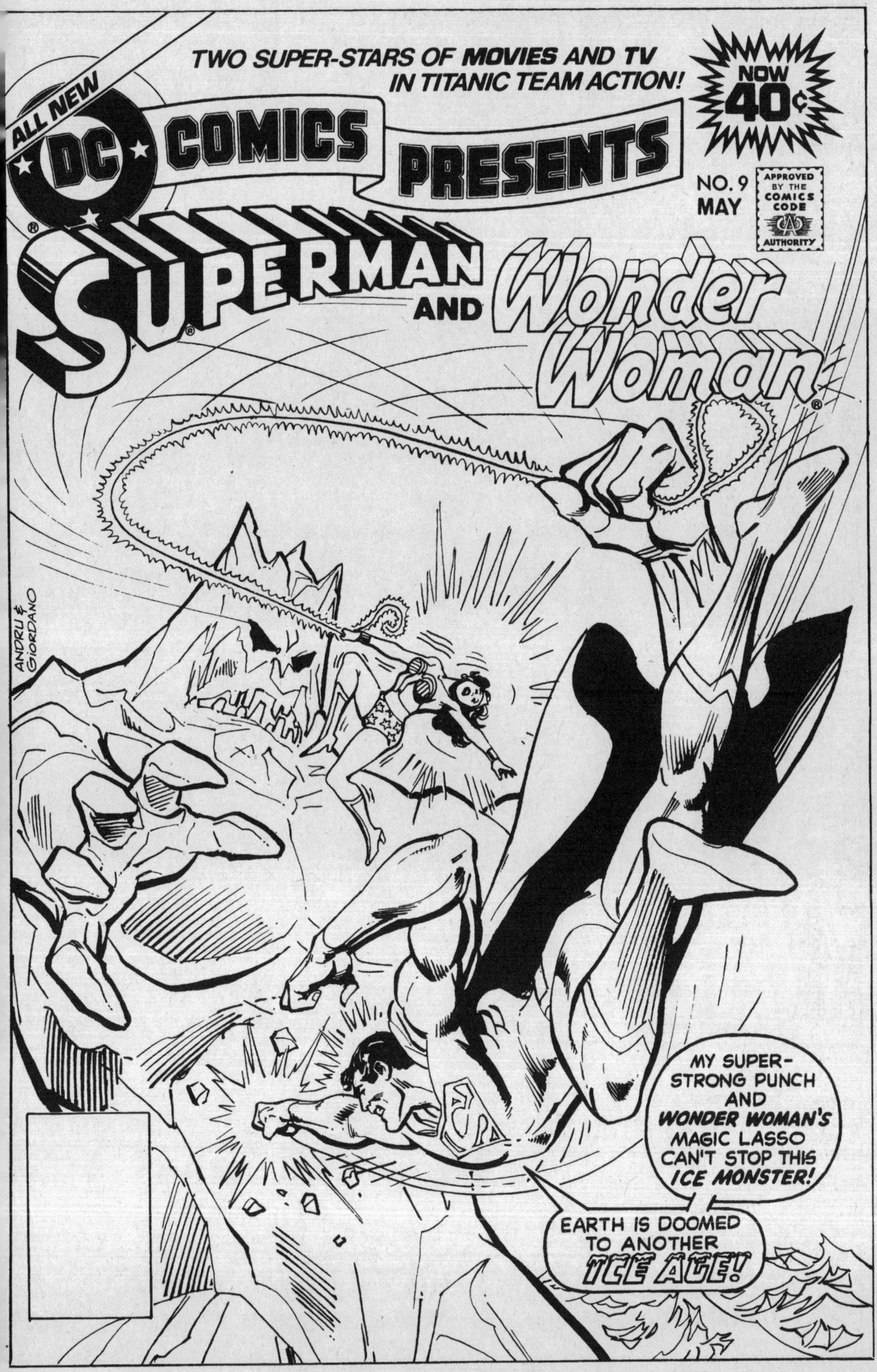
TWO SUPER-STARS OF MOVIES AND TV IN TITANIC TEAM ACTION!
NOW 40¢
ALL NEW
DC COMICS PRESENTS
NO. 9 MAY
APPROVED BY THE COMICS CODE AUTHORITY
SUPERMAN AND Wonder Woman
ANDRU & GIORDANO
MY SUPER-STRONG PUNCH AND WONDER WOMAN'S MAGIC LASSO CAN'T STOP THIS ICE MONSTER!
EARTH IS DOOMED TO ANOTHER ICE AGE!

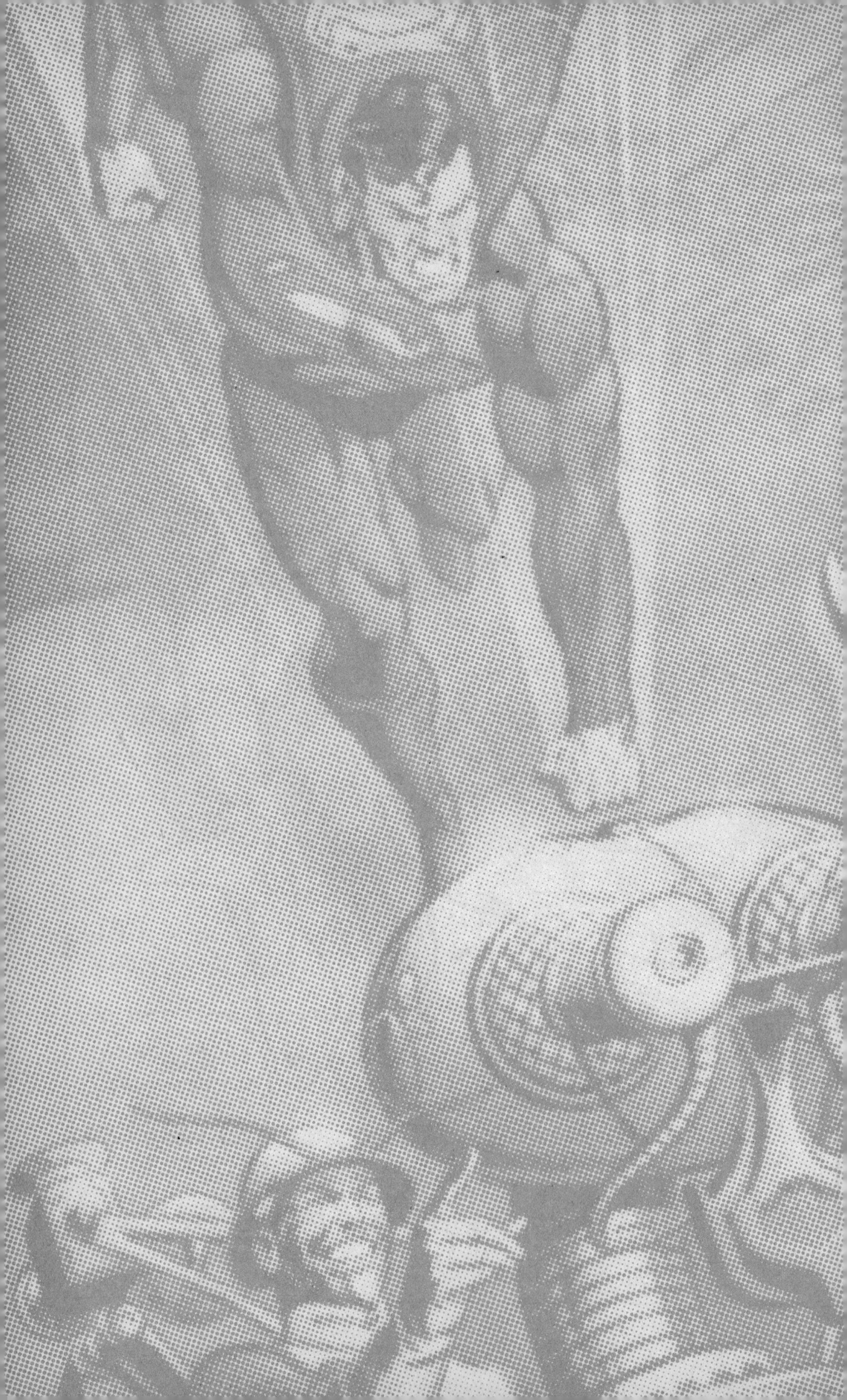

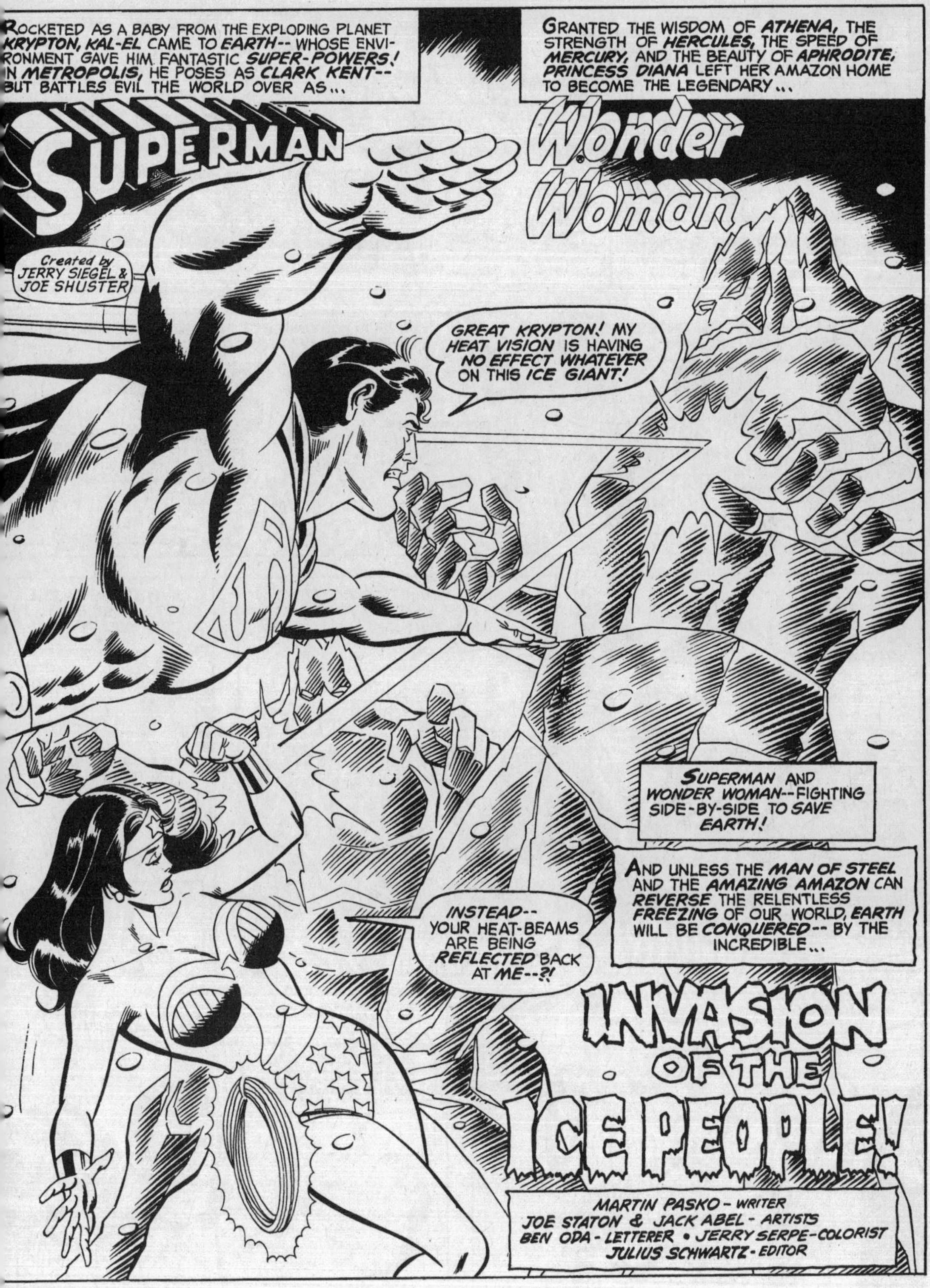
ROCKETED AS A BABY FROM THE EXPLODING PLANET KRYPTON, KAL-EL CAME TO EARTH-- WHOSE ENVIRONMENT GAVE HIM FANTASTIC SUPER-POWERS! IN METROPOLIS, HE POSES AS CLARK KENT-- BUT BATTLES EVIL THE WORLD OVER AS...
SUPERMAN
Created by JERRY SIEGEL & JOE SHUSTER
GRANTED THE WISDOM OF ATHENA, THE STRENGTH OF HERCULES, THE SPEED OF MERCURY, AND THE BEAUTY OF APHRODITE, PRINCESS DIANA LEFT HER AMAZON HOME TO BECOME THE LEGENDARY...
Wonder Woman
GREAT KRYPTON! MY HEAT VISION IS HAVING NO EFFECT WHATEVER ON THIS ICE GIANT!
INSTEAD-- YOUR HEAT-BEAMS ARE BEING REFLECTED BACK AT ME--?!
SUPERMAN AND WONDER WOMAN--FIGHTING SIDE-BY-SIDE TO SAVE EARTH!
AND UNLESS THE MAN OF STEEL AND THE AMAZING AMAZON CAN REVERSE THE RELENTLESS FREEZING OF OUR WORLD, EARTH WILL BE CONQUERED-- BY THE INCREDIBLE...
INVASION OF THE ICE PEOPLE!
MARTIN PASKO - WRITER
JOE STATON & JACK ABEL - ARTISTS
BEN ODA - LETTERER • JERRY SERPE - COLORIST
JULIUS SCHWARTZ - EDITOR

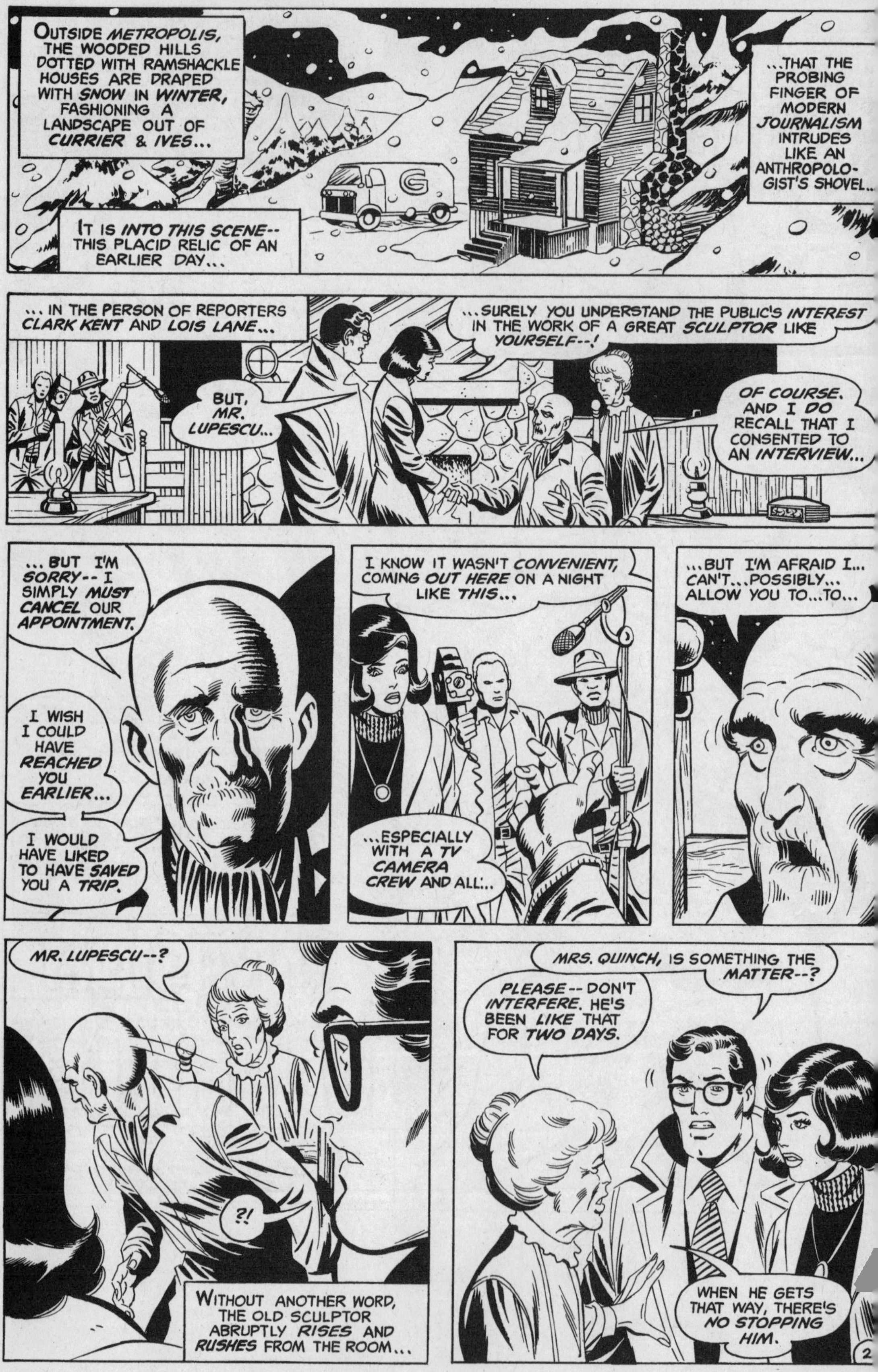
OUTSIDE METROPOLIS, THE WOODED HILLS DOTTED WITH RAMSHACKLE HOUSES ARE DRAPED WITH SNOW IN WINTER, FASHIONING A LANDSCAPE OUT OF CURRIER & IVES...
IT IS INTO THIS SCENE-- THIS PLACID RELIC OF AN EARLIER DAY...
...THAT THE PROBING FINGER OF MODERN JOURNALISM INTRUDES LIKE AN ANTHROPOLOGIST'S SHOVEL...
...IN THE PERSON OF REPORTERS CLARK KENT AND LOIS LANE...
...SURELY YOU UNDERSTAND THE PUBLIC'S INTEREST IN THE WORK OF A GREAT SCULPTOR LIKE YOURSELF--!
BUT, MR. LUPESCU...
OF COURSE. AND I DO RECALL THAT I CONSENTED TO AN INTERVIEW...
...BUT I'M SORRY-- I SIMPLY MUST CANCEL OUR APPOINTMENT.
I WISH I COULD HAVE REACHED YOU EARLIER...
I WOULD HAVE LIKED TO HAVE SAVED YOU A TRIP.
I KNOW IT WASN'T CONVENIENT, COMING OUT HERE ON A NIGHT LIKE THIS...
...ESPECIALLY WITH A TV CAMERA CREW AND ALL...
...BUT I'M AFRAID I... CAN'T...POSSIBLY... ALLOW YOU TO...TO...
MR. LUPESCU--?
?!
WITHOUT ANOTHER WORD, THE OLD SCULPTOR ABRUPTLY RISES AND RUSHES FROM THE ROOM...
MRS. QUINCH, IS SOMETHING THE MATTER--?
PLEASE-- DON'T INTERFERE. HE'S BEEN LIKE THAT FOR TWO DAYS.
WHEN HE GETS THAT WAY, THERE'S NO STOPPING HIM.
2

"EVERY SO OFTEN, A KIND OF... *TRANCE* COMES OVER HIM...

"...AND HE GOES OUT TO RESUME WORK ON THAT...THAT *THING!*

"HE *STARTED* IT AS A GIANT *SNOWMAN!* AT FIRST I THOUGHT HE WAS GOING *SENILE*, DOING SUCH A CHILDISH THING...

"...BUT THEN THE SNOW *FROZE* -- AND HE STARTED *CHISELING...*

"HE'S BEEN WORKING LIKE A *DEMON* -- AS IF UNDER A *SPELL* -- SLAVING TO COMPLETE IT AS *QUICKLY* AS POSSIBLE.

"HE'S CREATING AN *ICE-SCULPTURE* -- THAT'S ALL I KNOW!

"I TRY TO GET HIM TO *COME IN* TO WARM *UP* NOW AND THEN -- BUT HE *WON'T HEAR* OF IT..."

"...OR *CAN'T* HEAR! SO, YOU SEE, *MR. KENT*, YOU'VE COME HERE *IN VAIN...*

MAYBE *NOT.* HIS *STRANGE* BEHAVIOR IS A STORY IN ITSELF -- *EH?*

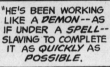
...IT'S... FINISHED.

FINALLY, IT'S...

AT LAST...

...FINISSSHHHH...

MR. LUPESCU --!

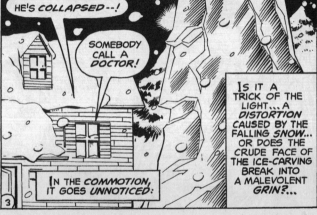

HE'S *COLLAPSED* --!

SOMEBODY CALL A *DOCTOR!*

IN THE *COMMOTION*, IT GOES *UNNOTICED:*

IS IT A TRICK OF THE LIGHT...A *DISTORTION* CAUSED BY THE FALLING *SNOW...* OR DOES THE CRUDE FACE OF THE ICE-CARVING BREAK INTO A MALEVOLENT *GRIN?...*

3

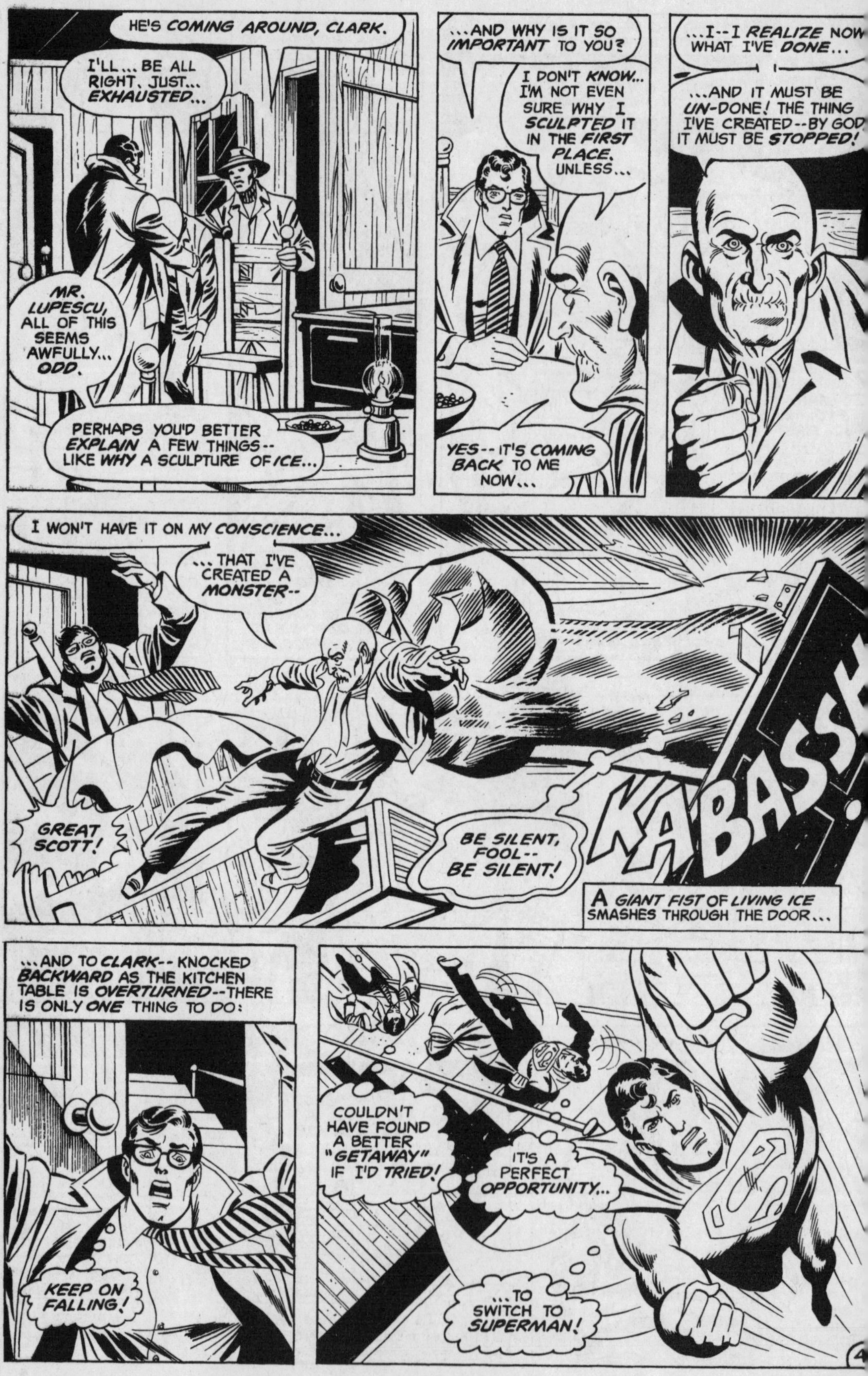
HE'S COMING AROUND, CLARK.
I'LL... BE ALL RIGHT, JUST... EXHAUSTED...
MR. LUPESCU, ALL OF THIS SEEMS AWFULLY... ODD.
PERHAPS YOU'D BETTER EXPLAIN A FEW THINGS-- LIKE WHY A SCULPTURE OF ICE...
...AND WHY IS IT SO IMPORTANT TO YOU?
I DON'T KNOW... I'M NOT EVEN SURE WHY I SCULPTED IT IN THE FIRST PLACE. UNLESS...
YES-- IT'S COMING BACK TO ME NOW...
...I--I REALIZE NOW WHAT I'VE DONE...
...AND IT MUST BE UN-DONE! THE THING I'VE CREATED--BY GOD IT MUST BE STOPPED!
I WON'T HAVE IT ON MY CONSCIENCE...
...THAT I'VE CREATED A MONSTER--
GREAT SCOTT!
BE SILENT, FOOL-- BE SILENT!
KABASSH
A GIANT FIST OF LIVING ICE SMASHES THROUGH THE DOOR...
...AND TO CLARK-- KNOCKED BACKWARD AS THE KITCHEN TABLE IS OVERTURNED--THERE IS ONLY ONE THING TO DO:
KEEP ON FALLING!
COULDN'T HAVE FOUND A BETTER "GETAWAY" IF I'D TRIED!
IT'S A PERFECT OPPORTUNITY...
...TO SWITCH TO SUPERMAN!
4

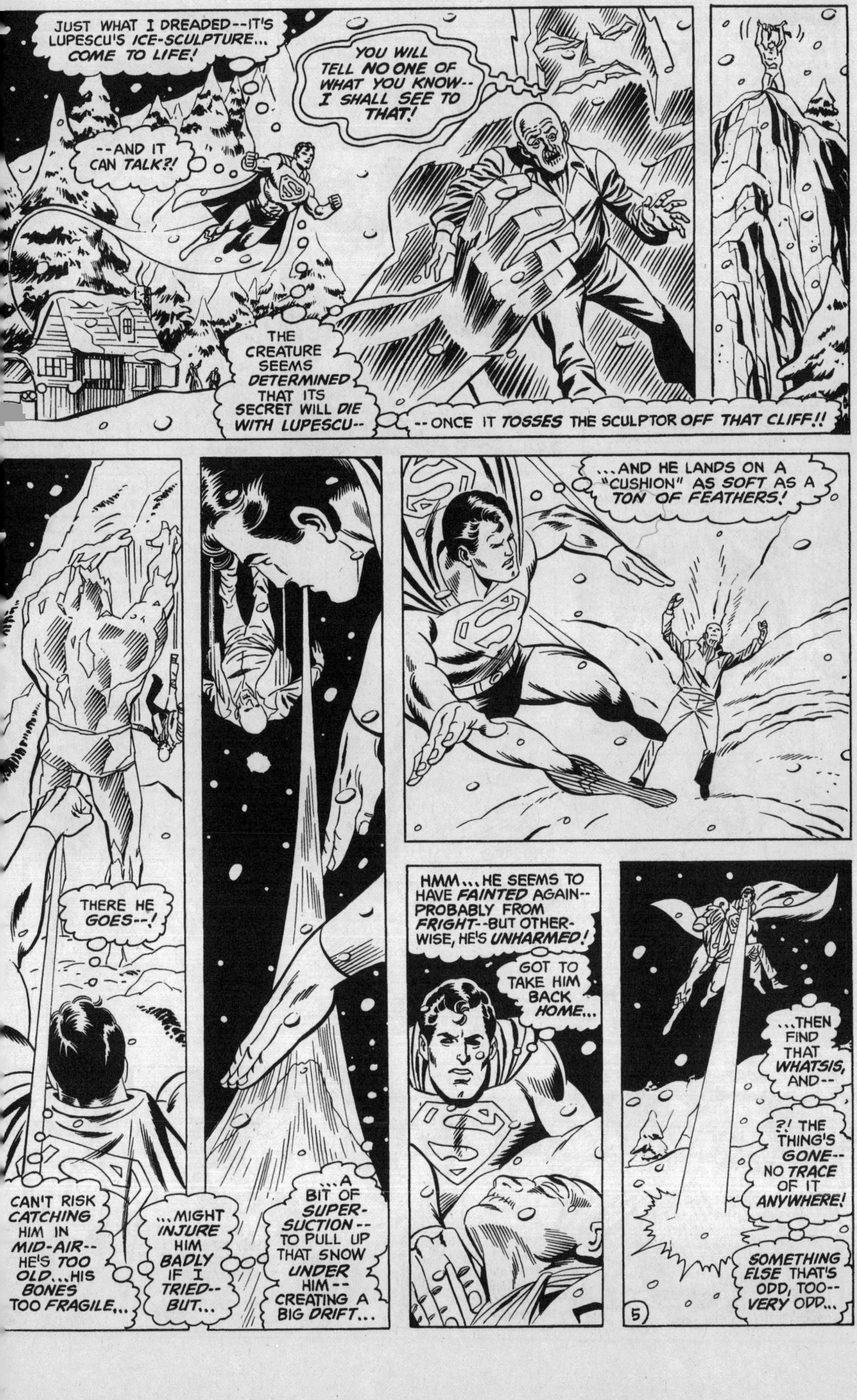
JUST WHAT I DREADED--IT'S LUPESCU'S ICE-SCULPTURE... COME TO LIFE!
--AND IT CAN TALK?!
YOU WILL TELL NO ONE OF WHAT YOU KNOW-- I SHALL SEE TO THAT!
THE CREATURE SEEMS DETERMINED THAT ITS SECRET WILL DIE WITH LUPESCU--
--ONCE IT TOSSES THE SCULPTOR OFF THAT CLIFF!!
THERE HE GOES--!
CAN'T RISK CATCHING HIM IN MID-AIR-- HE'S TOO OLD... HIS BONES TOO FRAGILE...
...MIGHT INJURE HIM BADLY IF I TRIED-- BUT...
...A BIT OF SUPER-SUCTION-- TO PULL UP THAT SNOW UNDER HIM-- CREATING A BIG DRIFT...
...AND HE LANDS ON A "CUSHION" AS SOFT AS A TON OF FEATHERS!
HMM... HE SEEMS TO HAVE FAINTED AGAIN-- PROBABLY FROM FRIGHT--BUT OTHERWISE, HE'S UNHARMED!
GOT TO TAKE HIM BACK HOME...
...THEN FIND THAT WHATSIS, AND--
?! THE THING'S GONE-- NO TRACE OF IT ANYWHERE!
SOMETHING ELSE THAT'S ODD, TOO-- VERY ODD...
5

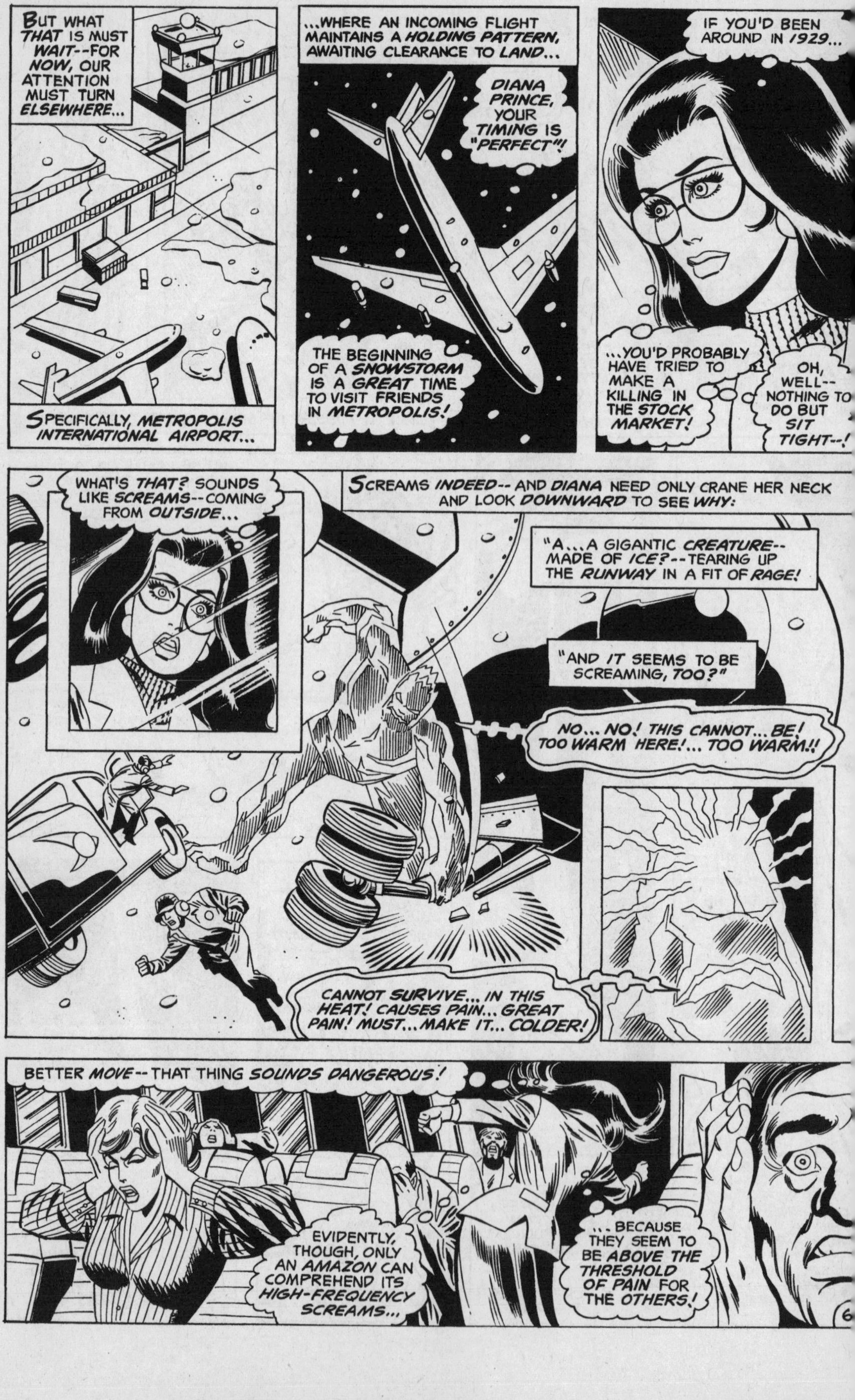
BUT WHAT THAT IS MUST WAIT--FOR NOW, OUR ATTENTION MUST TURN ELSEWHERE...
SPECIFICALLY, METROPOLIS INTERNATIONAL AIRPORT...
...WHERE AN INCOMING FLIGHT MAINTAINS A HOLDING PATTERN, AWAITING CLEARANCE TO LAND...
DIANA PRINCE, YOUR TIMING IS "PERFECT"!
THE BEGINNING OF A SNOWSTORM IS A GREAT TIME TO VISIT FRIENDS IN METROPOLIS!
IF YOU'D BEEN AROUND IN 1929...
...YOU'D PROBABLY HAVE TRIED TO MAKE A KILLING IN THE STOCK MARKET!
OH, WELL-- NOTHING TO DO BUT SIT TIGHT--!
WHAT'S THAT? SOUNDS LIKE SCREAMS--COMING FROM OUTSIDE...
SCREAMS INDEED-- AND DIANA NEED ONLY CRANE HER NECK AND LOOK DOWNWARD TO SEE WHY:
"A...A GIGANTIC CREATURE-- MADE OF ICE?--TEARING UP THE RUNWAY IN A FIT OF RAGE!
"AND IT SEEMS TO BE SCREAMING, TOO?"
NO... NO! THIS CANNOT... BE! TOO WARM HERE!... TOO WARM!!
CANNOT SURVIVE... IN THIS HEAT! CAUSES PAIN... GREAT PAIN! MUST... MAKE IT... COLDER!
BETTER MOVE--THAT THING SOUNDS DANGEROUS!
EVIDENTLY, THOUGH, ONLY AN AMAZON CAN COMPREHEND ITS HIGH-FREQUENCY SCREAMS...,
...BECAUSE THEY SEEM TO BE ABOVE THE THRESHOLD OF PAIN FOR THE OTHERS!
6

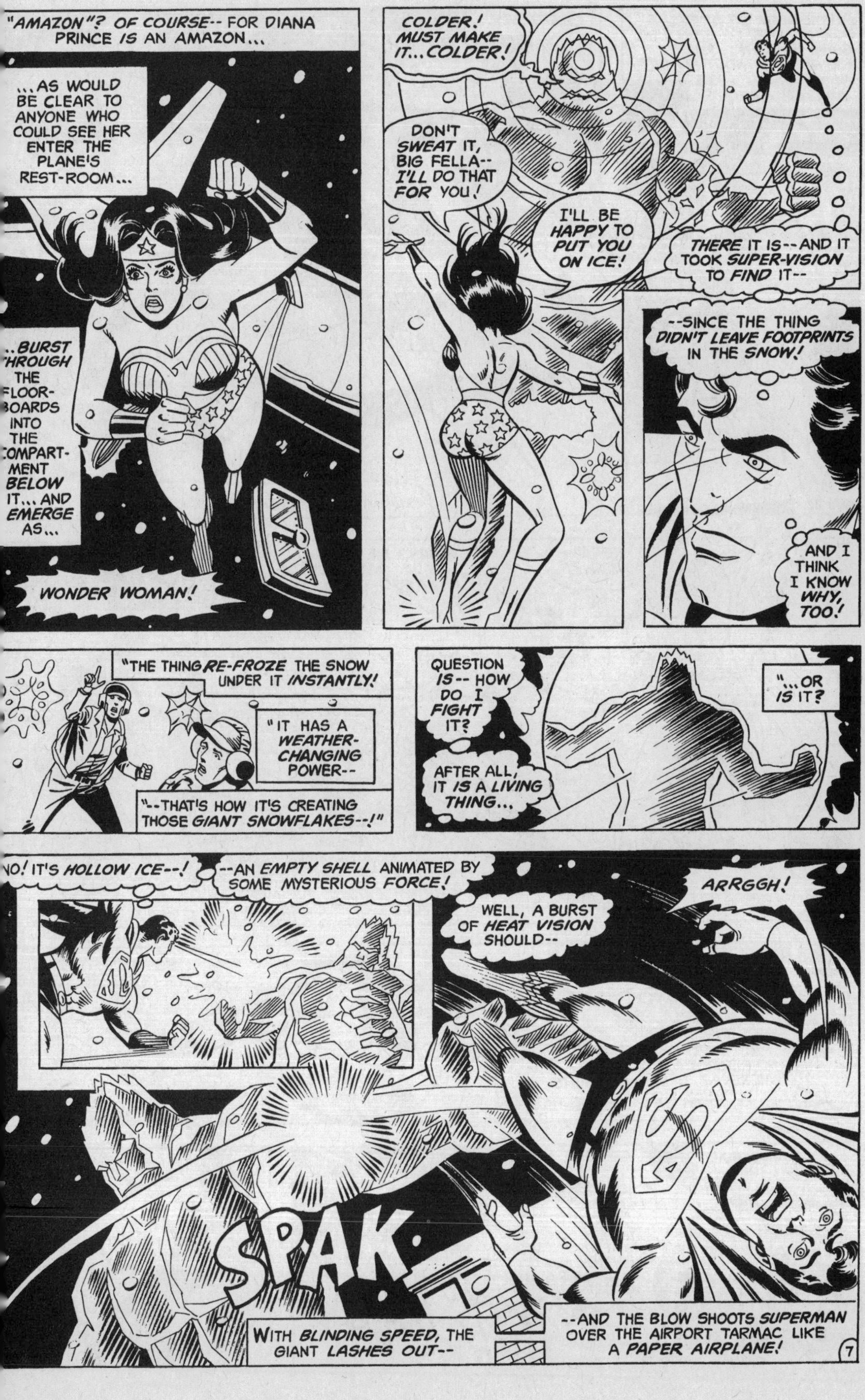
"AMAZON"? OF COURSE-- FOR DIANA PRINCE IS AN AMAZON...
...AS WOULD BE CLEAR TO ANYONE WHO COULD SEE HER ENTER THE PLANE'S REST-ROOM...
..BURST THROUGH THE FLOOR-BOARDS INTO THE COMPART-MENT BELOW IT... AND EMERGE AS...
WONDER WOMAN!
COLDER! MUST MAKE IT... COLDER!
DON'T SWEAT IT, BIG FELLA-- I'LL DO THAT FOR YOU!
I'LL BE HAPPY TO PUT YOU ON ICE!
THERE IT IS--AND IT TOOK SUPER-VISION TO FIND IT--
--SINCE THE THING DIDN'T LEAVE FOOTPRINTS IN THE SNOW!
AND I THINK I KNOW WHY, TOO!
"THE THING RE-FROZE THE SNOW UNDER IT INSTANTLY!
"IT HAS A WEATHER-CHANGING POWER--
"--THAT'S HOW IT'S CREATING THOSE GIANT SNOWFLAKES--!"
QUESTION IS-- HOW DO I FIGHT IT?
AFTER ALL, IT IS A LIVING THING...
"...OR IS IT?
NO! IT'S HOLLOW ICE--!
--AN EMPTY SHELL ANIMATED BY SOME MYSTERIOUS FORCE!
WELL, A BURST OF HEAT VISION SHOULD--
ARRGGH!
SPAK
WITH BLINDING SPEED, THE GIANT LASHES OUT--
--AND THE BLOW SHOOTS SUPERMAN OVER THE AIRPORT TARMAC LIKE A PAPER AIRPLANE!
7

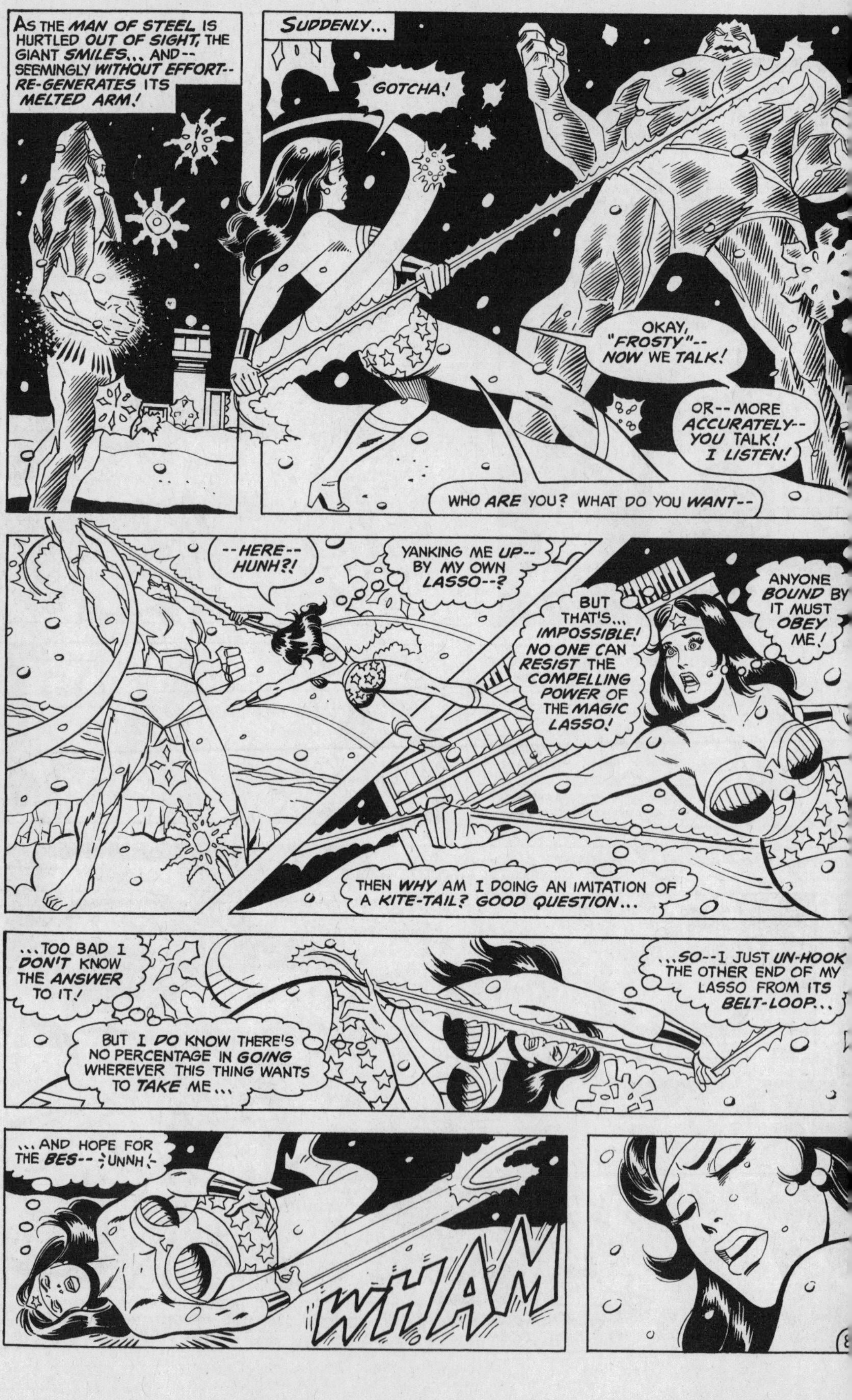
AS THE MAN OF STEEL IS HURTLED OUT OF SIGHT, THE GIANT SMILES... AND--SEEMINGLY WITHOUT EFFORT--RE-GENERATES ITS MELTED ARM!
SUDDENLY...
GOTCHA!
OKAY, "FROSTY"--NOW WE TALK!
OR--MORE ACCURATELY--YOU TALK! I LISTEN!
WHO ARE YOU? WHAT DO YOU WANT--
--HERE--HUNH?!
YANKING ME UP--BY MY OWN LASSO--?
BUT THAT'S... IMPOSSIBLE! NO ONE CAN RESIST THE COMPELLING POWER OF THE MAGIC LASSO!
ANYONE BOUND BY IT MUST OBEY ME!
THEN WHY AM I DOING AN IMITATION OF A KITE-TAIL? GOOD QUESTION...
...TOO BAD I DON'T KNOW THE ANSWER TO IT!
BUT I DO KNOW THERE'S NO PERCENTAGE IN GOING WHEREVER THIS THING WANTS TO TAKE ME...
...SO--I JUST UN-HOOK THE OTHER END OF MY LASSO FROM ITS BELT-LOOP...
...AND HOPE FOR THE BES-- UNNH!
WHAM

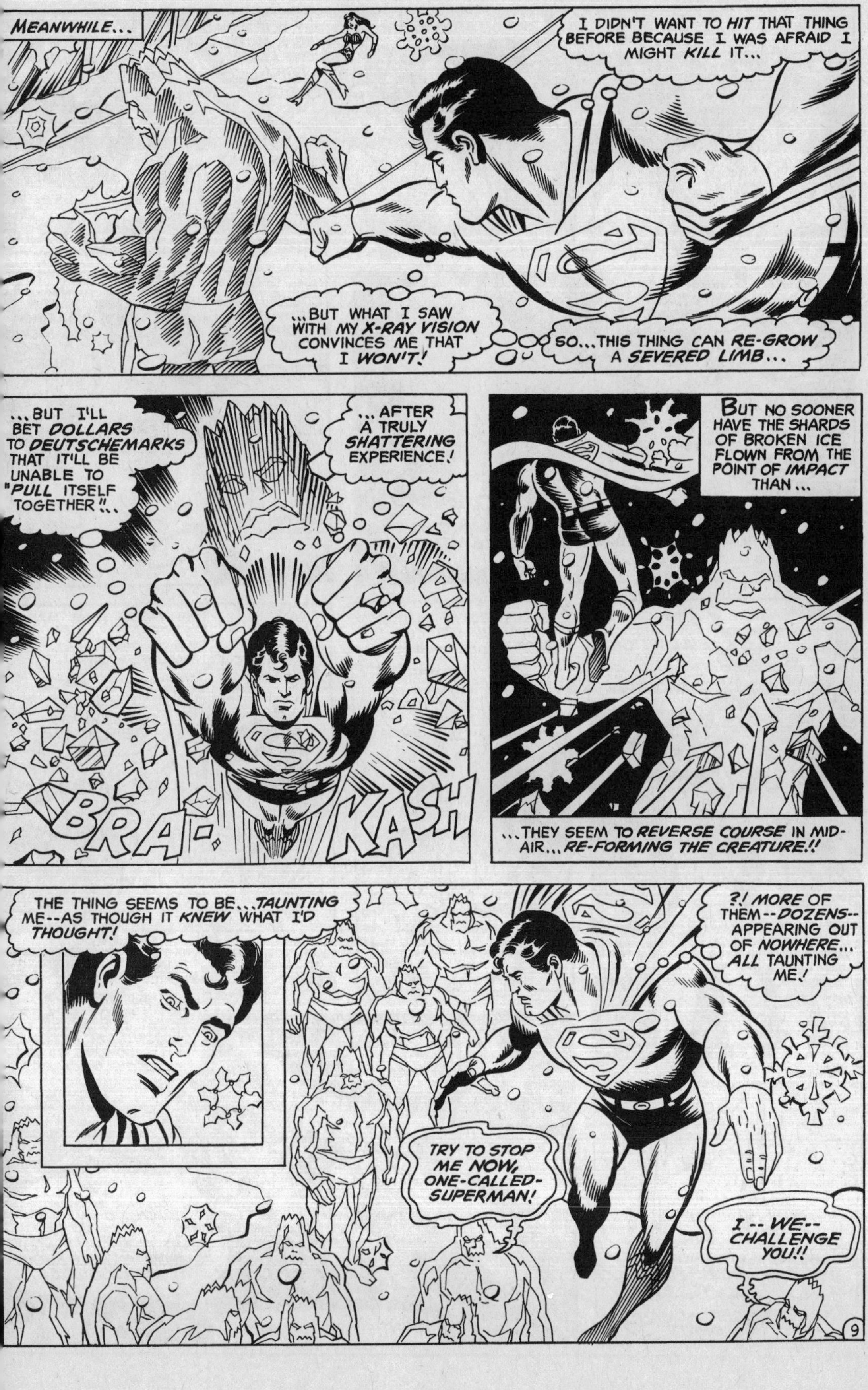
MEANWHILE...
I DIDN'T WANT TO HIT THAT THING BEFORE BECAUSE I WAS AFRAID I MIGHT KILL IT...
...BUT WHAT I SAW WITH MY X-RAY VISION CONVINCES ME THAT I WON'T!
SO...THIS THING CAN RE-GROW A SEVERED LIMB...
...BUT I'LL BET DOLLARS TO DEUTSCHEMARKS THAT IT'LL BE UNABLE TO "PULL ITSELF TOGETHER"!...
...AFTER A TRULY SHATTERING EXPERIENCE!
BRA-KASH
BUT NO SOONER HAVE THE SHARDS OF BROKEN ICE FLOWN FROM THE POINT OF IMPACT THAN...
...THEY SEEM TO REVERSE COURSE IN MID-AIR...RE-FORMING THE CREATURE!!
THE THING SEEMS TO BE...TAUNTING ME--AS THOUGH IT KNEW WHAT I'D THOUGHT!
?! MORE OF THEM--DOZENS--APPEARING OUT OF NOWHERE... ALL TAUNTING ME!
TRY TO STOP ME NOW, ONE-CALLED-SUPERMAN!
I -- WE-- CHALLENGE YOU!!
9

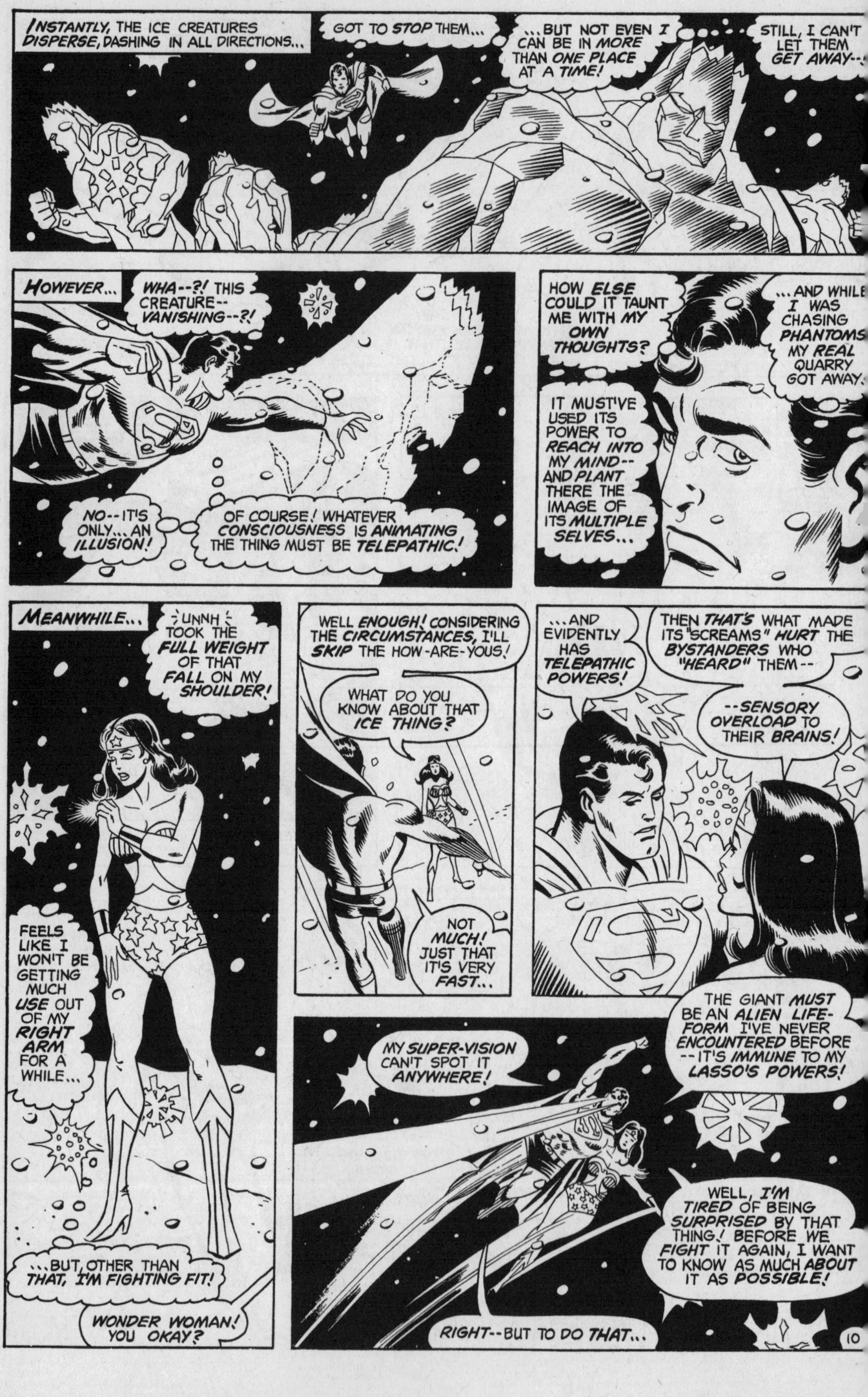
INSTANTLY, THE ICE CREATURES DISPERSE, DASHING IN ALL DIRECTIONS...
GOT TO STOP THEM...
...BUT NOT EVEN I CAN BE IN MORE THAN ONE PLACE AT A TIME!
STILL, I CAN'T LET THEM GET AWAY--
HOWEVER...
WHA--?! THIS CREATURE-- VANISHING--?!
NO--IT'S ONLY... AN ILLUSION!
OF COURSE! WHATEVER CONSCIOUSNESS IS ANIMATING THE THING MUST BE TELEPATHIC!
HOW ELSE COULD IT TAUNT ME WITH MY OWN THOUGHTS?
IT MUST'VE USED ITS POWER TO REACH INTO MY MIND--AND PLANT THERE THE IMAGE OF ITS MULTIPLE SELVES...
...AND WHILE I WAS CHASING PHANTOMS MY REAL QUARRY GOT AWAY.
MEANWHILE...
UNNH TOOK THE FULL WEIGHT OF THAT FALL ON MY SHOULDER!
FEELS LIKE I WON'T BE GETTING MUCH USE OUT OF MY RIGHT ARM FOR A WHILE...
...BUT, OTHER THAN THAT, I'M FIGHTING FIT!
WONDER WOMAN! YOU OKAY?
WELL ENOUGH! CONSIDERING THE CIRCUMSTANCES, I'LL SKIP THE HOW-ARE-YOUS!
WHAT DO YOU KNOW ABOUT THAT ICE THING?
NOT MUCH! JUST THAT IT'S VERY FAST...
...AND EVIDENTLY HAS TELEPATHIC POWERS!
THEN THAT'S WHAT MADE ITS "SCREAMS" HURT THE BYSTANDERS WHO "HEARD" THEM--
--SENSORY OVERLOAD TO THEIR BRAINS!
THE GIANT MUST BE AN ALIEN LIFE-FORM I'VE NEVER ENCOUNTERED BEFORE --IT'S IMMUNE TO MY LASSO'S POWERS!
MY SUPER-VISION CAN'T SPOT IT ANYWHERE!
WELL, I'M TIRED OF BEING SURPRISED BY THAT THING! BEFORE WE FIGHT IT AGAIN, I WANT TO KNOW AS MUCH ABOUT IT AS POSSIBLE!
RIGHT--BUT TO DO THAT...
10

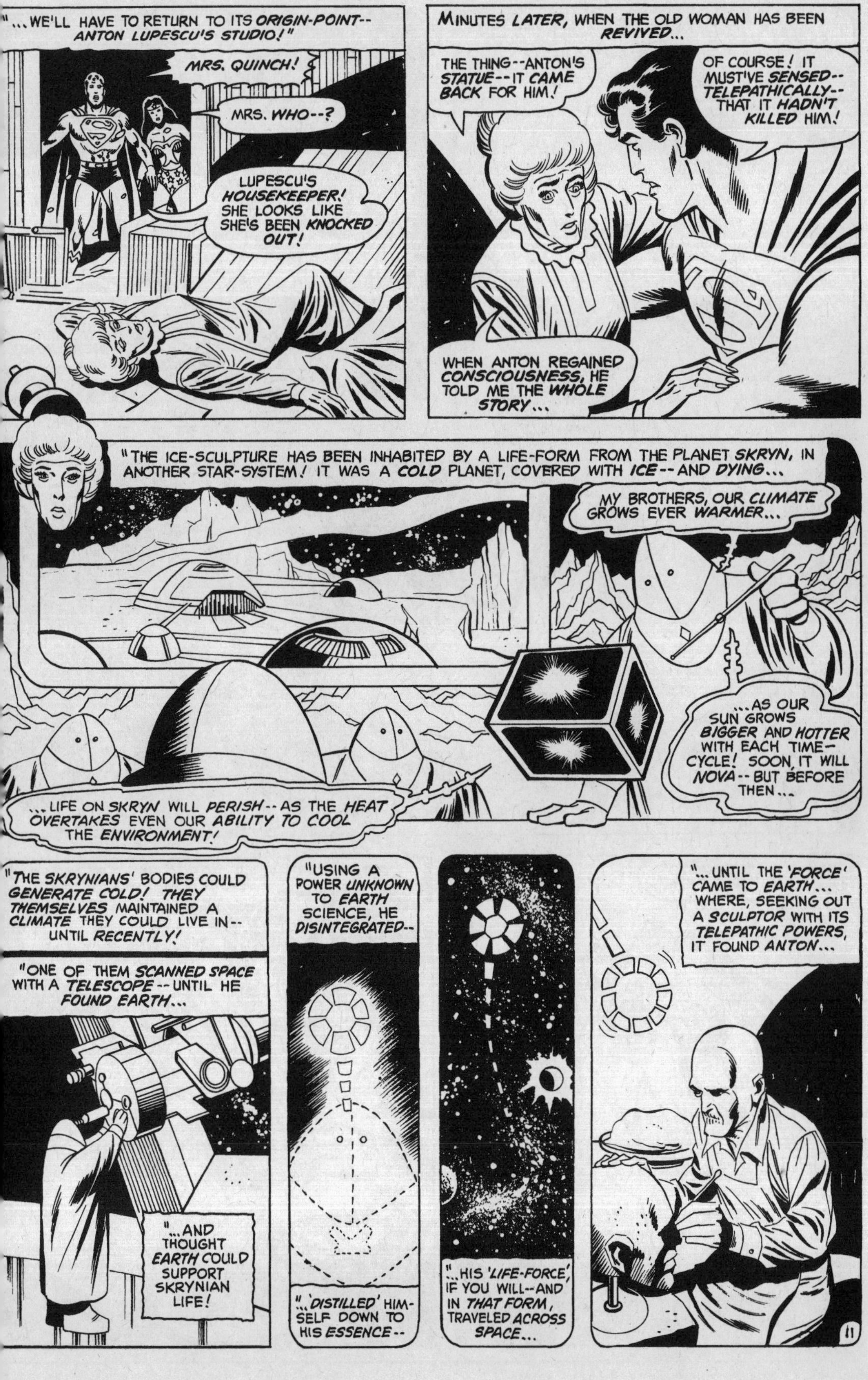
"...WE'LL HAVE TO RETURN TO ITS ORIGIN-POINT-- ANTON LUPESCU'S STUDIO!"
MRS. QUINCH!
MRS. WHO--?
LUPESCU'S HOUSEKEEPER! SHE LOOKS LIKE SHE'S BEEN KNOCKED OUT!
MINUTES LATER, WHEN THE OLD WOMAN HAS BEEN REVIVED...
THE THING--ANTON'S STATUE--IT CAME BACK FOR HIM!
OF COURSE! IT MUST'VE SENSED--TELEPATHICALLY--THAT IT HADN'T KILLED HIM!
WHEN ANTON REGAINED CONSCIOUSNESS, HE TOLD ME THE WHOLE STORY...
"THE ICE-SCULPTURE HAS BEEN INHABITED BY A LIFE-FORM FROM THE PLANET SKRYN, IN ANOTHER STAR-SYSTEM! IT WAS A COLD PLANET, COVERED WITH ICE--AND DYING...
MY BROTHERS, OUR CLIMATE GROWS EVER WARMER...
...AS OUR SUN GROWS BIGGER AND HOTTER WITH EACH TIME-CYCLE! SOON, IT WILL NOVA--BUT BEFORE THEN...
...LIFE ON SKRYN WILL PERISH--AS THE HEAT OVERTAKES EVEN OUR ABILITY TO COOL THE ENVIRONMENT!
"THE SKRYNIANS' BODIES COULD GENERATE COLD! THEY THEMSELVES MAINTAINED A CLIMATE THEY COULD LIVE IN--UNTIL RECENTLY!
"ONE OF THEM SCANNED SPACE WITH A TELESCOPE--UNTIL HE FOUND EARTH...
"...AND THOUGHT EARTH COULD SUPPORT SKRYNIAN LIFE!
"USING A POWER UNKNOWN TO EARTH SCIENCE, HE DISINTEGRATED--
"...'DISTILLED' HIMSELF DOWN TO HIS ESSENCE--
"...HIS 'LIFE-FORCE', IF YOU WILL--AND IN THAT FORM, TRAVELED ACROSS SPACE...
"...UNTIL THE 'FORCE' CAME TO EARTH... WHERE, SEEKING OUT A SCULPTOR WITH ITS TELEPATHIC POWERS, IT FOUND ANTON...
11

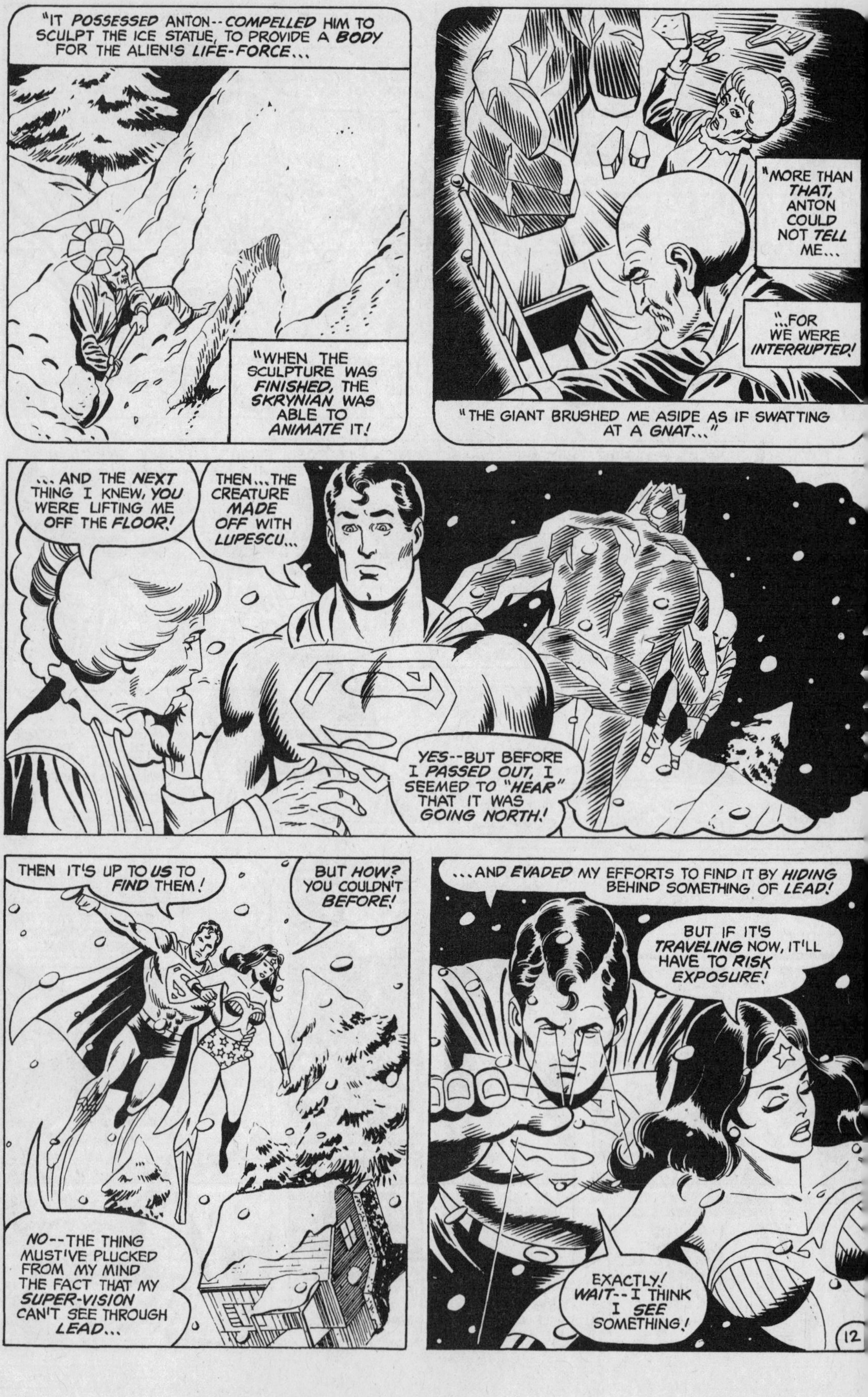
"IT POSSESSED ANTON--COMPELLED HIM TO SCULPT THE ICE STATUE, TO PROVIDE A BODY FOR THE ALIEN'S LIFE-FORCE...
"WHEN THE SCULPTURE WAS FINISHED, THE SKRYNIAN WAS ABLE TO ANIMATE IT!
"MORE THAN THAT, ANTON COULD NOT TELL ME...
"...FOR WE WERE INTERRUPTED!
"THE GIANT BRUSHED ME ASIDE AS IF SWATTING AT A GNAT..."
...AND THE NEXT THING I KNEW, YOU WERE LIFTING ME OFF THE FLOOR!
THEN...THE CREATURE MADE OFF WITH LUPESCU...
YES--BUT BEFORE I PASSED OUT, I SEEMED TO "HEAR" THAT IT WAS GOING NORTH!
THEN IT'S UP TO US TO FIND THEM!
BUT HOW? YOU COULDN'T BEFORE!
NO--THE THING MUST'VE PLUCKED FROM MY MIND THE FACT THAT MY SUPER-VISION CAN'T SEE THROUGH LEAD...
...AND EVADED MY EFFORTS TO FIND IT BY HIDING BEHIND SOMETHING OF LEAD!
BUT IF IT'S TRAVELING NOW, IT'LL HAVE TO RISK EXPOSURE!
EXACTLY! WAIT--I THINK I SEE SOMETHING!
12

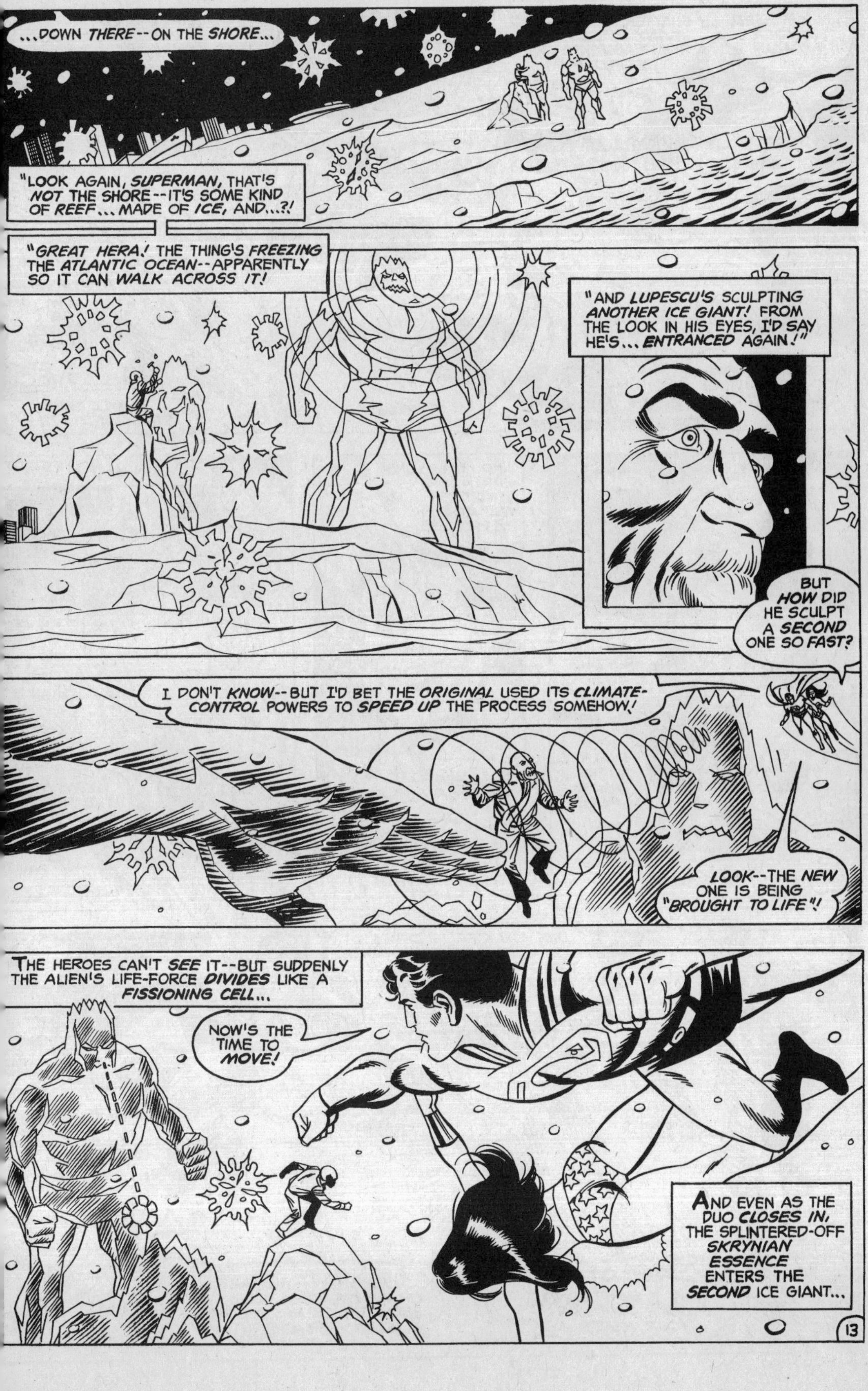
...DOWN THERE--ON THE SHORE...
"LOOK AGAIN, SUPERMAN, THAT'S NOT THE SHORE--IT'S SOME KIND OF REEF... MADE OF ICE, AND...?!
"GREAT HERA! THE THING'S FREEZING THE ATLANTIC OCEAN--APPARENTLY SO IT CAN WALK ACROSS IT!
"AND LUPESCU'S SCULPTING ANOTHER ICE GIANT! FROM THE LOOK IN HIS EYES, I'D SAY HE'S... ENTRANCED AGAIN!"
BUT HOW DID HE SCULPT A SECOND ONE SO FAST?
I DON'T KNOW--BUT I'D BET THE ORIGINAL USED ITS CLIMATE-CONTROL POWERS TO SPEED UP THE PROCESS SOMEHOW!
LOOK--THE NEW ONE IS BEING "BROUGHT TO LIFE"!
THE HEROES CAN'T SEE IT--BUT SUDDENLY THE ALIEN'S LIFE-FORCE DIVIDES LIKE A FISSIONING CELL...
NOW'S THE TIME TO MOVE!
AND EVEN AS THE DUO CLOSES IN, THE SPLINTERED-OFF SKRYNIAN ESSENCE ENTERS THE SECOND ICE GIANT...
13

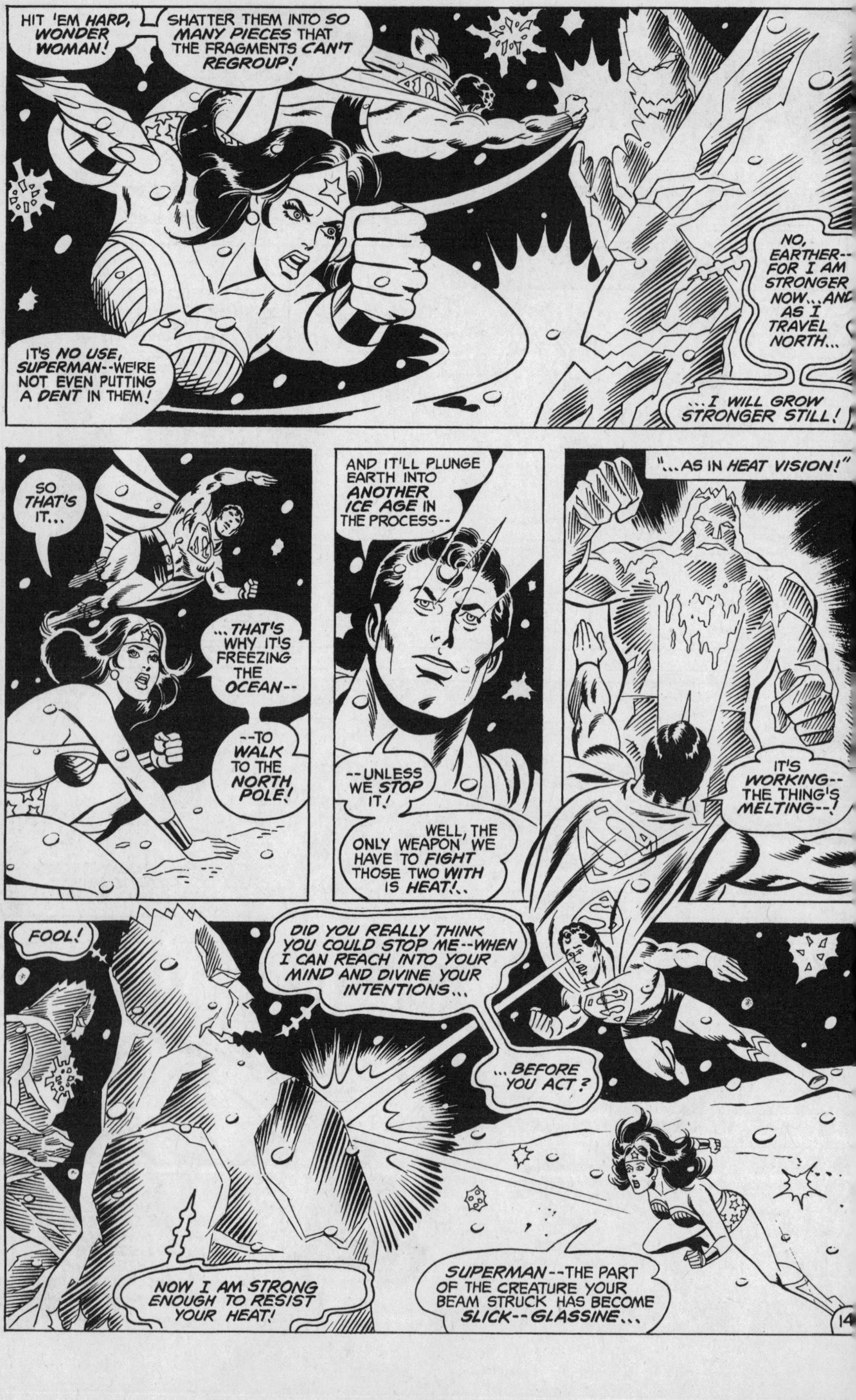
HIT 'EM HARD, WONDER WOMAN!
SHATTER THEM INTO SO MANY PIECES THAT THE FRAGMENTS CAN'T REGROUP!
IT'S NO USE, SUPERMAN--WE'RE NOT EVEN PUTTING A DENT IN THEM!
NO, EARTHER--FOR I AM STRONGER NOW...AND AS I TRAVEL NORTH...
...I WILL GROW STRONGER STILL!
SO THAT'S IT...
...THAT'S WHY IT'S FREEZING THE OCEAN--
--TO WALK TO THE NORTH POLE!
AND IT'LL PLUNGE EARTH INTO ANOTHER ICE AGE IN THE PROCESS--
--UNLESS WE STOP IT!
WELL, THE ONLY WEAPON WE HAVE TO FIGHT THOSE TWO WITH IS HEAT!..
"...AS IN HEAT VISION!"
IT'S WORKING--THE THING'S MELTING--!
FOOL!
DID YOU REALLY THINK YOU COULD STOP ME--WHEN I CAN REACH INTO YOUR MIND AND DIVINE YOUR INTENTIONS...
...BEFORE YOU ACT?
NOW I AM STRONG ENOUGH TO RESIST YOUR HEAT!
SUPERMAN--THE PART OF THE CREATURE YOUR BEAM STRUCK HAS BECOME SLICK--GLASSINE...
14

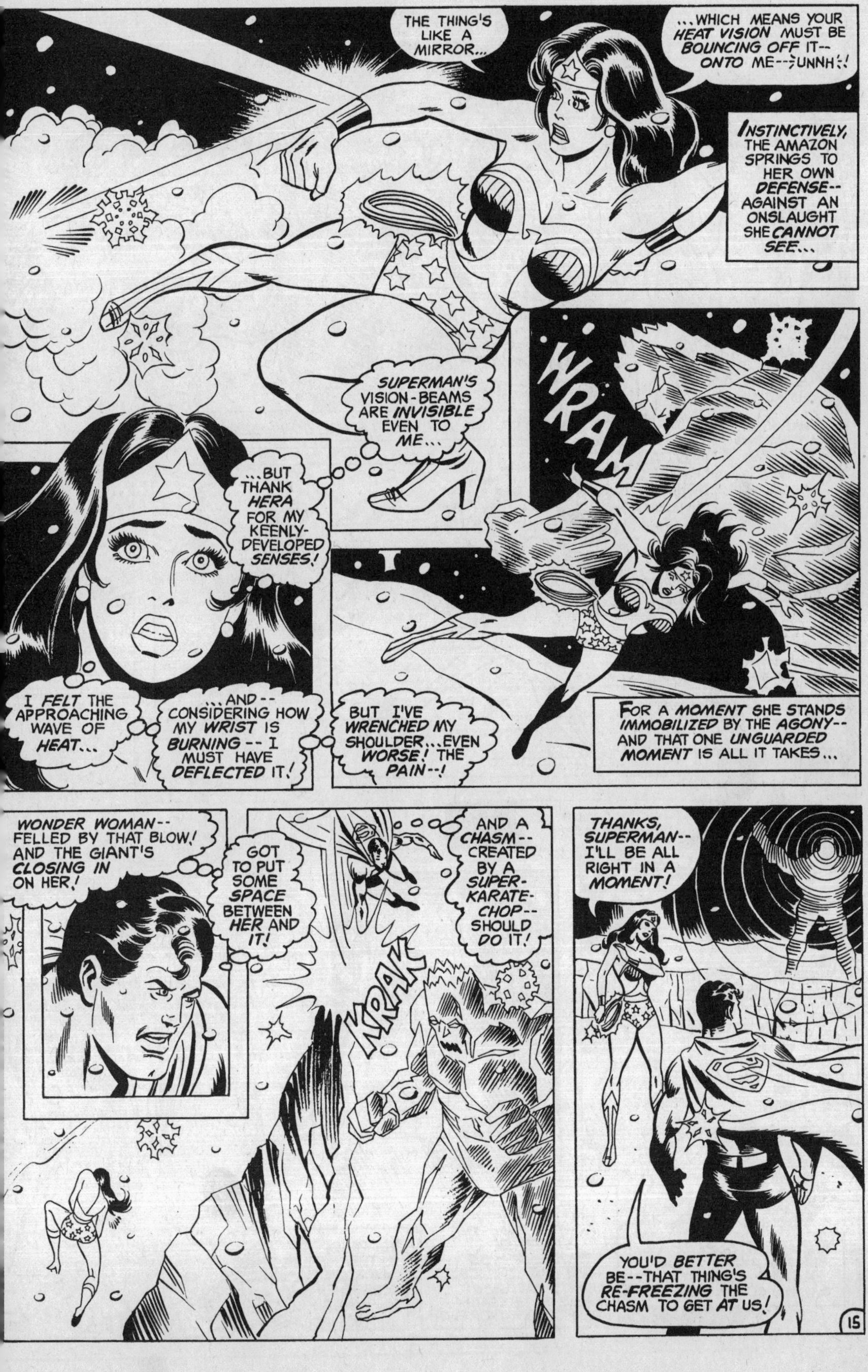
THE THING'S LIKE A MIRROR...
...WHICH MEANS YOUR HEAT VISION MUST BE BOUNCING OFF IT-- ONTO ME--UNNH!
INSTINCTIVELY, THE AMAZON SPRINGS TO HER OWN DEFENSE-- AGAINST AN ONSLAUGHT SHE CANNOT SEE...
SUPERMAN'S VISION-BEAMS ARE INVISIBLE EVEN TO ME...
...BUT THANK HERA FOR MY KEENLY-DEVELOPED SENSES!
WRAM
I FELT THE APPROACHING WAVE OF HEAT...
...AND-- CONSIDERING HOW MY WRIST IS BURNING -- I MUST HAVE DEFLECTED IT!
BUT I'VE WRENCHED MY SHOULDER...EVEN WORSE! THE PAIN--!
FOR A MOMENT SHE STANDS IMMOBILIZED BY THE AGONY-- AND THAT ONE UNGUARDED MOMENT IS ALL IT TAKES...
WONDER WOMAN-- FELLED BY THAT BLOW! AND THE GIANT'S CLOSING IN ON HER!
GOT TO PUT SOME SPACE BETWEEN HER AND IT!
AND A CHASM-- CREATED BY A SUPER-KARATE-CHOP-- SHOULD DO IT!
KRAK
THANKS, SUPERMAN-- I'LL BE ALL RIGHT IN A MOMENT!
YOU'D BETTER BE--THAT THING'S RE-FREEZING THE CHASM TO GET AT US!
15

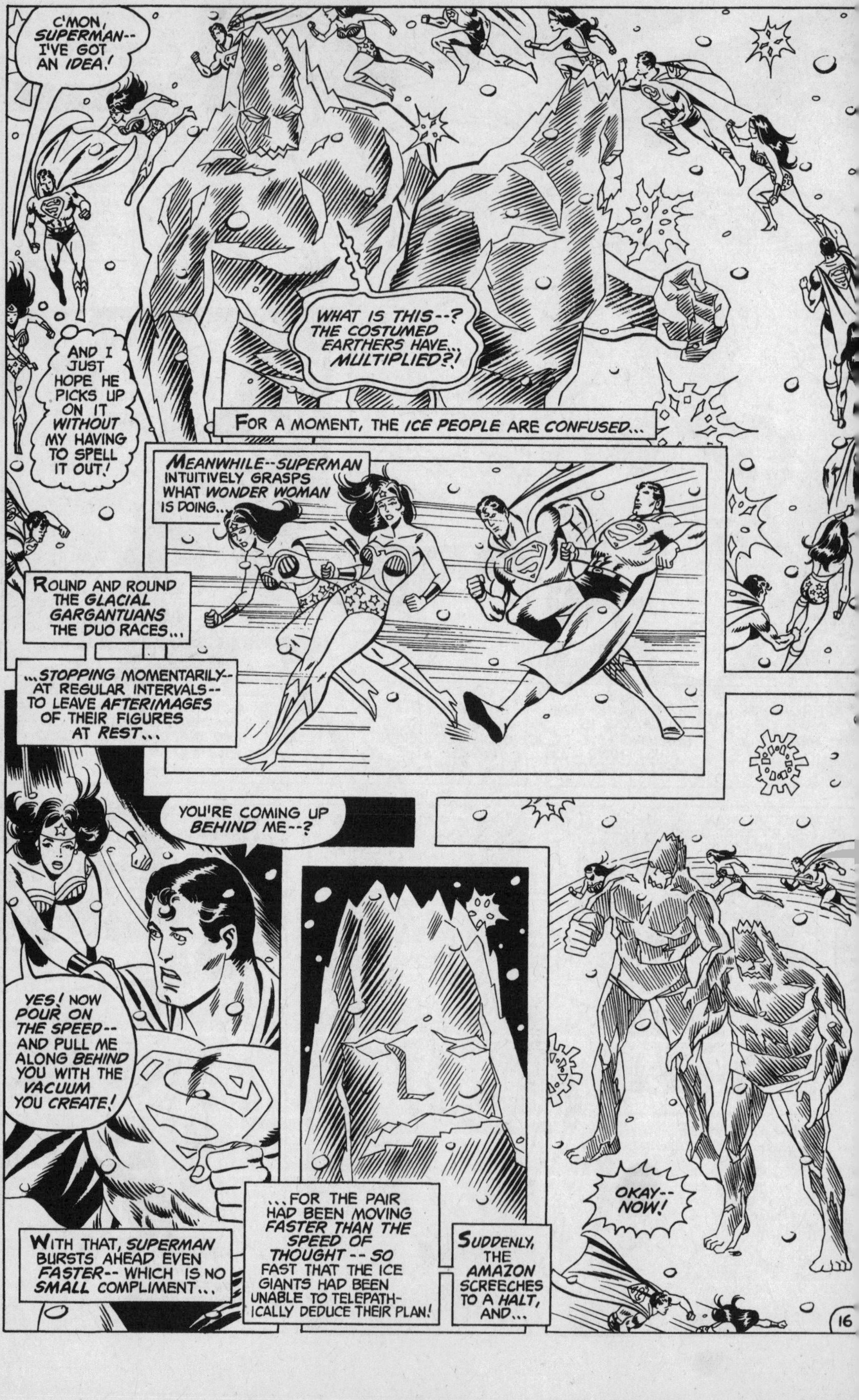
C'MON, SUPERMAN-- I'VE GOT AN IDEA!
WHAT IS THIS--? THE COSTUMED EARTHERS HAVE... MULTIPLIED?!
AND I JUST HOPE HE PICKS UP ON IT WITHOUT MY HAVING TO SPELL IT OUT!
FOR A MOMENT, THE ICE PEOPLE ARE CONFUSED...
MEANWHILE--SUPERMAN INTUITIVELY GRASPS WHAT WONDER WOMAN IS DOING...
ROUND AND ROUND THE GLACIAL GARGANTUANS THE DUO RACES...
...STOPPING MOMENTARILY-- AT REGULAR INTERVALS-- TO LEAVE AFTERIMAGES OF THEIR FIGURES AT REST...
YOU'RE COMING UP BEHIND ME--?
YES! NOW POUR ON THE SPEED-- AND PULL ME ALONG BEHIND YOU WITH THE VACUUM YOU CREATE!
WITH THAT, SUPERMAN BURSTS AHEAD EVEN FASTER-- WHICH IS NO SMALL COMPLIMENT...
...FOR THE PAIR HAD BEEN MOVING FASTER THAN THE SPEED OF THOUGHT -- SO FAST THAT THE ICE GIANTS HAD BEEN UNABLE TO TELEPATHICALLY DEDUCE THEIR PLAN!
SUDDENLY, THE AMAZON SCREECHES TO A HALT, AND...
OKAY-- NOW!
16

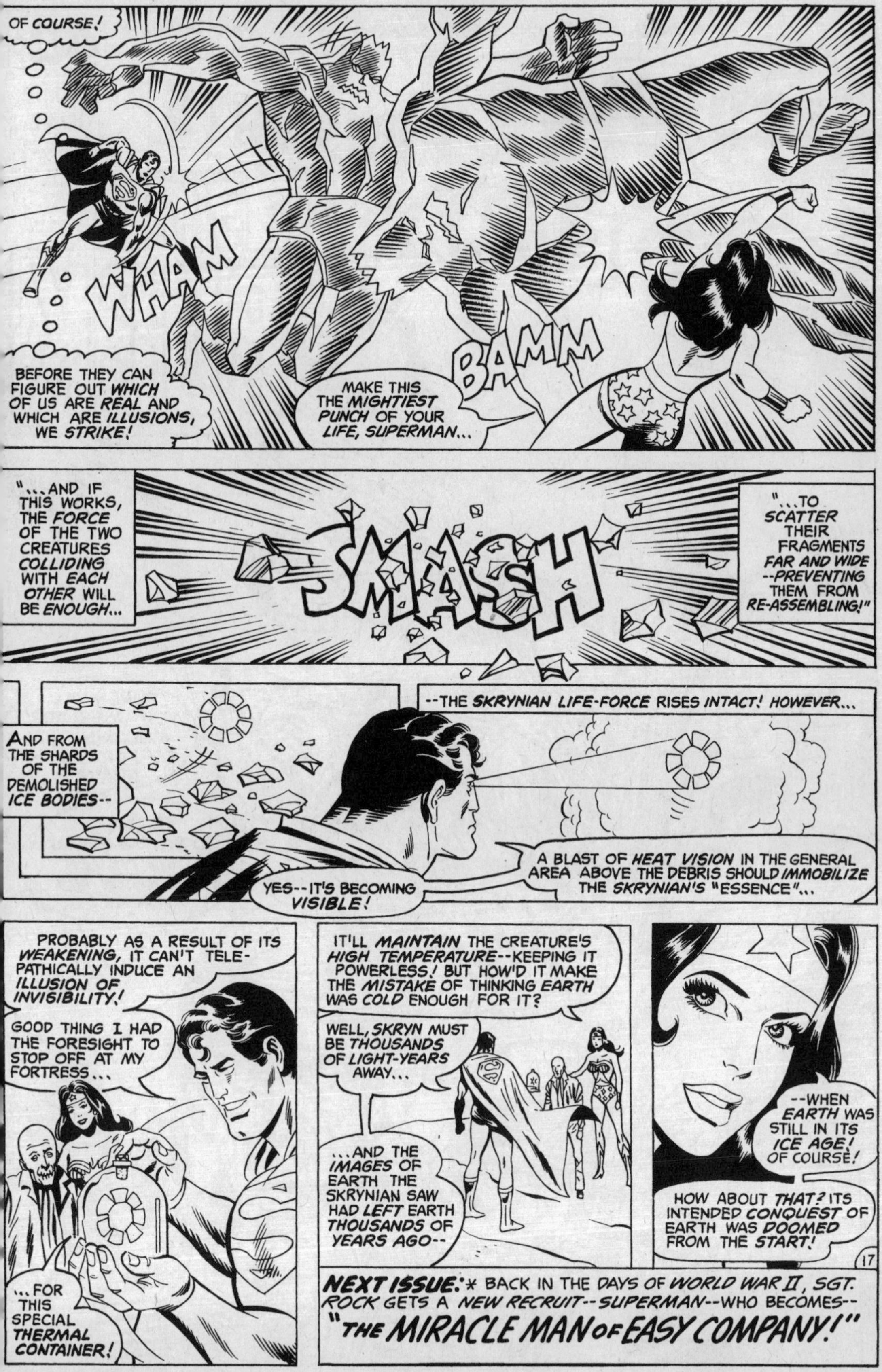
OF COURSE!
BEFORE THEY CAN FIGURE OUT WHICH OF US ARE REAL AND WHICH ARE ILLUSIONS, WE STRIKE!
WHAM
MAKE THIS THE MIGHTIEST PUNCH OF YOUR LIFE, SUPERMAN...
BAMM
"...AND IF THIS WORKS, THE FORCE OF THE TWO CREATURES COLLIDING WITH EACH OTHER WILL BE ENOUGH...
SMASH
"...TO SCATTER THEIR FRAGMENTS FAR AND WIDE --PREVENTING THEM FROM RE-ASSEMBLING!"
AND FROM THE SHARDS OF THE DEMOLISHED ICE BODIES--
--THE SKRYNIAN LIFE-FORCE RISES INTACT! HOWEVER...
A BLAST OF HEAT VISION IN THE GENERAL AREA ABOVE THE DEBRIS SHOULD IMMOBILIZE THE SKRYNIAN'S "ESSENCE"...
YES--IT'S BECOMING VISIBLE!
PROBABLY AS A RESULT OF ITS WEAKENING, IT CAN'T TELE-PATHICALLY INDUCE AN ILLUSION OF INVISIBILITY!
GOOD THING I HAD THE FORESIGHT TO STOP OFF AT MY FORTRESS...
...FOR THIS SPECIAL THERMAL CONTAINER!
IT'LL MAINTAIN THE CREATURE'S HIGH TEMPERATURE--KEEPING IT POWERLESS! BUT HOW'D IT MAKE THE MISTAKE OF THINKING EARTH WAS COLD ENOUGH FOR IT?
WELL, SKRYN MUST BE THOUSANDS OF LIGHT-YEARS AWAY...
...AND THE IMAGES OF EARTH THE SKRYNIAN SAW HAD LEFT EARTH THOUSANDS OF YEARS AGO--
--WHEN EARTH WAS STILL IN ITS ICE AGE! OF COURSE!
HOW ABOUT THAT? ITS INTENDED CONQUEST OF EARTH WAS DOOMED FROM THE START!
17
NEXT ISSUE: * BACK IN THE DAYS OF WORLD WAR II, SGT. ROCK GETS A NEW RECRUIT--SUPERMAN--WHO BECOMES--
"THE MIRACLE MAN OF EASY COMPANY!"

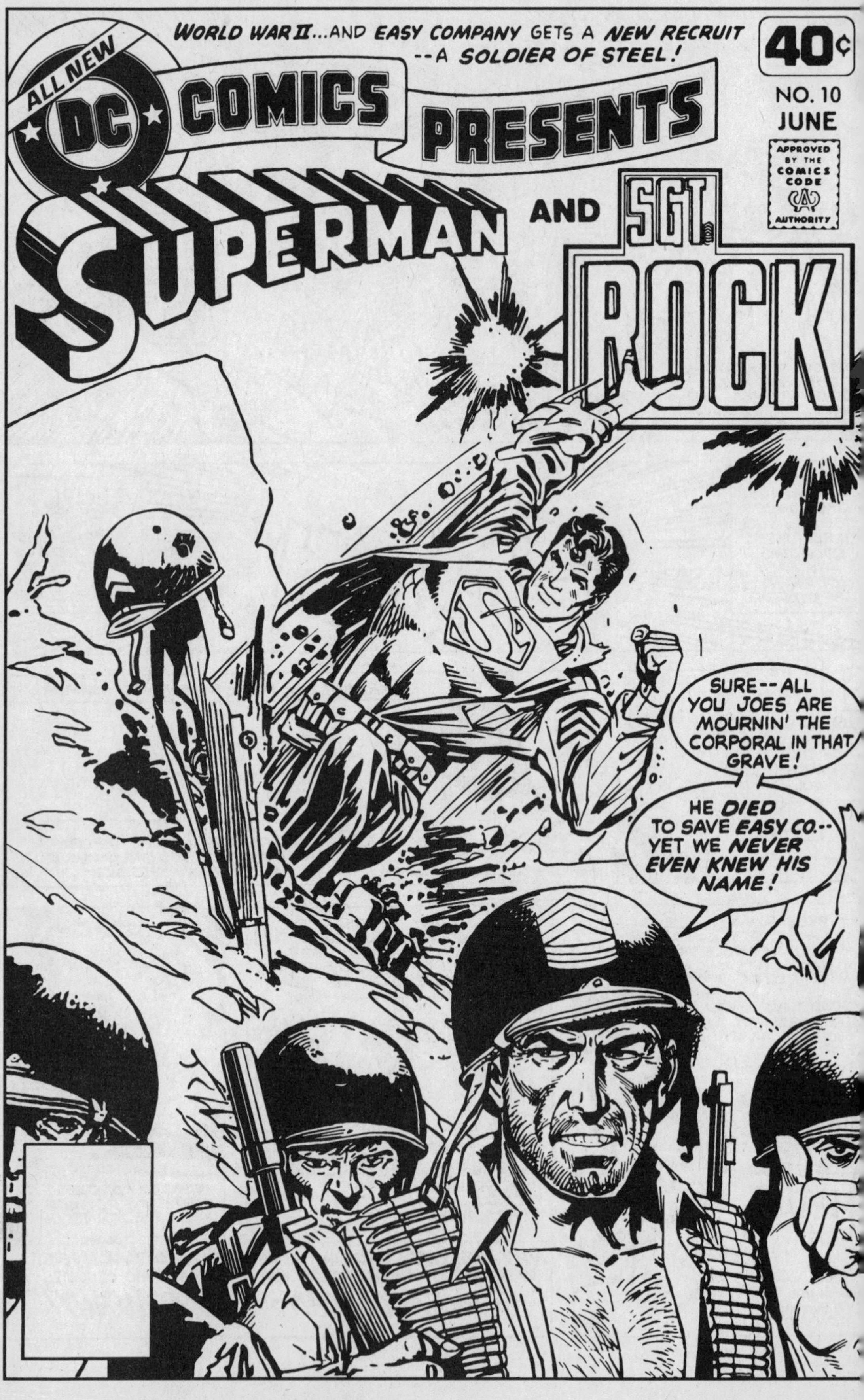
WORLD WAR II...AND EASY COMPANY GETS A NEW RECRUIT --A SOLDIER OF STEEL!
40¢
ALL NEW
DC
COMICS PRESENTS
NO. 10
JUNE
APPROVED BY THE COMICS CODE AUTHORITY
SUPERMAN AND SGT. ROCK
SURE--ALL YOU JOES ARE MOURNIN' THE CORPORAL IN THAT GRAVE!
HE DIED TO SAVE EASY CO.--YET WE NEVER EVEN KNEW HIS NAME!

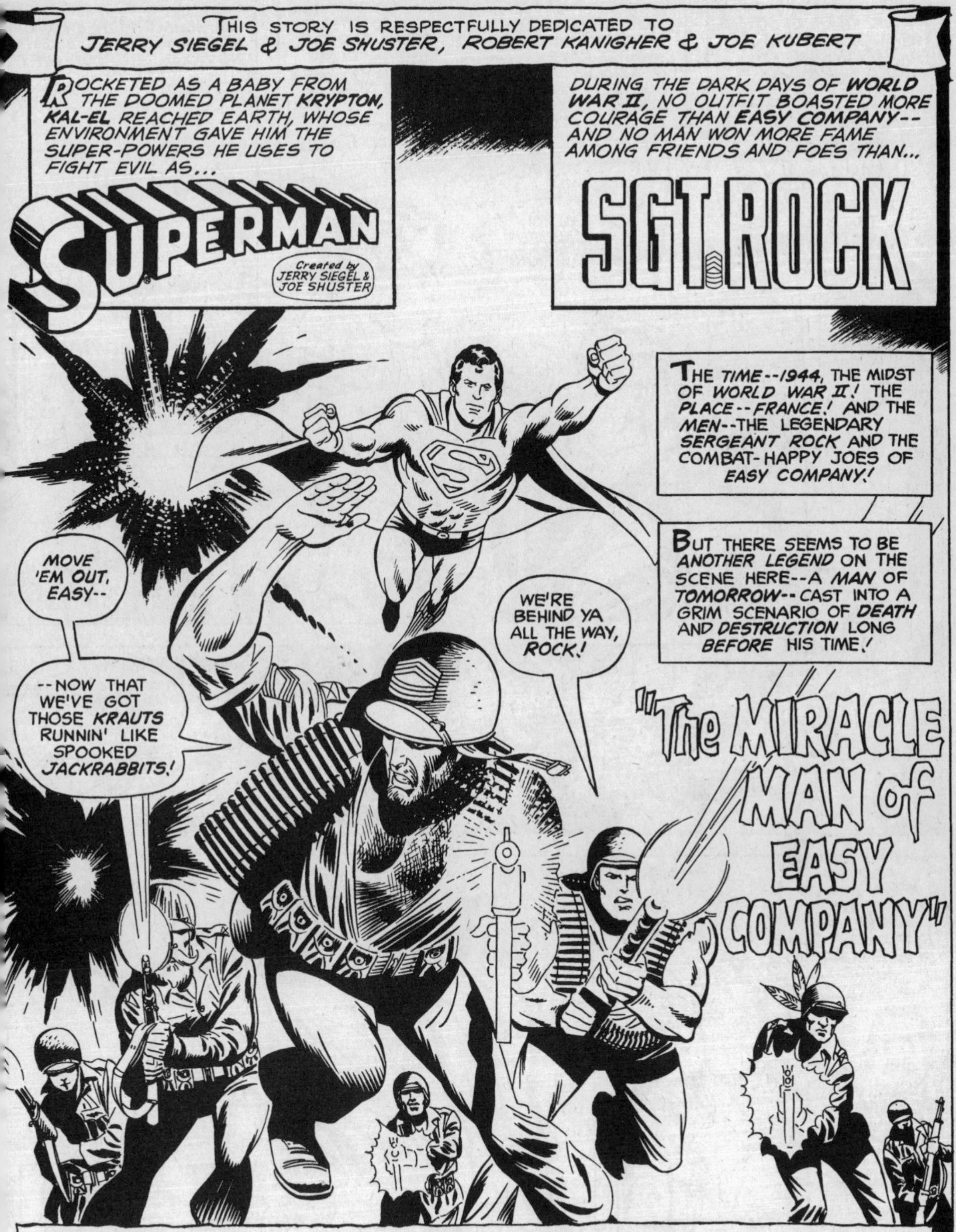
THIS STORY IS RESPECTFULLY DEDICATED TO JERRY SIEGEL & JOE SHUSTER, ROBERT KANIGHER & JOE KUBERT
ROCKETED AS A BABY FROM THE DOOMED PLANET KRYPTON, KAL-EL REACHED EARTH, WHOSE ENVIRONMENT GAVE HIM THE SUPER-POWERS HE USES TO FIGHT EVIL AS...
SUPERMAN
Created by JERRY SIEGEL & JOE SHUSTER
DURING THE DARK DAYS OF WORLD WAR II, NO OUTFIT BOASTED MORE COURAGE THAN EASY COMPANY-- AND NO MAN WON MORE FAME AMONG FRIENDS AND FOES THAN...
SGT. ROCK
THE TIME--1944, THE MIDST OF WORLD WAR II! THE PLACE--FRANCE! AND THE MEN--THE LEGENDARY SERGEANT ROCK AND THE COMBAT-HAPPY JOES OF EASY COMPANY!
BUT THERE SEEMS TO BE ANOTHER LEGEND ON THE SCENE HERE--A MAN OF TOMORROW--CAST INTO A GRIM SCENARIO OF DEATH AND DESTRUCTION LONG BEFORE HIS TIME!
MOVE 'EM OUT, EASY--
--NOW THAT WE'VE GOT THOSE KRAUTS RUNNIN' LIKE SPOOKED JACKRABBITS!
WE'RE BEHIND YA ALL THE WAY, ROCK!
"The MIRACLE MAN of EASY COMPANY"
WRITER – CARY BATES / PENCILLER – JOE STATON / INKER – JACK ABEL
LETTERER – BEN ODA / COLORIST – ADRIENNE ROY / EDITOR – JULIUS SCHWARTZ

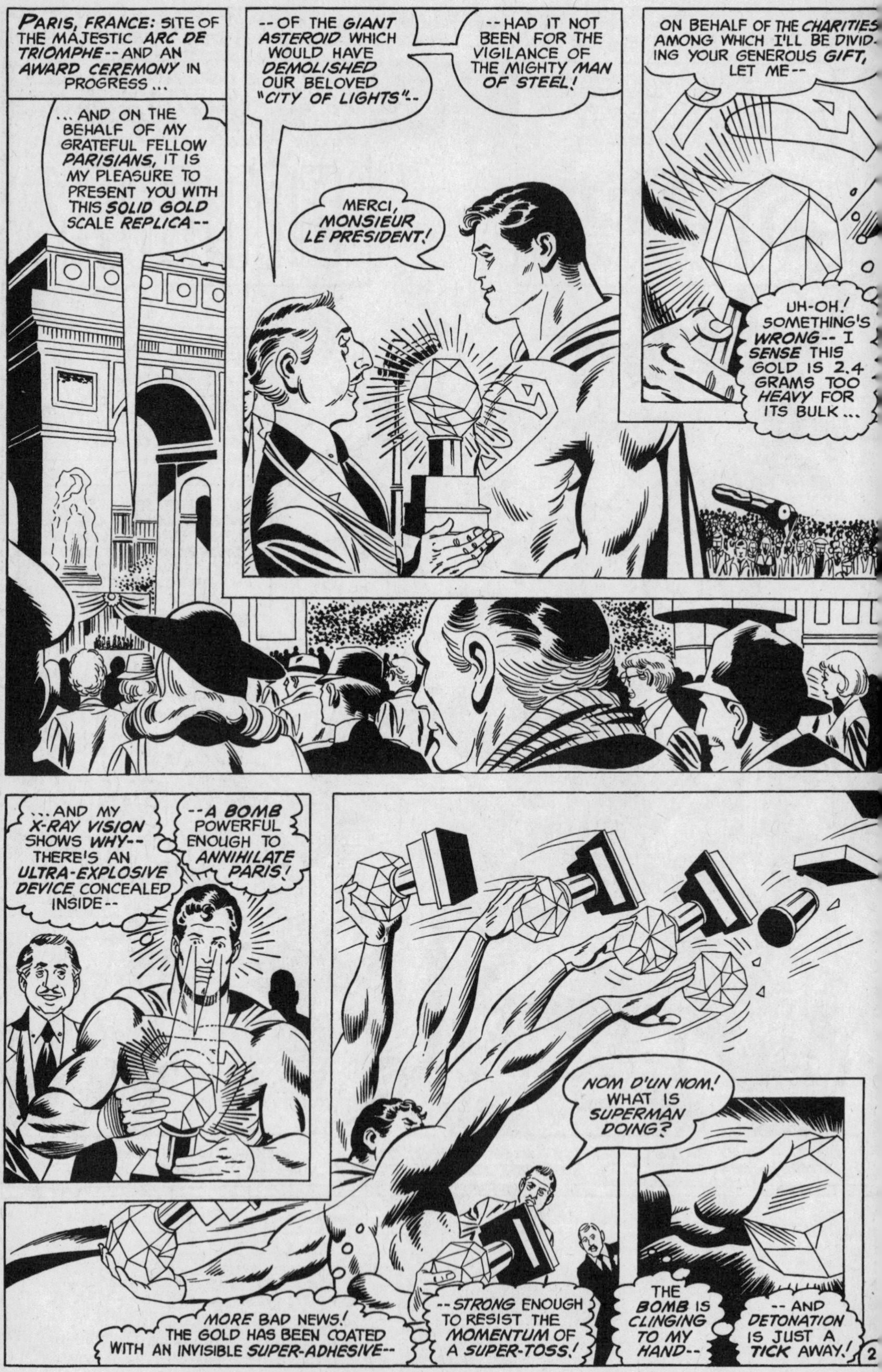
PARIS, FRANCE: SITE OF THE MAJESTIC ARC DE TRIOMPHE -- AND AN AWARD CEREMONY IN PROGRESS...
...AND ON THE BEHALF OF MY GRATEFUL FELLOW PARISIANS, IT IS MY PLEASURE TO PRESENT YOU WITH THIS SOLID GOLD SCALE REPLICA --
-- OF THE GIANT ASTEROID WHICH WOULD HAVE DEMOLISHED OUR BELOVED "CITY OF LIGHTS"--
-- HAD IT NOT BEEN FOR THE VIGILANCE OF THE MIGHTY MAN OF STEEL!
MERCI, MONSIEUR LE PRESIDENT!
ON BEHALF OF THE CHARITIES AMONG WHICH I'LL BE DIVIDING YOUR GENEROUS GIFT, LET ME --
UH-OH! SOMETHING'S WRONG -- I SENSE THIS GOLD IS 2.4 GRAMS TOO HEAVY FOR ITS BULK...
...AND MY X-RAY VISION SHOWS WHY -- THERE'S AN ULTRA-EXPLOSIVE DEVICE CONCEALED INSIDE --
-- A BOMB POWERFUL ENOUGH TO ANNIHILATE PARIS!
NOM D'UN NOM! WHAT IS SUPERMAN DOING?
MORE BAD NEWS! THE GOLD HAS BEEN COATED WITH AN INVISIBLE SUPER-ADHESIVE --
-- STRONG ENOUGH TO RESIST THE MOMENTUM OF A SUPER-TOSS!
THE BOMB IS CLINGING TO MY HAND --
-- AND DETONATION IS JUST A TICK AWAY!
2

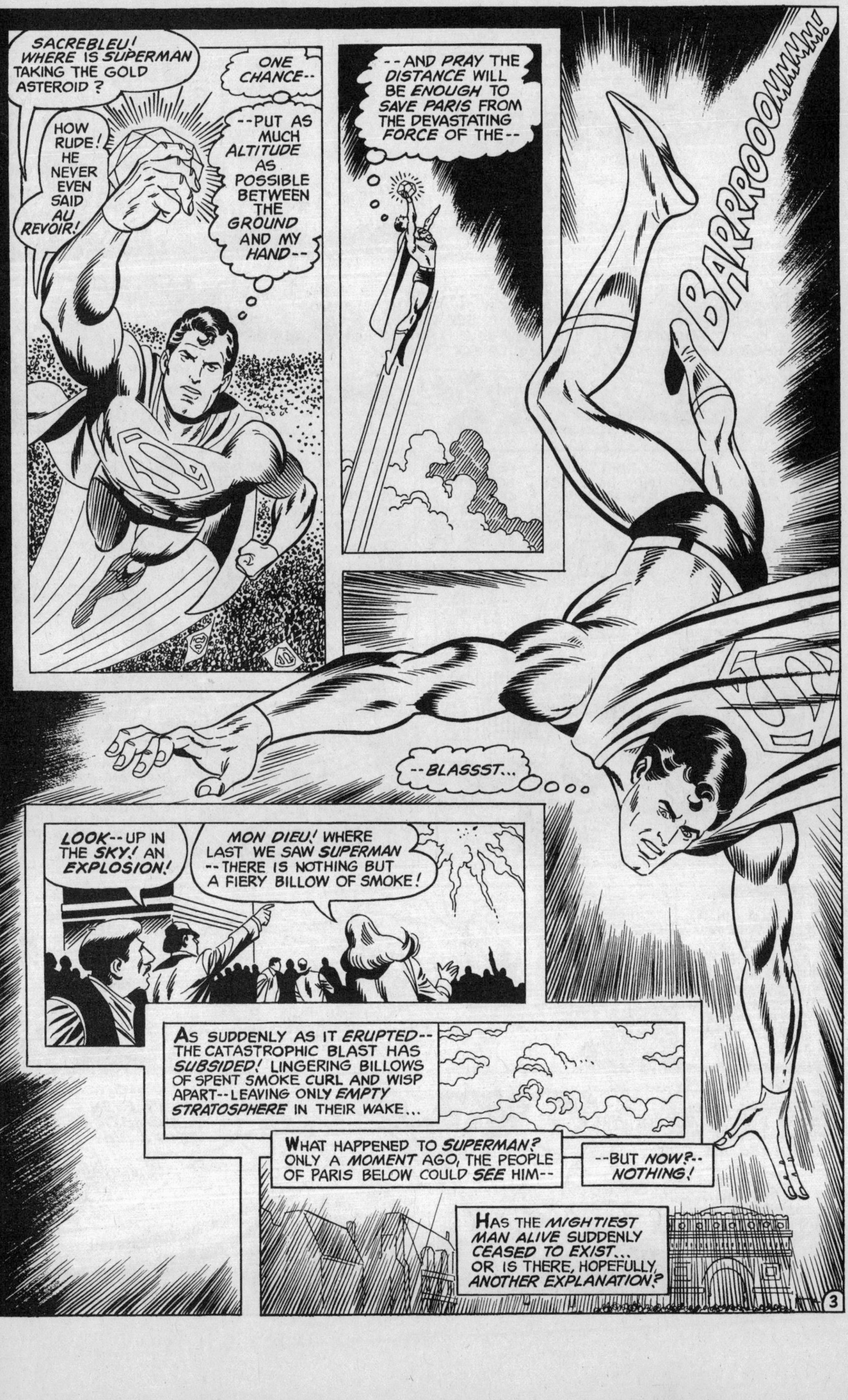
SACREBLEU! WHERE IS SUPERMAN TAKING THE GOLD ASTEROID?
HOW RUDE! HE NEVER EVEN SAID AU REVOIR!
ONE CHANCE--
--PUT AS MUCH ALTITUDE AS POSSIBLE BETWEEN THE GROUND AND MY HAND--
--AND PRAY THE DISTANCE WILL BE ENOUGH TO SAVE PARIS FROM THE DEVASTATING FORCE OF THE--
BARROOOMMM!
--BLASSST...
LOOK--UP IN THE SKY! AN EXPLOSION!
MON DIEU! WHERE LAST WE SAW SUPERMAN --THERE IS NOTHING BUT A FIERY BILLOW OF SMOKE!
AS SUDDENLY AS IT ERUPTED--THE CATASTROPHIC BLAST HAS SUBSIDED! LINGERING BILLOWS OF SPENT SMOKE CURL AND WISP APART--LEAVING ONLY EMPTY STRATOSPHERE IN THEIR WAKE...
WHAT HAPPENED TO SUPERMAN? ONLY A MOMENT AGO, THE PEOPLE OF PARIS BELOW COULD SEE HIM--
--BUT NOW?--NOTHING!
HAS THE MIGHTIEST MAN ALIVE SUDDENLY CEASED TO EXIST... OR IS THERE, HOPEFULLY, ANOTHER EXPLANATION?
3

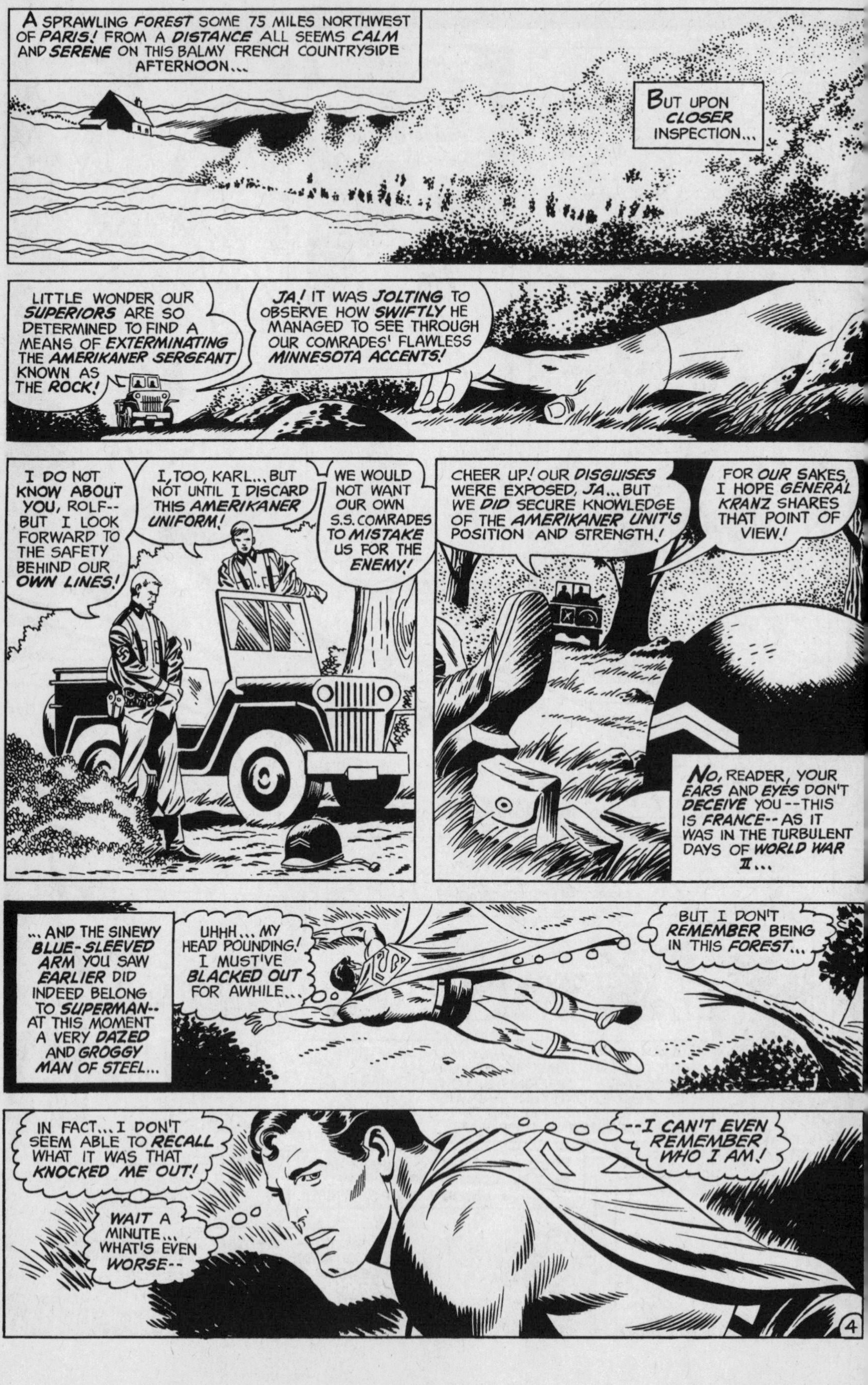
A SPRAWLING FOREST SOME 75 MILES NORTHWEST OF PARIS! FROM A DISTANCE ALL SEEMS CALM AND SERENE ON THIS BALMY FRENCH COUNTRYSIDE AFTERNOON...
BUT UPON CLOSER INSPECTION...
LITTLE WONDER OUR SUPERIORS ARE SO DETERMINED TO FIND A MEANS OF EXTERMINATING THE AMERIKANER SERGEANT KNOWN AS THE ROCK!
JA! IT WAS JOLTING TO OBSERVE HOW SWIFTLY HE MANAGED TO SEE THROUGH OUR COMRADES' FLAWLESS MINNESOTA ACCENTS!
I DO NOT KNOW ABOUT YOU, ROLF-- BUT I LOOK FORWARD TO THE SAFETY BEHIND OUR OWN LINES!
I, TOO, KARL... BUT NOT UNTIL I DISCARD THIS AMERIKANER UNIFORM!
WE WOULD NOT WANT OUR OWN S.S. COMRADES TO MISTAKE US FOR THE ENEMY!
CHEER UP! OUR DISGUISES WERE EXPOSED, JA... BUT WE DID SECURE KNOWLEDGE OF THE AMERIKANER UNIT'S POSITION AND STRENGTH!
FOR OUR SAKES, I HOPE GENERAL KRANZ SHARES THAT POINT OF VIEW!
NO, READER, YOUR EARS AND EYES DON'T DECEIVE YOU --THIS IS FRANCE-- AS IT WAS IN THE TURBULENT DAYS OF WORLD WAR II...
... AND THE SINEWY BLUE-SLEEVED ARM YOU SAW EARLIER DID INDEED BELONG TO SUPERMAN-- AT THIS MOMENT A VERY DAZED AND GROGGY MAN OF STEEL...
UHHH... MY HEAD POUNDING! I MUST'VE BLACKED OUT FOR AWHILE...
BUT I DON'T REMEMBER BEING IN THIS FOREST...
IN FACT... I DON'T SEEM ABLE TO RECALL WHAT IT WAS THAT KNOCKED ME OUT!
WAIT A MINUTE... WHAT'S EVEN WORSE--
--I CAN'T EVEN REMEMBER WHO I AM!
4

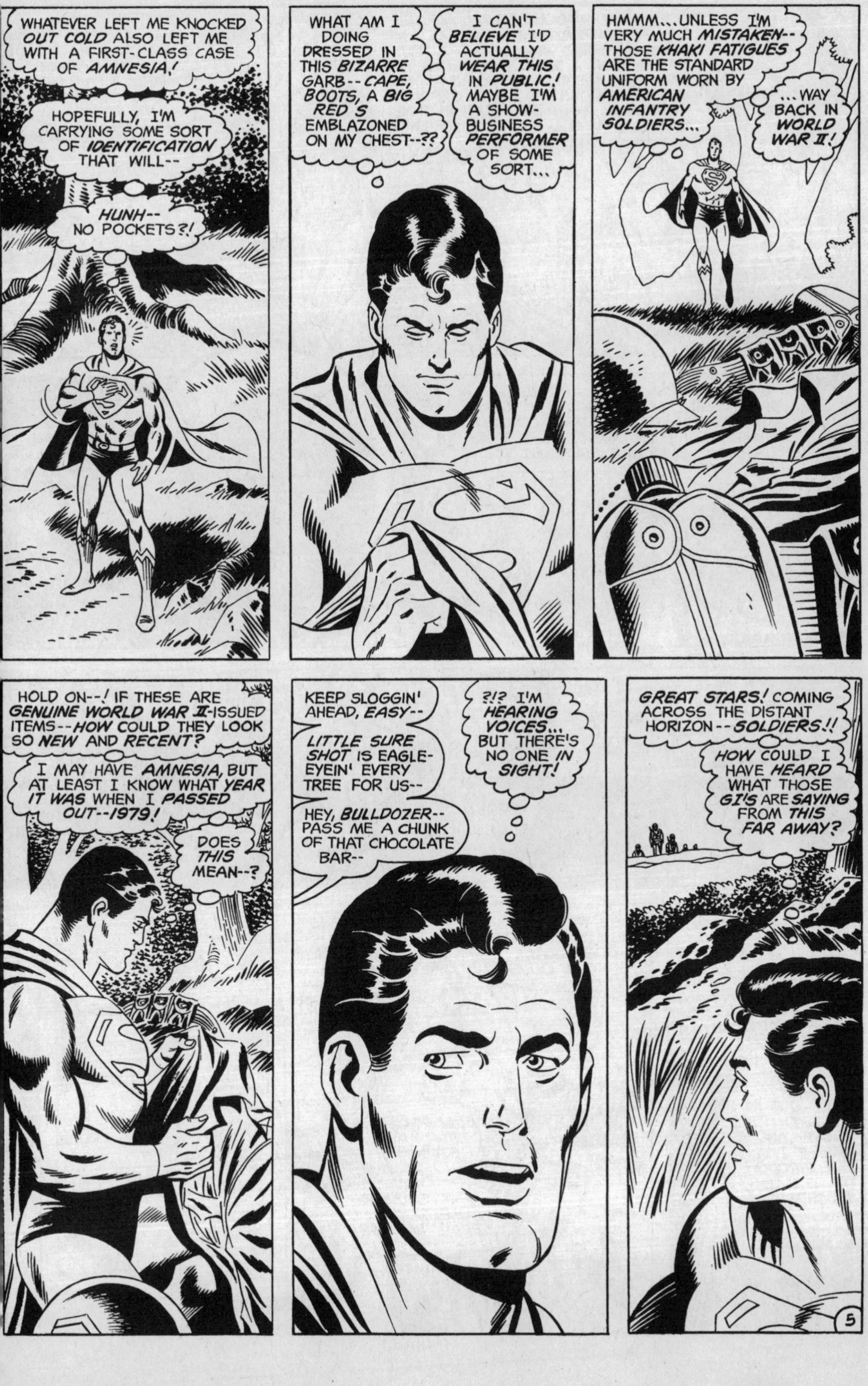
WHATEVER LEFT ME KNOCKED OUT COLD ALSO LEFT ME WITH A FIRST-CLASS CASE OF AMNESIA!
HOPEFULLY, I'M CARRYING SOME SORT OF IDENTIFICATION THAT WILL--
HUNH-- NO POCKETS?!
WHAT AM I DOING DRESSED IN THIS BIZARRE GARB--CAPE, BOOTS, A BIG RED S EMBLAZONED ON MY CHEST--??
I CAN'T BELIEVE I'D ACTUALLY WEAR THIS IN PUBLIC! MAYBE I'M A SHOW-BUSINESS PERFORMER OF SOME SORT...
HMMM...UNLESS I'M VERY MUCH MISTAKEN--THOSE KHAKI FATIGUES ARE THE STANDARD UNIFORM WORN BY AMERICAN INFANTRY SOLDIERS...
...WAY BACK IN WORLD WAR II!
HOLD ON--! IF THESE ARE GENUINE WORLD WAR II-ISSUED ITEMS--HOW COULD THEY LOOK SO NEW AND RECENT?
I MAY HAVE AMNESIA, BUT AT LEAST I KNOW WHAT YEAR IT WAS WHEN I PASSED OUT--1979!
DOES THIS MEAN--?
KEEP SLOGGIN' AHEAD, EASY--
LITTLE SURE SHOT IS EAGLE-EYEIN' EVERY TREE FOR US--
HEY, BULLDOZER--PASS ME A CHUNK OF THAT CHOCOLATE BAR--
?!? I'M HEARING VOICES... BUT THERE'S NO ONE IN SIGHT!
GREAT STARS! COMING ACROSS THE DISTANT HORIZON--SOLDIERS!!
HOW COULD I HAVE HEARD WHAT THOSE GI'S ARE SAYING FROM THIS FAR AWAY?
5

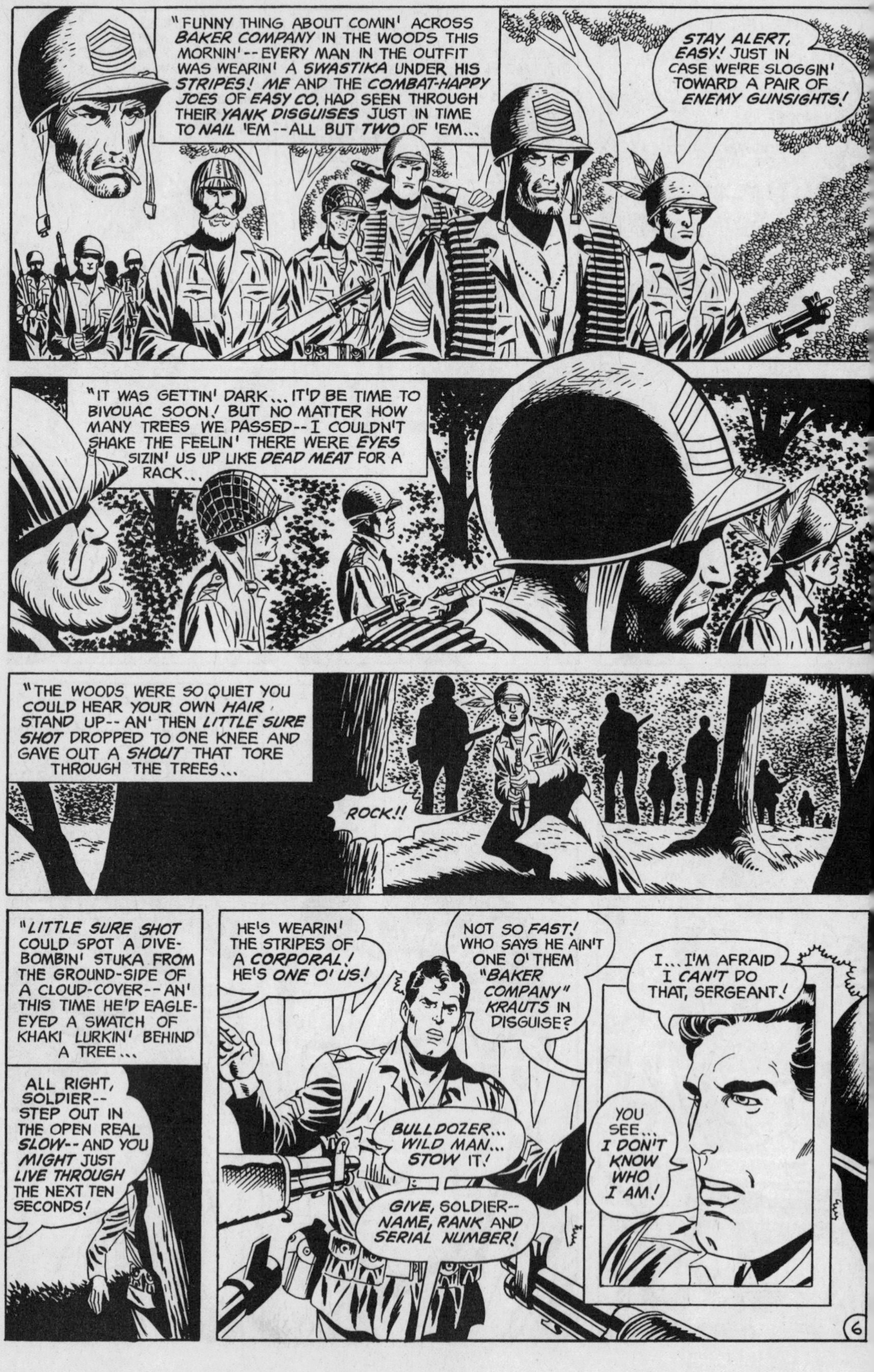
"FUNNY THING ABOUT COMIN' ACROSS BAKER COMPANY IN THE WOODS THIS MORNIN' -- EVERY MAN IN THE OUTFIT WAS WEARIN' A SWASTIKA UNDER HIS STRIPES! ME AND THE COMBAT-HAPPY JOES OF EASY CO. HAD SEEN THROUGH THEIR YANK DISGUISES JUST IN TIME TO NAIL 'EM -- ALL BUT TWO OF 'EM...
STAY ALERT, EASY! JUST IN CASE WE'RE SLOGGIN' TOWARD A PAIR OF ENEMY GUNSIGHTS!
"IT WAS GETTIN' DARK... IT'D BE TIME TO BIVOUAC SOON! BUT NO MATTER HOW MANY TREES WE PASSED -- I COULDN'T SHAKE THE FEELIN' THERE WERE EYES SIZIN' US UP LIKE DEAD MEAT FOR A RACK...
"THE WOODS WERE SO QUIET YOU COULD HEAR YOUR OWN HAIR STAND UP -- AN' THEN LITTLE SURE SHOT DROPPED TO ONE KNEE AND GAVE OUT A SHOUT THAT TORE THROUGH THE TREES...
ROCK!!
"LITTLE SURE SHOT COULD SPOT A DIVE-BOMBIN' STUKA FROM THE GROUND-SIDE OF A CLOUD-COVER -- AN' THIS TIME HE'D EAGLE-EYED A SWATCH OF KHAKI LURKIN' BEHIND A TREE...
ALL RIGHT, SOLDIER -- STEP OUT IN THE OPEN REAL SLOW -- AND YOU MIGHT JUST LIVE THROUGH THE NEXT TEN SECONDS!
HE'S WEARIN' THE STRIPES OF A CORPORAL! HE'S ONE O' US!
NOT SO FAST! WHO SAYS HE AIN'T ONE O' THEM "BAKER COMPANY" KRAUTS IN DISGUISE?
BULLDOZER... WILD MAN... STOW IT!
GIVE, SOLDIER -- NAME, RANK AND SERIAL NUMBER!
I... I'M AFRAID I CAN'T DO THAT, SERGEANT!
YOU SEE... I DON'T KNOW WHO I AM!
6

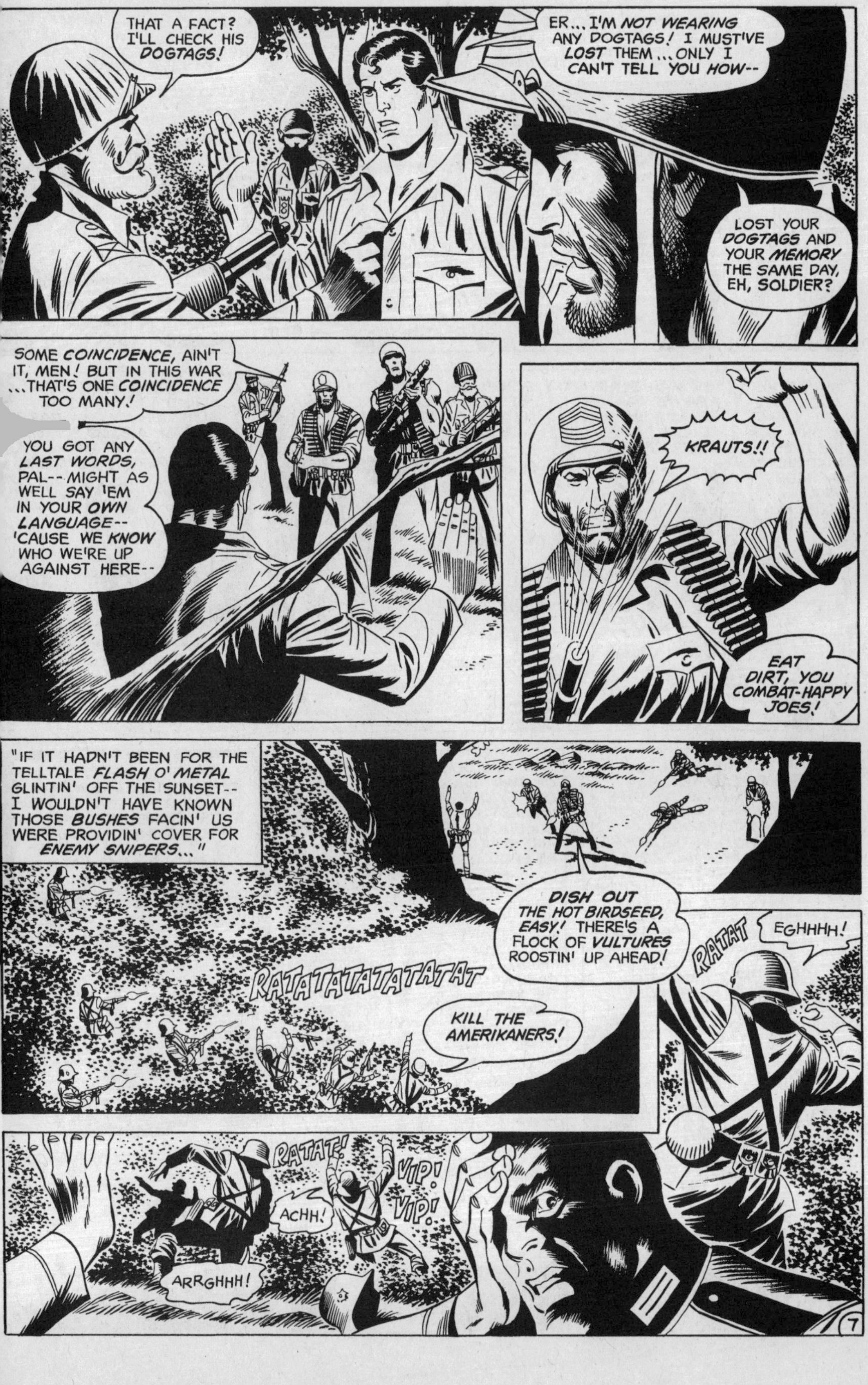
THAT A FACT? I'LL CHECK HIS DOGTAGS!
ER... I'M NOT WEARING ANY DOGTAGS! I MUST'VE LOST THEM... ONLY I CAN'T TELL YOU HOW--
LOST YOUR DOGTAGS AND YOUR MEMORY THE SAME DAY, EH, SOLDIER?
SOME COINCIDENCE, AIN'T IT, MEN! BUT IN THIS WAR ...THAT'S ONE COINCIDENCE TOO MANY!
YOU GOT ANY LAST WORDS, PAL--MIGHT AS WELL SAY 'EM IN YOUR OWN LANGUAGE-- 'CAUSE WE KNOW WHO WE'RE UP AGAINST HERE--
KRAUTS!!
EAT DIRT, YOU COMBAT-HAPPY JOES!
"IF IT HADN'T BEEN FOR THE TELLTALE FLASH O' METAL GLINTIN' OFF THE SUNSET-- I WOULDN'T HAVE KNOWN THOSE BUSHES FACIN' US WERE PROVIDIN' COVER FOR ENEMY SNIPERS..."
DISH OUT THE HOT BIRDSEED, EASY! THERE'S A FLOCK OF VULTURES ROOSTIN' UP AHEAD!
RATATATATATATATAT
KILL THE AMERIKANERS!
RATAT
EGHHHH!
RATAT!
VIP!
VIP!
ACHH!
ARRGHHH!
7

"THE *ENEMY* NEVER GOT TO GO TO THE PLATE! IT WAS A *ONE-INNIN'* GAME... AND WE'D KNOCKED THE OPPOSIN' BATTERS *OUT*...

LOOK WHO'S *STILL STANDIN'*, SARGE!

SO I SEE -- ALONG WITH *EVERYTHIN'* ELSE, IT LOOKS LIKE HE'S *FORGOTTEN* HOW TO *TAKE ORDERS!*

MAYBE HE *IS* ON THE LEVEL! IF IT WASN'T FOR THE *TREE*-- THAT ENEMY BARRAGE WOULDA KILLED HIM FOR SURE!

OR MAYBE THE *KRAUTS* WANTED TO PLUG 'IM SO HE COULDN'T SPILL THEIR *SECRETS!*

EITHER ONE O' YOU COULD BE *RIGHT*-- SO WE'RE GONNA PLAY A GAME OF *EASY* QUESTIONS-AND-ANSWERS!

LUCKILY MY *AMNESIA* SEEMS TO BE *PARTIAL*. ALTHOUGH MY *OWN* PAST IS ONLY A *BLUR*, SOMEHOW I CAN *SENSE* I'M A *UNITED STATES CITIZEN!*

BUT MY CAPED *CIRCUS SUIT* WOULD JUST RAISE *QUESTIONS* I STILL CAN'T *ANSWER*-- SO WEARING THIS *G.I. UNIFORM* DISCARDED BY THE *GERMAN SPIES* SEEMED LIKE A GOOD IDEA!

I CAN'T BEGIN TO *EXPLAIN* IT... BUT *SOMEHOW* I'VE BEEN TRANSPORTED ABOUT *35 YEARS* INTO THE *PAST*-- IN THE MIDST OF *WORLD WAR II!*

UNTIL I CAN THINK OF A *BETTER* COURSE OF ACTION, I'LL KEEP PLAYING THE ROLE OF A *G.I.* WITHOUT A *NAME* OR *NUMBER!*

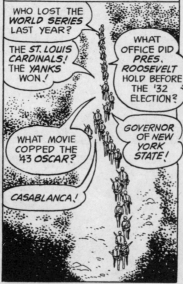

"AS WE SLOGGED ANOTHER MILE OR TWO THROUGH THE WOODS-- ONE BY ONE, WE FIRED OUR CAGIEST *RED-WHITE-AND-BLUE* QUESTIONS AT OUR *STRAGGLER!* AND WOULDN'T YOU KNOW IT-- HE SPOUTED BACK WITH ALL THE *RIGHT ANSWERS!*

WHO LOST THE *WORLD SERIES* LAST YEAR?

THE *ST. LOUIS CARDINALS!* THE *YANKS* WON!

WHAT OFFICE DID *PRES. ROOSEVELT* HOLD BEFORE THE '32 ELECTION?

GOVERNOR OF NEW YORK STATE!

WHAT MOVIE COPPED THE '43 OSCAR?

CASABLANCA!

"BY THE TIME WE FOUND A *SAFE* SPOT TO *DIG IN* FOR THE NIGHT-- ALL OF US WERE *SATISFIED* THE NEW MAN WAS JUST WHAT HE *SAID* HE WAS--A *G.I.* WITH A *HEAD- INJURY* THAT SENT HIS *MEMORY A.W.O.L....*

RECKON IT'S ABOUT TIME FOR *INTRODUCTIONS*, CORPORAL-- I'M *SGT. FRANK ROCK!*

AND THESE ARE THE *COMBAT- HAPPY JOES* OF *EASY CO....*

8

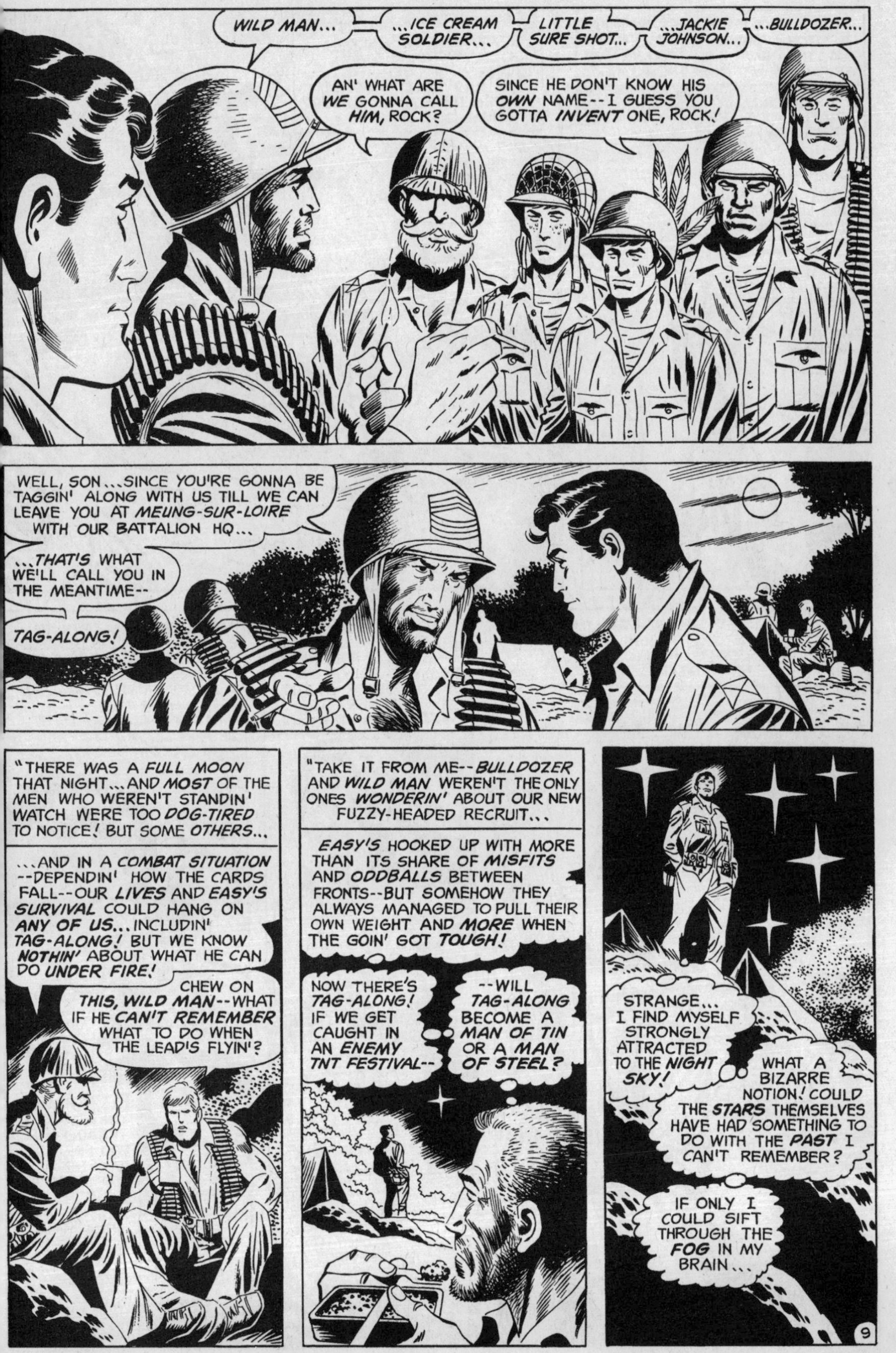
WILD MAN...
...ICE CREAM SOLDIER...
LITTLE SURE SHOT...
...JACKIE JOHNSON...
...BULLDOZER...
AN' WHAT ARE WE GONNA CALL HIM, ROCK?
SINCE HE DON'T KNOW HIS OWN NAME--I GUESS YOU GOTTA INVENT ONE, ROCK!
WELL, SON...SINCE YOU'RE GONNA BE TAGGIN' ALONG WITH US TILL WE CAN LEAVE YOU AT MEUNG-SUR-LOIRE WITH OUR BATTALION HQ...
...THAT'S WHAT WE'LL CALL YOU IN THE MEANTIME--
TAG-ALONG!
"THERE WAS A FULL MOON THAT NIGHT...AND MOST OF THE MEN WHO WEREN'T STANDIN' WATCH WERE TOO DOG-TIRED TO NOTICE! BUT SOME OTHERS...
...AND IN A COMBAT SITUATION --DEPENDIN' HOW THE CARDS FALL--OUR LIVES AND EASY'S SURVIVAL COULD HANG ON ANY OF US...INCLUDIN' TAG-ALONG! BUT WE KNOW NOTHIN' ABOUT WHAT HE CAN DO UNDER FIRE!
CHEW ON THIS, WILD MAN--WHAT IF HE CAN'T REMEMBER WHAT TO DO WHEN THE LEAD'S FLYIN'?
"TAKE IT FROM ME--BULLDOZER AND WILD MAN WEREN'T THE ONLY ONES WONDERIN' ABOUT OUR NEW FUZZY-HEADED RECRUIT...
EASY'S HOOKED UP WITH MORE THAN ITS SHARE OF MISFITS AND ODDBALLS BETWEEN FRONTS--BUT SOMEHOW THEY ALWAYS MANAGED TO PULL THEIR OWN WEIGHT AND MORE WHEN THE GOIN' GOT TOUGH!
NOW THERE'S TAG-ALONG! IF WE GET CAUGHT IN AN ENEMY TNT FESTIVAL--
--WILL TAG-ALONG BECOME A MAN OF TIN OR A MAN OF STEEL?
STRANGE... I FIND MYSELF STRONGLY ATTRACTED TO THE NIGHT SKY!
WHAT A BIZARRE NOTION! COULD THE STARS THEMSELVES HAVE HAD SOMETHING TO DO WITH THE PAST I CAN'T REMEMBER?
IF ONLY I COULD SIFT THROUGH THE FOG IN MY BRAIN...
9

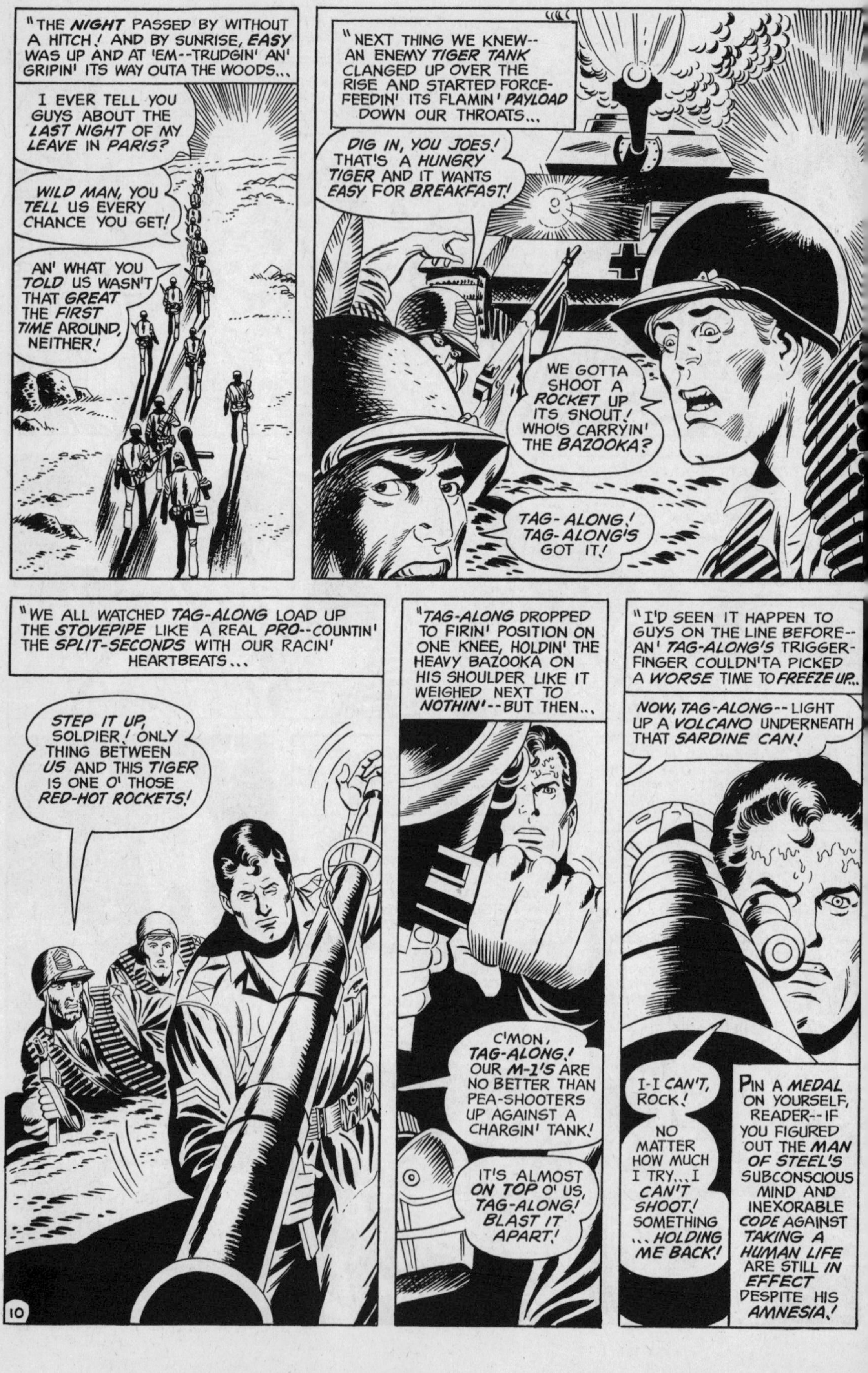
"THE NIGHT PASSED BY WITHOUT A HITCH! AND BY SUNRISE, EASY WAS UP AND AT 'EM--TRUDGIN' AN' GRIPIN' ITS WAY OUTA THE WOODS...
I EVER TELL YOU GUYS ABOUT THE LAST NIGHT OF MY LEAVE IN PARIS?
WILD MAN, YOU TELL US EVERY CHANCE YOU GET!
AN' WHAT YOU TOLD US WASN'T THAT GREAT THE FIRST TIME AROUND, NEITHER!
"NEXT THING WE KNEW-- AN ENEMY TIGER TANK CLANGED UP OVER THE RISE AND STARTED FORCE-FEEDIN' ITS FLAMIN' PAYLOAD DOWN OUR THROATS...
DIG IN, YOU JOES! THAT'S A HUNGRY TIGER AND IT WANTS EASY FOR BREAKFAST!
WE GOTTA SHOOT A ROCKET UP ITS SNOUT! WHO'S CARRYIN' THE BAZOOKA?
TAG-ALONG! TAG-ALONG'S GOT IT!
"WE ALL WATCHED TAG-ALONG LOAD UP THE STOVEPIPE LIKE A REAL PRO--COUNTIN' THE SPLIT-SECONDS WITH OUR RACIN' HEARTBEATS...
STEP IT UP, SOLDIER! ONLY THING BETWEEN US AND THIS TIGER IS ONE O' THOSE RED-HOT ROCKETS!
"TAG-ALONG DROPPED TO FIRIN' POSITION ON ONE KNEE, HOLDIN' THE HEAVY BAZOOKA ON HIS SHOULDER LIKE IT WEIGHED NEXT TO NOTHIN'--BUT THEN...
C'MON, TAG-ALONG! OUR M-1'S ARE NO BETTER THAN PEA-SHOOTERS UP AGAINST A CHARGIN' TANK!
IT'S ALMOST ON TOP O' US, TAG-ALONG! BLAST IT APART!
"I'D SEEN IT HAPPEN TO GUYS ON THE LINE BEFORE-- AN' TAG-ALONG'S TRIGGER-FINGER COULDN'TA PICKED A WORSE TIME TO FREEZE UP...
NOW, TAG-ALONG-- LIGHT UP A VOLCANO UNDERNEATH THAT SARDINE CAN!
I-I CAN'T, ROCK!
NO MATTER HOW MUCH I TRY... I CAN'T SHOOT! SOMETHING ... HOLDING ME BACK!
PIN A MEDAL ON YOURSELF, READER--IF YOU FIGURED OUT THE MAN OF STEEL'S SUBCONSCIOUS MIND AND INEXORABLE CODE AGAINST TAKING A HUMAN LIFE ARE STILL IN EFFECT DESPITE HIS AMNESIA!
10

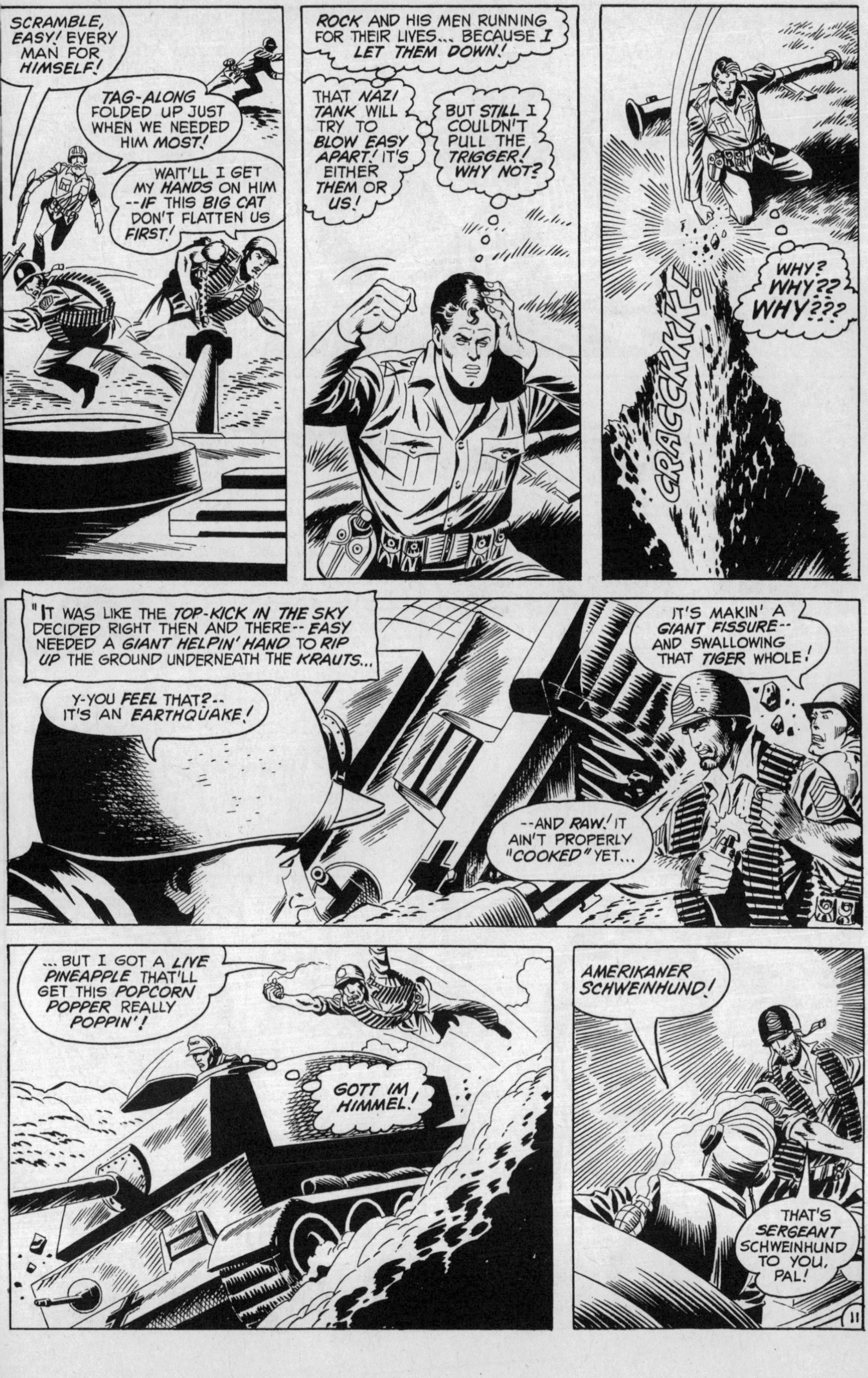
SCRAMBLE, EASY! EVERY MAN FOR HIMSELF!
TAG-ALONG FOLDED UP JUST WHEN WE NEEDED HIM MOST!
WAIT'LL I GET MY HANDS ON HIM --IF THIS BIG CAT DON'T FLATTEN US FIRST!
ROCK AND HIS MEN RUNNING FOR THEIR LIVES... BECAUSE I LET THEM DOWN!
THAT NAZI TANK WILL TRY TO BLOW EASY APART! IT'S EITHER THEM OR US!
BUT STILL I COULDN'T PULL THE TRIGGER! WHY NOT?
WHY? WHY?? WHY???
CRACCKKK!
"IT WAS LIKE THE TOP-KICK IN THE SKY DECIDED RIGHT THEN AND THERE-- EASY NEEDED A GIANT HELPIN' HAND TO RIP UP THE GROUND UNDERNEATH THE KRAUTS...
Y-YOU FEEL THAT?-- IT'S AN EARTHQUAKE!
IT'S MAKIN' A GIANT FISSURE-- AND SWALLOWING THAT TIGER WHOLE!
--AND RAW! IT AIN'T PROPERLY "COOKED" YET...
...BUT I GOT A LIVE PINEAPPLE THAT'LL GET THIS POPCORN POPPER REALLY POPPIN'!
GOTT IM HIMMEL!
AMERIKANER SCHWEINHUND!
THAT'S SERGEANT SCHWEINHUND TO YOU, PAL!
11

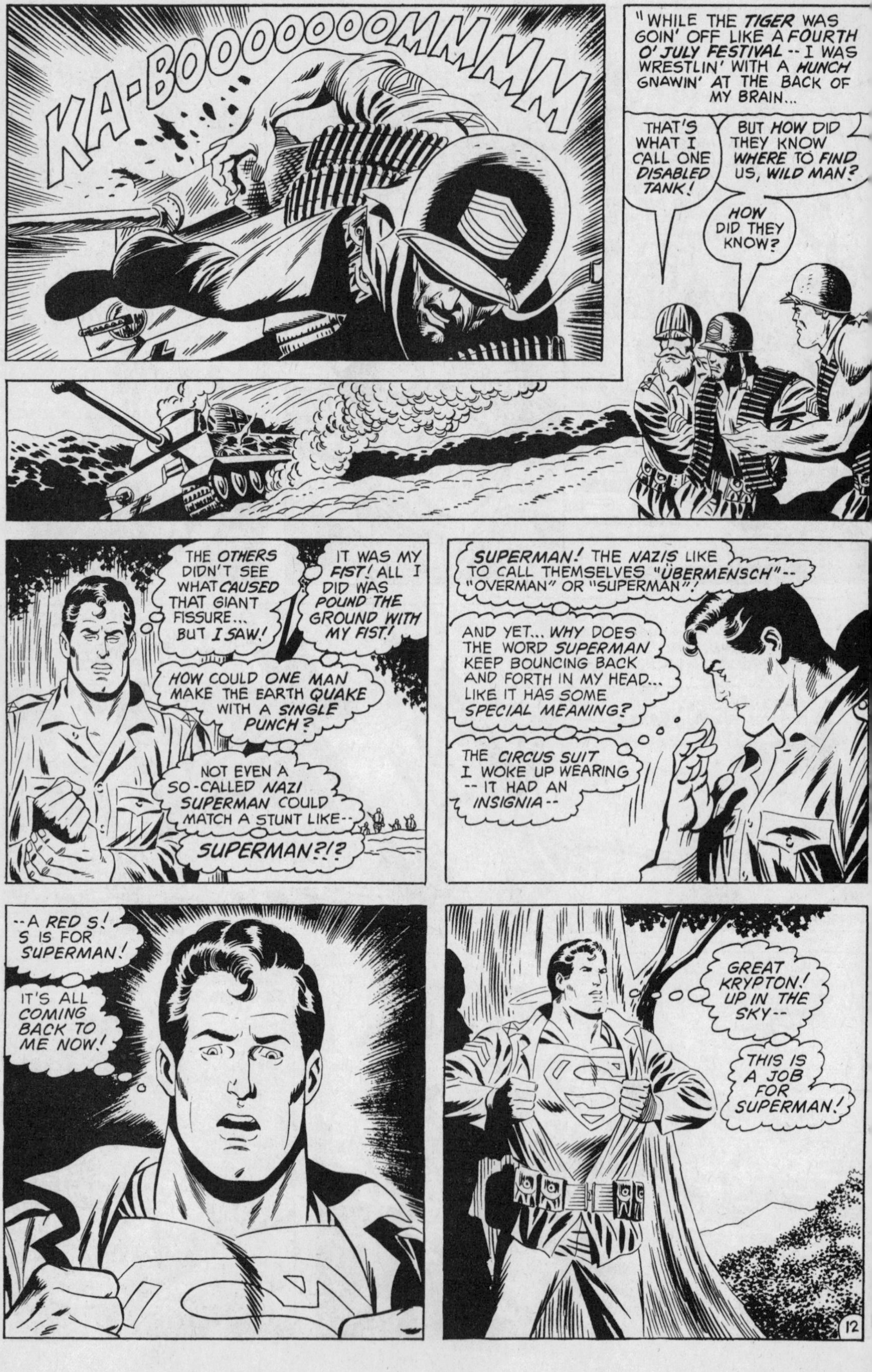
KA-BOOOOOOOOMMMMM
"WHILE THE TIGER WAS GOIN' OFF LIKE A FOURTH O' JULY FESTIVAL -- I WAS WRESTLIN' WITH A HUNCH GNAWIN' AT THE BACK OF MY BRAIN...
THAT'S WHAT I CALL ONE DISABLED TANK!
BUT HOW DID THEY KNOW WHERE TO FIND US, WILD MAN?
HOW DID THEY KNOW?
THE OTHERS DIDN'T SEE WHAT CAUSED THAT GIANT FISSURE... BUT I SAW!
IT WAS MY FIST! ALL I DID WAS POUND THE GROUND WITH MY FIST!
HOW COULD ONE MAN MAKE THE EARTH QUAKE WITH A SINGLE PUNCH?
NOT EVEN A SO-CALLED NAZI SUPERMAN COULD MATCH A STUNT LIKE--
SUPERMAN?!?
SUPERMAN! THE NAZIS LIKE TO CALL THEMSELVES "ÜBERMENSCH"-- "OVERMAN" OR "SUPERMAN"!
AND YET... WHY DOES THE WORD SUPERMAN KEEP BOUNCING BACK AND FORTH IN MY HEAD... LIKE IT HAS SOME SPECIAL MEANING?
THE CIRCUS SUIT I WOKE UP WEARING -- IT HAD AN INSIGNIA--
--A RED S! S IS FOR SUPERMAN!
IT'S ALL COMING BACK TO ME NOW!
GREAT KRYPTON! UP IN THE SKY--
THIS IS A JOB FOR SUPERMAN!
12

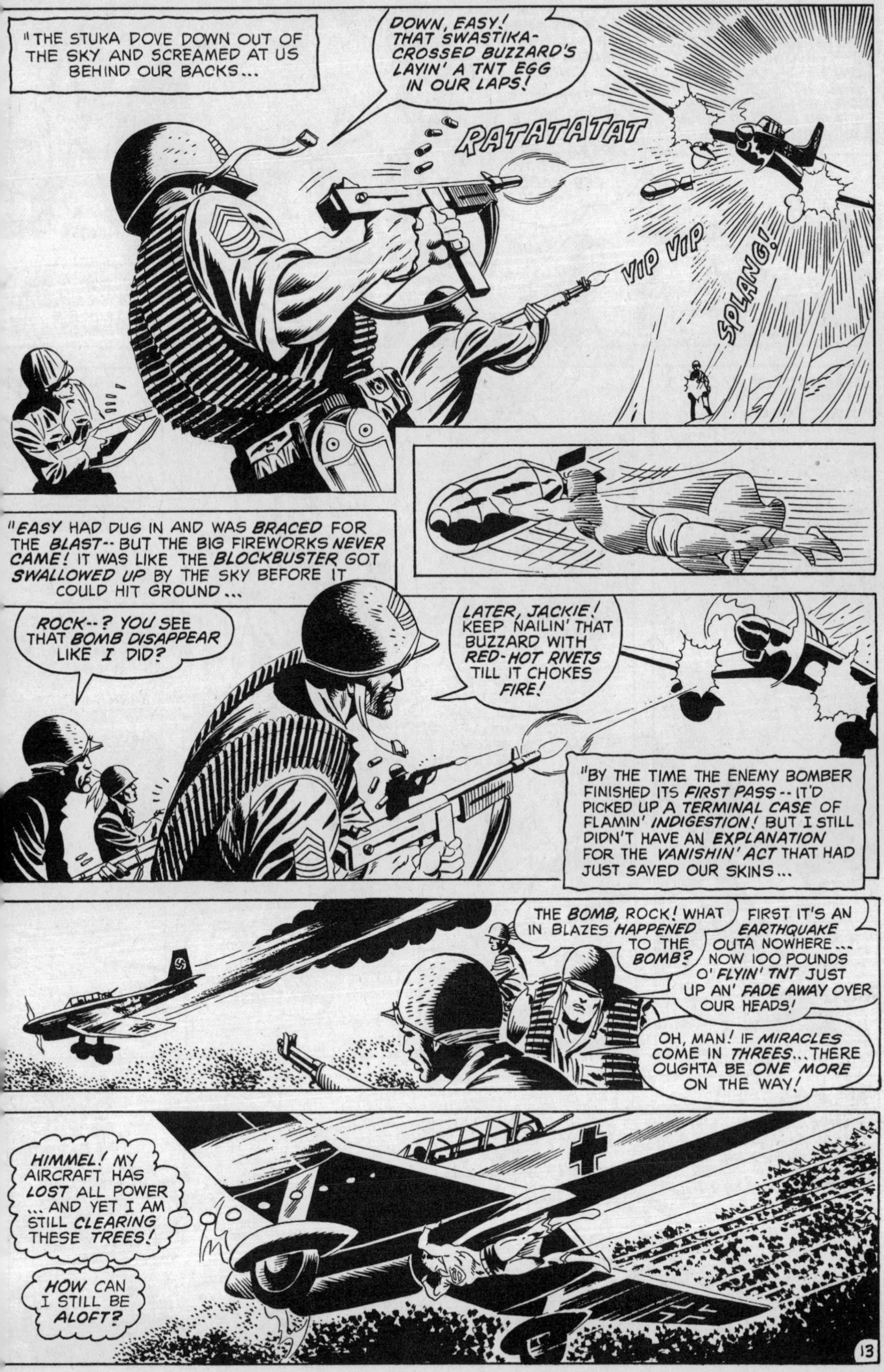
"THE STUKA DOVE DOWN OUT OF THE SKY AND SCREAMED AT US BEHIND OUR BACKS...
DOWN, EASY! THAT SWASTIKA-CROSSED BUZZARD'S LAYIN' A TNT EGG IN OUR LAPS!
RATATATAT
VIP VIP
SPLANG!
"EASY HAD DUG IN AND WAS BRACED FOR THE BLAST-- BUT THE BIG FIREWORKS NEVER CAME! IT WAS LIKE THE BLOCKBUSTER GOT SWALLOWED UP BY THE SKY BEFORE IT COULD HIT GROUND...
ROCK--? YOU SEE THAT BOMB DISAPPEAR LIKE I DID?
LATER, JACKIE! KEEP NAILIN' THAT BUZZARD WITH RED-HOT RIVETS TILL IT CHOKES FIRE!
"BY THE TIME THE ENEMY BOMBER FINISHED ITS FIRST PASS -- IT'D PICKED UP A TERMINAL CASE OF FLAMIN' INDIGESTION! BUT I STILL DIDN'T HAVE AN EXPLANATION FOR THE VANISHIN' ACT THAT HAD JUST SAVED OUR SKINS...
THE BOMB, ROCK! WHAT IN BLAZES HAPPENED TO THE BOMB?
FIRST IT'S AN EARTHQUAKE OUTA NOWHERE... NOW 100 POUNDS O' FLYIN' TNT JUST UP AN' FADE AWAY OVER OUR HEADS!
OH, MAN! IF MIRACLES COME IN THREES... THERE OUGHTA BE ONE MORE ON THE WAY!
HIMMEL! MY AIRCRAFT HAS LOST ALL POWER ... AND YET I AM STILL CLEARING THESE TREES!
HOW CAN I STILL BE ALOFT?
13

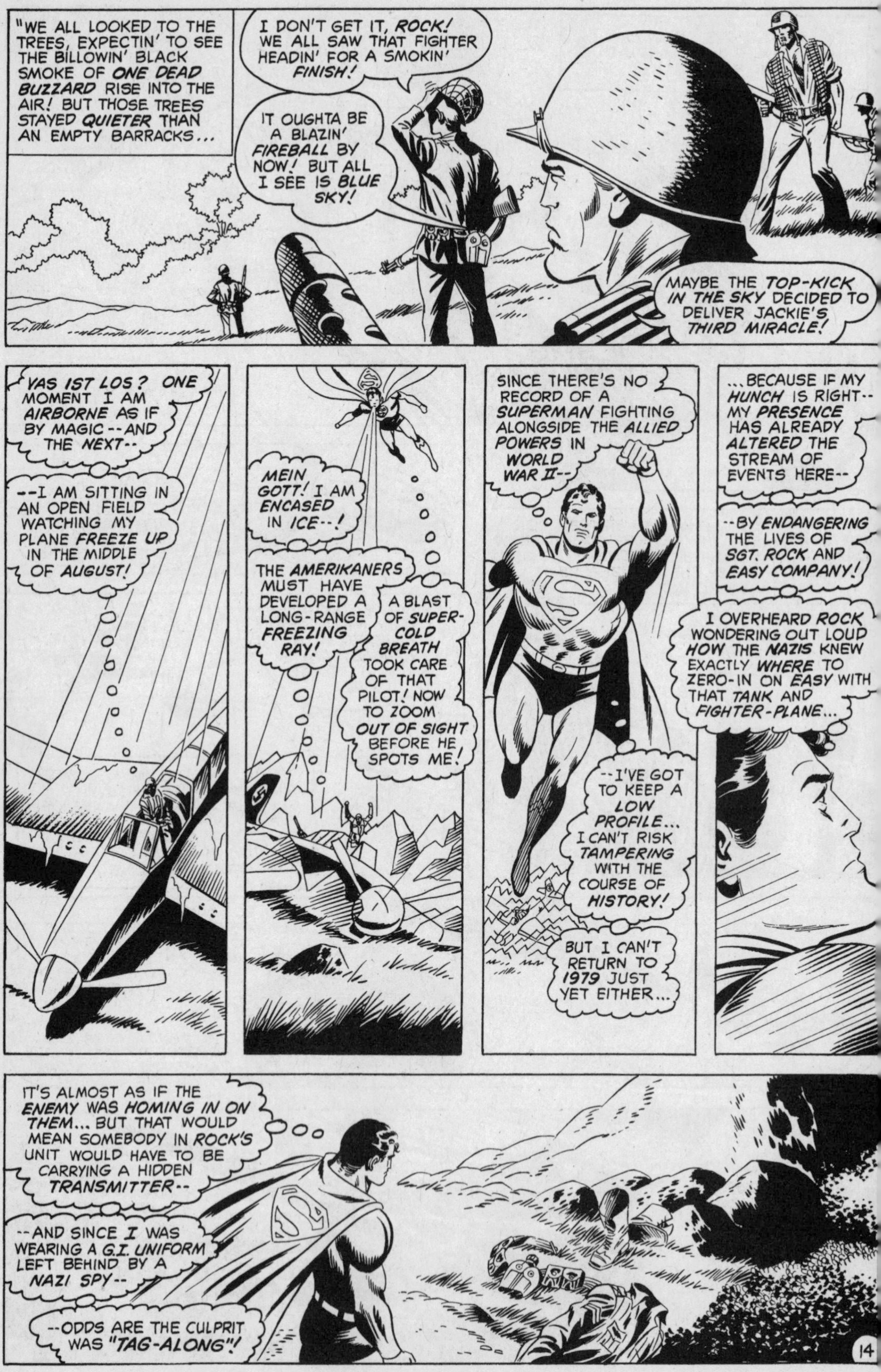
"WE ALL LOOKED TO THE TREES, EXPECTIN' TO SEE THE BILLOWIN' BLACK SMOKE OF ONE DEAD BUZZARD RISE INTO THE AIR! BUT THOSE TREES STAYED QUIETER THAN AN EMPTY BARRACKS...
I DON'T GET IT, ROCK! WE ALL SAW THAT FIGHTER HEADIN' FOR A SMOKIN' FINISH!
IT OUGHTA BE A BLAZIN' FIREBALL BY NOW! BUT ALL I SEE IS BLUE SKY!
MAYBE THE TOP-KICK IN THE SKY DECIDED TO DELIVER JACKIE'S THIRD MIRACLE!
VAS IST LOS? ONE MOMENT I AM AIRBORNE AS IF BY MAGIC--AND THE NEXT--
--I AM SITTING IN AN OPEN FIELD WATCHING MY PLANE FREEZE UP IN THE MIDDLE OF AUGUST!
MEIN GOTT! I AM ENCASED IN ICE--!
THE AMERIKANERS MUST HAVE DEVELOPED A LONG-RANGE FREEZING RAY!
A BLAST OF SUPER-COLD BREATH TOOK CARE OF THAT PILOT! NOW TO ZOOM OUT OF SIGHT BEFORE HE SPOTS ME!
SINCE THERE'S NO RECORD OF A SUPERMAN FIGHTING ALONGSIDE THE ALLIED POWERS IN WORLD WAR II--
--I'VE GOT TO KEEP A LOW PROFILE... I CAN'T RISK TAMPERING WITH THE COURSE OF HISTORY!
BUT I CAN'T RETURN TO 1979 JUST YET EITHER...
...BECAUSE IF MY HUNCH IS RIGHT--MY PRESENCE HAS ALREADY ALTERED THE STREAM OF EVENTS HERE--
--BY ENDANGERING THE LIVES OF SGT. ROCK AND EASY COMPANY!
I OVERHEARD ROCK WONDERING OUT LOUD HOW THE NAZIS KNEW EXACTLY WHERE TO ZERO-IN ON EASY WITH THAT TANK AND FIGHTER-PLANE...
IT'S ALMOST AS IF THE ENEMY WAS HOMING IN ON THEM... BUT THAT WOULD MEAN SOMEBODY IN ROCK'S UNIT WOULD HAVE TO BE CARRYING A HIDDEN TRANSMITTER--
--AND SINCE I WAS WEARING A G.I. UNIFORM LEFT BEHIND BY A NAZI SPY--
--ODDS ARE THE CULPRIT WAS "TAG-ALONG"!
14

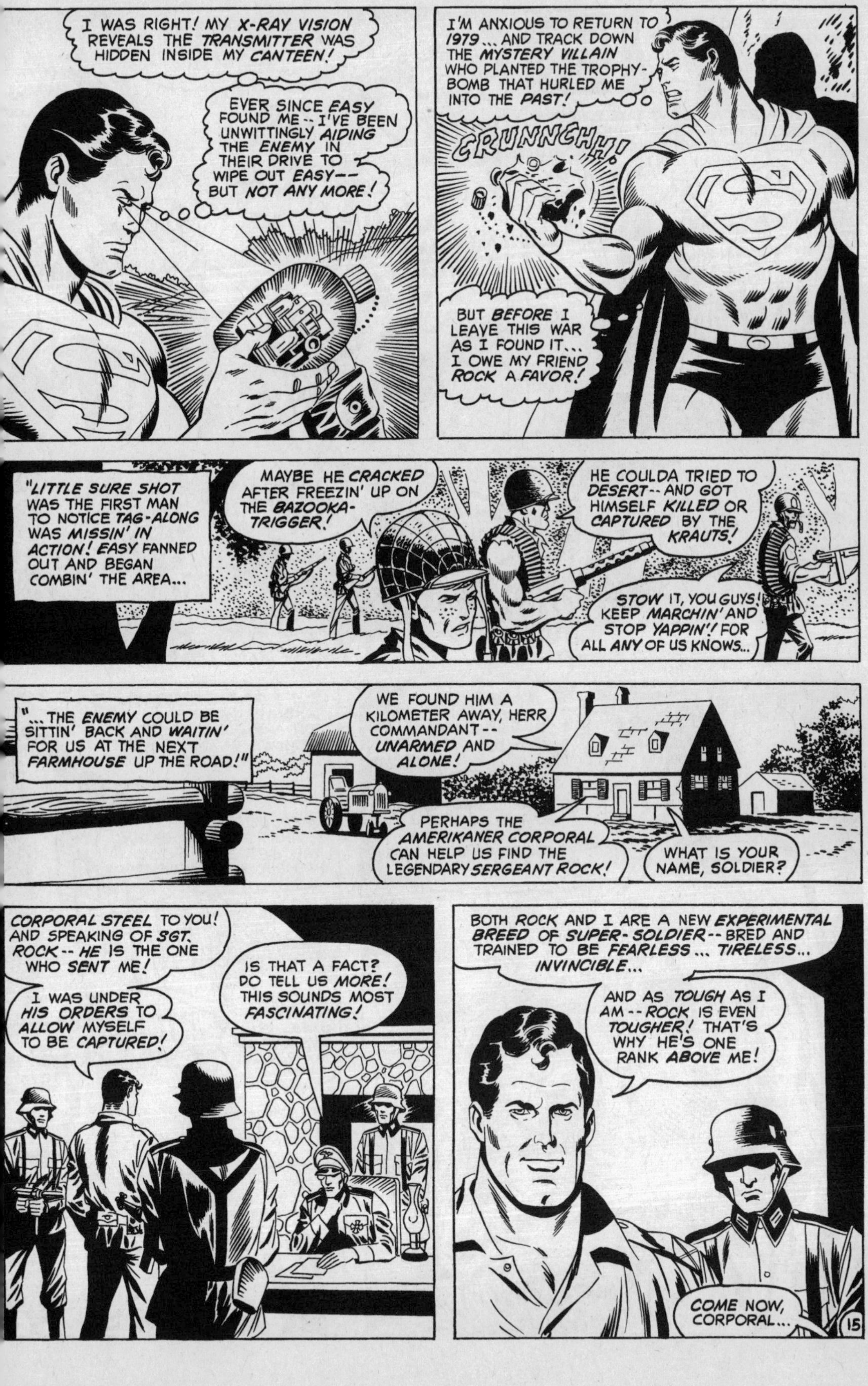
I WAS RIGHT! MY X-RAY VISION REVEALS THE TRANSMITTER WAS HIDDEN INSIDE MY CANTEEN!
EVER SINCE EASY FOUND ME -- I'VE BEEN UNWITTINGLY AIDING THE ENEMY IN THEIR DRIVE TO WIPE OUT EASY-- BUT NOT ANY MORE!
I'M ANXIOUS TO RETURN TO 1979... AND TRACK DOWN THE MYSTERY VILLAIN WHO PLANTED THE TROPHY-BOMB THAT HURLED ME INTO THE PAST!
CRUNNCHH!
BUT BEFORE I LEAVE THIS WAR AS I FOUND IT... I OWE MY FRIEND ROCK A FAVOR!
"LITTLE SURE SHOT WAS THE FIRST MAN TO NOTICE TAG-ALONG WAS MISSIN' IN ACTION! EASY FANNED OUT AND BEGAN COMBIN' THE AREA...
MAYBE HE CRACKED AFTER FREEZIN' UP ON THE BAZOOKA-TRIGGER!
HE COULDA TRIED TO DESERT-- AND GOT HIMSELF KILLED OR CAPTURED BY THE KRAUTS!
STOW IT, YOU GUYS! KEEP MARCHIN' AND STOP YAPPIN'! FOR ALL ANY OF US KNOWS...
"... THE ENEMY COULD BE SITTIN' BACK AND WAITIN' FOR US AT THE NEXT FARMHOUSE UP THE ROAD!"
WE FOUND HIM A KILOMETER AWAY, HERR COMMANDANT-- UNARMED AND ALONE!
PERHAPS THE AMERIKANER CORPORAL CAN HELP US FIND THE LEGENDARY SERGEANT ROCK!
WHAT IS YOUR NAME, SOLDIER?
CORPORAL STEEL TO YOU! AND SPEAKING OF SGT. ROCK-- HE IS THE ONE WHO SENT ME!
I WAS UNDER HIS ORDERS TO ALLOW MYSELF TO BE CAPTURED!
IS THAT A FACT? DO TELL US MORE! THIS SOUNDS MOST FASCINATING!
BOTH ROCK AND I ARE A NEW EXPERIMENTAL BREED OF SUPER-SOLDIER-- BRED AND TRAINED TO BE FEARLESS... TIRELESS... INVINCIBLE...
AND AS TOUGH AS I AM-- ROCK IS EVEN TOUGHER! THAT'S WHY HE'S ONE RANK ABOVE ME!
COME NOW, CORPORAL...
15

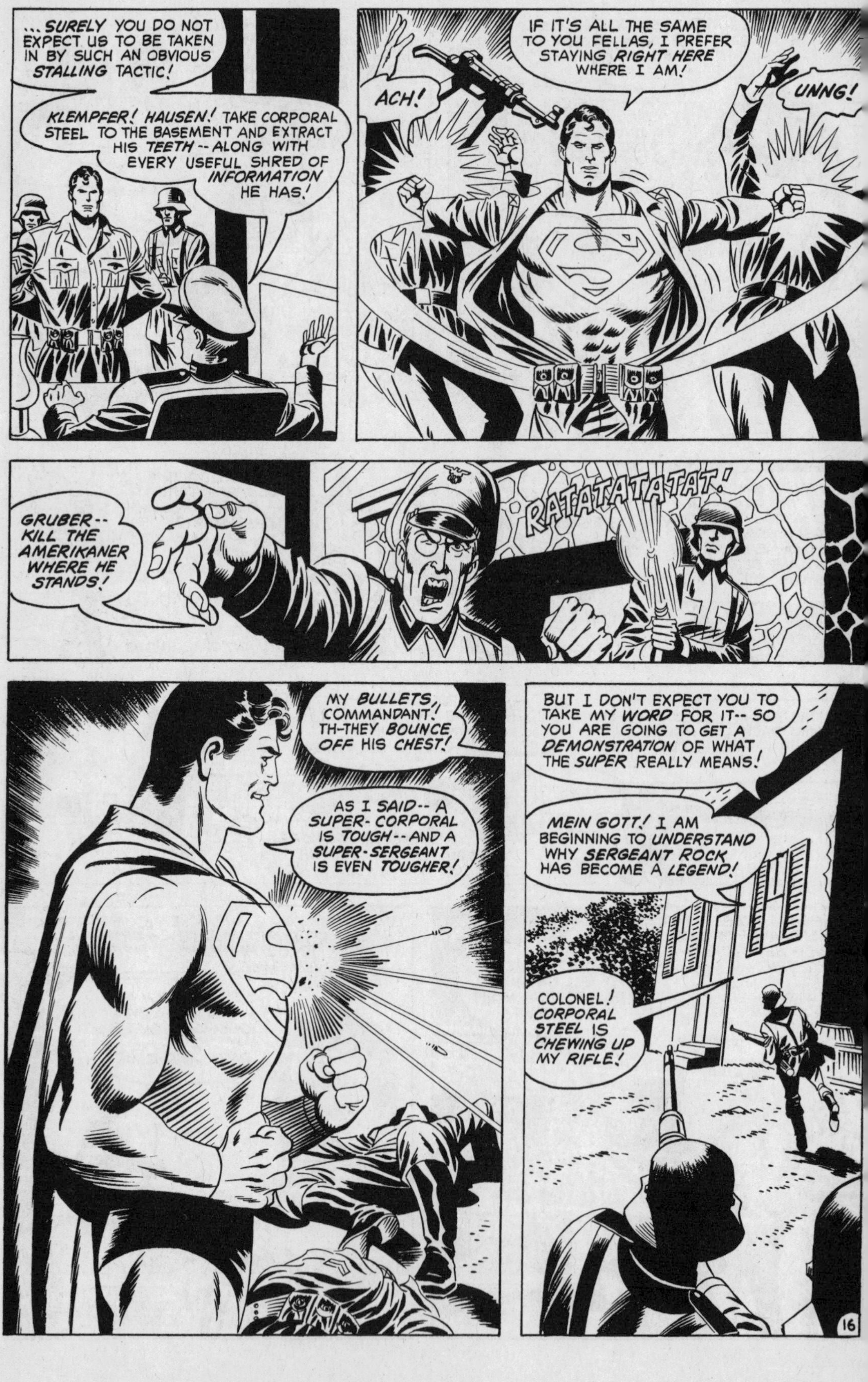
...SURELY YOU DO NOT EXPECT US TO BE TAKEN IN BY SUCH AN OBVIOUS STALLING TACTIC!
KLEMPFER! HAUSEN! TAKE CORPORAL STEEL TO THE BASEMENT AND EXTRACT HIS TEETH -- ALONG WITH EVERY USEFUL SHRED OF INFORMATION HE HAS!
IF IT'S ALL THE SAME TO YOU FELLAS, I PREFER STAYING RIGHT HERE WHERE I AM!
ACH!
UNNG!
GRUBER -- KILL THE AMERIKANER WHERE HE STANDS!
RATATATATAT!
MY BULLETS, COMMANDANT! TH-THEY BOUNCE OFF HIS CHEST!
AS I SAID -- A SUPER-CORPORAL IS TOUGH -- AND A SUPER-SERGEANT IS EVEN TOUGHER!
BUT I DON'T EXPECT YOU TO TAKE MY WORD FOR IT -- SO YOU ARE GOING TO GET A DEMONSTRATION OF WHAT THE SUPER REALLY MEANS!
MEIN GOTT! I AM BEGINNING TO UNDERSTAND WHY SERGEANT ROCK HAS BECOME A LEGEND!
COLONEL! CORPORAL STEEL IS CHEWING UP MY RIFLE!
16

"WE FOUND *TAG-ALONG* LATER THAT DAY -- WITHOUT A MARK ON 'IM! NOT ONE *CUT, BRUISE,* OR *BURN!* BUT *STILL,* HIS CHEST WOULDN'T MAKE A *SOUND...*"

NO *HEARTBEAT,* ROCK! *TAG-ALONG'S* OUT OF ACTION -- *PERMANENTLY!*

THOSE LOUSY *KRAUTS!* THEY GOT WAYS OF *TORTURIN'* THAT DON'T *SHOW!*

"WE KNEW THE *KRAUTS* HAD BEEN HOLED-UP THERE 'CAUSE WE FOUND THEIR CIGARETTE BUTTS ALL OVER THE GROUND! BUT THE *FARMHOUSE* LOOKED LIKE IT'D BEEN TORN APART BY A RAMPAGIN' *TORNADO...*"

WHAT DO YOU FIGURE IT WAS, ROCK? WE DIDN'T HEAR ANY *EXPLOSIONS!*

YOU GOT ME! ONE THING'S FOR SURE -- WHATEVER *TAG-ALONG* TOLD THE *ENEMY* --

--IT SENT 'EM *SCUTTLIN'* AWAY TOWARD THEIR OWN LINES WITH THEIR *TAILS* BETWEEN THEIR *LEGS!* ALL THE TRACKS *POINT* TO *ONE SCARED DIVISION!*

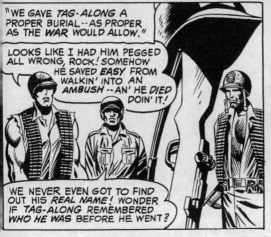

"WE GAVE *TAG-ALONG* A PROPER BURIAL -- AS PROPER AS THE *WAR* WOULD ALLOW."

LOOKS LIKE I HAD HIM PEGGED ALL WRONG, ROCK! SOMEHOW HE *SAVED* EASY FROM WALKIN' INTO AN *AMBUSH* -- AN' HE *DIED* DOIN' IT!

WE NEVER EVEN GOT TO FIND OUT HIS *REAL NAME!* WONDER IF *TAG-ALONG* REMEMBERED WHO HE WAS BEFORE HE WENT?

ONE THING ABOUT *EASY CO,* AND THIS WAR -- EVERY MAN FINDS OUT JUST *WHO* HE IS -- WHETHER HE *WANTS* TO OR NOT!

WHEREVER HE IS NOW -- LET'S HOPE *TAG-ALONG* CAN SAY THE *SAME!*

MOVE 'EM OUT, EASY --

-- THERE'S STILL A WAR ON!

NEXT ISSUE: *SUPERMAN* SETS OUT TO FIND WHO PLANTED THE BOMB IN HIS TROPHY -- AND WINDS UP IN A DEATH-BATTLE WITH *HAWKMAN!* ALSO -- THE WINNER OF OUR LETTER-COLUMN CONTEST APPEARS IN THE STORY!

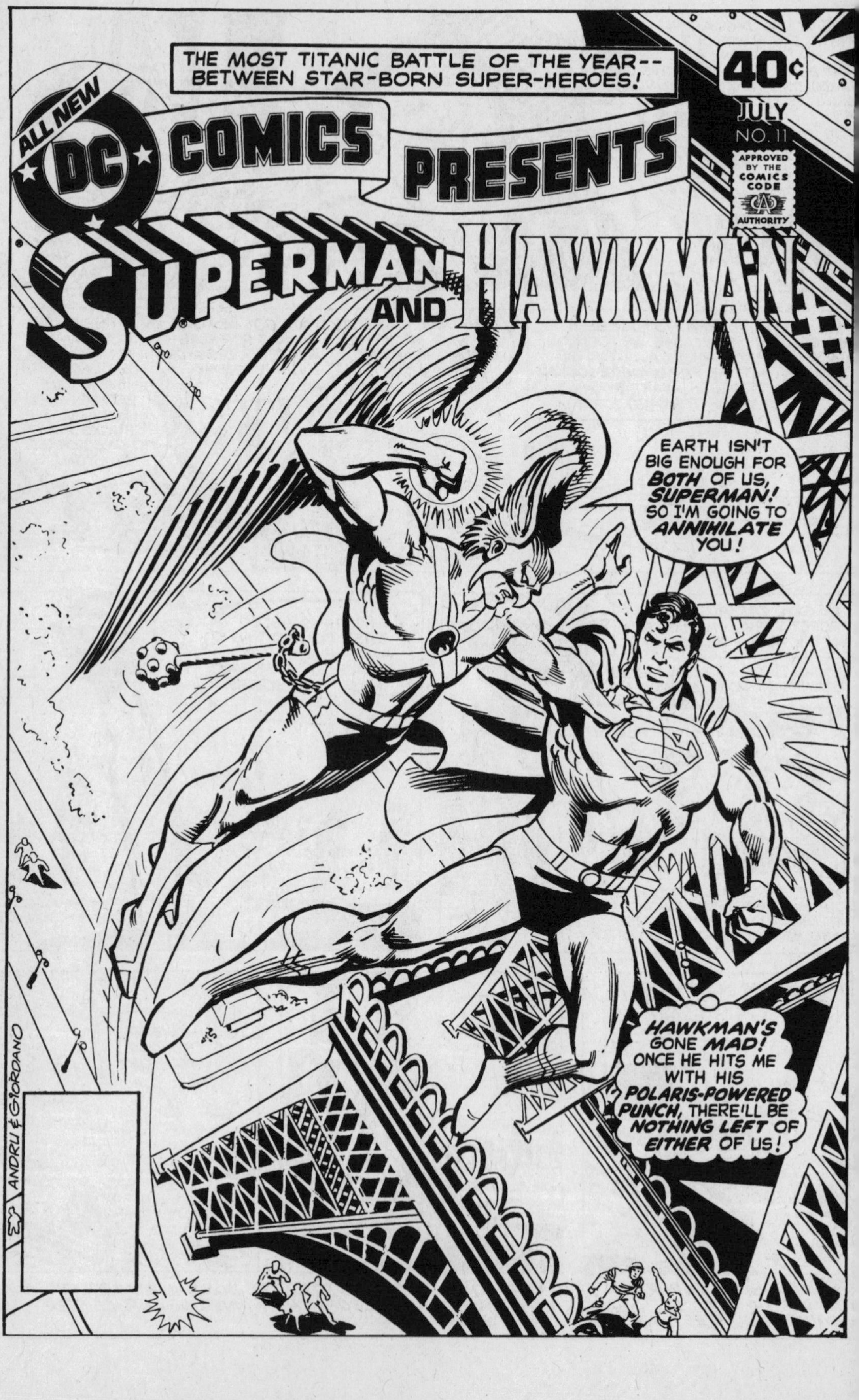
THE MOST TITANIC BATTLE OF THE YEAR--
BETWEEN STAR-BORN SUPER-HEROES!
40¢
JULY
NO. 11
APPROVED BY THE COMICS CODE AUTHORITY
ALL NEW
DC COMICS PRESENTS
SUPERMAN AND HAWKMAN
EARTH ISN'T BIG ENOUGH FOR BOTH OF US, SUPERMAN! SO I'M GOING TO ANNIHILATE YOU!
HAWKMAN'S GONE MAD! ONCE HE HITS ME WITH HIS POLARIS-POWERED PUNCH, THERE'LL BE NOTHING LEFT OF EITHER OF US!
ANDRU & GIORDANO

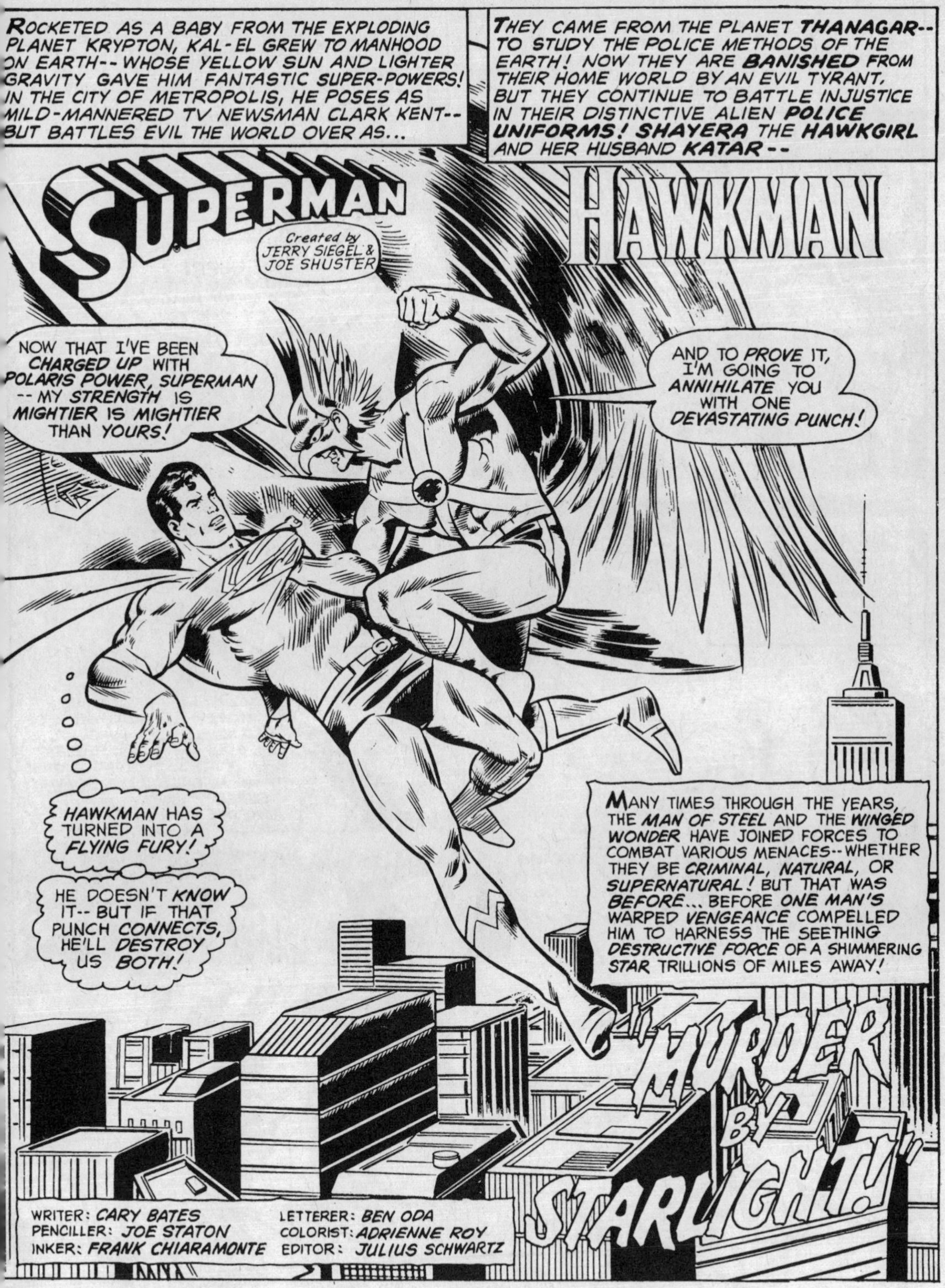
ROCKETED AS A BABY FROM THE EXPLODING PLANET KRYPTON, KAL-EL GREW TO MANHOOD ON EARTH-- WHOSE YELLOW SUN AND LIGHTER GRAVITY GAVE HIM FANTASTIC SUPER-POWERS! IN THE CITY OF METROPOLIS, HE POSES AS MILD-MANNERED TV NEWSMAN CLARK KENT-- BUT BATTLES EVIL THE WORLD OVER AS...
THEY CAME FROM THE PLANET THANAGAR-- TO STUDY THE POLICE METHODS OF THE EARTH! NOW THEY ARE BANISHED FROM THEIR HOME WORLD BY AN EVIL TYRANT, BUT THEY CONTINUE TO BATTLE INJUSTICE IN THEIR DISTINCTIVE ALIEN POLICE UNIFORMS! SHAYERA THE HAWKGIRL AND HER HUSBAND KATAR--
SUPERMAN
Created by JERRY SIEGEL & JOE SHUSTER
HAWKMAN
NOW THAT I'VE BEEN CHARGED UP WITH POLARIS POWER, SUPERMAN -- MY STRENGTH IS MIGHTIER IS MIGHTIER THAN YOURS!
AND TO PROVE IT, I'M GOING TO ANNIHILATE YOU WITH ONE DEVASTATING PUNCH!
HAWKMAN HAS TURNED INTO A FLYING FURY!
HE DOESN'T KNOW IT-- BUT IF THAT PUNCH CONNECTS, HE'LL DESTROY US BOTH!
MANY TIMES THROUGH THE YEARS, THE MAN OF STEEL AND THE WINGED WONDER HAVE JOINED FORCES TO COMBAT VARIOUS MENACES--WHETHER THEY BE CRIMINAL, NATURAL, OR SUPERNATURAL! BUT THAT WAS BEFORE... BEFORE ONE MAN'S WARPED VENGEANCE COMPELLED HIM TO HARNESS THE SEETHING DESTRUCTIVE FORCE OF A SHIMMERING STAR TRILLIONS OF MILES AWAY!
"MURDER BY STARLIGHT!"
WRITER: CARY BATES
PENCILLER: JOE STATON
INKER: FRANK CHIARAMONTE
LETTERER: BEN ODA
COLORIST: ADRIENNE ROY
EDITOR: JULIUS SCHWARTZ

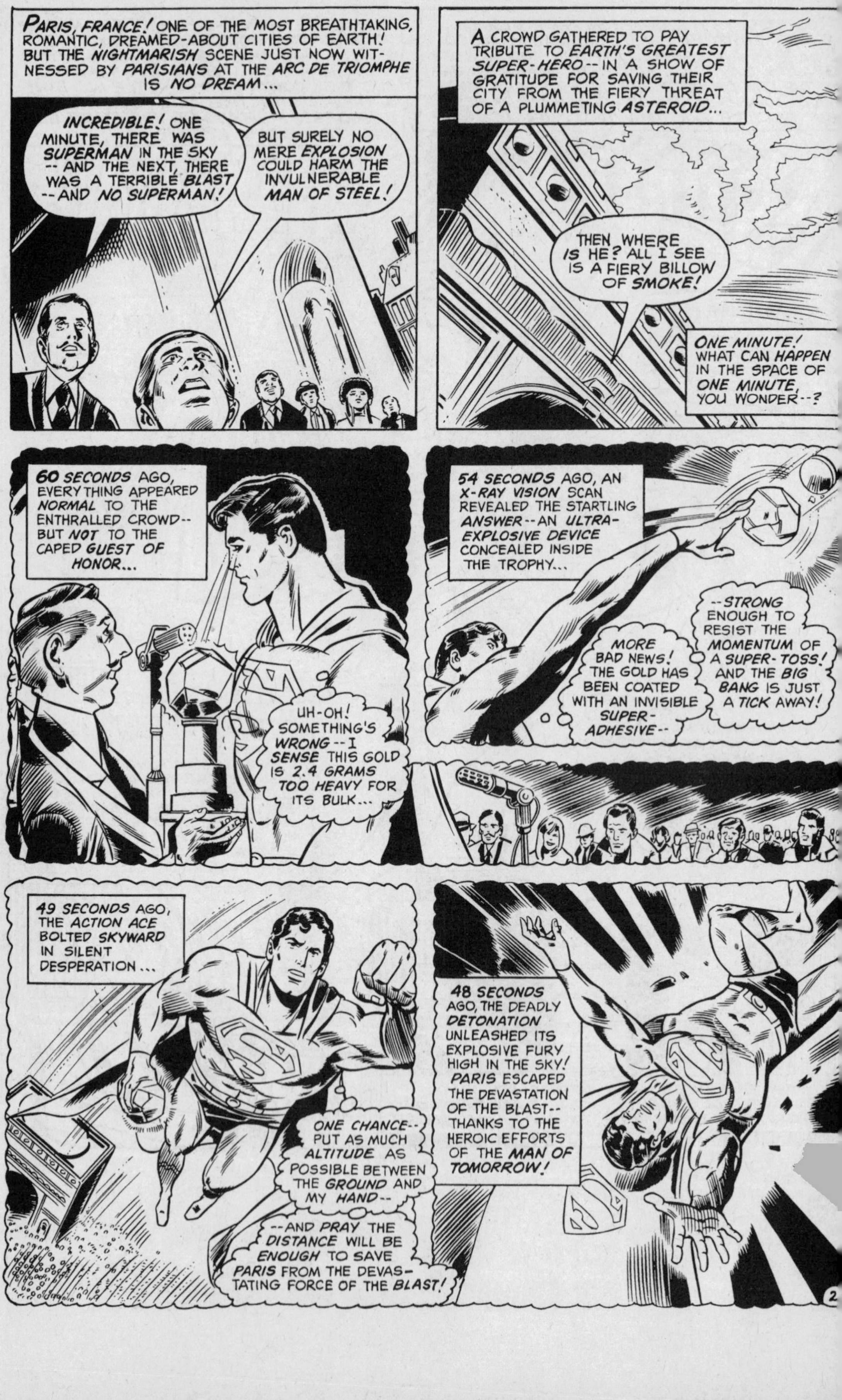

PARIS, FRANCE! ONE OF THE MOST BREATHTAKING, ROMANTIC, DREAMED-ABOUT CITIES OF EARTH! BUT THE NIGHTMARISH SCENE JUST NOW WITNESSED BY PARISIANS AT THE ARC DE TRIOMPHE IS NO DREAM...
INCREDIBLE! ONE MINUTE, THERE WAS SUPERMAN IN THE SKY -- AND THE NEXT, THERE WAS A TERRIBLE BLAST -- AND NO SUPERMAN!
BUT SURELY NO MERE EXPLOSION COULD HARM THE INVULNERABLE MAN OF STEEL!
A CROWD GATHERED TO PAY TRIBUTE TO EARTH'S GREATEST SUPER-HERO -- IN A SHOW OF GRATITUDE FOR SAVING THEIR CITY FROM THE FIERY THREAT OF A PLUMMETING ASTEROID...
THEN WHERE IS HE? ALL I SEE IS A FIERY BILLOW OF SMOKE!
ONE MINUTE! WHAT CAN HAPPEN IN THE SPACE OF ONE MINUTE, YOU WONDER--?
60 SECONDS AGO, EVERYTHING APPEARED NORMAL TO THE ENTHRALLED CROWD-- BUT NOT TO THE CAPED GUEST OF HONOR...
UH-OH! SOMETHING'S WRONG -- I SENSE THIS GOLD IS 2.4 GRAMS TOO HEAVY FOR ITS BULK...
54 SECONDS AGO, AN X-RAY VISION SCAN REVEALED THE STARTLING ANSWER -- AN ULTRA-EXPLOSIVE DEVICE CONCEALED INSIDE THE TROPHY...
MORE BAD NEWS! THE GOLD HAS BEEN COATED WITH AN INVISIBLE SUPER-ADHESIVE--
--STRONG ENOUGH TO RESIST THE MOMENTUM OF A SUPER-TOSS! AND THE BIG BANG IS JUST A TICK AWAY!
49 SECONDS AGO, THE ACTION ACE BOLTED SKYWARD IN SILENT DESPERATION...
ONE CHANCE-- PUT AS MUCH ALTITUDE AS POSSIBLE BETWEEN THE GROUND AND MY HAND--
--AND PRAY THE DISTANCE WILL BE ENOUGH TO SAVE PARIS FROM THE DEVASTATING FORCE OF THE BLAST!
48 SECONDS AGO, THE DEADLY DETONATION UNLEASHED ITS EXPLOSIVE FURY HIGH IN THE SKY! PARIS ESCAPED THE DEVASTATION OF THE BLAST-- THANKS TO THE HEROIC EFFORTS OF THE MAN OF TOMORROW!

25 SECONDS AGO, THE SMOKE FINALLY CLEARED -- REVEALING ONLY EMPTY SKY!

WHILE THE PARISIANS BELOW WERE FEARING THE WORST -- NONE OF THEM HAD THE FAINTEST INKLING OF THE ASTOUNDING TRUTH!

THE TREMENDOUS FORCE OF THE EXPLOSION HAD HURTLED SUPERMAN THROUGH THE TIME BARRIER -- BACK TO THE CHAOTIC PANORAMA OF WORLD WAR II!

NOW WE RETURN TO THE PRESENT -- AS A FAMILIAR CAPED CHAMPION SUDDENLY REMATERIALIZES PRECISELY WHERE HE HAD VANISHED...

LOOK! THERE HE IS AGAIN -- AS IF NOTHING HAD HAPPENED!

I TOLD YOU SO! NO MERE EXPLOSION CAN HARM THE MAN OF STEEL!

AMAZING! EVEN THOUGH MY ADVENTURE WITH SGT. ROCK LASTED A FULL TWO DAYS IN 1944 --

-- I'VE RE-EMERGED HERE IN 1979 SCANT SECONDS AFTER I LEFT!

YOU HAVE MY DEEPEST APOLOGY, SUPERMAN! I CANNOT IMAGINE WHO COULD HAVE -- HOW DO YOU SAY -- "BOOBY-TRAPPED" OUR GOLD TROPHY!

SOMEONE EXTREMELY DANGEROUS, MONSIEUR LE PRESIDENT...

... SOMEONE WITH A TECHNOLOGY ADVANCED ENOUGH TO CONSTRUCT A BOMB CAPABLE OF DOING SERIOUS DAMAGE EVEN TO ME!

BUT WHO, SUPERMAN? ONE OF YOUR SUPER-FOES, PERHAPS?

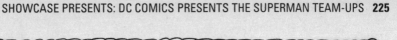

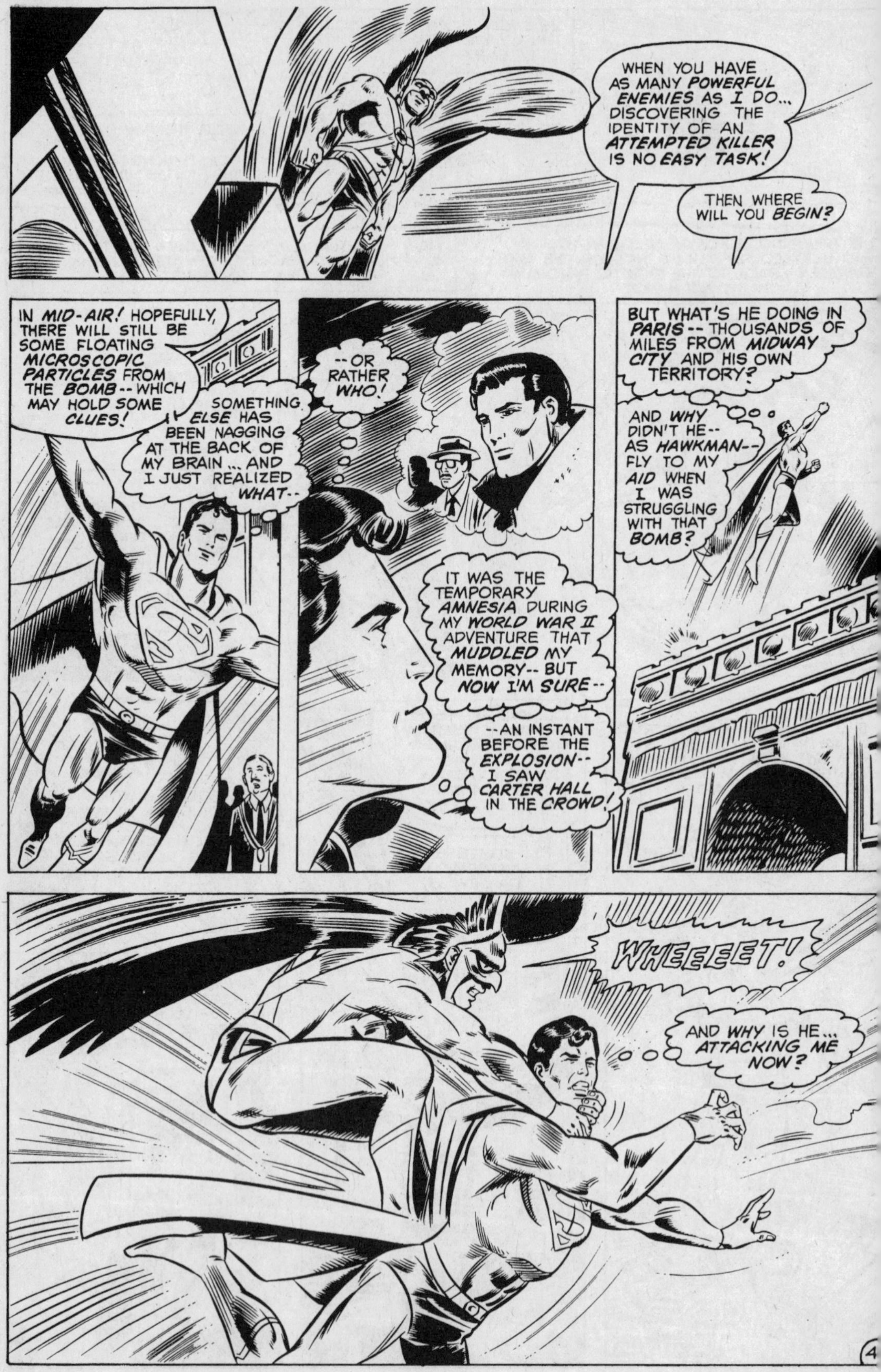
WHEN YOU HAVE AS MANY POWERFUL ENEMIES AS I DO... DISCOVERING THE IDENTITY OF AN ATTEMPTED KILLER IS NO EASY TASK!
THEN WHERE WILL YOU BEGIN?
IN MID-AIR! HOPEFULLY, THERE WILL STILL BE SOME FLOATING MICROSCOPIC PARTICLES FROM THE BOMB--WHICH MAY HOLD SOME CLUES!
SOMETHING ELSE HAS BEEN NAGGING AT THE BACK OF MY BRAIN ... AND I JUST REALIZED WHAT--
--OR RATHER WHO!
IT WAS THE TEMPORARY AMNESIA DURING MY WORLD WAR II ADVENTURE THAT MUDDLED MY MEMORY--BUT NOW I'M SURE--
--AN INSTANT BEFORE THE EXPLOSION--I SAW CARTER HALL IN THE CROWD!
BUT WHAT'S HE DOING IN PARIS--THOUSANDS OF MILES FROM MIDWAY CITY AND HIS OWN TERRITORY?
AND WHY DIDN'T HE--AS HAWKMAN--FLY TO MY AID WHEN I WAS STRUGGLING WITH THAT BOMB?
WHEEEET!
AND WHY IS HE... ATTACKING ME NOW?
4

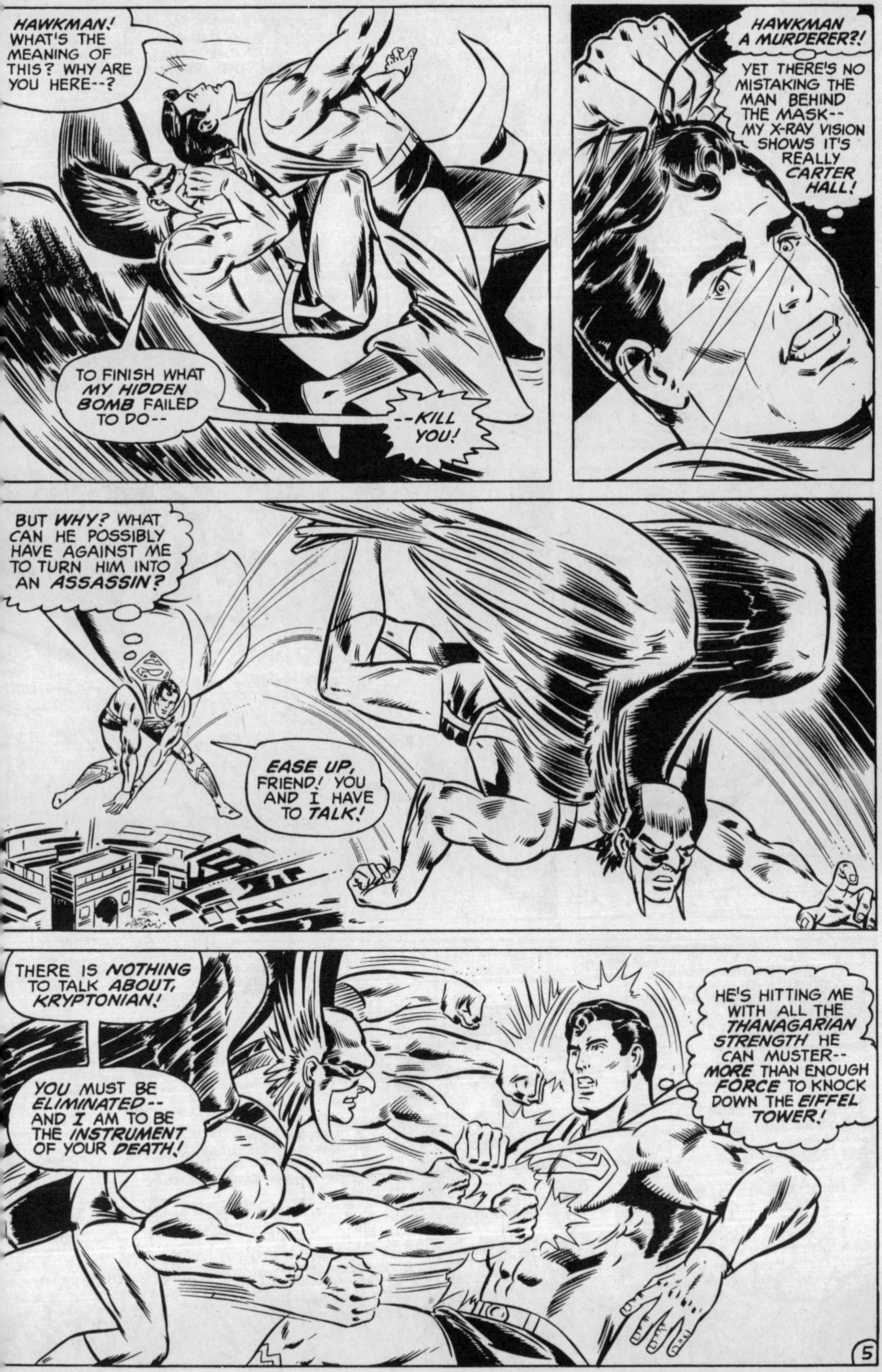
HAWKMAN! WHAT'S THE MEANING OF THIS? WHY ARE YOU HERE--?
TO FINISH WHAT MY HIDDEN BOMB FAILED TO DO--
--KILL YOU!
HAWKMAN A MURDERER?!
YET THERE'S NO MISTAKING THE MAN BEHIND THE MASK-- MY X-RAY VISION SHOWS IT'S REALLY CARTER HALL!
BUT WHY? WHAT CAN HE POSSIBLY HAVE AGAINST ME TO TURN HIM INTO AN ASSASSIN?
EASE UP, FRIEND! YOU AND I HAVE TO TALK!
THERE IS NOTHING TO TALK ABOUT, KRYPTONIAN!
YOU MUST BE ELIMINATED-- AND I AM TO BE THE INSTRUMENT OF YOUR DEATH!
HE'S HITTING ME WITH ALL THE THANAGARIAN STRENGTH HE CAN MUSTER-- MORE THAN ENOUGH FORCE TO KNOCK DOWN THE EIFFEL TOWER!
5

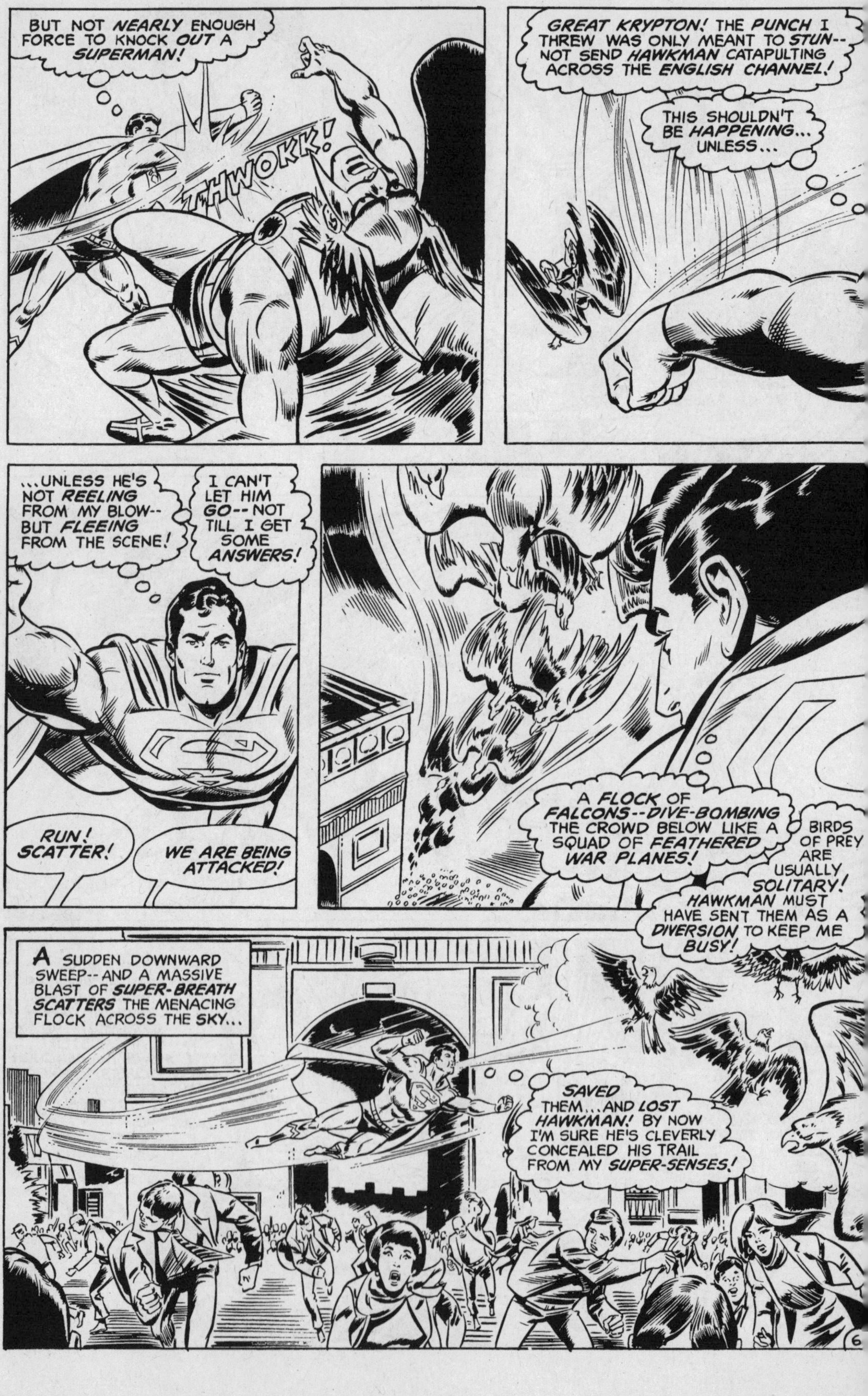
BUT NOT NEARLY ENOUGH FORCE TO KNOCK OUT A SUPERMAN!
THWOKK!
GREAT KRYPTON! THE PUNCH I THREW WAS ONLY MEANT TO STUN-- NOT SEND HAWKMAN CATAPULTING ACROSS THE ENGLISH CHANNEL!
THIS SHOULDN'T BE HAPPENING... UNLESS...
...UNLESS HE'S NOT REELING FROM MY BLOW-- BUT FLEEING FROM THE SCENE!
I CAN'T LET HIM GO-- NOT TILL I GET SOME ANSWERS!
RUN! SCATTER!
WE ARE BEING ATTACKED!
A FLOCK OF FALCONS--DIVE-BOMBING THE CROWD BELOW LIKE A SQUAD OF FEATHERED WAR PLANES!
BIRDS OF PREY ARE USUALLY SOLITARY! HAWKMAN MUST HAVE SENT THEM AS A DIVERSION TO KEEP ME BUSY!
A SUDDEN DOWNWARD SWEEP-- AND A MASSIVE BLAST OF SUPER-BREATH SCATTERS THE MENACING FLOCK ACROSS THE SKY...
SAVED THEM... AND LOST HAWKMAN! BY NOW I'M SURE HE'S CLEVERLY CONCEALED HIS TRAIL FROM MY SUPER-SENSES!
6

THIS IS MY *LUCKY* DAY!

NEWSPAPERS WILL PAY ME A *FORTUNE* FOR THESE SPECTACULAR SHOTS OF *SUPERMAN* AND *HAWKMAN* IN *BATTLE!*

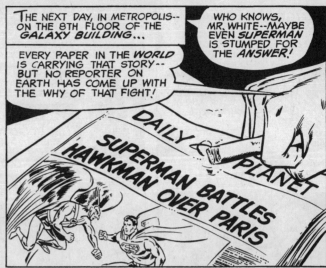

THE NEXT DAY, IN METROPOLIS-- ON THE 8TH FLOOR OF THE *GALAXY BUILDING...*

EVERY PAPER IN THE *WORLD* IS CARRYING THAT STORY-- BUT NO REPORTER ON EARTH HAS COME UP WITH THE *WHY* OF THAT FIGHT!

WHO KNOWS, MR. WHITE--MAYBE EVEN *SUPERMAN* IS STUMPED FOR THE *ANSWER!*

DAILY PLANET

SUPERMAN BATTLES HAWKMAN OVER PARIS

AND *WHO* MIGHT *YOU* BE, YOUNG MAN?

PERRY, MEET *MARC TEICHMAN*-- FIRST-PRIZE *WINNER* IN THE *DAILY PLANET'S* CHARITY *LOTTERY DRAWING!*

IT'S A *PLEASURE,* MR. WHITE...

...TO MEET THE EDITOR OF MY *FAVORITE* NEWSPAPER!

NICE OF YOU TO COME ALL THE WAY UP TO MY OFFICE TO *TELL* ME THAT... BUT... I'M VERY *BUSY,* SO IF YOU DON'T MIND...

DAILY PLANET
SUPERMAN BATTLES HAWKMAN OVER PARIS

ER... *CHIEF*--

--I THINK YOU'VE *FORGOTTEN* THE *RULES* OF THE *CONTEST!* THE *WINNER* IS SUPPOSED TO REPORT TO *YOUR* OFFICE AT 10 A.M. ON THE MORNING OF THE 27TH--AND THAT'S WHERE HIS *HALF-DAY* WITH *SUPERMAN* IS TO *BEGIN!*

WGBS

AHEM--PERHAPS I *DID* FORGET, JIMMY... BUT *YOU* FORGOT SOMETHING, *TOO*--

--*DON'T* CALL ME *CHIEF!*

QUIET, EVERYONE! I *HEAR* SOMETHING--

--A *WHOOSHING* SOUND! AND IT'S GETTING *LOUDER!*

IT'S *HIM*--!

7

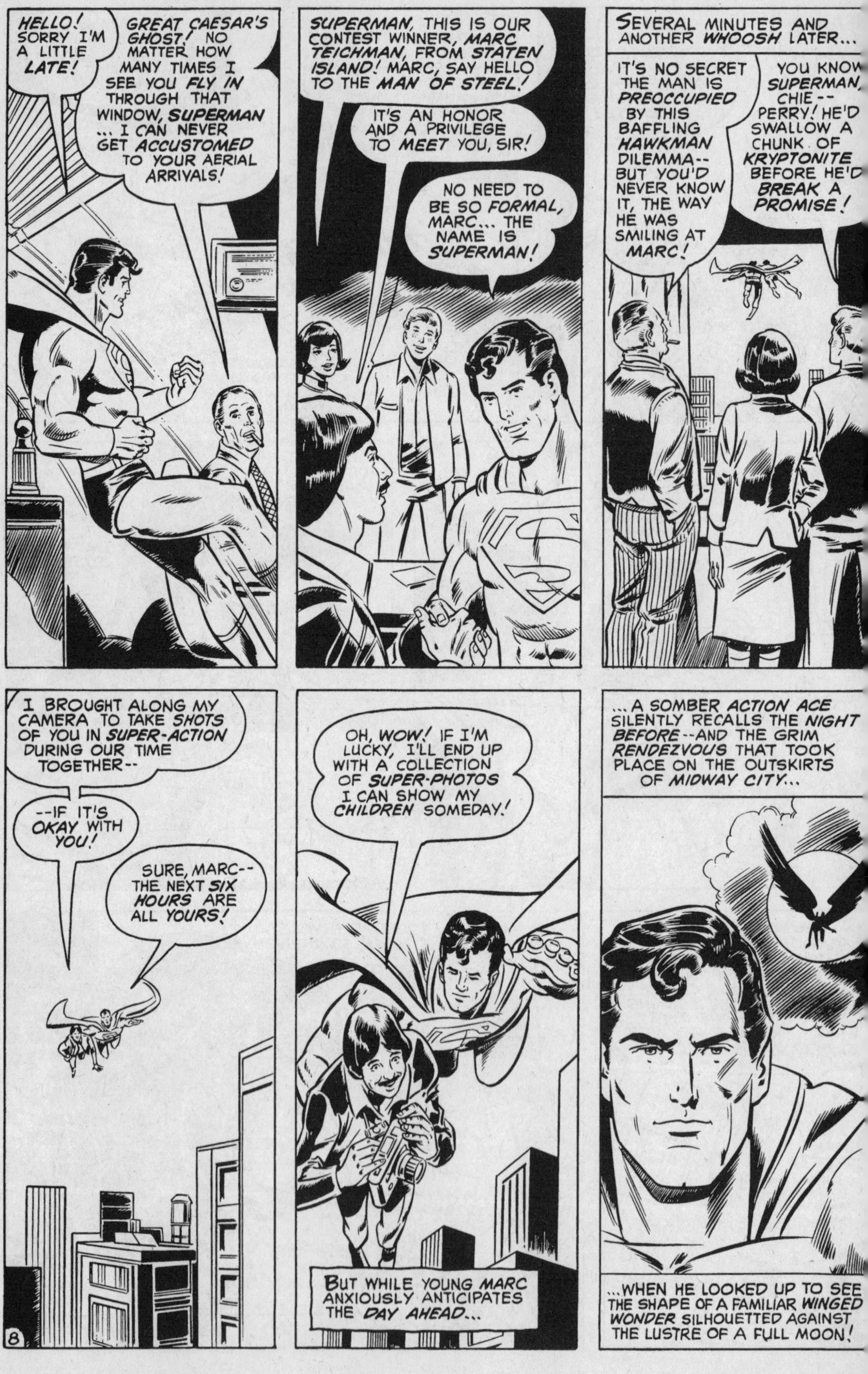
HELLO! SORRY I'M A LITTLE LATE!
GREAT CAESAR'S GHOST! NO MATTER HOW MANY TIMES I SEE YOU FLY IN THROUGH THAT WINDOW, SUPERMAN ... I CAN NEVER GET ACCUSTOMED TO YOUR AERIAL ARRIVALS!
SUPERMAN, THIS IS OUR CONTEST WINNER, MARC TEICHMAN, FROM STATEN ISLAND! MARC, SAY HELLO TO THE MAN OF STEEL!
IT'S AN HONOR AND A PRIVILEGE TO MEET YOU, SIR!
NO NEED TO BE SO FORMAL, MARC... THE NAME IS SUPERMAN!
SEVERAL MINUTES AND ANOTHER WHOOSH LATER...
IT'S NO SECRET THE MAN IS PREOCCUPIED BY THIS BAFFLING HAWKMAN DILEMMA-- BUT YOU'D NEVER KNOW IT, THE WAY HE WAS SMILING AT MARC!
YOU KNOW SUPERMAN, CHIE-- PERRY! HE'D SWALLOW A CHUNK OF KRYPTONITE BEFORE HE'D BREAK A PROMISE!
I BROUGHT ALONG MY CAMERA TO TAKE SHOTS OF YOU IN SUPER-ACTION DURING OUR TIME TOGETHER--
--IF IT'S OKAY WITH YOU!
SURE, MARC-- THE NEXT SIX HOURS ARE ALL YOURS!
8
OH, WOW! IF I'M LUCKY, I'LL END UP WITH A COLLECTION OF SUPER-PHOTOS I CAN SHOW MY CHILDREN SOMEDAY!
BUT WHILE YOUNG MARC ANXIOUSLY ANTICIPATES THE DAY AHEAD...
...A SOMBER ACTION ACE SILENTLY RECALLS THE NIGHT BEFORE--AND THE GRIM RENDEZVOUS THAT TOOK PLACE ON THE OUTSKIRTS OF MIDWAY CITY...
...WHEN HE LOOKED UP TO SEE THE SHAPE OF A FAMILIAR WINGED WONDER SILHOUETTED AGAINST THE LUSTRE OF A FULL MOON!

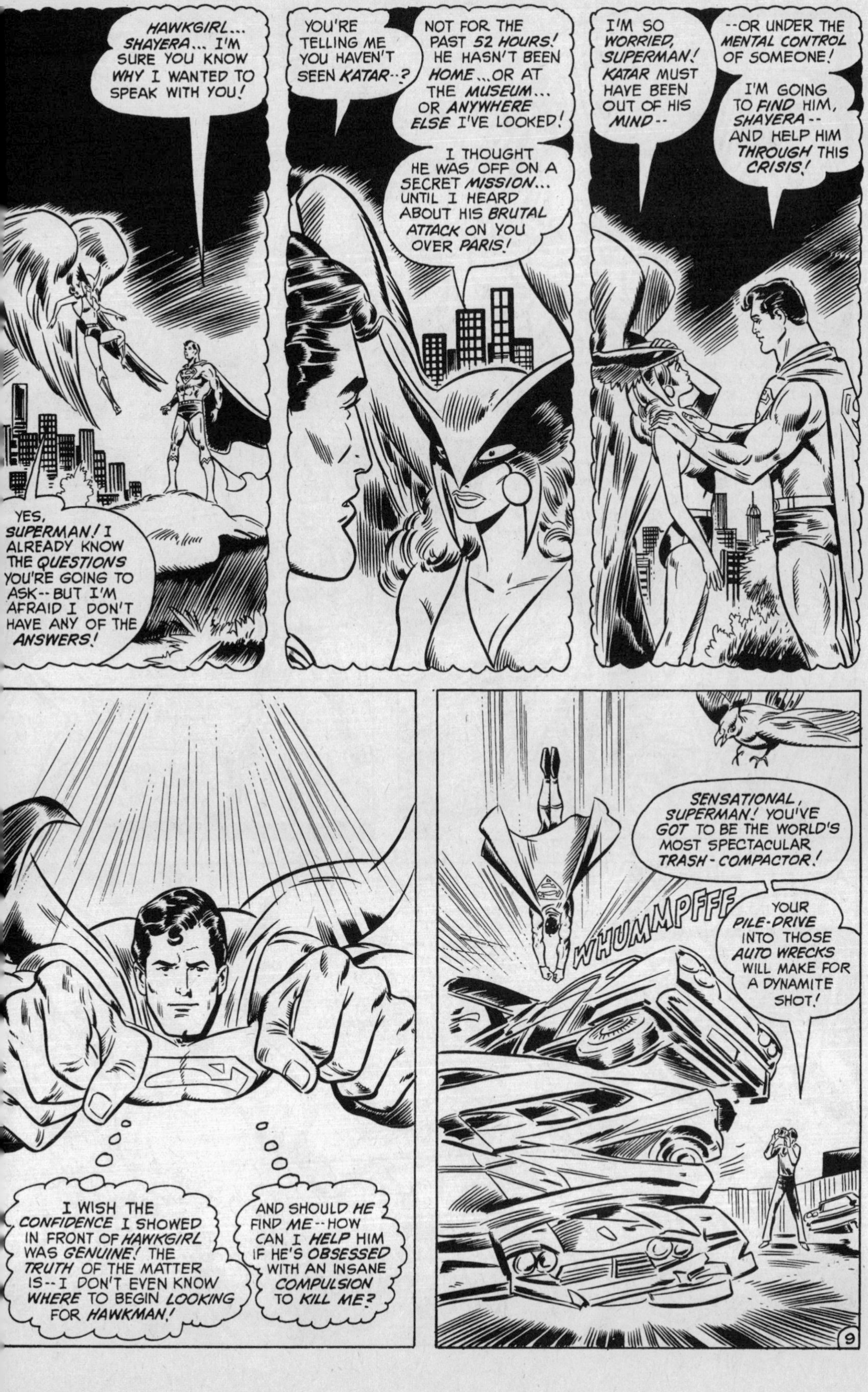
HAWKGIRL... SHAYERA... I'M SURE YOU KNOW WHY I WANTED TO SPEAK WITH YOU!
YES, SUPERMAN! I ALREADY KNOW THE QUESTIONS YOU'RE GOING TO ASK--BUT I'M AFRAID I DON'T HAVE ANY OF THE ANSWERS!
YOU'RE TELLING ME YOU HAVEN'T SEEN KATAR--?
NOT FOR THE PAST 52 HOURS! HE HASN'T BEEN HOME...OR AT THE MUSEUM... OR ANYWHERE ELSE I'VE LOOKED!
I THOUGHT HE WAS OFF ON A SECRET MISSION... UNTIL I HEARD ABOUT HIS BRUTAL ATTACK ON YOU OVER PARIS!
I'M SO WORRIED, SUPERMAN! KATAR MUST HAVE BEEN OUT OF HIS MIND--
--OR UNDER THE MENTAL CONTROL OF SOMEONE!
I'M GOING TO FIND HIM, SHAYERA--AND HELP HIM THROUGH THIS CRISIS!
I WISH THE CONFIDENCE I SHOWED IN FRONT OF HAWKGIRL WAS GENUINE! THE TRUTH OF THE MATTER IS--I DON'T EVEN KNOW WHERE TO BEGIN LOOKING FOR HAWKMAN!
AND SHOULD HE FIND ME--HOW CAN I HELP HIM IF HE'S OBSESSED WITH AN INSANE COMPULSION TO KILL ME?
SENSATIONAL, SUPERMAN! YOU'VE GOT TO BE THE WORLD'S MOST SPECTACULAR TRASH-COMPACTOR!
WHUMMPFFF
YOUR PILE-DRIVE INTO THOSE AUTO WRECKS WILL MAKE FOR A DYNAMITE SHOT!
9

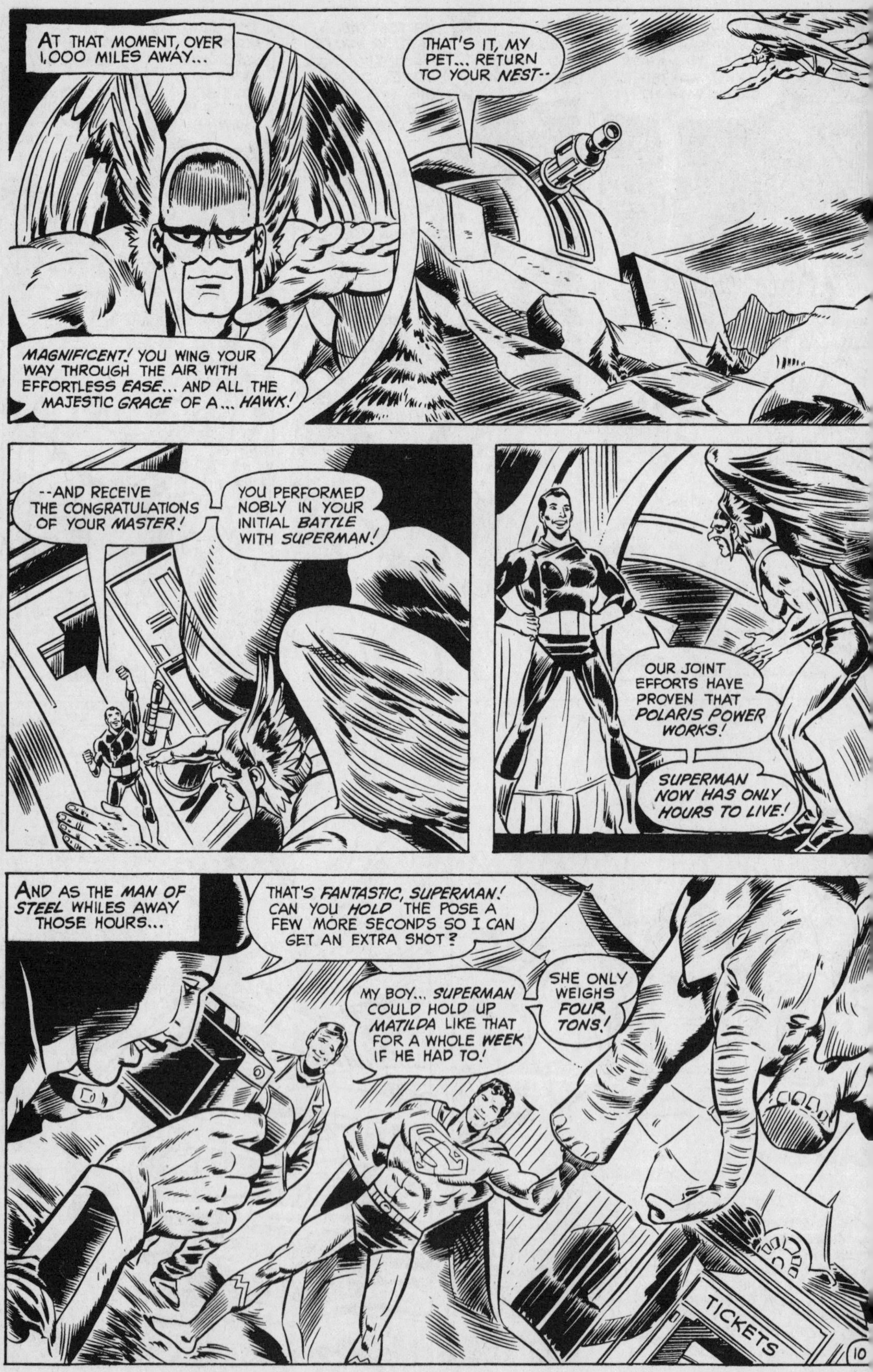
AT THAT MOMENT, OVER 1,000 MILES AWAY...
THAT'S IT, MY PET... RETURN TO YOUR NEST--
MAGNIFICENT! YOU WING YOUR WAY THROUGH THE AIR WITH EFFORTLESS EASE... AND ALL THE MAJESTIC GRACE OF A... HAWK!
--AND RECEIVE THE CONGRATULATIONS OF YOUR MASTER!
YOU PERFORMED NOBLY IN YOUR INITIAL BATTLE WITH SUPERMAN!
OUR JOINT EFFORTS HAVE PROVEN THAT POLARIS POWER WORKS!
SUPERMAN NOW HAS ONLY HOURS TO LIVE!
AND AS THE MAN OF STEEL WHILES AWAY THOSE HOURS...
THAT'S FANTASTIC, SUPERMAN! CAN YOU HOLD THE POSE A FEW MORE SECONDS SO I CAN GET AN EXTRA SHOT?
MY BOY... SUPERMAN COULD HOLD UP MATILDA LIKE THAT FOR A WHOLE WEEK IF HE HAD TO!
SHE ONLY WEIGHS FOUR TONS!
TICKETS
10

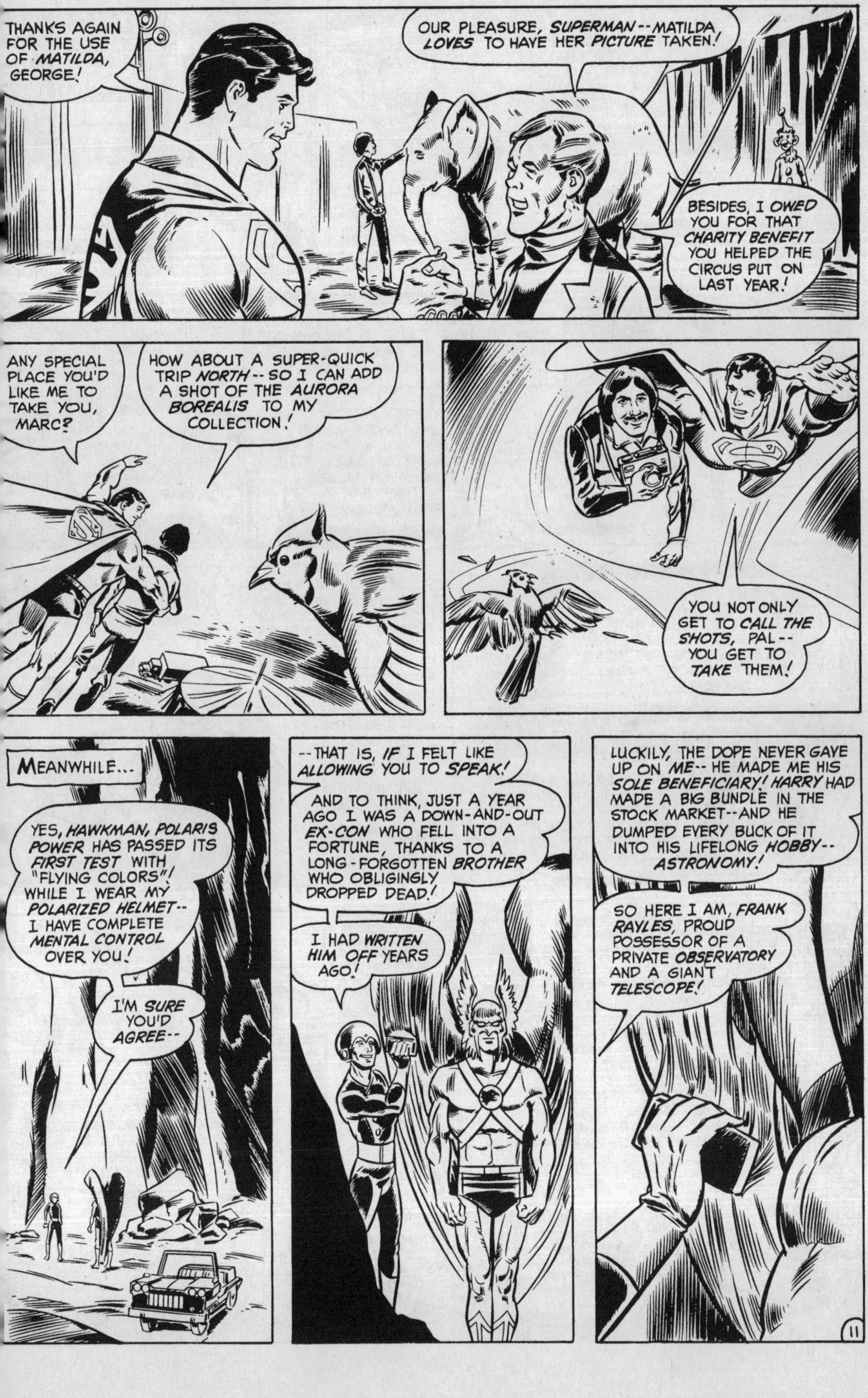
THANKS AGAIN FOR THE USE OF MATILDA, GEORGE!
OUR PLEASURE, SUPERMAN--MATILDA LOVES TO HAVE HER PICTURE TAKEN!
BESIDES, I OWED YOU FOR THAT CHARITY BENEFIT YOU HELPED THE CIRCUS PUT ON LAST YEAR!
ANY SPECIAL PLACE YOU'D LIKE ME TO TAKE YOU, MARC?
HOW ABOUT A SUPER-QUICK TRIP NORTH--SO I CAN ADD A SHOT OF THE AURORA BOREALIS TO MY COLLECTION!
YOU NOT ONLY GET TO CALL THE SHOTS, PAL--YOU GET TO TAKE THEM!
MEANWHILE...
YES, HAWKMAN, POLARIS POWER HAS PASSED ITS FIRST TEST WITH "FLYING COLORS"! WHILE I WEAR MY POLARIZED HELMET--I HAVE COMPLETE MENTAL CONTROL OVER YOU!
I'M SURE YOU'D AGREE--
--THAT IS, IF I FELT LIKE ALLOWING YOU TO SPEAK!
AND TO THINK, JUST A YEAR AGO I WAS A DOWN-AND-OUT EX-CON WHO FELL INTO A FORTUNE, THANKS TO A LONG-FORGOTTEN BROTHER WHO OBLIGINGLY DROPPED DEAD!
I HAD WRITTEN HIM OFF YEARS AGO!
LUCKILY, THE DOPE NEVER GAVE UP ON ME--HE MADE ME HIS SOLE BENEFICIARY! HARRY HAD MADE A BIG BUNDLE IN THE STOCK MARKET--AND HE DUMPED EVERY BUCK OF IT INTO HIS LIFELONG HOBBY--ASTRONOMY!
SO HERE I AM, FRANK RAYLES, PROUD POSSESSOR OF A PRIVATE OBSERVATORY AND A GIANT TELESCOPE!
11

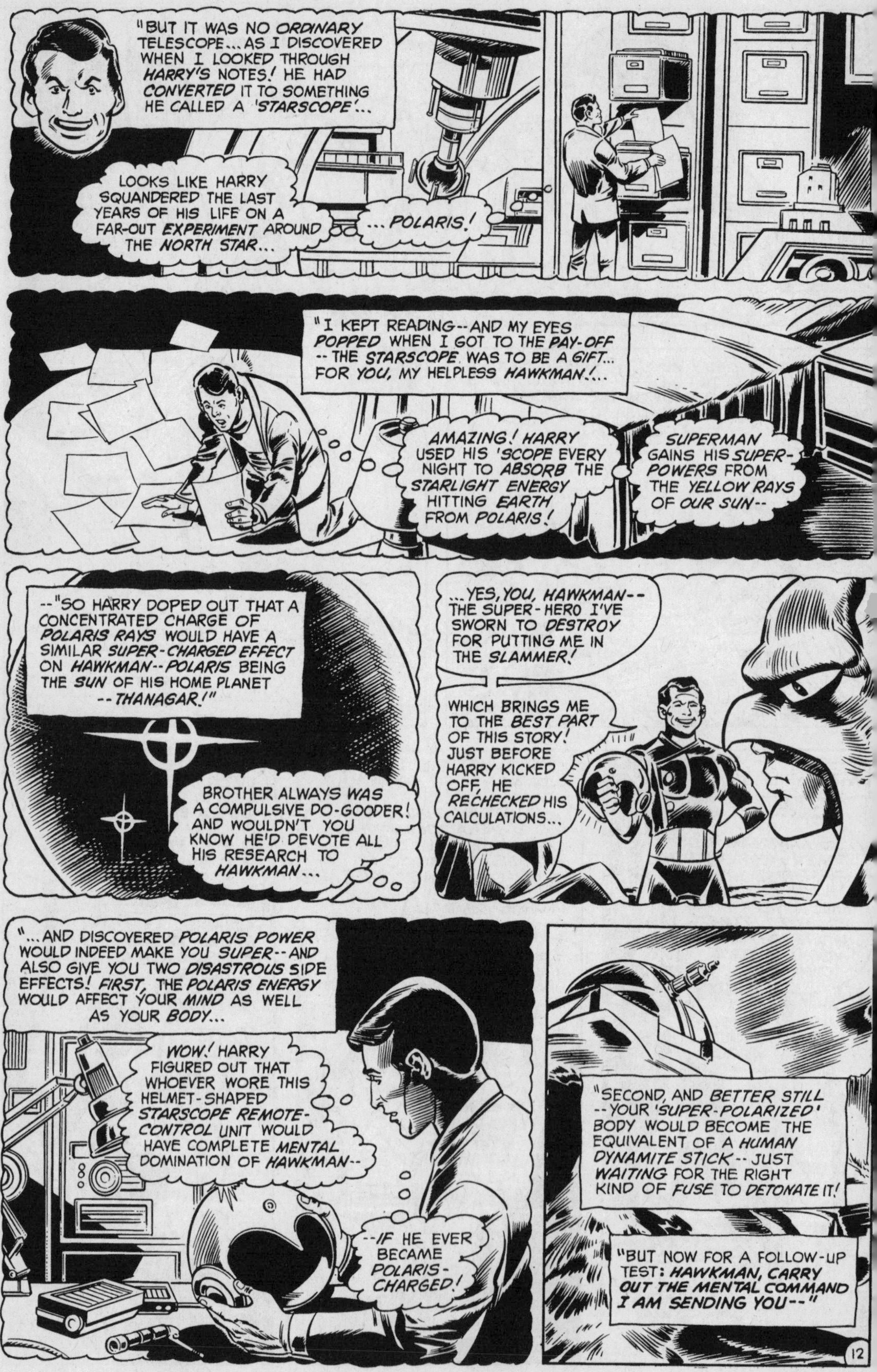
"BUT IT WAS NO ORDINARY TELESCOPE... AS I DISCOVERED WHEN I LOOKED THROUGH HARRY'S NOTES! HE HAD CONVERTED IT TO SOMETHING HE CALLED A 'STARSCOPE'...
LOOKS LIKE HARRY SQUANDERED THE LAST YEARS OF HIS LIFE ON A FAR-OUT EXPERIMENT AROUND THE NORTH STAR...
...POLARIS!
"I KEPT READING--AND MY EYES POPPED WHEN I GOT TO THE PAY-OFF --THE STARSCOPE WAS TO BE A GIFT... FOR YOU, MY HELPLESS HAWKMAN!...
AMAZING! HARRY USED HIS 'SCOPE EVERY NIGHT TO ABSORB THE STARLIGHT ENERGY HITTING EARTH FROM POLARIS!
SUPERMAN GAINS HIS SUPER-POWERS FROM THE YELLOW RAYS OF OUR SUN--
--"SO HARRY DOPED OUT THAT A CONCENTRATED CHARGE OF POLARIS RAYS WOULD HAVE A SIMILAR SUPER-CHARGED EFFECT ON HAWKMAN--POLARIS BEING THE SUN OF HIS HOME PLANET --THANAGAR!"
BROTHER ALWAYS WAS A COMPULSIVE DO-GOODER! AND WOULDN'T YOU KNOW HE'D DEVOTE ALL HIS RESEARCH TO HAWKMAN...
...YES, YOU, HAWKMAN-- THE SUPER-HERO I'VE SWORN TO DESTROY FOR PUTTING ME IN THE SLAMMER!
WHICH BRINGS ME TO THE BEST PART OF THIS STORY! JUST BEFORE HARRY KICKED OFF, HE RECHECKED HIS CALCULATIONS...
"...AND DISCOVERED POLARIS POWER WOULD INDEED MAKE YOU SUPER--AND ALSO GIVE YOU TWO DISASTROUS SIDE EFFECTS! FIRST, THE POLARIS ENERGY WOULD AFFECT YOUR MIND AS WELL AS YOUR BODY...
WOW! HARRY FIGURED OUT THAT WHOEVER WORE THIS HELMET-SHAPED STARSCOPE REMOTE-CONTROL UNIT WOULD HAVE COMPLETE MENTAL DOMINATION OF HAWKMAN--
--IF HE EVER BECAME POLARIS-CHARGED!
"SECOND, AND BETTER STILL --YOUR 'SUPER-POLARIZED' BODY WOULD BECOME THE EQUIVALENT OF A HUMAN DYNAMITE STICK--JUST WAITING FOR THE RIGHT KIND OF FUSE TO DETONATE IT!
"BUT NOW FOR A FOLLOW-UP TEST: HAWKMAN, CARRY OUT THE MENTAL COMMAND I AM SENDING YOU--"
12

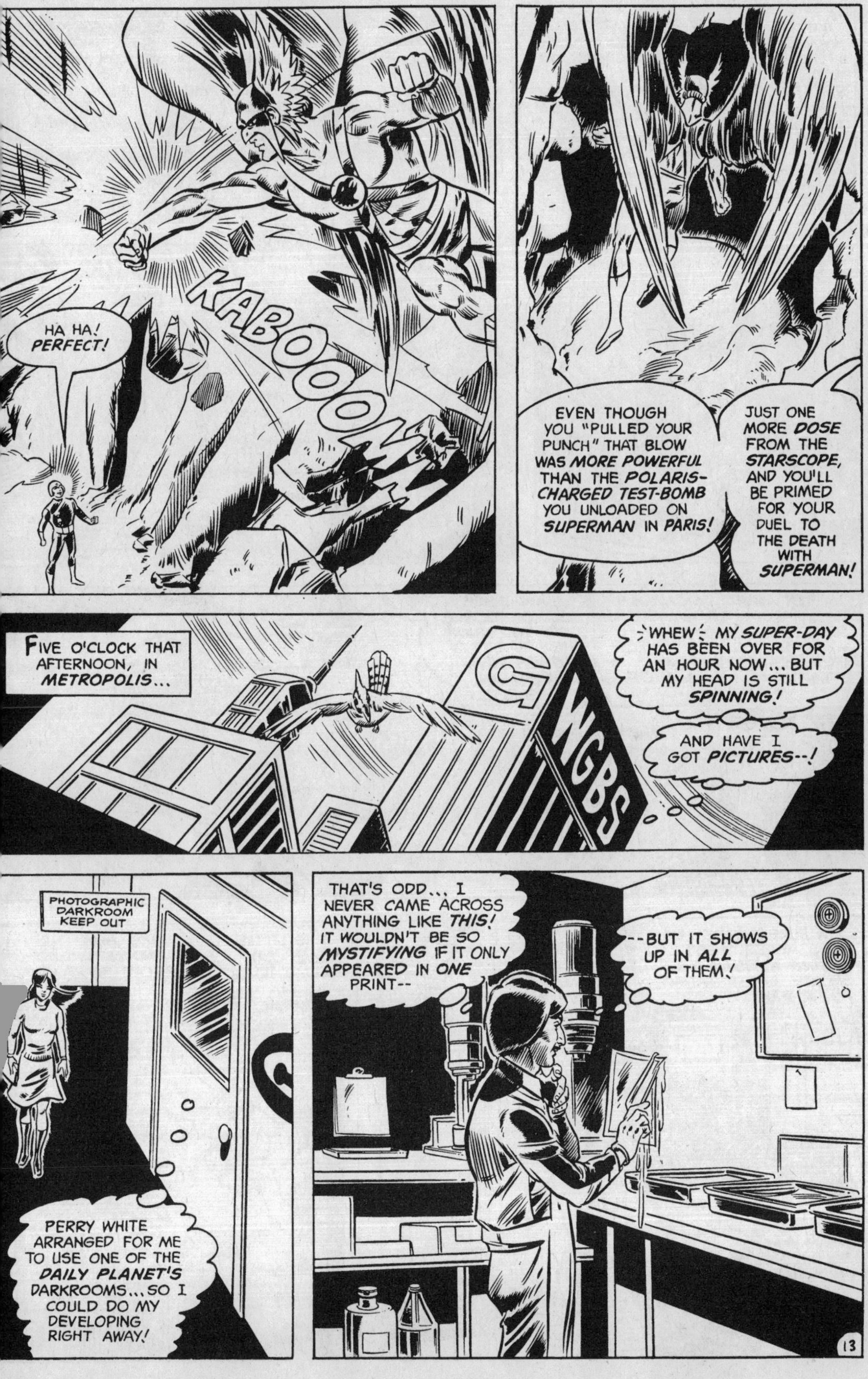
HA HA! PERFECT!
KABOOOOM
EVEN THOUGH YOU "PULLED YOUR PUNCH" THAT BLOW WAS MORE POWERFUL THAN THE POLARIS-CHARGED TEST-BOMB YOU UNLOADED ON SUPERMAN IN PARIS!
JUST ONE MORE DOSE FROM THE STARSCOPE, AND YOU'LL BE PRIMED FOR YOUR DUEL TO THE DEATH WITH SUPERMAN!
FIVE O'CLOCK THAT AFTERNOON, IN METROPOLIS...
WHEW! MY SUPER-DAY HAS BEEN OVER FOR AN HOUR NOW... BUT MY HEAD IS STILL SPINNING!
AND HAVE I GOT PICTURES--!
WGBS
PHOTOGRAPHIC DARKROOM KEEP OUT
PERRY WHITE ARRANGED FOR ME TO USE ONE OF THE DAILY PLANET'S DARKROOMS... SO I COULD DO MY DEVELOPING RIGHT AWAY!
THAT'S ODD... I NEVER CAME ACROSS ANYTHING LIKE THIS! IT WOULDN'T BE SO MYSTIFYING IF IT ONLY APPEARED IN ONE PRINT--
--BUT IT SHOWS UP IN ALL OF THEM!
13

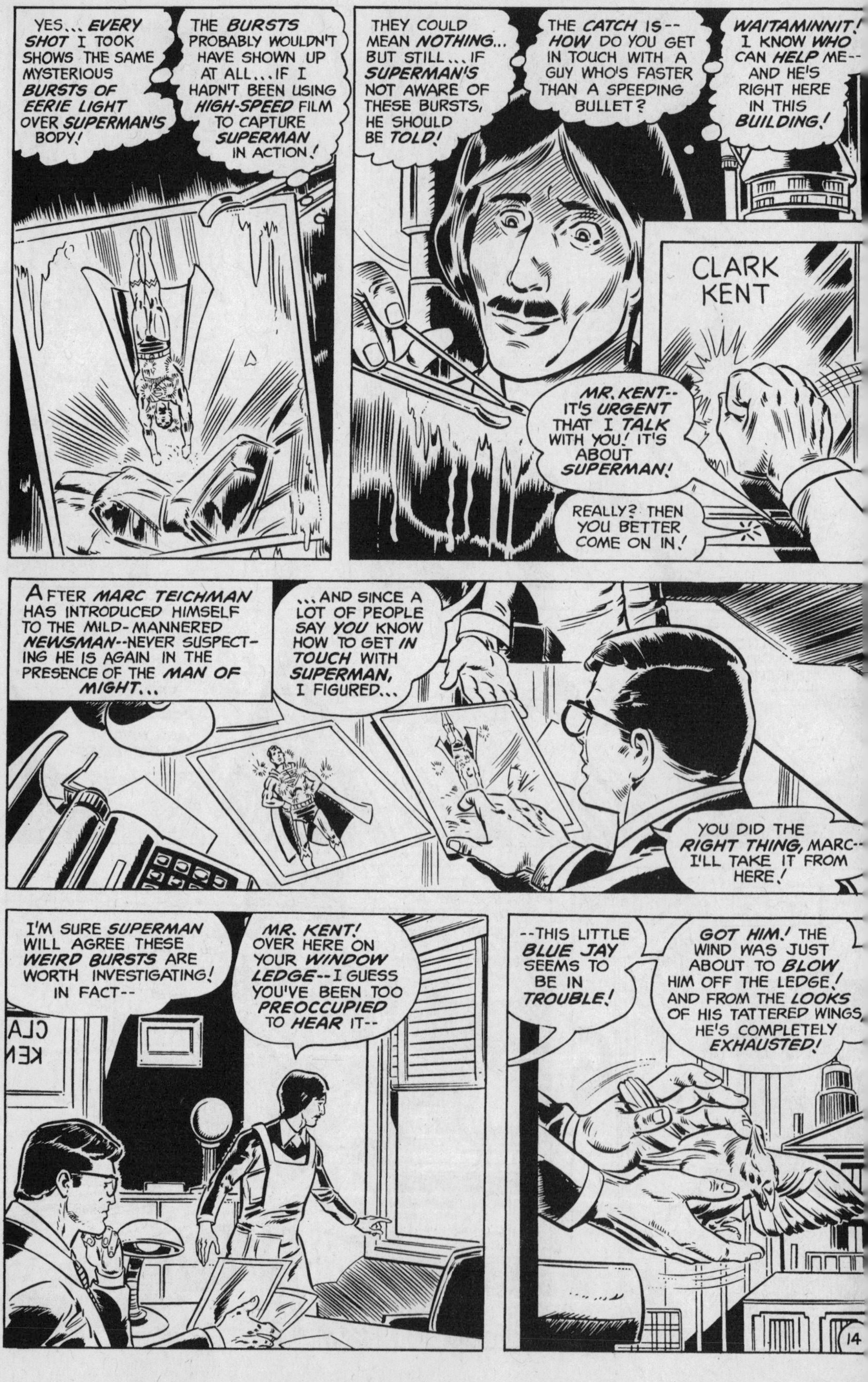
YES... EVERY SHOT I TOOK SHOWS THE SAME MYSTERIOUS BURSTS OF EERIE LIGHT OVER SUPERMAN'S BODY!
THE BURSTS PROBABLY WOULDN'T HAVE SHOWN UP AT ALL... IF I HADN'T BEEN USING HIGH-SPEED FILM TO CAPTURE SUPERMAN IN ACTION!
THEY COULD MEAN NOTHING... BUT STILL... IF SUPERMAN'S NOT AWARE OF THESE BURSTS, HE SHOULD BE TOLD!
THE CATCH IS-- HOW DO YOU GET IN TOUCH WITH A GUY WHO'S FASTER THAN A SPEEDING BULLET?
WAITAMINNIT! I KNOW WHO CAN HELP ME-- AND HE'S RIGHT HERE IN THIS BUILDING!
CLARK KENT
MR. KENT-- IT'S URGENT THAT I TALK WITH YOU! IT'S ABOUT SUPERMAN!
REALLY? THEN YOU BETTER COME ON IN!
AFTER MARC TEICHMAN HAS INTRODUCED HIMSELF TO THE MILD-MANNERED NEWSMAN--NEVER SUSPECTING HE IS AGAIN IN THE PRESENCE OF THE MAN OF MIGHT...
...AND SINCE A LOT OF PEOPLE SAY YOU KNOW HOW TO GET IN TOUCH WITH SUPERMAN, I FIGURED...
YOU DID THE RIGHT THING, MARC-- I'LL TAKE IT FROM HERE!
I'M SURE SUPERMAN WILL AGREE THESE WEIRD BURSTS ARE WORTH INVESTIGATING! IN FACT--
MR. KENT! OVER HERE ON YOUR WINDOW LEDGE--I GUESS YOU'VE BEEN TOO PREOCCUPIED TO HEAR IT--
--THIS LITTLE BLUE JAY SEEMS TO BE IN TROUBLE!
GOT HIM! THE WIND WAS JUST ABOUT TO BLOW HIM OFF THE LEDGE! AND FROM THE LOOKS OF HIS TATTERED WINGS, HE'S COMPLETELY EXHAUSTED!
14

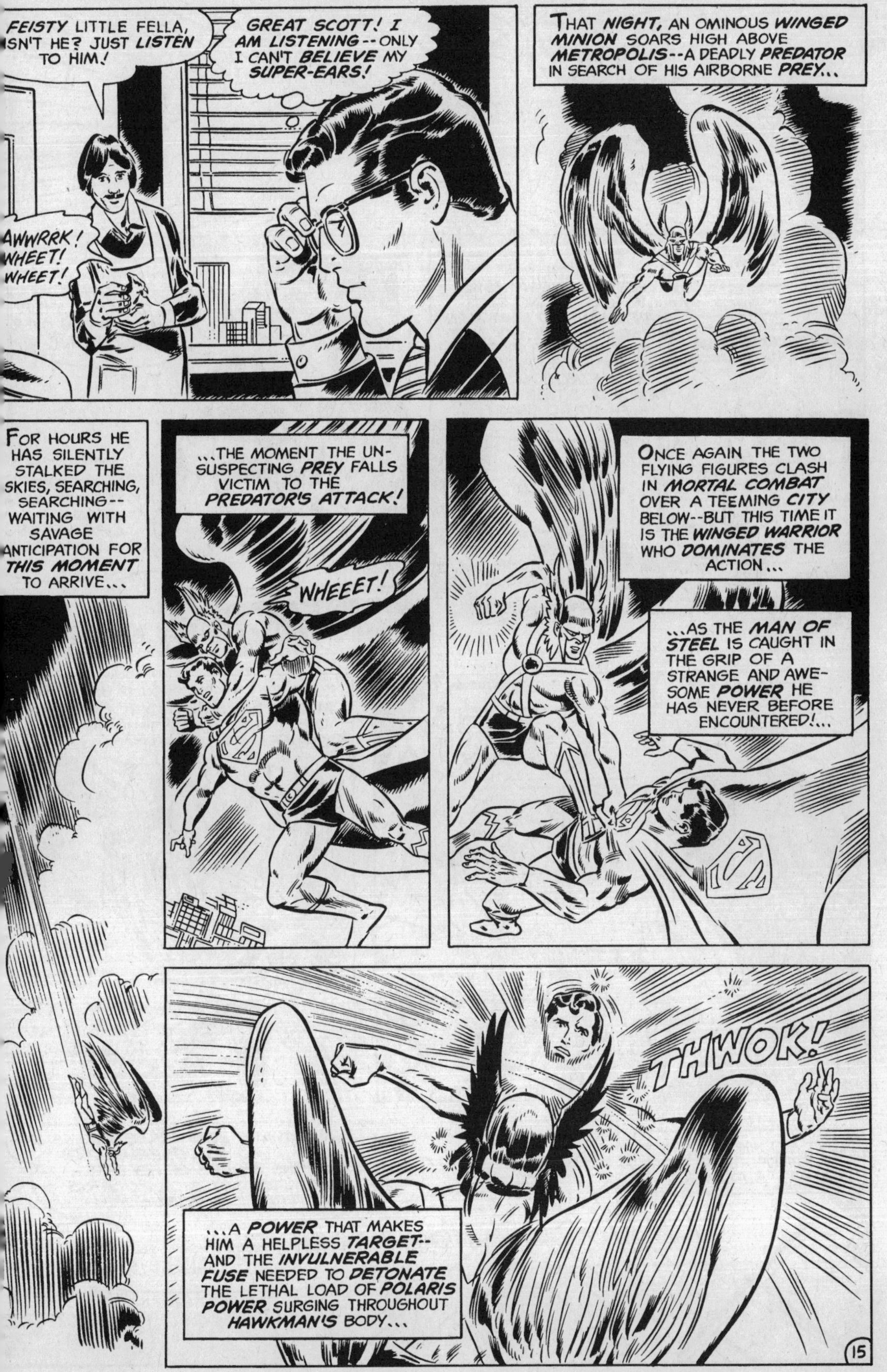
FEISTY LITTLE FELLA, ISN'T HE? JUST LISTEN TO HIM!
GREAT SCOTT! I AM LISTENING -- ONLY I CAN'T BELIEVE MY SUPER-EARS!
AWWRRK! WHEET! WHEET!
THAT NIGHT, AN OMINOUS WINGED MINION SOARS HIGH ABOVE METROPOLIS--A DEADLY PREDATOR IN SEARCH OF HIS AIRBORNE PREY...
FOR HOURS HE HAS SILENTLY STALKED THE SKIES, SEARCHING, SEARCHING--WAITING WITH SAVAGE ANTICIPATION FOR THIS MOMENT TO ARRIVE...
...THE MOMENT THE UN-SUSPECTING PREY FALLS VICTIM TO THE PREDATOR'S ATTACK!
WHEEET!
ONCE AGAIN THE TWO FLYING FIGURES CLASH IN MORTAL COMBAT OVER A TEEMING CITY BELOW--BUT THIS TIME IT IS THE WINGED WARRIOR WHO DOMINATES THE ACTION...
...AS THE MAN OF STEEL IS CAUGHT IN THE GRIP OF A STRANGE AND AWE-SOME POWER HE HAS NEVER BEFORE ENCOUNTERED!...
THWOK!
...A POWER THAT MAKES HIM A HELPLESS TARGET--AND THE INVULNERABLE FUSE NEEDED TO DETONATE THE LETHAL LOAD OF POLARIS POWER SURGING THROUGHOUT HAWKMAN'S BODY...
15

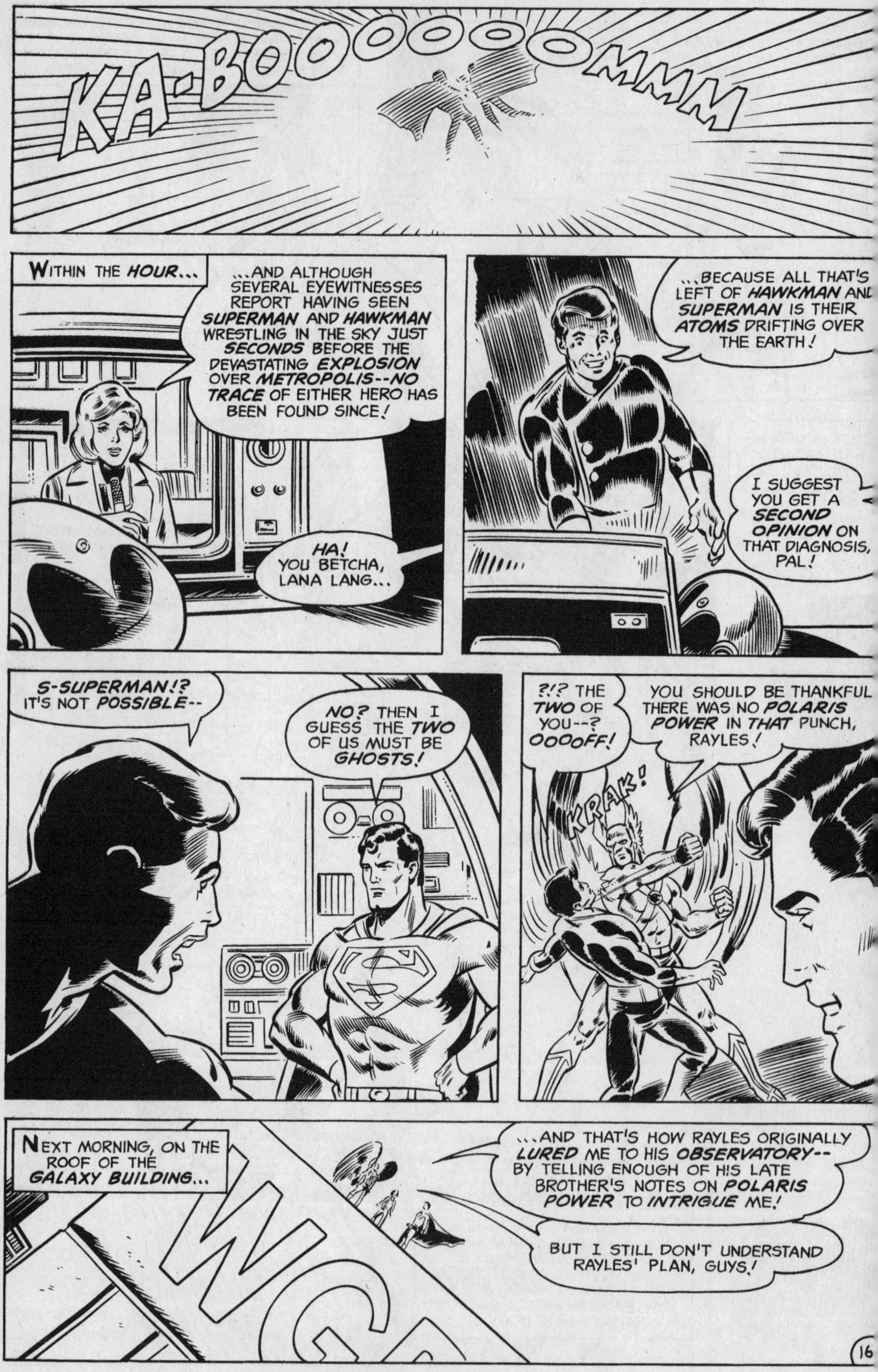
KA-BOOOOOOOMMMM
WITHIN THE HOUR...
...AND ALTHOUGH SEVERAL EYEWITNESSES REPORT HAVING SEEN SUPERMAN AND HAWKMAN WRESTLING IN THE SKY JUST SECONDS BEFORE THE DEVASTATING EXPLOSION OVER METROPOLIS--NO TRACE OF EITHER HERO HAS BEEN FOUND SINCE!
HA! YOU BETCHA, LANA LANG...
...BECAUSE ALL THAT'S LEFT OF HAWKMAN AND SUPERMAN IS THEIR ATOMS DRIFTING OVER THE EARTH!
I SUGGEST YOU GET A SECOND OPINION ON THAT DIAGNOSIS, PAL!
S-SUPERMAN!? IT'S NOT POSSIBLE--
NO? THEN I GUESS THE TWO OF US MUST BE GHOSTS!
?!? THE TWO OF YOU--? OOOOFF!
YOU SHOULD BE THANKFUL THERE WAS NO POLARIS POWER IN THAT PUNCH, RAYLES!
KRAK!
NEXT MORNING, ON THE ROOF OF THE GALAXY BUILDING...
...AND THAT'S HOW RAYLES ORIGINALLY LURED ME TO HIS OBSERVATORY-- BY TELLING ENOUGH OF HIS LATE BROTHER'S NOTES ON POLARIS POWER TO INTRIGUE ME!
BUT I STILL DON'T UNDERSTAND RAYLES' PLAN, GUYS!
16

RAYLES' THEORY WAS SOUND-- IF HAWKMAN'S POLARIS-POWERED FIST HAD MADE CONTACT WITH MY INVULNERABLE BODY, A FATAL BLAST WOULD INDEED HAVE RESULTED!

SO I "ROLLED" WITH THE PUNCH... AND THE "BLAST" METROPOLIS SAW WAS MERELY PHOSPHORESCENT SPECIAL EFFECTS!

BUT WHAT TIPPED YOU OFF, SUPERMAN? SURELY YOU COULDN'T HAVE FIGURED ALL THAT OUT FROM MY FILM AND THE RADIATION-RESIDUE LEFT ON YOUR BODY FROM HAWKMAN'S FIRST ATTACK!

A LITTLE BIRDIE TOLD ME THE REST OF IT, MARC --CHATTERING AWAY IN BIRD LANGUAGE... WHICH HAWKMAN HAD TAUGHT ME ENOUGH OF SO I COULD GET THE GIST OF HIS MESSAGE!

"JUST BEFORE MY MIND BECAME HELPLESSLY POLARIS-CHARGED, I SPOKE IN BIRD LANGUAGE WITH ONE OF MY LOYAL FEATHERED FRIENDS-- ASKING HIM TO FIND SUPERMAN!

~WHEEET!~ GET A MESSAGE TO SUPERMAN...

"THE BLUE JAY APPARENTLY WORE ITSELF OUT TRYING TO KEEP UP WITH YOUR SUPER-DAY ACTIVITIES, MARC -- BUT LUCKILY YOU FINALLY SPOTTED HIM IN TIME!"

SUPERMAN HAD TO MAKE RAYLES BELIEVE HIS "EXPLOSION" DESTROYED US--SO HE'D REMOVE THE REMOTE-CONTROL HELMET THAT GAVE HIM MENTAL CONTROL OVER ME!

AND ACCORDING TO HIS BROTHER'S NOTES--THE POLARIS POWER WILL SEEP HARMLESSLY OUT OF MY BODY OVER THE NEXT FEW DAYS!

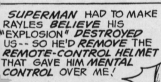

NO WONDER THEY CALL YOU GUYS SUPER-HEROES!

AS FAR AS SUPERMAN AND I ARE CONCERNED, THIS WAS A THREE-WAY TEAM-UP, MARC!

THAT'S FOR SURE! YOU WERE INSTRUMENTAL TO OUR SURVIVAL, PAL!

AND NOW HAWKMAN AND I ARE GOING TO GIVE YOU A DOUBLE-FLYING ESCORT--

--ALL THE WAY BACK TO STATEN ISLAND!

YOU GUYS ARE TOO MUCH! IF ONLY MY FRIENDS COULD SEE ME NOW!

NEXT ISSUE: SUPERMAN FIGHTS A FANTASTIC BATTLE AGAINST MISTER MIRACLE... "WINNER TAKE METROPOLIS!"

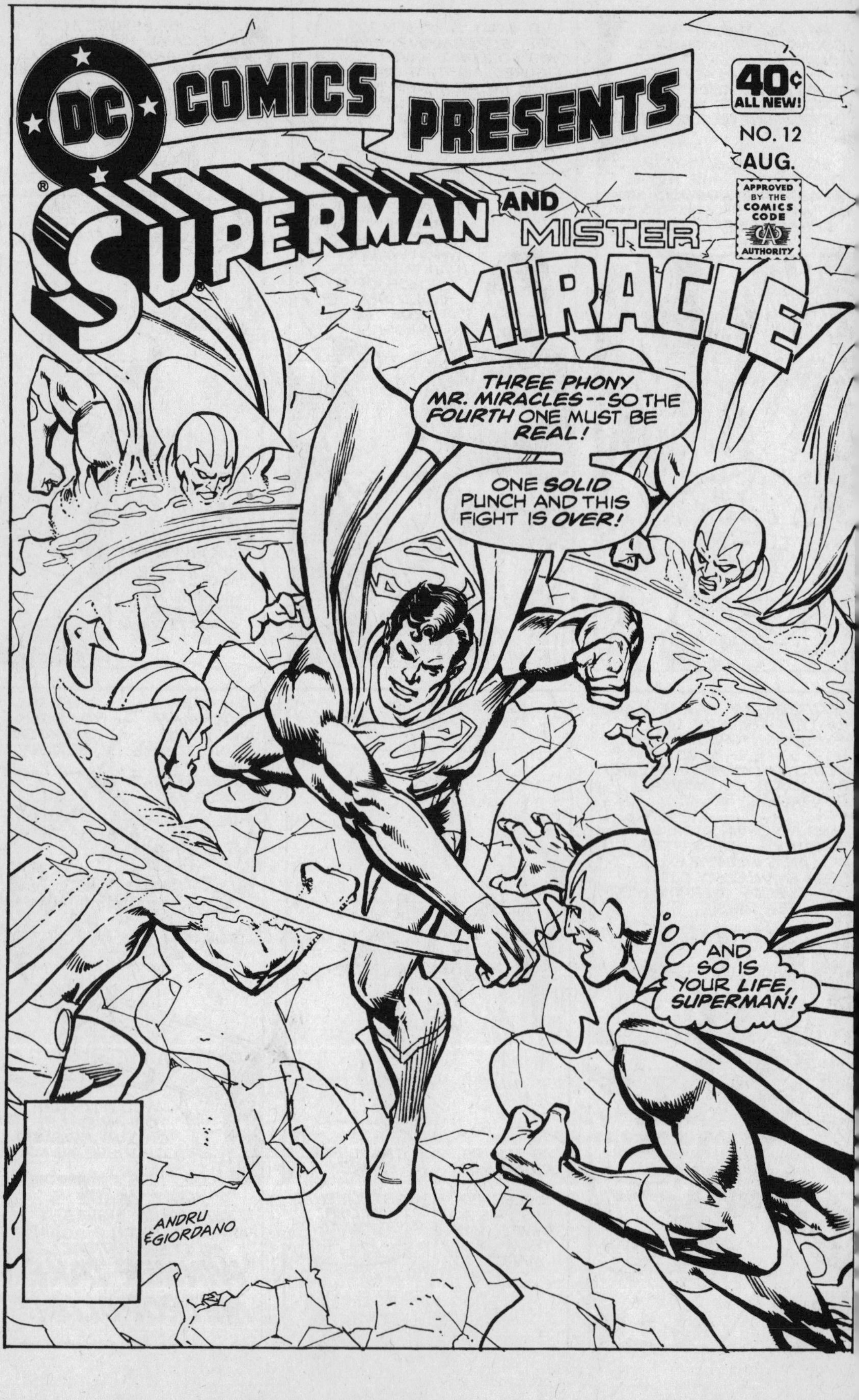
DC
COMICS PRESENTS
40¢ ALL NEW!
NO. 12
AUG.
APPROVED BY THE COMICS CODE AUTHORITY
SUPERMAN AND MISTER MIRACLE
THREE PHONY MR. MIRACLES--SO THE FOURTH ONE MUST BE REAL!
ONE SOLID PUNCH AND THIS FIGHT IS OVER!
AND SO IS YOUR LIFE, SUPERMAN!
ANDRU &GIORDANO

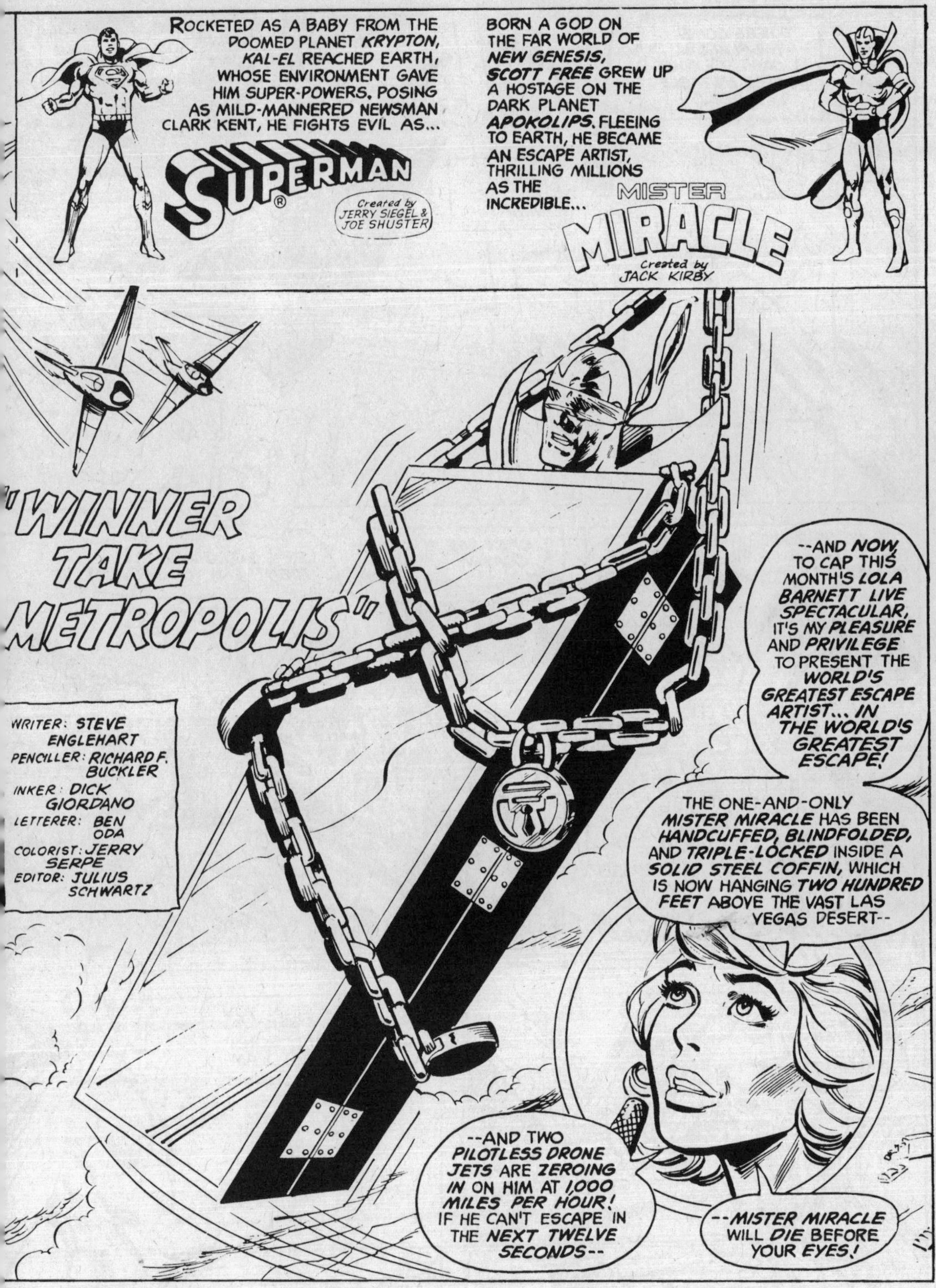
ROCKETED AS A BABY FROM THE DOOMED PLANET KRYPTON, KAL-EL REACHED EARTH, WHOSE ENVIRONMENT GAVE HIM SUPER-POWERS. POSING AS MILD-MANNERED NEWSMAN CLARK KENT, HE FIGHTS EVIL AS...
SUPERMAN®
Created by JERRY SIEGEL & JOE SHUSTER
BORN A GOD ON THE FAR WORLD OF NEW GENESIS, SCOTT FREE GREW UP A HOSTAGE ON THE DARK PLANET APOKOLIPS. FLEEING TO EARTH, HE BECAME AN ESCAPE ARTIST, THRILLING MILLIONS AS THE INCREDIBLE...
MISTER MIRACLE
Created by JACK KIRBY
"WINNER TAKE METROPOLIS"
WRITER: STEVE ENGLEHART
PENCILLER: RICHARD F. BUCKLER
INKER: DICK GIORDANO
LETTERER: BEN ODA
COLORIST: JERRY SERPE
EDITOR: JULIUS SCHWARTZ
--AND NOW, TO CAP THIS MONTH'S LOLA BARNETT LIVE SPECTACULAR, IT'S MY PLEASURE AND PRIVILEGE TO PRESENT THE WORLD'S GREATEST ESCAPE ARTIST... IN THE WORLD'S GREATEST ESCAPE!
THE ONE-AND-ONLY MISTER MIRACLE HAS BEEN HANDCUFFED, BLINDFOLDED, AND TRIPLE-LOCKED INSIDE A SOLID STEEL COFFIN, WHICH IS NOW HANGING TWO HUNDRED FEET ABOVE THE VAST LAS VEGAS DESERT--
--AND TWO PILOTLESS DRONE JETS ARE ZEROING IN ON HIM AT 1,000 MILES PER HOUR! IF HE CAN'T ESCAPE IN THE NEXT TWELVE SECONDS--
--MISTER MIRACLE WILL DIE BEFORE YOUR EYES!

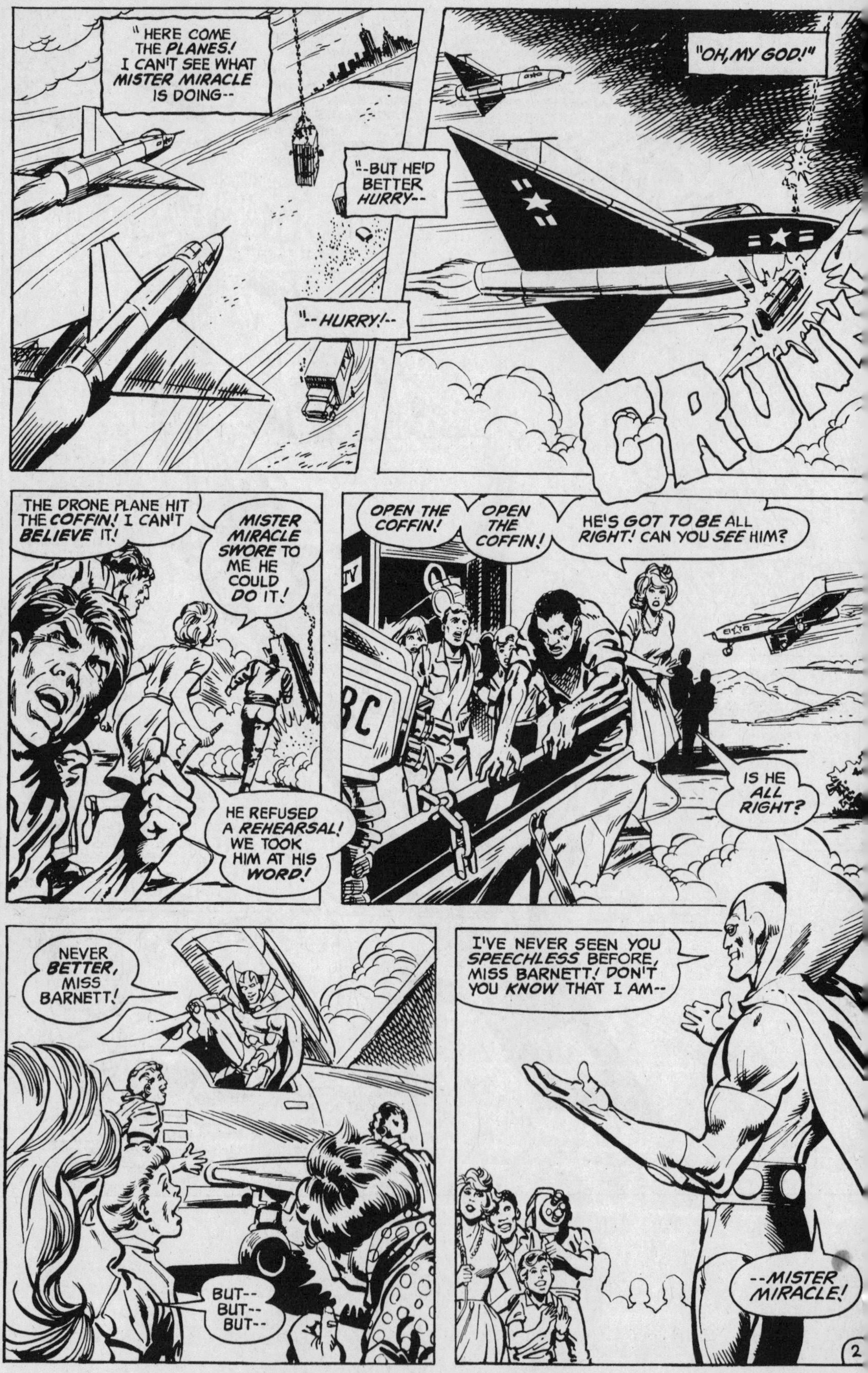
"HERE COME THE PLANES! I CAN'T SEE WHAT MISTER MIRACLE IS DOING--
"--BUT HE'D BETTER HURRY--
"--HURRY!--
"OH, MY GOD!"
CRUN
THE DRONE PLANE HIT THE COFFIN! I CAN'T BELIEVE IT!
MISTER MIRACLE SWORE TO ME HE COULD DO IT!
HE REFUSED A REHEARSAL! WE TOOK HIM AT HIS WORD!
OPEN THE COFFIN!
OPEN THE COFFIN!
HE'S GOT TO BE ALL RIGHT! CAN YOU SEE HIM?
IS HE ALL RIGHT?
NEVER BETTER, MISS BARNETT!
BUT-- BUT-- BUT--
I'VE NEVER SEEN YOU SPEECHLESS BEFORE, MISS BARNETT! DON'T YOU KNOW THAT I AM--
--MISTER MIRACLE!
2

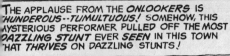

THE APPLAUSE FROM THE *ONLOOKERS* IS *THUNDEROUS--TUMULTUOUS!* SOMEHOW, THIS *MYSTERIOUS* PERFORMER PULLED OFF THE *MOST DAZZLING STUNT* EVER *SEEN* IN THIS TOWN THAT *THRIVES* ON DAZZLING STUNTS!

BUT HOW MUCH *GRANDER* WOULD BE THEIR AMAZEMENT IF THEY KNEW THAT THIS *"PERFORMER"* IS ACTUALLY ONE OF THE AWESOME *NEW GODS*--

--SON OF *HIGHFATHER*, AND PRINCE OF THE PLANET *NEW GENESIS!*

IT'S A *SHAME* SO FEW PEOPLE SAW YOU *DO* THAT, SCOTT!*

WHAT DO YOU *MEAN*, MISS BARNETT? THE ENTIRE *UBC* NETWORK CARRIES YOUR SHOW!

* MISTER MIRACLE'S REAL NAME IS *SCOTT FREE.* --JULIE

TRUE-- BUT *GALAXY BROADCASTING* IS AIRING A DOCUMENTARY ON *SUPERMAN!* WE DON'T EXPECT TO GET MORE THAN A *15 RATING* AGAINST THAT!

EVER SINCE I *LEFT* THEM FOR *UBC*, THEY'VE TRIED TO *UNDERCUT* ME!

SUPERMAN --AGAIN!

"EVEN *BARDA*"!

HI, SCOTT! BOY, WAS THAT *SOMETHING!* EVEN *BARDA** WAS WORRIED ABOUT *THAT* ONE!

AS IF *YOU* WEREN'T HIDING YOUR EYES IN MY *SKIRTS*, OBERON!

* THE STATUESQUE BEAUTY WHO IS MRS. SCOTT FREE. --JULIE

SCOTT? IS SOMETHING *WRONG?*

SUPERMAN! I AM A *GOD*, AND HE IS *NOT*--

--BUT NO MATTER *WHAT* I'VE DONE IN MY TIME ON EARTH, I'VE COME *NOWHERE NEAR* ATTAINING *HIS* POPULARITY!

MY *BEST* EFFORTS-- MY *MOST BRILLIANT ILLUSIONS*--ALL FOR *NAUGHT!*

WONDER PUP

3

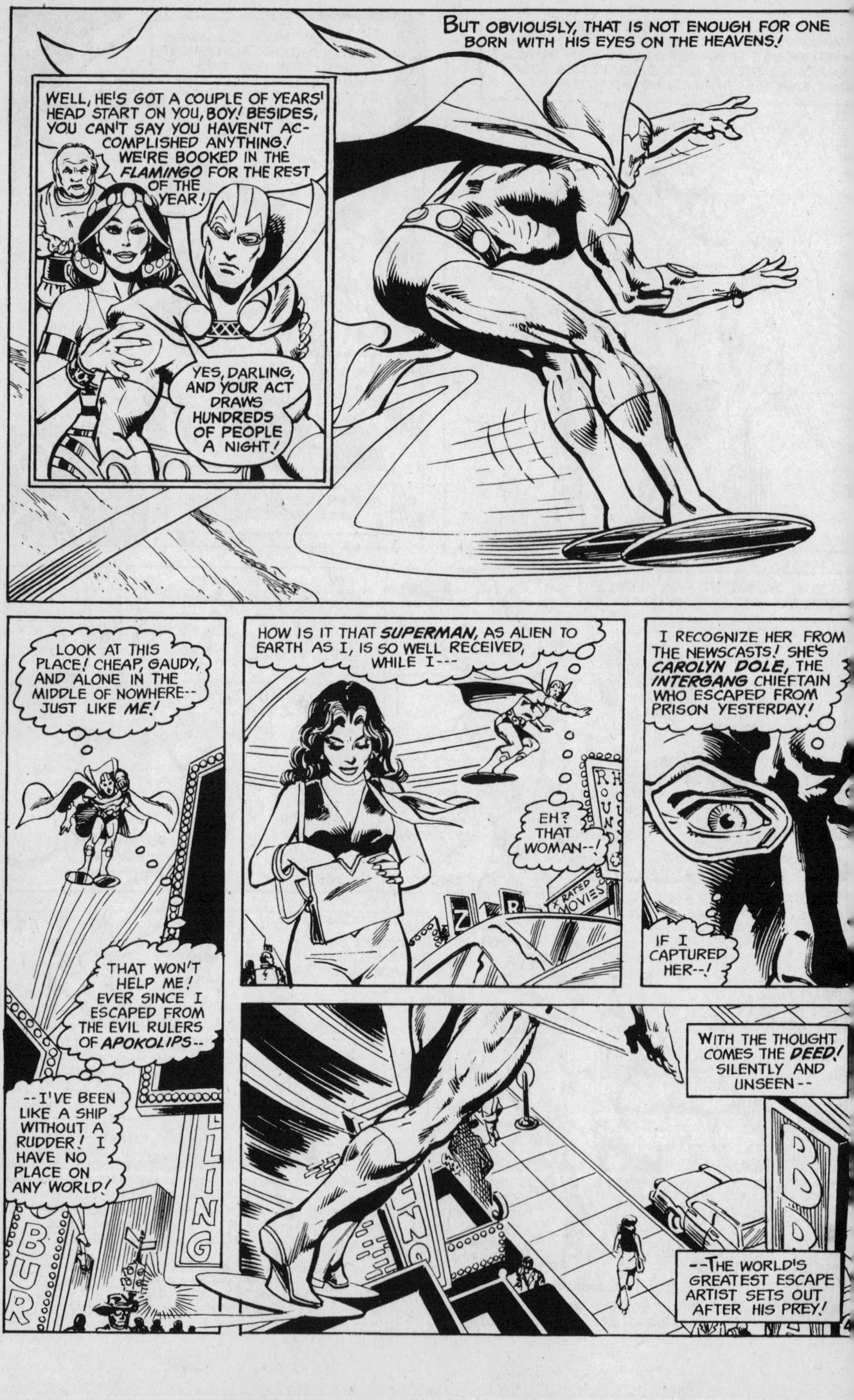
BUT OBVIOUSLY, THAT IS NOT ENOUGH FOR ONE BORN WITH HIS EYES ON THE HEAVENS!
WELL, HE'S GOT A COUPLE OF YEARS' HEAD START ON YOU, BOY! BESIDES, YOU CAN'T SAY YOU HAVEN'T ACCOMPLISHED ANYTHING! WE'RE BOOKED IN THE FLAMINGO FOR THE REST OF THE YEAR!
YES, DARLING, AND YOUR ACT DRAWS HUNDREDS OF PEOPLE A NIGHT!
LOOK AT THIS PLACE! CHEAP, GAUDY, AND ALONE IN THE MIDDLE OF NOWHERE-- JUST LIKE ME!
THAT WON'T HELP ME! EVER SINCE I ESCAPED FROM THE EVIL RULERS OF APOKOLIPS--
--I'VE BEEN LIKE A SHIP WITHOUT A RUDDER! I HAVE NO PLACE ON ANY WORLD!
HOW IS IT THAT SUPERMAN, AS ALIEN TO EARTH AS I, IS SO WELL RECEIVED, WHILE I---
EH? THAT WOMAN--!
X RATED MOVIES
I RECOGNIZE HER FROM THE NEWSCASTS! SHE'S CAROLYN DOLE, THE INTERGANG CHIEFTAIN WHO ESCAPED FROM PRISON YESTERDAY!
IF I CAPTURED HER--!
WITH THE THOUGHT COMES THE DEED! SILENTLY AND UNSEEN--
--THE WORLD'S GREATEST ESCAPE ARTIST SETS OUT AFTER HIS PREY!

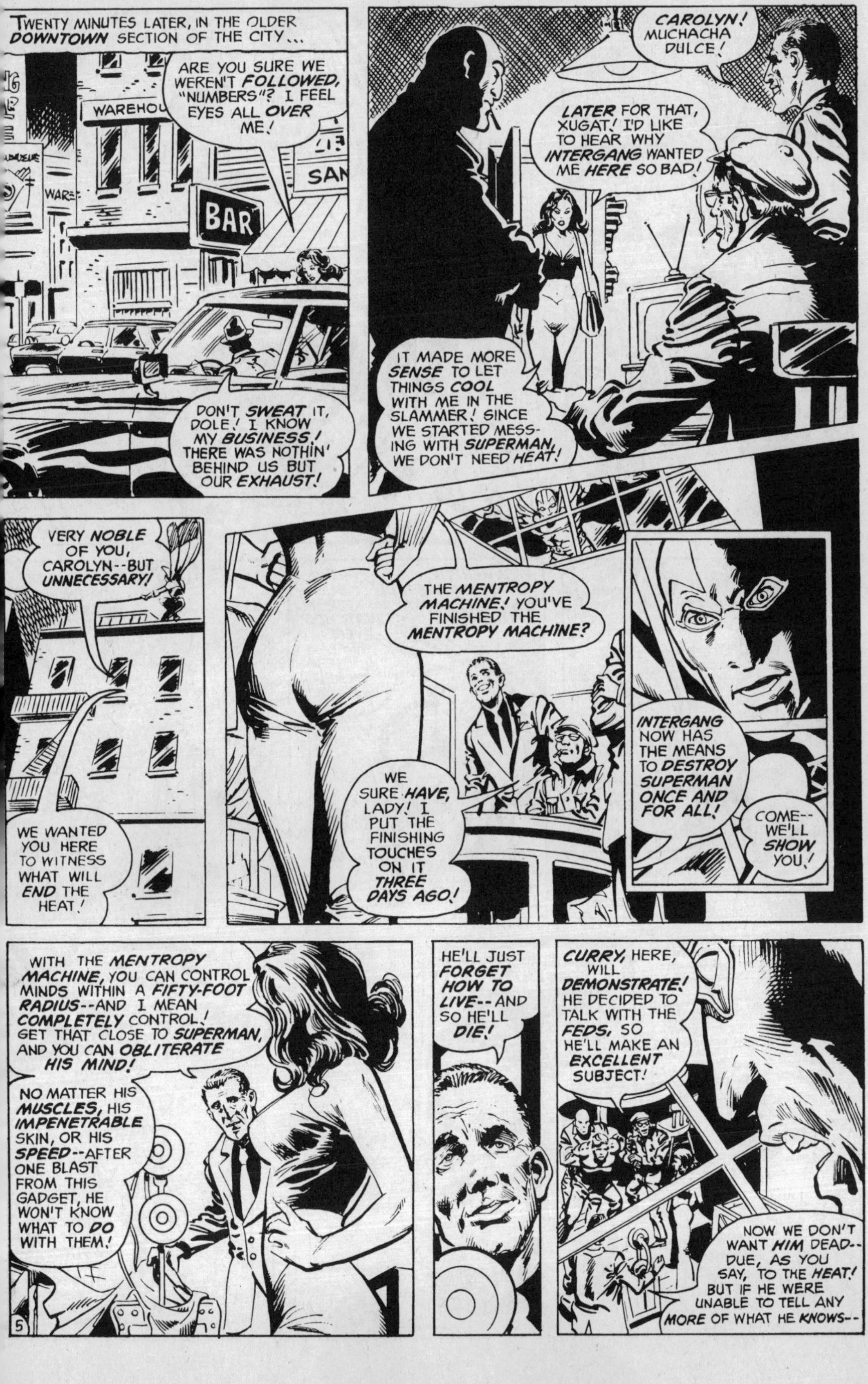
TWENTY MINUTES LATER, IN THE OLDER DOWNTOWN SECTION OF THE CITY...
WAREHOU
BAR
SAN
ARE YOU SURE WE WEREN'T FOLLOWED, "NUMBERS"? I FEEL EYES ALL OVER ME!
DON'T SWEAT IT, DOLE! I KNOW MY BUSINESS! THERE WAS NOTHIN' BEHIND US BUT OUR EXHAUST!
CAROLYN! MUCHACHA DULCE!
LATER FOR THAT, XUGAT! I'D LIKE TO HEAR WHY INTERGANG WANTED ME HERE SO BAD!
IT MADE MORE SENSE TO LET THINGS COOL WITH ME IN THE SLAMMER! SINCE WE STARTED MESSING WITH SUPERMAN, WE DON'T NEED HEAT!
VERY NOBLE OF YOU, CAROLYN--BUT UNNECESSARY!
WE WANTED YOU HERE TO WITNESS WHAT WILL END THE HEAT!
THE MENTROPY MACHINE! YOU'VE FINISHED THE MENTROPY MACHINE?
WE SURE HAVE, LADY! I PUT THE FINISHING TOUCHES ON IT THREE DAYS AGO!
INTERGANG NOW HAS THE MEANS TO DESTROY SUPERMAN ONCE AND FOR ALL!
COME--WE'LL SHOW YOU!
WITH THE MENTROPY MACHINE, YOU CAN CONTROL MINDS WITHIN A FIFTY-FOOT RADIUS--AND I MEAN COMPLETELY CONTROL! GET THAT CLOSE TO SUPERMAN, AND YOU CAN OBLITERATE HIS MIND!
NO MATTER HIS MUSCLES, HIS IMPENETRABLE SKIN, OR HIS SPEED--AFTER ONE BLAST FROM THIS GADGET, HE WON'T KNOW WHAT TO DO WITH THEM!
5
HE'LL JUST FORGET HOW TO LIVE--AND SO HE'LL DIE!
CURRY, HERE, WILL DEMONSTRATE! HE DECIDED TO TALK WITH THE FEDS, SO HE'LL MAKE AN EXCELLENT SUBJECT!
NOW WE DON'T WANT HIM DEAD--DUE, AS YOU SAY, TO THE HEAT! BUT IF HE WERE UNABLE TO TELL ANY MORE OF WHAT HE KNOWS--

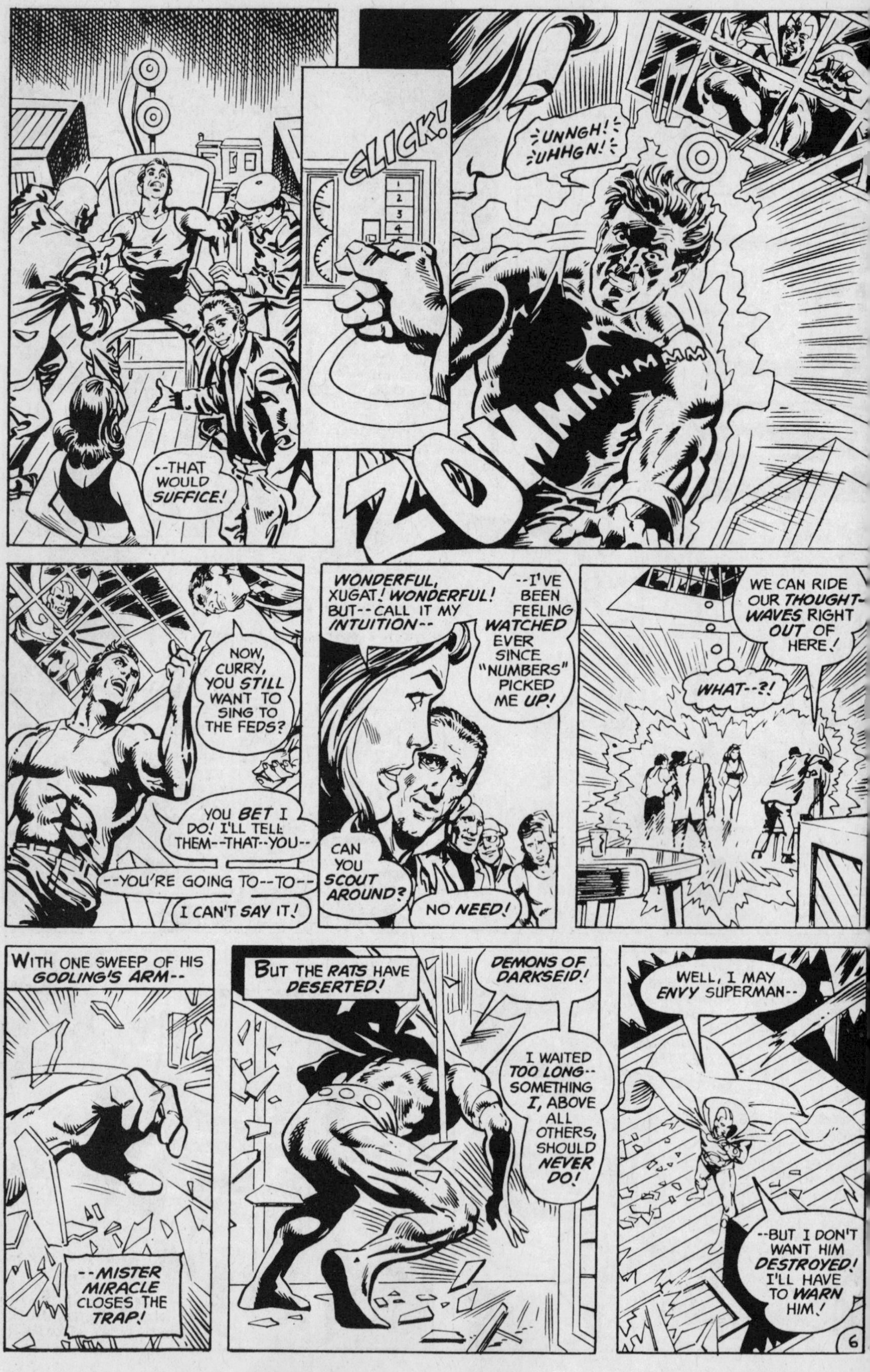
--THAT WOULD SUFFICE!
CLICK!
UNNGH! UHHGN!
ZOMMMMMMMM
NOW, CURRY, YOU STILL WANT TO SING TO THE FEDS?
YOU BET I DO! I'LL TELL THEM--THAT--YOU--
--YOU'RE GOING TO--TO--
I CAN'T SAY IT!
WONDERFUL, XUGAT! WONDERFUL! BUT--CALL IT MY INTUITION--
--I'VE BEEN FEELING WATCHED EVER SINCE "NUMBERS" PICKED ME UP!
CAN YOU SCOUT AROUND?
NO NEED!
WE CAN RIDE OUR THOUGHT-WAVES RIGHT OUT OF HERE!
WHAT--?!
WITH ONE SWEEP OF HIS GODLING'S ARM--
--MISTER MIRACLE CLOSES THE TRAP!
BUT THE RATS HAVE DESERTED!
DEMONS OF DARKSEID!
I WAITED TOO LONG-- SOMETHING I, ABOVE ALL OTHERS, SHOULD NEVER DO!
WELL, I MAY ENVY SUPERMAN--
--BUT I DON'T WANT HIM DESTROYED! I'LL HAVE TO WARN HIM!
6

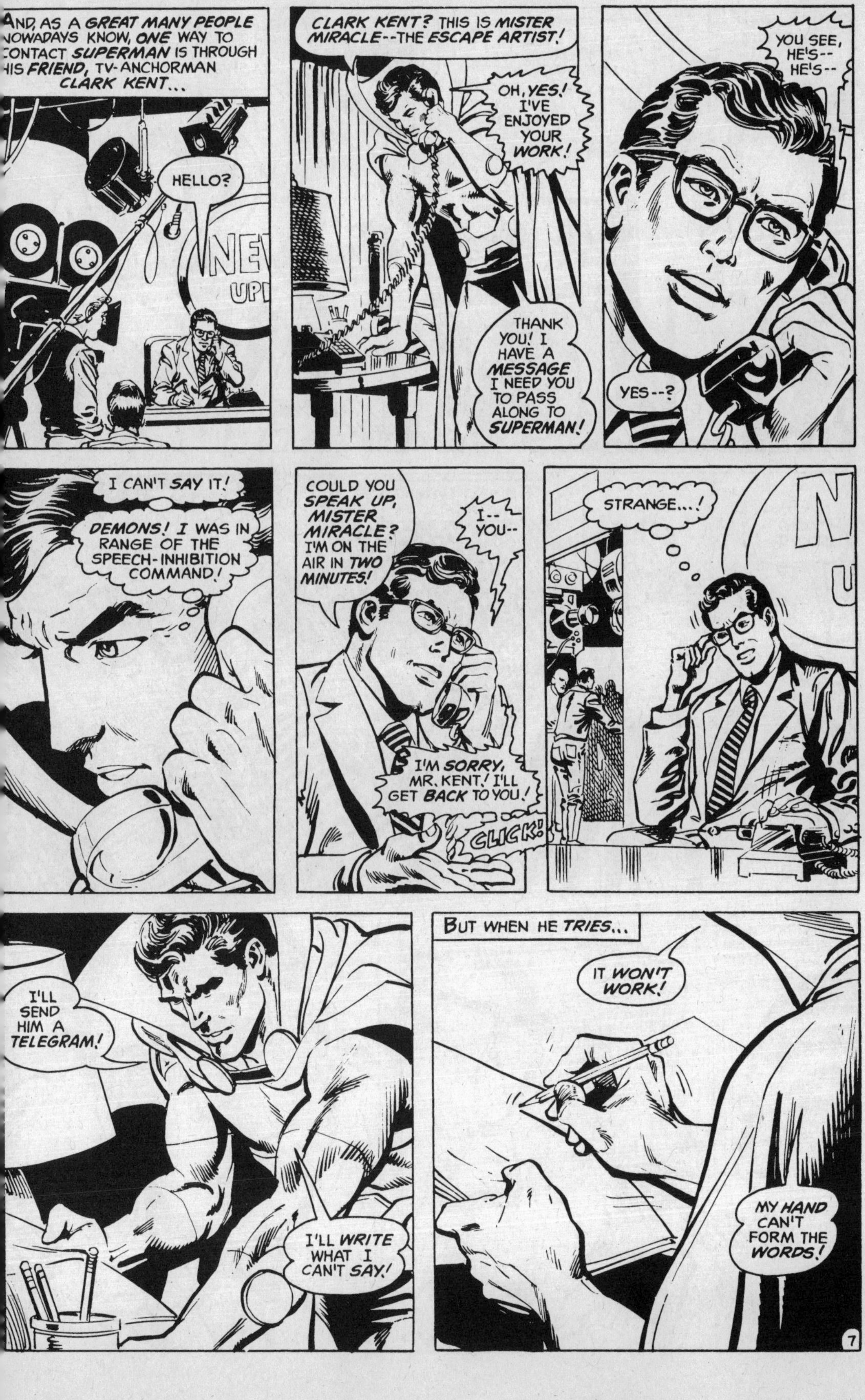
AND, AS A GREAT MANY PEOPLE NOWADAYS KNOW, ONE WAY TO CONTACT SUPERMAN IS THROUGH HIS FRIEND, TV-ANCHORMAN CLARK KENT...
HELLO?
CLARK KENT? THIS IS MISTER MIRACLE--THE ESCAPE ARTIST!
OH, YES! I'VE ENJOYED YOUR WORK!
THANK YOU! I HAVE A MESSAGE I NEED YOU TO PASS ALONG TO SUPERMAN!
YOU SEE, HE'S-- HE'S--
YES--?
I CAN'T SAY IT!
DEMONS! I WAS IN RANGE OF THE SPEECH-INHIBITION COMMAND!
COULD YOU SPEAK UP, MISTER MIRACLE? I'M ON THE AIR IN TWO MINUTES!
I-- YOU--
I'M SORRY, MR. KENT! I'LL GET BACK TO YOU!
CLICK!
STRANGE...!
I'LL SEND HIM A TELEGRAM!
I'LL WRITE WHAT I CAN'T SAY!
BUT WHEN HE TRIES...
IT WON'T WORK!
MY HAND CAN'T FORM THE WORDS!

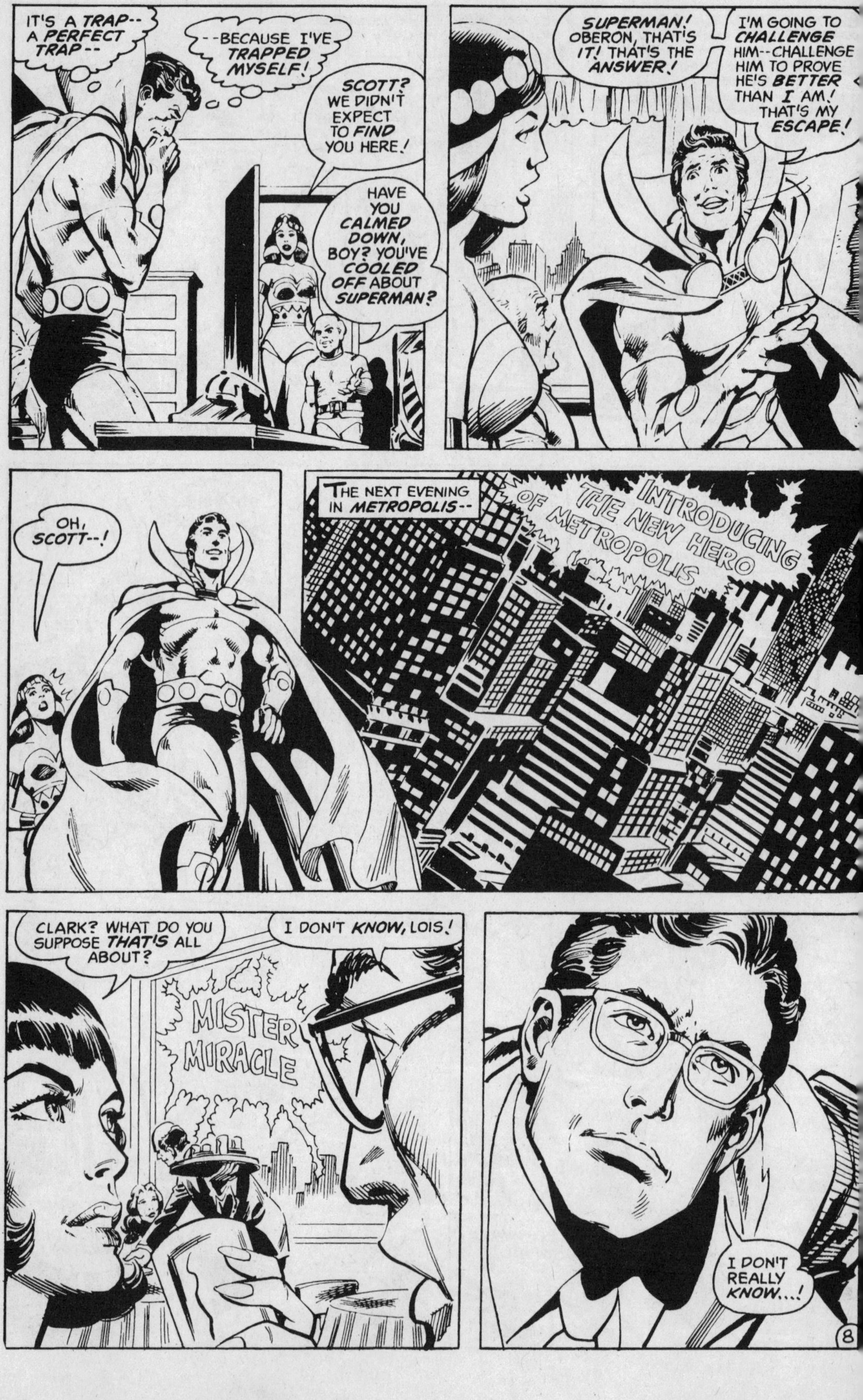
IT'S A TRAP-- A PERFECT TRAP--
--BECAUSE I'VE TRAPPED MYSELF!
SCOTT? WE DIDN'T EXPECT TO FIND YOU HERE!
HAVE YOU CALMED DOWN, BOY? YOU'VE COOLED OFF ABOUT SUPERMAN?
SUPERMAN! OBERON, THAT'S IT! THAT'S THE ANSWER!
I'M GOING TO CHALLENGE HIM--CHALLENGE HIM TO PROVE HE'S BETTER THAN I AM! THAT'S MY ESCAPE!
OH, SCOTT--!
THE NEXT EVENING IN METROPOLIS--
INTRODUCING THE NEW HERO OF METROPOLIS
CLARK? WHAT DO YOU SUPPOSE THAT'S ALL ABOUT?
I DON'T KNOW, LOIS!
MISTER MIRACLE
I DON'T REALLY KNOW...!
8

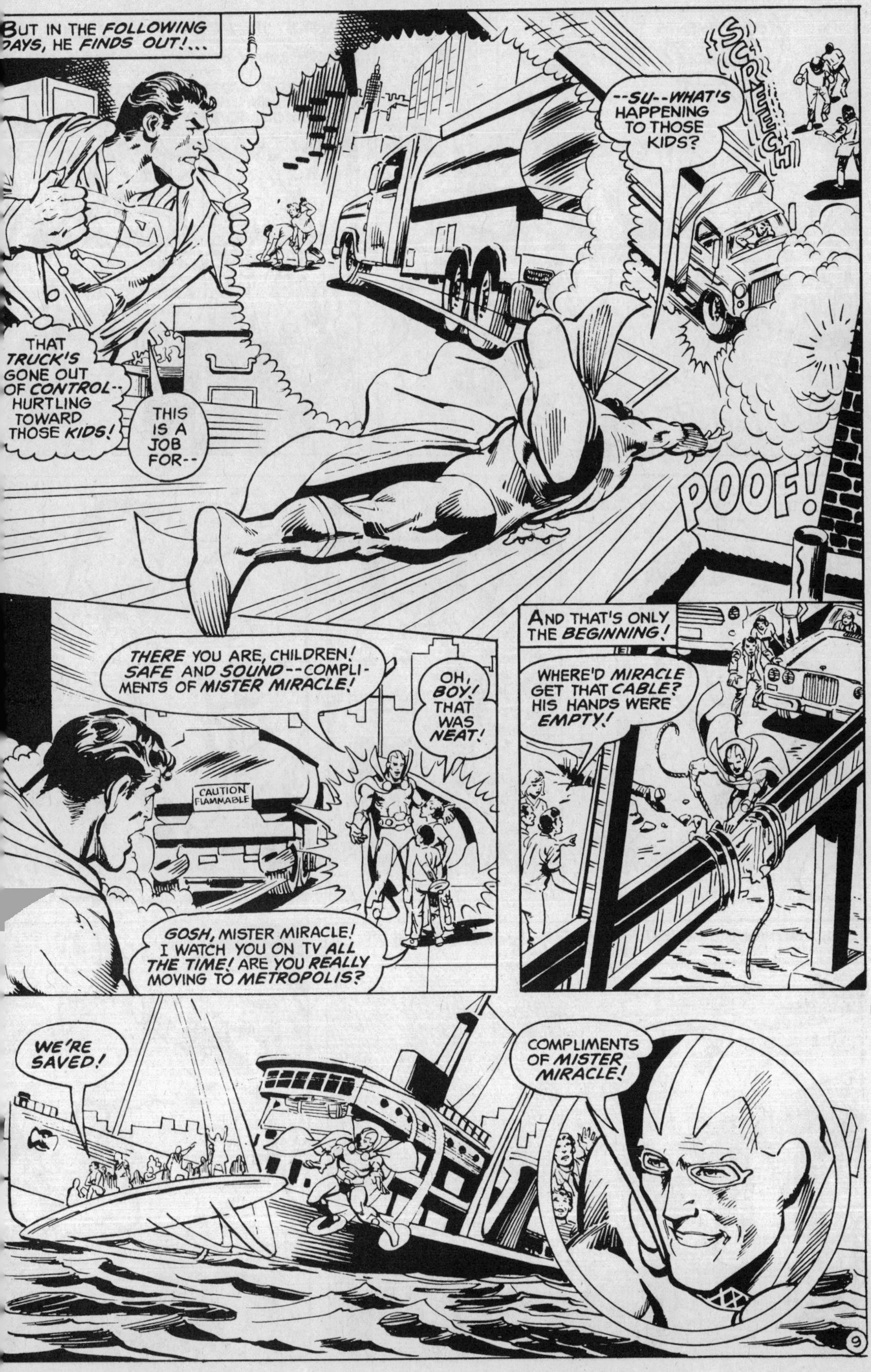
BUT IN THE FOLLOWING DAYS, HE FINDS OUT!...
SCREECH
--SU--WHAT'S HAPPENING TO THOSE KIDS?
THAT TRUCK'S GONE OUT OF CONTROL-- HURTLING TOWARD THOSE KIDS!
THIS IS A JOB FOR--
POOF!
THERE YOU ARE, CHILDREN! SAFE AND SOUND--COMPLIMENTS OF MISTER MIRACLE!
OH, BOY! THAT WAS NEAT!
CAUTION FLAMMABLE
GOSH, MISTER MIRACLE! I WATCH YOU ON TV ALL THE TIME! ARE YOU REALLY MOVING TO METROPOLIS?
AND THAT'S ONLY THE BEGINNING!
WHERE'D MIRACLE GET THAT CABLE? HIS HANDS WERE EMPTY!
WE'RE SAVED!
COMPLIMENTS OF MISTER MIRACLE!
9

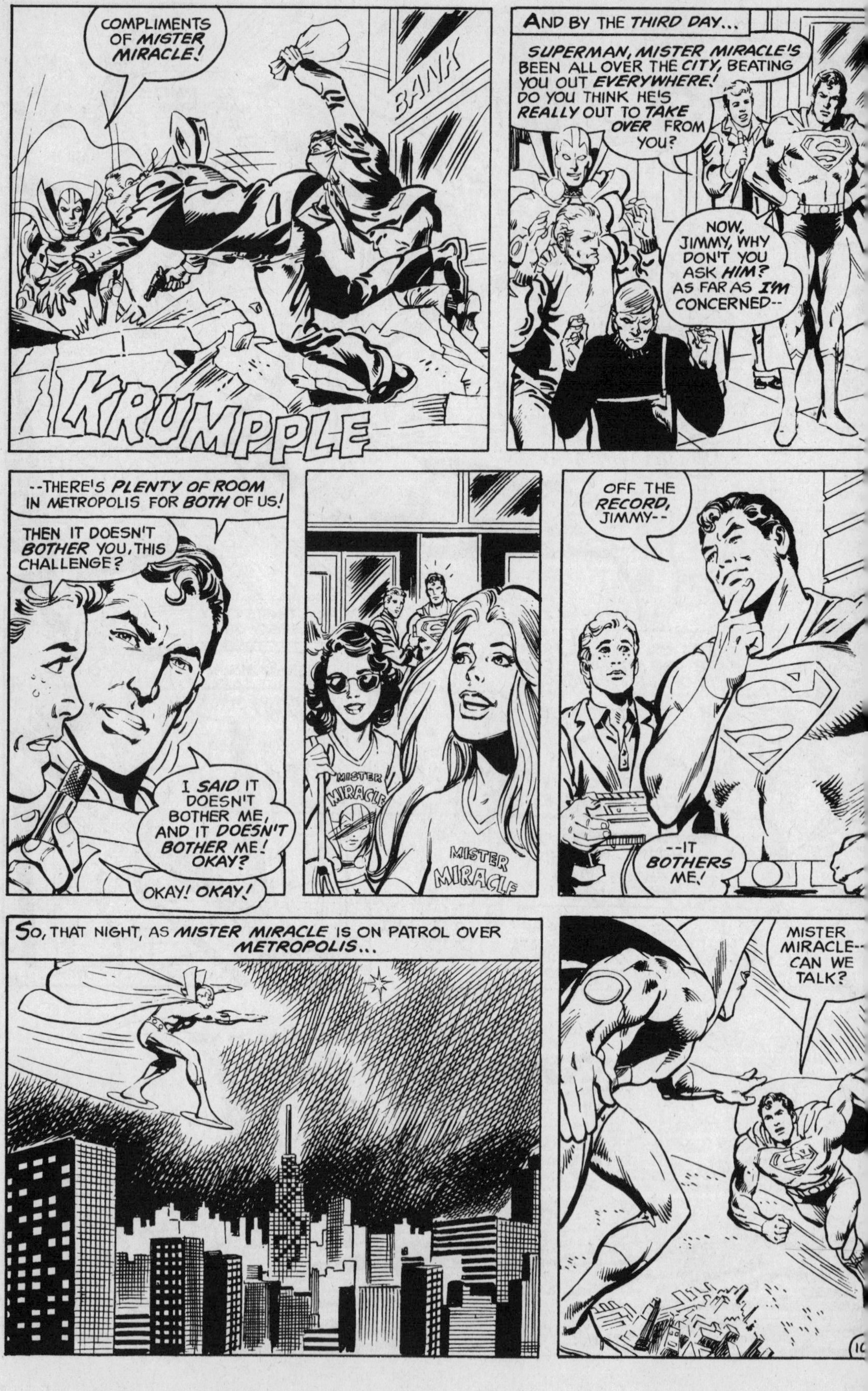
COMPLIMENTS OF MISTER MIRACLE!
BANK
KRUMPPLE
AND BY THE THIRD DAY...
SUPERMAN, MISTER MIRACLE'S BEEN ALL OVER THE CITY, BEATING YOU OUT EVERYWHERE! DO YOU THINK HE'S REALLY OUT TO TAKE OVER FROM YOU?
NOW, JIMMY, WHY DON'T YOU ASK HIM? AS FAR AS I'M CONCERNED--
--THERE'S PLENTY OF ROOM IN METROPOLIS FOR BOTH OF US!
THEN IT DOESN'T BOTHER YOU, THIS CHALLENGE?
I SAID IT DOESN'T BOTHER ME, AND IT DOESN'T BOTHER ME! OKAY?
OKAY! OKAY!
MISTER MIRACLE
MISTER MIRACLE
OFF THE RECORD, JIMMY--
--IT BOTHERS ME!
SO, THAT NIGHT, AS MISTER MIRACLE IS ON PATROL OVER METROPOLIS...
MISTER MIRACLE-- CAN WE TALK?

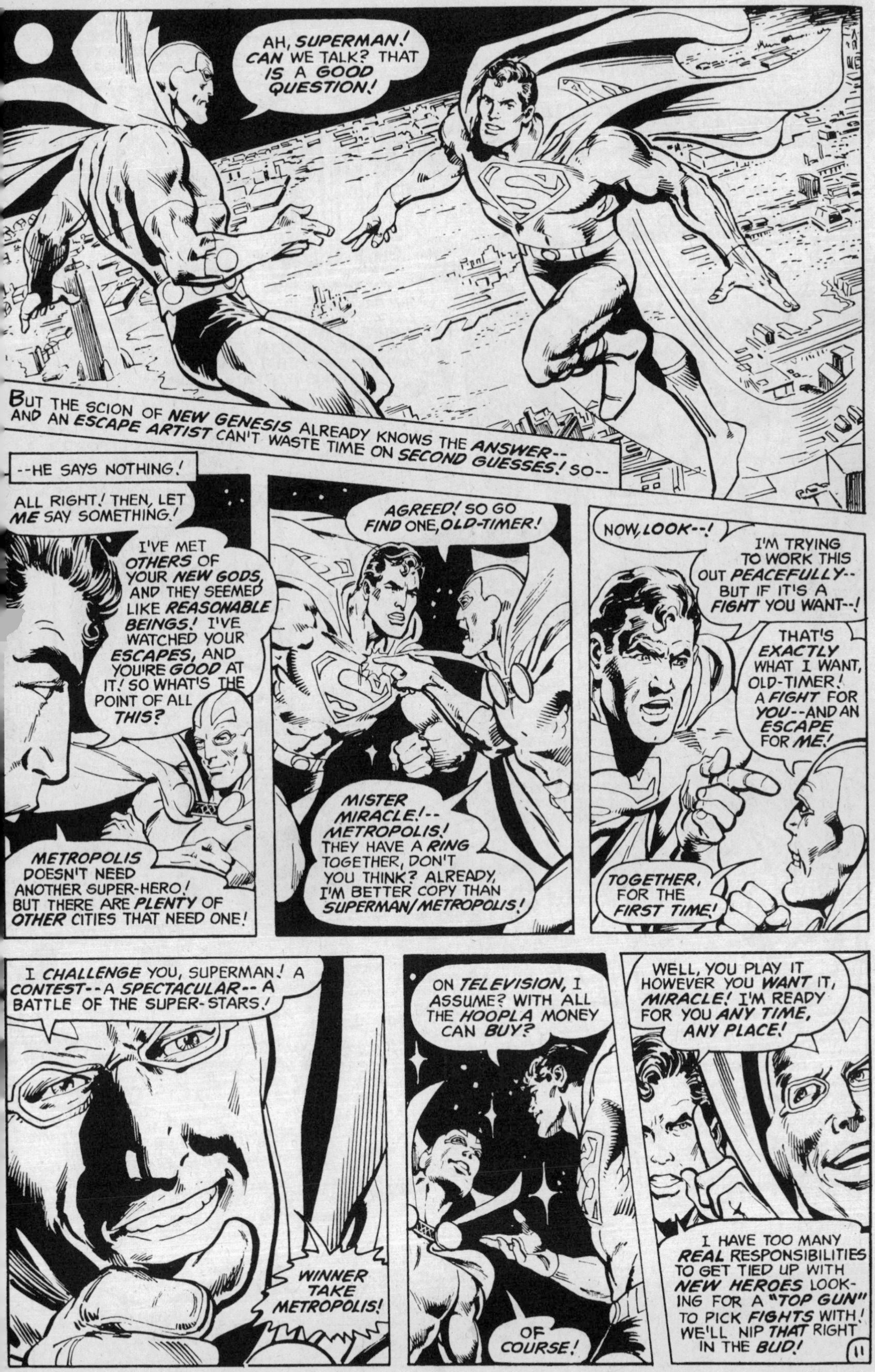
AH, SUPERMAN! CAN WE TALK? THAT IS A GOOD QUESTION!
BUT THE SCION OF NEW GENESIS ALREADY KNOWS THE ANSWER-- AND AN ESCAPE ARTIST CAN'T WASTE TIME ON SECOND GUESSES! SO--
--HE SAYS NOTHING!
ALL RIGHT! THEN, LET ME SAY SOMETHING!
I'VE MET OTHERS OF YOUR NEW GODS, AND THEY SEEMED LIKE REASONABLE BEINGS! I'VE WATCHED YOUR ESCAPES, AND YOU'RE GOOD AT IT! SO WHAT'S THE POINT OF ALL THIS?
METROPOLIS DOESN'T NEED ANOTHER SUPER-HERO! BUT THERE ARE PLENTY OF OTHER CITIES THAT NEED ONE!
AGREED! SO GO FIND ONE, OLD-TIMER!
MISTER MIRACLE!-- METROPOLIS! THEY HAVE A RING TOGETHER, DON'T YOU THINK? ALREADY, I'M BETTER COPY THAN SUPERMAN/METROPOLIS!
NOW, LOOK--!
I'M TRYING TO WORK THIS OUT PEACEFULLY-- BUT IF IT'S A FIGHT YOU WANT--!
THAT'S EXACTLY WHAT I WANT, OLD-TIMER! A FIGHT FOR YOU--AND AN ESCAPE FOR ME!
TOGETHER, FOR THE FIRST TIME!
I CHALLENGE YOU, SUPERMAN! A CONTEST--A SPECTACULAR--A BATTLE OF THE SUPER-STARS!
WINNER TAKE METROPOLIS!
ON TELEVISION, I ASSUME? WITH ALL THE HOOPLA MONEY CAN BUY?
OF COURSE!
WELL, YOU PLAY IT HOWEVER YOU WANT IT, MIRACLE! I'M READY FOR YOU ANY TIME, ANY PLACE!
I HAVE TOO MANY REAL RESPONSIBILITIES TO GET TIED UP WITH NEW HEROES LOOKING FOR A "TOP GUN" TO PICK FIGHTS WITH! WE'LL NIP THAT RIGHT IN THE BUD!
11

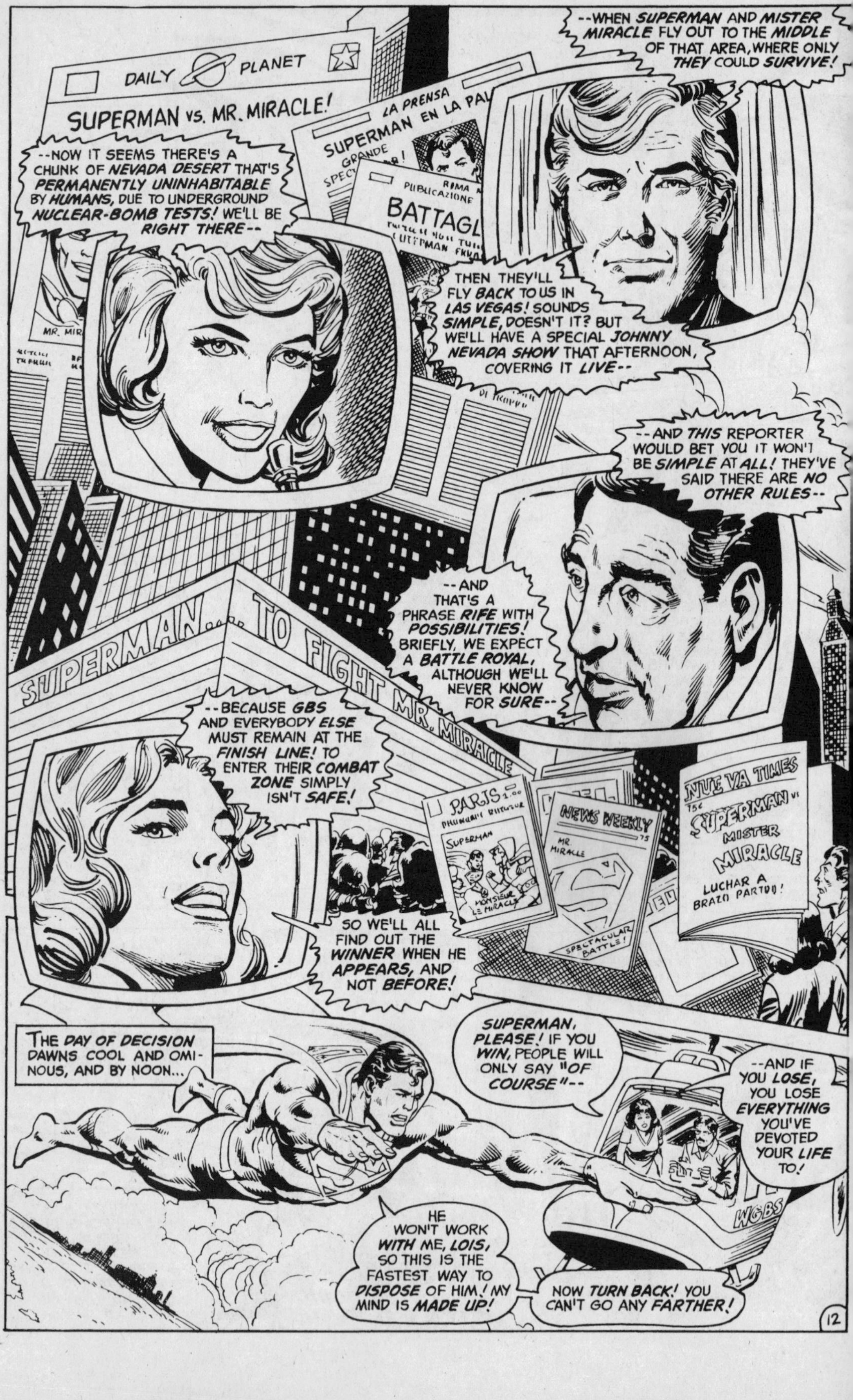
DAILY PLANET
SUPERMAN VS. MR. MIRACLE!
LA PRENSA
SUPERMAN EN LA PA
BATTAGL
--WHEN SUPERMAN AND MISTER MIRACLE FLY OUT TO THE MIDDLE OF THAT AREA, WHERE ONLY THEY COULD SURVIVE!
--NOW IT SEEMS THERE'S A CHUNK OF NEVADA DESERT THAT'S PERMANENTLY UNINHABITABLE BY HUMANS, DUE TO UNDERGROUND NUCLEAR-BOMB TESTS! WE'LL BE RIGHT THERE--
THEN THEY'LL FLY BACK TO US IN LAS VEGAS! SOUNDS SIMPLE, DOESN'T IT? BUT WE'LL HAVE A SPECIAL JOHNNY NEVADA SHOW THAT AFTERNOON, COVERING IT LIVE--
--AND THIS REPORTER WOULD BET YOU IT WON'T BE SIMPLE AT ALL! THEY'VE SAID THERE ARE NO OTHER RULES--
--AND THAT'S A PHRASE RIFE WITH POSSIBILITIES! BRIEFLY, WE EXPECT A BATTLE ROYAL, ALTHOUGH WE'LL NEVER KNOW FOR SURE--
SUPERMAN... TO FIGHT MR. MIRACLE
--BECAUSE GBS AND EVERYBODY ELSE MUST REMAIN AT THE FINISH LINE! TO ENTER THEIR COMBAT ZONE SIMPLY ISN'T SAFE!
SO WE'LL ALL FIND OUT THE WINNER WHEN HE APPEARS, AND NOT BEFORE!
PARIS
SUPERMAN
MONSIEUR LE MIRACLE
NEWS WEEKLY
MR. MIRACLE
SPECTACULAR BATTLE!
SUPERMAN VS MISTER MIRACLE
LUCHAR A BRAZO PARTIDO!
THE DAY OF DECISION DAWNS COOL AND OMINOUS, AND BY NOON...
SUPERMAN, PLEASE! IF YOU WIN, PEOPLE WILL ONLY SAY "OF COURSE"--
--AND IF YOU LOSE, YOU LOSE EVERYTHING YOU'VE DEVOTED YOUR LIFE TO!
HE WON'T WORK WITH ME, LOIS, SO THIS IS THE FASTEST WAY TO DISPOSE OF HIM! MY MIND IS MADE UP!
NOW TURN BACK! YOU CAN'T GO ANY FARTHER!
WGBS
12

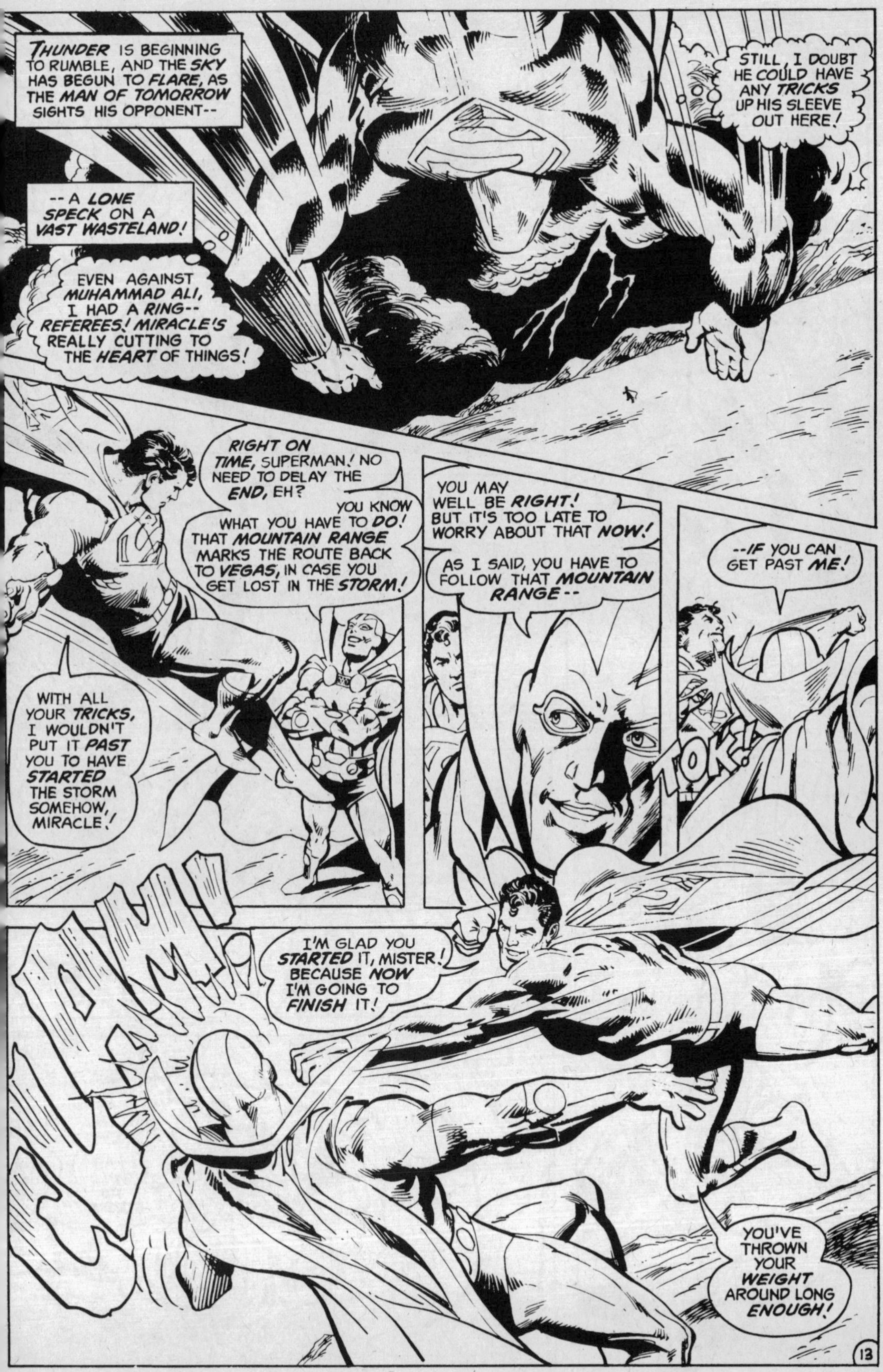
THUNDER IS BEGINNING TO RUMBLE, AND THE SKY HAS BEGUN TO FLARE, AS THE MAN OF TOMORROW SIGHTS HIS OPPONENT--
STILL, I DOUBT HE COULD HAVE ANY TRICKS UP HIS SLEEVE OUT HERE!
--A LONE SPECK ON A VAST WASTELAND!
EVEN AGAINST MUHAMMAD ALI, I HAD A RING--REFEREES! MIRACLE'S REALLY CUTTING TO THE HEART OF THINGS!
RIGHT ON TIME, SUPERMAN! NO NEED TO DELAY THE END, EH?
YOU KNOW WHAT YOU HAVE TO DO! THAT MOUNTAIN RANGE MARKS THE ROUTE BACK TO VEGAS, IN CASE YOU GET LOST IN THE STORM!
WITH ALL YOUR TRICKS, I WOULDN'T PUT IT PAST YOU TO HAVE STARTED THE STORM SOMEHOW, MIRACLE!
YOU MAY WELL BE RIGHT! BUT IT'S TOO LATE TO WORRY ABOUT THAT NOW!
AS I SAID, YOU HAVE TO FOLLOW THAT MOUNTAIN RANGE--
--IF YOU CAN GET PAST ME!
TOK!
I'M GLAD YOU STARTED IT, MISTER! BECAUSE NOW I'M GOING TO FINISH IT!
YOU'VE THROWN YOUR WEIGHT AROUND LONG ENOUGH!
13

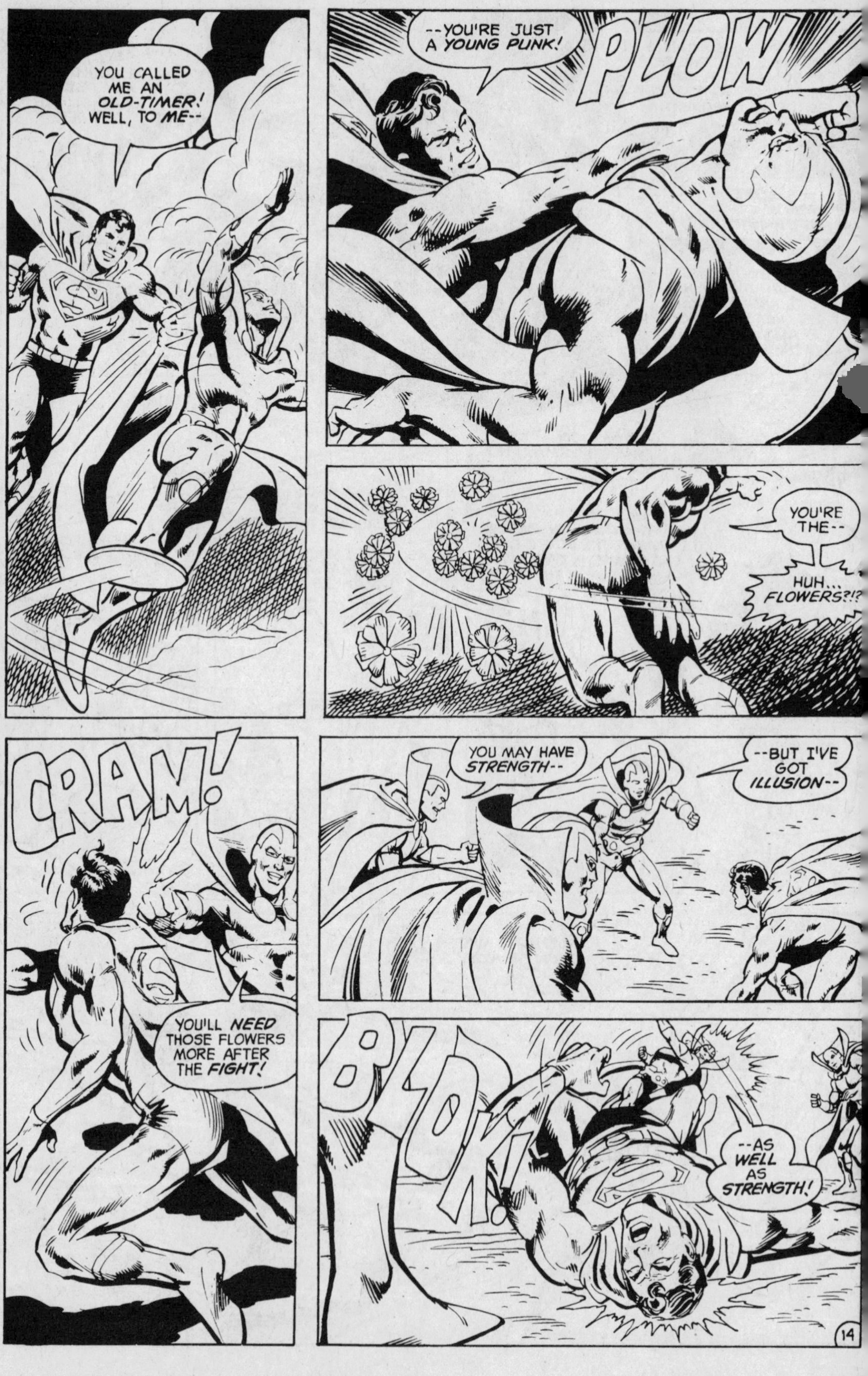

YOU CALLED ME AN OLD-TIMER! WELL, TO ME--
--YOU'RE JUST A YOUNG PUNK!
PLOW
YOU'RE THE--
HUH... FLOWERS?!?
CRAM!
YOU'LL NEED THOSE FLOWERS MORE AFTER THE FIGHT!
YOU MAY HAVE STRENGTH--
--BUT I'VE GOT ILLUSION--
BLOK!
--AS WELL AS STRENGTH!
14

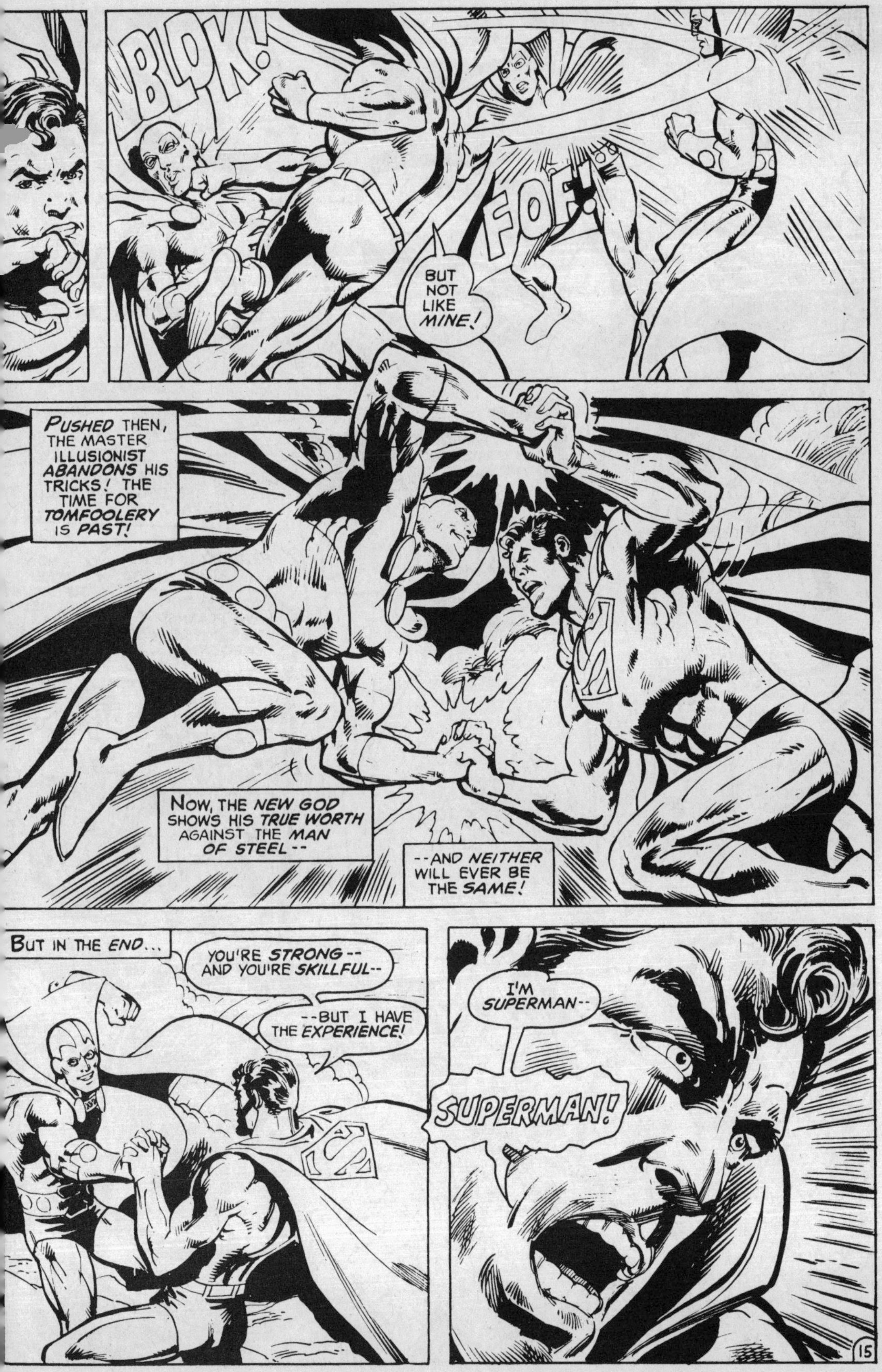
BLOK!
FOF!
BUT NOT LIKE MINE!
PUSHED THEN, THE MASTER ILLUSIONIST ABANDONS HIS TRICKS! THE TIME FOR TOMFOOLERY IS PAST!
NOW, THE NEW GOD SHOWS HIS TRUE WORTH AGAINST THE MAN OF STEEL --
--AND NEITHER WILL EVER BE THE SAME!
BUT IN THE END...
YOU'RE STRONG -- AND YOU'RE SKILLFUL--
--BUT I HAVE THE EXPERIENCE!
I'M SUPERMAN--
SUPERMAN!
15

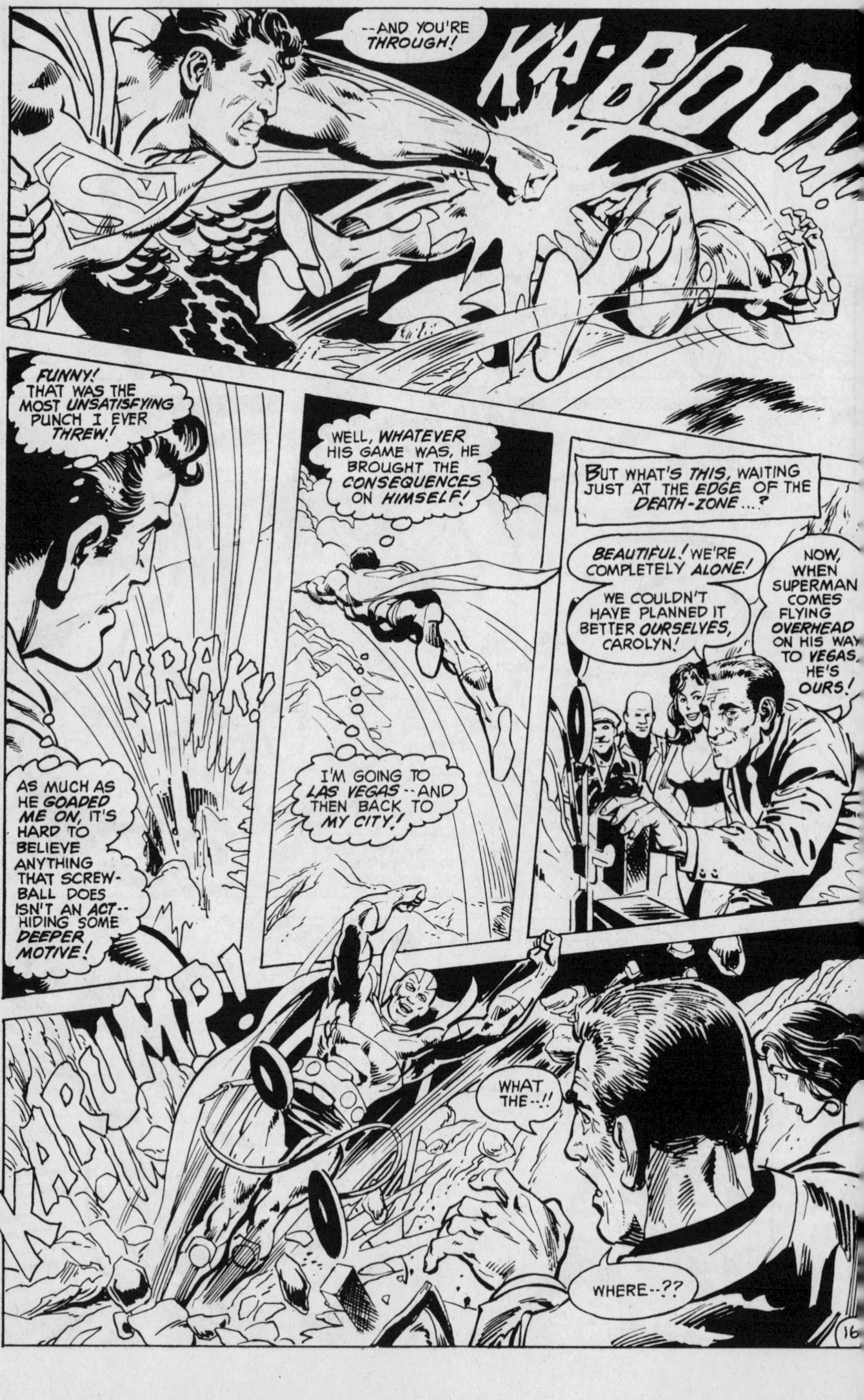
--AND YOU'RE THROUGH!
KA-BOOM!
FUNNY! THAT WAS THE MOST UNSATISFYING PUNCH I EVER THREW!
KRAK!
AS MUCH AS HE GOADED ME ON, IT'S HARD TO BELIEVE ANYTHING THAT SCREW-BALL DOES ISN'T AN ACT--HIDING SOME DEEPER MOTIVE!
WELL, WHATEVER HIS GAME WAS, HE BROUGHT THE CONSEQUENCES ON HIMSELF!
I'M GOING TO LAS VEGAS--AND THEN BACK TO MY CITY!
BUT WHAT'S THIS, WAITING JUST AT THE EDGE OF THE DEATH-ZONE...?
BEAUTIFUL! WE'RE COMPLETELY ALONE!
WE COULDN'T HAVE PLANNED IT BETTER OURSELVES, CAROLYN!
NOW, WHEN SUPERMAN COMES FLYING OVERHEAD ON HIS WAY TO VEGAS, HE'S OURS!
KA-RUMP!
WHAT THE--!!
WHERE--??
16

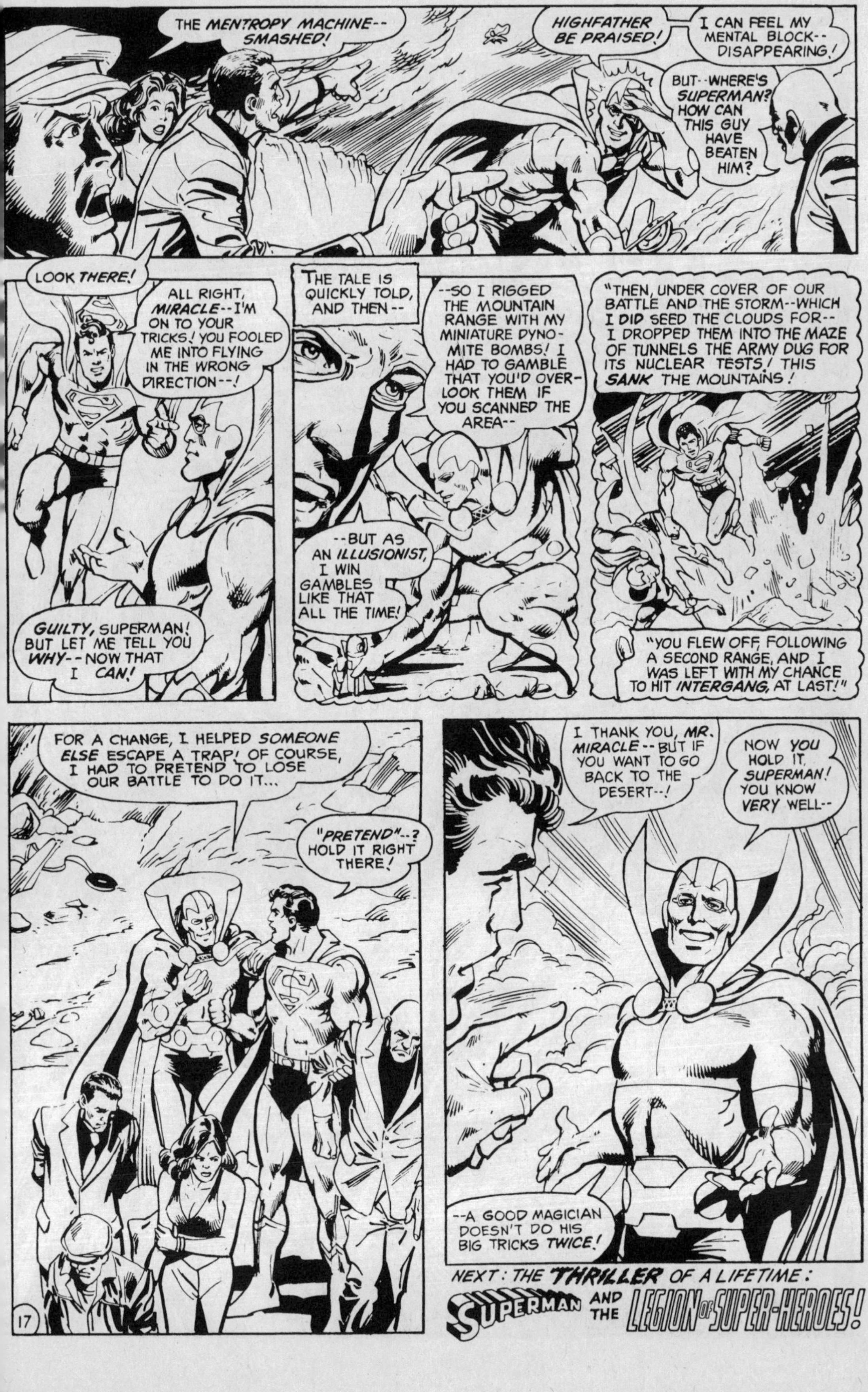
THE MENTROPY MACHINE-- SMASHED!
HIGHFATHER BE PRAISED!
I CAN FEEL MY MENTAL BLOCK-- DISAPPEARING!
BUT--WHERE'S SUPERMAN? HOW CAN THIS GUY HAVE BEATEN HIM?
LOOK THERE!
ALL RIGHT, MIRACLE--I'M ON TO YOUR TRICKS! YOU FOOLED ME INTO FLYING IN THE WRONG DIRECTION--!
GUILTY, SUPERMAN! BUT LET ME TELL YOU WHY--NOW THAT I CAN!
THE TALE IS QUICKLY TOLD, AND THEN--
--SO I RIGGED THE MOUNTAIN RANGE WITH MY MINIATURE DYNO-MITE BOMBS! I HAD TO GAMBLE THAT YOU'D OVER-LOOK THEM IF YOU SCANNED THE AREA--
--BUT AS AN ILLUSIONIST, I WIN GAMBLES LIKE THAT ALL THE TIME!
"THEN, UNDER COVER OF OUR BATTLE AND THE STORM--WHICH I DID SEED THE CLOUDS FOR--I DROPPED THEM INTO THE MAZE OF TUNNELS THE ARMY DUG FOR ITS NUCLEAR TESTS! THIS SANK THE MOUNTAINS!
"YOU FLEW OFF, FOLLOWING A SECOND RANGE, AND I WAS LEFT WITH MY CHANCE TO HIT INTERGANG, AT LAST!"
FOR A CHANGE, I HELPED SOMEONE ELSE ESCAPE A TRAP! OF COURSE, I HAD TO PRETEND TO LOSE OUR BATTLE TO DO IT...
"PRETEND"--? HOLD IT RIGHT THERE!
17
I THANK YOU, MR. MIRACLE--BUT IF YOU WANT TO GO BACK TO THE DESERT--!
NOW YOU HOLD IT, SUPERMAN! YOU KNOW VERY WELL--
--A GOOD MAGICIAN DOESN'T DO HIS BIG TRICKS TWICE!
NEXT: THE THRILLER OF A LIFETIME:
SUPERMAN AND THE LEGION OF SUPER-HEROES!

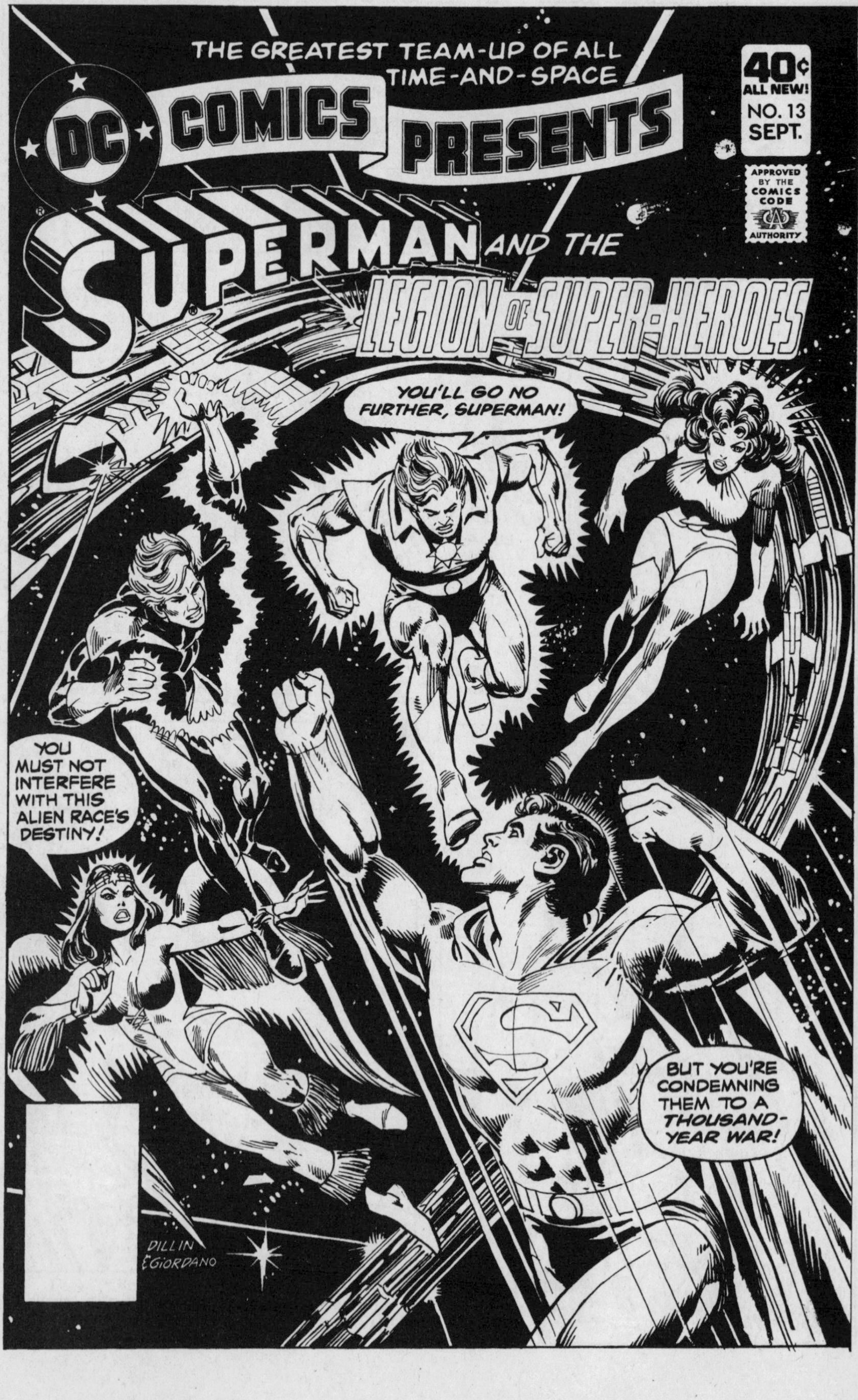
THE GREATEST TEAM-UP OF ALL TIME-AND-SPACE
DC COMICS PRESENTS
40¢ ALL NEW!
NO. 13 SEPT.
APPROVED BY THE COMICS CODE AUTHORITY
SUPERMAN AND THE LEGION OF SUPER-HEROES
YOU'LL GO NO FURTHER, SUPERMAN!
YOU MUST NOT INTERFERE WITH THIS ALIEN RACE'S DESTINY!
BUT YOU'RE CONDEMNING THEM TO A THOUSAND-YEAR WAR!
DILLIN &GIORDANO

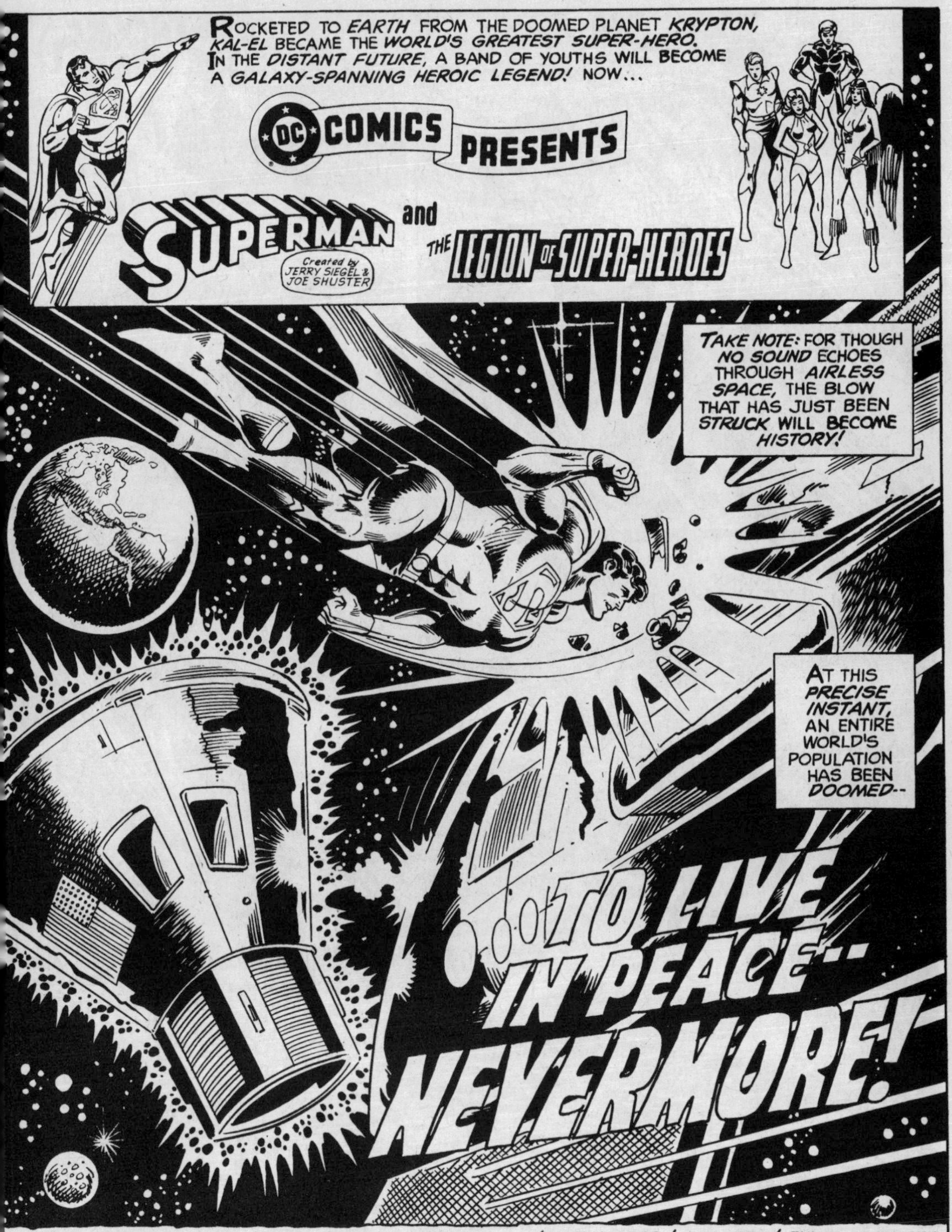
ROCKETED TO EARTH FROM THE DOOMED PLANET KRYPTON, KAL-EL BECAME THE WORLD'S GREATEST SUPER-HERO. IN THE DISTANT FUTURE, A BAND OF YOUTHS WILL BECOME A GALAXY-SPANNING HEROIC LEGEND! NOW...
DC COMICS PRESENTS
SUPERMAN and THE LEGION OF SUPER-HEROES
Created by JERRY SIEGEL & JOE SHUSTER
TAKE NOTE: FOR THOUGH NO SOUND ECHOES THROUGH AIRLESS SPACE, THE BLOW THAT HAS JUST BEEN STRUCK WILL BECOME HISTORY!
AT THIS PRECISE INSTANT, AN ENTIRE WORLD'S POPULATION HAS BEEN DOOMED--
...TO LIVE IN PEACE... NEVERMORE!
PAUL LEVITZ WRITER / DICK DILLIN & DICK GIORDANO ARTISTS / JERRY SERPE COLORIST / BEN ODA LETTERER / JULIUS SCHWARTZ EDITOR

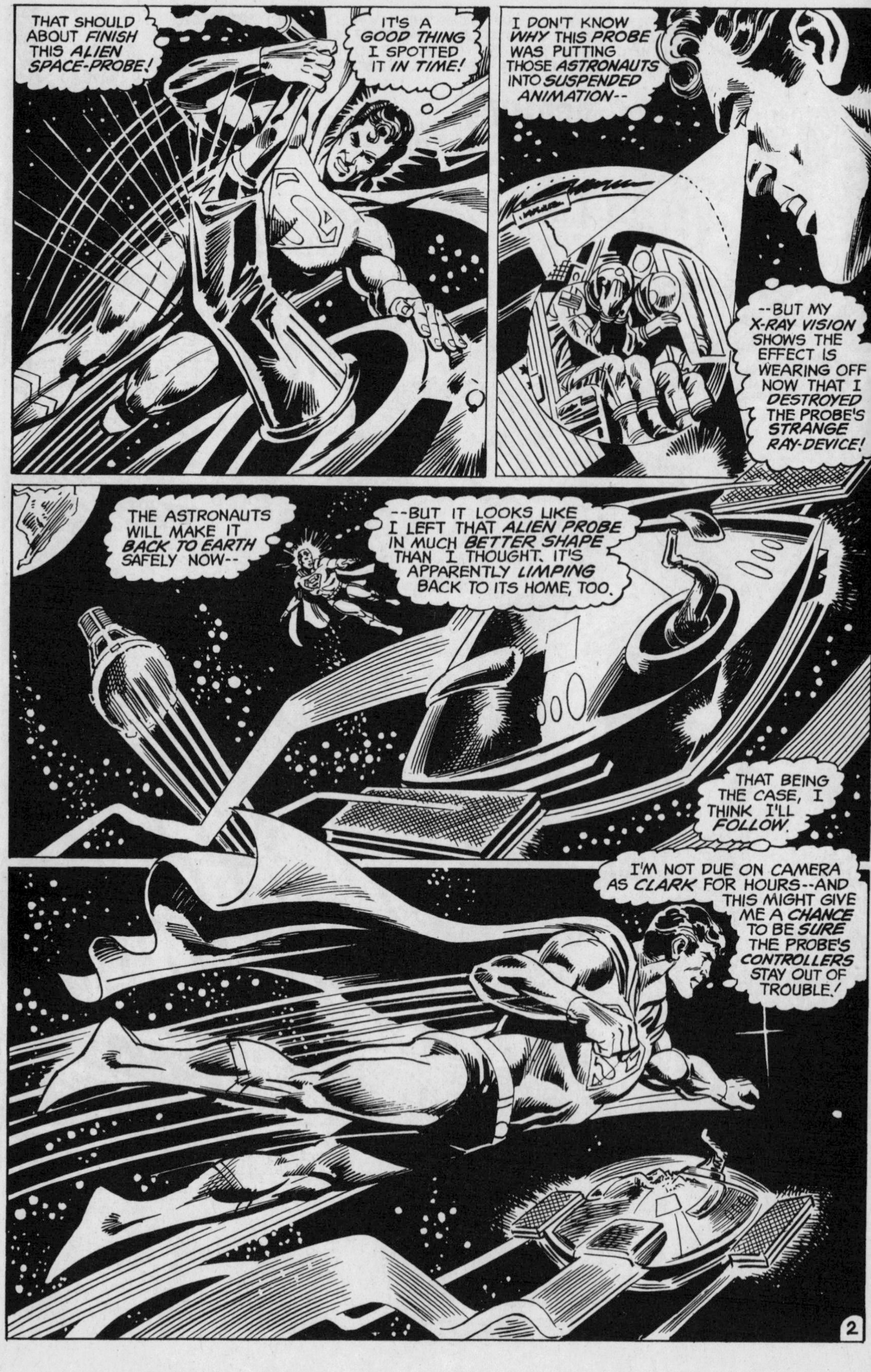
THAT SHOULD ABOUT FINISH THIS ALIEN SPACE-PROBE!
IT'S A GOOD THING I SPOTTED IT IN TIME!
I DON'T KNOW WHY THIS PROBE WAS PUTTING THOSE ASTRONAUTS INTO SUSPENDED ANIMATION--
--BUT MY X-RAY VISION SHOWS THE EFFECT IS WEARING OFF NOW THAT I DESTROYED THE PROBE'S STRANGE RAY-DEVICE!
THE ASTRONAUTS WILL MAKE IT BACK TO EARTH SAFELY NOW--
--BUT IT LOOKS LIKE I LEFT THAT ALIEN PROBE IN MUCH BETTER SHAPE THAN I THOUGHT. IT'S APPARENTLY LIMPING BACK TO ITS HOME, TOO.
THAT BEING THE CASE, I THINK I'LL FOLLOW.
I'M NOT DUE ON CAMERA AS CLARK FOR HOURS--AND THIS MIGHT GIVE ME A CHANCE TO BE SURE THE PROBE'S CONTROLLERS STAY OUT OF TROUBLE!
2

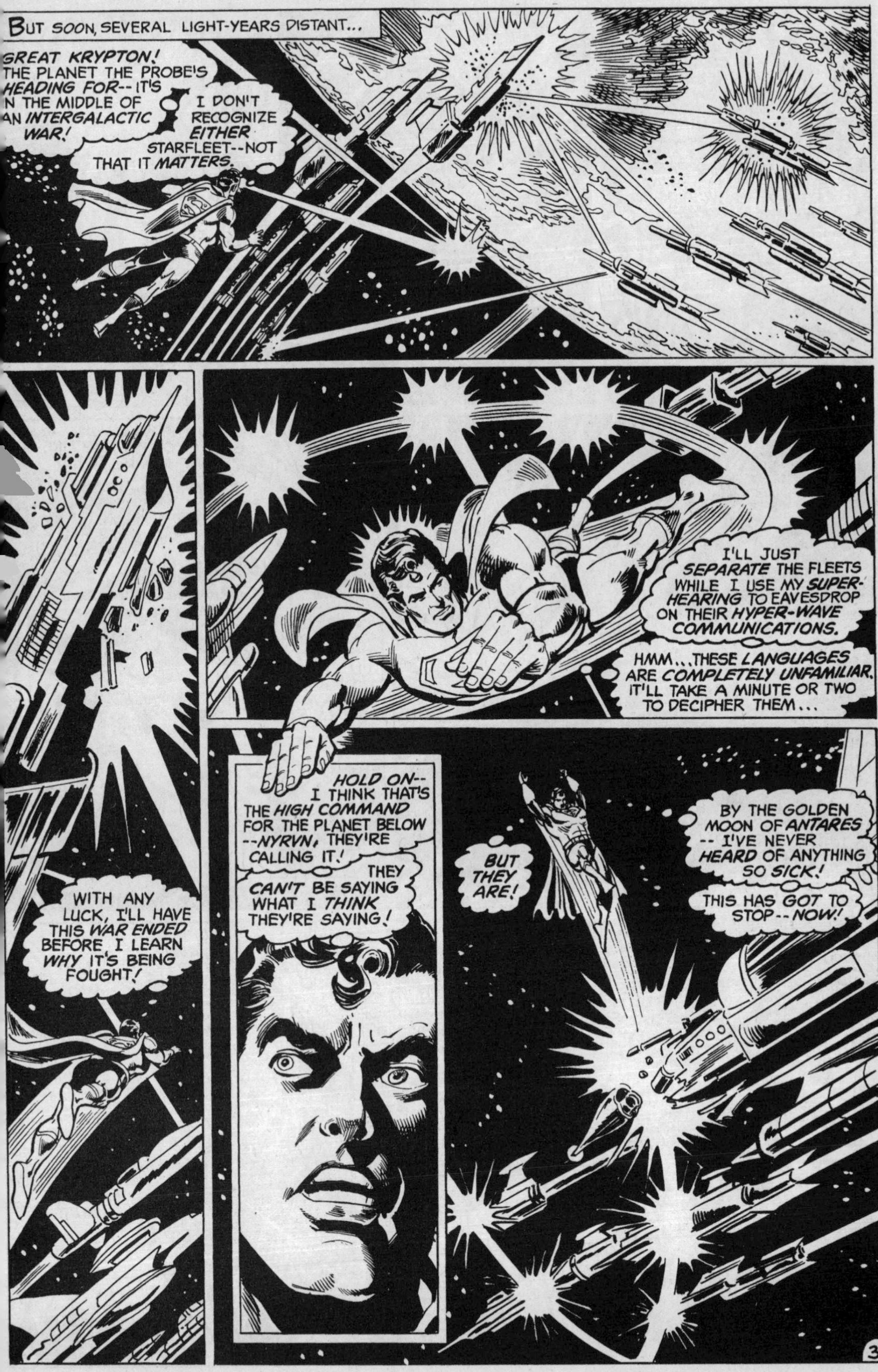
BUT SOON, SEVERAL LIGHT-YEARS DISTANT...
GREAT KRYPTON! THE PLANET THE PROBE'S HEADING FOR-- IT'S IN THE MIDDLE OF AN INTERGALACTIC WAR!
I DON'T RECOGNIZE EITHER STARFLEET--NOT THAT IT MATTERS.
I'LL JUST SEPARATE THE FLEETS WHILE I USE MY SUPER-HEARING TO EAVESDROP ON THEIR HYPER-WAVE COMMUNICATIONS.
HMM...THESE LANGUAGES ARE COMPLETELY UNFAMILIAR. IT'LL TAKE A MINUTE OR TWO TO DECIPHER THEM...
WITH ANY LUCK, I'LL HAVE THIS WAR ENDED BEFORE I LEARN WHY IT'S BEING FOUGHT!
HOLD ON-- I THINK THAT'S THE HIGH COMMAND FOR THE PLANET BELOW --NYRVN, THEY'RE CALLING IT!
THEY CAN'T BE SAYING WHAT I THINK THEY'RE SAYING!
BUT THEY ARE!
BY THE GOLDEN MOON OF ANTARES -- I'VE NEVER HEARD OF ANYTHING SO SICK!
THIS HAS GOT TO STOP -- NOW!
3

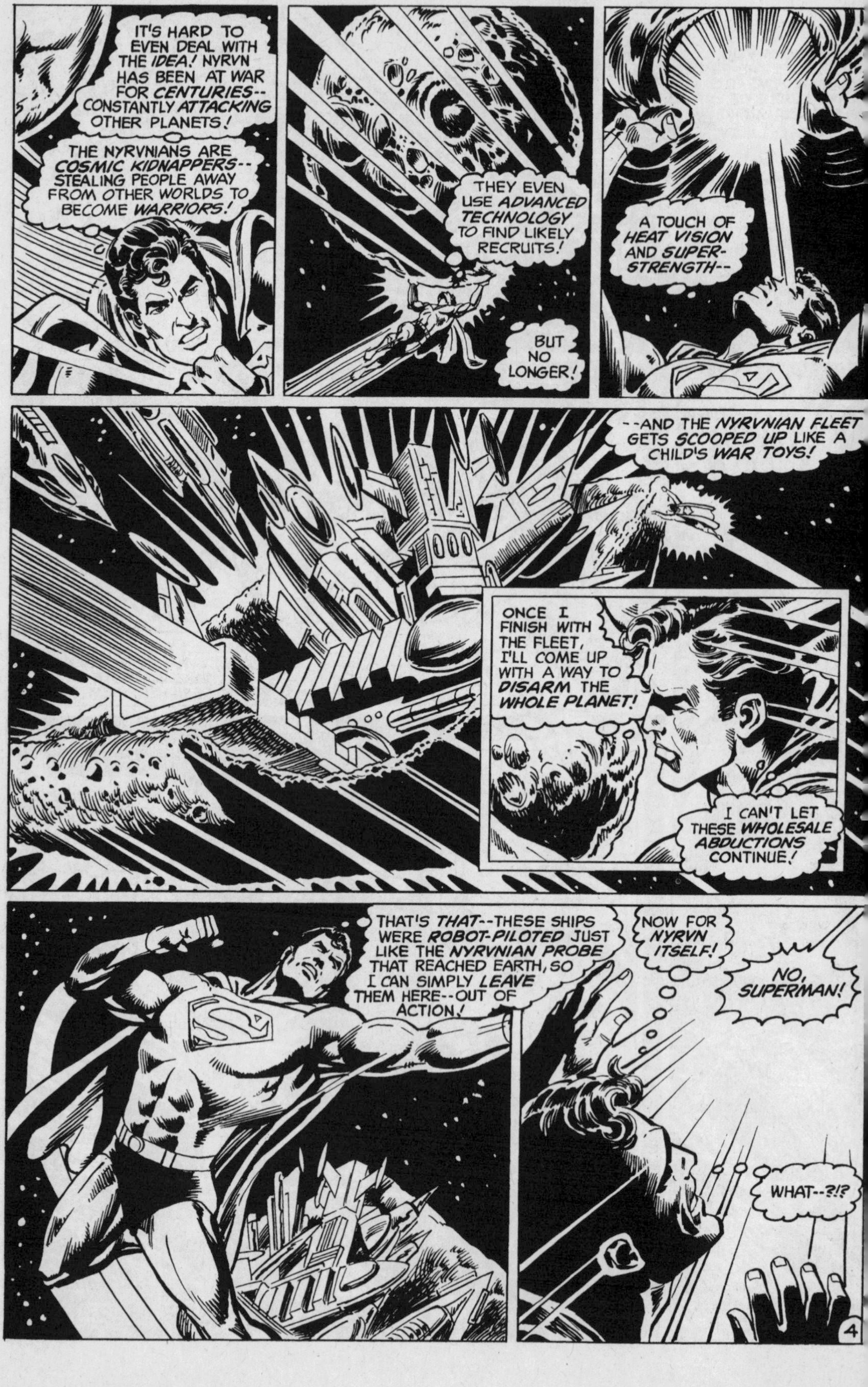
IT'S HARD TO EVEN DEAL WITH THE IDEA! NYRVN HAS BEEN AT WAR FOR CENTURIES-- CONSTANTLY ATTACKING OTHER PLANETS!
THE NYRVNIANS ARE COSMIC KIDNAPPERS-- STEALING PEOPLE AWAY FROM OTHER WORLDS TO BECOME WARRIORS!
THEY EVEN USE ADVANCED TECHNOLOGY TO FIND LIKELY RECRUITS!
BUT NO LONGER!
A TOUCH OF HEAT VISION AND SUPER-STRENGTH--
--AND THE NYRVNIAN FLEET GETS SCOOPED UP LIKE A CHILD'S WAR TOYS!
ONCE I FINISH WITH THE FLEET, I'LL COME UP WITH A WAY TO DISARM THE WHOLE PLANET!
I CAN'T LET THESE WHOLESALE ABDUCTIONS CONTINUE!
THAT'S THAT--THESE SHIPS WERE ROBOT-PILOTED JUST LIKE THE NYRVNIAN PROBE THAT REACHED EARTH, SO I CAN SIMPLY LEAVE THEM HERE--OUT OF ACTION!
NOW FOR NYRVN ITSELF!
NO, SUPERMAN!
WHAT--?!?
4

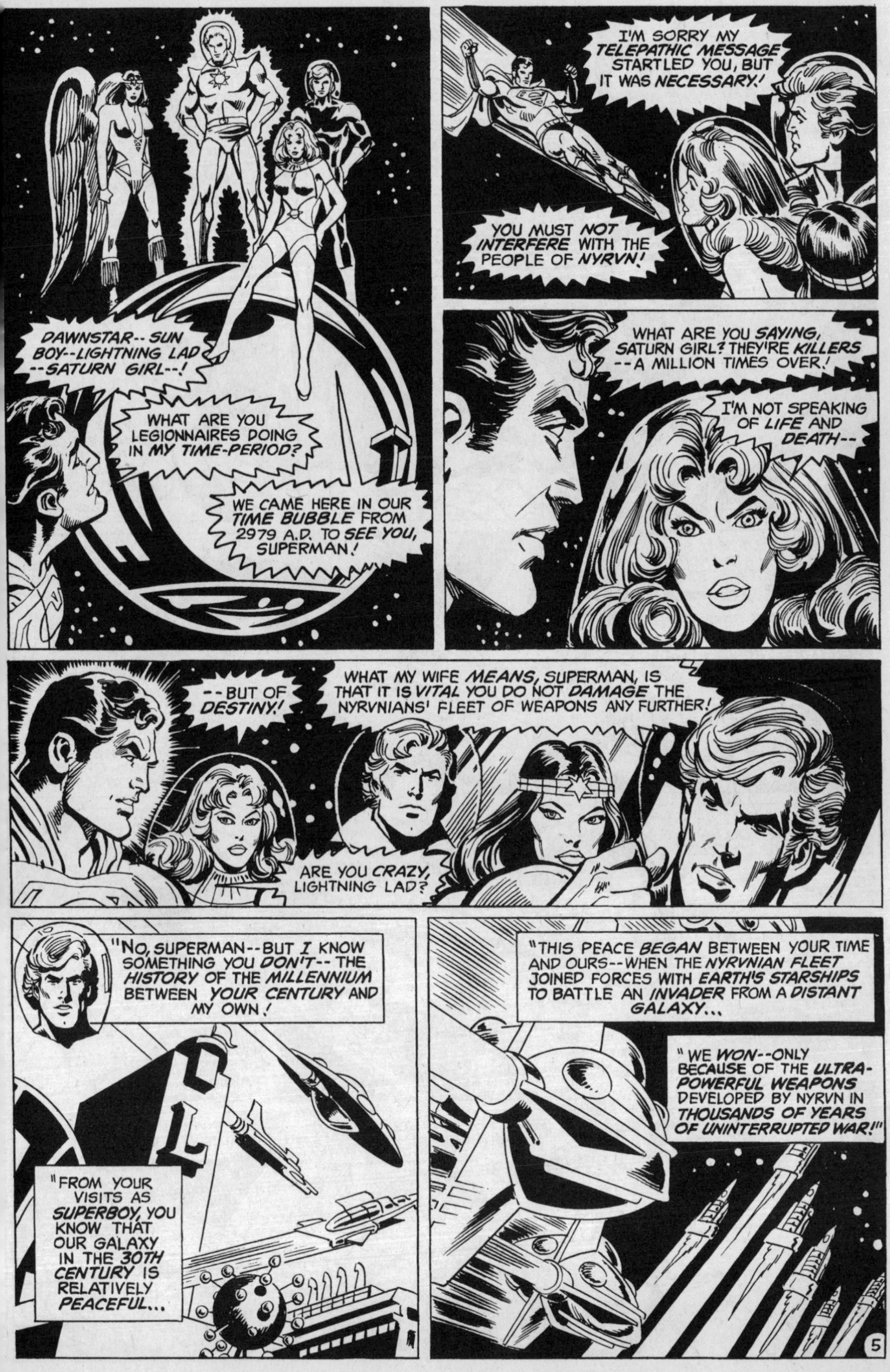
DAWNSTAR-- SUN BOY--LIGHTNING LAD --SATURN GIRL--!
WHAT ARE YOU LEGIONNAIRES DOING IN MY TIME-PERIOD?
WE CAME HERE IN OUR TIME BUBBLE FROM 2979 A.D. TO SEE YOU, SUPERMAN!
I'M SORRY MY TELEPATHIC MESSAGE STARTLED YOU, BUT IT WAS NECESSARY!
YOU MUST NOT INTERFERE WITH THE PEOPLE OF NYRVN!
WHAT ARE YOU SAYING, SATURN GIRL? THEY'RE KILLERS --A MILLION TIMES OVER!
I'M NOT SPEAKING OF LIFE AND DEATH--
--BUT OF DESTINY!
WHAT MY WIFE MEANS, SUPERMAN, IS THAT IT IS VITAL YOU DO NOT DAMAGE THE NYRVNIANS' FLEET OF WEAPONS ANY FURTHER!
ARE YOU CRAZY, LIGHTNING LAD?
"NO, SUPERMAN--BUT I KNOW SOMETHING YOU DON'T-- THE HISTORY OF THE MILLENNIUM BETWEEN YOUR CENTURY AND MY OWN!
"FROM YOUR VISITS AS SUPERBOY, YOU KNOW THAT OUR GALAXY IN THE 30TH CENTURY IS RELATIVELY PEACEFUL...
"THIS PEACE BEGAN BETWEEN YOUR TIME AND OURS--WHEN THE NYRVNIAN FLEET JOINED FORCES WITH EARTH'S STARSHIPS TO BATTLE AN INVADER FROM A DISTANT GALAXY...
"WE WON--ONLY BECAUSE OF THE ULTRA-POWERFUL WEAPONS DEVELOPED BY NYRVN IN THOUSANDS OF YEARS OF UNINTERRUPTED WAR!"
5

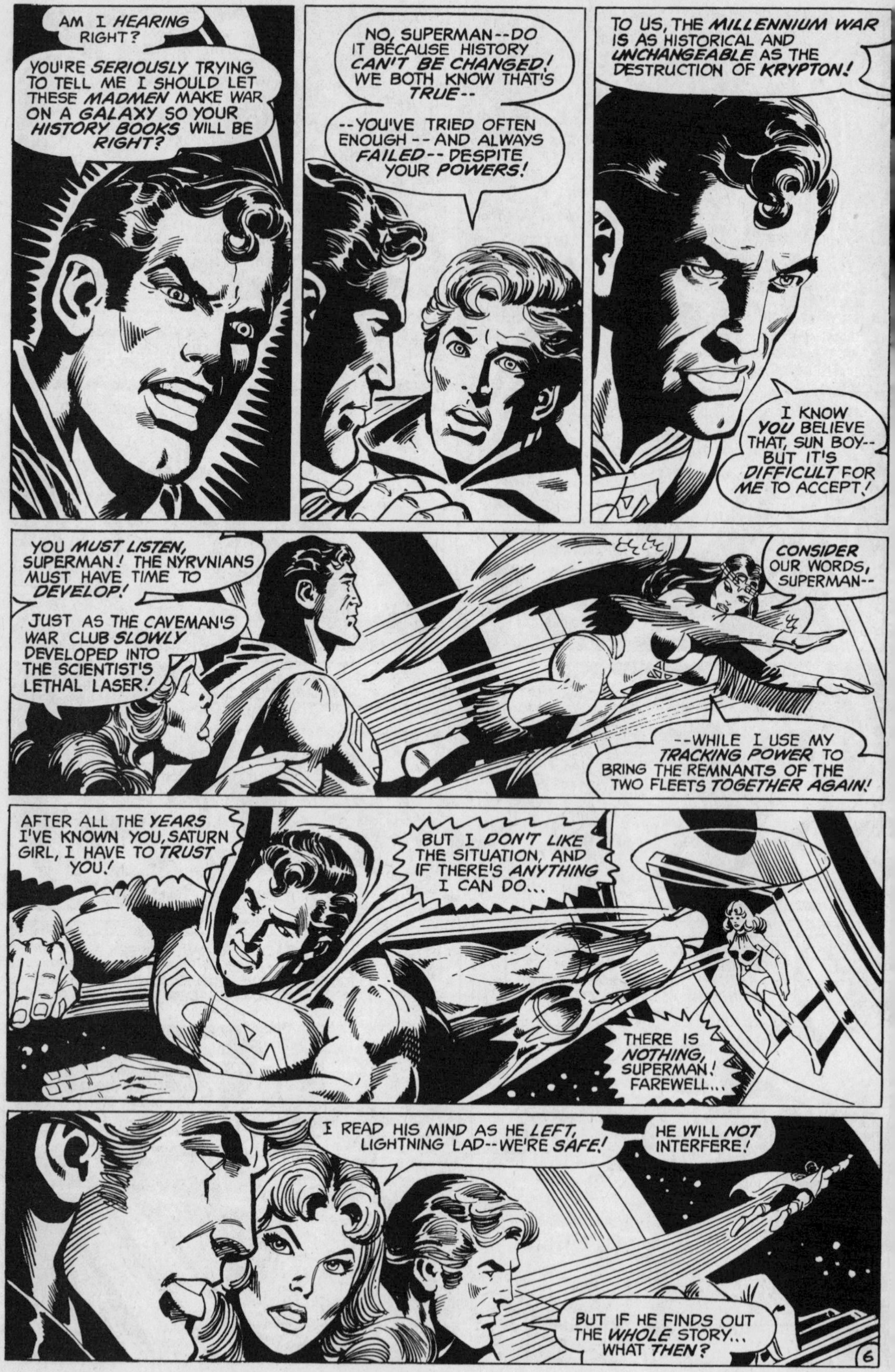
AM I HEARING RIGHT?
YOU'RE SERIOUSLY TRYING TO TELL ME I SHOULD LET THESE MADMEN MAKE WAR ON A GALAXY SO YOUR HISTORY BOOKS WILL BE RIGHT?
NO, SUPERMAN--DO IT BECAUSE HISTORY CAN'T BE CHANGED! WE BOTH KNOW THAT'S TRUE--
--YOU'VE TRIED OFTEN ENOUGH--AND ALWAYS FAILED--DESPITE YOUR POWERS!
TO US, THE MILLENNIUM WAR IS AS HISTORICAL AND UNCHANGEABLE AS THE DESTRUCTION OF KRYPTON!
I KNOW YOU BELIEVE THAT, SUN BOY--BUT IT'S DIFFICULT FOR ME TO ACCEPT!
YOU MUST LISTEN, SUPERMAN! THE NYRVNIANS MUST HAVE TIME TO DEVELOP!
JUST AS THE CAVEMAN'S WAR CLUB SLOWLY DEVELOPED INTO THE SCIENTIST'S LETHAL LASER!
CONSIDER OUR WORDS, SUPERMAN--
--WHILE I USE MY TRACKING POWER TO BRING THE REMNANTS OF THE TWO FLEETS TOGETHER AGAIN!
AFTER ALL THE YEARS I'VE KNOWN YOU, SATURN GIRL, I HAVE TO TRUST YOU!
BUT I DON'T LIKE THE SITUATION, AND IF THERE'S ANYTHING I CAN DO...
THERE IS NOTHING, SUPERMAN! FAREWELL...
I READ HIS MIND AS HE LEFT, LIGHTNING LAD--WE'RE SAFE!
HE WILL NOT INTERFERE!
BUT IF HE FINDS OUT THE WHOLE STORY... WHAT THEN?
6

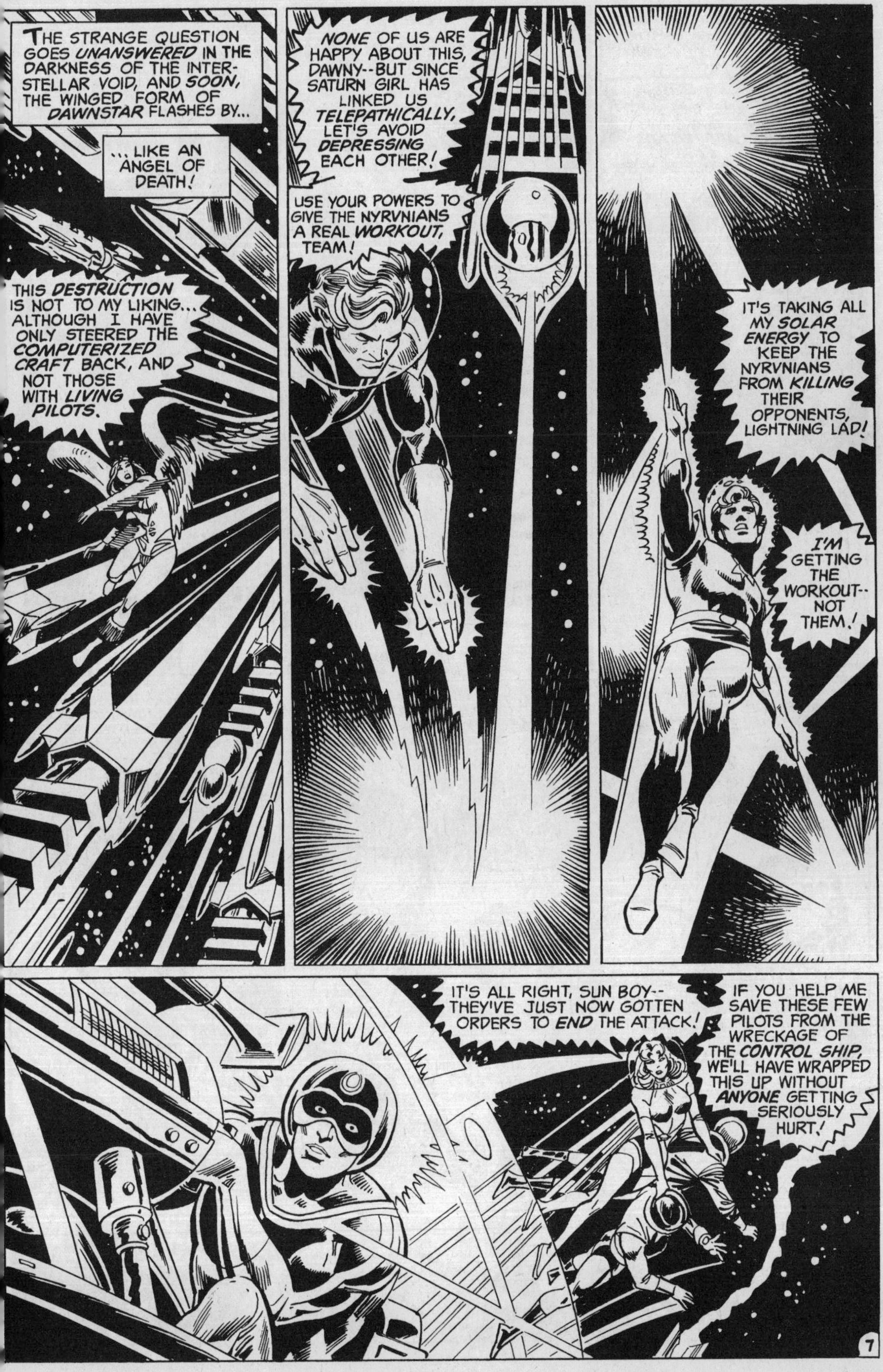
THE STRANGE QUESTION GOES UNANSWERED IN THE DARKNESS OF THE INTERSTELLAR VOID, AND SOON, THE WINGED FORM OF DAWNSTAR FLASHES BY...
...LIKE AN ANGEL OF DEATH!
THIS DESTRUCTION IS NOT TO MY LIKING... ALTHOUGH I HAVE ONLY STEERED THE COMPUTERIZED CRAFT BACK, AND NOT THOSE WITH LIVING PILOTS.
NONE OF US ARE HAPPY ABOUT THIS, DAWNY--BUT SINCE SATURN GIRL HAS LINKED US TELEPATHICALLY, LET'S AVOID DEPRESSING EACH OTHER!
USE YOUR POWERS TO GIVE THE NYRVNIANS A REAL WORKOUT, TEAM!
IT'S TAKING ALL MY SOLAR ENERGY TO KEEP THE NYRVNIANS FROM KILLING THEIR OPPONENTS, LIGHTNING LAD!
I'M GETTING THE WORKOUT--NOT THEM!
IT'S ALL RIGHT, SUN BOY--THEY'VE JUST NOW GOTTEN ORDERS TO END THE ATTACK!
IF YOU HELP ME SAVE THESE FEW PILOTS FROM THE WRECKAGE OF THE CONTROL SHIP, WE'LL HAVE WRAPPED THIS UP WITHOUT ANYONE GETTING SERIOUSLY HURT!
7

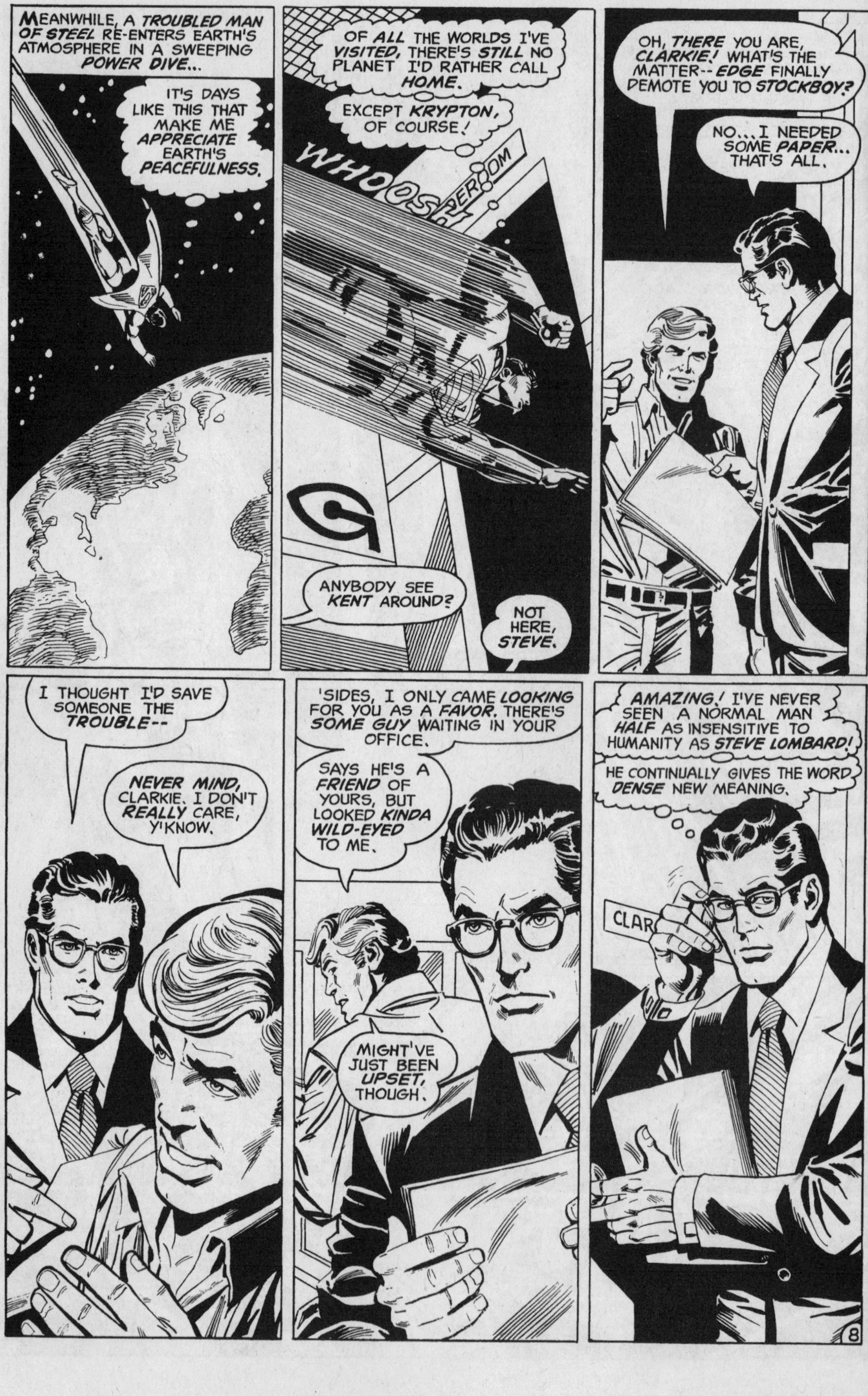

MEANWHILE, A TROUBLED MAN OF STEEL RE-ENTERS EARTH'S ATMOSPHERE IN A SWEEPING POWER DIVE...
IT'S DAYS LIKE THIS THAT MAKE ME APPRECIATE EARTH'S PEACEFULNESS.
OF ALL THE WORLDS I'VE VISITED, THERE'S STILL NO PLANET I'D RATHER CALL HOME.
EXCEPT KRYPTON, OF COURSE!
WHOOSH
ANYBODY SEE KENT AROUND?
NOT HERE, STEVE.
OH, THERE YOU ARE, CLARKIE! WHAT'S THE MATTER-- EDGE FINALLY DEMOTE YOU TO STOCKBOY?
NO... I NEEDED SOME PAPER... THAT'S ALL.
I THOUGHT I'D SAVE SOMEONE THE TROUBLE--
NEVER MIND, CLARKIE. I DON'T REALLY CARE, Y'KNOW.
'SIDES, I ONLY CAME LOOKING FOR YOU AS A FAVOR. THERE'S SOME GUY WAITING IN YOUR OFFICE.
SAYS HE'S A FRIEND OF YOURS, BUT LOOKED KINDA WILD-EYED TO ME.
MIGHT'VE JUST BEEN UPSET, THOUGH.
AMAZING! I'VE NEVER SEEN A NORMAL MAN HALF AS INSENSITIVE TO HUMANITY AS STEVE LOMBARD!
HE CONTINUALLY GIVES THE WORD DENSE NEW MEANING.
CLAR
8

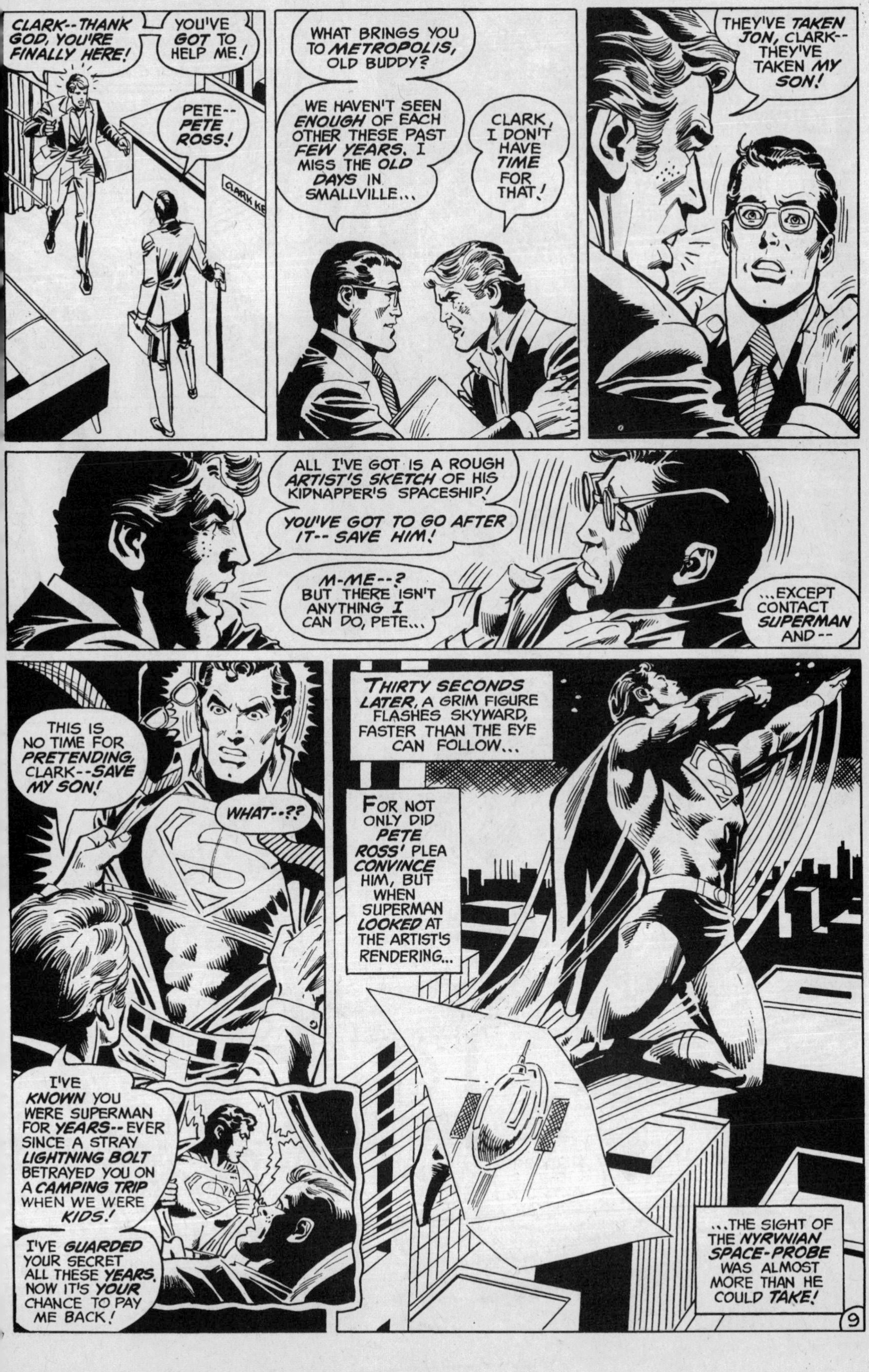
CLARK--THANK GOD, YOU'RE FINALLY HERE!
YOU'VE GOT TO HELP ME!
PETE--PETE ROSS!
CLARK KE
WHAT BRINGS YOU TO METROPOLIS, OLD BUDDY?
WE HAVEN'T SEEN ENOUGH OF EACH OTHER THESE PAST FEW YEARS. I MISS THE OLD DAYS IN SMALLVILLE...
CLARK, I DON'T HAVE TIME FOR THAT!
THEY'VE TAKEN JON, CLARK--THEY'VE TAKEN MY SON!
ALL I'VE GOT IS A ROUGH ARTIST'S SKETCH OF HIS KIDNAPPER'S SPACESHIP!
YOU'VE GOT TO GO AFTER IT-- SAVE HIM!
M-ME--? BUT THERE ISN'T ANYTHING I CAN DO, PETE...
...EXCEPT CONTACT SUPERMAN AND--
THIS IS NO TIME FOR PRETENDING, CLARK--SAVE MY SON!
WHAT--??
I'VE KNOWN YOU WERE SUPERMAN FOR YEARS-- EVER SINCE A STRAY LIGHTNING BOLT BETRAYED YOU ON A CAMPING TRIP WHEN WE WERE KIDS!
I'VE GUARDED YOUR SECRET ALL THESE YEARS. NOW IT'S YOUR CHANCE TO PAY ME BACK!
THIRTY SECONDS LATER, A GRIM FIGURE FLASHES SKYWARD, FASTER THAN THE EYE CAN FOLLOW...
FOR NOT ONLY DID PETE ROSS' PLEA CONVINCE HIM, BUT WHEN SUPERMAN LOOKED AT THE ARTIST'S RENDERING...
...THE SIGHT OF THE NYRVNIAN SPACE-PROBE WAS ALMOST MORE THAN HE COULD TAKE!
9

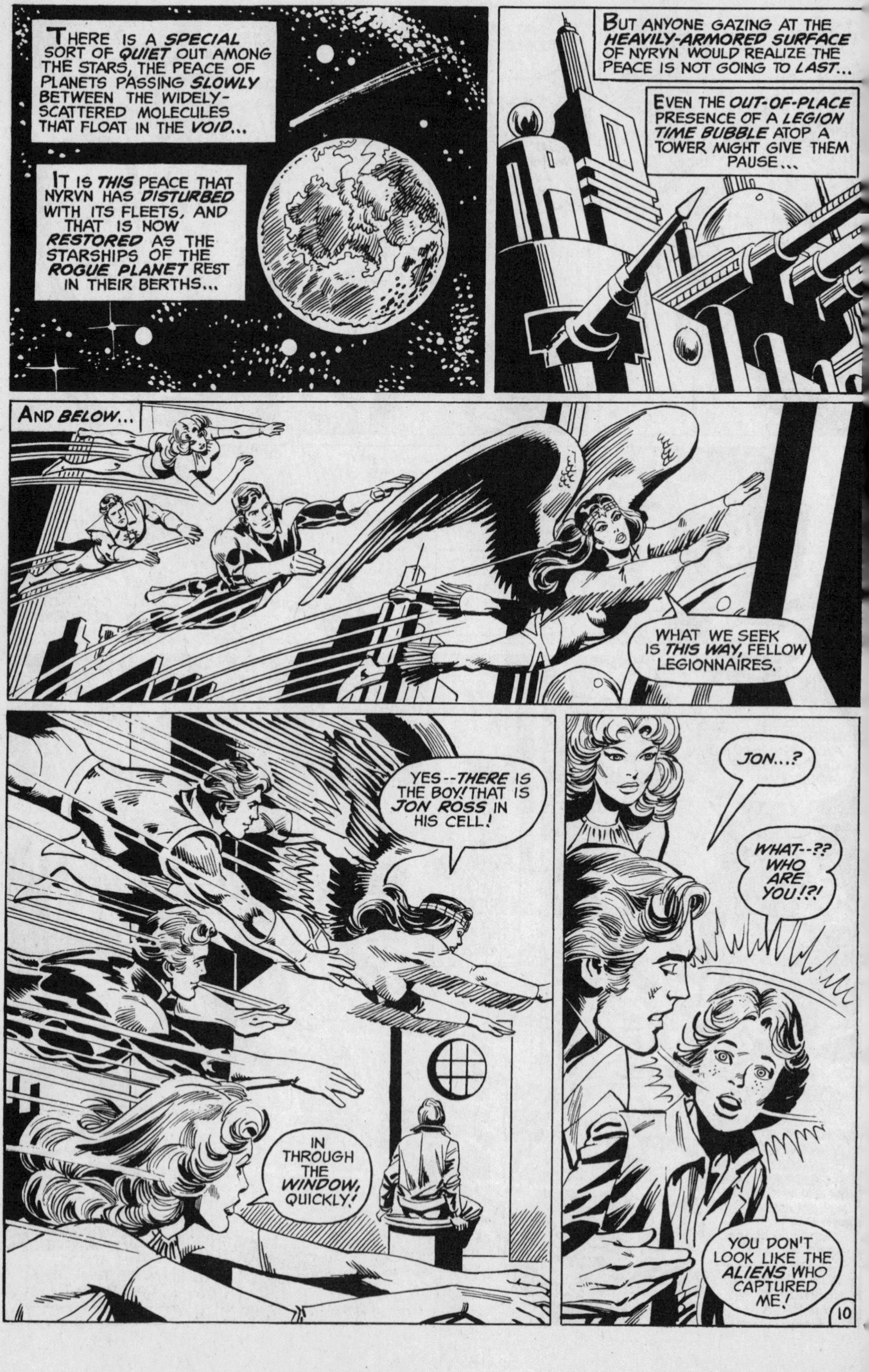
THERE IS A SPECIAL SORT OF QUIET OUT AMONG THE STARS, THE PEACE OF PLANETS PASSING SLOWLY BETWEEN THE WIDELY-SCATTERED MOLECULES THAT FLOAT IN THE VOID...
IT IS THIS PEACE THAT NYRVN HAS DISTURBED WITH ITS FLEETS, AND THAT IS NOW RESTORED AS THE STARSHIPS OF THE ROGUE PLANET REST IN THEIR BERTHS...
BUT ANYONE GAZING AT THE HEAVILY-ARMORED SURFACE OF NYRYN WOULD REALIZE THE PEACE IS NOT GOING TO LAST...
EVEN THE OUT-OF-PLACE PRESENCE OF A LEGION TIME BUBBLE ATOP A TOWER MIGHT GIVE THEM PAUSE...
AND BELOW...
WHAT WE SEEK IS THIS WAY, FELLOW LEGIONNAIRES.
YES--THERE IS THE BOY! THAT IS JON ROSS IN HIS CELL!
IN THROUGH THE WINDOW, QUICKLY!
JON...?
WHAT--?? WHO ARE YOU!?!
YOU DON'T LOOK LIKE THE ALIENS WHO CAPTURED ME!
10

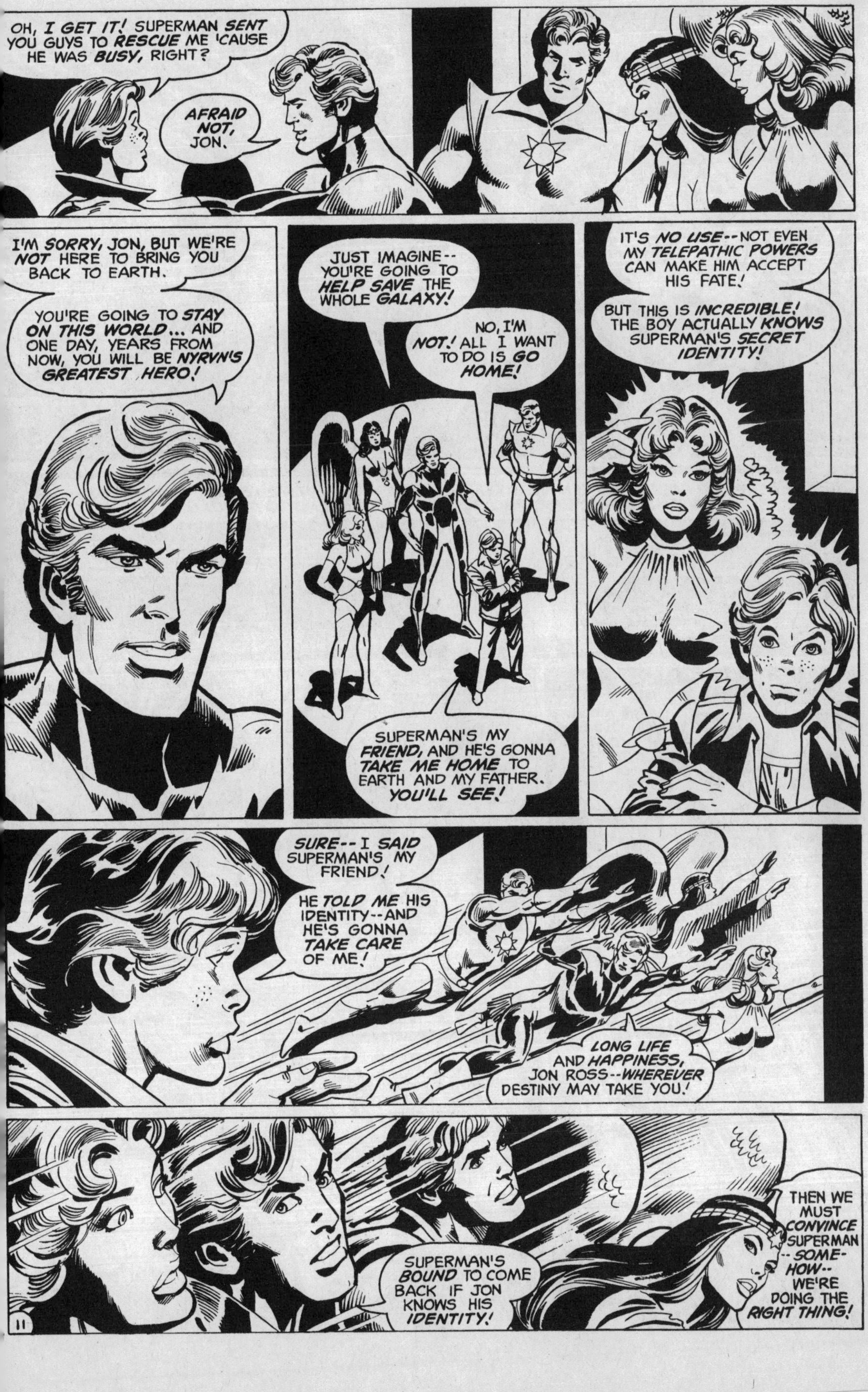
OH, I GET IT! SUPERMAN SENT YOU GUYS TO RESCUE ME 'CAUSE HE WAS BUSY, RIGHT?
AFRAID NOT, JON.
I'M SORRY, JON, BUT WE'RE NOT HERE TO BRING YOU BACK TO EARTH.
YOU'RE GOING TO STAY ON THIS WORLD... AND ONE DAY, YEARS FROM NOW, YOU WILL BE NYRVN'S GREATEST HERO!
JUST IMAGINE-- YOU'RE GOING TO HELP SAVE THE WHOLE GALAXY!
NO, I'M NOT! ALL I WANT TO DO IS GO HOME!
SUPERMAN'S MY FRIEND, AND HE'S GONNA TAKE ME HOME TO EARTH AND MY FATHER. YOU'LL SEE!
IT'S NO USE--NOT EVEN MY TELEPATHIC POWERS CAN MAKE HIM ACCEPT HIS FATE!
BUT THIS IS INCREDIBLE! THE BOY ACTUALLY KNOWS SUPERMAN'S SECRET IDENTITY!
SURE--I SAID SUPERMAN'S MY FRIEND!
HE TOLD ME HIS IDENTITY--AND HE'S GONNA TAKE CARE OF ME!
LONG LIFE AND HAPPINESS, JON ROSS--WHEREVER DESTINY MAY TAKE YOU!
SUPERMAN'S BOUND TO COME BACK IF JON KNOWS HIS IDENTITY!
THEN WE MUST CONVINCE SUPERMAN --SOME-HOW-- WE'RE DOING THE RIGHT THING!
11

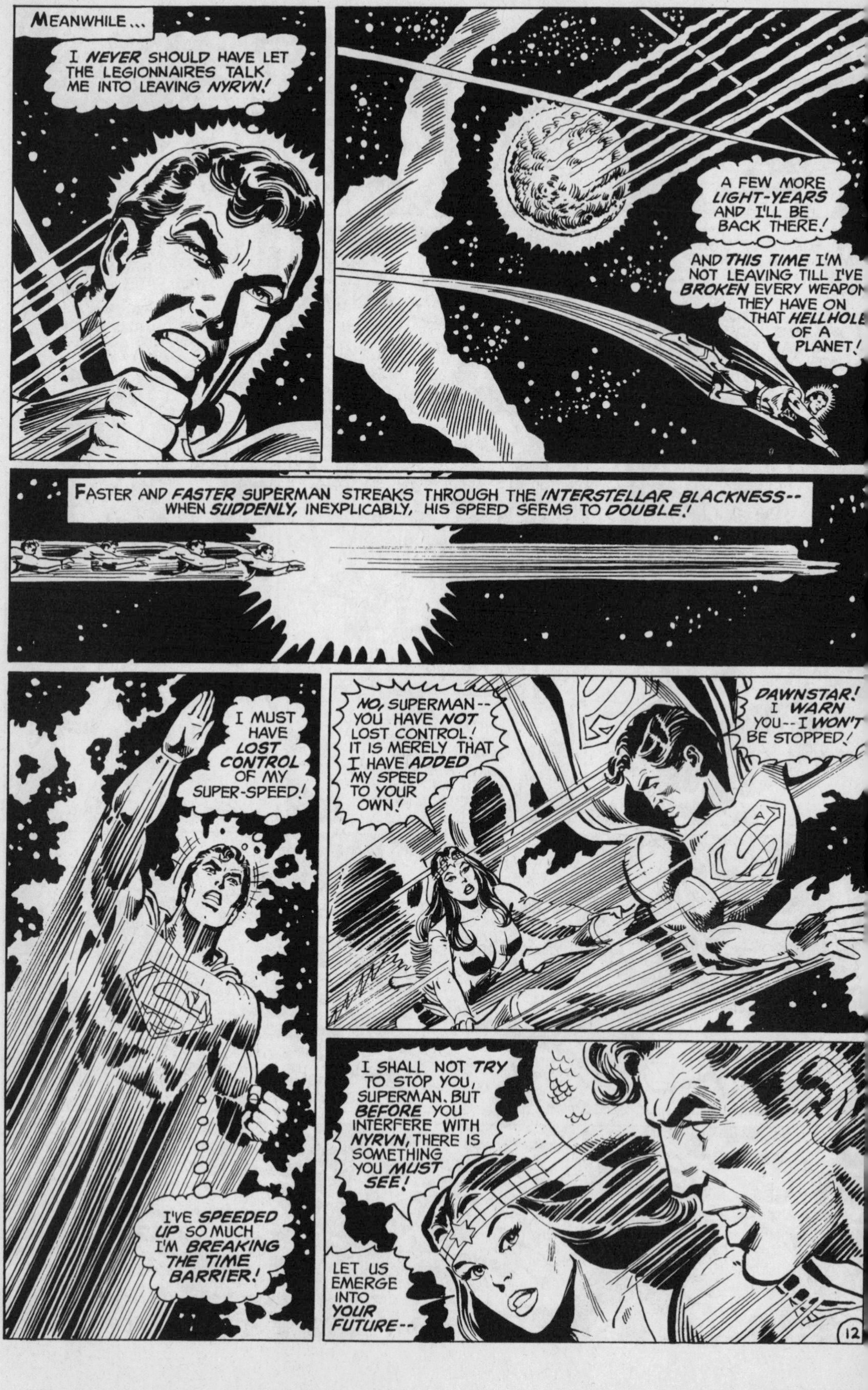
MEANWHILE...
I NEVER SHOULD HAVE LET THE LEGIONNAIRES TALK ME INTO LEAVING NYRVN!
A FEW MORE LIGHT-YEARS AND I'LL BE BACK THERE!
AND THIS TIME I'M NOT LEAVING TILL I'VE BROKEN EVERY WEAPON THEY HAVE ON THAT HELLHOLE OF A PLANET!
FASTER AND FASTER SUPERMAN STREAKS THROUGH THE INTERSTELLAR BLACKNESS-- WHEN SUDDENLY, INEXPLICABLY, HIS SPEED SEEMS TO DOUBLE!
I MUST HAVE LOST CONTROL OF MY SUPER-SPEED!
I'VE SPEEDED UP SO MUCH I'M BREAKING THE TIME BARRIER!
NO, SUPERMAN-- YOU HAVE NOT LOST CONTROL! IT IS MERELY THAT I HAVE ADDED MY SPEED TO YOUR OWN!
DAWNSTAR! I WARN YOU--I WON'T BE STOPPED!
I SHALL NOT TRY TO STOP YOU, SUPERMAN. BUT BEFORE YOU INTERFERE WITH NYRVN, THERE IS SOMETHING YOU MUST SEE!
LET US EMERGE INTO YOUR FUTURE--
12

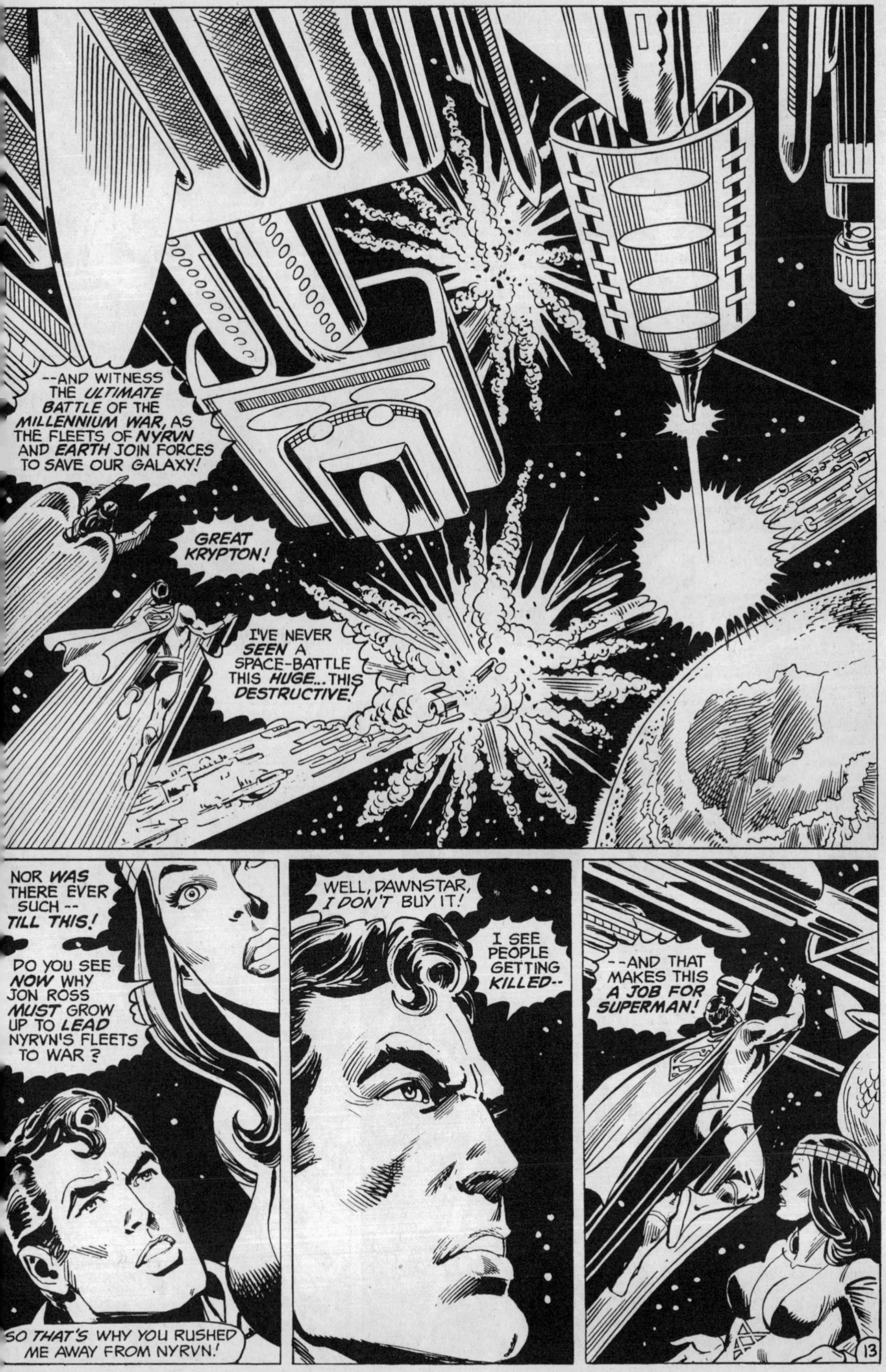
--AND WITNESS THE ULTIMATE BATTLE OF THE MILLENNIUM WAR, AS THE FLEETS OF NYRVN AND EARTH JOIN FORCES TO SAVE OUR GALAXY!
GREAT KRYPTON!
I'VE NEVER SEEN A SPACE-BATTLE THIS HUGE... THIS DESTRUCTIVE!
NOR WAS THERE EVER SUCH -- TILL THIS!
DO YOU SEE NOW WHY JON ROSS MUST GROW UP TO LEAD NYRVN'S FLEETS TO WAR?
SO THAT'S WHY YOU RUSHED ME AWAY FROM NYRVN!
WELL, DAWNSTAR, I DON'T BUY IT!
I SEE PEOPLE GETTING KILLED--
--AND THAT MAKES THIS A JOB FOR SUPERMAN!
13

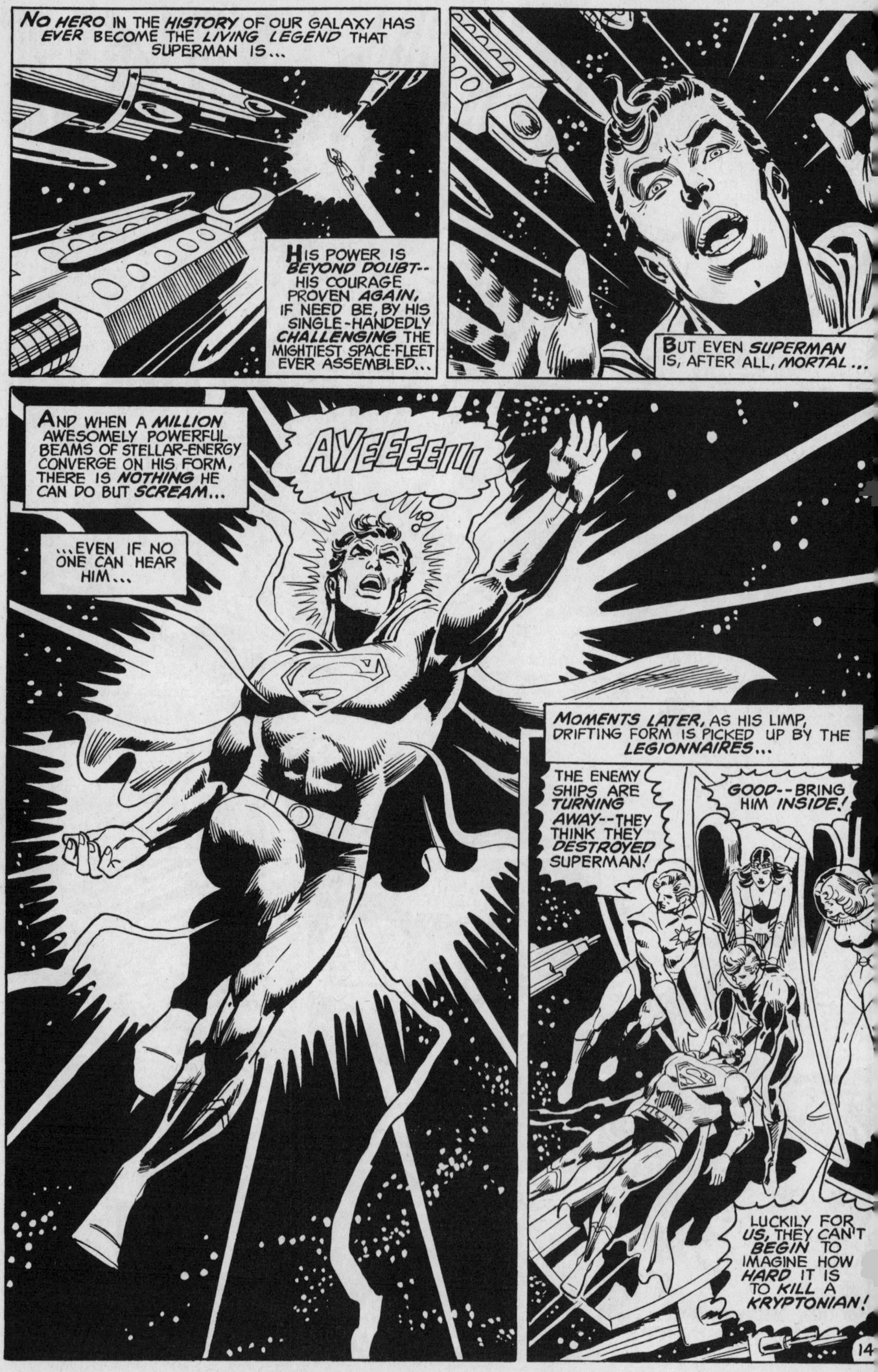
NO HERO IN THE HISTORY OF OUR GALAXY HAS EVER BECOME THE LIVING LEGEND THAT SUPERMAN IS...
HIS POWER IS BEYOND DOUBT-- HIS COURAGE PROVEN AGAIN, IF NEED BE, BY HIS SINGLE-HANDEDLY CHALLENGING THE MIGHTIEST SPACE-FLEET EVER ASSEMBLED...
BUT EVEN SUPERMAN IS, AFTER ALL, MORTAL...
AND WHEN A MILLION AWESOMELY POWERFUL BEAMS OF STELLAR-ENERGY CONVERGE ON HIS FORM, THERE IS NOTHING HE CAN DO BUT SCREAM...
AYEEEEE!!!
...EVEN IF NO ONE CAN HEAR HIM...
MOMENTS LATER, AS HIS LIMP, DRIFTING FORM IS PICKED UP BY THE LEGIONNAIRES...
THE ENEMY SHIPS ARE TURNING AWAY--THEY THINK THEY DESTROYED SUPERMAN!
GOOD--BRING HIM INSIDE!
LUCKILY FOR US, THEY CAN'T BEGIN TO IMAGINE HOW HARD IT IS TO KILL A KRYPTONIAN!
14

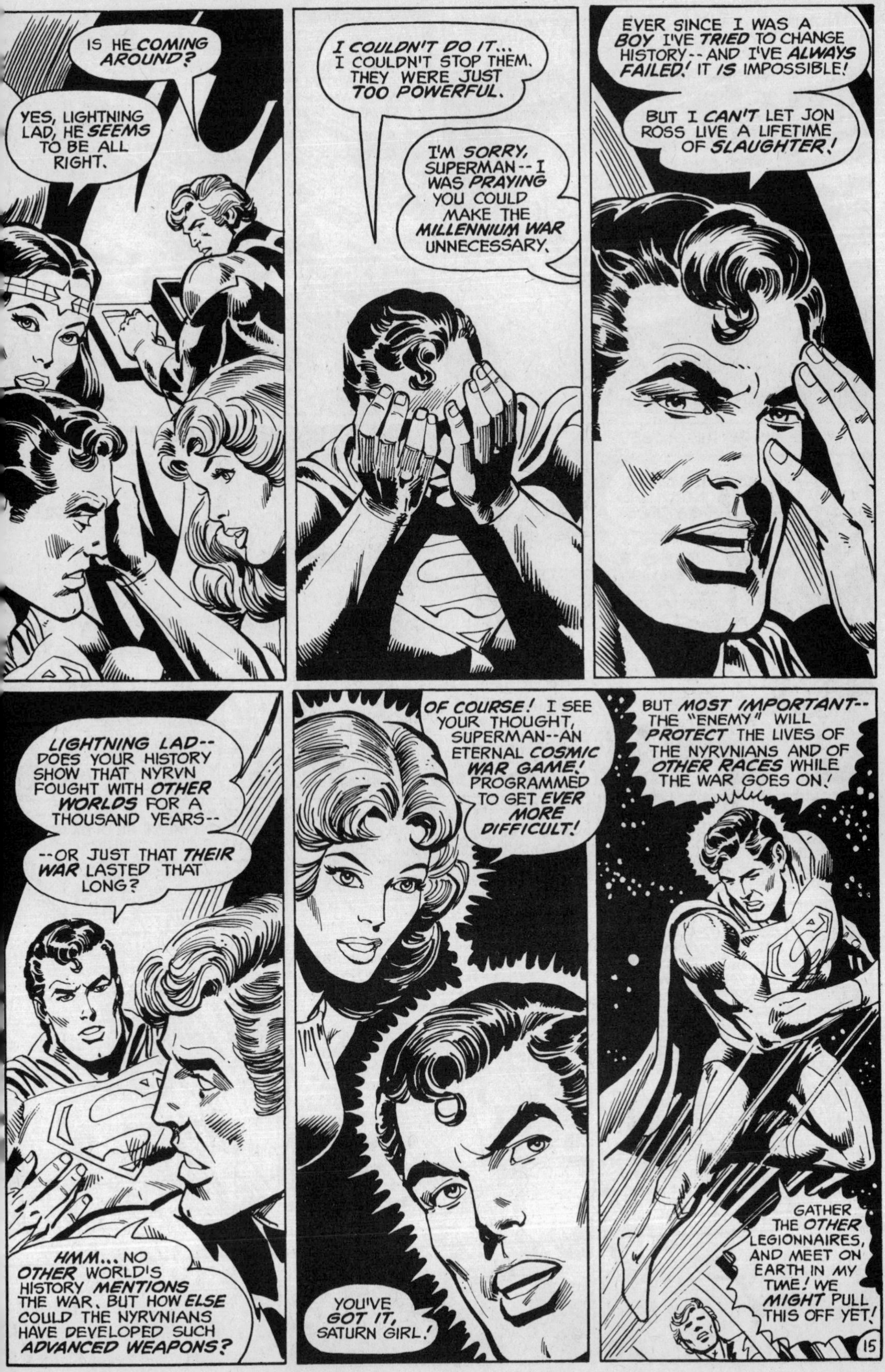
IS HE COMING AROUND?
YES, LIGHTNING LAD, HE SEEMS TO BE ALL RIGHT.
I COULDN'T DO IT... I COULDN'T STOP THEM. THEY WERE JUST TOO POWERFUL.
I'M SORRY, SUPERMAN -- I WAS PRAYING YOU COULD MAKE THE MILLENNIUM WAR UNNECESSARY.
EVER SINCE I WAS A BOY I'VE TRIED TO CHANGE HISTORY -- AND I'VE ALWAYS FAILED! IT IS IMPOSSIBLE!
BUT I CAN'T LET JON ROSS LIVE A LIFETIME OF SLAUGHTER!
LIGHTNING LAD -- DOES YOUR HISTORY SHOW THAT NYRVN FOUGHT WITH OTHER WORLDS FOR A THOUSAND YEARS --
-- OR JUST THAT THEIR WAR LASTED THAT LONG?
HMM... NO OTHER WORLD'S HISTORY MENTIONS THE WAR. BUT HOW ELSE COULD THE NYRVNIANS HAVE DEVELOPED SUCH ADVANCED WEAPONS?
OF COURSE! I SEE YOUR THOUGHT, SUPERMAN -- AN ETERNAL COSMIC WAR GAME! PROGRAMMED TO GET EVER MORE DIFFICULT!
YOU'VE GOT IT, SATURN GIRL!
BUT MOST IMPORTANT -- THE "ENEMY" WILL PROTECT THE LIVES OF THE NYRVNIANS AND OF OTHER RACES WHILE THE WAR GOES ON!
GATHER THE OTHER LEGIONNAIRES, AND MEET ON EARTH IN MY TIME! WE MIGHT PULL THIS OFF YET!
15

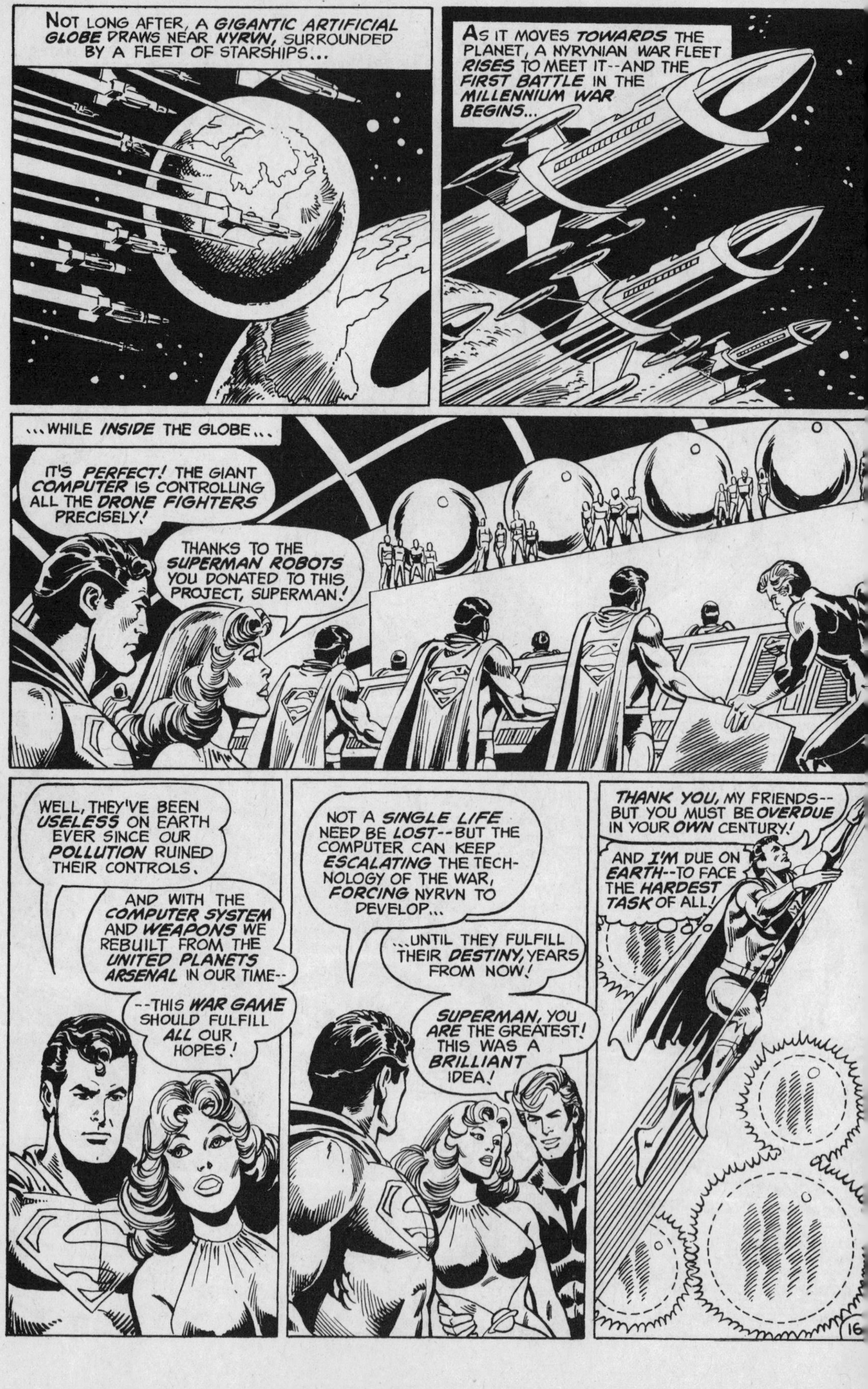
NOT LONG AFTER, A GIGANTIC ARTIFICIAL GLOBE DRAWS NEAR NYRVN, SURROUNDED BY A FLEET OF STARSHIPS...
AS IT MOVES TOWARDS THE PLANET, A NYRVNIAN WAR FLEET RISES TO MEET IT--AND THE FIRST BATTLE IN THE MILLENNIUM WAR BEGINS...
...WHILE INSIDE THE GLOBE...
IT'S PERFECT! THE GIANT COMPUTER IS CONTROLLING ALL THE DRONE FIGHTERS PRECISELY!
THANKS TO THE SUPERMAN ROBOTS YOU DONATED TO THIS PROJECT, SUPERMAN!
WELL, THEY'VE BEEN USELESS ON EARTH EVER SINCE OUR POLLUTION RUINED THEIR CONTROLS.
AND WITH THE COMPUTER SYSTEM AND WEAPONS WE REBUILT FROM THE UNITED PLANETS ARSENAL IN OUR TIME--
--THIS WAR GAME SHOULD FULFILL ALL OUR HOPES!
NOT A SINGLE LIFE NEED BE LOST--BUT THE COMPUTER CAN KEEP ESCALATING THE TECHNOLOGY OF THE WAR, FORCING NYRVN TO DEVELOP...
...UNTIL THEY FULFILL THEIR DESTINY, YEARS FROM NOW!
SUPERMAN, YOU ARE THE GREATEST! THIS WAS A BRILLIANT IDEA!
THANK YOU, MY FRIENDS--BUT YOU MUST BE OVERDUE IN YOUR OWN CENTURY!
AND I'M DUE ON EARTH--TO FACE THE HARDEST TASK OF ALL!
16

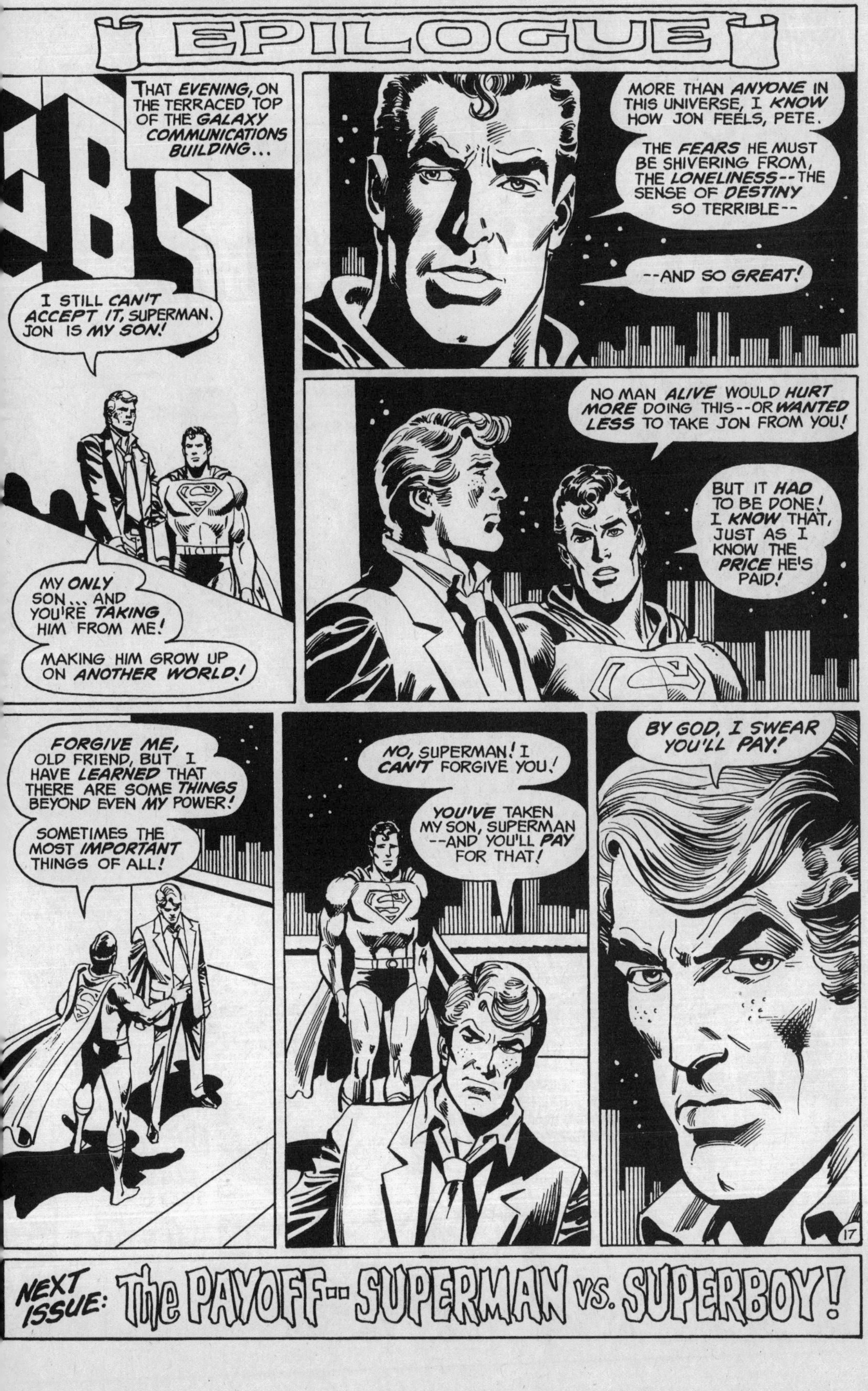
EPILOGUE
THAT EVENING, ON THE TERRACED TOP OF THE GALAXY COMMUNICATIONS BUILDING...
GBS
I STILL CAN'T ACCEPT IT, SUPERMAN. JON IS MY SON!
MY ONLY SON... AND YOU'RE TAKING HIM FROM ME!
MAKING HIM GROW UP ON ANOTHER WORLD!
MORE THAN ANYONE IN THIS UNIVERSE, I KNOW HOW JON FEELS, PETE.
THE FEARS HE MUST BE SHIVERING FROM, THE LONELINESS--THE SENSE OF DESTINY SO TERRIBLE--
--AND SO GREAT!
NO MAN ALIVE WOULD HURT MORE DOING THIS--OR WANTED LESS TO TAKE JON FROM YOU!
BUT IT HAD TO BE DONE! I KNOW THAT, JUST AS I KNOW THE PRICE HE'S PAID!
FORGIVE ME, OLD FRIEND, BUT I HAVE LEARNED THAT THERE ARE SOME THINGS BEYOND EVEN MY POWER!
SOMETIMES THE MOST IMPORTANT THINGS OF ALL!
NO, SUPERMAN! I CAN'T FORGIVE YOU!
YOU'VE TAKEN MY SON, SUPERMAN --AND YOU'LL PAY FOR THAT!
BY GOD, I SWEAR YOU'LL PAY!
17
NEXT ISSUE: The PAYOFF-- SUPERMAN vs. SUPERBOY!

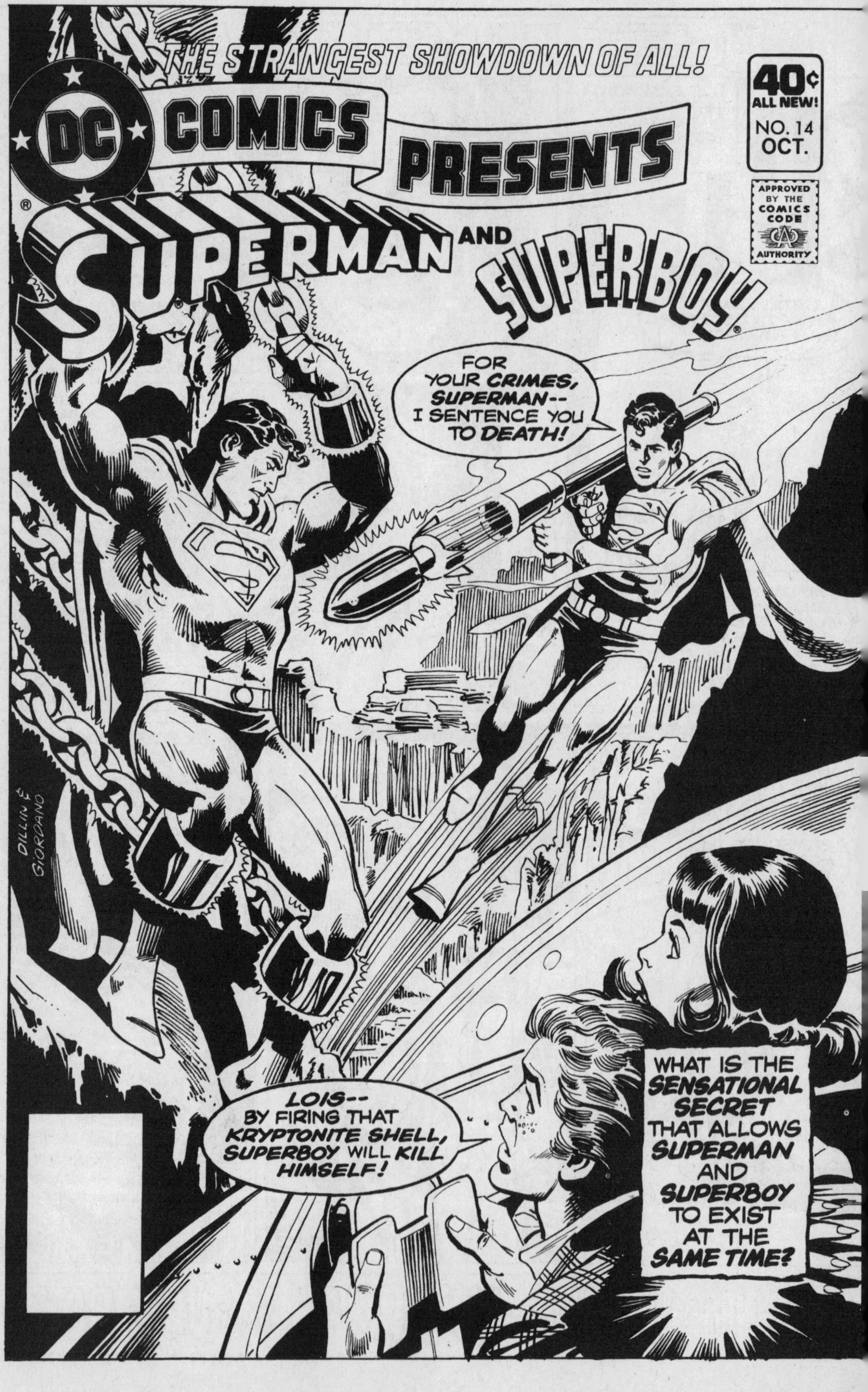
THE STRANGEST SHOWDOWN OF ALL!
DC COMICS PRESENTS
40¢ ALL NEW!
NO. 14 OCT.
APPROVED BY THE COMICS CODE AUTHORITY
SUPERMAN AND SUPERBOY
FOR YOUR CRIMES, SUPERMAN-- I SENTENCE YOU TO DEATH!
DILLIN & GIORDANO
LOIS-- BY FIRING THAT KRYPTONITE SHELL, SUPERBOY WILL KILL HIMSELF!
WHAT IS THE SENSATIONAL SECRET THAT ALLOWS SUPERMAN AND SUPERBOY TO EXIST AT THE SAME TIME?

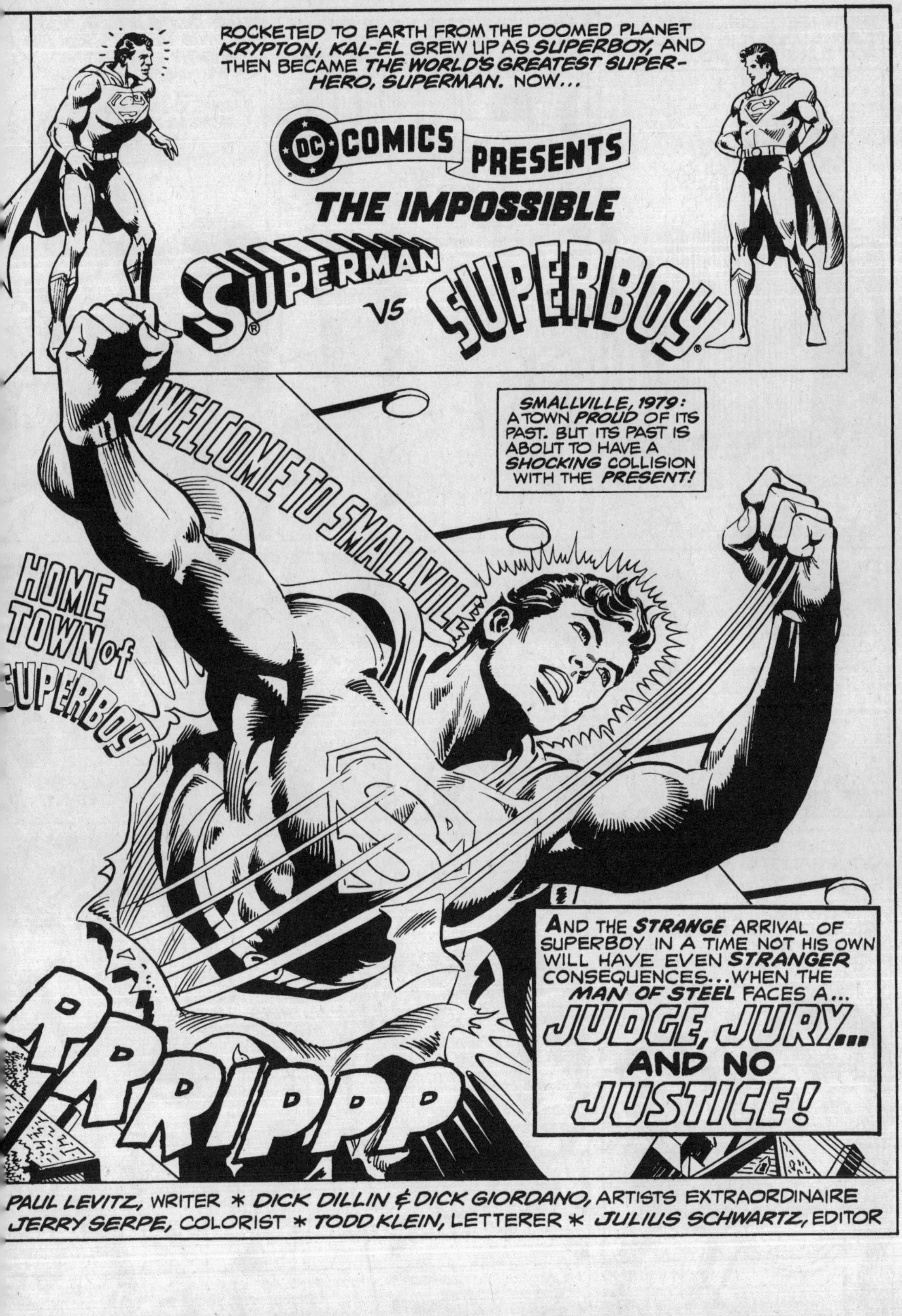
ROCKETED TO EARTH FROM THE DOOMED PLANET KRYPTON, KAL-EL GREW UP AS SUPERBOY, AND THEN BECAME THE WORLD'S GREATEST SUPER-HERO, SUPERMAN. NOW...
DC COMICS PRESENTS
THE IMPOSSIBLE
SUPERMAN VS SUPERBOY
WELCOME TO SMALLVILLE
HOME TOWN of SUPERBOY
SMALLVILLE, 1979: A TOWN PROUD OF ITS PAST. BUT ITS PAST IS ABOUT TO HAVE A SHOCKING COLLISION WITH THE PRESENT!
RRRIPPP
AND THE STRANGE ARRIVAL OF SUPERBOY IN A TIME NOT HIS OWN WILL HAVE EVEN STRANGER CONSEQUENCES...WHEN THE MAN OF STEEL FACES A...
JUDGE, JURY... AND NO JUSTICE!
PAUL LEVITZ, WRITER * DICK DILLIN & DICK GIORDANO, ARTISTS EXTRAORDINAIRE
JERRY SERPE, COLORIST * TODD KLEIN, LETTERER * JULIUS SCHWARTZ, EDITOR

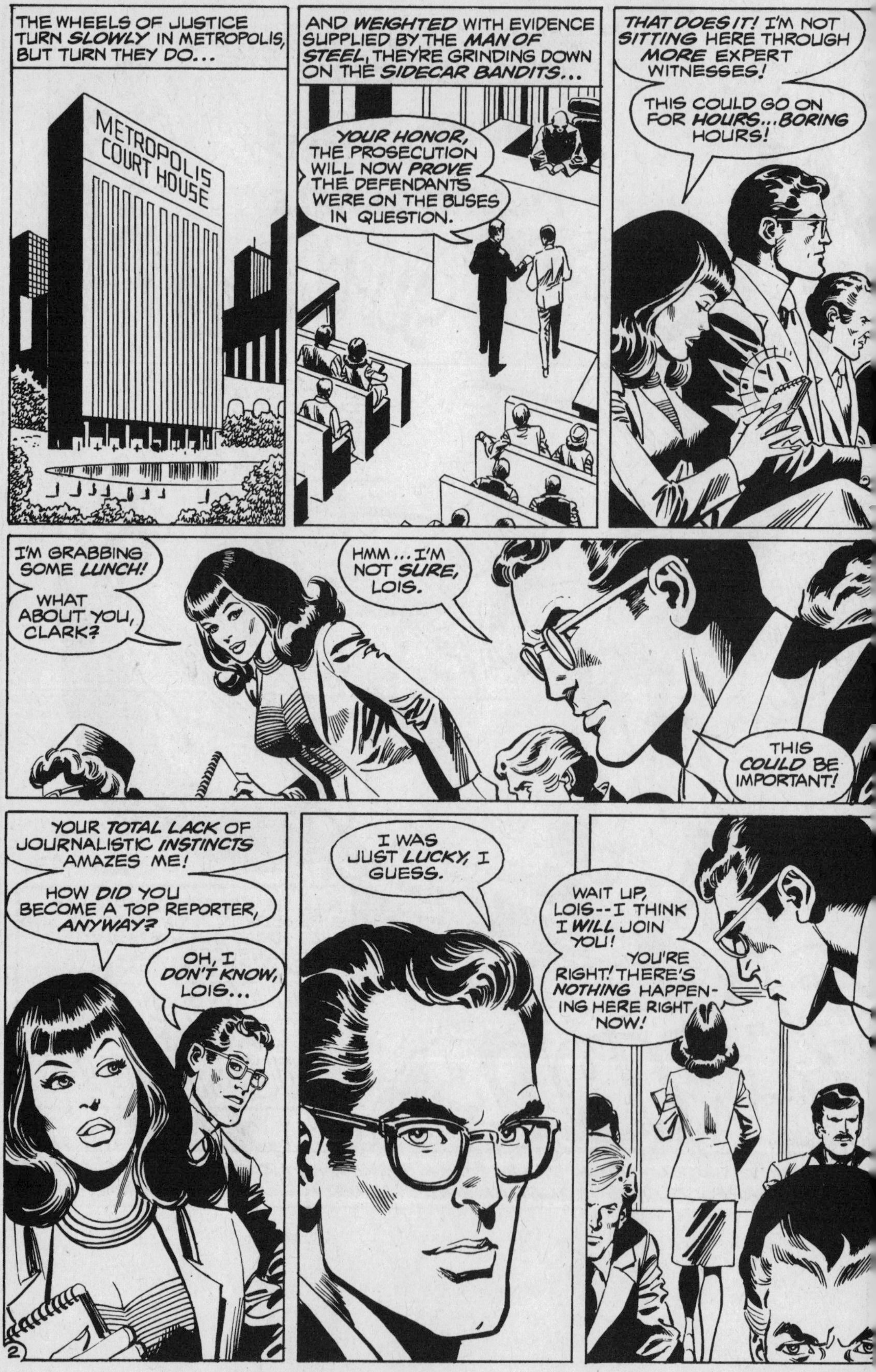
THE WHEELS OF JUSTICE TURN SLOWLY IN METROPOLIS, BUT TURN THEY DO...
METROPOLIS COURT HOUSE
AND WEIGHTED WITH EVIDENCE SUPPLIED BY THE MAN OF STEEL, THEY'RE GRINDING DOWN ON THE SIDECAR BANDITS...
YOUR HONOR, THE PROSECUTION WILL NOW PROVE THE DEFENDANTS WERE ON THE BUSES IN QUESTION.
THAT DOES IT! I'M NOT SITTING HERE THROUGH MORE EXPERT WITNESSES!
THIS COULD GO ON FOR HOURS...BORING HOURS!
I'M GRABBING SOME LUNCH!
WHAT ABOUT YOU, CLARK?
HMM...I'M NOT SURE, LOIS.
THIS COULD BE IMPORTANT!
YOUR TOTAL LACK OF JOURNALISTIC INSTINCTS AMAZES ME!
HOW DID YOU BECOME A TOP REPORTER, ANYWAY?
OH, I DON'T KNOW, LOIS...
I WAS JUST LUCKY, I GUESS.
WAIT UP, LOIS--I THINK I WILL JOIN YOU!
YOU'RE RIGHT! THERE'S NOTHING HAPPENING HERE RIGHT NOW!
2

KWAM

WRONG, CLARK KENT!

THERE *IS* SOMETHING HAPPENING HERE!

AND IT'S GOING TO HAPPEN TO *YOU!*

SUPERBOY--??

...THAT'S *IMPOSSIBLE!*

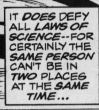

IT *DOES* DEFY ALL *LAWS OF SCIENCE*--FOR CERTAINLY THE *SAME* PERSON CAN'T BE IN *TWO* PLACES AT THE *SAME* TIME...

BUT TO ALL APPEARANCES, THAT'S *EXACTLY* WHAT'S OCCURRING!

THUD

THIS IS *INCREDIBLE!*

THAT CAN'T BE *SUPERBOY* BECAUSE *I'M SUPERMAN*--AND WE CAN'T *BOTH* BE HERE--NOT UNLESS *TIME'S* GONE MAD!

BUT THAT *PUNCH* HAD REAL *SUPER-STRENGTH* BEHIND IT--AND THAT MEANS *CLARK KENT* HAS TO *VANISH* IN THIS RUBBLE--

--SO I CAN FLY OUT OF THE COURT-ROOM AT *SUPER-SPEED*--

"--AND RETURN AS *SUPERMAN!*"

FIRST SUPERBOY, NOW *YOU*, SUPERMAN! WHAT'S GOING ON?

I'M *NOT SURE*, LOIS.

BUT I'M GOING TO *FIND OUT*--COUNT ON IT!

③

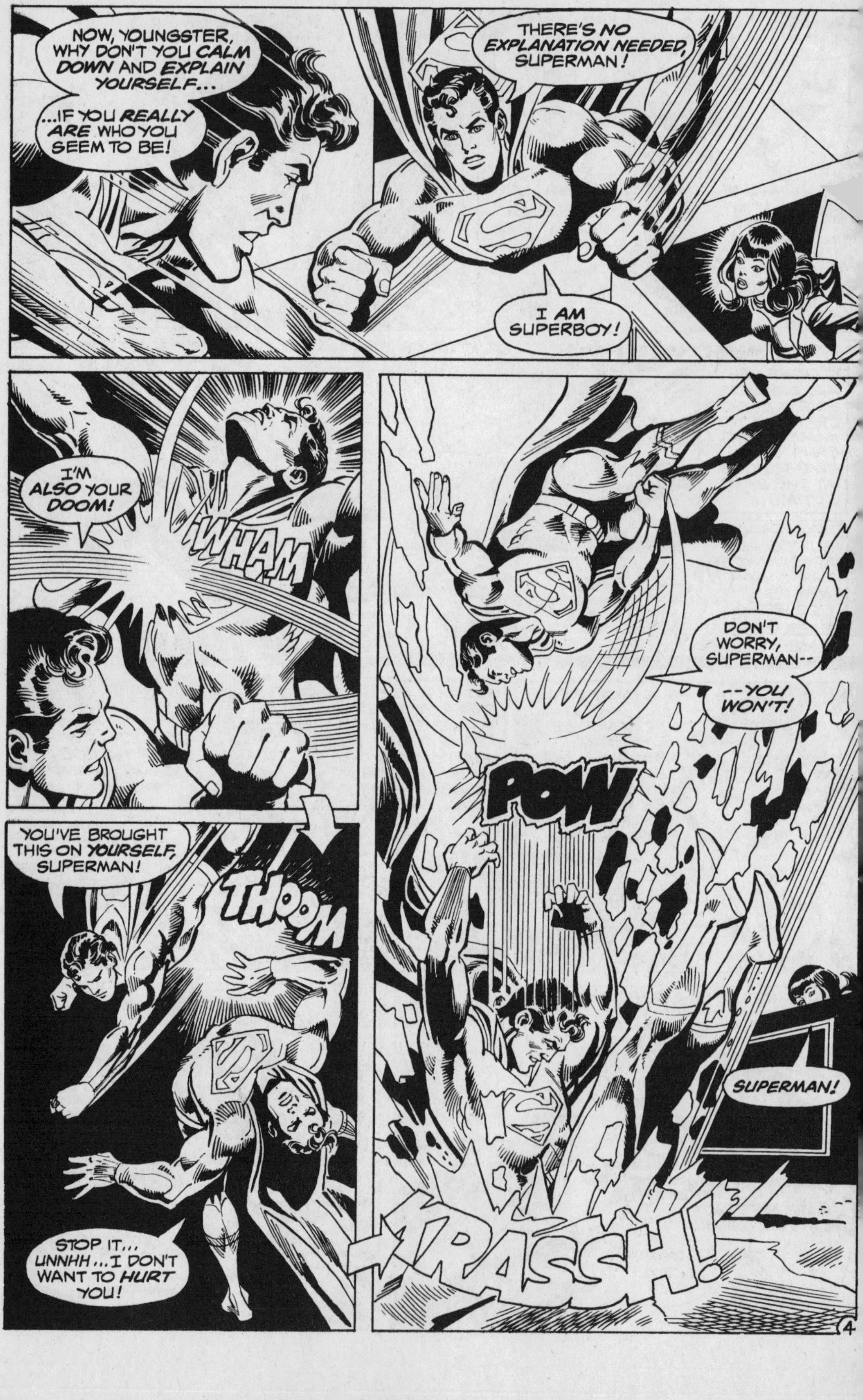
NOW, YOUNGSTER, WHY DON'T YOU CALM DOWN AND EXPLAIN YOURSELF...
...IF YOU REALLY ARE WHO YOU SEEM TO BE!
THERE'S NO EXPLANATION NEEDED, SUPERMAN!
I AM SUPERBOY!
I'M ALSO YOUR DOOM!
WHAM
YOU'VE BROUGHT THIS ON YOURSELF, SUPERMAN!
THOOM
STOP IT... UNNHH... I DON'T WANT TO HURT YOU!
DON'T WORRY, SUPERMAN--
--YOU WON'T!
POW
SUPERMAN!
KRASSH!
4

ARE YOU HURT?

LOIS-- GET BACK!

SHE'S COMING OUT OF THE *JURY BOX* TO *HELP* YOU, SUPERMAN.

AND, BELIEVE ME, YOU'LL *NEED* THAT HELP! BUT NOT NOW-- NOT *YET!*

BECAUSE SHE'S GIVEN *ME* AN *IDEA*-- A *VERY IMPORTANT* IDEA!

I'M *LEAVING*, SUPERMAN--BUT I'LL BE *BACK*.

BACK TO *SETTLE* OUR *ACCOUNT!*

SMASH

SUPERMAN-- AREN'T YOU GOING TO *CHASE* HIM?

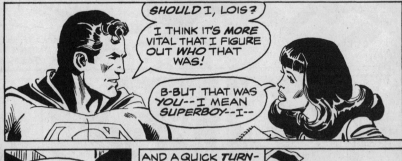

SHOULD I, LOIS?

I THINK IT'S *MORE* VITAL THAT I FIGURE OUT *WHO* THAT WAS!

B-BUT THAT WAS *YOU*-- I MEAN SUPERBOY--I--

YOU'RE GETTING THE *POINT*, LOIS!

WHOOSH

AND A QUICK *TURN-AROUND* LATER...

IT'S *SIMPLER* TO *DRILL* BACK *UNDER* THE RUBBLE THAN TO *SNEAK* IN AT SUPER-SPEED. AND IT *IS* TIME FOR CLARK TO MAKE HIS *REAPPEARANCE*...

UH, LOIS...?

CLARK--ARE YOU ALL *RIGHT?*

WELL....I *COULD* USE A HAND...

5

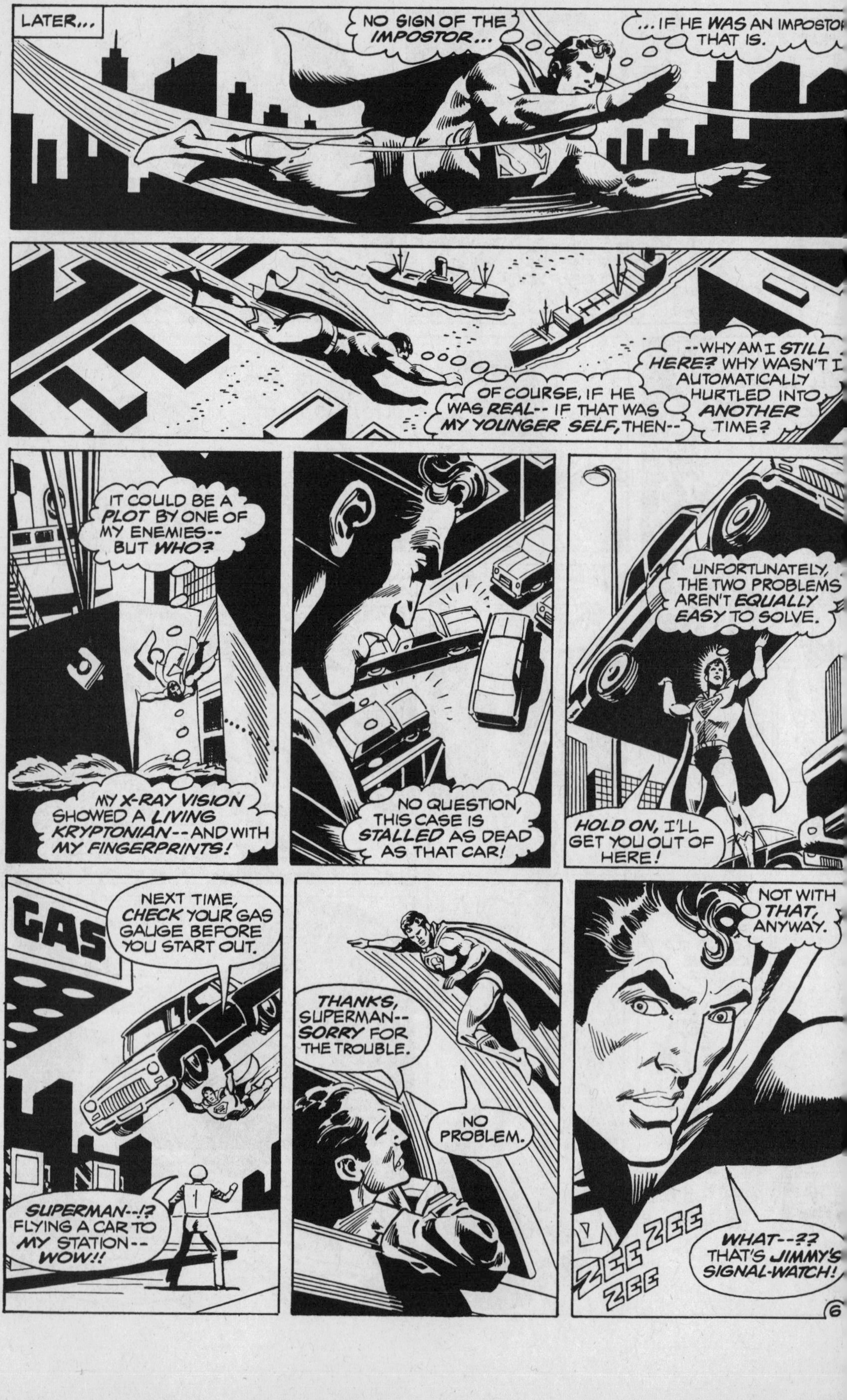
LATER...
NO SIGN OF THE IMPOSTOR...
...IF HE WAS AN IMPOSTOR THAT IS.
OF COURSE, IF HE WAS REAL-- IF THAT WAS MY YOUNGER SELF, THEN--
--WHY AM I STILL HERE? WHY WASN'T I AUTOMATICALLY HURTLED INTO ANOTHER TIME?
IT COULD BE A PLOT BY ONE OF MY ENEMIES-- BUT WHO?
MY X-RAY VISION SHOWED A LIVING KRYPTONIAN--AND WITH MY FINGERPRINTS!
NO QUESTION, THIS CASE IS STALLED AS DEAD AS THAT CAR!
UNFORTUNATELY, THE TWO PROBLEMS AREN'T EQUALLY EASY TO SOLVE.
HOLD ON, I'LL GET YOU OUT OF HERE!
GAS
NEXT TIME, CHECK YOUR GAS GAUGE BEFORE YOU START OUT.
SUPERMAN--!? FLYING A CAR TO MY STATION-- WOW!!
THANKS, SUPERMAN-- SORRY FOR THE TROUBLE.
NO PROBLEM.
NOT WITH THAT, ANYWAY.
ZEE ZEE ZEE
WHAT--?? THAT'S JIMMY'S SIGNAL-WATCH!
6

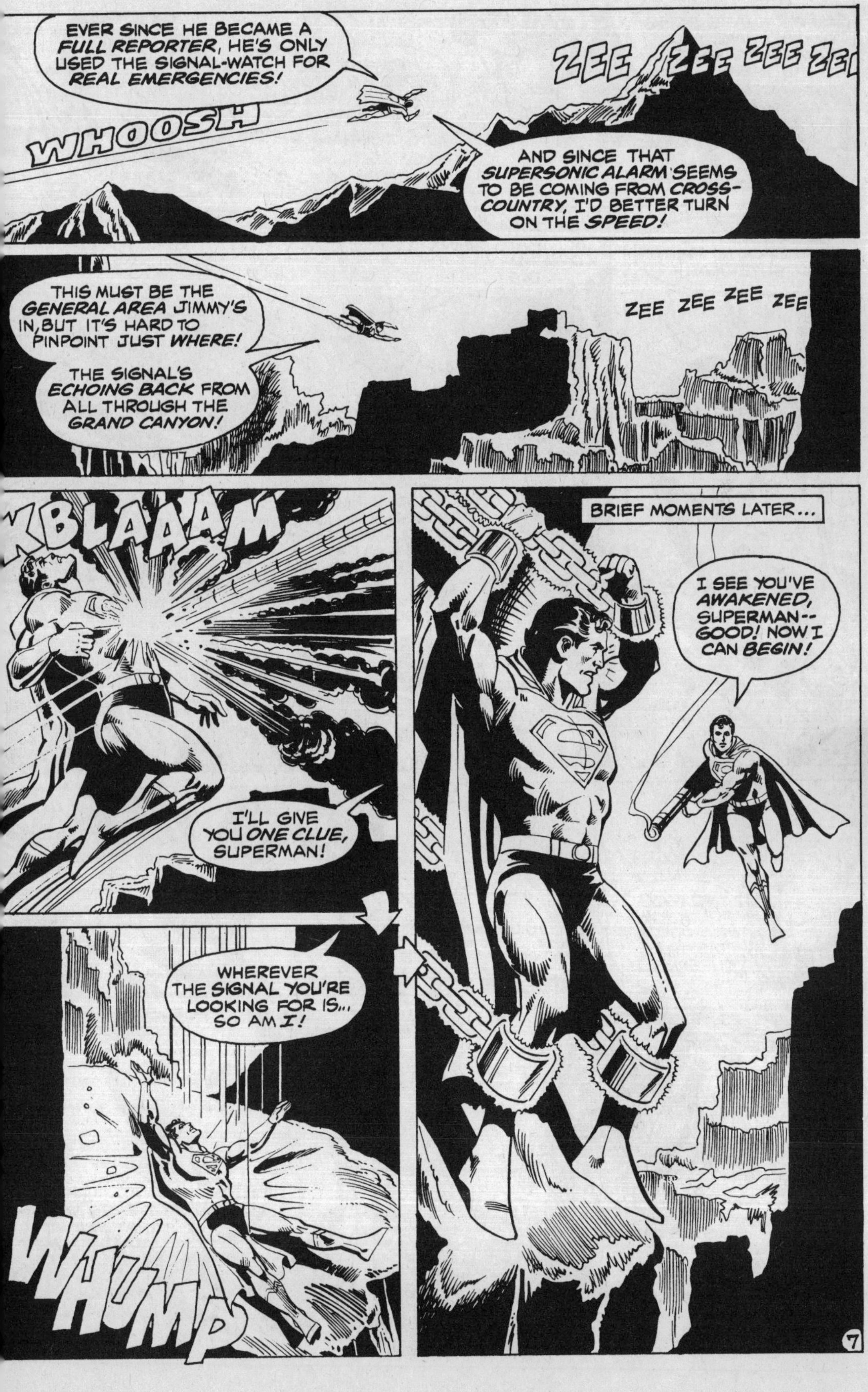
EVER SINCE HE BECAME A FULL REPORTER, HE'S ONLY USED THE SIGNAL-WATCH FOR REAL EMERGENCIES!
ZEE ZEE ZEE ZEE
WHOOSH
AND SINCE THAT SUPERSONIC ALARM SEEMS TO BE COMING FROM CROSS-COUNTRY, I'D BETTER TURN ON THE SPEED!
THIS MUST BE THE GENERAL AREA JIMMY'S IN, BUT IT'S HARD TO PINPOINT JUST WHERE!
THE SIGNAL'S ECHOING BACK FROM ALL THROUGH THE GRAND CANYON!
ZEE ZEE ZEE ZEE
KBLAAAM
I'LL GIVE YOU ONE CLUE, SUPERMAN!
WHEREVER THE SIGNAL YOU'RE LOOKING FOR IS... SO AM I!
WHUMP
BRIEF MOMENTS LATER...
I SEE YOU'VE AWAKENED, SUPERMAN-- GOOD! NOW I CAN BEGIN!
7

BEGIN? WHAT'S GOING ON--WHY HAVE YOU *CHAINED* ME HERE LIKE THIS?

HEE HEE HEE... THOSE KRYPTONITE CHAINS ARE JUST FOR *STARTERS!*

YOUR *SINS* HAVE COME BACK TO *HAUNT* YOU, SUPERMAN--

--AND *THIS* IS THE JURY THAT'S GOING TO CONDEMN YOU TO *DIE!*

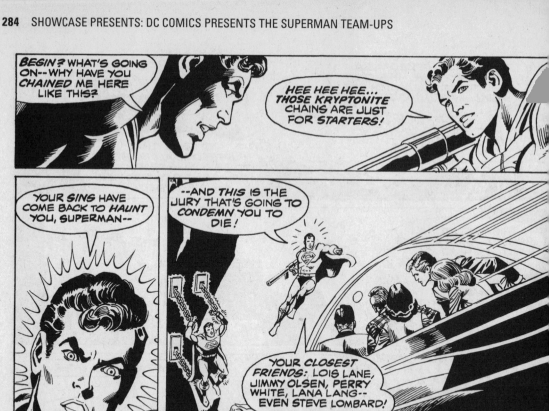

YOUR *CLOSEST* FRIENDS: LOIS LANE, JIMMY OLSEN, PERRY WHITE, LANA LANG-- EVEN STEVE LOMBARD!

THEY'LL MAKE ME YOUR *EXECUTIONER!*

NO WAY! YOU *KNOW* WE WOULDN'T DO THAT, SUPERMAN!

THIS IS *CRAZY!*

SILENCE!

SHUT UP OR I'LL KILL HIM *WITHOUT* A TRIAL--

--AND ALL OF *YOU* AS WELL!

YOU *CAN'T* BE SUPERBOY-- THERE'S *NOTHING* THAT EVIL--THAT *MAD*-- IN ME!

WHO ARE YOU --*REALLY?*

8

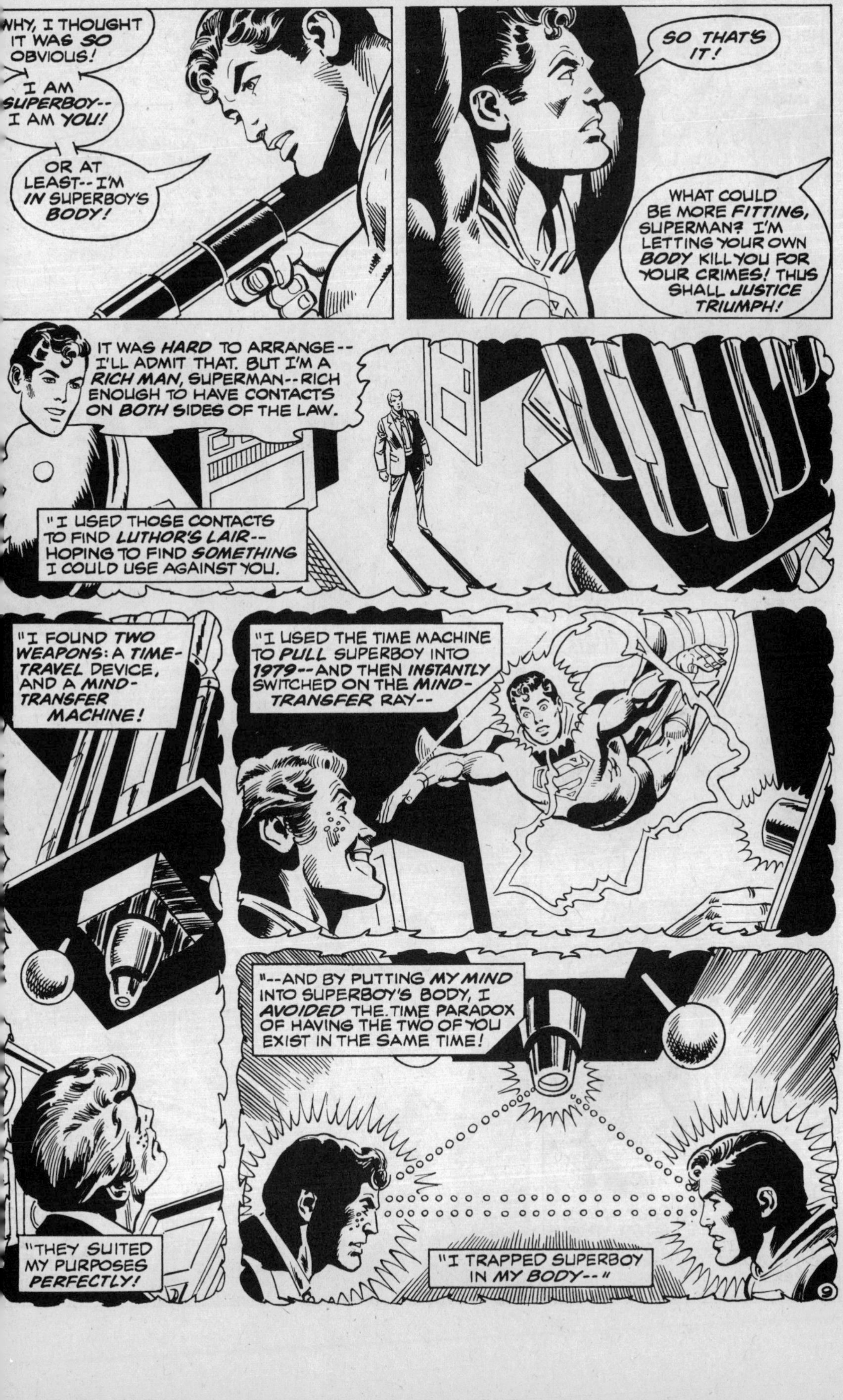
WHY, I THOUGHT IT WAS SO OBVIOUS!
I AM SUPERBOY-- I AM YOU!
OR AT LEAST-- I'M IN SUPERBOY'S BODY!
SO THAT'S IT!
WHAT COULD BE MORE FITTING, SUPERMAN? I'M LETTING YOUR OWN BODY KILL YOU FOR YOUR CRIMES! THUS SHALL JUSTICE TRIUMPH!
IT WAS HARD TO ARRANGE-- I'LL ADMIT THAT. BUT I'M A RICH MAN, SUPERMAN--RICH ENOUGH TO HAVE CONTACTS ON BOTH SIDES OF THE LAW.
"I USED THOSE CONTACTS TO FIND LUTHOR'S LAIR-- HOPING TO FIND SOMETHING I COULD USE AGAINST YOU.
"I FOUND TWO WEAPONS: A TIME-TRAVEL DEVICE, AND A MIND-TRANSFER MACHINE!
"I USED THE TIME MACHINE TO PULL SUPERBOY INTO 1979--AND THEN INSTANTLY SWITCHED ON THE MIND-TRANSFER RAY--
"--AND BY PUTTING MY MIND INTO SUPERBOY'S BODY, I AVOIDED THE TIME PARADOX OF HAVING THE TWO OF YOU EXIST IN THE SAME TIME!
"THEY SUITED MY PURPOSES PERFECTLY!
"I TRAPPED SUPERBOY IN MY BODY--"
9

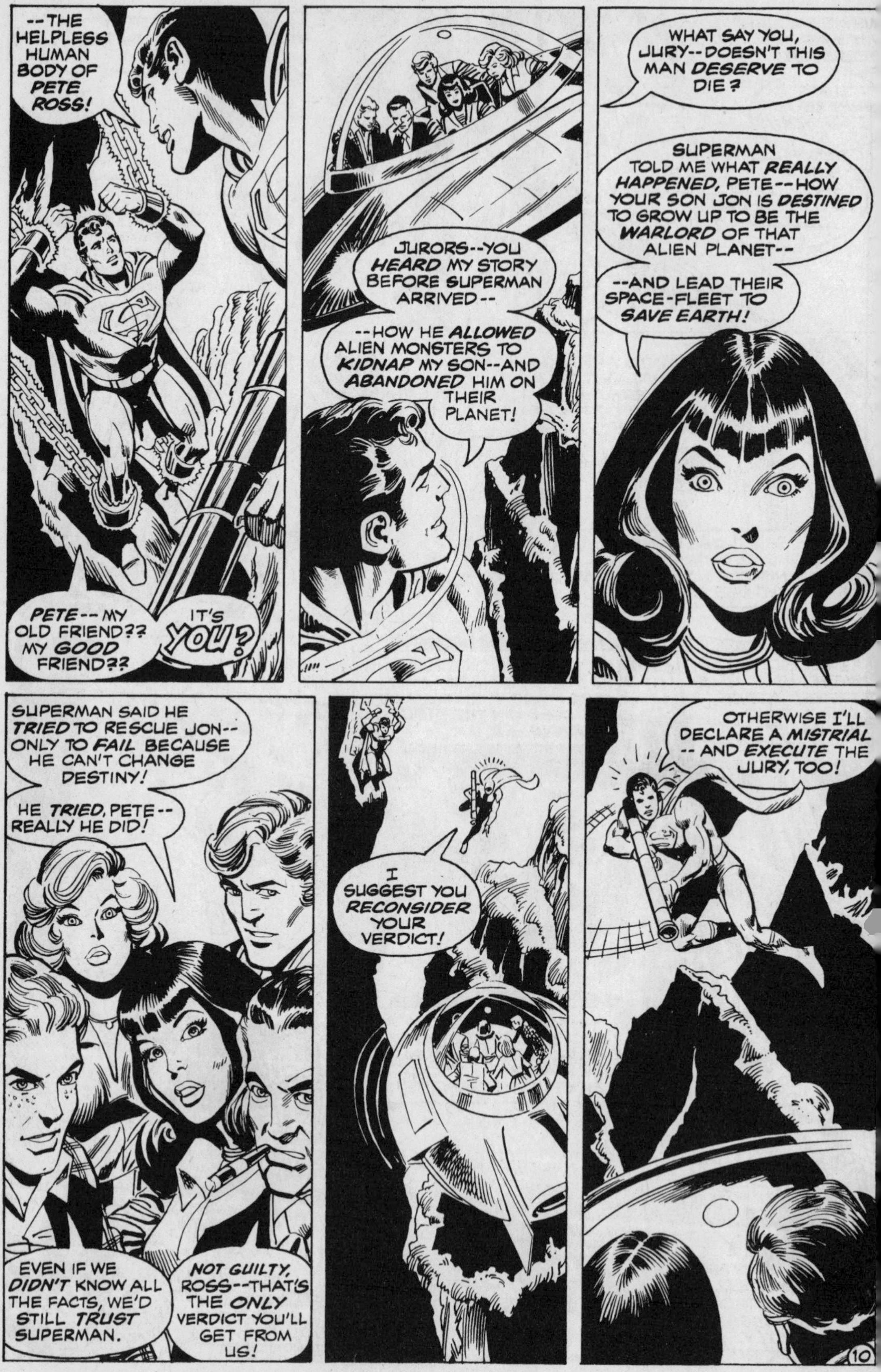
--THE HELPLESS HUMAN BODY OF PETE ROSS!
PETE--MY OLD FRIEND?? MY GOOD FRIEND??
IT'S YOU?
JURORS--YOU HEARD MY STORY BEFORE SUPERMAN ARRIVED--
--HOW HE ALLOWED ALIEN MONSTERS TO KIDNAP MY SON--AND ABANDONED HIM ON THEIR PLANET!
WHAT SAY YOU, JURY--DOESN'T THIS MAN DESERVE TO DIE?
SUPERMAN TOLD ME WHAT REALLY HAPPENED, PETE--HOW YOUR SON JON IS DESTINED TO GROW UP TO BE THE WARLORD OF THAT ALIEN PLANET--
--AND LEAD THEIR SPACE-FLEET TO SAVE EARTH!
SUPERMAN SAID HE TRIED TO RESCUE JON--ONLY TO FAIL BECAUSE HE CAN'T CHANGE DESTINY!
HE TRIED, PETE--REALLY HE DID!
EVEN IF WE DIDN'T KNOW ALL THE FACTS, WE'D STILL TRUST SUPERMAN.
NOT GUILTY, ROSS--THAT'S THE ONLY VERDICT YOU'LL GET FROM US!
I SUGGEST YOU RECONSIDER YOUR VERDICT!
OTHERWISE I'LL DECLARE A MISTRIAL--AND EXECUTE THE JURY, TOO!
10

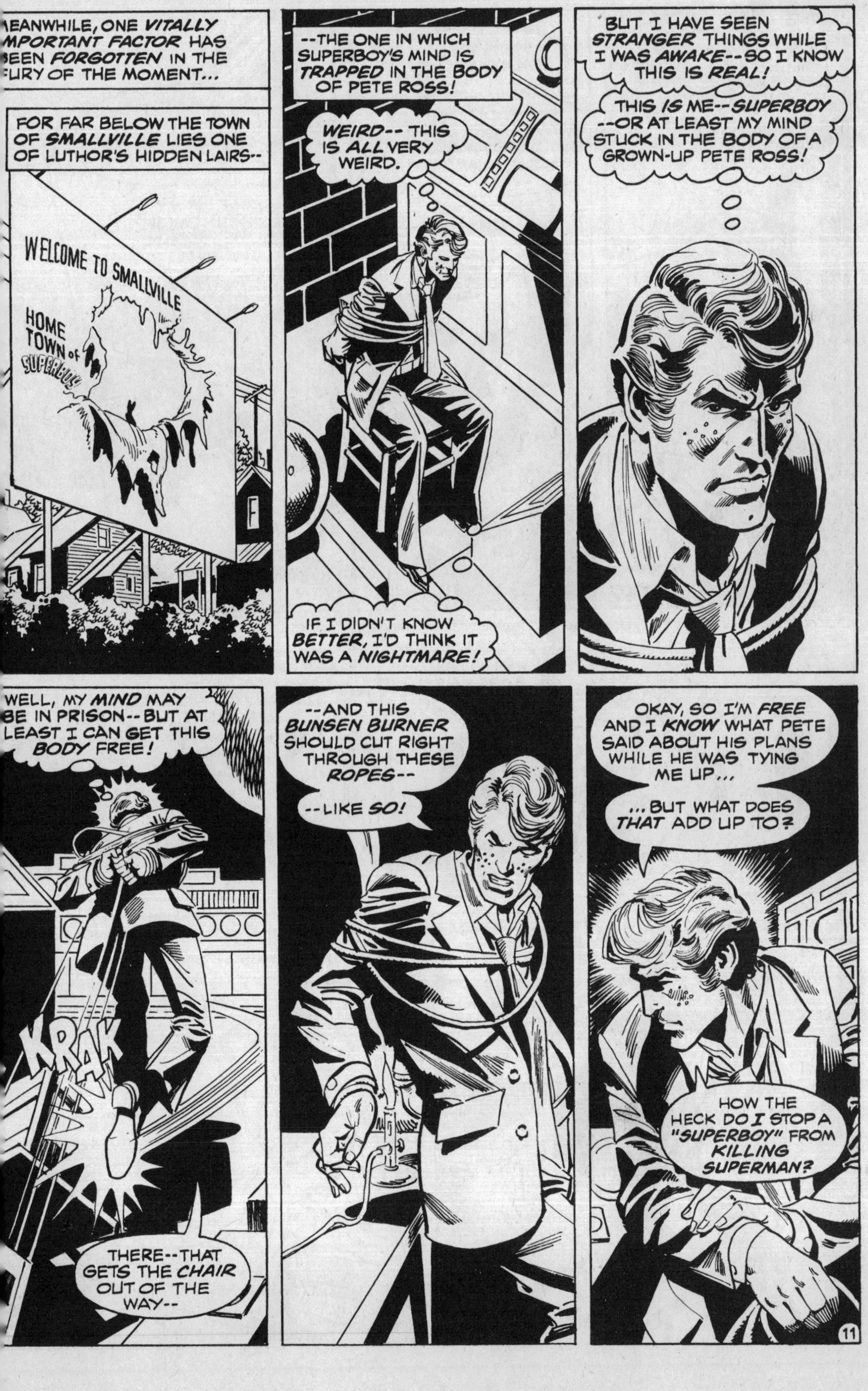
MEANWHILE, ONE VITALLY IMPORTANT FACTOR HAS BEEN FORGOTTEN IN THE FURY OF THE MOMENT...
FOR FAR BELOW THE TOWN OF SMALLVILLE LIES ONE OF LUTHOR'S HIDDEN LAIRS--
WELCOME TO SMALLVILLE
HOME TOWN of SUPERBOY
--THE ONE IN WHICH SUPERBOY'S MIND IS TRAPPED IN THE BODY OF PETE ROSS!
WEIRD-- THIS IS ALL VERY WEIRD.
IF I DIDN'T KNOW BETTER, I'D THINK IT WAS A NIGHTMARE!
BUT I HAVE SEEN STRANGER THINGS WHILE I WAS AWAKE--SO I KNOW THIS IS REAL!
THIS IS ME--SUPERBOY --OR AT LEAST MY MIND STUCK IN THE BODY OF A GROWN-UP PETE ROSS!
WELL, MY MIND MAY BE IN PRISON--BUT AT LEAST I CAN GET THIS BODY FREE!
KRAK
THERE--THAT GETS THE CHAIR OUT OF THE WAY--
--AND THIS BUNSEN BURNER SHOULD CUT RIGHT THROUGH THESE ROPES--
--LIKE SO!
OKAY, SO I'M FREE AND I KNOW WHAT PETE SAID ABOUT HIS PLANS WHILE HE WAS TYING ME UP...
...BUT WHAT DOES THAT ADD UP TO?
HOW THE HECK DO I STOP A "SUPERBOY" FROM KILLING SUPERMAN?
11

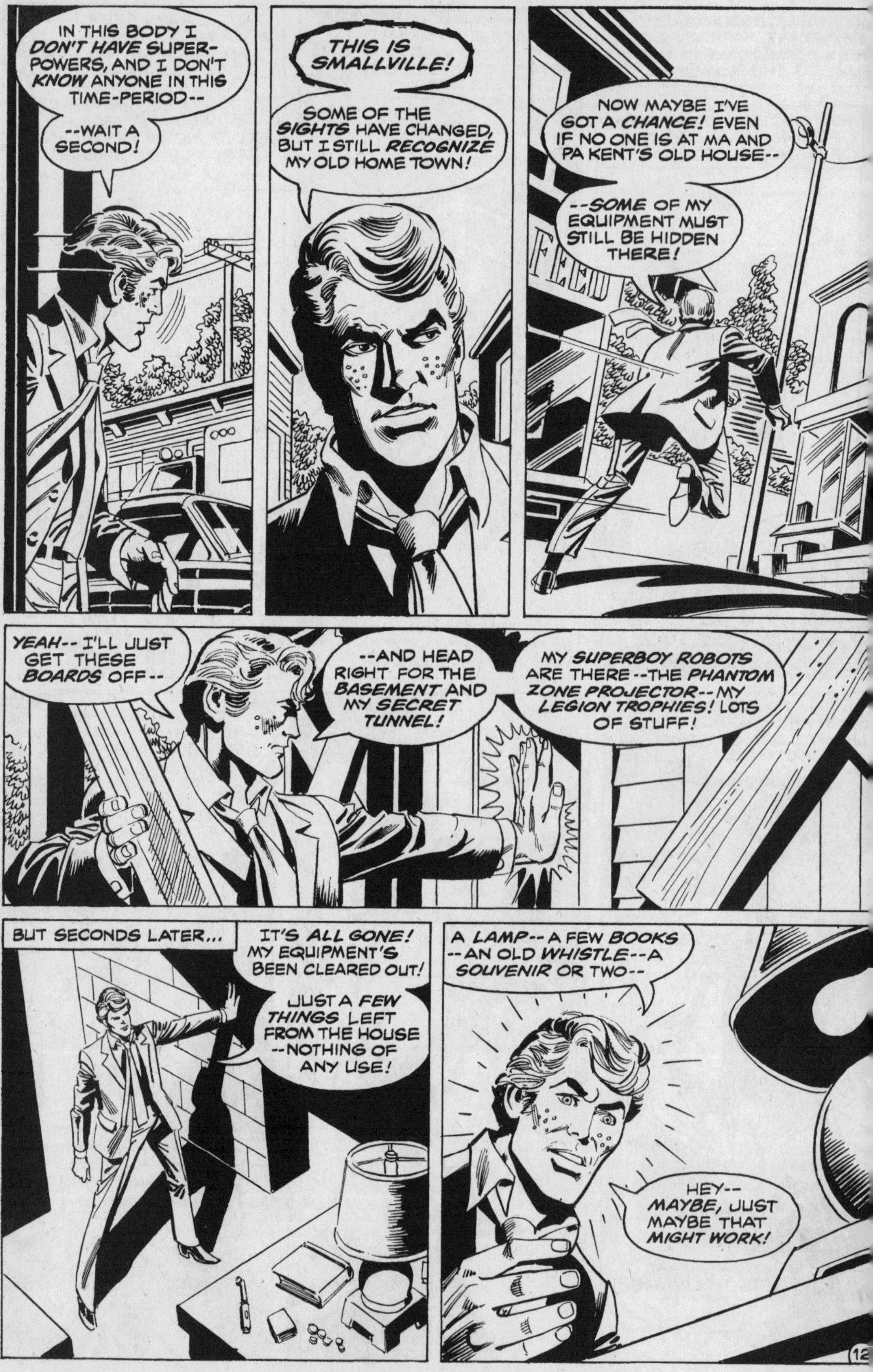
IN THIS BODY I DON'T HAVE SUPER-POWERS, AND I DON'T KNOW ANYONE IN THIS TIME-PERIOD--
--WAIT A SECOND!
THIS IS SMALLVILLE!
SOME OF THE SIGHTS HAVE CHANGED, BUT I STILL RECOGNIZE MY OLD HOME TOWN!
NOW MAYBE I'VE GOT A CHANCE! EVEN IF NO ONE IS AT MA AND PA KENT'S OLD HOUSE--
--SOME OF MY EQUIPMENT MUST STILL BE HIDDEN THERE!
FEED
YEAH-- I'LL JUST GET THESE BOARDS OFF--
--AND HEAD RIGHT FOR THE BASEMENT AND MY SECRET TUNNEL!
MY SUPERBOY ROBOTS ARE THERE--THE PHANTOM ZONE PROJECTOR--MY LEGION TROPHIES! LOTS OF STUFF!
BUT SECONDS LATER...
IT'S ALL GONE! MY EQUIPMENT'S BEEN CLEARED OUT!
JUST A FEW THINGS LEFT FROM THE HOUSE --NOTHING OF ANY USE!
A LAMP--A FEW BOOKS --AN OLD WHISTLE--A SOUVENIR OR TWO--
HEY-- MAYBE, JUST MAYBE THAT MIGHT WORK!
12

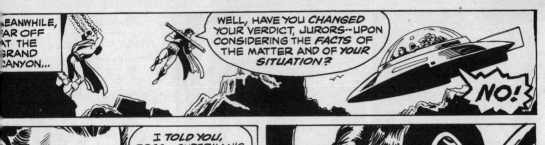

MEANWHILE, FAR OFF AT THE GRAND CANYON...

WELL, HAVE YOU *CHANGED* YOUR *VERDICT*, JURORS--UPON CONSIDERING THE *FACTS* OF THE MATTER AND OF *YOUR* SITUATION?

NO!

I *TOLD* YOU, ROSS--SUPERMAN'S *NOT GUILTY!*

NOW GET US *OUT* OF THIS FLYING SAUCER, YOU *LUNATIC!*

NO, MISTER WHITE--YOU'RE *NOT GOING ANYWHERE!*

YOU'RE MY *WITNESSES*--

--TO SUPERMAN'S *EXECUTION!*

BLAM

THE *GREEN KRYPTONITE SHELL* BURSTS FROM THE *LEADEN* BAZOOKA-- ITS *RADIATION* SPELLING CERTAIN DOOM FOR THE MAN OF STEEL!...

BUT AS THE SHELL SPEEDS *CLOSER,* THE STRAINING SUPERMAN GIVES ONE LAST HEROIC *BURST* OF STRENGTH--

SNAP

KRAK

--AND IT IS THE *MAN* IN HIM-- *NOT* THE SUPERMAN --THAT FINDS THE STRENGTH TO *BREAK FREE*--

KABLAM

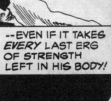

--EVEN IF IT TAKES *EVERY* LAST ERG OF STRENGTH LEFT IN HIS BODY!

NO! I DON'T BELIEVE IT--HE *SNAPPED* THE CHAINS!

IT *DOESN'T MATTER,* THOUGH -- HE'S LYING ON THE GROUND UNCONSCIOUS AND *HELPLESS*--

13

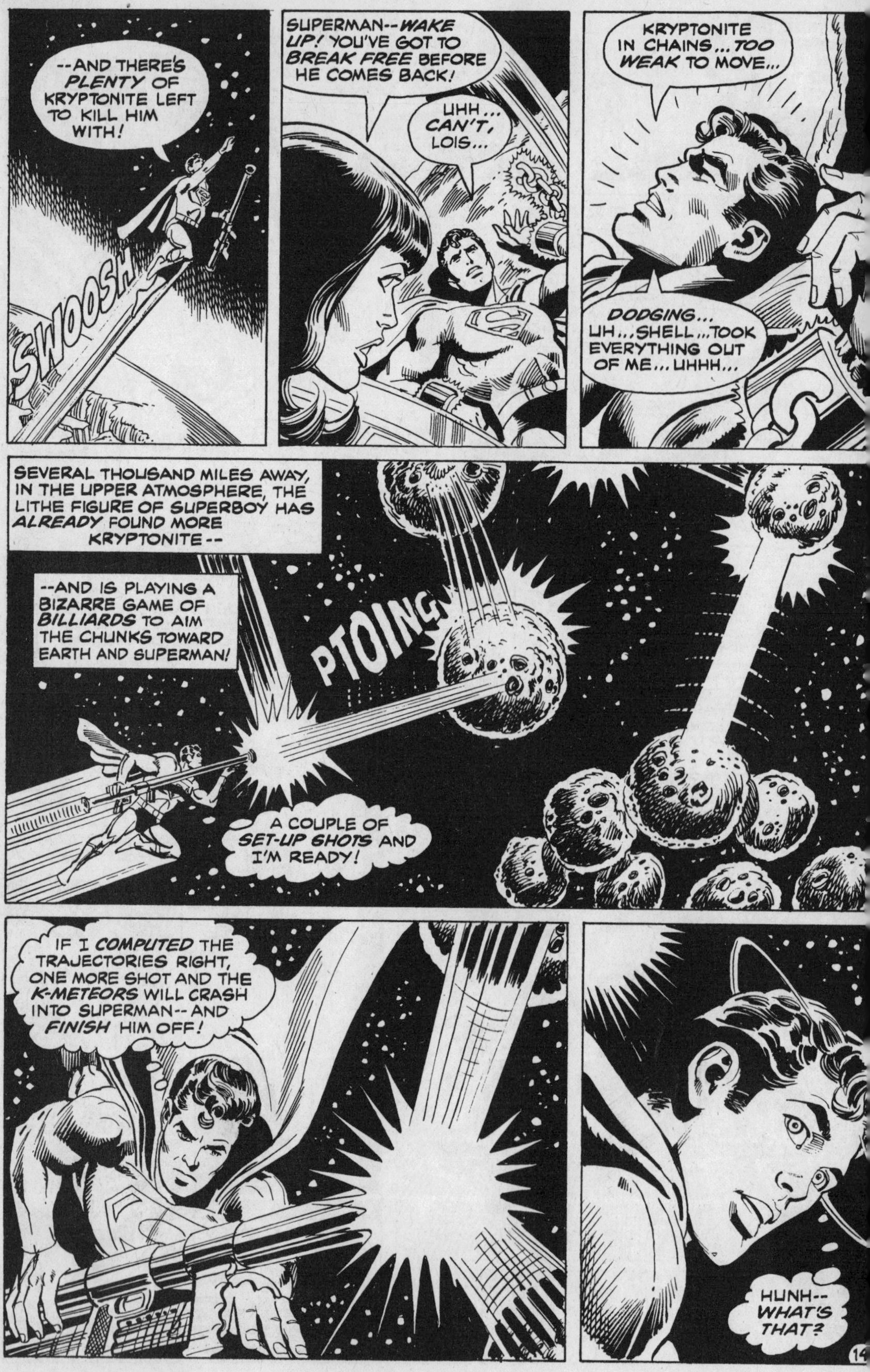
--AND THERE'S PLENTY OF KRYPTONITE LEFT TO KILL HIM WITH!
SWOOSH
SUPERMAN--WAKE UP! YOU'VE GOT TO BREAK FREE BEFORE HE COMES BACK!
UHH... CAN'T, LOIS...
KRYPTONITE IN CHAINS... TOO WEAK TO MOVE...
DODGING... UH... SHELL... TOOK EVERYTHING OUT OF ME... UHHH...
SEVERAL THOUSAND MILES AWAY, IN THE UPPER ATMOSPHERE, THE LITHE FIGURE OF SUPERBOY HAS ALREADY FOUND MORE KRYPTONITE--
--AND IS PLAYING A BIZARRE GAME OF BILLIARDS TO AIM THE CHUNKS TOWARD EARTH AND SUPERMAN!
PTOING
A COUPLE OF SET-UP SHOTS AND I'M READY!
IF I COMPUTED THE TRAJECTORIES RIGHT, ONE MORE SHOT AND THE K-METEORS WILL CRASH INTO SUPERMAN-- AND FINISH HIM OFF!
HUNH-- WHAT'S THAT?
14

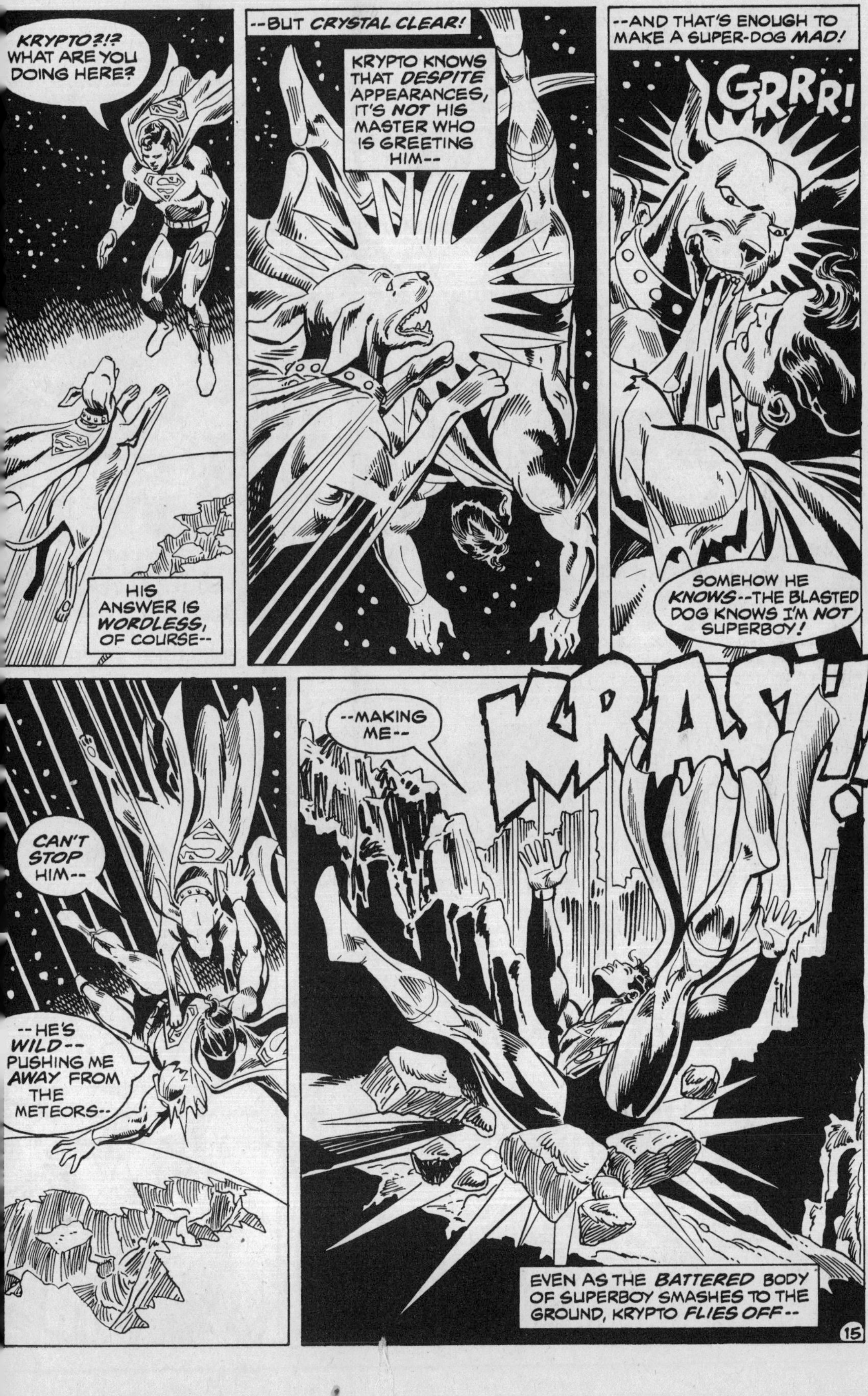
KRYPTO?!? WHAT ARE YOU DOING HERE?
HIS ANSWER IS WORDLESS, OF COURSE--
--BUT CRYSTAL CLEAR!
KRYPTO KNOWS THAT DESPITE APPEARANCES, IT'S NOT HIS MASTER WHO IS GREETING HIM--
--AND THAT'S ENOUGH TO MAKE A SUPER-DOG MAD!
GRRR!
SOMEHOW HE KNOWS--THE BLASTED DOG KNOWS I'M NOT SUPERBOY!
CAN'T STOP HIM--
--HE'S WILD--PUSHING ME AWAY FROM THE METEORS--
--MAKING ME--
KRASH!!
EVEN AS THE BATTERED BODY OF SUPERBOY SMASHES TO THE GROUND, KRYPTO FLIES OFF--
15

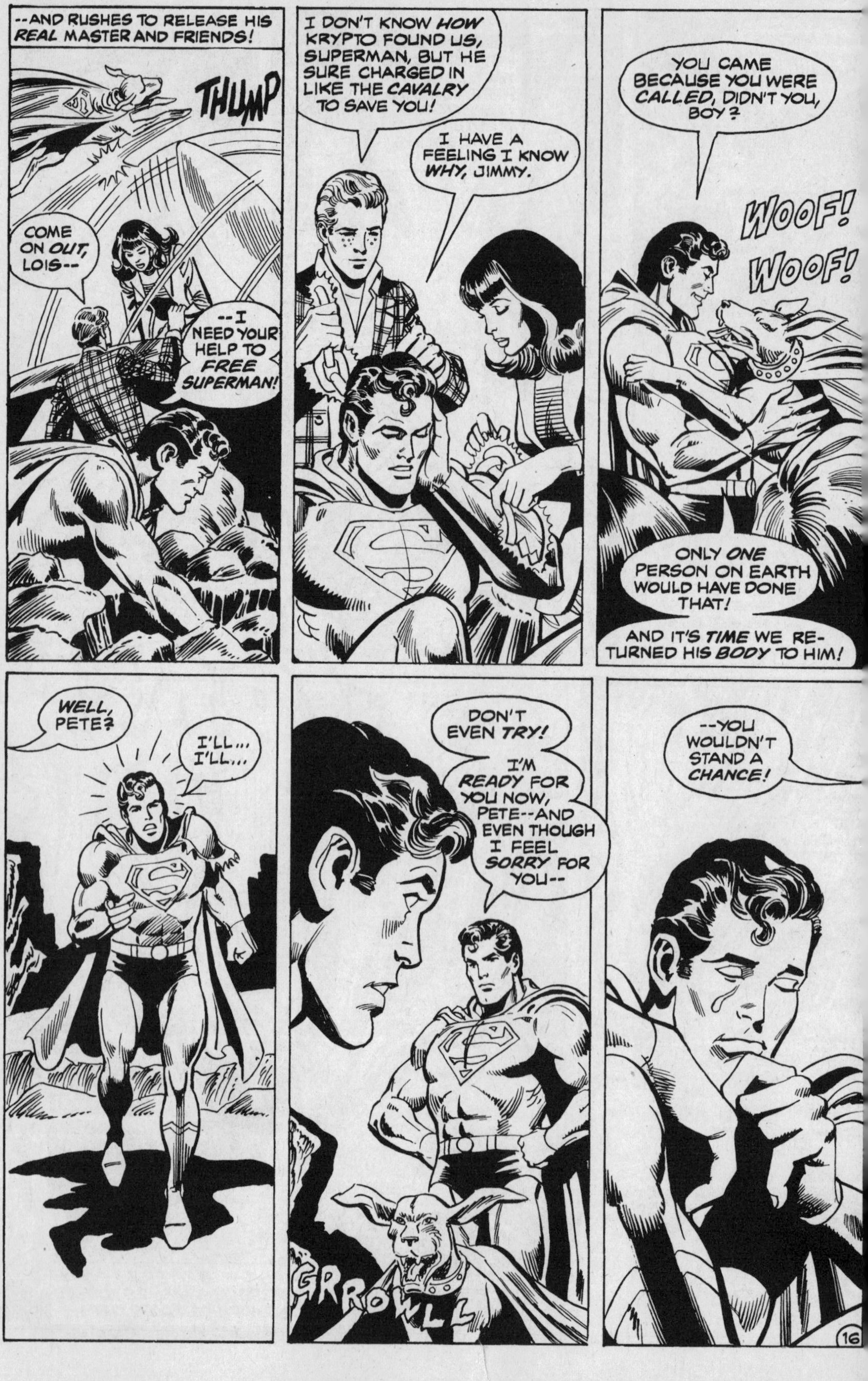
--AND RUSHES TO RELEASE HIS REAL MASTER AND FRIENDS!
THUMP
COME ON OUT, LOIS--
--I NEED YOUR HELP TO FREE SUPERMAN!
I DON'T KNOW HOW KRYPTO FOUND US, SUPERMAN, BUT HE SURE CHARGED IN LIKE THE CAVALRY TO SAVE YOU!
I HAVE A FEELING I KNOW WHY, JIMMY.
YOU CAME BECAUSE YOU WERE CALLED, DIDN'T YOU, BOY?
WOOF! WOOF!
ONLY ONE PERSON ON EARTH WOULD HAVE DONE THAT!
AND IT'S TIME WE RE-TURNED HIS BODY TO HIM!
WELL, PETE?
I'LL... I'LL...
DON'T EVEN TRY!
I'M READY FOR YOU NOW, PETE--AND EVEN THOUGH I FEEL SORRY FOR YOU--
GRROWLL
--YOU WOULDN'T STAND A CHANCE!
16

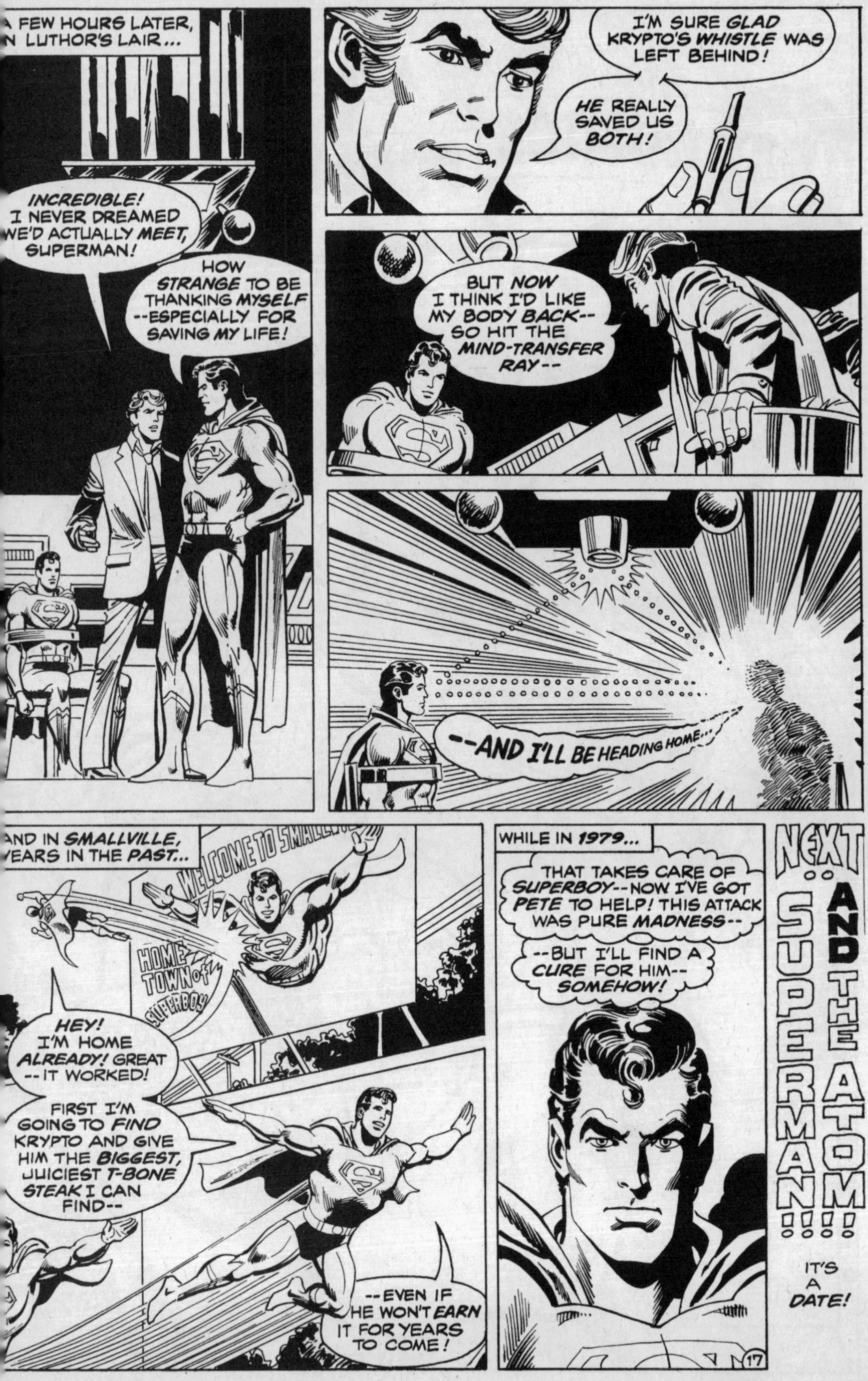
A FEW HOURS LATER, IN LUTHOR'S LAIR...
INCREDIBLE! I NEVER DREAMED WE'D ACTUALLY MEET, SUPERMAN!
HOW STRANGE TO BE THANKING MYSELF --ESPECIALLY FOR SAVING MY LIFE!
I'M SURE GLAD KRYPTO'S WHISTLE WAS LEFT BEHIND!
HE REALLY SAVED US BOTH!
BUT NOW I THINK I'D LIKE MY BODY BACK-- SO HIT THE MIND-TRANSFER RAY--
--AND I'LL BE HEADING HOME...
AND IN SMALLVILLE, YEARS IN THE PAST...
WELCOME TO SMALLVILLE
HOME TOWN of SUPERBOY
HEY! I'M HOME ALREADY! GREAT --IT WORKED!
FIRST I'M GOING TO FIND KRYPTO AND GIVE HIM THE BIGGEST, JUICIEST T-BONE STEAK I CAN FIND--
--EVEN IF HE WON'T EARN IT FOR YEARS TO COME!
WHILE IN 1979...
THAT TAKES CARE OF SUPERBOY--NOW I'VE GOT PETE TO HELP! THIS ATTACK WAS PURE MADNESS--
--BUT I'LL FIND A CURE FOR HIM--SOMEHOW!
17
NEXT: SUPERMAN AND THE ATOM!!!
IT'S A DATE!

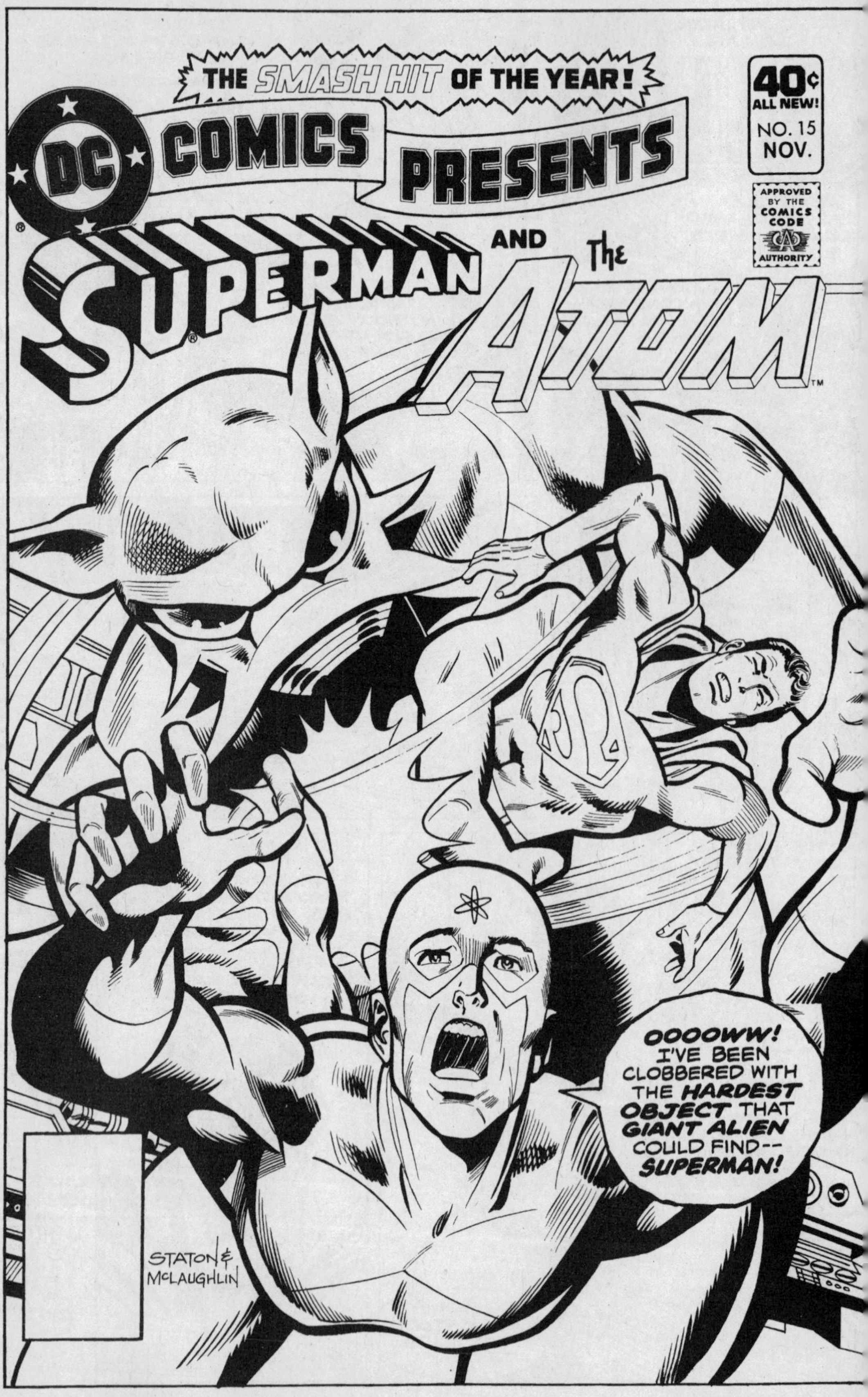
THE SMASH HIT OF THE YEAR!
DC COMICS PRESENTS
40¢ ALL NEW!
NO. 15 NOV.
APPROVED BY THE COMICS CODE AUTHORITY
SUPERMAN AND The ATOM
OOOOWW! I'VE BEEN CLOBBERED WITH THE HARDEST OBJECT THAT GIANT ALIEN COULD FIND-- SUPERMAN!
STATON & McLAUGHLIN

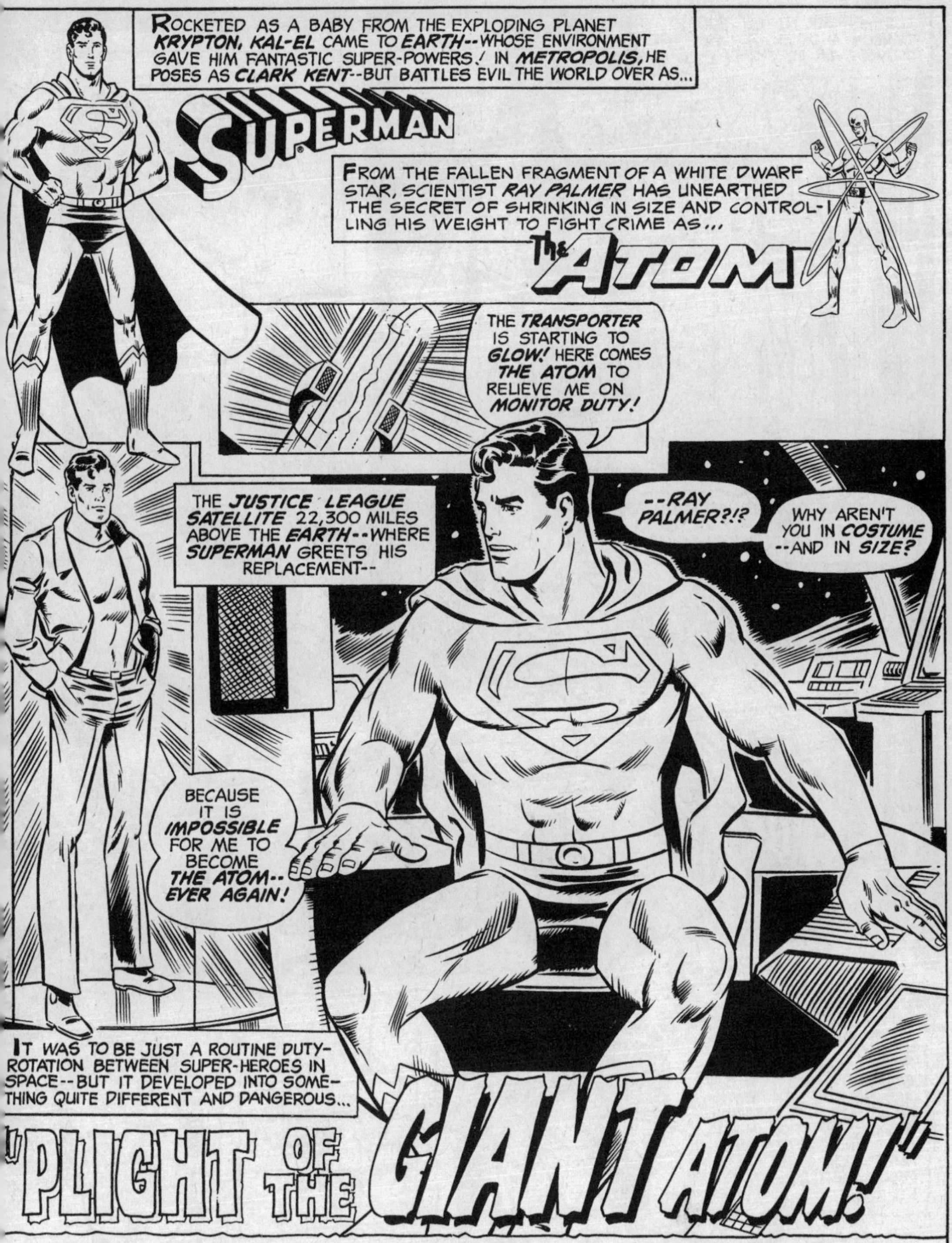
ROCKETED AS A BABY FROM THE EXPLODING PLANET KRYPTON, KAL-EL CAME TO EARTH--WHOSE ENVIRONMENT GAVE HIM FANTASTIC SUPER-POWERS! IN METROPOLIS, HE POSES AS CLARK KENT--BUT BATTLES EVIL THE WORLD OVER AS...
SUPERMAN
FROM THE FALLEN FRAGMENT OF A WHITE DWARF STAR, SCIENTIST RAY PALMER HAS UNEARTHED THE SECRET OF SHRINKING IN SIZE AND CONTROL-LING HIS WEIGHT TO FIGHT CRIME AS...
The ATOM
THE TRANSPORTER IS STARTING TO GLOW! HERE COMES THE ATOM TO RELIEVE ME ON MONITOR DUTY!
THE JUSTICE LEAGUE SATELLITE 22,300 MILES ABOVE THE EARTH--WHERE SUPERMAN GREETS HIS REPLACEMENT--
--RAY PALMER?!?
WHY AREN'T YOU IN COSTUME --AND IN SIZE?
BECAUSE IT IS IMPOSSIBLE FOR ME TO BECOME THE ATOM--EVER AGAIN!
IT WAS TO BE JUST A ROUTINE DUTY-ROTATION BETWEEN SUPER-HEROES IN SPACE--BUT IT DEVELOPED INTO SOME-THING QUITE DIFFERENT AND DANGEROUS...
"PLIGHT OF THE GIANT ATOM!"
WRITER: CARY BATES * PENCILLER: JOE STATON * INKER: FRANK CHIARAMONTE
LETTERER: BEN ODA * COLORIST: JERRY SERPE * EDITOR: JULIUS SCHWARTZ

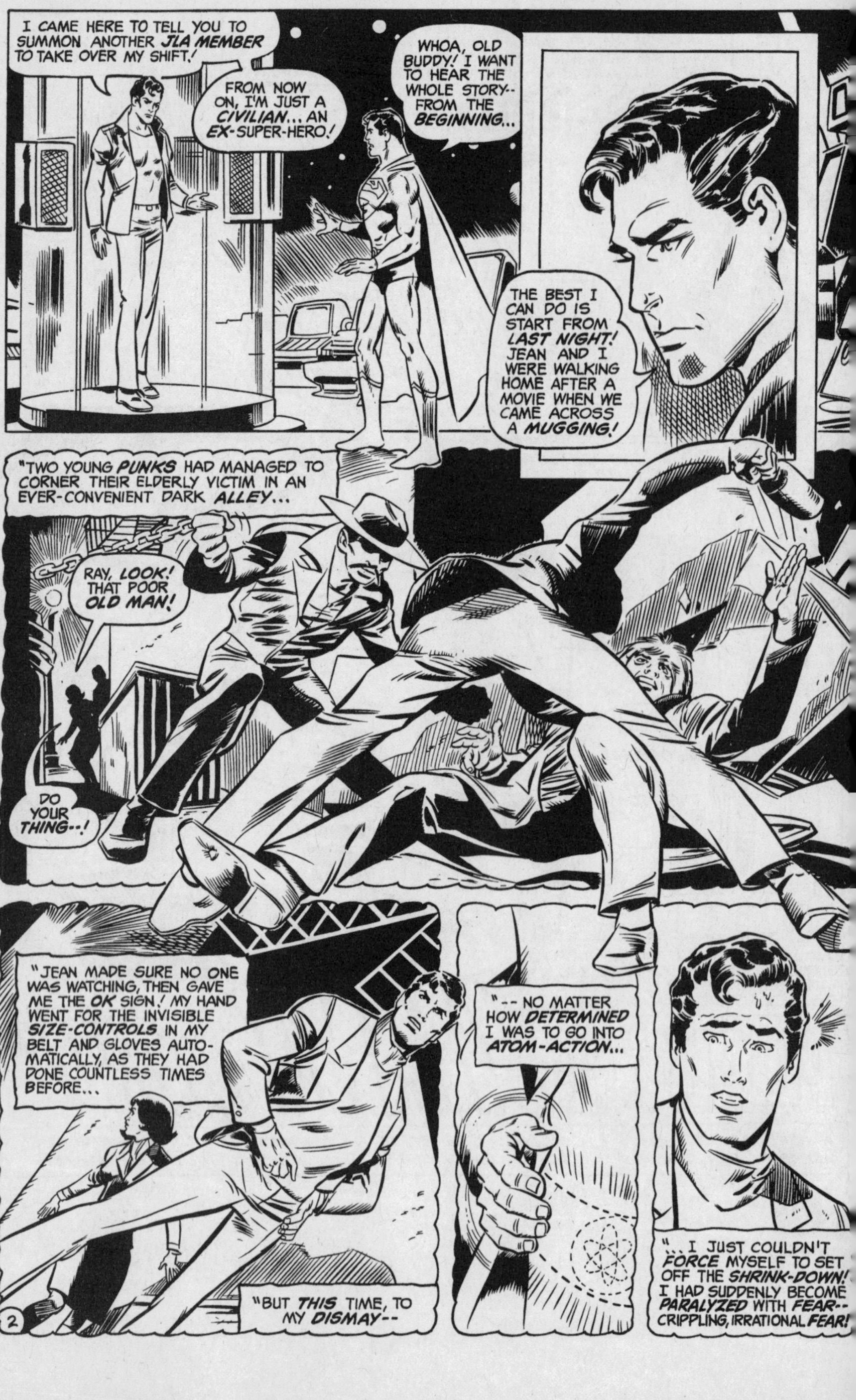
I CAME HERE TO TELL YOU TO SUMMON ANOTHER JLA MEMBER TO TAKE OVER MY SHIFT!
FROM NOW ON, I'M JUST A CIVILIAN... AN EX-SUPER-HERO!
WHOA, OLD BUDDY! I WANT TO HEAR THE WHOLE STORY-- FROM THE BEGINNING...
THE BEST I CAN DO IS START FROM LAST NIGHT! JEAN AND I WERE WALKING HOME AFTER A MOVIE WHEN WE CAME ACROSS A MUGGING!
"TWO YOUNG PUNKS HAD MANAGED TO CORNER THEIR ELDERLY VICTIM IN AN EVER-CONVENIENT DARK ALLEY...
RAY, LOOK! THAT POOR OLD MAN!
DO YOUR THING--!
"JEAN MADE SURE NO ONE WAS WATCHING, THEN GAVE ME THE OK SIGN! MY HAND WENT FOR THE INVISIBLE SIZE-CONTROLS IN MY BELT AND GLOVES AUTOMATICALLY, AS THEY HAD DONE COUNTLESS TIMES BEFORE...
"BUT THIS TIME, TO MY DISMAY--
"-- NO MATTER HOW DETERMINED I WAS TO GO INTO ATOM-ACTION...
"...I JUST COULDN'T FORCE MYSELF TO SET OFF THE SHRINK-DOWN! I HAD SUDDENLY BECOME PARALYZED WITH FEAR-- CRIPPLING, IRRATIONAL FEAR!
2

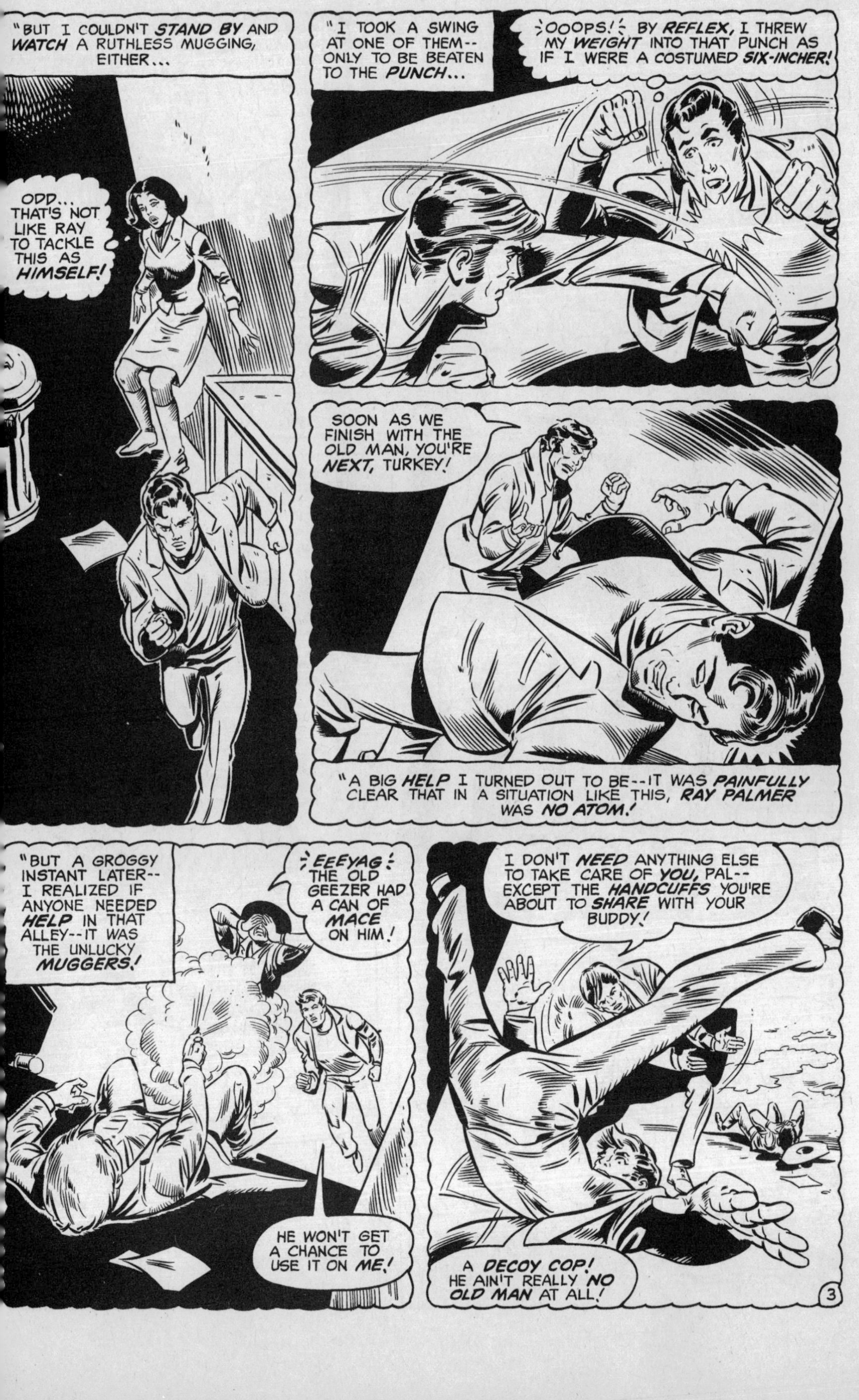
"BUT I COULDN'T STAND BY AND WATCH A RUTHLESS MUGGING, EITHER...
ODD... THAT'S NOT LIKE RAY TO TACKLE THIS AS HIMSELF!
"I TOOK A SWING AT ONE OF THEM-- ONLY TO BE BEATEN TO THE PUNCH...
OOOPS! BY REFLEX, I THREW MY WEIGHT INTO THAT PUNCH AS IF I WERE A COSTUMED SIX-INCHER!
SOON AS WE FINISH WITH THE OLD MAN, YOU'RE NEXT, TURKEY!
"A BIG HELP I TURNED OUT TO BE--IT WAS PAINFULLY CLEAR THAT IN A SITUATION LIKE THIS, RAY PALMER WAS NO ATOM!
"BUT A GROGGY INSTANT LATER-- I REALIZED IF ANYONE NEEDED HELP IN THAT ALLEY--IT WAS THE UNLUCKY MUGGERS!
EEEYAG! THE OLD GEEZER HAD A CAN OF MACE ON HIM!
HE WON'T GET A CHANCE TO USE IT ON ME!
I DON'T NEED ANYTHING ELSE TO TAKE CARE OF YOU, PAL-- EXCEPT THE HANDCUFFS YOU'RE ABOUT TO SHARE WITH YOUR BUDDY!
A DECOY COP! HE AIN'T REALLY NO OLD MAN AT ALL!
3

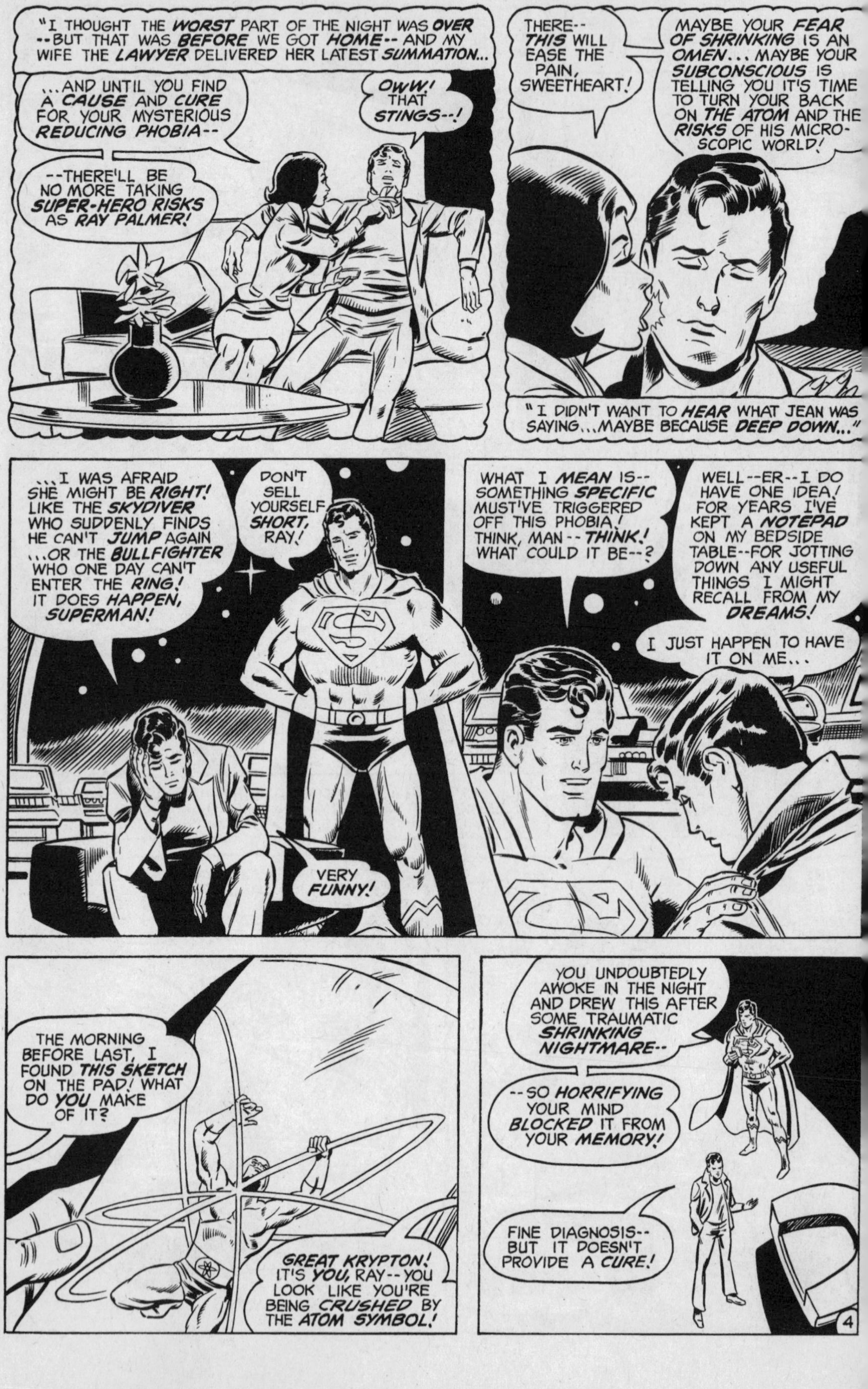
"I THOUGHT THE WORST PART OF THE NIGHT WAS OVER --BUT THAT WAS BEFORE WE GOT HOME-- AND MY WIFE THE LAWYER DELIVERED HER LATEST SUMMATION...
...AND UNTIL YOU FIND A CAUSE AND CURE FOR YOUR MYSTERIOUS REDUCING PHOBIA--
OWW! THAT STINGS--!
--THERE'LL BE NO MORE TAKING SUPER-HERO RISKS AS RAY PALMER!
THERE-- THIS WILL EASE THE PAIN, SWEETHEART!
MAYBE YOUR FEAR OF SHRINKING IS AN OMEN... MAYBE YOUR SUBCONSCIOUS IS TELLING YOU IT'S TIME TO TURN YOUR BACK ON THE ATOM AND THE RISKS OF HIS MICRO-SCOPIC WORLD!
"I DIDN'T WANT TO HEAR WHAT JEAN WAS SAYING...MAYBE BECAUSE DEEP DOWN..."
...I WAS AFRAID SHE MIGHT BE RIGHT! LIKE THE SKYDIVER WHO SUDDENLY FINDS HE CAN'T JUMP AGAIN ...OR THE BULLFIGHTER WHO ONE DAY CAN'T ENTER THE RING! IT DOES HAPPEN, SUPERMAN!
DON'T SELL YOURSELF SHORT, RAY!
VERY FUNNY!
WHAT I MEAN IS-- SOMETHING SPECIFIC MUST'VE TRIGGERED OFF THIS PHOBIA! THINK, MAN -- THINK! WHAT COULD IT BE--?
WELL --ER-- I DO HAVE ONE IDEA! FOR YEARS I'VE KEPT A NOTEPAD ON MY BEDSIDE TABLE--FOR JOTTING DOWN ANY USEFUL THINGS I MIGHT RECALL FROM MY DREAMS!
I JUST HAPPEN TO HAVE IT ON ME...
THE MORNING BEFORE LAST, I FOUND THIS SKETCH ON THE PAD! WHAT DO YOU MAKE OF IT?
GREAT KRYPTON! IT'S YOU, RAY-- YOU LOOK LIKE YOU'RE BEING CRUSHED BY THE ATOM SYMBOL!
YOU UNDOUBTEDLY AWOKE IN THE NIGHT AND DREW THIS AFTER SOME TRAUMATIC SHRINKING NIGHTMARE--
--SO HORRIFYING YOUR MIND BLOCKED IT FROM YOUR MEMORY!
FINE DIAGNOSIS-- BUT IT DOESN'T PROVIDE A CURE!
4

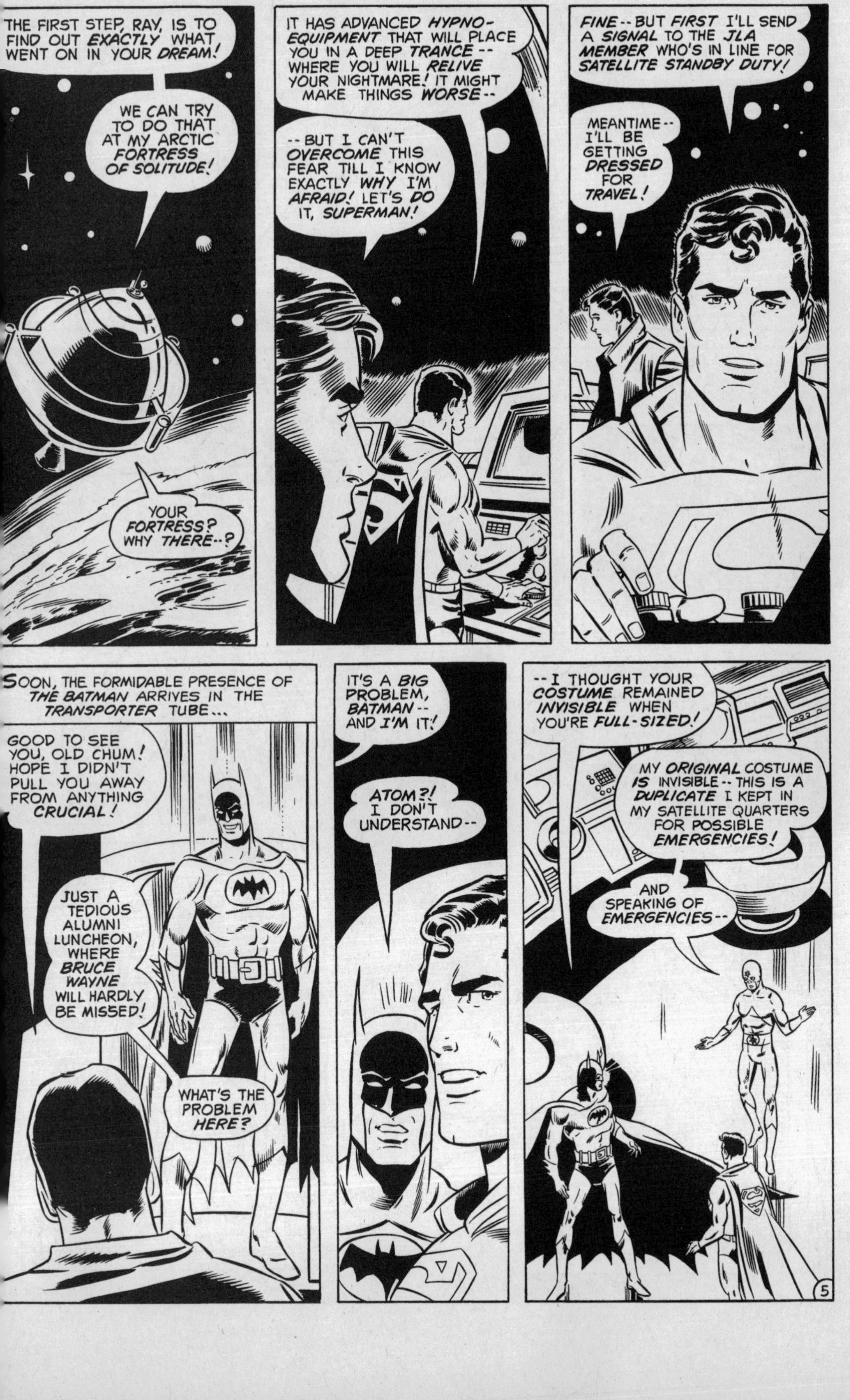
THE FIRST STEP, RAY, IS TO FIND OUT EXACTLY WHAT WENT ON IN YOUR DREAM!
WE CAN TRY TO DO THAT AT MY ARCTIC FORTRESS OF SOLITUDE!
YOUR FORTRESS? WHY THERE--?
IT HAS ADVANCED HYPNO-EQUIPMENT THAT WILL PLACE YOU IN A DEEP TRANCE -- WHERE YOU WILL RELIVE YOUR NIGHTMARE! IT MIGHT MAKE THINGS WORSE--
-- BUT I CAN'T OVERCOME THIS FEAR TILL I KNOW EXACTLY WHY I'M AFRAID! LET'S DO IT, SUPERMAN!
FINE -- BUT FIRST I'LL SEND A SIGNAL TO THE JLA MEMBER WHO'S IN LINE FOR SATELLITE STANDBY DUTY!
MEANTIME -- I'LL BE GETTING DRESSED FOR TRAVEL!
SOON, THE FORMIDABLE PRESENCE OF THE BATMAN ARRIVES IN THE TRANSPORTER TUBE...
GOOD TO SEE YOU, OLD CHUM! HOPE I DIDN'T PULL YOU AWAY FROM ANYTHING CRUCIAL!
JUST A TEDIOUS ALUMNI LUNCHEON, WHERE BRUCE WAYNE WILL HARDLY BE MISSED!
WHAT'S THE PROBLEM HERE?
IT'S A BIG PROBLEM, BATMAN -- AND I'M IT!
ATOM?! I DON'T UNDERSTAND--
-- I THOUGHT YOUR COSTUME REMAINED INVISIBLE WHEN YOU'RE FULL-SIZED!
MY ORIGINAL COSTUME IS INVISIBLE -- THIS IS A DUPLICATE I KEPT IN MY SATELLITE QUARTERS FOR POSSIBLE EMERGENCIES!
AND SPEAKING OF EMERGENCIES--
5

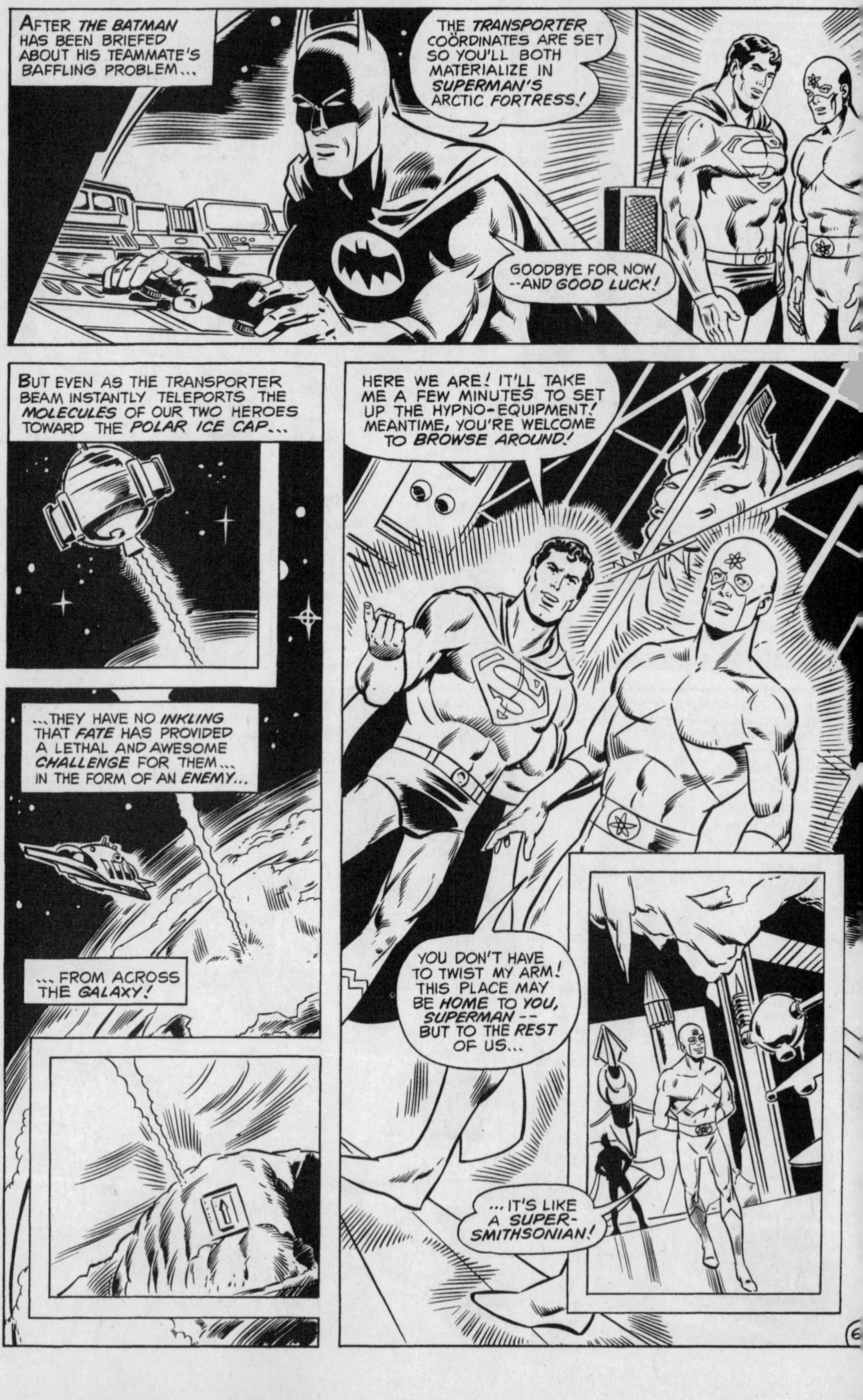
AFTER THE BATMAN HAS BEEN BRIEFED ABOUT HIS TEAMMATE'S BAFFLING PROBLEM...
THE TRANSPORTER COÖRDINATES ARE SET SO YOU'LL BOTH MATERIALIZE IN SUPERMAN'S ARCTIC FORTRESS!
GOODBYE FOR NOW --AND GOOD LUCK!
BUT EVEN AS THE TRANSPORTER BEAM INSTANTLY TELEPORTS THE MOLECULES OF OUR TWO HEROES TOWARD THE POLAR ICE CAP...
...THEY HAVE NO INKLING THAT FATE HAS PROVIDED A LETHAL AND AWESOME CHALLENGE FOR THEM... IN THE FORM OF AN ENEMY...
... FROM ACROSS THE GALAXY!
HERE WE ARE! IT'LL TAKE ME A FEW MINUTES TO SET UP THE HYPNO-EQUIPMENT! MEANTIME, YOU'RE WELCOME TO BROWSE AROUND!
YOU DON'T HAVE TO TWIST MY ARM! THIS PLACE MAY BE HOME TO YOU, SUPERMAN -- BUT TO THE REST OF US...
...IT'S LIKE A SUPER-SMITHSONIAN!
6

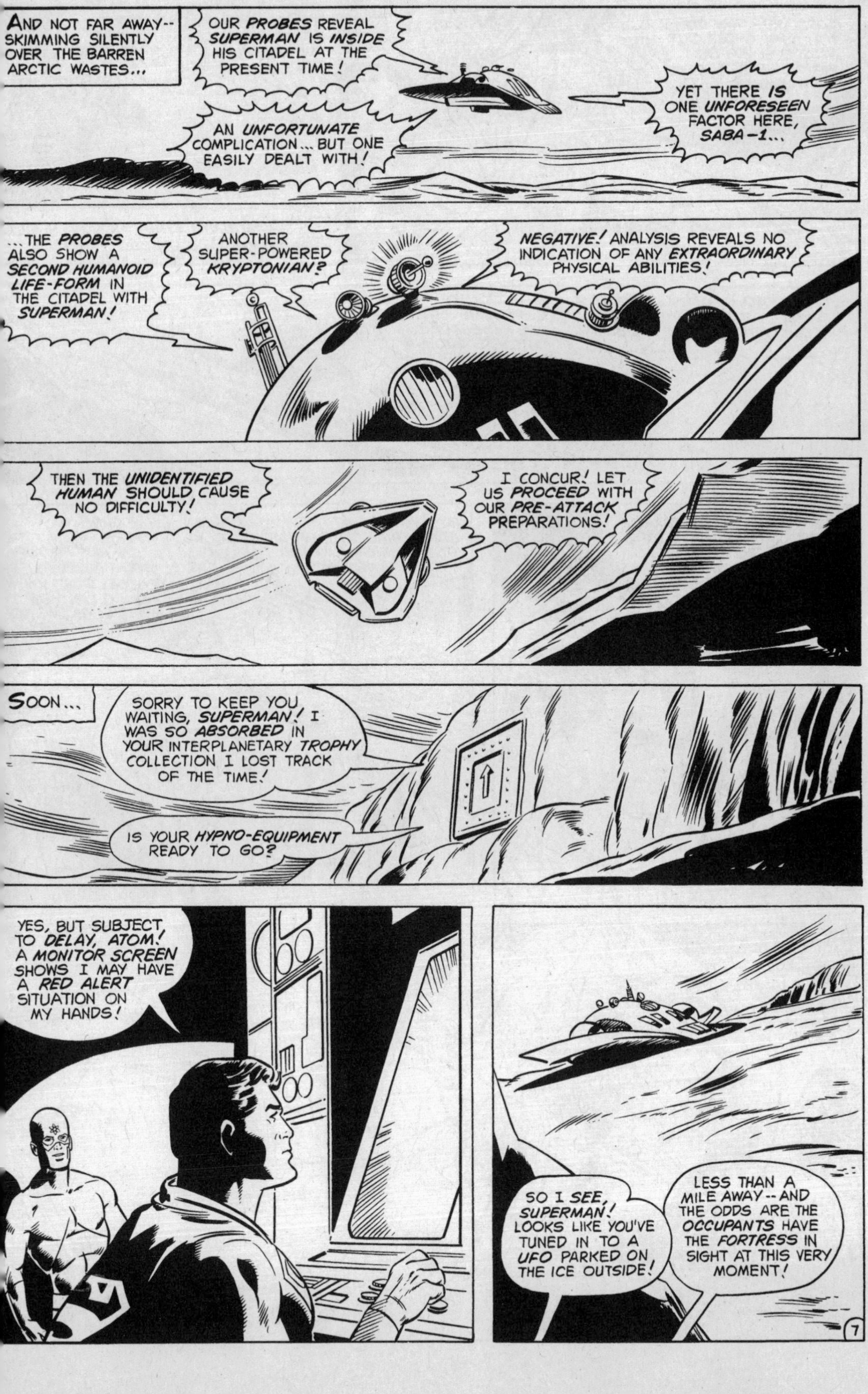
AND NOT FAR AWAY-- SKIMMING SILENTLY OVER THE BARREN ARCTIC WASTES...
OUR PROBES REVEAL SUPERMAN IS INSIDE HIS CITADEL AT THE PRESENT TIME!
AN UNFORTUNATE COMPLICATION... BUT ONE EASILY DEALT WITH!
YET THERE IS ONE UNFORESEEN FACTOR HERE, SABA-1...
...THE PROBES ALSO SHOW A SECOND HUMANOID LIFE-FORM IN THE CITADEL WITH SUPERMAN!
ANOTHER SUPER-POWERED KRYPTONIAN?
NEGATIVE! ANALYSIS REVEALS NO INDICATION OF ANY EXTRAORDINARY PHYSICAL ABILITIES!
THEN THE UNIDENTIFIED HUMAN SHOULD CAUSE NO DIFFICULTY!
I CONCUR! LET US PROCEED WITH OUR PRE-ATTACK PREPARATIONS!
SOON...
SORRY TO KEEP YOU WAITING, SUPERMAN! I WAS SO ABSORBED IN YOUR INTERPLANETARY TROPHY COLLECTION I LOST TRACK OF THE TIME!
IS YOUR HYPNO-EQUIPMENT READY TO GO?
YES, BUT SUBJECT TO DELAY, ATOM! A MONITOR SCREEN SHOWS I MAY HAVE A RED ALERT SITUATION ON MY HANDS!
SO I SEE, SUPERMAN! LOOKS LIKE YOU'VE TUNED IN TO A UFO PARKED ON THE ICE OUTSIDE!
LESS THAN A MILE AWAY -- AND THE ODDS ARE THE OCCUPANTS HAVE THE FORTRESS IN SIGHT AT THIS VERY MOMENT!
7

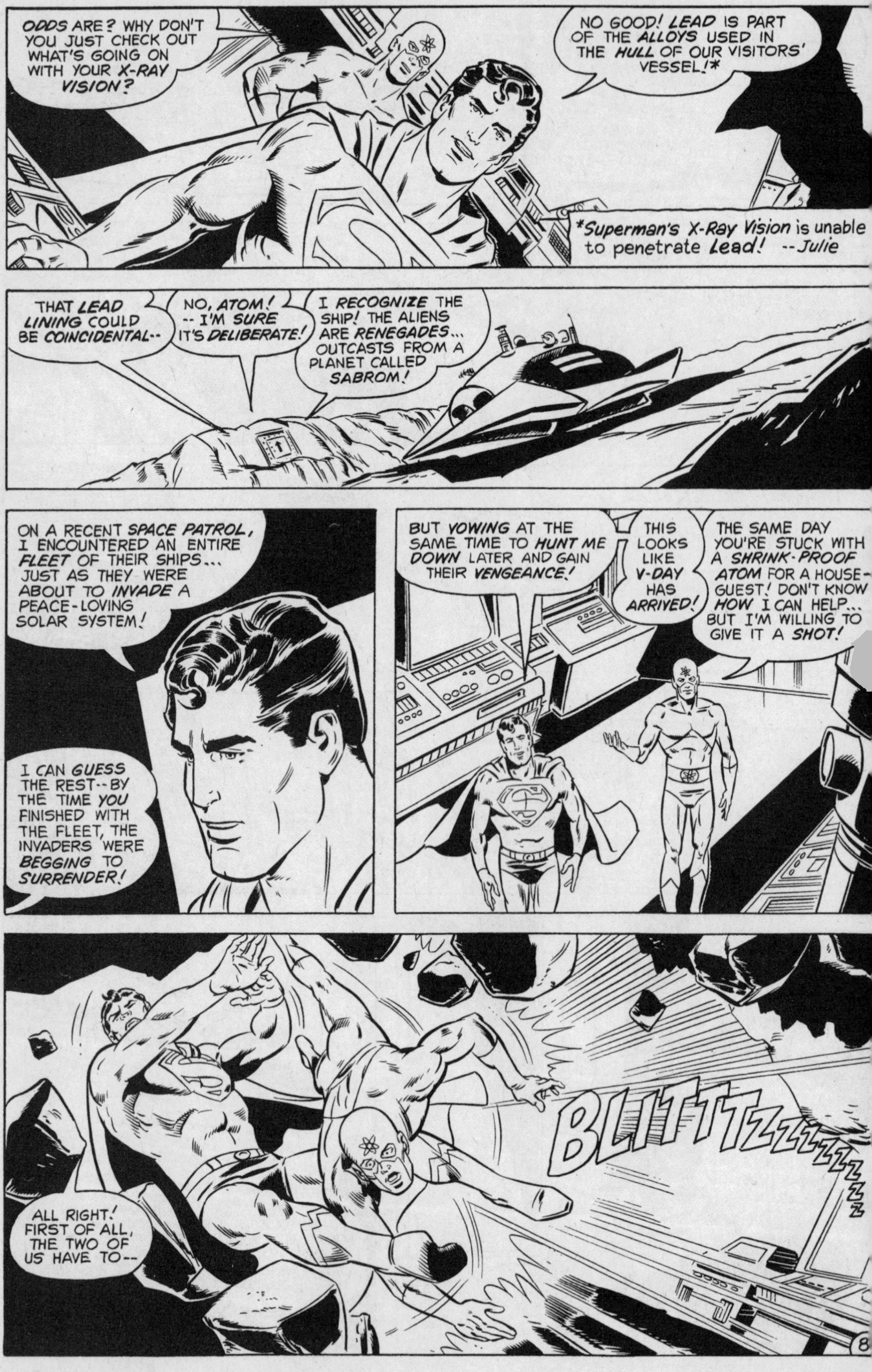
ODDS ARE? WHY DON'T YOU JUST CHECK OUT WHAT'S GOING ON WITH YOUR X-RAY VISION?
NO GOOD! LEAD IS PART OF THE ALLOYS USED IN THE HULL OF OUR VISITORS' VESSEL!*
*Superman's X-Ray Vision is unable to penetrate Lead! --Julie
THAT LEAD LINING COULD BE COINCIDENTAL--
NO, ATOM! -- I'M SURE IT'S DELIBERATE!
I RECOGNIZE THE SHIP! THE ALIENS ARE RENEGADES... OUTCASTS FROM A PLANET CALLED SABROM!
ON A RECENT SPACE PATROL, I ENCOUNTERED AN ENTIRE FLEET OF THEIR SHIPS... JUST AS THEY WERE ABOUT TO INVADE A PEACE-LOVING SOLAR SYSTEM!
I CAN GUESS THE REST--BY THE TIME YOU FINISHED WITH THE FLEET, THE INVADERS WERE BEGGING TO SURRENDER!
BUT VOWING AT THE SAME TIME TO HUNT ME DOWN LATER AND GAIN THEIR VENGEANCE!
THIS LOOKS LIKE V-DAY HAS ARRIVED!
THE SAME DAY YOU'RE STUCK WITH A SHRINK-PROOF ATOM FOR A HOUSE-GUEST! DON'T KNOW HOW I CAN HELP... BUT I'M WILLING TO GIVE IT A SHOT!
BLITTTZZZZZZZ
ALL RIGHT! FIRST OF ALL, THE TWO OF US HAVE TO--
8

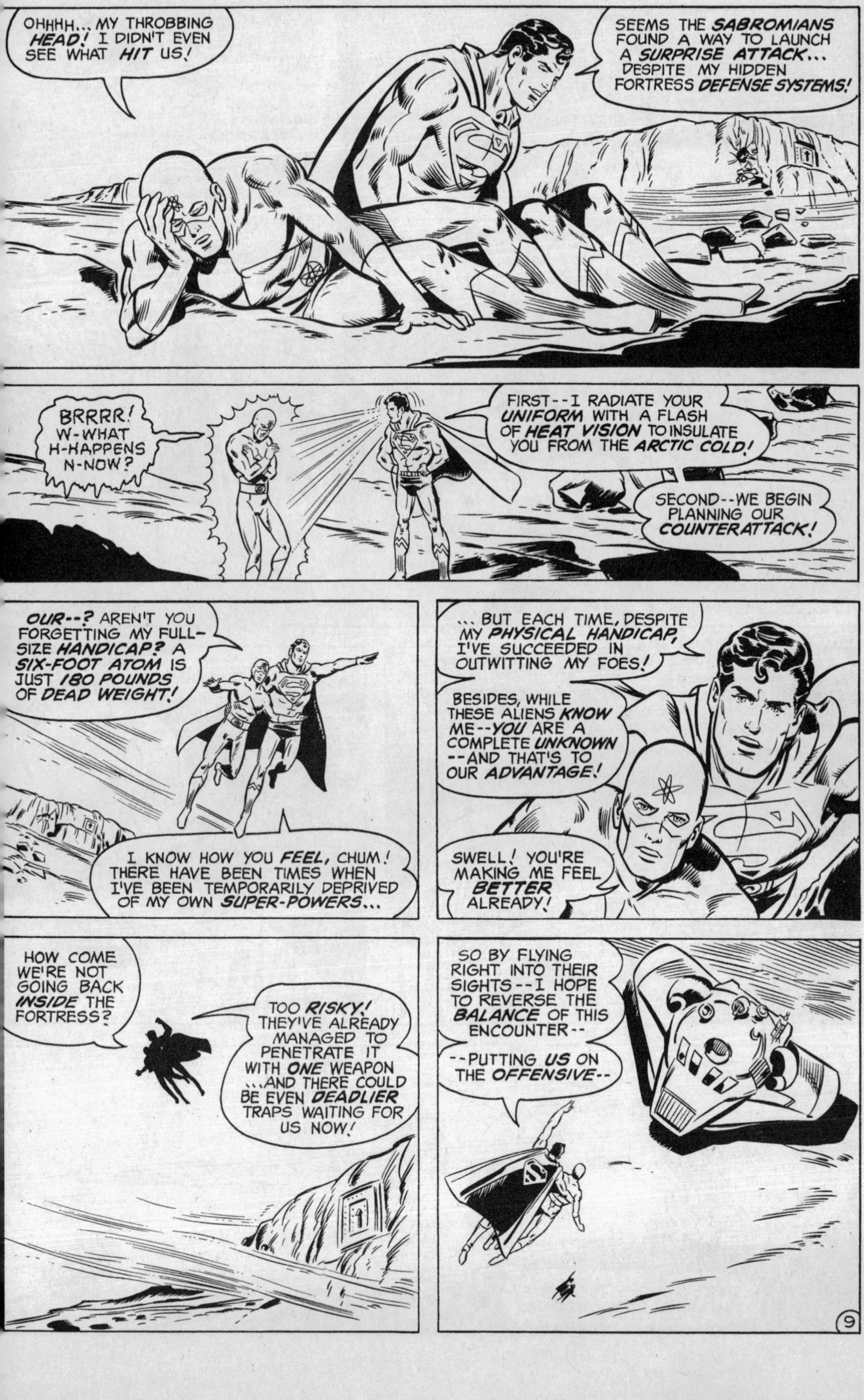
OHHHH... MY THROBBING HEAD! I DIDN'T EVEN SEE WHAT HIT US!
SEEMS THE SABROMIANS FOUND A WAY TO LAUNCH A SURPRISE ATTACK... DESPITE MY HIDDEN FORTRESS DEFENSE SYSTEMS!
BRRRR! W-WHAT H-HAPPENS N-NOW?
FIRST--I RADIATE YOUR UNIFORM WITH A FLASH OF HEAT VISION TO INSULATE YOU FROM THE ARCTIC COLD!
SECOND--WE BEGIN PLANNING OUR COUNTERATTACK!
OUR--? AREN'T YOU FORGETTING MY FULL-SIZE HANDICAP? A SIX-FOOT ATOM IS JUST 180 POUNDS OF DEAD WEIGHT!
I KNOW HOW YOU FEEL, CHUM! THERE HAVE BEEN TIMES WHEN I'VE BEEN TEMPORARILY DEPRIVED OF MY OWN SUPER-POWERS...
... BUT EACH TIME, DESPITE MY PHYSICAL HANDICAP, I'VE SUCCEEDED IN OUTWITTING MY FOES!
BESIDES, WHILE THESE ALIENS KNOW ME--YOU ARE A COMPLETE UNKNOWN --AND THAT'S TO OUR ADVANTAGE!
SWELL! YOU'RE MAKING ME FEEL BETTER ALREADY!
HOW COME WE'RE NOT GOING BACK INSIDE THE FORTRESS?
TOO RISKY! THEY'VE ALREADY MANAGED TO PENETRATE IT WITH ONE WEAPON ...AND THERE COULD BE EVEN DEADLIER TRAPS WAITING FOR US NOW!
SO BY FLYING RIGHT INTO THEIR SIGHTS--I HOPE TO REVERSE THE BALANCE OF THIS ENCOUNTER--
--PUTTING US ON THE OFFENSIVE--
9

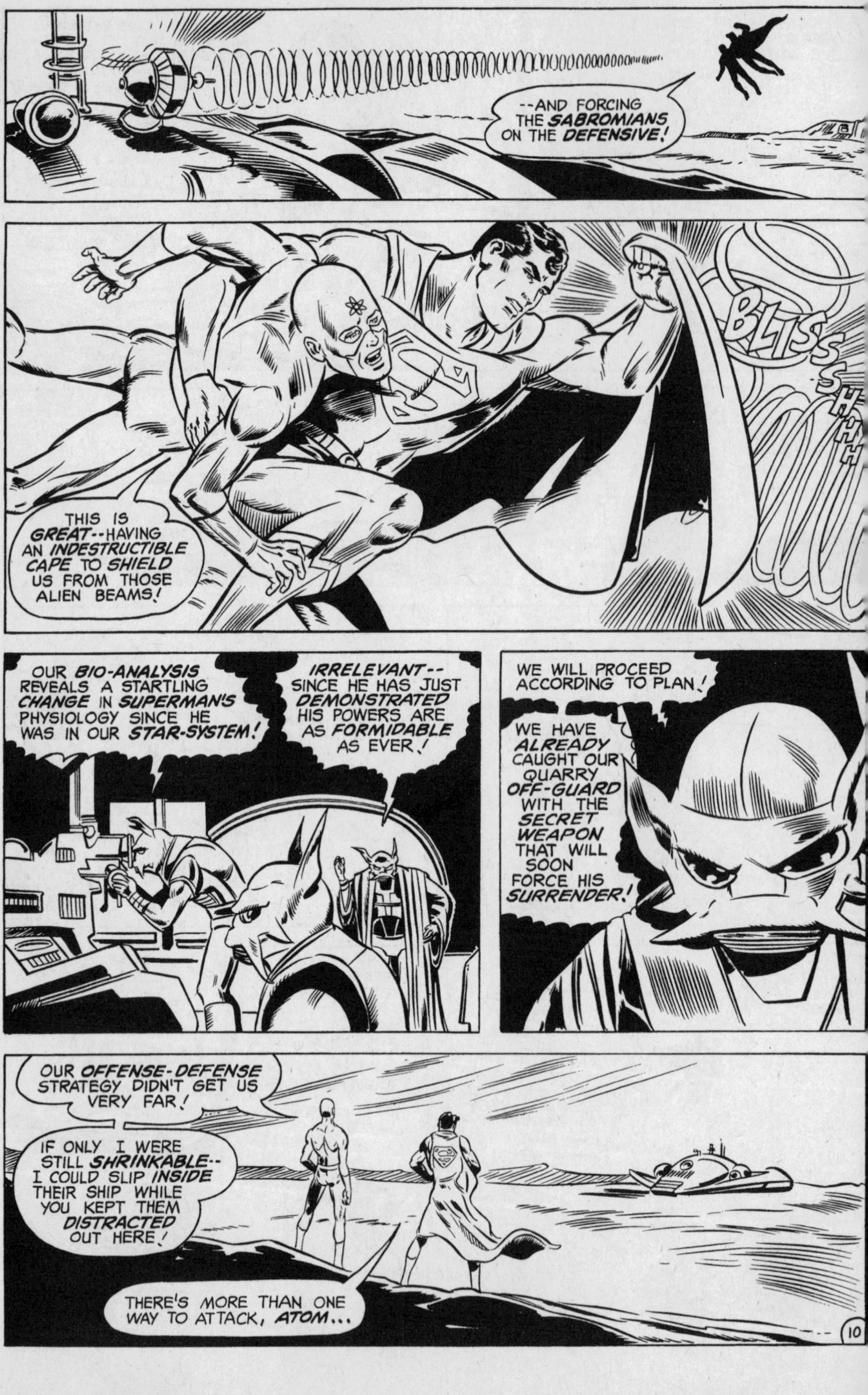
--AND FORCING THE SABROMIANS ON THE DEFENSIVE!
BLISSSHHH
THIS IS GREAT--HAVING AN INDESTRUCTIBLE CAPE TO SHIELD US FROM THOSE ALIEN BEAMS!
OUR BIO-ANALYSIS REVEALS A STARTLING CHANGE IN SUPERMAN'S PHYSIOLOGY SINCE HE WAS IN OUR STAR-SYSTEM!
IRRELEVANT--SINCE HE HAS JUST DEMONSTRATED HIS POWERS ARE AS FORMIDABLE AS EVER!
WE WILL PROCEED ACCORDING TO PLAN!
WE HAVE ALREADY CAUGHT OUR QUARRY OFF-GUARD WITH THE SECRET WEAPON THAT WILL SOON FORCE HIS SURRENDER!
OUR OFFENSE-DEFENSE STRATEGY DIDN'T GET US VERY FAR!
IF ONLY I WERE STILL SHRINKABLE--I COULD SLIP INSIDE THEIR SHIP WHILE YOU KEPT THEM DISTRACTED OUT HERE!
THERE'S MORE THAN ONE WAY TO ATTACK, ATOM...
10

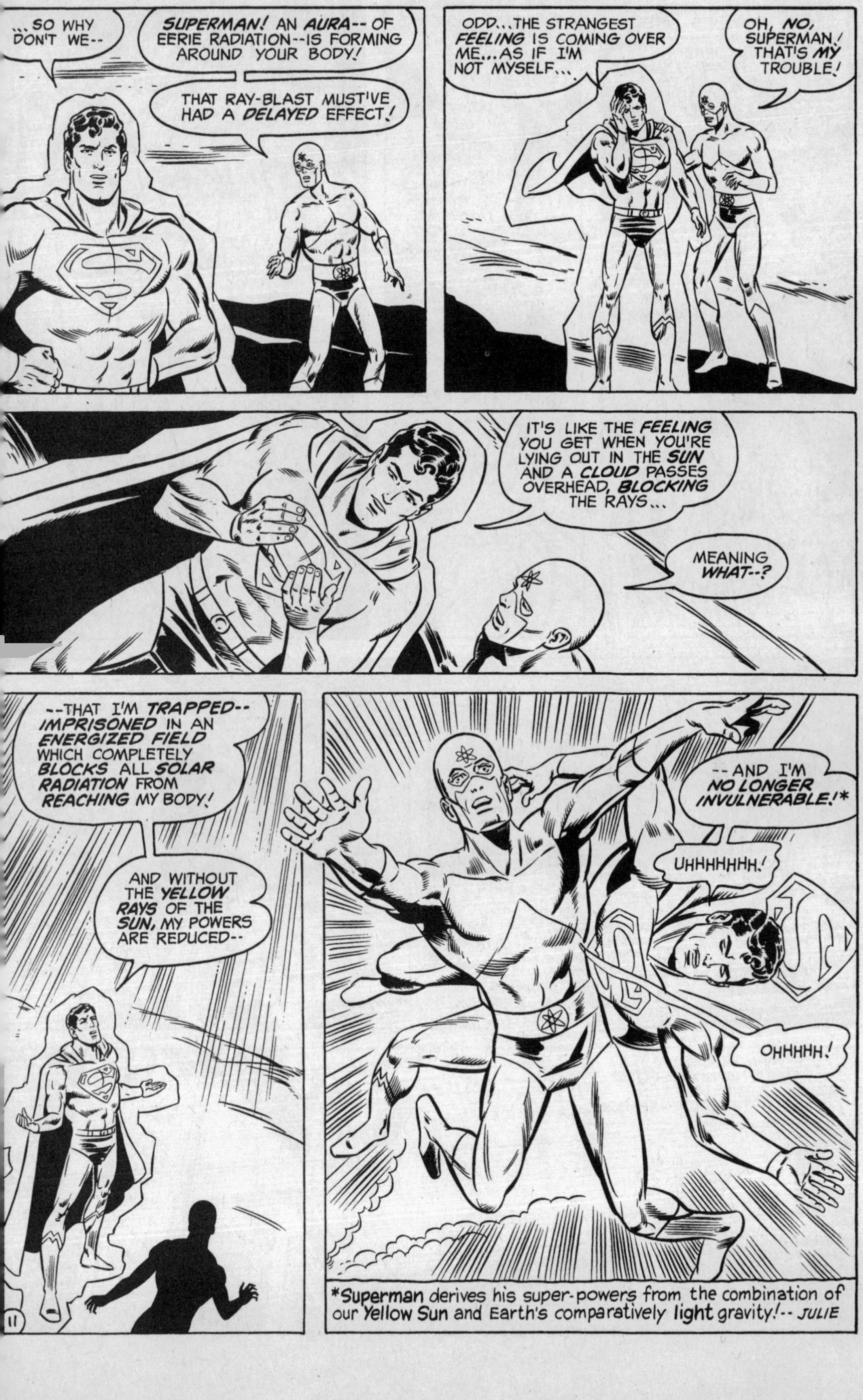
...SO WHY DON'T WE--
SUPERMAN! AN AURA-- OF EERIE RADIATION--IS FORMING AROUND YOUR BODY!
THAT RAY-BLAST MUST'VE HAD A DELAYED EFFECT!
ODD...THE STRANGEST FEELING IS COMING OVER ME...AS IF I'M NOT MYSELF...
OH, NO, SUPERMAN! THAT'S MY TROUBLE!
IT'S LIKE THE FEELING YOU GET WHEN YOU'RE LYING OUT IN THE SUN AND A CLOUD PASSES OVERHEAD, BLOCKING THE RAYS...
MEANING WHAT--?
--THAT I'M TRAPPED-- IMPRISONED IN AN ENERGIZED FIELD WHICH COMPLETELY BLOCKS ALL SOLAR RADIATION FROM REACHING MY BODY!
AND WITHOUT THE YELLOW RAYS OF THE SUN, MY POWERS ARE REDUCED--
11
--AND I'M NO LONGER INVULNERABLE!*
UHHHHHHH!
OHHHHH!
*Superman derives his super-powers from the combination of our Yellow Sun and Earth's comparatively light gravity!-- JULIE

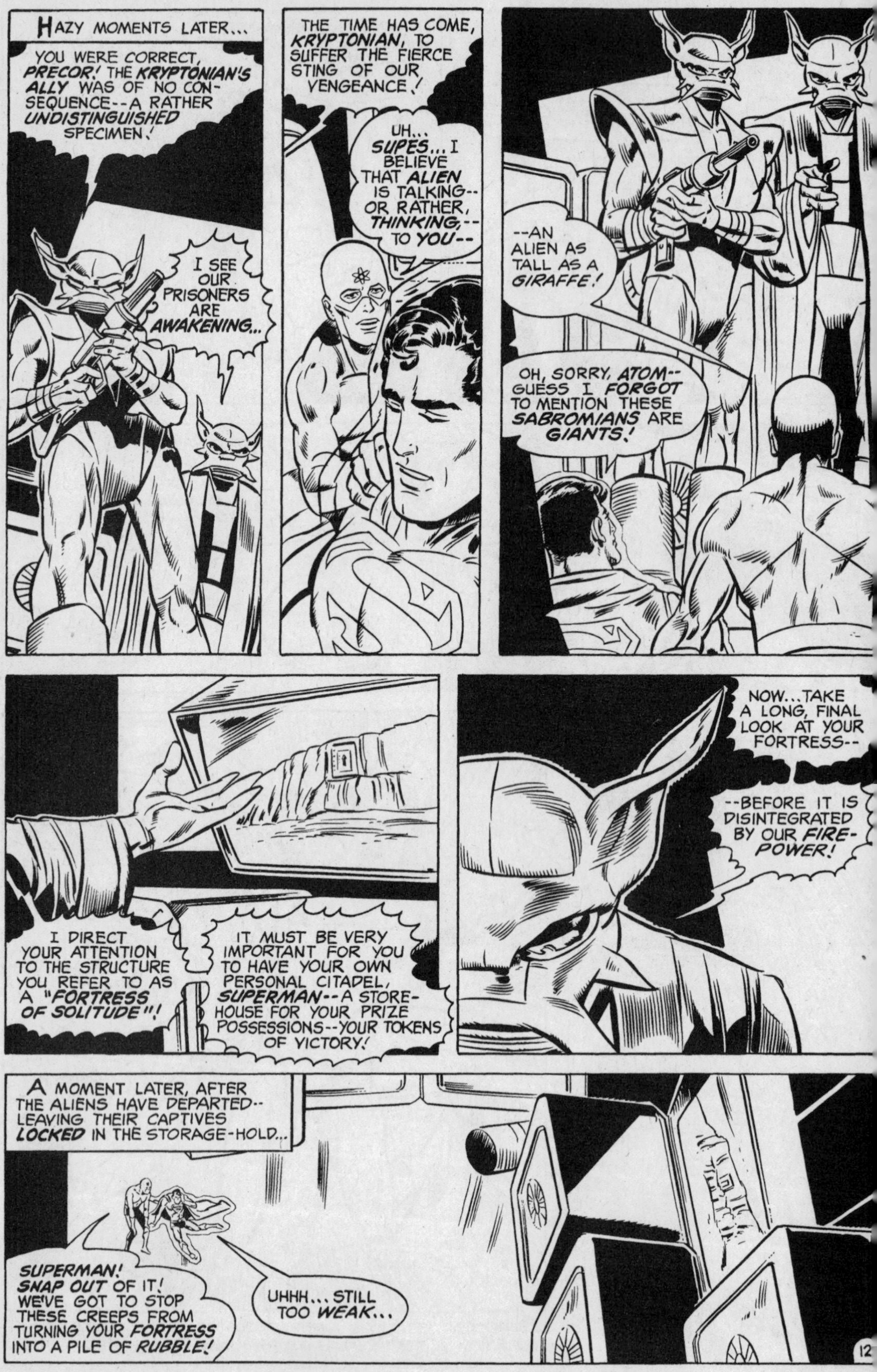
HAZY MOMENTS LATER...
YOU WERE CORRECT, PRECOR! THE KRYPTONIAN'S ALLY WAS OF NO CONSEQUENCE--A RATHER UNDISTINGUISHED SPECIMEN!
I SEE OUR PRISONERS ARE AWAKENING...
THE TIME HAS COME, KRYPTONIAN, TO SUFFER THE FIERCE STING OF OUR VENGEANCE!
UH... SUPES... I BELIEVE THAT ALIEN IS TALKING--OR RATHER, THINKING,--TO YOU--
--AN ALIEN AS TALL AS A GIRAFFE!
OH, SORRY, ATOM--GUESS I FORGOT TO MENTION THESE SABROMIANS ARE GIANTS!
I DIRECT YOUR ATTENTION TO THE STRUCTURE YOU REFER TO AS A "FORTRESS OF SOLITUDE"!
IT MUST BE VERY IMPORTANT FOR YOU TO HAVE YOUR OWN PERSONAL CITADEL, SUPERMAN--A STOREHOUSE FOR YOUR PRIZE POSSESSIONS--YOUR TOKENS OF VICTORY!
NOW...TAKE A LONG, FINAL LOOK AT YOUR FORTRESS--
--BEFORE IT IS DISINTEGRATED BY OUR FIREPOWER!
A MOMENT LATER, AFTER THE ALIENS HAVE DEPARTED--LEAVING THEIR CAPTIVES LOCKED IN THE STORAGE-HOLD...
SUPERMAN! SNAP OUT OF IT! WE'VE GOT TO STOP THESE CREEPS FROM TURNING YOUR FORTRESS INTO A PILE OF RUBBLE!
UHHH... STILL TOO WEAK...
12

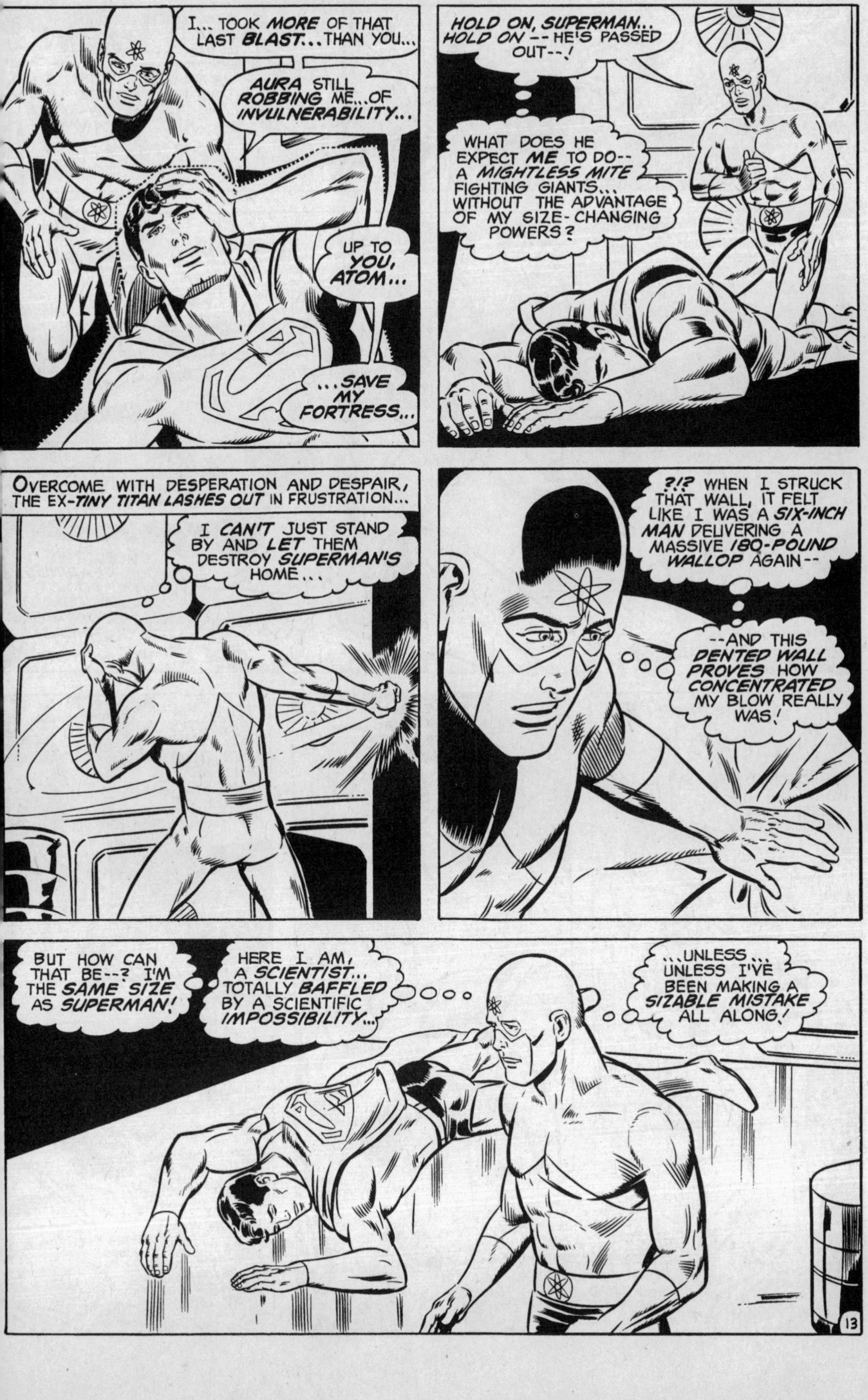
I... TOOK MORE OF THAT LAST BLAST...THAN YOU...
AURA STILL ROBBING ME...OF INVULNERABILITY...
UP TO YOU, ATOM...
...SAVE MY FORTRESS...
HOLD ON, SUPERMAN... HOLD ON -- HE'S PASSED OUT--!
WHAT DOES HE EXPECT ME TO DO-- A MIGHTLESS MITE FIGHTING GIANTS... WITHOUT THE ADVANTAGE OF MY SIZE-CHANGING POWERS?
OVERCOME WITH DESPERATION AND DESPAIR, THE EX-TINY TITAN LASHES OUT IN FRUSTRATION...
I CAN'T JUST STAND BY AND LET THEM DESTROY SUPERMAN'S HOME...
?!? WHEN I STRUCK THAT WALL, IT FELT LIKE I WAS A SIX-INCH MAN DELIVERING A MASSIVE 180-POUND WALLOP AGAIN--
--AND THIS DENTED WALL PROVES HOW CONCENTRATED MY BLOW REALLY WAS!
BUT HOW CAN THAT BE--? I'M THE SAME SIZE AS SUPERMAN!
HERE I AM, A SCIENTIST... TOTALLY BAFFLED BY A SCIENTIFIC IMPOSSIBILITY...
...UNLESS... UNLESS I'VE BEEN MAKING A SIZABLE MISTAKE ALL ALONG!
13

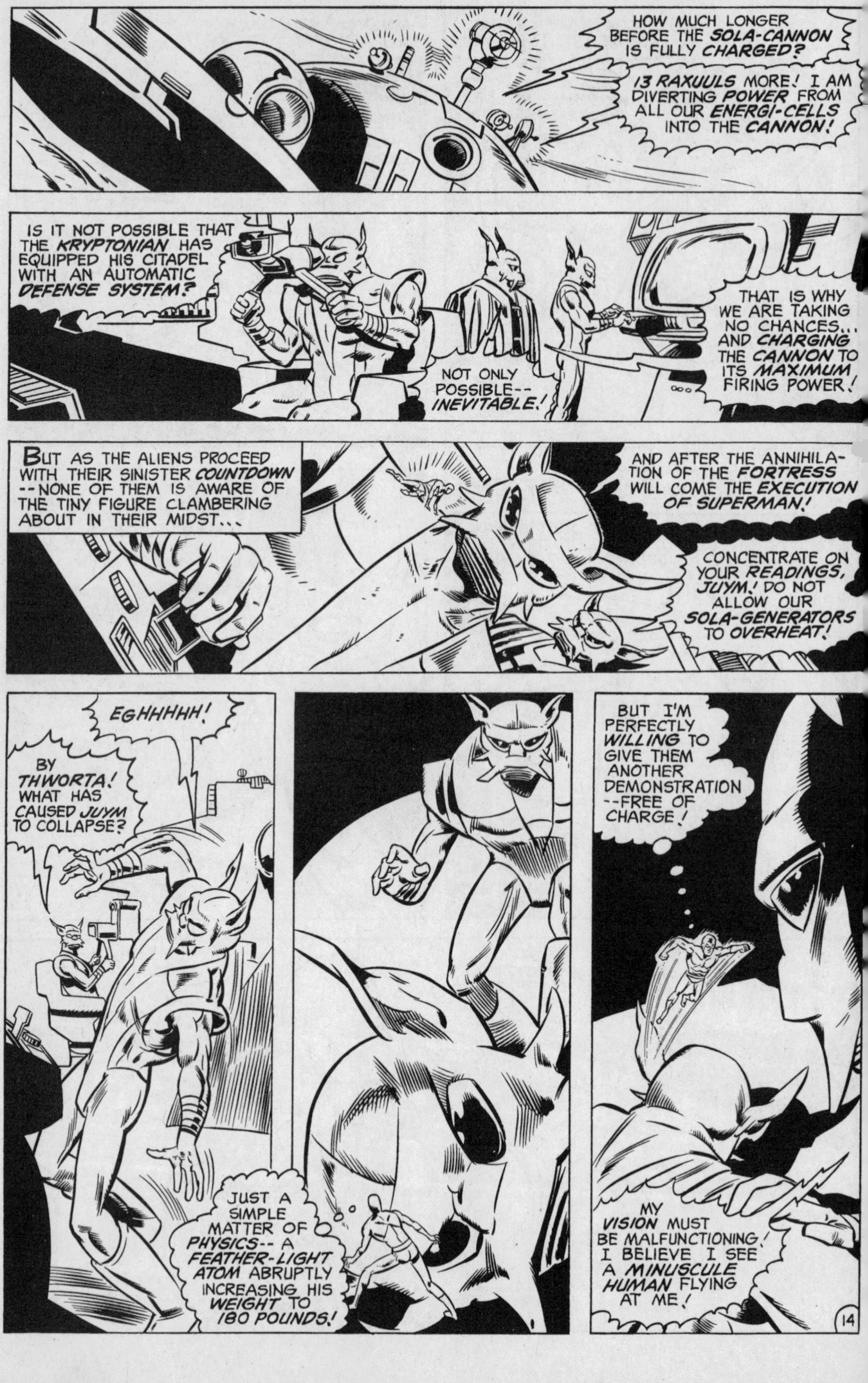
HOW MUCH LONGER BEFORE THE SOLA-CANNON IS FULLY CHARGED?
13 RAXUULS MORE! I AM DIVERTING POWER FROM ALL OUR ENERGI-CELLS INTO THE CANNON!
IS IT NOT POSSIBLE THAT THE KRYPTONIAN HAS EQUIPPED HIS CITADEL WITH AN AUTOMATIC DEFENSE SYSTEM?
NOT ONLY POSSIBLE-- INEVITABLE!
THAT IS WHY WE ARE TAKING NO CHANCES... AND CHARGING THE CANNON TO ITS MAXIMUM FIRING POWER!
BUT AS THE ALIENS PROCEED WITH THEIR SINISTER COUNTDOWN --NONE OF THEM IS AWARE OF THE TINY FIGURE CLAMBERING ABOUT IN THEIR MIDST...
AND AFTER THE ANNIHILATION OF THE FORTRESS WILL COME THE EXECUTION OF SUPERMAN!
CONCENTRATE ON YOUR READINGS, JUYM! DO NOT ALLOW OUR SOLA-GENERATORS TO OVERHEAT!
EGHHHHH!
BY THWORTA! WHAT HAS CAUSED JUYM TO COLLAPSE?
JUST A SIMPLE MATTER OF PHYSICS-- A FEATHER-LIGHT ATOM ABRUPTLY INCREASING HIS WEIGHT TO 180 POUNDS!
BUT I'M PERFECTLY WILLING TO GIVE THEM ANOTHER DEMONSTRATION --FREE OF CHARGE!
MY VISION MUST BE MALFUNCTIONING! I BELIEVE I SEE A MINUSCULE HUMAN FLYING AT ME!
14

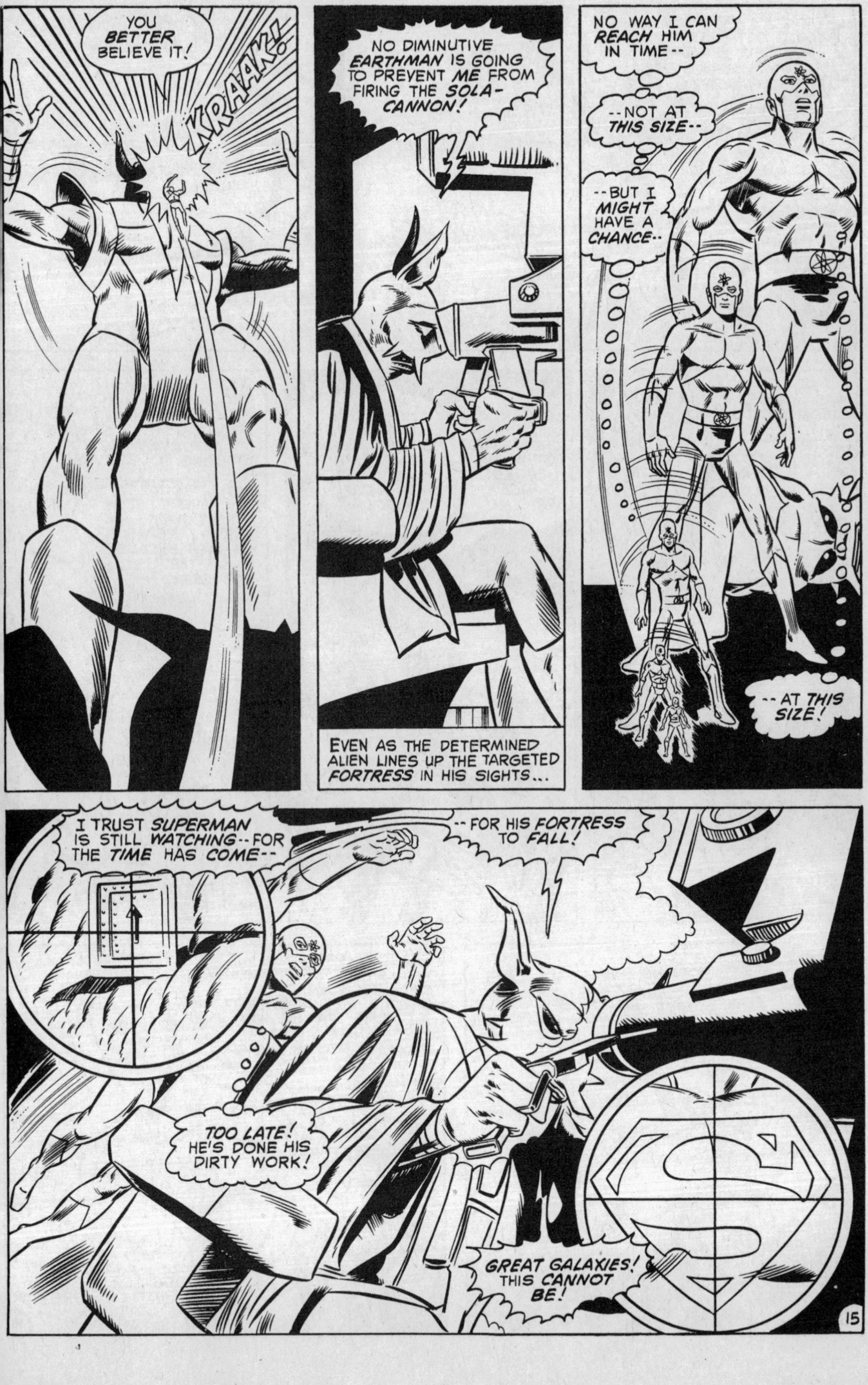
YOU BETTER BELIEVE IT!
KRAAK!
NO DIMINUTIVE EARTHMAN IS GOING TO PREVENT ME FROM FIRING THE SOLA-CANNON!
EVEN AS THE DETERMINED ALIEN LINES UP THE TARGETED FORTRESS IN HIS SIGHTS...
NO WAY I CAN REACH HIM IN TIME--
--NOT AT THIS SIZE--
--BUT I MIGHT HAVE A CHANCE--
--AT THIS SIZE!
I TRUST SUPERMAN IS STILL WATCHING--FOR THE TIME HAS COME--
--FOR HIS FORTRESS TO FALL!
TOO LATE! HE'S DONE HIS DIRTY WORK!
GREAT GALAXIES! THIS CANNOT BE!
15

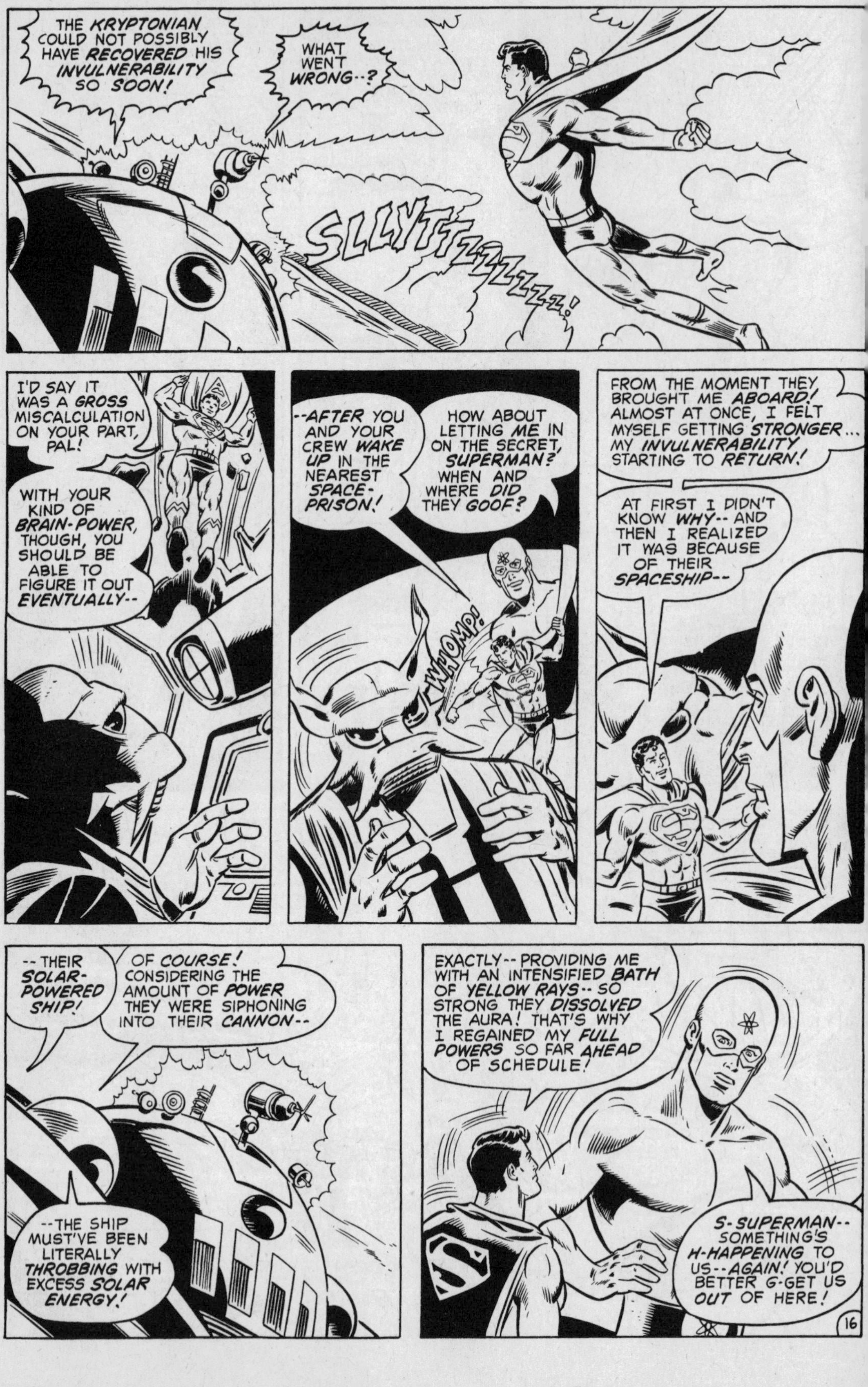
THE KRYPTONIAN COULD NOT POSSIBLY HAVE RECOVERED HIS INVULNERABILITY SO SOON!
WHAT WENT WRONG--?
SLLYTTTZZZZZZZZ!
I'D SAY IT WAS A GROSS MISCALCULATION ON YOUR PART, PAL!
WITH YOUR KIND OF BRAIN-POWER, THOUGH, YOU SHOULD BE ABLE TO FIGURE IT OUT EVENTUALLY--
--AFTER YOU AND YOUR CREW WAKE UP IN THE NEAREST SPACE-PRISON!
HOW ABOUT LETTING ME IN ON THE SECRET, SUPERMAN? WHEN AND WHERE DID THEY GOOF?
WHOMP!
FROM THE MOMENT THEY BROUGHT ME ABOARD! ALMOST AT ONCE, I FELT MYSELF GETTING STRONGER... MY INVULNERABILITY STARTING TO RETURN!
AT FIRST I DIDN'T KNOW WHY-- AND THEN I REALIZED IT WAS BECAUSE OF THEIR SPACESHIP--
--THEIR SOLAR-POWERED SHIP!
OF COURSE! CONSIDERING THE AMOUNT OF POWER THEY WERE SIPHONING INTO THEIR CANNON--
--THE SHIP MUST'VE BEEN LITERALLY THROBBING WITH EXCESS SOLAR ENERGY!
EXACTLY--PROVIDING ME WITH AN INTENSIFIED BATH OF YELLOW RAYS-- SO STRONG THEY DISSOLVED THE AURA! THAT'S WHY I REGAINED MY FULL POWERS SO FAR AHEAD OF SCHEDULE!
S-SUPERMAN-- SOMETHING'S H-HAPPENING TO US--AGAIN! YOU'D BETTER G-GET US OUT OF HERE!
16

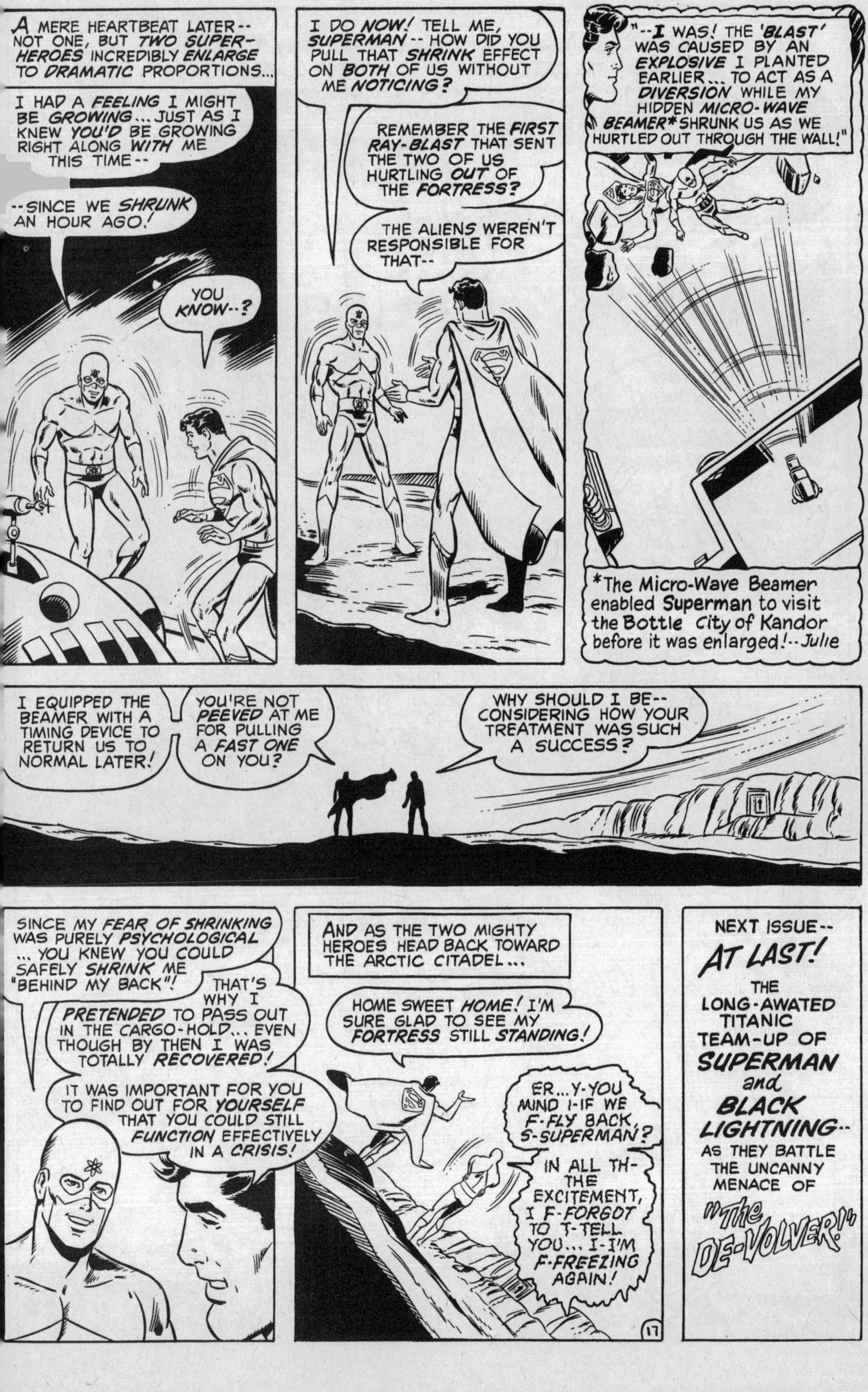
A MERE HEARTBEAT LATER-- NOT ONE, BUT TWO SUPER-HEROES INCREDIBLY ENLARGE TO DRAMATIC PROPORTIONS...
I HAD A FEELING I MIGHT BE GROWING... JUST AS I KNEW YOU'D BE GROWING RIGHT ALONG WITH ME THIS TIME--
--SINCE WE SHRUNK AN HOUR AGO!
YOU KNOW--?
I DO NOW! TELL ME, SUPERMAN -- HOW DID YOU PULL THAT SHRINK EFFECT ON BOTH OF US WITHOUT ME NOTICING?
REMEMBER THE FIRST RAY-BLAST THAT SENT THE TWO OF US HURTLING OUT OF THE FORTRESS?
THE ALIENS WEREN'T RESPONSIBLE FOR THAT--
"--I WAS! THE 'BLAST' WAS CAUSED BY AN EXPLOSIVE I PLANTED EARLIER... TO ACT AS A DIVERSION WHILE MY HIDDEN MICRO-WAVE BEAMER* SHRUNK US AS WE HURTLED OUT THROUGH THE WALL!"
*The Micro-Wave Beamer enabled Superman to visit the Bottle City of Kandor before it was enlarged! --Julie
I EQUIPPED THE BEAMER WITH A TIMING DEVICE TO RETURN US TO NORMAL LATER!
YOU'RE NOT PEEVED AT ME FOR PULLING A FAST ONE ON YOU?
WHY SHOULD I BE-- CONSIDERING HOW YOUR TREATMENT WAS SUCH A SUCCESS?
SINCE MY FEAR OF SHRINKING WAS PURELY PSYCHOLOGICAL ... YOU KNEW YOU COULD SAFELY SHRINK ME "BEHIND MY BACK"!
THAT'S WHY I PRETENDED TO PASS OUT IN THE CARGO-HOLD... EVEN THOUGH BY THEN I WAS TOTALLY RECOVERED!
IT WAS IMPORTANT FOR YOU TO FIND OUT FOR YOURSELF THAT YOU COULD STILL FUNCTION EFFECTIVELY IN A CRISIS!
AND AS THE TWO MIGHTY HEROES HEAD BACK TOWARD THE ARCTIC CITADEL...
HOME SWEET HOME! I'M SURE GLAD TO SEE MY FORTRESS STILL STANDING!
ER... Y-YOU MIND I-IF WE F-FLY BACK, S-SUPERMAN?
IN ALL TH-THE EXCITEMENT, I F-FORGOT TO T-TELL YOU... I-I'M F-FREEZING AGAIN!
17
NEXT ISSUE-- AT LAST! THE LONG-AWATED TITANIC TEAM-UP OF SUPERMAN and BLACK LIGHTNING-- AS THEY BATTLE THE UNCANNY MENACE OF "The DE-VOLVER!"

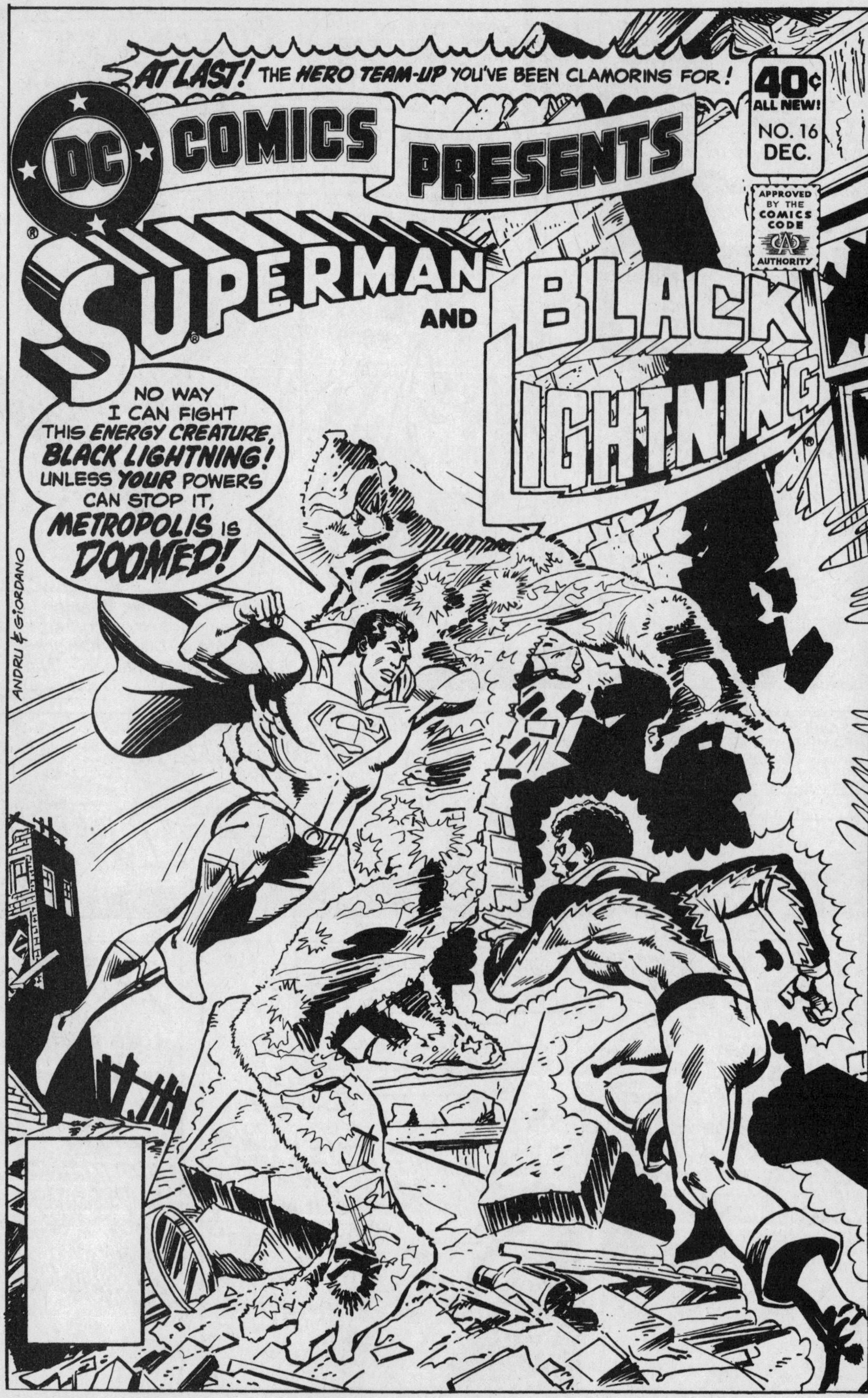
AT LAST! THE HERO TEAM-UP YOU'VE BEEN CLAMORINS FOR!
DC COMICS PRESENTS
40¢ ALL NEW!
NO. 16 DEC.
APPROVED BY THE COMICS CODE AUTHORITY
SUPERMAN AND BLACK LIGHTNING
NO WAY I CAN FIGHT THIS ENERGY CREATURE, BLACK LIGHTNING! UNLESS YOUR POWERS CAN STOP IT, METROPOLIS IS DOOMED!
ANDRU & GIORDANO

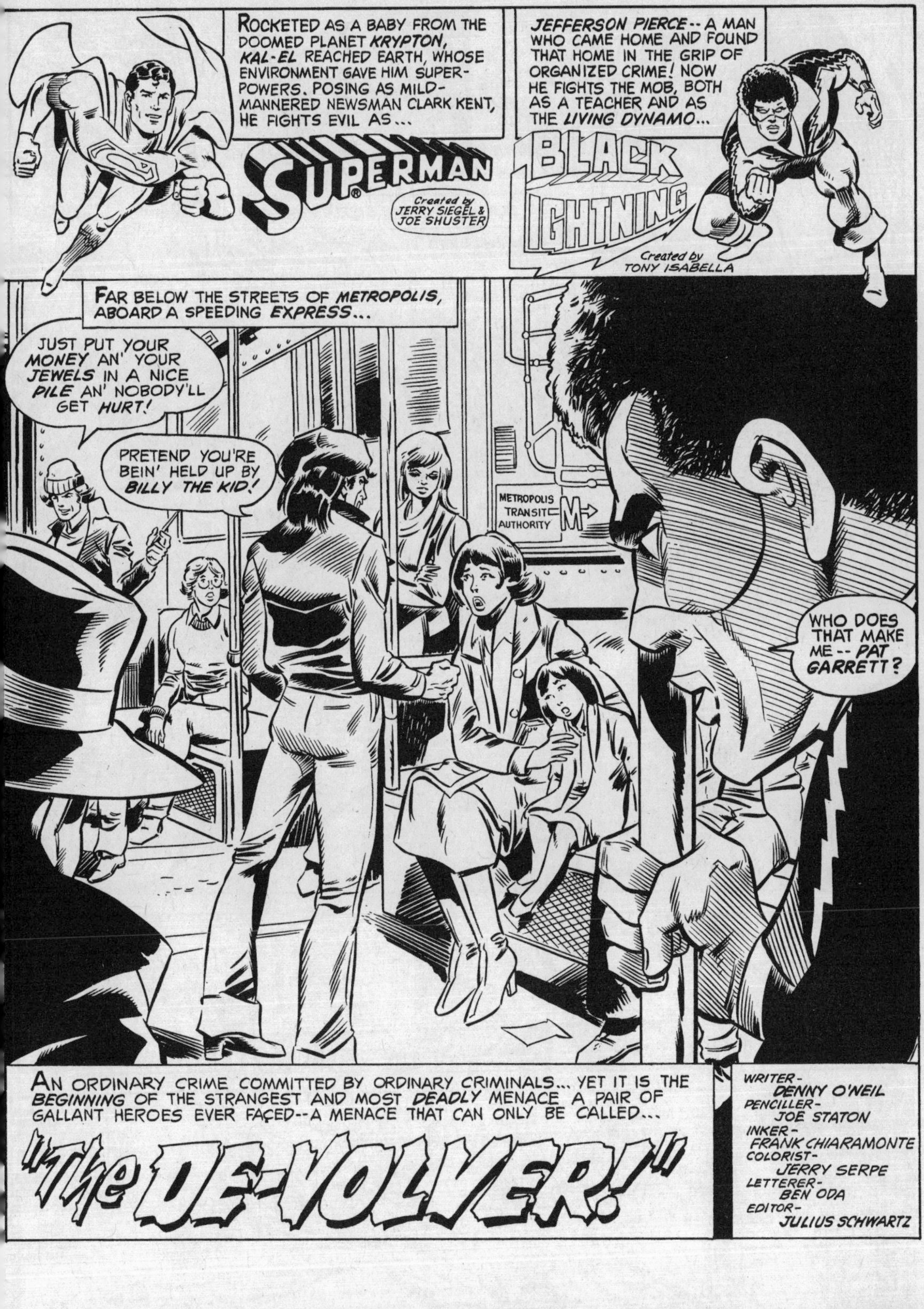
ROCKETED AS A BABY FROM THE DOOMED PLANET KRYPTON, KAL-EL REACHED EARTH, WHOSE ENVIRONMENT GAVE HIM SUPER-POWERS. POSING AS MILD-MANNERED NEWSMAN CLARK KENT, HE FIGHTS EVIL AS...
SUPERMAN
Created by JERRY SIEGEL & JOE SHUSTER
JEFFERSON PIERCE -- A MAN WHO CAME HOME AND FOUND THAT HOME IN THE GRIP OF ORGANIZED CRIME! NOW HE FIGHTS THE MOB, BOTH AS A TEACHER AND AS THE LIVING DYNAMO...
BLACK LIGHTNING
Created by TONY ISABELLA
FAR BELOW THE STREETS OF METROPOLIS, ABOARD A SPEEDING EXPRESS...
JUST PUT YOUR MONEY AN' YOUR JEWELS IN A NICE PILE AN' NOBODY'LL GET HURT!
PRETEND YOU'RE BEIN' HELD UP BY BILLY THE KID!
METROPOLIS TRANSIT AUTHORITY
WHO DOES THAT MAKE ME -- PAT GARRETT?
AN ORDINARY CRIME COMMITTED BY ORDINARY CRIMINALS... YET IT IS THE BEGINNING OF THE STRANGEST AND MOST DEADLY MENACE A PAIR OF GALLANT HEROES EVER FACED--A MENACE THAT CAN ONLY BE CALLED...
"The DE-VOLVER!"
WRITER- DENNY O'NEIL
PENCILLER- JOE STATON
INKER- FRANK CHIARAMONTE
COLORIST- JERRY SERPE
LETTERER- BEN ODA
EDITOR- JULIUS SCHWARTZ

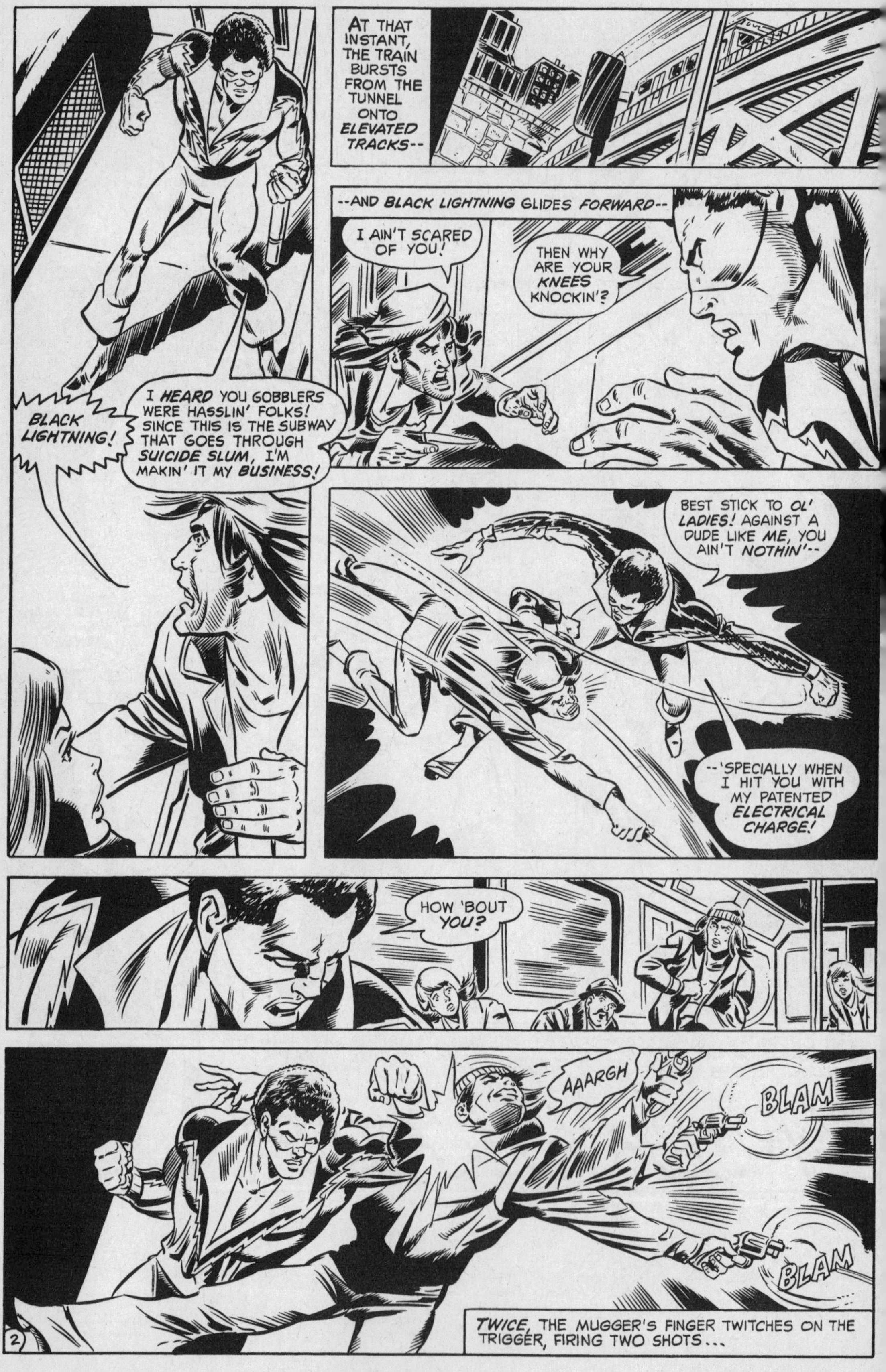
AT THAT INSTANT, THE TRAIN BURSTS FROM THE TUNNEL ONTO ELEVATED TRACKS--
BLACK LIGHTNING!
I HEARD YOU GOBBLERS WERE HASSLIN' FOLKS! SINCE THIS IS THE SUBWAY THAT GOES THROUGH SUICIDE SLUM, I'M MAKIN' IT MY BUSINESS!
--AND BLACK LIGHTNING GLIDES FORWARD--
I AIN'T SCARED OF YOU!
THEN WHY ARE YOUR KNEES KNOCKIN'?
BEST STICK TO OL' LADIES! AGAINST A DUDE LIKE ME, YOU AIN'T NOTHIN'--
--'SPECIALLY WHEN I HIT YOU WITH MY PATENTED ELECTRICAL CHARGE!
HOW 'BOUT YOU?
AAARGH
BLAM
BLAM
TWICE, THE MUGGER'S FINGER TWITCHES ON THE TRIGGER, FIRING TWO SHOTS...
2

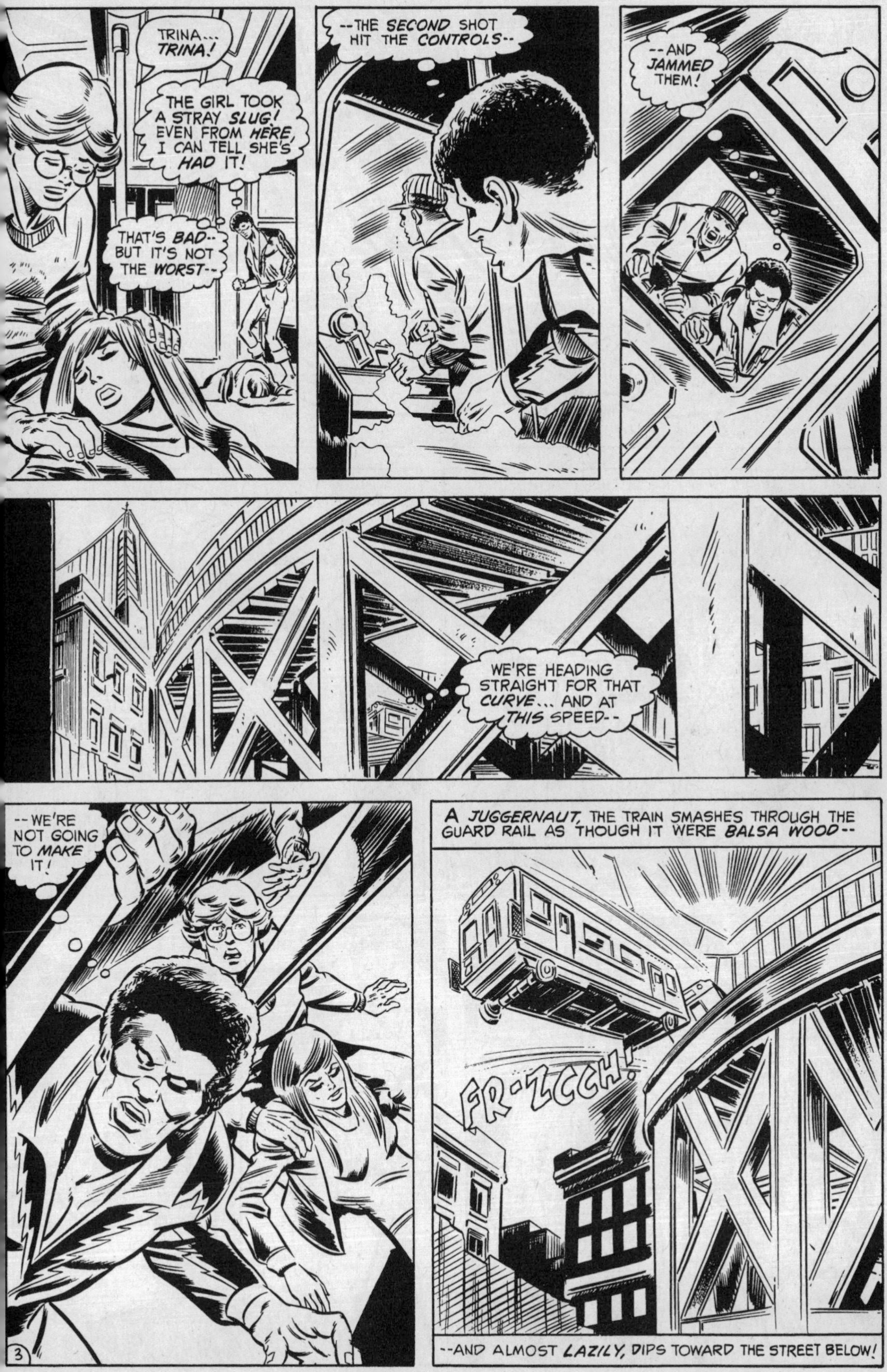
TRINA... TRINA!
THE GIRL TOOK A STRAY SLUG! EVEN FROM HERE, I CAN TELL SHE'S HAD IT!
THAT'S BAD-- BUT IT'S NOT THE WORST--
--THE SECOND SHOT HIT THE CONTROLS--
--AND JAMMED THEM!
WE'RE HEADING STRAIGHT FOR THAT CURVE... AND AT THIS SPEED--
--WE'RE NOT GOING TO MAKE IT!
A JUGGERNAUT, THE TRAIN SMASHES THROUGH THE GUARD RAIL AS THOUGH IT WERE BALSA WOOD--
FR-ZCCH!
--AND ALMOST LAZILY, DIPS TOWARD THE STREET BELOW!
3

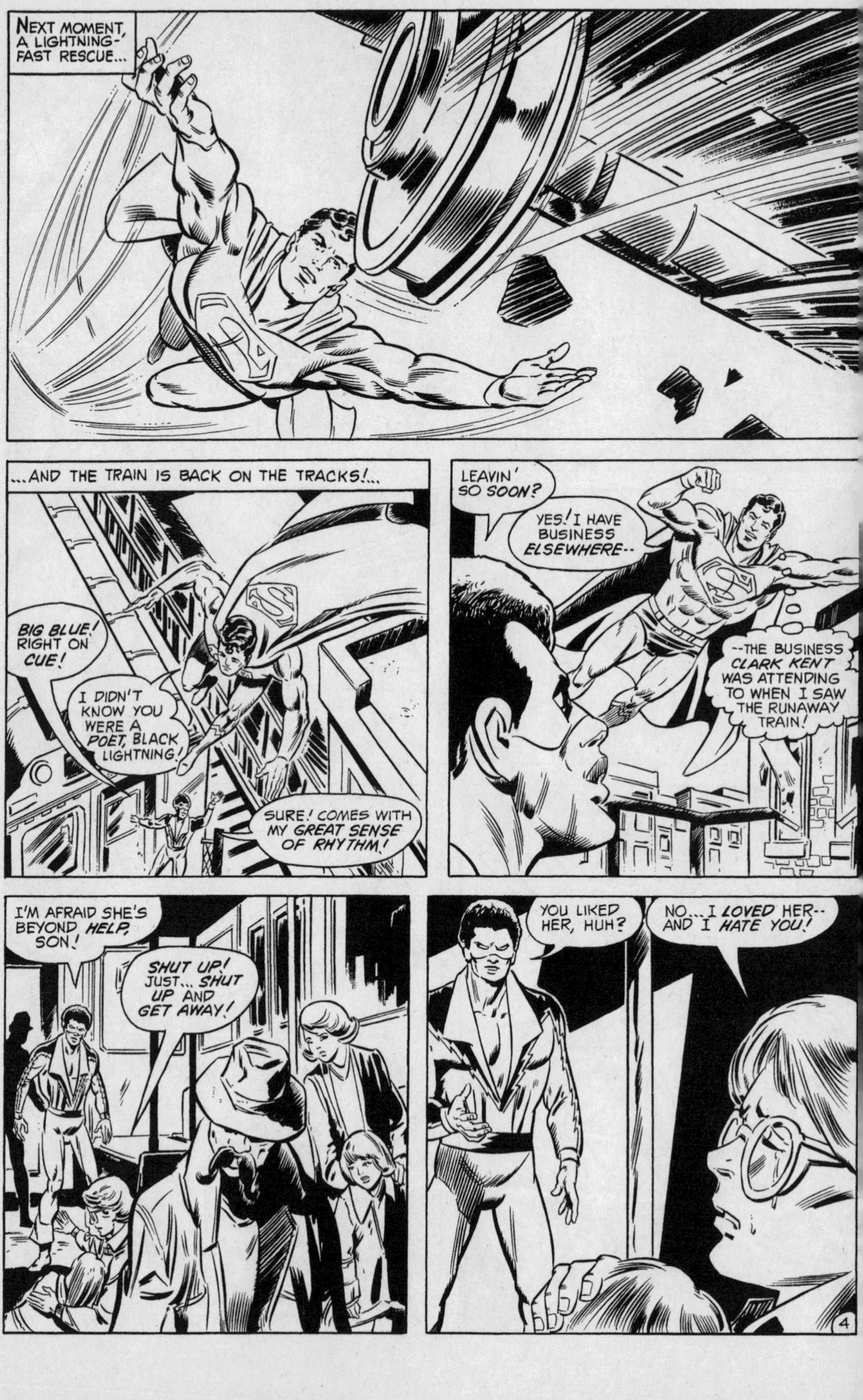
NEXT MOMENT, A LIGHTNING-FAST RESCUE...
...AND THE TRAIN IS BACK ON THE TRACKS!...
BIG BLUE! RIGHT ON CUE!
I DIDN'T KNOW YOU WERE A POET, BLACK LIGHTNING!
SURE! COMES WITH MY GREAT SENSE OF RHYTHM!
LEAVIN' SO SOON?
YES! I HAVE BUSINESS ELSEWHERE--
--THE BUSINESS CLARK KENT WAS ATTENDING TO WHEN I SAW THE RUNAWAY TRAIN!
I'M AFRAID SHE'S BEYOND HELP, SON!
SHUT UP! JUST... SHUT UP AND GET AWAY!
YOU LIKED HER, HUH?
NO...I LOVED HER--AND I HATE YOU!
4

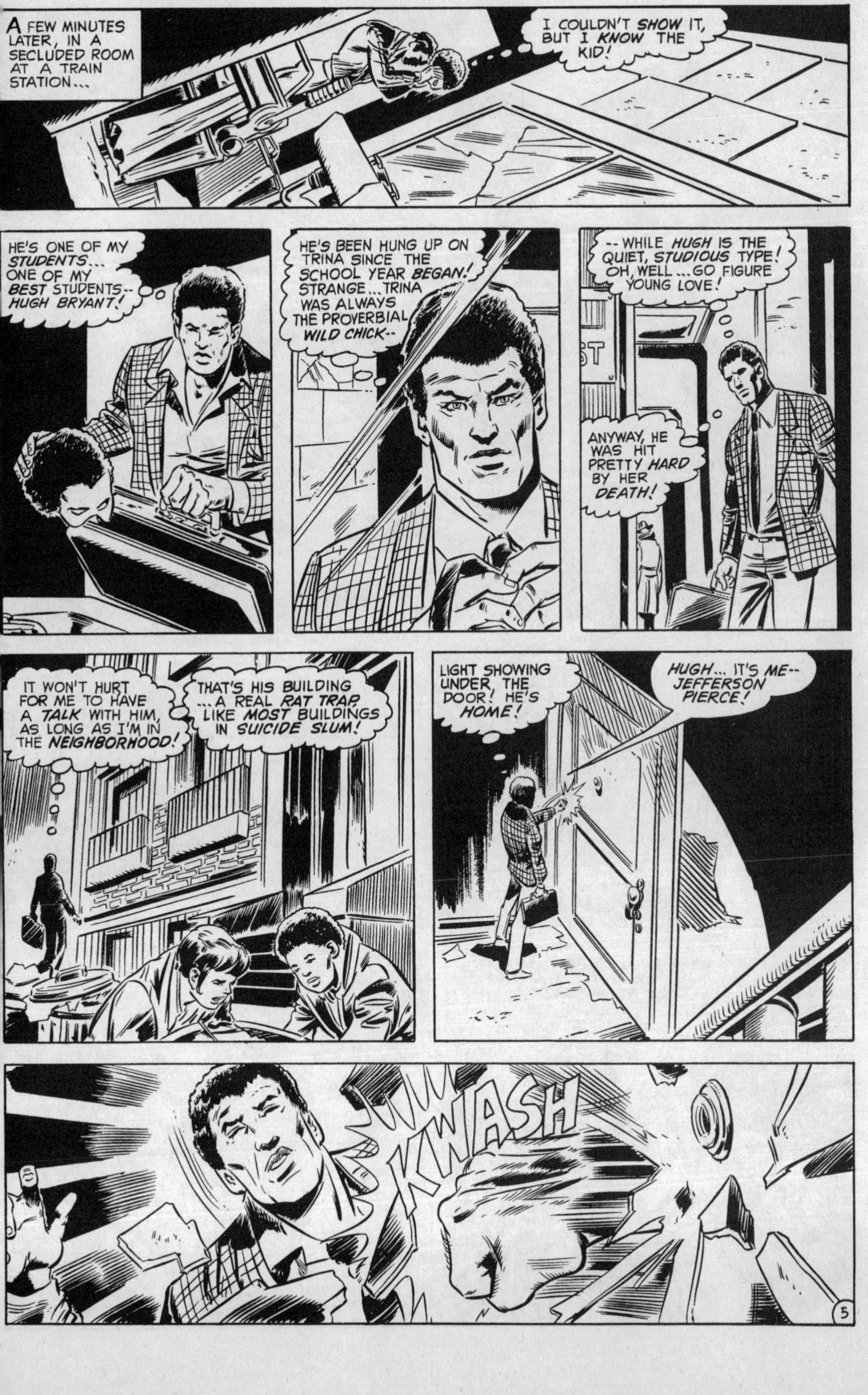
A FEW MINUTES LATER, IN A SECLUDED ROOM AT A TRAIN STATION...
I COULDN'T SHOW IT, BUT I KNOW THE KID!
HE'S ONE OF MY STUDENTS... ONE OF MY BEST STUDENTS-- HUGH BRYANT!
HE'S BEEN HUNG UP ON TRINA SINCE THE SCHOOL YEAR BEGAN! STRANGE...TRINA WAS ALWAYS THE PROVERBIAL WILD CHICK--
--WHILE HUGH IS THE QUIET, STUDIOUS TYPE! OH, WELL...GO FIGURE YOUNG LOVE!
ANYWAY, HE WAS HIT PRETTY HARD BY HER DEATH!
IT WON'T HURT FOR ME TO HAVE A TALK WITH HIM, AS LONG AS I'M IN THE NEIGHBORHOOD!
THAT'S HIS BUILDING ...A REAL RAT TRAP, LIKE MOST BUILDINGS IN SUICIDE SLUM!
LIGHT SHOWING UNDER THE DOOR! HE'S HOME!
HUGH... IT'S ME-- JEFFERSON PIERCE!
KWASH
5

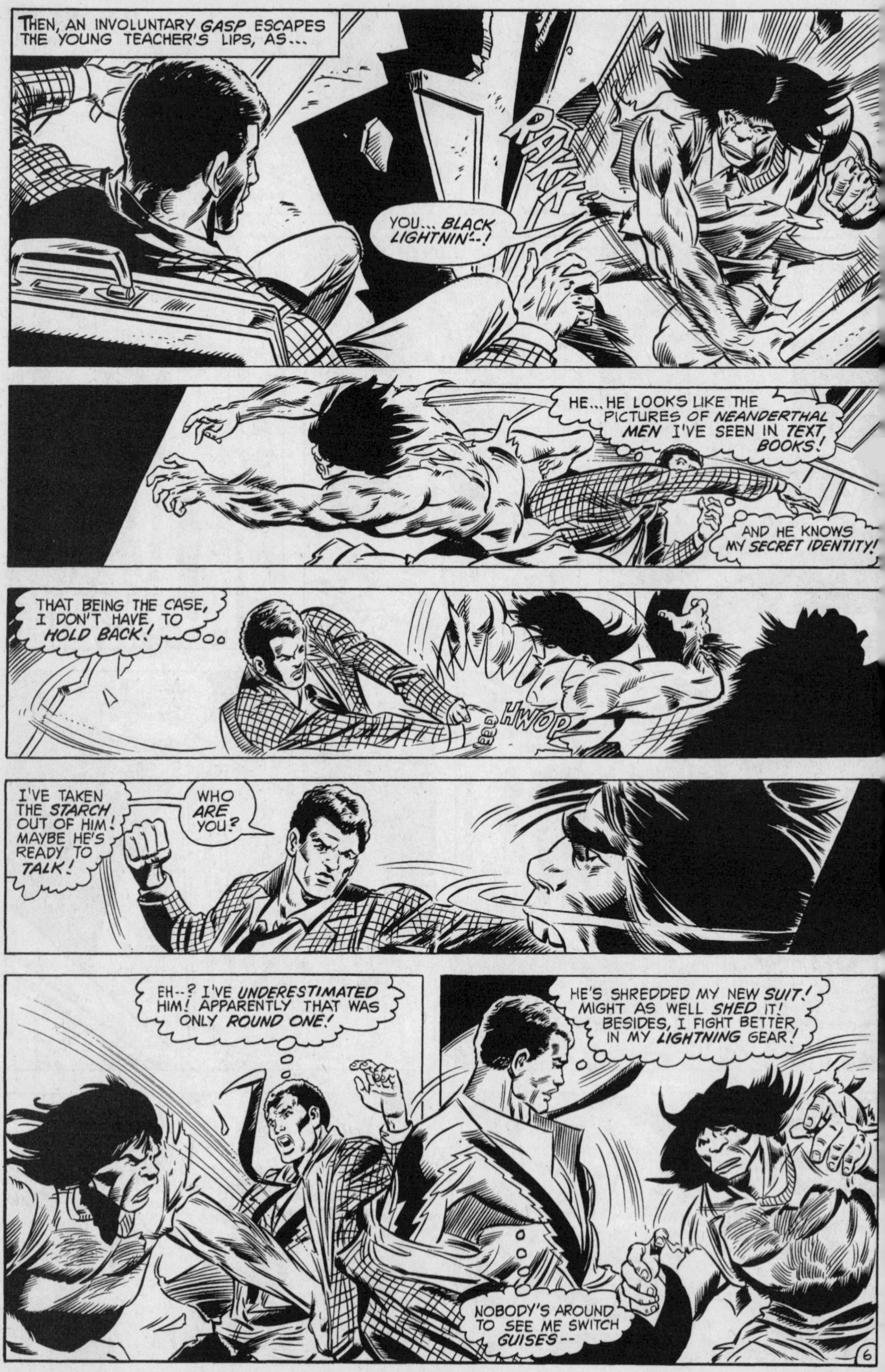
THEN, AN INVOLUNTARY GASP ESCAPES THE YOUNG TEACHER'S LIPS, AS...
RAKK
YOU... BLACK LIGHTNIN'--!
HE... HE LOOKS LIKE THE PICTURES OF NEANDERTHAL MEN I'VE SEEN IN TEXT BOOKS!
AND HE KNOWS MY SECRET IDENTITY!
THAT BEING THE CASE, I DON'T HAVE TO HOLD BACK!
HWOP
I'VE TAKEN THE STARCH OUT OF HIM! MAYBE HE'S READY TO TALK!
WHO ARE YOU?
EH--? I'VE UNDERESTIMATED HIM! APPARENTLY THAT WAS ONLY ROUND ONE!
HE'S SHREDDED MY NEW SUIT! MIGHT AS WELL SHED IT! BESIDES, I FIGHT BETTER IN MY LIGHTNING GEAR!
NOBODY'S AROUND TO SEE ME SWITCH GUISES--
6

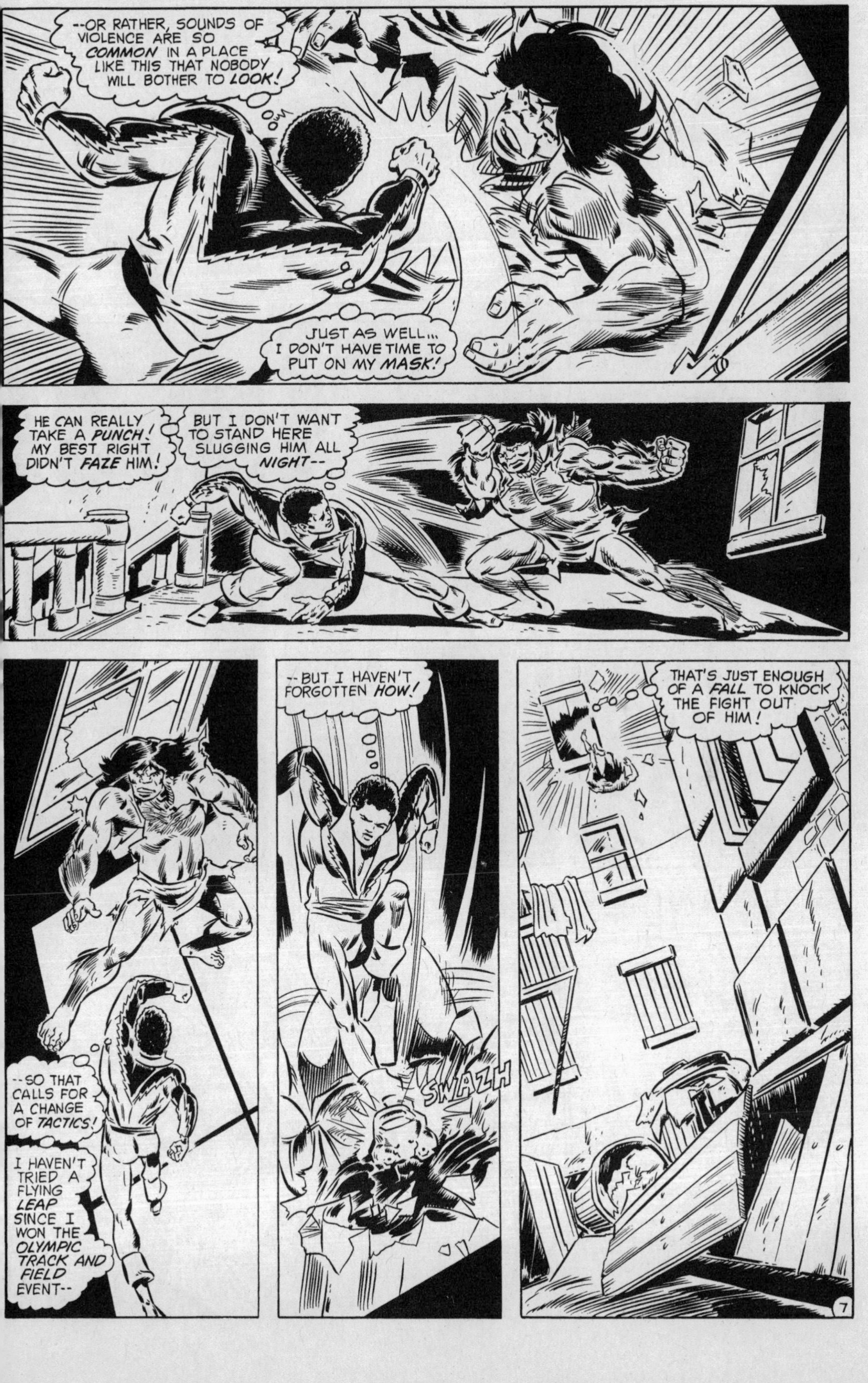
--OR RATHER, SOUNDS OF VIOLENCE ARE SO COMMON IN A PLACE LIKE THIS THAT NOBODY WILL BOTHER TO LOOK!
JUST AS WELL... I DON'T HAVE TIME TO PUT ON MY MASK!
HE CAN REALLY TAKE A PUNCH! MY BEST RIGHT DIDN'T FAZE HIM!
BUT I DON'T WANT TO STAND HERE SLUGGING HIM ALL NIGHT--
--SO THAT CALLS FOR A CHANGE OF TACTICS!
I HAVEN'T TRIED A FLYING LEAP SINCE I WON THE OLYMPIC TRACK AND FIELD EVENT--
--BUT I HAVEN'T FORGOTTEN HOW!
SWAZH
THAT'S JUST ENOUGH OF A FALL TO KNOCK THE FIGHT OUT OF HIM!
7

HOWEVER, WHEN BLACK LIGHTNING RACES DOWN TO THE YARD...

NO *SIGN* OF HIM--?!

I CAN'T BOTHER *SEARCHING* FOR HIM! I'VE GOT TO FIND OUT WHAT HAPPENED TO *HUGH!*

As BLACK LIGHTNING MOVES AWAY, A FIGURE *STIRS* IN THE GLOOM OF THE CELLAR DOORWAY...

...STIRS AND BEGINS TO *CHANGE*...

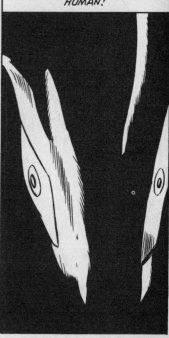

...CHANGE INTO SOMETHING NOT *HUMAN!*

AND, IN HUGH BRYANT'S *APARTMENT*--

FOOD ON THE *BURNER*...YET HUGH ISN'T *HERE!*

Relvenator

THAT PREHISTORIC *GOON* I BATTLED SURELY WOULDN'T BE HEATING SOME *SOUP*--

--OR *WOULD* HE? YEAH...IF HE *WAS* HUGH, HE WOULD!

IT'S *NUTTY*... BUT COME TO THINK OF IT, HE *WAS* WEARING THE REMAINS OF HUGH'S SWEATER AND JEANS!

WHATEVER'S GOING ON, IT MAY BE TOO MUCH FOR ME TO HANDLE *ALONE!*

8

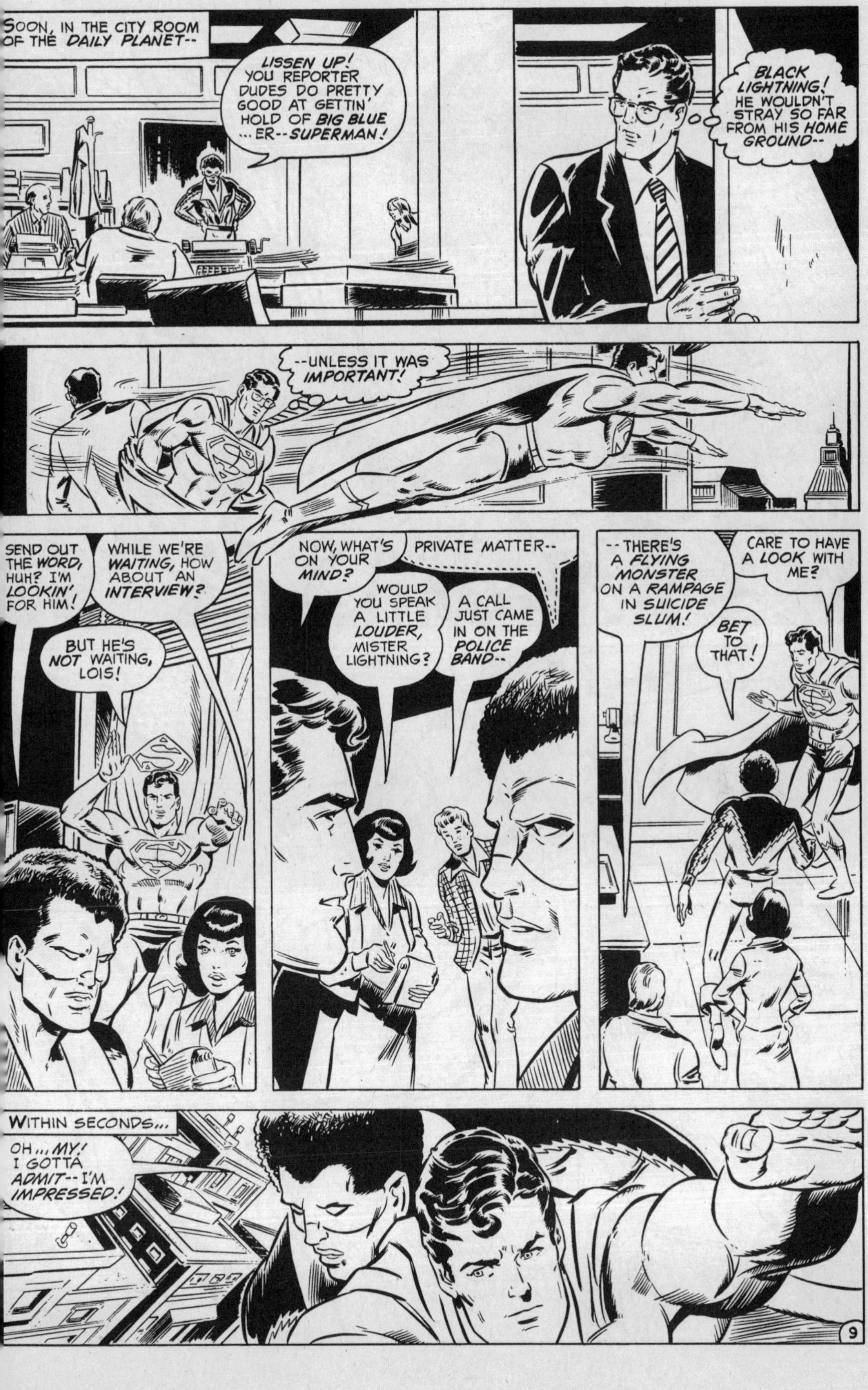
SOON, IN THE CITY ROOM OF THE DAILY PLANET--
LISSEN UP! YOU REPORTER DUDES DO PRETTY GOOD AT GETTIN' HOLD OF BIG BLUE ...ER--SUPERMAN!
BLACK LIGHTNING! HE WOULDN'T STRAY SO FAR FROM HIS HOME GROUND--
--UNLESS IT WAS IMPORTANT!
SEND OUT THE WORD, HUH? I'M LOOKIN' FOR HIM!
WHILE WE'RE WAITING, HOW ABOUT AN INTERVIEW?
BUT HE'S NOT WAITING, LOIS!
NOW, WHAT'S ON YOUR MIND?
PRIVATE MATTER--
WOULD YOU SPEAK A LITTLE LOUDER, MISTER LIGHTNING?
A CALL JUST CAME IN ON THE POLICE BAND--
--THERE'S A FLYING MONSTER ON A RAMPAGE IN SUICIDE SLUM!
CARE TO HAVE A LOOK WITH ME?
BET TO THAT!
WITHIN SECONDS...
OH... MY! I GOTTA ADMIT--I'M IMPRESSED!
9

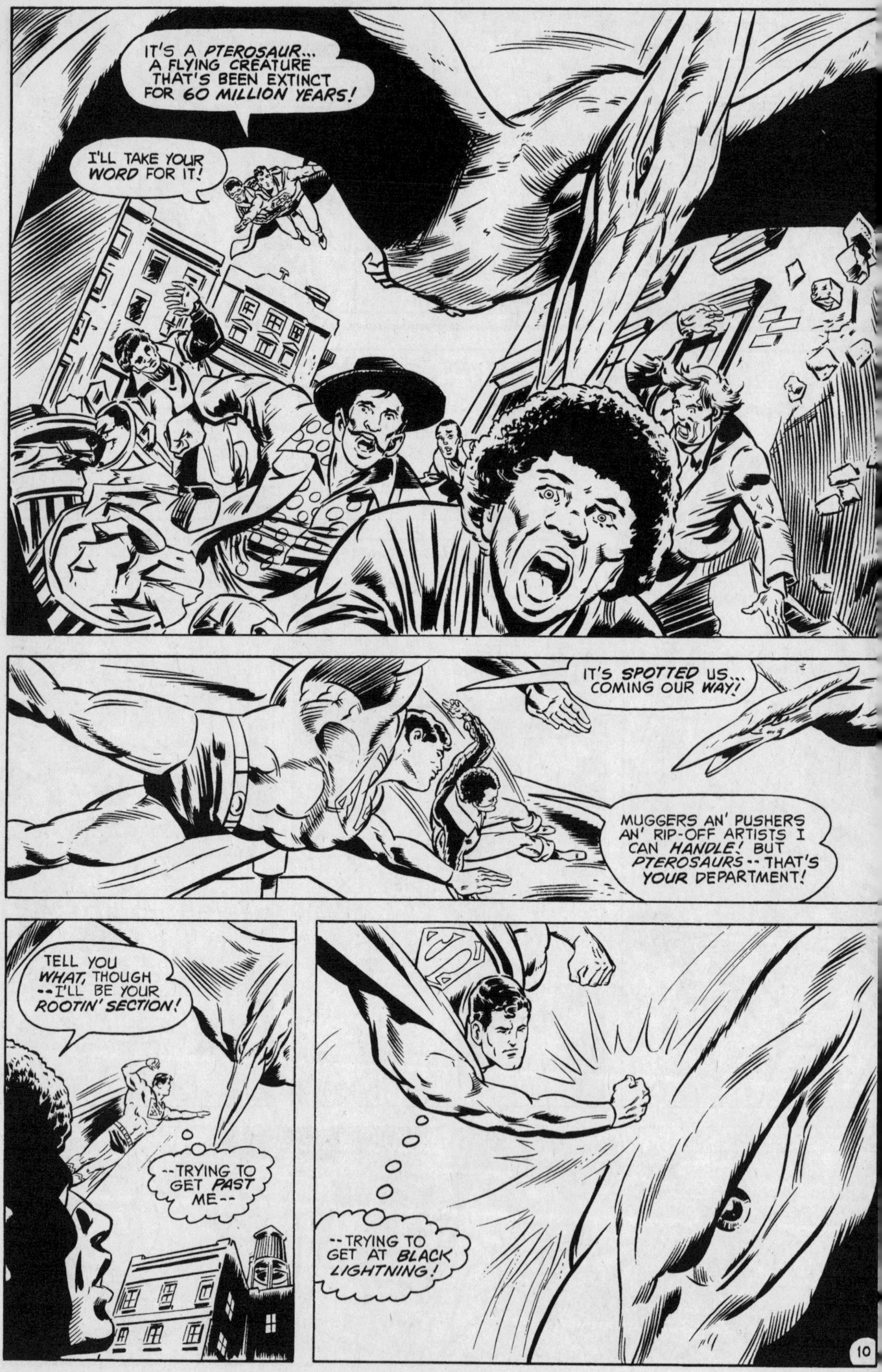
IT'S A PTEROSAUR... A FLYING CREATURE THAT'S BEEN EXTINCT FOR 60 MILLION YEARS!
I'LL TAKE YOUR WORD FOR IT!
IT'S SPOTTED US... COMING OUR WAY!
MUGGERS AN' PUSHERS AN' RIP-OFF ARTISTS I CAN HANDLE! BUT PTEROSAURS -- THAT'S YOUR DEPARTMENT!
TELL YOU WHAT, THOUGH --I'LL BE YOUR ROOTIN' SECTION!
--TRYING TO GET PAST ME--
--TRYING TO GET AT BLACK LIGHTNING!
10

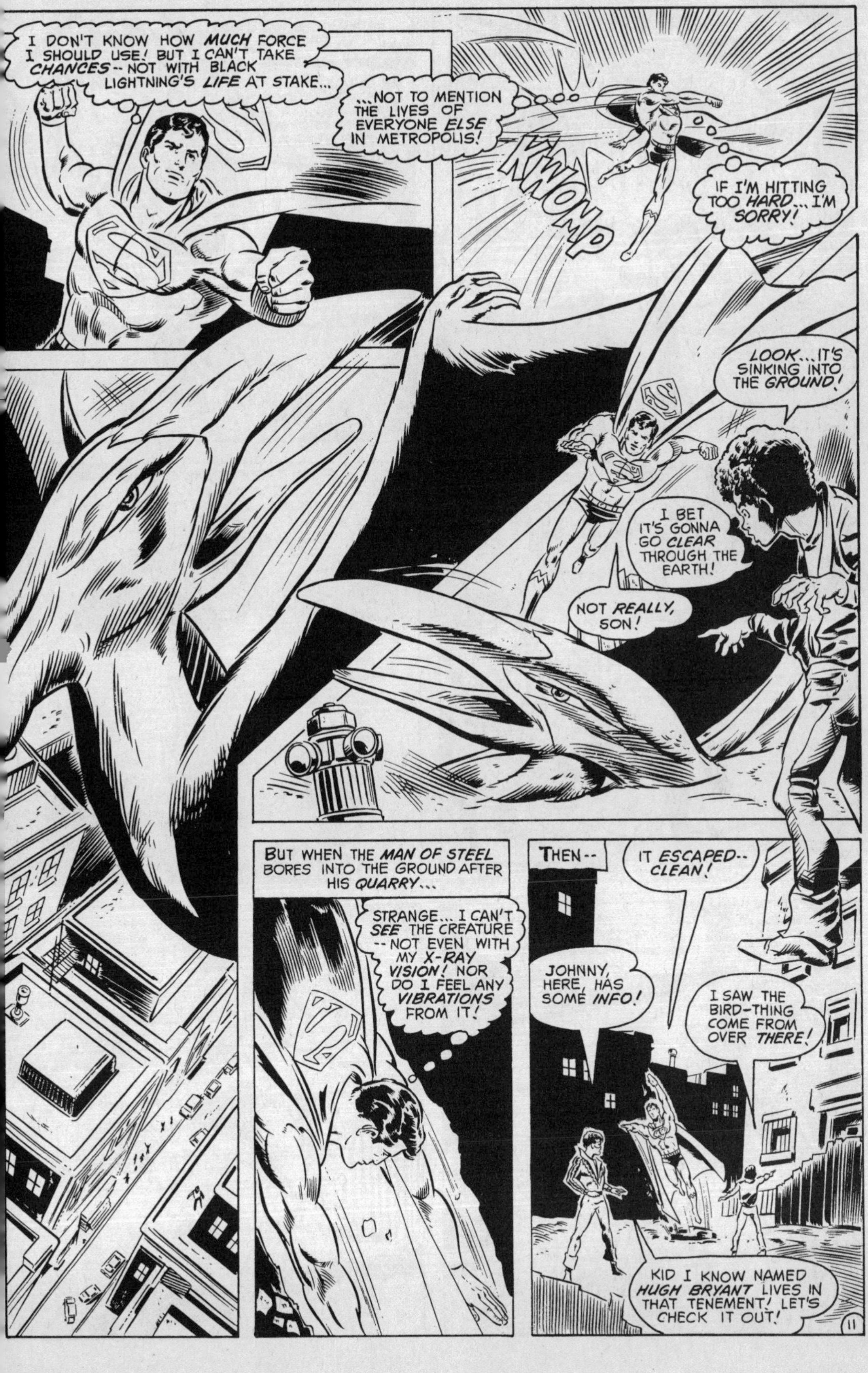
I DON'T KNOW HOW MUCH FORCE I SHOULD USE! BUT I CAN'T TAKE CHANCES-- NOT WITH BLACK LIGHTNING'S LIFE AT STAKE...
...NOT TO MENTION THE LIVES OF EVERYONE ELSE IN METROPOLIS!
KWOMP
IF I'M HITTING TOO HARD... I'M SORRY!
LOOK... IT'S SINKING INTO THE GROUND!
I BET IT'S GONNA GO CLEAR THROUGH THE EARTH!
NOT REALLY, SON!
BUT WHEN THE MAN OF STEEL BORES INTO THE GROUND AFTER HIS QUARRY...
STRANGE... I CAN'T SEE THE CREATURE -- NOT EVEN WITH MY X-RAY VISION! NOR DO I FEEL ANY VIBRATIONS FROM IT!
THEN--
IT ESCAPED-- CLEAN!
JOHNNY, HERE, HAS SOME INFO!
I SAW THE BIRD-THING COME FROM OVER THERE!
KID I KNOW NAMED HUGH BRYANT LIVES IN THAT TENEMENT! LET'S CHECK IT OUT!
11

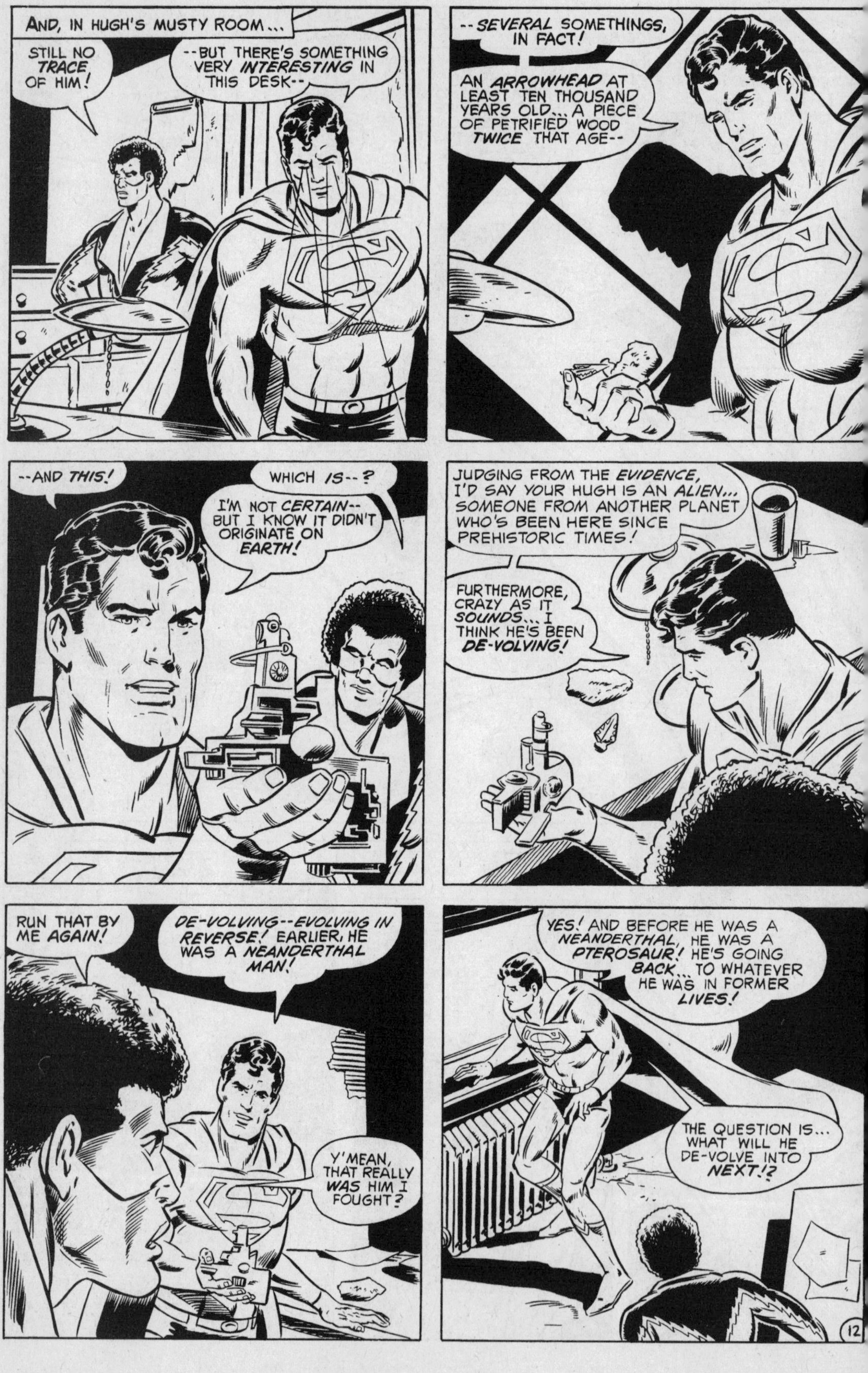
AND, IN HUGH'S MUSTY ROOM...
STILL NO TRACE OF HIM!
--BUT THERE'S SOMETHING VERY INTERESTING IN THIS DESK--
--SEVERAL SOMETHINGS, IN FACT!
AN ARROWHEAD AT LEAST TEN THOUSAND YEARS OLD... A PIECE OF PETRIFIED WOOD TWICE THAT AGE--
--AND THIS!
WHICH IS--?
I'M NOT CERTAIN-- BUT I KNOW IT DIDN'T ORIGINATE ON EARTH!
JUDGING FROM THE EVIDENCE, I'D SAY YOUR HUGH IS AN ALIEN... SOMEONE FROM ANOTHER PLANET WHO'S BEEN HERE SINCE PREHISTORIC TIMES!
FURTHERMORE, CRAZY AS IT SOUNDS... I THINK HE'S BEEN DE-VOLVING!
RUN THAT BY ME AGAIN!
DE-VOLVING--EVOLVING IN REVERSE! EARLIER, HE WAS A NEANDERTHAL MAN!
Y'MEAN, THAT REALLY WAS HIM I FOUGHT?
YES! AND BEFORE HE WAS A NEANDERTHAL, HE WAS A PTEROSAUR! HE'S GOING BACK... TO WHATEVER HE WAS IN FORMER LIVES!
THE QUESTION IS... WHAT WILL HE DE-VOLVE INTO NEXT!?
12

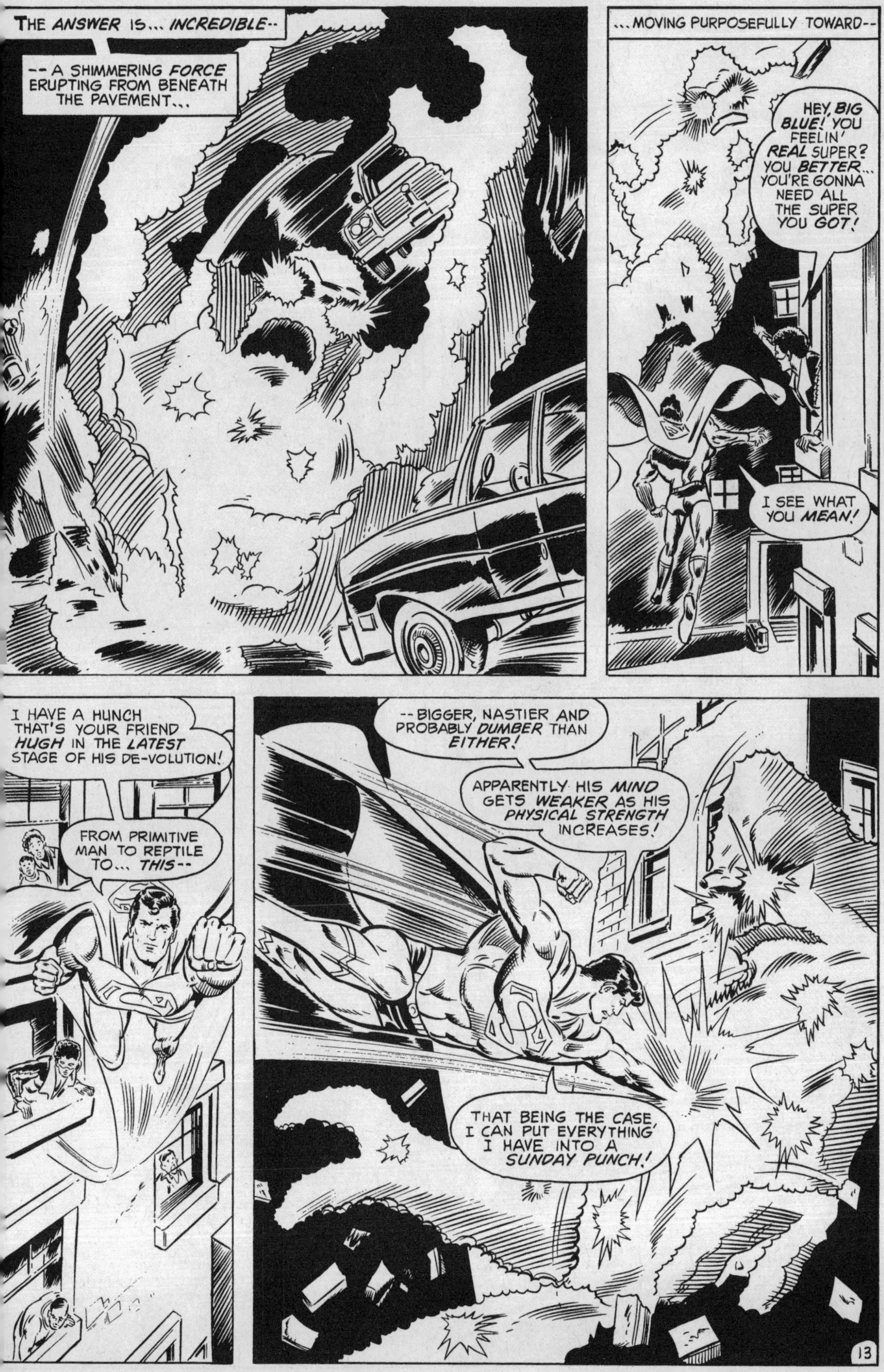
THE ANSWER IS... INCREDIBLE--
-- A SHIMMERING FORCE ERUPTING FROM BENEATH THE PAVEMENT...
...MOVING PURPOSEFULLY TOWARD--
HEY, BIG BLUE! YOU FEELIN' REAL SUPER? YOU BETTER... YOU'RE GONNA NEED ALL THE SUPER YOU GOT!
I SEE WHAT YOU MEAN!
I HAVE A HUNCH THAT'S YOUR FRIEND HUGH IN THE LATEST STAGE OF HIS DE-VOLUTION!
FROM PRIMITIVE MAN TO REPTILE TO... THIS--
--BIGGER, NASTIER AND PROBABLY DUMBER THAN EITHER!
APPARENTLY HIS MIND GETS WEAKER AS HIS PHYSICAL STRENGTH INCREASES!
THAT BEING THE CASE, I CAN PUT EVERYTHING I HAVE INTO A SUNDAY PUNCH!
13

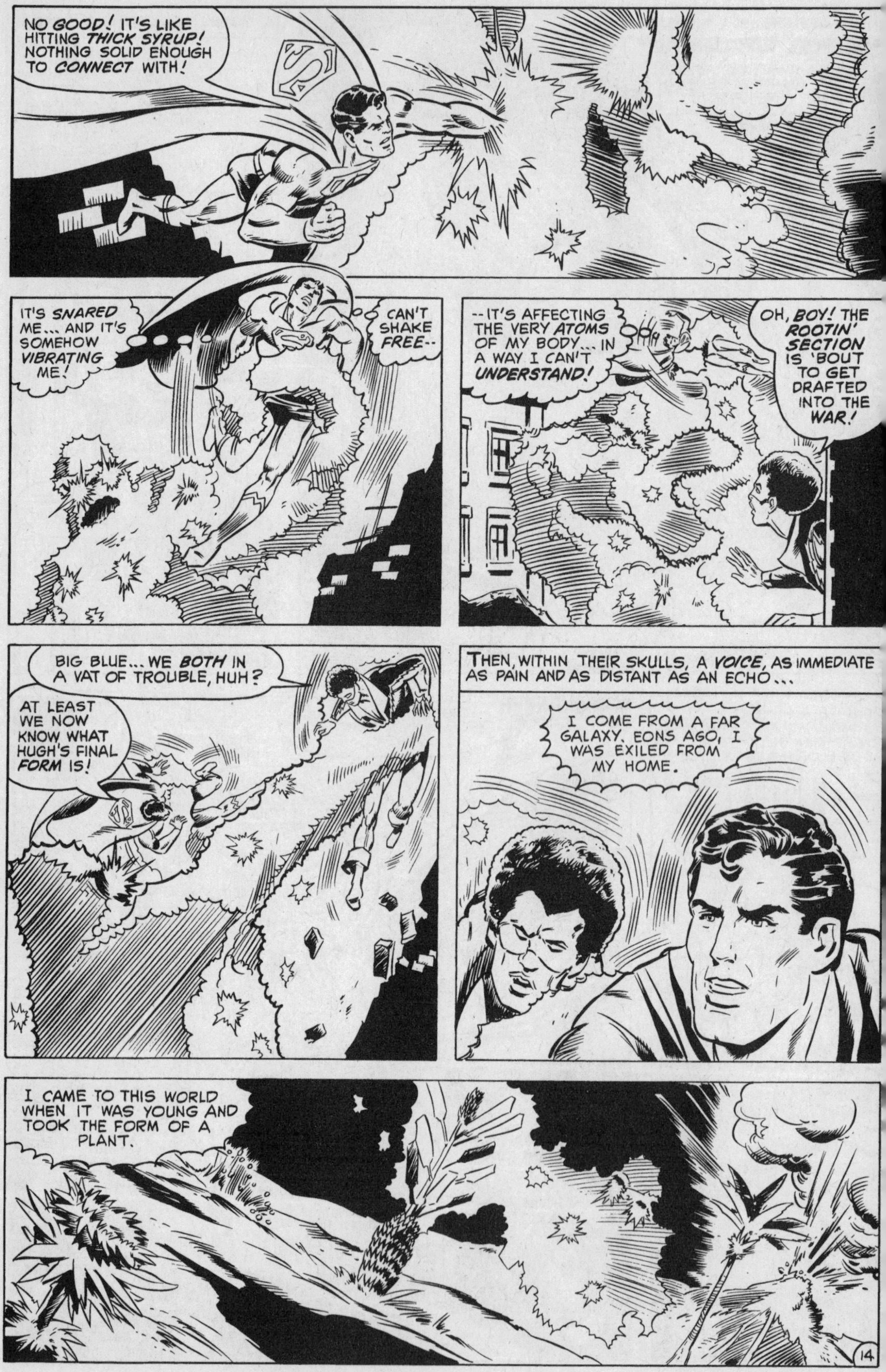
NO GOOD! IT'S LIKE HITTING THICK SYRUP! NOTHING SOLID ENOUGH TO CONNECT WITH!
IT'S SNARED ME... AND IT'S SOMEHOW VIBRATING ME!
CAN'T SHAKE FREE--
--IT'S AFFECTING THE VERY ATOMS OF MY BODY... IN A WAY I CAN'T UNDERSTAND!
OH, BOY! THE ROOTIN' SECTION IS 'BOUT TO GET DRAFTED INTO THE WAR!
BIG BLUE... WE BOTH IN A VAT OF TROUBLE, HUH?
AT LEAST WE NOW KNOW WHAT HUGH'S FINAL FORM IS!
THEN, WITHIN THEIR SKULLS, A VOICE, AS IMMEDIATE AS PAIN AND AS DISTANT AS AN ECHO...
I COME FROM A FAR GALAXY. EONS AGO, I WAS EXILED FROM MY HOME.
I CAME TO THIS WORLD WHEN IT WAS YOUNG AND TOOK THE FORM OF A PLANT.
14

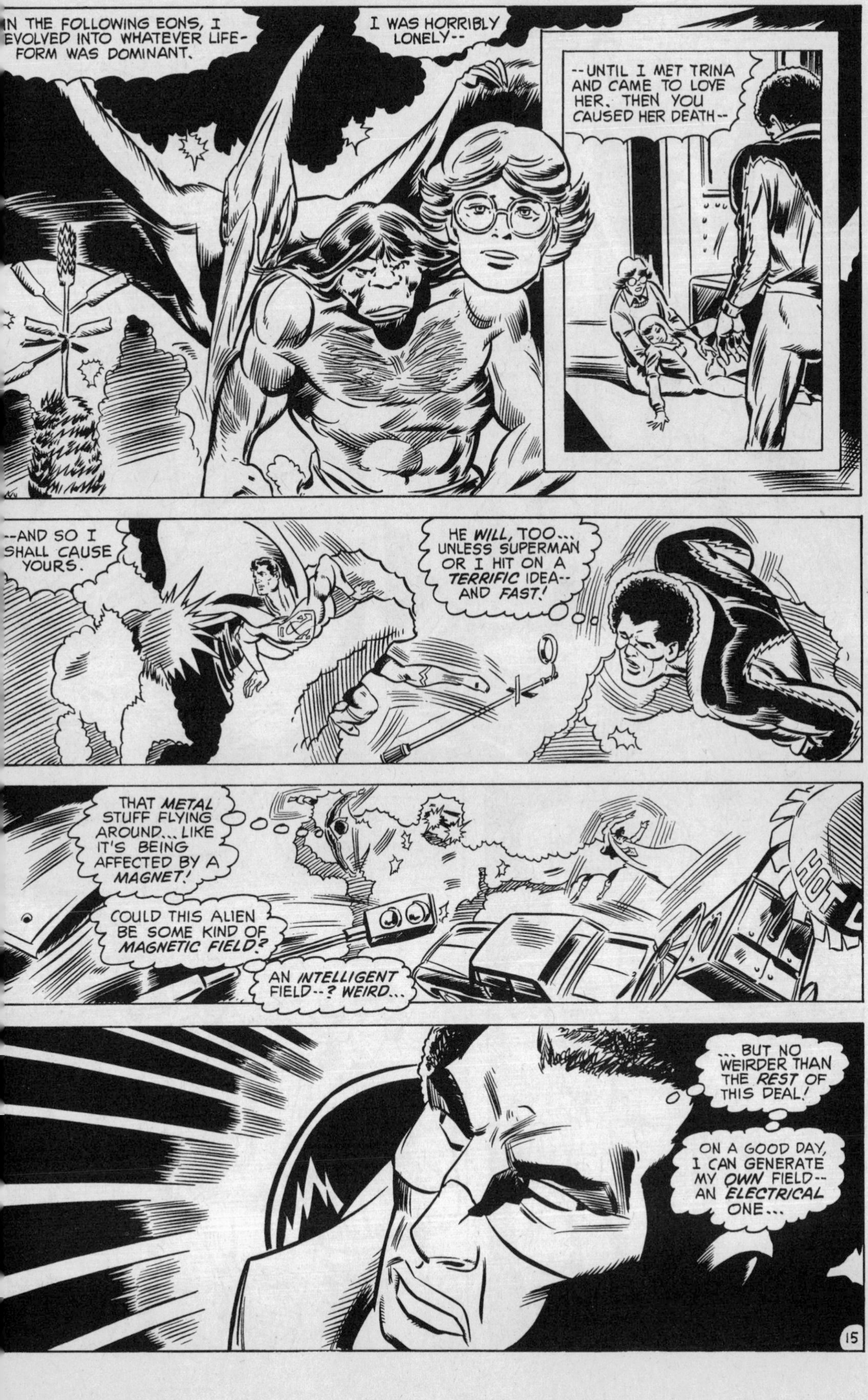

IN THE FOLLOWING EONS, I EVOLVED INTO WHATEVER LIFE-FORM WAS DOMINANT.
I WAS HORRIBLY LONELY--
--UNTIL I MET TRINA AND CAME TO LOVE HER. THEN YOU CAUSED HER DEATH--
--AND SO I SHALL CAUSE YOURS.
HE WILL, TOO... UNLESS SUPERMAN OR I HIT ON A TERRIFIC IDEA--AND FAST!
THAT METAL STUFF FLYING AROUND... LIKE IT'S BEING AFFECTED BY A MAGNET!
COULD THIS ALIEN BE SOME KIND OF MAGNETIC FIELD?
AN INTELLIGENT FIELD--? WEIRD...
HOT
... BUT NO WEIRDER THAN THE REST OF THIS DEAL!
ON A GOOD DAY, I CAN GENERATE MY OWN FIELD--AN ELECTRICAL ONE...
15

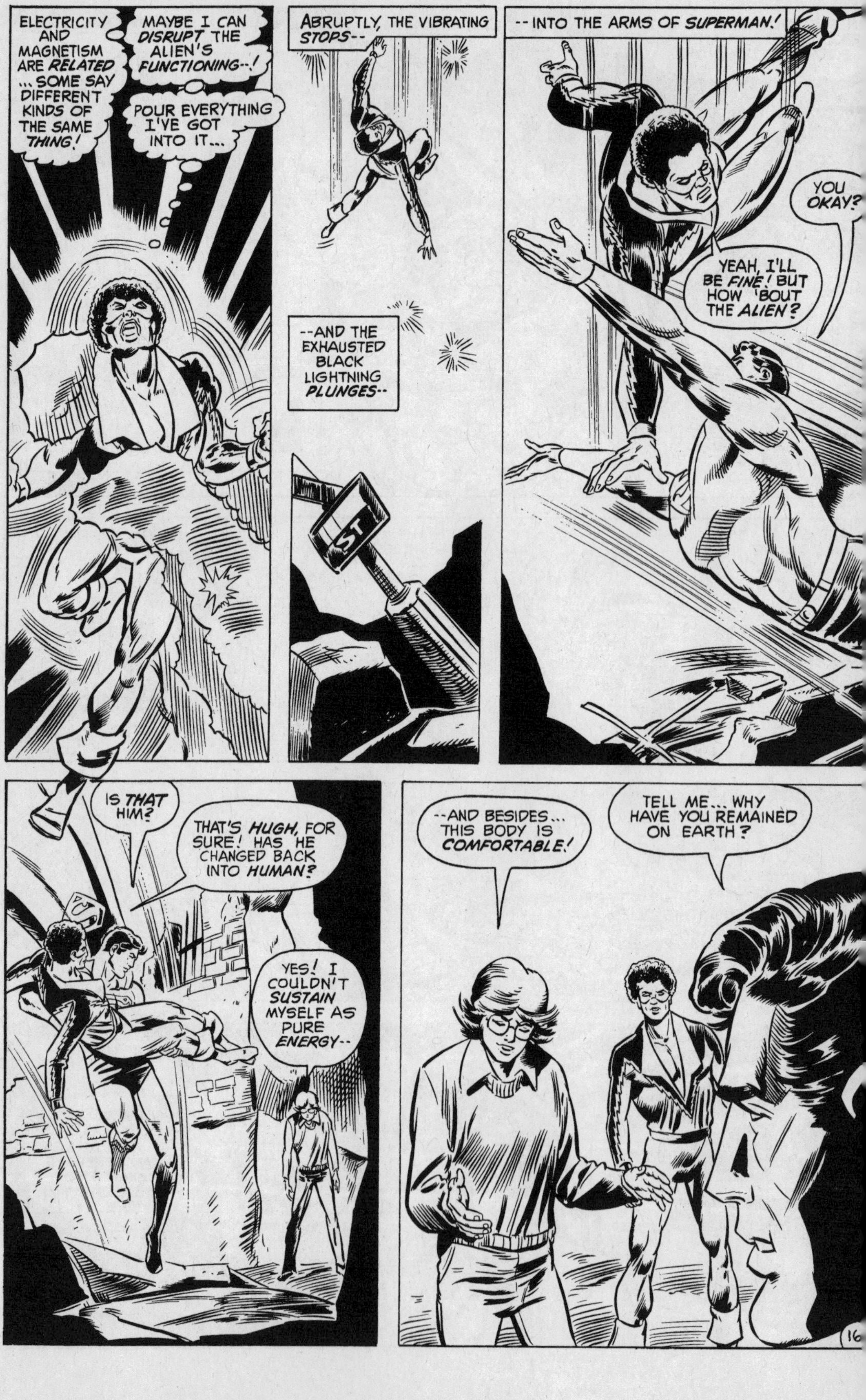
ELECTRICITY AND MAGNETISM ARE RELATED ... SOME SAY DIFFERENT KINDS OF THE SAME THING!
MAYBE I CAN DISRUPT THE ALIEN'S FUNCTIONING--!
POUR EVERYTHING I'VE GOT INTO IT...
ABRUPTLY, THE VIBRATING STOPS--
--AND THE EXHAUSTED BLACK LIGHTNING PLUNGES--
ST
-- INTO THE ARMS OF SUPERMAN!
YOU OKAY?
YEAH, I'LL BE FINE! BUT HOW 'BOUT THE ALIEN?
IS THAT HIM?
THAT'S HUGH, FOR SURE! HAS HE CHANGED BACK INTO HUMAN?
YES! I COULDN'T SUSTAIN MYSELF AS PURE ENERGY--
--AND BESIDES... THIS BODY IS COMFORTABLE!
TELL ME... WHY HAVE YOU REMAINED ON EARTH?
16

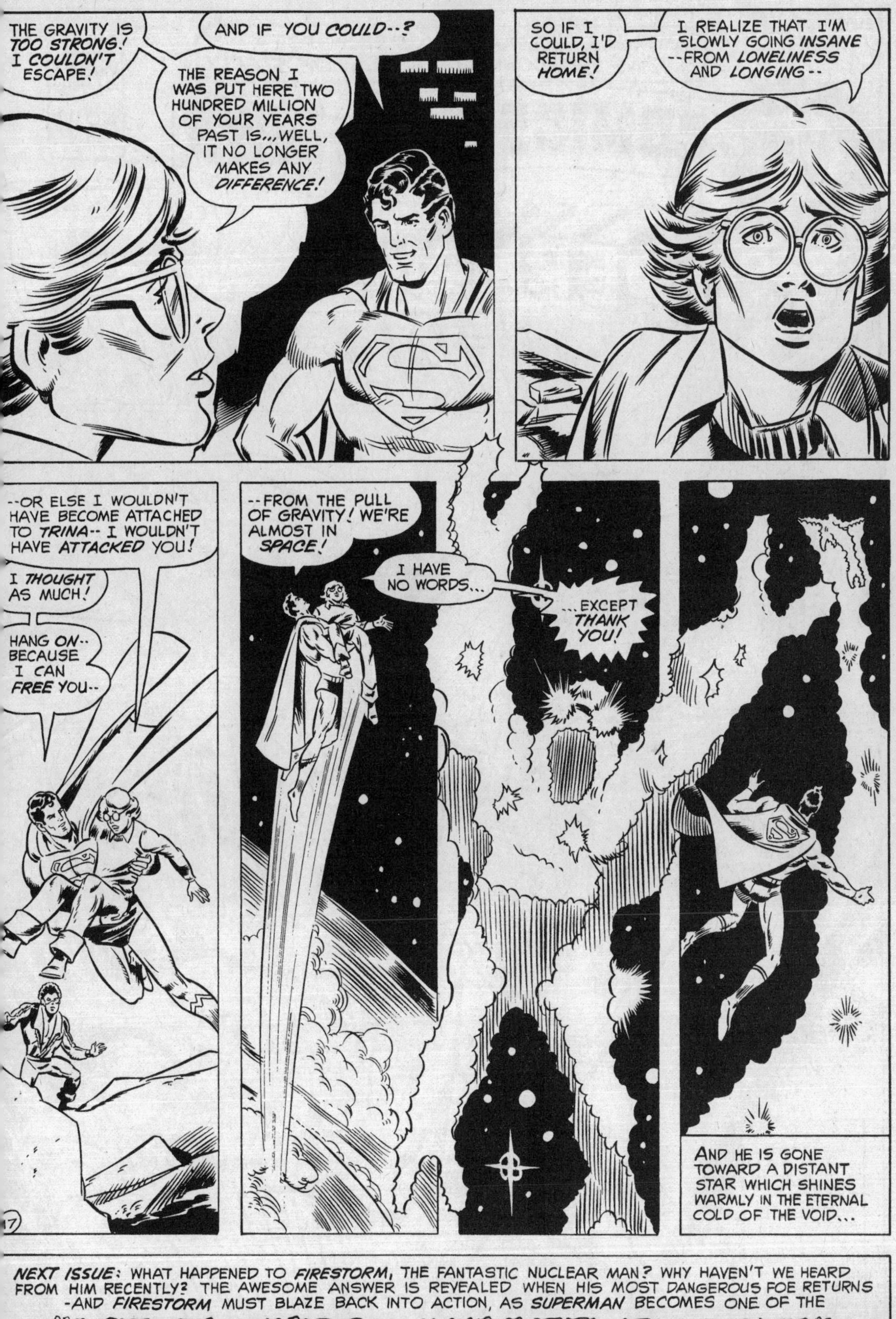
THE GRAVITY IS TOO STRONG! I COULDN'T ESCAPE!
AND IF YOU COULD--?
THE REASON I WAS PUT HERE TWO HUNDRED MILLION OF YOUR YEARS PAST IS...WELL, IT NO LONGER MAKES ANY DIFFERENCE!
SO IF I COULD, I'D RETURN HOME!
I REALIZE THAT I'M SLOWLY GOING INSANE --FROM LONELINESS AND LONGING--
--OR ELSE I WOULDN'T HAVE BECOME ATTACHED TO TRINA-- I WOULDN'T HAVE ATTACKED YOU!
I THOUGHT AS MUCH!
HANG ON-- BECAUSE I CAN FREE YOU--
--FROM THE PULL OF GRAVITY! WE'RE ALMOST IN SPACE!
I HAVE NO WORDS...
...EXCEPT THANK YOU!
AND HE IS GONE TOWARD A DISTANT STAR WHICH SHINES WARMLY IN THE ETERNAL COLD OF THE VOID...
NEXT ISSUE: WHAT HAPPENED TO FIRESTORM, THE FANTASTIC NUCLEAR MAN? WHY HAVEN'T WE HEARD FROM HIM RECENTLY? THE AWESOME ANSWER IS REVEALED WHEN HIS MOST DANGEROUS FOE RETURNS -AND FIRESTORM MUST BLAZE BACK INTO ACTION, AS SUPERMAN BECOMES ONE OF THE
"ICE SLAVES OF KILLER FROST!"

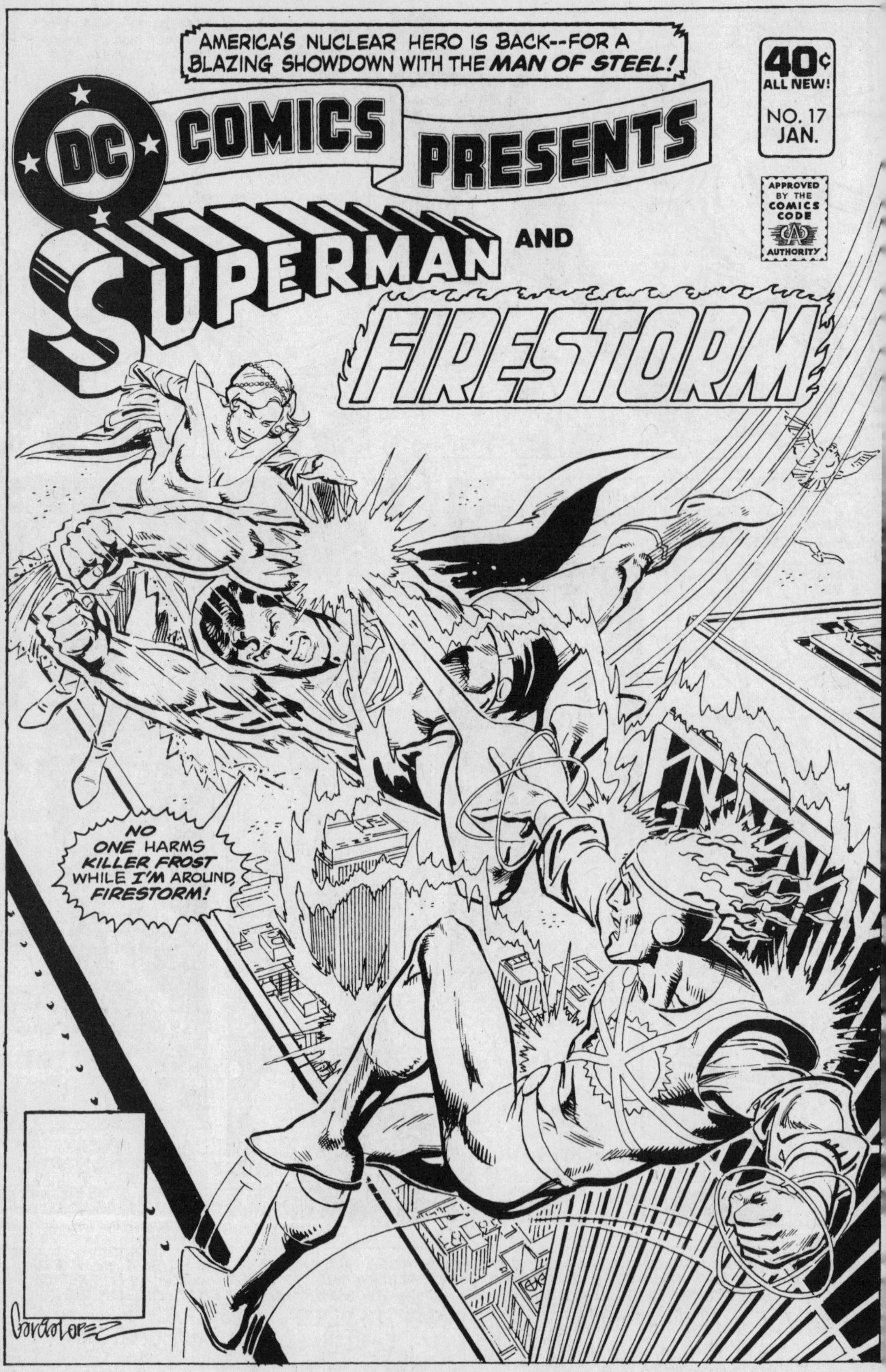
AMERICA'S NUCLEAR HERO IS BACK--FOR A BLAZING SHOWDOWN WITH THE MAN OF STEEL!
40¢ ALL NEW!
NO. 17 JAN.
DC COMICS PRESENTS
APPROVED BY THE COMICS CODE AUTHORITY
SUPERMAN AND FIRESTORM
NO ONE HARMS KILLER FROST WHILE I'M AROUND, FIRESTORM!
GarciaLopez

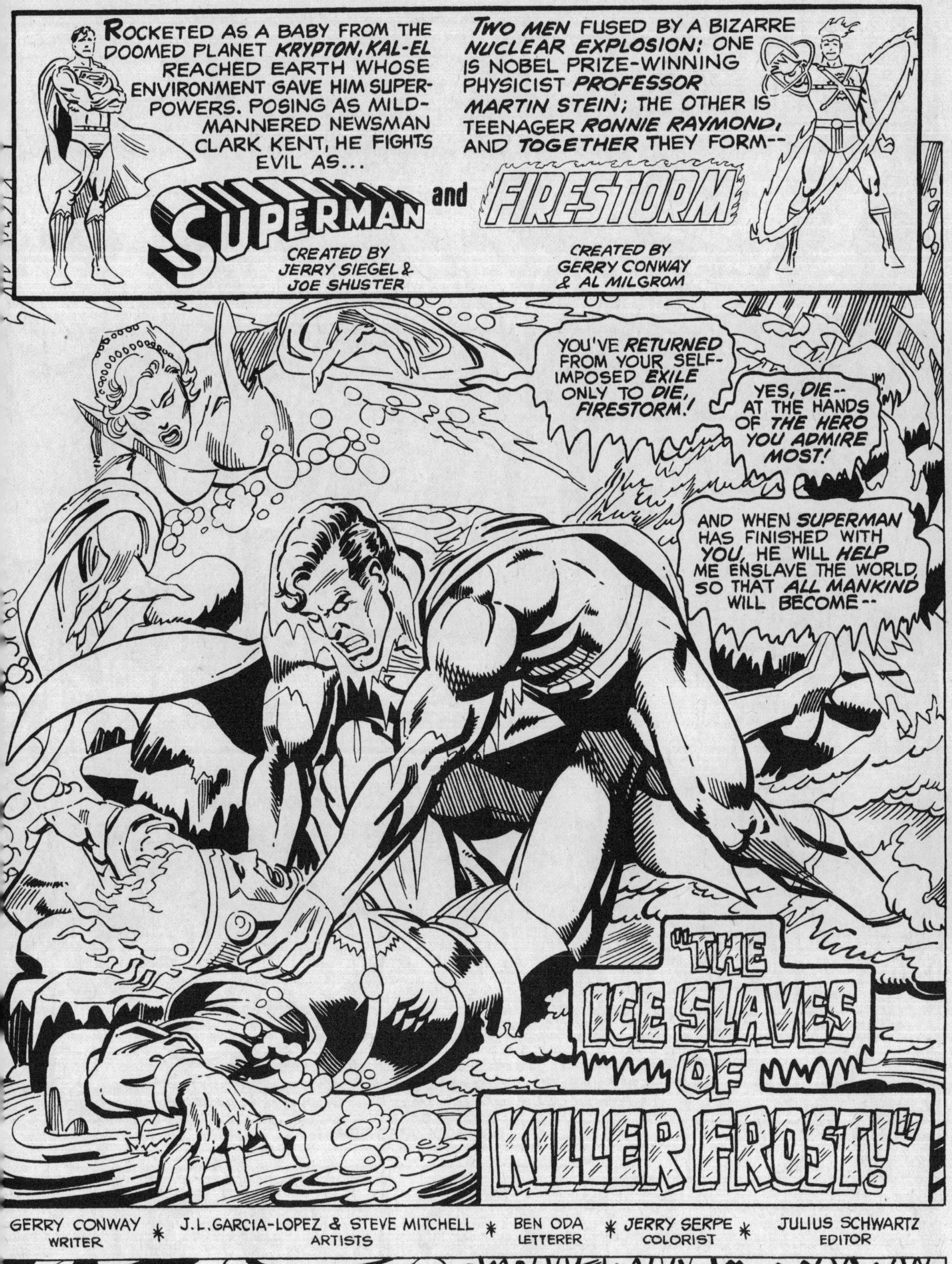
ROCKETED AS A BABY FROM THE DOOMED PLANET KRYPTON, KAL-EL REACHED EARTH WHOSE ENVIRONMENT GAVE HIM SUPER-POWERS. POSING AS MILD-MANNERED NEWSMAN CLARK KENT, HE FIGHTS EVIL AS...
TWO MEN FUSED BY A BIZARRE NUCLEAR EXPLOSION: ONE IS NOBEL PRIZE-WINNING PHYSICIST PROFESSOR MARTIN STEIN; THE OTHER IS TEENAGER RONNIE RAYMOND, AND TOGETHER THEY FORM--
SUPERMAN and FIRESTORM
CREATED BY JERRY SIEGEL & JOE SHUSTER
CREATED BY GERRY CONWAY & AL MILGROM
YOU'VE RETURNED FROM YOUR SELF-IMPOSED EXILE ONLY TO DIE, FIRESTORM!
YES, DIE-- AT THE HANDS OF THE HERO YOU ADMIRE MOST!
AND WHEN SUPERMAN HAS FINISHED WITH YOU, HE WILL HELP ME ENSLAVE THE WORLD, SO THAT ALL MANKIND WILL BECOME--
"THE ICE SLAVES OF KILLER FROST!"
GERRY CONWAY WRITER * J.L.GARCIA-LOPEZ & STEVE MITCHELL ARTISTS * BEN ODA LETTERER * JERRY SERPE COLORIST * JULIUS SCHWARTZ EDITOR

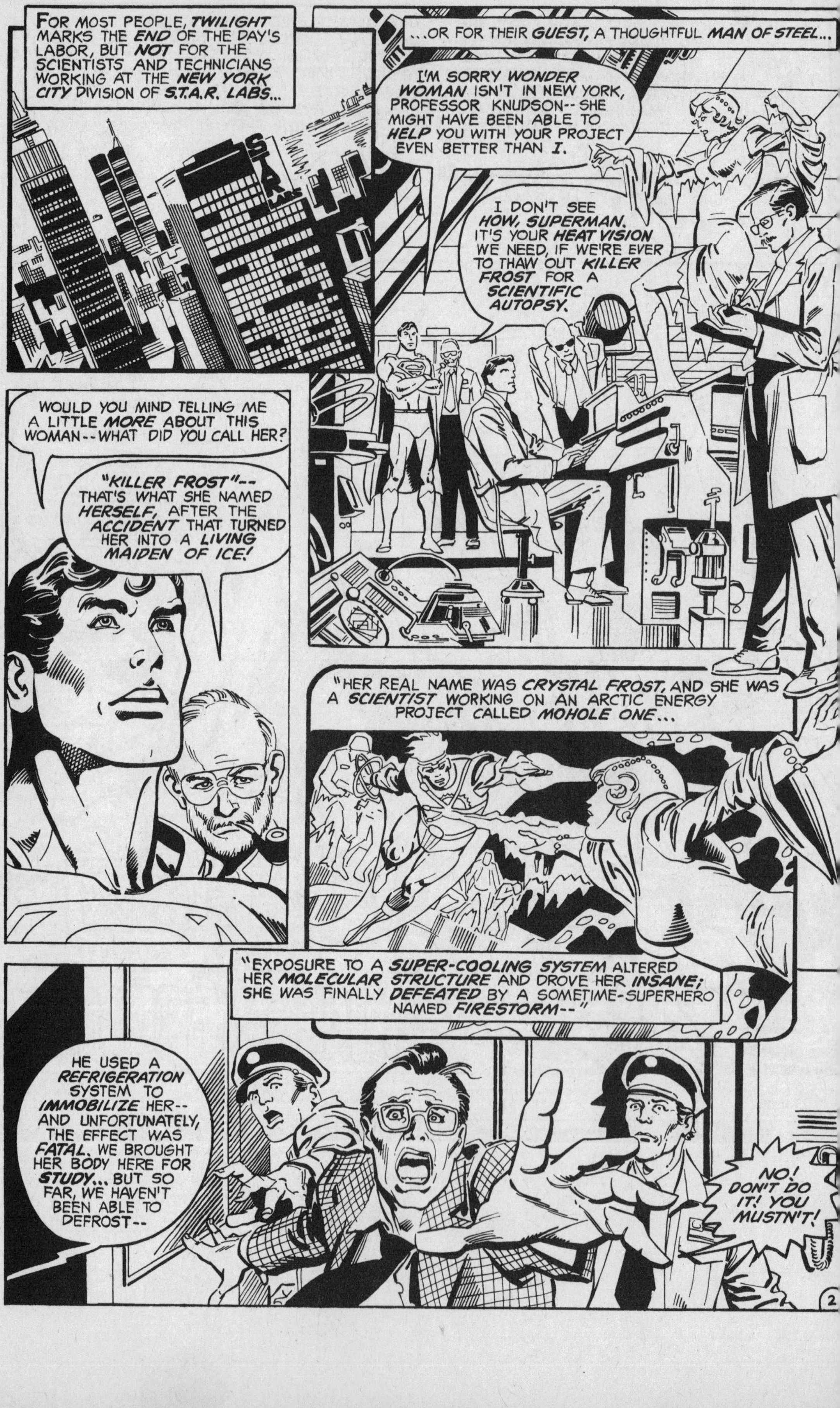
FOR MOST PEOPLE, TWILIGHT MARKS THE END OF THE DAY'S LABOR, BUT NOT FOR THE SCIENTISTS AND TECHNICIANS WORKING AT THE NEW YORK CITY DIVISION OF S.T.A.R. LABS...
...OR FOR THEIR GUEST, A THOUGHTFUL MAN OF STEEL...
I'M SORRY WONDER WOMAN ISN'T IN NEW YORK, PROFESSOR KNUDSON-- SHE MIGHT HAVE BEEN ABLE TO HELP YOU WITH YOUR PROJECT EVEN BETTER THAN I.
I DON'T SEE HOW, SUPERMAN. IT'S YOUR HEAT VISION WE NEED, IF WE'RE EVER TO THAW OUT KILLER FROST FOR A SCIENTIFIC AUTOPSY.
WOULD YOU MIND TELLING ME A LITTLE MORE ABOUT THIS WOMAN--WHAT DID YOU CALL HER?
"KILLER FROST"-- THAT'S WHAT SHE NAMED HERSELF, AFTER THE ACCIDENT THAT TURNED HER INTO A LIVING MAIDEN OF ICE!
"HER REAL NAME WAS CRYSTAL FROST, AND SHE WAS A SCIENTIST WORKING ON AN ARCTIC ENERGY PROJECT CALLED MOHOLE ONE...
"EXPOSURE TO A SUPER-COOLING SYSTEM ALTERED HER MOLECULAR STRUCTURE AND DROVE HER INSANE; SHE WAS FINALLY DEFEATED BY A SOMETIME-SUPERHERO NAMED FIRESTORM--"
HE USED A REFRIGERATION SYSTEM TO IMMOBILIZE HER-- AND UNFORTUNATELY, THE EFFECT WAS FATAL. WE BROUGHT HER BODY HERE FOR STUDY... BUT SO FAR, WE HAVEN'T BEEN ABLE TO DEFROST--
NO! DON'T DO IT! YOU MUSTN'T!
2

YOU *CAN'T* DEFROST HER--YOU DON'T *REALIZE* WHAT A *MONSTER* SHE IS!

SHE HATES MEN-- *ALL MEN*--SHE'LL *KILL* US! *SHE'LL DESTROY* US ALL!

SORRY, PROFESSOR, THIS *FRUITCAKE* JUST BUSTED IN BEFORE WE COULD *GRAB* HIM!

C'MON, FELLA...YOU'RE *GOIN'* TO *BELLEVUE!*

I *RECOGNIZE* THAT MAN-- *MARTIN STEIN*, THE NOBEL PRIZE WINNER!

A MAN WITH A *BRILLIANT* FUTURE --UNTIL *LAST YEAR*, WHEN HE SUDDENLY *WENT TO PIECES!*

"I SUPPOSE IT *STARTED* WHEN HIS PET PROJECT--A FULLY-AUTO-MATED *NUCLEAR PLANT* ON THE *HUDSON RIVER*--WAS CLOSED DOWN BY THE *GOVERNOR'S OFFICE*...

"*SOON* AFTER, STEIN STARTED *DRINKING*...BEGAN HAVING *BLACKOUTS*..."

A COUPLE OF TIMES HE *DISAPPEARED* FROM HIS LAB... WAS GONE FOR *HOURS!* HE ALIENATED ALL HIS FRIENDS AND *COLLEAGUES.*

NOW HE'S JUST A *BROKEN MAN* ...A *SHADOW* OF HIMSELF. *TRAGIC.*

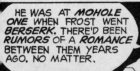

HE WAS AT *MOHOLE ONE* WHEN FROST WENT *BERSERK.* THERE'D BEEN *RUMORS* OF A *ROMANCE* BETWEEN THEM YEARS AGO. NO MATTER.

SUPERMAN, IF YOU'LL DO THE *HONORS*...

VERY WELL, PROFESSOR. *STAND BACK*... IT'S GOING TO GET *VERY HOT* IN HERE!

FOR LONG MOMENTS, THERE IS *NO SOUND* IN THE CHAMBER EXCEPT FOR THE *HUM* OF ELECTRONIC EQUIPMENT AND THE *SOFT CRACKLE* OF MELTING ICE...

AND THEN, *SUDDENLY...*

K-RRAKOOM

LOOK OUT! HER ICE SHEATH-- *EXPLODING!*

③

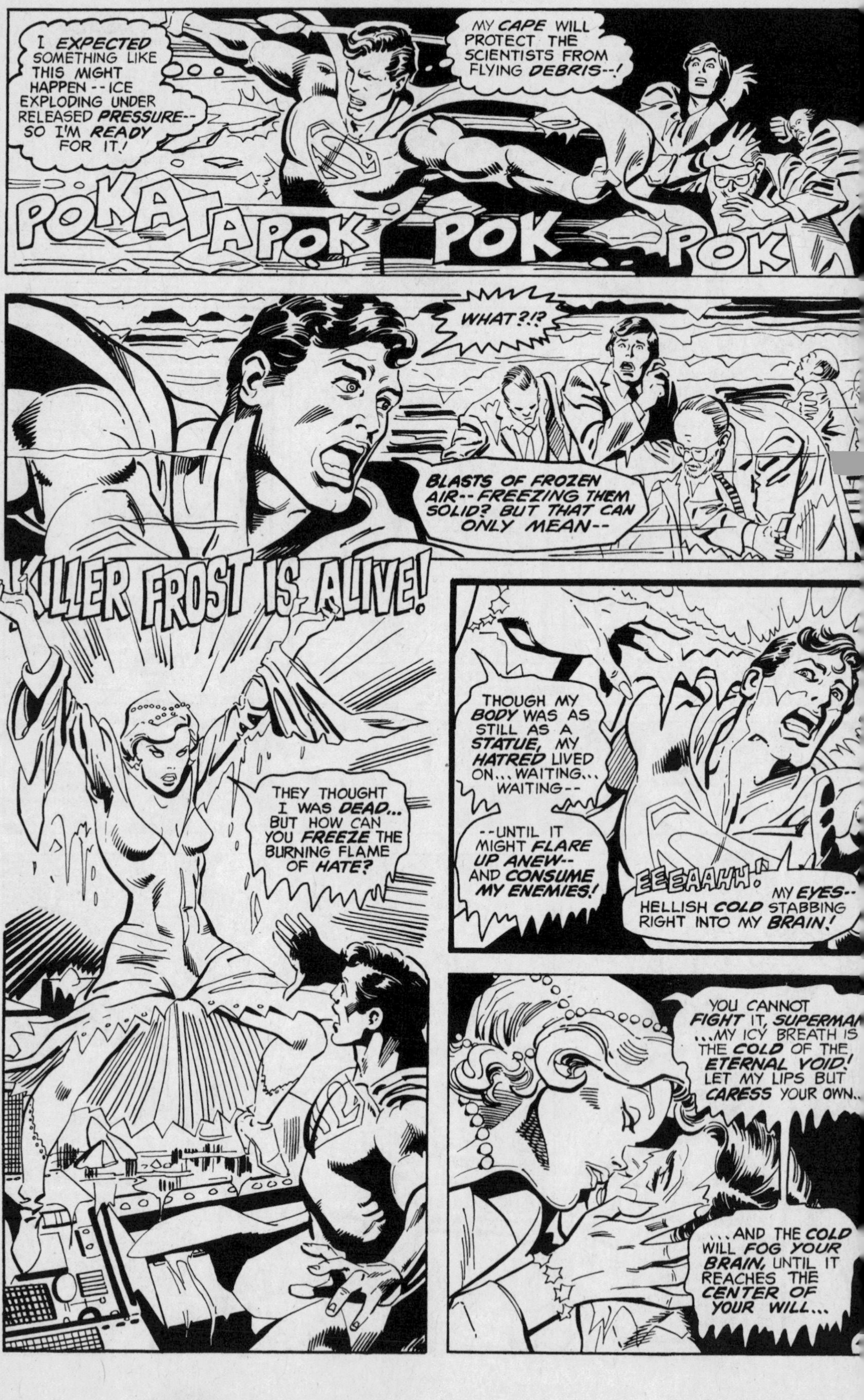
I EXPECTED SOMETHING LIKE THIS MIGHT HAPPEN -- ICE EXPLODING UNDER RELEASED PRESSURE-- SO I'M READY FOR IT!
MY CAPE WILL PROTECT THE SCIENTISTS FROM FLYING DEBRIS--!
POKATAPOK POK POK
WHAT?!?
BLASTS OF FROZEN AIR-- FREEZING THEM SOLID? BUT THAT CAN ONLY MEAN--
KILLER FROST IS ALIVE!
THEY THOUGHT I WAS DEAD... BUT HOW CAN YOU FREEZE THE BURNING FLAME OF HATE?
THOUGH MY BODY WAS AS STILL AS A STATUE, MY HATRED LIVED ON... WAITING... WAITING--
--UNTIL IT MIGHT FLARE UP ANEW-- AND CONSUME MY ENEMIES!
EEEAAHH! MY EYES-- HELLISH COLD STABBING RIGHT INTO MY BRAIN!
YOU CANNOT FIGHT IT, SUPERMAN ...MY ICY BREATH IS THE COLD OF THE ETERNAL VOID! LET MY LIPS BUT CARESS YOUR OWN...
...AND THE COLD WILL FOG YOUR BRAIN, UNTIL IT REACHES THE CENTER OF YOUR WILL...

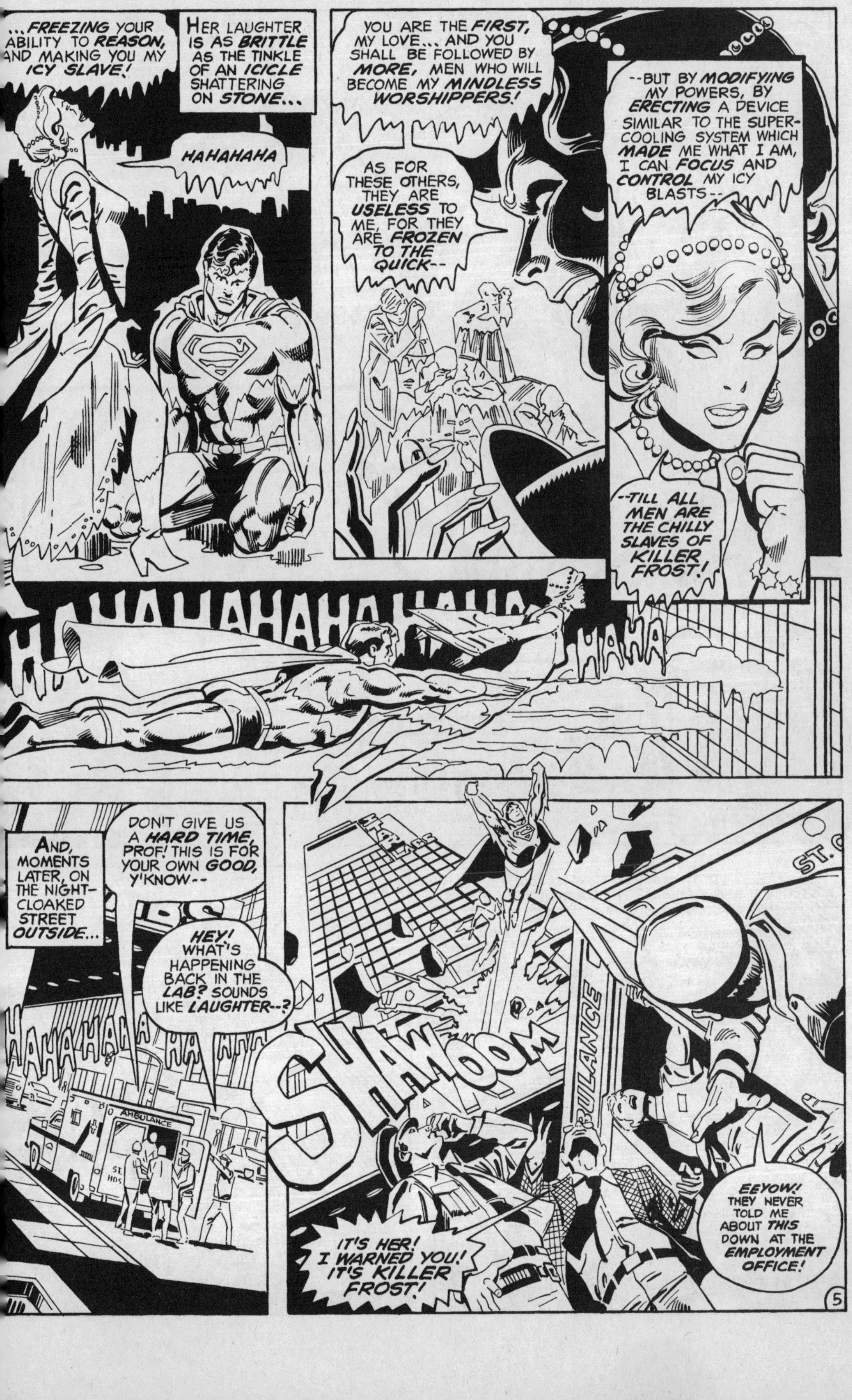
...FREEZING YOUR ABILITY TO REASON, AND MAKING YOU MY ICY SLAVE!
HER LAUGHTER IS AS BRITTLE AS THE TINKLE OF AN ICICLE SHATTERING ON STONE...
HAHAHAHA
YOU ARE THE FIRST, MY LOVE... AND YOU SHALL BE FOLLOWED BY MORE, MEN WHO WILL BECOME MY MINDLESS WORSHIPPERS!
AS FOR THESE OTHERS, THEY ARE USELESS TO ME, FOR THEY ARE FROZEN TO THE QUICK--
--BUT BY MODIFYING MY POWERS, BY ERECTING A DEVICE SIMILAR TO THE SUPER-COOLING SYSTEM WHICH MADE ME WHAT I AM, I CAN FOCUS AND CONTROL MY ICY BLASTS--
--TILL ALL MEN ARE THE CHILLY SLAVES OF KILLER FROST!
HAHAHAHAHAHA
HAHA
AND, MOMENTS LATER, ON THE NIGHT-CLOAKED STREET OUTSIDE...
DON'T GIVE US A HARD TIME, PROF! THIS IS FOR YOUR OWN GOOD, Y'KNOW--
HEY! WHAT'S HAPPENING BACK IN THE LAB? SOUNDS LIKE LAUGHTER--?
HAHAHAHAHA
AMBULANCE
SHAWOOM
IT'S HER! I WARNED YOU! IT'S KILLER FROST!
EEYOW! THEY NEVER TOLD ME ABOUT THIS DOWN AT THE EMPLOYMENT OFFICE!
5

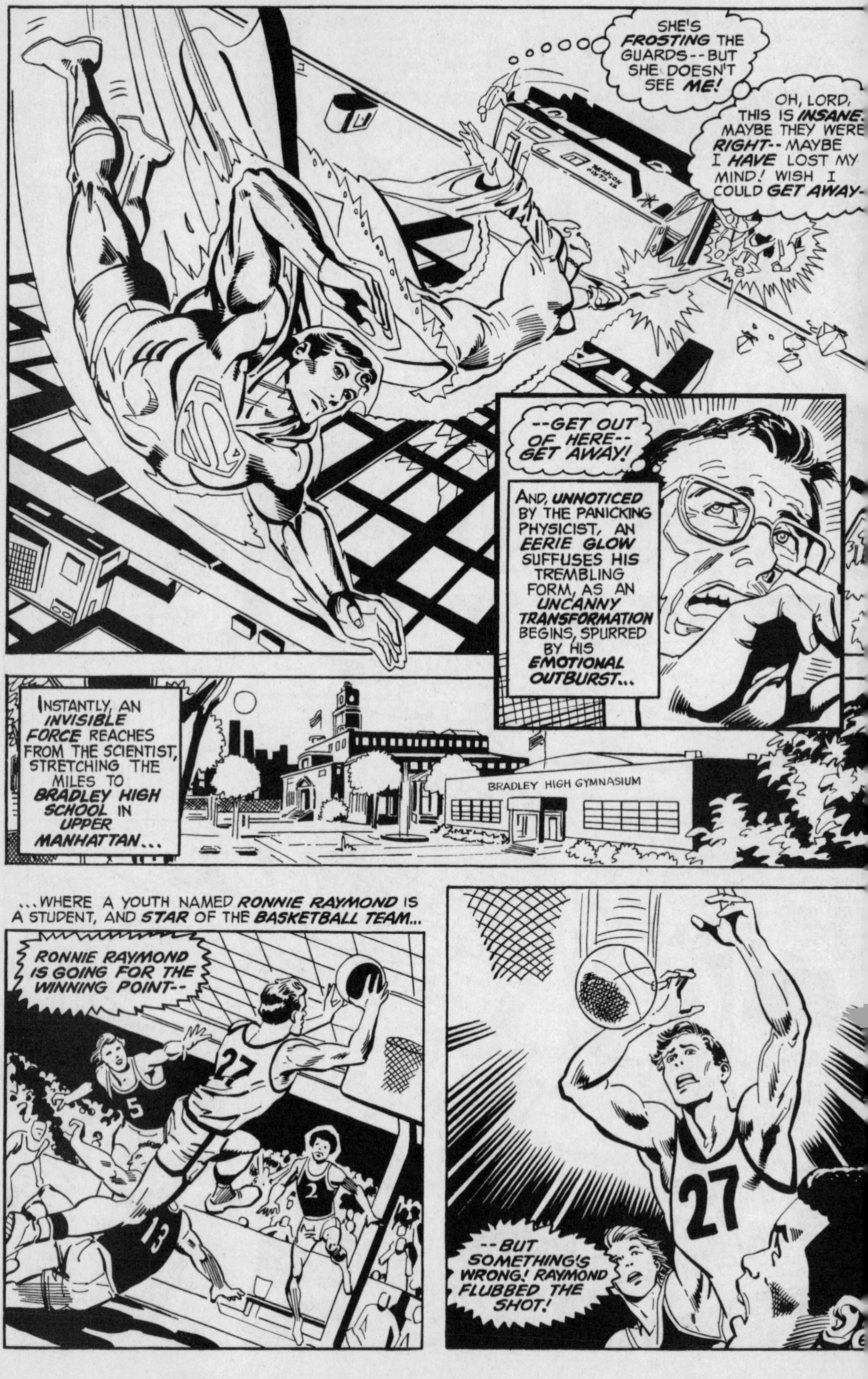
SHE'S FROSTING THE GUARDS--BUT SHE DOESN'T SEE ME!
OH, LORD, THIS IS INSANE. MAYBE THEY WERE RIGHT-- MAYBE I HAVE LOST MY MIND! WISH I COULD GET AWAY-
--GET OUT OF HERE-- GET AWAY!
AND, UNNOTICED BY THE PANICKING PHYSICIST, AN EERIE GLOW SUFFUSES HIS TREMBLING FORM, AS AN UNCANNY TRANSFORMATION BEGINS, SPURRED BY HIS EMOTIONAL OUTBURST...
INSTANTLY, AN INVISIBLE FORCE REACHES FROM THE SCIENTIST, STRETCHING THE MILES TO BRADLEY HIGH SCHOOL IN UPPER MANHATTAN...
BRADLEY HIGH GYMNASIUM
...WHERE A YOUTH NAMED RONNIE RAYMOND IS A STUDENT, AND STAR OF THE BASKETBALL TEAM...
RONNIE RAYMOND IS GOING FOR THE WINNING POINT--
--BUT SOMETHING'S WRONG! RAYMOND FLUBBED THE SHOT!

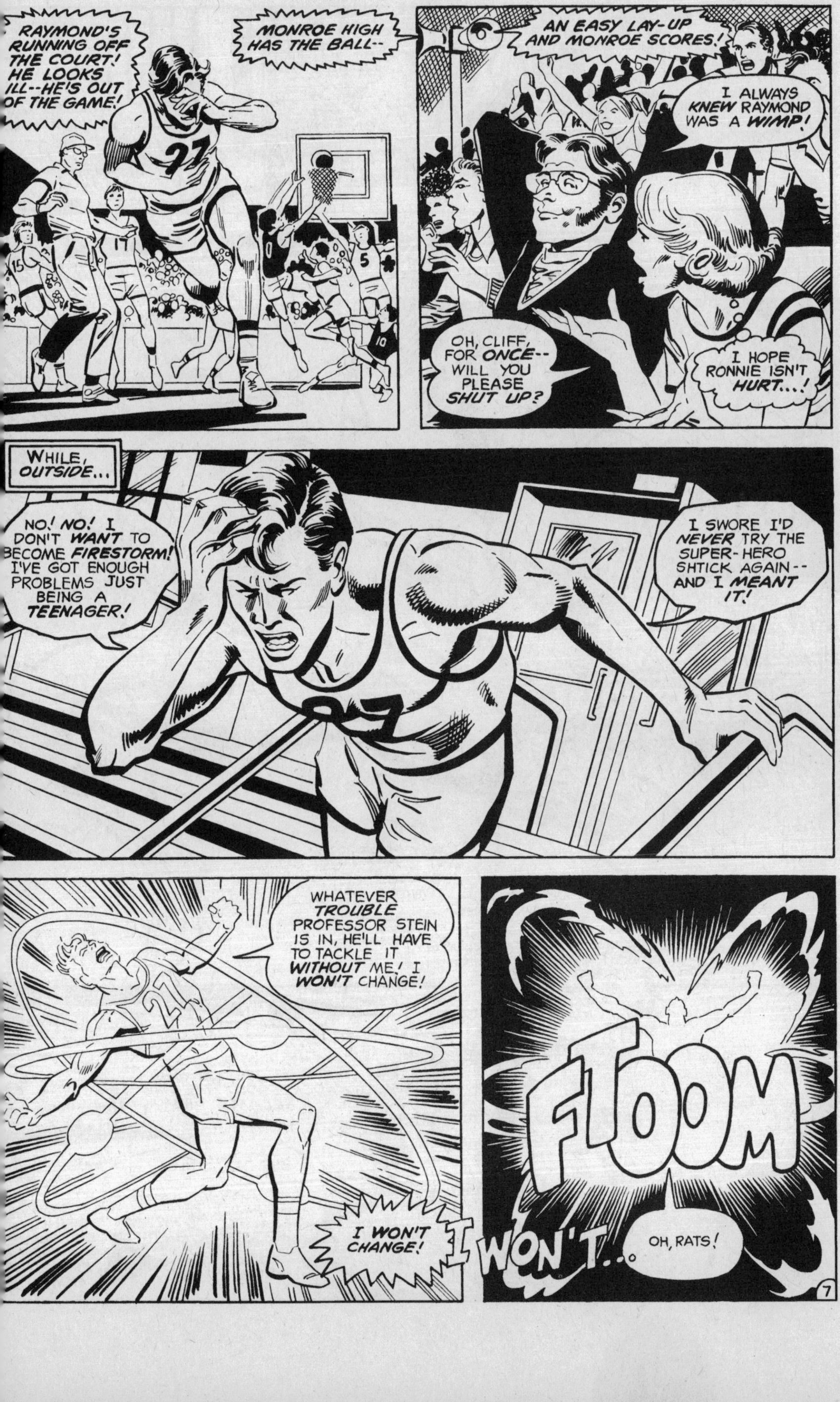
RAYMOND'S RUNNING OFF THE COURT! HE LOOKS ILL--HE'S OUT OF THE GAME!
MONROE HIGH HAS THE BALL--
AN EASY LAY-UP AND MONROE SCORES!
I ALWAYS KNEW RAYMOND WAS A WIMP!
OH, CLIFF, FOR ONCE-- WILL YOU PLEASE SHUT UP?
I HOPE RONNIE ISN'T HURT...!
WHILE, OUTSIDE...
NO! NO! I DON'T WANT TO BECOME FIRESTORM! I'VE GOT ENOUGH PROBLEMS JUST BEING A TEENAGER!
I SWORE I'D NEVER TRY THE SUPER-HERO SHTICK AGAIN-- AND I MEANT IT!
WHATEVER TROUBLE PROFESSOR STEIN IS IN, HE'LL HAVE TO TACKLE IT WITHOUT ME! I WON'T CHANGE!
I WON'T CHANGE!
I WON'T...
FTOOM
OH, RATS!
7

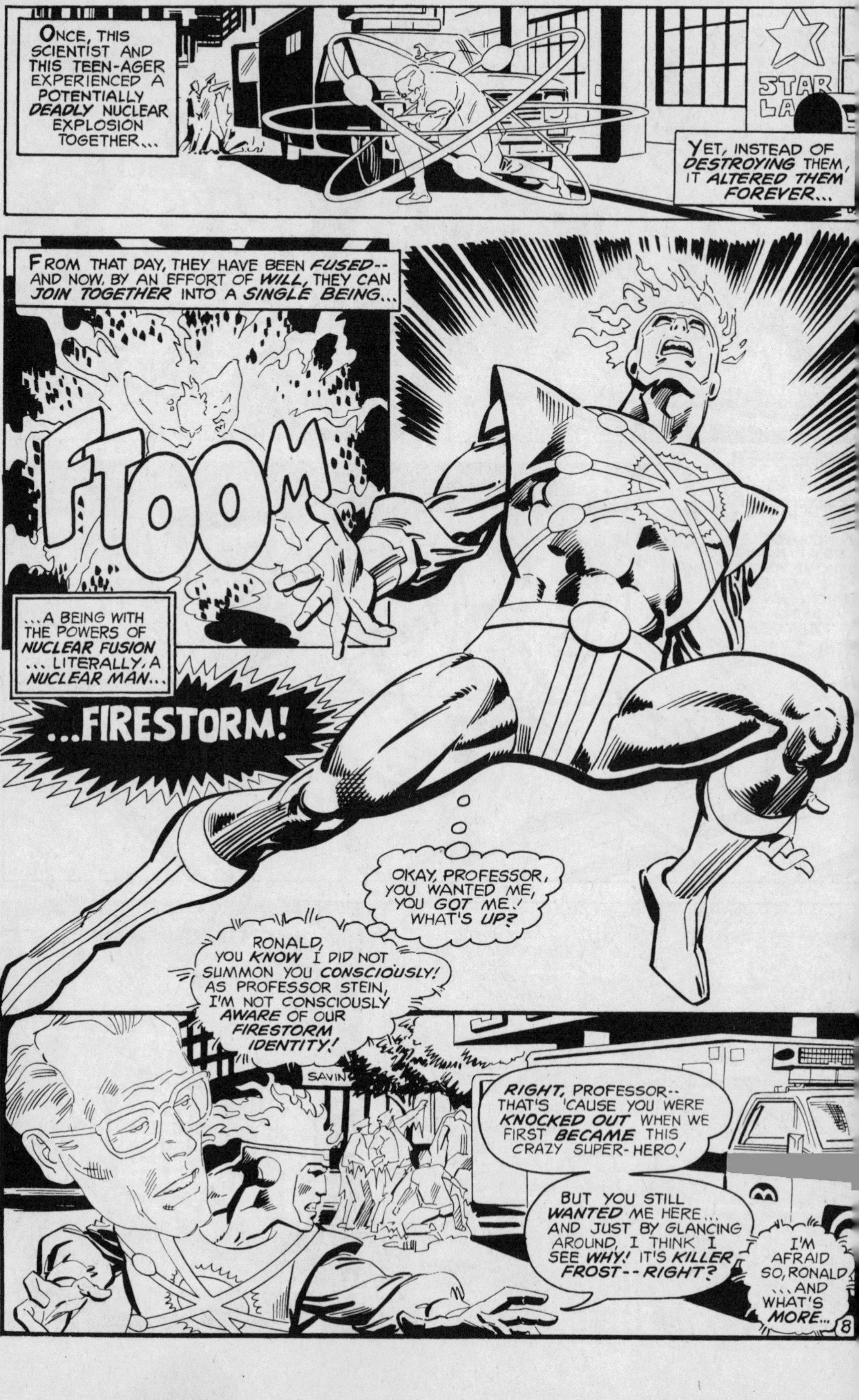
ONCE, THIS SCIENTIST AND THIS TEEN-AGER EXPERIENCED A POTENTIALLY DEADLY NUCLEAR EXPLOSION TOGETHER...
STAR LA
YET, INSTEAD OF DESTROYING THEM, IT ALTERED THEM FOREVER...
FROM THAT DAY, THEY HAVE BEEN FUSED-- AND NOW, BY AN EFFORT OF WILL, THEY CAN JOIN TOGETHER INTO A SINGLE BEING...
FTOOM
...A BEING WITH THE POWERS OF NUCLEAR FUSION ... LITERALLY, A NUCLEAR MAN...
...FIRESTORM!
OKAY, PROFESSOR, YOU WANTED ME, YOU GOT ME.! WHAT'S UP?
RONALD, YOU KNOW I DID NOT SUMMON YOU CONSCIOUSLY! AS PROFESSOR STEIN, I'M NOT CONSCIOUSLY AWARE OF OUR FIRESTORM IDENTITY!
SAVIN
RIGHT, PROFESSOR-- THAT'S 'CAUSE YOU WERE KNOCKED OUT WHEN WE FIRST BECAME THIS CRAZY SUPER-HERO!
BUT YOU STILL WANTED ME HERE... AND JUST BY GLANCING AROUND, I THINK I SEE WHY! IT'S KILLER FROST-- RIGHT?
I'M AFRAID SO, RONALD ... AND WHAT'S MORE...
8

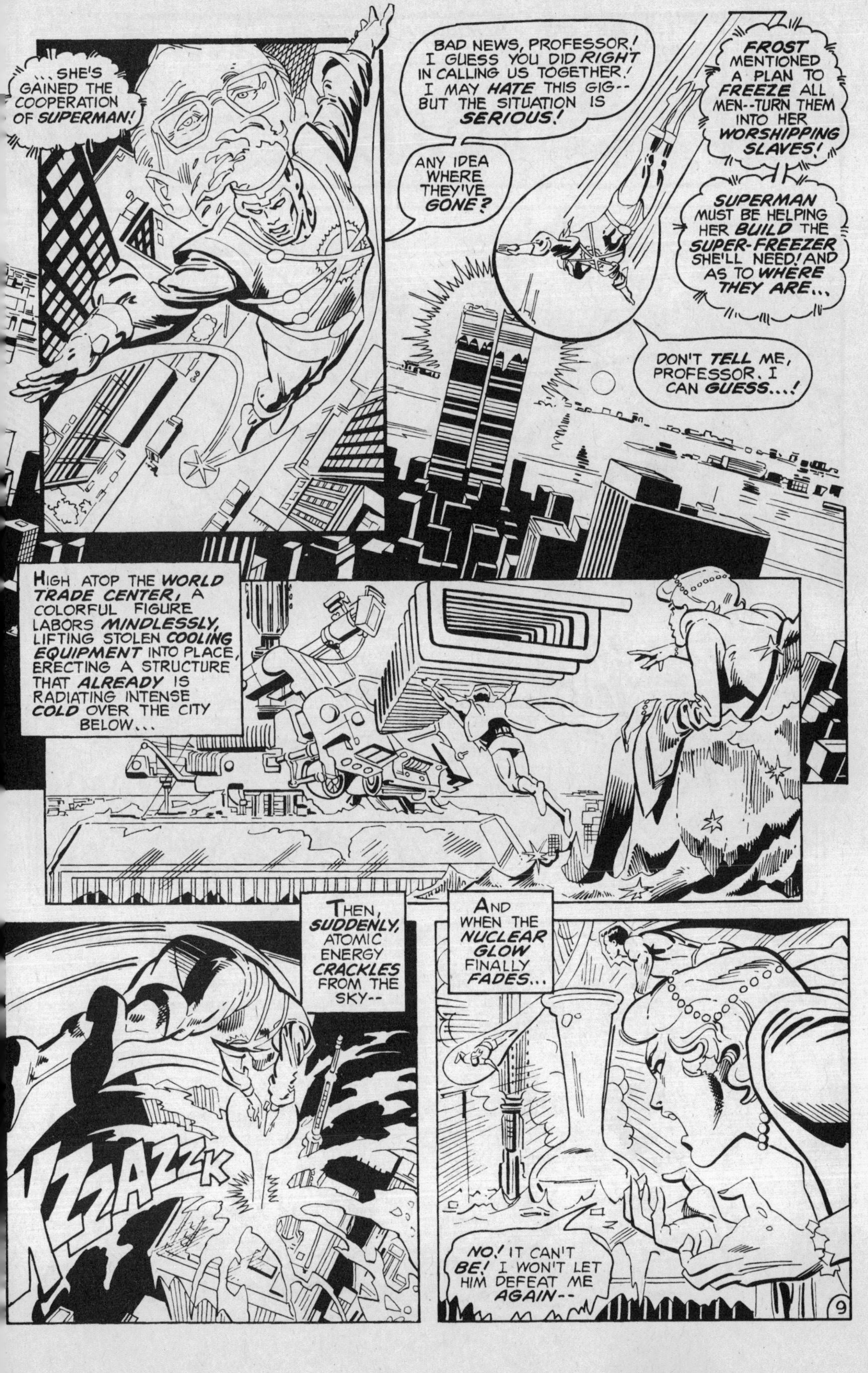
...SHE'S GAINED THE COOPERATION OF SUPERMAN!
BAD NEWS, PROFESSOR! I GUESS YOU DID RIGHT IN CALLING US TOGETHER! I MAY HATE THIS GIG-- BUT THE SITUATION IS SERIOUS!
ANY IDEA WHERE THEY'VE GONE?
FROST MENTIONED A PLAN TO FREEZE ALL MEN--TURN THEM INTO HER WORSHIPPING SLAVES!
SUPERMAN MUST BE HELPING HER BUILD THE SUPER-FREEZER SHE'LL NEED! AND AS TO WHERE THEY ARE...
DON'T TELL ME, PROFESSOR. I CAN GUESS...!
HIGH ATOP THE WORLD TRADE CENTER, A COLORFUL FIGURE LABORS MINDLESSLY, LIFTING STOLEN COOLING EQUIPMENT INTO PLACE, ERECTING A STRUCTURE THAT ALREADY IS RADIATING INTENSE COLD OVER THE CITY BELOW...
THEN, SUDDENLY, ATOMIC ENERGY CRACKLES FROM THE SKY--
KZZAZZK
AND WHEN THE NUCLEAR GLOW FINALLY FADES...
NO! IT CAN'T BE! I WON'T LET HIM DEFEAT ME AGAIN--
9

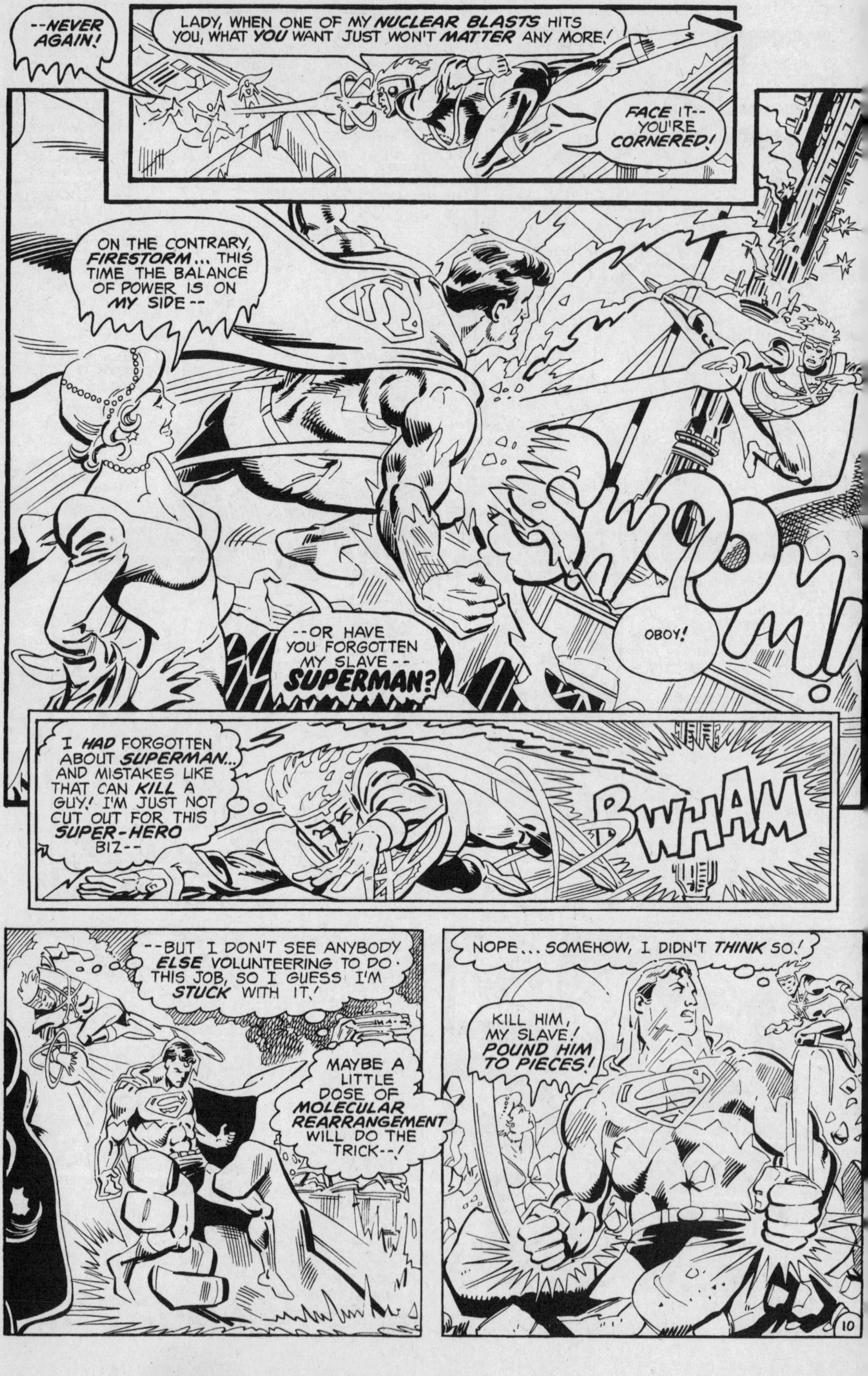
--NEVER AGAIN!
LADY, WHEN ONE OF MY NUCLEAR BLASTS HITS YOU, WHAT YOU WANT JUST WON'T MATTER ANY MORE!
FACE IT-- YOU'RE CORNERED!
ON THE CONTRARY, FIRESTORM... THIS TIME THE BALANCE OF POWER IS ON MY SIDE--
--OR HAVE YOU FORGOTTEN MY SLAVE-- SUPERMAN?
OBOY!
I HAD FORGOTTEN ABOUT SUPERMAN... AND MISTAKES LIKE THAT CAN KILL A GUY! I'M JUST NOT CUT OUT FOR THIS SUPER-HERO BIZ--
BWHAM
--BUT I DON'T SEE ANYBODY ELSE VOLUNTEERING TO DO THIS JOB, SO I GUESS I'M STUCK WITH IT!
MAYBE A LITTLE DOSE OF MOLECULAR REARRANGEMENT WILL DO THE TRICK--!
NOPE... SOMEHOW, I DIDN'T THINK SO!
KILL HIM, MY SLAVE! POUND HIM TO PIECES!
10

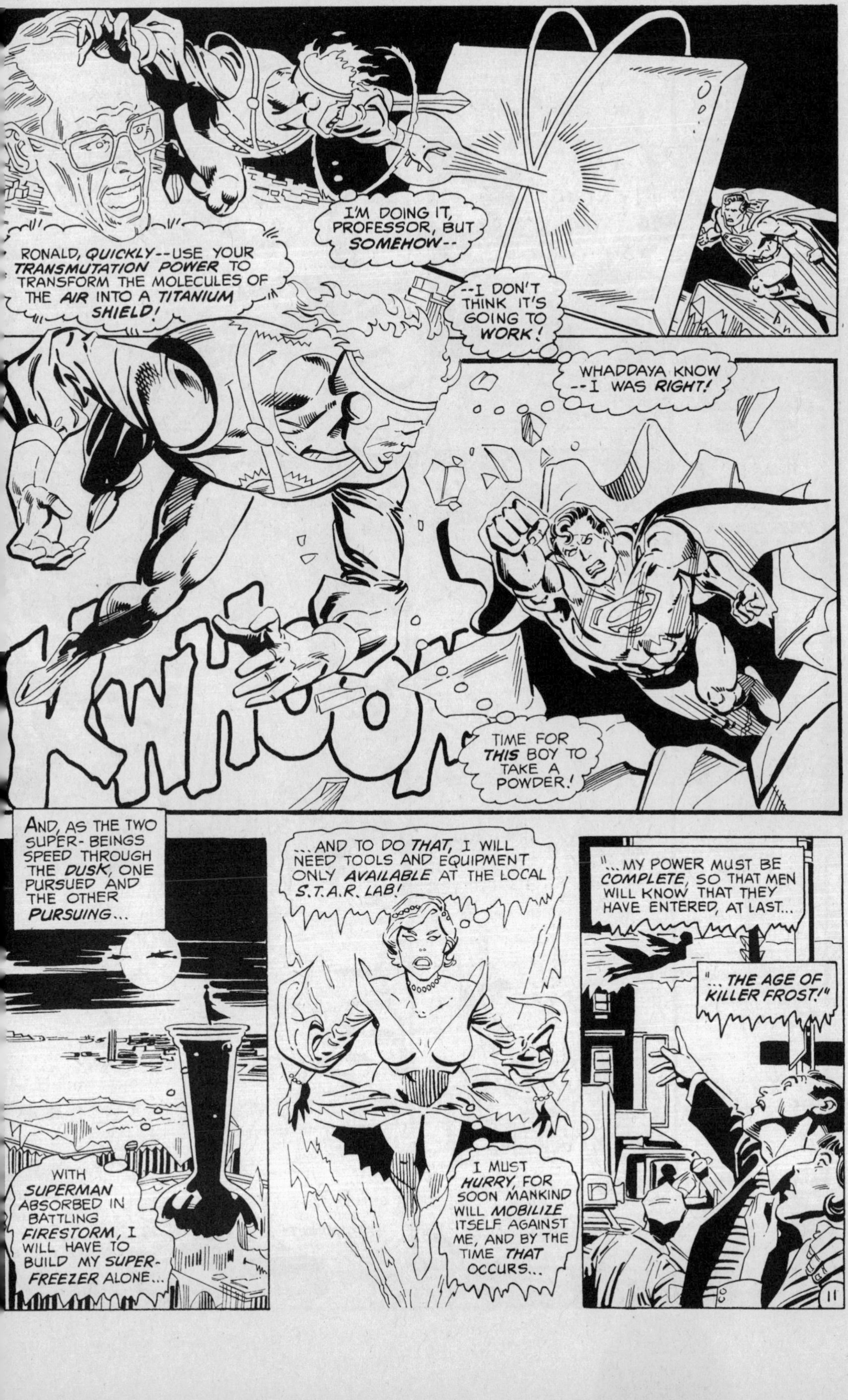
RONALD, QUICKLY--USE YOUR TRANSMUTATION POWER TO TRANSFORM THE MOLECULES OF THE AIR INTO A TITANIUM SHIELD!
I'M DOING IT, PROFESSOR, BUT SOMEHOW--
--I DON'T THINK IT'S GOING TO WORK!
WHADDAYA KNOW --I WAS RIGHT!
KWHOOM
TIME FOR THIS BOY TO TAKE A POWDER!
AND, AS THE TWO SUPER-BEINGS SPEED THROUGH THE DUSK, ONE PURSUED AND THE OTHER PURSUING...
WITH SUPERMAN ABSORBED IN BATTLING FIRESTORM, I WILL HAVE TO BUILD MY SUPER-FREEZER ALONE...
...AND TO DO THAT, I WILL NEED TOOLS AND EQUIPMENT ONLY AVAILABLE AT THE LOCAL S.T.A.R. LAB!
I MUST HURRY, FOR SOON MANKIND WILL MOBILIZE ITSELF AGAINST ME, AND BY THE TIME THAT OCCURS...
"...MY POWER MUST BE COMPLETE, SO THAT MEN WILL KNOW THAT THEY HAVE ENTERED, AT LAST...
"...THE AGE OF KILLER FROST!"
11

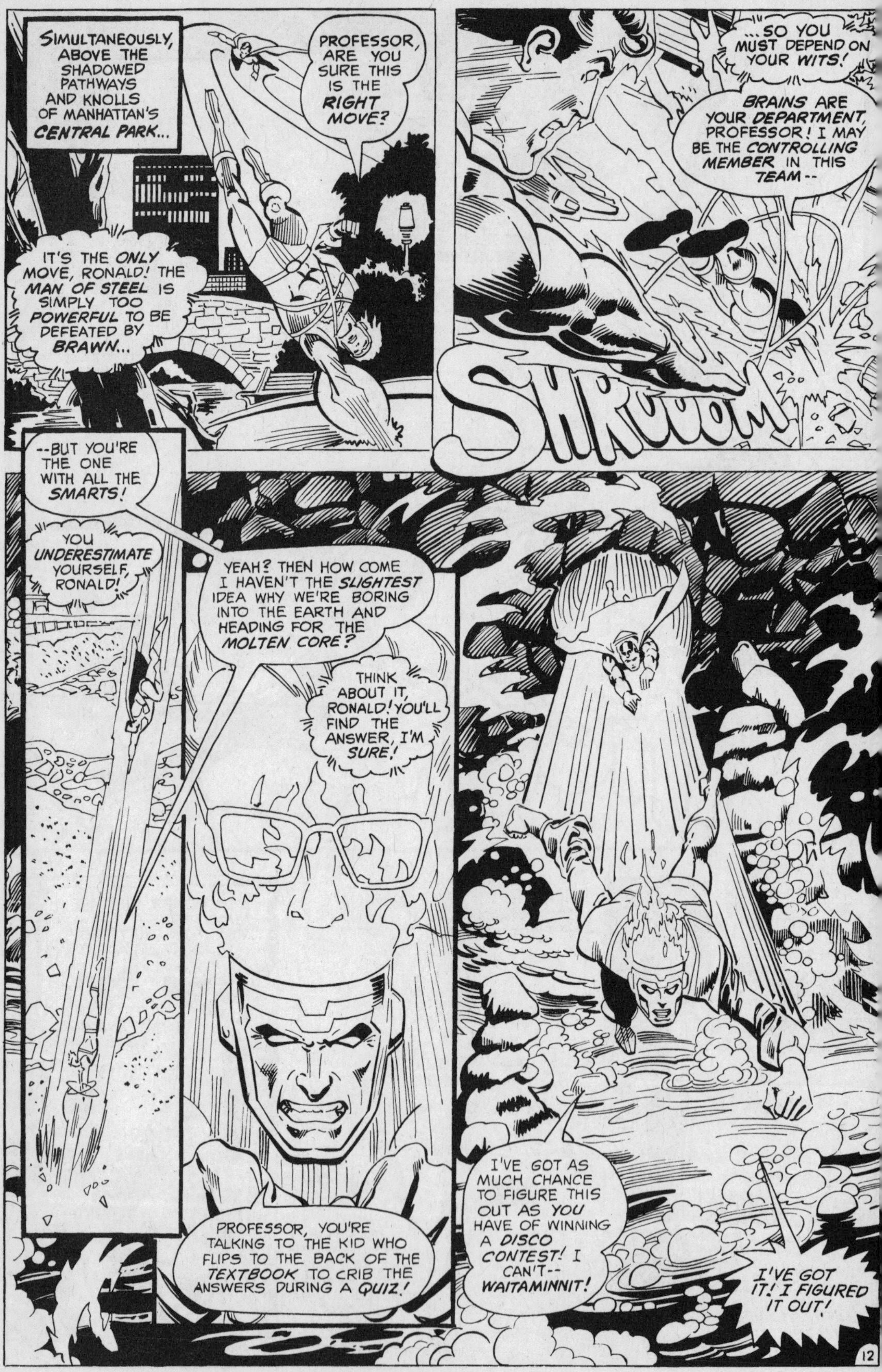
SIMULTANEOUSLY, ABOVE THE SHADOWED PATHWAYS AND KNOLLS OF MANHATTAN'S CENTRAL PARK...
PROFESSOR, ARE YOU SURE THIS IS THE RIGHT MOVE?
IT'S THE ONLY MOVE, RONALD! THE MAN OF STEEL IS SIMPLY TOO POWERFUL TO BE DEFEATED BY BRAWN...
...SO YOU MUST DEPEND ON YOUR WITS!
BRAINS ARE YOUR DEPARTMENT, PROFESSOR! I MAY BE THE CONTROLLING MEMBER IN THIS TEAM--
SHROOOOM
--BUT YOU'RE THE ONE WITH ALL THE SMARTS!
YOU UNDERESTIMATE YOURSELF, RONALD!
YEAH? THEN HOW COME I HAVEN'T THE SLIGHTEST IDEA WHY WE'RE BORING INTO THE EARTH AND HEADING FOR THE MOLTEN CORE?
THINK ABOUT IT, RONALD! YOU'LL FIND THE ANSWER, I'M SURE!
PROFESSOR, YOU'RE TALKING TO THE KID WHO FLIPS TO THE BACK OF THE TEXTBOOK TO CRIB THE ANSWERS DURING A QUIZ!
I'VE GOT AS MUCH CHANCE TO FIGURE THIS OUT AS YOU HAVE OF WINNING A DISCO CONTEST! I CAN'T-- WAITAMINNIT!
I'VE GOT IT! I FIGURED IT OUT!
12

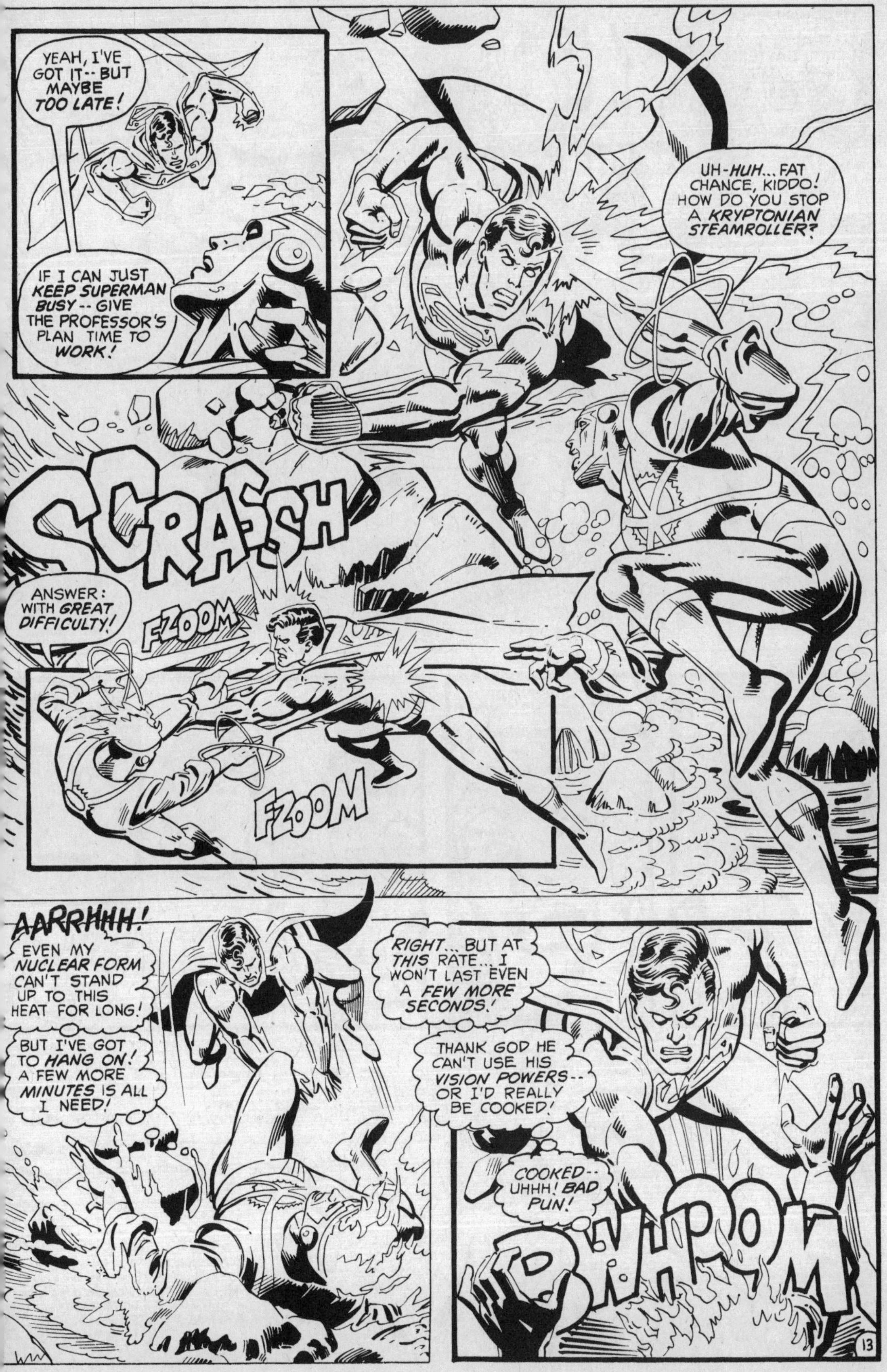
YEAH, I'VE GOT IT-- BUT MAYBE TOO LATE!
IF I CAN JUST KEEP SUPERMAN BUSY-- GIVE THE PROFESSOR'S PLAN TIME TO WORK!
UH-HUH... FAT CHANCE, KIDDO! HOW DO YOU STOP A KRYPTONIAN STEAMROLLER?
SCRASSH
ANSWER: WITH GREAT DIFFICULTY!
FZOOM
FZOOM
AARRHHH!
EVEN MY NUCLEAR FORM CAN'T STAND UP TO THIS HEAT FOR LONG!
BUT I'VE GOT TO HANG ON! A FEW MORE MINUTES IS ALL I NEED!
RIGHT... BUT AT THIS RATE... I WON'T LAST EVEN A FEW MORE SECONDS!
THANK GOD HE CAN'T USE HIS VISION POWERS-- OR I'D REALLY BE COOKED!
COOKED-- UHHH! BAD PUN!
DWHROOM
13

THAT'S IT... I'M TOO BATTERED AND WEAK TO MOVE. IT WAS A NICE TRY... BUT I GUESS I WAS JUST PLAIN OUTCLASSED...
HERE HE COMES... FOR THE FINISH...
CAN'T LOOK...!
WHAT'S TAKING HIM SO LONG?
LET'S JUST GET IT OVER WITH SO... HUH?
IT WORKED!
WHAT...
...HAPPENED...
...TO ME?
THE LAST THING I REMEMBER... KILLER FROST WAS--KISSING ME?
YOUR MIND WAS IN A DEEP FREEZE, PAL, BUT THANKS TO THE INCREDIBLE HEAT DOWN HERE, YOU'RE ALL THAWED OUT...
...JUST LIKE I EXPECTED!
NOW, LET'S GET OUT OF HERE --I FEEL LIKE I'VE JUST SPENT A WEEKEND IN A SAUNA! I'LL EXPLAIN ON THE WAY...
14

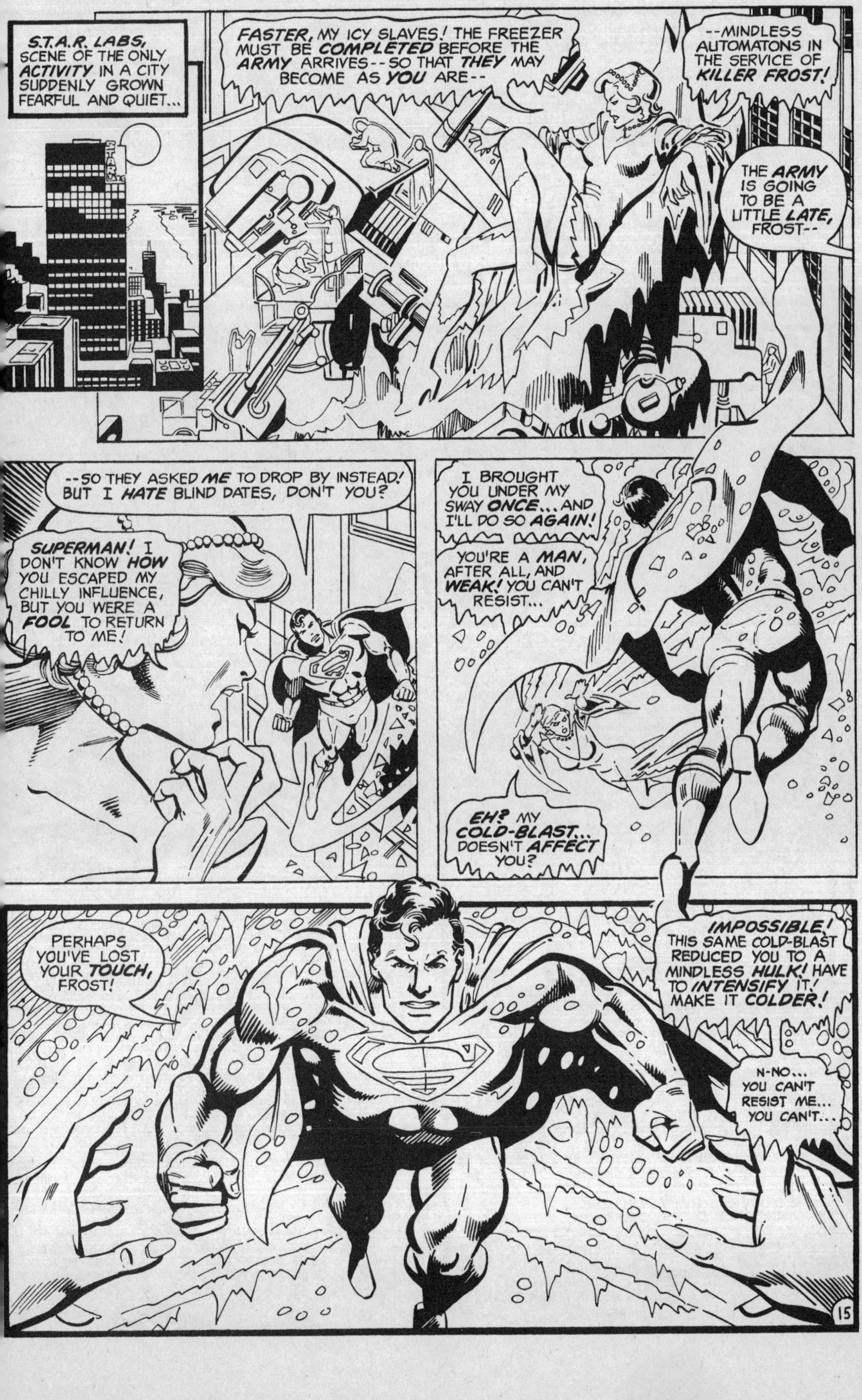
S.T.A.R. LABS, SCENE OF THE ONLY ACTIVITY IN A CITY SUDDENLY GROWN FEARFUL AND QUIET...
FASTER, MY ICY SLAVES! THE FREEZER MUST BE COMPLETED BEFORE THE ARMY ARRIVES--SO THAT THEY MAY BECOME AS YOU ARE--
--MINDLESS AUTOMATONS IN THE SERVICE OF KILLER FROST!
THE ARMY IS GOING TO BE A LITTLE LATE, FROST--
--SO THEY ASKED ME TO DROP BY INSTEAD! BUT I HATE BLIND DATES, DON'T YOU?
SUPERMAN! I DON'T KNOW HOW YOU ESCAPED MY CHILLY INFLUENCE, BUT YOU WERE A FOOL TO RETURN TO ME!
I BROUGHT YOU UNDER MY SWAY ONCE... AND I'LL DO SO AGAIN!
YOU'RE A MAN, AFTER ALL, AND WEAK! YOU CAN'T RESIST...
EH? MY COLD-BLAST... DOESN'T AFFECT YOU?
PERHAPS YOU'VE LOST YOUR TOUCH, FROST!
IMPOSSIBLE! THIS SAME COLD-BLAST REDUCED YOU TO A MINDLESS HULK! HAVE TO INTENSIFY IT! MAKE IT COLDER!
N-NO... YOU CAN'T RESIST ME... YOU CAN'T...
15

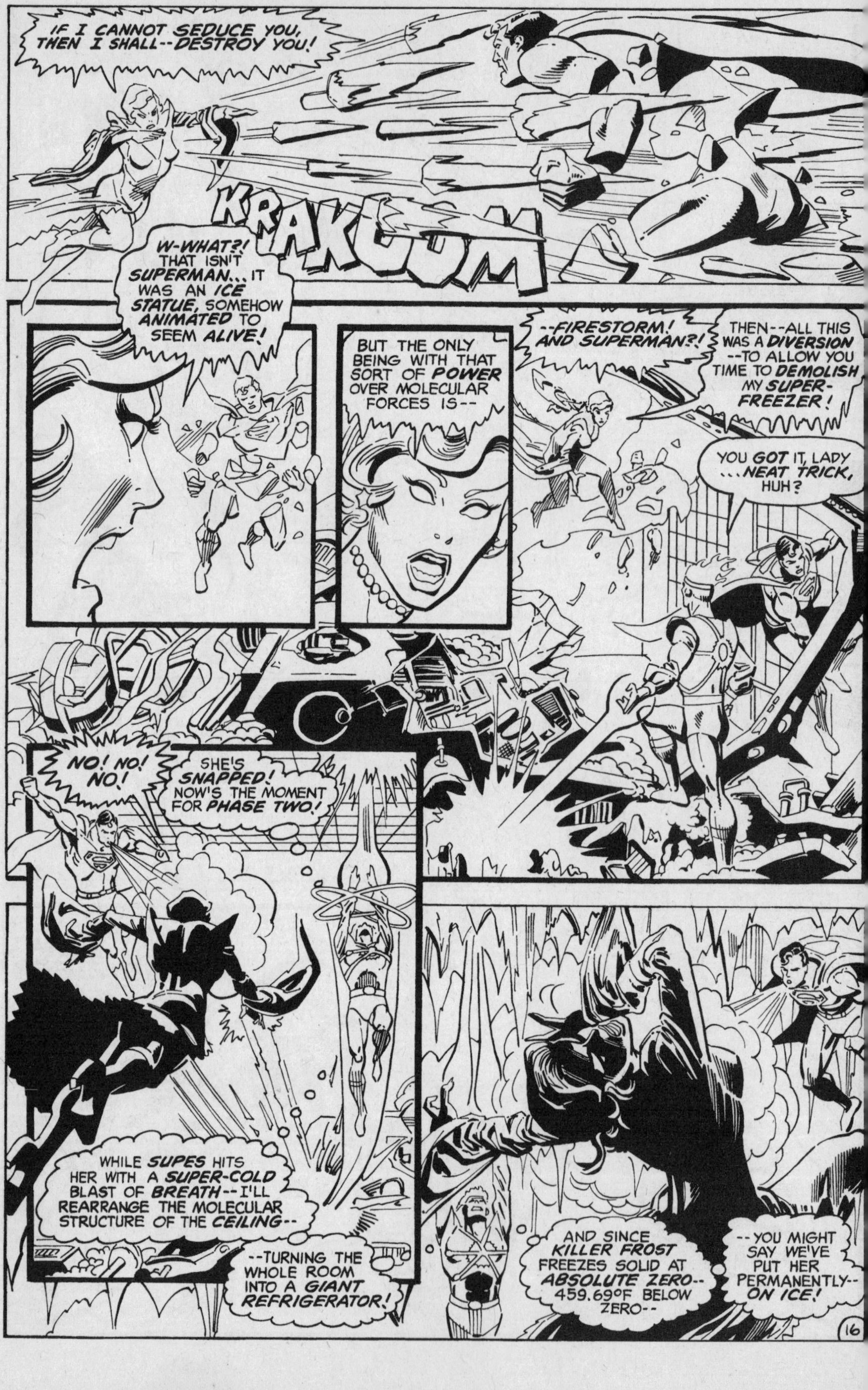
IF I CANNOT SEDUCE YOU, THEN I SHALL--DESTROY YOU!
KRAKOOM
W-WHAT?! THAT ISN'T SUPERMAN... IT WAS AN ICE STATUE, SOMEHOW ANIMATED TO SEEM ALIVE!
BUT THE ONLY BEING WITH THAT SORT OF POWER OVER MOLECULAR FORCES IS--
--FIRESTORM! AND SUPERMAN?!
THEN--ALL THIS WAS A DIVERSION --TO ALLOW YOU TIME TO DEMOLISH MY SUPER-FREEZER!
YOU GOT IT, LADY ...NEAT TRICK, HUH?
NO! NO! NO!
SHE'S SNAPPED! NOW'S THE MOMENT FOR PHASE TWO!
WHILE SUPES HITS HER WITH A SUPER-COLD BLAST OF BREATH--I'LL REARRANGE THE MOLECULAR STRUCTURE OF THE CEILING--
--TURNING THE WHOLE ROOM INTO A GIANT REFRIGERATOR!
AND SINCE KILLER FROST FREEZES SOLID AT ABSOLUTE ZERO-- 459.69°F BELOW ZERO--
--YOU MIGHT SAY WE'VE PUT HER PERMANENTLY-- ON ICE!
16

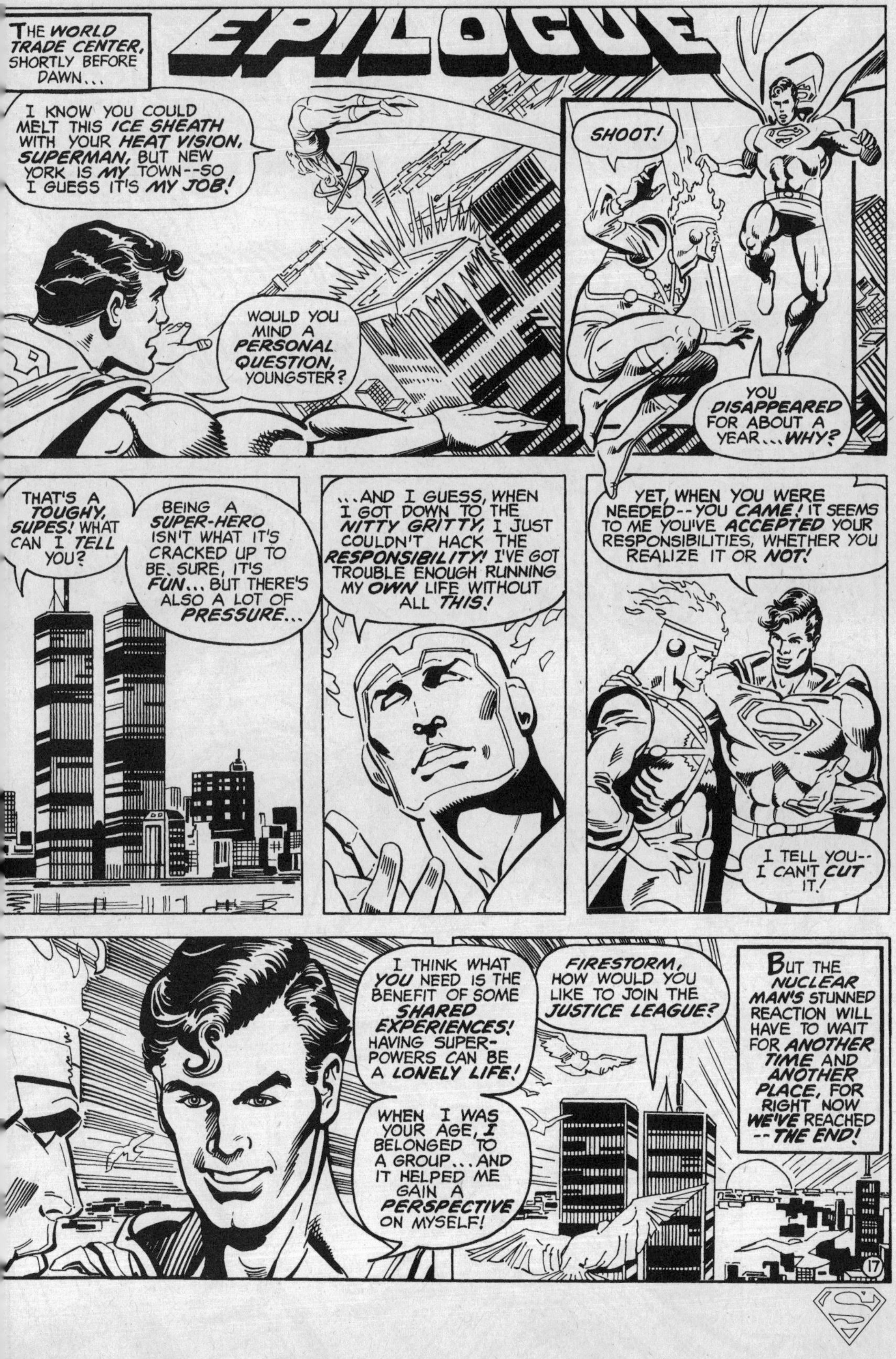
THE WORLD TRADE CENTER, SHORTLY BEFORE DAWN...
EPILOGUE
I KNOW YOU COULD MELT THIS ICE SHEATH WITH YOUR HEAT VISION, SUPERMAN, BUT NEW YORK IS MY TOWN--SO I GUESS IT'S MY JOB!
SHOOT!
WOULD YOU MIND A PERSONAL QUESTION, YOUNGSTER?
YOU DISAPPEARED FOR ABOUT A YEAR...WHY?
THAT'S A TOUGHY, SUPES! WHAT CAN I TELL YOU?
BEING A SUPER-HERO ISN'T WHAT IT'S CRACKED UP TO BE. SURE, IT'S FUN... BUT THERE'S ALSO A LOT OF PRESSURE...
...AND I GUESS, WHEN I GOT DOWN TO THE NITTY GRITTY, I JUST COULDN'T HACK THE RESPONSIBILITY! I'VE GOT TROUBLE ENOUGH RUNNING MY OWN LIFE WITHOUT ALL THIS!
YET, WHEN YOU WERE NEEDED--YOU CAME! IT SEEMS TO ME YOU'VE ACCEPTED YOUR RESPONSIBILITIES, WHETHER YOU REALIZE IT OR NOT!
I TELL YOU--I CAN'T CUT IT!
I THINK WHAT YOU NEED IS THE BENEFIT OF SOME SHARED EXPERIENCES! HAVING SUPER-POWERS CAN BE A LONELY LIFE!
WHEN I WAS YOUR AGE, I BELONGED TO A GROUP...AND IT HELPED ME GAIN A PERSPECTIVE ON MYSELF!
FIRESTORM, HOW WOULD YOU LIKE TO JOIN THE JUSTICE LEAGUE?
BUT THE NUCLEAR MAN'S STUNNED REACTION WILL HAVE TO WAIT FOR ANOTHER TIME AND ANOTHER PLACE, FOR RIGHT NOW WE'VE REACHED --THE END!
17

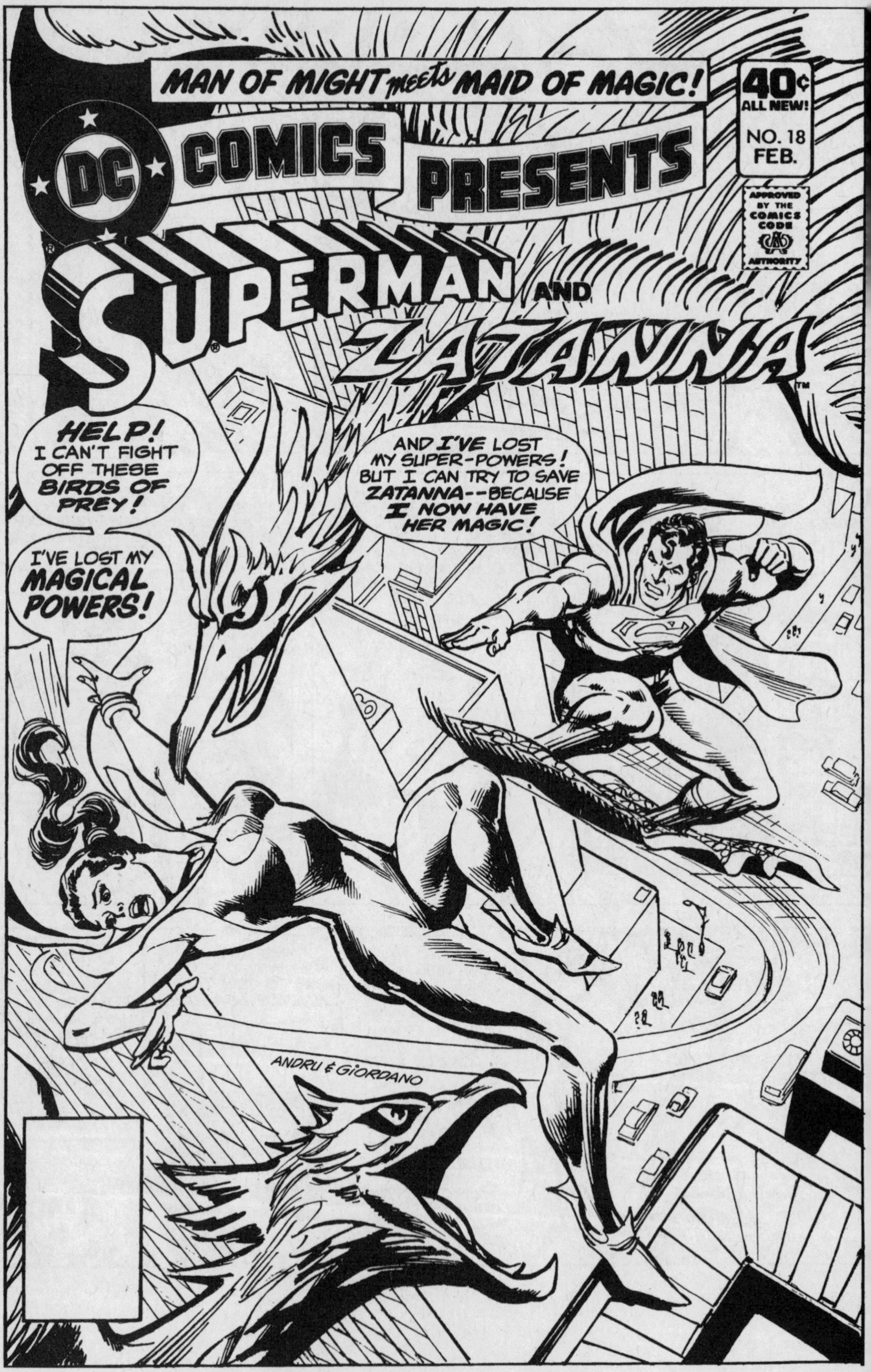
MAN OF MIGHT meets MAID OF MAGIC!
40¢ ALL NEW!
NO. 18 FEB.
APPROVED BY THE COMICS CODE AUTHORITY
DC COMICS PRESENTS
SUPERMAN AND ZATANNA
HELP! I CAN'T FIGHT OFF THESE BIRDS OF PREY!
I'VE LOST MY MAGICAL POWERS!
AND I'VE LOST MY SUPER-POWERS! BUT I CAN TRY TO SAVE ZATANNA--BECAUSE I NOW HAVE HER MAGIC!
ANDRU & GIORDANO

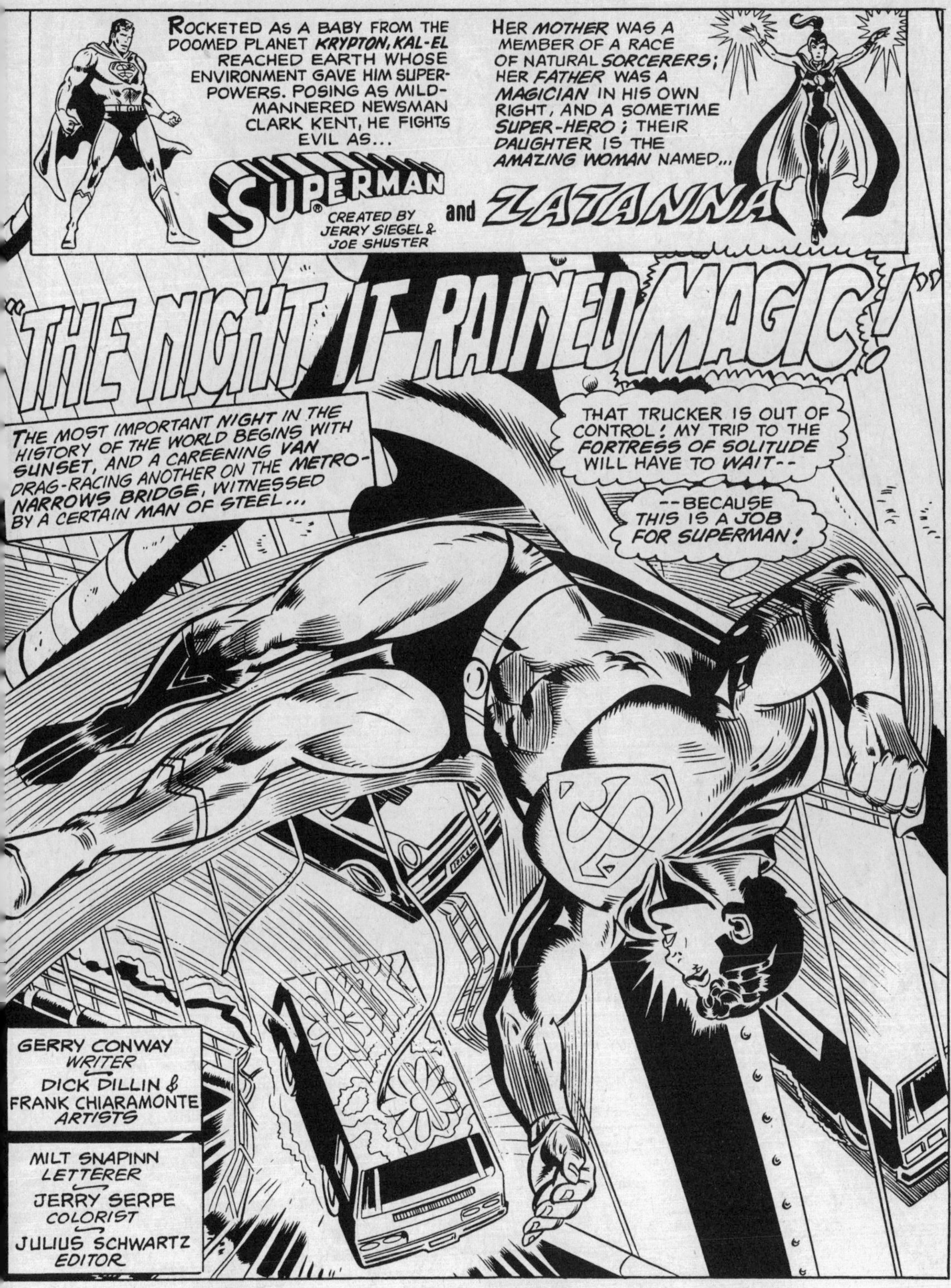
ROCKETED AS A BABY FROM THE DOOMED PLANET KRYPTON, KAL-EL REACHED EARTH WHOSE ENVIRONMENT GAVE HIM SUPER-POWERS. POSING AS MILD-MANNERED NEWSMAN CLARK KENT, HE FIGHTS EVIL AS...
HER MOTHER WAS A MEMBER OF A RACE OF NATURAL SORCERERS; HER FATHER WAS A MAGICIAN IN HIS OWN RIGHT, AND A SOMETIME SUPER-HERO; THEIR DAUGHTER IS THE AMAZING WOMAN NAMED...
SUPERMAN®
CREATED BY JERRY SIEGEL & JOE SHUSTER
and ZATANNA
"THE NIGHT IT RAINED MAGIC!"
THE MOST IMPORTANT NIGHT IN THE HISTORY OF THE WORLD BEGINS WITH SUNSET, AND A CAREENING VAN DRAG-RACING ANOTHER ON THE METRO-NARROWS BRIDGE, WITNESSED BY A CERTAIN MAN OF STEEL...
THAT TRUCKER IS OUT OF CONTROL! MY TRIP TO THE FORTRESS OF SOLITUDE WILL HAVE TO WAIT--
--BECAUSE THIS IS A JOB FOR SUPERMAN!
GERRY CONWAY WRITER
DICK DILLIN & FRANK CHIARAMONTE ARTISTS
MILT SNAPINN LETTERER
JERRY SERPE COLORIST
JULIUS SCHWARTZ EDITOR

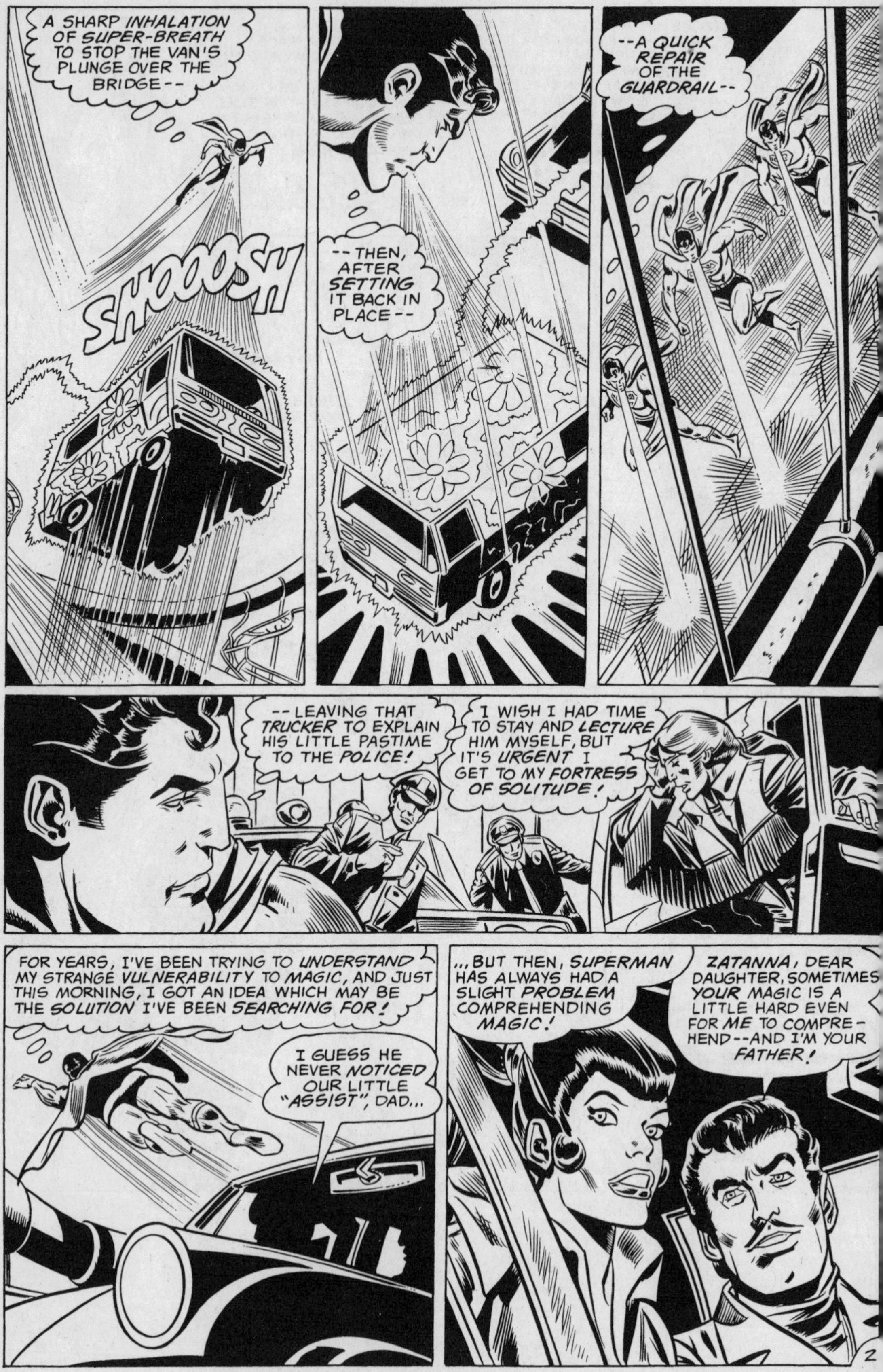
A SHARP INHALATION OF SUPER-BREATH TO STOP THE VAN'S PLUNGE OVER THE BRIDGE--
SHOOOSH
--THEN, AFTER SETTING IT BACK IN PLACE--
--A QUICK REPAIR OF THE GUARDRAIL--
--LEAVING THAT TRUCKER TO EXPLAIN HIS LITTLE PASTIME TO THE POLICE!
I WISH I HAD TIME TO STAY AND LECTURE HIM MYSELF, BUT IT'S URGENT I GET TO MY FORTRESS OF SOLITUDE!
FOR YEARS, I'VE BEEN TRYING TO UNDERSTAND MY STRANGE VULNERABILITY TO MAGIC, AND JUST THIS MORNING, I GOT AN IDEA WHICH MAY BE THE SOLUTION I'VE BEEN SEARCHING FOR!
I GUESS HE NEVER NOTICED OUR LITTLE "ASSIST", DAD...
...BUT THEN, SUPERMAN HAS ALWAYS HAD A SLIGHT PROBLEM COMPREHENDING MAGIC!
ZATANNA, DEAR DAUGHTER, SOMETIMES YOUR MAGIC IS A LITTLE HARD EVEN FOR ME TO COMPRE-HEND--AND I'M YOUR FATHER!
2

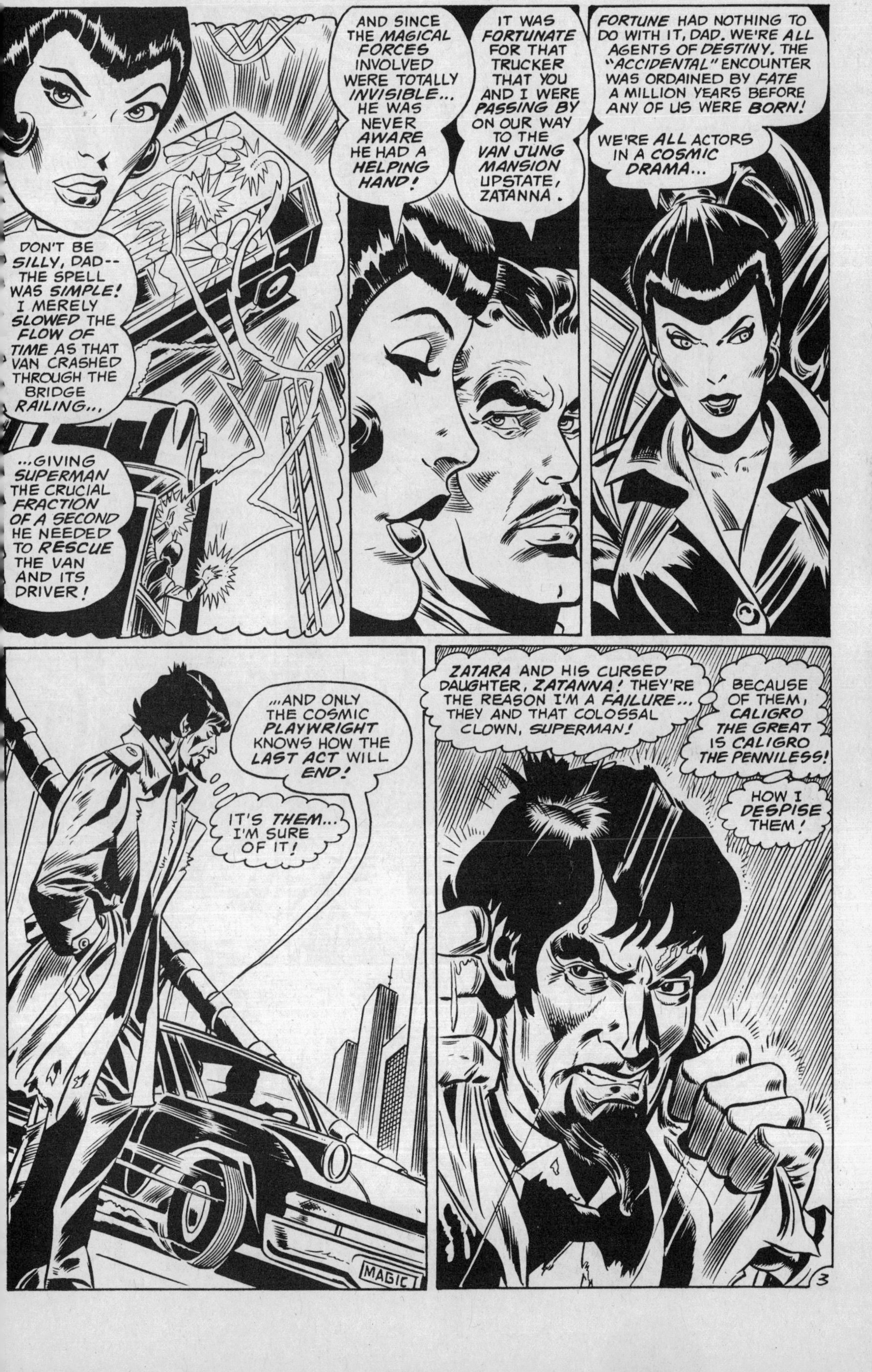
DON'T BE SILLY, DAD-- THE SPELL WAS SIMPLE! I MERELY SLOWED THE FLOW OF TIME AS THAT VAN CRASHED THROUGH THE BRIDGE RAILING...
...GIVING SUPERMAN THE CRUCIAL FRACTION OF A SECOND HE NEEDED TO RESCUE THE VAN AND ITS DRIVER!
AND SINCE THE MAGICAL FORCES INVOLVED WERE TOTALLY INVISIBLE... HE WAS NEVER AWARE HE HAD A HELPING HAND!
IT WAS FORTUNATE FOR THAT TRUCKER THAT YOU AND I WERE PASSING BY ON OUR WAY TO THE VAN JUNG MANSION UPSTATE, ZATANNA.
FORTUNE HAD NOTHING TO DO WITH IT, DAD. WE'RE ALL AGENTS OF DESTINY. THE "ACCIDENTAL" ENCOUNTER WAS ORDAINED BY FATE A MILLION YEARS BEFORE ANY OF US WERE BORN!
WE'RE ALL ACTORS IN A COSMIC DRAMA...
...AND ONLY THE COSMIC PLAYWRIGHT KNOWS HOW THE LAST ACT WILL END!
IT'S THEM... I'M SURE OF IT!
MAGIC
ZATARA AND HIS CURSED DAUGHTER, ZATANNA! THEY'RE THE REASON I'M A FAILURE... THEY AND THAT COLOSSAL CLOWN, SUPERMAN!
BECAUSE OF THEM, CALIGRO THE GREAT IS CALIGRO THE PENNILESS!
HOW I DESPISE THEM!
3

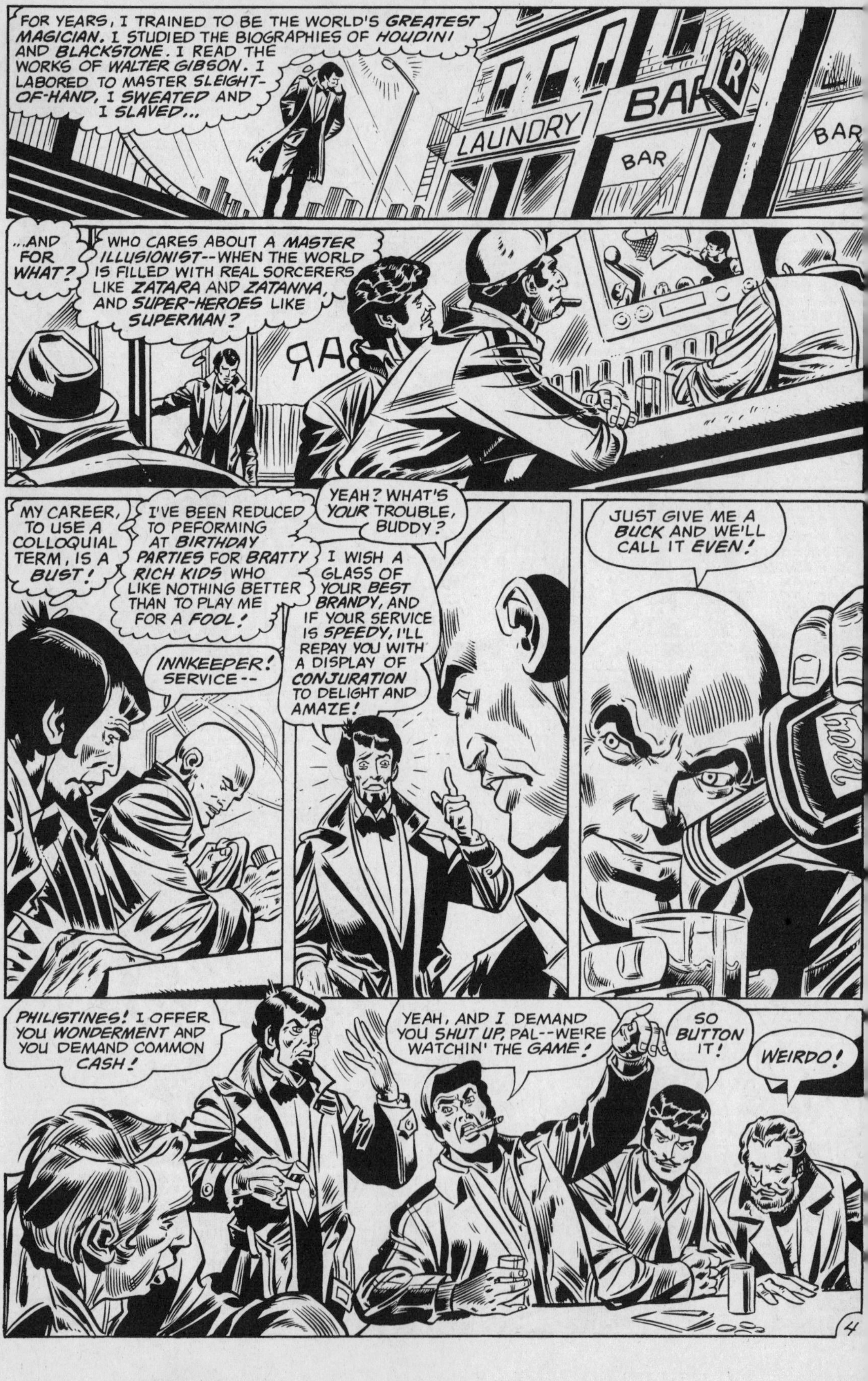
FOR YEARS, I TRAINED TO BE THE WORLD'S GREATEST MAGICIAN. I STUDIED THE BIOGRAPHIES OF HOUDINI AND BLACKSTONE. I READ THE WORKS OF WALTER GIBSON. I LABORED TO MASTER SLEIGHT-OF-HAND, I SWEATED AND I SLAVED...
LAUNDRY
BAR
BAR
BAR
R
...AND FOR WHAT?
WHO CARES ABOUT A MASTER ILLUSIONIST--WHEN THE WORLD IS FILLED WITH REAL SORCERERS LIKE ZATARA AND ZATANNA, AND SUPER-HEROES LIKE SUPERMAN?
MY CAREER, TO USE A COLLOQUIAL TERM, IS A BUST!
I'VE BEEN REDUCED TO PEFORMING AT BIRTHDAY PARTIES FOR BRATTY RICH KIDS WHO LIKE NOTHING BETTER THAN TO PLAY ME FOR A FOOL!
INNKEEPER! SERVICE--
YEAH? WHAT'S YOUR TROUBLE, BUDDY?
I WISH A GLASS OF YOUR BEST BRANDY, AND IF YOUR SERVICE IS SPEEDY, I'LL REPAY YOU WITH A DISPLAY OF CONJURATION TO DELIGHT AND AMAZE!
JUST GIVE ME A BUCK AND WE'LL CALL IT EVEN!
PHILISTINES! I OFFER YOU WONDERMENT AND YOU DEMAND COMMON CASH!
YEAH, AND I DEMAND YOU SHUT UP, PAL--WE'RE WATCHIN' THE GAME!
SO BUTTON IT!
WEIRDO!
4

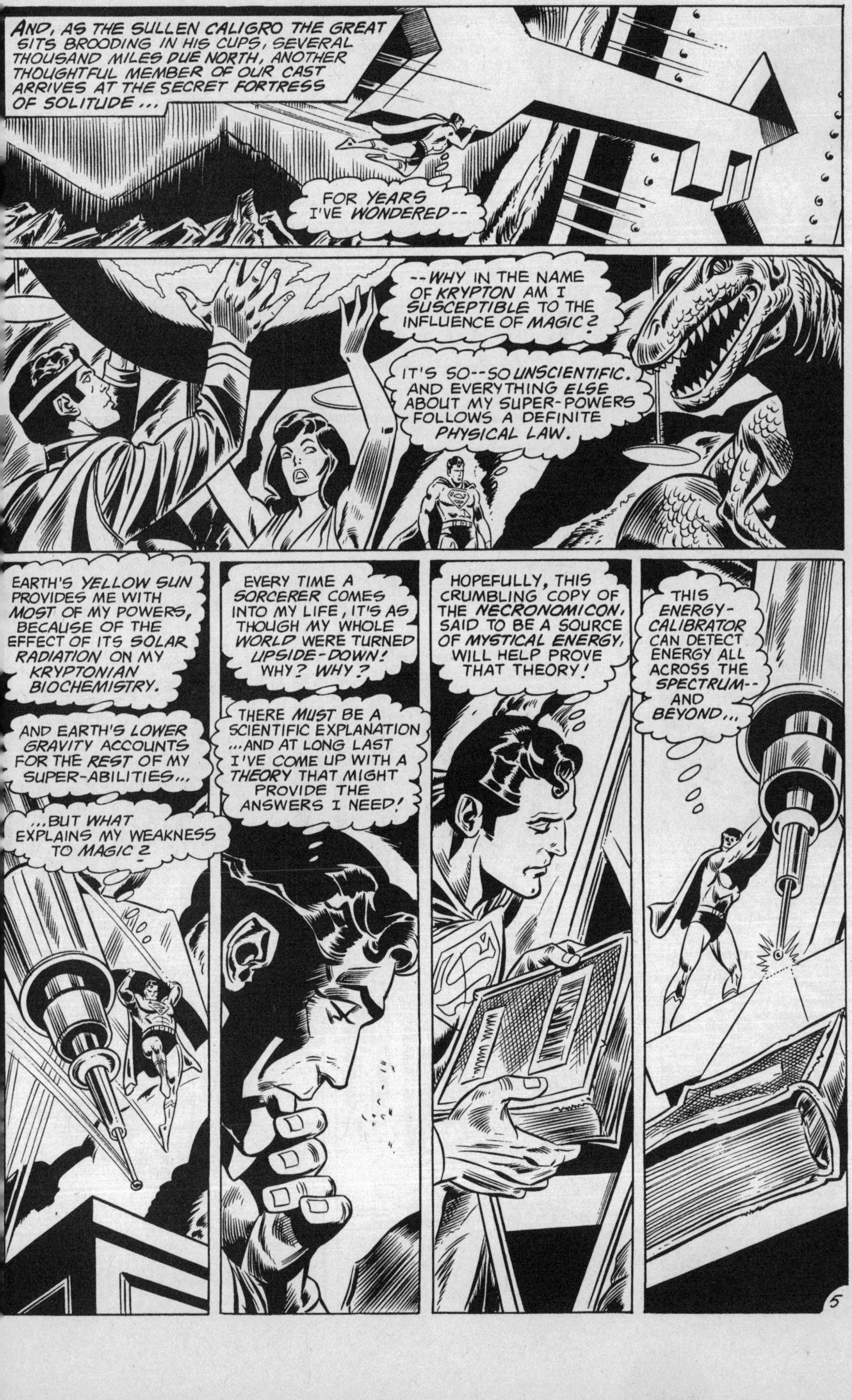
AND, AS THE SULLEN CALIGRO THE GREAT SITS BROODING IN HIS CUPS, SEVERAL THOUSAND MILES DUE NORTH, ANOTHER THOUGHTFUL MEMBER OF OUR CAST ARRIVES AT THE SECRET FORTRESS OF SOLITUDE ...
FOR YEARS I'VE WONDERED--
--WHY IN THE NAME OF KRYPTON AM I SUSCEPTIBLE TO THE INFLUENCE OF MAGIC?
IT'S SO--SO UNSCIENTIFIC. AND EVERYTHING ELSE ABOUT MY SUPER-POWERS FOLLOWS A DEFINITE PHYSICAL LAW.
EARTH'S YELLOW SUN PROVIDES ME WITH MOST OF MY POWERS, BECAUSE OF THE EFFECT OF ITS SOLAR RADIATION ON MY KRYPTONIAN BIOCHEMISTRY.
AND EARTH'S LOWER GRAVITY ACCOUNTS FOR THE REST OF MY SUPER-ABILITIES...
...BUT WHAT EXPLAINS MY WEAKNESS TO MAGIC?
EVERY TIME A SORCERER COMES INTO MY LIFE, IT'S AS THOUGH MY WHOLE WORLD WERE TURNED UPSIDE-DOWN! WHY? WHY?
THERE MUST BE A SCIENTIFIC EXPLANATION ...AND AT LONG LAST I'VE COME UP WITH A THEORY THAT MIGHT PROVIDE THE ANSWERS I NEED!
HOPEFULLY, THIS CRUMBLING COPY OF THE NECRONOMICON, SAID TO BE A SOURCE OF MYSTICAL ENERGY, WILL HELP PROVE THAT THEORY!
THIS ENERGY-CALIBRATOR CAN DETECT ENERGY ALL ACROSS THE SPECTRUM--AND BEYOND...
5

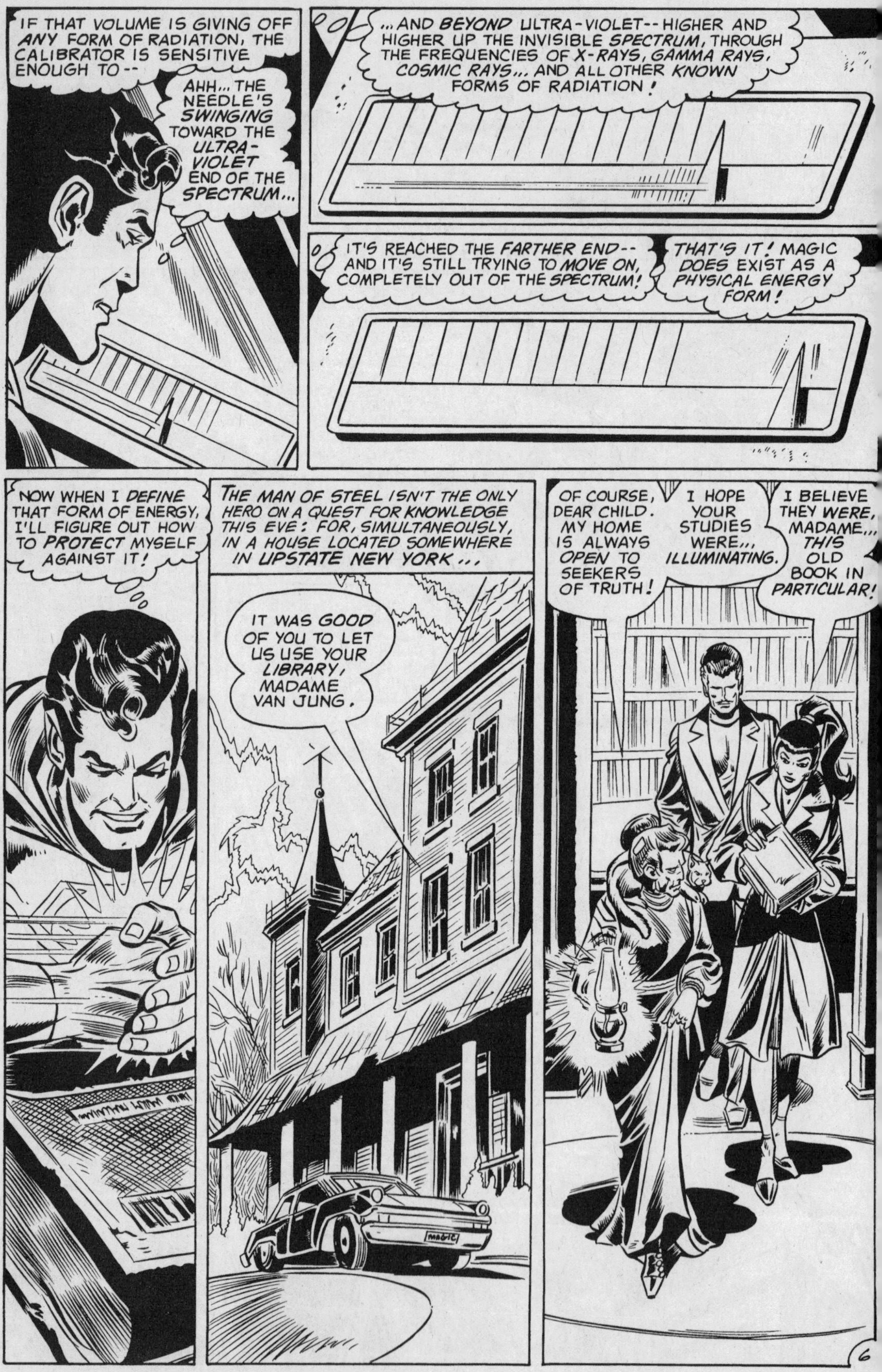

IF THAT VOLUME IS GIVING OFF ANY FORM OF RADIATION, THE CALIBRATOR IS SENSITIVE ENOUGH TO --
AHH... THE NEEDLE'S SWINGING TOWARD THE ULTRA-VIOLET END OF THE SPECTRUM...
...AND BEYOND ULTRA-VIOLET--HIGHER AND HIGHER UP THE INVISIBLE SPECTRUM, THROUGH THE FREQUENCIES OF X-RAYS, GAMMA RAYS, COSMIC RAYS... AND ALL OTHER KNOWN FORMS OF RADIATION!
IT'S REACHED THE FARTHER END-- AND IT'S STILL TRYING TO MOVE ON, COMPLETELY OUT OF THE SPECTRUM!
THAT'S IT! MAGIC DOES EXIST AS A PHYSICAL ENERGY FORM!
NOW WHEN I DEFINE THAT FORM OF ENERGY, I'LL FIGURE OUT HOW TO PROTECT MYSELF AGAINST IT!
THE MAN OF STEEL ISN'T THE ONLY HERO ON A QUEST FOR KNOWLEDGE THIS EVE: FOR, SIMULTANEOUSLY, IN A HOUSE LOCATED SOMEWHERE IN UPSTATE NEW YORK...
IT WAS GOOD OF YOU TO LET US USE YOUR LIBRARY, MADAME VAN JUNG.
MAGIC
OF COURSE, DEAR CHILD. MY HOME IS ALWAYS OPEN TO SEEKERS OF TRUTH!
I HOPE YOUR STUDIES WERE... ILLUMINATING.
I BELIEVE THEY WERE, MADAME... THIS OLD BOOK IN PARTICULAR!
6

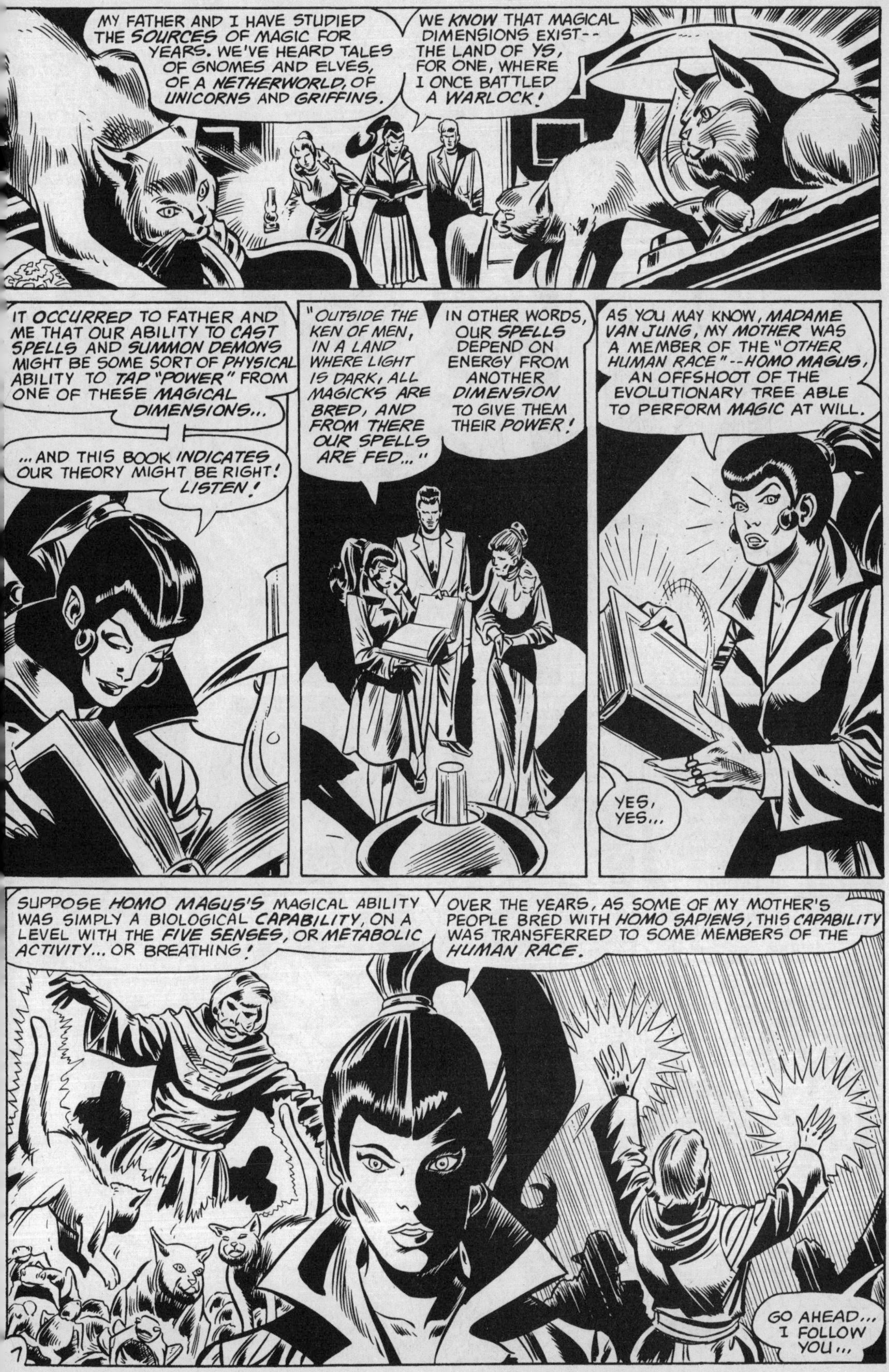
MY FATHER AND I HAVE STUDIED THE SOURCES OF MAGIC FOR YEARS. WE'VE HEARD TALES OF GNOMES AND ELVES, OF A NETHERWORLD, OF UNICORNS AND GRIFFINS.
WE KNOW THAT MAGICAL DIMENSIONS EXIST-- THE LAND OF YS, FOR ONE, WHERE I ONCE BATTLED A WARLOCK!
IT OCCURRED TO FATHER AND ME THAT OUR ABILITY TO CAST SPELLS AND SUMMON DEMONS MIGHT BE SOME SORT OF PHYSICAL ABILITY TO TAP "POWER" FROM ONE OF THESE MAGICAL DIMENSIONS...
...AND THIS BOOK INDICATES OUR THEORY MIGHT BE RIGHT! LISTEN!
"OUTSIDE THE KEN OF MEN, IN A LAND WHERE LIGHT IS DARK, ALL MAGICKS ARE BRED, AND FROM THERE OUR SPELLS ARE FED..."
IN OTHER WORDS, OUR SPELLS DEPEND ON ENERGY FROM ANOTHER DIMENSION TO GIVE THEM THEIR POWER!
AS YOU MAY KNOW, MADAME VAN JUNG, MY MOTHER WAS A MEMBER OF THE "OTHER HUMAN RACE"--HOMO MAGUS, AN OFFSHOOT OF THE EVOLUTIONARY TREE ABLE TO PERFORM MAGIC AT WILL.
YES, YES...
SUPPOSE HOMO MAGUS'S MAGICAL ABILITY WAS SIMPLY A BIOLOGICAL CAPABILITY, ON A LEVEL WITH THE FIVE SENSES, OR METABOLIC ACTIVITY... OR BREATHING!
OVER THE YEARS, AS SOME OF MY MOTHER'S PEOPLE BRED WITH HOMO SAPIENS, THIS CAPABILITY WAS TRANSFERRED TO SOME MEMBERS OF THE HUMAN RACE.
GO AHEAD... I FOLLOW YOU...
7

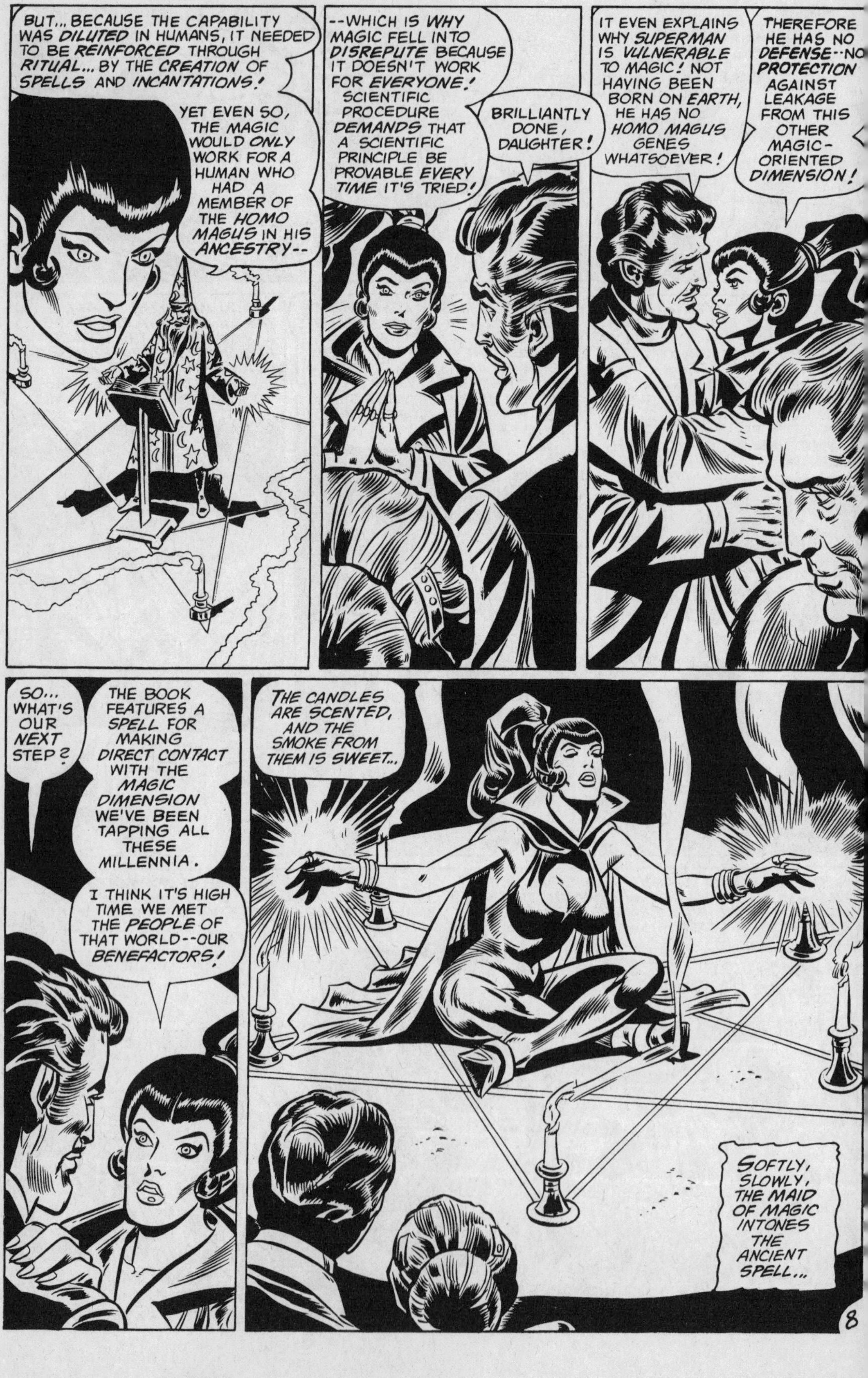
BUT... BECAUSE THE CAPABILITY WAS DILUTED IN HUMANS, IT NEEDED TO BE REINFORCED THROUGH RITUAL... BY THE CREATION OF SPELLS AND INCANTATIONS!
YET EVEN SO, THE MAGIC WOULD ONLY WORK FOR A HUMAN WHO HAD A MEMBER OF THE HOMO MAGUS IN HIS ANCESTRY--
--WHICH IS WHY MAGIC FELL INTO DISREPUTE BECAUSE IT DOESN'T WORK FOR EVERYONE! SCIENTIFIC PROCEDURE DEMANDS THAT A SCIENTIFIC PRINCIPLE BE PROVABLE EVERY TIME IT'S TRIED!
BRILLIANTLY DONE, DAUGHTER!
IT EVEN EXPLAINS WHY SUPERMAN IS VULNERABLE TO MAGIC! NOT HAVING BEEN BORN ON EARTH, HE HAS NO HOMO MAGUS GENES WHATSOEVER!
THEREFORE HE HAS NO DEFENSE--NO PROTECTION AGAINST LEAKAGE FROM THIS OTHER MAGIC-ORIENTED DIMENSION!
SO... WHAT'S OUR NEXT STEP?
THE BOOK FEATURES A SPELL FOR MAKING DIRECT CONTACT WITH THE MAGIC DIMENSION WE'VE BEEN TAPPING ALL THESE MILLENNIA.
I THINK IT'S HIGH TIME WE MET THE PEOPLE OF THAT WORLD--OUR BENEFACTORS!
THE CANDLES ARE SCENTED, AND THE SMOKE FROM THEM IS SWEET...
SOFTLY, SLOWLY, THE MAID OF MAGIC INTONES THE ANCIENT SPELL...
8

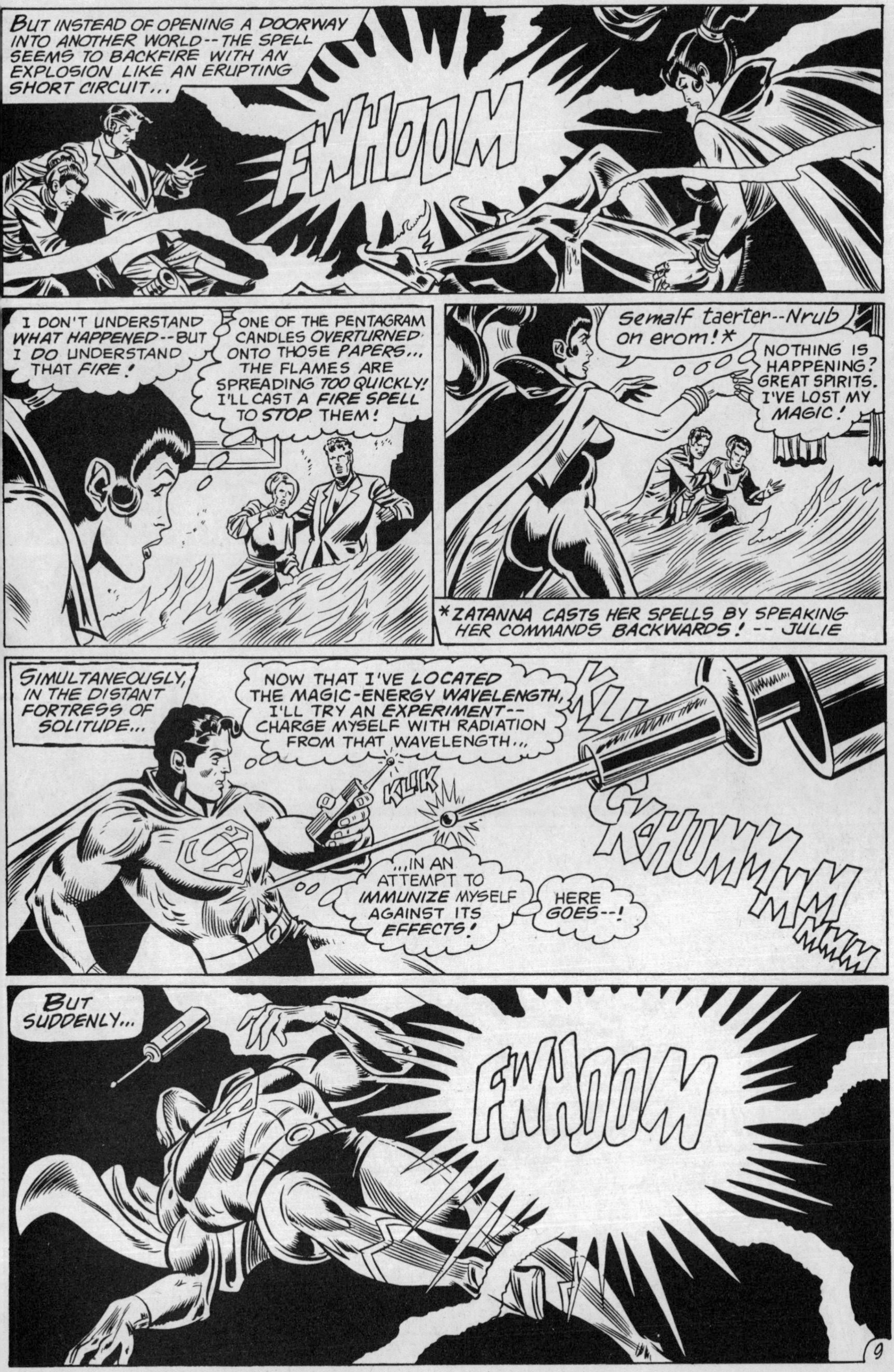
BUT INSTEAD OF OPENING A DOORWAY INTO ANOTHER WORLD--THE SPELL SEEMS TO BACKFIRE WITH AN EXPLOSION LIKE AN ERUPTING SHORT CIRCUIT...
FWHOOM
I DON'T UNDERSTAND WHAT HAPPENED--BUT I DO UNDERSTAND THAT FIRE!
ONE OF THE PENTAGRAM CANDLES OVERTURNED ONTO THOSE PAPERS... THE FLAMES ARE SPREADING TOO QUICKLY! I'LL CAST A FIRE SPELL TO STOP THEM!
Semalf taerter--Nrub on erom!*
NOTHING IS HAPPENING? GREAT SPIRITS. I'VE LOST MY MAGIC!
*ZATANNA CASTS HER SPELLS BY SPEAKING HER COMMANDS BACKWARDS! -- JULIE
SIMULTANEOUSLY, IN THE DISTANT FORTRESS OF SOLITUDE...
NOW THAT I'VE LOCATED THE MAGIC-ENERGY WAVELENGTH, I'LL TRY AN EXPERIMENT-- CHARGE MYSELF WITH RADIATION FROM THAT WAVELENGTH...
KLIK
KLIK
KKHUMMMMMMMM
...IN AN ATTEMPT TO IMMUNIZE MYSELF AGAINST ITS EFFECTS!
HERE GOES--!
BUT SUDDENLY...
FWHOOM
9

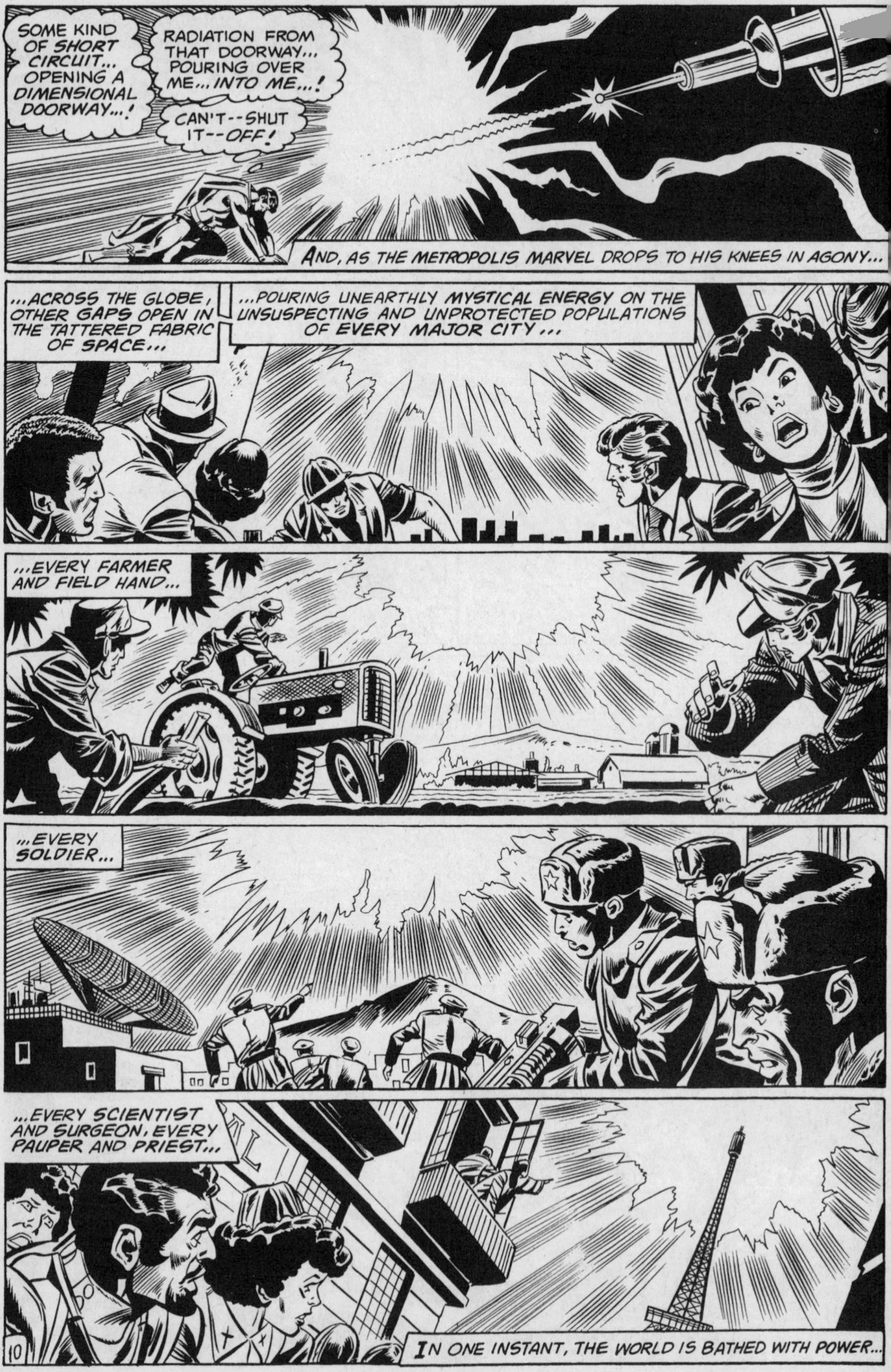
SOME KIND OF SHORT CIRCUIT... OPENING A DIMENSIONAL DOORWAY...!
RADIATION FROM THAT DOORWAY... POURING OVER ME... INTO ME...!
CAN'T--SHUT IT--OFF!
AND, AS THE METROPOLIS MARVEL DROPS TO HIS KNEES IN AGONY...
...ACROSS THE GLOBE, OTHER GAPS OPEN IN THE TATTERED FABRIC OF SPACE...
...POURING UNEARTHLY MYSTICAL ENERGY ON THE UNSUSPECTING AND UNPROTECTED POPULATIONS OF EVERY MAJOR CITY...
...EVERY FARMER AND FIELD HAND...
...EVERY SOLDIER...
...EVERY SCIENTIST AND SURGEON, EVERY PAUPER AND PRIEST...
10
IN ONE INSTANT, THE WORLD IS BATHED WITH POWER...

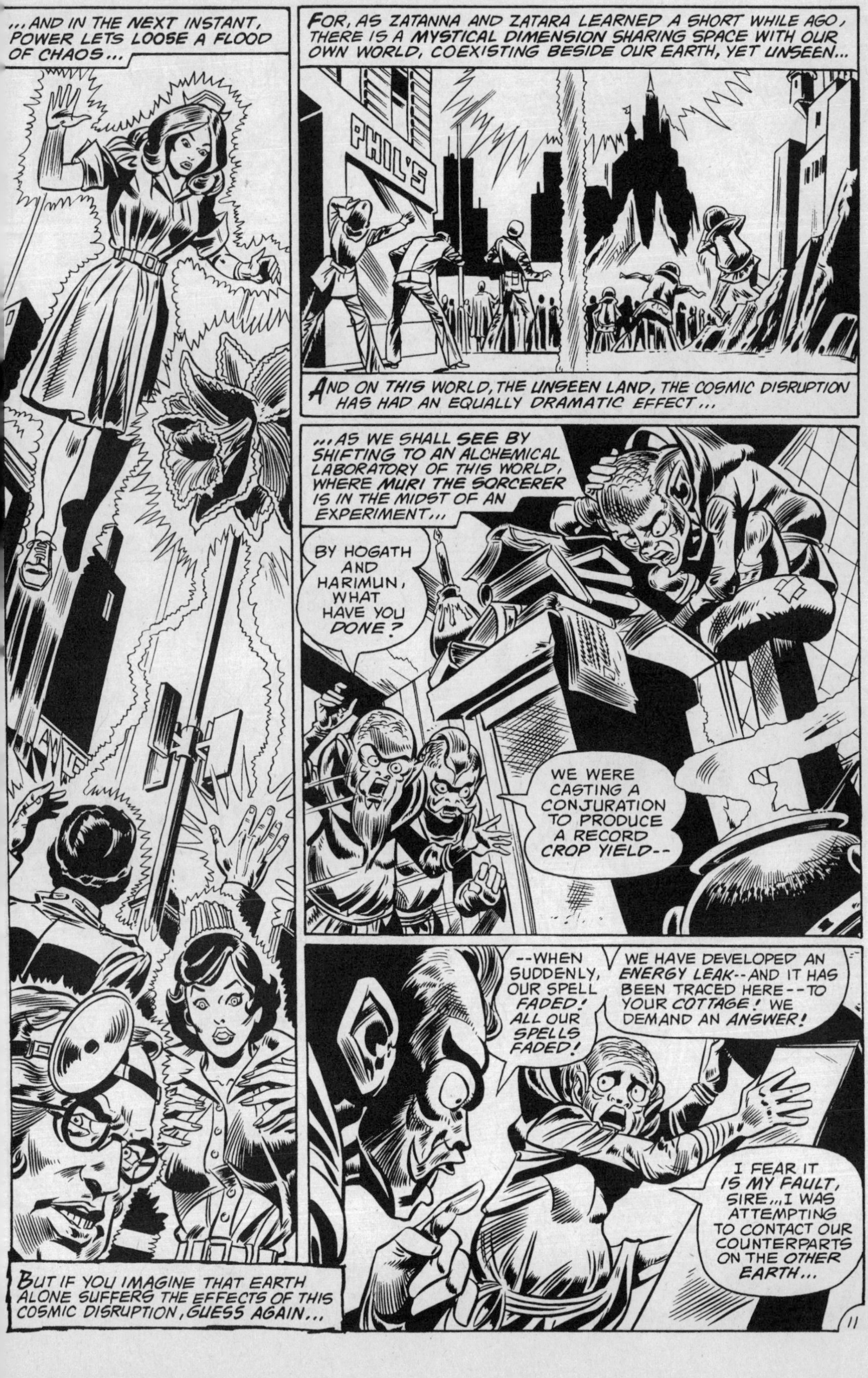
...AND IN THE NEXT INSTANT, POWER LETS LOOSE A FLOOD OF CHAOS...
FOR, AS ZATANNA AND ZATARA LEARNED A SHORT WHILE AGO, THERE IS A MYSTICAL DIMENSION SHARING SPACE WITH OUR OWN WORLD, COEXISTING BESIDE OUR EARTH, YET UNSEEN...
PHIL'S
AND ON THIS WORLD, THE UNSEEN LAND, THE COSMIC DISRUPTION HAS HAD AN EQUALLY DRAMATIC EFFECT...
...AS WE SHALL SEE BY SHIFTING TO AN ALCHEMICAL LABORATORY OF THIS WORLD, WHERE MURI THE SORCERER IS IN THE MIDST OF AN EXPERIMENT...
BY HOGATH AND HARIMUN, WHAT HAVE YOU DONE?
WE WERE CASTING A CONJURATION TO PRODUCE A RECORD CROP YIELD--
--WHEN SUDDENLY, OUR SPELL FADED! ALL OUR SPELLS FADED!
WE HAVE DEVELOPED AN ENERGY LEAK--AND IT HAS BEEN TRACED HERE--TO YOUR COTTAGE! WE DEMAND AN ANSWER!
I FEAR IT IS MY FAULT, SIRE...I WAS ATTEMPTING TO CONTACT OUR COUNTERPARTS ON THE OTHER EARTH...
BUT IF YOU IMAGINE THAT EARTH ALONE SUFFERS THE EFFECTS OF THIS COSMIC DISRUPTION, GUESS AGAIN...
11

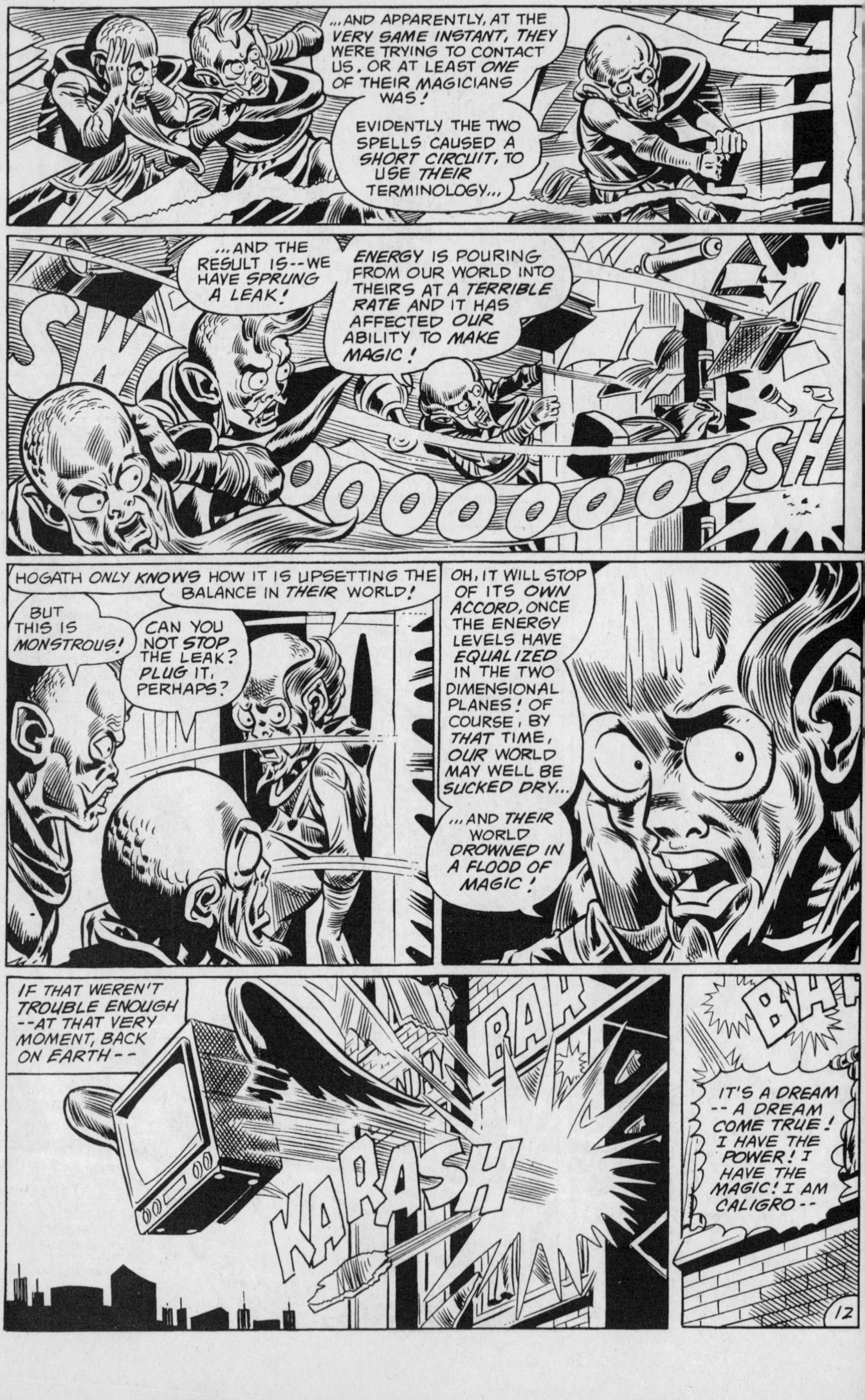
...AND APPARENTLY, AT THE VERY SAME INSTANT, THEY WERE TRYING TO CONTACT US. OR AT LEAST ONE OF THEIR MAGICIANS WAS!
EVIDENTLY THE TWO SPELLS CAUSED A SHORT CIRCUIT, TO USE THEIR TERMINOLOGY...
...AND THE RESULT IS--WE HAVE SPRUNG A LEAK!
ENERGY IS POURING FROM OUR WORLD INTO THEIRS AT A TERRIBLE RATE AND IT HAS AFFECTED OUR ABILITY TO MAKE MAGIC!
SWOOOOOOOOOOSH
HOGATH ONLY KNOWS HOW IT IS UPSETTING THE BALANCE IN THEIR WORLD!
BUT THIS IS MONSTROUS!
CAN YOU NOT STOP THE LEAK? PLUG IT, PERHAPS?
OH, IT WILL STOP OF ITS OWN ACCORD, ONCE THE ENERGY LEVELS HAVE EQUALIZED IN THE TWO DIMENSIONAL PLANES! OF COURSE, BY THAT TIME, OUR WORLD MAY WELL BE SUCKED DRY...
...AND THEIR WORLD DROWNED IN A FLOOD OF MAGIC!
IF THAT WEREN'T TROUBLE ENOUGH --AT THAT VERY MOMENT, BACK ON EARTH--
BAH
KARASH
IT'S A DREAM -- A DREAM COME TRUE! I HAVE THE POWER! I HAVE THE MAGIC! I AM CALIGRO--
12

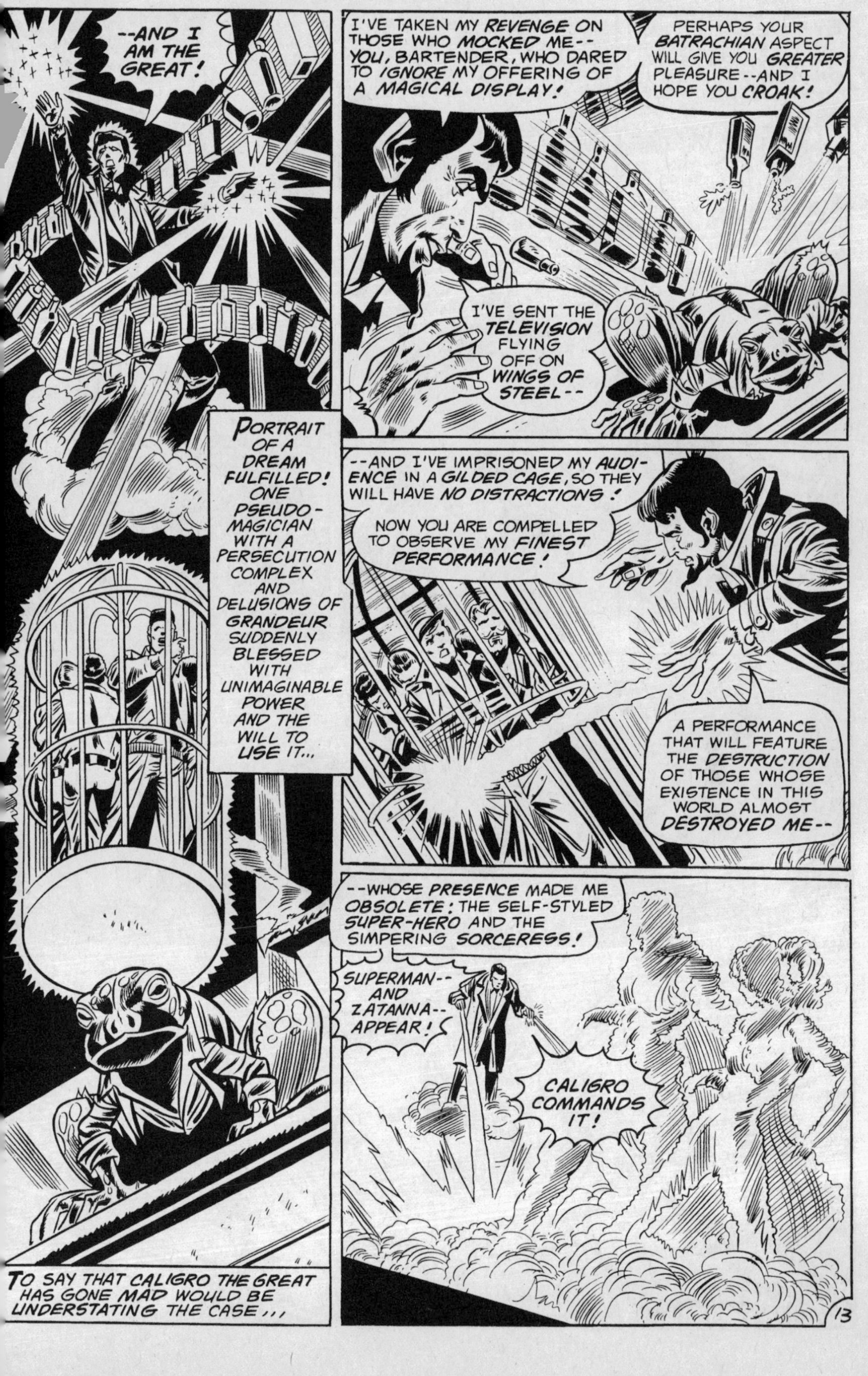
--AND I AM THE GREAT!
PORTRAIT OF A DREAM FULFILLED! ONE PSEUDO-MAGICIAN WITH A PERSECUTION COMPLEX AND DELUSIONS OF GRANDEUR SUDDENLY BLESSED WITH UNIMAGINABLE POWER AND THE WILL TO USE IT...
TO SAY THAT CALIGRO THE GREAT HAS GONE MAD WOULD BE UNDERSTATING THE CASE...
I'VE TAKEN MY REVENGE ON THOSE WHO MOCKED ME-- YOU, BARTENDER, WHO DARED TO IGNORE MY OFFERING OF A MAGICAL DISPLAY!
PERHAPS YOUR BATRACHIAN ASPECT WILL GIVE YOU GREATER PLEASURE--AND I HOPE YOU CROAK!
I'VE SENT THE TELEVISION FLYING OFF ON WINGS OF STEEL--
--AND I'VE IMPRISONED MY AUDIENCE IN A GILDED CAGE, SO THEY WILL HAVE NO DISTRACTIONS!
NOW YOU ARE COMPELLED TO OBSERVE MY FINEST PERFORMANCE!
A PERFORMANCE THAT WILL FEATURE THE DESTRUCTION OF THOSE WHOSE EXISTENCE IN THIS WORLD ALMOST DESTROYED ME--
--WHOSE PRESENCE MADE ME OBSOLETE: THE SELF-STYLED SUPER-HERO AND THE SIMPERING SORCERESS!
SUPERMAN-- AND ZATANNA-- APPEAR!
CALIGRO COMMANDS IT!
13

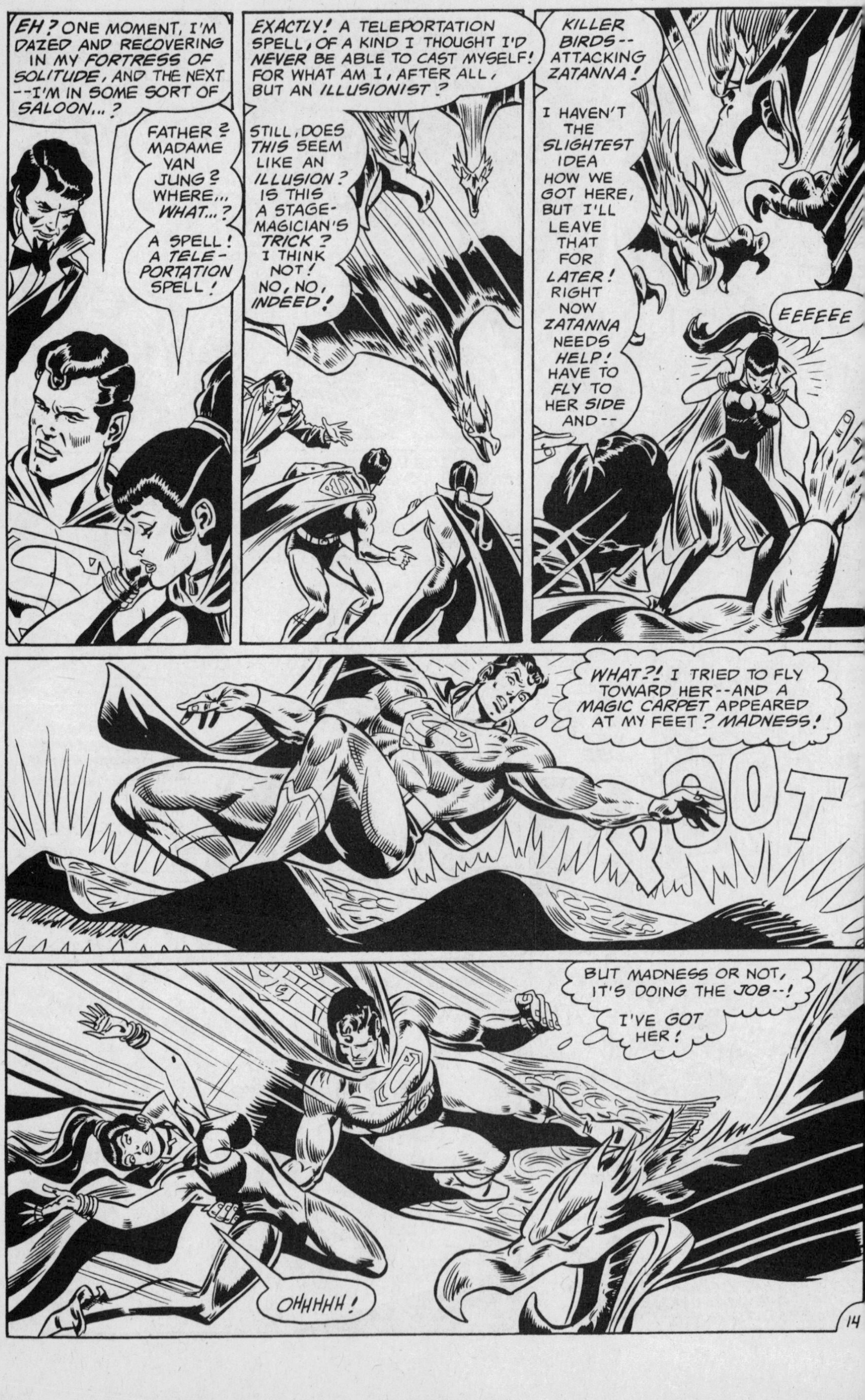
EH? ONE MOMENT, I'M DAZED AND RECOVERING IN MY FORTRESS OF SOLITUDE, AND THE NEXT --I'M IN SOME SORT OF SALOON...?
FATHER? MADAME VAN JUNG? WHERE... WHAT...?
A SPELL! A TELE-PORTATION SPELL!
EXACTLY! A TELEPORTATION SPELL, OF A KIND I THOUGHT I'D NEVER BE ABLE TO CAST MYSELF! FOR WHAT AM I, AFTER ALL, BUT AN ILLUSIONIST?
STILL, DOES THIS SEEM LIKE AN ILLUSION? IS THIS A STAGE-MAGICIAN'S TRICK? I THINK NOT! NO, NO, INDEED!
KILLER BIRDS-- ATTACKING ZATANNA!
I HAVEN'T THE SLIGHTEST IDEA HOW WE GOT HERE, BUT I'LL LEAVE THAT FOR LATER! RIGHT NOW ZATANNA NEEDS HELP! HAVE TO FLY TO HER SIDE AND--
EEEEEE
WHAT?! I TRIED TO FLY TOWARD HER--AND A MAGIC CARPET APPEARED AT MY FEET? MADNESS!
POOT
BUT MADNESS OR NOT, IT'S DOING THE JOB--!
I'VE GOT HER!
OHHHHH!
14

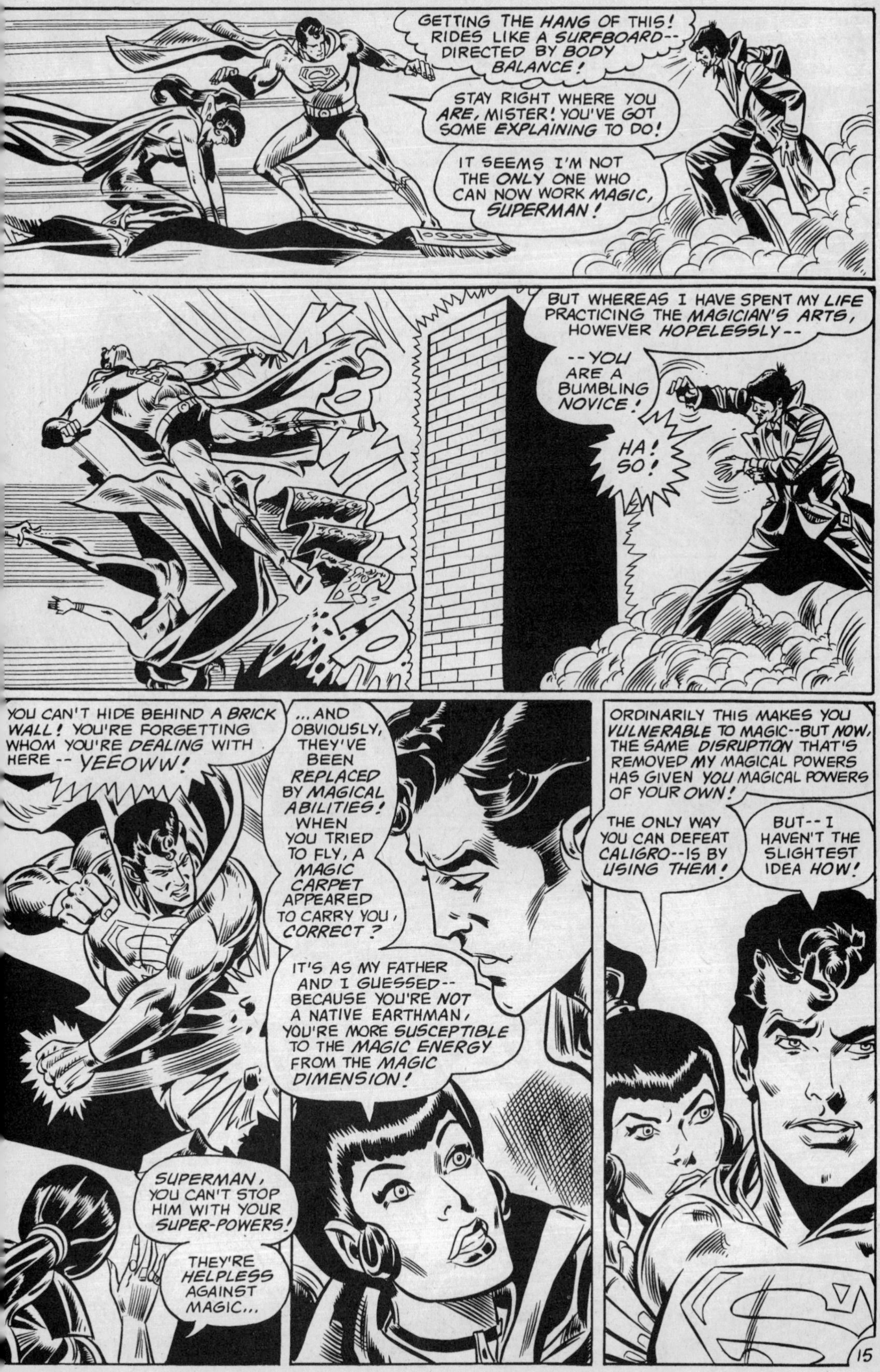
GETTING THE HANG OF THIS! RIDES LIKE A SURFBOARD-- DIRECTED BY BODY BALANCE!
STAY RIGHT WHERE YOU ARE, MISTER! YOU'VE GOT SOME EXPLAINING TO DO!
IT SEEMS I'M NOT THE ONLY ONE WHO CAN NOW WORK MAGIC, SUPERMAN!
BUT WHEREAS I HAVE SPENT MY LIFE PRACTICING THE MAGICIAN'S ARTS, HOWEVER HOPELESSLY--
--YOU ARE A BUMBLING NOVICE!
HA! SO!
KWMP
YOU CAN'T HIDE BEHIND A BRICK WALL! YOU'RE FORGETTING WHOM YOU'RE DEALING WITH HERE -- YEEOWW!
SUPERMAN, YOU CAN'T STOP HIM WITH YOUR SUPER-POWERS!
THEY'RE HELPLESS AGAINST MAGIC...
...AND OBVIOUSLY, THEY'VE BEEN REPLACED BY MAGICAL ABILITIES! WHEN YOU TRIED TO FLY, A MAGIC CARPET APPEARED TO CARRY YOU, CORRECT?
IT'S AS MY FATHER AND I GUESSED-- BECAUSE YOU'RE NOT A NATIVE EARTHMAN, YOU'RE MORE SUSCEPTIBLE TO THE MAGIC ENERGY FROM THE MAGIC DIMENSION!
ORDINARILY THIS MAKES YOU VULNERABLE TO MAGIC--BUT NOW, THE SAME DISRUPTION THAT'S REMOVED MY MAGICAL POWERS HAS GIVEN YOU MAGICAL POWERS OF YOUR OWN!
THE ONLY WAY YOU CAN DEFEAT CALIGRO--IS BY USING THEM!
BUT--I HAVEN'T THE SLIGHTEST IDEA HOW!
15

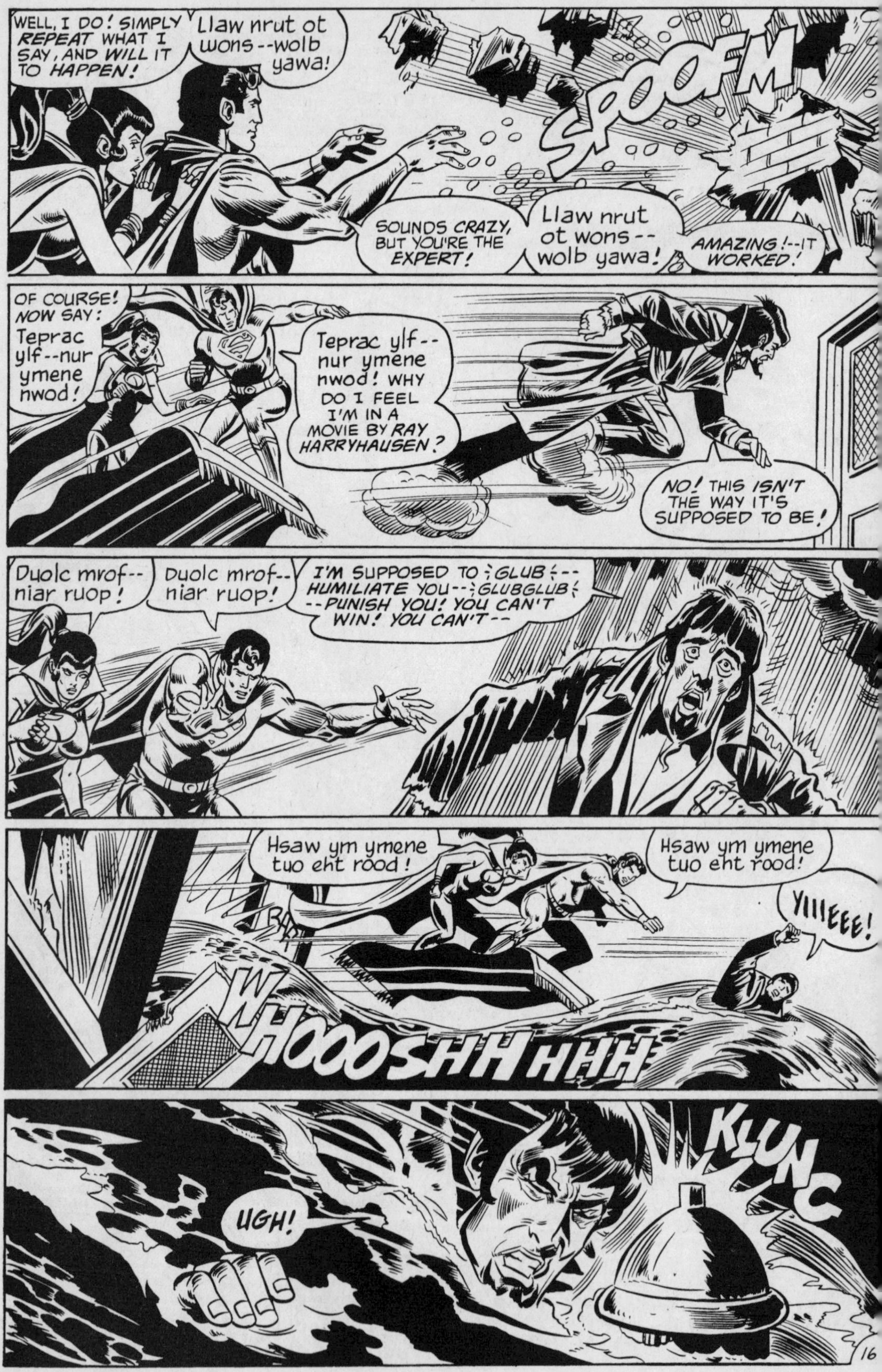
WELL, I DO! SIMPLY REPEAT WHAT I SAY, AND WILL IT TO HAPPEN!
Llaw nrut ot wons--wolb yawa!
SOUNDS CRAZY, BUT YOU'RE THE EXPERT!
Llaw nrut ot wons--wolb yawa!
SPOOFM
AMAZING!--IT WORKED!
OF COURSE! NOW SAY: Teprac ylf--nur ymene nwod!
Teprac ylf--nur ymene nwod! WHY DO I FEEL I'M IN A MOVIE BY RAY HARRYHAUSEN?
NO! THIS ISN'T THE WAY IT'S SUPPOSED TO BE!
Duolc mrof--niar ruop!
Duolc mrof--niar ruop!
I'M SUPPOSED TO GLUB--HUMILIATE YOU--GLUBGLUB--PUNISH YOU! YOU CAN'T WIN! YOU CAN'T--
Hsaw ym ymene tuo eht rood!
Hsaw ym ymene tuo eht rood!
YIIIEEE!
WHOOOSHHHHH
KLUNC
UGH!
16

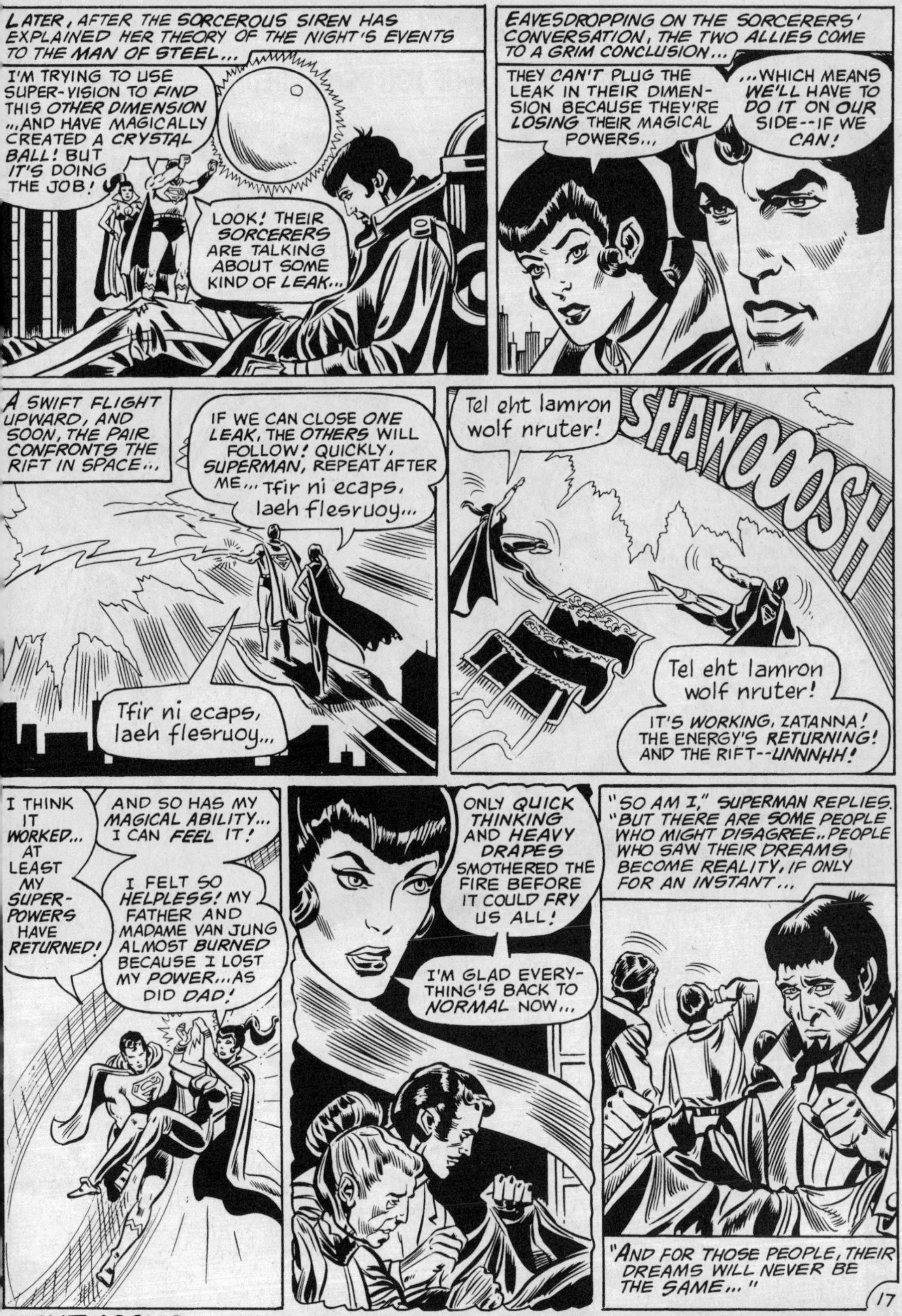
LATER, AFTER THE SORCEROUS SIREN HAS EXPLAINED HER THEORY OF THE NIGHT'S EVENTS TO THE MAN OF STEEL...
I'M TRYING TO USE SUPER-VISION TO FIND THIS OTHER DIMENSION ...AND HAVE MAGICALLY CREATED A CRYSTAL BALL! BUT IT'S DOING THE JOB!
LOOK! THEIR SORCERERS ARE TALKING ABOUT SOME KIND OF LEAK...
EAVESDROPPING ON THE SORCERERS' CONVERSATION, THE TWO ALLIES COME TO A GRIM CONCLUSION...
THEY CAN'T PLUG THE LEAK IN THEIR DIMENSION BECAUSE THEY'RE LOSING THEIR MAGICAL POWERS...
...WHICH MEANS WE'LL HAVE TO DO IT ON OUR SIDE--IF WE CAN!
A SWIFT FLIGHT UPWARD, AND SOON, THE PAIR CONFRONTS THE RIFT IN SPACE...
IF WE CAN CLOSE ONE LEAK, THE OTHERS WILL FOLLOW! QUICKLY, SUPERMAN, REPEAT AFTER ME... Tfir ni ecaps, laeh flesruoy...
Tfir ni ecaps, laeh flesruoy...
Tel eht lamron wolf nruter!
SHAWOOOSH
Tel eht lamron wolf nruter!
IT'S WORKING, ZATANNA! THE ENERGY'S RETURNING! AND THE RIFT--UNNNHH!
I THINK IT WORKED... AT LEAST MY SUPER-POWERS HAVE RETURNED!
AND SO HAS MY MAGICAL ABILITY... I CAN FEEL IT!
I FELT SO HELPLESS! MY FATHER AND MADAME VAN JUNG ALMOST BURNED BECAUSE I LOST MY POWER... AS DID DAD!
ONLY QUICK THINKING AND HEAVY DRAPES SMOTHERED THE FIRE BEFORE IT COULD FRY US ALL!
I'M GLAD EVERYTHING'S BACK TO NORMAL NOW...
"SO AM I," SUPERMAN REPLIES. "BUT THERE ARE SOME PEOPLE WHO MIGHT DISAGREE.. PEOPLE WHO SAW THEIR DREAMS BECOME REALITY, IF ONLY FOR AN INSTANT...
"AND FOR THOSE PEOPLE, THEIR DREAMS WILL NEVER BE THE SAME..."
17

NEXT ISSUE: SUPERMAN TEAMS WITH ANOTHER FAVORITE HEROINE--BATGIRL--TO ASK THE QUESTION... "WHO HAUNTS THIS HOUSE?"

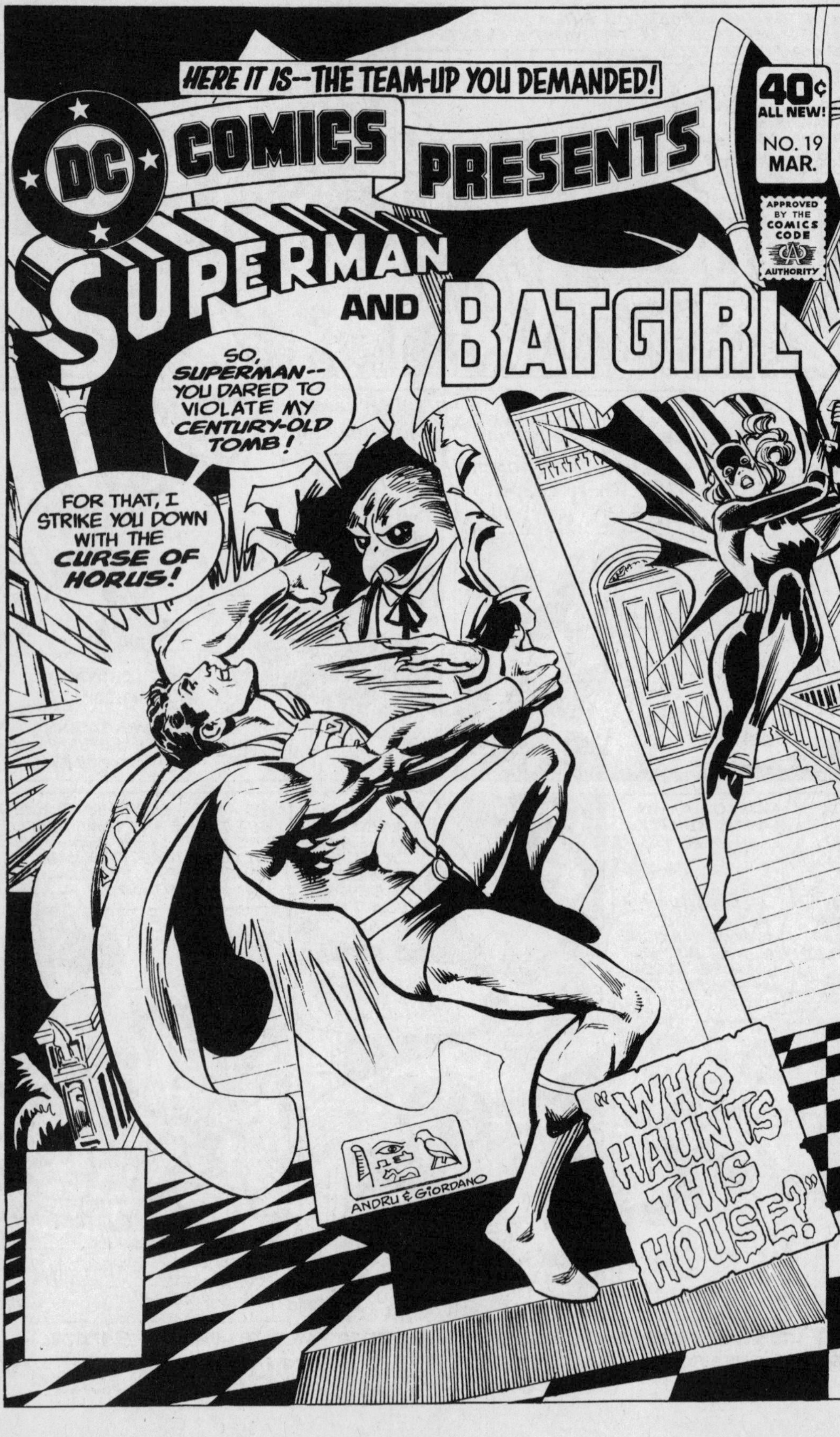
HERE IT IS--THE TEAM-UP YOU DEMANDED!
DC COMICS PRESENTS
40¢ ALL NEW!
NO. 19 MAR.
APPROVED BY THE COMICS CODE AUTHORITY
SUPERMAN AND BATGIRL
SO, SUPERMAN-- YOU DARED TO VIOLATE MY CENTURY-OLD TOMB!
FOR THAT, I STRIKE YOU DOWN WITH THE CURSE OF HORUS!
ANDRU & GIORDANO
"WHO HAUNTS THIS HOUSE?"

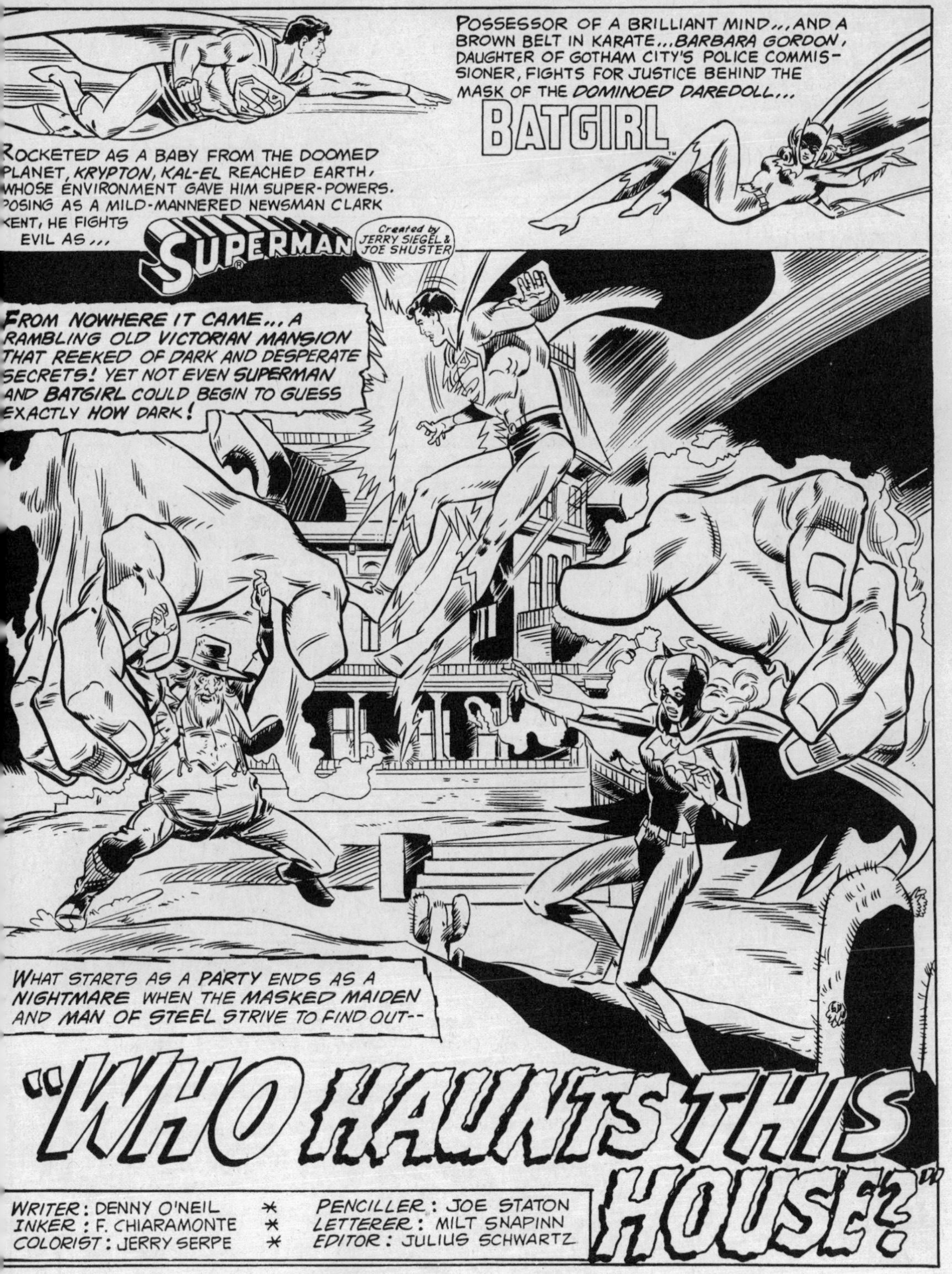
ROCKETED AS A BABY FROM THE DOOMED PLANET, KRYPTON, KAL-EL REACHED EARTH, WHOSE ENVIRONMENT GAVE HIM SUPER-POWERS. POSING AS A MILD-MANNERED NEWSMAN CLARK KENT, HE FIGHTS EVIL AS...
SUPERMAN
Created by JERRY SIEGEL & JOE SHUSTER
POSSESSOR OF A BRILLIANT MIND... AND A BROWN BELT IN KARATE... BARBARA GORDON, DAUGHTER OF GOTHAM CITY'S POLICE COMMISSIONER, FIGHTS FOR JUSTICE BEHIND THE MASK OF THE DOMINOED DAREDOLL...
BATGIRL
FROM NOWHERE IT CAME... A RAMBLING OLD VICTORIAN MANSION THAT REEKED OF DARK AND DESPERATE SECRETS! YET NOT EVEN SUPERMAN AND BATGIRL COULD BEGIN TO GUESS EXACTLY HOW DARK!
WHAT STARTS AS A PARTY ENDS AS A NIGHTMARE WHEN THE MASKED MAIDEN AND MAN OF STEEL STRIVE TO FIND OUT--
"WHO HAUNTS THIS HOUSE?"
WRITER: DENNY O'NEIL * PENCILLER: JOE STATON
INKER: F. CHIARAMONTE * LETTERER: MILT SNAPINN
COLORIST: JERRY SERPE * EDITOR: JULIUS SCHWARTZ

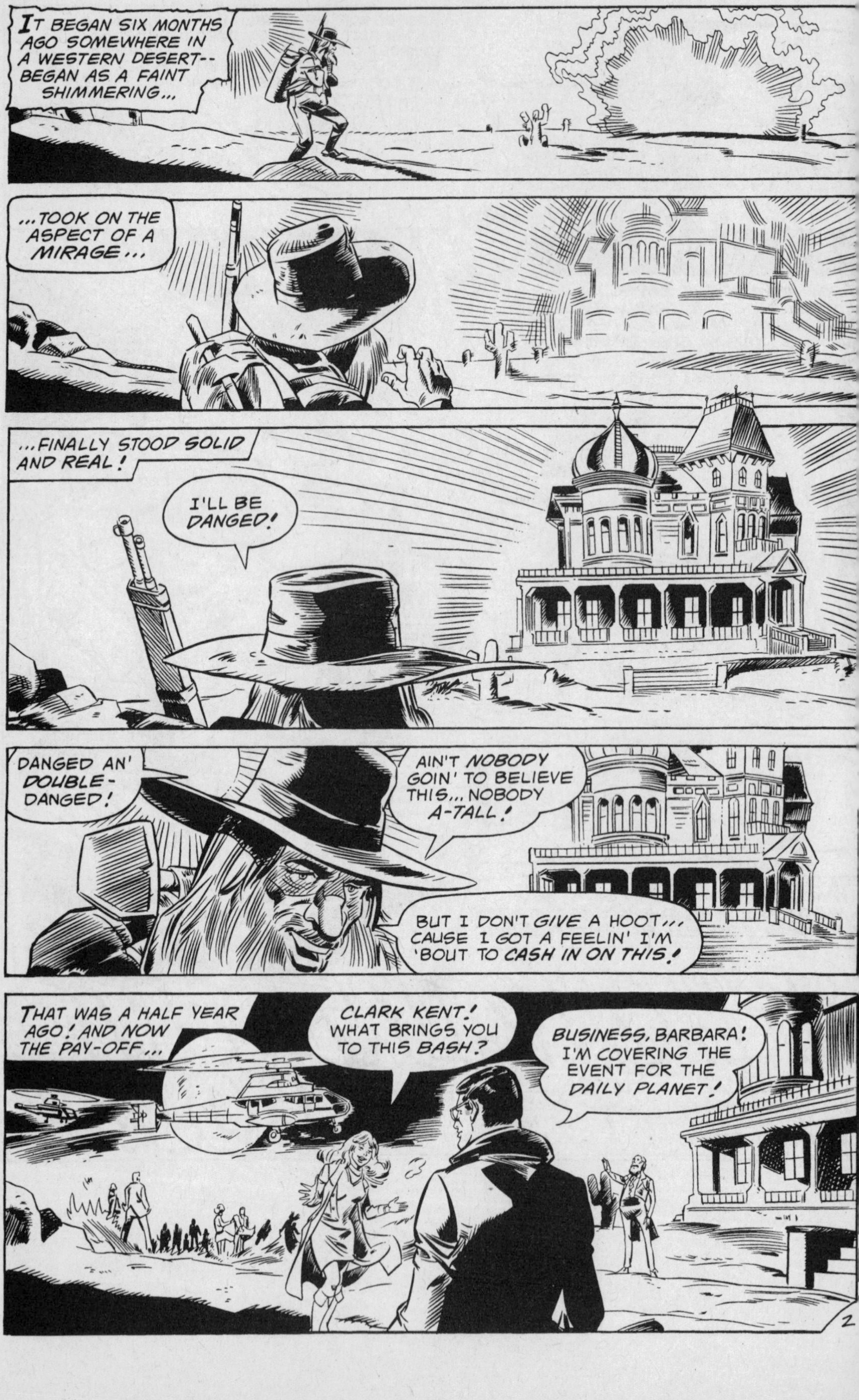
IT BEGAN SIX MONTHS AGO SOMEWHERE IN A WESTERN DESERT-- BEGAN AS A FAINT SHIMMERING...
...TOOK ON THE ASPECT OF A MIRAGE...
...FINALLY STOOD SOLID AND REAL!
I'LL BE DANGED!
DANGED AN' DOUBLE-DANGED!
AIN'T NOBODY GOIN' TO BELIEVE THIS... NOBODY A-TALL!
BUT I DON'T GIVE A HOOT... CAUSE I GOT A FEELIN' I'M 'BOUT TO CASH IN ON THIS!
THAT WAS A HALF YEAR AGO! AND NOW THE PAY-OFF...
CLARK KENT! WHAT BRINGS YOU TO THIS BASH?
BUSINESS, BARBARA! I'M COVERING THE EVENT FOR THE DAILY PLANET!
2

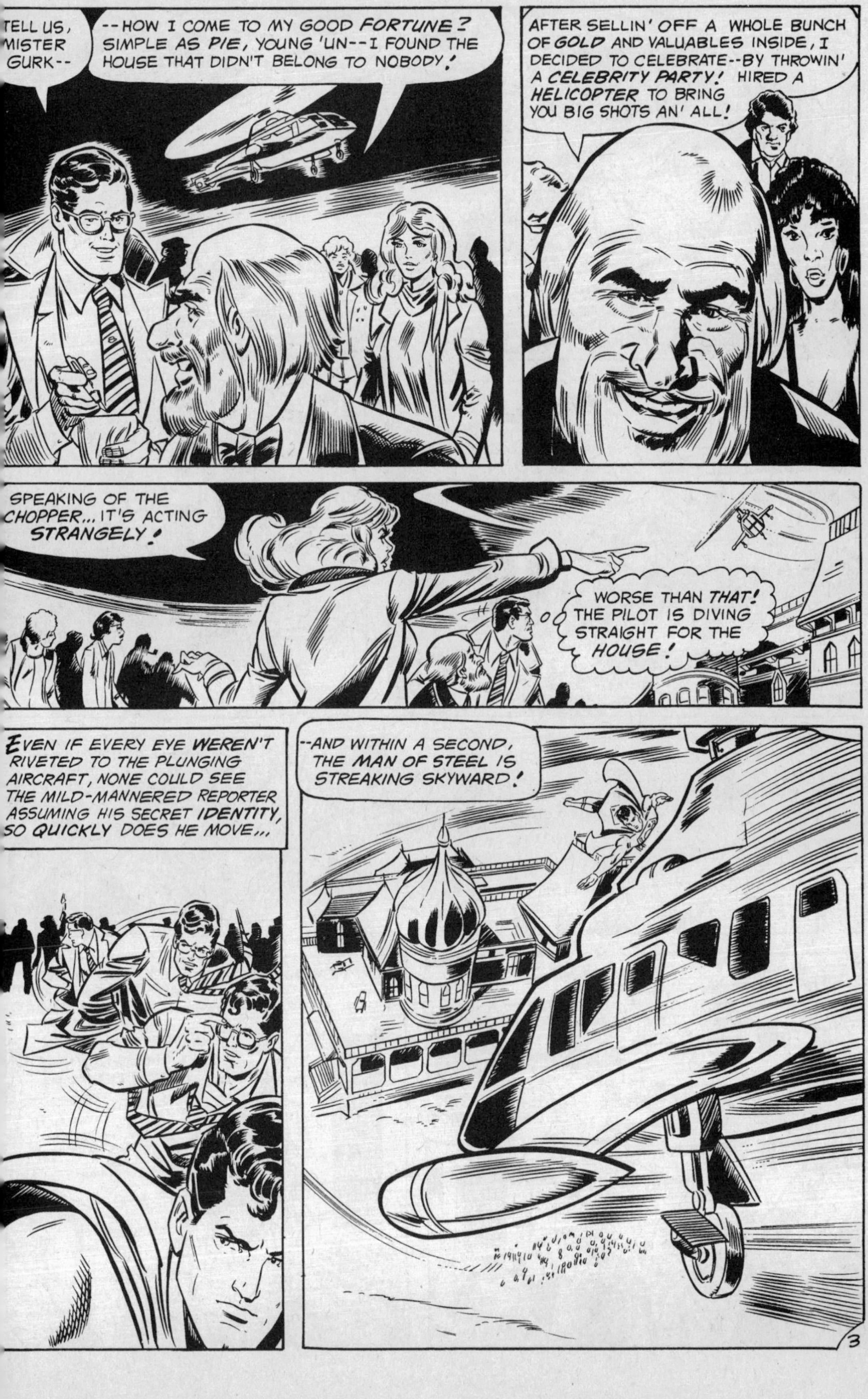
TELL US, MISTER GURK--
--HOW I COME TO MY GOOD FORTUNE? SIMPLE AS PIE, YOUNG 'UN--I FOUND THE HOUSE THAT DIDN'T BELONG TO NOBODY!
AFTER SELLIN' OFF A WHOLE BUNCH OF GOLD AND VALUABLES INSIDE, I DECIDED TO CELEBRATE--BY THROWIN' A CELEBRITY PARTY! HIRED A HELICOPTER TO BRING YOU BIG SHOTS AN' ALL!
SPEAKING OF THE CHOPPER... IT'S ACTING STRANGELY!
WORSE THAN THAT! THE PILOT IS DIVING STRAIGHT FOR THE HOUSE!
EVEN IF EVERY EYE WEREN'T RIVETED TO THE PLUNGING AIRCRAFT, NONE COULD SEE THE MILD-MANNERED REPORTER ASSUMING HIS SECRET IDENTITY, SO QUICKLY DOES HE MOVE...
--AND WITHIN A SECOND, THE MAN OF STEEL IS STREAKING SKYWARD!
3

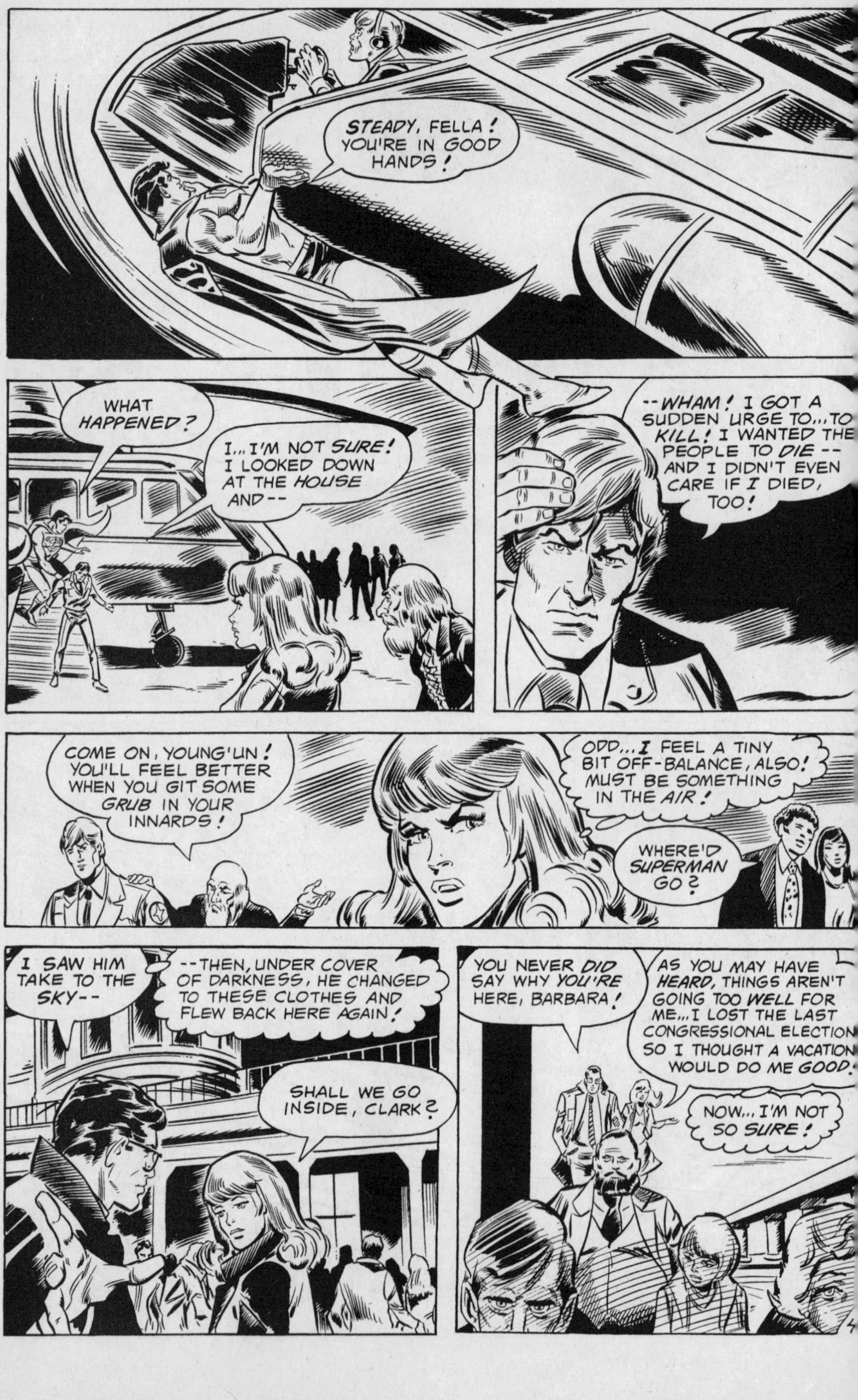
STEADY, FELLA! YOU'RE IN GOOD HANDS!
WHAT HAPPENED?
I...I'M NOT SURE! I LOOKED DOWN AT THE HOUSE AND--
--WHAM! I GOT A SUDDEN URGE TO...TO KILL! I WANTED THE PEOPLE TO DIE -- AND I DIDN'T EVEN CARE IF I DIED, TOO!
COME ON, YOUNG'UN! YOU'LL FEEL BETTER WHEN YOU GIT SOME GRUB IN YOUR INNARDS!
ODD...I FEEL A TINY BIT OFF-BALANCE, ALSO! MUST BE SOMETHING IN THE AIR!
WHERE'D SUPERMAN GO?
I SAW HIM TAKE TO THE SKY--
--THEN, UNDER COVER OF DARKNESS, HE CHANGED TO THESE CLOTHES AND FLEW BACK HERE AGAIN!
SHALL WE GO INSIDE, CLARK?
YOU NEVER DID SAY WHY YOU'RE HERE, BARBARA!
AS YOU MAY HAVE HEARD, THINGS AREN'T GOING TOO WELL FOR ME...I LOST THE LAST CONGRESSIONAL ELECTION SO I THOUGHT A VACATION WOULD DO ME GOOD.
NOW...I'M NOT SO SURE!

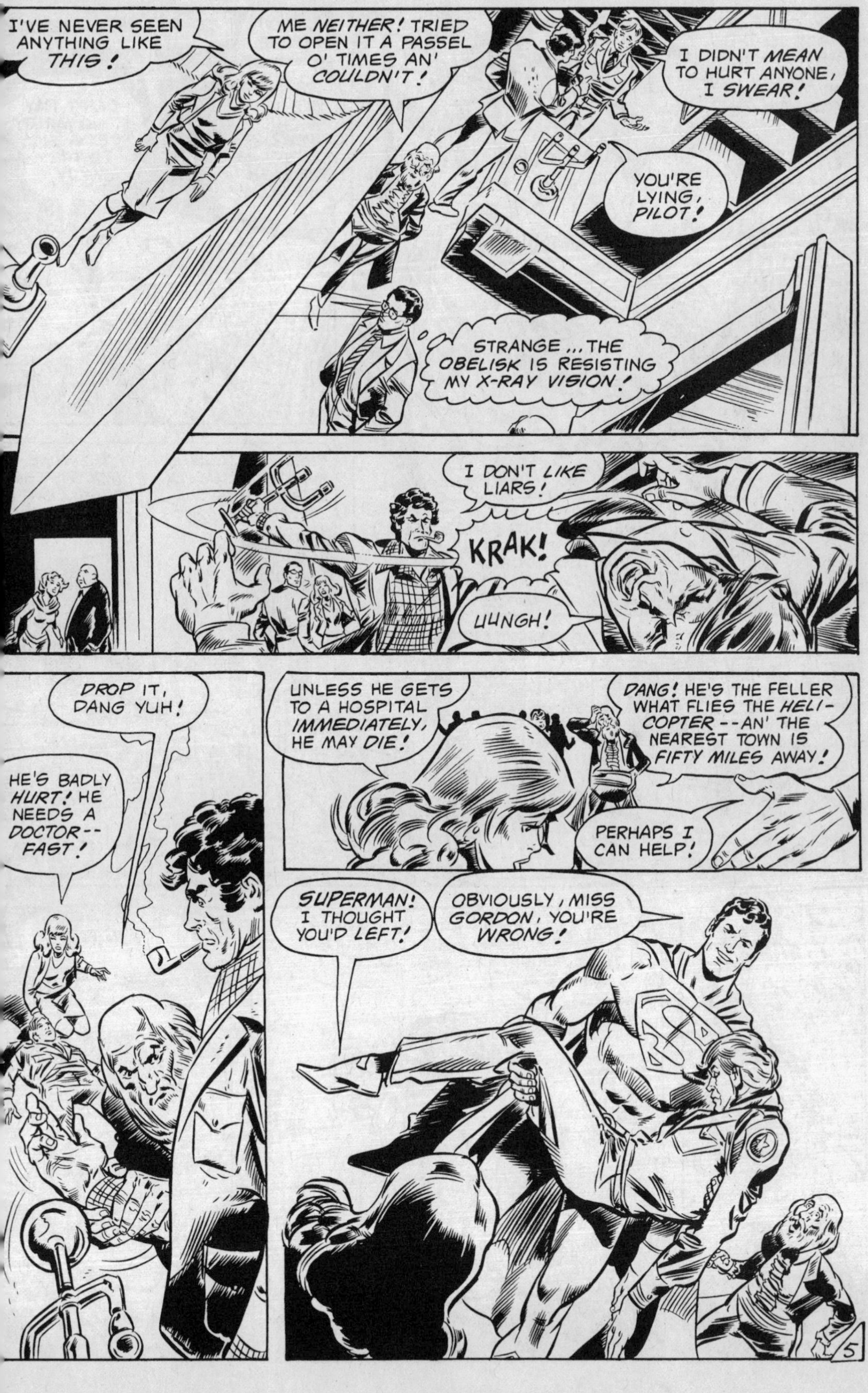
I'VE NEVER SEEN ANYTHING LIKE THIS!
ME NEITHER! TRIED TO OPEN IT A PASSEL O' TIMES AN' COULDN'T!
I DIDN'T MEAN TO HURT ANYONE, I SWEAR!
YOU'RE LYING, PILOT!
STRANGE ... THE OBELISK IS RESISTING MY X-RAY VISION!
I DON'T LIKE LIARS!
KRAK!
UUNGH!
DROP IT, DANG YUH!
HE'S BADLY HURT! HE NEEDS A DOCTOR-- FAST!
UNLESS HE GETS TO A HOSPITAL IMMEDIATELY, HE MAY DIE!
DANG! HE'S THE FELLER WHAT FLIES THE HELI-COPTER --AN' THE NEAREST TOWN IS FIFTY MILES AWAY!
PERHAPS I CAN HELP!
SUPERMAN! I THOUGHT YOU'D LEFT!
OBVIOUSLY, MISS GORDON, YOU'RE WRONG!
5

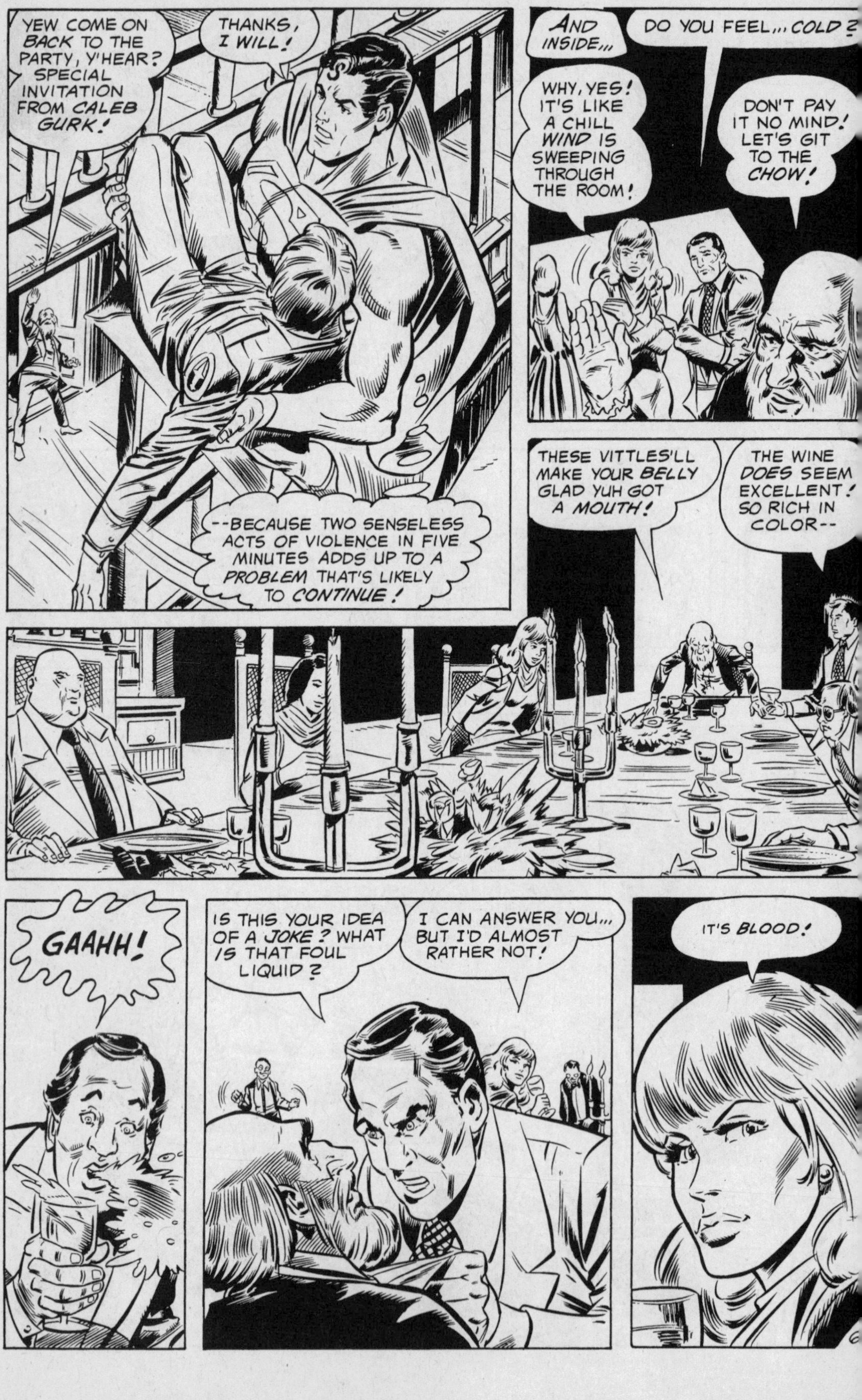
YEW COME ON BACK TO THE PARTY, Y'HEAR? SPECIAL INVITATION FROM CALEB GURK!
THANKS, I WILL!
--BECAUSE TWO SENSELESS ACTS OF VIOLENCE IN FIVE MINUTES ADDS UP TO A PROBLEM THAT'S LIKELY TO CONTINUE!
AND INSIDE...
DO YOU FEEL... COLD?
WHY, YES! IT'S LIKE A CHILL WIND IS SWEEPING THROUGH THE ROOM!
DON'T PAY IT NO MIND! LET'S GIT TO THE CHOW!
THESE VITTLES'LL MAKE YOUR BELLY GLAD YUH GOT A MOUTH!
THE WINE DOES SEEM EXCELLENT! SO RICH IN COLOR--
GAAHH!
IS THIS YOUR IDEA OF A JOKE? WHAT IS THAT FOUL LIQUID?
I CAN ANSWER YOU... BUT I'D ALMOST RATHER NOT!
IT'S BLOOD!
6

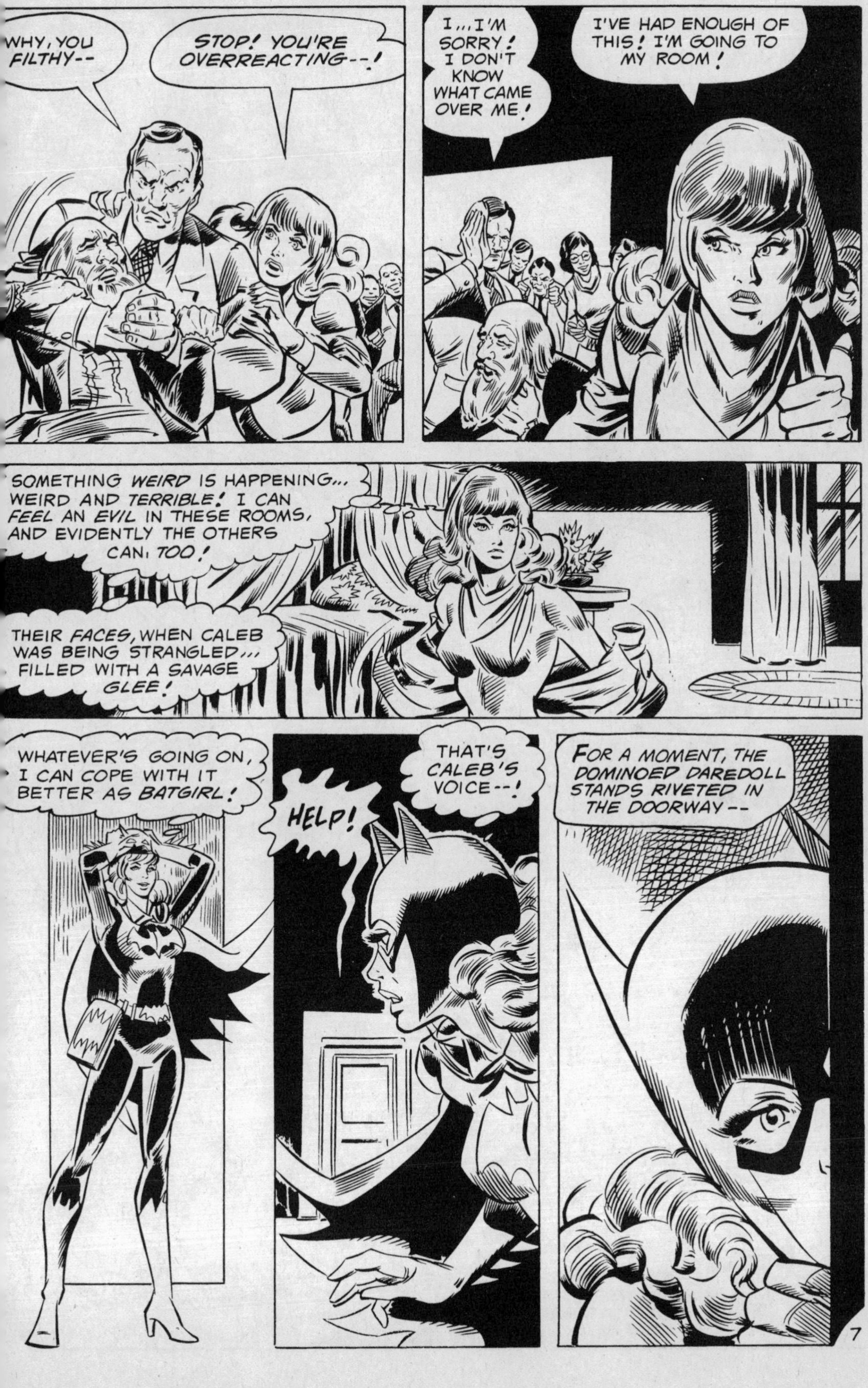
WHY, YOU FILTHY--
STOP! YOU'RE OVERREACTING--!
I...I'M SORRY! I DON'T KNOW WHAT CAME OVER ME!
I'VE HAD ENOUGH OF THIS! I'M GOING TO MY ROOM!
SOMETHING WEIRD IS HAPPENING... WEIRD AND TERRIBLE! I CAN FEEL AN EVIL IN THESE ROOMS, AND EVIDENTLY THE OTHERS CAN, TOO!
THEIR FACES, WHEN CALEB WAS BEING STRANGLED... FILLED WITH A SAVAGE GLEE!
WHATEVER'S GOING ON, I CAN COPE WITH IT BETTER AS BATGIRL!
HELP!
THAT'S CALEB'S VOICE--!
FOR A MOMENT, THE DOMINOED DAREDOLL STANDS RIVETED IN THE DOORWAY--
7

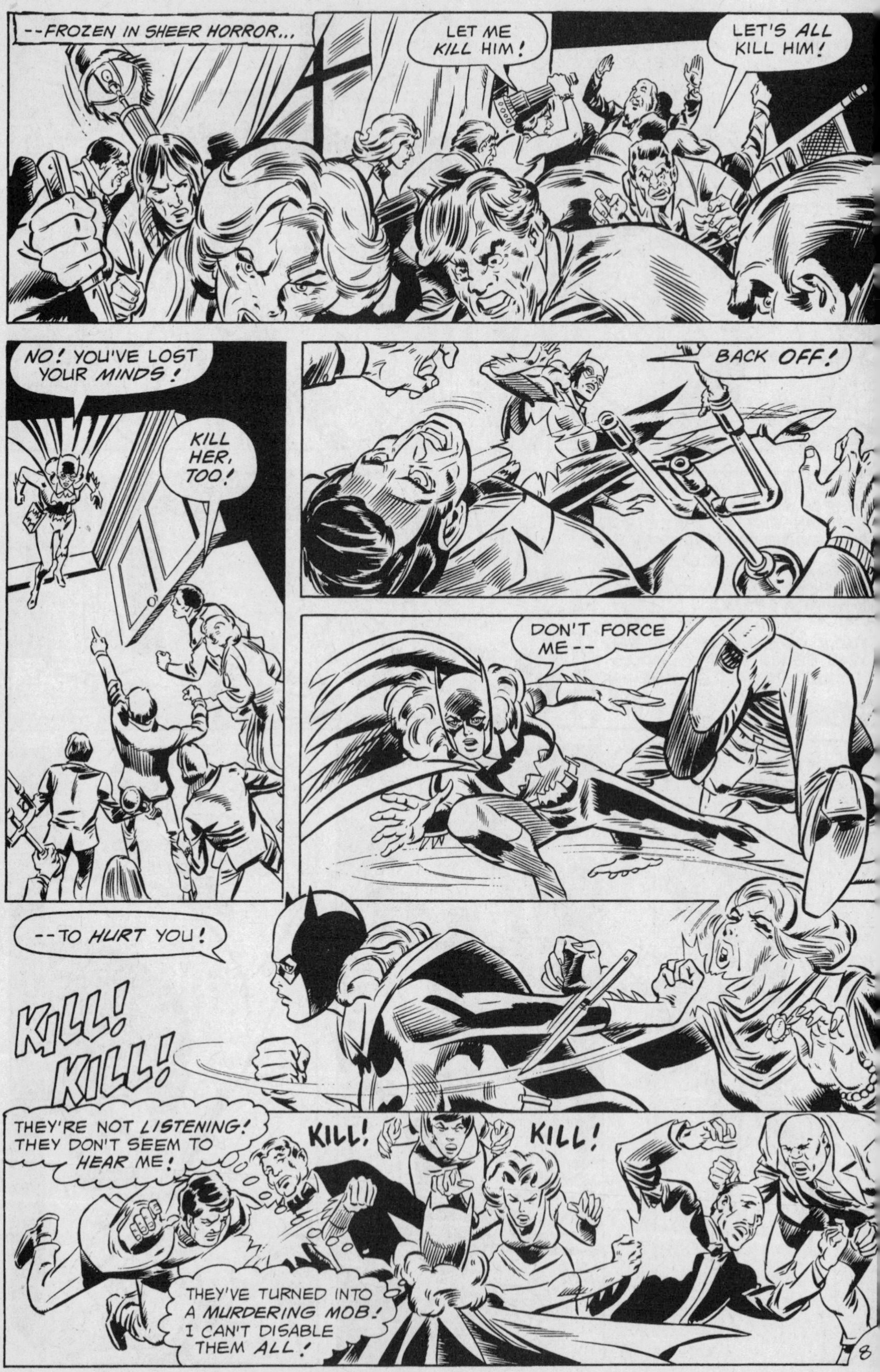
--FROZEN IN SHEER HORROR...
LET ME KILL HIM!
LET'S ALL KILL HIM!
NO! YOU'VE LOST YOUR MINDS!
KILL HER, TOO!
BACK OFF!
DON'T FORCE ME--
--TO HURT YOU!
KILL! KILL!
THEY'RE NOT LISTENING! THEY DON'T SEEM TO HEAR ME!
KILL!
KILL!
THEY'VE TURNED INTO A MURDERING MOB! I CAN'T DISABLE THEM ALL!
8

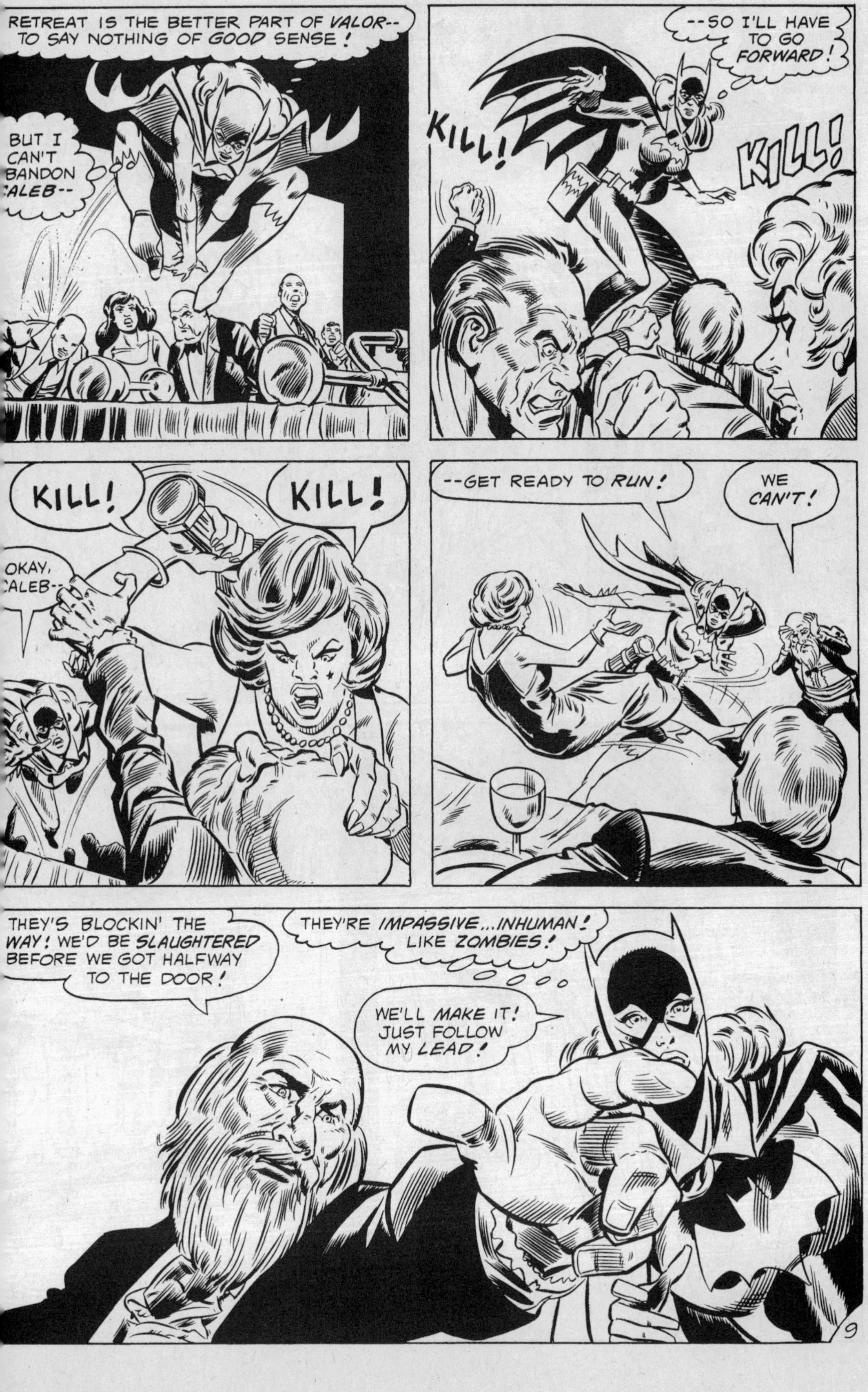
RETREAT IS THE BETTER PART OF VALOR-- TO SAY NOTHING OF GOOD SENSE!
BUT I CAN'T BANDON CALEB--
--SO I'LL HAVE TO GO FORWARD!
KILL!
KILL!
KILL!
KILL!
OKAY, CALEB--
--GET READY TO RUN!
WE CAN'T!
THEY'S BLOCKIN' THE WAY! WE'D BE SLAUGHTERED BEFORE WE GOT HALFWAY TO THE DOOR!
THEY'RE IMPASSIVE... INHUMAN! LIKE ZOMBIES!
WE'LL MAKE IT! JUST FOLLOW MY LEAD!
9

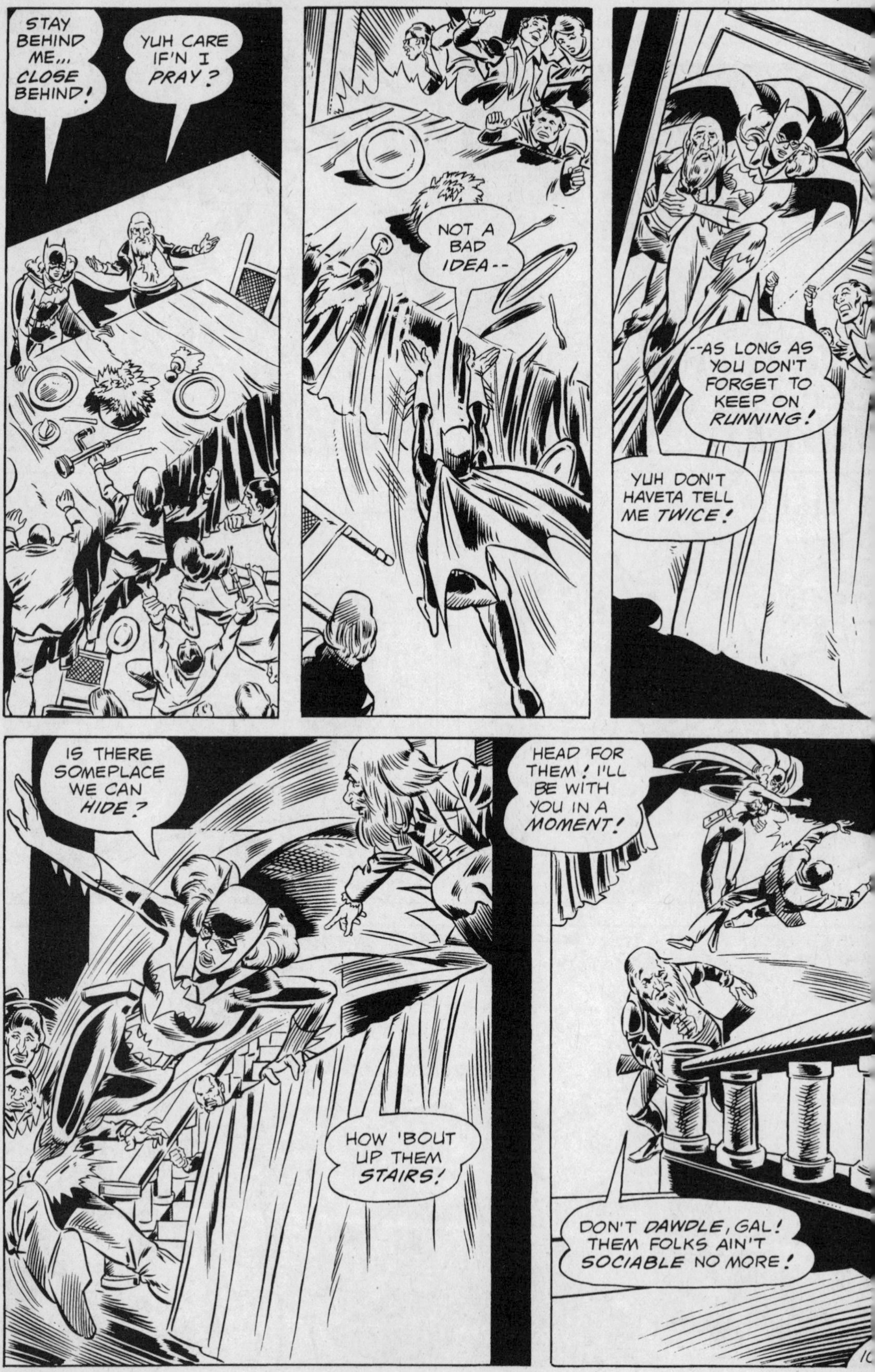
STAY BEHIND ME... CLOSE BEHIND!
YUH CARE IF'N I PRAY?
NOT A BAD IDEA--
--AS LONG AS YOU DON'T FORGET TO KEEP ON RUNNING!
YUH DON'T HAVETA TELL ME TWICE!
IS THERE SOMEPLACE WE CAN HIDE?
HOW 'BOUT UP THEM STAIRS!
HEAD FOR THEM! I'LL BE WITH YOU IN A MOMENT!
DON'T DAWDLE, GAL! THEM FOLKS AIN'T SOCIABLE NO MORE!

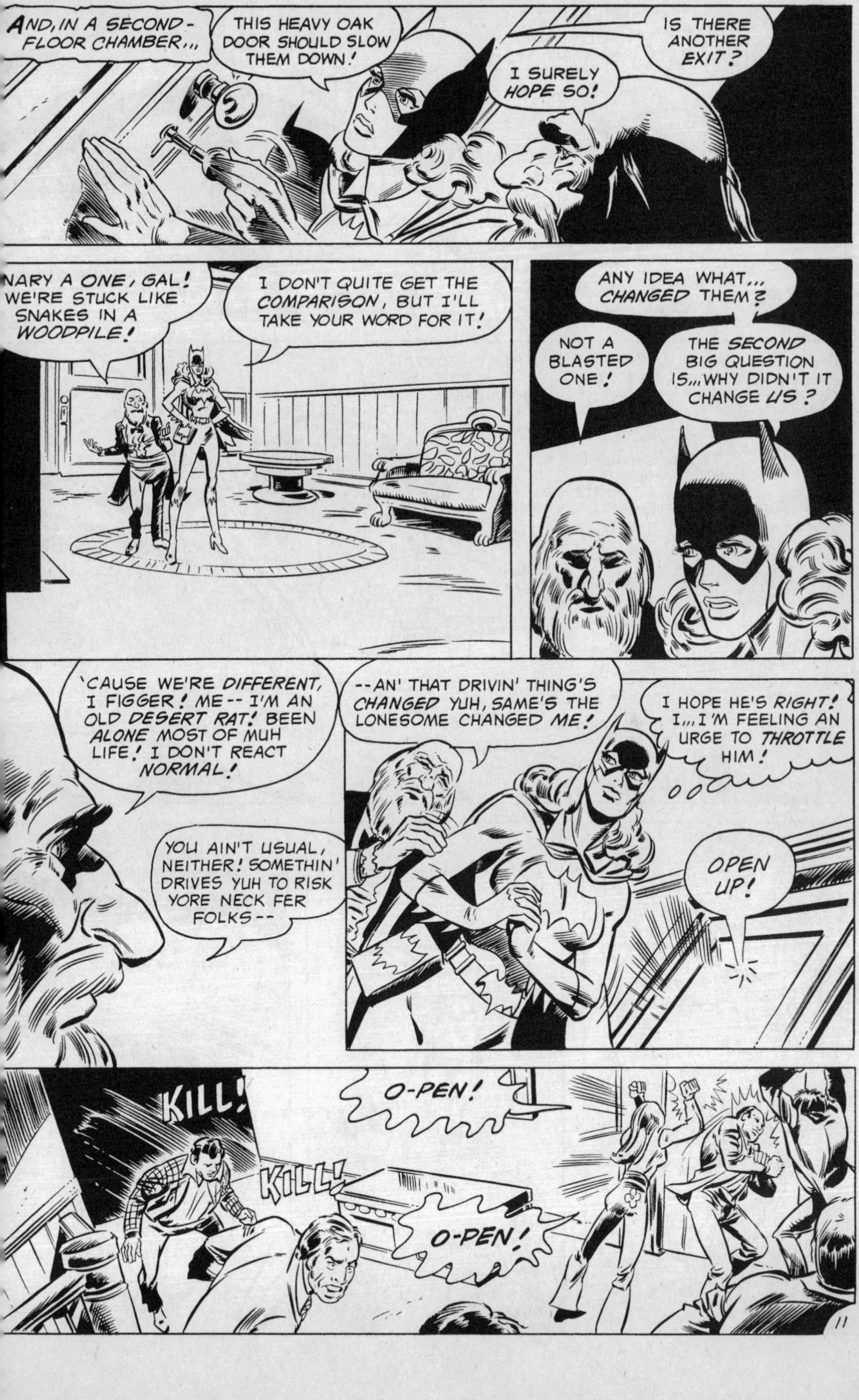
AND, IN A SECOND-FLOOR CHAMBER...
THIS HEAVY OAK DOOR SHOULD SLOW THEM DOWN!
IS THERE ANOTHER EXIT?
I SURELY HOPE SO!
NARY A ONE, GAL! WE'RE STUCK LIKE SNAKES IN A WOODPILE!
I DON'T QUITE GET THE COMPARISON, BUT I'LL TAKE YOUR WORD FOR IT!
ANY IDEA WHAT... CHANGED THEM?
NOT A BLASTED ONE!
THE SECOND BIG QUESTION IS... WHY DIDN'T IT CHANGE US?
'CAUSE WE'RE DIFFERENT, I FIGGER! ME-- I'M AN OLD DESERT RAT! BEEN ALONE MOST OF MUH LIFE! I DON'T REACT NORMAL!
YOU AIN'T USUAL, NEITHER! SOMETHIN' DRIVES YUH TO RISK YORE NECK FER FOLKS--
--AN' THAT DRIVIN' THING'S CHANGED YUH, SAME'S THE LONESOME CHANGED ME!
I HOPE HE'S RIGHT! I... I'M FEELING AN URGE TO THROTTLE HIM!
OPEN UP!
KILL!
O-PEN!
KILL!
O-PEN!
11

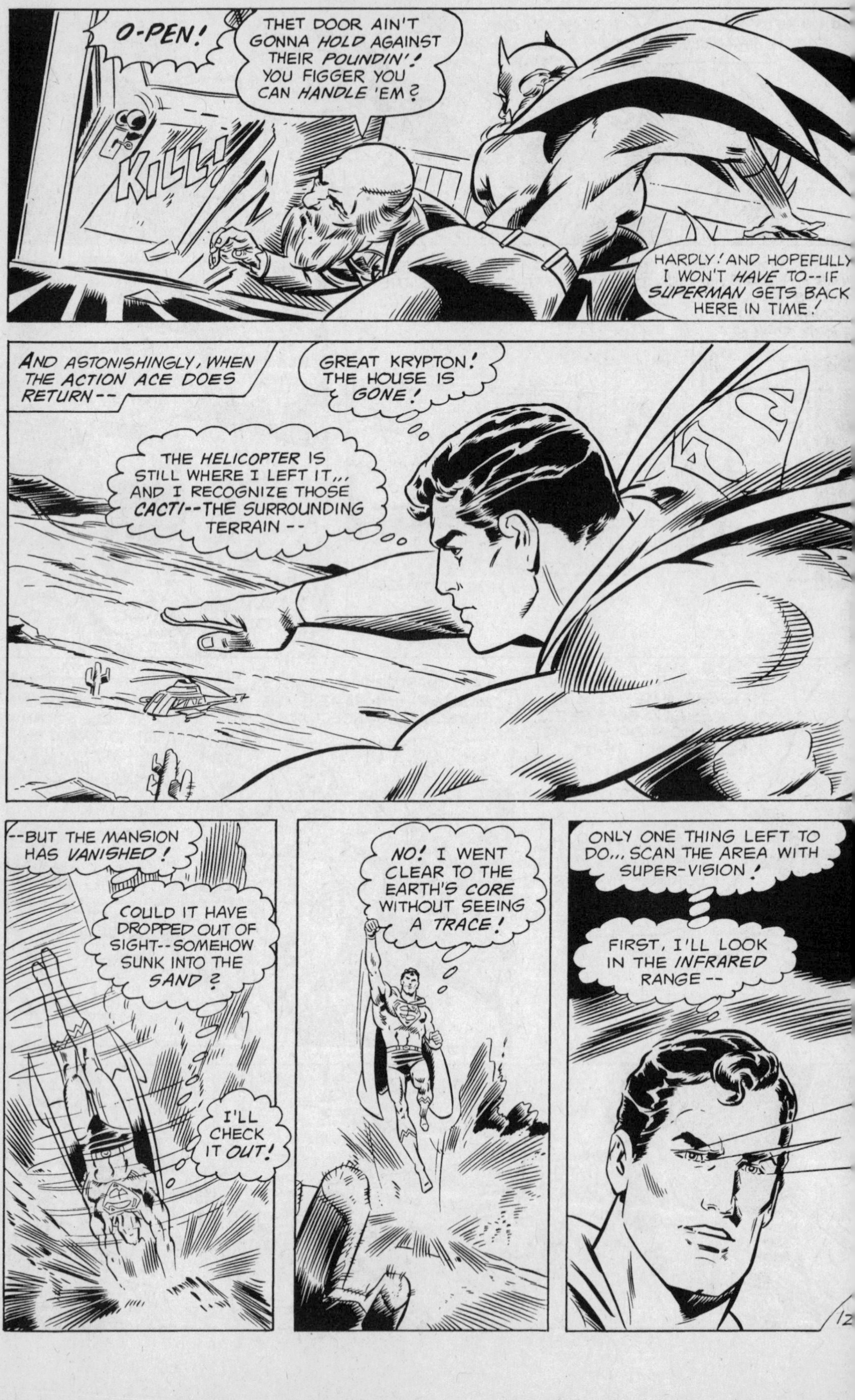
O-PEN!
THET DOOR AIN'T GONNA HOLD AGAINST THEIR POUNDIN'! YOU FIGGER YOU CAN HANDLE 'EM?
KILL!
HARDLY! AND HOPEFULLY I WON'T HAVE TO--IF SUPERMAN GETS BACK HERE IN TIME!
AND ASTONISHINGLY, WHEN THE ACTION ACE DOES RETURN--
GREAT KRYPTON! THE HOUSE IS GONE!
THE HELICOPTER IS STILL WHERE I LEFT IT,,, AND I RECOGNIZE THOSE CACTI--THE SURROUNDING TERRAIN--
--BUT THE MANSION HAS VANISHED!
COULD IT HAVE DROPPED OUT OF SIGHT--SOMEHOW SUNK INTO THE SAND?
I'LL CHECK IT OUT!
NO! I WENT CLEAR TO THE EARTH'S CORE WITHOUT SEEING A TRACE!
ONLY ONE THING LEFT TO DO... SCAN THE AREA WITH SUPER-VISION!
FIRST, I'LL LOOK IN THE INFRARED RANGE--
12

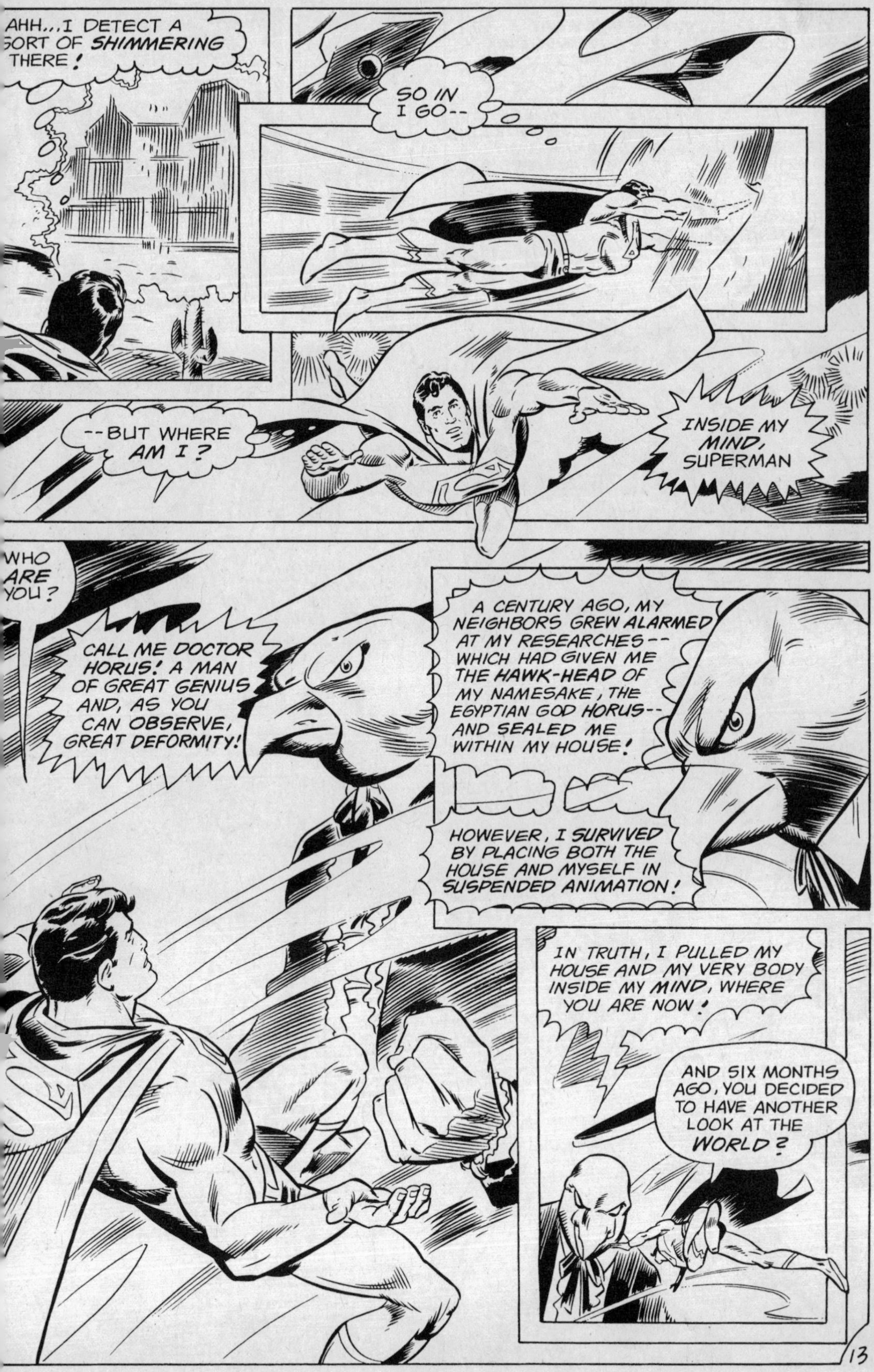
AHH...I DETECT A SORT OF SHIMMERING THERE!
SO IN I GO--
--BUT WHERE AM I?
INSIDE MY MIND, SUPERMAN
WHO ARE YOU?
CALL ME DOCTOR HORUS! A MAN OF GREAT GENIUS AND, AS YOU CAN OBSERVE, GREAT DEFORMITY!
A CENTURY AGO, MY NEIGHBORS GREW ALARMED AT MY RESEARCHES--WHICH HAD GIVEN ME THE HAWK-HEAD OF MY NAMESAKE, THE EGYPTIAN GOD HORUS--AND SEALED ME WITHIN MY HOUSE!
HOWEVER, I SURVIVED BY PLACING BOTH THE HOUSE AND MYSELF IN SUSPENDED ANIMATION!
IN TRUTH, I PULLED MY HOUSE AND MY VERY BODY INSIDE MY MIND, WHERE YOU ARE NOW!
AND SIX MONTHS AGO, YOU DECIDED TO HAVE ANOTHER LOOK AT THE WORLD?
13

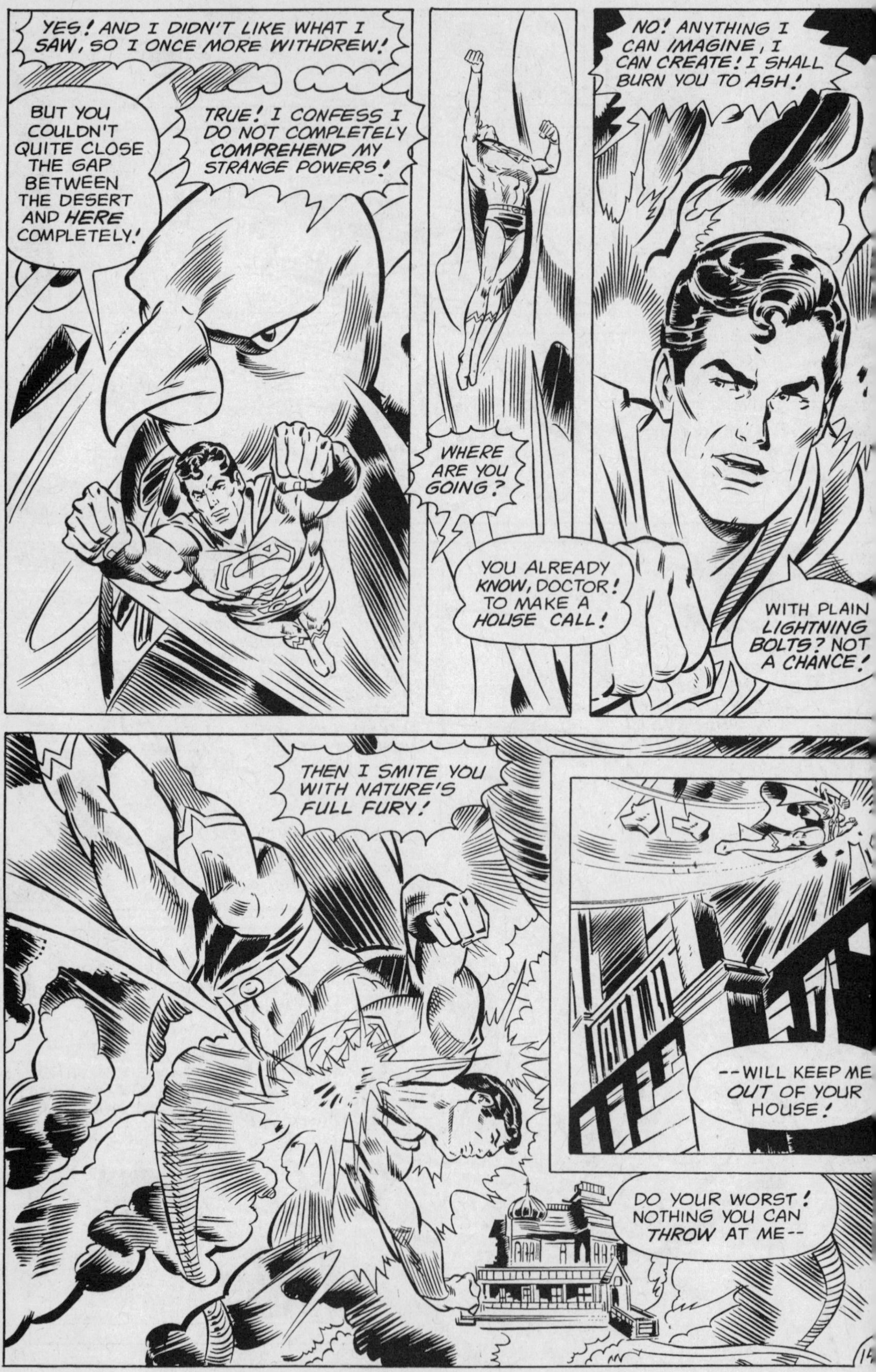
YES! AND I DIDN'T LIKE WHAT I SAW, SO I ONCE MORE WITHDREW!
BUT YOU COULDN'T QUITE CLOSE THE GAP BETWEEN THE DESERT AND HERE COMPLETELY!
TRUE! I CONFESS I DO NOT COMPLETELY COMPREHEND MY STRANGE POWERS!
WHERE ARE YOU GOING?
YOU ALREADY KNOW, DOCTOR! TO MAKE A HOUSE CALL!
NO! ANYTHING I CAN IMAGINE, I CAN CREATE! I SHALL BURN YOU TO ASH!
WITH PLAIN LIGHTNING BOLTS? NOT A CHANCE!
THEN I SMITE YOU WITH NATURE'S FULL FURY!
DO YOUR WORST! NOTHING YOU CAN THROW AT ME--
--WILL KEEP ME OUT OF YOUR HOUSE!

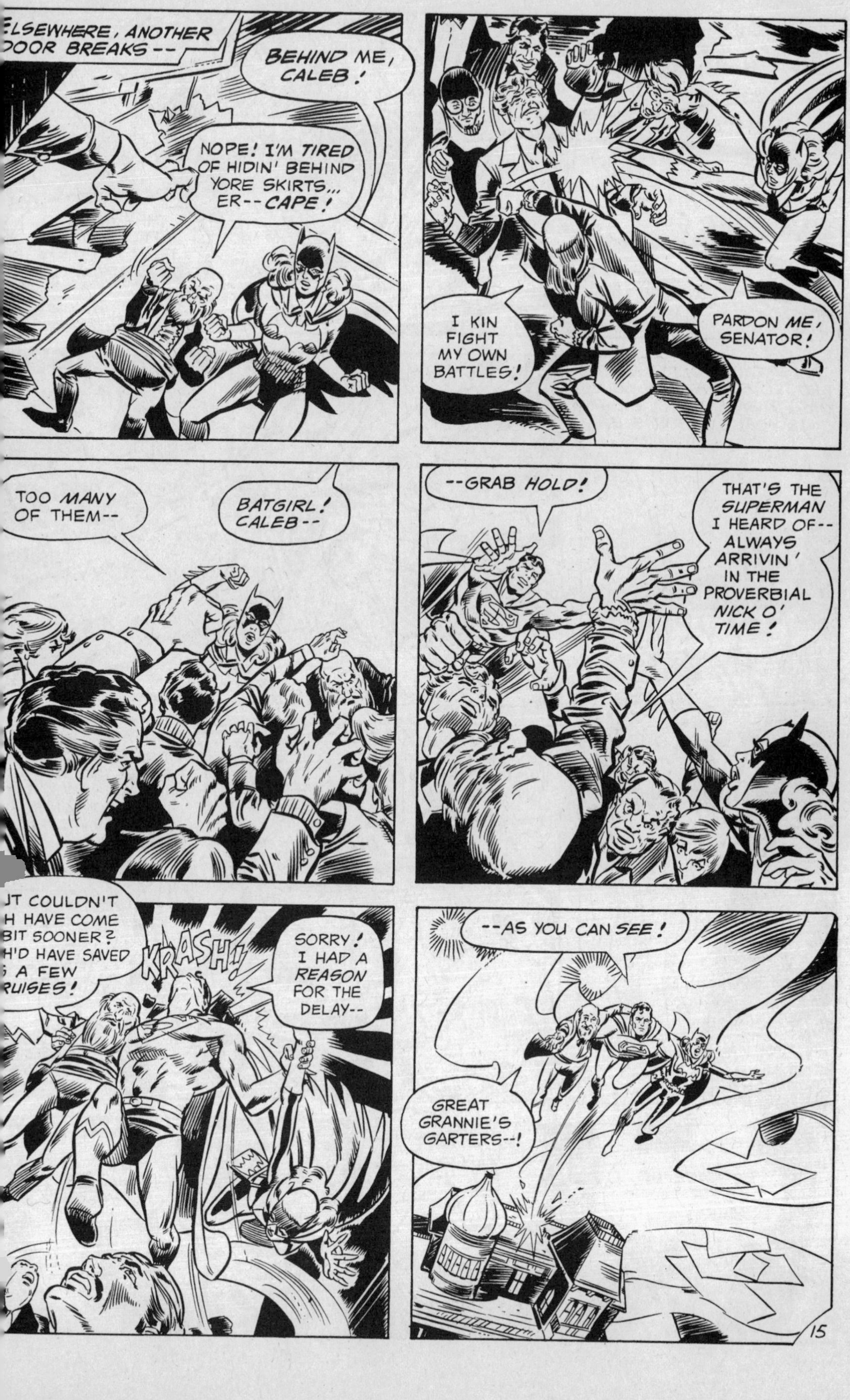
ELSEWHERE, ANOTHER DOOR BREAKS--
BEHIND ME, CALEB!
NOPE! I'M TIRED OF HIDIN' BEHIND YORE SKIRTS... ER--CAPE!
I KIN FIGHT MY OWN BATTLES!
PARDON ME, SENATOR!
TOO MANY OF THEM--
BATGIRL! CALEB--
--GRAB HOLD!
THAT'S THE SUPERMAN I HEARD OF--ALWAYS ARRIVIN' IN THE PROVERBIAL NICK O' TIME!
UT COULDN'T H HAVE COME BIT SOONER? H'D HAVE SAVED A FEW RUISES!
KRASH!
SORRY! I HAD A REASON FOR THE DELAY--
--AS YOU CAN SEE!
GREAT GRANNIE'S GARTERS--!
15

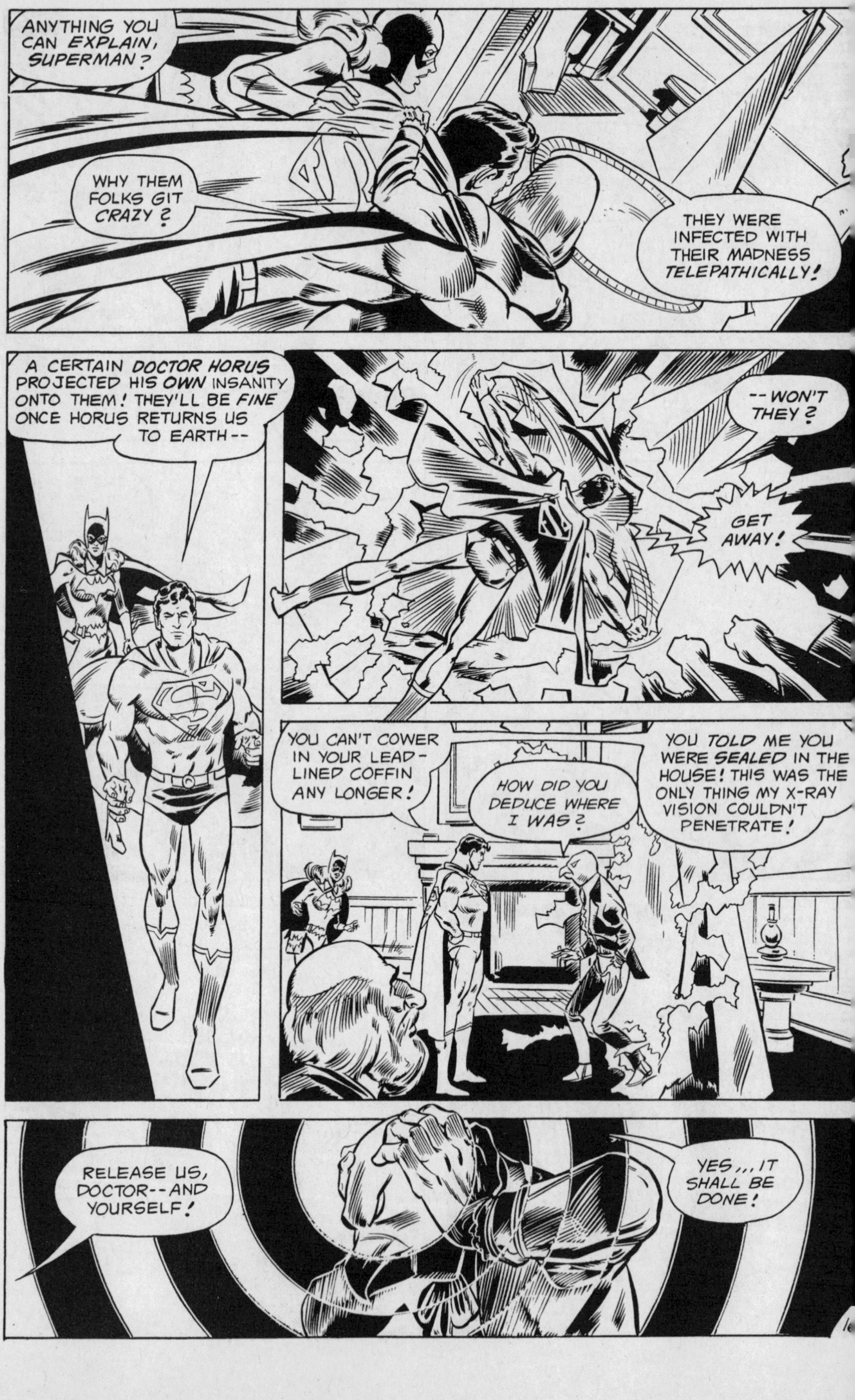
ANYTHING YOU CAN EXPLAIN, SUPERMAN?
WHY THEM FOLKS GIT CRAZY?
THEY WERE INFECTED WITH THEIR MADNESS TELEPATHICALLY!
A CERTAIN DOCTOR HORUS PROJECTED HIS OWN INSANITY ONTO THEM! THEY'LL BE FINE ONCE HORUS RETURNS US TO EARTH--
--WON'T THEY?
GET AWAY!
YOU CAN'T COWER IN YOUR LEAD-LINED COFFIN ANY LONGER!
HOW DID YOU DEDUCE WHERE I WAS?
YOU TOLD ME YOU WERE SEALED IN THE HOUSE! THIS WAS THE ONLY THING MY X-RAY VISION COULDN'T PENETRATE!
RELEASE US, DOCTOR--AND YOURSELF!
YES... IT SHALL BE DONE!

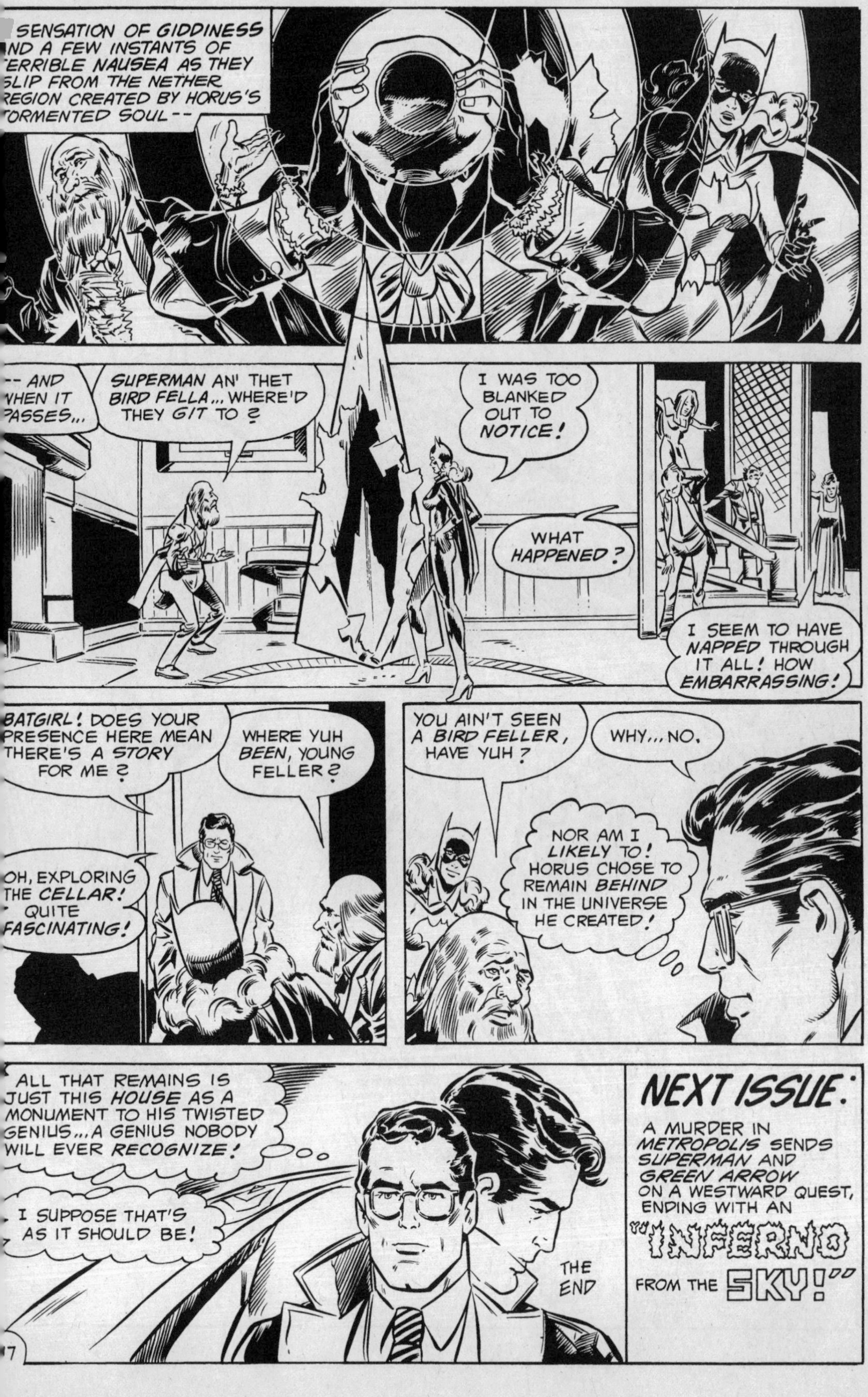
SENSATION OF GIDDINESS
ND A FEW INSTANTS OF
ERRIBLE NAUSEA AS THEY
SLIP FROM THE NETHER
REGION CREATED BY HORUS'S
ORMENTED SOUL--
-- AND
HEN IT
ASSES...
SUPERMAN AN' THET BIRD FELLA... WHERE'D THEY GIT TO ?
I WAS TOO BLANKED OUT TO NOTICE!
WHAT HAPPENED ?
I SEEM TO HAVE NAPPED THROUGH IT ALL! HOW EMBARRASSING!
BATGIRL! DOES YOUR PRESENCE HERE MEAN THERE'S A STORY FOR ME ?
WHERE YUH BEEN, YOUNG FELLER ?
OH, EXPLORING THE CELLAR! QUITE FASCINATING!
YOU AIN'T SEEN A BIRD FELLER, HAVE YUH ?
WHY... NO.
NOR AM I LIKELY TO! HORUS CHOSE TO REMAIN BEHIND IN THE UNIVERSE HE CREATED!
ALL THAT REMAINS IS JUST THIS HOUSE AS A MONUMENT TO HIS TWISTED GENIUS... A GENIUS NOBODY WILL EVER RECOGNIZE!
I SUPPOSE THAT'S AS IT SHOULD BE!
THE END
NEXT ISSUE:
A MURDER IN METROPOLIS SENDS SUPERMAN AND GREEN ARROW ON A WESTWARD QUEST, ENDING WITH AN
"INFERNO FROM THE SKY!"

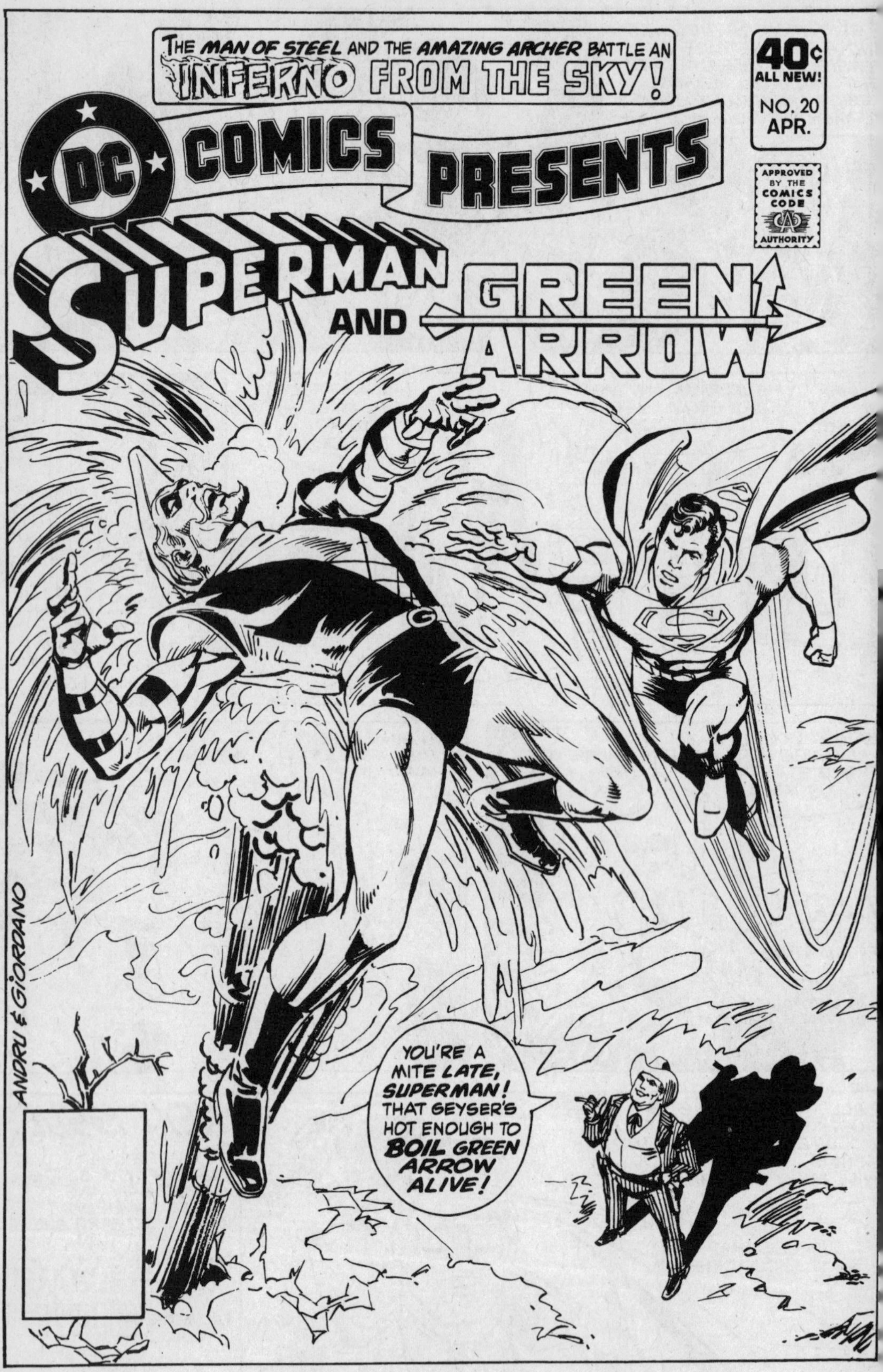
THE MAN OF STEEL AND THE AMAZING ARCHER BATTLE AN
INFERNO FROM THE SKY!
40¢
ALL NEW!
NO. 20
APR.
APPROVED BY THE COMICS CODE AUTHORITY
DC COMICS PRESENTS
SUPERMAN AND GREEN ARROW
ANDRU & GIORDANO
YOU'RE A MITE LATE, SUPERMAN! THAT GEYSER'S HOT ENOUGH TO BOIL GREEN ARROW ALIVE!

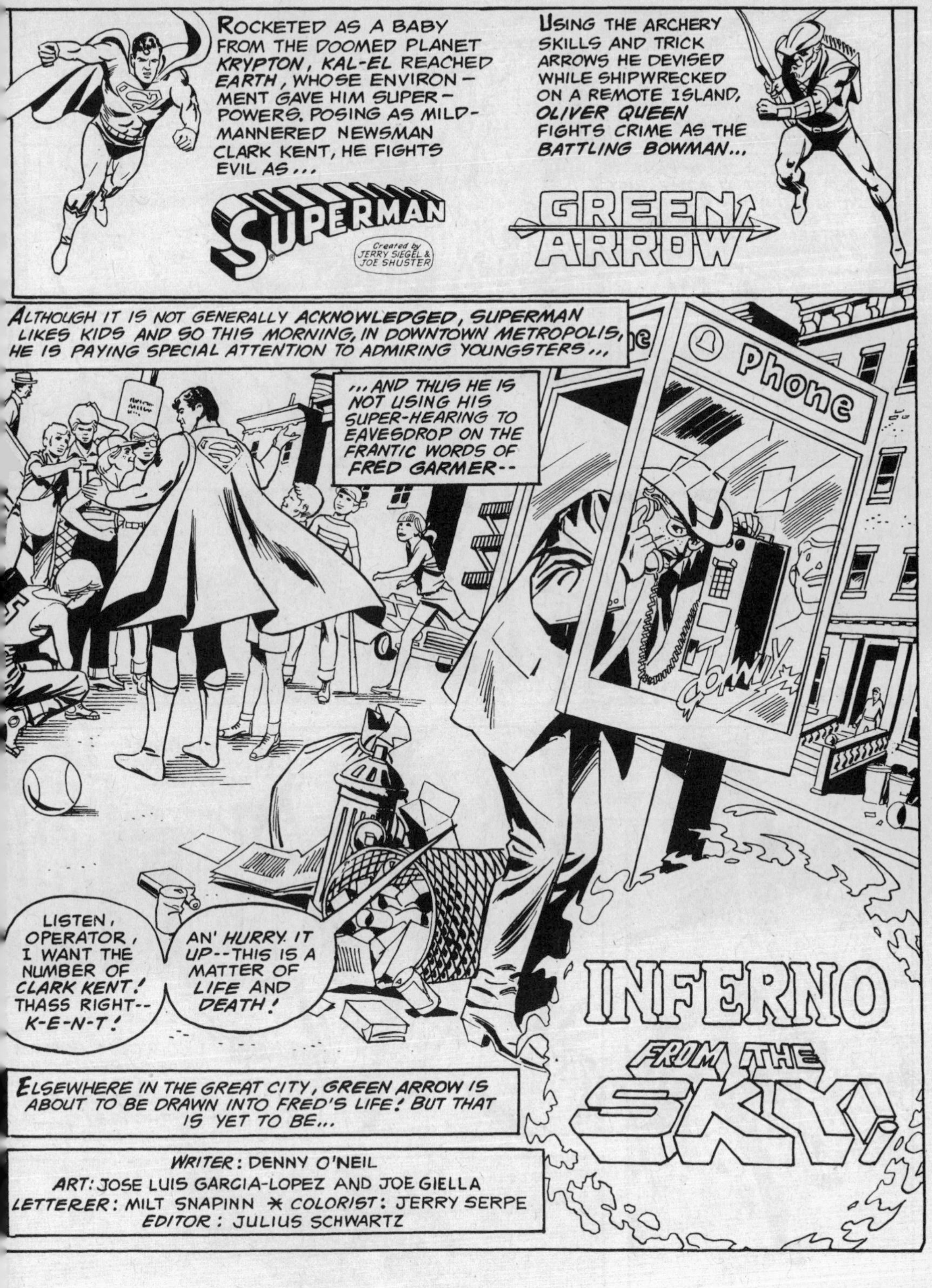
ROCKETED AS A BABY FROM THE DOOMED PLANET KRYPTON, KAL-EL REACHED EARTH, WHOSE ENVIRON-MENT GAVE HIM SUPER-POWERS. POSING AS MILD-MANNERED NEWSMAN CLARK KENT, HE FIGHTS EVIL AS...
SUPERMAN
Created by JERRY SIEGEL & JOE SHUSTER
USING THE ARCHERY SKILLS AND TRICK ARROWS HE DEVISED WHILE SHIPWRECKED ON A REMOTE ISLAND, OLIVER QUEEN FIGHTS CRIME AS THE BATTLING BOWMAN...
GREEN ARROW
ALTHOUGH IT IS NOT GENERALLY ACKNOWLEDGED, SUPERMAN LIKES KIDS AND SO THIS MORNING, IN DOWNTOWN METROPOLIS, HE IS PAYING SPECIAL ATTENTION TO ADMIRING YOUNGSTERS...
...AND THUS HE IS NOT USING HIS SUPER-HEARING TO EAVESDROP ON THE FRANTIC WORDS OF FRED GARMER--
Phone
LISTEN, OPERATOR, I WANT THE NUMBER OF CLARK KENT! THASS RIGHT-- K-E-N-T!
AN' HURRY IT UP--THIS IS A MATTER OF LIFE AND DEATH!
INFERNO FROM THE SKY!
ELSEWHERE IN THE GREAT CITY, GREEN ARROW IS ABOUT TO BE DRAWN INTO FRED'S LIFE! BUT THAT IS YET TO BE...
WRITER: DENNY O'NEIL
ART: JOSE LUIS GARCIA-LOPEZ AND JOE GIELLA
LETTERER: MILT SNAPINN * COLORIST: JERRY SERPE
EDITOR: JULIUS SCHWARTZ

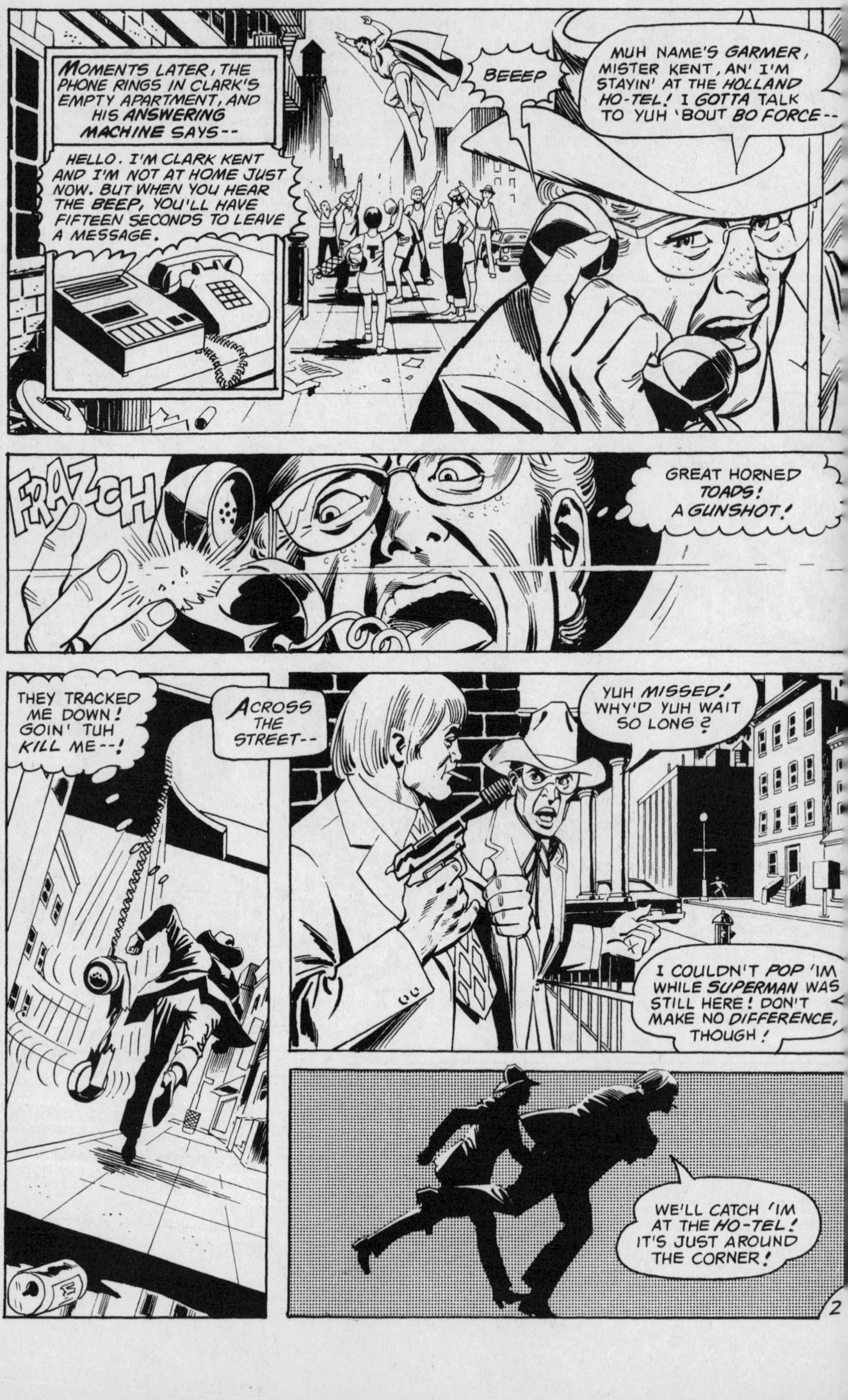
MOMENTS LATER, THE PHONE RINGS IN CLARK'S EMPTY APARTMENT, AND HIS ANSWERING MACHINE SAYS--
HELLO. I'M CLARK KENT AND I'M NOT AT HOME JUST NOW. BUT WHEN YOU HEAR THE BEEP, YOU'LL HAVE FIFTEEN SECONDS TO LEAVE A MESSAGE.
BEEEP
MUH NAME'S GARMER, MISTER KENT, AN' I'M STAYIN' AT THE HOLLAND HO-TEL! I GOTTA TALK TO YUH 'BOUT BO FORCE--
FRAZCH
GREAT HORNED TOADS! A GUNSHOT!
THEY TRACKED ME DOWN! GOIN' TUH KILL ME--!
ACROSS THE STREET--
YUH MISSED! WHY'D YUH WAIT SO LONG?
I COULDN'T POP 'IM WHILE SUPERMAN WAS STILL HERE! DON'T MAKE NO DIFFERENCE, THOUGH!
WE'LL CATCH 'IM AT THE HO-TEL! IT'S JUST AROUND THE CORNER!
2

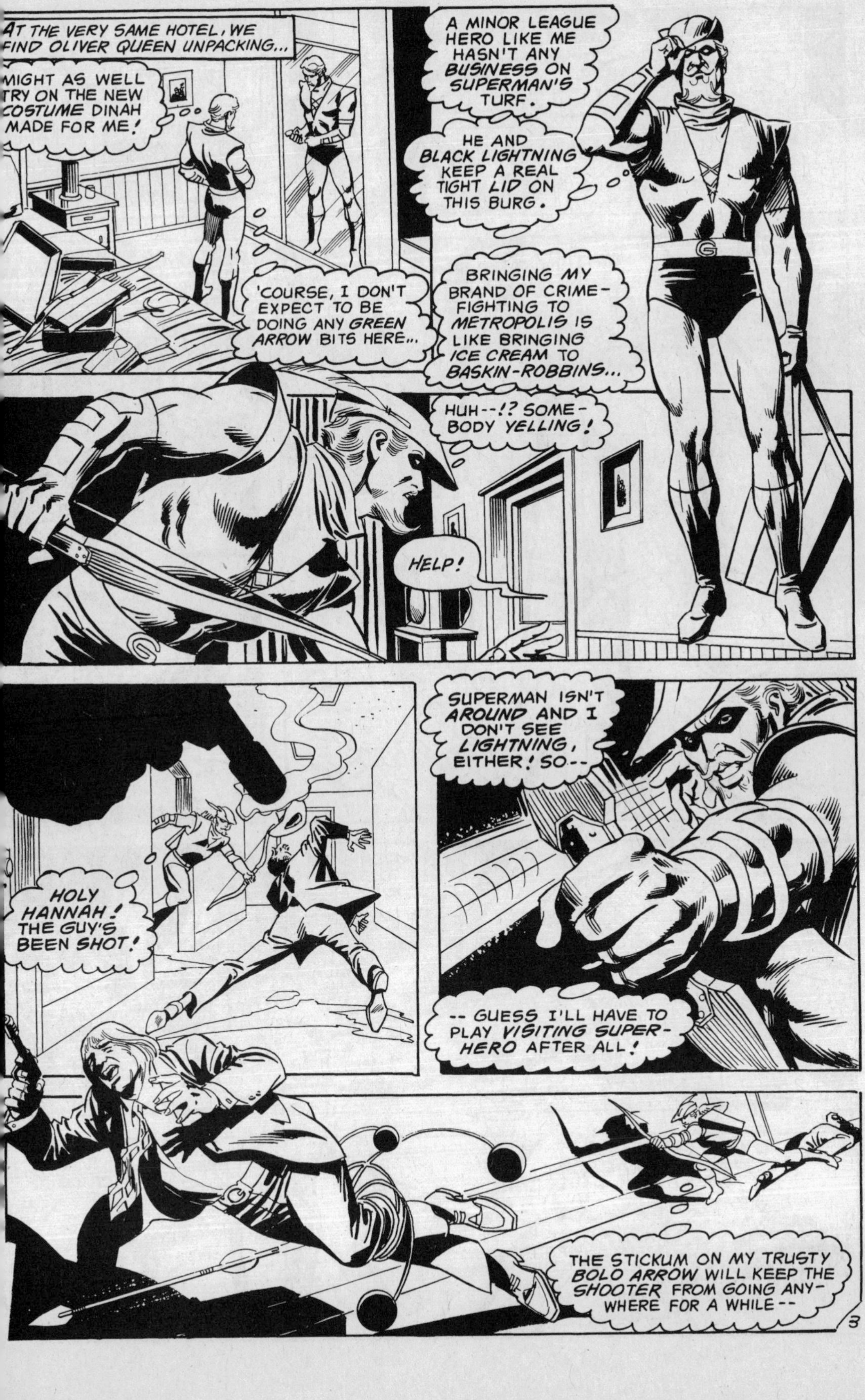
AT THE VERY SAME HOTEL, WE FIND OLIVER QUEEN UNPACKING...
MIGHT AS WELL TRY ON THE NEW COSTUME DINAH MADE FOR ME!
'COURSE, I DON'T EXPECT TO BE DOING ANY GREEN ARROW BITS HERE...
A MINOR LEAGUE HERO LIKE ME HASN'T ANY BUSINESS ON SUPERMAN'S TURF.
HE AND BLACK LIGHTNING KEEP A REAL TIGHT LID ON THIS BURG.
BRINGING MY BRAND OF CRIME-FIGHTING TO METROPOLIS IS LIKE BRINGING ICE CREAM TO BASKIN-ROBBINS...
HUH--!? SOME-BODY YELLING!
HELP!
HOLY HANNAH! THE GUY'S BEEN SHOT!
SUPERMAN ISN'T AROUND AND I DON'T SEE LIGHTNING, EITHER! SO--
-- GUESS I'LL HAVE TO PLAY VISITING SUPER-HERO AFTER ALL!
THE STICKUM ON MY TRUSTY BOLO ARROW WILL KEEP THE SHOOTER FROM GOING ANY-WHERE FOR A WHILE--
3

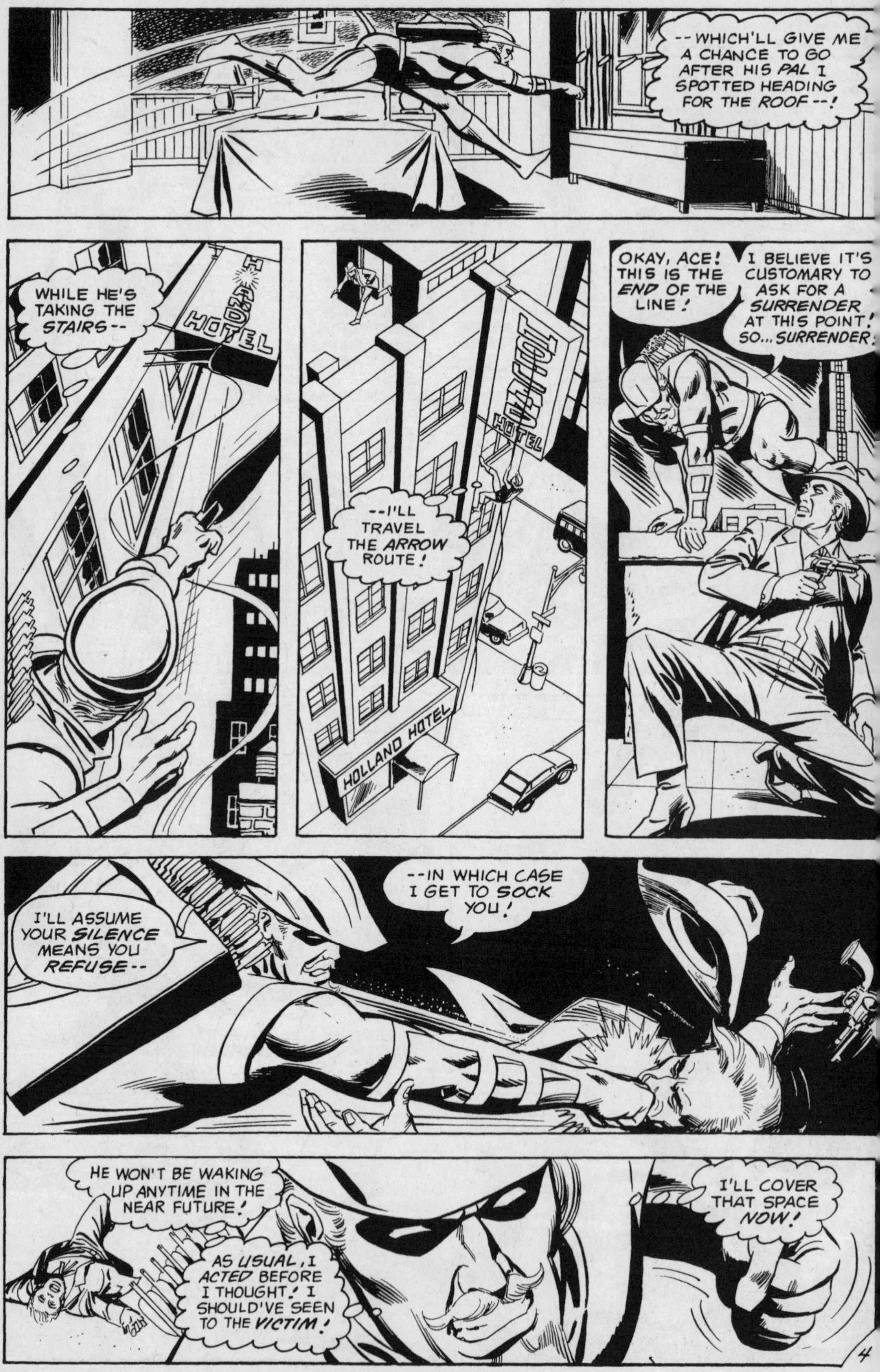
--WHICH'LL GIVE ME A CHANCE TO GO AFTER HIS PAL I SPOTTED HEADING FOR THE ROOF--!
WHILE HE'S TAKING THE STAIRS--
HOTEL
--I'LL TRAVEL THE ARROW ROUTE!
HOTEL
HOLLAND HOTEL
OKAY, ACE! THIS IS THE END OF THE LINE!
I BELIEVE IT'S CUSTOMARY TO ASK FOR A SURRENDER AT THIS POINT! SO...SURRENDER!
I'LL ASSUME YOUR SILENCE MEANS YOU REFUSE--
--IN WHICH CASE I GET TO SOCK YOU!
HE WON'T BE WAKING UP ANYTIME IN THE NEAR FUTURE!
AS USUAL, I ACTED BEFORE I THOUGHT! I SHOULD'VE SEEN TO THE VICTIM!
I'LL COVER THAT SPACE NOW!
4

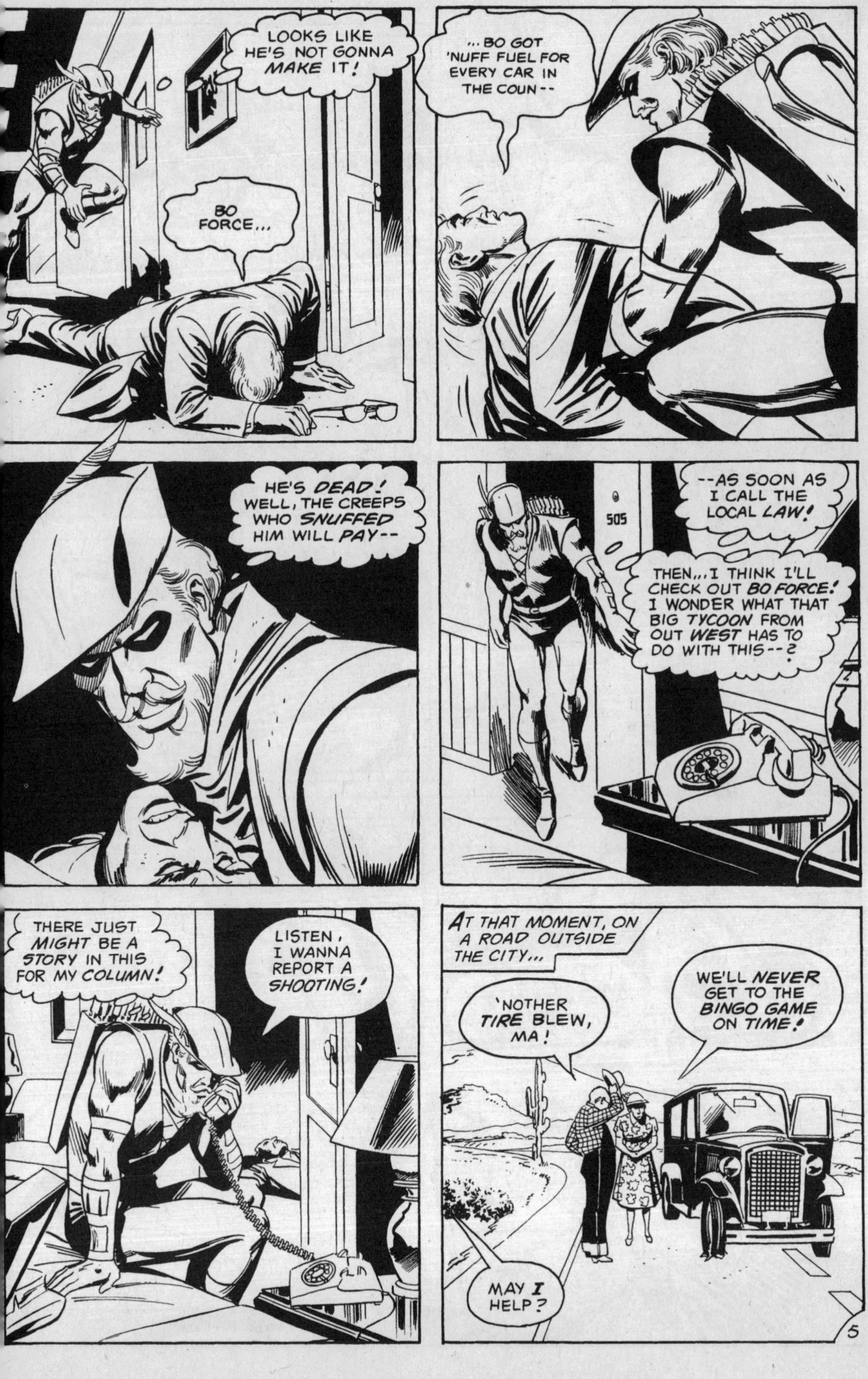
LOOKS LIKE HE'S NOT GONNA MAKE IT!
BO FORCE...
...BO GOT 'NUFF FUEL FOR EVERY CAR IN THE COUN--
HE'S DEAD! WELL, THE CREEPS WHO SNUFFED HIM WILL PAY--
505
--AS SOON AS I CALL THE LOCAL LAW!
THEN...I THINK I'LL CHECK OUT BO FORCE! I WONDER WHAT THAT BIG TYCOON FROM OUT WEST HAS TO DO WITH THIS--?
THERE JUST MIGHT BE A STORY IN THIS FOR MY COLUMN!
LISTEN, I WANNA REPORT A SHOOTING!
AT THAT MOMENT, ON A ROAD OUTSIDE THE CITY...
'NOTHER TIRE BLEW, MA!
WE'LL NEVER GET TO THE BINGO GAME ON TIME!
MAY I HELP?
5

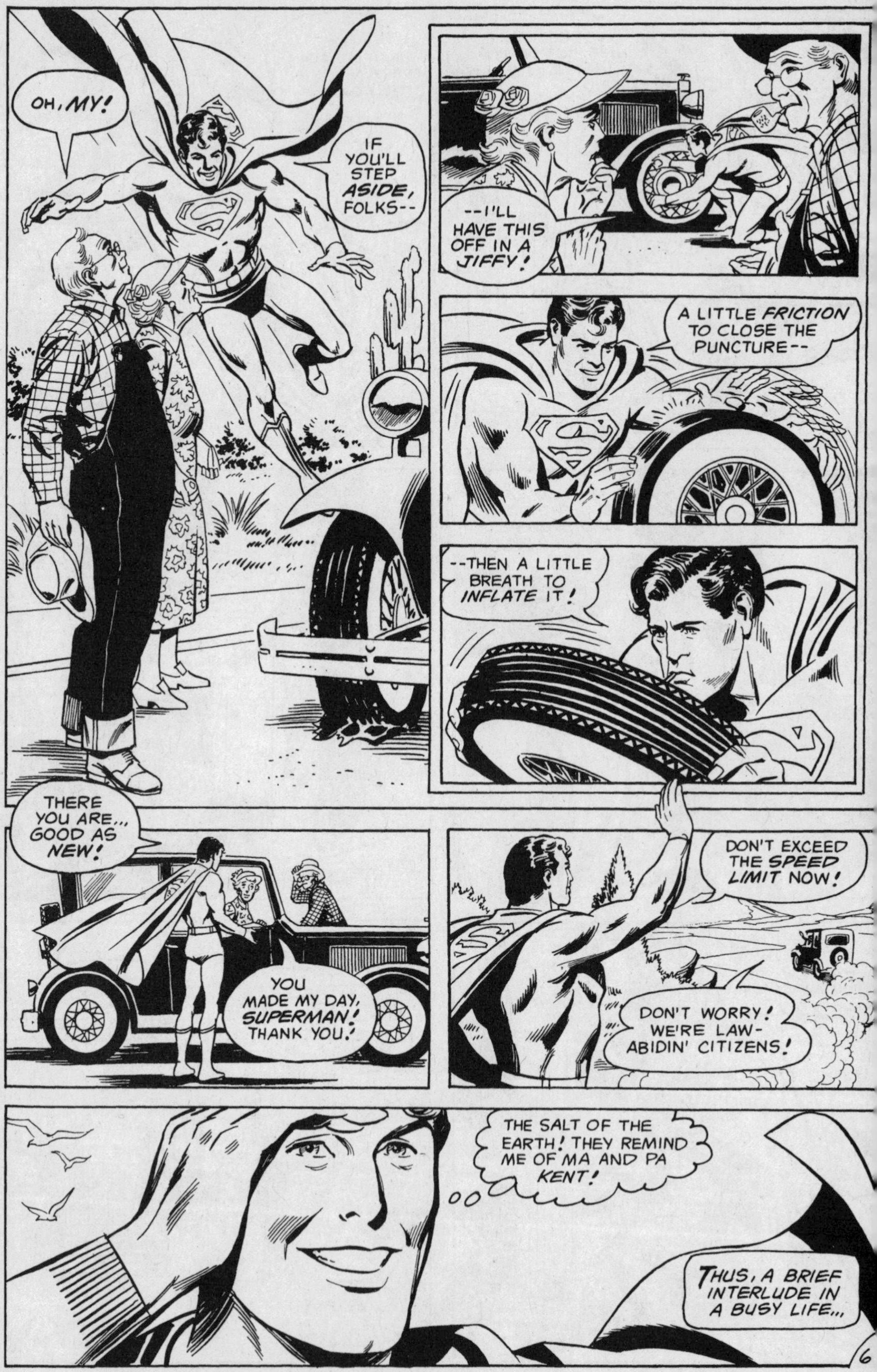
OH, MY!
IF YOU'LL STEP ASIDE, FOLKS--
--I'LL HAVE THIS OFF IN A JIFFY!
A LITTLE FRICTION TO CLOSE THE PUNCTURE--
--THEN A LITTLE BREATH TO INFLATE IT!
THERE YOU ARE... GOOD AS NEW!
YOU MADE MY DAY, SUPERMAN! THANK YOU!
DON'T EXCEED THE SPEED LIMIT NOW!
DON'T WORRY! WE'RE LAW-ABIDIN' CITIZENS!
THE SALT OF THE EARTH! THEY REMIND ME OF MA AND PA KENT!
THUS, A BRIEF INTERLUDE IN A BUSY LIFE...
6

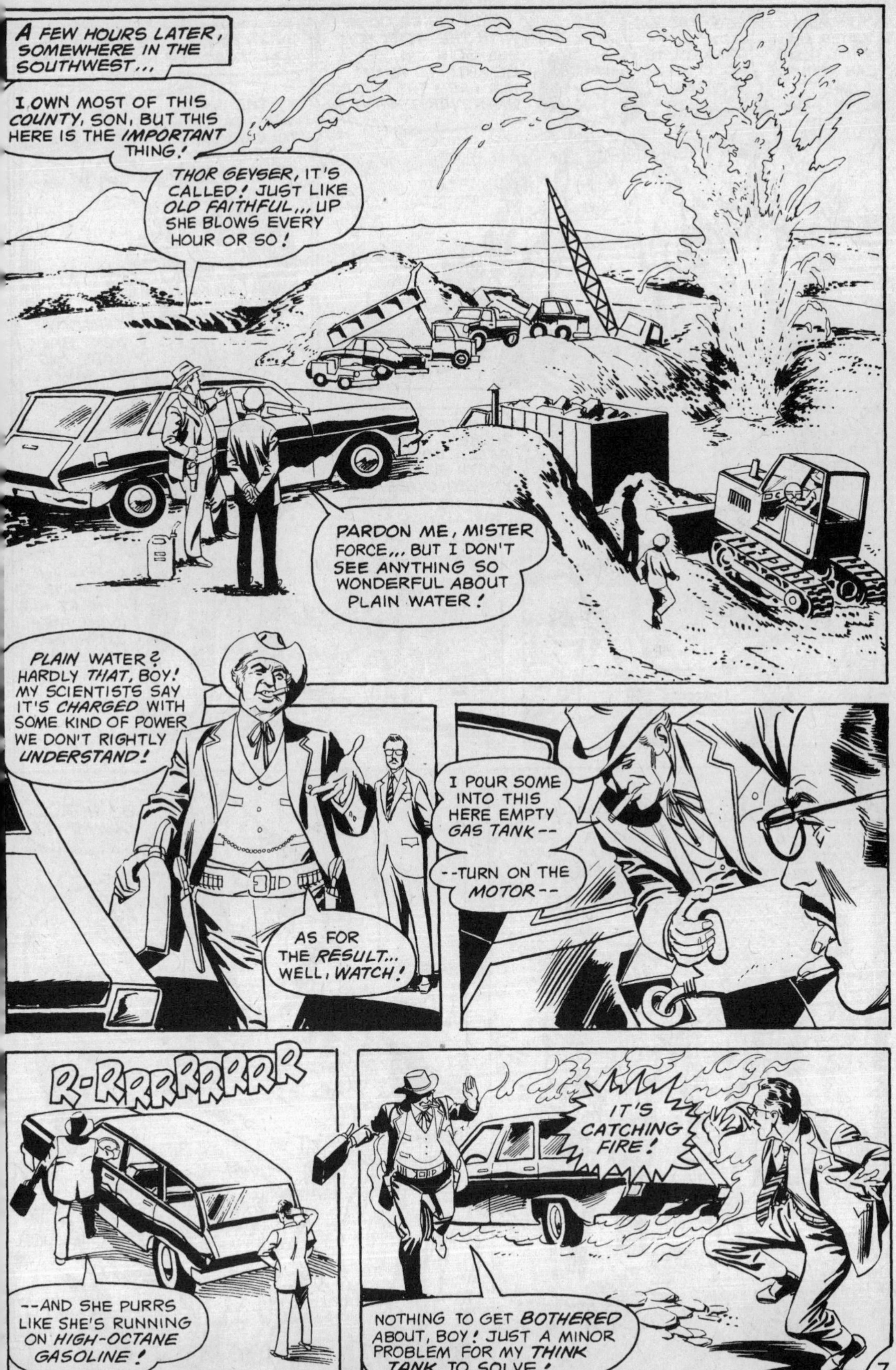
A FEW HOURS LATER, SOMEWHERE IN THE SOUTHWEST...
I OWN MOST OF THIS COUNTY, SON, BUT THIS HERE IS THE IMPORTANT THING!
THOR GEYSER, IT'S CALLED! JUST LIKE OLD FAITHFUL... UP SHE BLOWS EVERY HOUR OR SO!
PARDON ME, MISTER FORCE... BUT I DON'T SEE ANYTHING SO WONDERFUL ABOUT PLAIN WATER!
PLAIN WATER? HARDLY THAT, BOY! MY SCIENTISTS SAY IT'S CHARGED WITH SOME KIND OF POWER WE DON'T RIGHTLY UNDERSTAND!
AS FOR THE RESULT... WELL, WATCH!
I POUR SOME INTO THIS HERE EMPTY GAS TANK--
--TURN ON THE MOTOR--
R-RRRRRRRR
--AND SHE PURRS LIKE SHE'S RUNNING ON HIGH-OCTANE GASOLINE!
IT'S CATCHING FIRE!
NOTHING TO GET BOTHERED ABOUT, BOY! JUST A MINOR PROBLEM FOR MY THINK TANK TO SOLVE!
7

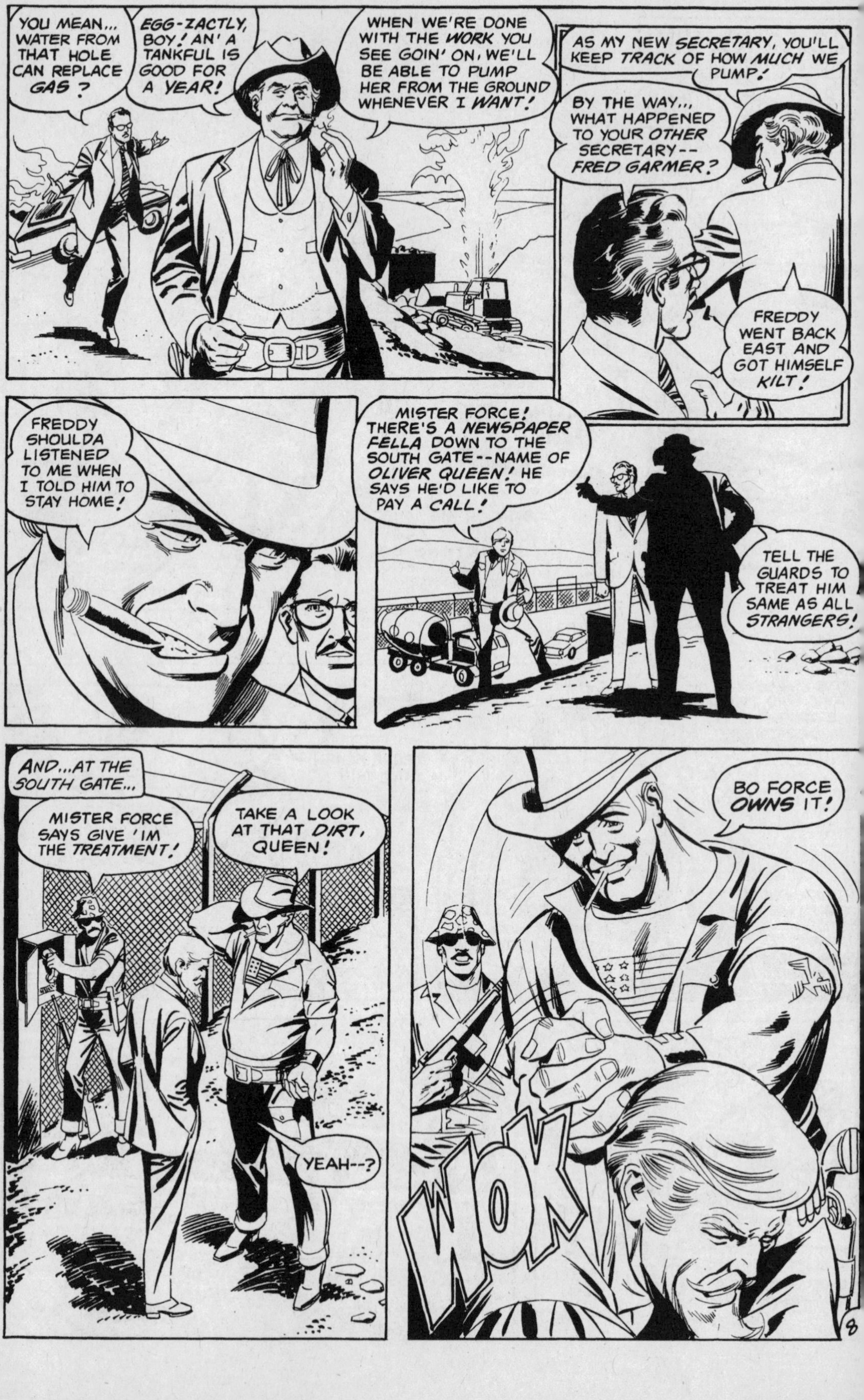
YOU MEAN... WATER FROM THAT HOLE CAN REPLACE GAS?
EGG-ZACTLY, BOY! AN' A TANKFUL IS GOOD FOR A YEAR!
WHEN WE'RE DONE WITH THE WORK YOU SEE GOIN' ON, WE'LL BE ABLE TO PUMP HER FROM THE GROUND WHENEVER I WANT!
AS MY NEW SECRETARY, YOU'LL KEEP TRACK OF HOW MUCH WE PUMP!
BY THE WAY... WHAT HAPPENED TO YOUR OTHER SECRETARY-- FRED GARMER?
FREDDY WENT BACK EAST AND GOT HIMSELF KILT!
FREDDY SHOULDA LISTENED TO ME WHEN I TOLD HIM TO STAY HOME!
MISTER FORCE! THERE'S A NEWSPAPER FELLA DOWN TO THE SOUTH GATE--NAME OF OLIVER QUEEN! HE SAYS HE'D LIKE TO PAY A CALL!
TELL THE GUARDS TO TREAT HIM SAME AS ALL STRANGERS!
AND...AT THE SOUTH GATE...
MISTER FORCE SAYS GIVE 'IM THE TREATMENT!
TAKE A LOOK AT THAT DIRT, QUEEN!
YEAH--?
BO FORCE OWNS IT!
WOK
8

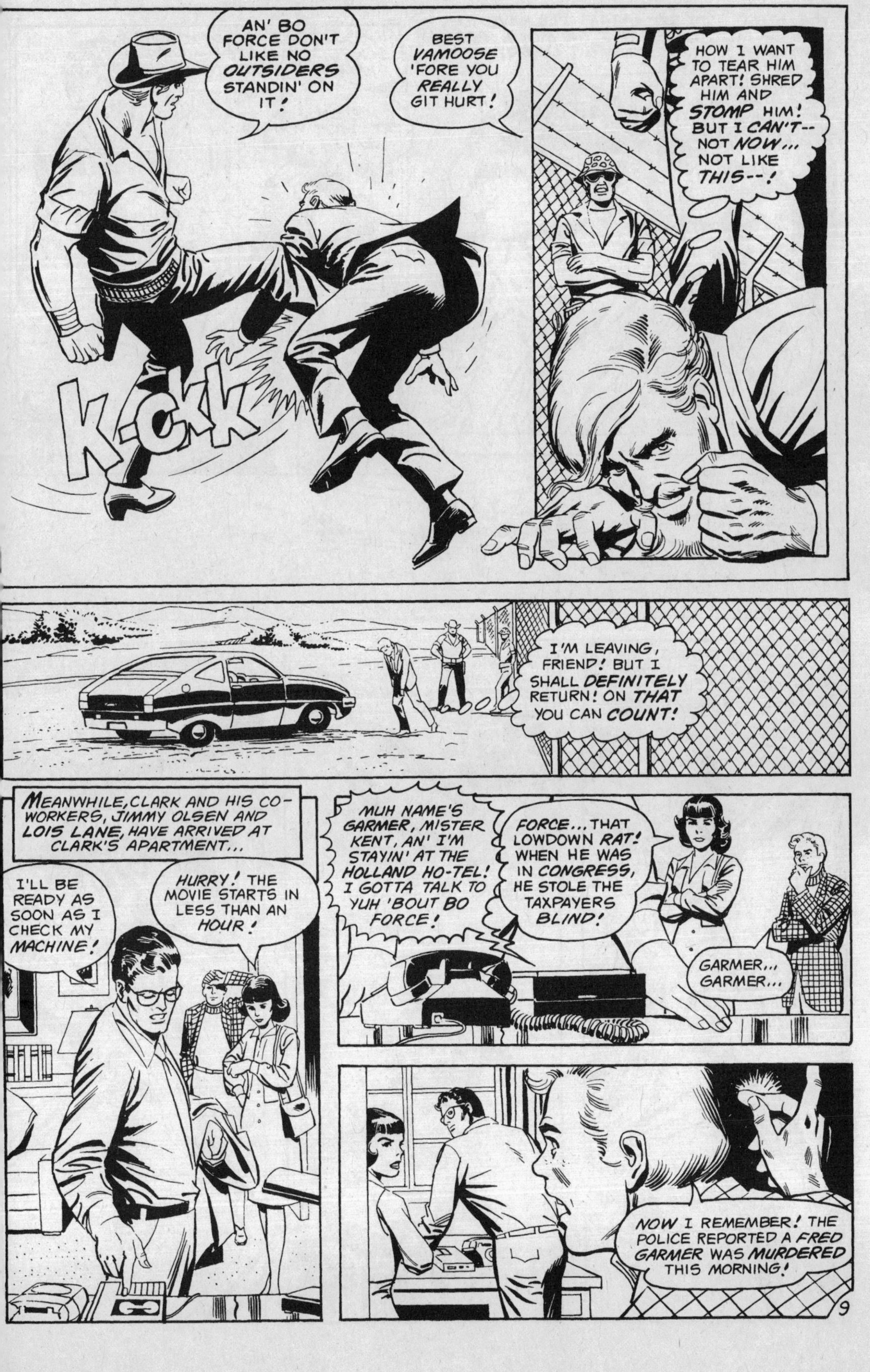
AN' BO FORCE DON'T LIKE NO OUTSIDERS STANDIN' ON IT!
BEST VAMOOSE 'FORE YOU REALLY GIT HURT!
K-CKK
HOW I WANT TO TEAR HIM APART! SHRED HIM AND STOMP HIM! BUT I CAN'T-- NOT NOW... NOT LIKE THIS--!
I'M LEAVING, FRIEND! BUT I SHALL DEFINITELY RETURN! ON THAT YOU CAN COUNT!
MEANWHILE, CLARK AND HIS CO-WORKERS, JIMMY OLSEN AND LOIS LANE, HAVE ARRIVED AT CLARK'S APARTMENT...
I'LL BE READY AS SOON AS I CHECK MY MACHINE!
HURRY! THE MOVIE STARTS IN LESS THAN AN HOUR!
MUH NAME'S GARMER, MISTER KENT, AN' I'M STAYIN' AT THE HOLLAND HO-TEL! I GOTTA TALK TO YUH 'BOUT BO FORCE!
FORCE... THAT LOWDOWN RAT! WHEN HE WAS IN CONGRESS, HE STOLE THE TAXPAYERS BLIND!
GARMER... GARMER...
NOW I REMEMBER! THE POLICE REPORTED A FRED GARMER WAS MURDERED THIS MORNING!
9

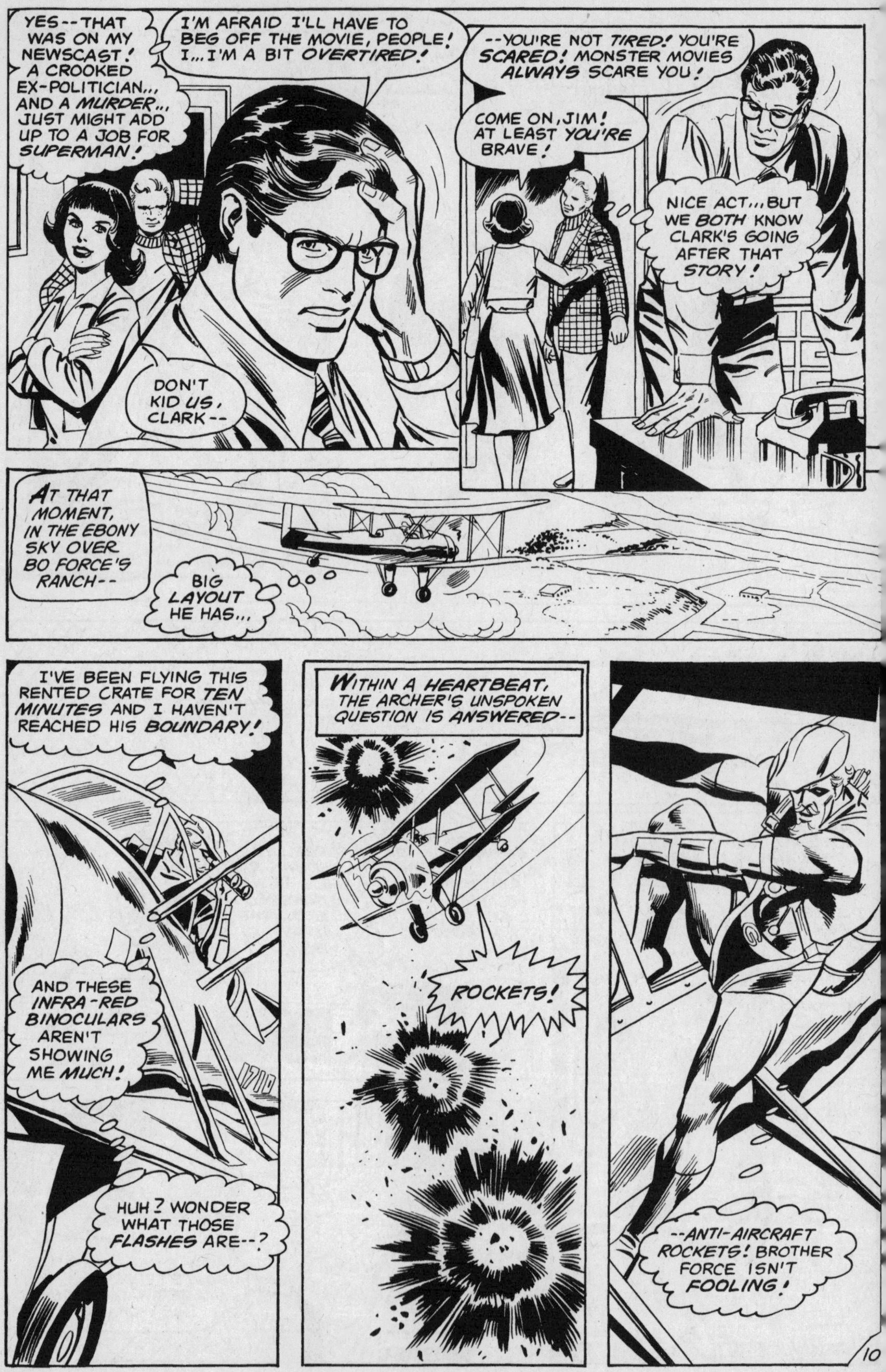
YES--THAT WAS ON MY NEWSCAST! A CROOKED EX-POLITICIAN... AND A MURDER... JUST MIGHT ADD UP TO A JOB FOR SUPERMAN!
I'M AFRAID I'LL HAVE TO BEG OFF THE MOVIE, PEOPLE! I... I'M A BIT OVERTIRED!
DON'T KID US, CLARK--
--YOU'RE NOT TIRED! YOU'RE SCARED! MONSTER MOVIES ALWAYS SCARE YOU!
COME ON, JIM! AT LEAST YOU'RE BRAVE!
NICE ACT... BUT WE BOTH KNOW CLARK'S GOING AFTER THAT STORY!
AT THAT MOMENT, IN THE EBONY SKY OVER BO FORCE'S RANCH--
BIG LAYOUT HE HAS...
I'VE BEEN FLYING THIS RENTED CRATE FOR TEN MINUTES AND I HAVEN'T REACHED HIS BOUNDARY!
AND THESE INFRA-RED BINOCULARS AREN'T SHOWING ME MUCH!
HUH? WONDER WHAT THOSE FLASHES ARE--?
WITHIN A HEARTBEAT, THE ARCHER'S UNSPOKEN QUESTION IS ANSWERED--
ROCKETS!
--ANTI-AIRCRAFT ROCKETS! BROTHER FORCE ISN'T FOOLING!
10

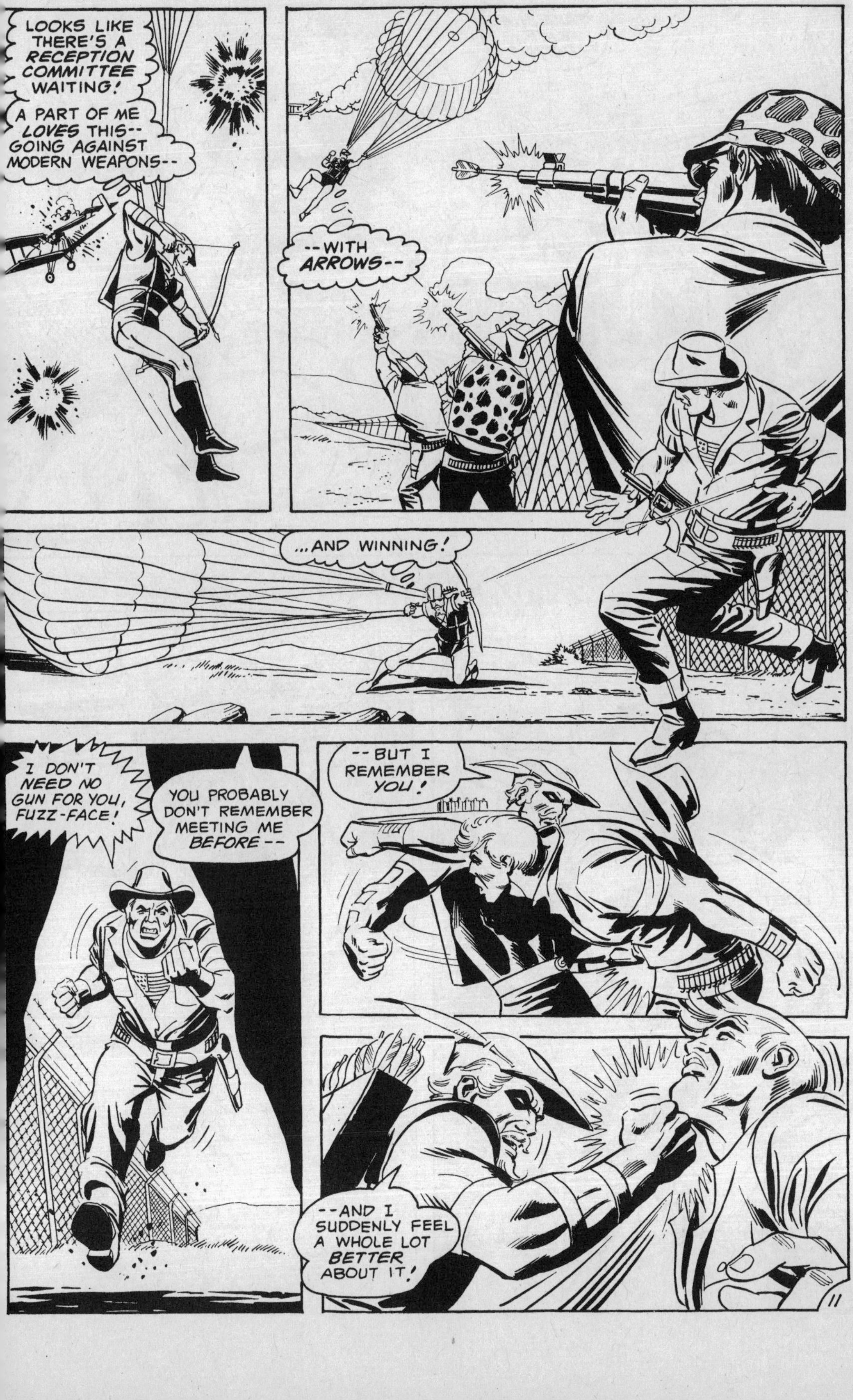
LOOKS LIKE THERE'S A RECEPTION COMMITTEE WAITING!
A PART OF ME LOVES THIS-- GOING AGAINST MODERN WEAPONS--
--WITH ARROWS--
...AND WINNING!
I DON'T NEED NO GUN FOR YOU, FUZZ-FACE!
YOU PROBABLY DON'T REMEMBER MEETING ME BEFORE--
--BUT I REMEMBER YOU!
--AND I SUDDENLY FEEL A WHOLE LOT BETTER ABOUT IT!
11

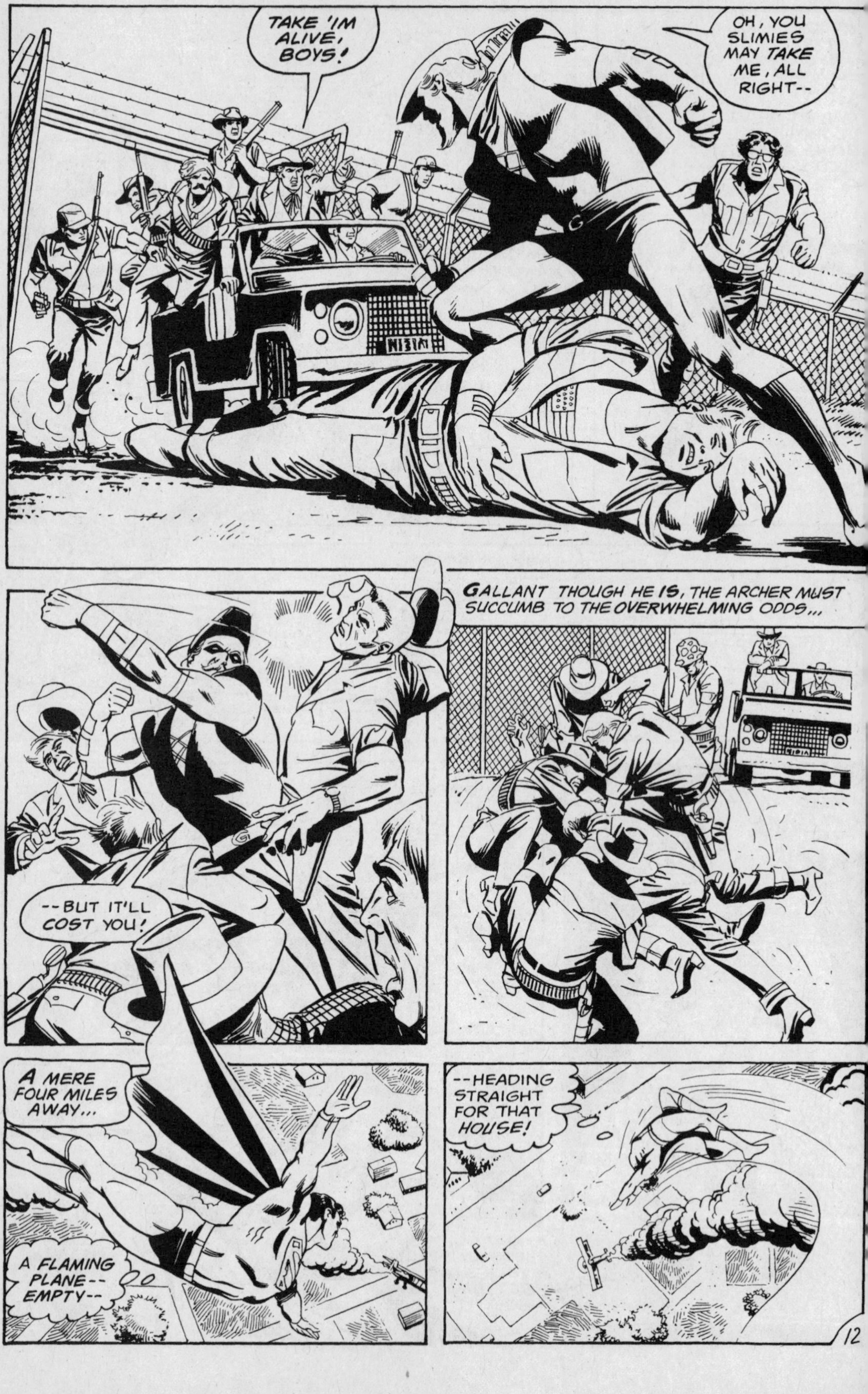
TAKE 'IM ALIVE, BOYS!
OH, YOU SLIMIES MAY TAKE ME, ALL RIGHT--
GALLANT THOUGH HE IS, THE ARCHER MUST SUCCUMB TO THE OVERWHELMING ODDS...
--BUT IT'LL COST YOU!
A MERE FOUR MILES AWAY...
A FLAMING PLANE-- EMPTY--
--HEADING STRAIGHT FOR THAT HOUSE!
12

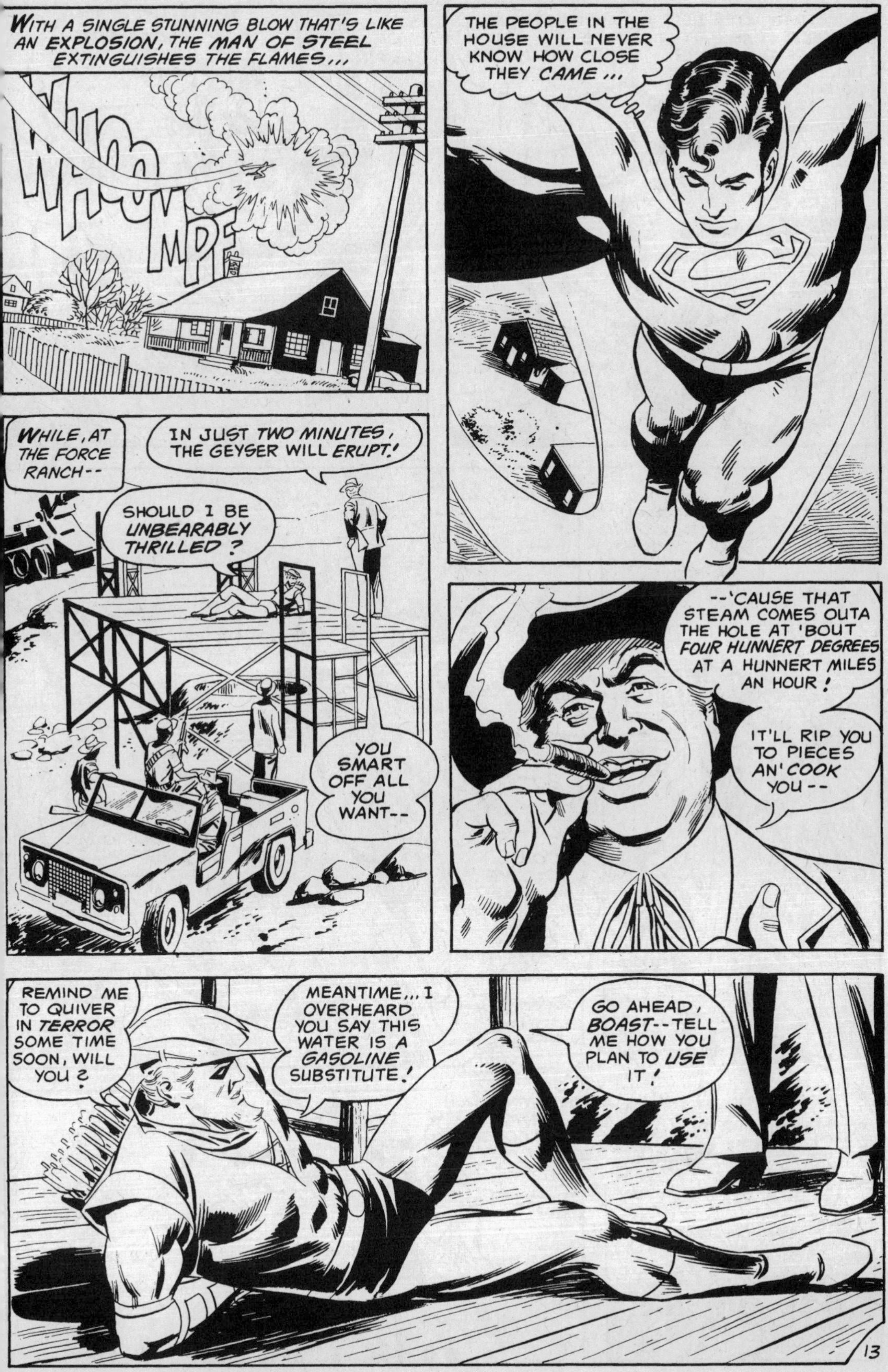
WITH A SINGLE STUNNING BLOW THAT'S LIKE AN EXPLOSION, THE MAN OF STEEL EXTINGUISHES THE FLAMES...
WHOOOMPF
THE PEOPLE IN THE HOUSE WILL NEVER KNOW HOW CLOSE THEY CAME...
WHILE, AT THE FORCE RANCH--
IN JUST TWO MINUTES, THE GEYSER WILL ERUPT!
SHOULD I BE UNBEARABLY THRILLED?
YOU SMART OFF ALL YOU WANT--
--'CAUSE THAT STEAM COMES OUTA THE HOLE AT 'BOUT FOUR HUNNERT DEGREES AT A HUNNERT MILES AN HOUR!
IT'LL RIP YOU TO PIECES AN' COOK YOU--
REMIND ME TO QUIVER IN TERROR SOME TIME SOON, WILL YOU?
MEANTIME... I OVERHEARD YOU SAY THIS WATER IS A GASOLINE SUBSTITUTE!
GO AHEAD, BOAST--TELL ME HOW YOU PLAN TO USE IT!
13

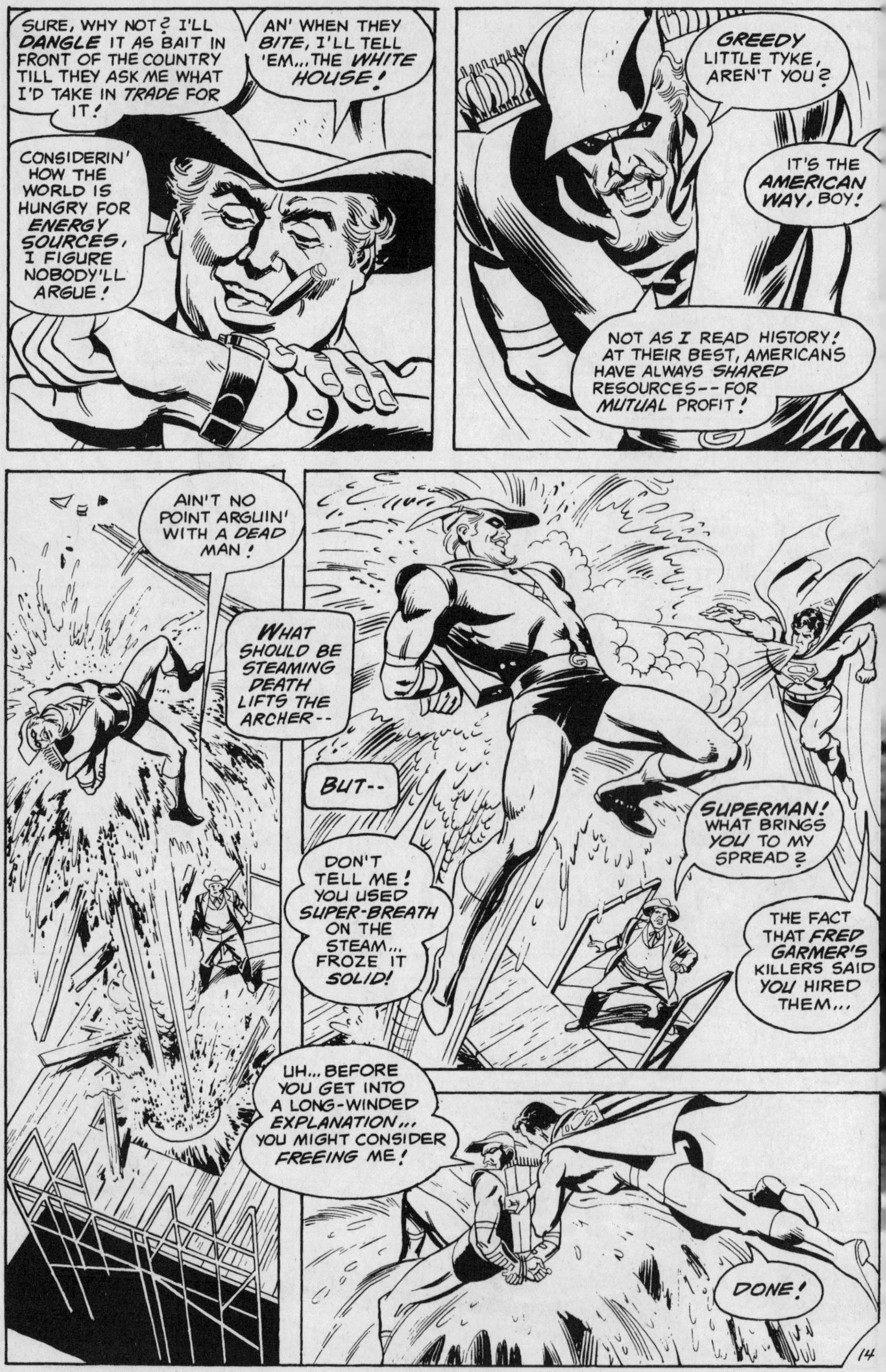
SURE, WHY NOT? I'LL DANGLE IT AS BAIT IN FRONT OF THE COUNTRY TILL THEY ASK ME WHAT I'D TAKE IN TRADE FOR IT!
AN' WHEN THEY BITE, I'LL TELL 'EM... THE WHITE HOUSE!
CONSIDERIN' HOW THE WORLD IS HUNGRY FOR ENERGY SOURCES, I FIGURE NOBODY'LL ARGUE!
GREEDY LITTLE TYKE, AREN'T YOU?
IT'S THE AMERICAN WAY, BOY!
NOT AS I READ HISTORY! AT THEIR BEST, AMERICANS HAVE ALWAYS SHARED RESOURCES-- FOR MUTUAL PROFIT!
AIN'T NO POINT ARGUIN' WITH A DEAD MAN!
WHAT SHOULD BE STEAMING DEATH LIFTS THE ARCHER--
BUT--
DON'T TELL ME! YOU USED SUPER-BREATH ON THE STEAM... FROZE IT SOLID!
SUPERMAN! WHAT BRINGS YOU TO MY SPREAD?
THE FACT THAT FRED GARMER'S KILLERS SAID YOU HIRED THEM...
UH... BEFORE YOU GET INTO A LONG-WINDED EXPLANATION... YOU MIGHT CONSIDER FREEING ME!
DONE!
14

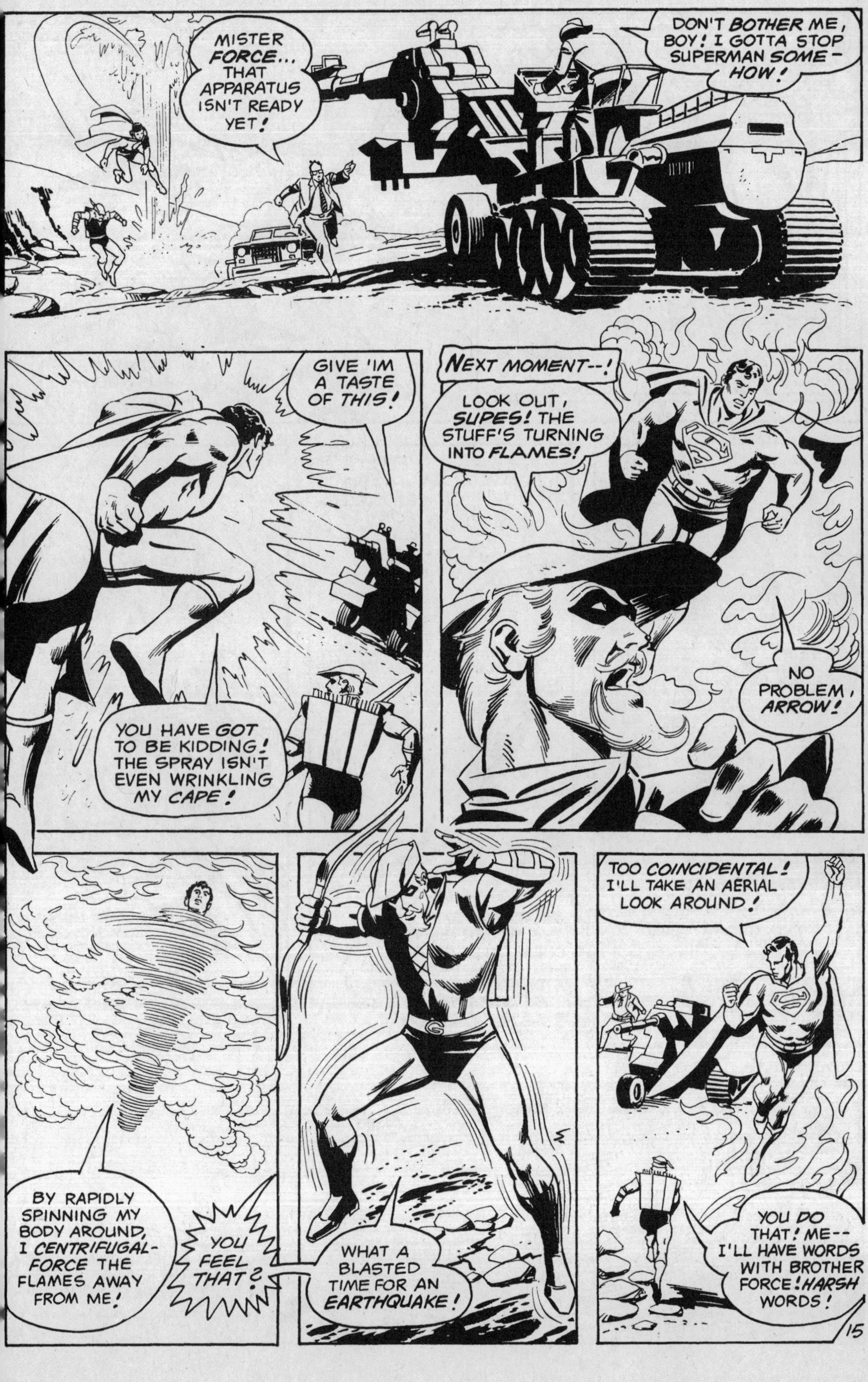
MISTER FORCE... THAT APPARATUS ISN'T READY YET!
DON'T BOTHER ME, BOY! I GOTTA STOP SUPERMAN SOME-HOW!
GIVE 'IM A TASTE OF THIS!
YOU HAVE GOT TO BE KIDDING! THE SPRAY ISN'T EVEN WRINKLING MY CAPE!
NEXT MOMENT--!
LOOK OUT, SUPES! THE STUFF'S TURNING INTO FLAMES!
NO PROBLEM, ARROW!
BY RAPIDLY SPINNING MY BODY AROUND, I CENTRIFUGAL-FORCE THE FLAMES AWAY FROM ME!
YOU FEEL THAT?
WHAT A BLASTED TIME FOR AN EARTHQUAKE!
TOO COINCIDENTAL! I'LL TAKE AN AERIAL LOOK AROUND!
YOU DO THAT! ME-- I'LL HAVE WORDS WITH BROTHER FORCE! HARSH WORDS!
15

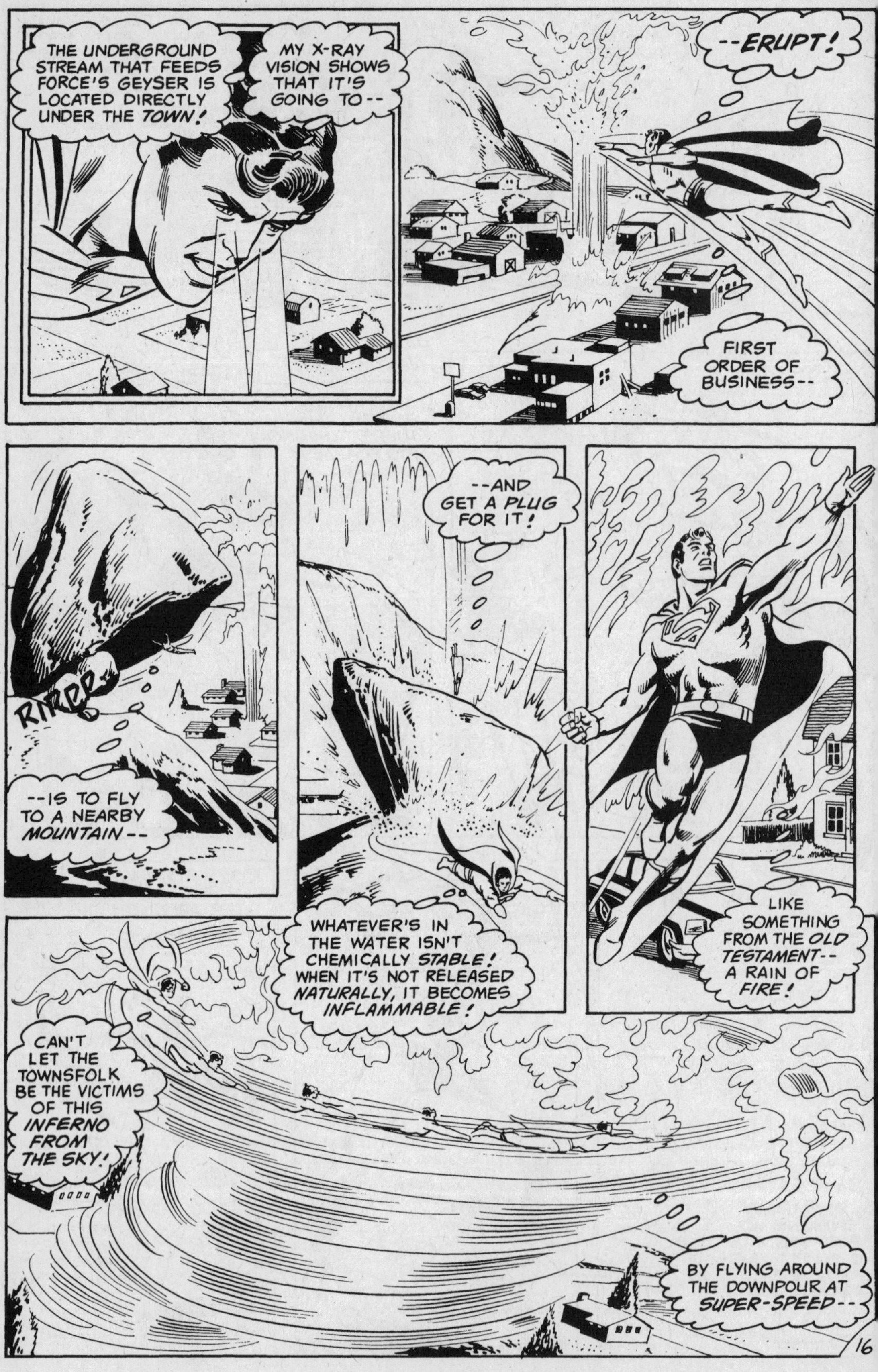
THE UNDERGROUND STREAM THAT FEEDS FORCE'S GEYSER IS LOCATED DIRECTLY UNDER THE TOWN!
MY X-RAY VISION SHOWS THAT IT'S GOING TO--
--ERUPT!
FIRST ORDER OF BUSINESS--
--IS TO FLY TO A NEARBY MOUNTAIN--
RIPPP
--AND GET A PLUG FOR IT!
WHATEVER'S IN THE WATER ISN'T CHEMICALLY STABLE! WHEN IT'S NOT RELEASED NATURALLY, IT BECOMES INFLAMMABLE!
LIKE SOMETHING FROM THE OLD TESTAMENT-- A RAIN OF FIRE!
CAN'T LET THE TOWNSFOLK BE THE VICTIMS OF THIS INFERNO FROM THE SKY!
BY FLYING AROUND THE DOWNPOUR AT SUPER-SPEED--
16

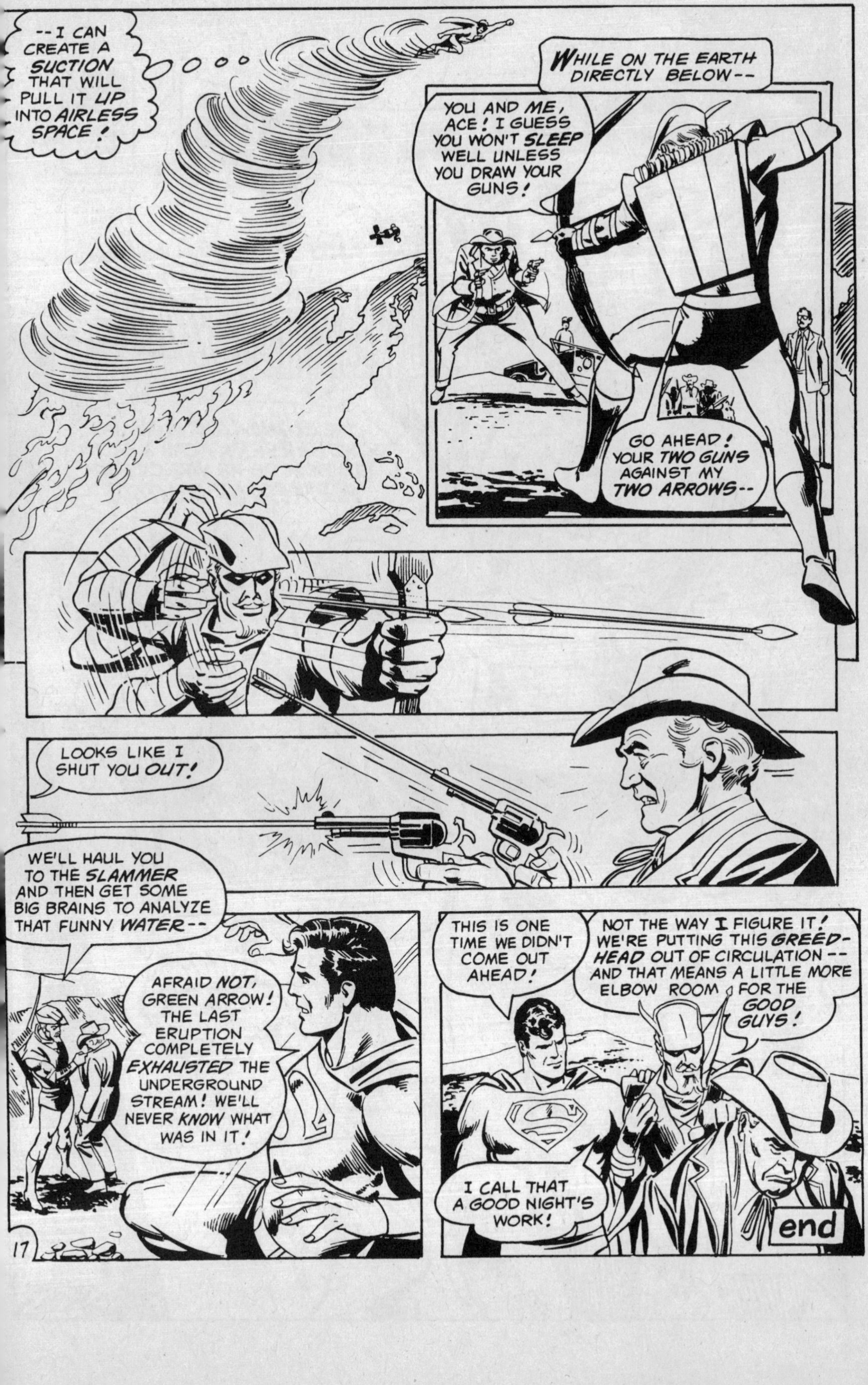
--I CAN CREATE A SUCTION THAT WILL PULL IT UP INTO AIRLESS SPACE!
WHILE ON THE EARTH DIRECTLY BELOW--
YOU AND ME, ACE! I GUESS YOU WON'T SLEEP WELL UNLESS YOU DRAW YOUR GUNS!
GO AHEAD! YOUR TWO GUNS AGAINST MY TWO ARROWS--
LOOKS LIKE I SHUT YOU OUT!
WE'LL HAUL YOU TO THE SLAMMER AND THEN GET SOME BIG BRAINS TO ANALYZE THAT FUNNY WATER--
AFRAID NOT, GREEN ARROW! THE LAST ERUPTION COMPLETELY EXHAUSTED THE UNDERGROUND STREAM! WE'LL NEVER KNOW WHAT WAS IN IT!
17
THIS IS ONE TIME WE DIDN'T COME OUT AHEAD!
NOT THE WAY I FIGURE IT! WE'RE PUTTING THIS GREED-HEAD OUT OF CIRCULATION -- AND THAT MEANS A LITTLE MORE ELBOW ROOM FOR THE GOOD GUYS!
I CALL THAT A GOOD NIGHT'S WORK!
end

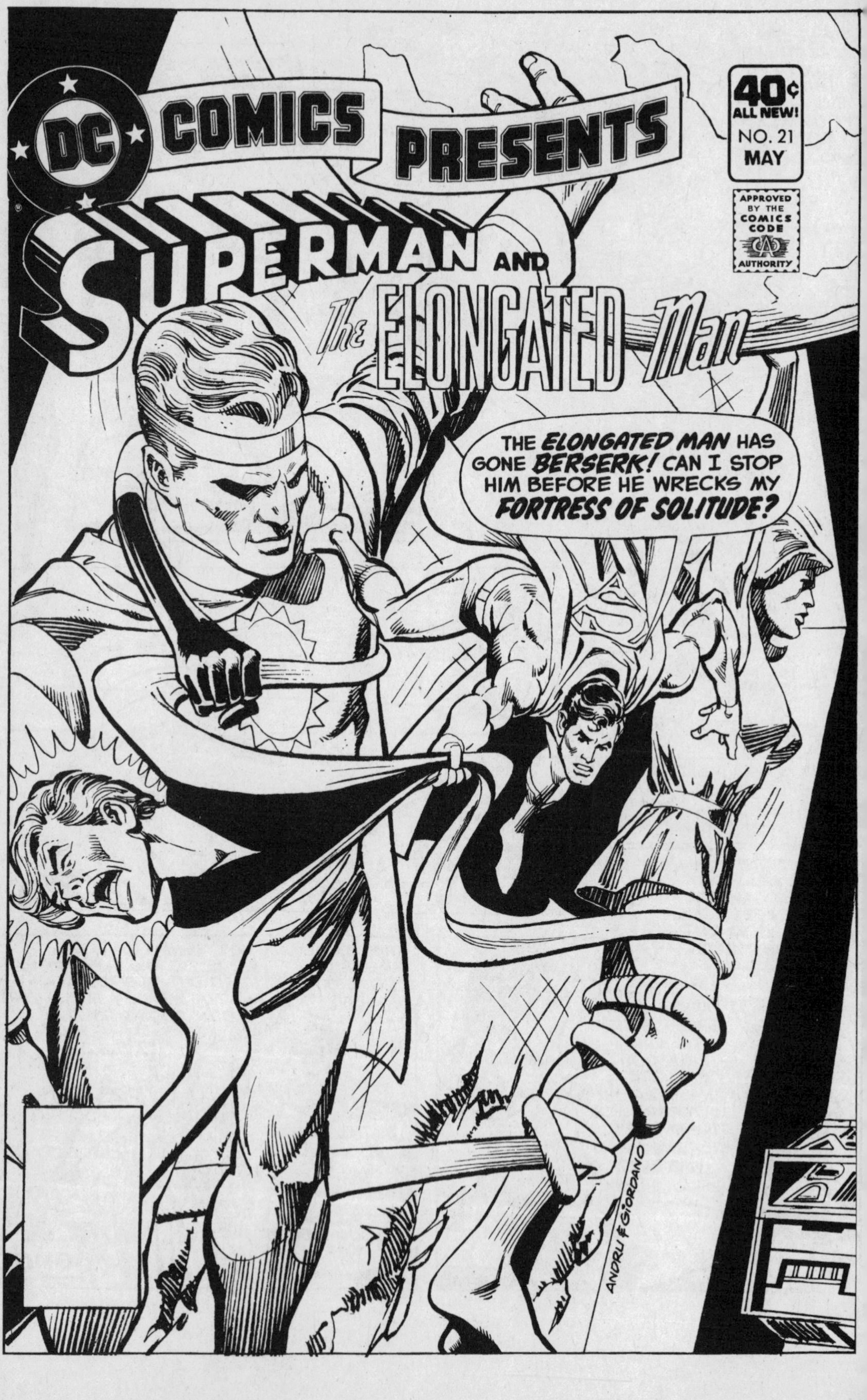
DC COMICS PRESENTS
40¢ ALL NEW!
NO. 21
MAY
APPROVED BY THE COMICS CODE AUTHORITY
SUPERMAN AND
The ELONGATED Man
THE ELONGATED MAN HAS GONE BERSERK! CAN I STOP HIM BEFORE HE WRECKS MY FORTRESS OF SOLITUDE?
ANDRU & GIORDANO

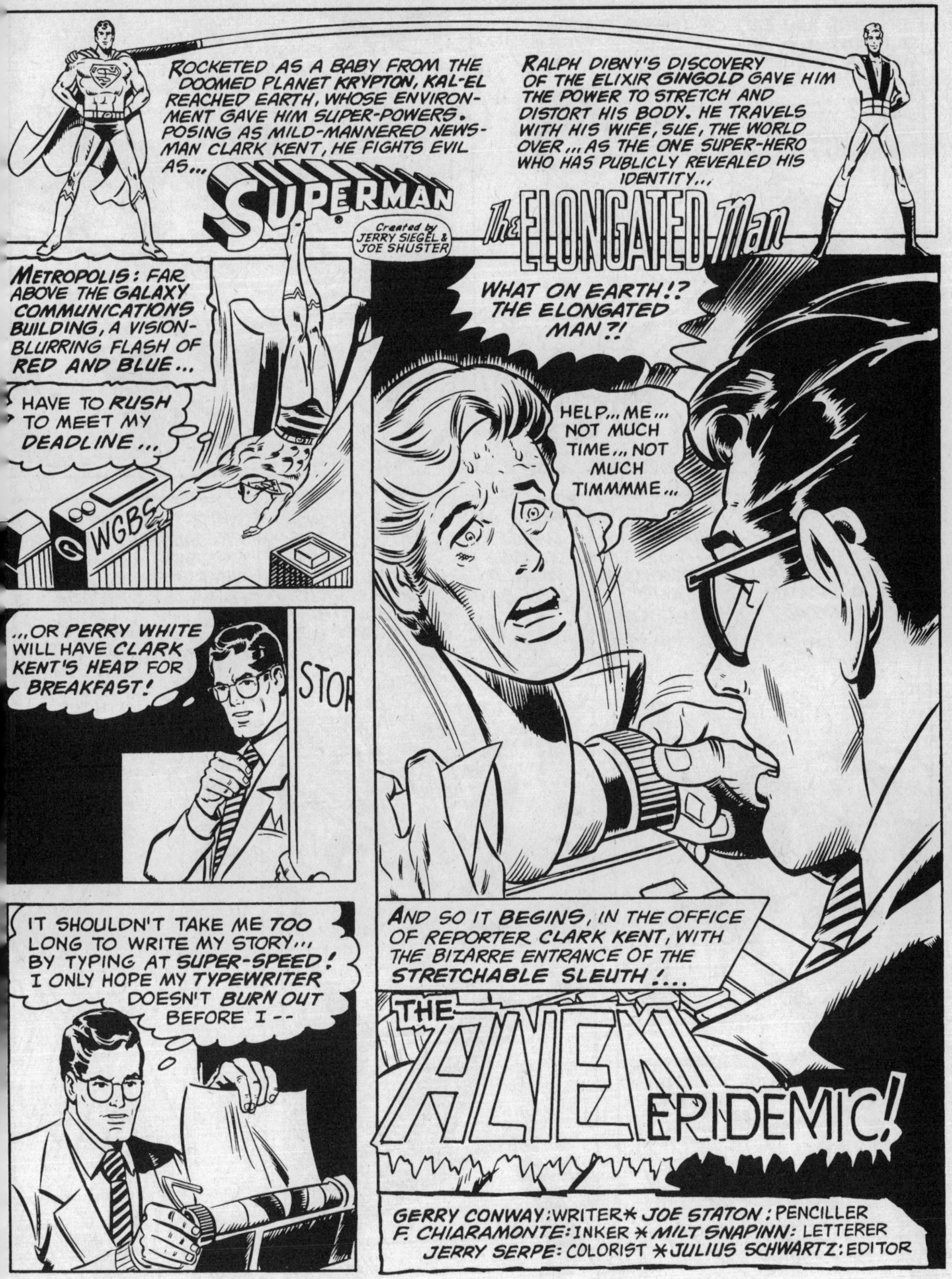
ROCKETED AS A BABY FROM THE DOOMED PLANET KRYPTON, KAL-EL REACHED EARTH, WHOSE ENVIRONMENT GAVE HIM SUPER-POWERS. POSING AS MILD-MANNERED NEWSMAN CLARK KENT, HE FIGHTS EVIL AS...
SUPERMAN
Created by JERRY SIEGEL & JOE SHUSTER
RALPH DIBNY'S DISCOVERY OF THE ELIXIR GINGOLD GAVE HIM THE POWER TO STRETCH AND DISTORT HIS BODY. HE TRAVELS WITH HIS WIFE, SUE, THE WORLD OVER... AS THE ONE SUPER-HERO WHO HAS PUBLICLY REVEALED HIS IDENTITY...
The ELONGATED Man
METROPOLIS: FAR ABOVE THE GALAXY COMMUNICATIONS BUILDING, A VISION-BLURRING FLASH OF RED AND BLUE...
HAVE TO RUSH TO MEET MY DEADLINE...
WGBS
...OR PERRY WHITE WILL HAVE CLARK KENT'S HEAD FOR BREAKFAST!
STOR
IT SHOULDN'T TAKE ME TOO LONG TO WRITE MY STORY... BY TYPING AT SUPER-SPEED! I ONLY HOPE MY TYPEWRITER DOESN'T BURN OUT BEFORE I --
WHAT ON EARTH!? THE ELONGATED MAN?!
HELP... ME... NOT MUCH TIME... NOT MUCH TIMMMME...
AND SO IT BEGINS, IN THE OFFICE OF REPORTER CLARK KENT, WITH THE BIZARRE ENTRANCE OF THE STRETCHABLE SLEUTH!...
THE ALIEN EPIDEMIC!
GERRY CONWAY: WRITER * JOE STATON: PENCILLER
F. CHIARAMONTE: INKER * MILT SNAPINN: LETTERER
JERRY SERPE: COLORIST * JULIUS SCHWARTZ: EDITOR

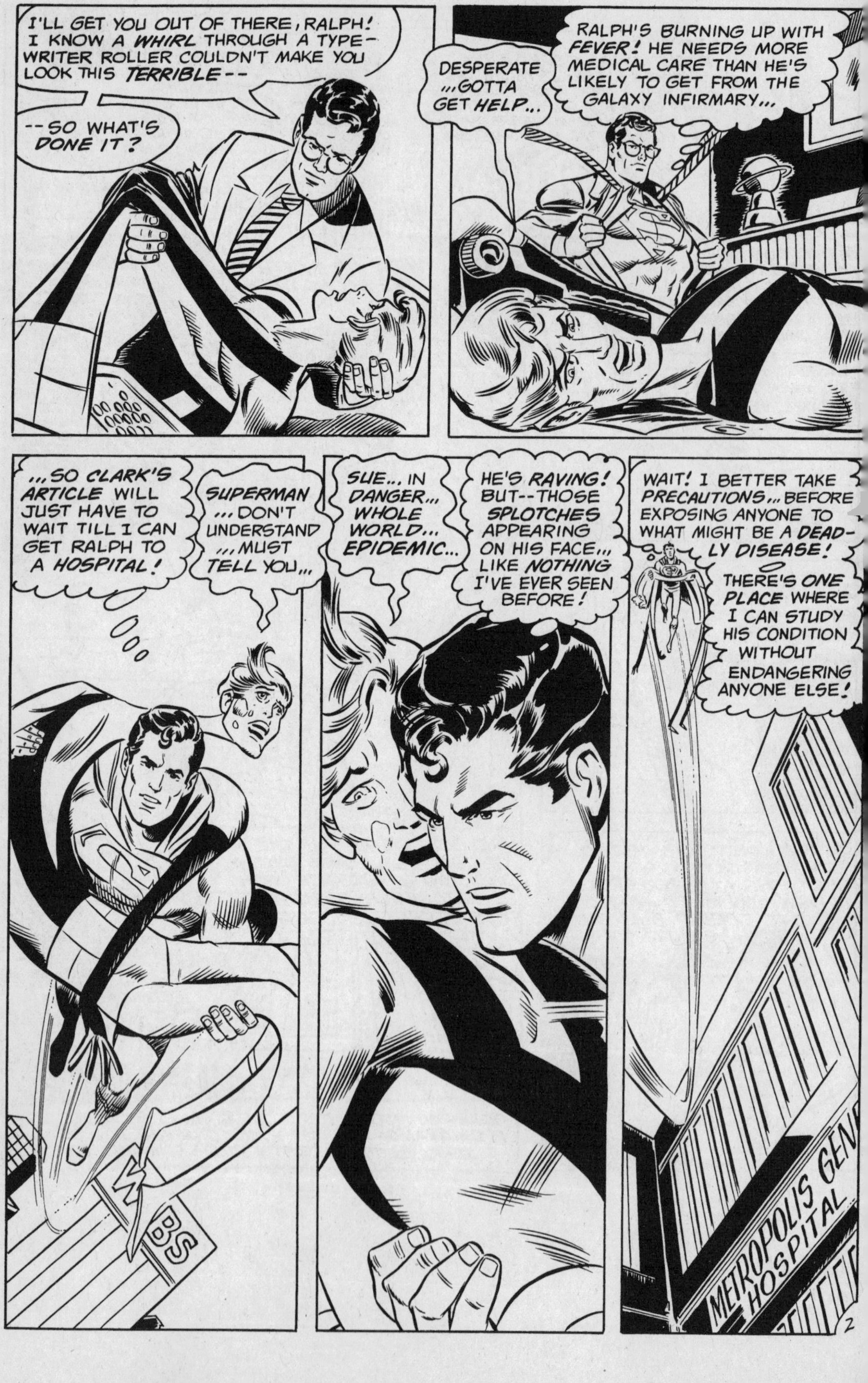
I'LL GET YOU OUT OF THERE, RALPH! I KNOW A WHIRL THROUGH A TYPE-WRITER ROLLER COULDN'T MAKE YOU LOOK THIS TERRIBLE--
--SO WHAT'S DONE IT?
DESPERATE ...GOTTA GET HELP...
RALPH'S BURNING UP WITH FEVER! HE NEEDS MORE MEDICAL CARE THAN HE'S LIKELY TO GET FROM THE GALAXY INFIRMARY...
...SO CLARK'S ARTICLE WILL JUST HAVE TO WAIT TILL I CAN GET RALPH TO A HOSPITAL!
SUPERMAN ...DON'T UNDERSTAND ...MUST TELL YOU...
SUE... IN DANGER... WHOLE WORLD... EPIDEMIC...
HE'S RAVING! BUT--THOSE SPLOTCHES APPEARING ON HIS FACE... LIKE NOTHING I'VE EVER SEEN BEFORE!
WAIT! I BETTER TAKE PRECAUTIONS... BEFORE EXPOSING ANYONE TO WHAT MIGHT BE A DEADLY DISEASE!
THERE'S ONE PLACE WHERE I CAN STUDY HIS CONDITION WITHOUT ENDANGERING ANYONE ELSE!
WBS
METROPOLIS GEN HOSPITAL
2

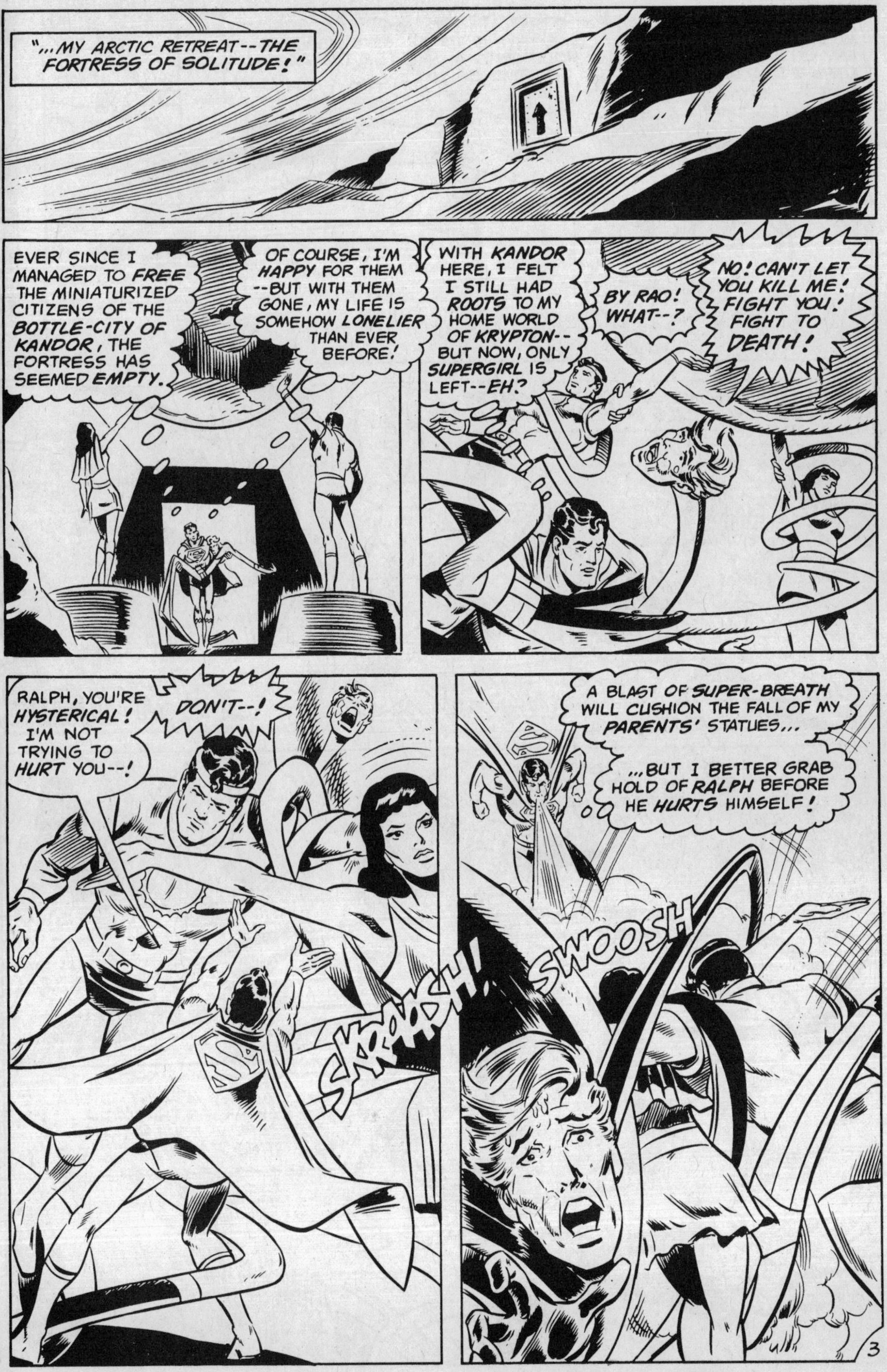
"...MY ARCTIC RETREAT--THE FORTRESS OF SOLITUDE!"
EVER SINCE I MANAGED TO FREE THE MINIATURIZED CITIZENS OF THE BOTTLE-CITY OF KANDOR, THE FORTRESS HAS SEEMED EMPTY.
OF COURSE, I'M HAPPY FOR THEM --BUT WITH THEM GONE, MY LIFE IS SOMEHOW LONELIER THAN EVER BEFORE!
WITH KANDOR HERE, I FELT I STILL HAD ROOTS TO MY HOME WORLD OF KRYPTON-- BUT NOW, ONLY SUPERGIRL IS LEFT--EH?
BY RAO! WHAT--?
NO! CAN'T LET YOU KILL ME! FIGHT YOU! FIGHT TO DEATH!
RALPH, YOU'RE HYSTERICAL! I'M NOT TRYING TO HURT YOU--!
DON'T--!
SKROOSH!
A BLAST OF SUPER-BREATH WILL CUSHION THE FALL OF MY PARENTS' STATUES...
...BUT I BETTER GRAB HOLD OF RALPH BEFORE HE HURTS HIMSELF!
SWOOSH
3

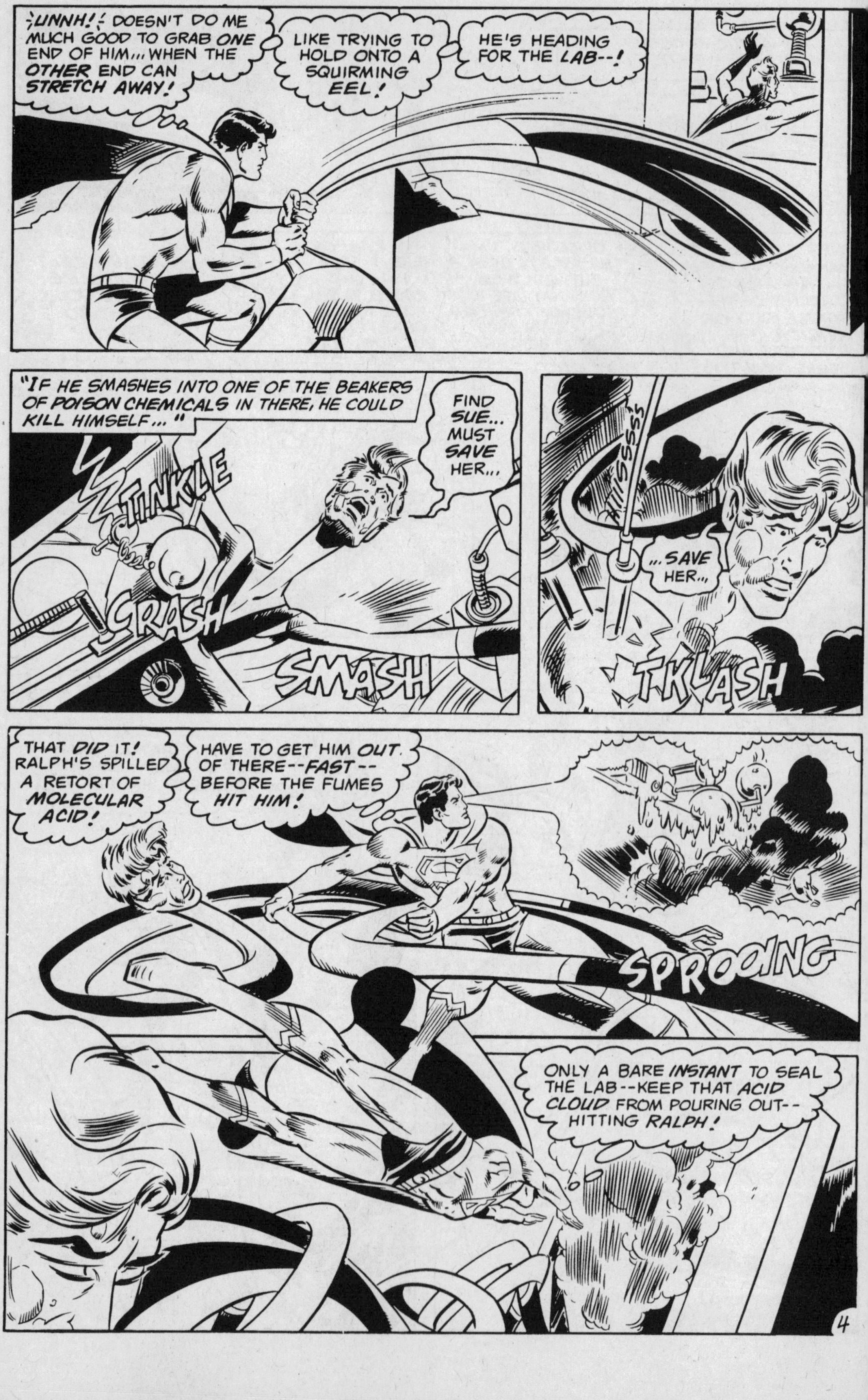
-UNNH!- DOESN'T DO ME MUCH GOOD TO GRAB ONE END OF HIM... WHEN THE OTHER END CAN STRETCH AWAY!
LIKE TRYING TO HOLD ONTO A SQUIRMING EEL!
HE'S HEADING FOR THE LAB--!
"IF HE SMASHES INTO ONE OF THE BEAKERS OF POISON CHEMICALS IN THERE, HE COULD KILL HIMSELF..."
FIND SUE... MUST SAVE HER...
TINKLE
CRASH
SMASH
HISSSSSS
...SAVE HER...
TKLASH
THAT DID IT! RALPH'S SPILLED A RETORT OF MOLECULAR ACID!
HAVE TO GET HIM OUT OF THERE--FAST--BEFORE THE FUMES HIT HIM!
SPROOING
ONLY A BARE INSTANT TO SEAL THE LAB--KEEP THAT ACID CLOUD FROM POURING OUT--HITTING RALPH!
4

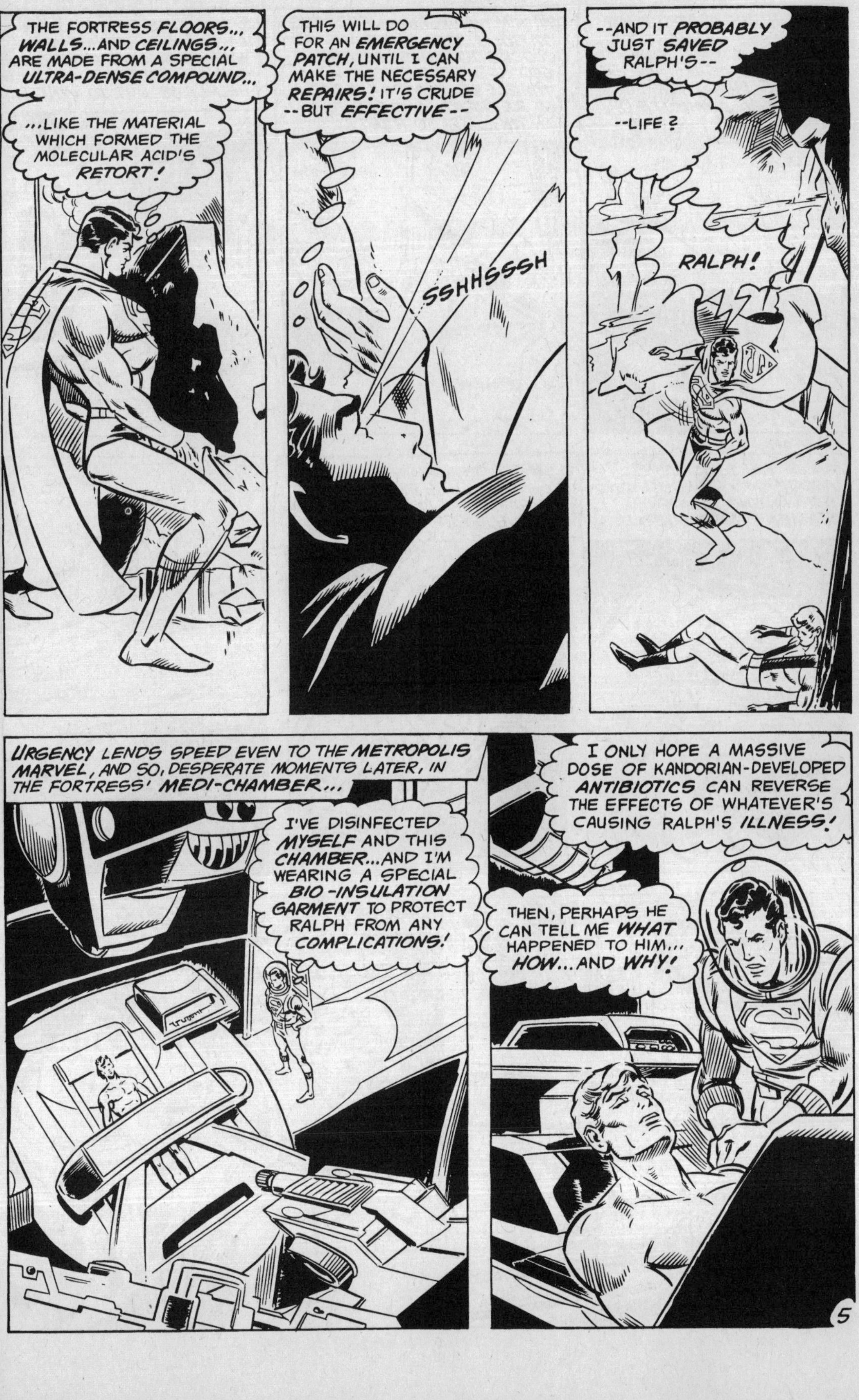
THE FORTRESS FLOORS... WALLS...AND CEILINGS... ARE MADE FROM A SPECIAL ULTRA-DENSE COMPOUND...
...LIKE THE MATERIAL WHICH FORMED THE MOLECULAR ACID'S RETORT!
THIS WILL DO FOR AN EMERGENCY PATCH, UNTIL I CAN MAKE THE NECESSARY REPAIRS! IT'S CRUDE --BUT EFFECTIVE--
SSHHSSSH
--AND IT PROBABLY JUST SAVED RALPH'S--
--LIFE?
RALPH!
URGENCY LENDS SPEED EVEN TO THE METROPOLIS MARVEL, AND SO, DESPERATE MOMENTS LATER, IN THE FORTRESS' MEDI-CHAMBER...
I'VE DISINFECTED MYSELF AND THIS CHAMBER...AND I'M WEARING A SPECIAL BIO-INSULATION GARMENT TO PROTECT RALPH FROM ANY COMPLICATIONS!
I ONLY HOPE A MASSIVE DOSE OF KANDORIAN-DEVELOPED ANTIBIOTICS CAN REVERSE THE EFFECTS OF WHATEVER'S CAUSING RALPH'S ILLNESS!
THEN, PERHAPS HE CAN TELL ME WHAT HAPPENED TO HIM... HOW...AND WHY!
5

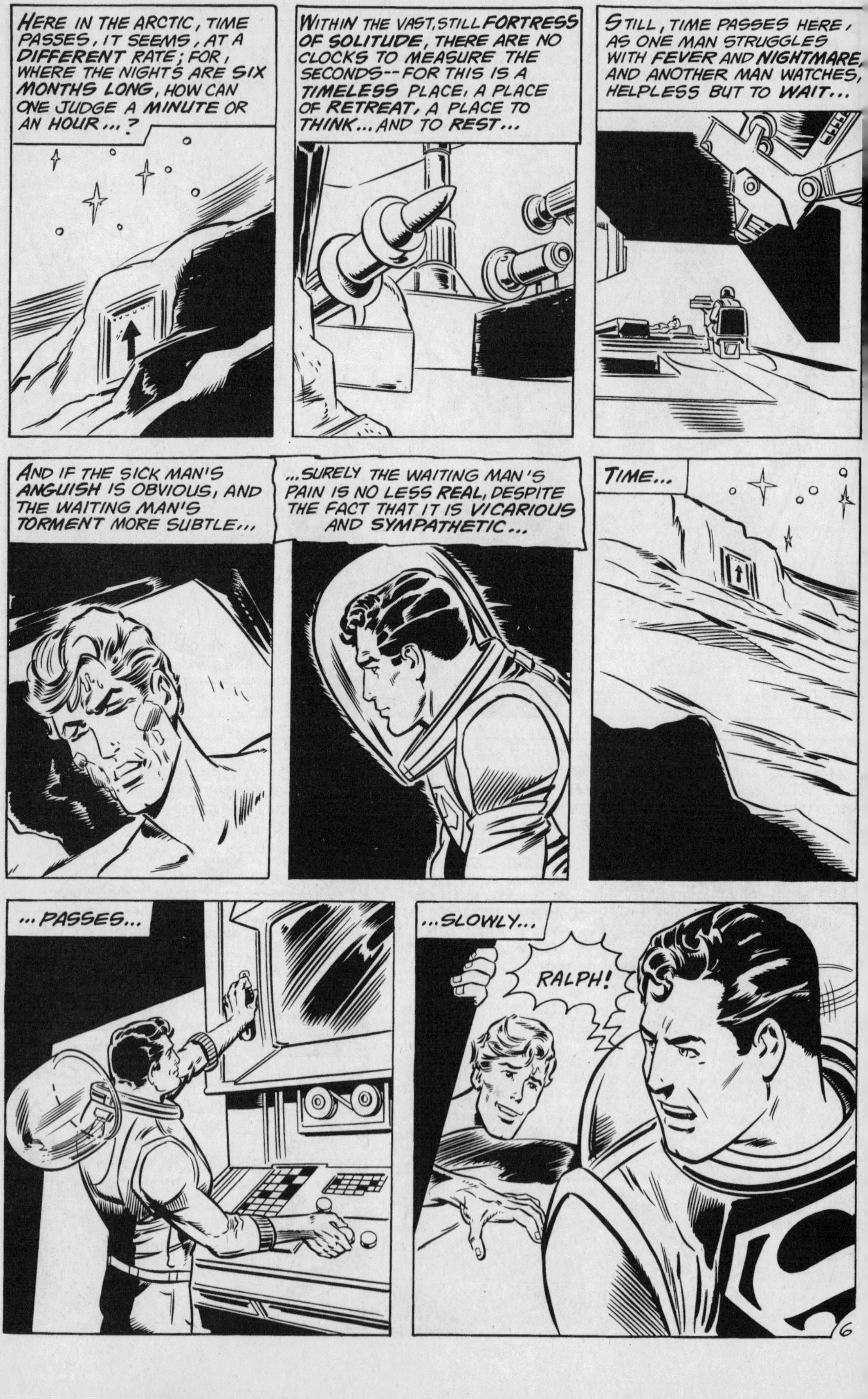
HERE IN THE ARCTIC, TIME PASSES, IT SEEMS, AT A DIFFERENT RATE; FOR, WHERE THE NIGHTS ARE SIX MONTHS LONG, HOW CAN ONE JUDGE A MINUTE OR AN HOUR...?
WITHIN THE VAST, STILL FORTRESS OF SOLITUDE, THERE ARE NO CLOCKS TO MEASURE THE SECONDS--FOR THIS IS A TIMELESS PLACE, A PLACE OF RETREAT, A PLACE TO THINK... AND TO REST...
STILL, TIME PASSES HERE, AS ONE MAN STRUGGLES WITH FEVER AND NIGHTMARE, AND ANOTHER MAN WATCHES, HELPLESS BUT TO WAIT...
AND IF THE SICK MAN'S ANGUISH IS OBVIOUS, AND THE WAITING MAN'S TORMENT MORE SUBTLE...
...SURELY THE WAITING MAN'S PAIN IS NO LESS REAL, DESPITE THE FACT THAT IT IS VICARIOUS AND SYMPATHETIC...
TIME...
...PASSES...
...SLOWLY...
RALPH!
6

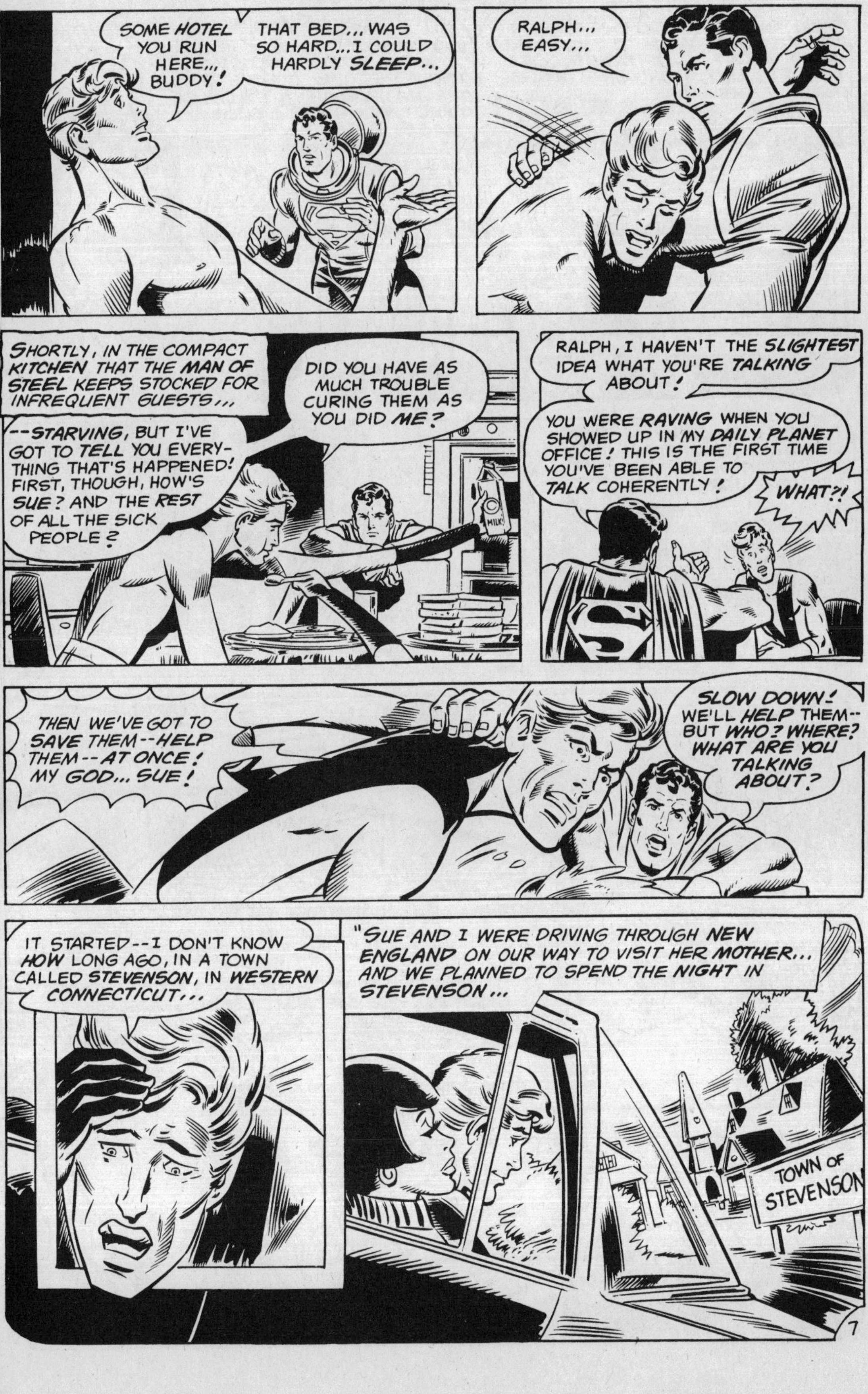
SOME HOTEL YOU RUN HERE... BUDDY!
THAT BED... WAS SO HARD... I COULD HARDLY SLEEP...
RALPH... EASY...
SHORTLY, IN THE COMPACT KITCHEN THAT THE MAN OF STEEL KEEPS STOCKED FOR INFREQUENT GUESTS...
--STARVING, BUT I'VE GOT TO TELL YOU EVERYTHING THAT'S HAPPENED! FIRST, THOUGH, HOW'S SUE? AND THE REST OF ALL THE SICK PEOPLE?
DID YOU HAVE AS MUCH TROUBLE CURING THEM AS YOU DID ME?
MILK
RALPH, I HAVEN'T THE SLIGHTEST IDEA WHAT YOU'RE TALKING ABOUT!
YOU WERE RAVING WHEN YOU SHOWED UP IN MY DAILY PLANET OFFICE! THIS IS THE FIRST TIME YOU'VE BEEN ABLE TO TALK COHERENTLY!
WHAT?!
THEN WE'VE GOT TO SAVE THEM--HELP THEM--AT ONCE! MY GOD... SUE!
SLOW DOWN! WE'LL HELP THEM-- BUT WHO? WHERE? WHAT ARE YOU TALKING ABOUT?
IT STARTED--I DON'T KNOW HOW LONG AGO, IN A TOWN CALLED STEVENSON, IN WESTERN CONNECTICUT...
"SUE AND I WERE DRIVING THROUGH NEW ENGLAND ON OUR WAY TO VISIT HER MOTHER... AND WE PLANNED TO SPEND THE NIGHT IN STEVENSON...
TOWN OF STEVENSON
7

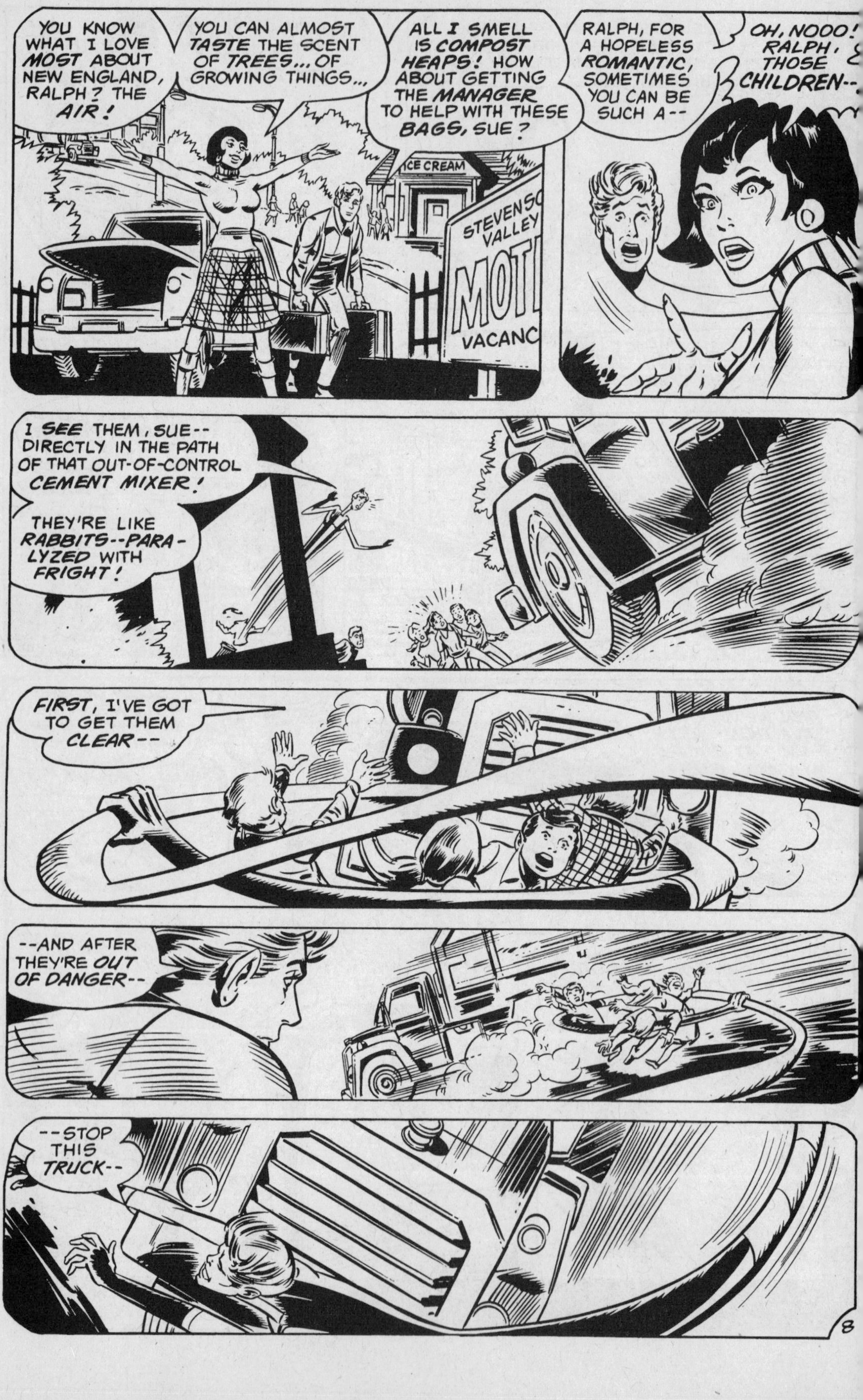
YOU KNOW WHAT I LOVE MOST ABOUT NEW ENGLAND, RALPH? THE AIR!
YOU CAN ALMOST TASTE THE SCENT OF TREES...OF GROWING THINGS...
ALL I SMELL IS COMPOST HEAPS! HOW ABOUT GETTING THE MANAGER TO HELP WITH THESE BAGS, SUE?
ICE CREAM
STEVENSO VALLEY
MOT
VACANC
RALPH, FOR A HOPELESS ROMANTIC, SOMETIMES YOU CAN BE SUCH A--
OH, NOOO! RALPH, THOSE CHILDREN--
I SEE THEM, SUE-- DIRECTLY IN THE PATH OF THAT OUT-OF-CONTROL CEMENT MIXER!
THEY'RE LIKE RABBITS--PARALYZED WITH FRIGHT!
FIRST, I'VE GOT TO GET THEM CLEAR--
--AND AFTER THEY'RE OUT OF DANGER--
--STOP THIS TRUCK--
8

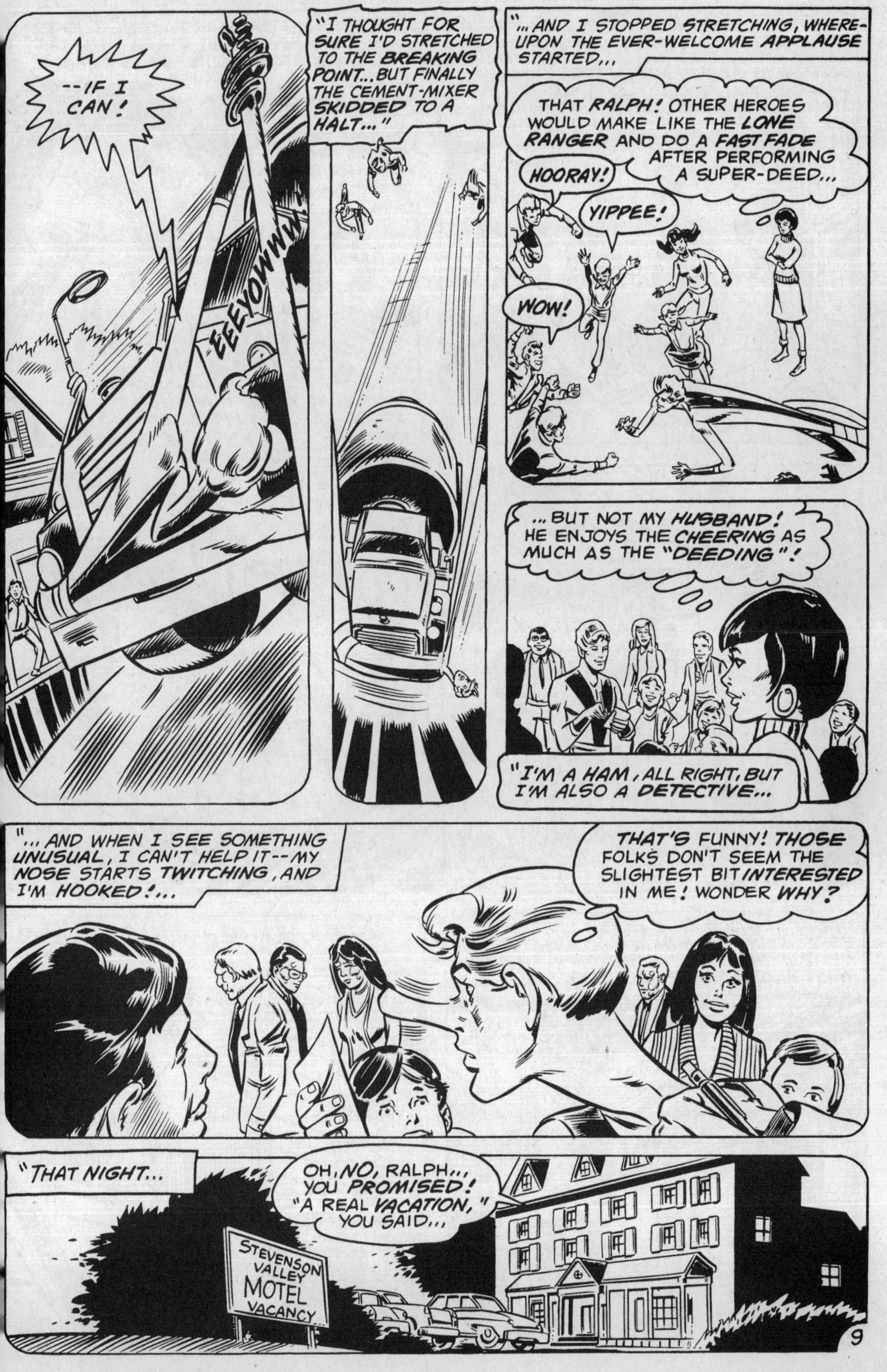
--IF I CAN!
EEEYOWWW!
"I THOUGHT FOR SURE I'D STRETCHED TO THE BREAKING POINT... BUT FINALLY THE CEMENT-MIXER SKIDDED TO A HALT..."
"...AND I STOPPED STRETCHING, WHEREUPON THE EVER-WELCOME APPLAUSE STARTED...
THAT RALPH! OTHER HEROES WOULD MAKE LIKE THE LONE RANGER AND DO A FAST FADE AFTER PERFORMING A SUPER-DEED...
HOORAY!
YIPPEE!
WOW!
...BUT NOT MY HUSBAND! HE ENJOYS THE CHEERING AS MUCH AS THE "DEEDING"!
"I'M A HAM, ALL RIGHT, BUT I'M ALSO A DETECTIVE...
"...AND WHEN I SEE SOMETHING UNUSUAL, I CAN'T HELP IT--MY NOSE STARTS TWITCHING, AND I'M HOOKED!...
THAT'S FUNNY! THOSE FOLKS DON'T SEEM THE SLIGHTEST BIT INTERESTED IN ME! WONDER WHY?
"THAT NIGHT...
OH, NO, RALPH... YOU PROMISED! "A REAL VACATION," YOU SAID...
STEVENSON VALLEY MOTEL VACANCY
9

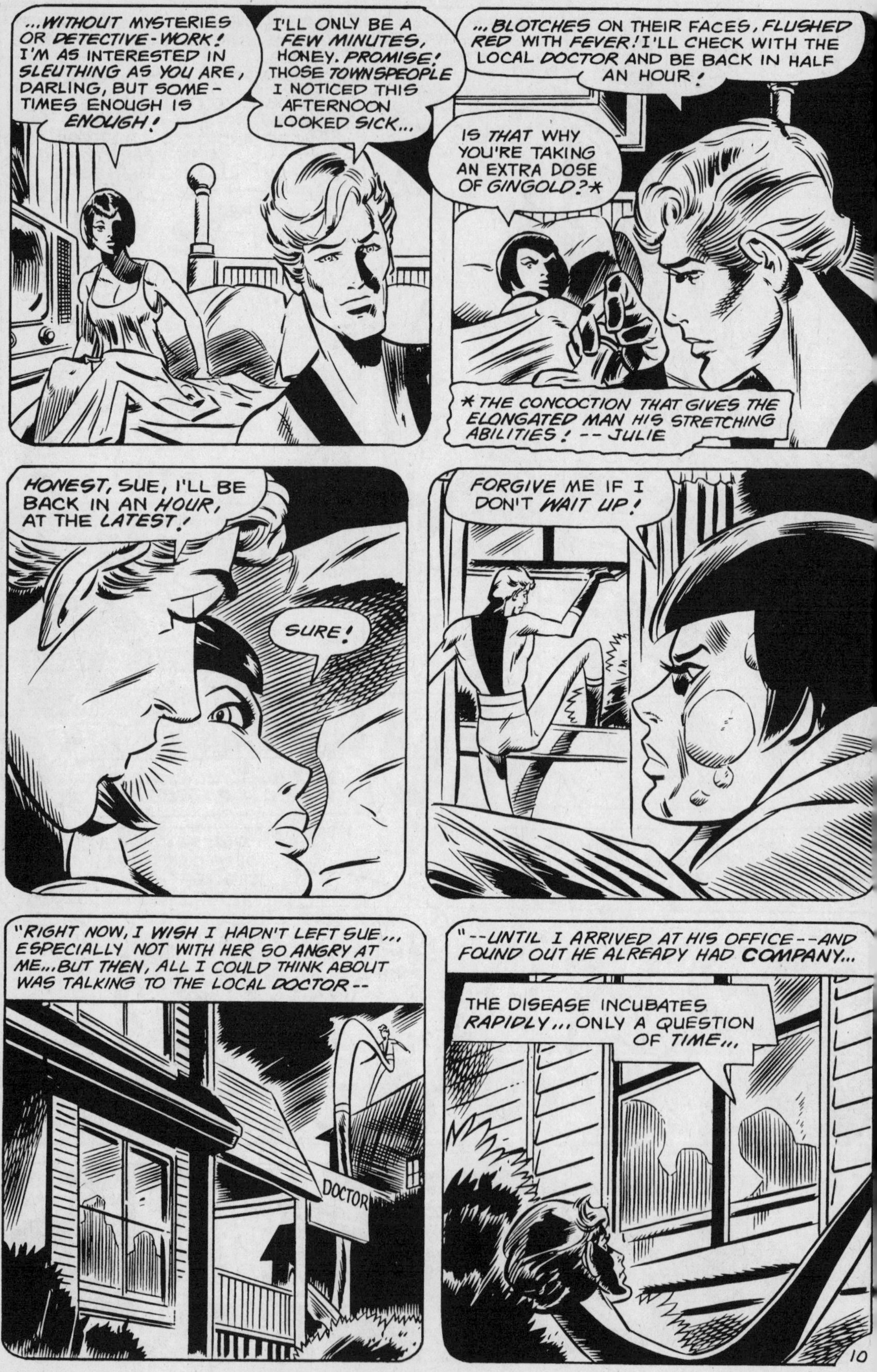
...WITHOUT MYSTERIES OR DETECTIVE-WORK! I'M AS INTERESTED IN SLEUTHING AS YOU ARE, DARLING, BUT SOME-TIMES ENOUGH IS ENOUGH!
I'LL ONLY BE A FEW MINUTES, HONEY. PROMISE! THOSE TOWNSPEOPLE I NOTICED THIS AFTERNOON LOOKED SICK...
...BLOTCHES ON THEIR FACES, FLUSHED RED WITH FEVER! I'LL CHECK WITH THE LOCAL DOCTOR AND BE BACK IN HALF AN HOUR!
IS THAT WHY YOU'RE TAKING AN EXTRA DOSE OF GINGOLD?*
*THE CONCOCTION THAT GIVES THE ELONGATED MAN HIS STRETCHING ABILITIES! --JULIE
HONEST, SUE, I'LL BE BACK IN AN HOUR, AT THE LATEST!
SURE!
FORGIVE ME IF I DON'T WAIT UP!
"RIGHT NOW, I WISH I HADN'T LEFT SUE... ESPECIALLY NOT WITH HER SO ANGRY AT ME...BUT THEN, ALL I COULD THINK ABOUT WAS TALKING TO THE LOCAL DOCTOR--
DOCTOR
"--UNTIL I ARRIVED AT HIS OFFICE--AND FOUND OUT HE ALREADY HAD COMPANY...
THE DISEASE INCUBATES RAPIDLY... ONLY A QUESTION OF TIME...
10

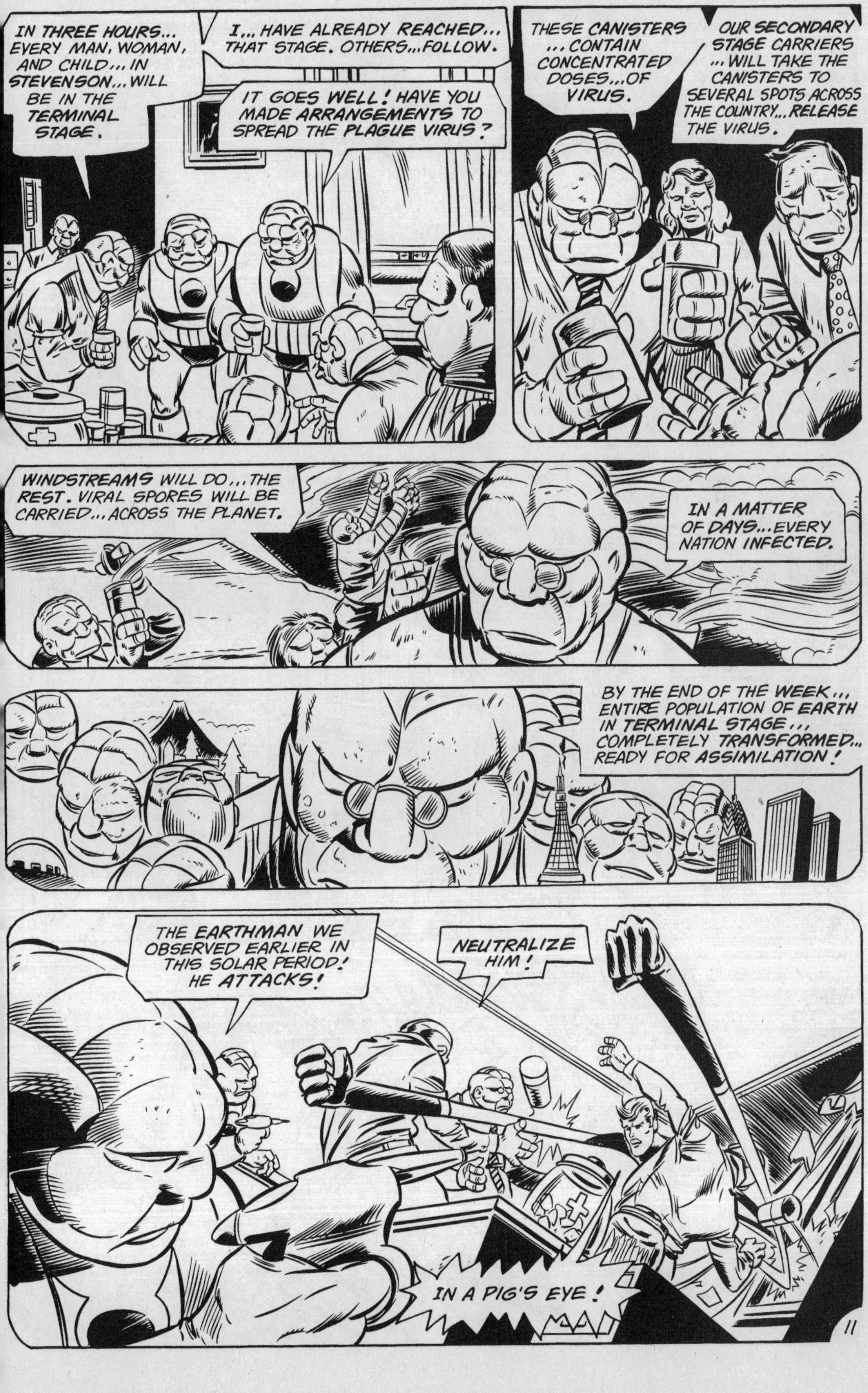
IN THREE HOURS... EVERY MAN, WOMAN, AND CHILD... IN STEVENSON... WILL BE IN THE TERMINAL STAGE.
I... HAVE ALREADY REACHED... THAT STAGE. OTHERS... FOLLOW.
IT GOES WELL! HAVE YOU MADE ARRANGEMENTS TO SPREAD THE PLAGUE VIRUS?
THESE CANISTERS ... CONTAIN CONCENTRATED DOSES... OF VIRUS.
OUR SECONDARY STAGE CARRIERS ... WILL TAKE THE CANISTERS TO SEVERAL SPOTS ACROSS THE COUNTRY... RELEASE THE VIRUS.
WINDSTREAMS WILL DO... THE REST. VIRAL SPORES WILL BE CARRIED... ACROSS THE PLANET.
IN A MATTER OF DAYS... EVERY NATION INFECTED.
BY THE END OF THE WEEK... ENTIRE POPULATION OF EARTH IN TERMINAL STAGE... COMPLETELY TRANSFORMED... READY FOR ASSIMILATION!
THE EARTHMAN WE OBSERVED EARLIER IN THIS SOLAR PERIOD! HE ATTACKS!
NEUTRALIZE HIM!
IN A PIG'S EYE!
11

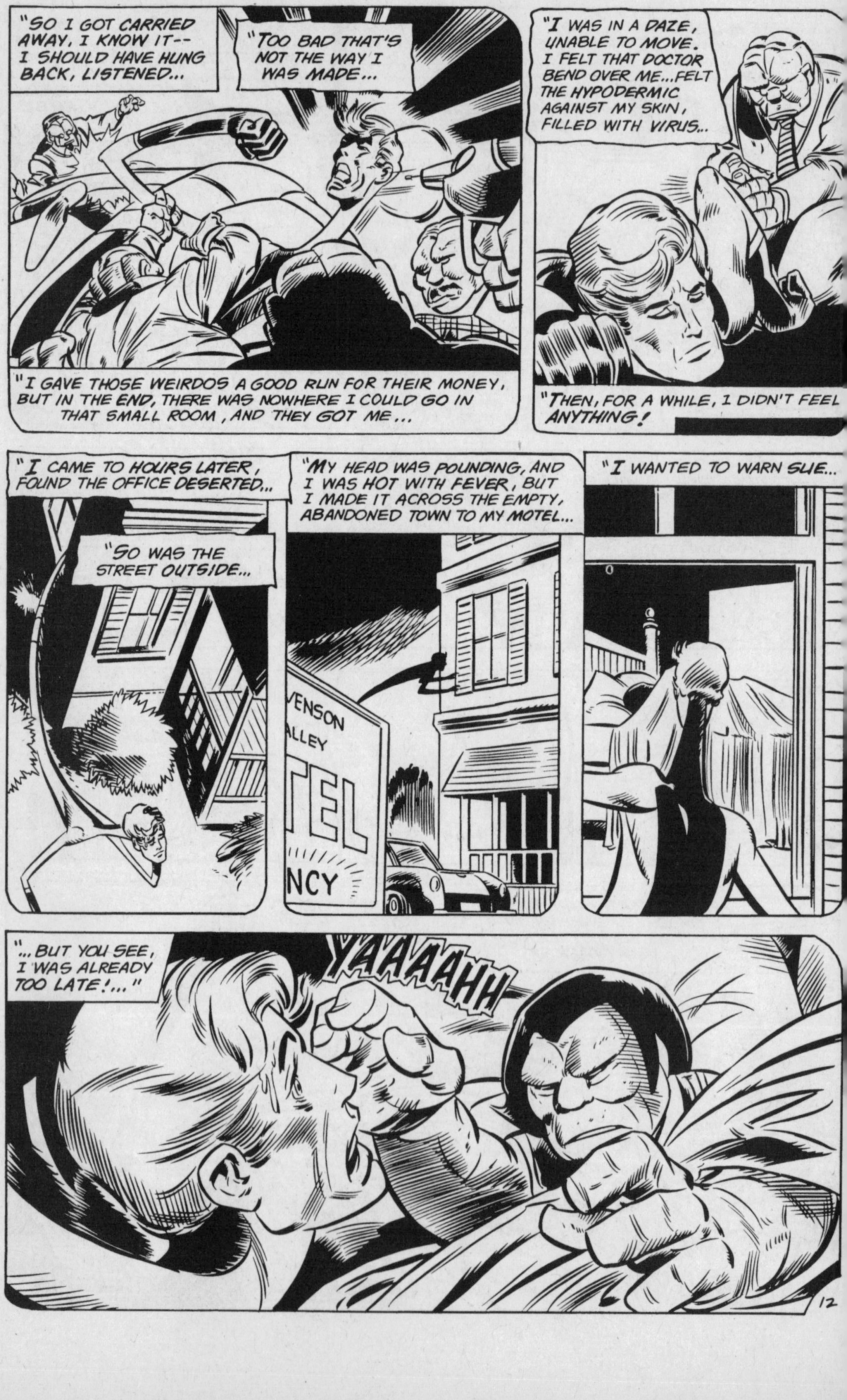
"SO I GOT CARRIED AWAY. I KNOW IT-- I SHOULD HAVE HUNG BACK, LISTENED...
"TOO BAD THAT'S NOT THE WAY I WAS MADE...
"I GAVE THOSE WEIRDOS A GOOD RUN FOR THEIR MONEY, BUT IN THE END, THERE WAS NOWHERE I COULD GO IN THAT SMALL ROOM, AND THEY GOT ME...
"I WAS IN A DAZE, UNABLE TO MOVE. I FELT THAT DOCTOR BEND OVER ME...FELT THE HYPODERMIC AGAINST MY SKIN, FILLED WITH VIRUS...
"THEN, FOR A WHILE, I DIDN'T FEEL ANYTHING!
"I CAME TO HOURS LATER, FOUND THE OFFICE DESERTED...
"SO WAS THE STREET OUTSIDE...
"MY HEAD WAS POUNDING, AND I WAS HOT WITH FEVER, BUT I MADE IT ACROSS THE EMPTY, ABANDONED TOWN TO MY MOTEL...
VENSON
ALLEY
TEL
NCY
"I WANTED TO WARN SUE...
"...BUT YOU SEE, I WAS ALREADY TOO LATE!..."
YAAAAAHH
12

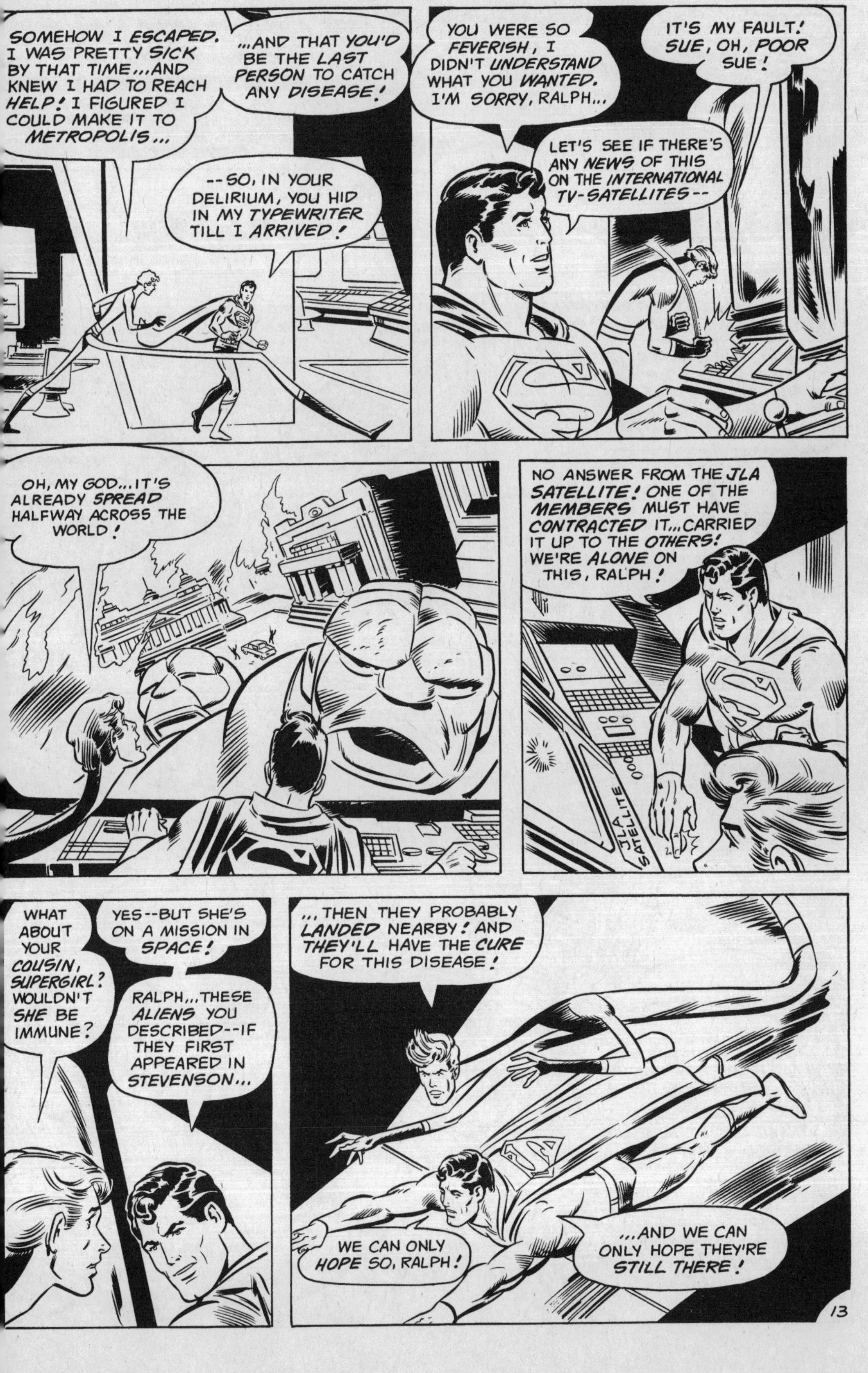
SOMEHOW I ESCAPED. I WAS PRETTY SICK BY THAT TIME... AND KNEW I HAD TO REACH HELP! I FIGURED I COULD MAKE IT TO METROPOLIS...
...AND THAT YOU'D BE THE LAST PERSON TO CATCH ANY DISEASE!
--SO, IN YOUR DELIRIUM, YOU HID IN MY TYPEWRITER TILL I ARRIVED!
YOU WERE SO FEVERISH, I DIDN'T UNDERSTAND WHAT YOU WANTED. I'M SORRY, RALPH...
IT'S MY FAULT! SUE, OH, POOR SUE!
LET'S SEE IF THERE'S ANY NEWS OF THIS ON THE INTERNATIONAL TV-SATELLITES--
OH, MY GOD... IT'S ALREADY SPREAD HALFWAY ACROSS THE WORLD!
NO ANSWER FROM THE JLA SATELLITE! ONE OF THE MEMBERS MUST HAVE CONTRACTED IT... CARRIED IT UP TO THE OTHERS! WE'RE ALONE ON THIS, RALPH!
JLA SATELLITE
WHAT ABOUT YOUR COUSIN, SUPERGIRL? WOULDN'T SHE BE IMMUNE?
YES--BUT SHE'S ON A MISSION IN SPACE!
RALPH... THESE ALIENS YOU DESCRIBED--IF THEY FIRST APPEARED IN STEVENSON...
...THEN THEY PROBABLY LANDED NEARBY! AND THEY'LL HAVE THE CURE FOR THIS DISEASE!
WE CAN ONLY HOPE SO, RALPH!
...AND WE CAN ONLY HOPE THEY'RE STILL THERE!
13

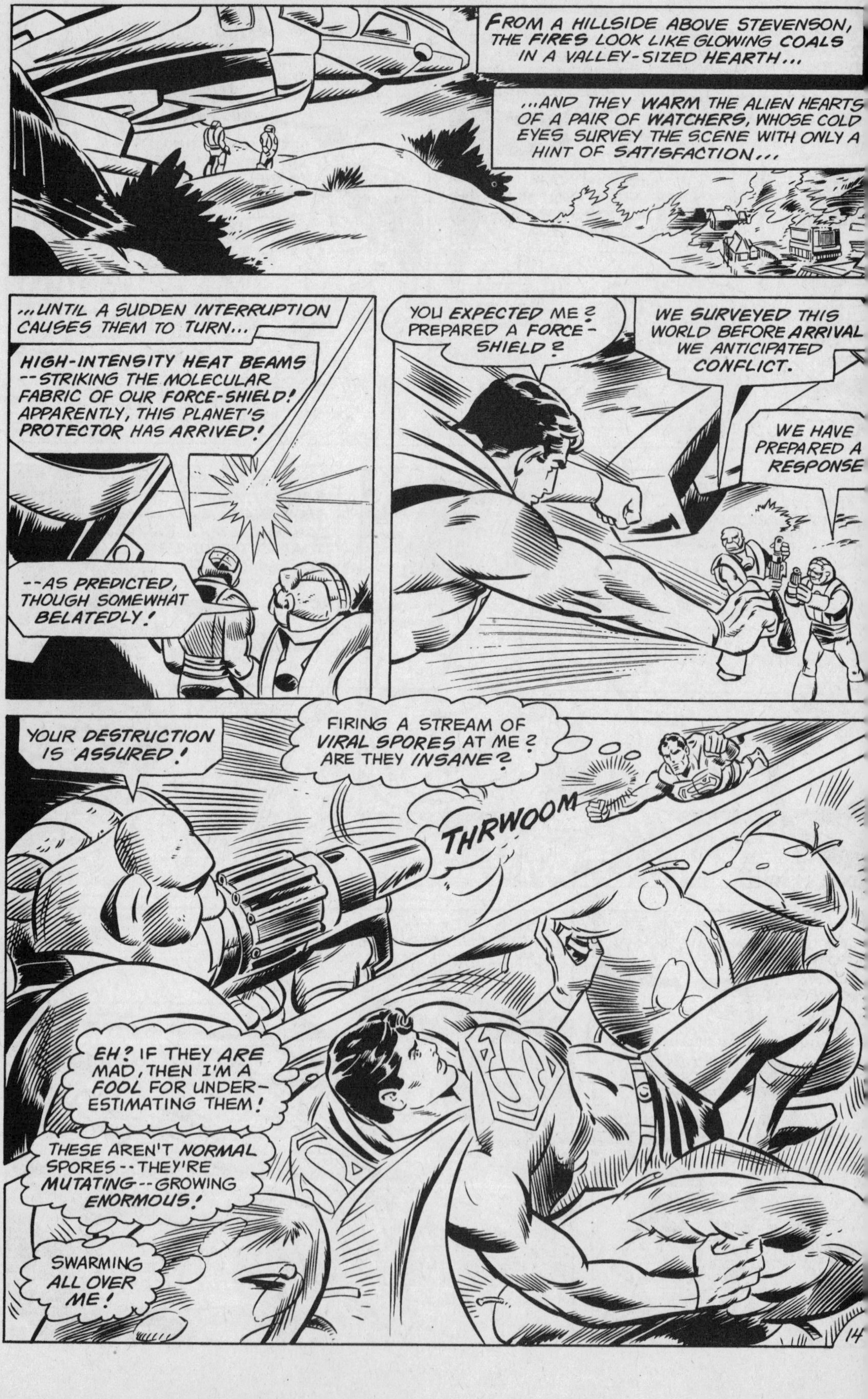
FROM A HILLSIDE ABOVE STEVENSON, THE FIRES LOOK LIKE GLOWING COALS IN A VALLEY-SIZED HEARTH...
...AND THEY WARM THE ALIEN HEARTS OF A PAIR OF WATCHERS, WHOSE COLD EYES SURVEY THE SCENE WITH ONLY A HINT OF SATISFACTION...
...UNTIL A SUDDEN INTERRUPTION CAUSES THEM TO TURN...
HIGH-INTENSITY HEAT BEAMS --STRIKING THE MOLECULAR FABRIC OF OUR FORCE-SHIELD! APPARENTLY, THIS PLANET'S PROTECTOR HAS ARRIVED!
--AS PREDICTED, THOUGH SOMEWHAT BELATEDLY!
YOU EXPECTED ME? PREPARED A FORCE-SHIELD?
WE SURVEYED THIS WORLD BEFORE ARRIVAL WE ANTICIPATED CONFLICT.
WE HAVE PREPARED A RESPONSE
YOUR DESTRUCTION IS ASSURED!
FIRING A STREAM OF VIRAL SPORES AT ME? ARE THEY INSANE?
THRWOOM
EH? IF THEY ARE MAD, THEN I'M A FOOL FOR UNDER-ESTIMATING THEM!
THESE AREN'T NORMAL SPORES--THEY'RE MUTATING--GROWING ENORMOUS!
SWARMING ALL OVER ME!
14

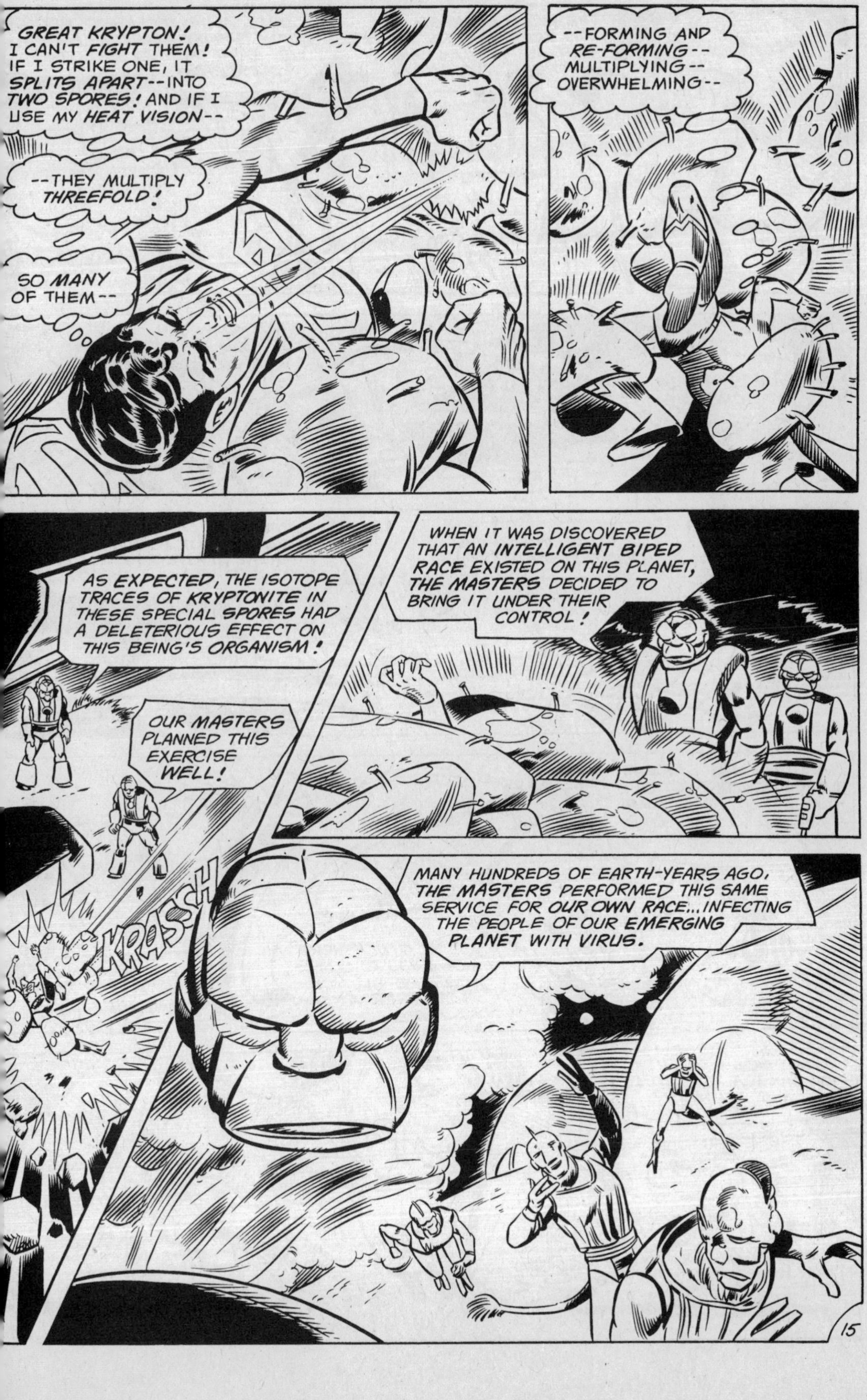
GREAT KRYPTON! I CAN'T FIGHT THEM! IF I STRIKE ONE, IT SPLITS APART--INTO TWO SPORES! AND IF I USE MY HEAT VISION--
--THEY MULTIPLY THREEFOLD!
SO MANY OF THEM--
--FORMING AND RE-FORMING--MULTIPLYING--OVERWHELMING--
AS EXPECTED, THE ISOTOPE TRACES OF KRYPTONITE IN THESE SPECIAL SPORES HAD A DELETERIOUS EFFECT ON THIS BEING'S ORGANISM!
OUR MASTERS PLANNED THIS EXERCISE WELL!
WHEN IT WAS DISCOVERED THAT AN INTELLIGENT BIPED RACE EXISTED ON THIS PLANET, THE MASTERS DECIDED TO BRING IT UNDER THEIR CONTROL!
KRASSH
MANY HUNDREDS OF EARTH-YEARS AGO, THE MASTERS PERFORMED THIS SAME SERVICE FOR OUR OWN RACE...INFECTING THE PEOPLE OF OUR EMERGING PLANET WITH VIRUS.
15

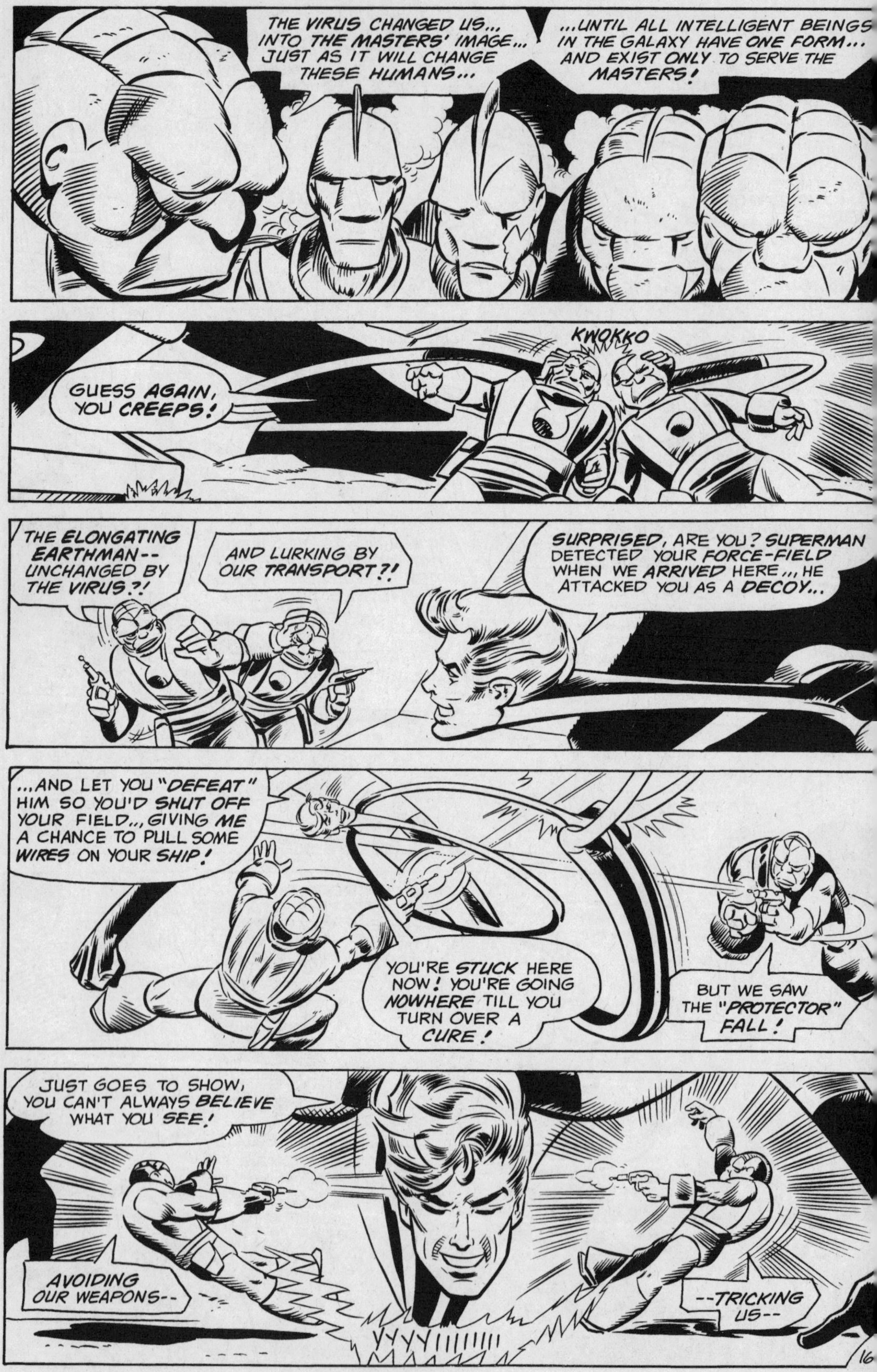
THE VIRUS CHANGED US... INTO THE MASTERS' IMAGE... JUST AS IT WILL CHANGE THESE HUMANS...
...UNTIL ALL INTELLIGENT BEINGS IN THE GALAXY HAVE ONE FORM... AND EXIST ONLY TO SERVE THE MASTERS!
KWOKKO
GUESS AGAIN, YOU CREEPS!
THE ELONGATING EARTHMAN-- UNCHANGED BY THE VIRUS?!
AND LURKING BY OUR TRANSPORT?!
SURPRISED, ARE YOU? SUPERMAN DETECTED YOUR FORCE-FIELD WHEN WE ARRIVED HERE... HE ATTACKED YOU AS A DECOY...
...AND LET YOU "DEFEAT" HIM SO YOU'D SHUT OFF YOUR FIELD... GIVING ME A CHANCE TO PULL SOME WIRES ON YOUR SHIP!
YOU'RE STUCK HERE NOW! YOU'RE GOING NOWHERE TILL YOU TURN OVER A CURE!
BUT WE SAW THE "PROTECTOR" FALL!
JUST GOES TO SHOW, YOU CAN'T ALWAYS BELIEVE WHAT YOU SEE!
AVOIDING OUR WEAPONS--
--TRICKING US--
16

OKAY, SUPERMAN ... YOU CAN *COME OUT* NOW! SUPERMAN--?

OH, GOOD LORD! WHAT IF HE REALLY *WAS*--

LIKE THE MAN SAID, *DON'T* ALWAYS BELIEVE WHAT YOU SEE!

THE DAY HASN'T *COME* WHEN I'LL BE DEFEATED *THAT* EASILY!

THE *KRYPTONITE* TRACES IN THOSE THINGS WEREN'T ENOUGH TO DO MUCH DAMAGE!

BUT THE MOMENTARY ELATION QUICKLY EVAPORATES, AS, MINUTES LATER...

NO GOOD! WE'VE BEEN OVER THIS SHIP WITH A *FINE-TOOTH COMB!*

NOT A *SIGN* OF A CURE...

...WHICH MEANS *SUE*... AND THE *OTHERS* ...ARE *DOOMED FOREVER!*

NOT *NECESSARILY*, RALPH! HAVEN'T YOU WONDERED WHY *YOU* WERE ABLE TO HOLD OUT AGAINST THE DISEASE AS LONG AS YOU *DID*?

AND WHY *SIMPLE ANTIBIOTICS* COULD CURE *YOU*-- AND NOT *OTHER* VICTIMS?

I CHECKED *METROPOLIS* WITH MY TELESCOPIC VISION--AND FOUND *JIMMY OLSEN* HAD RECOVERED, TOO!

HE USES *GINGOLD* TO BECOME *ELASTIC LAD*--MEANING THE CURE LIES *THERE!*

BUT--SUE IS *ALLERGIC* TO GINGOLD!

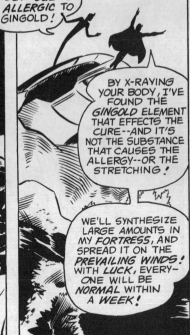

BY X-RAYING YOUR BODY, I'VE FOUND THE *GINGOLD* ELEMENT THAT EFFECTS THE CURE--AND IT'S NOT THE SUBSTANCE THAT CAUSES THE ALLERGY--OR THE STRETCHING!

WE'LL SYNTHESIZE LARGE AMOUNTS IN MY *FORTRESS*, AND SPREAD IT ON THE *PREVAILING WINDS!* WITH *LUCK*, EVERYONE WILL BE *NORMAL* WITHIN A *WEEK!*

AND *THEN*?

THEN, MY FRIEND, WE TRACK DOWN *THE MASTERS!*

--AND THAT'S WHEN OUR FIGHT WILL *REALLY* BEGIN!

FOR NOW-- THE END!

NEXT ISSUE: SUPERMAN TEAMS UP WITH *CAPT. COMET* TO BATTLE THE MUTANT MARVEL--

STARSTRIKER!!

17

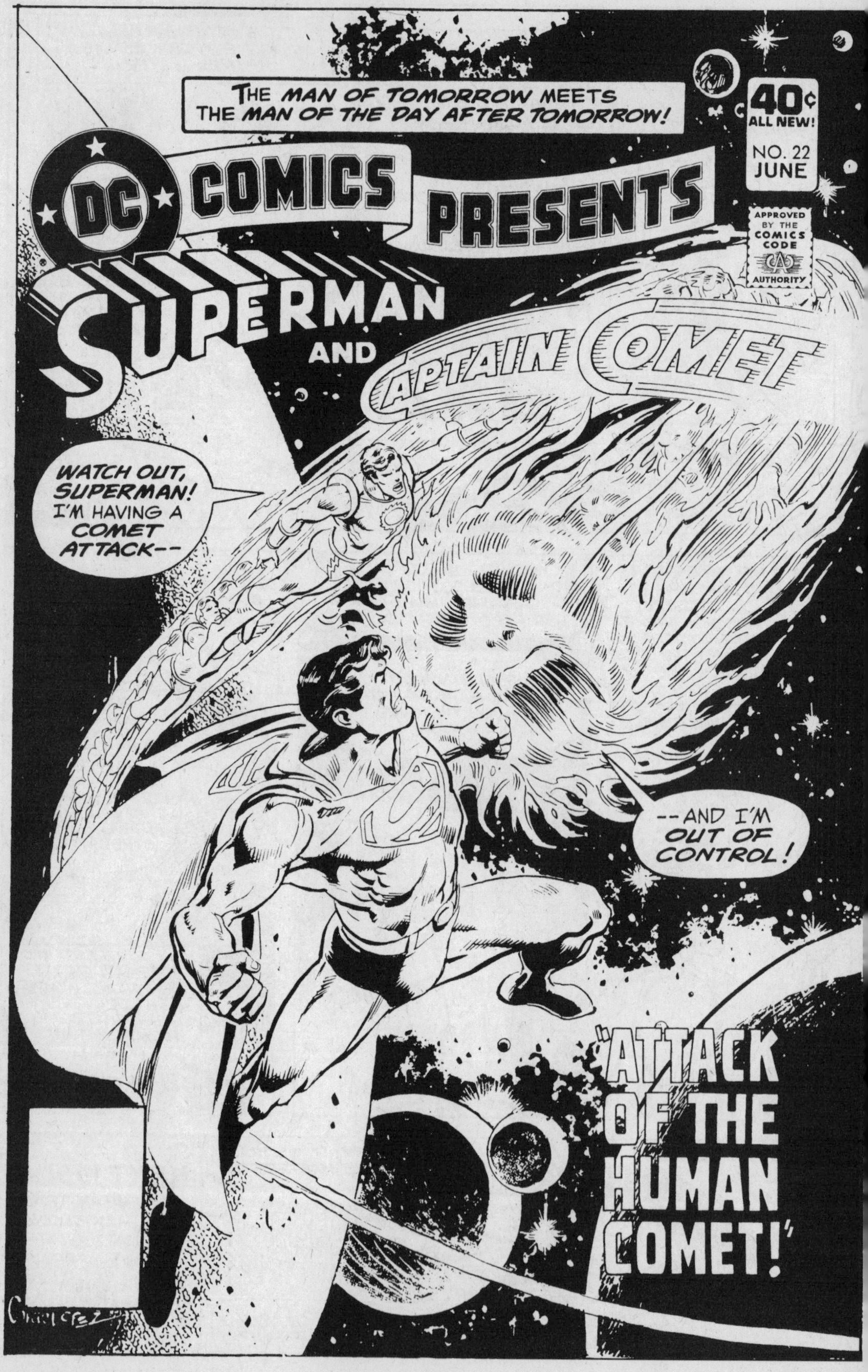
THE MAN OF TOMORROW MEETS THE MAN OF THE DAY AFTER TOMORROW!
40¢ ALL NEW!
NO. 22 JUNE
DC COMICS PRESENTS
APPROVED BY THE COMICS CODE AUTHORITY
SUPERMAN AND CAPTAIN COMET
WATCH OUT, SUPERMAN! I'M HAVING A COMET ATTACK--
--AND I'M OUT OF CONTROL!
"ATTACK OF THE HUMAN COMET!"

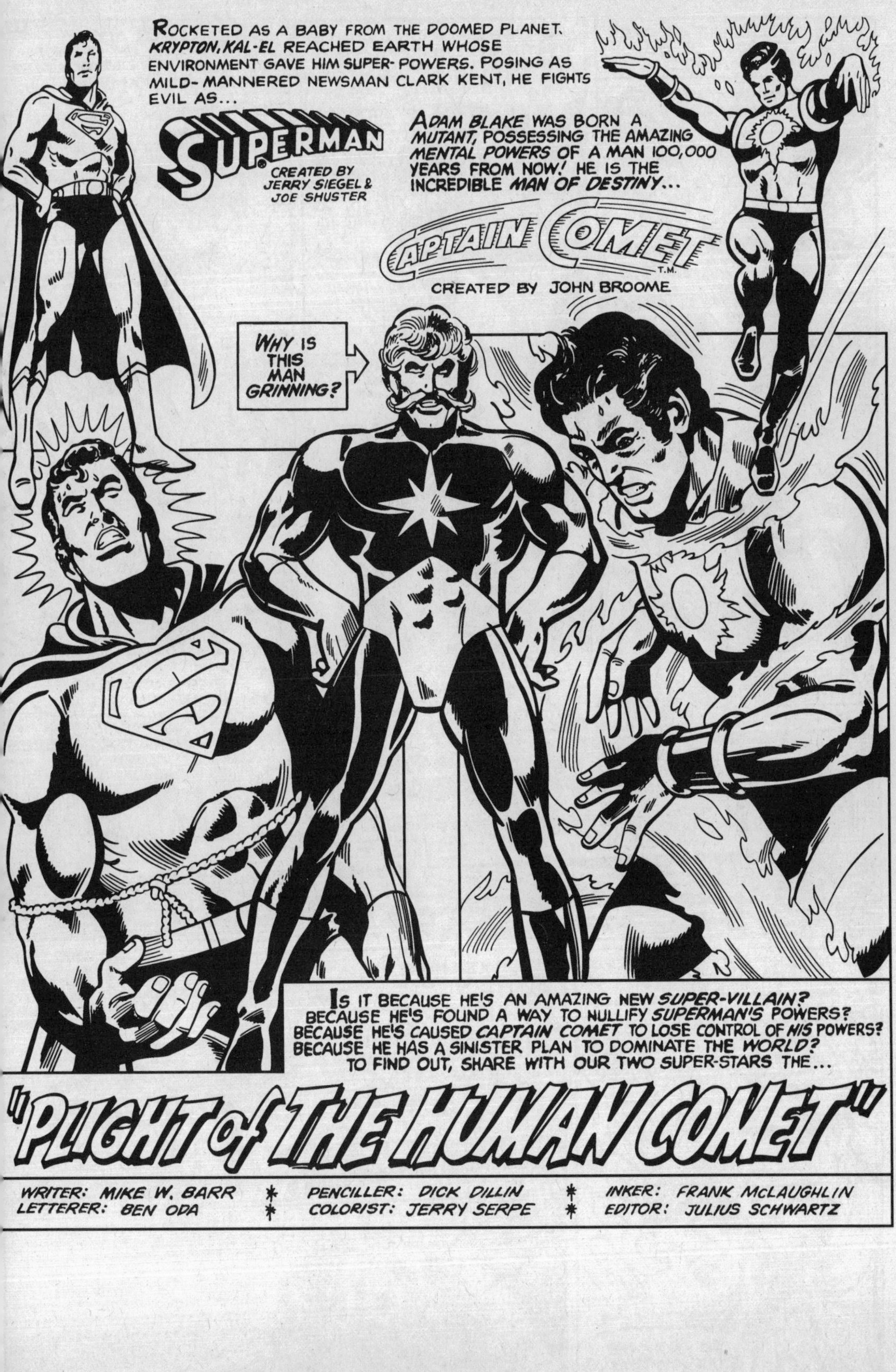
ROCKETED AS A BABY FROM THE DOOMED PLANET. KRYPTON, KAL-EL REACHED EARTH WHOSE ENVIRONMENT GAVE HIM SUPER-POWERS. POSING AS MILD-MANNERED NEWSMAN CLARK KENT, HE FIGHTS EVIL AS...
SUPERMAN
CREATED BY JERRY SIEGEL & JOE SHUSTER
ADAM BLAKE WAS BORN A MUTANT, POSSESSING THE AMAZING MENTAL POWERS OF A MAN 100,000 YEARS FROM NOW! HE IS THE INCREDIBLE MAN OF DESTINY...
CAPTAIN COMET T.M.
CREATED BY JOHN BROOME
WHY IS THIS MAN GRINNING?
IS IT BECAUSE HE'S AN AMAZING NEW SUPER-VILLAIN? BECAUSE HE'S FOUND A WAY TO NULLIFY SUPERMAN'S POWERS? BECAUSE HE'S CAUSED CAPTAIN COMET TO LOSE CONTROL OF HIS POWERS? BECAUSE HE HAS A SINISTER PLAN TO DOMINATE THE WORLD? TO FIND OUT, SHARE WITH OUR TWO SUPER-STARS THE...
"PLIGHT OF THE HUMAN COMET"
WRITER: MIKE W. BARR * PENCILLER: DICK DILLIN * INKER: FRANK McLAUGHLIN
LETTERER: BEN ODA * COLORIST: JERRY SERPE * EDITOR: JULIUS SCHWARTZ

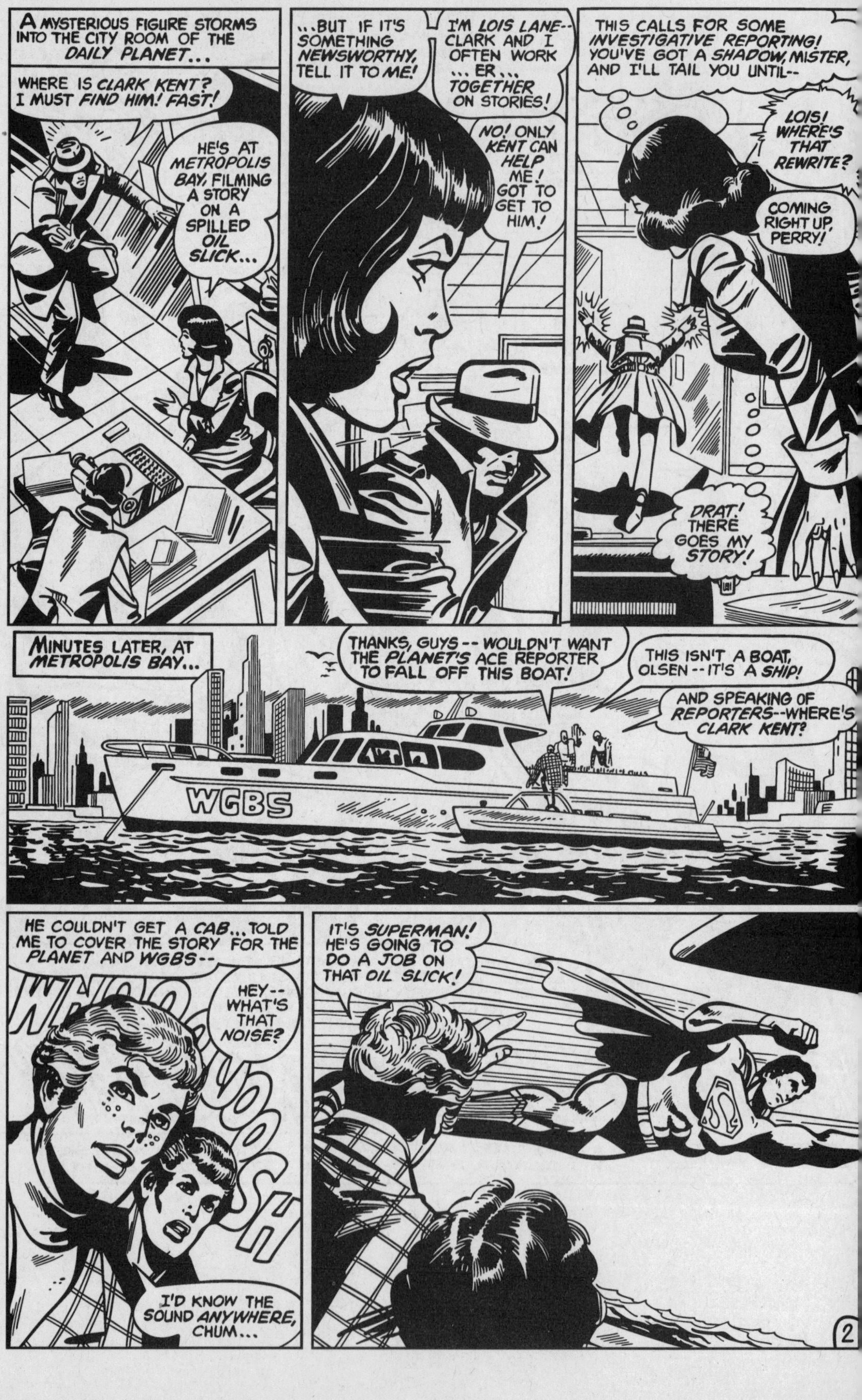
A MYSTERIOUS FIGURE STORMS INTO THE CITY ROOM OF THE DAILY PLANET...
WHERE IS CLARK KENT? I MUST FIND HIM! FAST!
HE'S AT METROPOLIS BAY, FILMING A STORY ON A SPILLED OIL SLICK...
...BUT IF IT'S SOMETHING NEWSWORTHY, TELL IT TO ME!
I'M LOIS LANE-- CLARK AND I OFTEN WORK ... ER... TOGETHER ON STORIES!
NO! ONLY KENT CAN HELP ME! GOT TO GET TO HIM!
THIS CALLS FOR SOME INVESTIGATIVE REPORTING! YOU'VE GOT A SHADOW, MISTER, AND I'LL TAIL YOU UNTIL--
LOIS! WHERE'S THAT REWRITE?
COMING RIGHT UP, PERRY!
DRAT! THERE GOES MY STORY!
MINUTES LATER, AT METROPOLIS BAY...
THANKS, GUYS -- WOULDN'T WANT THE PLANET'S ACE REPORTER TO FALL OFF THIS BOAT!
THIS ISN'T A BOAT, OLSEN -- IT'S A SHIP!
AND SPEAKING OF REPORTERS--WHERE'S CLARK KENT?
WGBS
HE COULDN'T GET A CAB... TOLD ME TO COVER THE STORY FOR THE PLANET AND WGBS--
WHOOOOOSH
HEY-- WHAT'S THAT NOISE?
I'D KNOW THE SOUND ANYWHERE, CHUM...
IT'S SUPERMAN! HE'S GOING TO DO A JOB ON THAT OIL SLICK!
2

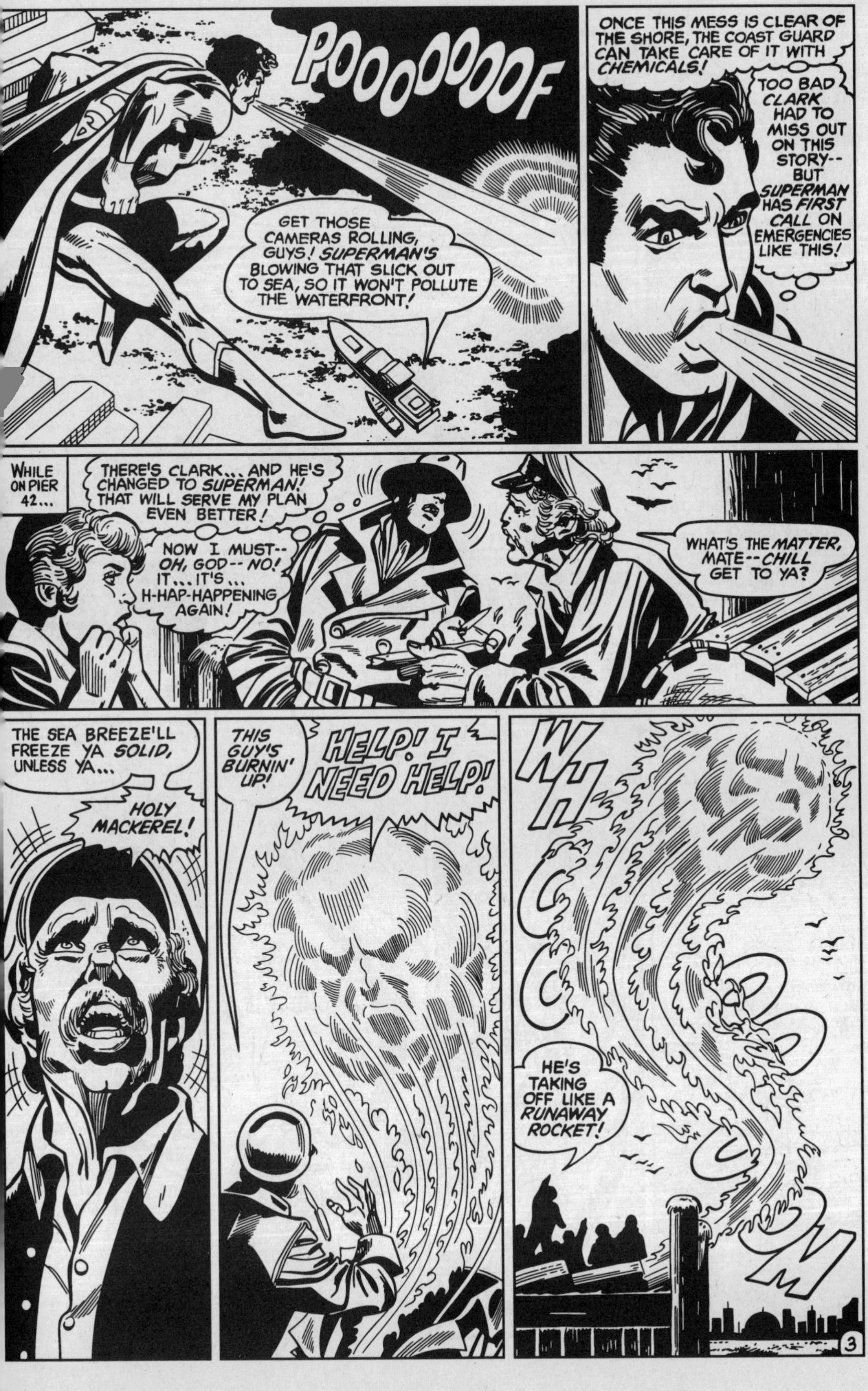
POOOOOOOF
GET THOSE CAMERAS ROLLING, GUYS! SUPERMAN'S BLOWING THAT SLICK OUT TO SEA, SO IT WON'T POLLUTE THE WATERFRONT!
ONCE THIS MESS IS CLEAR OF THE SHORE, THE COAST GUARD CAN TAKE CARE OF IT WITH CHEMICALS!
TOO BAD CLARK HAD TO MISS OUT ON THIS STORY-- BUT SUPERMAN HAS FIRST CALL ON EMERGENCIES LIKE THIS!
WHILE ON PIER 42...
THERE'S CLARK... AND HE'S CHANGED TO SUPERMAN! THAT WILL SERVE MY PLAN EVEN BETTER!
NOW I MUST-- OH, GOD-- NO! IT... IT'S... H-HAP-HAPPENING AGAIN!
WHAT'S THE MATTER, MATE--CHILL GET TO YA?
THE SEA BREEZE'LL FREEZE YA SOLID, UNLESS YA...
HOLY MACKEREL!
THIS GUY'S BURNIN' UP!
HELP! I NEED HELP!
WH
HE'S TAKING OFF LIKE A RUNAWAY ROCKET!
3

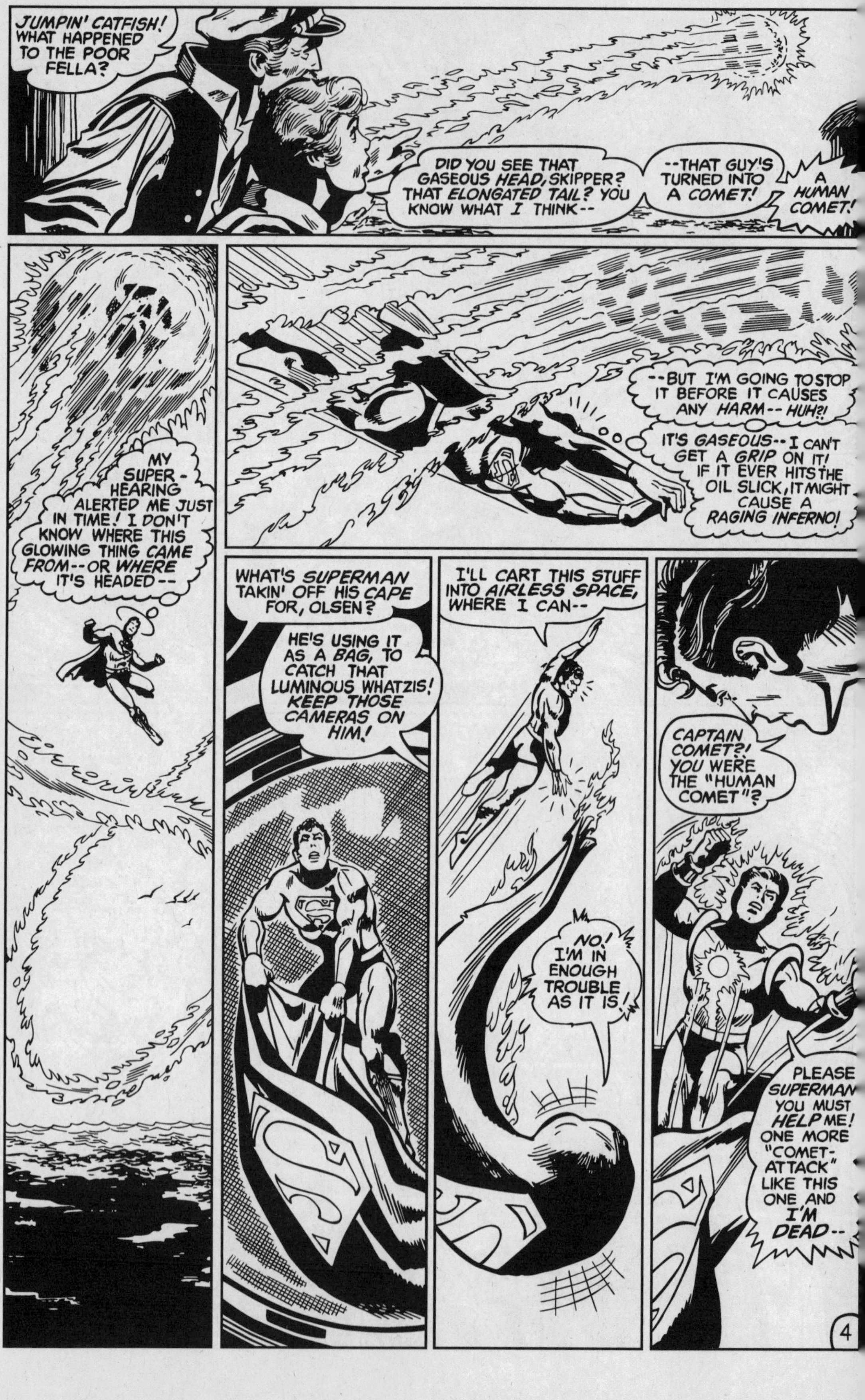
JUMPIN' CATFISH! WHAT HAPPENED TO THE POOR FELLA?
DID YOU SEE THAT GASEOUS HEAD, SKIPPER? THAT ELONGATED TAIL? YOU KNOW WHAT I THINK--
--THAT GUY'S TURNED INTO A COMET!
A HUMAN COMET!
MY SUPER-HEARING ALERTED ME JUST IN TIME! I DON'T KNOW WHERE THIS GLOWING THING CAME FROM--OR WHERE IT'S HEADED--
--BUT I'M GOING TO STOP IT BEFORE IT CAUSES ANY HARM--HUH?!
IT'S GASEOUS--I CAN'T GET A GRIP ON IT! IF IT EVER HITS THE OIL SLICK, IT MIGHT CAUSE A RAGING INFERNO!
WHAT'S SUPERMAN TAKIN' OFF HIS CAPE FOR, OLSEN?
HE'S USING IT AS A BAG, TO CATCH THAT LUMINOUS WHATZIS! KEEP THOSE CAMERAS ON HIM!
I'LL CART THIS STUFF INTO AIRLESS SPACE, WHERE I CAN--
NO! I'M IN ENOUGH TROUBLE AS IT IS!
CAPTAIN COMET?! YOU WERE THE "HUMAN COMET"?
PLEASE SUPERMAN YOU MUST HELP ME! ONE MORE "COMET-ATTACK" LIKE THIS ONE AND I'M DEAD--
4

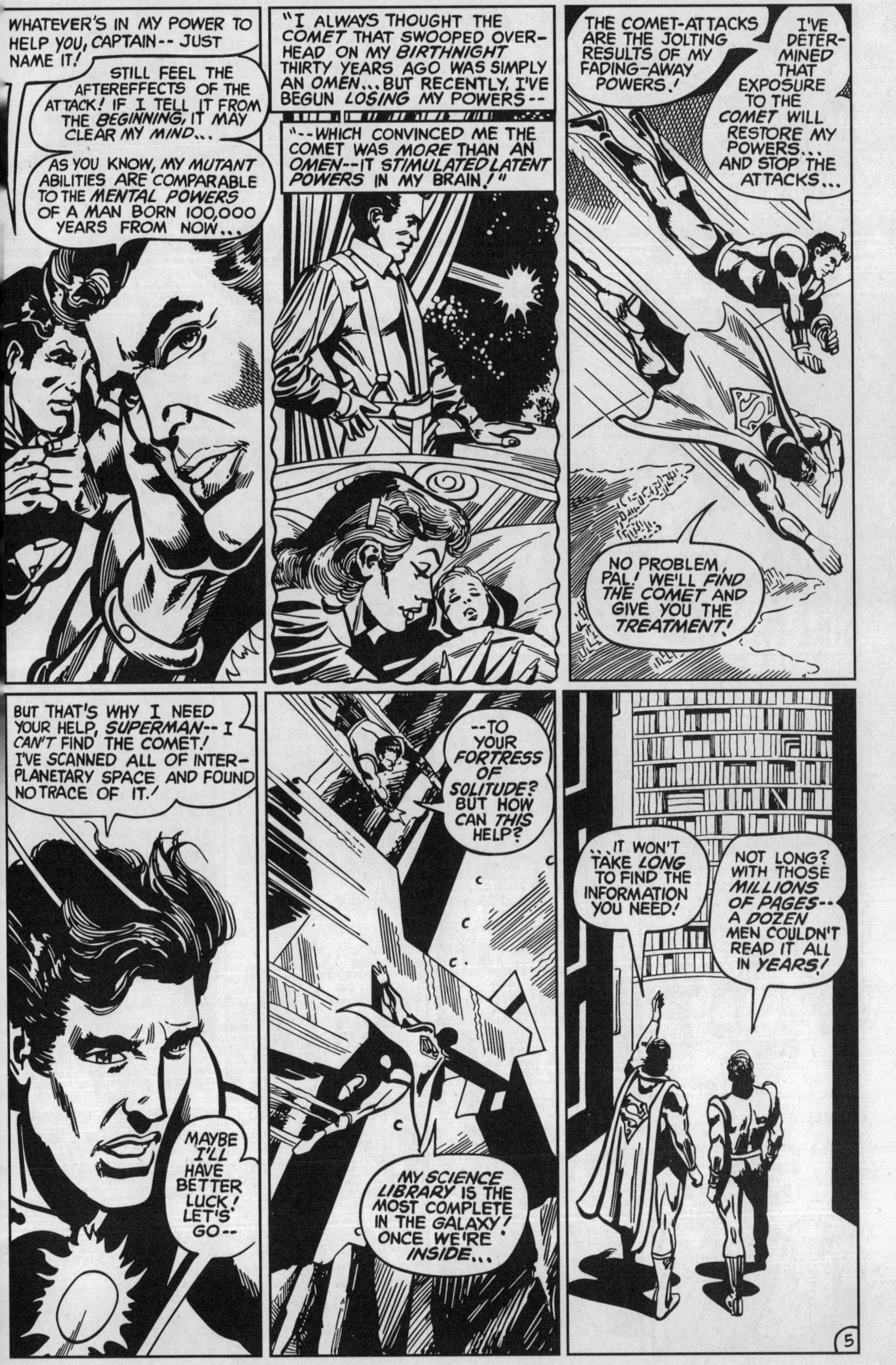
WHATEVER'S IN MY POWER TO HELP YOU, CAPTAIN-- JUST NAME IT!
STILL FEEL THE AFTEREFFECTS OF THE ATTACK! IF I TELL IT FROM THE BEGINNING, IT MAY CLEAR MY MIND...
AS YOU KNOW, MY MUTANT ABILITIES ARE COMPARABLE TO THE MENTAL POWERS OF A MAN BORN 100,000 YEARS FROM NOW...
"I ALWAYS THOUGHT THE COMET THAT SWOOPED OVERHEAD ON MY BIRTHNIGHT THIRTY YEARS AGO WAS SIMPLY AN OMEN... BUT RECENTLY, I'VE BEGUN LOSING MY POWERS--
"--WHICH CONVINCED ME THE COMET WAS MORE THAN AN OMEN--IT STIMULATED LATENT POWERS IN MY BRAIN!"
THE COMET-ATTACKS ARE THE JOLTING RESULTS OF MY FADING-AWAY POWERS!
I'VE DETERMINED THAT EXPOSURE TO THE COMET WILL RESTORE MY POWERS... AND STOP THE ATTACKS...
NO PROBLEM, PAL! WE'LL FIND THE COMET AND GIVE YOU THE TREATMENT!
BUT THAT'S WHY I NEED YOUR HELP, SUPERMAN-- I CAN'T FIND THE COMET! I'VE SCANNED ALL OF INTERPLANETARY SPACE AND FOUND NO TRACE OF IT!
MAYBE I'LL HAVE BETTER LUCK! LET'S GO--
--TO YOUR FORTRESS OF SOLITUDE? BUT HOW CAN THIS HELP?
MY SCIENCE LIBRARY IS THE MOST COMPLETE IN THE GALAXY! ONCE WE'RE INSIDE...
...IT WON'T TAKE LONG TO FIND THE INFORMATION YOU NEED!
NOT LONG? WITH THOSE MILLIONS OF PAGES-- A DOZEN MEN COULDN'T READ IT ALL IN YEARS!
5

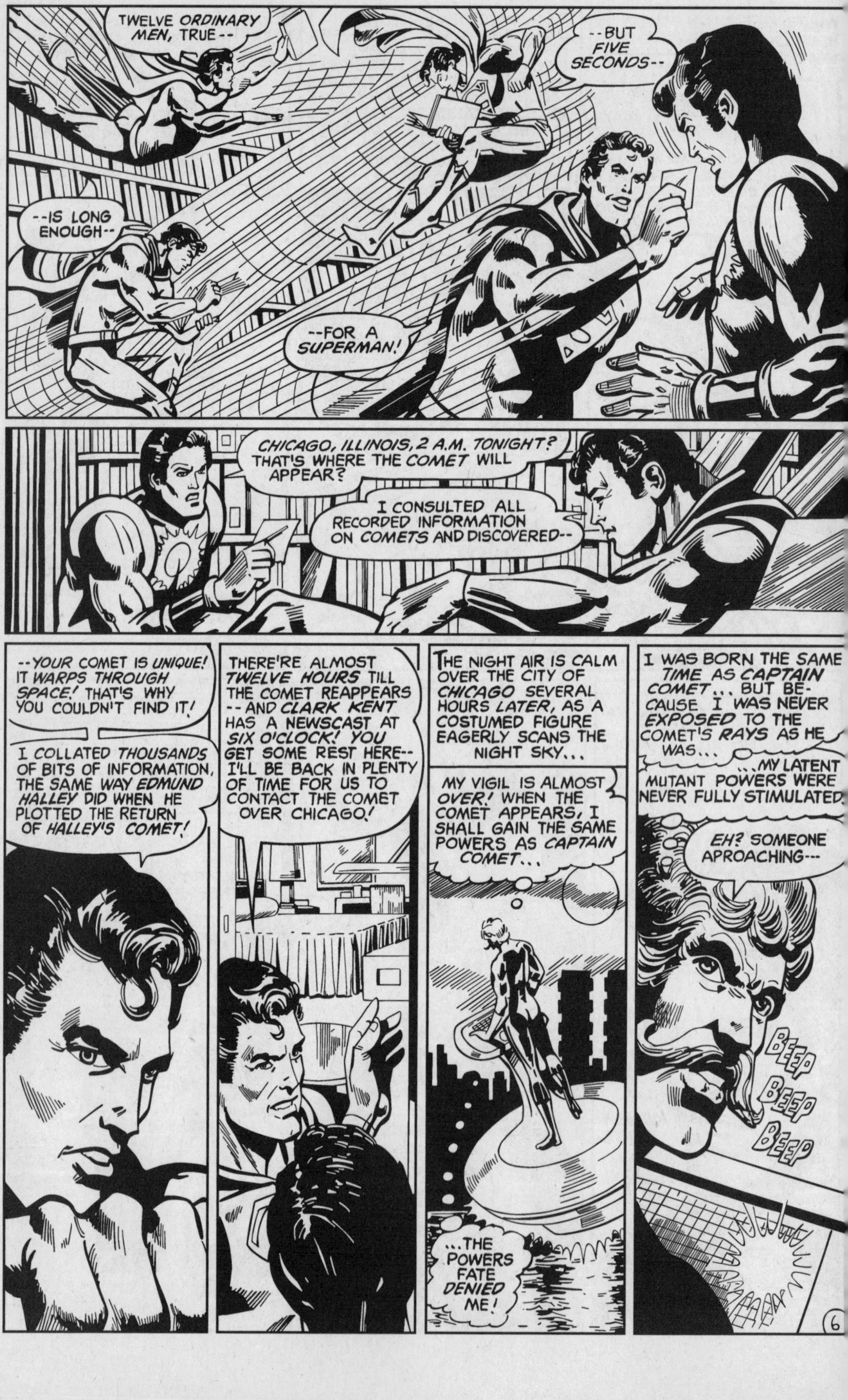
TWELVE ORDINARY MEN, TRUE--
--BUT FIVE SECONDS--
--IS LONG ENOUGH--
--FOR A SUPERMAN!
CHICAGO, ILLINOIS, 2 A.M. TONIGHT? THAT'S WHERE THE COMET WILL APPEAR?
I CONSULTED ALL RECORDED INFORMATION ON COMETS AND DISCOVERED--
--YOUR COMET IS UNIQUE! IT WARPS THROUGH SPACE! THAT'S WHY YOU COULDN'T FIND IT!
I COLLATED THOUSANDS OF BITS OF INFORMATION, THE SAME WAY EDMUND HALLEY DID WHEN HE PLOTTED THE RETURN OF HALLEY'S COMET!
THERE'RE ALMOST TWELVE HOURS TILL THE COMET REAPPEARS --AND CLARK KENT HAS A NEWSCAST AT SIX O'CLOCK! YOU GET SOME REST HERE-- I'LL BE BACK IN PLENTY OF TIME FOR US TO CONTACT THE COMET OVER CHICAGO!
THE NIGHT AIR IS CALM OVER THE CITY OF CHICAGO SEVERAL HOURS LATER, AS A COSTUMED FIGURE EAGERLY SCANS THE NIGHT SKY...
MY VIGIL IS ALMOST OVER! WHEN THE COMET APPEARS, I SHALL GAIN THE SAME POWERS AS CAPTAIN COMET...
...THE POWERS FATE DENIED ME!
I WAS BORN THE SAME TIME AS CAPTAIN COMET... BUT BE-CAUSE I WAS NEVER EXPOSED TO THE COMET'S RAYS AS HE WAS...
...MY LATENT MUTANT POWERS WERE NEVER FULLY STIMULATED.
EH? SOMEONE APROACHING---
BEEP BEEP BEEP
6

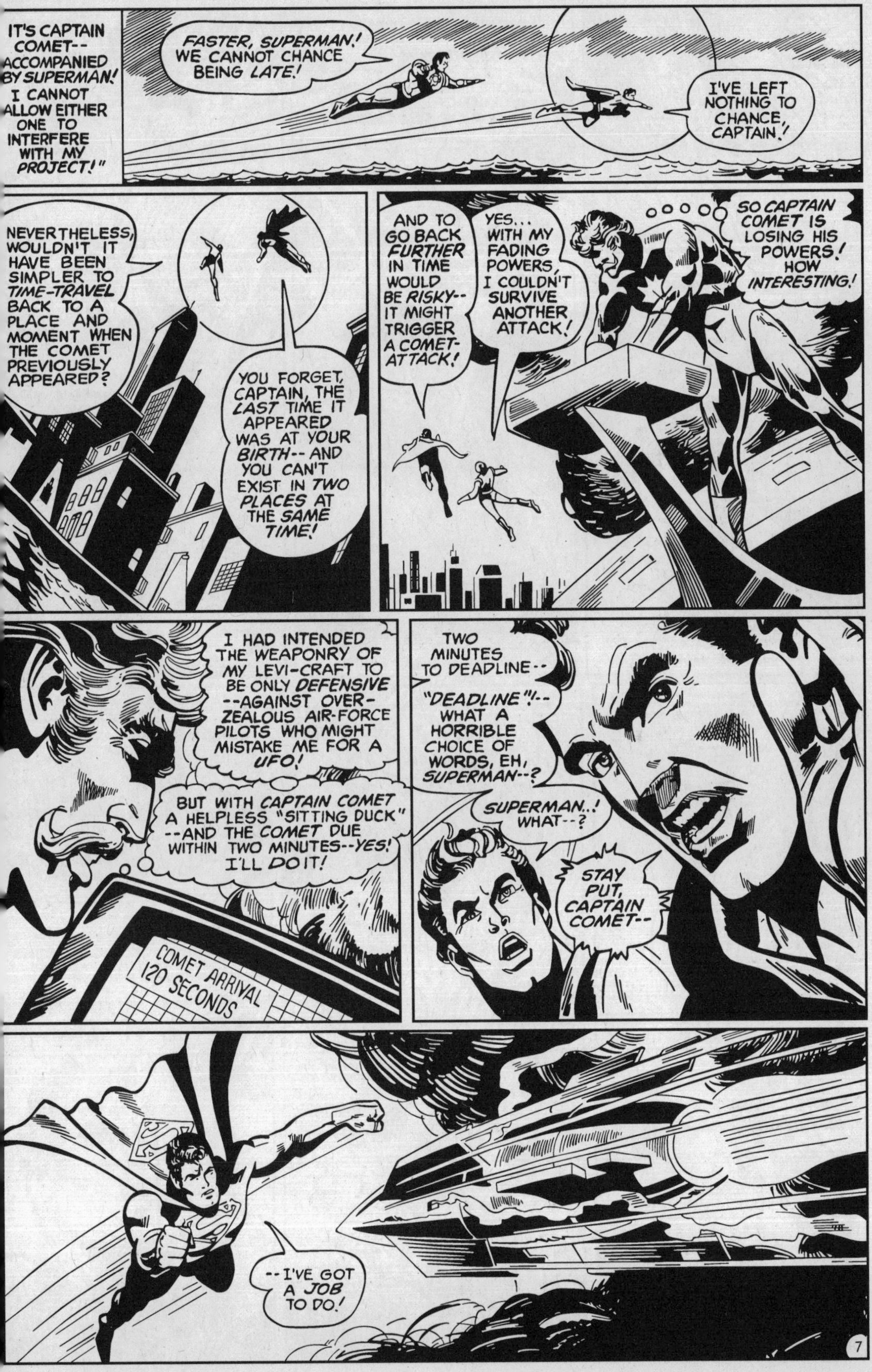
IT'S CAPTAIN COMET-- ACCOMPANIED BY SUPERMAN! I CANNOT ALLOW EITHER ONE TO INTERFERE WITH MY PROJECT!"
FASTER, SUPERMAN! WE CANNOT CHANCE BEING LATE!
I'VE LEFT NOTHING TO CHANCE, CAPTAIN!
NEVERTHELESS, WOULDN'T IT HAVE BEEN SIMPLER TO TIME-TRAVEL BACK TO A PLACE AND MOMENT WHEN THE COMET PREVIOUSLY APPEARED?
YOU FORGET, CAPTAIN, THE LAST TIME IT APPEARED WAS AT YOUR BIRTH-- AND YOU CAN'T EXIST IN TWO PLACES AT THE SAME TIME!
AND TO GO BACK FURTHER IN TIME WOULD BE RISKY-- IT MIGHT TRIGGER A COMET-ATTACK!
YES... WITH MY FADING POWERS, I COULDN'T SURVIVE ANOTHER ATTACK!
SO CAPTAIN COMET IS LOSING HIS POWERS! HOW INTERESTING!
I HAD INTENDED THE WEAPONRY OF MY LEVI-CRAFT TO BE ONLY DEFENSIVE --AGAINST OVER-ZEALOUS AIR-FORCE PILOTS WHO MIGHT MISTAKE ME FOR A UFO!
BUT WITH CAPTAIN COMET A HELPLESS "SITTING DUCK" --AND THE COMET DUE WITHIN TWO MINUTES--YES! I'LL DO IT!
COMET ARRIVAL 120 SECONDS
TWO MINUTES TO DEADLINE--
"DEADLINE"!-- WHAT A HORRIBLE CHOICE OF WORDS, EH, SUPERMAN--?
SUPERMAN..! WHAT--?
STAY PUT, CAPTAIN COMET--
--I'VE GOT A JOB TO DO!
7

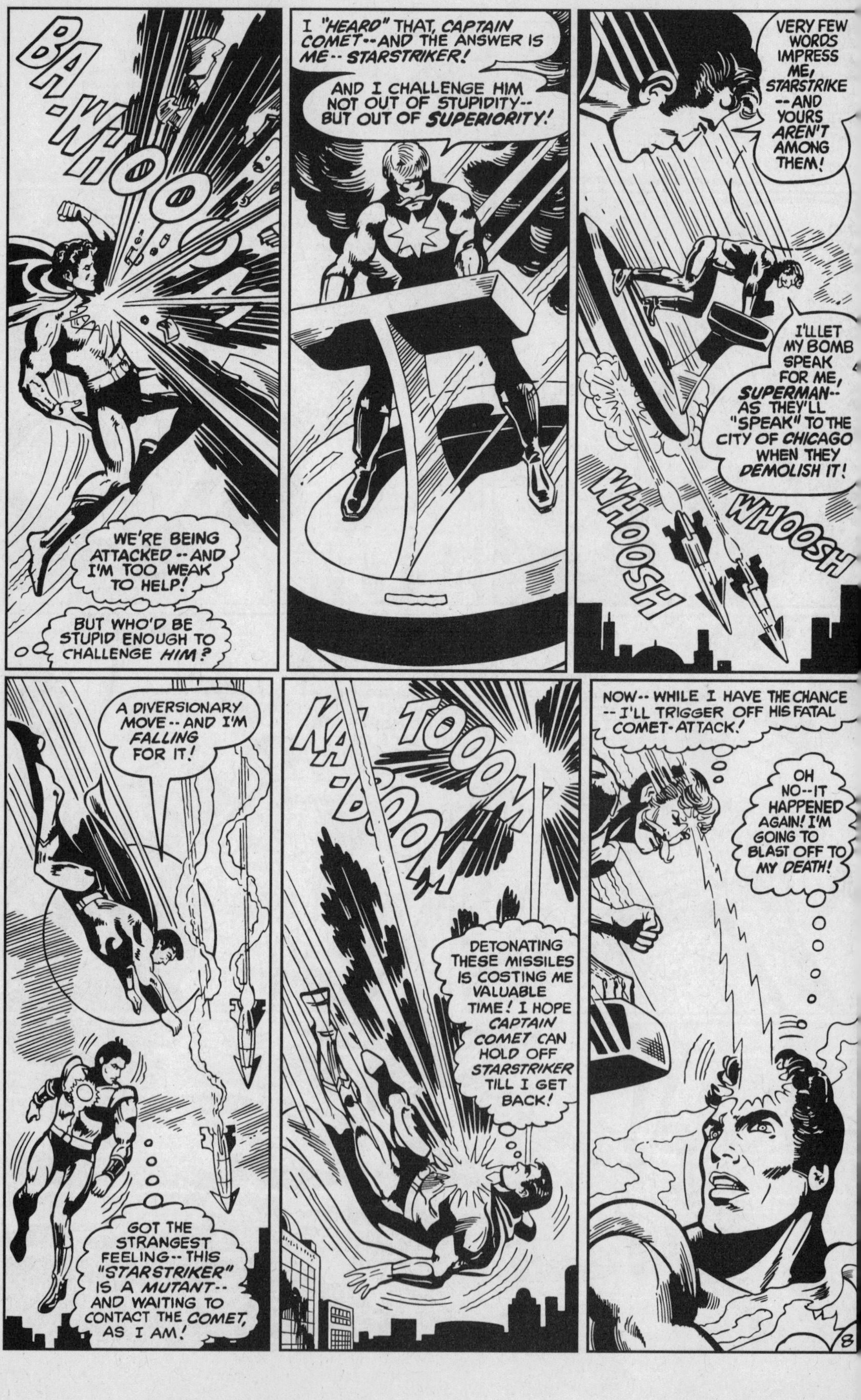
BA-WHOOOM
WE'RE BEING ATTACKED -- AND I'M TOO WEAK TO HELP!
BUT WHO'D BE STUPID ENOUGH TO CHALLENGE HIM?
I "HEARD" THAT, CAPTAIN COMET -- AND THE ANSWER IS ME -- STARSTRIKER!
AND I CHALLENGE HIM NOT OUT OF STUPIDITY -- BUT OUT OF SUPERIORITY!
VERY FEW WORDS IMPRESS ME, STARSTRIKE -- AND YOURS AREN'T AMONG THEM!
I'LL LET MY BOMB SPEAK FOR ME, SUPERMAN -- AS THEY'LL "SPEAK" TO THE CITY OF CHICAGO WHEN THEY DEMOLISH IT!
WHOOSH
WHOOSH
A DIVERSIONARY MOVE -- AND I'M FALLING FOR IT!
GOT THE STRANGEST FEELING -- THIS "STARSTRIKER" IS A MUTANT -- AND WAITING TO CONTACT THE COMET, AS I AM!
KA-TOOOM
KA-BOOOM
DETONATING THESE MISSILES IS COSTING ME VALUABLE TIME! I HOPE CAPTAIN COMET CAN HOLD OFF STARSTRIKER TILL I GET BACK!
NOW -- WHILE I HAVE THE CHANCE -- I'LL TRIGGER OFF HIS FATAL COMET-ATTACK!
OH NO -- IT HAPPENED AGAIN! I'M GOING TO BLAST OFF TO MY DEATH!
8

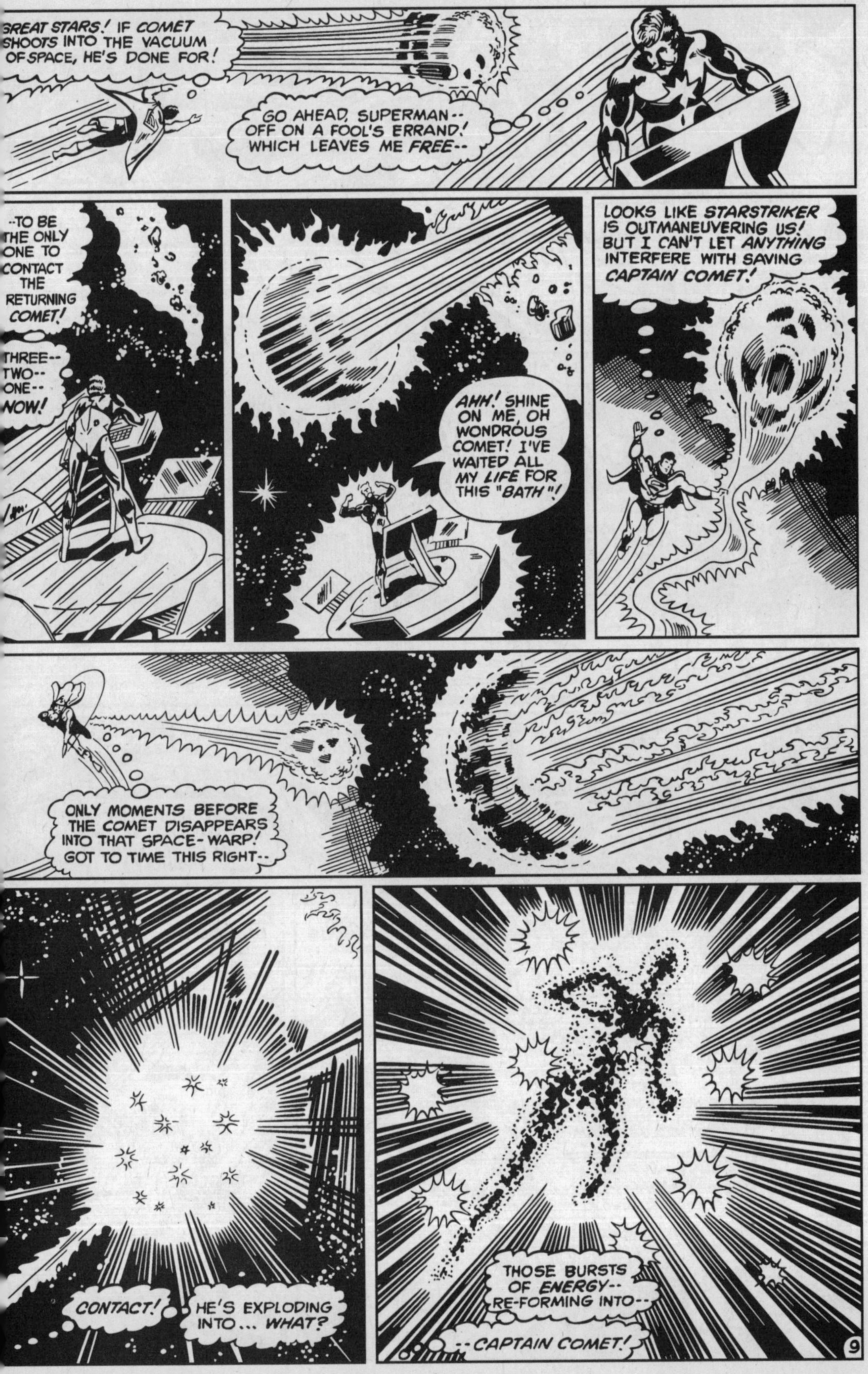
GREAT STARS! IF COMET SHOOTS INTO THE VACUUM OF SPACE, HE'S DONE FOR!
GO AHEAD, SUPERMAN-- OFF ON A FOOL'S ERRAND! WHICH LEAVES ME FREE--
--TO BE THE ONLY ONE TO CONTACT THE RETURNING COMET!
THREE-- TWO-- ONE-- NOW!
AHH! SHINE ON ME, OH WONDROUS COMET! I'VE WAITED ALL MY LIFE FOR THIS "BATH"!
LOOKS LIKE STARSTRIKER IS OUTMANEUVERING US! BUT I CAN'T LET ANYTHING INTERFERE WITH SAVING CAPTAIN COMET!
ONLY MOMENTS BEFORE THE COMET DISAPPEARS INTO THAT SPACE-WARP! GOT TO TIME THIS RIGHT--
CONTACT!
HE'S EXPLODING INTO... WHAT?
THOSE BURSTS OF ENERGY-- RE-FORMING INTO--
--CAPTAIN COMET!
9

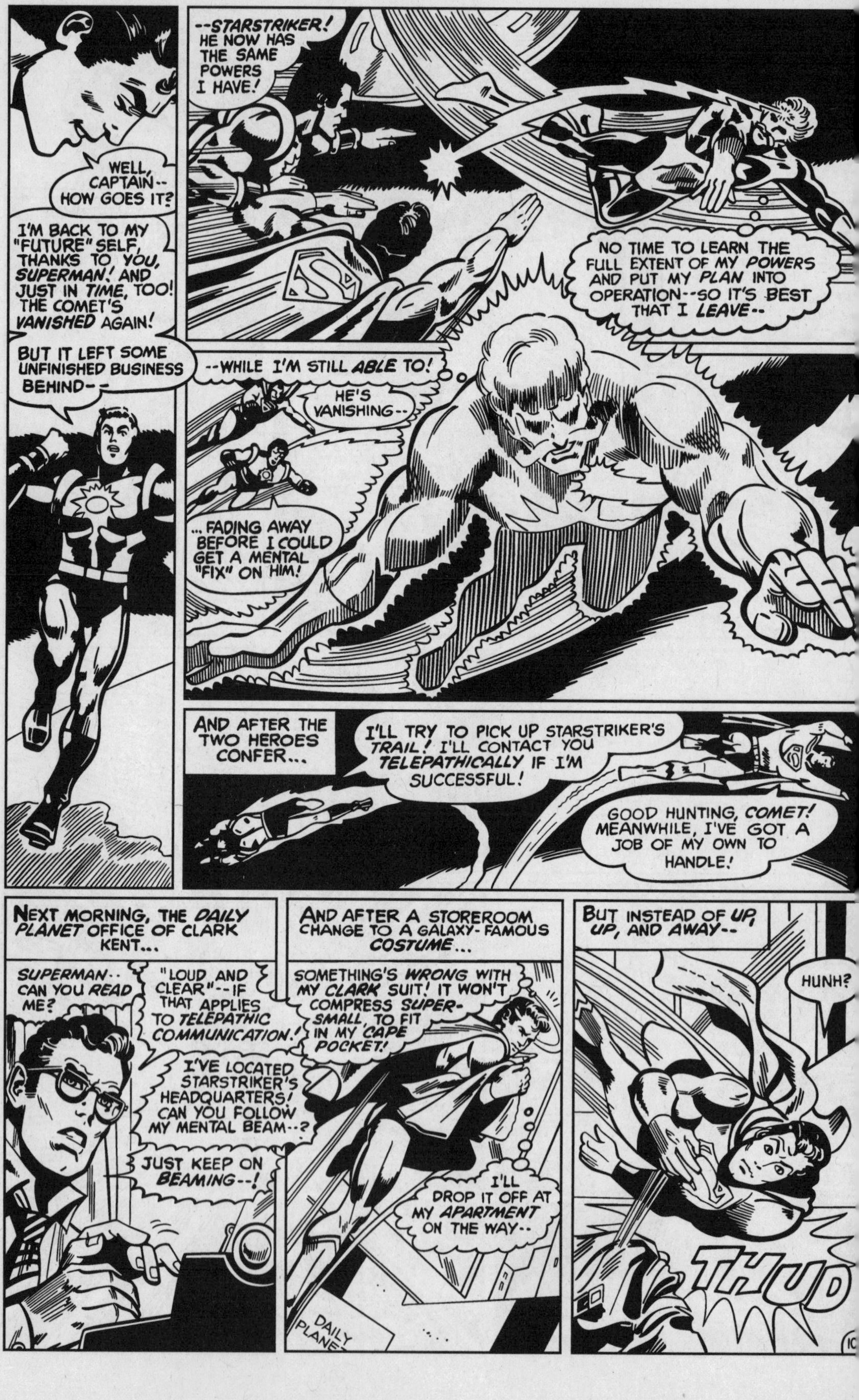

WELL, CAPTAIN-- HOW GOES IT?
I'M BACK TO MY "FUTURE" SELF, THANKS TO YOU, SUPERMAN! AND JUST IN TIME, TOO! THE COMET'S VANISHED AGAIN!
BUT IT LEFT SOME UNFINISHED BUSINESS BEHIND--
--STARSTRIKER! HE NOW HAS THE SAME POWERS I HAVE!
NO TIME TO LEARN THE FULL EXTENT OF MY POWERS AND PUT MY PLAN INTO OPERATION--SO IT'S BEST THAT I LEAVE--
--WHILE I'M STILL ABLE TO!
HE'S VANISHING--
...FADING AWAY BEFORE I COULD GET A MENTAL "FIX" ON HIM!
AND AFTER THE TWO HEROES CONFER...
I'LL TRY TO PICK UP STARSTRIKER'S TRAIL! I'LL CONTACT YOU TELEPATHICALLY IF I'M SUCCESSFUL!
GOOD HUNTING, COMET! MEANWHILE, I'VE GOT A JOB OF MY OWN TO HANDLE!
NEXT MORNING, THE DAILY PLANET OFFICE OF CLARK KENT...
SUPERMAN.. CAN YOU READ ME?
"LOUD AND CLEAR"--IF THAT APPLIES TO TELEPATHIC COMMUNICATION!
I'VE LOCATED STARSTRIKER'S HEADQUARTERS! CAN YOU FOLLOW MY MENTAL BEAM--?
JUST KEEP ON BEAMING--!
AND AFTER A STOREROOM CHANGE TO A GALAXY-FAMOUS COSTUME...
SOMETHING'S WRONG WITH MY CLARK SUIT! IT WON'T COMPRESS SUPER-SMALL, TO FIT IN MY CAPE POCKET!
I'LL DROP IT OFF AT MY APARTMENT ON THE WAY--
DAILY PLANE
BUT INSTEAD OF UP, UP, AND AWAY--
HUNH?
THUD
10

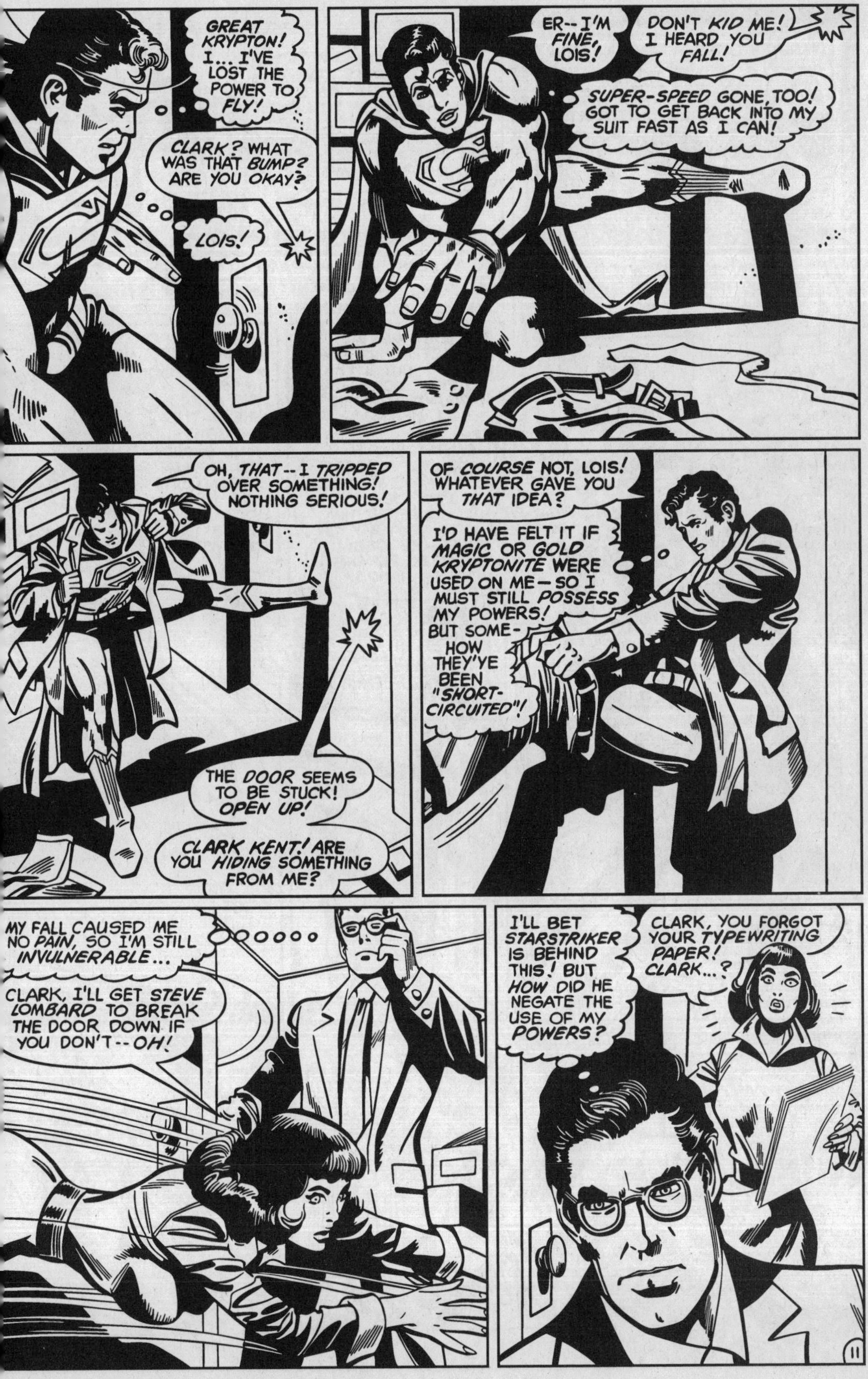
GREAT KRYPTON! I... I'VE LOST THE POWER TO FLY!
CLARK? WHAT WAS THAT BUMP? ARE YOU OKAY?
LOIS!
ER--I'M FINE, LOIS!
DON'T KID ME! I HEARD YOU FALL!
SUPER-SPEED GONE, TOO! GOT TO GET BACK INTO MY SUIT FAST AS I CAN!
OH, THAT--I TRIPPED OVER SOMETHING! NOTHING SERIOUS!
THE DOOR SEEMS TO BE STUCK! OPEN UP!
CLARK KENT! ARE YOU HIDING SOMETHING FROM ME?
OF COURSE NOT, LOIS! WHATEVER GAVE YOU THAT IDEA?
I'D HAVE FELT IT IF MAGIC OR GOLD KRYPTONITE WERE USED ON ME—SO I MUST STILL POSSESS MY POWERS! BUT SOME-HOW THEY'VE BEEN "SHORT-CIRCUITED"!
MY FALL CAUSED ME NO PAIN, SO I'M STILL INVULNERABLE...
CLARK, I'LL GET STEVE LOMBARD TO BREAK THE DOOR DOWN IF YOU DON'T--OH!
I'LL BET STARSTRIKER IS BEHIND THIS! BUT HOW DID HE NEGATE THE USE OF MY POWERS?
CLARK, YOU FORGOT YOUR TYPEWRITING PAPER! CLARK...?
11

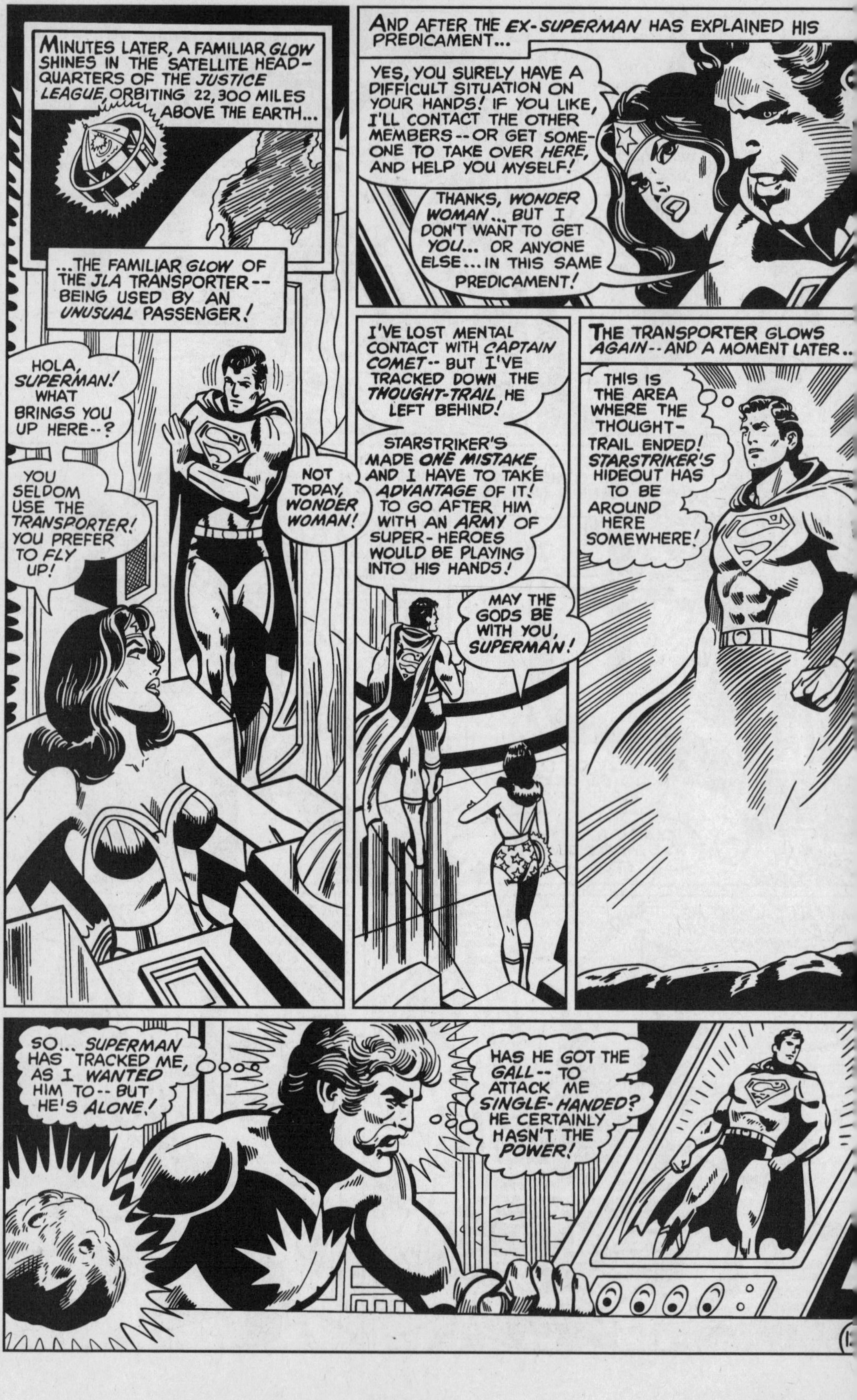
MINUTES LATER, A FAMILIAR GLOW SHINES IN THE SATELLITE HEAD-QUARTERS OF THE JUSTICE LEAGUE, ORBITING 22,300 MILES ABOVE THE EARTH...
...THE FAMILIAR GLOW OF THE JLA TRANSPORTER -- BEING USED BY AN UNUSUAL PASSENGER!
HOLA, SUPERMAN! WHAT BRINGS YOU UP HERE--?
YOU SELDOM USE THE TRANSPORTER! YOU PREFER TO FLY UP!
NOT TODAY, WONDER WOMAN!
AND AFTER THE EX-SUPERMAN HAS EXPLAINED HIS PREDICAMENT...
YES, YOU SURELY HAVE A DIFFICULT SITUATION ON YOUR HANDS! IF YOU LIKE, I'LL CONTACT THE OTHER MEMBERS--OR GET SOME-ONE TO TAKE OVER HERE, AND HELP YOU MYSELF!
THANKS, WONDER WOMAN... BUT I DON'T WANT TO GET YOU... OR ANYONE ELSE... IN THIS SAME PREDICAMENT!
I'VE LOST MENTAL CONTACT WITH CAPTAIN COMET-- BUT I'VE TRACKED DOWN THE THOUGHT-TRAIL HE LEFT BEHIND!
STARSTRIKER'S MADE ONE MISTAKE, AND I HAVE TO TAKE ADVANTAGE OF IT! TO GO AFTER HIM WITH AN ARMY OF SUPER-HEROES WOULD BE PLAYING INTO HIS HANDS!
MAY THE GODS BE WITH YOU, SUPERMAN!
THE TRANSPORTER GLOWS AGAIN--AND A MOMENT LATER...
THIS IS THE AREA WHERE THE THOUGHT-TRAIL ENDED! STARSTRIKER'S HIDEOUT HAS TO BE AROUND HERE SOMEWHERE!
SO... SUPERMAN HAS TRACKED ME, AS I WANTED HIM TO--BUT HE'S ALONE!
HAS HE GOT THE GALL-- TO ATTACK ME SINGLE-HANDED? HE CERTAINLY HASN'T THE POWER!

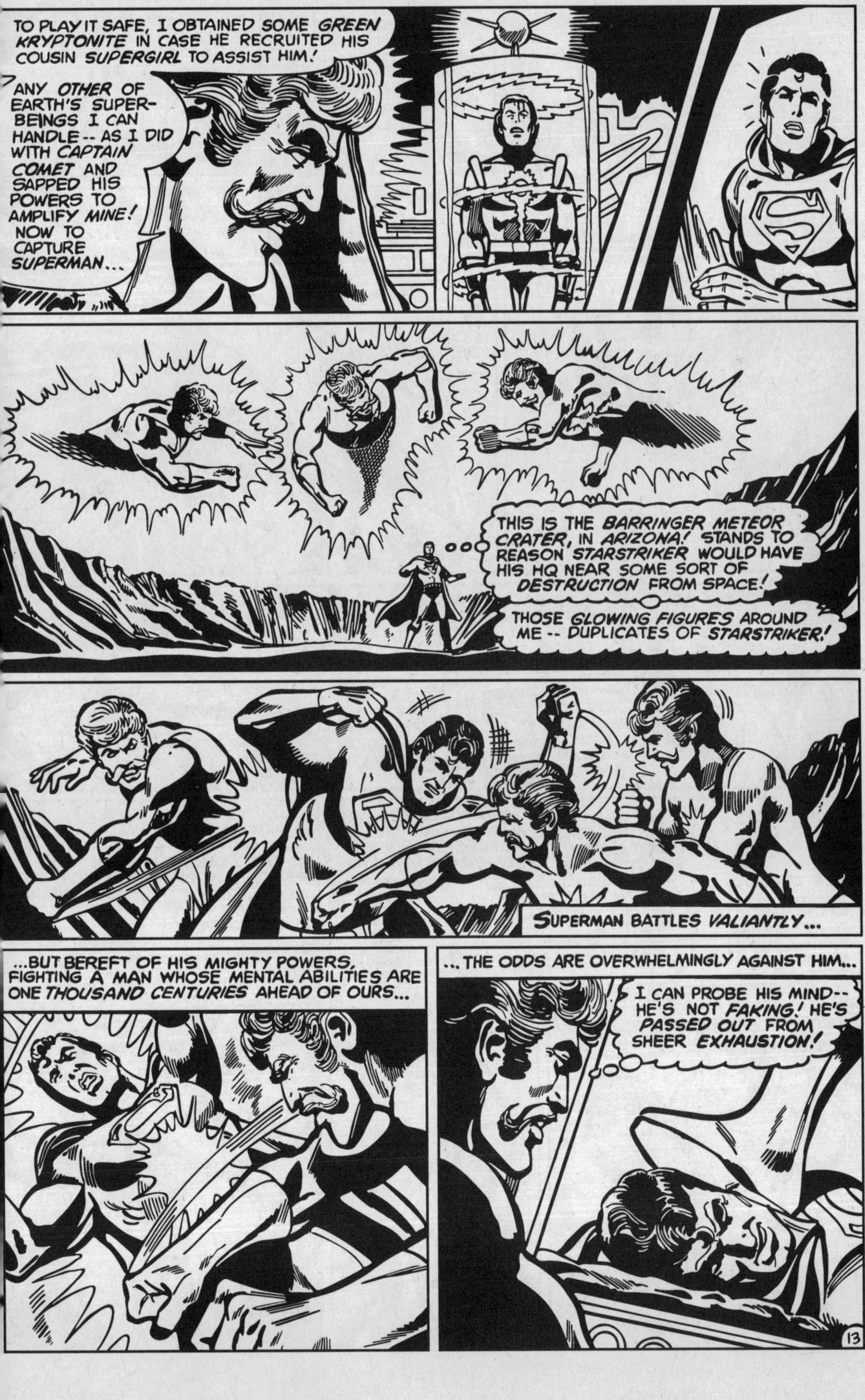
TO PLAY IT SAFE, I OBTAINED SOME GREEN KRYPTONITE IN CASE HE RECRUITED HIS COUSIN SUPERGIRL TO ASSIST HIM!
ANY OTHER OF EARTH'S SUPER-BEINGS I CAN HANDLE -- AS I DID WITH CAPTAIN COMET AND SAPPED HIS POWERS TO AMPLIFY MINE! NOW TO CAPTURE SUPERMAN...
THIS IS THE BARRINGER METEOR CRATER, IN ARIZONA! STANDS TO REASON STARSTRIKER WOULD HAVE HIS HQ NEAR SOME SORT OF DESTRUCTION FROM SPACE!
THOSE GLOWING FIGURES AROUND ME -- DUPLICATES OF STARSTRIKER!
SUPERMAN BATTLES VALIANTLY...
...BUT BEREFT OF HIS MIGHTY POWERS, FIGHTING A MAN WHOSE MENTAL ABILITIES ARE ONE THOUSAND CENTURIES AHEAD OF OURS...
...THE ODDS ARE OVERWHELMINGLY AGAINST HIM...
I CAN PROBE HIS MIND-- HE'S NOT FAKING! HE'S PASSED OUT FROM SHEER EXHAUSTION!
13

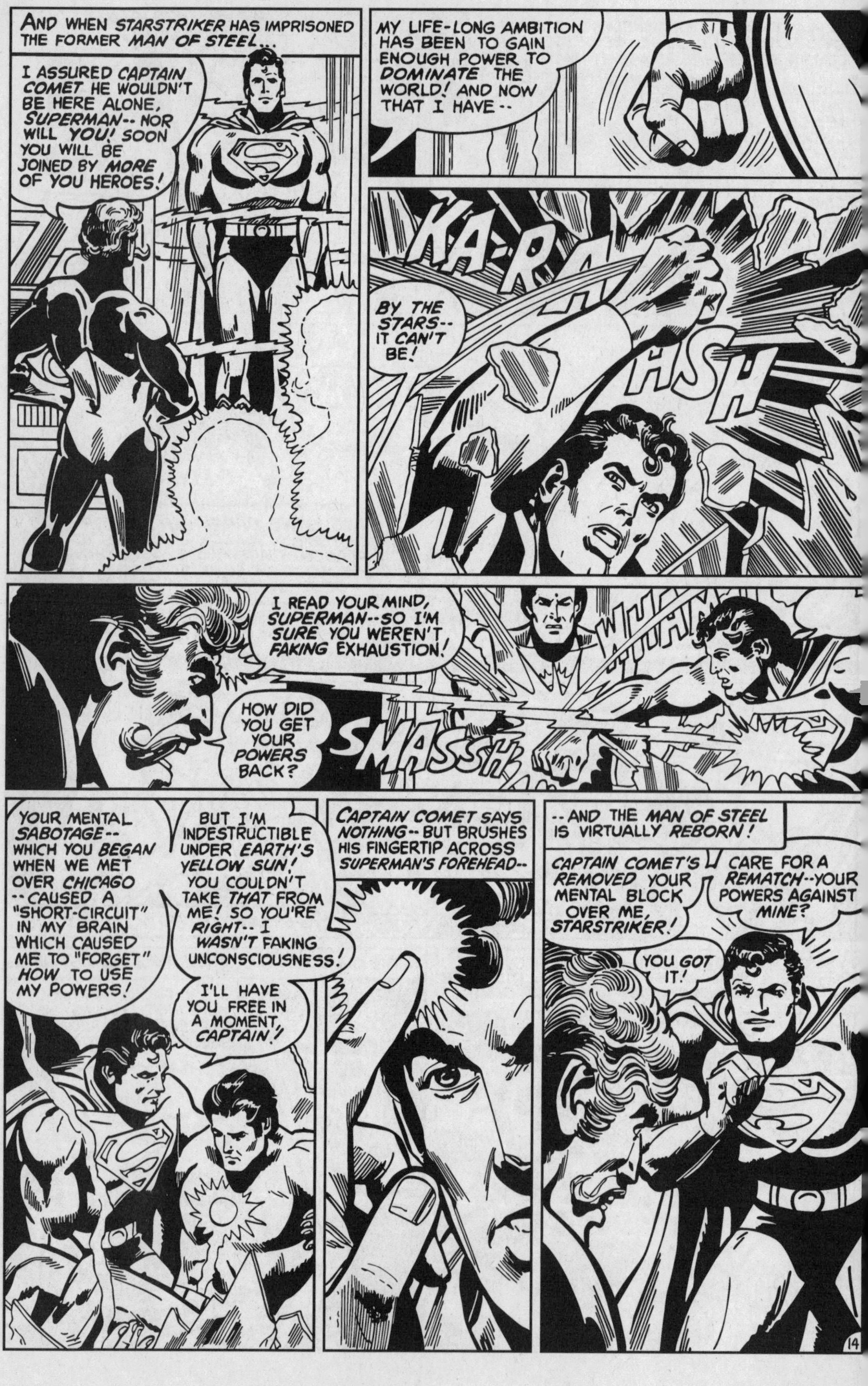
AND WHEN STARSTRIKER HAS IMPRISONED THE FORMER MAN OF STEEL...
I ASSURED CAPTAIN COMET HE WOULDN'T BE HERE ALONE, SUPERMAN-- NOR WILL YOU! SOON YOU WILL BE JOINED BY MORE OF YOU HEROES!
MY LIFE-LONG AMBITION HAS BEEN TO GAIN ENOUGH POWER TO DOMINATE THE WORLD! AND NOW THAT I HAVE --
KA-RA
HSH
BY THE STARS-- IT CAN'T BE!
I READ YOUR MIND, SUPERMAN--SO I'M SURE YOU WEREN'T FAKING EXHAUSTION!
HOW DID YOU GET YOUR POWERS BACK?
SMASSH
YOUR MENTAL SABOTAGE-- WHICH YOU BEGAN WHEN WE MET OVER CHICAGO --CAUSED A "SHORT-CIRCUIT" IN MY BRAIN WHICH CAUSED ME TO "FORGET" HOW TO USE MY POWERS!
BUT I'M INDESTRUCTIBLE UNDER EARTH'S YELLOW SUN! YOU COULDN'T TAKE THAT FROM ME! SO YOU'RE RIGHT-- I WASN'T FAKING UNCONSCIOUSNESS!
I'LL HAVE YOU FREE IN A MOMENT, CAPTAIN!
CAPTAIN COMET SAYS NOTHING-- BUT BRUSHES HIS FINGERTIP ACROSS SUPERMAN'S FOREHEAD--
--AND THE MAN OF STEEL IS VIRTUALLY REBORN!
CAPTAIN COMET'S REMOVED YOUR MENTAL BLOCK OVER ME, STARSTRIKER!
CARE FOR A REMATCH--YOUR POWERS AGAINST MINE?
YOU GOT IT!
14

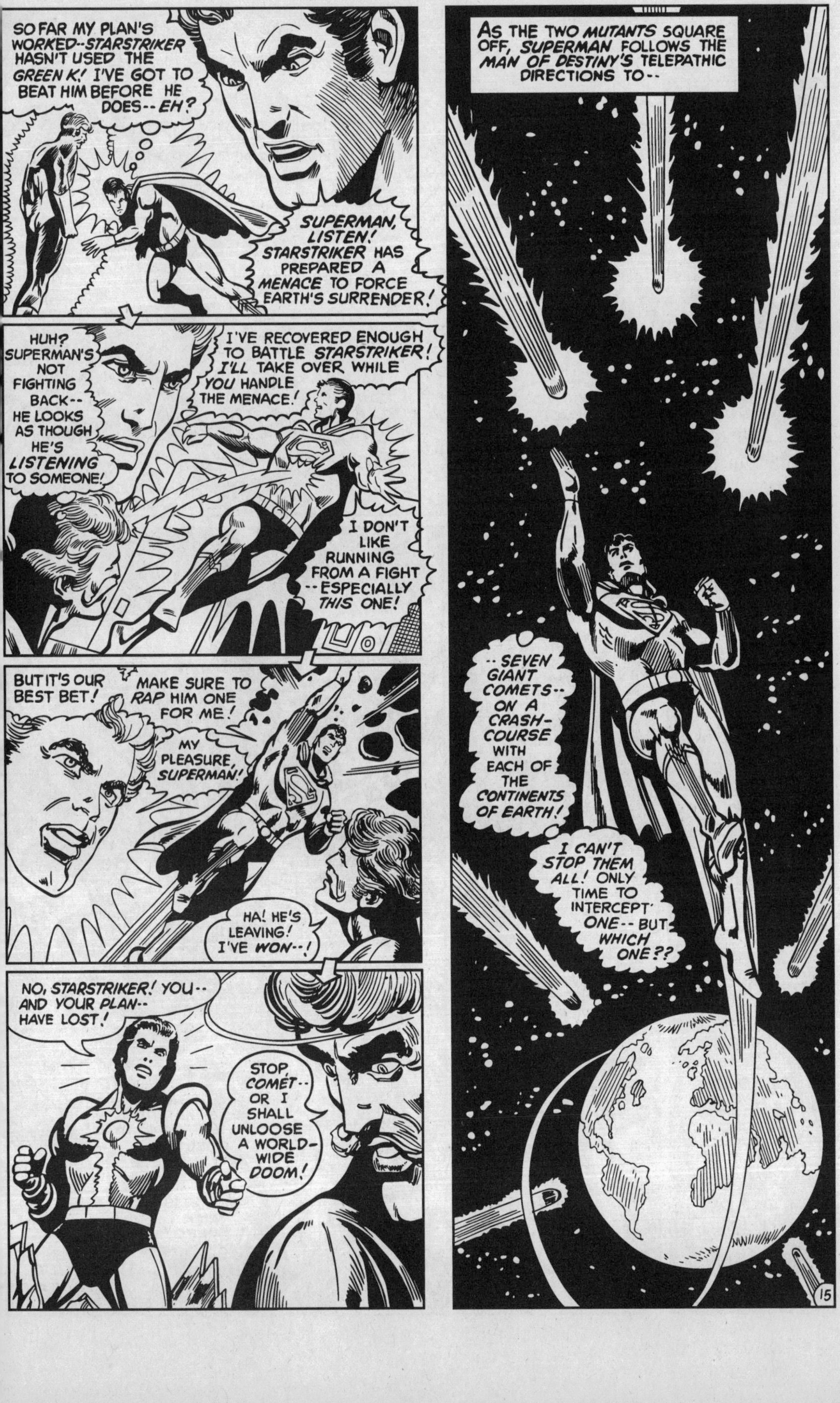
SO FAR MY PLAN'S WORKED--STARSTRIKER HASN'T USED THE GREEN K! I'VE GOT TO BEAT HIM BEFORE HE DOES--EH?
SUPERMAN, LISTEN! STARSTRIKER HAS PREPARED A MENACE TO FORCE EARTH'S SURRENDER!
HUH? SUPERMAN'S NOT FIGHTING BACK--HE LOOKS AS THOUGH HE'S LISTENING TO SOMEONE!
I'VE RECOVERED ENOUGH TO BATTLE STARSTRIKER! I'LL TAKE OVER WHILE YOU HANDLE THE MENACE!
I DON'T LIKE RUNNING FROM A FIGHT --ESPECIALLY THIS ONE!
BUT IT'S OUR BEST BET!
MAKE SURE TO RAP HIM ONE FOR ME!
MY PLEASURE, SUPERMAN!
HA! HE'S LEAVING! I'VE WON--!
NO, STARSTRIKER! YOU--AND YOUR PLAN--HAVE LOST!
STOP, COMET--OR I SHALL UNLOOSE A WORLD-WIDE DOOM!
AS THE TWO MUTANTS SQUARE OFF, SUPERMAN FOLLOWS THE MAN OF DESTINY'S TELEPATHIC DIRECTIONS TO--
--SEVEN GIANT COMETS--ON A CRASH-COURSE WITH EACH OF THE CONTINENTS OF EARTH!
I CAN'T STOP THEM ALL! ONLY TIME TO INTERCEPT ONE--BUT WHICH ONE??
15

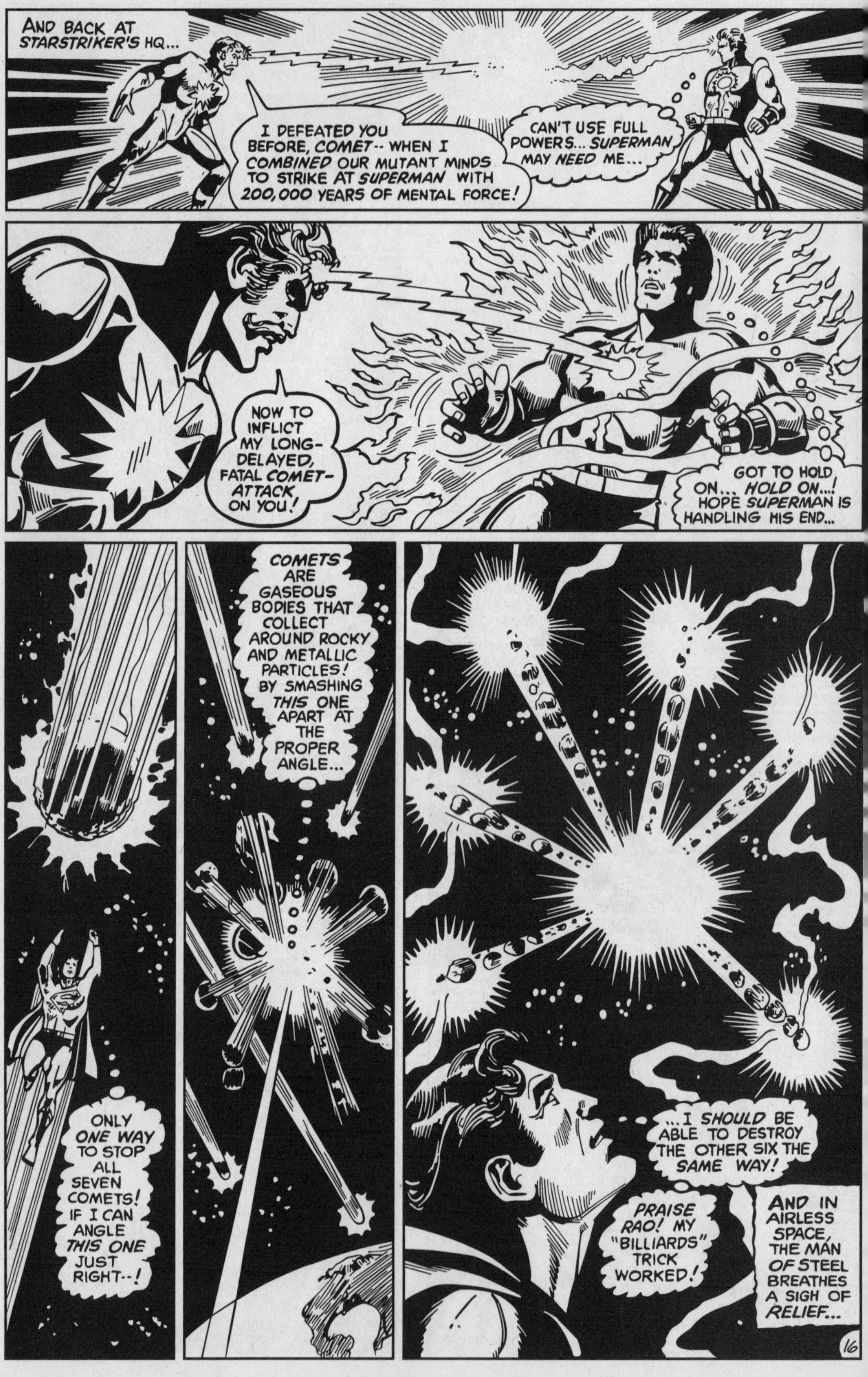
AND BACK AT STARSTRIKER'S HQ...
I DEFEATED YOU BEFORE, COMET-- WHEN I COMBINED OUR MUTANT MINDS TO STRIKE AT SUPERMAN WITH 200,000 YEARS OF MENTAL FORCE!
CAN'T USE FULL POWERS... SUPERMAN MAY NEED ME...
NOW TO INFLICT MY LONG-DELAYED, FATAL COMET-ATTACK ON YOU!
GOT TO HOLD ON... HOLD ON...! HOPE SUPERMAN IS HANDLING HIS END...
ONLY ONE WAY TO STOP ALL SEVEN COMETS! IF I CAN ANGLE THIS ONE JUST RIGHT--!
COMETS ARE GASEOUS BODIES THAT COLLECT AROUND ROCKY AND METALLIC PARTICLES! BY SMASHING THIS ONE APART AT THE PROPER ANGLE...
...I SHOULD BE ABLE TO DESTROY THE OTHER SIX THE SAME WAY!
PRAISE RAO! MY "BILLIARDS" TRICK WORKED!
AND IN AIRLESS SPACE, THE MAN OF STEEL BREATHES A SIGH OF RELIEF...
16

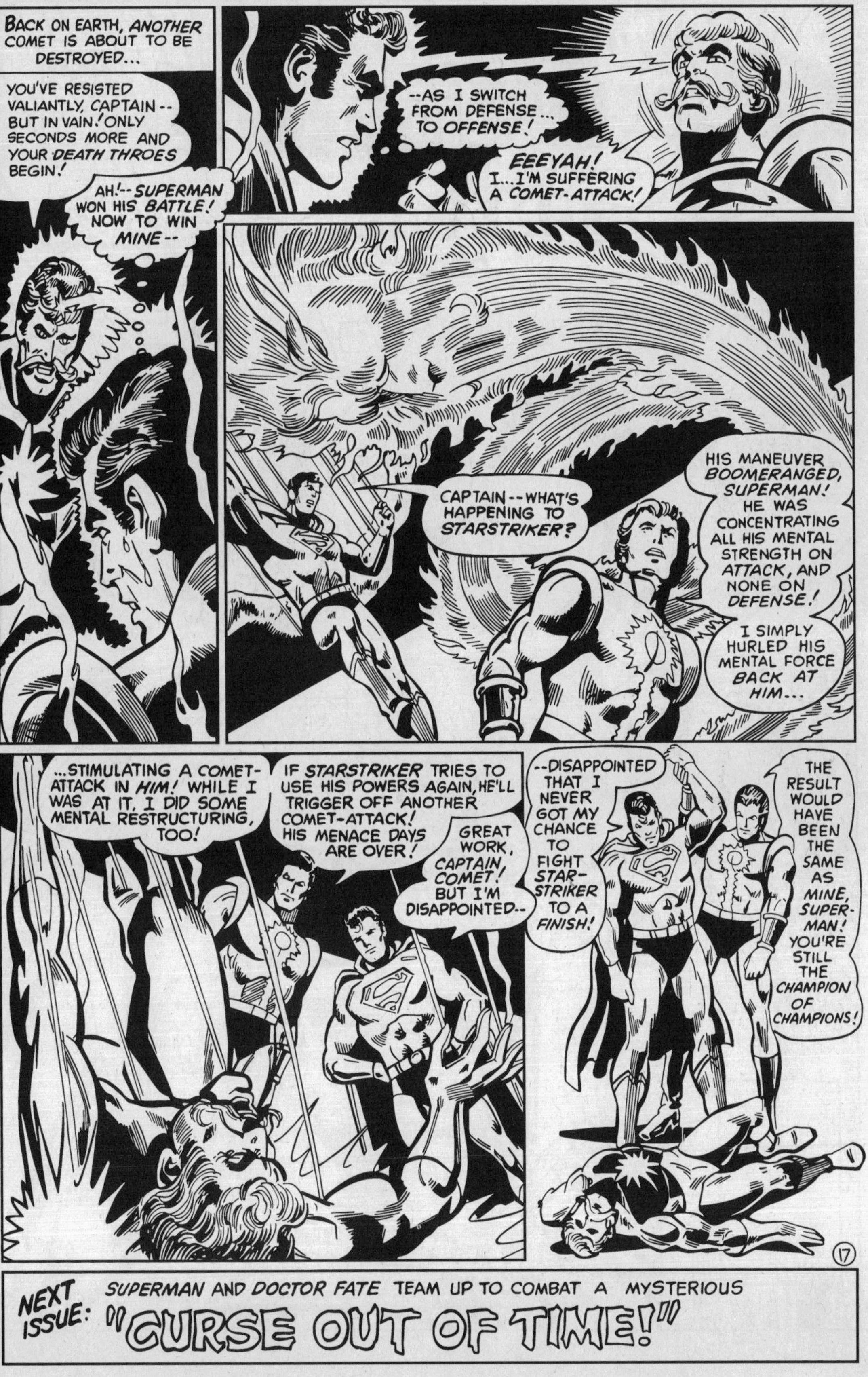
BACK ON EARTH, ANOTHER COMET IS ABOUT TO BE DESTROYED...
YOU'VE RESISTED VALIANTLY, CAPTAIN -- BUT IN VAIN! ONLY SECONDS MORE AND YOUR DEATH THROES BEGIN!
AH!-- SUPERMAN WON HIS BATTLE! NOW TO WIN MINE --
--AS I SWITCH FROM DEFENSE... TO OFFENSE!
EEEYAH! I...I'M SUFFERING A COMET-ATTACK!
CAPTAIN -- WHAT'S HAPPENING TO STARSTRIKER?
HIS MANEUVER BOOMERANGED, SUPERMAN! HE WAS CONCENTRATING ALL HIS MENTAL STRENGTH ON ATTACK, AND NONE ON DEFENSE!
I SIMPLY HURLED HIS MENTAL FORCE BACK AT HIM...
...STIMULATING A COMET-ATTACK IN HIM! WHILE I WAS AT IT, I DID SOME MENTAL RESTRUCTURING, TOO!
IF STARSTRIKER TRIES TO USE HIS POWERS AGAIN, HE'LL TRIGGER OFF ANOTHER COMET-ATTACK! HIS MENACE DAYS ARE OVER!
GREAT WORK, CAPTAIN COMET! BUT I'M DISAPPOINTED--
--DISAPPOINTED THAT I NEVER GOT MY CHANCE TO FIGHT STAR-STRIKER TO A FINISH!
THE RESULT WOULD HAVE BEEN THE SAME AS MINE, SUPER-MAN! YOU'RE STILL THE CHAMPION OF CHAMPIONS!
17
NEXT ISSUE: SUPERMAN AND DOCTOR FATE TEAM UP TO COMBAT A MYSTERIOUS
"CURSE OUT OF TIME!"

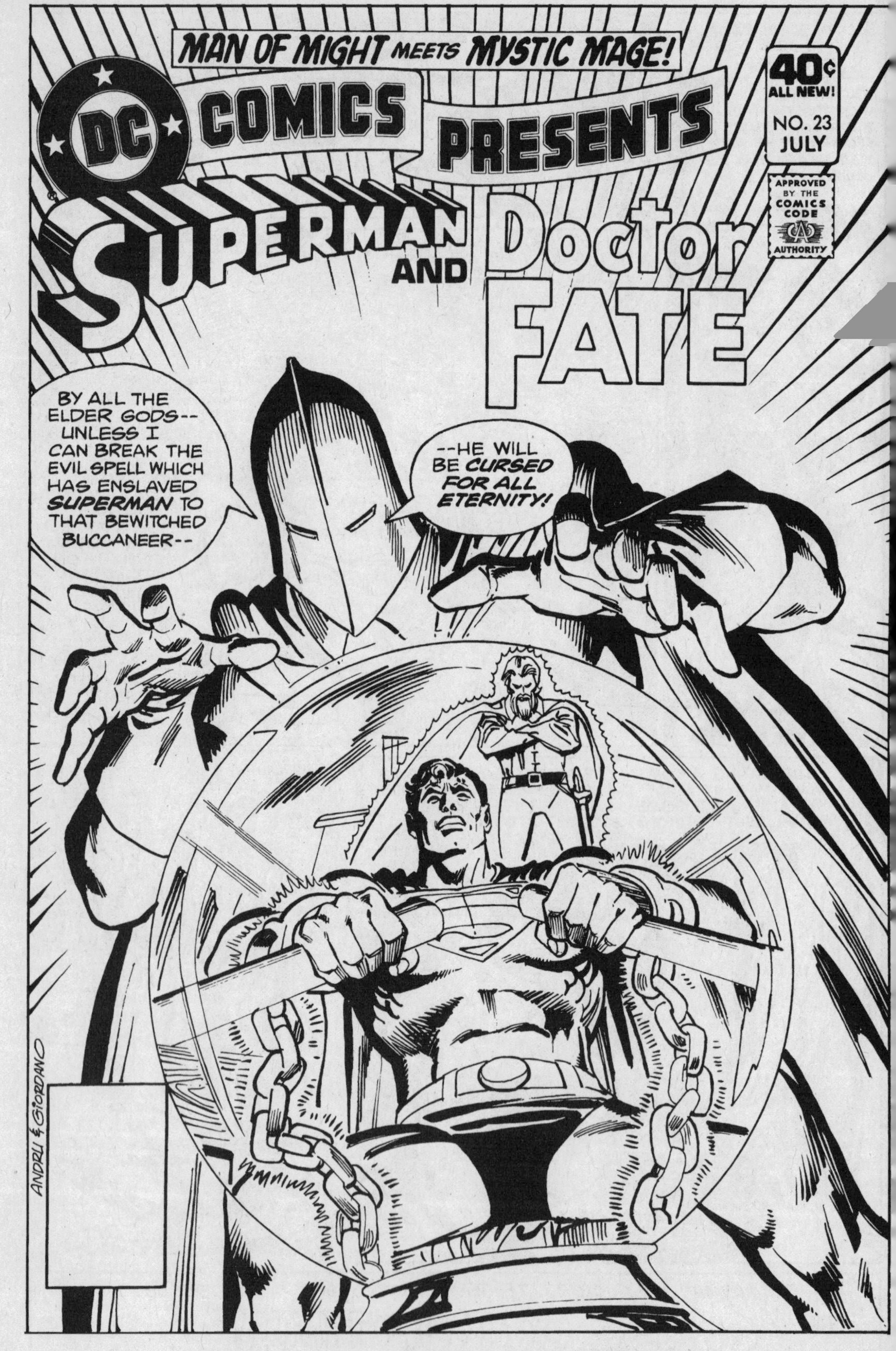
MAN OF MIGHT MEETS MYSTIC MAGE!
DC COMICS PRESENTS
40¢ ALL NEW!
NO. 23 JULY
APPROVED BY THE COMICS CODE AUTHORITY
SUPERMAN AND Doctor FATE
BY ALL THE ELDER GODS-- UNLESS I CAN BREAK THE EVIL SPELL WHICH HAS ENSLAVED SUPERMAN TO THAT BEWITCHED BUCCANEER--
--HE WILL BE CURSED FOR ALL ETERNITY!
ANDRU & GIORDANO

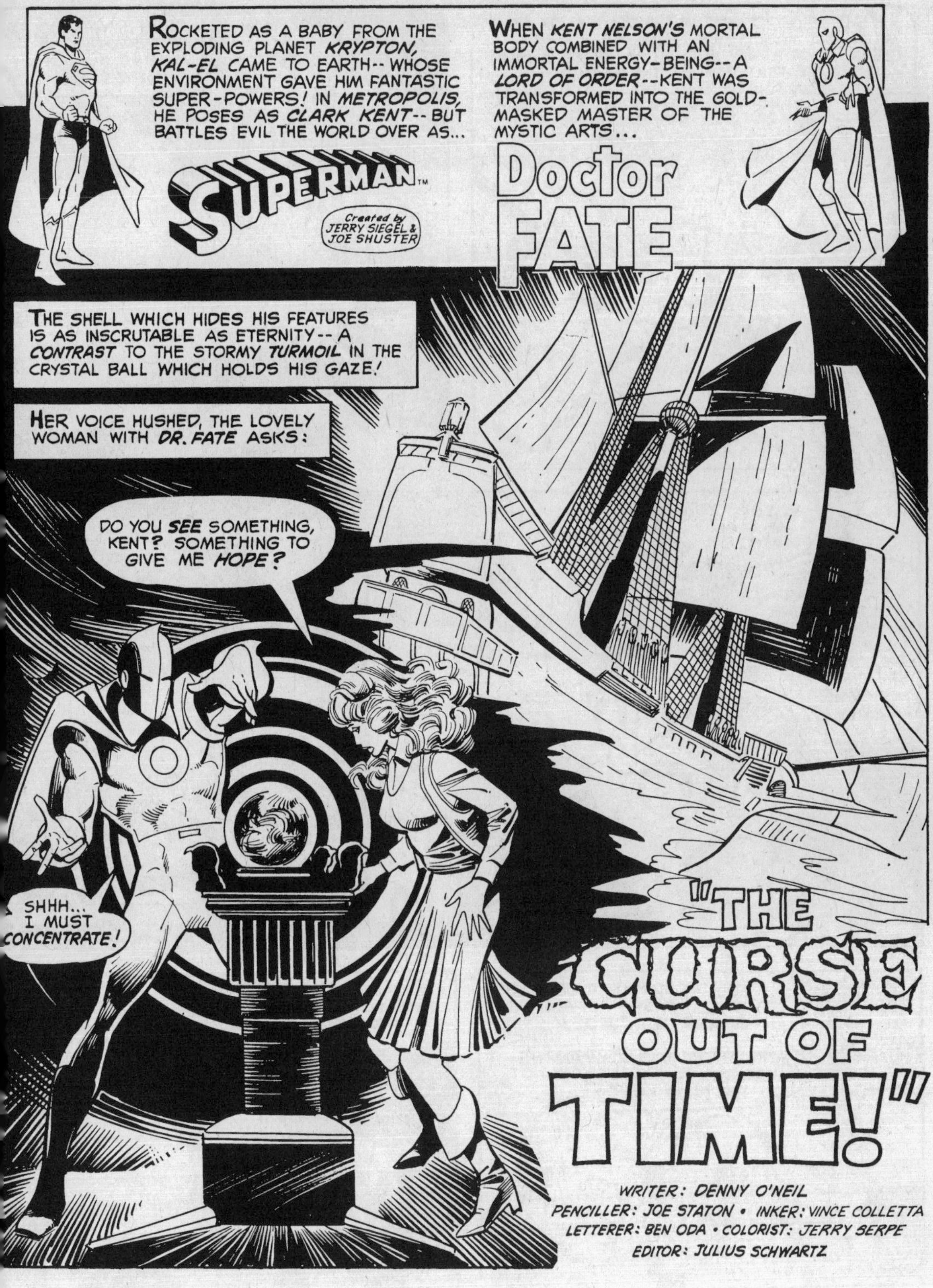
ROCKETED AS A BABY FROM THE EXPLODING PLANET KRYPTON, KAL-EL CAME TO EARTH-- WHOSE ENVIRONMENT GAVE HIM FANTASTIC SUPER-POWERS! IN METROPOLIS, HE POSES AS CLARK KENT-- BUT BATTLES EVIL THE WORLD OVER AS...
SUPERMAN
Created by JERRY SIEGEL & JOE SHUSTER
WHEN KENT NELSON'S MORTAL BODY COMBINED WITH AN IMMORTAL ENERGY-BEING-- A LORD OF ORDER --KENT WAS TRANSFORMED INTO THE GOLD-MASKED MASTER OF THE MYSTIC ARTS...
Doctor FATE
THE SHELL WHICH HIDES HIS FEATURES IS AS INSCRUTABLE AS ETERNITY-- A CONTRAST TO THE STORMY TURMOIL IN THE CRYSTAL BALL WHICH HOLDS HIS GAZE!
HER VOICE HUSHED, THE LOVELY WOMAN WITH DR. FATE ASKS:
DO YOU SEE SOMETHING, KENT? SOMETHING TO GIVE ME HOPE?
SHHH... I MUST CONCENTRATE!
"THE CURSE OUT OF TIME!"
WRITER: DENNY O'NEIL
PENCILLER: JOE STATON • INKER: VINCE COLLETTA
LETTERER: BEN ODA • COLORIST: JERRY SERPE
EDITOR: JULIUS SCHWARTZ

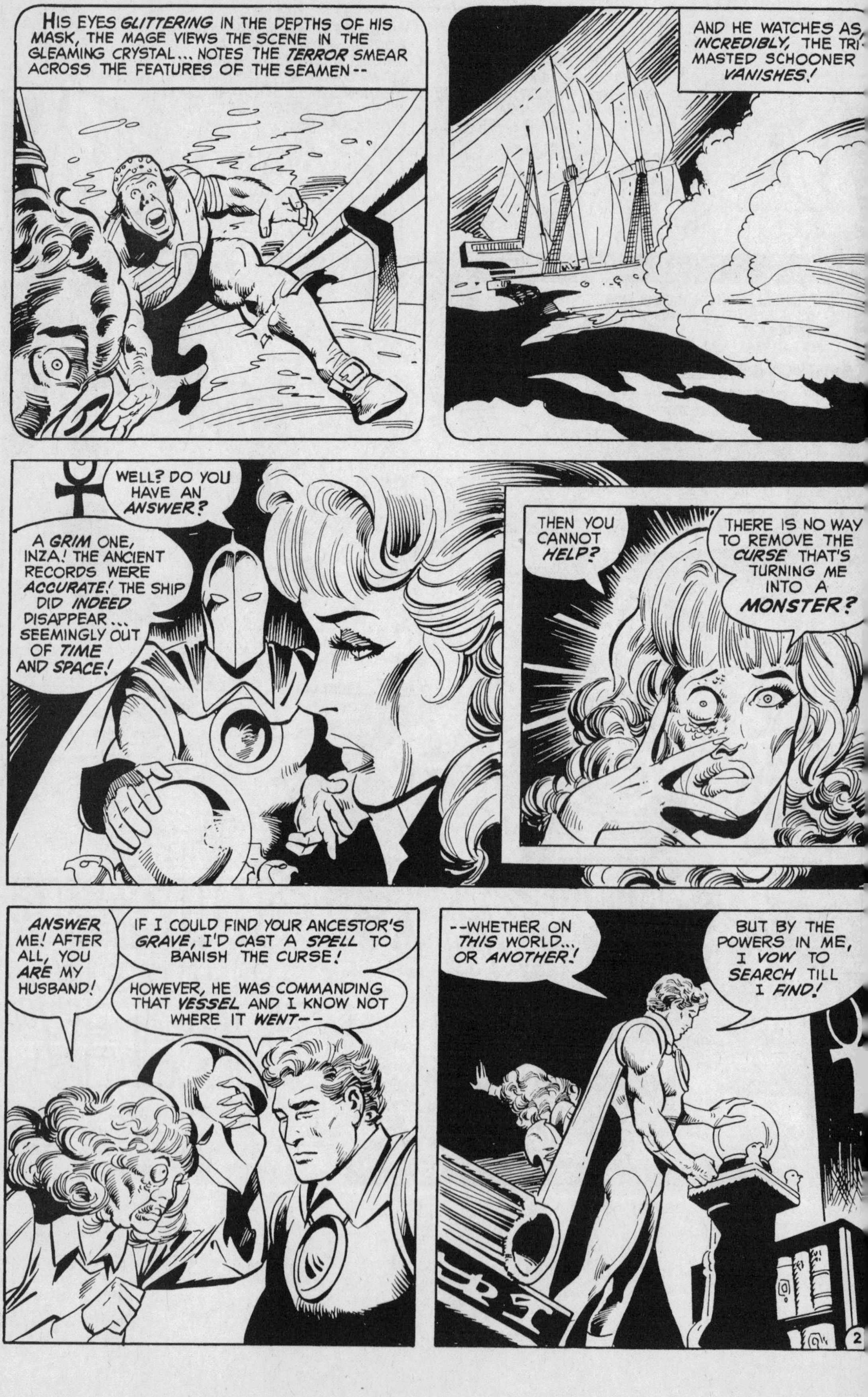
HIS EYES GLITTERING IN THE DEPTHS OF HIS MASK, THE MAGE VIEWS THE SCENE IN THE GLEAMING CRYSTAL... NOTES THE TERROR SMEAR ACROSS THE FEATURES OF THE SEAMEN--
AND HE WATCHES AS, INCREDIBLY, THE TRI-MASTED SCHOONER VANISHES!
WELL? DO YOU HAVE AN ANSWER?
A GRIM ONE, INZA! THE ANCIENT RECORDS WERE ACCURATE! THE SHIP DID INDEED DISAPPEAR... SEEMINGLY OUT OF TIME AND SPACE!
THEN YOU CANNOT HELP?
THERE IS NO WAY TO REMOVE THE CURSE THAT'S TURNING ME INTO A MONSTER?
ANSWER ME! AFTER ALL, YOU ARE MY HUSBAND!
IF I COULD FIND YOUR ANCESTOR'S GRAVE, I'D CAST A SPELL TO BANISH THE CURSE!
HOWEVER, HE WAS COMMANDING THAT VESSEL AND I KNOW NOT WHERE IT WENT--
--WHETHER ON THIS WORLD... OR ANOTHER!
BUT BY THE POWERS IN ME, I VOW TO SEARCH TILL I FIND!
2

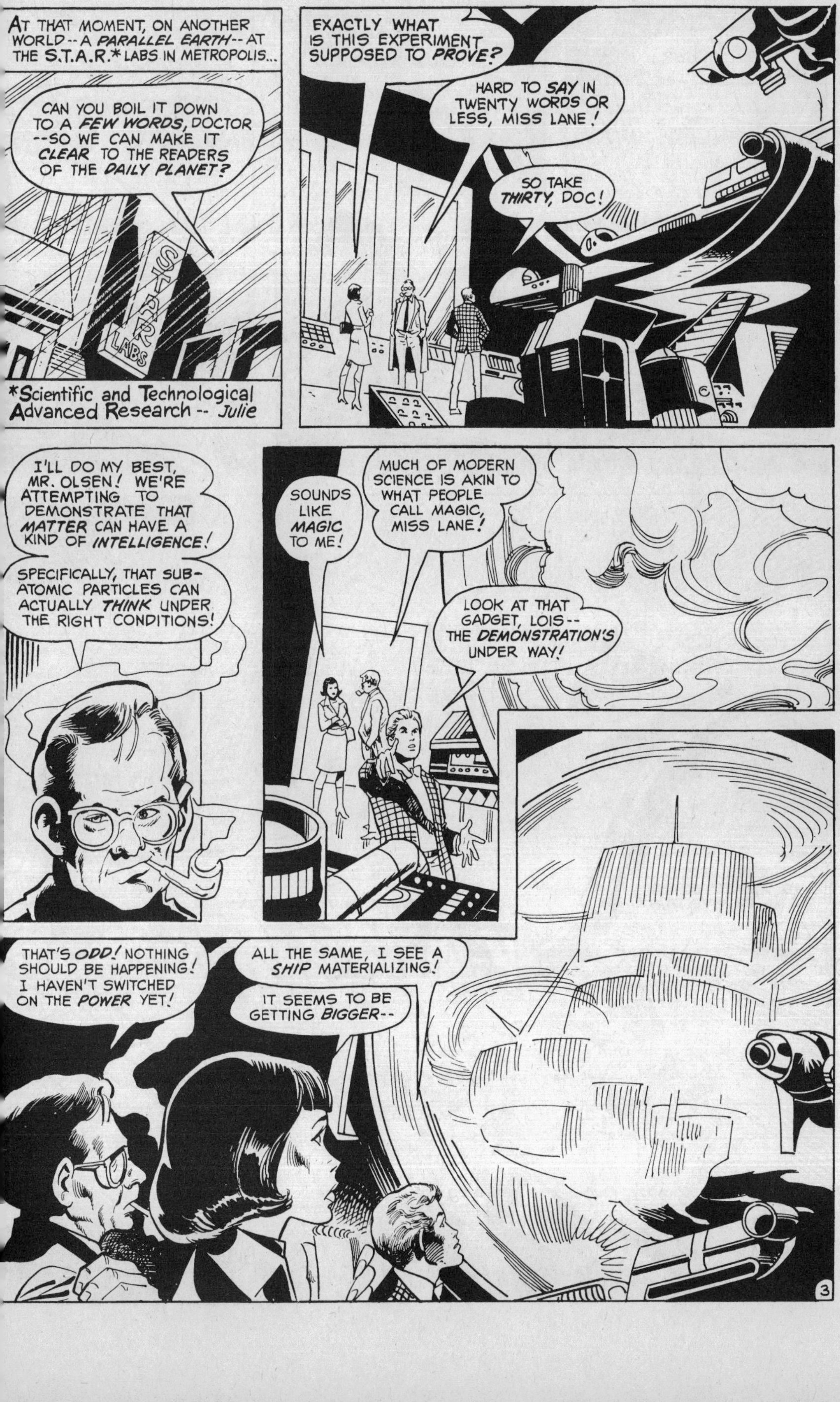
AT THAT MOMENT, ON ANOTHER WORLD -- A PARALLEL EARTH -- AT THE S.T.A.R.* LABS IN METROPOLIS...
CAN YOU BOIL IT DOWN TO A FEW WORDS, DOCTOR --SO WE CAN MAKE IT CLEAR TO THE READERS OF THE DAILY PLANET?
S.T.A.R. LABS
*Scientific and Technological Advanced Research -- Julie
EXACTLY WHAT IS THIS EXPERIMENT SUPPOSED TO PROVE?
HARD TO SAY IN TWENTY WORDS OR LESS, MISS LANE!
SO TAKE THIRTY, DOC!
I'LL DO MY BEST, MR. OLSEN! WE'RE ATTEMPTING TO DEMONSTRATE THAT MATTER CAN HAVE A KIND OF INTELLIGENCE!
SPECIFICALLY, THAT SUB-ATOMIC PARTICLES CAN ACTUALLY THINK UNDER THE RIGHT CONDITIONS!
SOUNDS LIKE MAGIC TO ME!
MUCH OF MODERN SCIENCE IS AKIN TO WHAT PEOPLE CALL MAGIC, MISS LANE!
LOOK AT THAT GADGET, LOIS-- THE DEMONSTRATION'S UNDER WAY!
THAT'S ODD! NOTHING SHOULD BE HAPPENING! I HAVEN'T SWITCHED ON THE POWER YET!
ALL THE SAME, I SEE A SHIP MATERIALIZING!
IT SEEMS TO BE GETTING BIGGER--
3

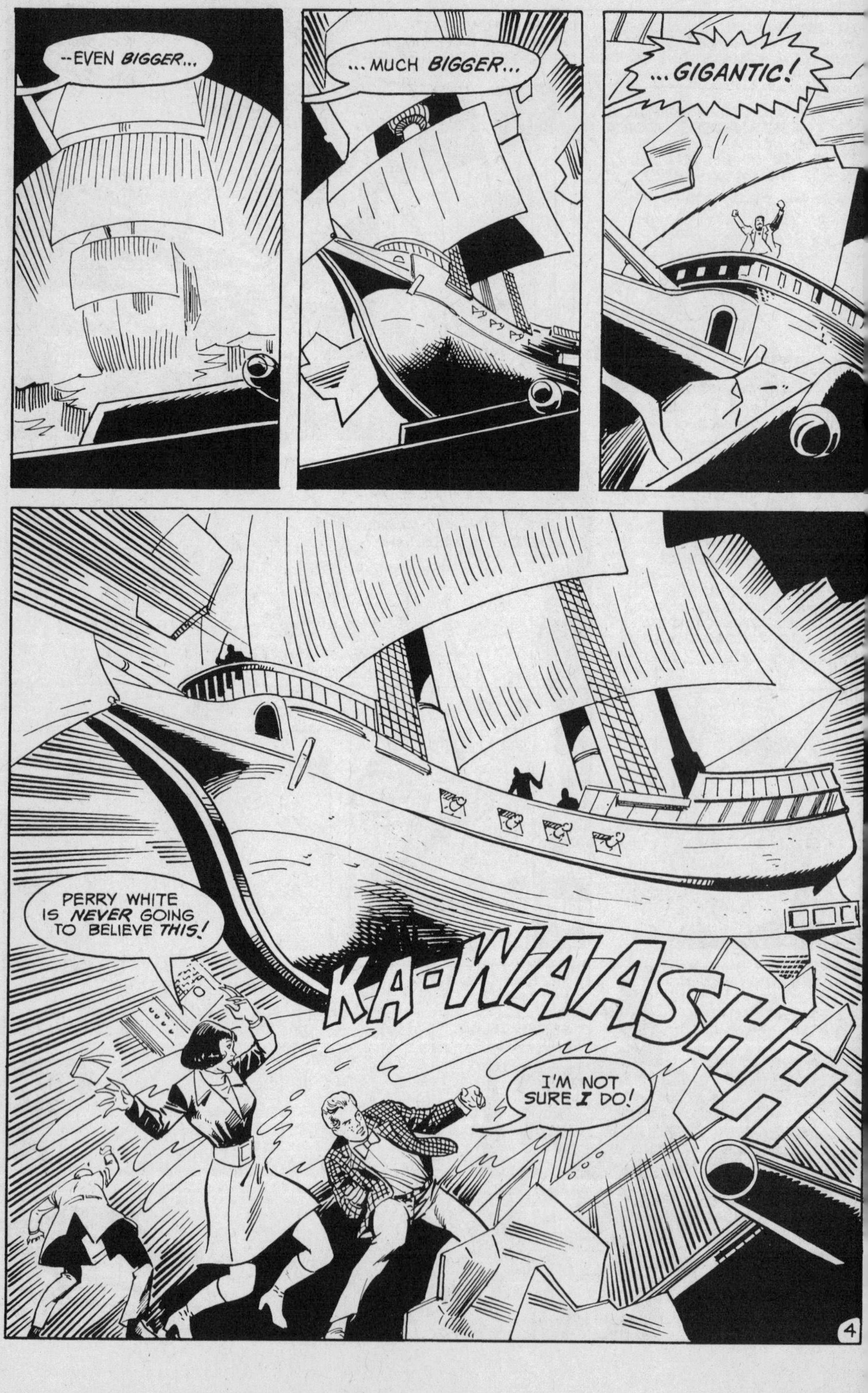
--EVEN BIGGER...
...MUCH BIGGER...
...GIGANTIC!
PERRY WHITE IS NEVER GOING TO BELIEVE THIS!
KA-WAASHH
I'M NOT SURE I DO!
4

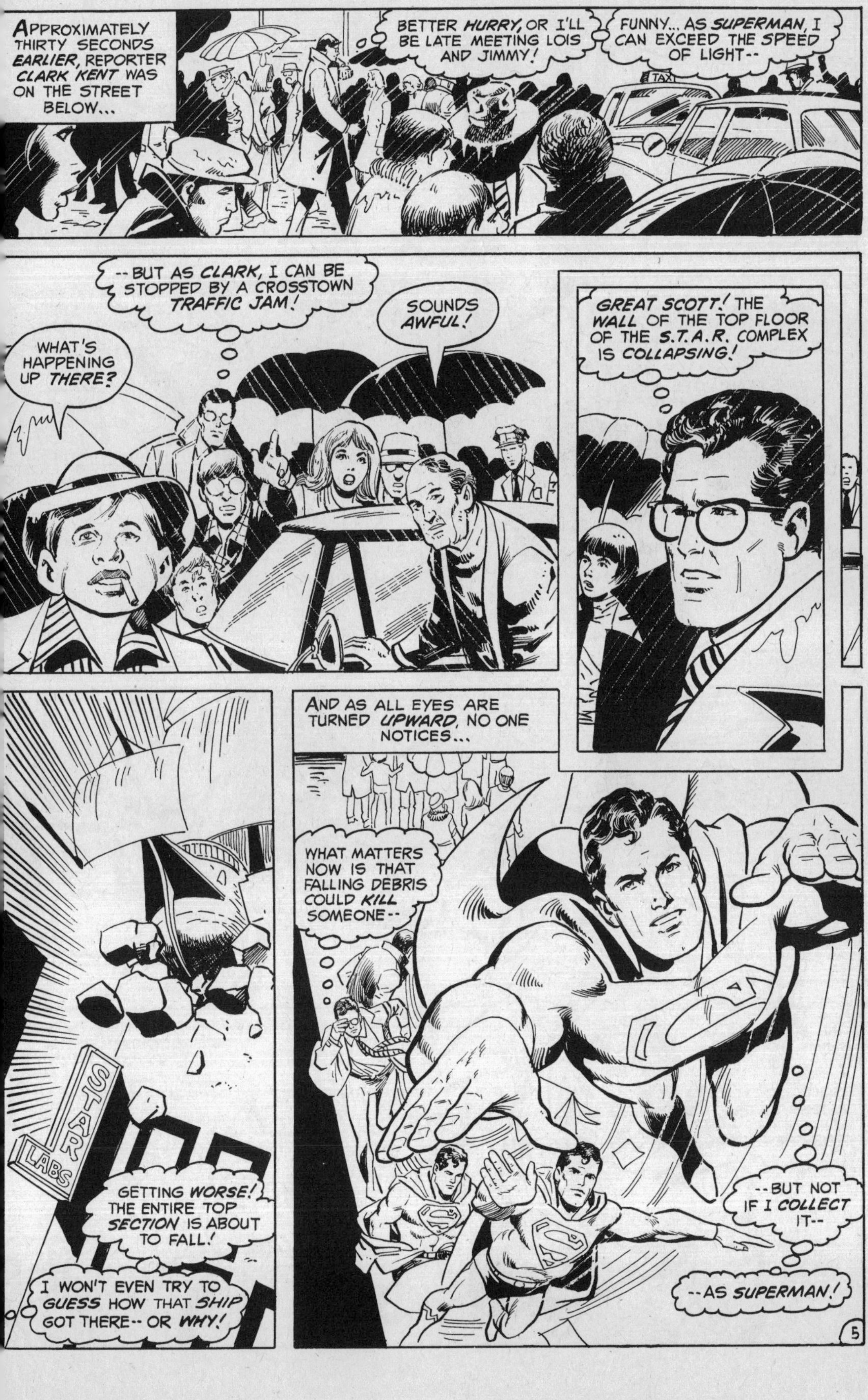
APPROXIMATELY THIRTY SECONDS EARLIER, REPORTER CLARK KENT WAS ON THE STREET BELOW...
BETTER HURRY, OR I'LL BE LATE MEETING LOIS AND JIMMY!
FUNNY... AS SUPERMAN, I CAN EXCEED THE SPEED OF LIGHT--
TAXI
--BUT AS CLARK, I CAN BE STOPPED BY A CROSSTOWN TRAFFIC JAM!
WHAT'S HAPPENING UP THERE?
SOUNDS AWFUL!
GREAT SCOTT! THE WALL OF THE TOP FLOOR OF THE S.T.A.R. COMPLEX IS COLLAPSING!
STAR LABS
GETTING WORSE! THE ENTIRE TOP SECTION IS ABOUT TO FALL!
I WON'T EVEN TRY TO GUESS HOW THAT SHIP GOT THERE-- OR WHY!
AND AS ALL EYES ARE TURNED UPWARD, NO ONE NOTICES...
WHAT MATTERS NOW IS THAT FALLING DEBRIS COULD KILL SOMEONE--
--BUT NOT IF I COLLECT IT--
--AS SUPERMAN!
5

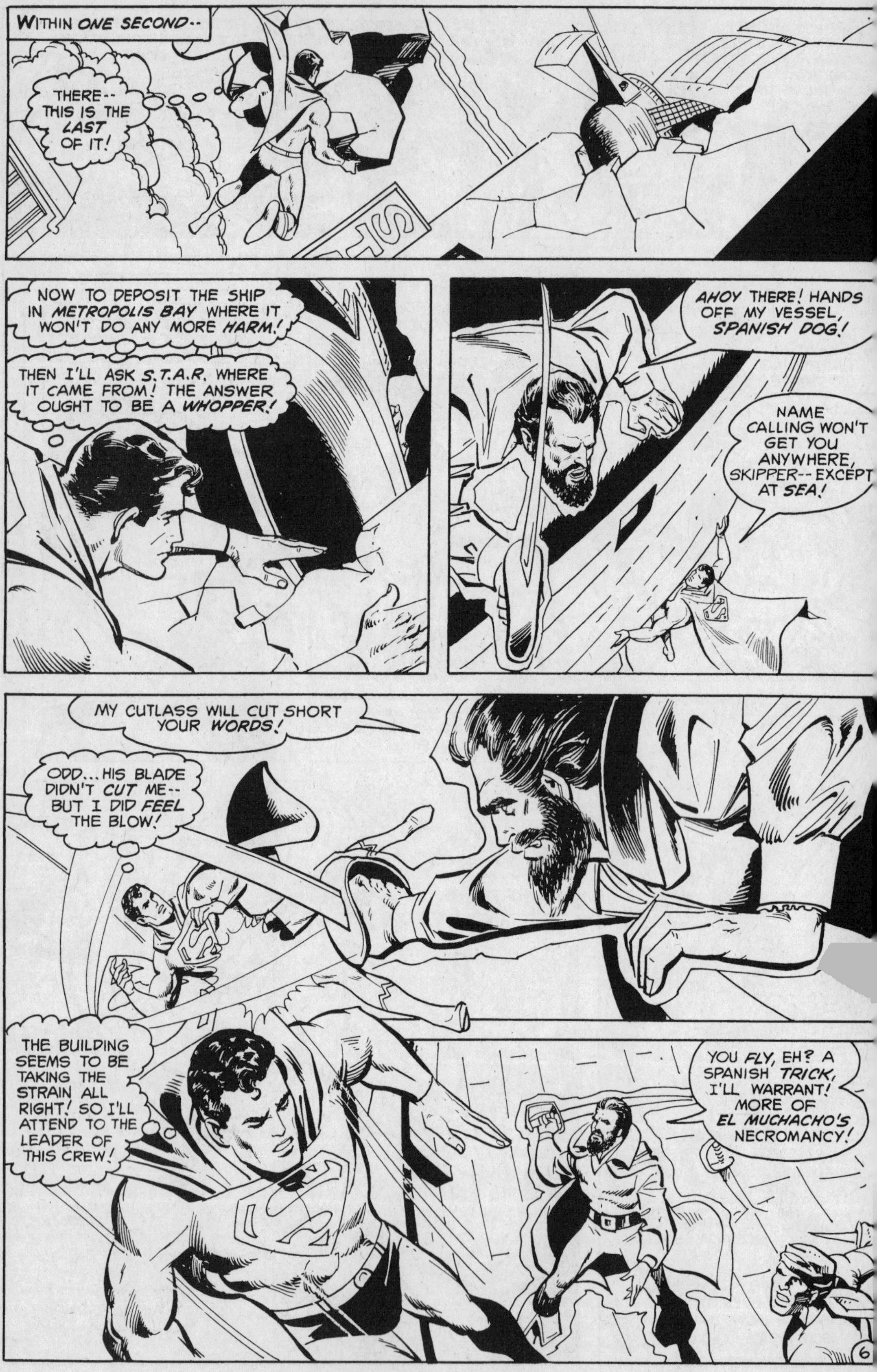
WITHIN ONE SECOND--
THERE-- THIS IS THE LAST OF IT!
NOW TO DEPOSIT THE SHIP IN METROPOLIS BAY WHERE IT WON'T DO ANY MORE HARM!
THEN I'LL ASK S.T.A.R. WHERE IT CAME FROM! THE ANSWER OUGHT TO BE A WHOPPER!
AHOY THERE! HANDS OFF MY VESSEL, SPANISH DOG!
NAME CALLING WON'T GET YOU ANYWHERE, SKIPPER-- EXCEPT AT SEA!
MY CUTLASS WILL CUT SHORT YOUR WORDS!
ODD... HIS BLADE DIDN'T CUT ME-- BUT I DID FEEL THE BLOW!
THE BUILDING SEEMS TO BE TAKING THE STRAIN ALL RIGHT! SO I'LL ATTEND TO THE LEADER OF THIS CREW!
YOU FLY, EH? A SPANISH TRICK, I'LL WARRANT! MORE OF EL MUCHACHO'S NECROMANCY!
6

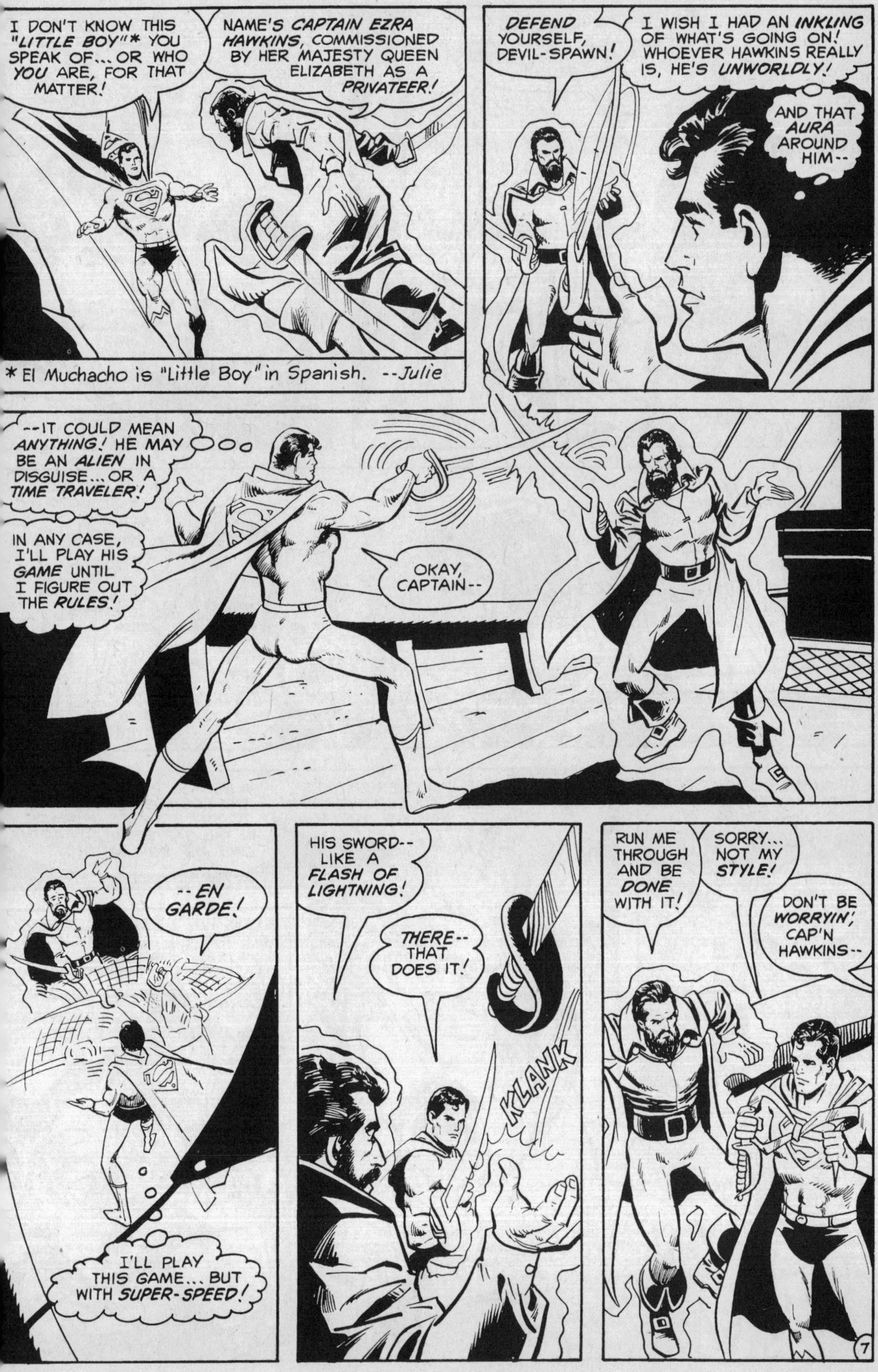
I DON'T KNOW THIS "LITTLE BOY"* YOU SPEAK OF... OR WHO YOU ARE, FOR THAT MATTER!
NAME'S CAPTAIN EZRA HAWKINS, COMMISSIONED BY HER MAJESTY QUEEN ELIZABETH AS A PRIVATEER!
* El Muchacho is "Little Boy" in Spanish. --Julie
DEFEND YOURSELF, DEVIL-SPAWN!
I WISH I HAD AN INKLING OF WHAT'S GOING ON! WHOEVER HAWKINS REALLY IS, HE'S UNWORLDLY!
AND THAT AURA AROUND HIM--
--IT COULD MEAN ANYTHING! HE MAY BE AN ALIEN IN DISGUISE... OR A TIME TRAVELER!
IN ANY CASE, I'LL PLAY HIS GAME UNTIL I FIGURE OUT THE RULES!
OKAY, CAPTAIN--
--EN GARDE!
I'LL PLAY THIS GAME... BUT WITH SUPER-SPEED!
HIS SWORD-- LIKE A FLASH OF LIGHTNING!
THERE-- THAT DOES IT!
KLANK
RUN ME THROUGH AND BE DONE WITH IT!
SORRY... NOT MY STYLE!
DON'T BE WORRYIN', CAP'N HAWKINS--
7

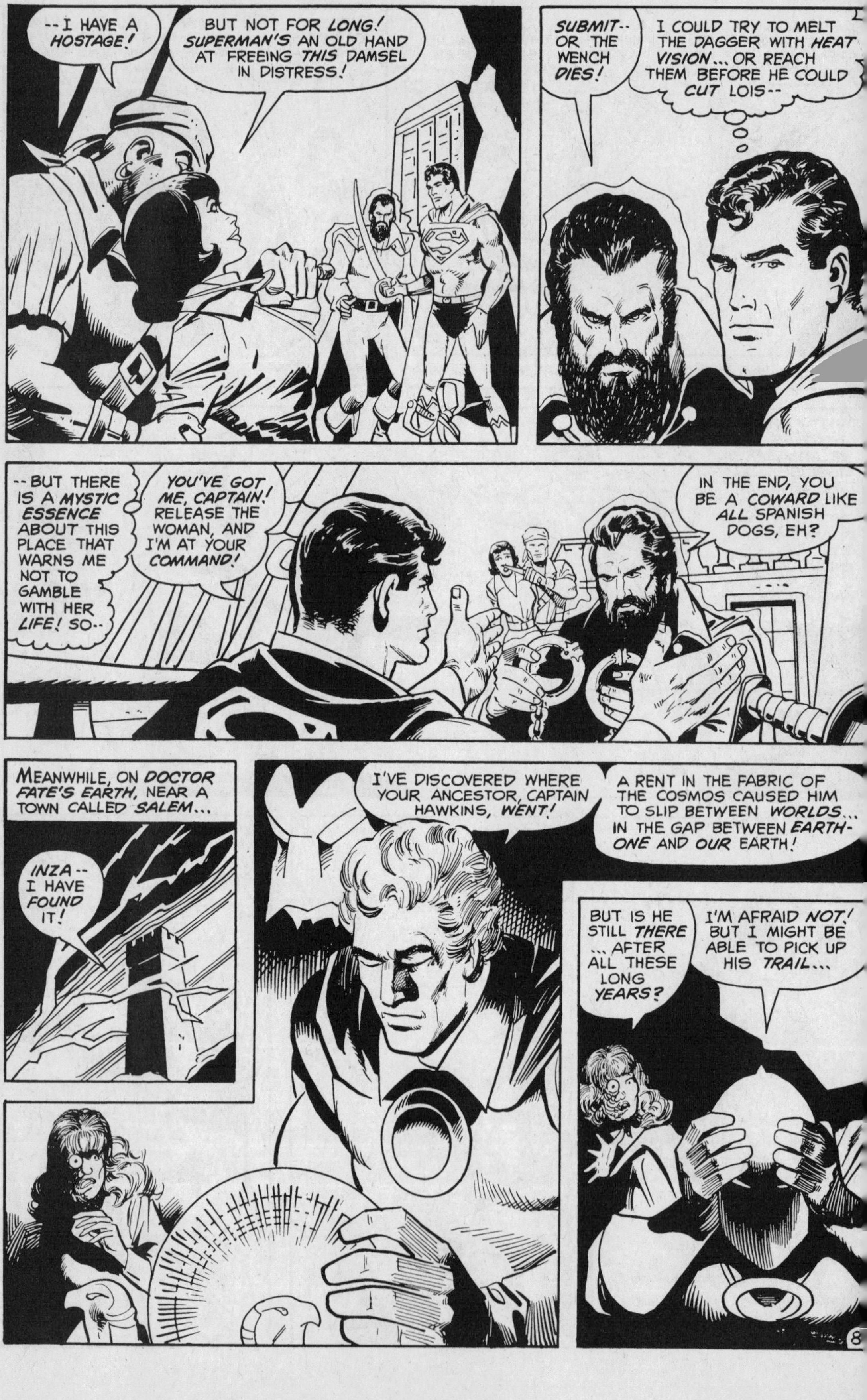
--I HAVE A HOSTAGE!
BUT NOT FOR LONG! SUPERMAN'S AN OLD HAND AT FREEING THIS DAMSEL IN DISTRESS!
SUBMIT-- OR THE WENCH DIES!
I COULD TRY TO MELT THE DAGGER WITH HEAT VISION... OR REACH THEM BEFORE HE COULD CUT LOIS--
--BUT THERE IS A MYSTIC ESSENCE ABOUT THIS PLACE THAT WARNS ME NOT TO GAMBLE WITH HER LIFE! SO--
YOU'VE GOT ME, CAPTAIN! RELEASE THE WOMAN, AND I'M AT YOUR COMMAND!
IN THE END, YOU BE A COWARD LIKE ALL SPANISH DOGS, EH?
MEANWHILE, ON DOCTOR FATE'S EARTH, NEAR A TOWN CALLED SALEM...
INZA-- I HAVE FOUND IT!
I'VE DISCOVERED WHERE YOUR ANCESTOR, CAPTAIN HAWKINS, WENT!
A RENT IN THE FABRIC OF THE COSMOS CAUSED HIM TO SLIP BETWEEN WORLDS... IN THE GAP BETWEEN EARTH-ONE AND OUR EARTH!
BUT IS HE STILL THERE ... AFTER ALL THESE LONG YEARS?
I'M AFRAID NOT! BUT I MIGHT BE ABLE TO PICK UP HIS TRAIL...
8

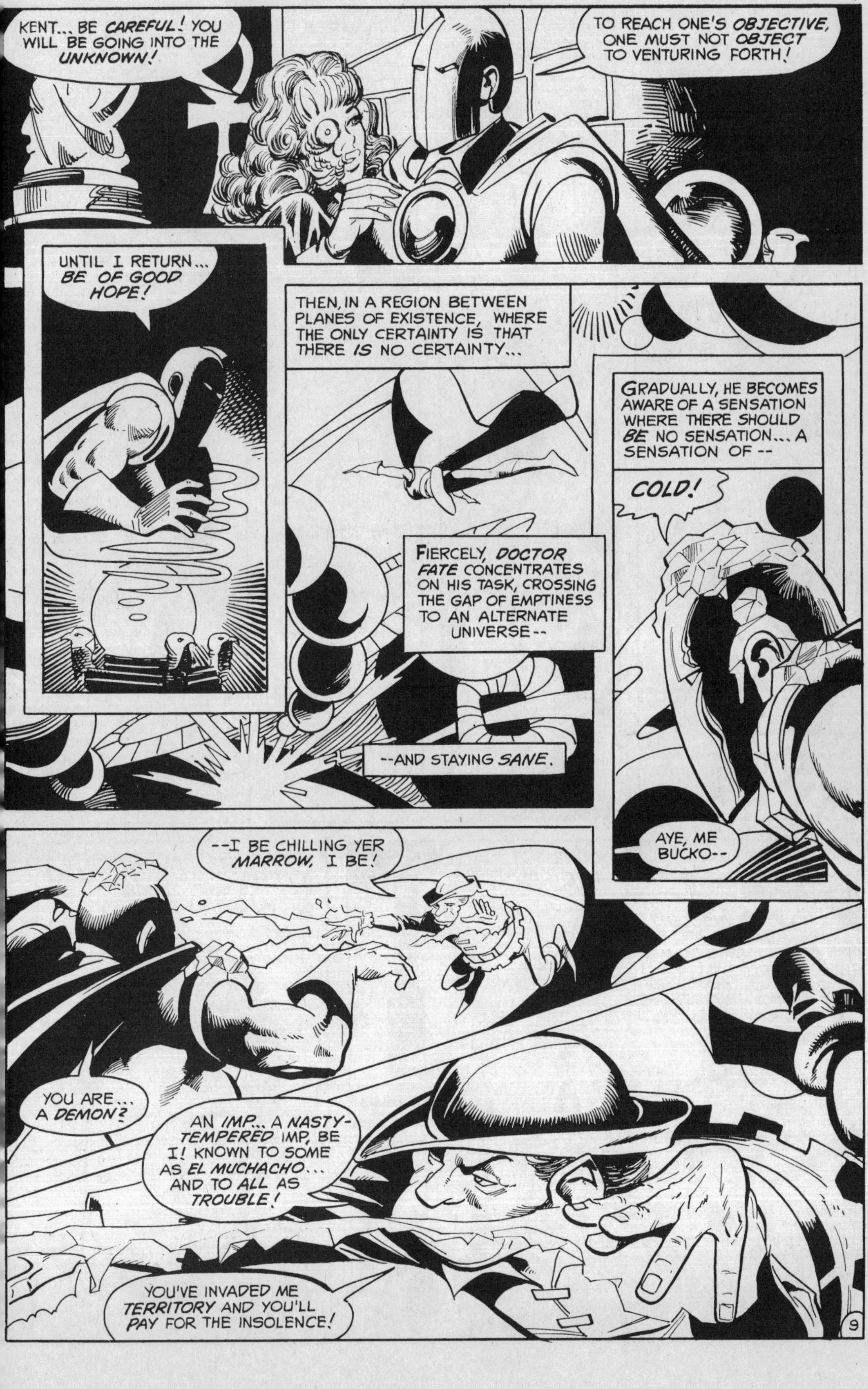
KENT... BE CAREFUL! YOU WILL BE GOING INTO THE UNKNOWN!
TO REACH ONE'S OBJECTIVE, ONE MUST NOT OBJECT TO VENTURING FORTH!
UNTIL I RETURN... BE OF GOOD HOPE!
THEN, IN A REGION BETWEEN PLANES OF EXISTENCE, WHERE THE ONLY CERTAINTY IS THAT THERE IS NO CERTAINTY...
FIERCELY, DOCTOR FATE CONCENTRATES ON HIS TASK, CROSSING THE GAP OF EMPTINESS TO AN ALTERNATE UNIVERSE--
--AND STAYING SANE.
GRADUALLY, HE BECOMES AWARE OF A SENSATION WHERE THERE SHOULD BE NO SENSATION... A SENSATION OF --
COLD!
AYE, ME BUCKO--
--I BE CHILLING YER MARROW, I BE!
YOU ARE... A DEMON?
AN IMP... A NASTY-TEMPERED IMP, BE I! KNOWN TO SOME AS EL MUCHACHO... AND TO ALL AS TROUBLE!
YOU'VE INVADED ME TERRITORY AND YOU'LL PAY FOR THE INSOLENCE!
9

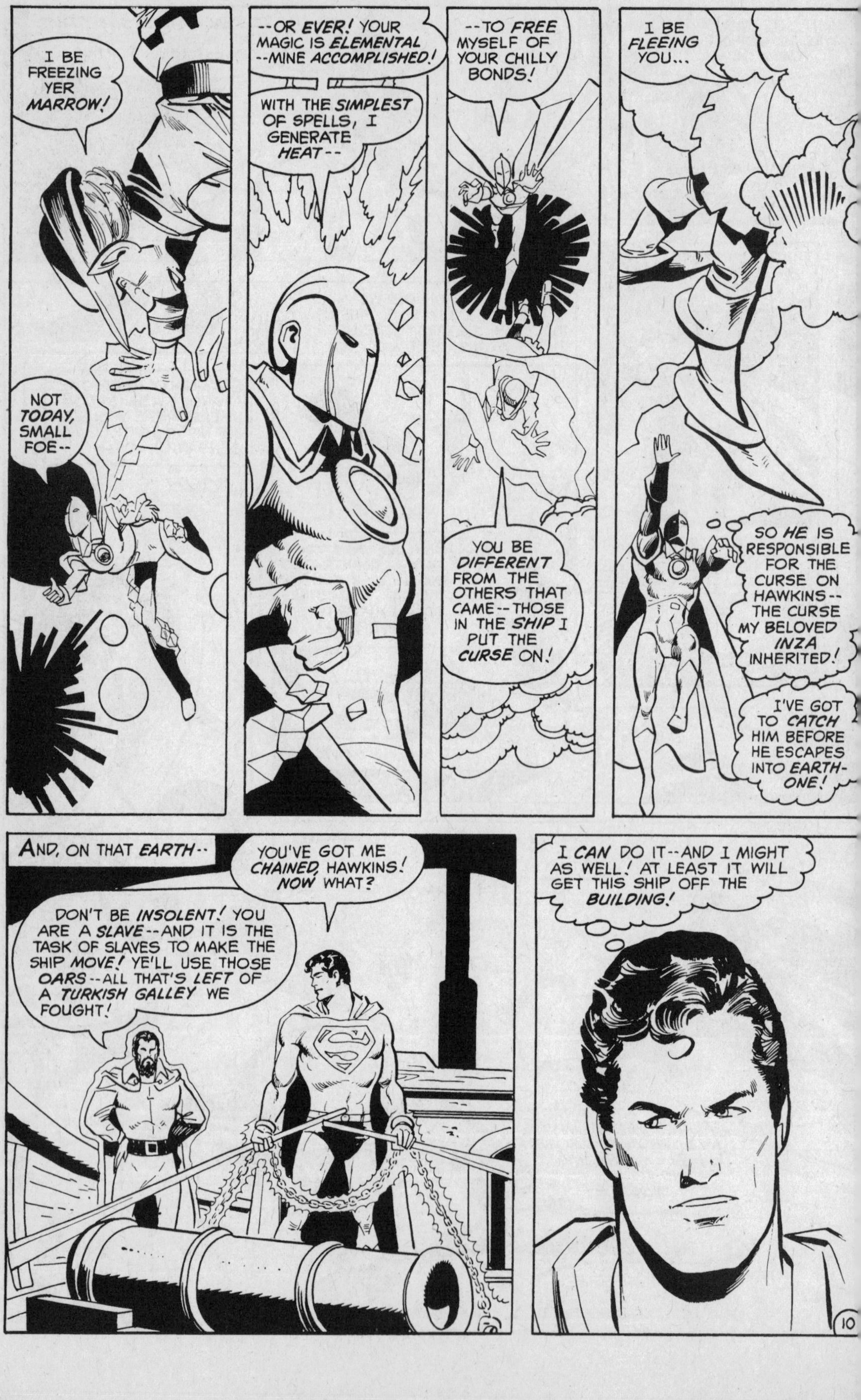
I BE FREEZING YER MARROW!
NOT TODAY, SMALL FOE--
--OR EVER! YOUR MAGIC IS ELEMENTAL --MINE ACCOMPLISHED!
WITH THE SIMPLEST OF SPELLS, I GENERATE HEAT--
--TO FREE MYSELF OF YOUR CHILLY BONDS!
YOU BE DIFFERENT FROM THE OTHERS THAT CAME--THOSE IN THE SHIP I PUT THE CURSE ON!
I BE FLEEING YOU...
SO HE IS RESPONSIBLE FOR THE CURSE ON HAWKINS--THE CURSE MY BELOVED INZA INHERITED!
I'VE GOT TO CATCH HIM BEFORE HE ESCAPES INTO EARTH-ONE!
AND, ON THAT EARTH--
YOU'VE GOT ME CHAINED, HAWKINS! NOW WHAT?
DON'T BE INSOLENT! YOU ARE A SLAVE--AND IT IS THE TASK OF SLAVES TO MAKE THE SHIP MOVE! YE'LL USE THOSE OARS--ALL THAT'S LEFT OF A TURKISH GALLEY WE FOUGHT!
I CAN DO IT--AND I MIGHT AS WELL! AT LEAST IT WILL GET THIS SHIP OFF THE BUILDING!
10

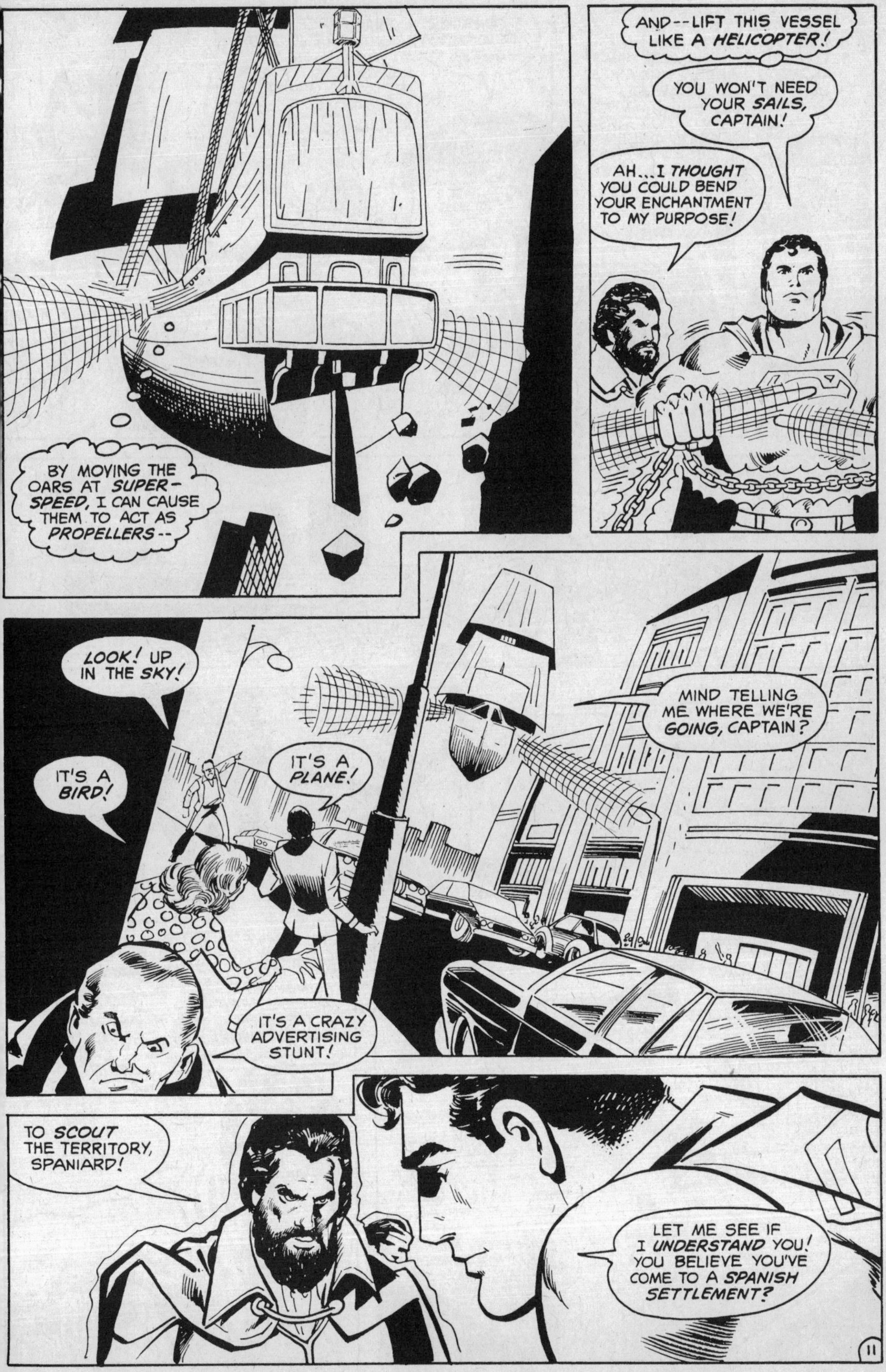

BY MOVING THE OARS AT SUPER-SPEED, I CAN CAUSE THEM TO ACT AS PROPELLERS--
AND--LIFT THIS VESSEL LIKE A HELICOPTER!
YOU WON'T NEED YOUR SAILS, CAPTAIN!
AH...I THOUGHT YOU COULD BEND YOUR ENCHANTMENT TO MY PURPOSE!
LOOK! UP IN THE SKY!
IT'S A BIRD!
IT'S A PLANE!
IT'S A CRAZY ADVERTISING STUNT!
MIND TELLING ME WHERE WE'RE GOING, CAPTAIN?
TO SCOUT THE TERRITORY, SPANIARD!
LET ME SEE IF I UNDERSTAND YOU! YOU BELIEVE YOU'VE COME TO A SPANISH SETTLEMENT?
11

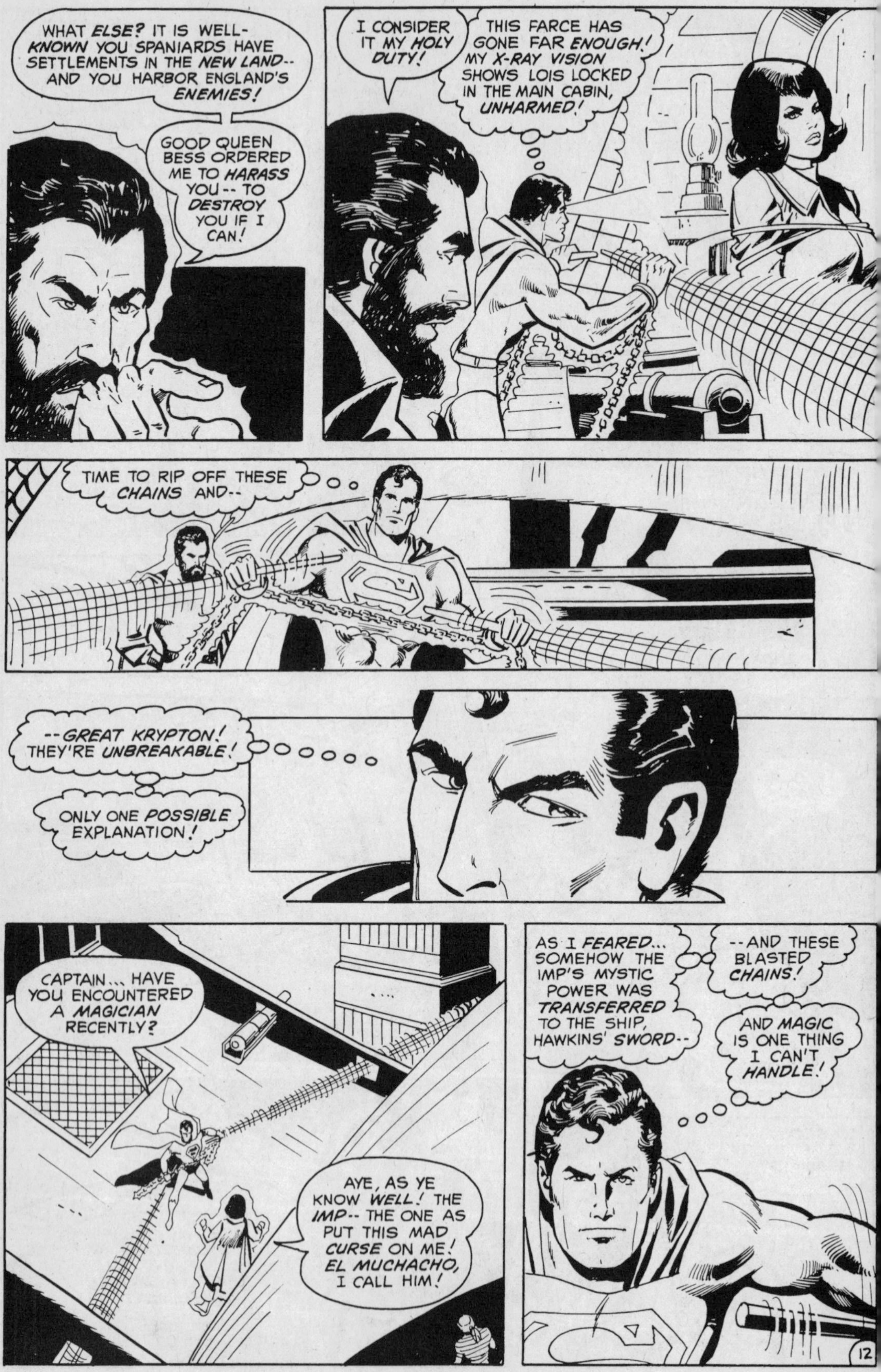
WHAT ELSE? IT IS WELL-KNOWN YOU SPANIARDS HAVE SETTLEMENTS IN THE NEW LAND-- AND YOU HARBOR ENGLAND'S ENEMIES!
GOOD QUEEN BESS ORDERED ME TO HARASS YOU -- TO DESTROY YOU IF I CAN!
I CONSIDER IT MY HOLY DUTY!
THIS FARCE HAS GONE FAR ENOUGH! MY X-RAY VISION SHOWS LOIS LOCKED IN THE MAIN CABIN, UNHARMED!
TIME TO RIP OFF THESE CHAINS AND--
--GREAT KRYPTON! THEY'RE UNBREAKABLE!
ONLY ONE POSSIBLE EXPLANATION!
CAPTAIN... HAVE YOU ENCOUNTERED A MAGICIAN RECENTLY?
AYE, AS YE KNOW WELL! THE IMP-- THE ONE AS PUT THIS MAD CURSE ON ME! EL MUCHACHO, I CALL HIM!
AS I FEARED... SOMEHOW THE IMP'S MYSTIC POWER WAS TRANSFERRED TO THE SHIP, HAWKINS' SWORD--
--AND THESE BLASTED CHAINS!
AND MAGIC IS ONE THING I CAN'T HANDLE!
12

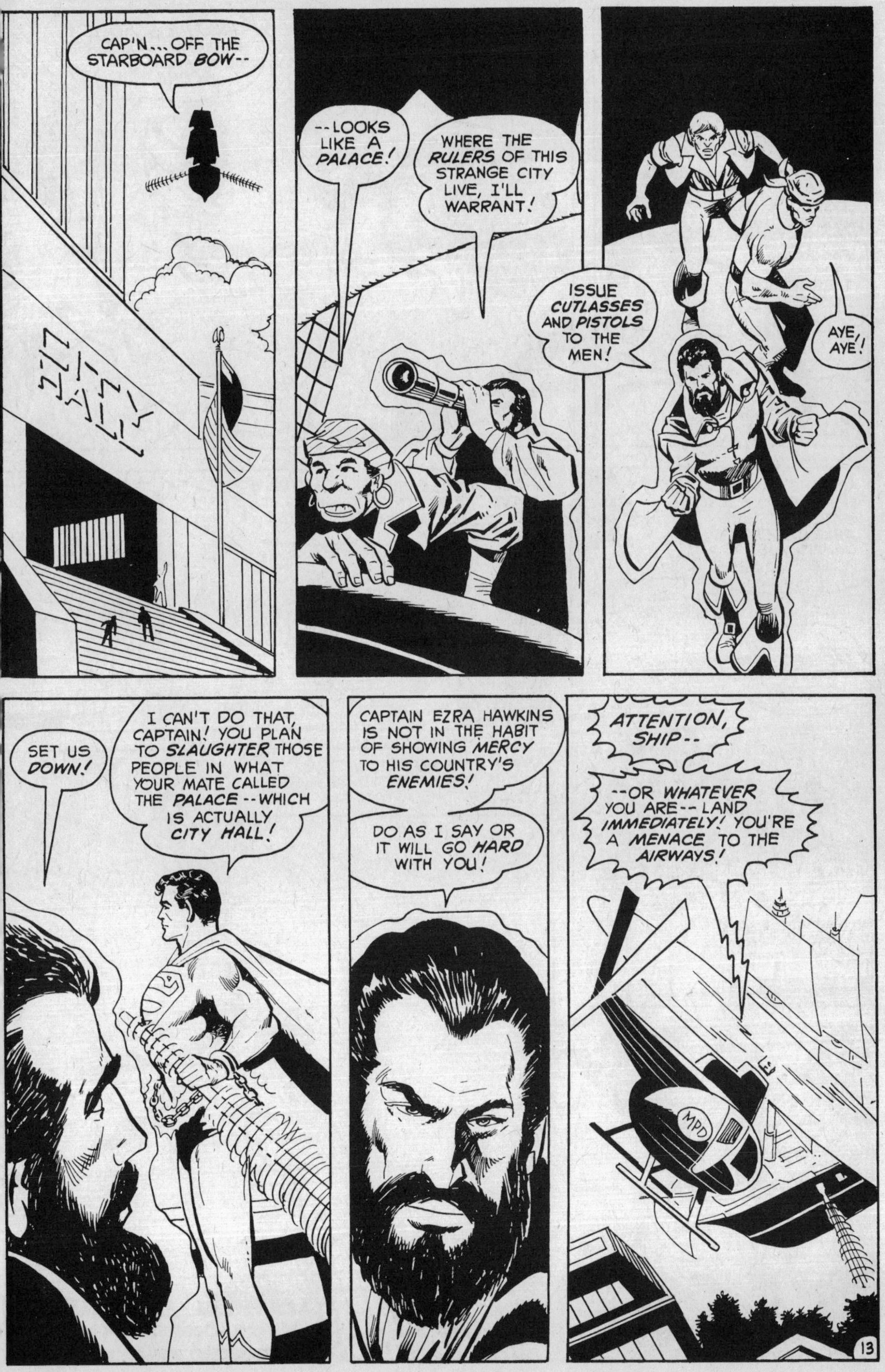
CAP'N... OFF THE STARBOARD BOW--
CITY HALL
--LOOKS LIKE A PALACE!
WHERE THE RULERS OF THIS STRANGE CITY LIVE, I'LL WARRANT!
ISSUE CUTLASSES AND PISTOLS TO THE MEN!
AYE, AYE!
SET US DOWN!
I CAN'T DO THAT, CAPTAIN! YOU PLAN TO SLAUGHTER THOSE PEOPLE IN WHAT YOUR MATE CALLED THE PALACE--WHICH IS ACTUALLY CITY HALL!
CAPTAIN EZRA HAWKINS IS NOT IN THE HABIT OF SHOWING MERCY TO HIS COUNTRY'S ENEMIES!
DO AS I SAY OR IT WILL GO HARD WITH YOU!
ATTENTION, SHIP--
--OR WHATEVER YOU ARE--LAND IMMEDIATELY! YOU'RE A MENACE TO THE AIRWAYS!
MPD
13

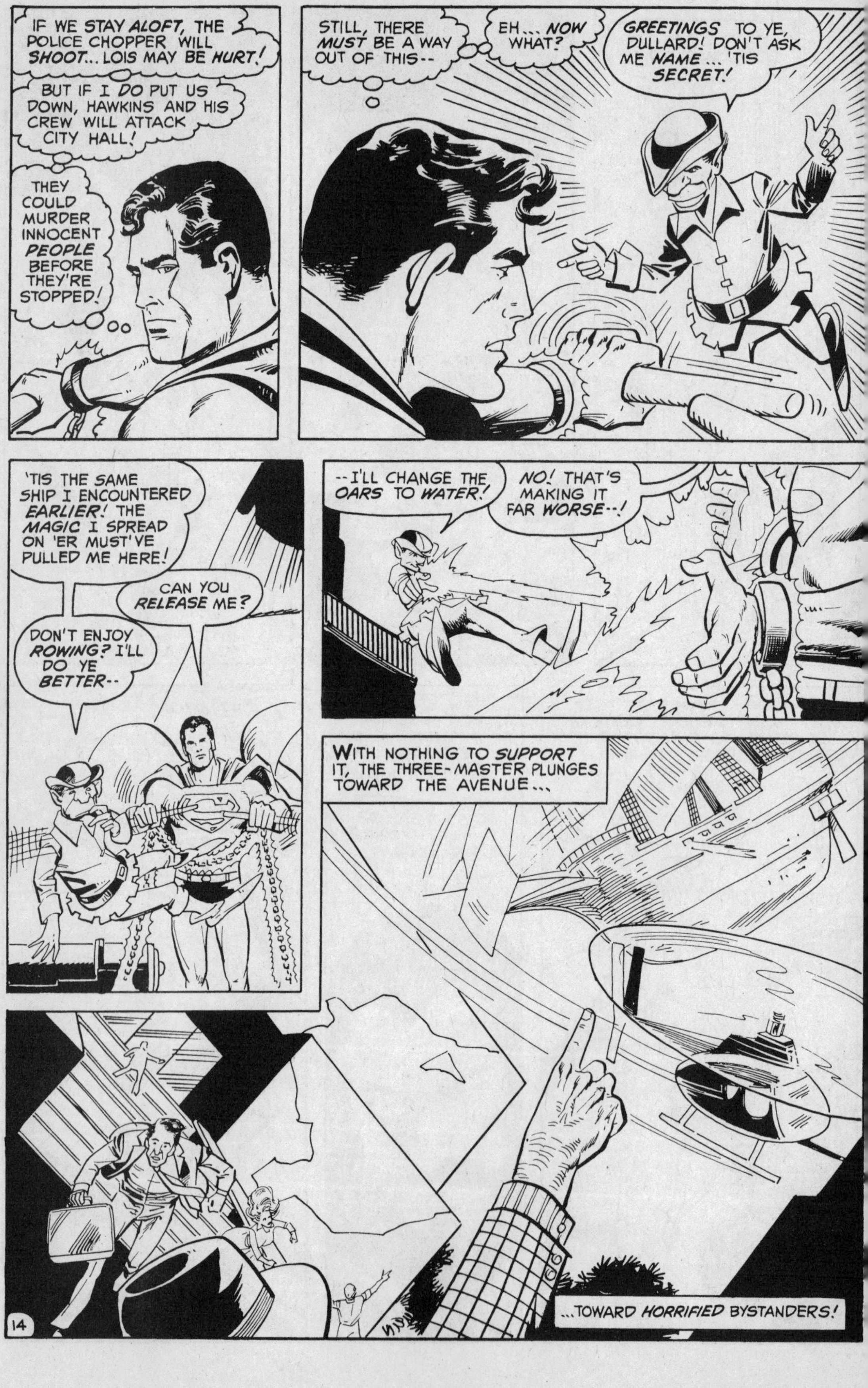
IF WE STAY ALOFT, THE POLICE CHOPPER WILL SHOOT... LOIS MAY BE HURT!
BUT IF I DO PUT US DOWN, HAWKINS AND HIS CREW WILL ATTACK CITY HALL!
THEY COULD MURDER INNOCENT PEOPLE BEFORE THEY'RE STOPPED!
STILL, THERE MUST BE A WAY OUT OF THIS--
EH... NOW WHAT?
GREETINGS TO YE, DULLARD! DON'T ASK ME NAME... 'TIS SECRET!
'TIS THE SAME SHIP I ENCOUNTERED EARLIER! THE MAGIC I SPREAD ON 'ER MUST'VE PULLED ME HERE!
CAN YOU RELEASE ME?
DON'T ENJOY ROWING? I'LL DO YE BETTER--
--I'LL CHANGE THE OARS TO WATER!
NO! THAT'S MAKING IT FAR WORSE--!
WITH NOTHING TO SUPPORT IT, THE THREE-MASTER PLUNGES TOWARD THE AVENUE...
...TOWARD HORRIFIED BYSTANDERS!
14

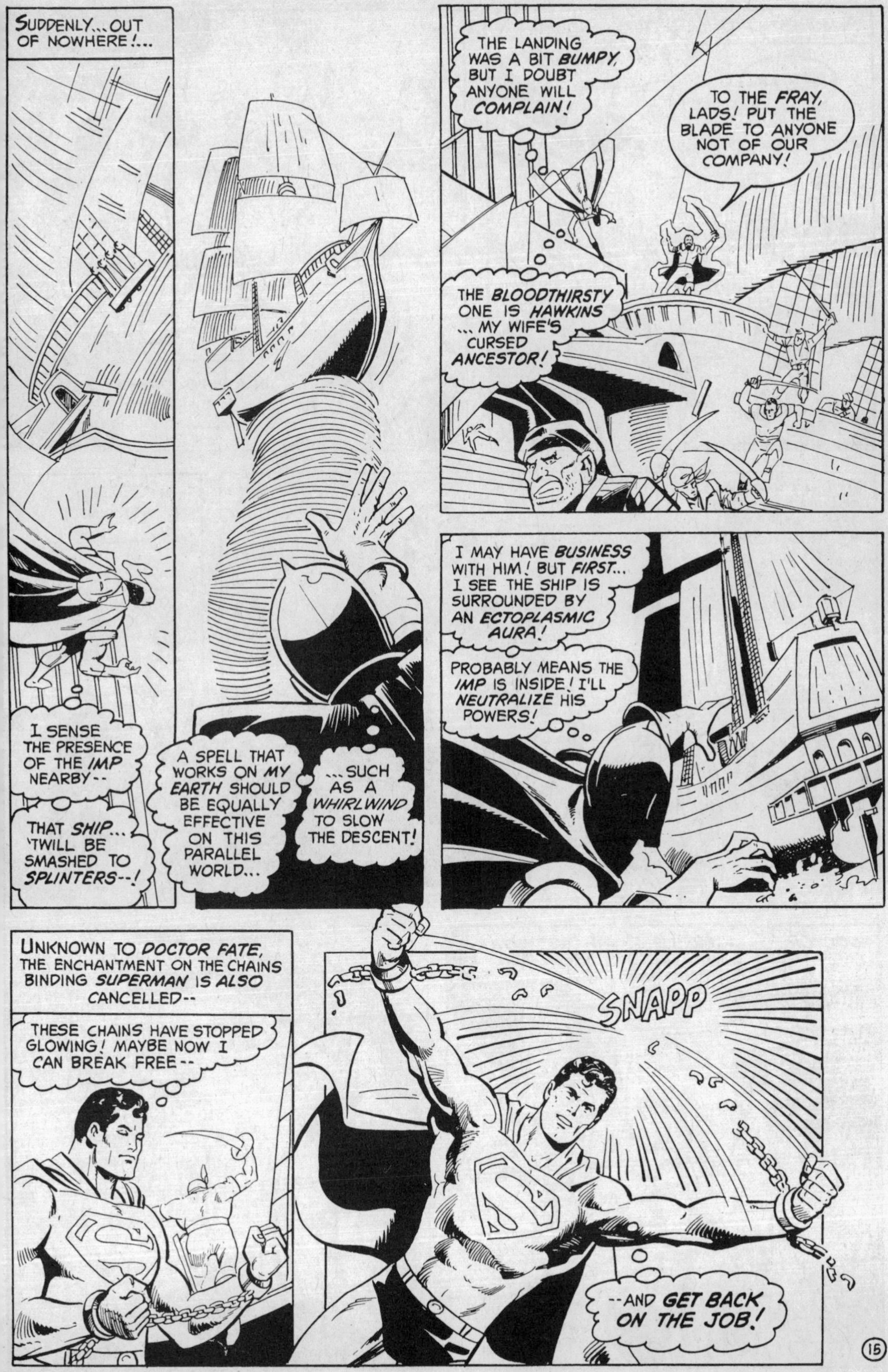
SUDDENLY... OUT OF NOWHERE!...
I SENSE THE PRESENCE OF THE IMP NEARBY--
THAT SHIP... 'TWILL BE SMASHED TO SPLINTERS--!
A SPELL THAT WORKS ON MY EARTH SHOULD BE EQUALLY EFFECTIVE ON THIS PARALLEL WORLD...
...SUCH AS A WHIRLWIND TO SLOW THE DESCENT!
THE LANDING WAS A BIT BUMPY, BUT I DOUBT ANYONE WILL COMPLAIN!
TO THE FRAY, LADS! PUT THE BLADE TO ANYONE NOT OF OUR COMPANY!
THE BLOODTHIRSTY ONE IS HAWKINS ... MY WIFE'S CURSED ANCESTOR!
I MAY HAVE BUSINESS WITH HIM! BUT FIRST... I SEE THE SHIP IS SURROUNDED BY AN ECTOPLASMIC AURA!
PROBABLY MEANS THE IMP IS INSIDE! I'LL NEUTRALIZE HIS POWERS!
UNKNOWN TO DOCTOR FATE, THE ENCHANTMENT ON THE CHAINS BINDING SUPERMAN IS ALSO CANCELLED--
THESE CHAINS HAVE STOPPED GLOWING! MAYBE NOW I CAN BREAK FREE--
SNAPP
--AND GET BACK ON THE JOB!
15

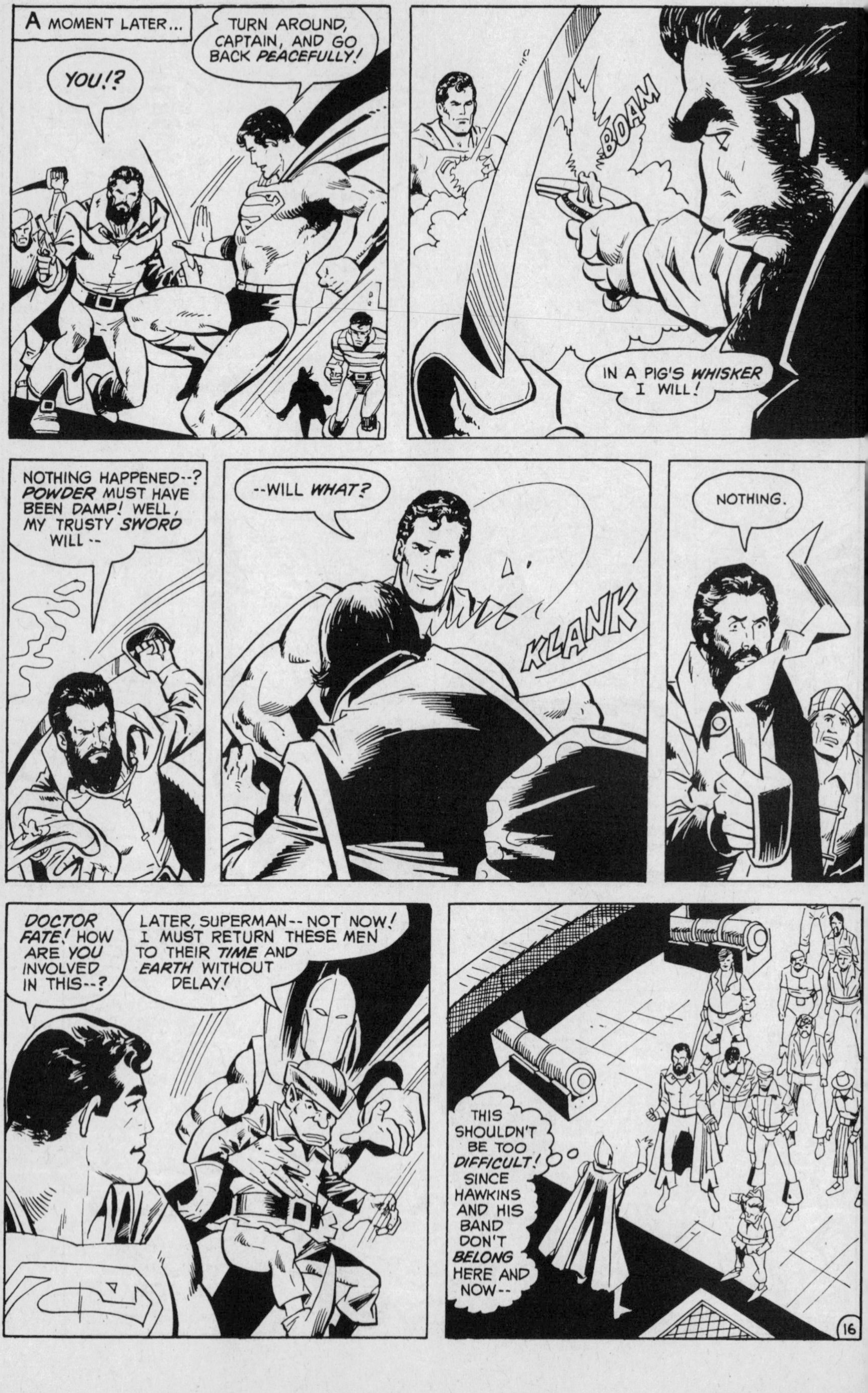
A MOMENT LATER...
YOU!?
TURN AROUND, CAPTAIN, AND GO BACK *PEACEFULLY!*
BOAM
IN A PIG'S *WHISKER* I WILL!
NOTHING HAPPENED--? *POWDER* MUST HAVE BEEN DAMP! WELL, MY TRUSTY *SWORD* WILL--
--WILL *WHAT?*
KLANK
NOTHING.
DOCTOR FATE! HOW ARE *YOU* INVOLVED IN THIS--?
LATER, SUPERMAN-- NOT NOW! I MUST RETURN THESE MEN TO THEIR *TIME* AND *EARTH* WITHOUT DELAY!
THIS SHOULDN'T BE TOO *DIFFICULT!* SINCE HAWKINS AND HIS BAND DON'T *BELONG* HERE AND NOW--
16

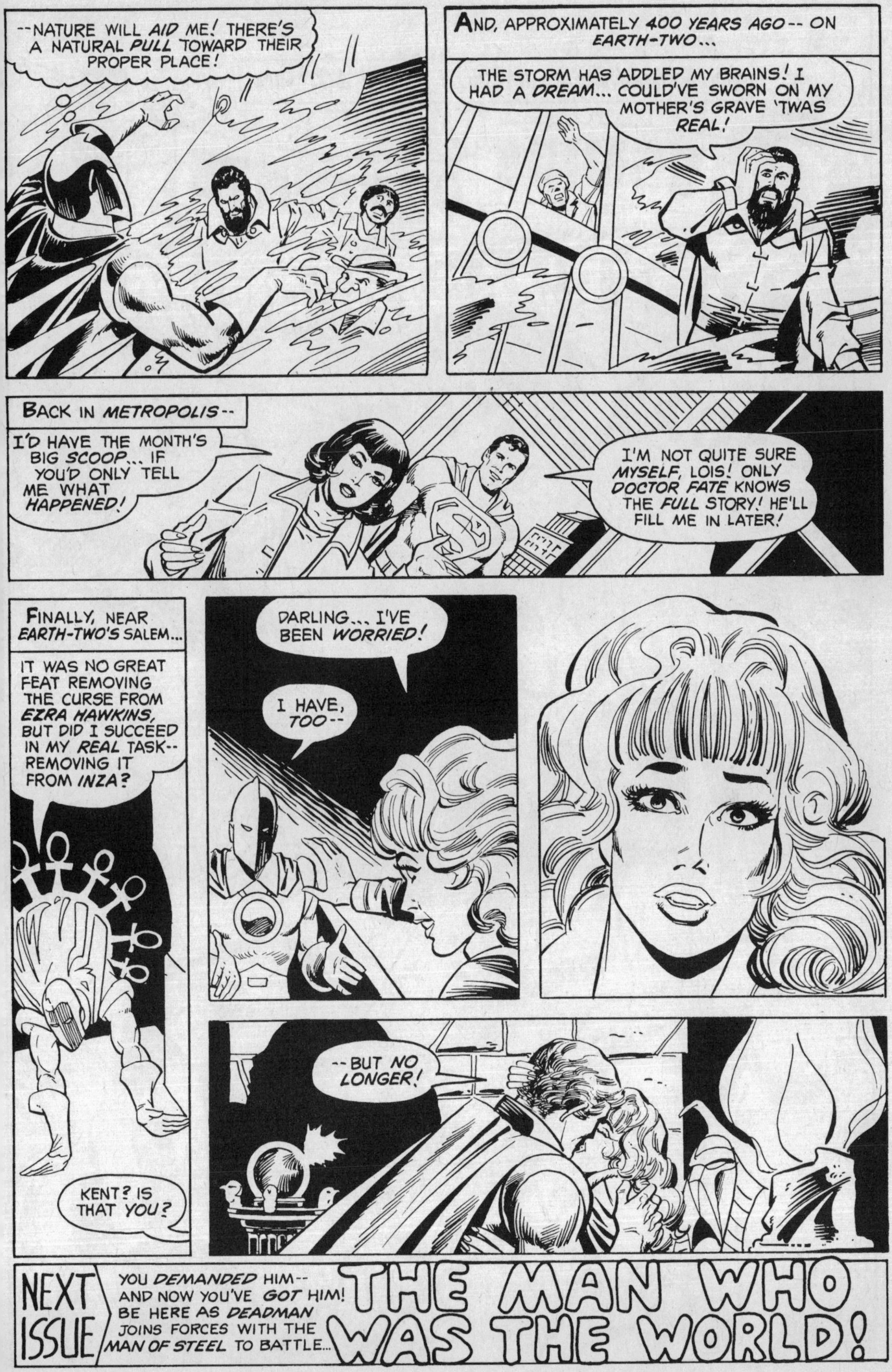
--NATURE WILL AID ME! THERE'S A NATURAL PULL TOWARD THEIR PROPER PLACE!
AND, APPROXIMATELY 400 YEARS AGO-- ON EARTH-TWO...
THE STORM HAS ADDLED MY BRAINS! I HAD A DREAM... COULD'VE SWORN ON MY MOTHER'S GRAVE 'TWAS REAL!
BACK IN METROPOLIS--
I'D HAVE THE MONTH'S BIG SCOOP... IF YOU'D ONLY TELL ME WHAT HAPPENED!
I'M NOT QUITE SURE MYSELF, LOIS! ONLY DOCTOR FATE KNOWS THE FULL STORY! HE'LL FILL ME IN LATER!
FINALLY, NEAR EARTH-TWO'S SALEM...
IT WAS NO GREAT FEAT REMOVING THE CURSE FROM EZRA HAWKINS, BUT DID I SUCCEED IN MY REAL TASK-- REMOVING IT FROM INZA?
KENT? IS THAT YOU?
DARLING... I'VE BEEN WORRIED!
I HAVE, TOO--
--BUT NO LONGER!
NEXT ISSUE
YOU DEMANDED HIM-- AND NOW YOU'VE GOT HIM! BE HERE AS DEADMAN JOINS FORCES WITH THE MAN OF STEEL TO BATTLE...
THE MAN WHO WAS THE WORLD!

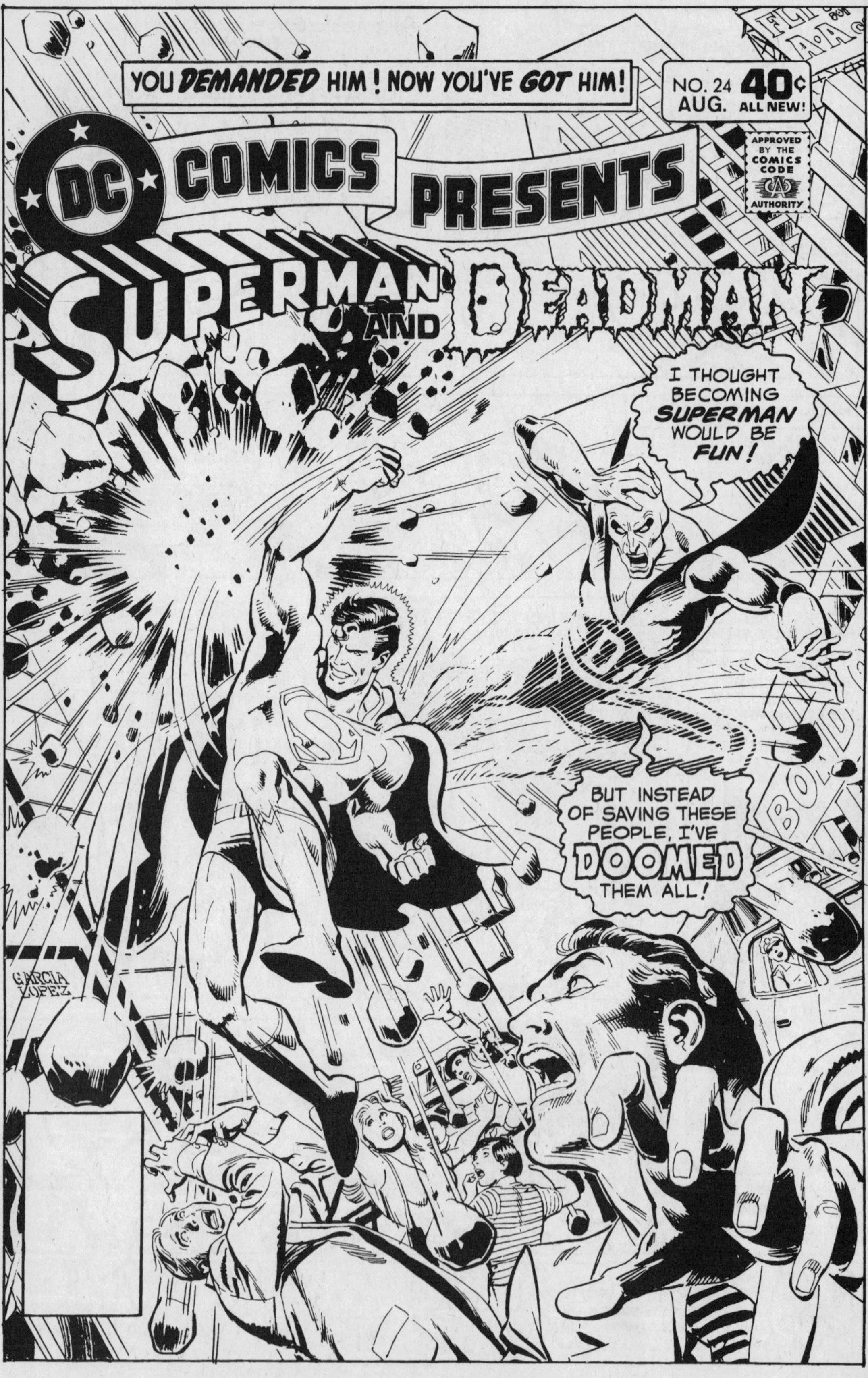

YOU DEMANDED HIM! NOW YOU'VE GOT HIM!
NO. 24 AUG. 40¢ ALL NEW!
DC COMICS PRESENTS
APPROVED BY THE COMICS CODE AUTHORITY
SUPERMAN AND DEADMAN
I THOUGHT BECOMING SUPERMAN WOULD BE FUN!
BUT INSTEAD OF SAVING THESE PEOPLE, I'VE DOOMED THEM ALL!
GARCIA LOPEZ

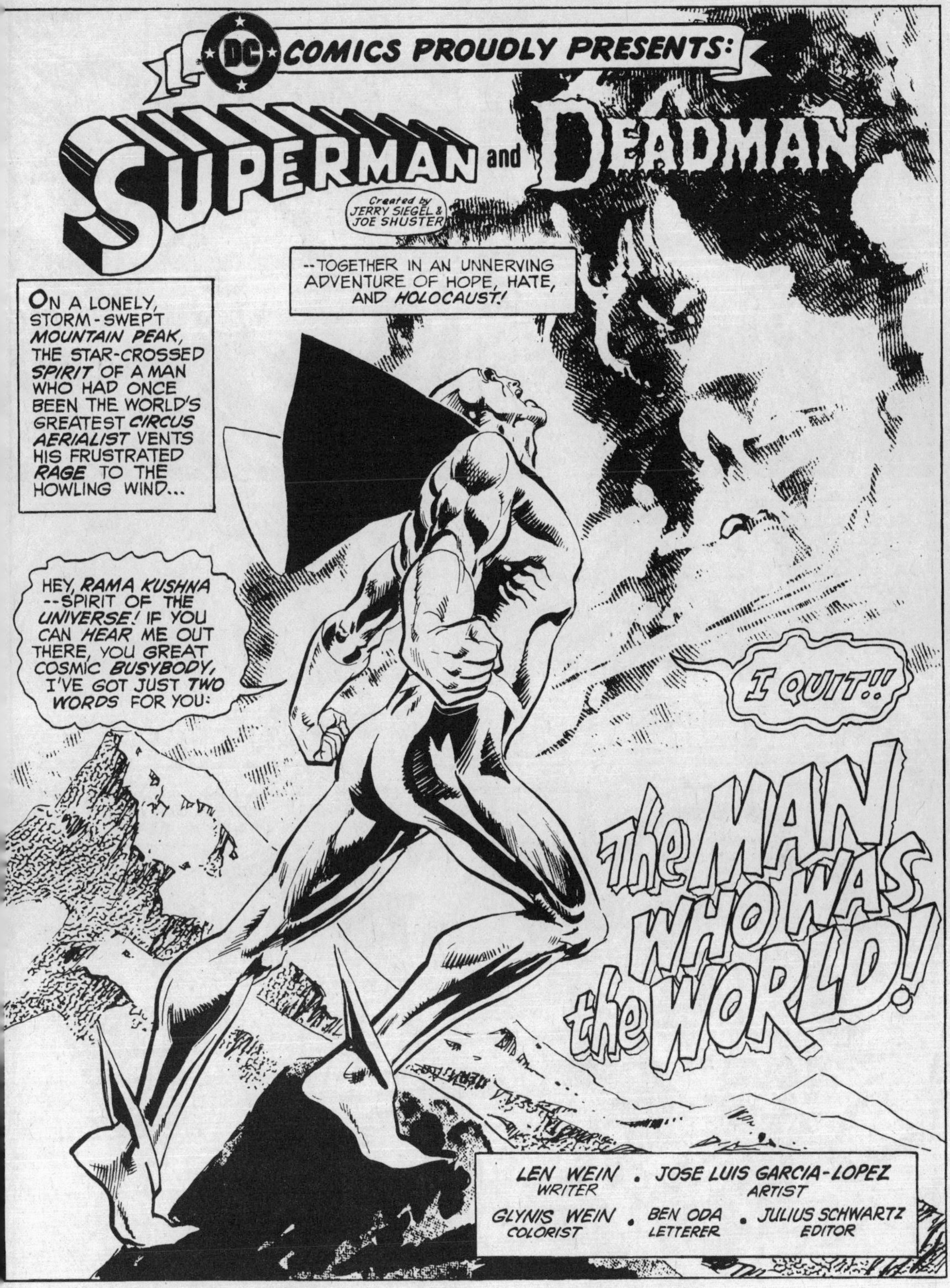
DC COMICS PROUDLY PRESENTS:
SUPERMAN and DEADMAN
Created by JERRY SIEGEL & JOE SHUSTER
--TOGETHER IN AN UNNERVING ADVENTURE OF HOPE, HATE, AND HOLOCAUST!
ON A LONELY, STORM-SWEPT MOUNTAIN PEAK, THE STAR-CROSSED SPIRIT OF A MAN WHO HAD ONCE BEEN THE WORLD'S GREATEST CIRCUS AERIALIST VENTS HIS FRUSTRATED RAGE TO THE HOWLING WIND...
HEY, RAMA KUSHNA --SPIRIT OF THE UNIVERSE! IF YOU CAN HEAR ME OUT THERE, YOU GREAT COSMIC BUSYBODY, I'VE GOT JUST TWO WORDS FOR YOU:
I QUIT!!
The MAN WHO WAS the WORLD!
LEN WEIN WRITER • JOSE LUIS GARCIA-LOPEZ ARTIST
GLYNIS WEIN COLORIST • BEN ODA LETTERER • JULIUS SCHWARTZ EDITOR

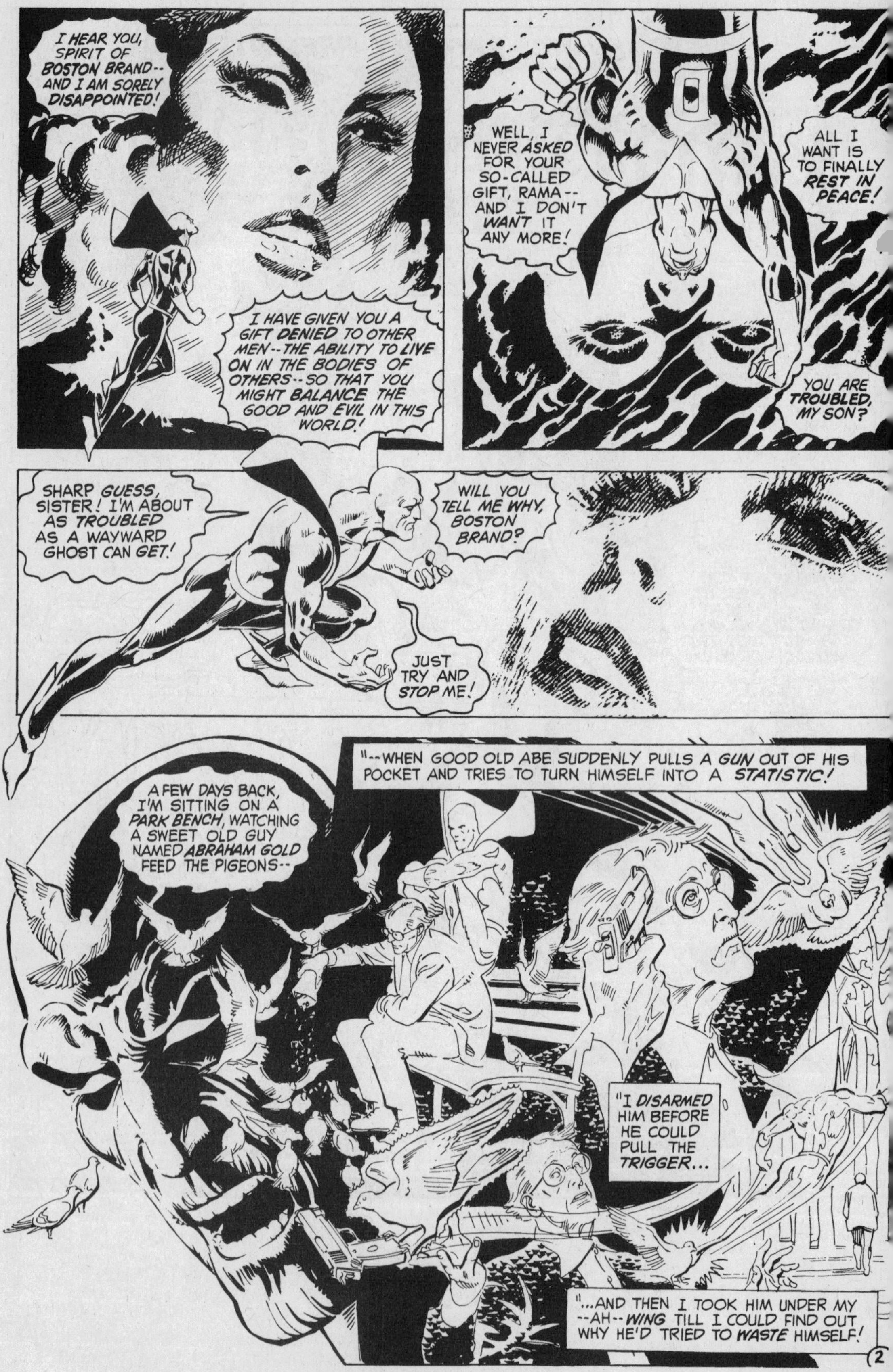

I HEAR YOU, SPIRIT OF BOSTON BRAND--AND I AM SORELY DISAPPOINTED!
I HAVE GIVEN YOU A GIFT DENIED TO OTHER MEN--THE ABILITY TO LIVE ON IN THE BODIES OF OTHERS--SO THAT YOU MIGHT BALANCE THE GOOD AND EVIL IN THIS WORLD!
WELL, I NEVER ASKED FOR YOUR SO-CALLED GIFT, RAMA--AND I DON'T WANT IT ANY MORE!
ALL I WANT IS TO FINALLY REST IN PEACE!
YOU ARE TROUBLED, MY SON?
SHARP GUESS, SISTER! I'M ABOUT AS TROUBLED AS A WAYWARD GHOST CAN GET!
WILL YOU TELL ME WHY, BOSTON BRAND?
JUST TRY AND STOP ME!
"--WHEN GOOD OLD ABE SUDDENLY PULLS A GUN OUT OF HIS POCKET AND TRIES TO TURN HIMSELF INTO A STATISTIC!
A FEW DAYS BACK, I'M SITTING ON A PARK BENCH, WATCHING A SWEET OLD GUY NAMED ABRAHAM GOLD FEED THE PIGEONS--
"I DISARMED HIM BEFORE HE COULD PULL THE TRIGGER...
"...AND THEN I TOOK HIM UNDER MY --AH--WING TILL I COULD FIND OUT WHY HE'D TRIED TO WASTE HIMSELF!
2

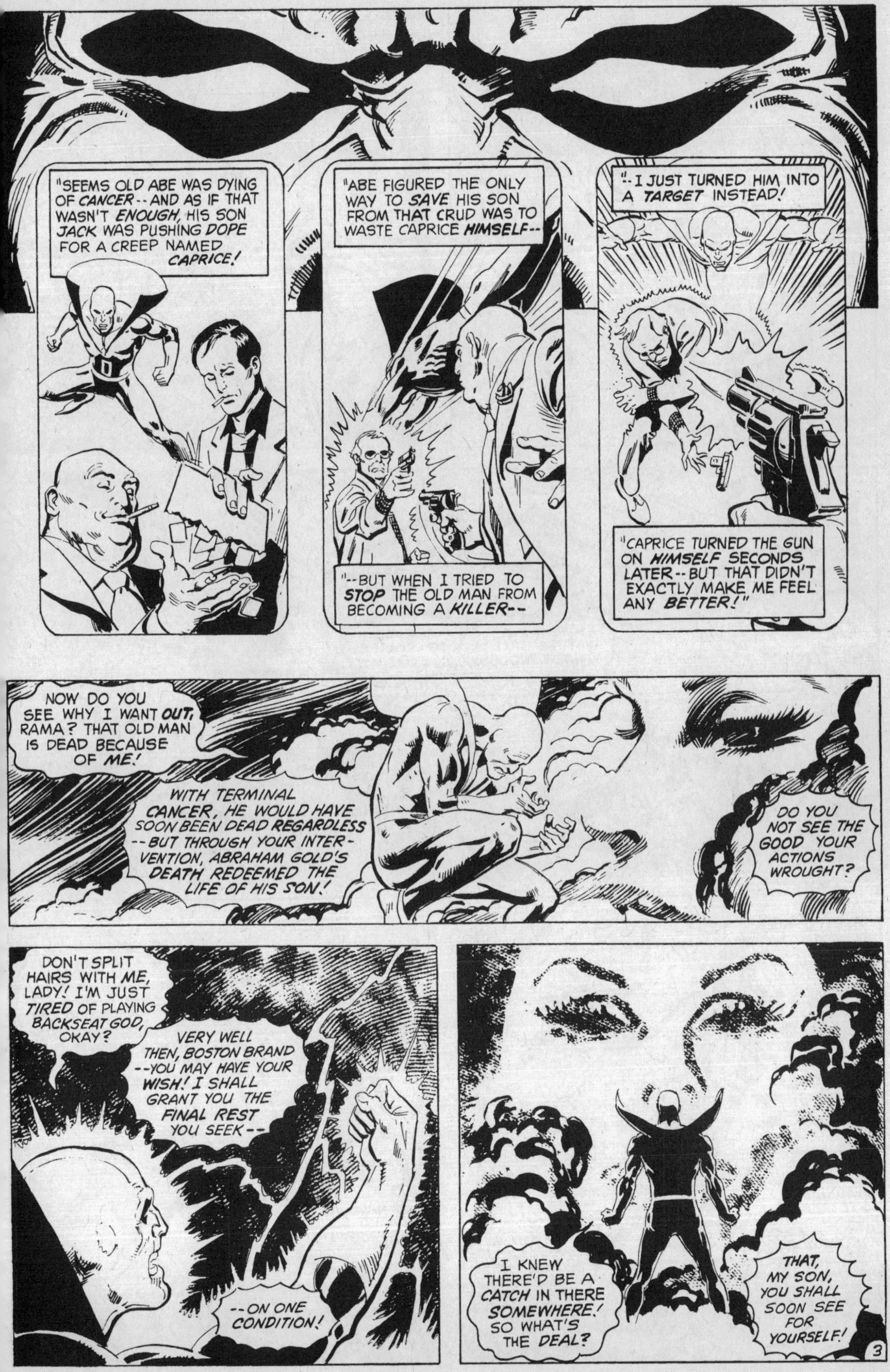
"SEEMS OLD ABE WAS DYING OF CANCER--AND AS IF THAT WASN'T ENOUGH, HIS SON JACK WAS PUSHING DOPE FOR A CREEP NAMED CAPRICE!
"ABE FIGURED THE ONLY WAY TO SAVE HIS SON FROM THAT CRUD WAS TO WASTE CAPRICE HIMSELF--
"--BUT WHEN I TRIED TO STOP THE OLD MAN FROM BECOMING A KILLER--
"--I JUST TURNED HIM INTO A TARGET INSTEAD!
"CAPRICE TURNED THE GUN ON HIMSELF SECONDS LATER--BUT THAT DIDN'T EXACTLY MAKE ME FEEL ANY BETTER!"
NOW DO YOU SEE WHY I WANT OUT, RAMA? THAT OLD MAN IS DEAD BECAUSE OF ME!
WITH TERMINAL CANCER, HE WOULD HAVE SOON BEEN DEAD REGARDLESS --BUT THROUGH YOUR INTER-VENTION, ABRAHAM GOLD'S DEATH REDEEMED THE LIFE OF HIS SON!
DO YOU NOT SEE THE GOOD YOUR ACTIONS WROUGHT?
DON'T SPLIT HAIRS WITH ME, LADY! I'M JUST TIRED OF PLAYING BACKSEAT GOD, OKAY?
VERY WELL THEN, BOSTON BRAND --YOU MAY HAVE YOUR WISH! I SHALL GRANT YOU THE FINAL REST YOU SEEK--
--ON ONE CONDITION!
I KNEW THERE'D BE A CATCH IN THERE SOMEWHERE! SO WHAT'S THE DEAL?
THAT, MY SON, YOU SHALL SOON SEE FOR YOURSELF!
3

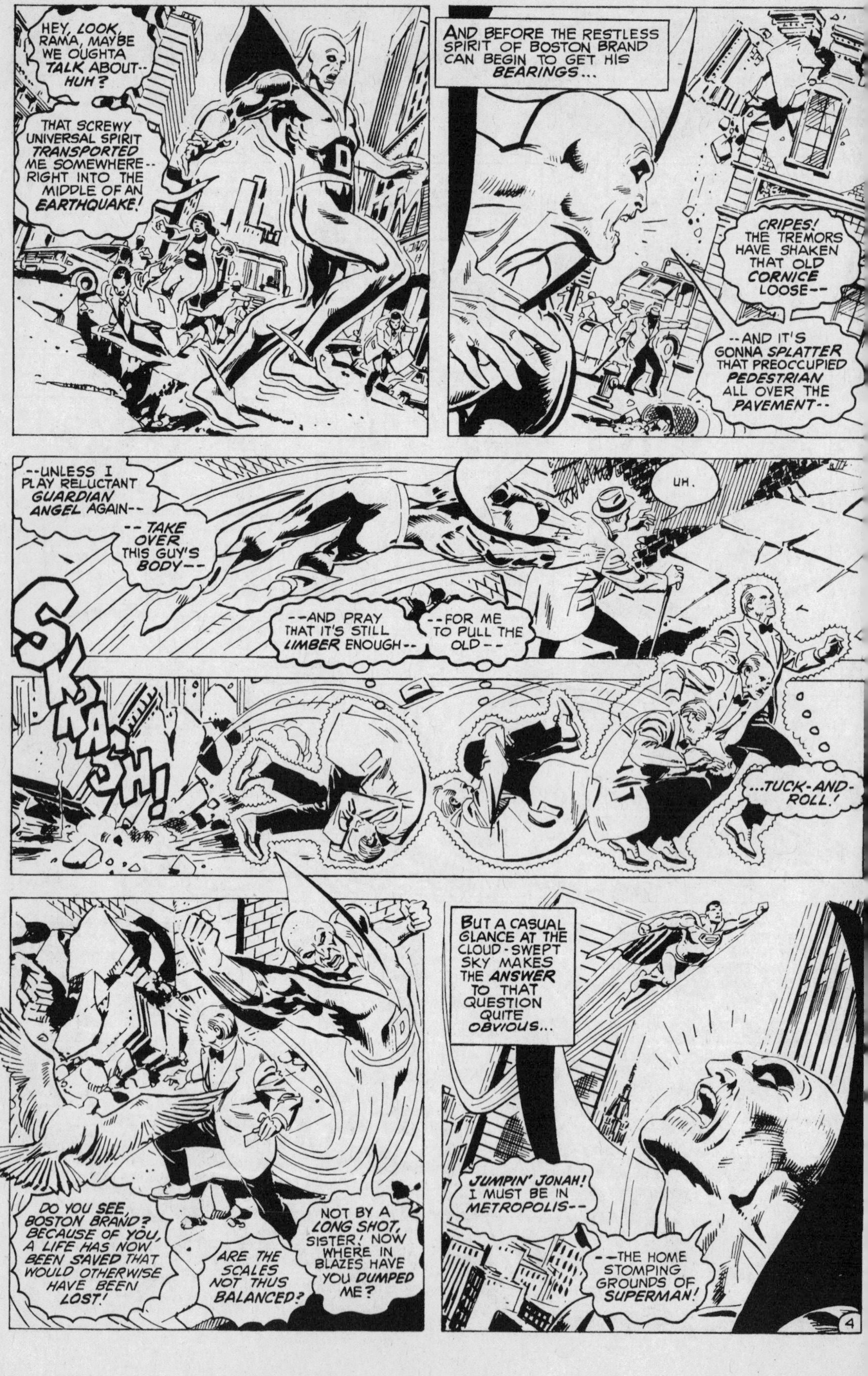
HEY, LOOK, RAMA, MAYBE WE OUGHTA TALK ABOUT-- HUH?
THAT SCREWY UNIVERSAL SPIRIT TRANSPORTED ME SOMEWHERE-- RIGHT INTO THE MIDDLE OF AN EARTHQUAKE!
AND BEFORE THE RESTLESS SPIRIT OF BOSTON BRAND CAN BEGIN TO GET HIS BEARINGS...
CRIPES! THE TREMORS HAVE SHAKEN THAT OLD CORNICE LOOSE--
--AND IT'S GONNA SPLATTER THAT PREOCCUPIED PEDESTRIAN ALL OVER THE PAVEMENT--
--UNLESS I PLAY RELUCTANT GUARDIAN ANGEL AGAIN--
--TAKE OVER THIS GUY'S BODY--
UH.
--AND PRAY THAT IT'S STILL LIMBER ENOUGH--
--FOR ME TO PULL THE OLD--
SKRASH!
...TUCK-AND-ROLL.!
DO YOU SEE, BOSTON BRAND? BECAUSE OF YOU, A LIFE HAS NOW BEEN SAVED THAT WOULD OTHERWISE HAVE BEEN LOST!
ARE THE SCALES NOT THUS BALANCED?
NOT BY A LONG SHOT, SISTER! NOW WHERE IN BLAZES HAVE YOU DUMPED ME?
BUT A CASUAL GLANCE AT THE CLOUD-SWEPT SKY MAKES THE ANSWER TO THAT QUESTION QUITE OBVIOUS...
JUMPIN' JONAH! I MUST BE IN METROPOLIS--
--THE HOME STOMPING GROUNDS OF SUPERMAN!
4

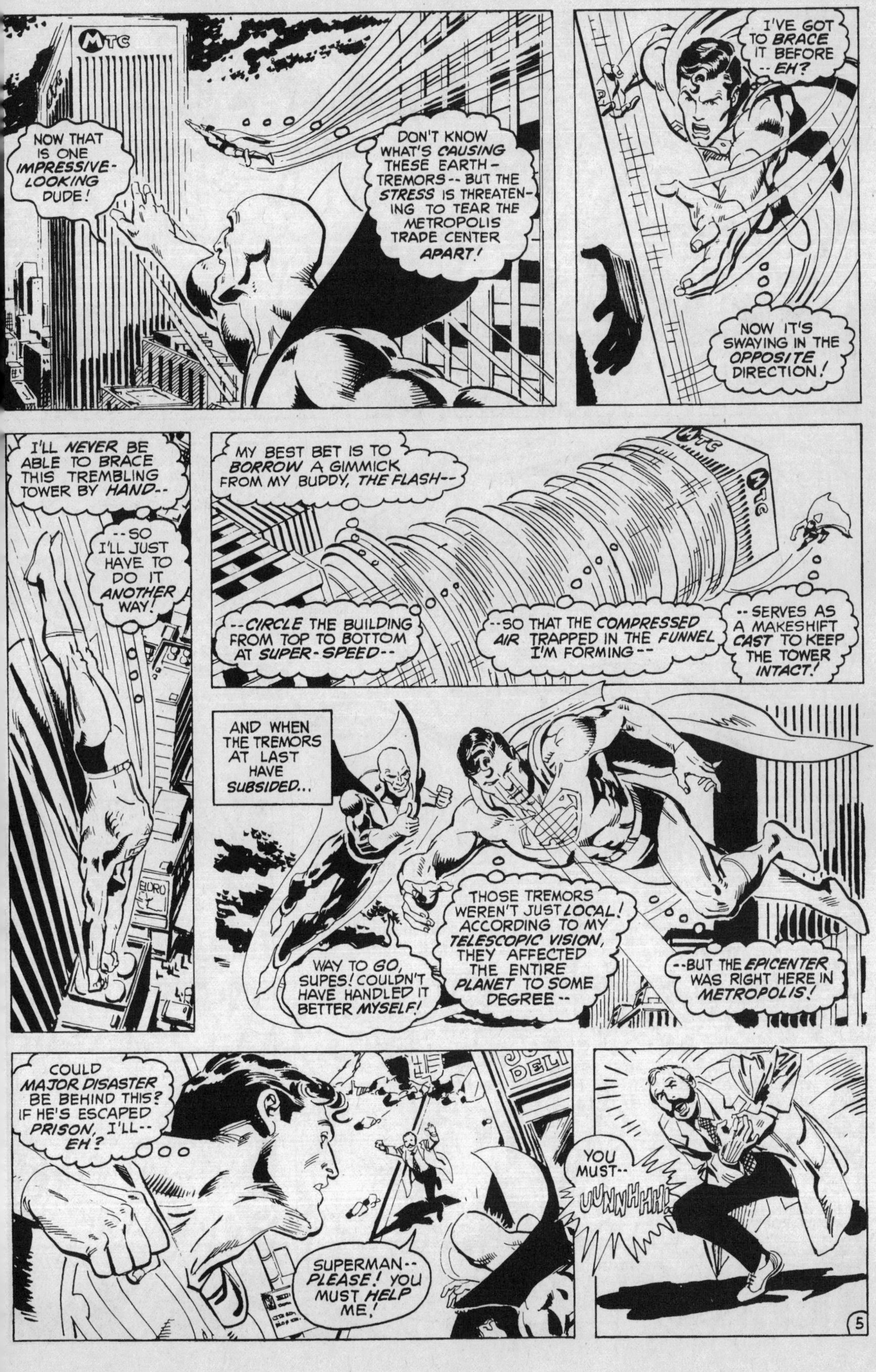
NOW THAT IS ONE IMPRESSIVE-LOOKING DUDE!
DON'T KNOW WHAT'S CAUSING THESE EARTH-TREMORS-- BUT THE STRESS IS THREATENING TO TEAR THE METROPOLIS TRADE CENTER APART!
I'VE GOT TO BRACE IT BEFORE --EH?
NOW IT'S SWAYING IN THE OPPOSITE DIRECTION!
I'LL NEVER BE ABLE TO BRACE THIS TREMBLING TOWER BY HAND--
--SO I'LL JUST HAVE TO DO IT ANOTHER WAY!
MY BEST BET IS TO BORROW A GIMMICK FROM MY BUDDY, THE FLASH--
--CIRCLE THE BUILDING FROM TOP TO BOTTOM AT SUPER-SPEED--
--SO THAT THE COMPRESSED AIR TRAPPED IN THE FUNNEL I'M FORMING--
--SERVES AS A MAKESHIFT CAST TO KEEP THE TOWER INTACT!
AND WHEN THE TREMORS AT LAST HAVE SUBSIDED...
WAY TO GO, SUPES! COULDN'T HAVE HANDLED IT BETTER MYSELF!
THOSE TREMORS WEREN'T JUST LOCAL! ACCORDING TO MY TELESCOPIC VISION, THEY AFFECTED THE ENTIRE PLANET TO SOME DEGREE--
--BUT THE EPICENTER WAS RIGHT HERE IN METROPOLIS!
COULD MAJOR DISASTER BE BEHIND THIS? IF HE'S ESCAPED PRISON, I'LL-- EH?
SUPERMAN-- PLEASE! YOU MUST HELP ME!
YOU MUST--
UUNNHHH!
5

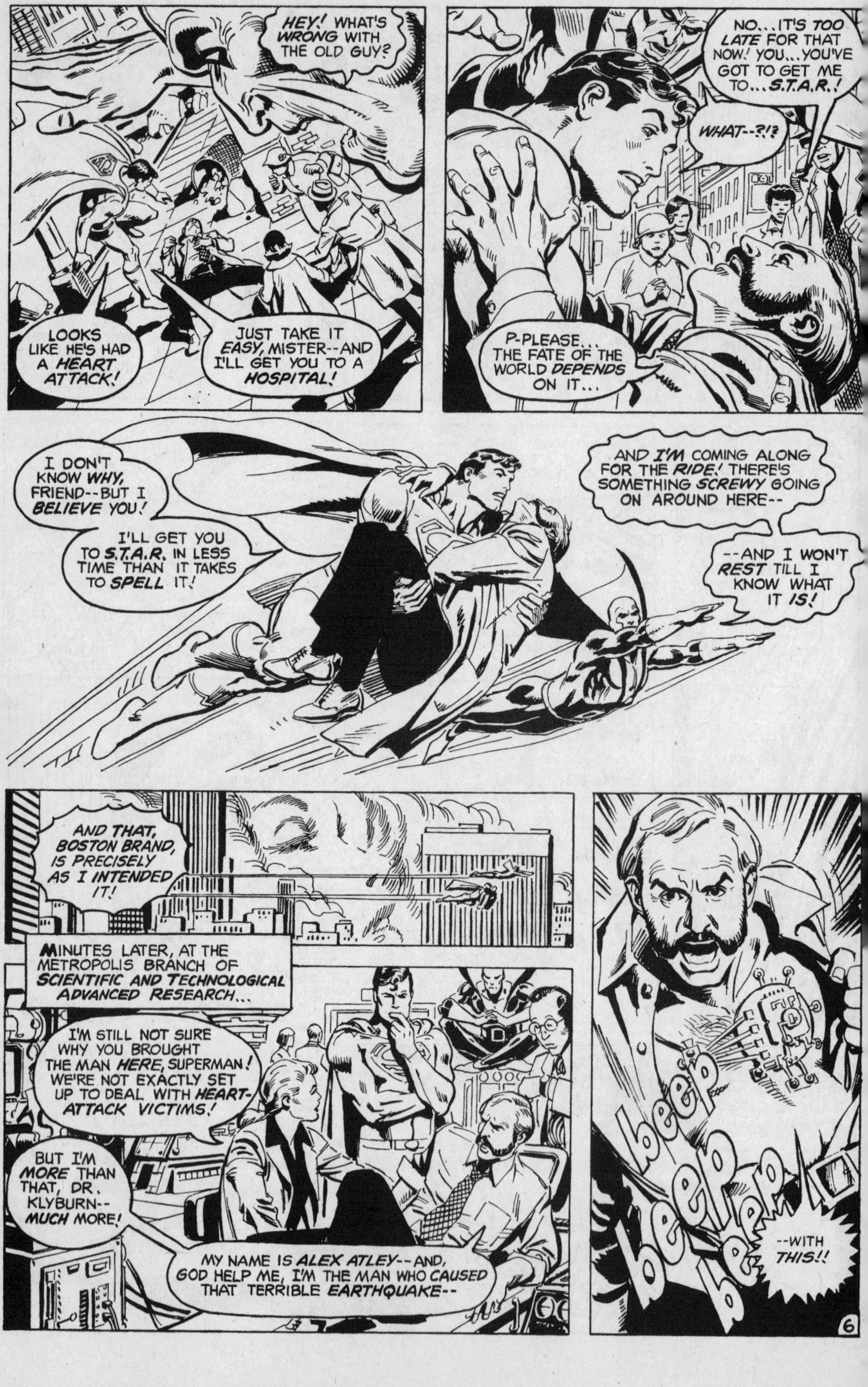
HEY! WHAT'S WRONG WITH THE OLD GUY?
LOOKS LIKE HE'S HAD A HEART ATTACK!
JUST TAKE IT EASY, MISTER--AND I'LL GET YOU TO A HOSPITAL!
NO...IT'S TOO LATE FOR THAT NOW! YOU...YOU'VE GOT TO GET ME TO...S.T.A.R.!
WHAT--?!?
P-PLEASE... THE FATE OF THE WORLD DEPENDS ON IT...
I DON'T KNOW WHY, FRIEND--BUT I BELIEVE YOU!
I'LL GET YOU TO S.T.A.R. IN LESS TIME THAN IT TAKES TO SPELL IT!
AND I'M COMING ALONG FOR THE RIDE! THERE'S SOMETHING SCREWY GOING ON AROUND HERE--
--AND I WON'T REST TILL I KNOW WHAT IT IS!
AND THAT, BOSTON BRAND, IS PRECISELY AS I INTENDED IT!
MINUTES LATER, AT THE METROPOLIS BRANCH OF SCIENTIFIC AND TECHNOLOGICAL ADVANCED RESEARCH...
I'M STILL NOT SURE WHY YOU BROUGHT THE MAN HERE, SUPERMAN! WE'RE NOT EXACTLY SET UP TO DEAL WITH HEART-ATTACK VICTIMS!
BUT I'M MORE THAN THAT, DR. KLYBURN--MUCH MORE!
MY NAME IS ALEX ATLEY--AND, GOD HELP ME, I'M THE MAN WHO CAUSED THAT TERRIBLE EARTHQUAKE--
--WITH THIS!!
beep beep beep
6

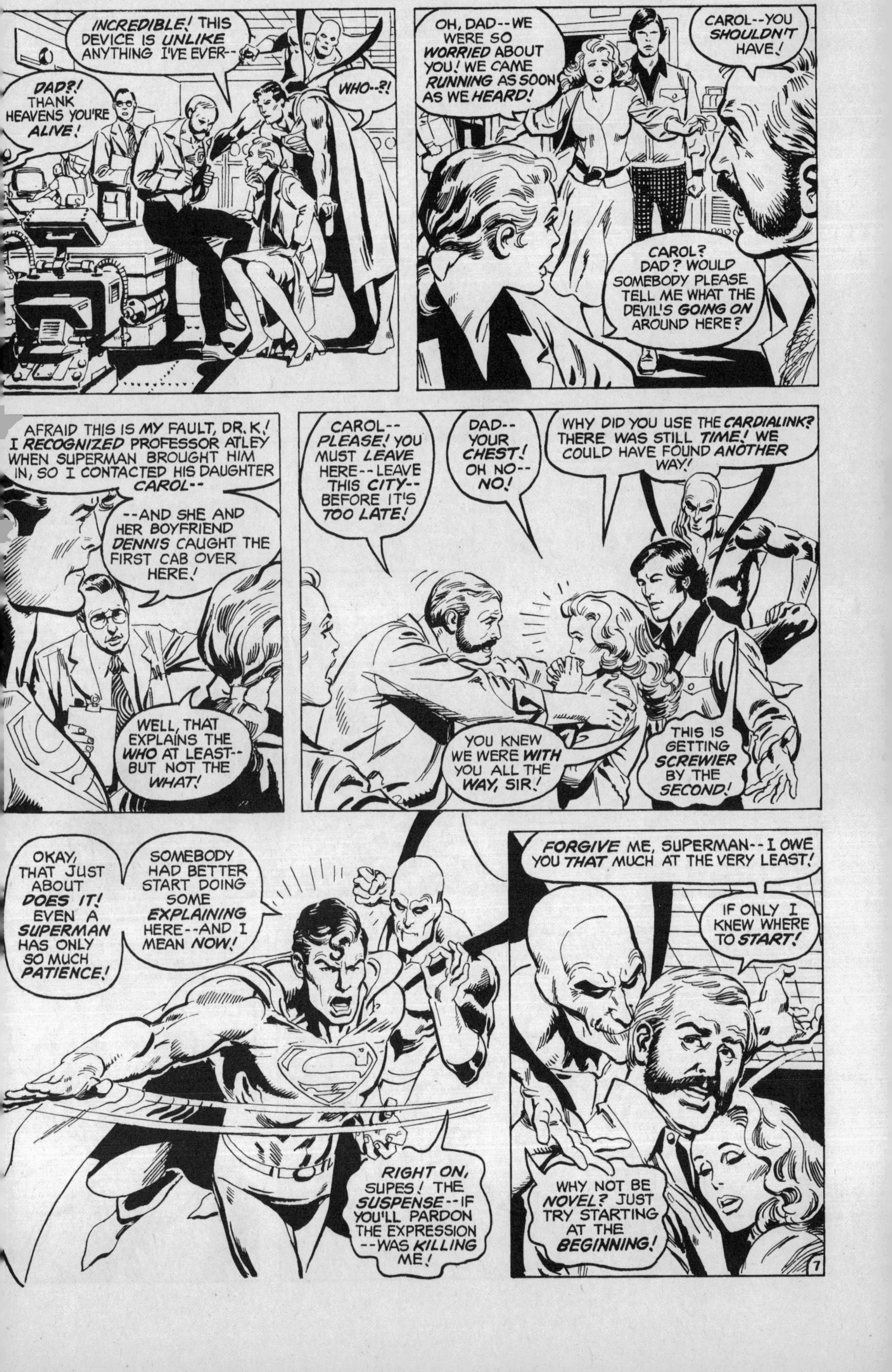
INCREDIBLE! THIS DEVICE IS UNLIKE ANYTHING I'VE EVER--
DAD?! THANK HEAVENS YOU'RE ALIVE!
WHO--?!
OH, DAD--WE WERE SO WORRIED ABOUT YOU! WE CAME RUNNING AS SOON AS WE HEARD!
CAROL--YOU SHOULDN'T HAVE!
CAROL? DAD? WOULD SOMEBODY PLEASE TELL ME WHAT THE DEVIL'S GOING ON AROUND HERE?
AFRAID THIS IS MY FAULT, DR. K.! I RECOGNIZED PROFESSOR ATLEY WHEN SUPERMAN BROUGHT HIM IN, SO I CONTACTED HIS DAUGHTER CAROL--
--AND SHE AND HER BOYFRIEND DENNIS CAUGHT THE FIRST CAB OVER HERE!
WELL, THAT EXPLAINS THE WHO AT LEAST--BUT NOT THE WHAT!
CAROL--PLEASE! YOU MUST LEAVE HERE--LEAVE THIS CITY--BEFORE IT'S TOO LATE!
DAD--YOUR CHEST! OH NO--NO!
WHY DID YOU USE THE CARDIALINK? THERE WAS STILL TIME! WE COULD HAVE FOUND ANOTHER WAY!
YOU KNEW WE WERE WITH YOU ALL THE WAY, SIR!
THIS IS GETTING SCREWIER BY THE SECOND!
OKAY, THAT JUST ABOUT DOES IT! EVEN A SUPERMAN HAS ONLY SO MUCH PATIENCE!
SOMEBODY HAD BETTER START DOING SOME EXPLAINING HERE--AND I MEAN NOW!
RIGHT ON, SUPES! THE SUSPENSE--IF YOU'LL PARDON THE EXPRESSION--WAS KILLING ME!
FORGIVE ME, SUPERMAN--I OWE YOU THAT MUCH AT THE VERY LEAST!
IF ONLY I KNEW WHERE TO START!
WHY NOT BE NOVEL? JUST TRY STARTING AT THE BEGINNING!
7

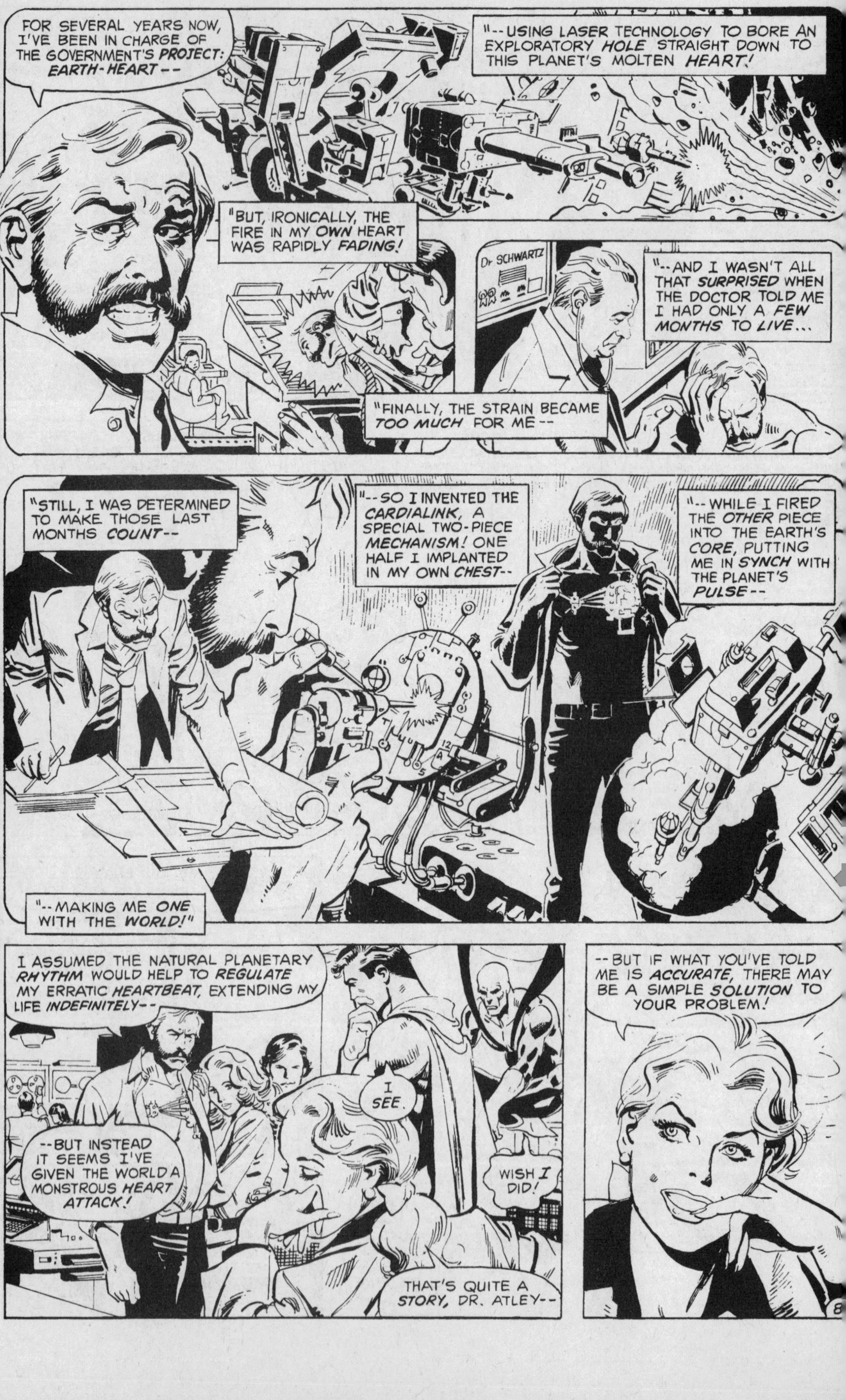
FOR SEVERAL YEARS NOW, I'VE BEEN IN CHARGE OF THE GOVERNMENT'S PROJECT: EARTH-HEART --
"-- USING LASER TECHNOLOGY TO BORE AN EXPLORATORY HOLE STRAIGHT DOWN TO THIS PLANET'S MOLTEN HEART!
"BUT, IRONICALLY, THE FIRE IN MY OWN HEART WAS RAPIDLY FADING!
"FINALLY, THE STRAIN BECAME TOO MUCH FOR ME --
Dr SCHWARTZ
"-- AND I WASN'T ALL THAT SURPRISED WHEN THE DOCTOR TOLD ME I HAD ONLY A FEW MONTHS TO LIVE...
"STILL, I WAS DETERMINED TO MAKE THOSE LAST MONTHS COUNT --
"-- SO I INVENTED THE CARDIALINK, A SPECIAL TWO-PIECE MECHANISM! ONE HALF I IMPLANTED IN MY OWN CHEST --
"-- WHILE I FIRED THE OTHER PIECE INTO THE EARTH'S CORE, PUTTING ME IN SYNCH WITH THE PLANET'S PULSE --
"-- MAKING ME ONE WITH THE WORLD!"
I ASSUMED THE NATURAL PLANETARY RHYTHM WOULD HELP TO REGULATE MY ERRATIC HEARTBEAT, EXTENDING MY LIFE INDEFINITELY --
-- BUT INSTEAD IT SEEMS I'VE GIVEN THE WORLD A MONSTROUS HEART ATTACK!
I SEE.
WISH I DID!
THAT'S QUITE A STORY, DR. ATLEY --
-- BUT IF WHAT YOU'VE TOLD ME IS ACCURATE, THERE MAY BE A SIMPLE SOLUTION TO YOUR PROBLEM!
8

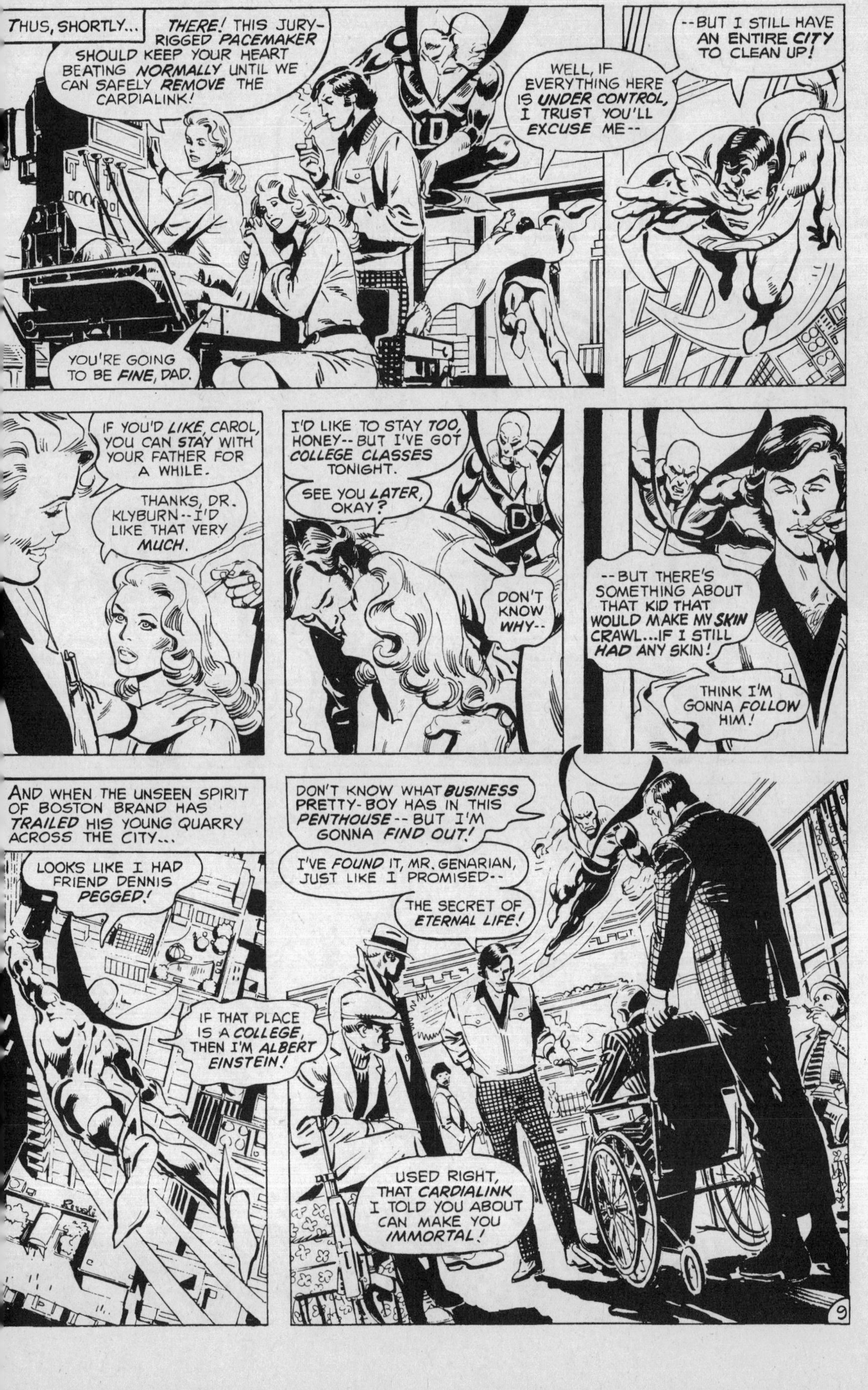
THUS, SHORTLY...
THERE! THIS JURY-RIGGED PACEMAKER SHOULD KEEP YOUR HEART BEATING NORMALLY UNTIL WE CAN SAFELY REMOVE THE CARDIALINK!
YOU'RE GOING TO BE FINE, DAD.
WELL, IF EVERYTHING HERE IS UNDER CONTROL, I TRUST YOU'LL EXCUSE ME--
--BUT I STILL HAVE AN ENTIRE CITY TO CLEAN UP!
IF YOU'D LIKE, CAROL, YOU CAN STAY WITH YOUR FATHER FOR A WHILE.
THANKS, DR. KLYBURN--I'D LIKE THAT VERY MUCH.
I'D LIKE TO STAY TOO, HONEY--BUT I'VE GOT COLLEGE CLASSES TONIGHT.
SEE YOU LATER, OKAY?
DON'T KNOW WHY--
--BUT THERE'S SOMETHING ABOUT THAT KID THAT WOULD MAKE MY SKIN CRAWL...IF I STILL HAD ANY SKIN!
THINK I'M GONNA FOLLOW HIM!
AND WHEN THE UNSEEN SPIRIT OF BOSTON BRAND HAS TRAILED HIS YOUNG QUARRY ACROSS THE CITY...
LOOKS LIKE I HAD FRIEND DENNIS PEGGED!
IF THAT PLACE IS A COLLEGE, THEN I'M ALBERT EINSTEIN!
DON'T KNOW WHAT BUSINESS PRETTY-BOY HAS IN THIS PENTHOUSE--BUT I'M GONNA FIND OUT!
I'VE FOUND IT, MR. GENARIAN, JUST LIKE I PROMISED--
THE SECRET OF ETERNAL LIFE!
USED RIGHT, THAT CARDIALINK I TOLD YOU ABOUT CAN MAKE YOU IMMORTAL!
9

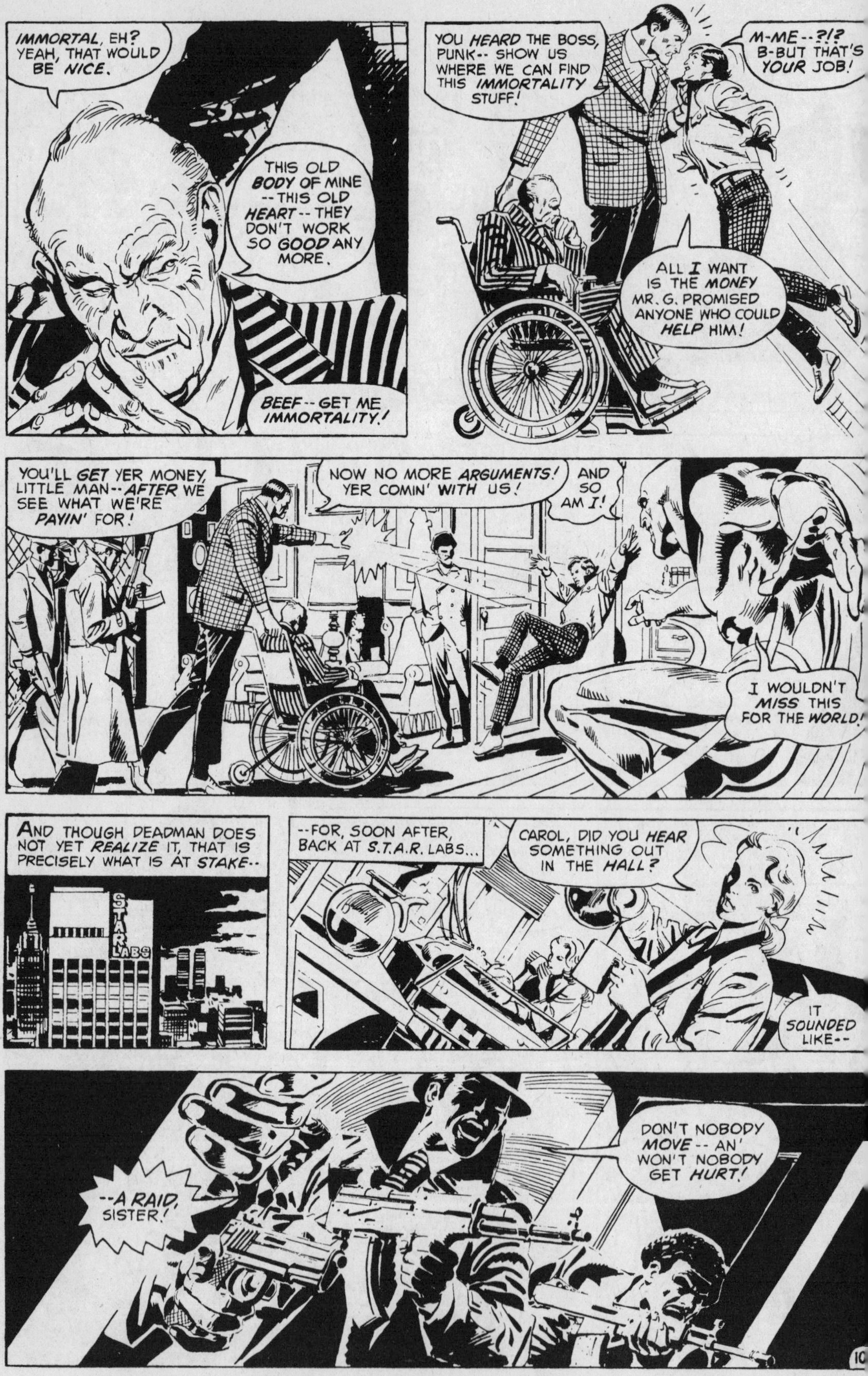
IMMORTAL, EH? YEAH, THAT WOULD BE NICE.
THIS OLD BODY OF MINE --THIS OLD HEART-- THEY DON'T WORK SO GOOD ANY MORE.
BEEF--GET ME IMMORTALITY!
YOU HEARD THE BOSS, PUNK-- SHOW US WHERE WE CAN FIND THIS IMMORTALITY STUFF!
M-ME--?!? B-BUT THAT'S YOUR JOB!
ALL I WANT IS THE MONEY MR. G. PROMISED ANYONE WHO COULD HELP HIM!
YOU'LL GET YER MONEY, LITTLE MAN--AFTER WE SEE WHAT WE'RE PAYIN' FOR!
NOW NO MORE ARGUMENTS! YER COMIN' WITH US!
AND SO AM I!
I WOULDN'T MISS THIS FOR THE WORLD!
AND THOUGH DEADMAN DOES NOT YET REALIZE IT, THAT IS PRECISELY WHAT IS AT STAKE--
S.T.A.R. LABS
--FOR, SOON AFTER, BACK AT S.T.A.R. LABS...
CAROL, DID YOU HEAR SOMETHING OUT IN THE HALL?
IT SOUNDED LIKE--
--A RAID, SISTER!
DON'T NOBODY MOVE-- AN' WON'T NOBODY GET HURT!
10

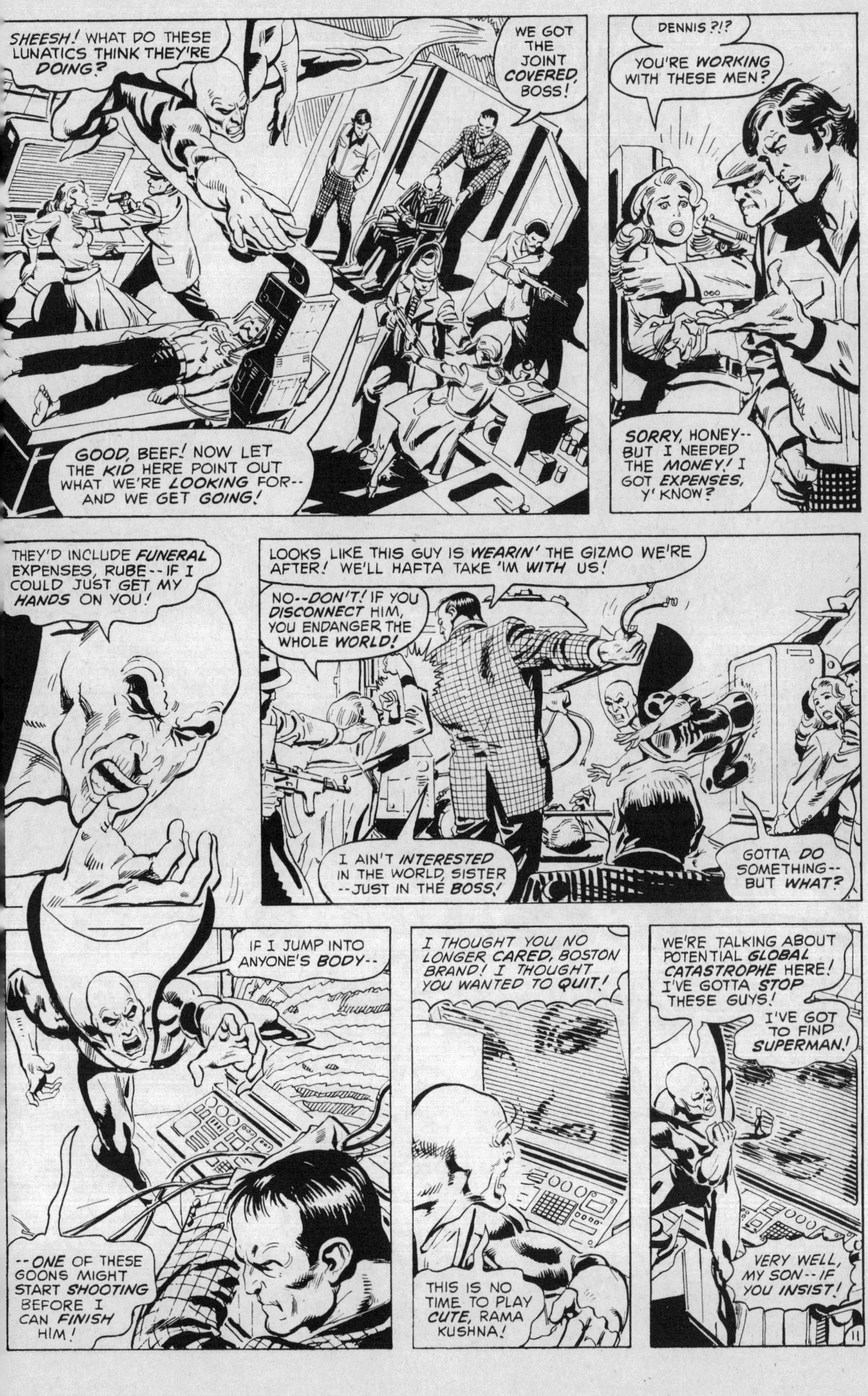
SHEESH! WHAT DO THESE LUNATICS THINK THEY'RE DOING?
WE GOT THE JOINT COVERED, BOSS!
GOOD, BEEF! NOW LET THE KID HERE POINT OUT WHAT WE'RE LOOKING FOR-- AND WE GET GOING!
DENNIS?!?
YOU'RE WORKING WITH THESE MEN?
SORRY, HONEY-- BUT I NEEDED THE MONEY! I GOT EXPENSES, Y' KNOW?
THEY'D INCLUDE FUNERAL EXPENSES, RUBE--IF I COULD JUST GET MY HANDS ON YOU!
LOOKS LIKE THIS GUY IS WEARIN' THE GIZMO WE'RE AFTER! WE'LL HAFTA TAKE 'IM WITH US!
NO--DON'T! IF YOU DISCONNECT HIM, YOU ENDANGER THE WHOLE WORLD!
I AIN'T INTERESTED IN THE WORLD, SISTER --JUST IN THE BOSS!
GOTTA DO SOMETHING-- BUT WHAT?
IF I JUMP INTO ANYONE'S BODY--
--ONE OF THESE GOONS MIGHT START SHOOTING BEFORE I CAN FINISH HIM!
I THOUGHT YOU NO LONGER CARED, BOSTON BRAND! I THOUGHT YOU WANTED TO QUIT!
THIS IS NO TIME TO PLAY CUTE, RAMA KUSHNA!
WE'RE TALKING ABOUT POTENTIAL GLOBAL CATASTROPHE HERE! I'VE GOTTA STOP THESE GUYS!
I'VE GOT TO FIND SUPERMAN!
VERY WELL, MY SON--IF YOU INSIST!
11

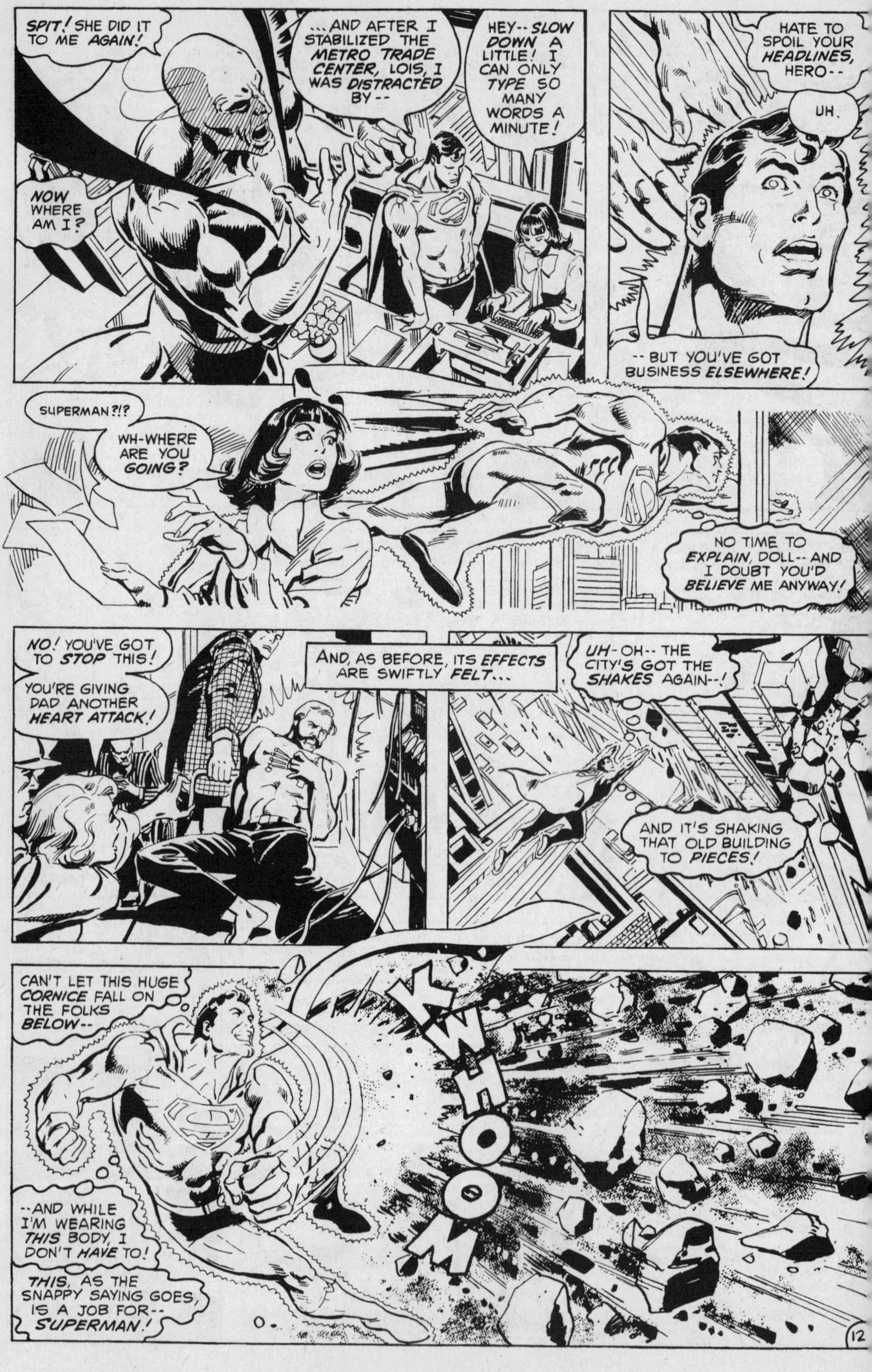
SPIT! SHE DID IT TO ME AGAIN!
NOW WHERE AM I?
...AND AFTER I STABILIZED THE METRO TRADE CENTER, LOIS, I WAS DISTRACTED BY--
HEY--SLOW DOWN A LITTLE! I CAN ONLY TYPE SO MANY WORDS A MINUTE!
HATE TO SPOIL YOUR HEADLINES, HERO--
UH.
--BUT YOU'VE GOT BUSINESS ELSEWHERE!
SUPERMAN?!?
WH-WHERE ARE YOU GOING?
NO TIME TO EXPLAIN, DOLL--AND I DOUBT YOU'D BELIEVE ME ANYWAY!
NO! YOU'VE GOT TO STOP THIS!
YOU'RE GIVING DAD ANOTHER HEART ATTACK!
AND, AS BEFORE, ITS EFFECTS ARE SWIFTLY FELT...
UH-OH--THE CITY'S GOT THE SHAKES AGAIN--!
AND IT'S SHAKING THAT OLD BUILDING TO PIECES!
CAN'T LET THIS HUGE CORNICE FALL ON THE FOLKS BELOW--
KWHOOM
--AND WHILE I'M WEARING THIS BODY, I DON'T HAVE TO!
THIS, AS THE SNAPPY SAYING GOES, IS A JOB FOR--SUPERMAN!
12

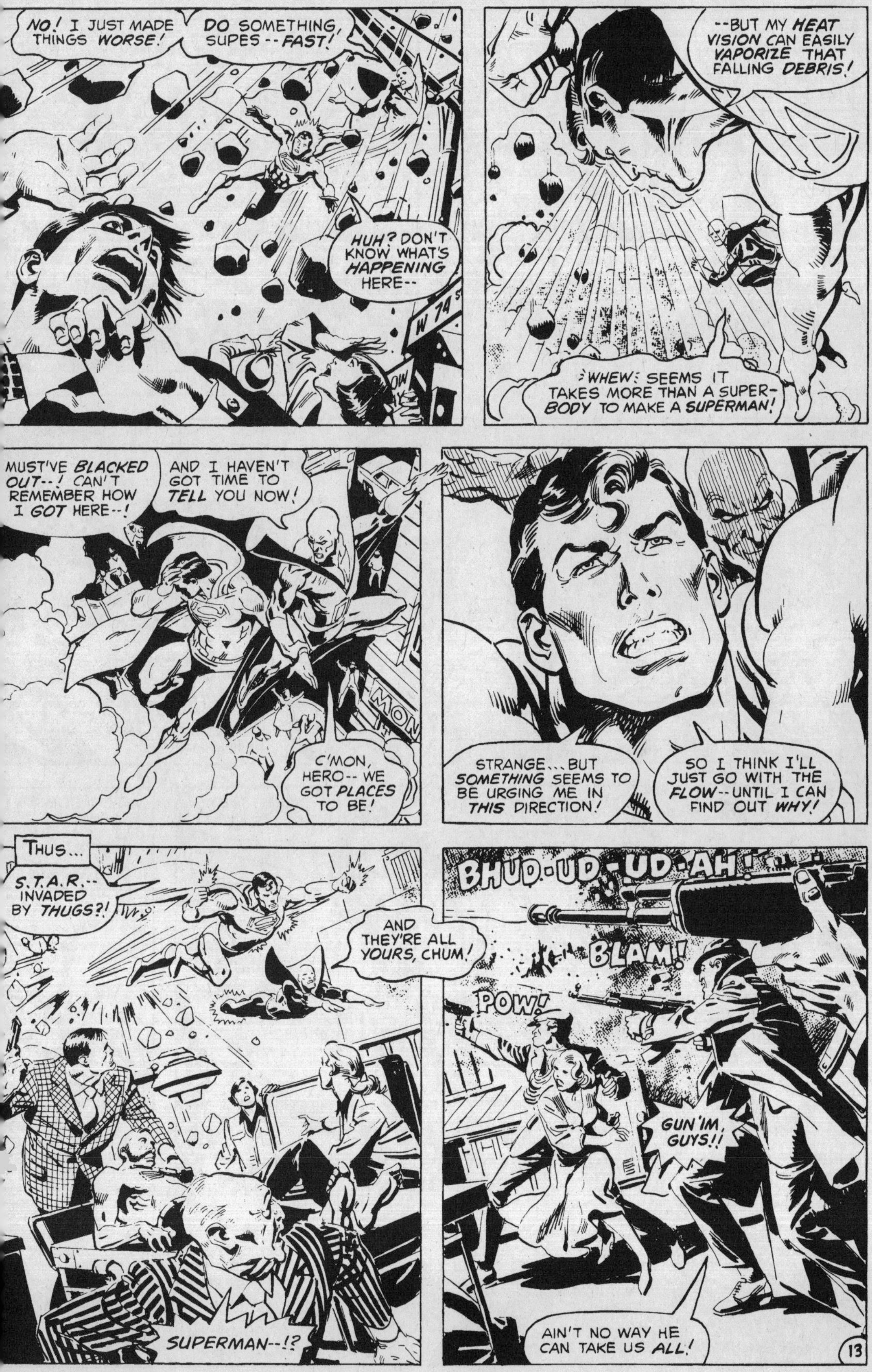
NO! I JUST MADE THINGS WORSE!
DO SOMETHING, SUPES--FAST!
HUH? DON'T KNOW WHAT'S HAPPENING HERE--
W 74
--BUT MY HEAT VISION CAN EASILY VAPORIZE THAT FALLING DEBRIS!
WHEW SEEMS IT TAKES MORE THAN A SUPER-BODY TO MAKE A SUPERMAN!
MUST'VE BLACKED OUT--! CAN'T REMEMBER HOW I GOT HERE--!
AND I HAVEN'T GOT TIME TO TELL YOU NOW!
C'MON, HERO-- WE GOT PLACES TO BE!
STRANGE... BUT SOMETHING SEEMS TO BE URGING ME IN THIS DIRECTION!
SO I THINK I'LL JUST GO WITH THE FLOW--UNTIL I CAN FIND OUT WHY!
THUS...
S.T.A.R.--INVADED BY THUGS?!
AND THEY'RE ALL YOURS, CHUM!
SUPERMAN--!?
BHUD-UD-UD-AH!
BLAM!
POW!
GUN'IM, GUYS!!
AIN'T NO WAY HE CAN TAKE US ALL!
13

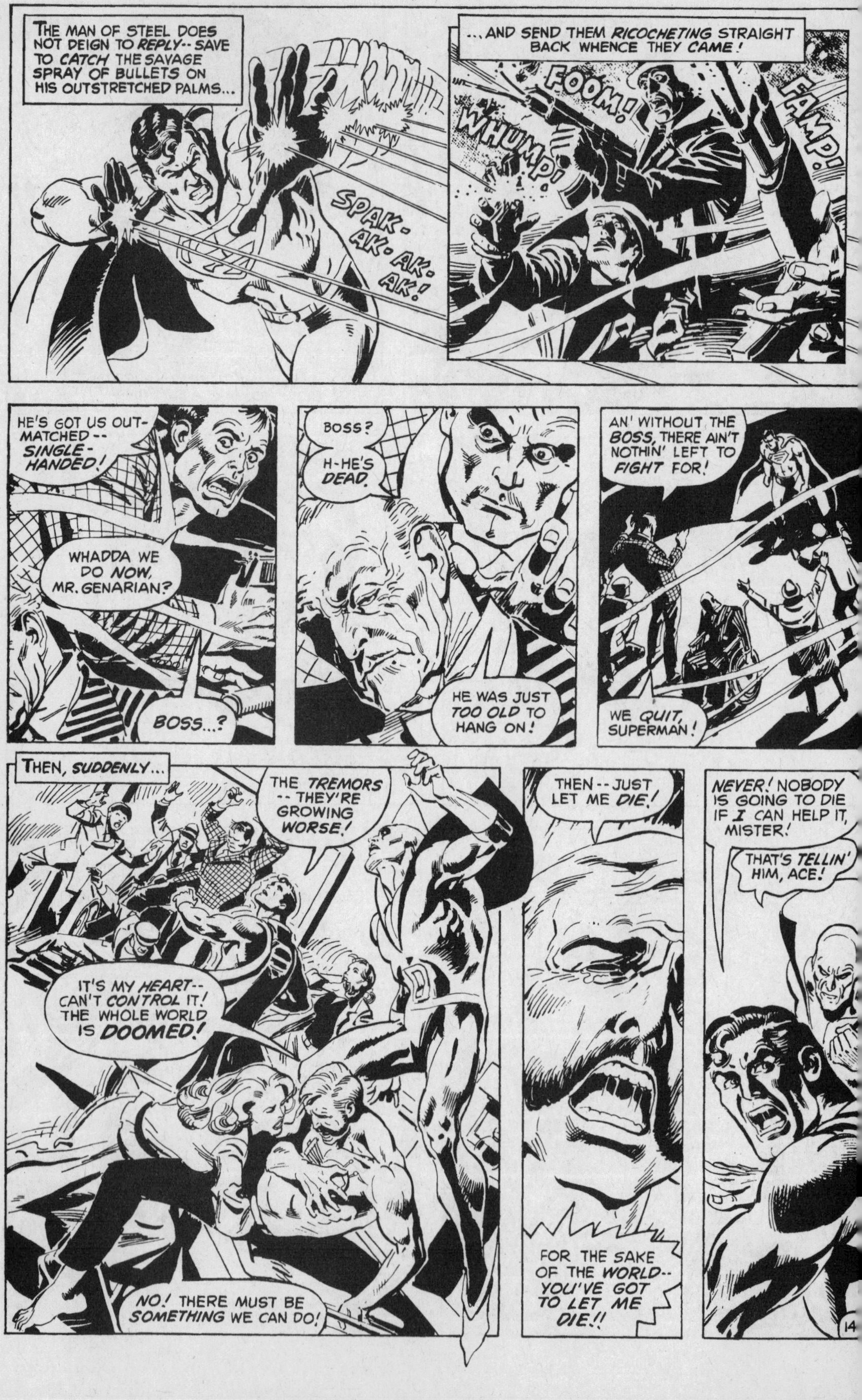
THE MAN OF STEEL DOES NOT DEIGN TO REPLY-- SAVE TO CATCH THE SAVAGE SPRAY OF BULLETS ON HIS OUTSTRETCHED PALMS...
SPAK-AK-AK-AK!
...AND SEND THEM RICOCHETING STRAIGHT BACK WHENCE THEY CAME!
FOOM!
WHUMP!
FAMP!
HE'S GOT US OUT-MATCHED -- SINGLE-HANDED!
WHADDA WE DO NOW, MR. GENARIAN?
BOSS...?
BOSS?
H-HE'S DEAD.
HE WAS JUST TOO OLD TO HANG ON!
AN' WITHOUT THE BOSS, THERE AIN'T NOTHIN' LEFT TO FIGHT FOR!
WE QUIT, SUPERMAN!
THEN, SUDDENLY...
THE TREMORS -- THEY'RE GROWING WORSE!
IT'S MY HEART-- CAN'T CONTROL IT! THE WHOLE WORLD IS DOOMED!
NO! THERE MUST BE SOMETHING WE CAN DO!
THEN -- JUST LET ME DIE!
FOR THE SAKE OF THE WORLD-- YOU'VE GOT TO LET ME DIE!!
NEVER! NOBODY IS GOING TO DIE IF I CAN HELP IT, MISTER!
THAT'S TELLIN' HIM, ACE!
14

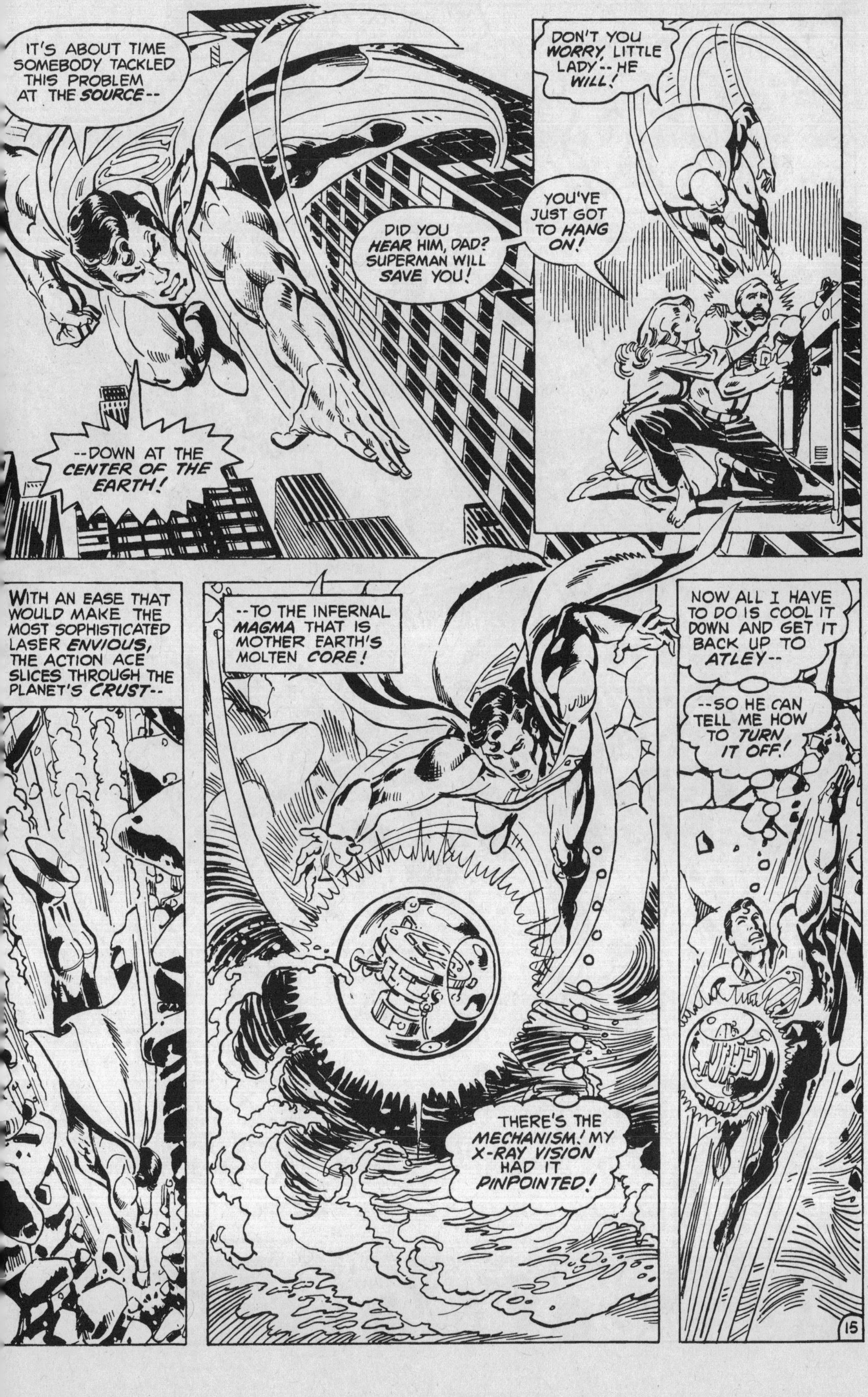
IT'S ABOUT TIME SOMEBODY TACKLED THIS PROBLEM AT THE SOURCE--
--DOWN AT THE CENTER OF THE EARTH!
DID YOU HEAR HIM, DAD? SUPERMAN WILL SAVE YOU!
YOU'VE JUST GOT TO HANG ON!
DON'T YOU WORRY, LITTLE LADY--HE WILL!
WITH AN EASE THAT WOULD MAKE THE MOST SOPHISTICATED LASER ENVIOUS, THE ACTION ACE SLICES THROUGH THE PLANET'S CRUST--
--TO THE INFERNAL MAGMA THAT IS MOTHER EARTH'S MOLTEN CORE!
THERE'S THE MECHANISM! MY X-RAY VISION HAD IT PINPOINTED!
NOW ALL I HAVE TO DO IS COOL IT DOWN AND GET IT BACK UP TO ATLEY--
--SO HE CAN TELL ME HOW TO TURN IT OFF!
15

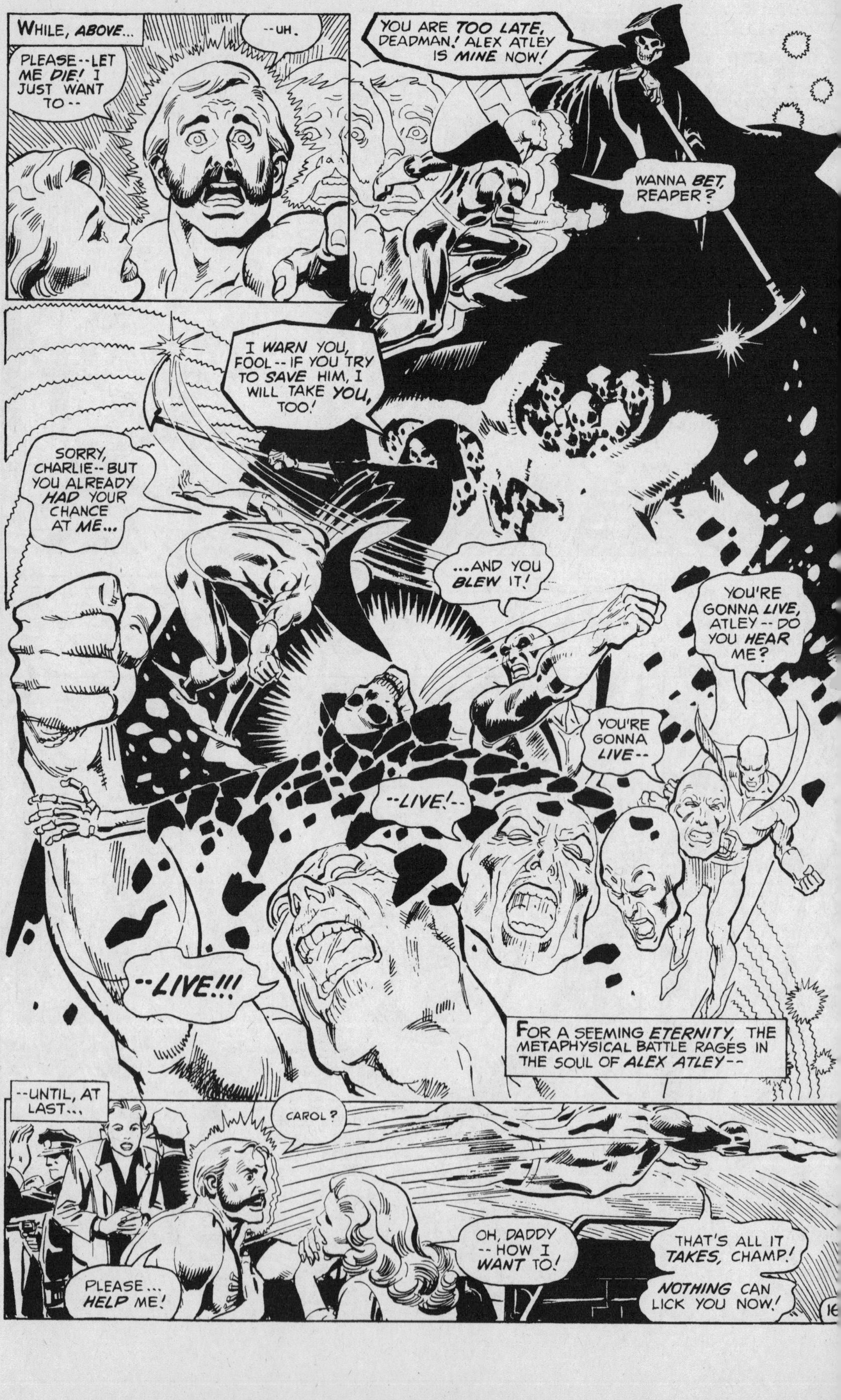

WHILE, ABOVE...
PLEASE--LET ME DIE! I JUST WANT TO--
--UH.
YOU ARE TOO LATE, DEADMAN! ALEX ATLEY IS MINE NOW!
WANNA BET, REAPER?
I WARN YOU, FOOL--IF YOU TRY TO SAVE HIM, I WILL TAKE YOU, TOO!
SORRY, CHARLIE--BUT YOU ALREADY HAD YOUR CHANCE AT ME...
...AND YOU BLEW IT!
YOU'RE GONNA LIVE, ATLEY--DO YOU HEAR ME?
YOU'RE GONNA LIVE--
--LIVE!--
--LIVE!!!
FOR A SEEMING ETERNITY, THE METAPHYSICAL BATTLE RAGES IN THE SOUL OF ALEX ATLEY--
--UNTIL, AT LAST...
CAROL?
PLEASE... HELP ME!
OH, DADDY --HOW I WANT TO!
THAT'S ALL IT TAKES, CHAMP!
NOTHING CAN LICK YOU NOW!
16

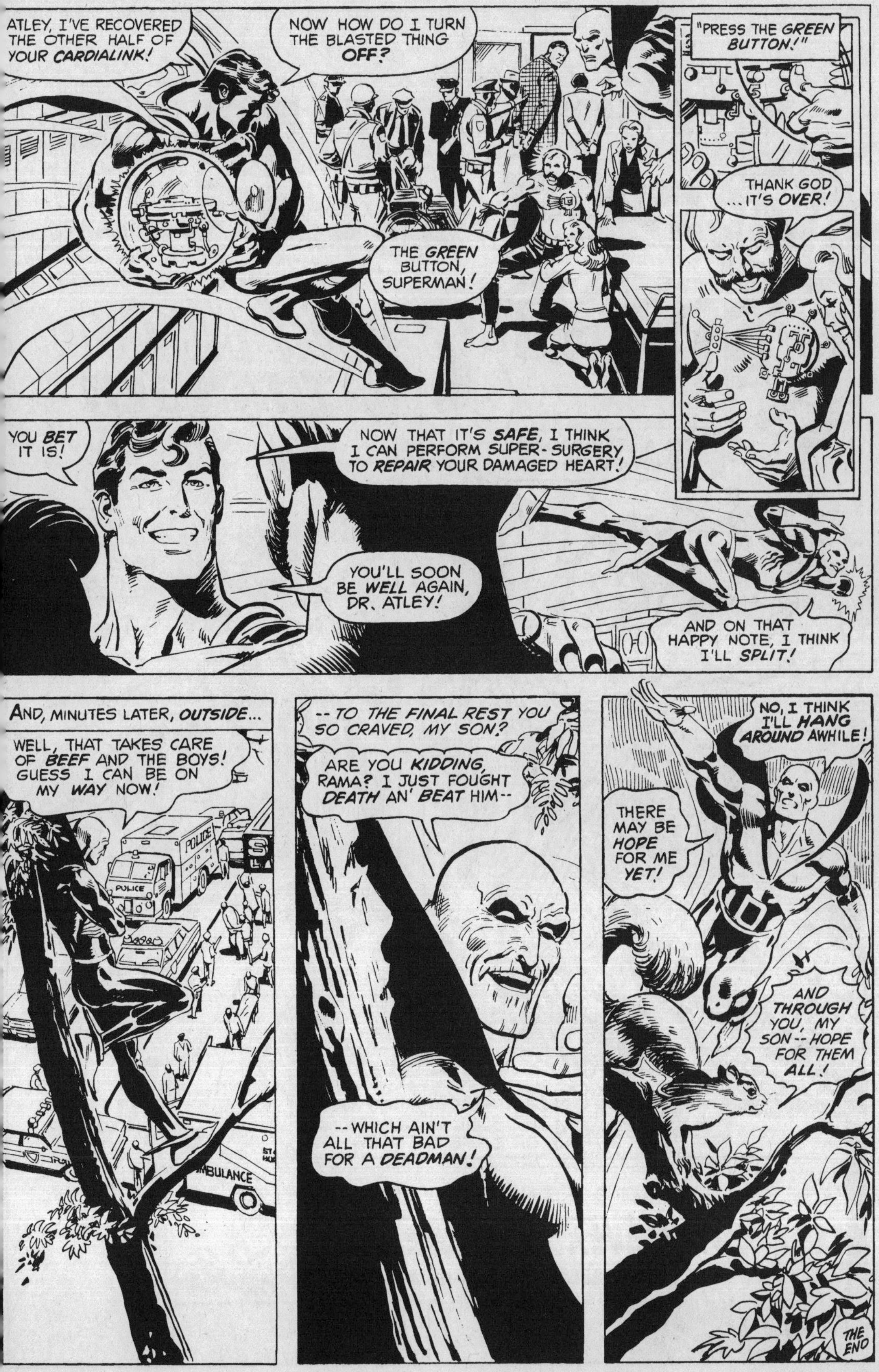
ATLEY, I'VE RECOVERED THE OTHER HALF OF YOUR CARDIALINK!
NOW HOW DO I TURN THE BLASTED THING OFF?
THE GREEN BUTTON, SUPERMAN!
"PRESS THE GREEN BUTTON!"
THANK GOD ...IT'S OVER!
YOU BET IT IS!
NOW THAT IT'S SAFE, I THINK I CAN PERFORM SUPER-SURGERY TO REPAIR YOUR DAMAGED HEART!
YOU'LL SOON BE WELL AGAIN, DR. ATLEY!
AND ON THAT HAPPY NOTE, I THINK I'LL SPLIT!
AND, MINUTES LATER, OUTSIDE...
WELL, THAT TAKES CARE OF BEEF AND THE BOYS! GUESS I CAN BE ON MY WAY NOW!
POLICE
POLICE
AMBULANCE
-- TO THE FINAL REST YOU SO CRAVED, MY SON?
ARE YOU KIDDING, RAMA? I JUST FOUGHT DEATH AN' BEAT HIM--
--WHICH AIN'T ALL THAT BAD FOR A DEADMAN!
NO, I THINK I'LL HANG AROUND AWHILE!
THERE MAY BE HOPE FOR ME YET!
AND THROUGH YOU, MY SON -- HOPE FOR THEM ALL!
THE END

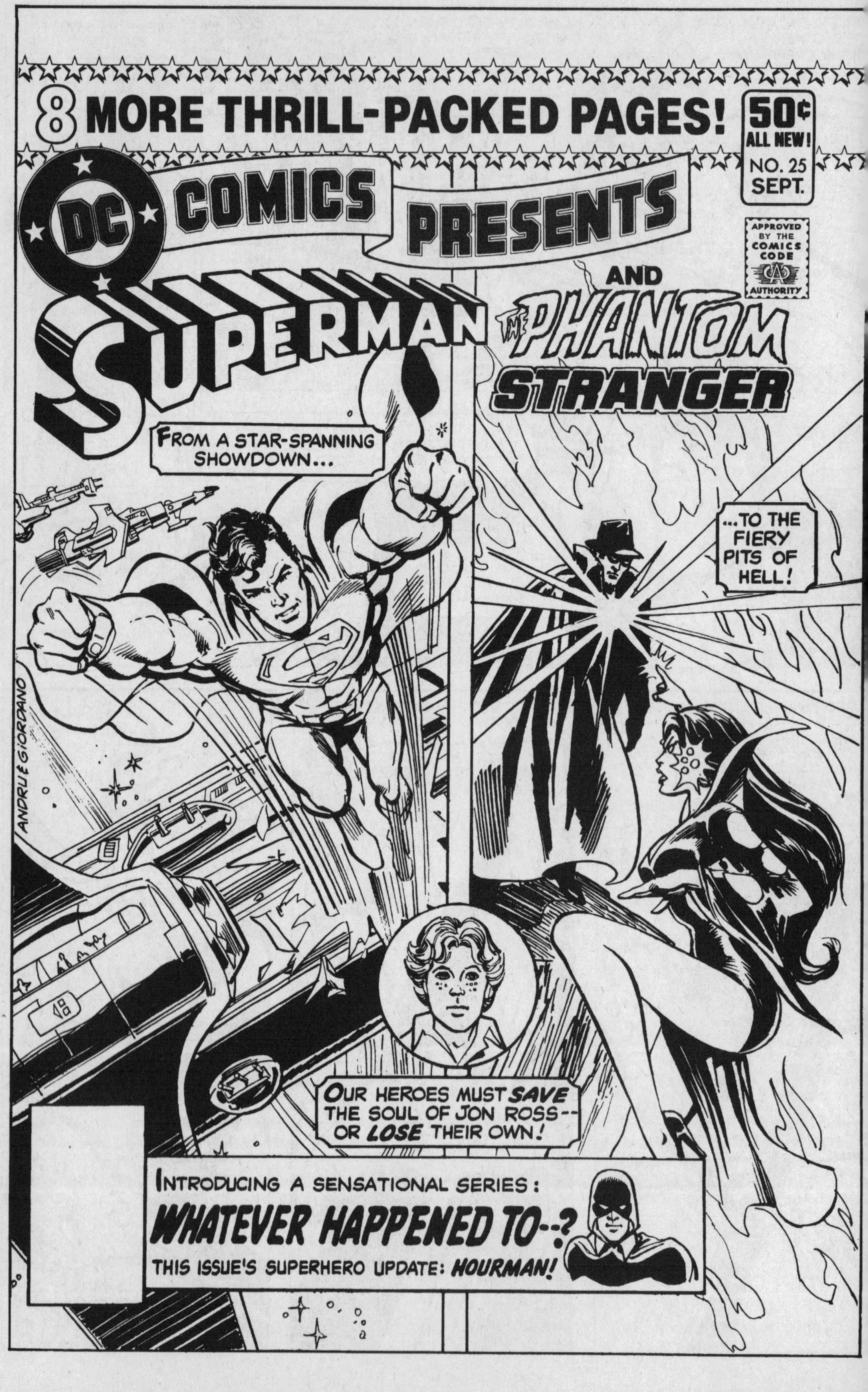
8 MORE THRILL-PACKED PAGES!
50¢ ALL NEW!
NO. 25 SEPT.
DC COMICS PRESENTS
APPROVED BY THE COMICS CODE AUTHORITY
SUPERMAN AND THE PHANTOM STRANGER
FROM A STAR-SPANNING SHOWDOWN...
...TO THE FIERY PITS OF HELL!
ANDRU & GIORDANO
OUR HEROES MUST SAVE THE SOUL OF JON ROSS-- OR LOSE THEIR OWN!
INTRODUCING A SENSATIONAL SERIES:
WHATEVER HAPPENED TO--?
THIS ISSUE'S SUPERHERO UPDATE: HOURMAN!

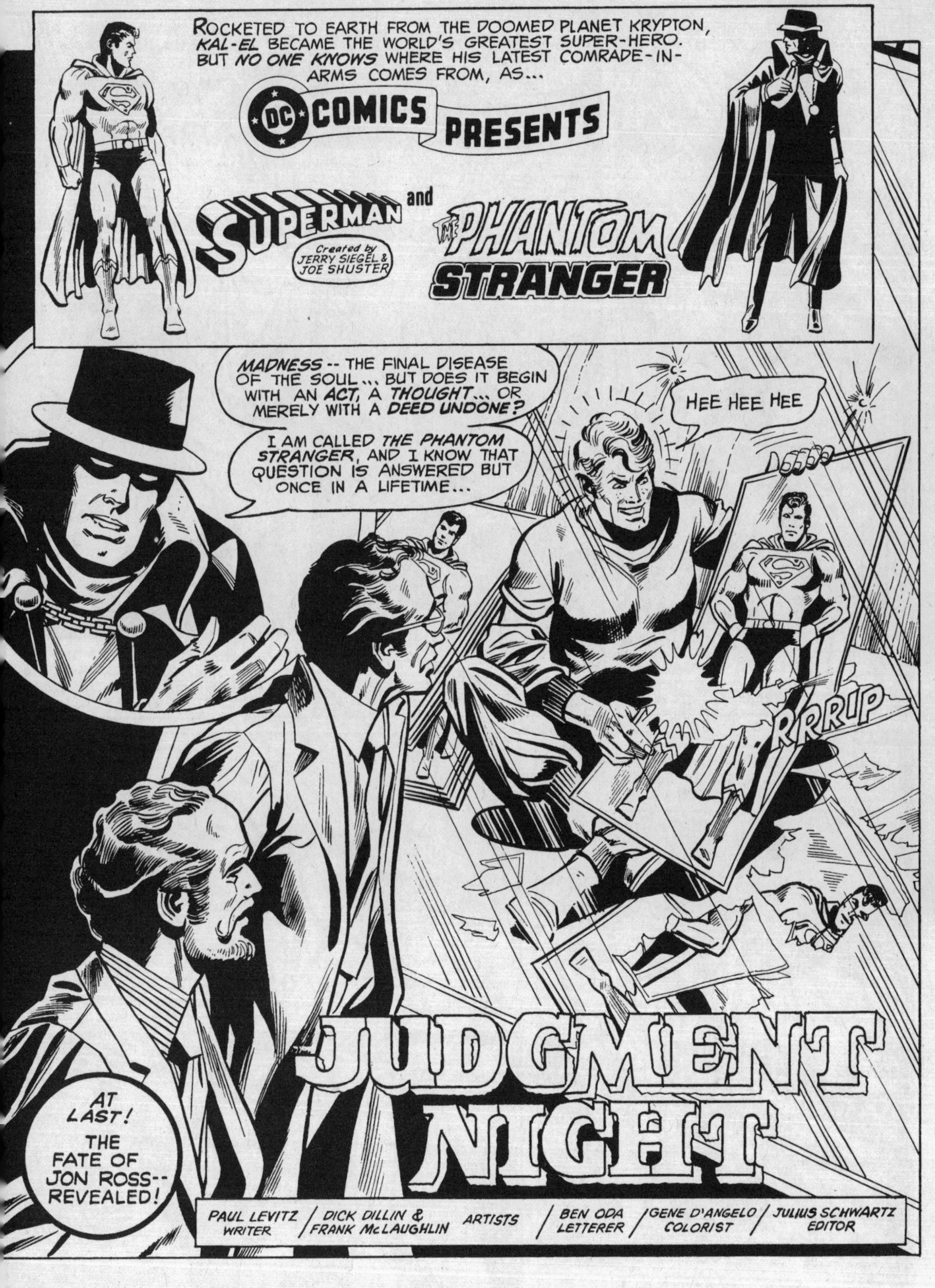
ROCKETED TO EARTH FROM THE DOOMED PLANET KRYPTON, KAL-EL BECAME THE WORLD'S GREATEST SUPER-HERO. BUT NO ONE KNOWS WHERE HIS LATEST COMRADE-IN-ARMS COMES FROM, AS...
DC COMICS PRESENTS
SUPERMAN and THE PHANTOM STRANGER
Created by JERRY SIEGEL & JOE SHUSTER
MADNESS -- THE FINAL DISEASE OF THE SOUL... BUT DOES IT BEGIN WITH AN ACT, A THOUGHT... OR MERELY WITH A DEED UNDONE?
I AM CALLED THE PHANTOM STRANGER, AND I KNOW THAT QUESTION IS ANSWERED BUT ONCE IN A LIFETIME...
HEE HEE HEE
RRRIP
JUDGMENT NIGHT
AT LAST! THE FATE OF JON ROSS-- REVEALED!
PAUL LEVITZ WRITER / DICK DILLIN & FRANK McLAUGHLIN ARTISTS / BEN ODA LETTERER / GENE D'ANGELO COLORIST / JULIUS SCHWARTZ EDITOR

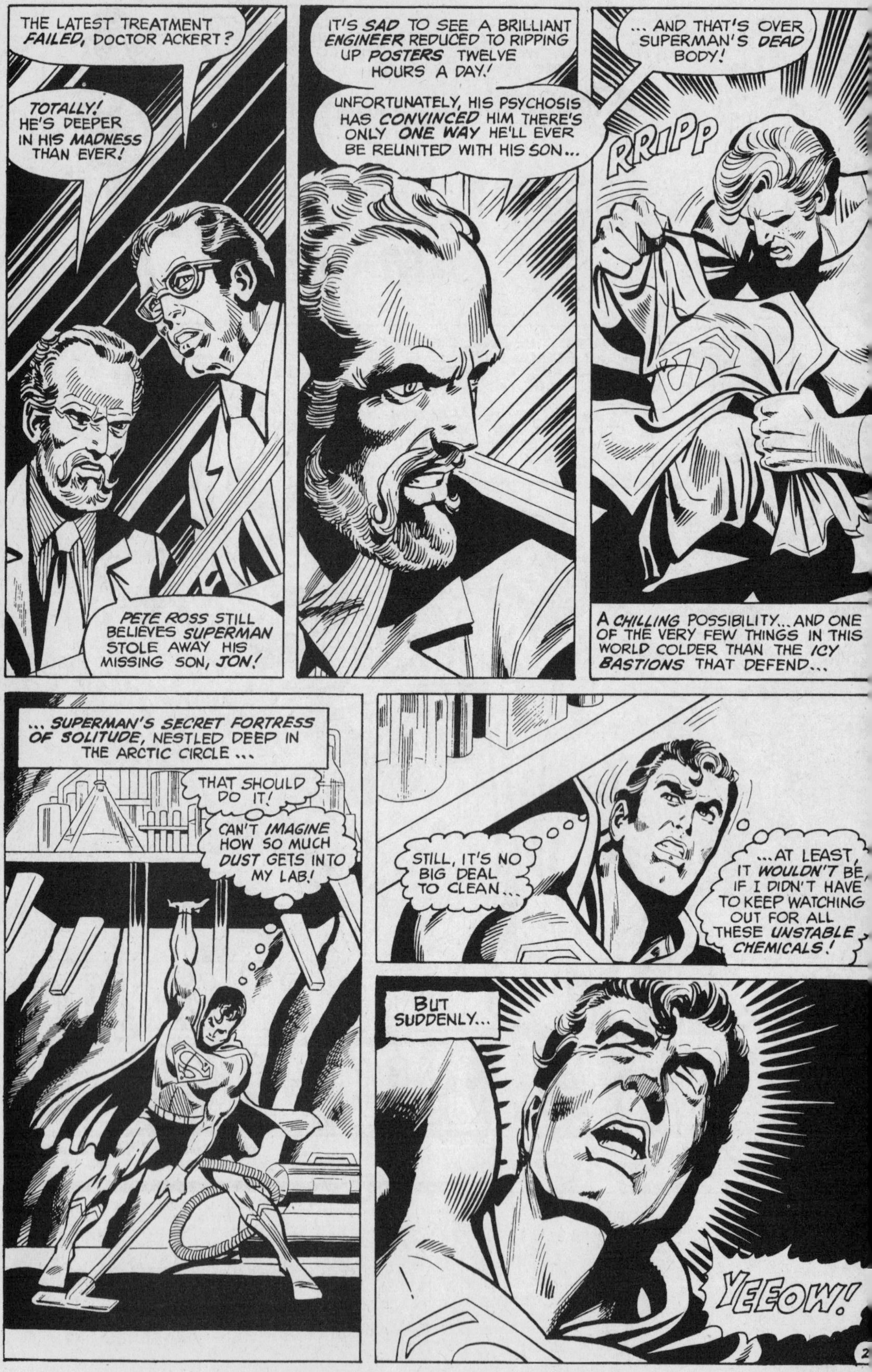
THE LATEST TREATMENT FAILED, DOCTOR ACKERT?
TOTALLY! HE'S DEEPER IN HIS MADNESS THAN EVER!
PETE ROSS STILL BELIEVES SUPERMAN STOLE AWAY HIS MISSING SON, JON!
IT'S SAD TO SEE A BRILLIANT ENGINEER REDUCED TO RIPPING UP POSTERS TWELVE HOURS A DAY!
UNFORTUNATELY, HIS PSYCHOSIS HAS CONVINCED HIM THERE'S ONLY ONE WAY HE'LL EVER BE REUNITED WITH HIS SON...
... AND THAT'S OVER SUPERMAN'S DEAD BODY!
RRIPP
A CHILLING POSSIBILITY... AND ONE OF THE VERY FEW THINGS IN THIS WORLD COLDER THAN THE ICY BASTIONS THAT DEFEND...
... SUPERMAN'S SECRET FORTRESS OF SOLITUDE, NESTLED DEEP IN THE ARCTIC CIRCLE ...
THAT SHOULD DO IT!
CAN'T IMAGINE HOW SO MUCH DUST GETS INTO MY LAB!
STILL, IT'S NO BIG DEAL TO CLEAN...
...AT LEAST, IT WOULDN'T BE, IF I DIDN'T HAVE TO KEEP WATCHING OUT FOR ALL THESE UNSTABLE CHEMICALS!
BUT SUDDENLY...
YEEOW!

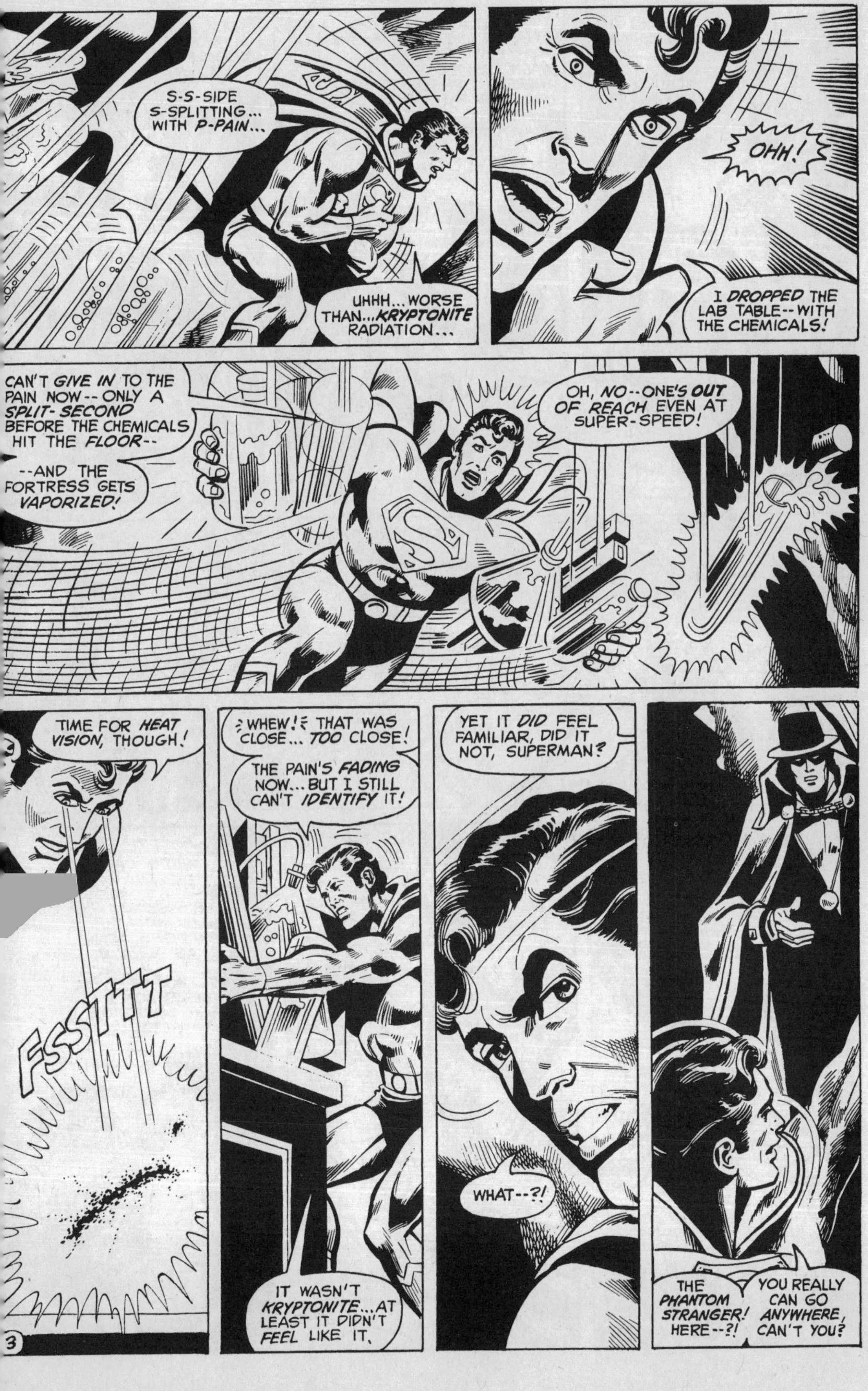
S-S-SIDE S-SPLITTING... WITH P-PAIN...
UHHH... WORSE THAN... KRYPTONITE RADIATION...
OHH!
I DROPPED THE LAB TABLE--WITH THE CHEMICALS!
CAN'T GIVE IN TO THE PAIN NOW--ONLY A SPLIT-SECOND BEFORE THE CHEMICALS HIT THE FLOOR--
--AND THE FORTRESS GETS VAPORIZED!
OH, NO--ONE'S OUT OF REACH EVEN AT SUPER-SPEED!
TIME FOR HEAT VISION, THOUGH!
FSSTTT
3
WHEW! THAT WAS CLOSE... TOO CLOSE!
THE PAIN'S FADING NOW... BUT I STILL CAN'T IDENTIFY IT!
IT WASN'T KRYPTONITE... AT LEAST IT DIDN'T FEEL LIKE IT.
YET IT DID FEEL FAMILIAR, DID IT NOT, SUPERMAN?
WHAT--?!
THE PHANTOM STRANGER! HERE--?!
YOU REALLY CAN GO ANYWHERE, CAN'T YOU?

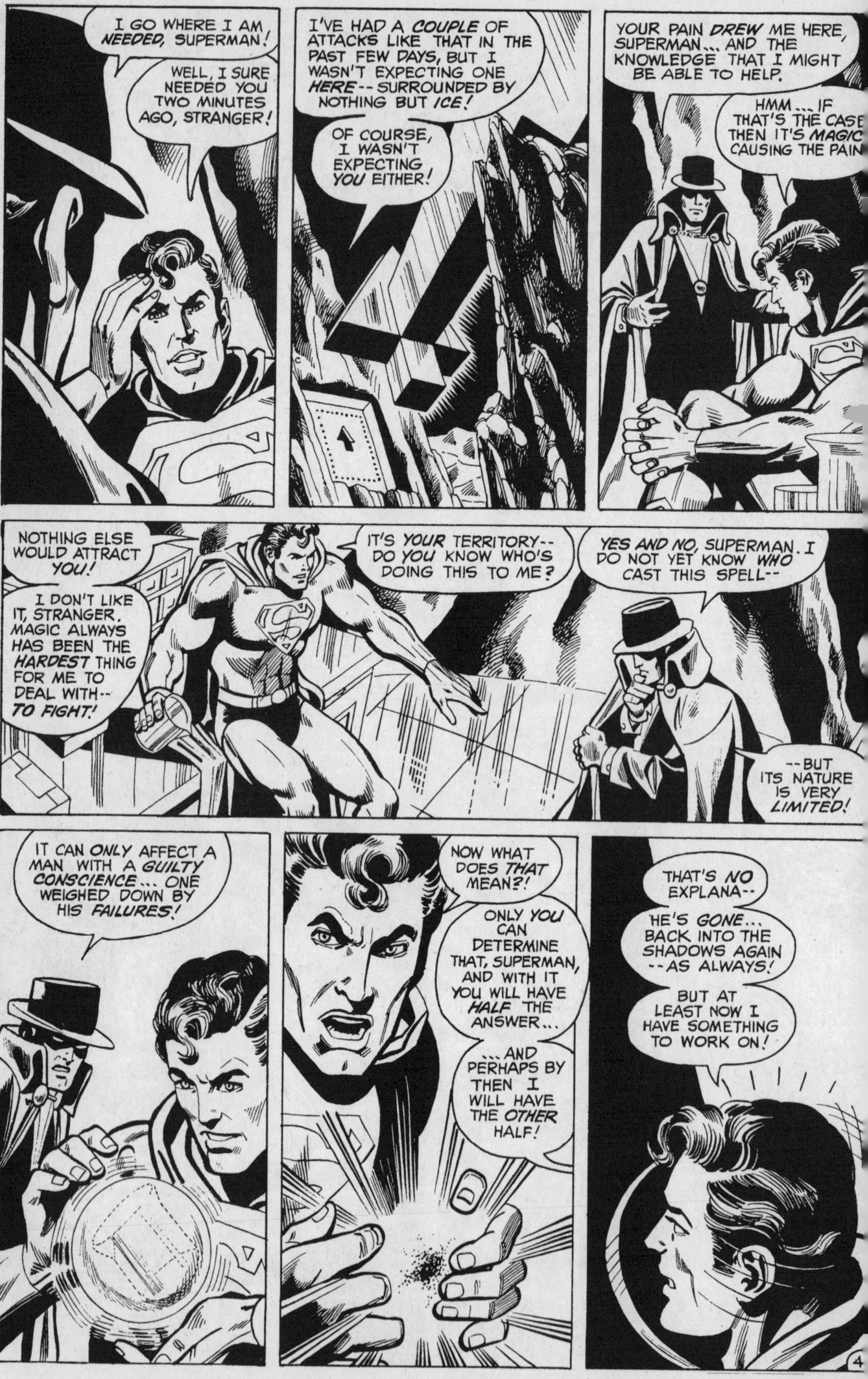
I GO WHERE I AM NEEDED, SUPERMAN!
WELL, I SURE NEEDED YOU TWO MINUTES AGO, STRANGER!
I'VE HAD A COUPLE OF ATTACKS LIKE THAT IN THE PAST FEW DAYS, BUT I WASN'T EXPECTING ONE HERE-- SURROUNDED BY NOTHING BUT ICE!
OF COURSE, I WASN'T EXPECTING YOU EITHER!
YOUR PAIN DREW ME HERE, SUPERMAN... AND THE KNOWLEDGE THAT I MIGHT BE ABLE TO HELP.
HMM... IF THAT'S THE CASE THEN IT'S MAGIC CAUSING THE PAIN
NOTHING ELSE WOULD ATTRACT YOU!
I DON'T LIKE IT, STRANGER. MAGIC ALWAYS HAS BEEN THE HARDEST THING FOR ME TO DEAL WITH-- TO FIGHT!
IT'S YOUR TERRITORY-- DO YOU KNOW WHO'S DOING THIS TO ME?
YES AND NO, SUPERMAN. I DO NOT YET KNOW WHO CAST THIS SPELL--
--BUT ITS NATURE IS VERY LIMITED!
IT CAN ONLY AFFECT A MAN WITH A GUILTY CONSCIENCE... ONE WEIGHED DOWN BY HIS FAILURES!
NOW WHAT DOES THAT MEAN?!
ONLY YOU CAN DETERMINE THAT, SUPERMAN, AND WITH IT YOU WILL HAVE HALF THE ANSWER...
...AND PERHAPS BY THEN I WILL HAVE THE OTHER HALF!
THAT'S NO EXPLANA--
HE'S GONE... BACK INTO THE SHADOWS AGAIN --AS ALWAYS!
BUT AT LEAST NOW I HAVE SOMETHING TO WORK ON!
4

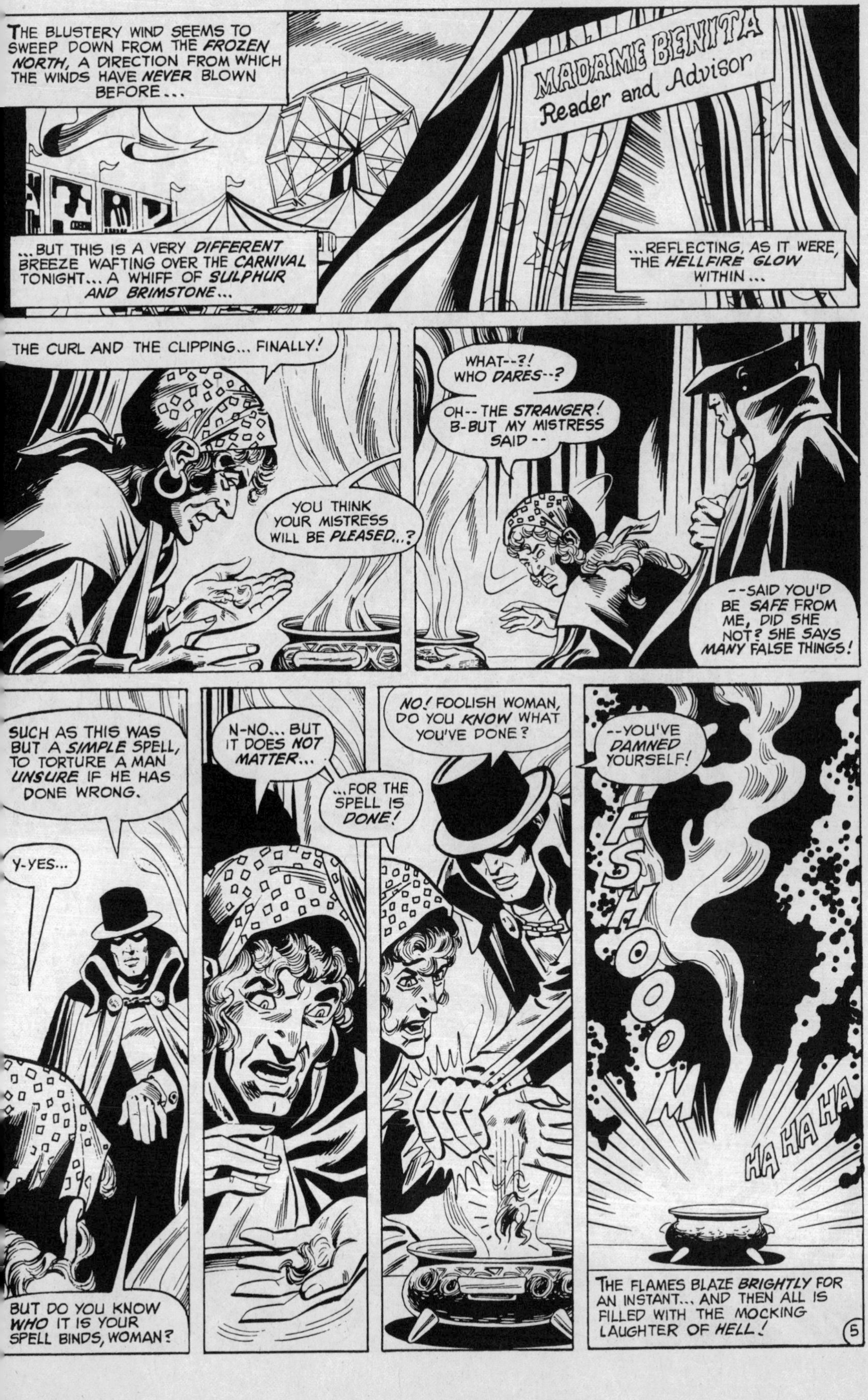
THE BLUSTERY WIND SEEMS TO SWEEP DOWN FROM THE FROZEN NORTH, A DIRECTION FROM WHICH THE WINDS HAVE NEVER BLOWN BEFORE...
MADAME BENITA
Reader and Advisor
...BUT THIS IS A VERY DIFFERENT BREEZE WAFTING OVER THE CARNIVAL TONIGHT... A WHIFF OF SULPHUR AND BRIMSTONE...
...REFLECTING, AS IT WERE, THE HELLFIRE GLOW WITHIN...
THE CURL AND THE CLIPPING... FINALLY!
YOU THINK YOUR MISTRESS WILL BE PLEASED...?
WHAT--?! WHO DARES--?
OH-- THE STRANGER! B-BUT MY MISTRESS SAID --
--SAID YOU'D BE SAFE FROM ME, DID SHE NOT? SHE SAYS MANY FALSE THINGS!
SUCH AS THIS WAS BUT A SIMPLE SPELL, TO TORTURE A MAN UNSURE IF HE HAS DONE WRONG.
Y-YES...
BUT DO YOU KNOW WHO IT IS YOUR SPELL BINDS, WOMAN?
N-NO... BUT IT DOES NOT MATTER...
...FOR THE SPELL IS DONE!
NO! FOOLISH WOMAN, DO YOU KNOW WHAT YOU'VE DONE?
--YOU'VE DAMNED YOURSELF!
FSHOOOOM
HA HA HA
THE FLAMES BLAZE BRIGHTLY FOR AN INSTANT... AND THEN ALL IS FILLED WITH THE MOCKING LAUGHTER OF HELL!
5

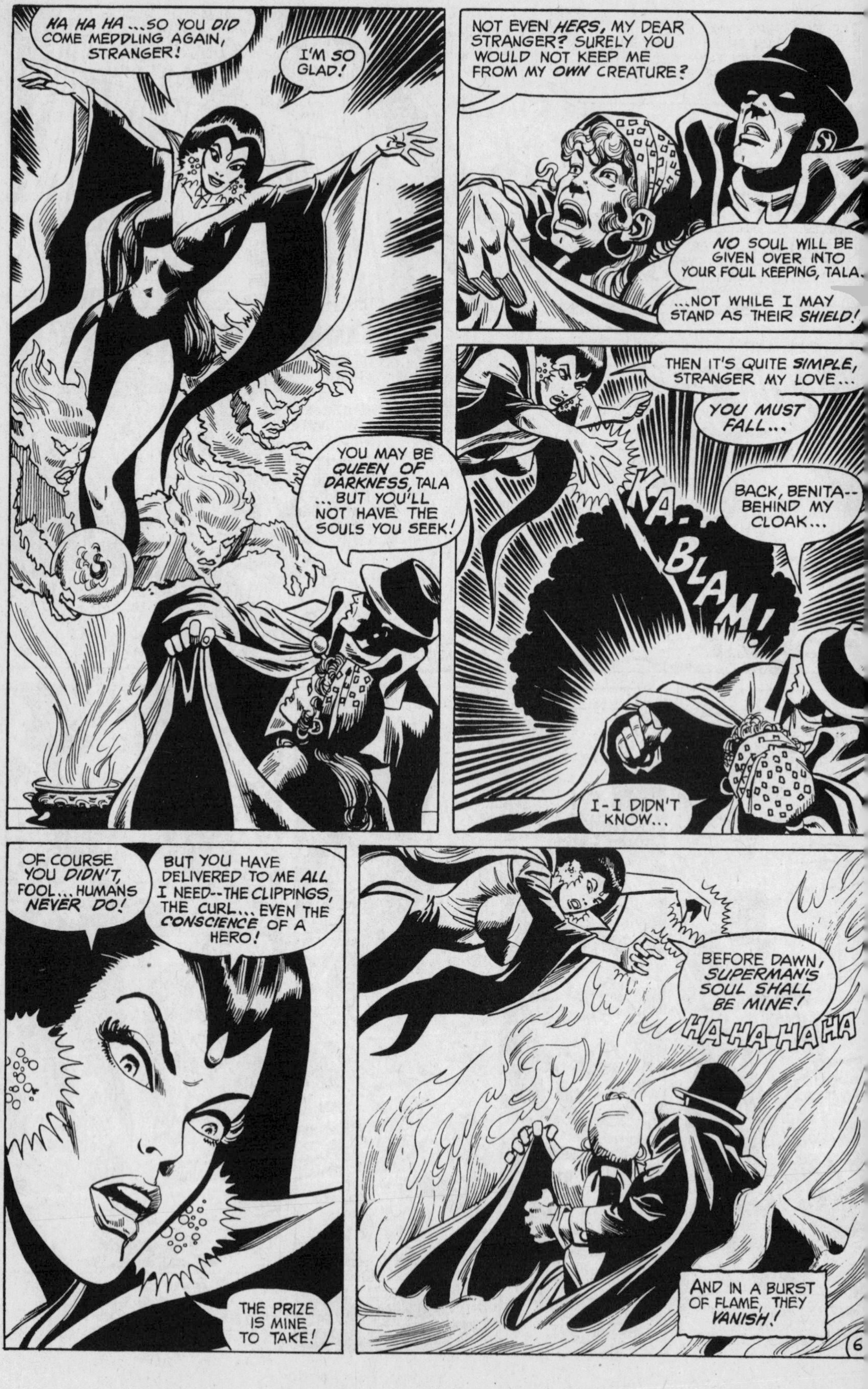
HA HA HA ...SO YOU DID COME MEDDLING AGAIN, STRANGER!
I'M SO GLAD!
YOU MAY BE QUEEN OF DARKNESS, TALA ... BUT YOU'LL NOT HAVE THE SOULS YOU SEEK!
NOT EVEN HERS, MY DEAR STRANGER? SURELY YOU WOULD NOT KEEP ME FROM MY OWN CREATURE?
NO SOUL WILL BE GIVEN OVER INTO YOUR FOUL KEEPING, TALA.
...NOT WHILE I MAY STAND AS THEIR SHIELD!
THEN IT'S QUITE SIMPLE, STRANGER MY LOVE...
YOU MUST FALL...
KA-BLAM!
BACK, BENITA-- BEHIND MY CLOAK...
I-I DIDN'T KNOW...
OF COURSE YOU DIDN'T, FOOL... HUMANS NEVER DO!
BUT YOU HAVE DELIVERED TO ME ALL I NEED--THE CLIPPINGS, THE CURL... EVEN THE CONSCIENCE OF A HERO!
THE PRIZE IS MINE TO TAKE!
BEFORE DAWN, SUPERMAN'S SOUL SHALL BE MINE!
HA-HA-HA-HAHA
AND IN A BURST OF FLAME, THEY VANISH!
6

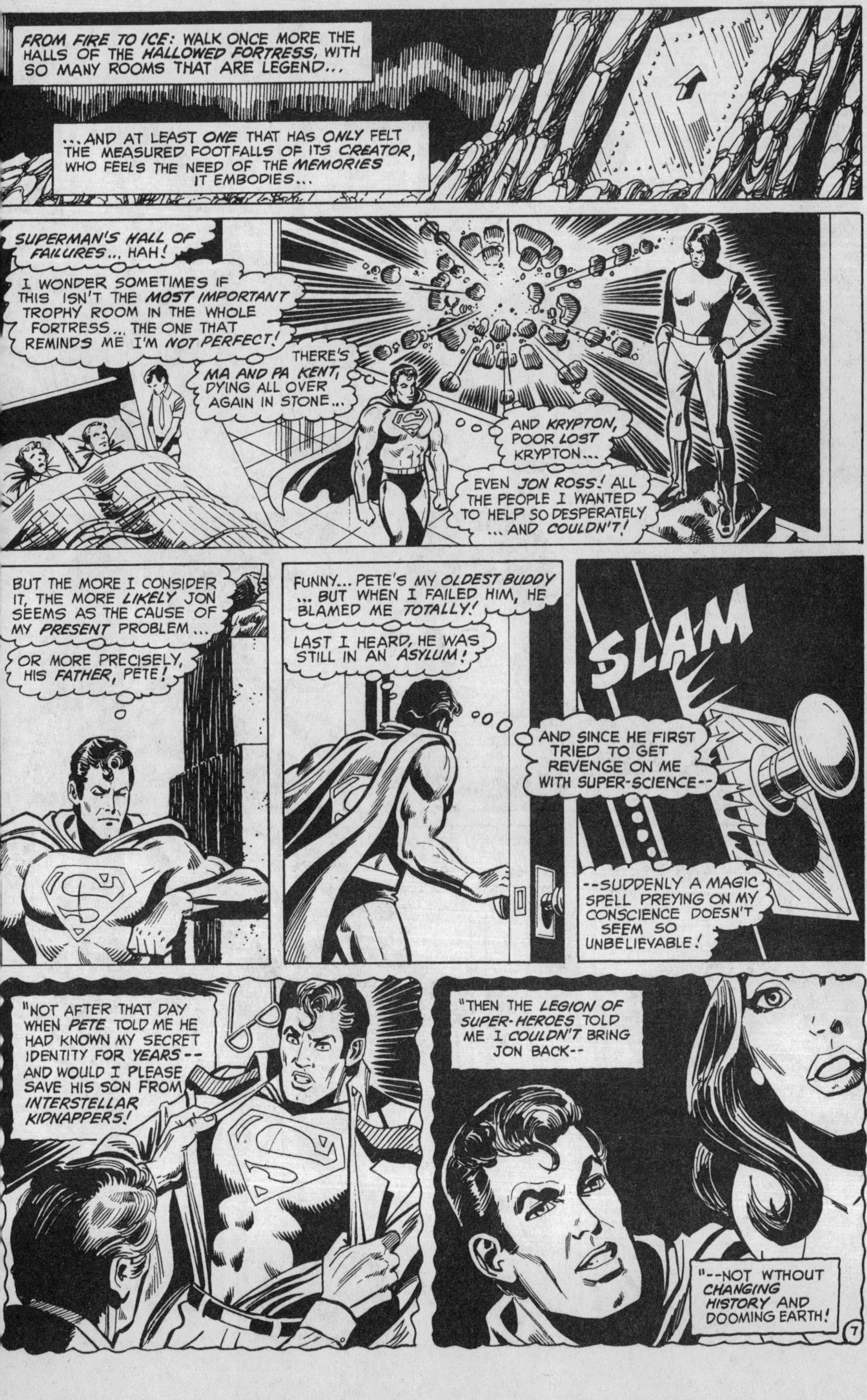
FROM FIRE TO ICE: WALK ONCE MORE THE HALLS OF THE HALLOWED FORTRESS, WITH SO MANY ROOMS THAT ARE LEGEND...
...AND AT LEAST ONE THAT HAS ONLY FELT THE MEASURED FOOTFALLS OF ITS CREATOR, WHO FEELS THE NEED OF THE MEMORIES IT EMBODIES...
SUPERMAN'S HALL OF FAILURES... HAH!
I WONDER SOMETIMES IF THIS ISN'T THE MOST IMPORTANT TROPHY ROOM IN THE WHOLE FORTRESS... THE ONE THAT REMINDS ME I'M NOT PERFECT!
THERE'S MA AND PA KENT, DYING ALL OVER AGAIN IN STONE...
AND KRYPTON, POOR LOST KRYPTON...
EVEN JON ROSS! ALL THE PEOPLE I WANTED TO HELP SO DESPERATELY ...AND COULDN'T!
BUT THE MORE I CONSIDER IT, THE MORE LIKELY JON SEEMS AS THE CAUSE OF MY PRESENT PROBLEM...
OR MORE PRECISELY, HIS FATHER, PETE!
FUNNY... PETE'S MY OLDEST BUDDY ...BUT WHEN I FAILED HIM, HE BLAMED ME TOTALLY!
LAST I HEARD, HE WAS STILL IN AN ASYLUM!
SLAM
AND SINCE HE FIRST TRIED TO GET REVENGE ON ME WITH SUPER-SCIENCE--
--SUDDENLY A MAGIC SPELL PREYING ON MY CONSCIENCE DOESN'T SEEM SO UNBELIEVABLE!
"NOT AFTER THAT DAY WHEN PETE TOLD ME HE HAD KNOWN MY SECRET IDENTITY FOR YEARS--AND WOULD I PLEASE SAVE HIS SON FROM INTERSTELLAR KIDNAPPERS!
"THEN THE LEGION OF SUPER-HEROES TOLD ME I COULDN'T BRING JON BACK--
"--NOT WTHOUT CHANGING HISTORY AND DOOMING EARTH!
7

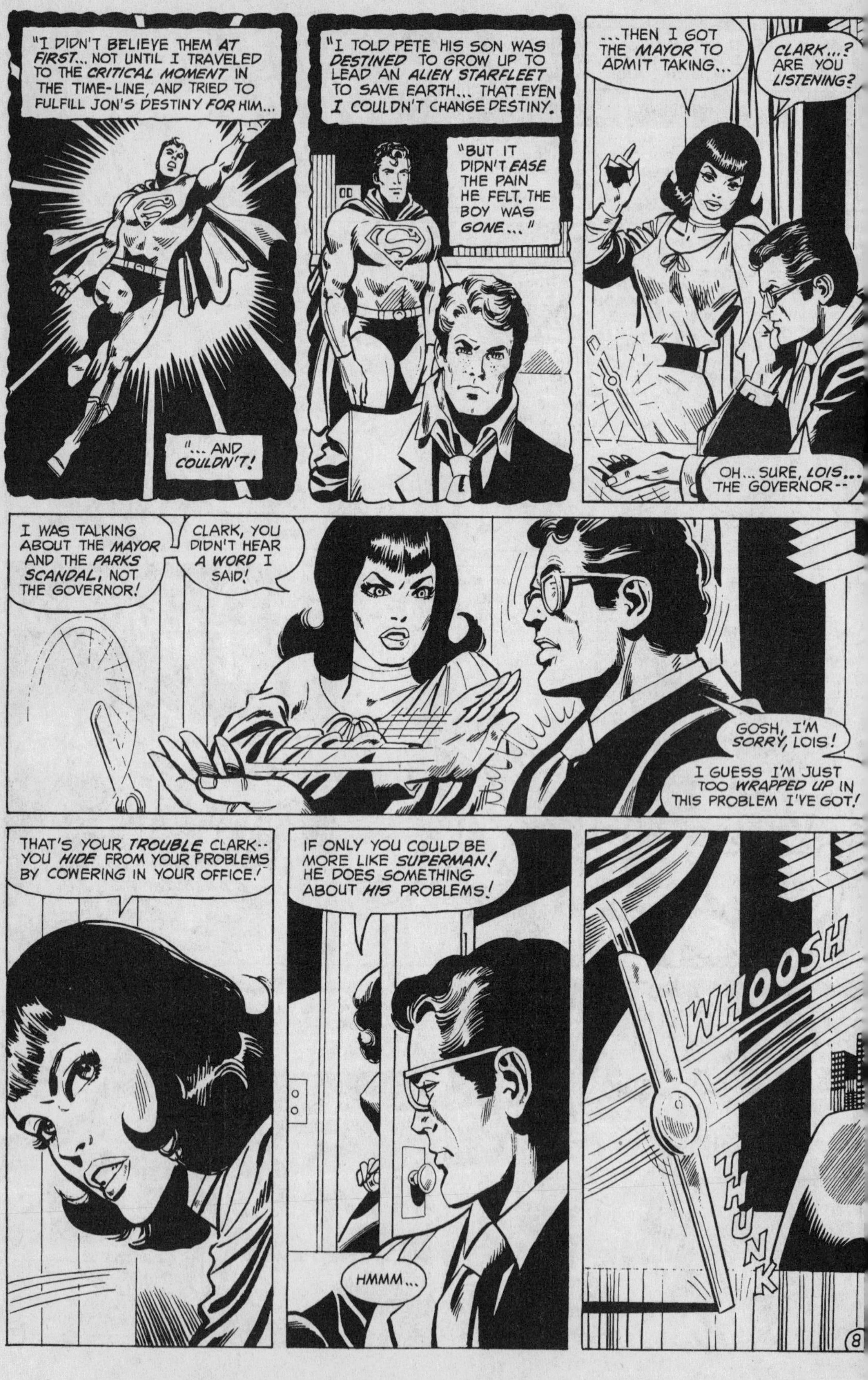
"I DIDN'T BELIEVE THEM AT FIRST... NOT UNTIL I TRAVELED TO THE CRITICAL MOMENT IN THE TIME-LINE, AND TRIED TO FULFILL JON'S DESTINY FOR HIM...
"... AND COULDN'T!
"I TOLD PETE HIS SON WAS DESTINED TO GROW UP TO LEAD AN ALIEN STARFLEET TO SAVE EARTH... THAT EVEN I COULDN'T CHANGE DESTINY.
"BUT IT DIDN'T EASE THE PAIN HE FELT. THE BOY WAS GONE..."
...THEN I GOT THE MAYOR TO ADMIT TAKING...
CLARK...? ARE YOU LISTENING?
OH... SURE, LOIS... THE GOVERNOR--
I WAS TALKING ABOUT THE MAYOR AND THE PARKS SCANDAL, NOT THE GOVERNOR!
CLARK, YOU DIDN'T HEAR A WORD I SAID!
GOSH, I'M SORRY, LOIS!
I GUESS I'M JUST TOO WRAPPED UP IN THIS PROBLEM I'VE GOT!
THAT'S YOUR TROUBLE CLARK-- YOU HIDE FROM YOUR PROBLEMS BY COWERING IN YOUR OFFICE!
IF ONLY YOU COULD BE MORE LIKE SUPERMAN! HE DOES SOMETHING ABOUT HIS PROBLEMS!
HMMM...
WHOOSH
THUNK
8

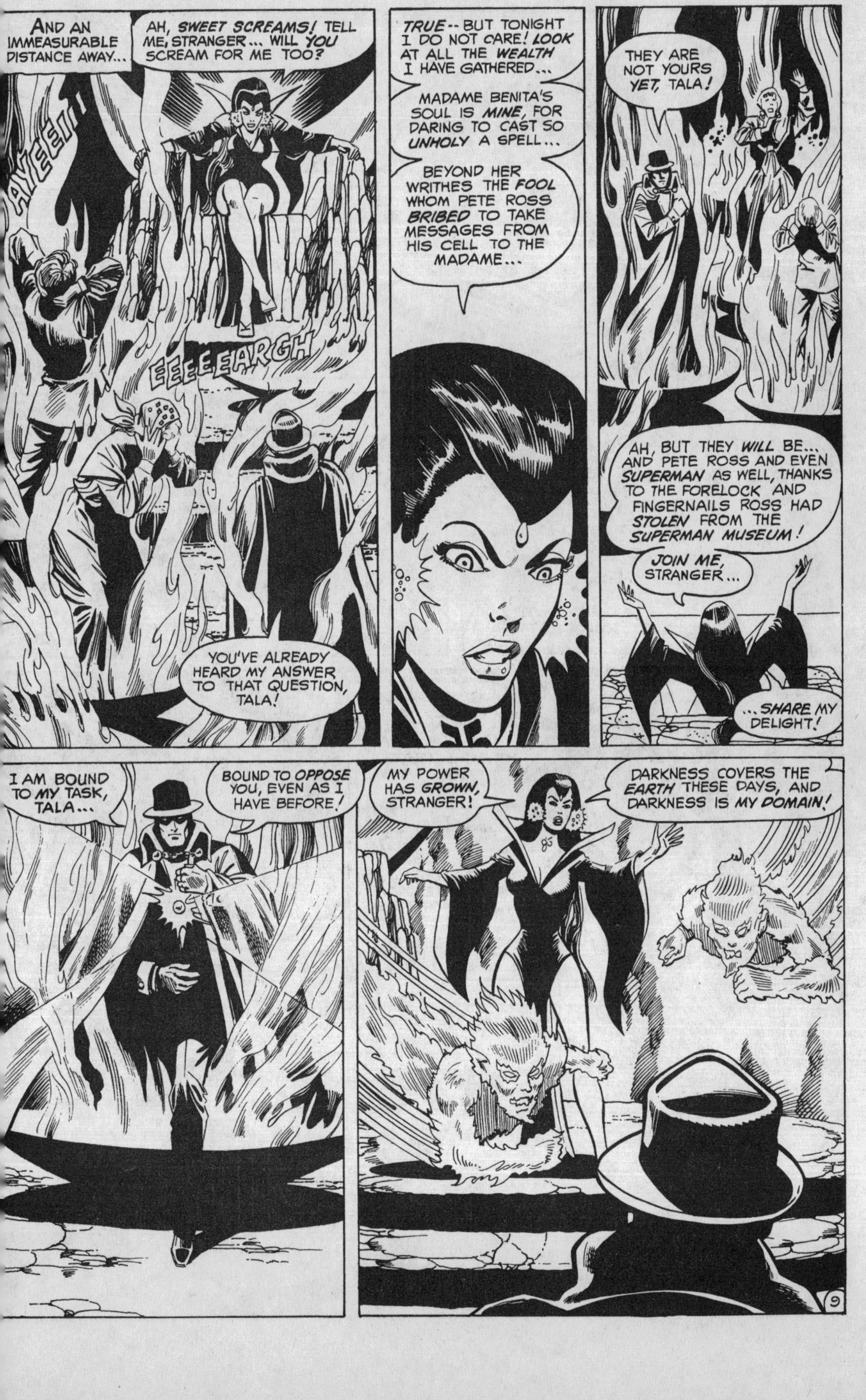
AND AN IMMEASURABLE DISTANCE AWAY...
AH, SWEET SCREAMS! TELL ME, STRANGER... WILL YOU SCREAM FOR ME TOO?
AYEE!!
EEEEEARGH
YOU'VE ALREADY HEARD MY ANSWER TO THAT QUESTION, TALA!
TRUE -- BUT TONIGHT I DO NOT CARE! LOOK AT ALL THE WEALTH I HAVE GATHERED...
MADAME BENITA'S SOUL IS MINE, FOR DARING TO CAST SO UNHOLY A SPELL...
BEYOND HER WRITHES THE FOOL WHOM PETE ROSS BRIBED TO TAKE MESSAGES FROM HIS CELL TO THE MADAME...
THEY ARE NOT YOURS YET, TALA!
AH, BUT THEY WILL BE... AND PETE ROSS AND EVEN SUPERMAN AS WELL, THANKS TO THE FORELOCK AND FINGERNAILS ROSS HAD STOLEN FROM THE SUPERMAN MUSEUM!
JOIN ME, STRANGER...
...SHARE MY DELIGHT!
I AM BOUND TO MY TASK, TALA...
BOUND TO OPPOSE YOU, EVEN AS I HAVE BEFORE!
MY POWER HAS GROWN, STRANGER!
DARKNESS COVERS THE EARTH THESE DAYS, AND DARKNESS IS MY DOMAIN!
9

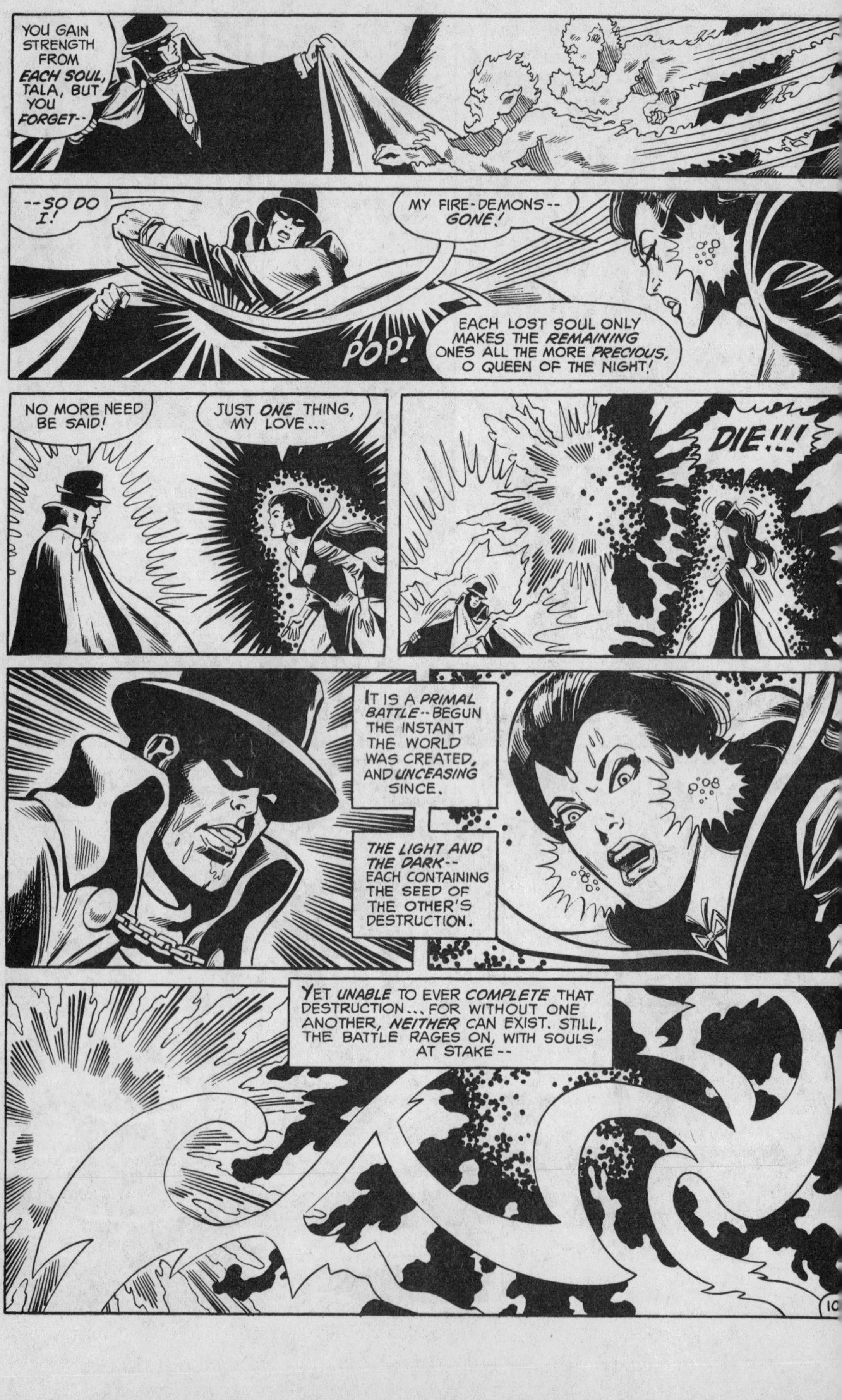
YOU GAIN STRENGTH FROM EACH SOUL, TALA, BUT YOU FORGET--
--SO DO I!
MY FIRE-DEMONS--GONE!
POP!
EACH LOST SOUL ONLY MAKES THE REMAINING ONES ALL THE MORE PRECIOUS, O QUEEN OF THE NIGHT!
NO MORE NEED BE SAID!
JUST ONE THING, MY LOVE...
DIE!!!
IT IS A PRIMAL BATTLE--BEGUN THE INSTANT THE WORLD WAS CREATED, AND UNCEASING SINCE.
THE LIGHT AND THE DARK--EACH CONTAINING THE SEED OF THE OTHER'S DESTRUCTION.
YET UNABLE TO EVER COMPLETE THAT DESTRUCTION... FOR WITHOUT ONE ANOTHER, NEITHER CAN EXIST. STILL, THE BATTLE RAGES ON, WITH SOULS AT STAKE--
10

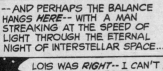

--AND PERHAPS THE BALANCE HANGS *HERE*-- WITH A MAN STREAKING AT THE SPEED OF LIGHT THROUGH THE ETERNAL NIGHT OF INTERSTELLAR SPACE...

LOIS WAS *RIGHT*-- I CAN'T LET THIS JON ROSS SITUATION GO ON!

AH, THERE'S THE PLANET *NYRVN* COMING UP-- COMPLETE WITH ITS WHOLE *FLEET* OF *ROBOT-DRONE WARSHIPS!*

JON ROSS IS DOWN ON THAT PLANET *SOMEWHERE*--

--AND *NOTHING* IS GOING TO STAND BETWEEN ME AND THE BOY...

NOT THIS TIME!

...RESHAPE THEM WITH *HEAT VISION* AND *SUPER-PRESSURE.*

HMM... EVEN AT *SUPER-SPEED* THIS COULD TAKE *HOURS!*

LET ME TAKE THESE *FRAGMENTS*...

NOW THIS WILL *SPEED UP* THE DISRUPTION OF THE ROBOT FLEET *CONSIDERABLY!*

11

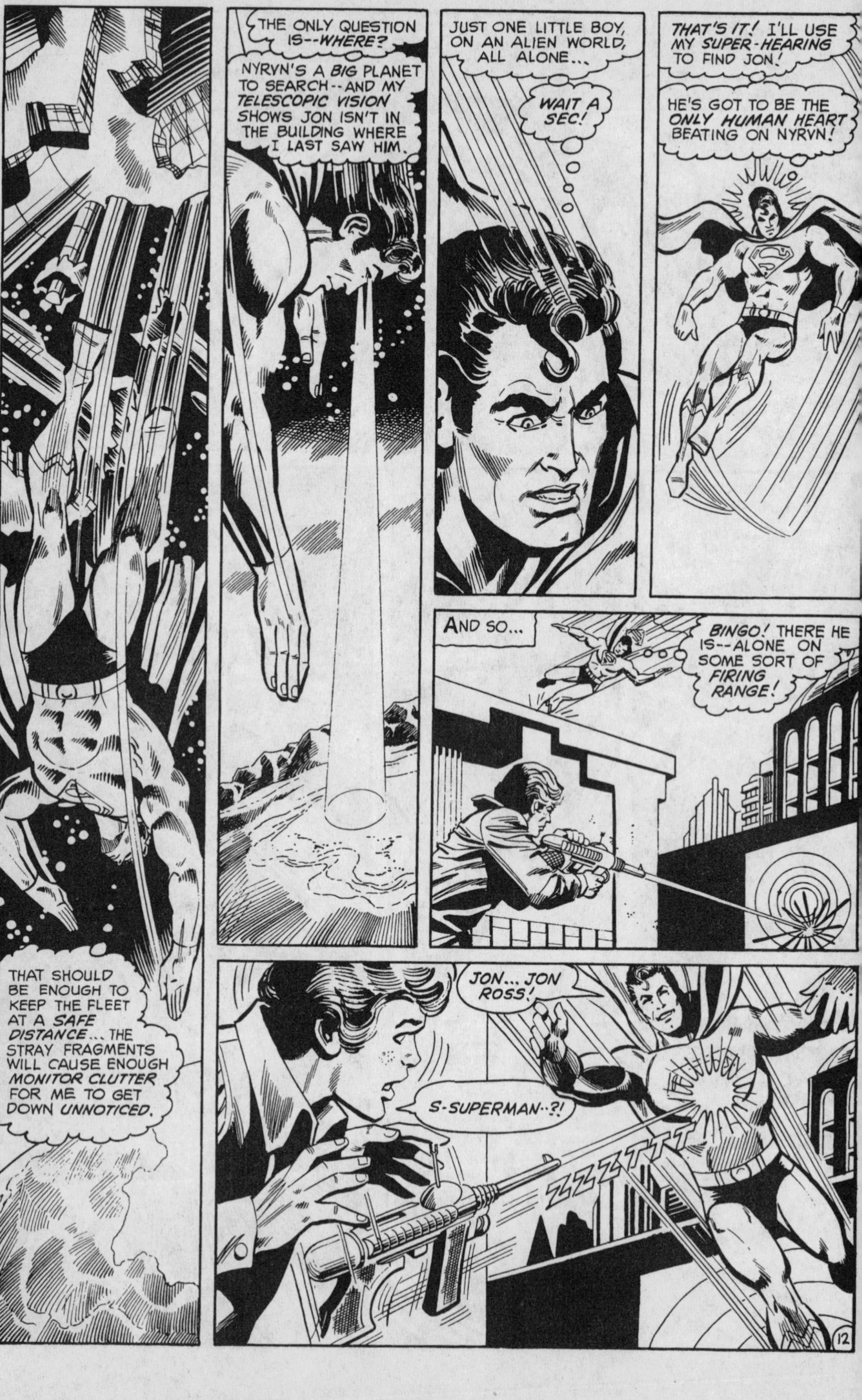
THE ONLY QUESTION IS--WHERE?
NYRYN'S A BIG PLANET TO SEARCH--AND MY TELESCOPIC VISION SHOWS JON ISN'T IN THE BUILDING WHERE I LAST SAW HIM.
JUST ONE LITTLE BOY, ON AN ALIEN WORLD, ALL ALONE...
WAIT A SEC!
THAT'S IT! I'LL USE MY SUPER-HEARING TO FIND JON!
HE'S GOT TO BE THE ONLY HUMAN HEART BEATING ON NYRVN!
AND SO...
BINGO! THERE HE IS--ALONE ON SOME SORT OF FIRING RANGE!
THAT SHOULD BE ENOUGH TO KEEP THE FLEET AT A SAFE DISTANCE... THE STRAY FRAGMENTS WILL CAUSE ENOUGH MONITOR CLUTTER FOR ME TO GET DOWN UNNOTICED.
JON... JON ROSS!
S-SUPERMAN..?!
ZZZZTTTT
12

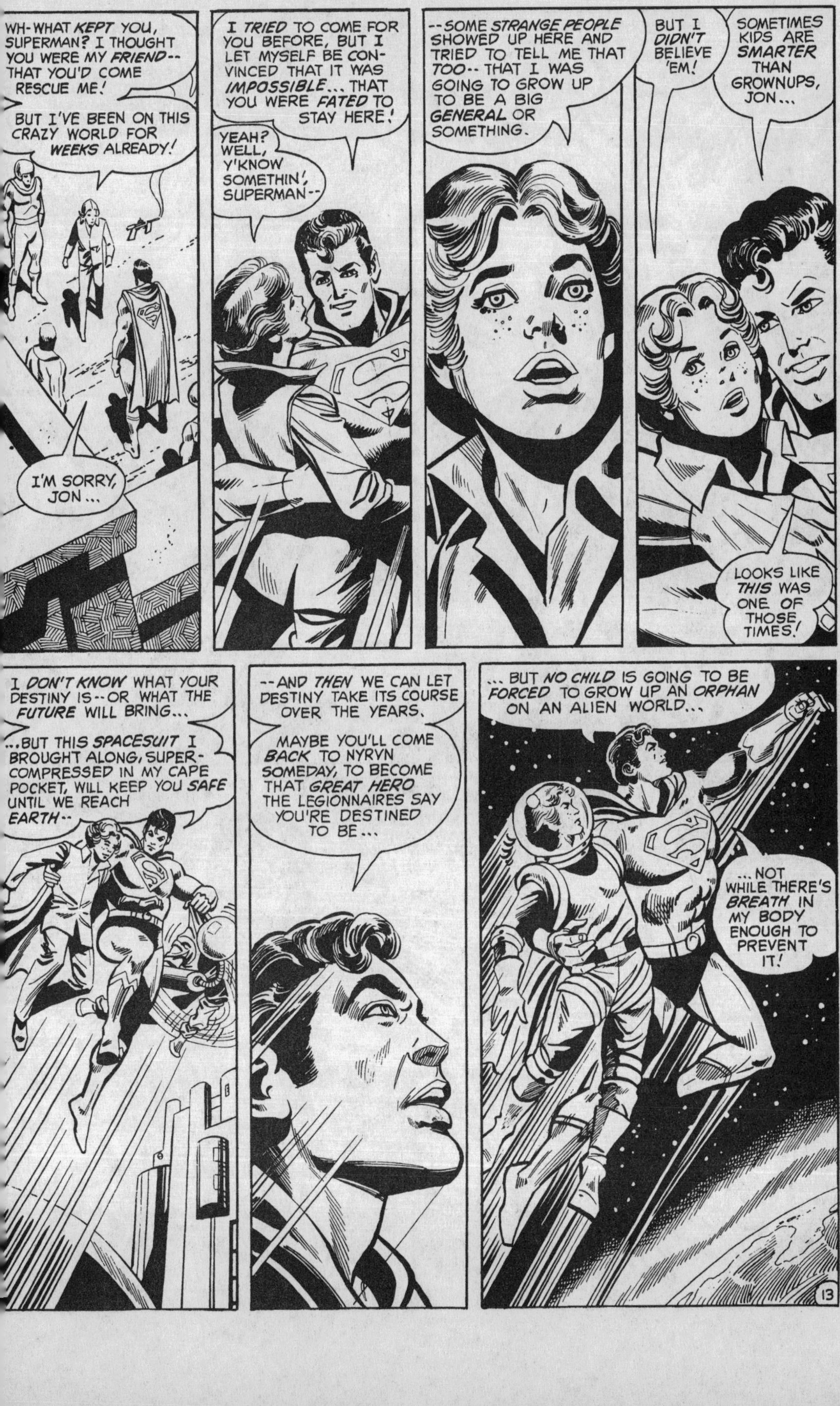
WH-WHAT KEPT YOU, SUPERMAN? I THOUGHT YOU WERE MY FRIEND-- THAT YOU'D COME RESCUE ME!
BUT I'VE BEEN ON THIS CRAZY WORLD FOR WEEKS ALREADY!
I'M SORRY, JON...
I TRIED TO COME FOR YOU BEFORE, BUT I LET MYSELF BE CONVINCED THAT IT WAS IMPOSSIBLE... THAT YOU WERE FATED TO STAY HERE!
YEAH? WELL, Y'KNOW SOMETHIN', SUPERMAN--
--SOME STRANGE PEOPLE SHOWED UP HERE AND TRIED TO TELL ME THAT TOO-- THAT I WAS GOING TO GROW UP TO BE A BIG GENERAL OR SOMETHING.
BUT I DIDN'T BELIEVE 'EM!
SOMETIMES KIDS ARE SMARTER THAN GROWNUPS, JON...
LOOKS LIKE THIS WAS ONE OF THOSE TIMES!
I DON'T KNOW WHAT YOUR DESTINY IS--OR WHAT THE FUTURE WILL BRING...
...BUT THIS SPACESUIT I BROUGHT ALONG, SUPER-COMPRESSED IN MY CAPE POCKET, WILL KEEP YOU SAFE UNTIL WE REACH EARTH--
--AND THEN WE CAN LET DESTINY TAKE ITS COURSE OVER THE YEARS.
MAYBE YOU'LL COME BACK TO NYRVN SOMEDAY, TO BECOME THAT GREAT HERO THE LEGIONNAIRES SAY YOU'RE DESTINED TO BE...
... BUT NO CHILD IS GOING TO BE FORCED TO GROW UP AN ORPHAN ON AN ALIEN WORLD...
... NOT WHILE THERE'S BREATH IN MY BODY ENOUGH TO PREVENT IT!
13

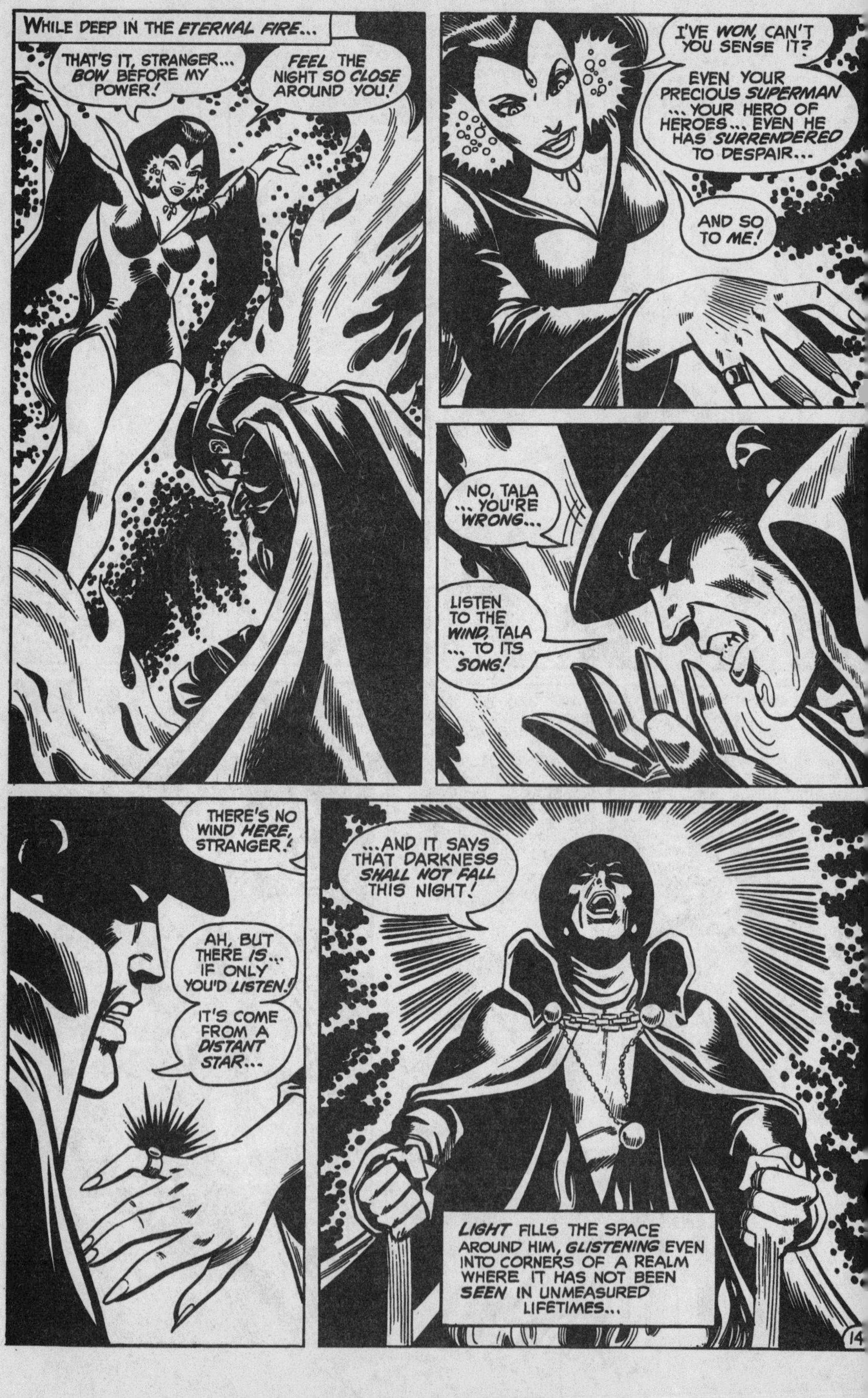
WHILE DEEP IN THE ETERNAL FIRE...
THAT'S IT, STRANGER... BOW BEFORE MY POWER!
FEEL THE NIGHT SO CLOSE AROUND YOU!
I'VE WON, CAN'T YOU SENSE IT?
EVEN YOUR PRECIOUS SUPERMAN ...YOUR HERO OF HEROES... EVEN HE HAS SURRENDERED TO DESPAIR...
AND SO TO ME!
NO, TALA ...YOU'RE WRONG...
LISTEN TO THE WIND, TALA ..., TO ITS SONG!
THERE'S NO WIND HERE, STRANGER!
AH, BUT THERE IS... IF ONLY YOU'D LISTEN!
IT'S COME FROM A DISTANT STAR...
...AND IT SAYS THAT DARKNESS SHALL NOT FALL THIS NIGHT!
LIGHT FILLS THE SPACE AROUND HIM, GLISTENING EVEN INTO CORNERS OF A REALM WHERE IT HAS NOT BEEN SEEN IN UNMEASURED LIFETIMES...
14

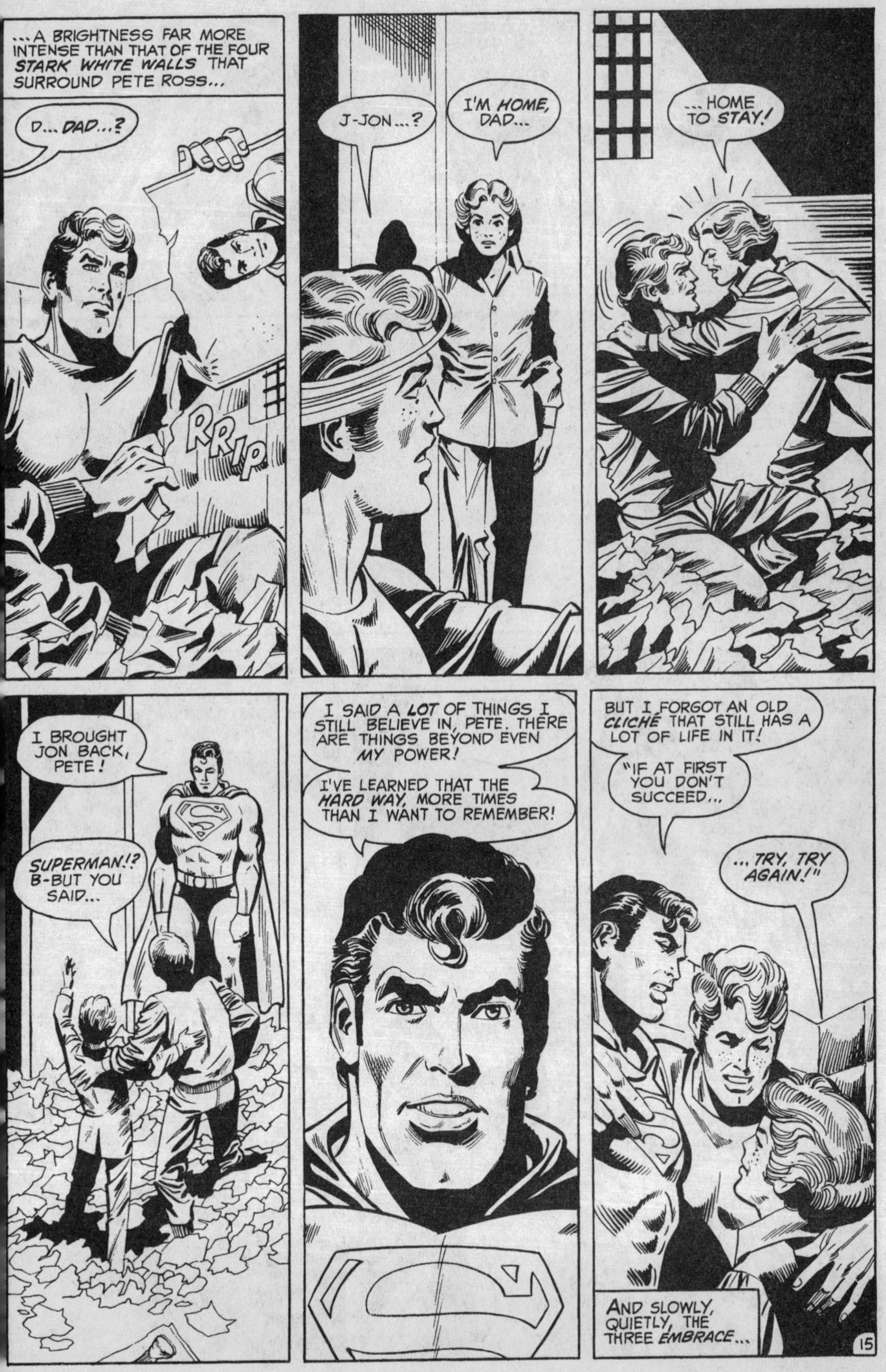
...A BRIGHTNESS FAR MORE INTENSE THAN THAT OF THE FOUR STARK WHITE WALLS THAT SURROUND PETE ROSS...
D... DAD...?
RRIP
J-JON...?
I'M HOME, DAD...
...HOME TO STAY!
I BROUGHT JON BACK, PETE!
SUPERMAN!? B-BUT YOU SAID...
I SAID A LOT OF THINGS I STILL BELIEVE IN, PETE. THERE ARE THINGS BEYOND EVEN MY POWER!
I'VE LEARNED THAT THE HARD WAY, MORE TIMES THAN I WANT TO REMEMBER!
BUT I FORGOT AN OLD CLICHÉ THAT STILL HAS A LOT OF LIFE IN IT!
"IF AT FIRST YOU DON'T SUCCEED...
...TRY, TRY AGAIN!"
AND SLOWLY, QUIETLY, THE THREE EMBRACE...
15

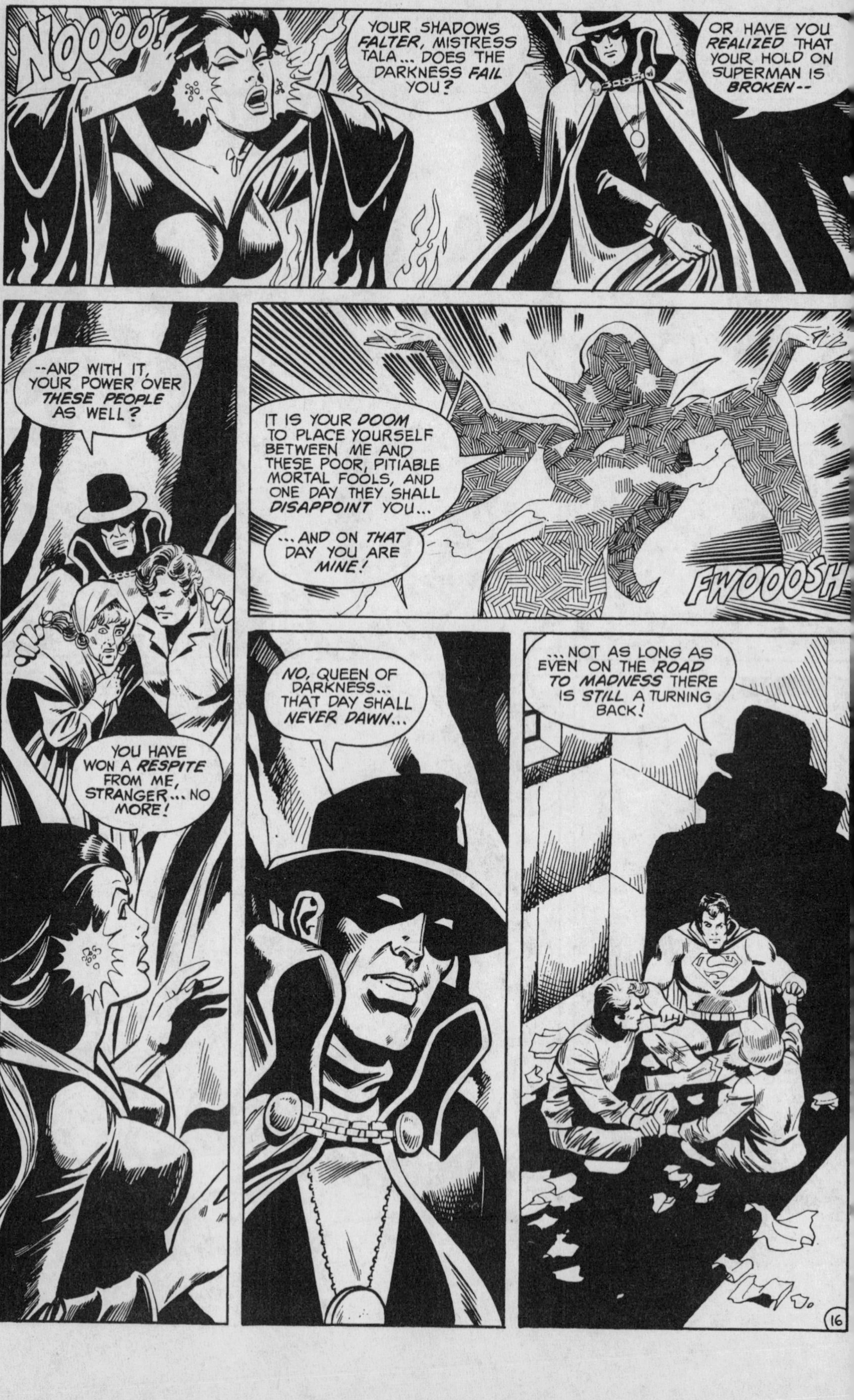
NOOOO!
YOUR SHADOWS FALTER, MISTRESS TALA... DOES THE DARKNESS FAIL YOU?
OR HAVE YOU REALIZED THAT YOUR HOLD ON SUPERMAN IS BROKEN--
--AND WITH IT, YOUR POWER OVER THESE PEOPLE AS WELL?
YOU HAVE WON A RESPITE FROM ME, STRANGER... NO MORE!
IT IS YOUR DOOM TO PLACE YOURSELF BETWEEN ME AND THESE POOR, PITIABLE MORTAL FOOLS, AND ONE DAY THEY SHALL DISAPPOINT YOU...
...AND ON THAT DAY YOU ARE MINE!
FWOOOSH
NO, QUEEN OF DARKNESS... THAT DAY SHALL NEVER DAWN...
...NOT AS LONG AS EVEN ON THE ROAD TO MADNESS THERE IS STILL A TURNING BACK!
16

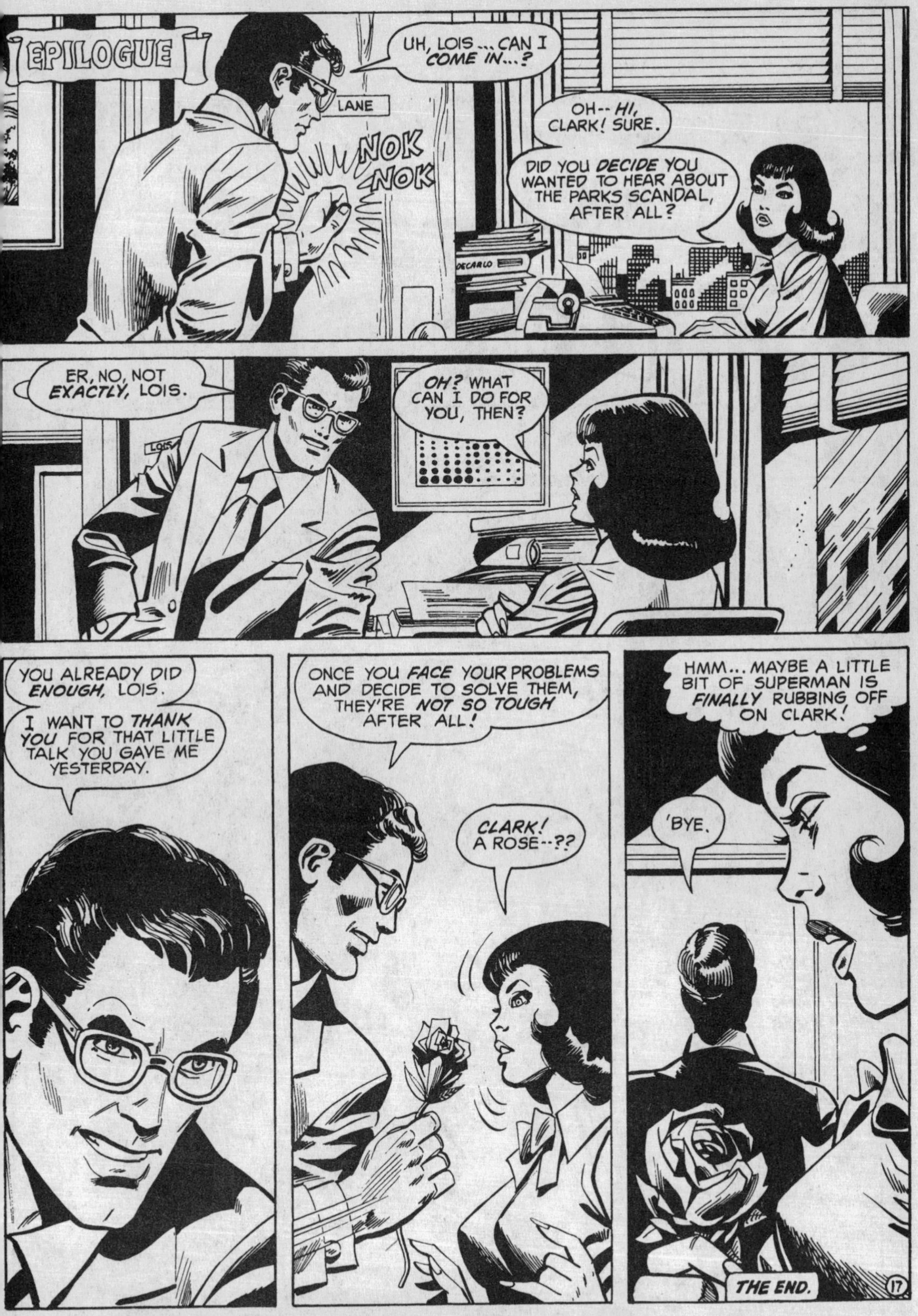
EPILOGUE
UH, LOIS ... CAN I COME IN...?
LANE
NOK NOK
OH-- HI, CLARK! SURE.
DID YOU DECIDE YOU WANTED TO HEAR ABOUT THE PARKS SCANDAL, AFTER ALL?
DECARLO
ER, NO, NOT EXACTLY, LOIS.
OH? WHAT CAN I DO FOR YOU, THEN?
LOIS
YOU ALREADY DID ENOUGH, LOIS.
I WANT TO THANK YOU FOR THAT LITTLE TALK YOU GAVE ME YESTERDAY.
ONCE YOU FACE YOUR PROBLEMS AND DECIDE TO SOLVE THEM, THEY'RE NOT SO TOUGH AFTER ALL!
CLARK! A ROSE--??
HMM... MAYBE A LITTLE BIT OF SUPERMAN IS FINALLY RUBBING OFF ON CLARK!
'BYE.
THE END.
17

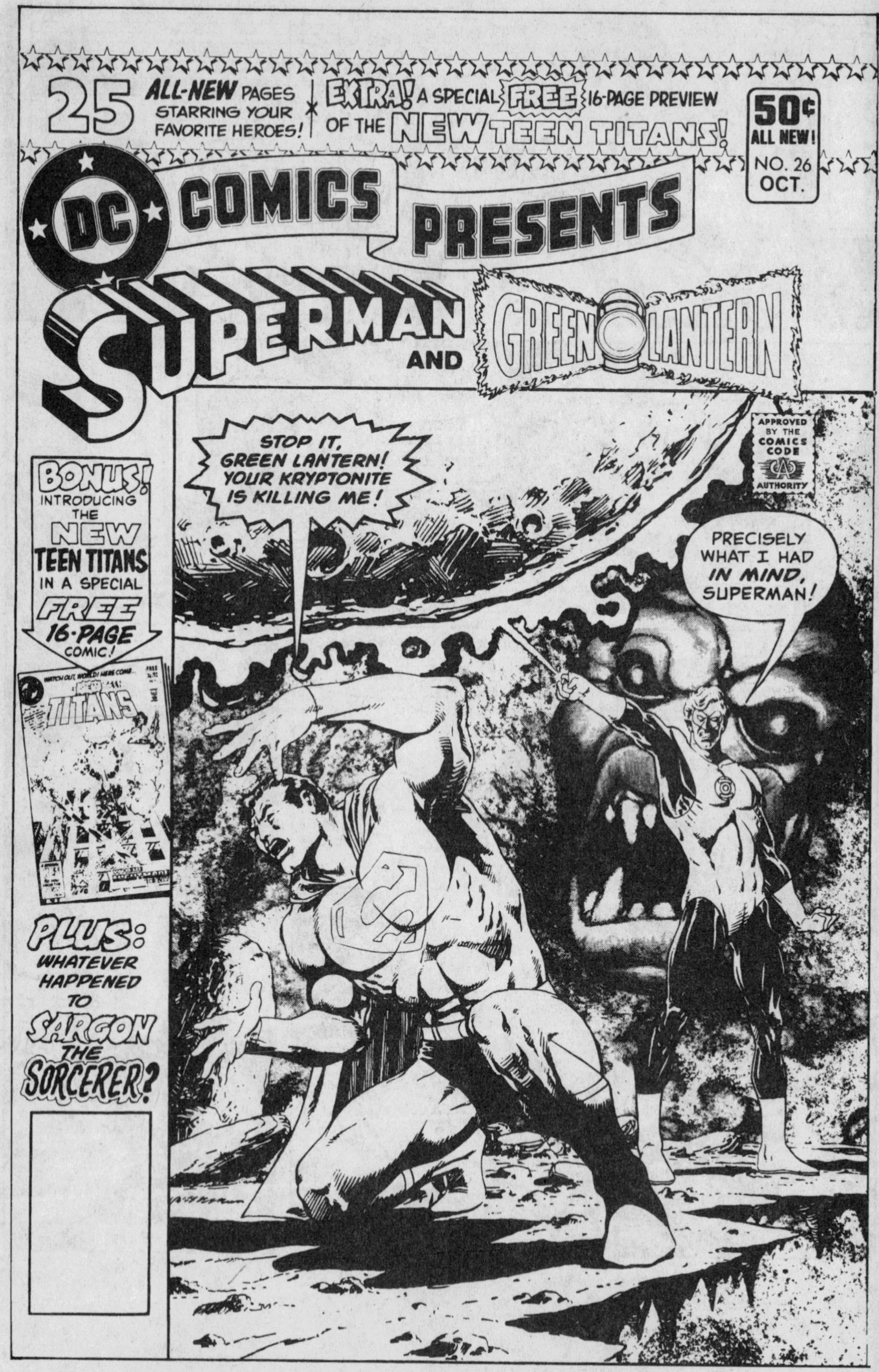
25 ALL-NEW PAGES STARRING YOUR FAVORITE HEROES!
EXTRA! A SPECIAL FREE 16-PAGE PREVIEW OF THE NEW TEEN TITANS!
50¢ ALL NEW!
NO. 26 OCT.
DC COMICS PRESENTS
SUPERMAN AND GREEN LANTERN
APPROVED BY THE COMICS CODE AUTHORITY
BONUS! INTRODUCING THE NEW TEEN TITANS IN A SPECIAL FREE 16-PAGE COMIC!
TITANS
STOP IT, GREEN LANTERN! YOUR KRYPTONITE IS KILLING ME!
PRECISELY WHAT I HAD IN MIND, SUPERMAN!
PLUS: WHATEVER HAPPENED TO SARGON THE SORCERER?

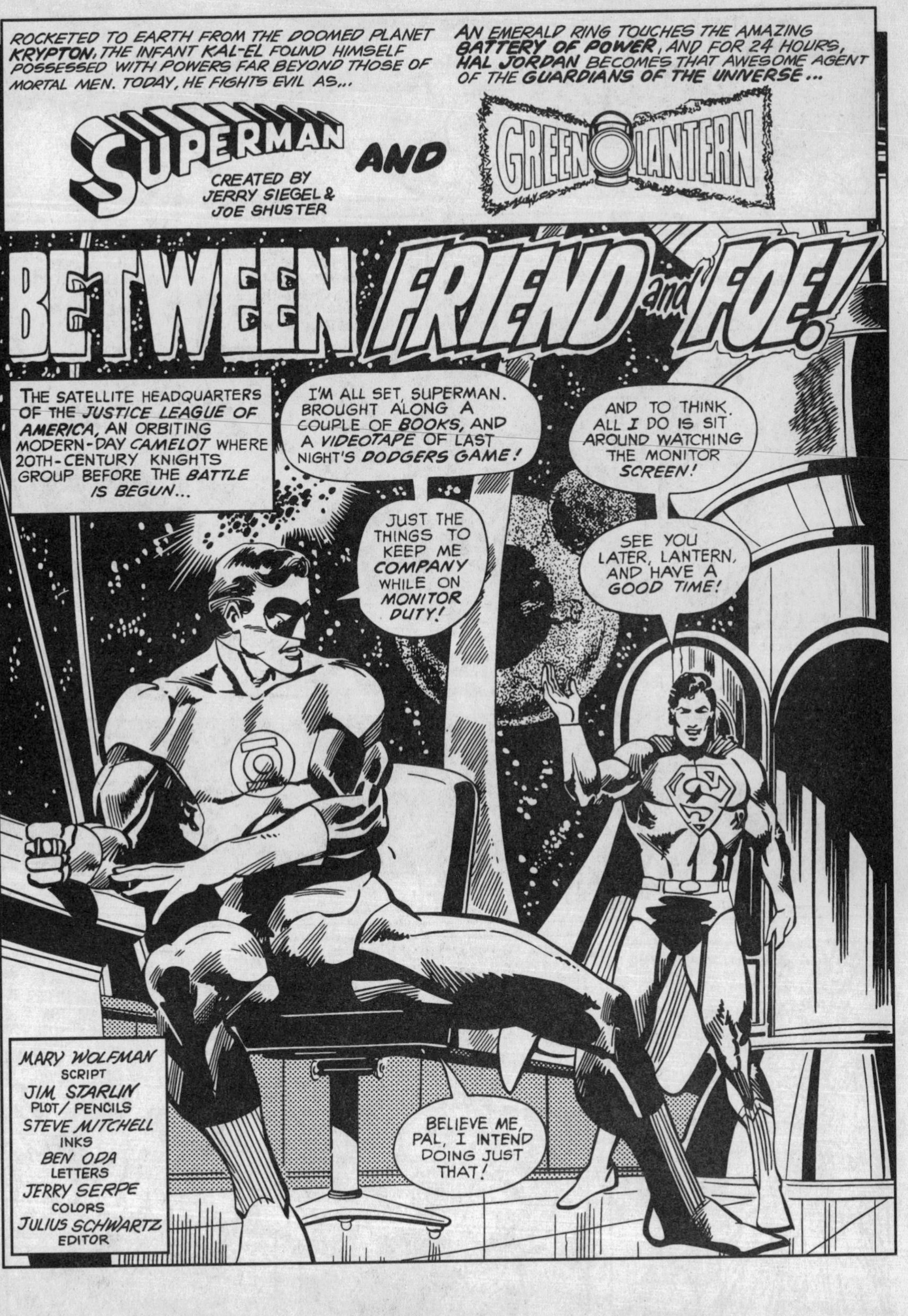
ROCKETED TO EARTH FROM THE DOOMED PLANET KRYPTON, THE INFANT KAL-EL FOUND HIMSELF POSSESSED WITH POWERS FAR BEYOND THOSE OF MORTAL MEN. TODAY, HE FIGHTS EVIL AS...
AN EMERALD RING TOUCHES THE AMAZING BATTERY OF POWER, AND FOR 24 HOURS, HAL JORDAN BECOMES THAT AWESOME AGENT OF THE GUARDIANS OF THE UNIVERSE...
SUPERMAN
CREATED BY JERRY SIEGEL & JOE SHUSTER
AND
GREEN LANTERN
BETWEEN FRIEND and FOE!
THE SATELLITE HEADQUARTERS OF THE JUSTICE LEAGUE OF AMERICA, AN ORBITING MODERN-DAY CAMELOT WHERE 20TH-CENTURY KNIGHTS GROUP BEFORE THE BATTLE IS BEGUN...
I'M ALL SET, SUPERMAN. BROUGHT ALONG A COUPLE OF BOOKS, AND A VIDEOTAPE OF LAST NIGHT'S DODGERS GAME!
JUST THE THINGS TO KEEP ME COMPANY WHILE ON MONITOR DUTY!
AND TO THINK, ALL I DO IS SIT AROUND WATCHING THE MONITOR SCREEN!
SEE YOU LATER, LANTERN, AND HAVE A GOOD TIME!
BELIEVE ME, PAL, I INTEND DOING JUST THAT!
MARV WOLFMAN SCRIPT
JIM STARLIN PLOT/ PENCILS
STEVE MITCHELL INKS
BEN ODA LETTERS
JERRY SERPE COLORS
JULIUS SCHWARTZ EDITOR

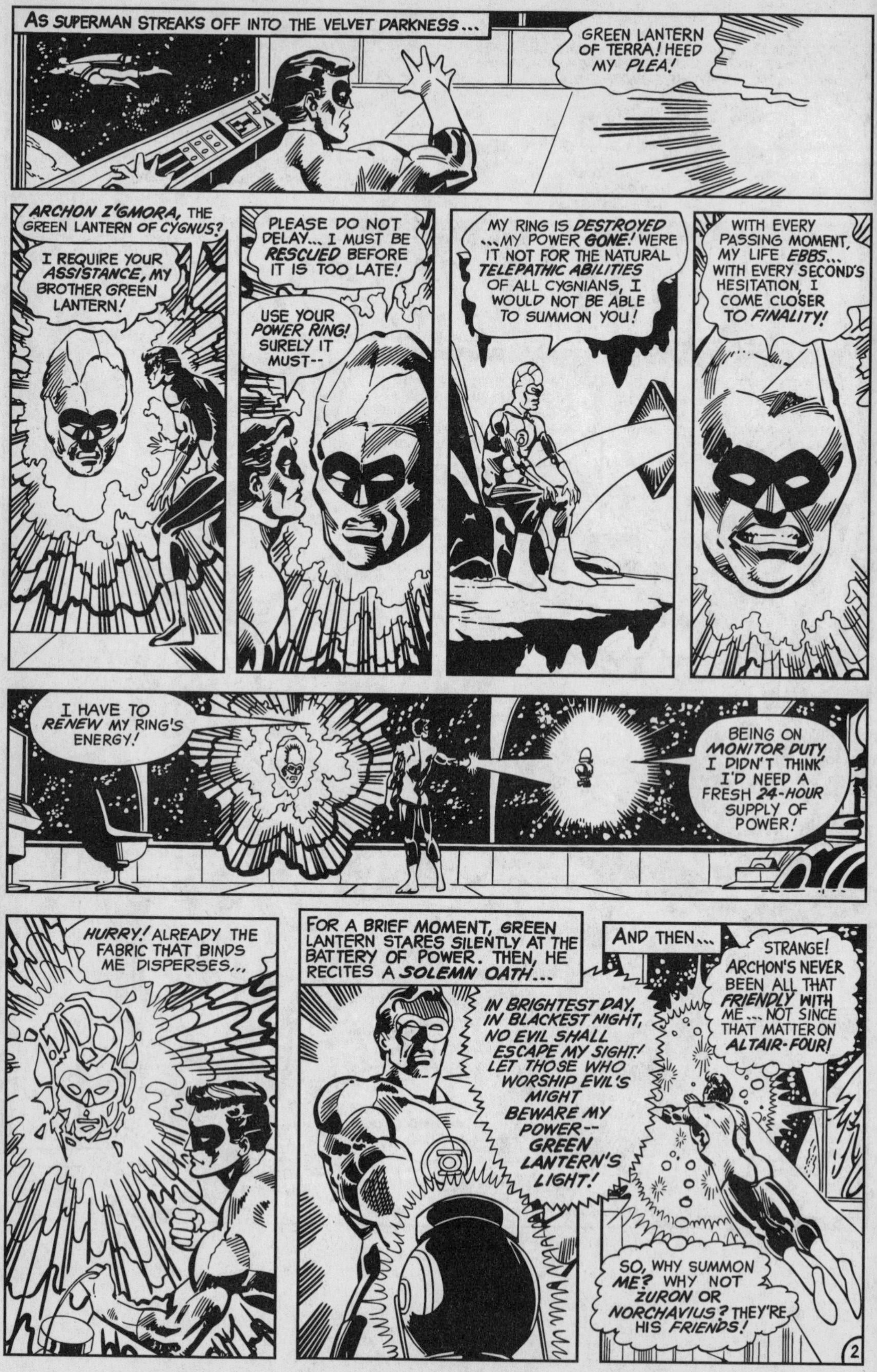
AS SUPERMAN STREAKS OFF INTO THE VELVET DARKNESS...
GREEN LANTERN OF TERRA! HEED MY PLEA!
ARCHON Z'GMORA, THE GREEN LANTERN OF CYGNUS?
I REQUIRE YOUR ASSISTANCE, MY BROTHER GREEN LANTERN!
PLEASE DO NOT DELAY... I MUST BE RESCUED BEFORE IT IS TOO LATE!
USE YOUR POWER RING! SURELY IT MUST--
MY RING IS DESTROYED ...MY POWER GONE! WERE IT NOT FOR THE NATURAL TELEPATHIC ABILITIES OF ALL CYGNIANS, I WOULD NOT BE ABLE TO SUMMON YOU!
WITH EVERY PASSING MOMENT, MY LIFE EBBS... WITH EVERY SECOND'S HESITATION, I COME CLOSER TO FINALITY!
I HAVE TO RENEW MY RING'S ENERGY!
BEING ON MONITOR DUTY I DIDN'T THINK I'D NEED A FRESH 24-HOUR SUPPLY OF POWER!
HURRY! ALREADY THE FABRIC THAT BINDS ME DISPERSES...
FOR A BRIEF MOMENT, GREEN LANTERN STARES SILENTLY AT THE BATTERY OF POWER. THEN, HE RECITES A SOLEMN OATH...
IN BRIGHTEST DAY, IN BLACKEST NIGHT, NO EVIL SHALL ESCAPE MY SIGHT! LET THOSE WHO WORSHIP EVIL'S MIGHT BEWARE MY POWER-- GREEN LANTERN'S LIGHT!
AND THEN...
STRANGE! ARCHON'S NEVER BEEN ALL THAT FRIENDLY WITH ME... NOT SINCE THAT MATTER ON ALTAIR-FOUR!
SO, WHY SUMMON ME? WHY NOT ZURON OR NORCHAVIUS? THEY'RE HIS FRIENDS!
2

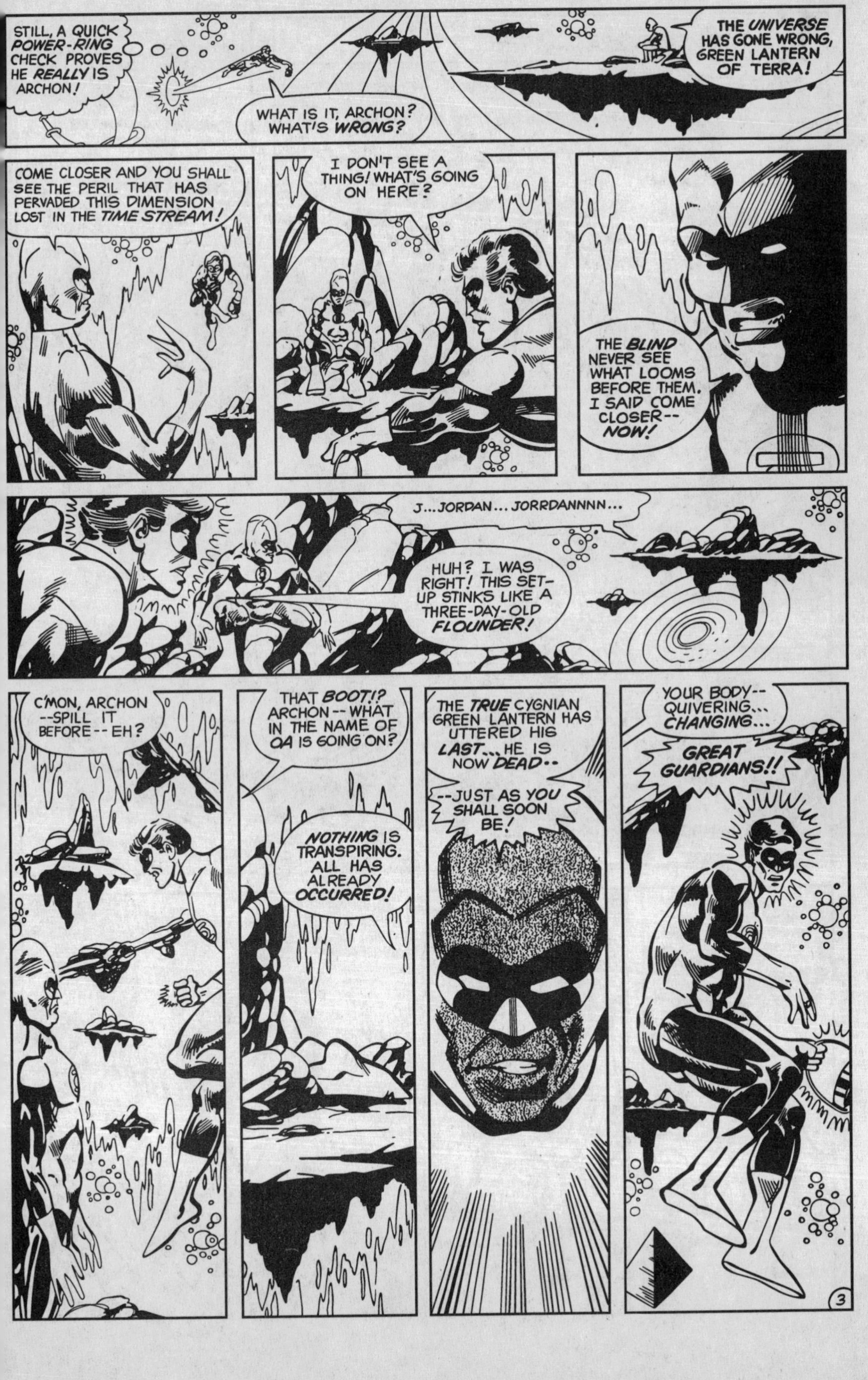
STILL, A QUICK POWER-RING CHECK PROVES HE REALLY IS ARCHON!
THE UNIVERSE HAS GONE WRONG, GREEN LANTERN OF TERRA!
WHAT IS IT, ARCHON? WHAT'S WRONG?
COME CLOSER AND YOU SHALL SEE THE PERIL THAT HAS PERVADED THIS DIMENSION LOST IN THE TIME STREAM!
I DON'T SEE A THING! WHAT'S GOING ON HERE?
THE BLIND NEVER SEE WHAT LOOMS BEFORE THEM. I SAID COME CLOSER-- NOW!
J...JORDAN... JORRDANNNN...
HUH? I WAS RIGHT! THIS SET-UP STINKS LIKE A THREE-DAY-OLD FLOUNDER!
C'MON, ARCHON --SPILL IT BEFORE--EH?
THAT BOOT!? ARCHON--WHAT IN THE NAME OF OA IS GOING ON?
NOTHING IS TRANSPIRING. ALL HAS ALREADY OCCURRED!
THE TRUE CYGNIAN GREEN LANTERN HAS UTTERED HIS LAST... HE IS NOW DEAD--
--JUST AS YOU SHALL SOON BE!
YOUR BODY-- QUIVERING... CHANGING...
GREAT GUARDIANS!!
3

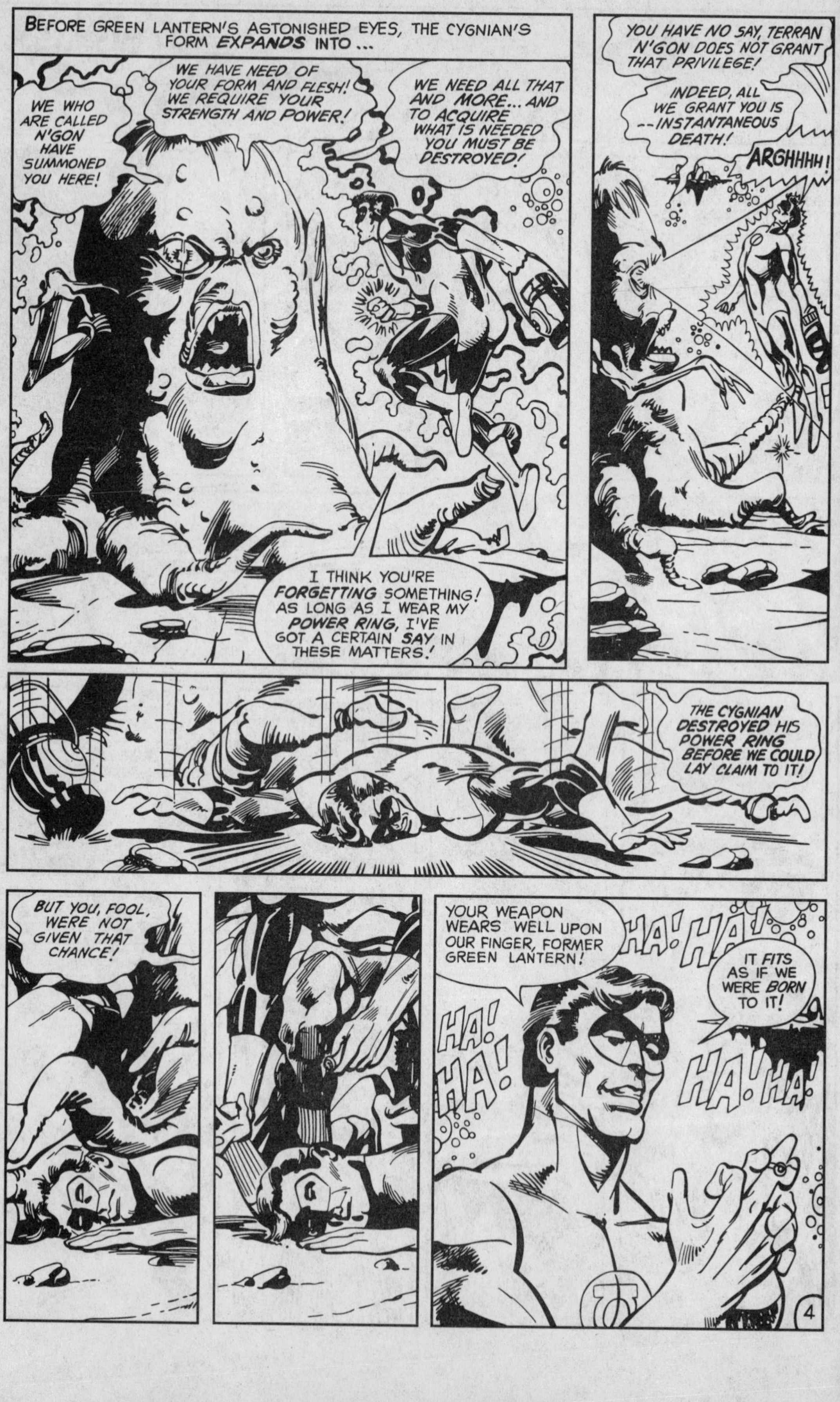
BEFORE GREEN LANTERN'S ASTONISHED EYES, THE CYGNIAN'S FORM EXPANDS INTO...
WE WHO ARE CALLED N'GON HAVE SUMMONED YOU HERE!
WE HAVE NEED OF YOUR FORM AND FLESH! WE REQUIRE YOUR STRENGTH AND POWER!
WE NEED ALL THAT AND MORE... AND TO ACQUIRE WHAT IS NEEDED YOU MUST BE DESTROYED!
I THINK YOU'RE FORGETTING SOMETHING! AS LONG AS I WEAR MY POWER RING, I'VE GOT A CERTAIN SAY IN THESE MATTERS!
YOU HAVE NO SAY, TERRAN N'GON DOES NOT GRANT THAT PRIVILEGE!
INDEED, ALL WE GRANT YOU IS --INSTANTANEOUS DEATH!
ARGHHHH!
THE CYGNIAN DESTROYED HIS POWER RING BEFORE WE COULD LAY CLAIM TO IT!
BUT YOU, FOOL, WERE NOT GIVEN THAT CHANCE!
YOUR WEAPON WEARS WELL UPON OUR FINGER, FORMER GREEN LANTERN!
HA! HA!
IT FITS AS IF WE WERE BORN TO IT!
HA! HA!
HA! HA!
4

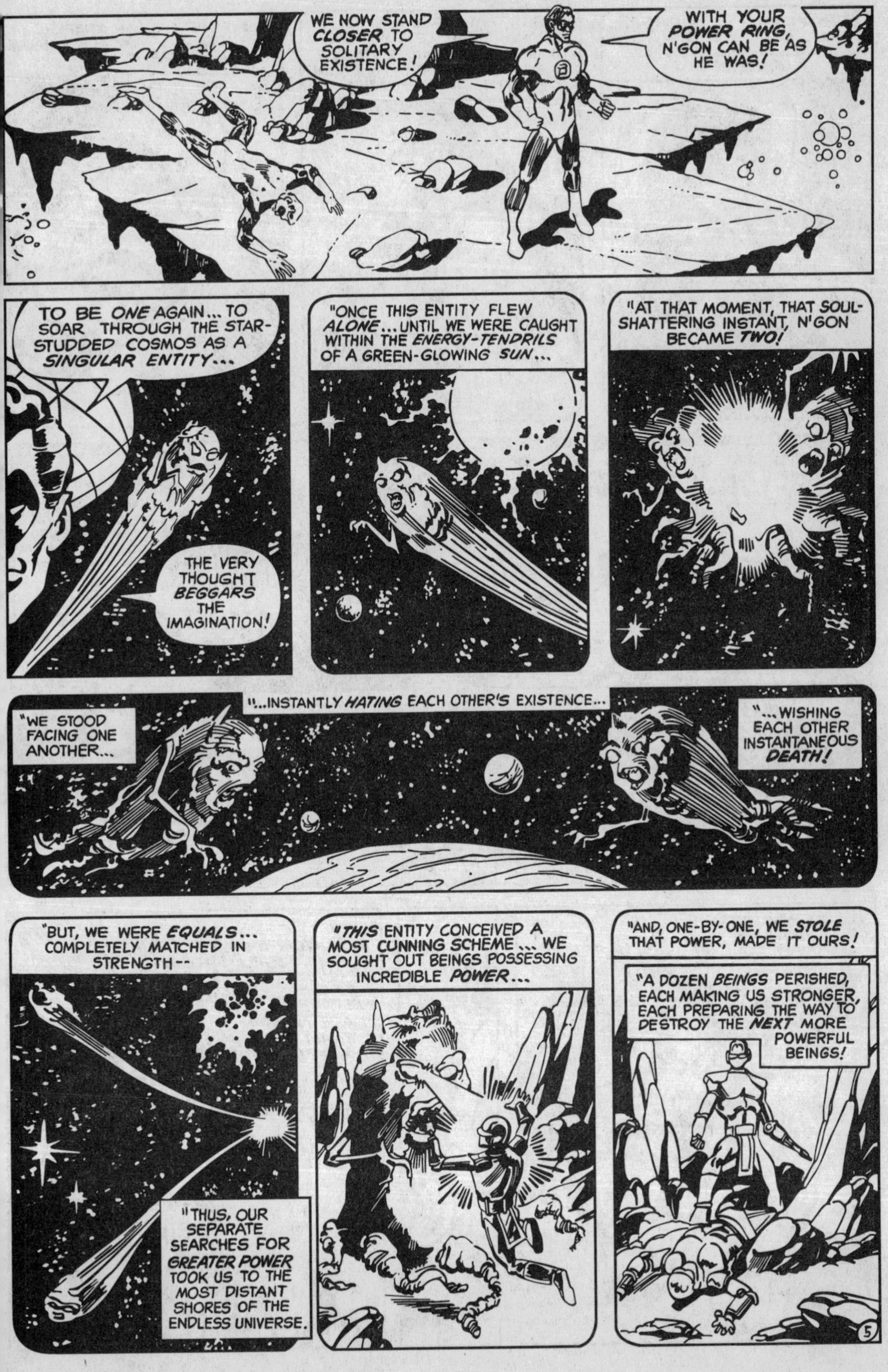

WE NOW STAND CLOSER TO SOLITARY EXISTENCE!
WITH YOUR POWER RING, N'GON CAN BE AS HE WAS!
TO BE ONE AGAIN... TO SOAR THROUGH THE STAR-STUDDED COSMOS AS A SINGULAR ENTITY...
THE VERY THOUGHT BEGGARS THE IMAGINATION!
"ONCE THIS ENTITY FLEW ALONE... UNTIL WE WERE CAUGHT WITHIN THE ENERGY-TENDRILS OF A GREEN-GLOWING SUN...
"AT THAT MOMENT, THAT SOUL-SHATTERING INSTANT, N'GON BECAME TWO!
"WE STOOD FACING ONE ANOTHER...
"...INSTANTLY HATING EACH OTHER'S EXISTENCE...
"...WISHING EACH OTHER INSTANTANEOUS DEATH!
"BUT, WE WERE EQUALS... COMPLETELY MATCHED IN STRENGTH--
"THUS, OUR SEPARATE SEARCHES FOR GREATER POWER TOOK US TO THE MOST DISTANT SHORES OF THE ENDLESS UNIVERSE.
"THIS ENTITY CONCEIVED A MOST CUNNING SCHEME... WE SOUGHT OUT BEINGS POSSESSING INCREDIBLE POWER...
"AND, ONE-BY-ONE, WE STOLE THAT POWER, MADE IT OURS!
"A DOZEN BEINGS PERISHED, EACH MAKING US STRONGER, EACH PREPARING THE WAY TO DESTROY THE NEXT MORE POWERFUL BEINGS!
5

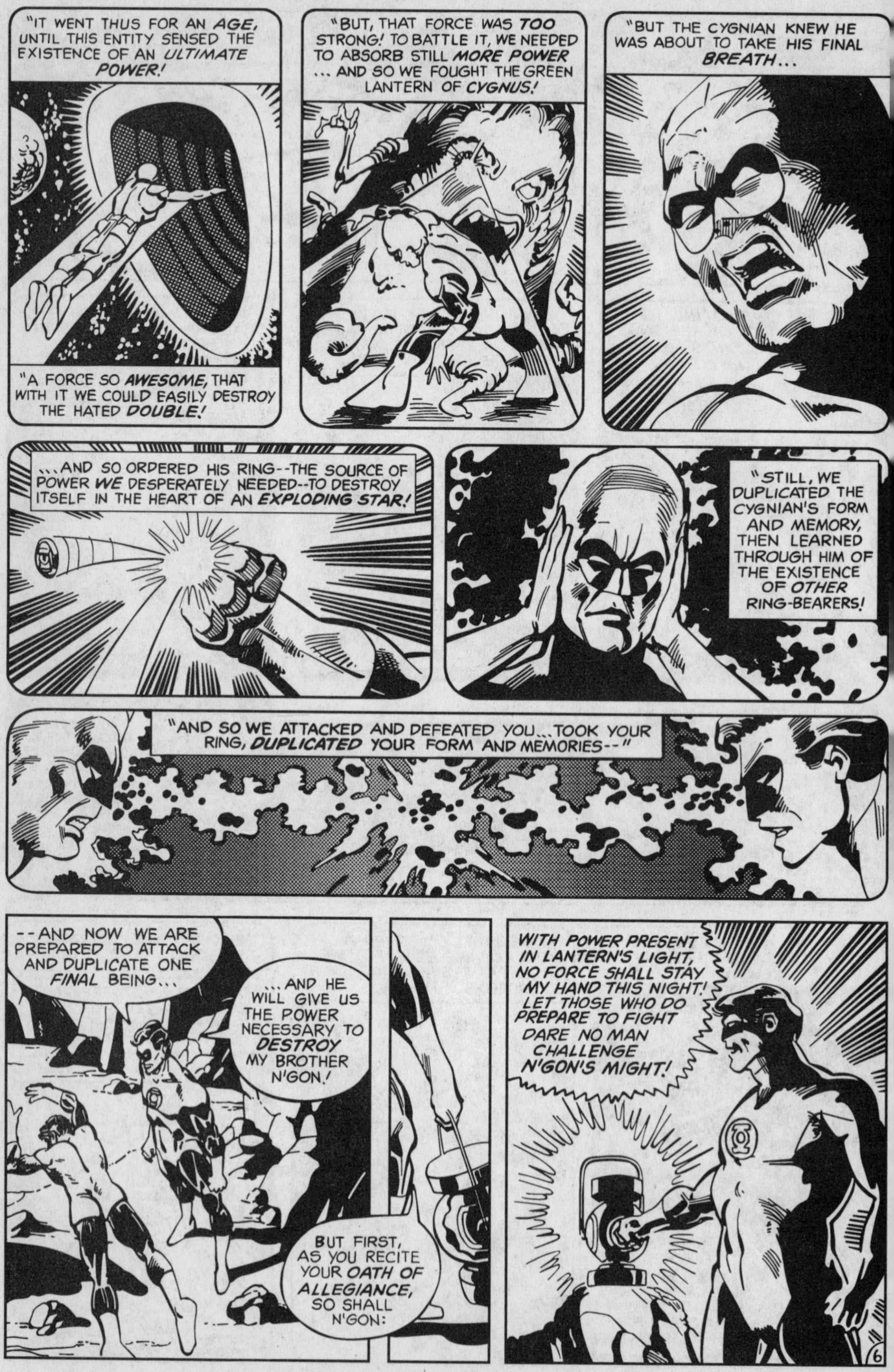
"IT WENT THUS FOR AN AGE, UNTIL THIS ENTITY SENSED THE EXISTENCE OF AN ULTIMATE POWER!
"A FORCE SO AWESOME, THAT WITH IT WE COULD EASILY DESTROY THE HATED DOUBLE!
"BUT, THAT FORCE WAS TOO STRONG! TO BATTLE IT, WE NEEDED TO ABSORB STILL MORE POWER ... AND SO WE FOUGHT THE GREEN LANTERN OF CYGNUS!
"BUT THE CYGNIAN KNEW HE WAS ABOUT TO TAKE HIS FINAL BREATH...
...AND SO ORDERED HIS RING--THE SOURCE OF POWER WE DESPERATELY NEEDED--TO DESTROY ITSELF IN THE HEART OF AN EXPLODING STAR!
"STILL, WE DUPLICATED THE CYGNIAN'S FORM AND MEMORY, THEN LEARNED THROUGH HIM OF THE EXISTENCE OF OTHER RING-BEARERS!
"AND SO WE ATTACKED AND DEFEATED YOU...TOOK YOUR RING, DUPLICATED YOUR FORM AND MEMORIES--"
--AND NOW WE ARE PREPARED TO ATTACK AND DUPLICATE ONE FINAL BEING...
...AND HE WILL GIVE US THE POWER NECESSARY TO DESTROY MY BROTHER N'GON!
BUT FIRST, AS YOU RECITE YOUR OATH OF ALLEGIANCE, SO SHALL N'GON:
WITH POWER PRESENT IN LANTERN'S LIGHT, NO FORCE SHALL STAY MY HAND THIS NIGHT! LET THOSE WHO DO PREPARE TO FIGHT DARE NO MAN CHALLENGE N'GON'S MIGHT!
6

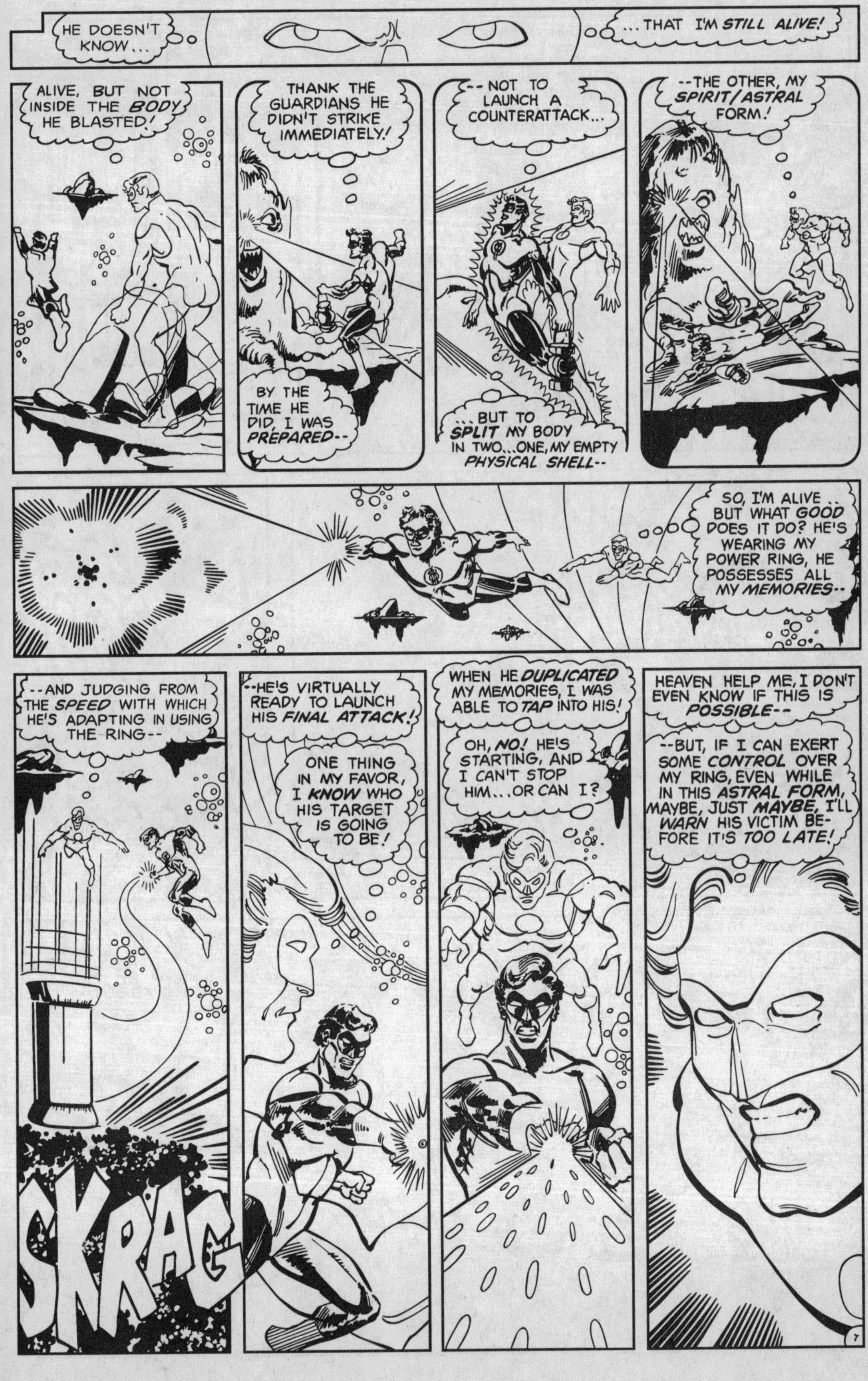
HE DOESN'T KNOW...
...THAT I'M STILL ALIVE!
ALIVE, BUT NOT INSIDE THE BODY HE BLASTED!
THANK THE GUARDIANS HE DIDN'T STRIKE IMMEDIATELY!
BY THE TIME HE DID, I WAS PREPARED--
--NOT TO LAUNCH A COUNTERATTACK...
...BUT TO SPLIT MY BODY IN TWO...ONE, MY EMPTY PHYSICAL SHELL--
--THE OTHER, MY SPIRIT/ASTRAL FORM!
SO, I'M ALIVE .. BUT WHAT GOOD DOES IT DO? HE'S WEARING MY POWER RING, HE POSSESSES ALL MY MEMORIES--
--AND JUDGING FROM THE SPEED WITH WHICH HE'S ADAPTING IN USING THE RING--
SKRAG
--HE'S VIRTUALLY READY TO LAUNCH HIS FINAL ATTACK!
ONE THING IN MY FAVOR, I KNOW WHO HIS TARGET IS GOING TO BE!
WHEN HE DUPLICATED MY MEMORIES, I WAS ABLE TO TAP INTO HIS!
OH, NO! HE'S STARTING, AND I CAN'T STOP HIM...OR CAN I?
HEAVEN HELP ME, I DON'T EVEN KNOW IF THIS IS POSSIBLE--
--BUT, IF I CAN EXERT SOME CONTROL OVER MY RING, EVEN WHILE IN THIS ASTRAL FORM, MAYBE, JUST MAYBE, I'LL WARN HIS VICTIM BEFORE IT'S TOO LATE!

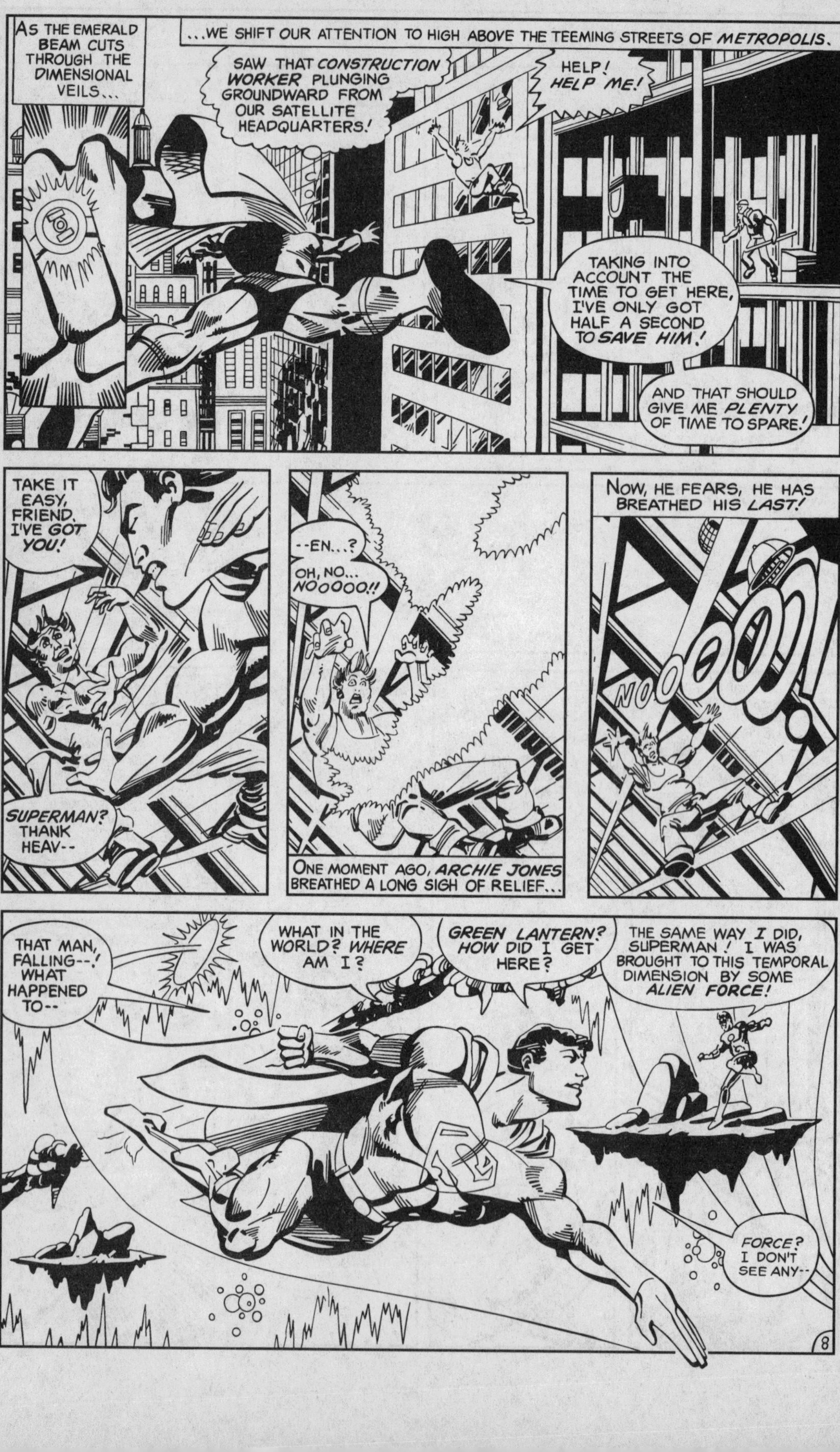
AS THE EMERALD BEAM CUTS THROUGH THE DIMENSIONAL VEILS...
...WE SHIFT OUR ATTENTION TO HIGH ABOVE THE TEEMING STREETS OF METROPOLIS.
SAW THAT CONSTRUCTION WORKER PLUNGING GROUNDWARD FROM OUR SATELLITE HEADQUARTERS!
HELP! HELP ME!
TAKING INTO ACCOUNT THE TIME TO GET HERE, I'VE ONLY GOT HALF A SECOND TO SAVE HIM!
AND THAT SHOULD GIVE ME PLENTY OF TIME TO SPARE!
TAKE IT EASY, FRIEND. I'VE GOT YOU!
SUPERMAN? THANK HEAV--
--EN...?
OH, NO... NOOOOO!!
ONE MOMENT AGO, ARCHIE JONES BREATHED A LONG SIGH OF RELIEF...
NOW, HE FEARS, HE HAS BREATHED HIS LAST!
NOOOOO!
THAT MAN, FALLING--! WHAT HAPPENED TO--
WHAT IN THE WORLD? WHERE AM I?
GREEN LANTERN? HOW DID I GET HERE?
THE SAME WAY I DID, SUPERMAN! I WAS BROUGHT TO THIS TEMPORAL DIMENSION BY SOME ALIEN FORCE!
FORCE? I DON'T SEE ANY--
8

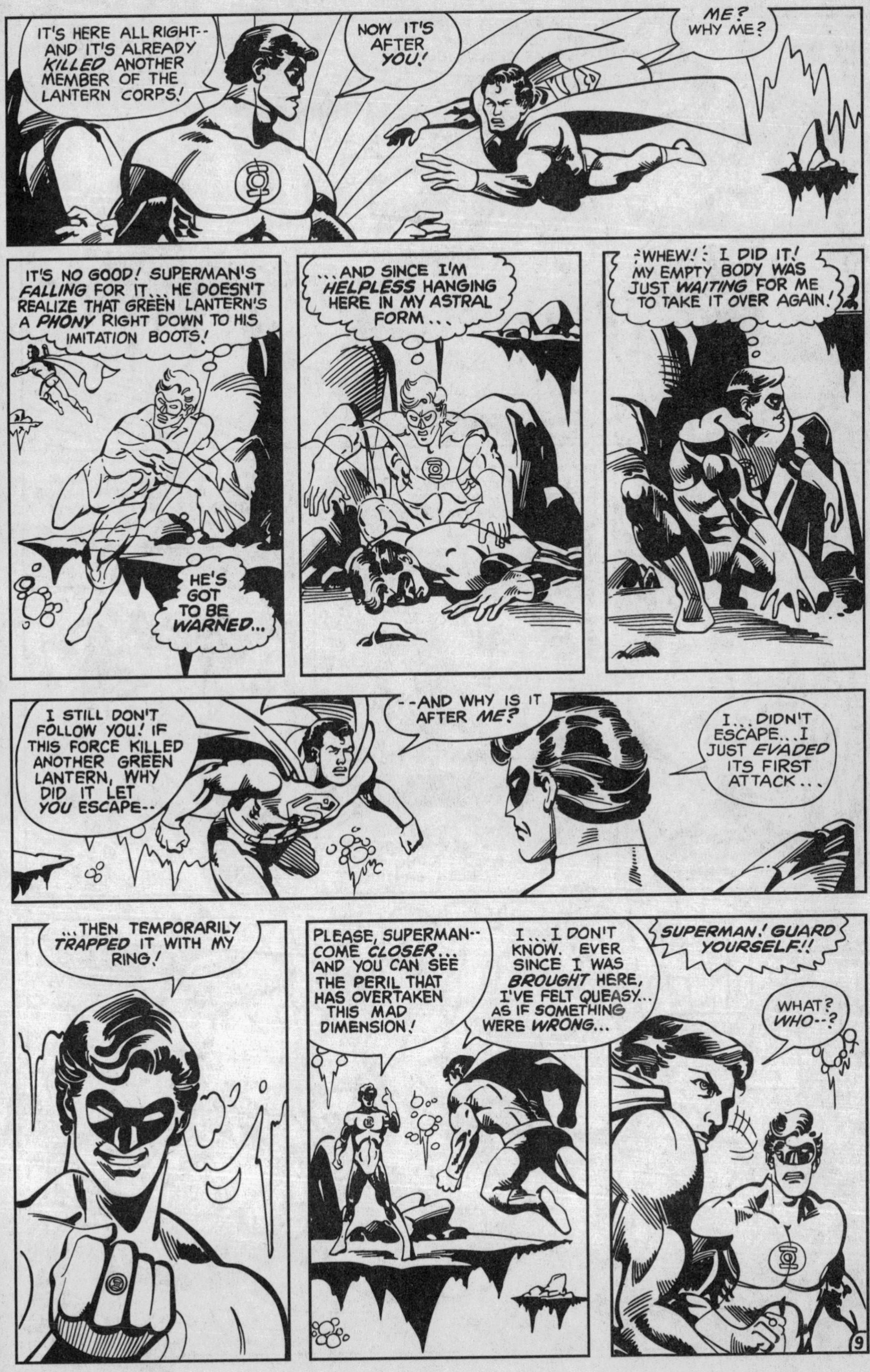
IT'S HERE ALL RIGHT-- AND IT'S ALREADY KILLED ANOTHER MEMBER OF THE LANTERN CORPS!
NOW IT'S AFTER YOU!
ME? WHY ME?
IT'S NO GOOD! SUPERMAN'S FALLING FOR IT... HE DOESN'T REALIZE THAT GREEN LANTERN'S A PHONY RIGHT DOWN TO HIS IMITATION BOOTS!
HE'S GOT TO BE WARNED...
...AND SINCE I'M HELPLESS HANGING HERE IN MY ASTRAL FORM...
-WHEW!- I DID IT! MY EMPTY BODY WAS JUST WAITING FOR ME TO TAKE IT OVER AGAIN!
I STILL DON'T FOLLOW YOU! IF THIS FORCE KILLED ANOTHER GREEN LANTERN, WHY DID IT LET YOU ESCAPE--
--AND WHY IS IT AFTER ME?
I... DIDN'T ESCAPE... I JUST EVADED ITS FIRST ATTACK...
...THEN TEMPORARILY TRAPPED IT WITH MY RING!
PLEASE, SUPERMAN-- COME CLOSER... AND YOU CAN SEE THE PERIL THAT HAS OVERTAKEN THIS MAD DIMENSION!
I... I DON'T KNOW. EVER SINCE I WAS BROUGHT HERE, I'VE FELT QUEASY... AS IF SOMETHING WERE WRONG...
SUPERMAN! GUARD YOURSELF!!
WHAT? WHO--?
9

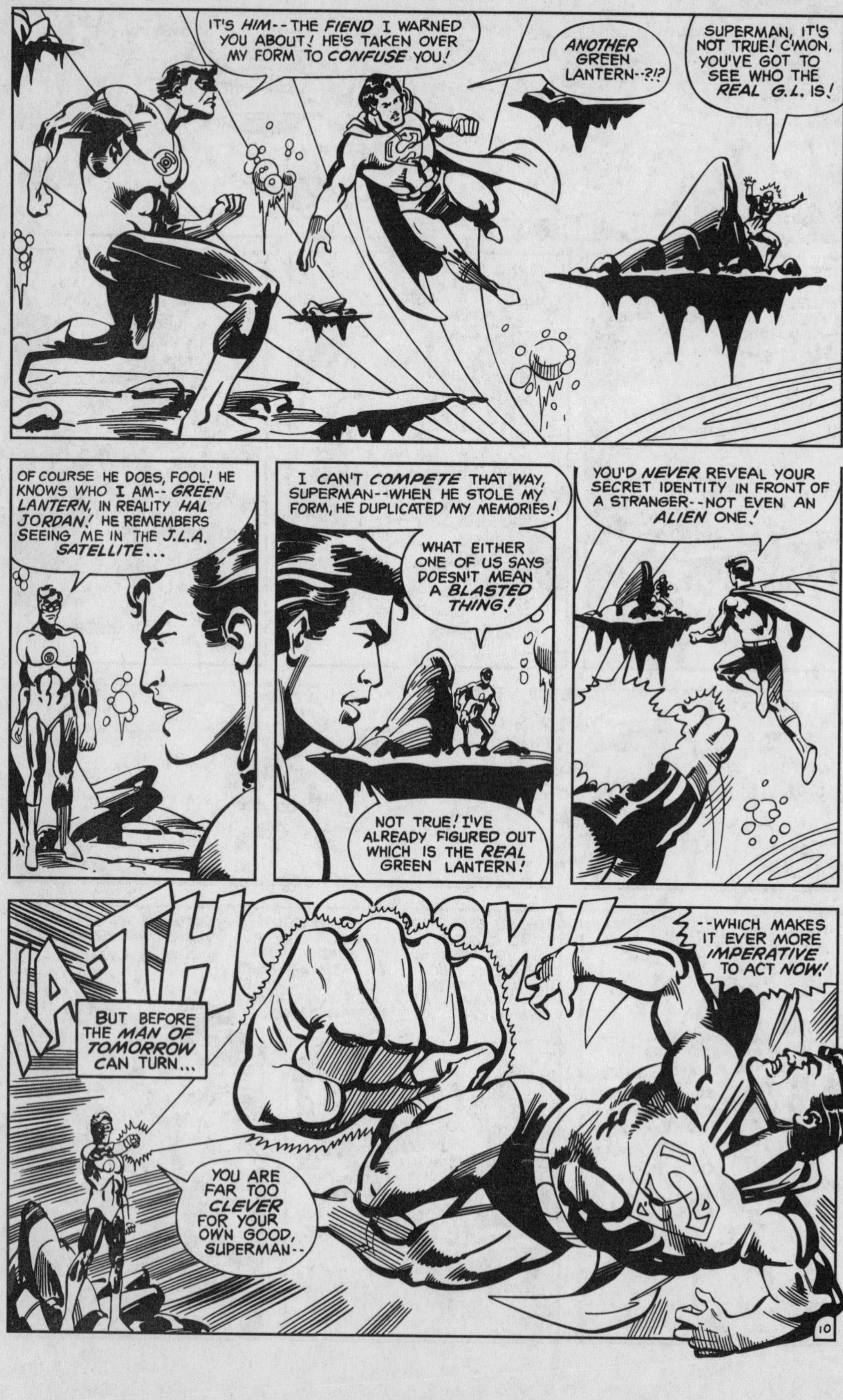
IT'S HIM--THE FIEND I WARNED YOU ABOUT! HE'S TAKEN OVER MY FORM TO CONFUSE YOU!
ANOTHER GREEN LANTERN--?!?
SUPERMAN, IT'S NOT TRUE! C'MON, YOU'VE GOT TO SEE WHO THE REAL G.L. IS!
OF COURSE HE DOES, FOOL! HE KNOWS WHO I AM--GREEN LANTERN, IN REALITY HAL JORDAN! HE REMEMBERS SEEING ME IN THE J.L.A. SATELLITE...
I CAN'T COMPETE THAT WAY, SUPERMAN--WHEN HE STOLE MY FORM, HE DUPLICATED MY MEMORIES!
WHAT EITHER ONE OF US SAYS DOESN'T MEAN A BLASTED THING!
NOT TRUE! I'VE ALREADY FIGURED OUT WHICH IS THE REAL GREEN LANTERN!
YOU'D NEVER REVEAL YOUR SECRET IDENTITY IN FRONT OF A STRANGER--NOT EVEN AN ALIEN ONE!
--WHICH MAKES IT EVER MORE IMPERATIVE TO ACT NOW!
BUT BEFORE THE MAN OF TOMORROW CAN TURN...
YOU ARE FAR TOO CLEVER FOR YOUR OWN GOOD, SUPERMAN--
10

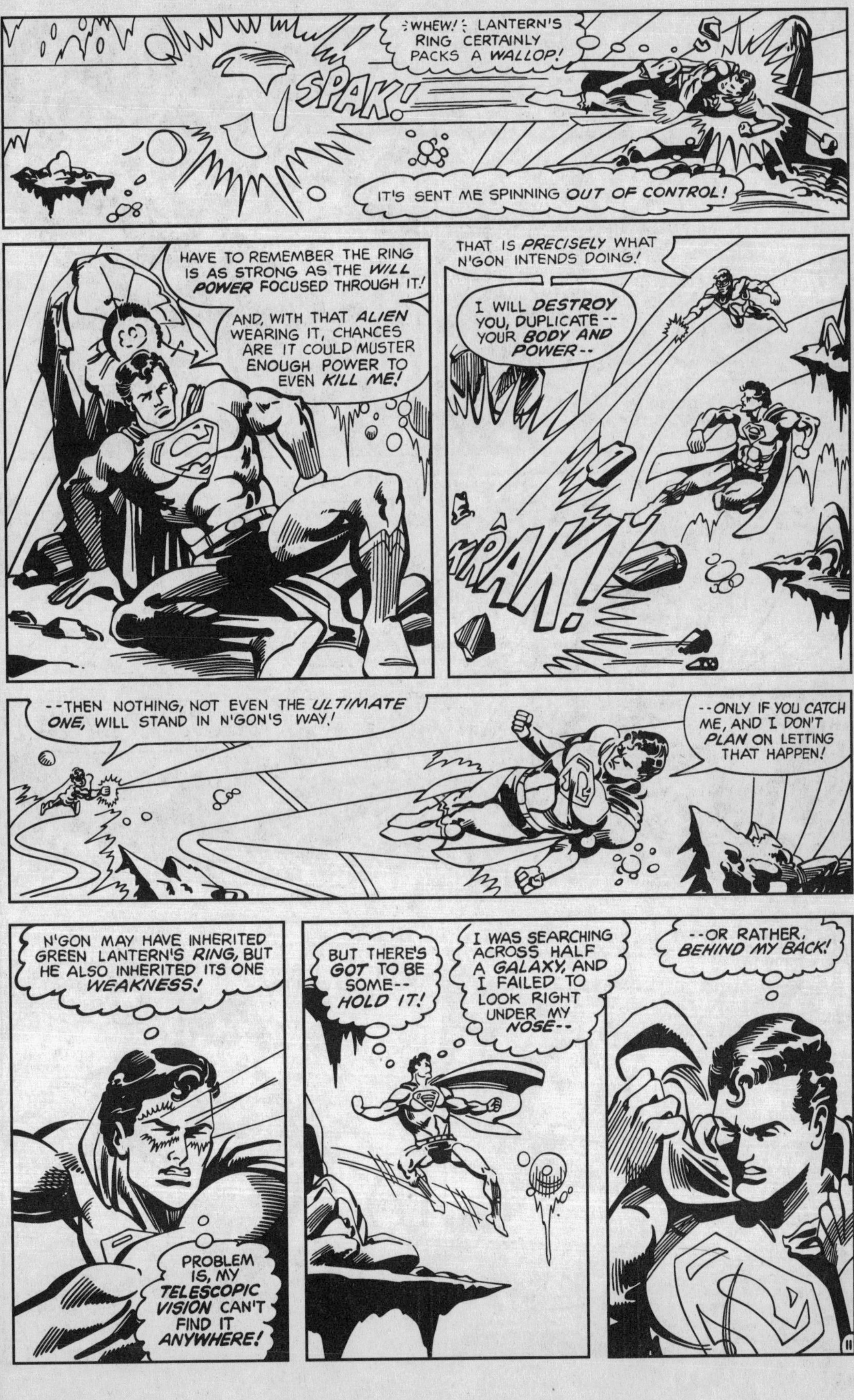
WHEW! LANTERN'S RING CERTAINLY PACKS A WALLOP!
SPAK!
IT'S SENT ME SPINNING OUT OF CONTROL!
HAVE TO REMEMBER THE RING IS AS STRONG AS THE WILL POWER FOCUSED THROUGH IT!
AND, WITH THAT ALIEN WEARING IT, CHANCES ARE IT COULD MUSTER ENOUGH POWER TO EVEN KILL ME!
THAT IS PRECISELY WHAT N'GON INTENDS DOING!
I WILL DESTROY YOU, DUPLICATE -- YOUR BODY AND POWER --
KRAK!
--THEN NOTHING, NOT EVEN THE ULTIMATE ONE, WILL STAND IN N'GON'S WAY!
--ONLY IF YOU CATCH ME, AND I DON'T PLAN ON LETTING THAT HAPPEN!
N'GON MAY HAVE INHERITED GREEN LANTERN'S RING, BUT HE ALSO INHERITED ITS ONE WEAKNESS!
PROBLEM IS, MY TELESCOPIC VISION CAN'T FIND IT ANYWHERE!
BUT THERE'S GOT TO BE SOME-- HOLD IT!
I WAS SEARCHING ACROSS HALF A GALAXY, AND I FAILED TO LOOK RIGHT UNDER MY NOSE--
--OR RATHER, BEHIND MY BACK!
11

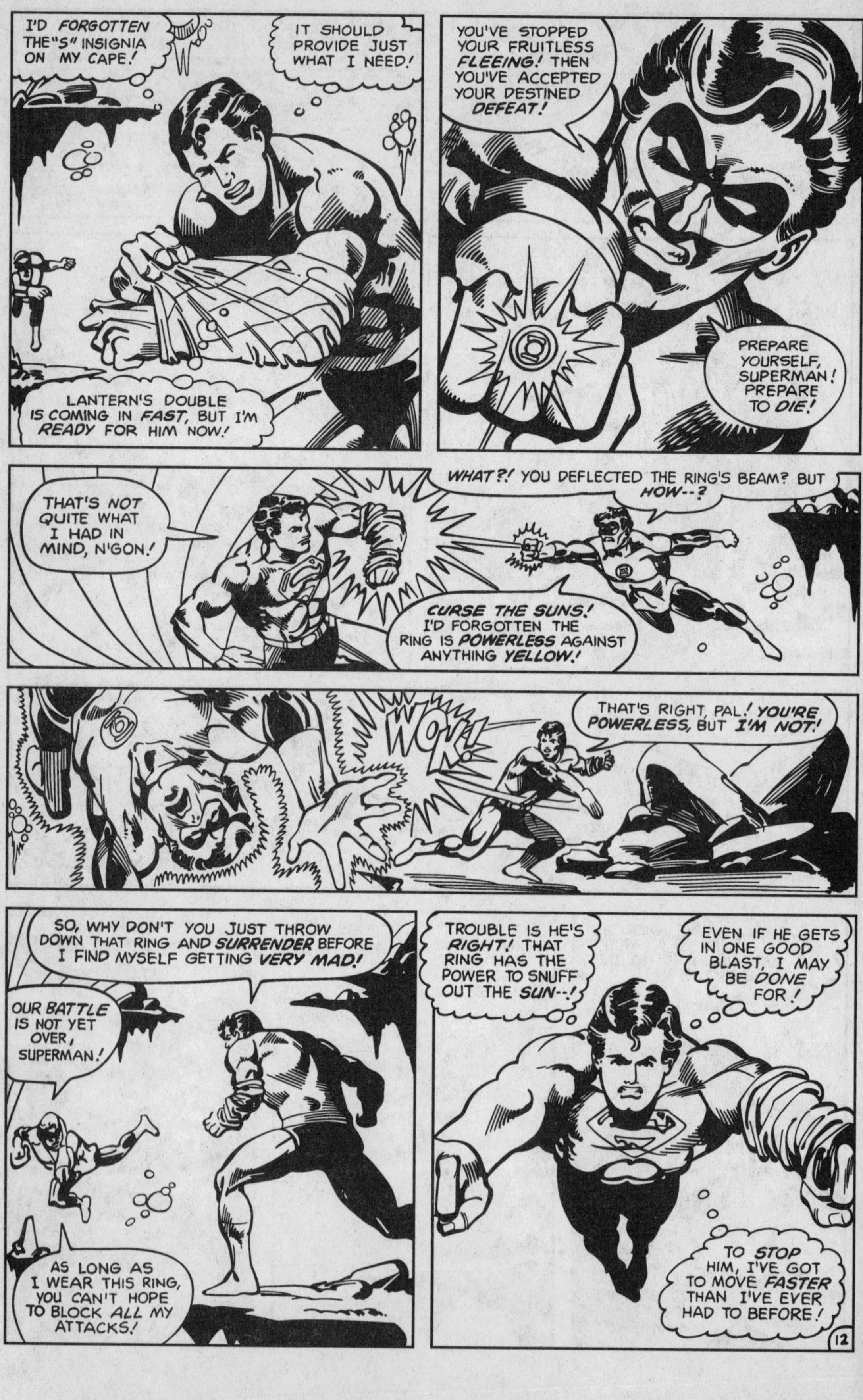
I'D FORGOTTEN THE "S" INSIGNIA ON MY CAPE!
IT SHOULD PROVIDE JUST WHAT I NEED!
LANTERN'S DOUBLE IS COMING IN FAST, BUT I'M READY FOR HIM NOW!
YOU'VE STOPPED YOUR FRUITLESS FLEEING! THEN YOU'VE ACCEPTED YOUR DESTINED DEFEAT!
PREPARE YOURSELF, SUPERMAN! PREPARE TO DIE!
THAT'S NOT QUITE WHAT I HAD IN MIND, N'GON!
WHAT?! YOU DEFLECTED THE RING'S BEAM? BUT HOW--?
CURSE THE SUNS! I'D FORGOTTEN THE RING IS POWERLESS AGAINST ANYTHING YELLOW!
WOK!
THAT'S RIGHT, PAL! YOU'RE POWERLESS, BUT I'M NOT!
SO, WHY DON'T YOU JUST THROW DOWN THAT RING AND SURRENDER BEFORE I FIND MYSELF GETTING VERY MAD!
OUR BATTLE IS NOT YET OVER, SUPERMAN!
AS LONG AS I WEAR THIS RING, YOU CAN'T HOPE TO BLOCK ALL MY ATTACKS!
TROUBLE IS HE'S RIGHT! THAT RING HAS THE POWER TO SNUFF OUT THE SUN--!
EVEN IF HE GETS IN ONE GOOD BLAST, I MAY BE DONE FOR!
TO STOP HIM, I'VE GOT TO MOVE FASTER THAN I'VE EVER HAD TO BEFORE!
12

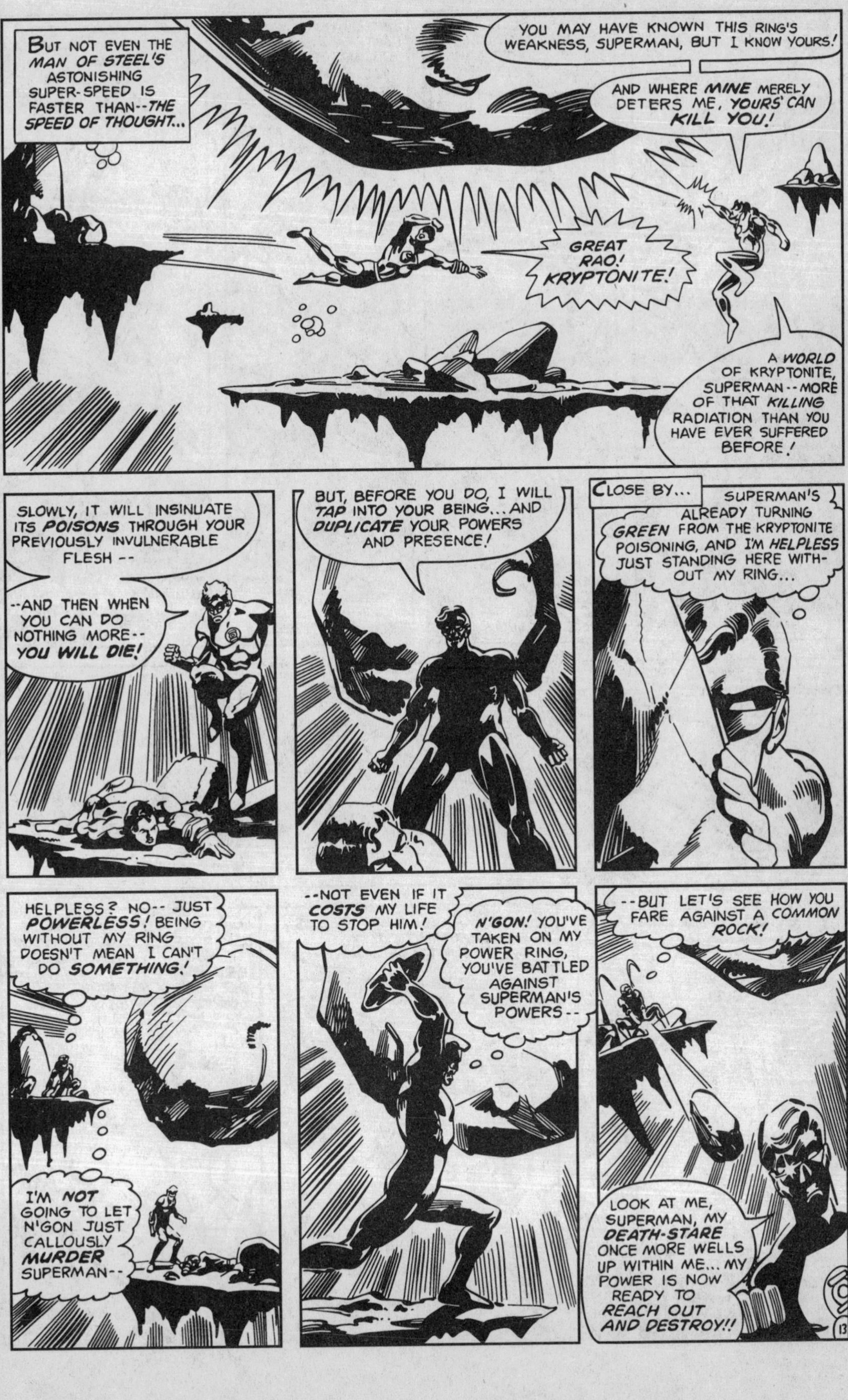
BUT NOT EVEN THE MAN OF STEEL'S ASTONISHING SUPER-SPEED IS FASTER THAN--THE SPEED OF THOUGHT...
YOU MAY HAVE KNOWN THIS RING'S WEAKNESS, SUPERMAN, BUT I KNOW YOURS!
AND WHERE MINE MERELY DETERS ME, YOURS' CAN KILL YOU!
GREAT RAO! KRYPTONITE!
A WORLD OF KRYPTONITE, SUPERMAN--MORE OF THAT KILLING RADIATION THAN YOU HAVE EVER SUFFERED BEFORE!
SLOWLY, IT WILL INSINUATE ITS POISONS THROUGH YOUR PREVIOUSLY INVULNERABLE FLESH --
--AND THEN WHEN YOU CAN DO NOTHING MORE-- YOU WILL DIE!
BUT, BEFORE YOU DO, I WILL TAP INTO YOUR BEING...AND DUPLICATE YOUR POWERS AND PRESENCE!
CLOSE BY...
SUPERMAN'S ALREADY TURNING GREEN FROM THE KRYPTONITE POISONING, AND I'M HELPLESS JUST STANDING HERE WITH-OUT MY RING...
HELPLESS? NO-- JUST POWERLESS! BEING WITHOUT MY RING DOESN'T MEAN I CAN'T DO SOMETHING!
I'M NOT GOING TO LET N'GON JUST CALLOUSLY MURDER SUPERMAN--
--NOT EVEN IF IT COSTS MY LIFE TO STOP HIM!
N'GON! YOU'VE TAKEN ON MY POWER RING, YOU'VE BATTLED AGAINST SUPERMAN'S POWERS--
--BUT LET'S SEE HOW YOU FARE AGAINST A COMMON ROCK!
LOOK AT ME, SUPERMAN, MY DEATH-STARE ONCE MORE WELLS UP WITHIN ME... MY POWER IS NOW READY TO REACH OUT AND DESTROY!!
13

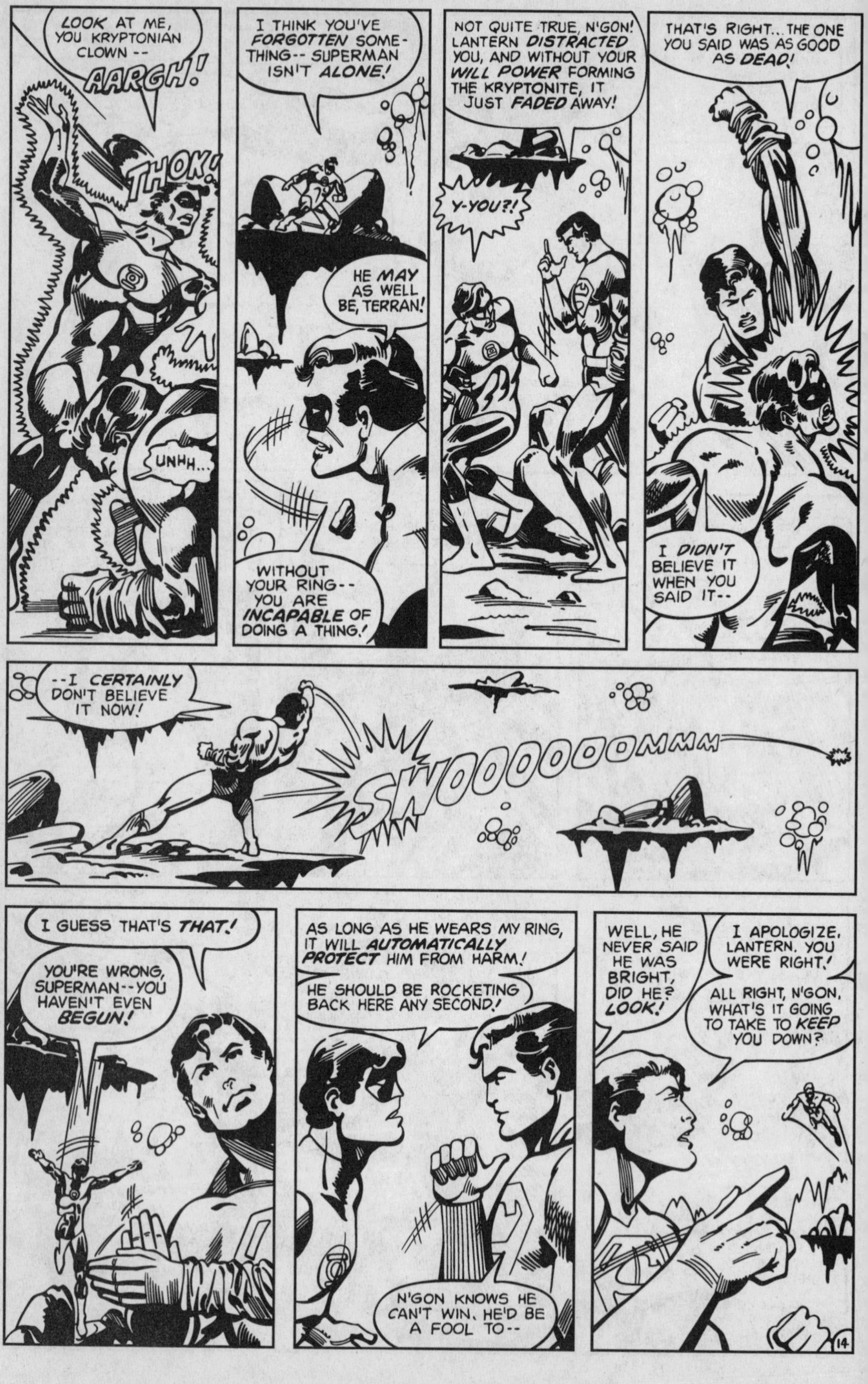
LOOK AT ME, YOU KRYPTONIAN CLOWN --
AARGH!
THOK!
UNHH...
I THINK YOU'VE FORGOTTEN SOME-THING-- SUPERMAN ISN'T ALONE!
HE MAY AS WELL BE, TERRAN!
WITHOUT YOUR RING-- YOU ARE INCAPABLE OF DOING A THING!
NOT QUITE TRUE, N'GON! LANTERN DISTRACTED YOU, AND WITHOUT YOUR WILL POWER FORMING THE KRYPTONITE, IT JUST FADED AWAY!
Y-YOU?!
THAT'S RIGHT... THE ONE YOU SAID WAS AS GOOD AS DEAD!
I DIDN'T BELIEVE IT WHEN YOU SAID IT--
--I CERTAINLY DON'T BELIEVE IT NOW!
SWOOOOOOOOMMM
I GUESS THAT'S THAT!
YOU'RE WRONG, SUPERMAN--YOU HAVEN'T EVEN BEGUN!
AS LONG AS HE WEARS MY RING, IT WILL AUTOMATICALLY PROTECT HIM FROM HARM!
HE SHOULD BE ROCKETING BACK HERE ANY SECOND!
N'GON KNOWS HE CAN'T WIN. HE'D BE A FOOL TO--
WELL, HE NEVER SAID HE WAS BRIGHT, DID HE? LOOK!
I APOLOGIZE, LANTERN. YOU WERE RIGHT!
ALL RIGHT, N'GON, WHAT'S IT GOING TO TAKE TO KEEP YOU DOWN?
14

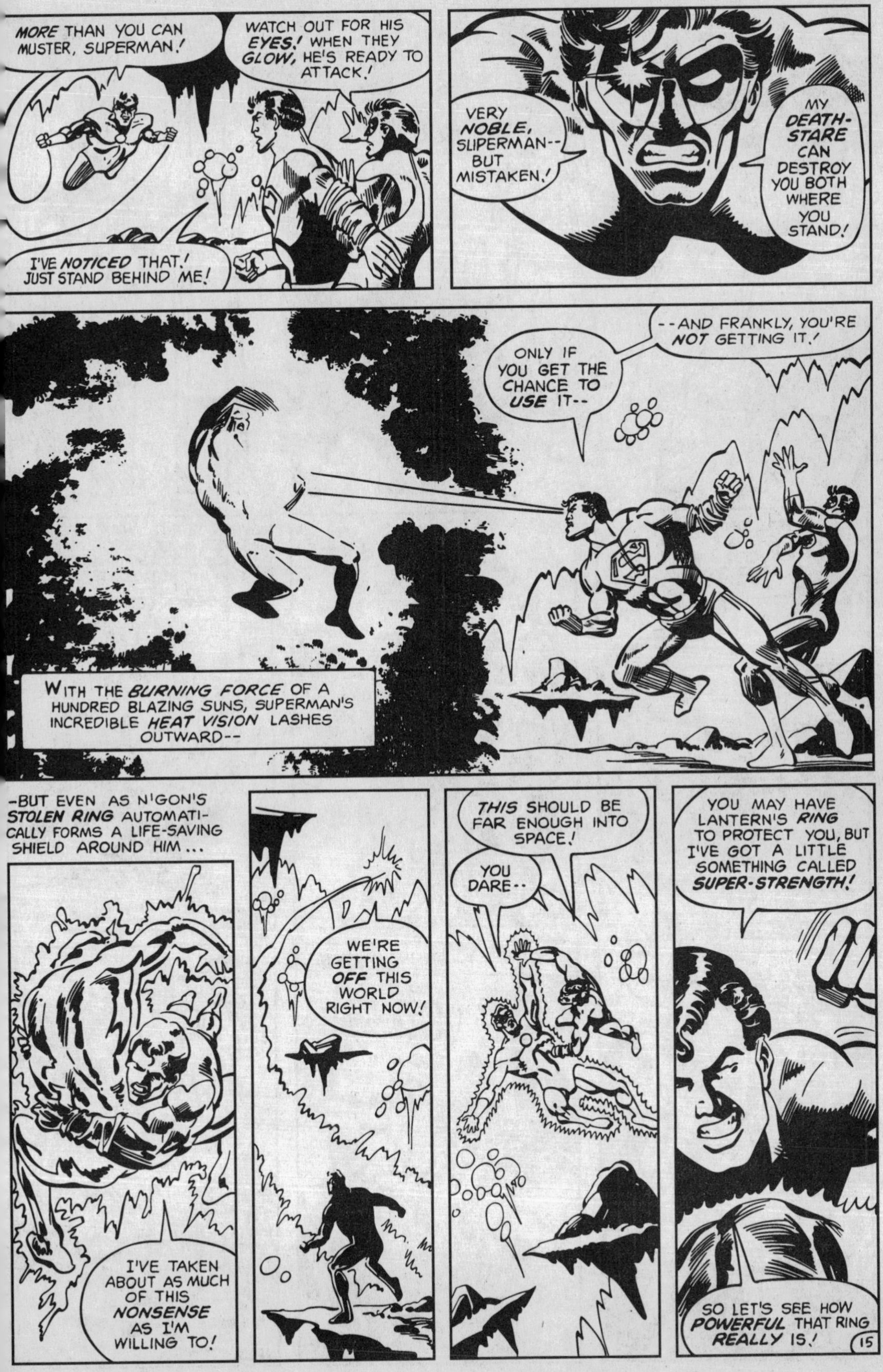
MORE THAN YOU CAN MUSTER, SUPERMAN!
WATCH OUT FOR HIS EYES! WHEN THEY GLOW, HE'S READY TO ATTACK!
I'VE NOTICED THAT! JUST STAND BEHIND ME!
VERY NOBLE, SUPERMAN-- BUT MISTAKEN!
MY DEATH-STARE CAN DESTROY YOU BOTH WHERE YOU STAND!
ONLY IF YOU GET THE CHANCE TO USE IT--
--AND FRANKLY, YOU'RE NOT GETTING IT!
WITH THE BURNING FORCE OF A HUNDRED BLAZING SUNS, SUPERMAN'S INCREDIBLE HEAT VISION LASHES OUTWARD--
-BUT EVEN AS N'GON'S STOLEN RING AUTOMATICALLY FORMS A LIFE-SAVING SHIELD AROUND HIM...
I'VE TAKEN ABOUT AS MUCH OF THIS NONSENSE AS I'M WILLING TO!
WE'RE GETTING OFF THIS WORLD RIGHT NOW!
THIS SHOULD BE FAR ENOUGH INTO SPACE!
YOU DARE--
YOU MAY HAVE LANTERN'S RING TO PROTECT YOU, BUT I'VE GOT A LITTLE SOMETHING CALLED SUPER-STRENGTH!
SO LET'S SEE HOW POWERFUL THAT RING REALLY IS!
15

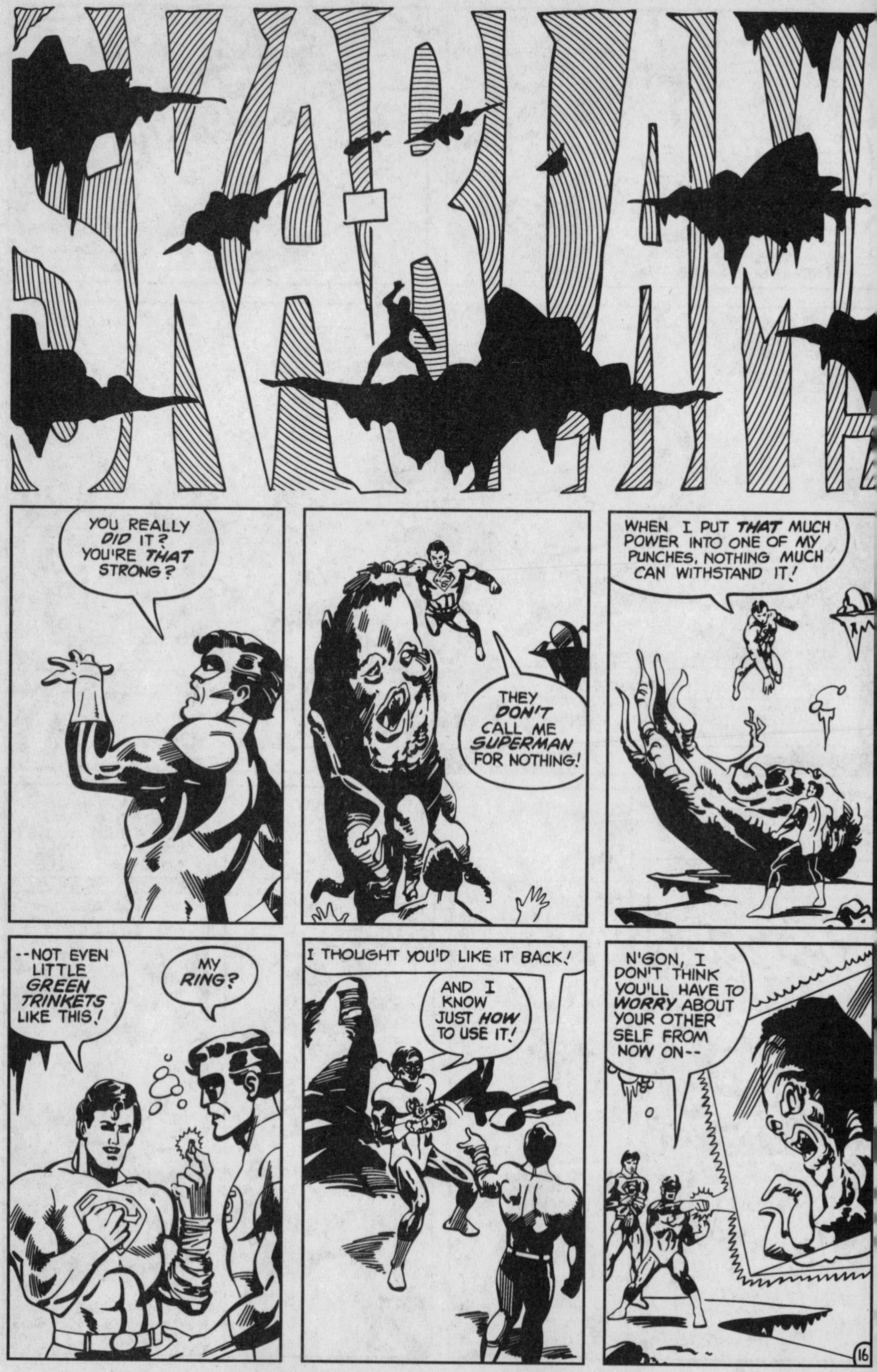
SKA-WHAM
YOU REALLY DID IT? YOU'RE THAT STRONG?
THEY DON'T CALL ME SUPERMAN FOR NOTHING!
WHEN I PUT THAT MUCH POWER INTO ONE OF MY PUNCHES, NOTHING MUCH CAN WITHSTAND IT!
--NOT EVEN LITTLE GREEN TRINKETS LIKE THIS!
MY RING?
I THOUGHT YOU'D LIKE IT BACK!
AND I KNOW JUST HOW TO USE IT!
N'GON, I DON'T THINK YOU'LL HAVE TO WORRY ABOUT YOUR OTHER SELF FROM NOW ON--
16

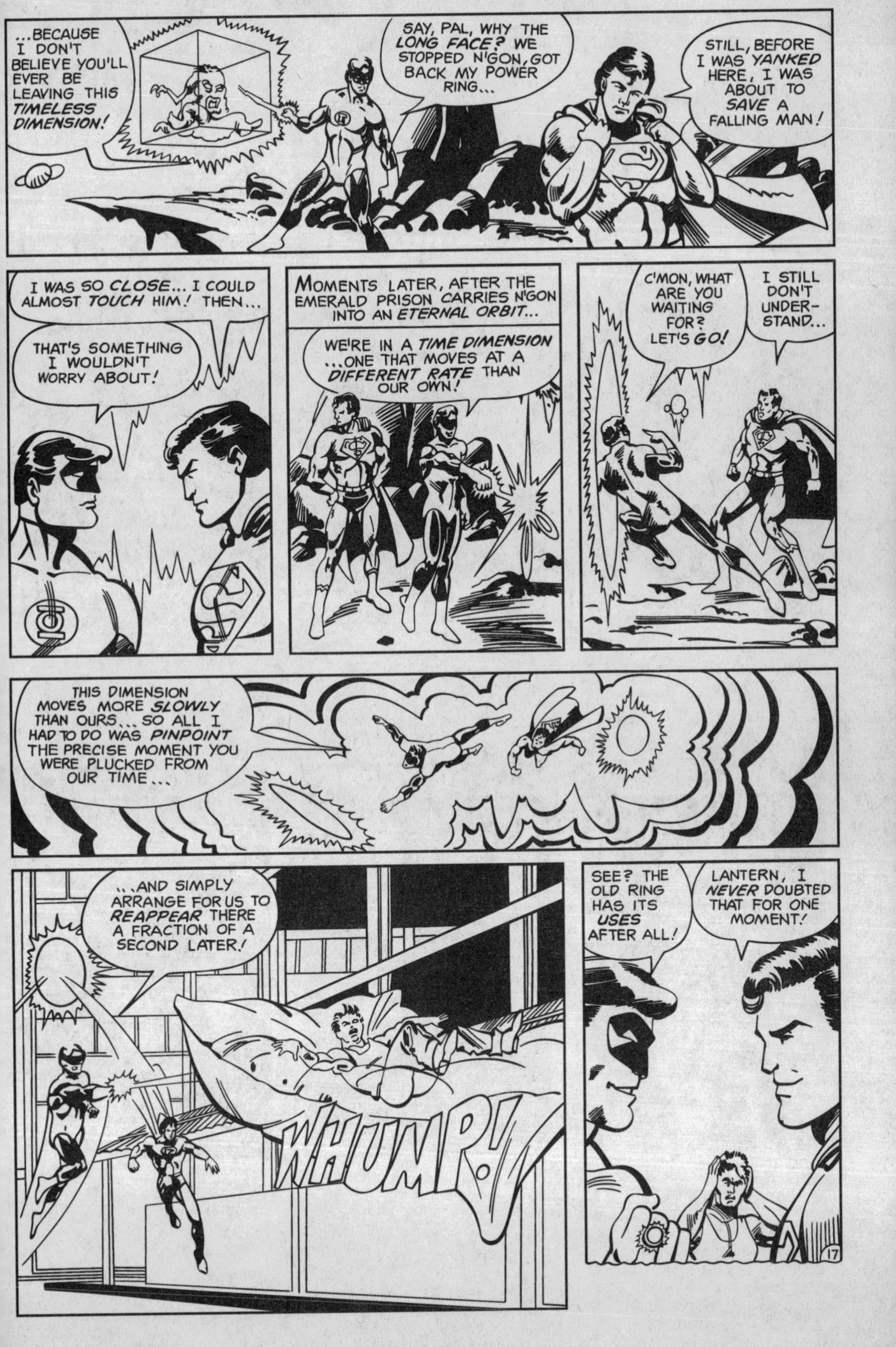
...BECAUSE I DON'T BELIEVE YOU'LL EVER BE LEAVING THIS TIMELESS DIMENSION!
SAY, PAL, WHY THE LONG FACE? WE STOPPED N'GON, GOT BACK MY POWER RING...
STILL, BEFORE I WAS YANKED HERE, I WAS ABOUT TO SAVE A FALLING MAN!
I WAS SO CLOSE... I COULD ALMOST TOUCH HIM! THEN...
THAT'S SOMETHING I WOULDN'T WORRY ABOUT!
MOMENTS LATER, AFTER THE EMERALD PRISON CARRIES N'GON INTO AN ETERNAL ORBIT...
WE'RE IN A TIME DIMENSION ...ONE THAT MOVES AT A DIFFERENT RATE THAN OUR OWN!
I STILL DON'T UNDER-STAND...
C'MON, WHAT ARE YOU WAITING FOR? LET'S GO!
THIS DIMENSION MOVES MORE SLOWLY THAN OURS... SO ALL I HAD TO DO WAS PINPOINT THE PRECISE MOMENT YOU WERE PLUCKED FROM OUR TIME...
...AND SIMPLY ARRANGE FOR US TO REAPPEAR THERE A FRACTION OF A SECOND LATER!
WHUMP!
SEE? THE OLD RING HAS ITS USES AFTER ALL!
LANTERN, I NEVER DOUBTED THAT FOR ONE MOMENT!
17

SHOWCASE PRESENTS

LOOK FOR THESE OTHER TITLES FEATURING CLASSIC TALES OF DC SUPER HEROES!

SHOWCASE PRESENTS
TEEN TITANS
OVER 500 PAGES OF COMICS!

SHOWCASE PRESENTS
BOOSTER GOLD

SHOWCASE PRESENTS
LEGION of SUPER-HEROES
COSMIC BOY
LIGHTNING BOY
SATURN GIRL
YES
NO
YES
NO
YES
NO

SHOWCASE PRESENTS
METAL MEN

SHOWCASE PRESENTS
SHAZAM!
OVER 500 PAGES OF COMICS!

SHOWCASE PRESENTS
THE PHANTOM STRANGER
OVER 500 PAGES OF COMICS!

SEARCH THE GRAPHIC NOVELS SECTION OF **DCCOMICS.COM**
FOR INFORMATION ON EVERY VOLUME IN THE **SHOWCASE** SERIES!

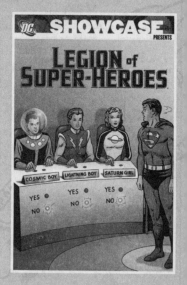